Contents

The content of each chapter is detailed on each chapter's first page.

For Sister Bridget Folkard and
her six thousand babies in Mubuga.

OXFORD HANDBOOK OF CLINICAL SPECIALTIES

SEVENTH EDITION

JUDITH COLLIER

MURRAY LONGMORE

MARK BRINSDEN

OXFORD

UNIVERSITY PRESS

OXFORD
UNIVERSITY PRESS

Great Clarendon Street, Oxford OX2 6DP.

Oxford University Press is a department of the University of Oxford.
It furthers the University's objective of excellence in research, scholarship,
and education by publishing worldwide in

Oxford New York

Auckland Cape Town Dar es Salaam Hong Kong Karachi
Kuala Lumpur Madrid Melbourne Mexico City Nairobi
New Delhi Shanghai Taipei Toronto

With offices in

Argentina Austria Brazil Chile Czech Republic France Greece
Gautemala Hungary Italy Japan Poland Portugal Singapore
South Korea Switzerland Thailan Turkey Ukraine Vietnam

Published in the United States
by Oxford University Press Inc., New York

First published 1987
Second edition 1989
Third edition 1991
Fourth edition 1995
Fifth edition 1999
Sixth edition 2003
Seventh edition 2006
Reprint 2006

Translations: Spanish
German
Hungarian
Polish
Romanian
Russian
Portugese

British Library Cataloguing in Publication Data
Data available

Library of Congress Cataloging in Publication Data
Data available

Typeset in JML and Newgen Imaging Systems (P) Ltd., Chennai, India
Printed and bound by Replika Press Pvt. Ltd., India

ISBN 0-19-920774-7 9780199207749

10 9 8 7 6 5 4 3 2 1

Preface to the seventh edition

As one St Anne's scholar exhorted herself half way through her 27th book: 'be calm, be patient, endure an infinite slowness, time spent checking a fact or a reference is not time wasted but an essential part of the sheer blank labour involved in scholarship'. We have been deeply involved in our own form of 'blank labour' for 3 years—trying to create more blank space. We have only been partly successful: as soon as a beautifully blank right-hand page is created, some vital new fact presents itself, and repopulates our pristine white deserts. All books should have as much blank space as possible, with the widest margins—at least an inch all round. In more leisurely days, OUP provided scholars with books which were *mostly* margin. The authors simply contributed a thin column of text which provided the fuel for readers digressions, speculations, expostulations, ruminations—and flashes of brilliance—all recorded for others' edification in the margins. If only the Greek text *Arithmetica* by Diophantus had had wider margins, the mystery surrounding Fermat's last theorem would have been easily solved—for in it he wrote 'I have discovered a truly marvellous demonstration of this proposition[1] that this margin is too narrow to contain.' We realize that our miserly margins are insufficient even for this comment—let alone enough for all the 'truly marvellous demonstrations' ('demonstrationem mirabilem' in Fermat's Latin) which our readers will wish to fix forever between our pages.

Our researches reveal that our blank pages are only used by half our readers—the remainder are too shy or too respectful of books to violate them with intellectual doodles and student scribbles. But we want to be violated! Without marginalia a book is a rather one-sided conversation. The processes of textual intercourse demand a two-way process. So do please use our Readers Comments Card to tell us where we have gone wrong and how we might improve. If some genius of a Reader were to send us their marginalia rivalling Fermat's, we will be only too pleased to pass on the gems for all to admire—provided we can read your writing, and providing that unlike Fermat you do not communicate entirely in Latin.

Taking up even more of our blank space are our new colour images, appearing for the first time in an Oxford Handbook along the side of the text to which they refer. On our necessarily thin paper they are inevitably something of an experiment. We cannot claim that all our pictures are worth a thousand words[2]—but some have replaced rather boring chunks of text.

In this edition, we have taken on specialist authors in the fields of Orthopaedics, Trauma, and Psychiatry—and it is a great pleasure to thank Mr Mark Brinsden and Dr Anish Patel for their help in these areas.

There are extensive changes in this edition particularly to Obstetrics, Gynaecology, Paediatrics, Orthopaedics, and Ophthalmology. So if you are thinking of using an old version of this book—it won't do! Not just out of considerations of clinical governance—but also because this edition is in fact *shorter* and *less wordy* than its predecessors. Why oppress yourself with the burdens of the past when the present is much more interesting? The only possible answer is that you will be jettisoning all those valuable marginalia referred to above. But even to this problem, there is a solution. Furnish yourself with the handheld electronic version of this text (see back cover)—and there you can go one step further than Fermat, and add marginalia *ad infinitum*.

Judith Collier & Murray Longmore—*Ferring*, 2006

1 This is the proof that the equation $x^n + y^n = z^n$ has no integer solutions for $n>2$. Pierre de Fermat (1601–65) was a French lawyer. He published practically nothing—but his marginalia elevated him, by general acclamation, to the status of 'one of the greatest mathematicians of all time'.
2 The phrase 'a picture is worth a thousand words' seems to embody some ancient Chinese wisdom. In fact the phrase was coined by a man keen to sell advertising space on trams in the 1920s.

Preface to the first edition

When someone says that he is 'doing obstetrics'—or whatever, this should not hide the fact that much more is being done besides, not just a little of each of medicine, psychiatry, gynaecology and paediatrics, but also a good deal of work to elicit and act upon the patient's unspoken hopes and fears. At the operating table he must concentrate minutely on the problem in hand; but later he must operate on other planes too, in social and psychological dimensions so as to understand how the patient came to need to be on the operating table, and how this might have been prevented. All the best specialists practise a holistic art, and our aim is to show how specialism and holism may be successfully interwoven, if not into a fully watertight garment, then at least into one which keeps out much of the criticism rained upon us by the proponents of alternative medicine.

We hope that by compiling this little volume we may make the arduous task of learning medicine a little less exhausting, so allowing more energy to be spent at the bedside, and on the wards. For a medical student coming fresh to a specialty the great tomes which mark the road to knowledge can numb the mind after a while, and what started out fresh is in danger of becoming exhausted by its own too much. It is not that we are against the great tomes themselves—we are simply against reading them too much and too soon. One starts off strong on 'care' and weak on knowledge, and the danger is that this state of affairs becomes reversed. It is easier to learn from books than from patients, yet what our patients teach us may be of more abiding significance: the value of sympathy, the uses of compassion and the limits of our human world. It is at the bedside that we learn how to be of practical help to people who are numbed by the mysterious disasters of womb or tomb, for which they are totally unprepared. If this small book enables those starting to explore the major specialties to learn all they can from their patients, it will have served its purpose—and can then be discarded.

Because of the page-a-subject format, the balance of topics in the following pages may at first strike the reader as being odd in places. However, it has been our intention to provide a maximally useful text rather than one which is perfectly balanced in apportioning space according to how common a particular topic is—just as the great *Terrestrial Globes* made by George Phillips in the 1960s may seem at first to provide an odd balance of place names, with Alice Springs appearing more prominently than Amsterdam. To chart a whole continent, and omit to name a single central location out of respect for 'balance' is to miss a good opportunity to be useful. George Phillips did not miss this opportunity, and neither we hope, have we. It is inevitable that some readers will be disappointed that we have left out their favoured subjects (the Phillips' Globe does not even mention Oxford!). To these readers we offer over 300 blank pages by way of apology.

Ferring J.A.B.C.
1987 J.M.L.

Conflicts of interest: none declared

Because of numerous and well-publicized occasions where writers of guidelines recommending certain drugs turn out to have undisclosed financial contacts with the pharmaceutical industries concerned, we wish to place on record that we have no contacts with any pharmaceutical company, and no pharmaceutical company employs us in any capacity, and neither have we received any financial input bearing upon our research for this publication. We have a policy of not seeing representatives from the pharmaceutical industry, or receiving their gifts or hospitality. We assert that the drugs recommended in this book have been selected on the basis of the best available evidence.

J.A.B.C. & J.M.L., principal authors

Drugs

While every effort has been made to check this text, it is still possible that drug or other errors have been missed. Also, dosage schedules are continually being revised and new side-effects recognized. Oxford University Press makes no representation, express or implied, that drug dosages in this book are correct. For these reasons, the reader is strongly urged to check with the most up to date published product information and *Data sheets* provided by the manufacturers, and the most recent codes of conduct and safety regulations. The authors and the publishers do not accept responsibility or legal liability for any errors in the text, or for the misuse or misapplication of material in this work.

Except where otherwise stated, drug doses and recommendations are for the **non-pregnant adult** who is **not breastfeeding**. To avoid excessive dosage in obese patients it may be best to calculate dosages on the basis of ideal body weight (IBW)—see p 621.

Readers are reminded of the need to keep up to date, and that this need can only ever be *partly* addressed by printed texts such as this.

Drug nomenclature

This book uses British[uk] approved names, followed, where there is a difference, by the recommended international non-proprietary name (rINN; usually there is no difference) as stipulated by European Directive. Exceptions to our rule of giving both names occur where the change is minute, eg amoxycillin[uk]/amoxicillin, where the rINN is used, to avoid tedious near-duplications. Among the new rINNs used are:

Alimemazine	(trimeprazine[uk])	Epinephrine	(adrenaline[uk])
Amoxicillin	(amoxycillin[uk])	Furosemide	(frusemide[uk])
Bendroflumethiazide	(bendrofluazide[uk])	Lidocaine	(lignocaine[uk])
Ciclosporin	(cyclosporin[uk])	Chlormethine	(mustine[uk])
Clomifene	(clomiphene[uk])	Norepinephrine	(noradrenaline[uk])
Diethylstilbestrol	(stilboestrol[uk])	Sulfonamides (all)	(sulphonamides[uk])
Dosulepin	(dothiepin[uk])	Trihexyphenidyl	(benzhexol[uk])

Acknowledgements

Specialist readers
These are thanked on the first page of each chapter.

We thank Dr Ahmad Mafi and Dr Steven Emmett for detailed help in reading the proofs.

We also thank all the authors who have joined us for previous editions: Judith Harvey, Tim Hodgetts, Torquil Duncan Brown, and Peter Scally.

Readers' participation We have been very fortunate to receive so many well considered communications via our reader's comments card (enclosed with this volume); these comments have contributed greatly to this edition. We acknowledge and thank them here: N Abcod; S Abedin; K Abou-Elhmd; A Adiele; R Adley; A Agbobee; M Al-Amin; A Alaraji; H Albrecht; Zulfiqar Ali; A Alwael; anonymous readers from Hinckley and District Hospital; V Atamyan; M Azam; N Balasuriyar; D Bansevicius; S Beasley; D Boddie; B Bourke; P Piotr Brykalski; C Budd; K Burn; I Cardozo; Tor Chiu, P Cliffe; P Collins; S Corcoran; H Constantinides; J Crane; D Dharmi; J Dart; T Davies; H Dormand; S Dunarchie; J Eduardien; S Eley; J Fagan; Faiz-ur-Rehman; O Fenton; P Fanagan; M Fry; D Foss; E France; D Groneberg; Z Gussanhamad; J Guznan; L Hansen; P Hausserman; J Hazlewood; J Heckmatt; S Helmy; T Hennigan; J Hill; S Holliday; R William Howe; G Hutchison; M Ip; J Jackson; F Jowett; A Juanroyee; H Kabil; B Kloft; A Kuber; P Lai; C Law; N Lees; J Lehane; R Lopez; A McBride; J McFazdean; R McLaughlin; S Mcpartlin; K Mandana; A Martin; C Maytum; E Miller; R Morley; D Moskopp; M Naraen; K Narayanan; A Navran; K Ngoo; M Norbrook; J Norman; K O'Driscoll; E Odumenya; H Okoi; E Olson; J Olson; M Omar; A Omorojor; A Madkhana; B & S Manidas; R Payne; G Porter; R Price; S Ranka; A Rees; J Rees; P Rees; R Reynolds; J Revilla; C Robertson; A Rodgers; E Russell; R Pyper; D Shukla; S Sobolewski; S Sohrabi; H Soren; S Stedman, M Stryan; S Swiig; L Tait; N Tseraidi; M Tsolaks; M Turur; F Udoh; A Uqaili; C Vandenbussche; M Wahba; D Warren; S Western; E Wright; P Zack.

We thank the following authors, publishers and editors for permission to reproduce images: JF Cullen; Freund; Ghorayeb; Alan Hutchings; D Kinshuck; A Land; K O'Driscoll; A Swain; the *British Journal of Hospital Medicine*; the *British Medical Journal*; *General Practitioner*; the *Journal of Paediatrics*; the Association for Consumer Research; Baillière Tindall; John Wright; Edward Arnold; Lange; Churchill Livingstone; Genesis Medical Ltd; Medtronics.

Pronouns For brevity, the pronoun '*he*' or '*she*' has been used in places where '*he or she*' would have been appropriate. Such circumlocutions do not aid the reader in forming a vivid visual impression, which is one of the leading aims of good authorship. Therefore, for balance and fairness, and where sense allows, we have tried alternating *he* with *she*.

Symbols and abbreviations

►	This is important
►►	Don't dawdle! Prompt action saves lives
●	Conflict (controversial topic)
ΔΔ	Differential diagnosis
♂/♀	Male to female ratio
#	Fracture
[1,2,etc]	Drug dose not in *BNF*; p 504
∵	On account of
~;≈	About; approximately equal to
-ve/+ve	Negative/positive
↓; ↑	Decreased; Increased
↔	Normal (eg plasma level)
A&E	Emergency department
Ac	Ante cibum (before food)
ACE(i)	Angiotensin-converting enzyme (inhibitor)
ACLS	Advanced cardiac life support
ACTH	Adrenocorticotrophic hormone
ADD	Attention deficit disorder
ADH	Antidiuretic hormone
ADNFLE	Autosomal-dominant nocturnal frontal lobe epilepsy
AFP	α-fetoprotein
AIDS	Acquired immunodeficiency syndrome
ALL	Acute lymphoblastic leukaemia
Alk	Alkaline (phos = phosphatase)
ALT	Alanine aminotransferase
ANA	Antinuclear antibody
ANF	Antinuclear factor
AP	Anteroposterior
APH	Antepartum haemorrhage
APLS	Advanced paediatric life support
APM	Auto-premotor syndrome
A(P)LS	Advanced (Paediatric) Life Support *Manuals* (269)
ARF	Acute renal failure
ARM	Artificial rupture of membranes
ASW	Approved social worker
ASO	Antistreptolysin O (titre)

ASD	Atrioseptal defect
ATLS	Advanced Trauma Life Support *Manual* reference
ATN	Acute tubular necrosis
AV	Atrioventricular
AVM	Arteriovenous malformation
BMJ	*British Medical Journal*
BP	Blood pressure
BJGP	*British Journal of General Practice*
BNA	Borderline nuclear abnormality
BNF	*British National Formulary*
C3	Complement
Ca	Carcinoma
CBT	Cognitive-behaviour therapy
CCF	Combined (right & left sided) cardiac failure
ChVS	Chorionic villus sampling
CI	Contraindications
CIN	Cervical intra-epithelial neoplasia
CMV	Cytomegalovirus
CNS	Central nervous system
CO	Cardiac output
CoC	Combined oral contraceptive
CPA	Care programme approach
CPR	Cardiopulmonary resuscitation
CPAP	Continuous positive airways pressure
CRP	C-reactive protein
CSF	Cerebrospinal fluid
CT	Computer tomography
CVP	Central venous pressure
CVS	Cardiovascular system
CXR	Chest x-ray
D	Dimension
D&C	Dilatation (cervix) & curettage
DB	Decibel
DHS	Dynamic hip screw
DIC	Disseminated intravascular coagulation
DIP	Distal interphalangeal
DKA	Diabetic ketoacidosis
dL	Decilitre
DM	Diabetes mellitus
DNA	Deoxyribonucleic acid
DoH	Department of Health

DPL	Diagnostic peritoneal lavage
DRG	Dorsal root ganglion
D&V	Diarrhoea and vomiting
DUB	Dysfunctional uterine bleeding
DVT	Deep venous thrombosis
E-BM	*Evidence-based Medicine* (journal)
EBV	Epstein-Barr virus
ECG	Electrocardiogram
ECT	Electroconvulsive therapy
EEG	Electroencephalogram
EIA	Enzyme immunoassay
ENT	Ear, nose and throat
EPDS	Edinburgh Postnatal Depression Scale
ERPC	Evacuation of retained products of conception
ESR	Erythrocyte sedimentation rate
ET	Endotracheal
FAST	Focused abdominal ultrasound for trauma
FB	Foreign body
FBC	Full blood count
FCR	Flexor carpi radials
FDP	Flexor digitorum profundis
FDS	Flexor digitorum sublimes
FH	Family history
FNT	Fetal nuchal translucency
FISH	Fluorescence *in situ* hybridization
FSH	Follicle-stimulating hormone
G	Gauge
g	Gram
G6PD	Glucose-6-phosphate dehydrogenase
GCS	Glasgow Coma Scale
GA	General anaesthesia
GFR	Glomerular filtration rate
GI	Gastrointestinal
GP	General practitioner
G(γ)GT	Gamma(γ)glutamyl transpeptidase
GTN	Gestational trophoblastic neoplasia

h	Hour
HAS	Human albumin solution
Hb	Haemoglobin
HBV	Hepatitis B virus
HBsAg	Hepatitis B surface antigen
HCG	Human chorionic gonadotrophin
HDL	High-density lipoprotein
HIV	Human immunodeficiency virus
HLA	Human leukocyte alleles
HPO	Hypothalamic-pituitary-ovarian
HPV	Human papiloma virus
HRT	Hormone replacement therapy
HVS	High vaginal swab
Ib/ibid	Ibidem (in the same place)
IBW	Ideal body weight
ICP	Intracranial pressure
IE	Infective endocarditis
Ig	Immunoglobulin
IHD	Ischaemic heart disease
IM	Intramuscular
INR	International normalized ratio of prothrombin time
IP	Interphalangeal
IPPV	Intermittent positive pressure ventilation
IPT	Interpersonal therapy
IQ	Intelligence quotient
Iu	International unit
IUCD	Intrauterine contraceptive device
IUI	Intrauterine insemination
ITP	Idiopathic thrombocytopenic purpura
ITU	Intensive therapy unit
IV	Intravenous
IVF	*In vitro* fertilization
IVI	Intravenous infusion
IVU	Intravenous urography
JVP	Jugular venous pressure
K^+	Potassium
Kg	Kilogram

KPa	Kilopascal
L	Litre
LA	Local anaesthesia
LBC	Liquid based cytology
LCR	Ligase chain reaction
LDH	Lactate dehydrogenase
LFT	Liver function test
LH	Luteinizing hormone
LHRH	Leutinizing hormone releasing hormone
LLETZ	Large loop excision of transformation zone
LMP	Day 1 of last menstrual period
LMWH	Low-molecular weight heparin
LP	Lumbar puncture
LVH	Left ventricular hypertrophy
μg	Microgram
MAP	Mean arterial pressure
MAOI	Monoamine oxidase inhibitor
MCP	Metacarpophalangeal
MCV	Mean cell volume
MEA	Microwave endometrial ablation
mg	Milligrams
MHA	Mental Health Act
mL	Millilitre
mmHg	Millimetres of mercury
MRI	Magnetic resonance imaging
MSU	Midstream urine culture
MTP	Metatarsophalangeal
mU	Milliunits
N=20*	Medline (p 504) reference to a randomized trial of 20 patients (* or whatever number follows N)
n=636*	Medline reference to a non-randomized trial of 636 patients
NaCl	Sodium chloride
NBM	Nil by mouth
NEJM	*New England Journal of Medicine*
NEPE	Non-epileptic paroxysmal events
NGT	Nasogastric tube
NHS	National Health Service
NICU	Neonatal intensive care unit
N_2O	Nitrous oxide
NSAIDs	Non-steroidal anti-inflammatory drugs
OED	*Oxford English Dictionary* 1st ed
OHCM	*Oxford Handbook of Clinical Medicine* 6th edition, OUP
ON	Omni nocte
β-HCG	β-Human-chorionic gonadotrophin
ORIF	Open reduction and internal fixation
ORh-ve	Blood group O, Rh negative
PA	Posteroanterior
PAN	Polyarteritis nodosa
pANCA	Perinuclear antineutrophil cytoplasmic antibody
P_aCO_2	Partial pressure of CO_2 in arterial blood
P_aO_2	Partial pressure of oxygen in arterial blood
pc	Post cibum (after food)
PCOS	Polycystic ovarian syndrome
PCR	Polymerase chain reaction
PCV	Packed cell volume
PDA	Patent ductus arteriosus
PE	Pulmonary embolus
PEDS	Parents' evaluation of developmental status
PET	Pre-eclamptic toxaemia
PG	Pemphigoid gestations
PGD	Preimplantation genetic diagnosis
PID	Pelvic inflammatory disease
PIP	Proximal interphalangeal
PKU	Phenylketonuria
PMB	Postmenopausal bleeding
PMS	Premenstrual syndrome
PO	Per os (by mouth)
PoP	Progesterone-only pill
PPH	Postpartum haemorrhage
PR	Per rectum
PTR	Prothrombin ratio
PE	Pulmonary embolism
PUO	Pyrexia of unknown origin
PV	Per vaginam (latin)
RA	Rheumatoid arthritis

RBC	Red blood cell
RCGP	Royal College of General Practitioners
RCOG	Royal College of Obstetricians and Gynaecologists
RMI	Risk of malignancy
RMO	Registered medical officer
RSI	Repetitive strain injury
RTA	Road traffic accident(s)
RUQ	Right upper quadrant
RVH	Right ventricular hypertrophy
Rx	Treatment (prescribing drugs)
S_1S_2	1st and 2nd heart sounds
SAD	Seasonal affective disorder
SALT	Speech and language therapist
SBE	Subacute bacterial endocarditis
SC	Subcutaneous
SCBU	Special care baby unit
SE	Side-effects
sec	Seconds
SERM	Selective oestrogen receptor modulator
SFH	Symphysis fundal height
SGA	Small-for-gestational age
SLE	Systemic lupus erythematosus
S_AO_2	Oximetry estimation of Capillary O_2 saturation; also S_aO_2
SSRI	Selective serotonin reuptake inhibitors
STD	Sexually transmitted disease
SUFE	Slipped upper femoral epiphysis
SVC	Superior vena cava
$t_{1/2}$	Half life
T°	Temperature
T_3	Triiodothyronine
T_4	Thyroxine
TB	Tuberculosis
TBW	Tension band wiring
TCRE	Transcervical resection of endometrium
TED	Transverse elastic graduated
TENS	Transcutaneous electrical nerve stimulation
TIA	Transient ischaemic attack
TFT	Thyroid function tests
ToP	Termination of pregnancy
TPH	Transplacental haemorrhage
TPR	Temperature, pulse, and respirations
TSH	Thyroid-stimulating hormone
TSOH	Transient synovitis of the hip
u (or U)	Units
U&E	Urea and electrolytes
UK	United Kingdom
URTI	Upper respiratory tract infection
Us(S)	Ultrasound (scan)
UTI	Urinary tract infection
UV	Ultraviolet
VLBW	Very low birth weight infants
VSD	Ventriculoseptal defect
VTE	Venous thromboembolism
VUR	Vesico-ureteric reflux
WCC	White blood cell count
wt	Weight
yrs	Years

Other abbreviations are given in full on the pages where they occur.

Understanding our patients

Most of the time we treat our patients quite well, without ever really understanding them. The idea that we should strive to understand and empathize with *all* our patients is unreasonable. Out-patient clinics and surgeries would grind to a halt, and urgent visits would never get done. It is also possible that to do so would be counter-productive from the patient's point of view. For two human beings to understand each other's inner life is a rare event, and if we offered this understanding to all our patients they might become addicted to us, and be unable to get on with the rest of their lives. Nevertheless, it is good practice to try to understand *some* patients. Doing so may entail swallowing an alien world and digesting it rather slowly. Paradoxically, to achieve this, we very often need to keep our mouths shut, particularly with those in whom we have reached a therapeutic impasse—for example if the illness is untreatable, or the patient has rejected our treatment, or if the patient seems to be asking or appealing for something more. Eye contact is important here. One of the authors (JML) recalls forever his very first patient—found on a surgical ward recovering from the repair of a perforated duodenal ulcer: a nice simple surgical patient, ideal for beginners. I asked all the questions in the book, and knew all his answers and his physical features: even the colour of his eyes. Luckily, the house officer who was really looking after him did not ask so many questions, and knew how to interpret the appeal for help behind those eyes, and in his busy day found space to receive the vital clue beyond my grasp—that my patient was a drug addict and under great stress as he could no longer finance his activity.

So, the first step in trying to understand a patient is to sit back and listen. Next, if possible, it is very helpful to see your patient often, to establish rapport, and mutual respect. If the relationship is all one way, with the doctor finding out all about the patient, but revealing nothing of him or herself, this mutual respect can take a very long time to grow. But beware of sharing too much of your own inner life with your patients: you may overburden them, or put them off. Different patients respond to different approaches. Understanding patients inevitably takes time, and it may be hard in a series of short appointments. A visit to the patient's home may be very revealing, but for many doctors trapped in hospital wards or clinics, this is impossible. But it is usually possible to have a longish, private interview, and take whatever opportunity arises. We once worked with a consultant who infuriated his junior staff on busy ward rounds by repeatedly selecting what seemed to us the most boring and commonplace medical 'cases' (such as someone with a stroke) and proceeding to draw the curtain around the patient's bed to exclude us, and engage in what seemed like a long chat with the patient, all in very hushed voices, so that we never knew what he said—until Sister told us that he never said anything much, and simply received anything that was on the patient's mind. For the most part, he was swallowing their world in silence. We came to realize that there was nothing that these patients, robbed as they were of health and wholeness, appreciated more in their entire hospital stay.

1 Obstetrics

Sources Royal College of Obstetricians and Gynaecologists; *BMJ*. *Cochrane childbirth & pregnancy database* (www.liv.ac.uk/lstm/ehcap/PC/nwc-pc1.html).

Relevant pages elsewhere: Neonatology p 107–22; breastfeeding p 124–6; rhesus disease p 116; ectopic pregnancy p 262; abortion and termination p 258–9; trophoblastic disease p 264; fibroids in pregnancy p 277; neonatal examination p 114; preterm and light-for-dates babies p 128; cystic fibrosis p 162; varicella (chickenpox) in pregnancy p 144; parvovirus B19 p 142; post-natal depression p 408.

1 The term *pregnancy-induced hypertension with proteinuria* is tending to replace the term *pre-eclampsia*. We have not followed this trend as to do so obscures the vital fact about pre-eclampsia: it may lead on to eclampsia. We favour *pre-eclampsia* because it is short and sends the shadow of a shiver down our spines, being a reminder of how dangerous it can be.

We thank Ms Alison Peattie—our Specialist Reader for this chapter.

The essence of reproductive health

Pregnancy is a risky affair, not only for babies, but also for mothers. The textbook causes of maternal mortality in the UK are pulmonary embolism, eclampsia, haemorrhage, and infection, with all the other causes being rare. But if an obstetrician could be granted one wish, it would not be to abolish these; rather it would be to make every pregnancy *planned* and *desired by the mother*. Worldwide, a woman dies every minute from the effects of pregnancy, and most of these women never wanted to be pregnant in the first place—but either had no means of contraception, or were without the skills, authority, and self-confidence to negotiate with their partners. So the real killers are poverty, ignorance, and the unwieldy desires of men, and the real solutions entail literacy, economic growth, and an equality of dialogue between the sexes. Any obstetric or governmental initiatives in reproductive health which do not recognize these facts are doomed.[1]

School-based sex education This *can* be effective, if linked to easy access to contraceptive services. This is the conclusion of a meta-analysis, taking into account cohort studies (if meta-analyses confine themselves to the 15-or so randomized studies, no benefit could be shown.)[2] It may be necessary to foster a knowledge-sharing, skill-promoting environment that is part of a continuing process, and not a 'one-off' affair—for educational programmes to work. ***Adolescent pregnancy rates:*** USA: 116/1000; UK: 57/1000; Canada: 50/1000.

In the UK, 2,027,900 babies were born in 2000–2 (live & stillbirths), and 563,379 pregnancies were legally terminated. The average age of a UK mother in 2002 was 29.3 years.

Definitions

Gravidity refers to the number of pregnancies that a woman has had (to any stage).

Parity refers to pregnancies that resulted in delivery beyond 28 weeks' gestation. An example of the shorthand way of expressing pregnancies before and after 28 weeks is: para 2+1. This means that she has had 2 pregnancies beyond 28 completed weeks' gestation, and 1 which terminated prior to 28 weeks. If she is not pregnant at the time of describing her she is gravida 3, but if she is pregnant now she is gravida 4. Twins present a problem as there is controversy as to whether they count as 1 for both parity and gravidity or should count as 2 for parity.

It is unclear whether the cut-off point in these definitions should now be 24 weeks, to harmonize with the new definition of stillbirth (p 82). In general, aim to use proper English rather than the shorthand described above, which is open to ambiguity. For example, when presenting a patient try something like: 'Mrs Cottard is a 32-year-old lady who is 15 weeks into her 4th pregnancy; the 3rd ended in a miscarriage at 17 weeks, and the others came to term with normal deliveries of children who are now 2 & 8.' The bald statement 'Para 2+1' is ambiguous, incomprehensible to the patient, and misses the point that the patient is now approaching the time when she lost her last baby.

Pre-pregnancy counselling

The aim is to help prospective parents embark upon pregnancy under conditions most likely to ensure optimal wellbeing for the fetus. Babies conceived 18–23 months after a live birth have the lowest rate of perinatal problems.[3] Ensure that a woman is rubella (and chickenpox, p 144) immune prior to pregnancy and all women should have their need for thromboprophylaxis in pregnancy considered (p 16). Other areas covered include:

- Optimal control of chronic disease (eg diabetes) before conception. This is also important for hypothyroidism as the fetus cannot make thyroxine until 12 weeks and under-replacement may affect neurodevelopment. Strict diet is essential peri-conceptually for women with phenylketonuria (PKU).
- Stop teratogens or seek expert advice prior to conception (p 29).
- Medication to protect the fetus from abnormality (eg folate supplements for neural tube defects, p 140 and below).
- Provide expert information for those at ↑risk of abnormality so pregnancy or its avoidance is an informed choice, and any tests needed (eg chorionic villus sampling, p 10) are planned. Regional genetic services give detailed pre-pregnancy counselling. See p 154. In relevant ethnic populations, take blood for thalassaemia and sickle-cell tests (p 22).
- If past/family history of thromboembolism, screen for thrombophilia.

Diet To prevent neural tube defects and cleft lip, all should have folate-rich foods and folic acid 0.4mg daily (eg Preconceive®) from before conception—until 13 weeks' gestation (5mg/day PO if history of neural tube defect, some epileptic drugs p 29). These foods have >0.1mg of folic acid per serving: Brussels sprouts, asparagus, spinach, black-eye beans, fortified breakfast cereals. Avoid liver and vitamin A (vitamin A embryopathy risk).

Smoking decreases ovulations, causes abnormal sperm production (± less penetrating capacity), ↑rates of miscarriage (×2), and is associated with preterm labour and lighter-for-dates babies (mean is 3376g in non-smoker; smoker: 3200g). Reduced reading ability in smokers' children up to 11yrs old shows that long-term effects are important. ~17% of smoking mothers stop before or in pregnancy.

Search for those who need counselling most:

- Diabetes mellitus
- Tropical travellers
- Frequent abortion
- Hypothyroidism
- Epilepsy
- Rubella-susceptible
- Pet-owners (toxoplasmosis risk is ↑)
- Phenylketonuria
- BP↑
- SLE
- Genetic history, eg:
  Spina bifida etc.
  Thalassaemia
  Duchenne's
  Cystic fibrosis
  Many others

Alcohol consumption High levels of consumption are known to cause the fetal alcohol syndrome (p 138). Moderate drinking has not been shown to adversely affect the fetus but alcohol does cross the placenta and may affect the fetal brain. Miscarriage rates are higher among drinkers of alcohol. NICE recommends <1unit/24h. To cut consumption: see p 513.

Spontaneous abortion (SA) At least 12% of first pregnancies spontaneously abort. Rates after 1 SA are increased to ~24%; after 2 SA to ~36%; after 3 to ~32% and after 4 to ~25%, so chances of a future pregnancy succeeding are ~2 in 3. Pregnancy order of SA/live pregnancies is also relevant: the more recent a live birth the more likely next time will be successful.

Recurrent spontaneous abortion/miscarriage See p 261.

Booking criteria and home delivery

Most women in the UK have 'shared' obstetric care—ie most of their antenatal care is from their GP and community midwife, with limited (often 1) visits (usually 2) to the hospital to see the consultant under whose care they are delivered, returning home 6–48h after birth for postnatal care. A minority receive their complete care from hospitals, and the usual reasons for this would be that their GP did not provide obstetric services, or that the complications of pregnancy made full consultant care more desirable. Some women are cared for by community midwifery staff and their GP, giving continuity to women. Women are receiving all their care from midwives—with medical staff involvement only if complications arise. Delivery may be at hospital in GP units (which may or may not be geographically isolated from consultant units) or at home. There is rigorous evidence that consultant input into antenatal care of normal pregnancies achieves no added benefits (p 8)—but risk factors making specialist visits and booking desirable are generally agreed (BOX).

Risk factors—vis à vis

The mother
- ≥40yrs old
- <20 or >35 years
- History of infertility
- past pregnancies
- Height <5ft
- Primip >35yrs old
- Very obese
- Spine deformation
- [illegible]

Past deliveries
- Preterm or small (<37 weeks, <2.5kg)
- Deformity, stillbirth or neonatal death
- Caesarean section or hysterotomy
- Retained placenta
- Placental abruption
- Bad postpartum haemorrhage
- Intrauterine growth retardation
- [illegible]
- Malpresentations after 36 weeks
- Serum α-fetoprotein ↑

This pregnancy
- Cardiac disease
- Thyroid disease
- Multiple pregnancy
- Rh antibodies (p 116)

Is it safe for low-risk mothers to deliver in high-technology hospitals? Here interventions, with their complications, are more common. In the UK, this question is usually academic as most GPs are reluctant to undertake births—and a 6-month Senior House Officer training in obstetrics gives scant skill. The rising birth rate and service pressures are driving these GP hospitals under great strain. In places (eg New Zealand, Holland) where delivery outside of big hospitals is the norm, there is fairly good (but not uncontested) evidence that on all measures, and in all but the highest risk groups, big hospitals come out less favourably. The few trials seeming to favour high-technology are now recognized to be seriously flawed.

Home delivery (Rare in the UK—1% of births; of these, only ⅔ are booked in advance for home delivery.) We cannot draw valid conclusions from the sparse data comparing morbidity and mortality in home vs hospital deliveries; home delivery is so rare. But an important observation is that rapid intervention is necessary to save life (maternal or fetal) in ~5% of low-risk pregnancies. This pinpoints the need for any domiciliary service to have good equipment available for home delivery and good emergency back-up (eg by emergency obstetric ambulance hosts—ie specially trained ambulance personnel who, it is to be hoped, will liaise directly with senior medical obstetric staff in hospital).

Birthroom birth This offers a homely birth in congenial surroundings with labour ward facilities nearby if needed. The mother is attended by her GP and community midwife. A randomized trial showed that mothers' satisfaction was greater, and nearly all requested this type of delivery for future births. GP units may offer a compromise to advocates of home delivery.

1 [illegible]

Booking criteria and home delivery

Most women in the UK have 'shared obstetric care'—ie most of their antenatal care is from the GP and community midwife, with limited (or no) visits (usually 2) to the hospital to see the consultant under whose care they are delivered, returning home (eg after 6–72h) for postnatal care. A minority receive their complete care from hospitals and the usual reasons for this would be that their GP did not provide obstetric services, or that the complications of pregnancy made full consultant care more desirable. Some women are cared for by community midwifery staff and their GP, but increasingly, low-risk women are receiving all their care from midwives, with medical staff involvement only if complications arise. Delivery may be at hospital, in GP units (which may or may not be geographically isolated from consultant units), or, rarely, at home. ►There is quite good evidence that consultant input into antenatal care of normal pregnancies achieves no added benefits (p 8)—but risk factors making specialist visits and booking desirable are generally agreed (BOX).

Is it safe for low-risk mothers to deliver in high-technology hospitals? Here interventions with their complications are more common. In the UK this question is usually academic as most GPs are reluctant to conduct births—and 6 months' Senior House Officer training in obstetrics gives scant skill. The rising birth rate and service pressures are putting these big hospitals under great strain. In places (eg New Zealand, Holland) where delivery outside of big hospitals is the norm, there is fairly clear (but not uncontested) evidence that on all measures, and in all but the highest risk groups, big hospitals come out less favourably. The few trials seeming to favour high-technology are now recognized to be seriously flawed.

Home delivery (Rare in the UK: ~1% of births, of these only ⅔ are booked in advance for home delivery). We cannot draw valid conclusions from the sparse data comparing morbidity and mortality in home *vs* hospital delivery, as home delivery is so rare. But an important observation is that rapid intervention is necessary to save life (maternal or fetal) in ~5% of low-risk pregnancies. This pinpoints the need for any domiciliary service to have good equipment available for home delivery and good emergency back-up (eg by emergency obstetric ambulance units—ie specially trained ambulance personnel who, it is to be hoped, will liaise directly with senior medical obstetric staff in hospital).

Risk factors—vis à vis:

The mother:
- >40yrs old
- Nullip <20 or >34yrs
- History of infertility
- ≥5 past pregnancies
- Multip <154cm tall
- Primip <158cm tall
- Very obese
- Social deprivation
- HBsAg or HIV+ve p 34

Past deliveries:
- Preterm or small (<37 weeks, <2.5kg)
- Deformity, stillbirth, or neonatal death
- Caesarean section[1]
- Hysterotomy
- Retained placenta/PPH
- Placental abruption
- Had pelvic floor repair
- Instrumental deliveries
- Poor fetal growth or wellbeing
- Diabetes, ↑BP, anaemia
- Malpresentations after 34 weeks
- Serum α-fetoprotein↑

This pregnancy:
- Cardiac disease
- Thyroid disease
- Multiple pregnancy
- Rh antibodies (p 116)

Birthroom birth This offers a homely birth in congenial surroundings with labour ward facilities nearby, if needed. The mother is attended by her GP and community midwife. A randomized trial showed that mothers' satisfaction is great, and nearly all requested this type of delivery for future births.[RCT 4] It may offer a compromise to adherents of home delivery.

1 R Windrim 2005 *Lancet* **365** 106 (the chief complication if past Caesar is uterine rupture)

Issues surrounding home delivery[1]

►*Remember that normal delivery is a retrospective diagnosis.*

- In the UK, because of past hospital experience of many abnormal labours, GPs are often *very* wary of home birth.
- Medico-legal aspects tend to dominate thoughts about worse-case scenarios—so that few GPs willingly take on intrapartum care.
- It's not clear who is to do the doctor's ordinary work when absent on a home delivery—if a mother particularly wants their GP present. Some small surgeries have had to close during delivery as no locum was available—an unacceptable consequence of offering mothers extra choice. NB: in the UK, midwives, but not GPs, have a statutory duty to help at home deliveries.
- It is not clear if there is a ready supply of doctors or midwives with the necessary experience in suturing and neonatal resuscitation. Where there is a good team, there is no doubt that home delivery can be a safe and rewarding experience.
- It has to be remembered that decisions about the place of labour are dynamic, and need revising (eg in 29%) as events in pregnancy unfold. It is not always clear how these decisions are to be taken, and how they are to be communicated.
- Necessary equipment is not readily available, eg Entonox®, —and we have not been able to get blood on site so as to be prepared for possible exsanguination.
- The key factor in increasing choice about home delivery is a good working relationship between the parents, the GP, and the midwife. Where this exists, ~70% of home delivery requests tend to come to fruition; where the GP is rated as being unsupportive, in a UK context, this figure drops to 54%.
- Everyone needs to know that transfer in labour is common in labours starting off as planned home deliveries (14%)—but that this need not mean that there is excess morbidity.
- It is salutary to note that in 1994–5 only 18.5% of pregnancies in England and Wales were considered 'normal' and without antenatal or postnatal complications.[5] If normal delivery is defined as delivery without use of general anaesthetic, induction, epidural, instrumentation or surgical intervention, the normal delivery rate in England in 2003 was 46%.[1]

1 *NHS Maternity Statistics, England:* 2003–04 available at www.dh.gov.uk

Physiological changes in pregnancy

Hormonal changes ***Progesterone***, synthesized by the corpus luteum until 35 post-conception days and by the placenta mainly thereafter, it decreases smooth muscle excitability (uterus, gut, ureters) and raises body temperature. ***Oestrogens*** (90% oestriol) increase breast and nipple growth, water retention and protein synthesis. The maternal thyroid often enlarges due to increased colloid production. Thyroxine levels, see p 25. Pituitary secretion of *prolactin* rises throughout pregnancy. Maternal *cortisol* output is increased but unbound levels remain constant.

Genital changes The 100g non-pregnant uterus weighs 1100g by term. Muscle hyperplasia occurs up to 20 weeks, with stretching after that. The cervix may develop ectropion ('erosions'). Late in pregnancy cervical collagen reduces. Vaginal discharge increases due to cervical ectopy, cell desquamation, and ↑ mucus production from a vasocongested vagina.

Haemodynamic changes ***Blood:*** From 10 weeks the plasma volume rises until 32 weeks when it is 3.8 litres (50% >non-pregnant). Red cell volume rises from 1.4 litres when non-pregnant to 1.64 litres at term if iron supplements not taken (↑18%), or 1.8 litres at term (↑30%) if supplements are taken—hence Hb falls due to dilution (physiological 'anaemia'). WCC (mean 10.5×10^9/L), platelets, ESR (up 4-fold), cholesterol, β-globulin, and fibrinogen are raised. Albumin and gamma-globulin fall.

Cardiovascular: Cardiac output rises from 5 litres/min to 6.5–7 litres/min in the first 10 weeks by increasing stroke volume (10%) and pulse rate (by ~15 beats/min). Peripheral resistance falls (due to hormonal changes). BP, particularly diastolic, falls during the first and second trimesters by 10–20mmHg, then rises to non-pregnant levels by term. With increased venous distensibility, and raised venous pressure (as occurs with any pelvic mass), varicose veins may form. Vasodilatation and hypotension stimulates renin and angiotensin release—an important feature of BP regulation in pregnancy.

Other changes Ventilation increases 40% (tidal volume rises from 500 to 700mL), the increased depth of breath being a progesterone effect. O_2 consumption increases only 20%. Breathlessness is common as maternal P_aCO_2 is set lower to allow the fetus to offload CO_2. Gut motility is reduced, resulting in constipation, delayed gastric emptying, and with a lax cardiac sphincter, heartburn. Renal size increases by ~1cm in length during pregnancy.

Frequency of micturition emerges early (glomerular filtration rate ↑ by 60%), later from bladder pressure by the fetal head. The bladder muscle is lax but residual urine after micturition is not normally present. Skin pigmentation (eg in linea nigra, nipples, or as chloasma—brown patches of pigmentation seen especially on the face), palmar erythema, spider naevi, and striae are common. Hair shedding from the head is reduced in pregnancy but the extra hairs are shed in the puerperium.

Pregnancy tests Positive eg from two weeks post-conception (or from the first day of the first missed period), until ~20 weeks of pregnancy, they remain positive for ~5 days after abortion or fetal death. Otherwise, the false +ve rate is low. They detect the β-subunit of human chorionic gonadotrophin in early morning urine, so are positive in trophoblastic disease (p 264).

Antenatal care

The aims of antenatal care are to: •Detect any disease in the mother •Ameliorate the discomforts of pregnancy •Monitor and promote fetal wellbeing •Prepare mother for birth •Monitor trends to prevent or detect any early complications of pregnancy (p48) (the most important variable [illegible], p 49) •Is thromboprophylaxis needed? (p 16).

Who should give antenatal care? Midwives may manage care, calling in doctors only if a specific need arises.

The 1st antenatal visit is very comprehensive: •Find a language interpreter if she needs one. Avoid using relatives (confidentiality issues). **History:** •Usual cycle length, LMP (and normal period?) Nägele's rule: expected delivery date: 9 months and 7 days after LMP (minus 3 months from first day of last period + 7 days). Pill withdrawal bleed for cycles shorter than 28 days subtract the difference from 28; if longer add the difference from 28. A revised rule suggests the addition of 10 days rather than 7 is more accurate.

•Contraception; drugs; past history eg surgery to abdomen or pelvis. •Any fertility problems, outcome and complications of past pregnancies. •Is there a family history of diabetes, BP↑, fetal abnormality, or twins? •Does she have concurrent illness (p 20–35)? If past or family history of DVT or embolism, test for thrombophilia.

•Does she have history of psychiatric illness? (esp. if severe or previous postnatal problems), arrange antenatal assessment and management plan, with easy access notes in case of relapse or recurrence.

•Is she poor (eg asylum seeker)? Is supply cut off? Unmarried? Unsupported? Subject to domestic violence? (Screen p 16.) A substance misuser? (See p 362.) •Advise on avoiding pâtés and blue and soft cheeses (Listeria) [illegible], Camembert; to avoid uncooked eggs (Salmonella p 511); avoid vitamin A tablets and liver (p 21). For prevention of toxoplasmosis advice see p 34.

Examination: Check heart, lungs, BP, weight (record BMI and advice on interventions if needed). Any varicose veins?

Tests: Blood: Hb, group, antibodies if Rh–ve (p 116); syphilis & rubella serology; HBsAg (p 26 & p 28); HIV test (counselling, p 26 & p 582); sickle test if black; thalassaemia if relevant (p 23). MSU for asymptomatic bacteriuria. Arrange tests to exclude Down's (p 12) if she is [illegible] or [illegible]. Use hospital/worker consider CXR after 14 weeks.

•Offer early ultrasound to establish dates, exclude multiple pregnancy and aid with Down's tests; and 18–20 week anomaly scans.

Suggest: Parentcraft/relaxation classes; dental visits (free); enquire about diet and smoking. Consider need for iron and folate (p 33 and p 24).

Advise on: Smoking, alcohol, diet, correct use of seat belt (straps over and below the bump, not over it), and exercise; lead safe sex. Enquire knowledge of social security benefits (used pregnancy and they are OK taking? make) travel up to 36 weeks (or most airlines) (see thromboprophylaxis p 16); intercourse is fine if no vaginal bleeding.

Later visits Check urine for albumin and fundal height. Check lie and presentation at 36 weeks. Do Hb and Rh antibodies at 28 & 34 weeks and give anti-D then if needed (p 9). Visits in low-risk women should be at 16, 18–20, 25, 28, 31, 34, 36, 38, 40 and 41 weeks (primips). Weigh only if clinically indicated.

The head is usually engaged (p 40) by 37 weeks in Caucasian primips. If not, consider large (or malpositioned) head, small pelvis or obstruction (placenta praevia) or wrong estimation of dates.

[illegible]

Antenatal care

The aims of antenatal care are to: •Detect any disease in the mother •Ameliorate the discomforts of pregnancy •Monitor and promote fetal well-being •Prepare mothers for birth •Monitor trends to prevent or detect any early complications of pregnancy: BP is the most important variable (eclampsia, p 48). •Is thromboprophylaxis needed? (p 16)

Who should give antenatal care? Midwives may manage care, calling in doctors *only if a specific need arises.*

The 1st antenatal visit is very comprehensive. ►Find a language interpreter if she needs one. Avoid using relatives (confidentiality issues). ***History:***

- Usual cycle length; LMP (a normal period?); Naegele's rule: expected delivery date ≈1yr and 7 days after LMP minus 3 months—(not if last period a Pill withdrawal bleed; for cycles shorter than 28 days subtract the difference from 28; if longer, add the difference from 28). A revised rule suggests the addition of 10 days rather than 7 is more accurate.
- Contraception; drugs; past history, eg surgery to abdomen or pelvis.
- Any fertility problems; outcome and complications of past pregnancies.
- Is there family history of diabetes, BP↑, fetal abnormality, or twins?
- Does she have concurrent illness (p 20–35)? If past or family history of DVT or embolism, screen for thrombophilia.
- Does she have history of psychiatric illness? If serious, or previous postnatal problems arrange antenatal assessment and management plan written in case notes in case of relapse or recurrence.[1]
- Is she *poor* (eg gas/electricity supply cut off)? *Unmarried? Unsupported? Subject to domestic violence*? (See p 514.) *A substance abuser*? (See p 362.)
- Advise on avoiding pâtés and blue and soft cheeses in mould rinds, eg Brie, Camembert (to avoid listeria, p 35 and *OHCM* p 591); avoid vitamin tablets and liver (p 2). Prevention of toxoplasmosis advice see p 34.

Examination: Check heart, lungs, BP, weight (record BMI), and abdomen. Is a cervical smear needed? Any varicose veins?

Tests: Blood: Hb, group (antibodies if Rh–ve, p 116), syphilis & rubella serology, HBsAg (p 36 & p 26) HIV test (counselling, *OHCM* p 582); sickle test if black, Hb electrophoresis if relevant (p 22). Take an MSU (protein; bacteria). Arrange tests to exclude Downs (p 12). If she is foreign or a TB contact or is a hospital worker, consider CXR after 14 weeks.

Offer early ultrasound to establish dates, exclude multiple pregnancy and aid with Downs tests and an 18–20 week anomaly scan.

Suggest: Parentcraft/relaxation classes; dental visit. Enquire about problems and anxieties. Consider need for *iron and folate* (p 85 and p 22).

Advise on: Smoking, alcohol, diet, correct use of seat belts (above the bump, below the bump, but not over it) and adequate rest. Ensure knowledge of social security benefits. Usual exercise and travel are OK (avoid malarious areas) up to 34 weeks on most airlines (see thromboprophylaxis, p 16). Intercourse is fine if no vaginal bleeding.

Later visits Check urine for albumin, BP, fundal height. Check lie and presentation at 36 weeks. Do Hb and Rh antibodies at 28 & 34 weeks and give anti-D then if needed (p 9). Visits are at <12 weeks then at 16, 18–20, 25, 28, 31, 34, 36, 38, 40 and 41 weeks (primip). Weigh only if clinically indicated.

The head is usually engaged (p 40) by 37 weeks in caucasian primips (if not, consider: large (or malpositioned) head, small pelvis or obstruction, placenta praevia, or wrong estimation of dates).

1 M Oates 2004 Chapter 11A in Why Mothers Die; *Confidential Enquiry into Maternal and Child Health* 2000-2

Using anti-D immunoglobulin

Dose 250U for gestations <20 weeks, 500U if >20 weeks. Give into deltoid (buttock absorption is too slow) as soon as possible after incident, at latest within 72h. After 20 weeks do Kleihauer test (FBC bottle of maternal blood; fetal RBCs therein are less susceptible to lysis, enabling them to be counted, so measuring the bleed's volume).

Postnatal use: 500U is the normal dose after 20 weeks' gestation. 37% of Rh-ve women give birth to Rh-ve babies and these women do not need anti-D.

- Anti-D should be given to all Rh-ve women where the baby's group cannot be determined (eg macerated stillbirths), or if circumstances are such that the baby's group is unknown 72h post delivery.
- Do a Kleihauer test on all eligible for anti-D. 500U anti-D can suppress immunization by up to 4mL of fetal red cells (8mL of fetal blood), but 1% of women have transplacental haemorrhage (TPH) of >4mL, especially after manual removal of placenta, and with caesarean section. A Kleihauer test is especially important in stillbirth, as massive spontaneous transplacental haemorrhage can be the cause of fetal death. Where >4mL TPH is suggested by the Kleihauer screen, a formal estimation of the TPH volume is required and 500U anti-D given for every 4mL fetal cells transfused (maximum 5000U anti-D at 2 IM sites/24h). Note: Kleihauer tests can be negative where there is ABO incompatibility as fetal cells are rapidly cleared from the maternal circulation. Liaise with the Transfusion Service. Check maternal blood every 48h to determine clearance of cells and need for continuing anti-D.
- Don't give prenatal anti-D if antibodies to anti-D are present.
- Any mother receiving anti-D prenatally (see below), should also receive it postnatally unless she delivers an Rh-negative baby.

Use of anti-D in abortion in rhesus negative mothers

1. Anti-D should be given to all having surgical or medical terminations of pregnancy unless they are already known to have anti-D antibodies. Give 250U if <20 weeks; 500U (and Kleihauer) if >20 weeks' gestation.
2. Anti-D should always be given where spontaneous abortion is followed by instrumentation.
3. Anti-D should be given where spontaneous complete abortion occurs after 12 weeks' gestation.
4. With threatened abortion after 12 weeks give anti-D; if bleeding continues intermittently give anti-D 6-weekly until delivery.
5. Routine anti-D is not recommended with threatened miscarriage before 12 weeks' gestation (but consider if viable fetus, heavy or repeated bleeding, and abdominal pain).

Use of anti-D in pregnancy in Rh–ve mothers

1. Give anti-D 500U at 28 and 34 weeks to rhesus negative women (primip antenatal sensitization falls from 1.5% to 0.2%).
   Anti-D may still be detectable in maternal blood at delivery. Still give postnatal anti-D, if indicated (as above).
2. When significant TPH may occur: with chorionic villus sampling; external cephalic version; APH; uterine procedures (eg amniocentesis, fetal blood sampling); abdominal trauma; intrauterine death. Use 250U before 20 weeks' gestation, 500U (and do Kleihauer) after 20 weeks.
3. Anti-D should be given in cases of ectopic pregnancy.
4. For threatened abortion see above.

Prenatal diagnosis

'The first half of pregnancy can become a time of constant 'exams' to see if the baby can be allowed to graduate to the second half of pregnancy'. Those at high and, increasingly, those at low risk of having an abnormal baby are offered prenatal diagnosis to allow better treatment of the expected defect, or (more often) if they would wish to terminate any abnormal fetus.

High-risk pregnancies • Maternal age >35 (chromosome defects).
• Previous abnormal baby or family history of inherited condition.

Problems ►*Anxiety while false +ve results are sorted out is a big problem.*
• Terminating normal fetuses, eg ♂ fetus of carriers of X-linked conditions.
• Most abnormalities are in low-risk groups (∴ missable by selective screening).
• Services available, their quality, and populations made eligible, vary widely.
• Termination of female fetuses in cultures valuing males more highly.
• Devaluation of positive view of handicapped or 'special needs' children.

Ultrasound At 11–14 weeks is useful for dating pregnancy and for nuchal translucency screening (see BOX). Further anomaly scan is at ~18 weeks. Skilled operators can detect many external and internal structural anomalies. See p 46, and opposite.

Ultrasound is best at detecting externally impinging structural abnormalities, eg anencephaly/spina bifida. Internal structural abnormality detection rate, eg for heart disease and diaphragmatic hernia, remains <50%. Fetuses with false +ve suggestion of abnormality are mostly associated with 'soft signs' on ultrasound, eg nuchal thickening (eg trisomy 21), choroid plexus cysts (trisomies 18 and 21), and echogenic bowel (trisomy 21 and cystic fibrosis). Use of 'soft signs' may increase false +ves 12-fold.

α-Fetoprotein (AFP) AFP is a glycoprotein synthesized by the fetal liver and GI tract. Fetal levels fall after 13 weeks, but maternal (transplacental) serum AFP continues to rise to 30 weeks. Maternal AFP is measured at 17 weeks. In 10% with a high AFP there is a fetal malformation, eg an open neural tube defect (but closed defects are missed), exomphalos, posterior urethral valves, nephrosis, GI obstruction, teratomas, Turner's syndrome (or normal twins). In ~30% of those with no malformation, there is an adverse outcome, eg placental abruption and third trimester deaths. ►Monitor closely. 1 in 40 with a low AFP have a chromosomal abnormality (eg Down's). AFP is lower in diabetic mothers. NB: as this test is nonspecific on its own, it is of use for preliminary screening; those with abnormal values may be offered further tests (see below, and p 12 for the 'quadruple test').

Amniocentesis is done under ultrasound guidance. Fetal loss rate is 0.5–1% at ~16 weeks' gestation, but ~5% for early amniocentesis at 10–13 weeks. Amniotic fluid AFP is measured (a more accurate screen for neural tube defects than maternal serum), and cells in the fluid are cultured for karyotyping (+enzyme and gene probe analysis). Cell culture takes 3wks, so an abnormal pregnancy must be terminated at a late stage.

Chorionic villus biopsy At 10+ weeks, placenta is sampled by transcervical catheter or transabdominal needle (favoured approach as less pregnancy loss and fewer multiple attempts)[1] under ultrasound guidance. Karyotyping takes 2 days, enzyme and gene probe analysis 3 weeks, so termination for abnormality is earlier, safer, and less distressing than after amniocentesis. Fetal loss rate is ~4%. Use up to 20 weeks (cordocentesis preferable thereafter). It does not detect neural tube defects—and may cause fetal malformation.

Fetoscopy is carried out at ~18wks with ultrasound guidance to find external malformations, do fetal blood samples, or biopsy. Fetal loss rate is ~4%.

1 Z Alfirevic 2003 *Cochrane Database Syst Rev* (3) CD003252

Obstetrics

High resolution ultrasound and fetal nuchal translucency

- Early scans (at 11-14 weeks) may detect 59% of those with structural abnormality and 78% of those with chromosome abnormality. It is especially good for detecting CNS defects, neck abnormalities, GI, and renal defects: less good for spina bifida, heart, and limb defects. With a combination of early and later scans up to 81% of malformations may be diagnosed.[7]
- Fluid accumulation in the neck at 10-14 weeks' gestation (increased fetal nuchal translucency, FNT) may reflect fetal heart failure,[8] and be seen in serious anomaly of the heart and great arteries.[9] Meta-analysis shows that taking the 99th percentile as a cut off for cardiac screening enables 33% of heart abnormalities to be detected antenatally.[1] Referring 99th percentile fetuses for echocardiography may show 106 cardiac abnormalities per 1000 fetuses examined.[2]
- There is a strong association between chromosomal abnormality and FNT. In one study, 84% of karyotypically proven trisomy 21 fetuses had a nuchal translucency >3mm at 10-13 weeks' gestation (as did 4.5% of chromosomally normal fetuses).
- The greater the extent of FNT, the greater the risk of abnormality.
- Nuchal translucency screening may be used to see who may benefit from more invasive chorionic villus sampling (or amniocentesis p 10, which may delineate the precise chromosomal abnormality, eg trisomies). Note: positive predictive value of screening is 4% so 96% of women with a 'positive' test undergo an 'unnecessary' invasive procedure (chorionic villus sampling in the first trimester or amniocentesis in the second trimester). If nuchal screening was used as the *only* screening test 2 or 3 normal pregnancies would be lost after chorionic villus sampling, and 1 after amniocentesis, for every 4 pregnancies correctly detected with trisomy 21.
- It is useful for screening twins as early detection is best, for if selective fetocide is to be used risk of miscarriage is 3-fold higher if done after 16 weeks. Monochorionic twins have a higher false +ve rate for nuchal translucency thickness than dichorionic twins or singletons.
- Note that the degree of neck flexion during the ultrasound examination may influence nuchal measurements.
- Adding nasal bone screening at 11-14 week ultrasound to increase sensitivity and reduce the false positive rate of screening for Down's syndrome has been suggested. Its use is currently only recommended in a research setting. In a general population setting, however, it is only measurable in 76% of fetuses and is felt to add little useful information.[3]
- Systematic review shows of all chromosomally normal fetuses (euploid) with significant nuchal thickening, 70-90% have normal outcome, 2.2-10.6% miscarry, 0.5-12.7% have neurodevelopmental problems, and 2.1-7.6% of malformations were undiagnosed before birth.[4]

1 G Makrydimas 2003 *Am J Obstet Gynecol* **189** 1330
2 F McAuliffe 2004 *Am J Obstet Gynecol* **191** 1486
3 F Malone 2004 *Obstet Gynecol* **104** 1222
4 R Maymon 2004 *Clin Genet* **66** 426

Tests to detect Down's syndrome

The first antenatal diagnosis of Down's syndrome was made in 1968. Initially there was amniocentesis for older mothers (Penrose noted association with maternal age in 1933; rates of Down's are 1:1500 babies if mother aged 20, 1:800 if aged 30, 1:270 if aged 35, 1:100 if aged 40, 1:50 if aged 45 or older.) Then screening by blood test was introduced, and nuchal screening (p 11). By 2007 the UK plans nationwide screening with tests giving detection rates of 75% with a false positive rate of <3% (and aims for 60% detection with <5% false positive from 2005). Tests aim to estimate the risk of Down's taking into consideration information from nuchal scanning, blood tests and the woman's age. Where risk of Down's is >1:250 (high risk-estimated to be 5% of pregnancies) she will be offered further tests such a chorionic villus sampling (p 46) and amniocentesis (p 10). Early ultrasound is vital for dating pregnancies for these tests.

The combined test This combines nuchal translucency (NT) + free β-human chorionic gonadotrophin (βHCG) + pregnancy associated plasma protein PrAP-A + the woman's age. Used between 10 weeks 3 days and 13 weeks 6 days. It can achieve detection rates of 95% of all aneuploides, 86% trisomy-21, and 100% of trisomy-18 and trisomy-13. In one study (n=4190), 97.6% took up screening; false positive screening occurred in 6.7%: 7 cases had neural tube defects, and 2 ventral wall defects were picked up on scan. 200 accepted chorionic villus sampling: there was fetal demise in 2 in next 28 days 1 of which had Down's.[1]

The integrated test This is better than the combined test if there are good facilities for nuchal translucency measurements available and the woman is prepared to wait for 2nd trimester results. It involves NT + PrAP-A in the first trimester + the quadruple test in the 2nd trimester.

The quadruple test This combines maternal α-fetoprotein (AFP) + unconjugated estriol + free βHCG or total βHCG + inhibin-A + the woman's age in the second trimester. This test is useful for women presenting in the second trimester.

The emotional cost to the mother is impossible to calculate: From the parents' point of view, a telling statistic is that 56 out of every 57 women under 37yrs old who had a +ve test, proved, after amniocentesis, *not* to have an affected fetus. Amniocentesis causes fetal loss, and these losses will usually be of normal babies. New screening regimens in the 1st trimester go some way to mitigating distress and anxiety.

We have no idea of the best way of counselling parents before the test. If you just hand out a leaflet, few will read it, and then when it comes to amniocentesis and termination, many will refuse—and the screening test wastes money, as well as laying health authorities open to litigation: 'I never understood that I might lose a normal baby…' The alternative is to provide full details at the time of the initial blood test. The irony is that gaining informed consent is then the most expensive part of the test, and one which itself could cause much distress. Imagine an overjoyed expectant mother arriving in the clinic serenely happy in fulfilling her reproductive potential: the quintessence of health. She leaves only after being handed ethical conundrums of quite staggering proportions, involving death, disease, and human sacrifices, and a timetable for their resolution that would leave even the most fast-moving philosopher breathless and disorientated, and which may leave her forever bereft of one of Nature's most generous gifts: the fundamental belief in one's own wholeness.

1 J Wise 2000 *BMJ* 320 733 [@10720346]

Preimplantation genetic diagnosis[1]

Preimplantation genetic diagnosis (PGD) is an early form of prenatal diagnosis in which embryos created *in vitro* are analysed for well-defined genetic defects. Defect free embryos are then used for implantation.

It is used in those with high risk of genetic disease eg carriers of monogenic disease or chromosome structural abnormalities (eg translocations) who have repeatedly terminated pregnancies due to prenatal tests showing abnormality, who have concurrent infertility, who have had recurrent miscarriage (as occurs with translocation carriers), and for those with moral or religious objections to termination.

It may also be used to screen for aneuploidy (PDG-AS) in those undergoing *in vitro* fertilization to enhance chance of ongoing pregnancy (sometimes the case for women >37–40 years old).

Pioneered in the early 1990s, by mid 2001, 3000 PGD cycles had been performed resulting in 700 pregnancies (pregnancy rate 24%), of which 5% of babies had some kind of abnormality. PGD selection of embryos by HLA type so that a child born after using this technology can be used as a stem cell donor to save a sibling from certain conditions is controversial but possible.

Genetic analysis at the single cell level occurs using 1st polar body of an egg, or 2nd polar body (extruded after fertilization and completion of second meiotic division), or using blastomeres from cleavage-stage embryos. The blastocyst is the latest stage from which cells can be used but is little used as it leaves little time for analysis as embryos must be transferred before day 5 or 6. Biopsied surplus embryos can be cryopreserved but implantation rate for these is only 12%.

Fluorescence *in situ* hybridisation (FISH) is used for analysis of chromosomes and polymerase chain reaction (PCR) for analysis of genes in monogenic diseases. PGD can currently be applied for detecting 33 monogenic diseases. Gene analysis for X-linked conditions has the advantage that healthy male embryos and non-carrier female embryos can be transferred. Sexing embryos for X-linked conditions remains useful for conditions where the single gene is not known (eg non-fragile-X X-linked mental retardation), has been judged too difficult a search, and for women eg over 37 who do not wish to wait for specific tests to be developed.

Pregnancy rates are 17% after testing for structural chromosome abnormality (including translocations), 16% after sexing, 21% after testing for monogenic diseases. This is lower than the expected rate of 20–25% expected for regular IVF. For PGD-AS 25% pregnancy rates are achieved overall for women of previously poor prognosis due to advanced maternal age, repeated IVF failure (but only 8% do get pregnant) and recurrent miscarriage (28% pregnancy rate achieved).

1 K Sermon 2004 *Lancet* **363** 1633

The placenta

The placenta is the organ of respiration, nutrition, and excretion for the fetus. It produces hormones for maternal wellbeing and immunologically protects the fetus by preventing rejection and allowing the passage of IgG antibodies from the mother.

Development At term the placenta weighs 1/7th the weight of the baby. It has a blood flow of 600mL/min. The placenta changes throughout pregnancy as calcium is deposited in the villi and fibrin on them. Excess fibrin may be deposited in diabetes and rhesus disease, so ↓ fetal nutrition.

Placental types ***Battledore*** insertion is where the umbilical cord inserts into the side of the placenta. ***Velamentous*** insertion (1%) is where the umbilical vessels pass within the membranes before insertion. If these vessels break (as in vasa praevia) it is fetal blood that is lost. ***Placenta succenturia:*** (5%) There is a separate (succenturiate) lobe away from the main placenta which may fail to separate normally and cause a PPH or puerperal sepsis. ***Placenta membranacea*** (1/3000) is a thin placenta all around the baby. As some is in the lower segment it predisposes to APH. It may fail to separate in the third stage of labour. ***Placenta accreta:*** There is abnormal adherence of all or part of the placenta to the uterus, termed ***placenta increta*** where there is placental infiltration of the myometrium or ***placenta percreta*** if penetration reaches the serosa. These latter 3 types predispose to PPH and may necessitate hysterectomy.

Placenta praevia The placenta lies in the lower uterine segment. It is found in ~0.5% of pregnancies. Risks are of significant haemorrhage by mother and fetus. ***Associations:*** Large placenta (eg twins); uterine abnormalities and fibroids; uterine damage, eg multiparity; former surgery (caesarean section, myomectomy); past infection. Ultrasound at <24 weeks' gestation shows a low-lying placenta in 28% but lower segment development later in pregnancy results in only 3% being low-lying at term. Transvaginal ultrasound is superior to transabdominal for localizing placentas accurately, and, if combined with Doppler, diagnose vasa praevia and placenta accreta. It has not been shown to increase bleeding.

Major (old III and IV degrees) with placenta covering the internal os requires caesarean section for delivery. Minor (old I and II) where the placenta is in the lower segment but not across the internal os: aim for normal delivery unless the placenta encroaches within 2cm of the internal os when vaginal delivery is contraindicated.[1] Presentation may be as APH (separation of the placenta as the lower segment stretches causes bleeding) or as failure for the head to engage ie a high presenting part. Problems are with bleeding and with mode of delivery as the placenta obstructs the os and may shear off during labour, or may be accreta (5%), especially after previous caesarean section (>24%). Poor lower segment contractility predisposes to postpartum haemorrhage. Caesarean section should be consultant-performed or supervised with consultant anaesthetic attendance. The rule of admitting those with major placenta praevia at ≤35 weeks' gestation so that immediate help is available, is controversial, and not practiced by many UK units.[2] Hospitalization is preferable if there is bleeding.[3]

After delivery Examine the placenta for abnormalities (clots, infarcts, amnion nodosum, vasa praevia, single umbilical artery). Weigh the placenta (weight >25% of the baby suggests congenital nephrotic syndrome). Blood may be taken from the cord for Hb, Coombs test, LFTs, and blood group (eg for rhesus disease), or for infection screens, if needed.

1 RCOG Clinical Guideline **27** 2001 Placenta praevia: diagnosis and management
2 Z Penn 2001 *BMJ* **ii** 165
3 M Hall 2004 Ch 4 in *Why Mothers Die; Confidential Enquiry into Maternal and Child Health* 2000-2

Plasma chemistry in pregnancy

Centile	Non-pregnant 2.5	Non-pregnant 97.5	Trimester 1 2.5	Trimester 1 97.5	Trimester 2 2.5	Trimester 2 97.5	Trimester 3 2.5	Trimester 3 97.5
Na^+ mmol/L	138	146	135	141	132	140	133	141
Ca^{2+} mmol/L	2	2.6	2.3	2.5	2.2	2.2	2.2	2.5
*corrected	2.3	2.6	2.25	2.57	2.3	2.5	2.3	2.59
Albumin g/L	44	50	39	49	36	44	33	41
$^{Free}T_4$ pmol/L	9	23	10	24	9	19	7	17
$^{Free}T_3$ pmol/L	4	9	4	8	4	7	3	5
TSH	0	4	0	1.6	1	1.8	7	7.3

Other plasma reference intervals (not analysed by trimester)

	Non-pregnant	*Pregnant*
Alkaline phosphatase IU/L	3-300	up to 450**
Bicarbonate mmol/L	24-30	20-25
Creatinine μmol/L	70-150	24-68
Urea mmol/L	2.5-6.7	2-4.2
Urate μmol/L	150-390	100-270

*Calcium corrected for plasma albumin (see *OHCM* p 694).
**Occasionally very much higher in apparently normal pregnancies.

C-reactive protein does not change much in pregnancy.
TSH may be low in the first half of a normal pregnancy (suppressed by HCG); for other thyroid changes see above and p 25.
Protein S falls in pregnancy, so protein S deficiency is difficult to diagnose. Activated protein C (APC) resistance is found in 40% of pregnancies so special tests are needed when looking for this. Genotyping for Factor V Leiden and prothrombin G20210A are unaffected by pregnancy.

Thromboprophylaxis

►Pregnancy is a hypercoagulable state: consider need for thromboprophylaxis pre-pregnancy, at booking, throughout the antenatal period, at start of labour and once delivered. See below. For caesarean section, see p 78.

Thromboprophylaxis after vaginal delivery:[1]
►In all pregnant women avoid immobility and dehydration.

Risk factors: (Thrombophilia/past thromboembolism considered separately). Women with any **two** of the risk factors opposite (RED BOX):

Treatment: Treat with low molecular weight heparin (LMWH) eg enoxaparin starting as soon as possible after delivery (as long as no postpartum haemorrhage and ≥4h after epidural catheter siting or removal—6h if that was traumatic). Continue for 3-5 days even if at home. Dose of enoxaparin: if the early pregnancy weight (EPW) is 50-90kg, give 40mg/24h SC; if EPW <50kg, give 20mg/24h SC; if EPW >90kg give 40mg/12h SC. If heparin is contra-indicated, use TED compression stockings (TED= transverse elastic graduated). For women with ≥3 persisting risk factors consider antenatal and postnatal prophylaxis, starting as early in pregnancy as possible as risk throughout. Continue normal dose prophylaxis when admitted in labour.

Risk factors:
- Age >35 years old
- BMI >35 or weight >90kg
- Parity ≥4
- Gross varicose veins
- Paraplegia
- Sickle cell disease
- Nephrotic syndrome
- Some cardiac causes
- Past thromboembolism
- Thrombophilia
- Myeloproliferative dis.
- Inflammatory bowel dis.
- Hyperemesis/dehydration
- Pre-eclampsia
- Immobility for ≥4 days
- Ovarian hyperstimulation
- Major infection (eg pyelonephritis)
- Labour lasting >12h
- Mid-cavity forceps
- Excessive blood loss
- Evacuation of retained products of conception
- Postpartum sterilization

Women with history of venous thromboembolism (VTE) ± thrombophilia: Action depends on risk, as follows: *VH* = very high; *HR* = high risk; *MR* = moderate risk.

- If previous VTE and already on long-term warfarin, use high-dose prophylactic LMWH, eg enoxaparin 40mg/12h SC—or a 12-hourly therapeutic dose, eg 1mg/kg (where kg is the early pregnancy weight). This is given prenatally. Withhold at the onset of labour (halve to /24h the day before and the day of induction) and revert to warfarin postpartum. ***(VH)***
- If recurrent VTE: previous VTE and 1st degree relative with VTE or thrombophilia: previous VTE and thrombophilia: or asymptomatic thrombophilia with antithrombin III deficiency, combined defects, homozygous factor V Leiden deficiency, or prothrombin gene defect: give LMWH antenatally and 6 weeks postpartum. ***(HR)***
- If asymptomatic thrombophilia other than types above: or if previous VTE in pregnancy and no other risk factors give LMWH for 6 weeks postpartum (PP) ± low dose aspirin antenatally. ***(MR)***

Air travel; thromboprophylaxis and pregnancy[2] For all gestations until 6 weeks postpartum advise isometric calf exercises good hydration in flight (avoid coffee/alcohol). If flight long-haul (>4h duration) wear knee length graduated compression stockings. If additional risk factors as above wear stockings for short flights and consider LMWH eg enoxaparin 40mg/24h SC pre-flight and next day. If heparin unsuitable use aspirin 75mg/24h PO for 3 days pre-travel and on day of travel.

1 RCOG 2004 Clinical Guideline **37** *Thromboprophylaxis*
2 2001 *Why Mothers Die* RCOG page 75

Minor symptoms of pregnancy

►Before prescribing any drug, think—Is it necessary. Is it safe? Consult *Data-sheets* ± a national teratology information service (0191 232 1525[uk]).

Symptoms and signs in the first 10 weeks: Early symptoms are amenorrhoea, nausea, vomiting, and bladder irritability. Breasts engorge, nipples enlarge (darken at 12 weeks), Montgomery's tubercles (sebaceous glands on nipples) become prominent. Vulval vascularity increases and the cervix softens and looks bluish (4 weeks). At 6–10 weeks the uterine body is more globular. Temperature rises (<37.8°C).

Headaches, palpitations, and fainting are all commoner in pregnancy. Sweating and feeling hot are also common, due to a dilated peripheral circulation. ***Management:*** Increase fluid intake and take showers.

Urinary frequency is due to pressure of the fetal head on the bladder in later pregnancy. Exclude UTI.

Abdominal pain: See p 38.

Breathlessness is common. See p 6.

Constipation tends to occur as gut motility decreases. Adequate oral fluids and a high fibre diet help combat it. Avoid stimulant laxatives—they increase uterine activity in some women. Increased venous distensibility and pelvic congestion predispose to ***haemorrhoids*** (if they prolapse, rest the mother head down, apply ice packs and replace them), and ***varicose veins***. Resting with feet up, and properly worn elastic stockings help.

Reflux oesophagitis and heartburn occur as pyloric sphincter relaxation allows irritant bile to reflux into the stomach. Cigarettes and spices should be avoided, small meals taken, and antacids may be used. Use more pillows, and a semi-recumbent position.

Third trimester backache: Due to pelvic ligament and muscle relaxation, pain tends to be worse at night. A firm mattress, flat shoes, standing with back straight, and pelvic support from physiotherapy all help.

Carpal tunnel syndrome (p 714) in pregnancy is due to fluid retention. Advise wrist splints until delivery cures the problem.

Itch/itchy rashes are common (up to 25%) and may be due to the usual causes (*OHCM* p 76, check LFT—see p 26) or to pruritic eruption of pregnancy (PEP = ***prurigo of pregnancy***)—an intensely itchy papular/plaque rash on the abdomen and limbs. PEP is most common in first pregnancies beyond 35 weeks' gestation. Emollients and weak topical steroids ease it. Delivery cures it. If vesicles are present, think of ***pemphigoid gestationis*** (PG): a rare (1:50,000) condition which may cause fatal heat loss and cardiac failure; the baby may be briefly affected; refer early (prednisolone may be needed). PG may recur in later pregnancies.

Ankle oedema: This is very common, almost normal manifestation of pregnancy. Measure BP and check urine for protein (pre-eclampsia, p 48). Check legs for DVT. It often responds to rest and leg elevation. Reassure that it is harmless (unless pre-eclampsia).

Leg cramps 33% get cramp, the latter half of pregnancy, severe in 5%, often worse at night. Raising the foot of the bed by 20cm will help.

Chloasma: This is a patch of darker pigmentation, eg on the face: p 586.

Nausea affects ~80%. ***Vomiting*** occurs in ~50%. It may start by 4 weeks and decline over the following weeks. At 20 weeks 20% may still vomit. Most respond to frequent small meals, reassurance, and a stress-free environment. It is associated with good outcome (fewer fetal losses).

Hyperemesis gravidarum

This is defined as persisting vomiting in pregnancy which causes weight loss (>15% of body mass) and ketosis. It affects 1% of pregnant women. Risk is increased in youth, non-smokers, primips, working outside home, in those with previous eating disorders and multiple, or molar pregnancy (hence the idea that excessively high HCG levels may be the cause—whereas steeply rising oestrogens may cause the very common feature of morning sickness). Rarely, hyperemesis has been fatal.

Presentation Inability to keep food or fluids down; weight↓ (2–5kg) ± nutritional deficiency, dehydration, hypovolaemia, tachycardia, postural hypotension, electrolyte disturbance with hypokalaemia and hyponatraemic shock, polyneuritis (B vitamins↓), behaviour disorders, liver and renal failure. There may be ptyalism (inability to swallow saliva) and spitting.

Tests Do PCV and U&E to help guide IV fluid regimen. 50% have abnormal LFTs (usually raised aminotransferase and bilirubin). TFTs are abnormal in 60% of those with hyperemesis. This is biochemical hyperthyroidism with raised free thyroxine and suppressed TSH. In women with hyperemesis thyroxine is converted to reverse tri-iodothyronine in the tissues which is physiologically inactive so stimulating metabolic rate less and conserving energy stores. The severity of hyperemesis correlates with the degree of biochemical hyperthyroidism, and those with abnormal TFTs require longer hospitalisation to prevent readmission. The biochemical hyperthyroidism settles as vomiting settles so does not require treatment in its own right. Chart losses, weigh, record pulse and standing and lying blood pressure. Exclude UTI. Do ultrasound scan to exclude twins or hydatidiform mole.

Treatment Admit to hospital. Give thromboprophylaxis (eg enoxaparin 40mg/24h/SC) and anti-embolic stockings. Spend time optimizing psychological wellbeing. Is she worried about how her other children are being cared for?

Most settle with due *care and attention*. If not too severe it may settle with rest, small carbohydrate meals, and carbonated drinks. Routine thiamine supplementation is wise for all women admitted (eg thiamine 25–50mg/8h PO) or if IV required 100mg diluted in 100mL normal saline given over 60minutes, repeated at weekly intervals.[1] This is to prevent development of Wernicke's encephalopathy (see *OHCM* p 738)—which is then associated with 40% fetal loss. Correct dehydration with IV infusion (eg with normal saline infusion with potassium added to each bag as guided by U&E). Beware rapid reversal of hyponatraemia which can cause fatal central pontine myelinosis.[11] If condition does not improve after rehydration anti-emetics may be needed eg cyclizine 50mg/8h PO/IM or IV. Phenothiazines can cause drowsiness, extrapyramidal side effects and oculogyric crisis. Those resistant to conventional treatments may respond to steroid treatment eg hydrocortisone 100mg twice daily followed by 10–40mg prednisolone/24h. Prednisolone can then usually be reduced to 2.5–10mg/24h by 20 weeks gestation. If it is needed long term screen for UTI, and gestational diabetes. Prednisolone is metabolized by the placenta, fetal blood levels are low and adverse fetal effects have not been reported.

Parenteral nutrition may, very rarely, be needed—*OHCM* p 468. If nutritional support is required both nasojejunal tube feeding and percutaneous endoscopic gastrostomy have been successfully used.[2] Parenteral nutrition has been found to be associated with serious complications (eg line sepsis).[3] ►Get a *dietician's help*.

1 A Neill 2003 *The Obstetrician and Gynaecologist* **5** 204

2 P Irving 2004 *Eur J Gastroenterol Hepatol* **16** 937

3 J Folk 2004 *J Reprod Med* **49** 497

Cardiac disease in pregnancy

In pregnancy cardiac output (CO) increases to a maximum of 30–40% > non-pregnant levels by ↑ heart rate and stroke volume. Twins ↑ CO 30% more.

Heart disease affects <1% of pregnant women. Examine the heart carefully early in all pregnancies. Ask the opinion of a cardiologist if there is doubt: •Past history (eg congenital heart disease, rheumatic fever). •Previous Kawasaki disease (now a more common cause of acquired heart disease than rheumatic fever). •Murmurs (other than 5-7 in the list below).

60% of maternal cardiac deaths occur after delivery. Cardiac failure can occur at any stage in pregnancy but risk increases as pregnancy advances and is greatest in the early puerperium. Eisenmenger's syndrome risks maternal mortality (MM) of 30%; pulmonary hypertension (MM = 30–50%); coarctation of the aorta (surges of BP↑ in the proximal segment), severe aortic or mitral stenosis and inoperable cyanotic heart disease are associated with ↑MM, so advise against pregnancy—or arrange meticulous specialist care. Seek pre-pregnancy advice for those with Marfan's or Ehlers-Danlos. Termination may be medically advised.

Prosthetic valve anticoagulation: Get expert help. Warfarin risks fetal harm (p 640); heparin risks valve thrombosis.[12] Some use IV heparin infusion weeks 6-12 and 37-term+7d; warfarin with target level of INR of 3 at other times.

Antenatal management Regular visits to cardiologist/obstetric combined clinic. Prevent anaemia, obesity, and smoking. Ensure sufficient rest. Treat hypertension. Treat infections early. Give antibiotic cover for dental treatment (*OHCM* p 154). Examine carefully to exclude pulmonary oedema and arrhythmias at all visits. Heart failure requires admission.

Labour If cardiac reserves are good before labour, risks during labour are low. Have O_2 and drugs to treat cardiac failure to hand. Avoid lithotomy position (dangerous ↑venous return after labour—the best position is semi-sitting). Aim for vaginal delivery at term with a short 2nd stage (lift out forceps or ventouse). Give antibiotic cover, eg ampicillin 500mg IV + gentamicin 80mg IV repeated twice at 8-hourly intervals, if valve or septal defect. Pain relief should be good. Epidurals are safe if hypotension is avoided. Beware large volumes of IV fluids. Avoid ergometrine (use syntocinon, if necessary). Caesarean section should not be done (except during eclampsia) if in heart failure. Heart failure is most likely within the first 24h after delivery, so ensure careful observations at this time.

Cardiac failure If symptoms or signs found, admit for bed rest, and treatment with diuretics ± digoxin. If acute failure develops, give 100% oxygen, nurse semi-recumbent, and give furosemide 40mg IV slowly (<4mg/min), morphine 10mg IV. Are vasodilators (nitrates or hydralazine) needed? Seek advice on ACE inhibitors. If there is no improvement, consider ventilation.

Arrhythmias ***Atrial fibrillation:*** Is there mitral stenosis?—admit. ℞ is as for the non-pregnant and may include digitalization or cardioversion. ***Narrow complex tachycardia:*** may precipitate cardiac failure. If Valsalva manoeuvre and carotid massage fail, anaesthetize and cardiovert.

These signs may be normal in pregnancy

1 Oedema and an increased pulse volume.
2 Vigorously pulsating neck veins (but JVP should not be ↑).
3 The apex beat is forceful (but <2cm lateral to midclavicular line).
4 The first heart sound is loud and a third heart sound can be heard in 84%.
5 An ejection systolic murmur is heard in 96% of women.
6 Systolic or continuous murmurs over either 2nd intercostal spaces 2cm from sternal edge, modified by pressure may be from mammary vessels.
7 Venous hums may be heard in the neck (modified by posture).
8 CXR may show slight cardiomegaly, ↑pulmonary vascular markings, distension of pulmonary veins due to ↑ cardiac output.

Psychopharmacology in pregnancy

For puerperal depression, see p 408.

We always try to avoid drugs in pregnancy, but sometimes psychotropics are essential, eg if the mother is neglecting herself or her pregnancy. When psychotropic drugs are used, they must be combined with well-planned psychosocial support from a trusted confidant of the patient.

Depression in pregnancy—*Unipolar:* For diagnosis, see p 336. Try to wait until the second trimester before prescribing. SSRIs should only be used with caution; avoid paroxetine (neonatal convulsions are a withdrawal reaction).[1] Most experience is with tricyclics such as amitriptyline—which are therefore the first choice when drugs are essential, despite warnings in naturally cautious *Data sheets* that read '*The safety of amitriptyline has not been established in pregnancy. It is not recommended during pregnancy, especially during the first and third trimesters unless there are compelling reasons, and, in these patients, the benefits should be weighed against the possible hazards to mother, fetus, and child... Animal experiments have shown harmful effects at exceptionally high doses...*' For these reasons, it is wise to discuss decisions with another doctor, or your local drug information service. Problems are unlikely, but the exact risk of teratogenesis is unknown. Withdrawal effects have been seen in neonates, eg agitation ± respiratory depression with amitriptyline, and colic, spasms, and hyper- or hypotension with imipramine, convulsions with clomipramine. Get a second opinion if ECT may be indicated. In general, breastfeeding is contraindicated, as metabolites pass to the baby.

Bipolar: Lithium (Li^+, p 354) is linked with teratogenicity (eg displacement of the tricuspid valve into the right ventricle). Offer specialist fetal echocardiography at 16 weeks in those women electing to stay on Li^+. Used outside the first trimester, lithium can still cause problems with the fetal renal and thyroid function. Monitor drug levels frequently (exactly 12h post-dose), and keep the dose as low as possible, and, in general, aim for a level of <0.4mmol/L. Do not change brands, as bioavailability varies. Do extra monitoring during intercurrent illness, D&V, and when poor compliance or toxicity is suspected (tremor, drowsiness, visual disturbance).

If lithium is stopped for a pregnancy or labour, restart it within a few days of birth. It is excreted in breast milk, so breastfeeding is contraindicated.

Phenothiazines in pregnant schizophrenics There is conflicting data on safety—but there is agreement that most pregnancies will be unaffected. Prebirth exposure may result in a syndrome of hyperreflexia, hypertonia, and tremor, which may persist for the first months of life. NB: rates of fetal abnormality are increased in schizophrenia, even in those taking no drugs. The *Data sheet* for chlorpromazine reads '*...There is inadequate evidence of safety in human pregnancy but it has been widely used for many years without apparent ill consequence. There is evidence of harmful effects in animals...It should be avoided in pregnancy unless the physician considers it essential. It may occasionally prolong labour, and at such a time should be withheld until the cervix is dilated 3–4cm. Possible adverse effects on the neonate include lethargy or paradoxical excitability, tremor, and low Apgar score. Being excreted in milk, breast feeding during treatment should be suspended...*'

Anxiety in pregnancy Temazepam has been used successfully in those where insomnia has been a real problem. Avoid diazepam around the time of delivery, as withdrawal may occur in the baby (floppy baby syndrome). Avoid β-blockers, as these retard fetal growth. Relaxation techniques (p 344) and supportive psychotherapy (p 380) are far more appropriate.

1 E Sanz 2005 *Lancet* **365** 482

Anaemia in pregnancy

►Even a small PPH may become life-threatening if the mother is anaemic. Anaemia predisposes to infection, and makes heart failure worse. Worn-out, anaemic mothers may not cope with their offspring. Anaemia is the main cause of perinatal problems associated with malaria; above all, anaemia is a leading mechanism by which poverty exacts its morbid toll in pregnancy.

WHO definition of anaemia of pregnancy Hb <11g/dL. By this standard 50% of women not on haematinics become anaemic. The fall in Hb is steepest around 20 weeks' gestation, and is physiological (p 6); indeed failure of Hb to fall below 10.5g/dL (but not further than ~9.5g/dL) indicates ↑risk of low birth weight or premature delivery.

Who is prone to anaemia? Those who start pregnancy anaemic, eg from menorrhagia, hookworm, malaria, with haemoglobinopathies; those with frequent pregnancies, twin pregnancy, or a poor diet.

Antenatal screening includes Hb estimation at booking, at 28 and 36 weeks. In black patients do sickle-cell tests, in others of foreign descent consider Hb electrophoresis for other haemoglobinopathies. From malarious areas consider malaria, and thick films. See p 27.

Treatment Pregnancy increases iron needs by 700–1400mg (per pregnancy), provided for by a pregnancy-induced 9-fold increase in iron absorption. Iron and folate supplements (and prevention against hookworm and malaria) are recommended in many developing countries.[13]

Offer iron to those likely to be iron deficient (see above) or who would refuse transfusion if haemorrhaging (p 85). ***Parenteral iron*** may be given (to those with iron deficiency anaemia not tolerating oral iron) as iron dextran or iron sucrose. Beware anaphylaxis. Use only if cardiopulmonary rescuscitation facilities to hand. Hb rises over 6 weeks, so late severe anaemia (Hb <9g/dL) may need blood transfusion. One unit of blood increases the Hb by ~0.7g/dL.

Thalassaemia These globin chain production disorders are found in Mediterranean, Indian, and South-east Asian populations. Although anaemic, never give parenteral iron as iron levels are high. Seek expert advice as to use of oral iron and folate. β-thalassaemia does not affect the fetus but in homozygotes regular transfusions sustain life only until young adulthood. There are α chains in fetal HbF, so in α-thalassaemias the fetus may be anaemic or, if severe, stillborn. Mothers carrying lethally affected hydropic fetuses risk severe pre-eclampsia, and delivery complications due to a large fetus and bulky placenta. Prenatal diagnosis is possible by chorionic villus sampling (p 10) for thalassaemias anticipated by parental blood studies.

Sickling disorders can affect people of African origin, Saudi Arabians, Indians, and Mediterranean populations. ***Sickle-cell trait*** is not usually a problem. ***Sickle-cell disease*** predisposes to abortion, preterm labour, stillbirth, crisis. There is a chronic haemolysis (eg Hb 6–9g/dL). Regular 3–4U blood transfusions every 6 weeks (so a problem is development of atypical antibodies) prevents crises. Infection may induce crises, and dehydration exacerbates them; treat with exchange transfusions (*OHCM* p 694). ***Sickle-cell haemoglobin c disease*** is a milder variant of sickle-cell disease. Hb levels usually near normal so women may be unaware they are affected. They are still susceptible to sickling crises in pregnancy and the puerperium, so antenatal diagnosis is essential. Prenatal sickle-cell diagnosis is possible by chorionic villus sampling.

►Aim for diagnosis at birth (cord blood) *at the latest* so that penicillin pneumococcal prophylaxis may be started (*OHCM* p 640).

HIV in pregnancy and labour

In sub-Saharan Africa HIV is common (prevalence ~24% in apparently well antenatal patients—and there are millions of AIDS orphans). In Zimbabwe 120,000 HIV+ve mothers give birth each year. Many babies are not infected *in utero* but become so during parturition. Most mothers at risk of passing on HIV to the next generation (vertical transmission) do not want to know their HIV status, or cannot afford to find out. (If their husband is uninfected, what is the chance of him remaining loyal?) In our section on perinatal HIV (p 34) we comment that anti-retrovirals and caesarean section can prevent vertical transmission—but this is not much help if the nearest hospital is 3h away by wheelbarrow, and has only basic drugs. What is needed is much more cost-effective advice.

- Only give blood transfusions if absolutely necessary.
- Avoid any procedure likely to lead to maternal cells contacting fetal blood—eg external cephalic version, and amniocentesis.
- In instrumental deliveries, try to avoid abrasions of the fetal skin. Vacuum extractors may be preferable to forceps.
- When you clamp the cord, ensure there is no maternal blood on it.
- Artificial rupture of membranes and episiotomies should be left to the last possible moment, or avoided altogether.
- Avoid fetal scalp electrodes, and doing fetal scalp blood samples.
- If the membranes have ruptured, avoid long labours—transmission risk doubles after ruptured for 4h and increases by 2%/h thereafter up to 24h.[MET 14]
- During caesarean sections, open the last layer by blunt dissection, to avoid minor cuts to the baby from the scalpel.
- Rinse the baby after birth; wipe the face away from mouth, eyes, and nostrils.
- Unless there is apnoea, avoid suction catheters to aspirate mucus from the nostrils. The baby's face is likely to be covered with the mother's blood at this stage, and you do not want to force HIV into nostrils.
- Health programmes are likely to end up encouraging breast feeding if there is no satisfactory alternative. Humanized milk is expensive, and may indicate to the mother's neighbours that she is HIV+ve. Using humanized milk might also compound problems by removing the one free method of contraception: lactational amenorrhoea. But studies from Nairobi showed 70% formula fed babies alive and disease-free at 2yrs *vs* 58% if breast fed. Most transmission occurred in the first 6 months. These babies had access to the city water supply.[RCT 15] Breast milk transmission was 16%. Also HIV+ve mothers in developing countries who breast feed may die sooner.
- Offer advice on avoiding future pregnancies. This is not an easy area. Encouraging the use of condoms is fine, but many will want the added protection of the Pill. IUCDs promote bleeding, and may increase spread to men. This may also be a problem with the progestogen-only Pill, but note that the latter may cause less ectropion than the combined Pill, and this might be advantageous. Sterilization is the hardest choice, especially when the mother now has no living children because of HIV.

Traditionally, drug therapy for HIV in pregnant patients consisted of monotherapy with zidovudine—in contrast to non-pregnant women treated with combination therapy. Combination therapies are recommended in pregnancy.[1] Antiretrovirals are becoming more available in many developing countries but there is a long way to go before all infected mothers will have access to them. Get expert advice.

1 RCOG *Clinical Guideline* 39 2004 Management of HIV in pregnancy

Diabetes mellitus (DM) in pregnancy

►Meticulous control around conception ↓malformation rates. Tell all diabetics about preconception services; they must know *before* pregnancy. Preconception change to insulin may help control. Treat retinopathy pre-pregnancy. Up to 20% may develop proliferative retinopathy so screen twice in pregnancy. If severe renal involvement; avoid pregnancy. DM may be pre-existing or appear in pregnancy; glycosuria unrelated to DM is common (glomerular filtration ↑ and tubular glucose reabsorption↓). Non-diabetic blood glucose levels in pregnancy are constant (3.5–4.5mmol/L) except after meals. Fetal glycaemia follows maternal, but compensatory fetal hyper-insulinaemia promotes fetal growth.

Complications ***Maternal:*** Hydramnios (25%—?due to fetal polyuria), preterm labour (17%—associated with hydramnios). Stillbirth near term was common. ***Fetal:*** Malformation rates ↑3–4-fold. Sacral agenesis, almost exclusive to diabetic offspring, is rare (CNS & CVS malformations are much commoner). Babies may be macrosomic (too large) or sometimes growth restricted. ***Neonatal risks:*** Hypoglycaemia, Ca^{2+}↓, Mg^{2+}↓, and RDS (p 118). They may be polycythaemic (29%)—so more neonatal jaundice.

Antenatal care Review in joint clinic with diabetologist. Confirm gestation with early ultrasound. Detailed abnormality scan at 19–20 weeks. Fetal echo at 22 weeks if early control poor. Educate about benefits of normoglycaemia and home glucose monitoring: regular postprandial monitoring *does* prevent harm to the baby. Insulin needs increase by 50–100% as pregnancy progresses so review regularly. Aim for fasting level <5.5mmol/L; 1h post-prandial level <7.5mmol/L. Give glucagon kit and ensure partner knows how to use it. Admit if adequate control impossible to achieve at home. Oral hypoglycaemics are currently avoided though glyburide does not cross placenta and may be safe.[16]

Monitor fetal growth and wellbeing by ultrasound and cardiotocography.

Delivery Timing takes into account control of diabetes, any pre-eclampsia, maturity and size of the baby, and with attention to fetal wellbeing. Delivery before 38 weeks may result in neonatal respiratory distress. Deliver the baby where there are good neonatal facilities. Traditionally, delivery was at 36–38 weeks to avoid stillbirth; but with close supervision pregnancies may go nearer to (but not beyond) term. ***In labour:*** Avoid acidosis and monitor the fetus (p 44). Avoid maternal hyperglycaemia (causes fetal hypoglycaemia). Monitor glucose; prevent hyperglycaemia with extra insulin (may need 5U/h) if β-sympathomimetics or glucocorticoids are used in preterm labour. Aim for vaginal delivery with a labour of <12h. Beware shoulder dystocia with macrosomic babies. With elective delivery, give normal insulin the evening before induction. During labour give 1L of 5–10% glucose/8h IVI with 1–2U insulin/h via a pump. Aim for a blood glucose of 4.5–5.5mmol/L (check hourly). Insulin needs fall as labour progresses and immediately postpartum. Stop infusions at delivery. Return to pre-pregnancy regimen. Do a caesarean section if labour is prolonged. Clamp cord early (as polycythaemia risk).

Postnatal • Encourage breast feeding (oral hypoglycaemics contraindicated). • Encourage pre-pregnancy counselling *before* next pregnancy (p 2) to transfer to insulin. • Do a postpartum glucose tolerance test at 6 weeks.

Gestational diabetes (OGTT glucose ≥7.8, *OHCM* p 294) *Incidence:* 3%.[17] 50% get full DM, so give lifelong dietary advice & follow-up.[18] Equations exist for giving risk of post-pregnancy DM from pre-pregnancy BMI (p 530), fasting plasma glucose, and months since delivery.[19] *Other risk factors:* age >30yrs; mothers who themselves have had low birth weights or IUGR (p 52); 1st-degree relative with DM; unexplained stillbirth;[20] gestational DM before 27 weeks (or if needing insulin).[21] [22] [n=1636]

►Exercise, a good diet, and no smoking all help lower this risk.

Thyroid disease in pregnancy (see also p 15)

►Whenever a mother isn't quite right postpartum, check her TSH & free T_4—but note that any apparent hypothyroidism may be transitory.

Biochemical changes in normal pregnancy NB: normal pregnancy mimics hyperthyroidism (pulse↑, warm moist skin, slight goitre, anxiety).

- Thyroid binding globulin & T_4 output rise to maintain free T_4 levels, p 15.
- High levels of HCG (p 14) mimic thyroid stimulating hormone (TSH).
- There is reduced availability of iodine (in iodine limited localities).
- TSH may fall below normal in the first trimester (suppressed by HCG).
- The best thyroid tests in pregnancy are free T_4, free T_3, and TSH.

Pre-pregnancy hyperthyroidism Treatment options include antithyroid drugs (but 60% relapse on stopping treatment), radioactive iodine (contra-indicated in pregnancy or breast feeding: avoid pregnancy for 4 months after use), or surgery. Fertility is reduced by hyperthyroidism.

Hyperthyroidism in pregnancy (Usually Graves' disease.) There is ↑risk of prematurity, fetal loss, and, possibly, malformations. Severity of hyperthyroidism often falls during pregnancy. Transient exacerbations may occur (1st trimester and postpartum). Treat with carbimazole or propylthiouracil. Keep dose as low as possible. Once under control, keep dose at ≤10mg/24h PO, keeping T_4 at the top of the normal range. Monitor at least monthly. Some advocate stopping antithyroid drugs in the last month of pregnancy. Propylthiouracil is preferred postpartum (less concentrated in breast milk). If hyperthyroidism cannot be controlled by drugs, partial thyroidectomy can be done in the second trimester. TRAb (TSH-receptor stimulating antibodies); high levels can cause fetal hyperthyroidism after 24 weeks causing premature delivery; craniosynostosis so intellectual impairment; goitre so polyhydramnios, extended neck in labour. Note labour, delivery, surgery, and anaesthesia can precipitate thyroid storm (fever, tachycardia, changed mental state—agitation, psychosis, coma) requiring urgent treatment.

Hypothyroidism is associated with relative infertility. In untreated hypothyroidism there are increased rates of miscarriage, stillbirth, premature labour, and abnormality. Optimize T_4 preconception (p 2). Requirements may increase by 50%. Monitor adequate replacement by T_4 and TSH measurements each trimester. Requirements return to pre-pregnancy levels postpartum.

Postpartum thyroiditis Prevalence: 5%. Hyperthyroidism is followed by hypothyroidism (~4 months postpartum). The hyperthyroid phase does not usually need treatment as it is self-limiting. If treatment is required β-blockers are usually sufficient. Antithyroid drugs are ineffective as thyrotoxicosis is from thyroid destruction releasing thyroxine, rather than increased synthesis. The hypothyroid phase is monitored for >6 months, and the woman treated if she becomes symptomatic. Withdraw treatment after 6-12 months for 4 weeks to see if long-term therapy is required. 90% have thyroid antiperoxidase antibodies; 5% of antibody positive women become permanently hypothyroid each year so monitor annually. Hypothyroidism may be associated with postpartum depression, so check thyroid status of women with postpartum depression.

Neonatal thyrotoxicosis Seen in 1% of babies of women with past Graves' disease, due to TRAb crossing the placenta. Signs: fetal tachycardia (>160/min) in late pregnancy ± intrauterine growth restriction. If mother has been on antithyroid drugs signs may not be manifest until the baby has metabolized the drug (7-10 days postpartum). Test thyroid function in affected babies frequently. Antithyroid drugs may be needed. It resolves spontaneously at 2-3 months, but perceptual motor difficulties, and hyperactivity can occur later in childhood.

Jaundice in pregnancy

►Get expert help *promptly*. Jaundice in pregnancy may be lethal. Know exactly what drugs were taken and when (*prescribed* or *over-the-counter*). Where has she travelled to? What life-style or occupational risks are there?

Jaundice occurs in 1 in 1500 pregnancies. Viral hepatitis and gallstones may cause jaundice in pregnancy and investigation is similar to the non-pregnant. Those with Gilbert's and Dubin-Johnson syndrome (*OHCM* p 722) do well in pregnancy (jaundice may be exacerbated with the latter).

Tests Do all the usual tests (*OHCM* p 222), eg urine tests for bile, serology, LFTs, and ultrasound.

Intrahepatic cholestasis of pregnancy Incidence 0.1–1.5% pregnancies in Europe. There is pruritus, especially of palms and soles in the second half of pregnancy. Liver transaminases are mildly ↑ (<300U/L) in 60%, ↑bilirubin in 25%. Exclude viral hepatitis. There is risk of preterm labour (60%), fetal distress (33%), and stillbirth (2%), so monitor fetal wellbeing; aim for delivery by 38 weeks. Give vitamin K 10mg PO/24h to the mother, and 1mg IM to the baby at birth. Ursodeoxycholic acid reduces pruritus and abnormal LFTs. Symptoms resolve within days of delivery. It is a contraindication to oestrogen-containing contraceptive Pills and recurs in 40% pregnancies.

Acute fatty liver of pregnancy Incidence: 1:6600–13,000 deliveries—so it is rare but grave. The mother develops abdominal pain, jaundice, headache, vomiting, ± thrombocytopenia, and pancreatitis. There is associated pre-eclampsia in 30–60% (±postpartum). It usually occurs after 30 weeks. There is hepatic steatosis with micro-droplets of fat in liver cells. Deep jaundice, uraemia, severe hypoglycaemia and clotting disorder may develop causing coma and death. Monitor BP. Give supportive treatment for liver and renal failure and treat hypoglycaemia vigorously (CVP line). Correct clotting disorders. Enlist haematologists help. Expedite delivery. Epidural and regional anaesthesia are CI. Monitor postpartum. Beware PPH and neonatal hypoglycaemia. Mortality can be as low as 18% maternal and 23% fetal.

Some other causes of jaundice in pregnancy

- Viral hepatitis; ALT↑, eg >200U/L; maternal mortality ↑ in E virus, *OHCM* p 576. Hepatitis C is thought to affect <1% of women in the UK at present. Vertical trasmission is thought to affect about 5% of babies, and transmission has not been shown to be reduced by caesarean section except in those also having HIV. Passive antibodies transferred from the mother wane by 18 months. Interferon treatment is not currently recommended for children under 3 years of age. Currently screening is not planned. Refer infected women for interferon and ribavirin treatment to clear the viral infection after childbirth.[1]
- The jaundice of severe pre-eclampsia (hepatic rupture and infarction can occur); ALT <500U/L; bilirubin <86μmol/L.
- Rarely complicating hyperemesis gravidarum (can be fatal); ALT <200U/L.
- Hepatitis may occur if halothane is used for anaesthesia (so avoid it).
- HELLP syndrome (haemolysis, elevated liver enzymes, and low platelet count). Incidence in pregnancy: 0.1–0.6%; in pre-eclampsia: 4–12%. It causes upper abdo pain, malaise, vomiting, headache, jaundice, microangiopathic haemolytic anaemia, DIC, LDH↑, ALT↑ <500U/L, bilirubin <86μmol/L. It recurs in 20%. Treatment: get expert help. Admit; deliver if severe.

Hepatitis B Check HBsAg in all women with jaundice and look for IgM anti-HBc to detect acute infection. Avoid contact with blood during delivery and be careful with disposal of 'sharps'. Babies need vaccination at birth (p 151). Offer vaccination to all the family.

1 L Pembrey 2003 *J Med Screen* **10** 161

Malaria in pregnancy

In any woman who presents with odd behaviour, fever, jaundice, sweating, DIC, fetal distress, premature labour, seizures, or loss of consciousness, always ask yourself: ►*Could this be malaria?* If so, do thick and thin films. Confirm (or exclude) pregnancy. Seek expert help, eg from Liverpool, below.

Falciparum malaria can be most dangerous (and complicated) in pregnancy, particularly in those with no malaria immunity. Cerebral malaria has a 50% mortality in pregnancy. Third stage placental autotransfusion may lead to fatal pulmonary oedema. Hypoglycaemia may be a feature (both of malaria itself and secondary to quinine). There is increased susceptibility to sepsis.[1] Women with co-existent HIV have less good pregnancy outcomes (both fetal and maternal).

Other associations between *falciparum* malaria and pregnancy are anaemia, abortion, stillbirth, low birth weight, and prematurity. PPH is also more common. Hyperreactive malaria splenomegaly (occurs typically where malaria is holoendemic) may contribute to anaemia via increased haemolysis.

Vivax malaria is less dangerous, but can cause anaemia and low birth weight.

Treating malaria ►*OHCM* p 562; ►►cerebral malaria, *OHCM* p 810. Quinine (full dosage), and artemesinin are reasonably safe in pregnancy; beware hypoglycaemia with IV quinine. In *falciparum* malaria, assume chloroquine resistance.

Quinine is used even in the 1st trimester. In many places (eg SE Asia) it must be combined with clindamycin 900mg/8h PO for 5 days. Avoid doxycycline.

Opinions on mefloquine in pregnancy are divided: some authorities do not use it (for treatment or prophylaxis)[23] citing a 4-fold increase in risk of stillbirth. But if the risk associated with malaria is considered high, then it could be used, for instance as IPT (intermittent preventive treatment), but more studies are needed. Mefloquine dose example (in 2nd and 3rd trimesters) for treating uncomplicated *falciparum* malaria: 25mg/kg plus artesunate, 4mg/day over 3 days. Appraise yourself of local guidelines.[2]

Transfer earlier rather than later to ITU. Women with a haematocrit <20% should get a slow transfusion of packed cells, if compatible, fresh, pathogen-free blood is available. Remember to include the volume of packed cells in calculations of fluid balance. Exchange transfusions may be needed (eg if 10% parasitaemia)—if facilities are available. Beware sepsis. Get expert help.

During labour, anticipate fetal distress, fluid-balance problems, and hypoglycaemia. Monitor appropriately. Send cord blood or heel prick sample of neonate to check if baby infected (0.3–4% are), and treat baby if infected.

Prevention in UK women Advise against visiting malarious areas. If it is unavoidable, give prophylaxis (*OHCM* p 562). Emphasize importance of preventive measures such as mosquito nets and insect repellents. Chloroquine and proguanil are used in normal doses if *P. falciparum* strains are sensitive—but with proguanil, concurrent folate supplements should be given.

Maloprim® (dapsone+pyrimethamine; not available in UK) is contraindicated in 1st trimester; if given in 2nd–3rd trimesters, give folate supplements too.

Mefloquine should generally be avoided as prophylaxis (exclude pregnancy before use, and avoid pregnancy for 3 months after use).

Mothers living in endemic areas Chemoprophylaxis improves birth weight (by ~250g, with fewer very low birth weight babies). Red cell mass also rises. WHO advises IPT (above), eg with 2 or 3 doses of sulfadoxine-pyrimethamine (SP) during pregnancy, which can compare favourably with weekly prophylaxis.[3] But SP causes Stevens-Johnson syndrome in 1 in 7000, and resistance to SP is spreading fast, so new IPT regimens need urgent evaluation in pregnancy.[24] Dihydroartemisinin-piperaquine (Artekin®) is a good candidate.[25]
►If in doubt, phone an expert, eg, in the UK, at Liverpool (0151 708 9393).

1 Gitau G 2005 The *Obstetrician and Gynaecologist* 7 5. See also White N 2005 *PLOS* **2** 1
2 Nosten F & N White 2005 *Lancet* **365** 653: lower doses are not recommended.
3 Kayentao K 2005 *J Infect Dis* **191** 109 & Greenwood 2004 *Am J Trop Med Hyg* **70** 1

Renal disease in pregnancy

Note: Values considered normal when not pregnant may reflect decreased renal function in pregnancy. Creatinine >75μmol/L and urea >4.5mmol/L merit further investigation. See p 15. Glycosuria in pregnancy may reflect altered renal physiology and not necessarily imply hyperglycaemia.

►Treat asymptomatic bacteriuria in pregnancy. Check that infection and bacteriuria clear with treatment.

Asymptomatic bacteriuria Found in 2% of sexually active women it is commoner (up to 7%) during pregnancy—especially in diabetics and in those with renal transplants. With the dilatation of the calyces and ureters that occurs in pregnancy, 25% will go on to develop pyelonephritis, which can cause fetal growth restriction, fetal death, and premature labour. This is the argument for screening all women for bacteriuria at booking. If present on 2 MSUs treatment is given (eg amoxicillin 250mg/8h PO with a high fluid intake). Test for cure after 1 and 2 weeks. If the organism is not sensitive to amoxicillin, consider nitrofurantoin 50mg/6h PO with food.

Pyelonephritis This may present as malaise with urinary frequency or as a more florid picture with raised temperature, tachycardia, vomiting, and loin pain. It is common at around 20 weeks and in the puerperium. Urinary infections should always be carefully excluded in those with hyperemesis gravidarum and in those admitted with premature labour. Treatment is with bed rest and plenty of fluids. After blood and urine culture give IV antibiotics (eg ampicillin 500mg/6h IV, according to sensitivities) if oral drugs cannot be used (eg if vomiting). Treat for 2–3 weeks. MSUs should be checked every fortnight for the rest of the pregnancy. 20% of women having pyelonephritis in pregnancy have underlying renal tract abnormalities and an IVU or ultrasound at 16 weeks' postpartum should be considered. In those who suffer repeated infection, nitrofurantoin (100mg/24h PO with food) may prevent recurrences. Avoid if the glomerular filtration rate is <50mL/min. SE: vomiting, peripheral neuropathy, pulmonary infiltration, and liver damage.

Chronic renal disease With mild renal impairment (pre-pregnancy creatinine <125mmol/L) without hypertension there is little evidence that pregnancy accelerates renal disorders. Patients with marked anaemia, hypertension, retinopathy, or heavy proteinuria should avoid pregnancy as further deterioration in renal function may be expected. Close collaboration between physicians and obstetricians during pregnancy in those with renal disease is the aim. Induction of labour may become advisable in those with hypertension and proteinuria, or if fetal growth is retarded.

Pregnancy for those on dialysis is fraught with problems (fluid overload, hypertension, pre-eclampsia, polyhydramnios). A 50% increase in dialysis is needed. Live birth outcome is 50–70%. Outcome is better for those with renal transplants; but 10% of mothers die within 7 years from birth.

Obstetric causes of acute tubular necrosis Acute tubular necrosis may be a complication of any of the following situations:

- Septicaemia (eg from septic abortion or pyelonephritis).
- Haemolysis (eg sickling crisis, malaria).
- Hypovolaemia, eg in pre-eclampsia; haemorrhage (APH, eg abruption, PPH, or intrapartum); DIC; abortion—or adrenal failure in those on steroids not receiving booster doses to cover labour.

Whenever these situations occur, monitor urine output carefully (catheterize the bladder). Aim for >30mL/h output. Monitor renal function (U&E, creatinine). Dialysis may be needed (*OHCM* p 278).

Epilepsy in pregnancy

►The key to successful pregnancy is access to good preconception counselling (p 2). Antiepileptic drugs are normally specialist initiated; ask for a review if pregnancy may be being considered.

►If seizures occur in pregnancy, think *could this be eclampsia?*

Epilepsy *de novo* is rare in pregnancy. Epilepsy affects ~0.5% of women of child-bearing age so a unit with 3000 deliveries per year has ~15 pregnant epileptic women at any one time. Seizure rates worsen in most women having >1 seizure/month. Sleep deprivation in the last month of pregnancy may contribute to seizures. It is unusual for seizures to recur in pregnancy when preceded by a long seizure-free period.

Complications—***Maternal:*** ↑Risk of 3rd trimester vaginal bleeding. 1% convulse in labour. ***Fetal:*** •Haemorrhagic disease of newborn can occur with enzyme inducers (below). •Congenital malformation (UK register suggests 5.9% affected with sodium valproate, 2.3% with carbamazepine, 2.1% with lamotrigine). Malformation is commoner if ≥2 anticonvulsants are used and with higher doses. ***Fetal valproate syndrome:*** Signs: major organ system anomalies ± autism ± small ears, small broad nose, a long upper lip, shallow philtrum & micro/retrognathia.[1] ***Cleft lip:*** Associated with maternal epilepsy only, the relative risk for a fetus having clefts compared to the non-epileptic population is 1.0 if the mother develops epilepsy after the pregnancy; 2.4 if she develops it after conception (but has no drugs); 4.7 if fetus is exposed to anticonvulsants. Phenytoin and phenobarbital cause clefts and congenital heart disease. ***Neural tube defects*** are commoner with valproate (& carbamazepine) so screen for these (p 10). ***Neurodevelopmental delay*** is seen with valproate, seen as lower verbal intelligence quotient (also seen in the offspring of those having frequent tonic clonic seizures in pregnancy.[2]

Management ►Get expert help (refer to epilepsy specialist to optimize and monitor medication: only make antiepileptic changes on expert advice). Avoid trimethadione and paramethadione (both very teratogenic). Where anticonvulsants are needed keep the dose of the chosen drug as low as possible. Aim for 1 drug only. Give folic acid supplements, eg 5mg/24h PO from prior to conception. Give vitamin K_1 20mg/24h PO to the mother from 36 weeks if she is taking enzyme inducers ie carbamazepine, ethosuximide, phenytoin, primidone, phenobarbitone (oxcarbazine and topiramate are subjects of debate).[3] Screen for neural tube defects and heart disease if relevant (above). Treat status epilepticus as in the non-pregnant but monitor the fetus. It is associated with significant fetal and maternal mortality. Deliver in hospital with resuscitation facilities (1–2% epileptic women convulse in labour and the subsequent 48 hours)—and avoid early discharge. Give baby vitamin K 1mg IM at birth. If seizures are likely, to avoid dropping the baby during a seizure, advise changing the baby on mat on floor, and feeding sitting on floor supported by cushions, and only bath the baby with supervision. Mothers may breast feed (phenobarbital can cause drowsiness in the baby). Ask for review of epilepsy drugs postnatally eg at 12 weeks.

Encourage mother to register pregnancy: tel 0800 389 1245 or www.epilepsyandpregnancy.co.uk. (NICE guideline, epilepsy, 2004).

1 D Renier 2001 *J Neurosurg* **95** 778 62% had musculoskeletal abnormalities, 26% had cardiovascular abnormalities, 22% had genital abnormalities, and 16% had pulmonary abnormalities.
2 N Adab 2004 *J Neurol Neurosurg Psychiatry* **75** 1575
3 Royal Society of Medicine Guideline 2004 *Managing epilepsy in women*

Connective tissue diseases in pregnancy

Rheumatoid arthritis is usually alleviated by pregnancy (but exacerbations may occur in the puerperium). Methotrexate use is contraindicated (teratogenic); sulfasalazine may be used (give extra folate). Azathioprine use may cause intrauterine growth restriction and penicillamine may weaken fetal collagen. Non-steroidal anti-inflammatories can be used in the first and second trimesters but are not recommended in the third as they can cause premature closure of the ductus arteriosus and late in pregnancy have been associated with renal impairment in the newborn. Congenital heart block is a rare fetal feature. Deliver babies with heart block as below.

Systemic lupus erythematosus SLE exacerbations are commoner in pregnancy and the puerperium. Most are mild to moderate involving skin, but those with renal involvement and hypertension may deteriorate and are prone to pre-eclampsia. Of those with SLE glomerulonephritis and a creatinine >130μmol prior to conception only 50% achieve a live birth. Pre-eclampsia, oligohydramnios, and intrauterine growth restriction may occur. Both hydralazine and methyldopa can be used in pre-eclampsia.

Planned pregnancy should be embarked on after 6 months stable disease without requiring cytotoxic suppression. Disease suppression may be maintained with azathioprine and hydroxychloroquine. Aspirin 75mg daily should be started prior to conception and continued throughout pregnancy and the fetus should be carefully monitored.

Rarely the fetus is affected by maternal antibodies that cause a self-limiting sunlight sensitive rash (usually face & scalp) for which no treatment is required; or anti-Ro or anti-La antibodies irreversibly damage the fetal heart conduction system causing congenital heart block (~65% require a pacemaker). Deliver by caesarean or monitor fetal blood gases in labour.

Mothers requiring ≥7.5mg daily prednisolone in the 2 weeks before delivery should receive hydrocortisone 100mg/6h IV in labour.

Antiphospholipid syndrome Those affected have antiphospholipid antibodies (lupus anticoagulant and/or anticardiolipin antibodies on 2 tests taken >8 weeks apart) ± past arterial thrombosis, venous thrombosis, or recurrent pregnancy loss. It may be primary, or follow other connective tissue disorder (usually SLE in which it occurs in 10%). ***Outcome:*** Untreated, <20% of pregnancies proceed to a live birth due to 1st trimester loss or placental thrombosis (causes placental insufficiency, leading to intrauterine growth restriction and fetal death).

Careful regular fetal assessment (Doppler flow studies and ultrasound for growth are required from 20 weeks) as appropriate obstetric intervention can substantially increase the number of live-born babies.

Management: Affected women are treated from conception with aspirin 75mg daily and heparin eg enoxaparin 40mg SC/24h from when fetal heart identified (~6weeks) until 34 weeks. Those who have suffered prior thromboses receive heparin throughout pregnancy. See p 33.

Postpartum use either heparin or warfarin (breastfeeding contraindicated with neither) as risk of thrombosis is high.

Pregnancies in those with SLE (especially with renal disease) and antiphospholipid syndrome require specialist management.

Venous thromboembolism (VTE) in pregnancy

Investigate any unexplained calf or chest symptoms swiftly. Thromboembolism is the chief UK cause of maternal death. VTE risk rises 6-fold in pregnancy ([illegible] of pregnancies; 20–40% occur antenatally (any trimester)). For those at special risk, see p 18. [illegible] of those with VTE have thrombophilia (p 33)—so check for this. Where clinical suspicion is strong but tests negative (scan/assessment), stop only after repeat negative tests 1 week later. Before starting treatment take blood for FBC, U&E, LFT, coagulation and thrombophilia screen.

Pulmonary embolism Small emboli may cause unexplained pyrexia, syncope, cough, chest pain, and breathlessness. Pleurisy should be considered due to embolism unless there is high fever or much purulent sputum. Large emboli present as collapse with chest pain, breathlessness and cyanosis. There will be a raised JVP, triple heart sound, and parasternal heave.

Tests: CXR and ECG may be normal (tachycardia is the most consistent finding). ECG changes of deep S wave in lead I and Q wave and inverted T wave in lead III can be caused by pregnancy alone. Blood gases may be [illegible]. CT pulmonary angiograms are better than ventilation/perfusion scans. Scan legs for venous thrombi.

Treatment: Massive embolism: require prolonged cardiac massage; thrombolysis, percutaneous catheter thrombus fragmentation, or pulmonary embolectomy. Give unfractionated heparin 5000U IV (10,000U IV if severe pulmonary embolism), then 1000U/h IV in 0.9% saline by syringe pump; monitor APTT at 6h, then 12h. Adjust dose as needed (usual 1000–2000U/h). After 3–7 days on IV heparin maintain on long-term heparin (eg 10,000U/12h SC) with careful monitoring. [illegible] thrombocytopenia, allergic skin rashes, alopecia, or [illegible] low molecular weight heparins eg enoxaparin (see below) is an [illegible] alternative. Warfarin is teratogenic [illegible] throughout pregnancy—Conradi–Hünermann syndrome, p [illegible]) and is used intrapartum up to 36 weeks only in those with artificial heart valves. SC heparin is continued through labour (see p [illegible] for dose and epidural conditions). Heparin postpartum is reduced (eg to 7500U/12h SC for unfractionated heparin) for at least 6 weeks postpartum and 3 months from embolus. Some choose warfarin therapy from 2 days postpartum.

Deep vein thrombosis (DVT) Suspect if leg pain, discomfort (especially left), swelling, oedema, [illegible], lower abdominal pain. Tests: Doppler ultrasound. Treatment: Elevate leg and use compression stockings. Give heparin throughout pregnancy eg enoxaparin 1mg/kg/12h SC (based on early pregnancy weight); measure peak anti-Xa activity 3h post-injection: aim for target between [illegible] (if above this reduce dose eg from 1mg/kg to [illegible]); repeat anti-Xa. Check platelets at 7 days and then monthly (if heparin-induced thrombocytopenia occurs use danaparoid sodium). After delivery warfarin may be used (breastfeeding is OK). [illegible] for at least 6 weeks postpartum and 3 months from thrombosis. Compression stockings should be worn for 2 years (reduces post-thrombotic syndrome incidence from 23% to 11%).

Prophylaxis see p 18.

Venous thromboembolism (VTE) in pregnancy

►*Investigate any unexplained calf or chest symptoms* **today**. Thromboembolism is the chief UK cause of maternal death. VTE risk rises 6-fold in pregnancy (~0.3–1.6% of pregnancies: 20–50% occur antenatally—in *any* trimester). For those at special risk see p 16. 50% of those with 1st VTE have *thrombophilia* (p 33), so check for this. Where clinical suspicion is strong but tests negative, start treatment, stop only after repeat negative tests 1 week later.[1] Before starting heparin take blood for FBC, U&E, LFTs, coagulation and thrombophilia screens.

Pulmonary embolism Small emboli may cause unexplained pyrexia, syncope, cough, chest pain, and breathlessness. Pleurisy should be considered due to embolism unless there is high fever or much purulent sputum. Large emboli present as collapse with chest pain, breathlessness, and cyanosis. There will be a raised JVP, third heart sound, and parasternal heave.

Tests: CXR and ECG may be normal (tachycardia is the most consistent finding). ECG changes of deep S-wave in lead I and Q-wave and inverted T-wave in lead III can be caused by pregnancy alone. Blood gases may be helpful ($P_aO_2\downarrow$; $P_aCO_2\downarrow$). CT pulmonary angiograms are better than ventilation/perfusion scans. Scan legs for venous thrombi.

Treatment: Massive emboli may require prolonged cardiac massage, thrombolysis, percutaneous catheter thrombus fragmentation or pulmonary embolectomy. Give unfractionated heparin 5000U IV, (10,000U IV in severe pulmonary embolism), then 1000U/h IVI in 0.9% saline by syringe pump. Monitor APTT at 6h, then /24h. Adjust dose as needed (usual 1000–2000U/h). After 3–7 days on IV heparin maintain on long-term heparin (eg 10,000U/12h SC) with careful monitoring. Problems: maternal osteopaenia (reversible on stopping); thrombocytopenia; allergic skin rashes; alopecia. For less massive emboli, low molecular weight heparin eg enoxaparin, (see below), is an alternative. Warfarin is teratogenic (in ~6.4% of those taking warfarin throughout pregnancy—Conradi-Hünermann syndrome, p 640) and is used antenatally up to 36 weeks only in those with artificial heart valves. SC heparin is continued through labour (see p 16 for dose and epidural conditions). Heparin postpartum is reduced (eg to 7500U/12h SC for unfractionated heparin). Treat for at least 6 weeks postpartum and 6 months from embolus. Some choose warfarin use from 2 days postpartum.

Deep vein thrombosis (DVT) Suspect if leg pain/discomfort (especially left); swelling; oedema; ↑T°; ↑WCC; lower abdominal pain. ***Tests:*** Doppler ultrasound. ***Treatment:*** Elevate leg and use compression stockings. Give heparin throughout pregnancy eg enoxaparin 1mg/kg/12h SC (based on early pregnancy weight); measure peak anti-Xa activity 3h post-injection; aim for level between 0.4–1U/mL (if above this reduce dose eg from 80mg/12h to 60mg/12h and repeat anti-Xa). Check platelets at 7 days and then monthly (if heparin-induced thrombocytopenia occurs use danaparoid sodium). After delivery warfarin may be used (breastfeeding is OK). Monitor INR meticulously. Treat for at least 6 weeks postpartum and 6 months from thrombosis. Compression stockings should be worn for 2 years (reduces post-thrombotic syndrome incidence from 23% to 11%).[1]

Prophylaxis See p 16.

1 RCOG *Clinical Guidelines* **28** 2001 Thromboembolic disease in pregnancy & puerperium: management

Thrombophilia in pregnancy[1,2]

Thrombophilia is a tendency to increased clotting and many underlying causes are now known to contribute. Collectively, the conditions below affect at least 15% of Western populations; but are found in 50% of those with episodes of venous thromboembolism. Factors include:

- Factor V Leiden mutation: This ↓ factor V breakdown by protein C (activated protein C (APC) resistance). This affects 4–10% of the population and increases thrombotic risk 3–8 times. Homozygous individuals have 80 times the risk of venous thromboembolism.
- Protein C deficiency (affects 0.3% of population; increasing thrombotic risk 10–15 times).
- Protein S deficiency (affects 2% of population; ↑thrombotic risk 10 times).
- Antithrombin III deficiency (affects 0.02% of population; thrombotic risk is increased 25–50 times).
- Lupus anticoagulant ± cardiolipin antibody. Women with lupus anticoagulant risk arterial and venous thrombosis; in atypical veins, eg portal or arm.
- G20210A mutation of the prothrombin gene (2% of the population).
- Homozygosity for the thermolabile variant of methylenetetrahydrofolate reductase (C677T MTHFR), which leads to homocysteinaemia (10% of the population).
- Dysfibrinogenaemia is rare, and the thrombotic risk variable.

Pregnancy is an acquired risk factor for venous thromboembolism. The difficulty is to know who has thrombophilia, and what risk this poses to a pregnant woman. Retrospective work from pregnancies complicated by thrombophilia (n=72,000), suggested risk of thromboembolism was 1:437 for women with factor V Leiden; 1:113 among those with protein C deficiency; 1:2.8 in those with type I (quantitative) antithrombin deficiency, and 1:42 amongst those with type II (qualitative) antithrombin deficiency. No association was found between venous thromboembolism and homozygosity for C677T MTHFR mutation, perhaps because plasma homocysteine reduces in pregnancy and folic acid supplements ameliorate hyperhomocysteinaemia.

Another study looking at relative risk of thromboembolism during pregnancy and postpartum suggests relative risk of thromboembolism is 9.3 for those with factor V Leiden; 15.2 for those with G20210A prothrombin gene mutation; relative risk for those affected by both was 107. By assuming an underlying rate of thromboembolism of 0.67 per 1000 pregnancies expected rates of thromboembolism of 1:500 was estimated for those with factor Leiden; 1:200 for those with G20210A prothrombin gene mutation and 4.6:100 for those with both. Being homozygous for the C677T MTHFR mutation was not associated with increased risk.

It is not felt that all women should be screened for thrombophilia; although screening is recommended for those with a family history of thromboembolism and those with past history of thromboembolism. Screening is also recommended in those with second-trimester pregnancy loss; severe or recurrent eclampsia and intrauterine growth restriction although it is not yet known how knowledge of thrombophilia will affect management. Those with thrombophilia but without previous history of thromboembolism require individualized assessment of the defect and additional risk factors by clinicians with expertise in this area. Drugs (eg low molecular weight heparin) are recommended for those with thrombophilia and past history of thromboembolism.

1 I Greer 2000 *NEJM* 342 424
2 British Heart Foundation *Factfile* 02/2002

Antenatal infection[1]

Rubella Childhood vaccination prevents rubella-susceptibility. ►Asymptomatic reinfection can occur making serology essential in all pregnant rubella contacts. Routine antenatal screening finds those needing puerperal vaccination (avoid pregnancy for 1 month: vaccine is live). Symptoms (p 142) are absent in 50%. The fetus is most at risk in the first 16 weeks' gestation. 50–60% of fetuses are affected if maternal primary infection is in the first month of gestation: <5% are affected if infection is at 16 weeks. Risk of fetal damage is much lower (<5%) with re-infection. Cataract is associated with infection at 8–9 weeks, deafness at 5–7 weeks (can occur with second trimester infection), cardiac lesions at 5–10 weeks. Other features: purpura, jaundice, hepatosplenomegaly, thrombocytopenia, cerebral palsy, microcephaly, mental retardation, cerebral calcification, microphthalmia, retinitis, growth disorder. Abortion or stillbirth may occur. If suspected in the mother seek expert help. Take antibody levels 10 days apart and look for IgM antibody 4–5 weeks from incubation period or date of contact.

Cytomegalovirus (CMV) In the UK, CMV is a commoner cause of congenital retardation than rubella. Maternal infection is usually mild or asymptomatic, or there is fever ± lymphadenopathy and sometimes sore throat. Up to 5/1000 live births are infected, of whom 5% will develop early multiple handicaps, and have cytomegalic inclusion disease (with non-specific features resembling rubella syndrome, plus microcephaly, choroidoretinitis). Another 5% later develop cerebral calcification (IQ↓); sensorineural deafness and psychomotor retardation. Diagnosis (paired sera) may be difficult. Amniocentesis at >20 weeks can detect fetal transmission.[27] Also test throat swabs, urine culture, and baby's serum after birth. Reducing women's exposure to toddlers' urine (the source of much infection) during pregnancy can limit spread. NB: reactivation of old CMV may occur in pregnancy; it rarely affects the baby. One way to know that +ve serology does not reflect old infection is to do serology (or freeze a sample) pre-pregnancy.

Toxoplasmosis 40% of fetuses are affected if the mother has the illness (2–7/1000 pregnancies); the earlier in pregnancy the more the damage. Symptoms are like glandular fever. Fever, rash, and eosinophilia also occur. If symptomatic, the CNS prognosis is poor. Diagnose by reference laboratory IgG and IgM tests. ***Maternal, ℞ (Royal College Regimen):*** Start spiramycin promptly in infected mothers, eg 1.5g/12h PO. In symptomatic non-immune women test every 10 weeks through pregnancy. If infected consider fetal cord blood sampling, eg at 21 weeks for IgM to see if the fetus is infected. If the fetus is infected, give the mother pyrimethamine 50mg/12h as loading doses on day 1, then 1mg/kg/day + sulfadiazine 50mg/kg/12h + calcium folinate 15mg twice weekly all until delivery. ***Affected babies:*** (diagnose by serology—>90% asymptomatic). Intracranial calcification, hydrocephalus, choroidoretinitis if severely affected. Encephalitis, epilepsy, mental and physical retardation, jaundice, hepatosplenomegaly, thrombocytopenia and skin rashes occur. Treat with 4-weekly courses of pyrimethamine, sulfadiazine and calcium folinate ×6, separated by 4 weeks of spiramycin. Prednisolone is given until signs of CNS inflammation or choroidoretinitis abate. ***Prevention:*** avoid eating raw meat, wash hands if raw meat touched, wear gloves if gardening or dealing with cat litter, and avoid sheep during lambing time.

HIV Without interventions ~15% babies acquire HIV if the mother is +ve (↑ risk in Africa; but HIV-2 transmitted less). Offer mothers tests for HIV, (see counselling *OHCM* p 582). Antenatal transmission is ≤2%. Maternal antiretroviral use, elective caesarean delivery and bottle feeding attains ≤2% risk.

►Vertical transmission occurs during vaginal delivery (1st twins are twice as commonly infected as 2nd); aim for elective caesarean section eg after 38 weeks (if undetectable viral load benefits less certain). HIV +ve women should be screened for genital infections early in pregnancy and at 28 weeks. All +ve mothers should take anti-retrovirals eg combinations of 3 or more HAART, *OHCM* p 584. Seek expert advice. Manage by multidisciplinary team work. If on these when conceives, continue but change if viral load not suppressed. If needed for maternal health ideally start at end of 1st trimester. If not needed for mother start HAART-like regime or zidovudine at 28–32 weeks,[2] continue through labour and stop when advised. For caesareans start zidovudine IVI 4h pre-op and continue until cord clamped. Take maternal blood at delivery to determine viral load. Clamp cord early. Wash baby at birth. Give neonate zidovudine for 4–6 weeks. Advise bottle feeding (↓ transmission ?by up to 50%, but beware if hygiene is a problem).RCT 28 29 If caesarean declined aim for short labour and other measures on p 23. Maternal antibodies persist up to 18 months in uninfected infants—but gene amplification by polymerase chain reaction can detect neonatal HIV proviral sequences.

Intrauterine HIV is associated with prematurity and growth restriction (in developing countries, but not in Europe). Clinical illness appears sooner than in adult AIDS (eg at aged 6 months)—with hepatosplenomegaly, failure to thrive, encephalopathy, recurrent fevers, respiratory diseases (interstitial lymphocytic pneumonitis), lymphadenopathy, salmonella septicaemia, pneumocystis, and CMV infection. Death is usually from respiratory failure or overwhelming infection. Mortality: 20% at 18 months. ►For treatment and advice on how to prevent transmission in labour, see p 23.

Intrauterine syphilis Maternal screening occurs (UK screen 55,700 to prevent 1 case. In some parts of London 2:1000 women are infected); if infection found treat the mother with procaine penicillin 600mg/24h IM daily for 10 days. ~1/3 are stillborn. Neonatal signs: rhinitis, snuffles, rash, hepatosplenomegaly, lymphadenopathy, anaemia, jaundice, ascites, hydrops, nephrosis, meningitis, ± keratitis, and nerve deafness. Nasal discharge exam: spirochaetes; x-rays: perichondritis; *CSF:* ↑Monocytes and protein with +ve serology. *Treatment:* Give procaine penicillin 37mg/kg/24h IM for 3 weeks.

Listeria Affects 6–15/100,000 pregnancies. Maternal symptoms: fever, shivering, myalgia, headache, sore throat, cough, vomiting, diarrhoea, vaginitis. Abortion (can be recurrent), premature labour, and stillbirth may occur. Infection is usually via infected food (eg milk, soft cheeses, pâté). ►Do blood cultures in any pregnant patient with unexplained fever for ≥48h. Serology, vaginal and rectal swabs do not help (can be commensal). See *OHCM* p 591.

Perinatal infection usually occurs in 2nd or 3rd trimester. 20% of affected fetuses are stillborn. Fetal distress in labour is common. An early postnatal feature is respiratory distress from pneumonia. There may be convulsions, hepatosplenomegaly, pustular or petechial rashes, conjunctivitis, fever, leucopenia. Meningitis is commoner after perinatal infection. Diagnose by culture of blood, CSF, meconium, and placenta. Infant mortality: 30%. Isolate baby (nosocomial spread can occur). Treat with ampicillin 50mg/kg/6h IV and gentamicin 3mg/kg/12h IV until 1 week after fever subsides. Monitor levels.

Sheep-borne conditions Listeriosis, toxoplasmosis, and ovine chlamydia (*Chlamydophila abortus*) can be contracted from sheep. Ovine chlamydial infection is rare; can cause DIC, septicaemia, and renal failure in pregnant women and abortion of the fetus. Diagnose by serology; treat with erythromycin or tetracycline. ►Pregnant women should not handle sheep or lambs.

1 Previously called 'TORCH' infections: toxoplasmosis, other (eg syphilis), rubella, CMV, herpes (and hepatitis). The 1st 4 are acquired antenatally—herpes & hepatitis usually perinatally. Other agents are important (chickenpox; HIV, p 144–5). *See also* Erythrovirus (=Parvovirus, p 142)—zoster reactivation in pregnancy is *not* a risk for the baby.

2 RCOG *Clinical Guideline* 39 2004 Management of HIV in pregnancy

Perinatal infection

Hepatitis B virus (HBV) All mothers should be screened for HBsAg. Carriers have persistent HBsAg for >6 months. High infectivity is associated with HBeAg so anti-HBe antibodies are negative. Without immunization 95% of babies born to these mothers might develop hepatitis B, and 93% of the babies would be chronic carriers at 6 months. If the mother develops acute infection in the mid- or third trimester there is high risk of perinatal infection. Her risk of death is 0.5–3%. Most neonatal infections occur at birth but some, (especially in the East) is transplacental—hence the seeming failure of vaccination in up to 15% of neonates adequately vaccinated. Most infected neonates will develop chronic infection and in infected males lifetime risk of developing hepatocellular cancer is 50%; 20% for ♀. Most will develop cirrhosis—so immunization is really important. ►Vaccinate babies of carriers and infected mothers at birth. See p 151.[30 31] In uncomplicated hepatitis HBV DNA is cleared, anti-core antibodies develop, followed by anti-HBe antibodies with the decline and disappearance of HBeAg and HBsAg at 3 months. Do serology of vaccinated baby at 12–15 months old. If HBsAg -ve and anti-HBs is present, the child has been protected

Hepatitis E Risk of maternal mortality is ↑; death is usually postpartum, preceded by coma and massive PPH. A vaccine is awaited.[32 33]

Herpes simplex Types I and II both cause problems. If mother develops primary genital infection in pregnancy refer to genitourinary clinic to screen for other infections. If in last trimester give aciclovir for 5 days to reduce virus shedding. Consider elective caesarean if primary infection in last 6 weeks of pregnancy (no maternal protective antibodies). If active primary infection lesions at time of delivery perform caesarean—if membranes rupture spontaneously still perform caesarean if within 4h of rupture. If mother with primary lesions does deliver vaginally risk of infection to the baby is 41%: so give mother (by IVI during labour) and newborn aciclovir and avoid fetal blood sampling, scalp electrodes and instrumental delivery if possible. Neonatal infection usually appears at 5–21 days with vesicular pustular lesions, often at the presenting part or sites of minor trauma (eg scalp electrode). Periocular and conjunctival lesions may occur. With systemic infection encephalitis (focal fits or CNS signs), jaundice, hepatosplenomegaly, collapse, and DIC may occur. Infected neonates should be isolated and treated with aciclovir (p 200). Seek expert help.

Chlamydia trachomatis Associations: low birth weight, premature membrane rupture, fetal death. ~30% of infected mothers have affected babies. Conjunctivitis develops 5–14 days after birth and may show minimal inflammation or purulent discharge. The cornea is not usually involved. ***Complications:*** Chlamydia pneumonitis, pharyngitis, or otitis media. ***Tests:*** Special swabs are available but may be unreliable. See p 285. ***Treatment:*** Local cleansing of eye and + erythromycin 12.5mg/kg/6h PO for ~3 weeks eliminates lung organisms. Give parents/partners erythromycin[34] or azithromycin 1g PO single dose.

Gonococcal conjunctivitis Occurs within ~4 days of birth, with purulent discharge and lid swelling, ± corneal hazing, corneal rupture, and panophthalmitis. Note, 50% will also have concurrent chlamydial infection. ***Treatment:*** Infants born to those with known gonorrhoea should have *cefotaxime* 100mg/kg IM stat, and *chloramphenicol* 0.5% eye-drops within 1h of birth. For active gonococcal infection give *benzylpenicillin* 50mg/kg/12h IM and 3-hourly 0.5% chloramphenicol drops for 7 days. Isolate the baby.

Ophthalmia neonatorum This is purulent discharge from the eye of a neonate <21 days old. Originally referring to *Neisseria gonorrhoea* there are many causes: chlamydiae, herpes virus, staphylococci, streptococci, pneumococci, *E. coli*, and other Gram -ve organisms. ***Tests:*** In a baby with a sticky eye take swabs for bacterial and viral culture, microscopy (look for intracellular gonococci) and chlamydia (eg immunofluorescence). Treat gonococcus and chlamydia as above; other infections with neomycin drops or ointment (allows chlamydia detection—not so with chloramphenicol).

Clostridium perfringens Suspect this in any complication of criminal abortion—and whenever intracellular encapsulated Gram +ve rods are seen on genital swabs. It may also complicate death *in utero*, and it may also infect haematomas, and other anaerobic sites. ***Clinical features:*** Endometritis → septicaemia/gangrene → myoglobinuria → renal failure → death.
Management: •Surgically debride all devitalized tissue. •Hyperbaric O_2. •High-dose IV benzylpenicillin (erythromycin if serious penicillin allergy). The use of gas gangrene antitoxin is controversial. Seek expert help.

Tuberculosis All babies born into families with a member who has TB, to immigrant mothers from communities with a high incidence of TB, or who will be travelling to areas with a high incidence of TB should be given BCG (Bacillus Calmette-Guérin) vaccination after birth 0.05mL intradermally at deltoid insertion: if using a multiple puncture gun dose is 0.03mL (percutaneous). Babies not vaccinated in hospital are unlikely to be vaccinated in the community.[1] Usual other childhood vaccinations should be given at the normal time but avoid using the BCG vaccinated arm for 3 months. Babies born to mothers with active or open TB should be separated from the mother until she has had 2 weeks of treatment and is sputum negative. BCG vaccinate the baby and treat with isoniazid until he or she has a positive skin reaction. Consider CXR in pregnant women with cough, fever or weight loss (especially if recent immigrant). Encourage breast feeding.

For perinatal **listeria** and **streptococcal infection**, see p 204.

1 D Bakshi 2004 *Acta Paediactr* **93** 1207

Abdominal pain in pregnancy

►With any pain in pregnancy think, could this be the onset of labour?

Abdominal pain may be from ligament stretching or from symphysis pubis strain. In early pregnancy remember miscarriage (p 260) and ectopics (p 262).

Abruption The triad of abdominal pain, uterine rigidity, and vaginal bleeding suggests this. It occurs in between 1 in 80 and 1 in 200 pregnancies. Fetal loss is high (up to 60%). A tender uterus is highly suggestive. Ultrasound may be diagnostic (but not necessarily so). A live viable fetus merits rapid delivery as demise can be sudden. Prepare for DIC, which complicates 33–50% of severe cases, and beware PPH, which is also common. See p 56.

Uterine rupture See p 80.

Uterine fibroids For torsion and red degeneration, see p 277.

Uterine torsion The uterus rotates axially 30–40° to the right in 80% of normal pregnancies. Rarely, it rotates >90° causing acute uterine torsion in mid or late pregnancy with abdominal pain, shock, a tense uterus, and urinary retention (catheterization may reveal a displaced urethra in twisted vagina). Fibroids, adnexal masses, or congenital asymmetrical uterine anomalies are present in 90%. Diagnosis is usually at laparotomy. Delivery is by caesarean section.

Ovarian tumours Torsion, rupture, see p 282. **Pyelonephritis** See p 28.

Appendicitis Incidence: ~1/1000 pregnancies. It is not commoner in pregnancy but mortality is higher (esp. from 20 weeks). Perforation is commoner (15–20%). Fetal mortality is ~1.5% for simple appendicitis; ~30% if perforation. The appendix migrates upwards, outwards and posteriorly as pregnancy progresses, so pain is less well localized (often paraumbilical or subcostal—but right lower quadrant still commonest)[35] and tenderness, rebound, and guarding less obvious. Peritonitis can make the uterus tense and woody-hard. Operative delay is dangerous. Laparotomy over site of maximal tenderness with patient tilted 30° to the left should be performed by an experienced obstetric surgeon (or by laparoscopy).[1]

Cholecystitis Incidence 1–6 per 10,000 pregnancies. Pregnancy encourages gallstone formation due to biliary stasis and increased cholesterol in bile. Symptoms are similar to the non-pregnant with subcostal pain, nausea, and vomiting. Jaundice is uncommon (5%). Ultrasound confirms the presence of stones. The main differential diagnosis is appendicitis, and laparotomy or laparoscopy is mandatory if this cannot be excluded. Surgery should be reserved for complicated non-resolving biliary tract disease during pregnancy as in >90% the acute process resolves with conservative management. For patients requiring surgery, laparoscopic cholecystectomy can be a safe and effective method of treatment,[1] but uterine perforation or injury is a risk.

Rectus sheath haematoma Very rarely, bleeding into the rectus sheath and haematoma formation can occur with coughing (or spontaneously) in late pregnancy causing swelling and tenderness. Ultrasound is helpful. ΔΔ: Abruption. ***Management:*** Laparotomy (or perhaps laparoscopy—but not in late pregnancy) is indicated if the diagnosis is in doubt or if there is shock.[36,37]

Abdominal pain may complicate pre-eclampsia by liver congestion. Rarely, in severe pre-eclampsia the liver perforates. Pancreatitis in pregnancy is rare; but mortality high (37% maternal; 5.6% fetal). Diagnose by urinary diastase in first trimester when amylase may be low.[38]

1 M Rollins 2004 *Surg Endosc* **18** 237

Abdominal palpation

The uterus occupies the pelvis and cannot be felt per abdomen until about 12 weeks' gestation. By 16 weeks it lies about halfway between the symphysis pubis and the umbilicus. By 20–24 weeks it has reached the umbilicus. In a primigravida, the fundus lies under the ribs by 36 weeks. At term the uterus tends to lie a little lower than at 36 weeks, due to the head descending into the pelvis. Some attendants prefer to measure the symphysis–fundal height (SFH) in cm from the symphysis pubis (after voiding urine). From ~16 weeks the SFH increases ~1cm/week:

As a rule of thumb, at 16–36 weeks the SFH (cm) ≈ dates (in weeks)
 36 weeks → the SFH (cm) ± 2cm = dates
 36 weeks to term: the SFH (cm) ± 3cm = dates

SFH is used as a rough guide to find babies small for gestational age (p 52). Suspect this if the measurement lies >2cm outside dates ranges given above. NB: more false positives with charts compared with the simple rule of weeks of gestation = cm from pubic symphysis to fundus.

Other reasons for discrepancy between fundal height and dates: uncertain menstrual history • Multiple gestation • Fibroids • Poly/oligohydramnios • Abnormal mass • Abnormal fetal size • Hydatidiform mole.

On inspecting the abdomen note any scars from previous operations. Caesarean section scars are usually transverse (Pfannenstiel). Laparoscopy scars are just below and parallel to the umbilicus or in the left upper quadrant (Palmer's point). It is common to see a line of pigmentation, the linea nigra, extending in the midline from pubic hair to umbilicus. This darkens during the first trimester (at about 12 weeks).

Palpating the abdomen Measure the SFH and listen to the fetal heart. After 32 weeks palpate laterally to assess the lie, then bimanually palpate over the lower uterine pole for presentation and degree of engagement. Pawlik's grip (examining the lower pole of the uterus between the thumb and index fingers of the right hand) can also be used for assessing the degree of engagement. Watch the patient's face during palpation and stop if it causes pain. Obesity, polyhydramnios and tense muscles make it difficult to feel the fetus. Midwives are skilled at palpation, so ask them if you need help.

It is important to determine the number of fetuses (p 67), the lie (longitudinal, oblique, or transverse), the presentation (cephalic or breech), and the engagement; ultrasound is useful here. Note the amount of liquor present, the apparent size of the fetus, and any contractions or fetal movements seen or felt.

Auscultation The fetal heart may be heard by Doppler ultrasound from ~12 weeks and with Pinard's stethoscope from ~24 weeks.

Engagement The level of the head is assessed in 5ths, with engagement at ≤2/5ths palpable abdominally. Engagement entails passage of the maximum diameter of the presenting part through the pelvic inlet. Fifths palpable abdominally states what you can feel, and makes no degree of judgment on degree of engagement of the head. In primigravidae the head is usually entering the pelvis by 37 weeks; otherwise causes must be excluded (eg placenta praevia or fetal abnormality). In multiparae the head may not enter the pelvis until the onset of labour.

[illegible]

Abdominal palpation

The uterus occupies the pelvis and cannot be felt *per abdomen* until about 12 weeks' gestation. By 16 weeks it lies about half way between the symphysis pubis and the umbilicus. By 20–24 weeks it has reached the umbilicus. In a primigravida, the fundus lies under the ribs by 36 weeks. At term the uterus tends to lie a little lower than at 36 weeks due to the head descending into the pelvis. Some attendants prefer to measure the symphysis fundal height (SFH) in cm from the symphysis pubis (after voiding urine). From 16 weeks the SFH increases ~1cm/week.

As a rule of thumb:	at 16–26 weeks	the SFH (cm) ≈ dates (in weeks)
	26–36 weeks	the SFH (cm) ± 2cm ≈ dates
	36 weeks to term	the SFH (cm) ± 3cm ≈ dates.

SFH is used as a rough guide to find babies small for gestational age (p 52). Suspect this if the measurement lies >1–2cm outside these ranges given above. NB: more false positives will occur with the simpler rule of *weeks of gestation = cm from pubic symphysis to fundus.*[1,2]

Other reasons for discrepancy between fundal height and dates: •Inaccurate menstrual history •Multiple gestation •Fibroids •Polyhydramnios •Adnexal mass •Maternal size •Hydatidiform mole.

On inspecting the abdomen note any scars from previous operations. Caesarean section scars are usually Pfannenstiel ('bikini-line'). Laparoscopy scars are just below and parallel to the umbilicus or in the left upper quadrant (Palmer's point). It is common to see a line of pigmentation, the linea nigra, extending in the midline from pubic hair to umbilicus. This darkens during the first trimester (the first 13 weeks).

Palpating the abdomen Measure the SFH and listen to the *fetal heart.* After 32 weeks palpate laterally to assess the lie, then bimanually palpate over the lower uterine pole for presentation and degree of engagement. Pawlik's grip (examining the lower pole of the uterus between the thumb and index fingers of the right hand) can also be used for assessing the degree of engagement. Watch the patient's face during palpation and stop if it causes pain. Obesity, polyhydramnios and tense muscles make it difficult to feel the fetus. Midwives are skilled at palpation, so ask them if you need help.

It is important to determine the *number of fetuses* (p 68), the *lie* (longitudinal, oblique, or transverse), the *presentation* (cephalic or breech), and the *engagement*. Ultrasound is useful here. Note the amount of liquor present, the apparent size of the fetus, and any contractions or fetal movements seen or felt.

Auscultation The fetal heart may be heard by Doppler ultrasound from ~12 weeks and with a Pinard stethoscope from ~24 weeks.

Engagement The level of the head is assessed in 2 ways—engagement, or fifths palpable abdominally. Engagement entails passage of the maximum diameter of the presenting part through the pelvic inlet. Fifths palpable abdominally states what you can feel, and makes no degree of judgment on degree of engagement of the head. In primigravida the head is usually entering the pelvis by 37 weeks, otherwise causes must be excluded (eg placenta praevia or fetal abnormality). In multips the head may not enter the pelvis until the onset of labour.

1 http://www.vh.org/Providers/ClinRef/FPHandbook/Chapter14/02-14.html
2 www.arcmesa.com/pdf/emerdeli/emerdeli_chap2.htm

Position

Occipitoanterior	*Occipitolateral*	*Occipitoposterior*
Back easily felt	Back can be felt	Back not felt
Limbs not easily felt	Limbs lateral	Limbs anterior
Shoulder lies 2cm from midline on opposite side from back	Midline shoulder	Shoulder 6–8cm lateral, same side as back
Back from midline=2–3cm	6–8cm	≥10cm

►The fetal heart is best heard over the baby's back (left scapula).

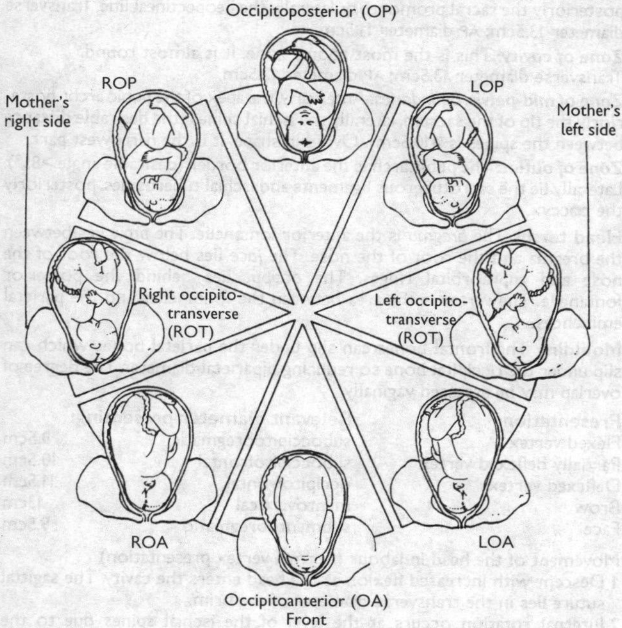

Pelvis and head

The ideal pelvis This has a rounded brim, a shallow cavity, non-prominent ischial spines, a curved sacrum with large sciatic notches and sacrospinous ligaments >3.5cm long. The angle of the brim is 55° to the horizontal, the AP diameter at least 12cm and transverse diameter at least 13.5cm. The subpubic arch should be rounded and the intertuberous distance at least 10cm. A *clinically favourable* pelvis is one where the sacral promontory cannot be felt, the ischial spines are not prominent, the subpubic arch and base of supraspinous ligaments both accept 2 fingers and the intertuberous diameter accepts 4 knuckles when the woman is examined.

The true pelvis Anteriorly there is the symphysis pubis (3.5cm long) and posteriorly the sacrum (12cm long).

Zone of inlet: *Boundaries:* Anteriorly lies the upper border of the pubis, posteriorly the sacral promontory, laterally the ileopectineal line. Transverse diameter 13.5cm; AP diameter 11.5cm.

Zone of cavity: This is the most roomy zone. It is almost round. Transverse diameter 13.5cm; AP diameter 12.5cm.

Zone of mid-pelvis: *Boundaries:* Anteriorly, the apex of the pubic arch; posteriorly the tip of the sacrum, laterally the ischial spines (the desirable distance between the spines is >10.5cm). Ovoid in shape, it is the narrowest part.

Zone of outlet: The pubic arch is the anterior border (desirable angle >85°). Laterally lie the sacrotuberous ligaments and ischial tuberosities, posteriorly the coccyx.

Head terms The *bregma* is the anterior fontanelle. The *brow* lies between the bregma and the root of the nose. The *face* lies below the root of the nose and supraorbital ridges. The *occiput* lies behind the posterior fontanelle. The *vertex* is the area between the fontanelles and the parietal eminences.

Moulding The frontal bones can slip under the parietal bones which can slip under the occipital bone so reducing biparietal diameter. The degree of overlap may be assessed vaginally.

Presentation:	**Relevant diameter presenting:**	
Flexed vertex	suboccipitobregmatic	9.5cm
Partially deflexed vertex	suboccipitofrontal	10.5cm
Deflexed vertex	occipitofrontal	11.5cm
Brow	mentovertical	13cm
Face	submentobregmatic	9.5cm

Movement of the head in labour (normal vertex presentation)

1. Descent with increased flexion as the head enters the cavity. The sagittal suture lies in the transverse diameter of the brim.
2. Internal rotation occurs at the level of the ischial spines due to the grooved gutter of the levator muscles. Head flexion increases. (The head rotates 90° if occipitolateral position, 45° if occipitoanterior, 135° if occipitoposterior.)
3. Disengagement by extension as the head comes out of the vulva.
4. Restitution: as the shoulders are rotated by the levators until the bisacromial diameter is anteroposterior, the head externally rotates the same amount as before but in opposite direction.
5. Delivery of anterior shoulder by lateral flexion of trunk posteriorly.
6. Delivery of posterior shoulder by lateral flexion of trunk anteriorly.
7. Delivery of buttocks and legs.

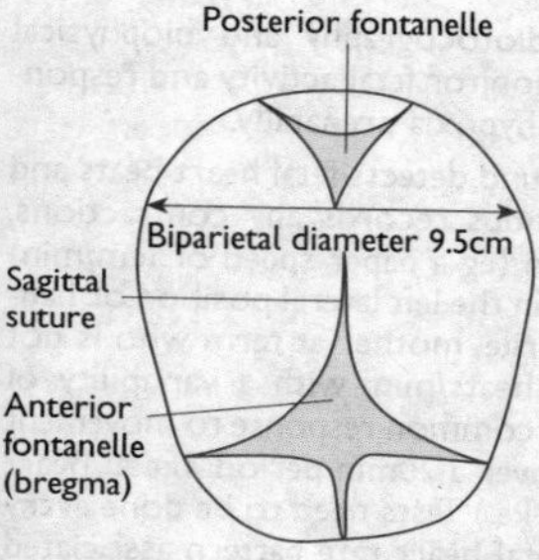

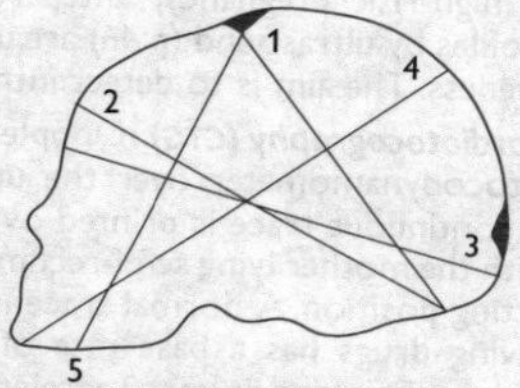

1 Suboccipitobregmatic 9.5cm flexed vertex presentation
2 Suboccipitofrontal 10.5cm partially deflexed vertex
3 Occipipitofrontal 11.5cm deflexed vertex
4 Mentovertical 13cm brow
5 Submentobregmatic 9.5cm face

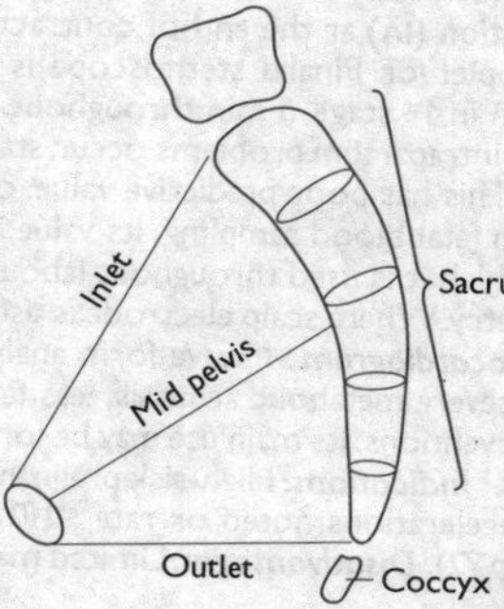

Life forced her through this gate of suffering

DH Lawrence, *Sons & Lovers*, JPS, 284

Fetal monitoring

In high-risk pregnancy, antepartum cardiotocography and biophysical profiles by ultrasound (p 46) are used to monitor fetal activity and responsiveness. The aim is to detect intrauterine hypoxia prenatally.

***Cardiotocography* (CTG) :** Doppler ultrasound detects fetal heart beats and a tocodynamometer over the uterine fundus records any contractions. A continuous trace is printed over ~30min (eg a paper speed of 1cm/min) with the mother lying semi-recumbent, or in the left lateral position or half-sitting position. A normal trace in an afebrile, mother at term who is not having drugs has a base rate of 110–160 beats/min, with a variability of >5 beats/min, and at least 2 accelerations (a common response to movement or noise) of an amplitude ≥15 beats/min over a 20min period. (Fetal heart rate falls by ~1 beat/min/week from 28 weeks.) Tests need to be done every 24h antenatally to identify the changing fetal heart rate pattern associated with hypoxia (loss of baseline variability with decelerations).

Intrapartum monitoring Death and disability due to complications of labour occur in <1:300 labours. Intrapartum fetal heart rate monitoring aims to detect patterns known to be associated with fetal distress—a diagnosis supported fetal hypoxia (acidosis) on blood sampling.

Intermittent auscultation* (IA)** at the end of contractions (to listen for decelerations) with doppler or Pinard stethoscope is used for low-risk labours. Use every 15min in 1st stage, 5 min throughout 2nd stage. If abnormality noted (below) or intrapartum problems occur, start ***continuous fetal heart rate monitoring. This has poor predictive value, overdiagnosing fetal distress even if used with fetal blood sampling. Its value is uncertain even in high-risk labours—for which it is used throughout labour, ideally with scalp electrode or pulse oximetry. Where scalp electrode is used it is also possible to monitor ***fetal electrocardiogram*** ST wave form analysis was associated with fewer babies with severe metabolic acidosis, less fetal blood sampling, and fewer operative interventions. Its main use may be for those labours with disquieting CTG patterns.[1] ***Indications:*** High-risk pregnancy; use of oxytocin; abnormality with IA (decelerations noted or rate <110 or >160 beats/min; fresh meconium passed, p 72). ***Disadvantages:*** Limited maternal mobility and discomfort.

Management of a poor trace:

1 Lie the mother on her left side and give O_2. Stop oxytocin. If there is uterine hypercontractility give tocolysis with 0.25mg terbutaline SC.

2 Take fetal blood sample. If you do not have this facility, consider rapid delivery if the trace does not improve.

Fetal blood sampling: Fetal acidosis reflects hypoxia. Scalp blood pH of 7.3–7.4 is normal. If 7.25–7.29 repeat after 45min. If 7.2–7.24 consider caesarean section. Levels <7.2 require immediate delivery unless in second stage when a level as low as 7.15 may be acceptable. CI maternal infection (HIV, hepatitis viruses and herpes), fetal suspected clotting disorder, <34 week's gestation.

1 Neilson 2003 Cochrane Database Syst Rev CD000116

Fetal heart rate patterns and their clinical significance
The normal pattern is described opposite. Accelerations suggest intact sympathetic activity and are rarely associated with hypoxia.

Loss of baseline variability Baseline variability of >5 beats/min shows response to vagal tone, sympathetic stimuli, and catecholamines in a well oxygenated fetal brainstem. Loss of baseline variability may reflect a preterm fetus who is sleeping, drug effects (eg diazepam, morphine, phenothiazine), or hypoxia.

Baseline tachycardia Heart rate >170 beats/min is associated with maternal fever, or β-sympathomimetic drug use, chorioamnionitis (loss of variation too), and acute/subacute hypoxia. Persistent rates >200 are associated with fetal cardiac arrhythmia.

Baseline bradycardia A heart rate <110 beats/min is rarely associated with fetal hypoxia (except in placental abruption). It may reflect ↑ fetal vagal tone, fetal heart block, or, if spasmodic, cord compression.

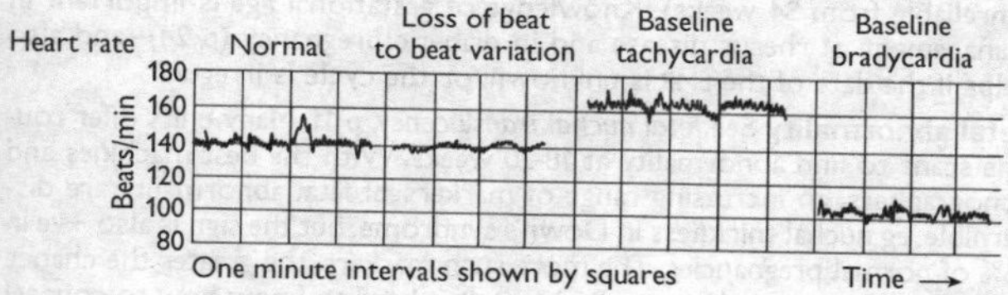

Early decelerations coinciding with uterine contractions reflect increased vagal tone as fetal intracranial pressure rises with the contraction. **Late decelerations**, when the nadir of the deceleration develops some 30sec after the peak of the uterine contraction, reflect fetal hypoxia, the degree and duration reflecting its severity. **Variable decelerations**, both in degree and relation to uterine contractions, may represent umbilical cord compression around the limbs or presenting part.

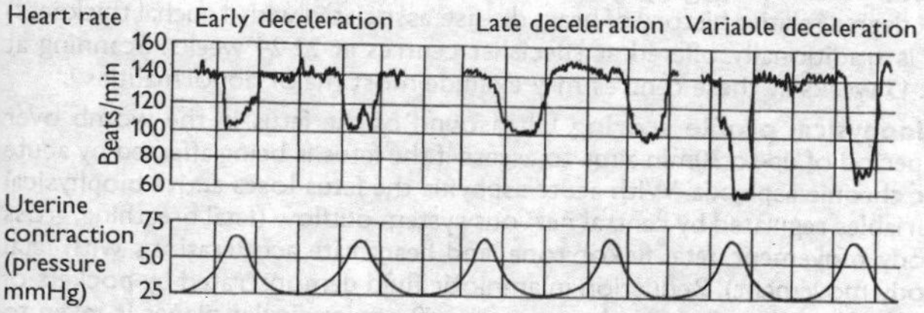

Pathological CTG pattern[1] This has 2 suspicious features (baseline rate 100–109 or 161–180 beats/minute; variability <5 beats/minute for ≥40 but <90 minutes; early, variable, or a prolonged deceleration of <3 minutes) or 1 abnormal feature (rate <100 or >180 beats/minute; sinusodial pattern for >10 minutes; variability <5 beats/minute for ≥90 minutes; atypical variable decelerations or a single deceleration of >3 minutes).

1 NICE Guideline 2001 *Electronic Fetal Monitoring*; see www.nice.org.uk

Ultrasound

In each ultrasound examination, examine placental site and structure, assess liquor volume and fetal structure, and wellbeing (see below).

Early in pregnancy If there is bleeding and pain, ultrasound can confirm intrauterine pregnancy—at 4 weeks + 3 days for regular 28 day cycle with transvaginal scan, (or ectopic) and the viability of the fetus. Where there is discrepancy between uterine size and dates, gestation can be estimated, a viable fetus ascertained (not missed abortion, p 260), or twins (and if monochorionic or dichorionic see p 68) diagnosed—especially important after the use of fertility drugs or in the presence of hyperemesis gravidarum (also to exclude hydatidiform mole).

Estimation of gestational age Crown-rump length is measured from 6 to 12 weeks (~10mm at 7 weeks; ~55mm at 12 weeks). From 12 weeks the biparietal diameter can be measured (and femur length from 14 weeks so that there are 2 independent estimations with each procedure). Biparietal diameter measurements to estimate age are most accurate up to 20 weeks (unreliable from 34 weeks). Knowledge of gestational age is important in management of rhesus disease and in diabetic pregnancy (p 24)—and also helps if the date of the LMP is unknown, or the cycle is irregular.

Fetal abnormality See *fetal nuchal translucency,* p 11. Many units offer routine scans to find abnormality at 18–20 weeks. With the best machines and sonographers, an increasing range of markers of fetal abnormality are discernible, eg nuchal thickness in Down's syndrome, but the sign is also +ve in ~6% of normal pregnancies. The more such markers, the greater the chance of abnormality (see p 10 for 'soft signs'). It is hard to know how to counsel women before these discerning scans: full informed consent is time-consuming, and itself causes psychopathology (p 12). Another problem is that many fetuses with chromosomal abnormalities suggested by early scans will spontaneously miscarry in subsequent weeks, and one will have overburdened the mother needlessly. Specific indications for scanning for abnormality include:

- Family history of neural tube defect
- Maternal diabetes or epilepsy
- AFP abnormal
- Oligohydramnios
- Twins
- Polyhydramnios

Fetal echocardiography Offered to high-risk groups (personal or 1st degree relative history of heart disease; associated with ↑nuchal thickness) it is traditionally offered at specialist centres at 22–24 weeks. Scanning at 12–15 weeks at these centres may exclude most major abnormalities.[1]

Biophysical profile scoring Ultrasound of the fetus in the womb over a period of up to 30min aims to assess if the fetus is being affected by acute or chronic asphyxia. With acute asphyxia the fetus loses active biophysical variables regulated by central nervous system outflow (fetal breathing, gross body movement, fetal flexor tone, and heart rate accelerations with fetal body movement). Reduction in amniotic fluid demonstrated by pockets of fluid of less than 1cm depth measured in 2 perpendicular planes is taken to indicate chronic asphyxia. By use of specific criteria for these 5 variables, a 'wellbeing' score can be reached. Management protocols according to score then help guide the obstetrician as to when intervention should take place.

Ultrasound is used as an adjunct to the diagnostic procedures of amniocentesis, fetoscopy, cordocentesis, and chorionic villus biopsy.

In pregnancies where fetal growth is of concern (p 52) growth can be monitored by regular scans; the abdominal to skull circumference ratio being of interest. Fetal weight can be estimated when planning vaginal delivery of breech presentation (but less accurate for larger fetuses).

In later pregnancy, the lie and presentation of the fetus can be determined. If there is APH, placenta praevia can be excluded and the placenta visualized to look for abruption. With secondary postpartum haemorrhage, retained products of conception may be visualized.

Side-effects Ultrasound is one of the safest tests ever invented; nevertheless, over the years, fears have been expressed about inducing childhood cancers. There is now good evidence that this does not occur. There is one randomized trial indicating that *repeated* ultrasound with Doppler is associated with an increased risk (1.65) of birth weights below the third centile.

Doppler ultrasound and fetal wellbeing Doppler ultrasound is a technique that can be used to assess circulation on both sides of the placenta. It has not been shown to be of use as a screening tool in routine antenatal care but it has been shown to be of use in high-risk pregnancies. Waveform outlines (velocimetry) have been seen to be abnormal in small babies who ultimately died or were severely ill perinatally, and babies known to be small from real-time ultrasound have been shown not to be at risk if umbilical artery waveforms were normal, but if end-diastolic signals are absent the baby is likely to be hypoxic and acidotic. In management of growth-retarded babies uncomplicated by other obstetric problems surveillance using Doppler velocimetry is more cost-effective than use of cardiotocography, and may be sufficient as the sole extra means of surveillance (in addition to ultrasound examination of biophysical parameters). ►Consider caesarean section if umbilical artery Doppler velocimetry shows absent or reversed end diastolic velocities in pregnancies complicated by intrauterine growth restriction and hypertension—to prevent postnatal problems such as cerebral haemorrhage, anaemia, and hypoglycaemia. These changes correlate with placental intervillous space ischaemia and spasm or occlusion of tertiary stem arterioles on the fetal side of the circulation. Placental intervillous ischaemia leads to centralization of fetal circulation so that blood returning from the placenta is shunted to fetal brain, coronary arteries and adrenals. Intervention studies based on knowledge of abnormal umbilical waveform patterns have resulted in babies small-for-gestational age (SGA) with abnormal waveform patterns being ~500g larger than expected when the mothers were given low-dose aspirin rather than placebo from the time of diagnosis. It is also the case that low-dose aspirin delays the onset of hypertension and reduces its severity in primiparous mothers whose babies had abnormal umbilical waveforms. However, aspirin has not been shown to be of benefit in low-risk pregnancies.

1 J Simpsom 2000 *BJOG* **107** 1492

Hypertension in pregnancy

Pre-existing essential hypertension Drugs may need modifying (some ↓ fetal growth).[MET 39] Risk of pre-eclampsia is raised ×5 (suspect if BP rises by 30/15mmHg from baseline or hyperuricaemia, proteinuria, or clotting activation). *If symptoms are episodic, think of phaeochromocytoma.*

Pre-eclampsia Terminology: see p 0. This is pregnancy-induced hypertension (PIH) with proteinuria ± oedema. It is a multisystem disorder originating in the placenta. The primary defect is failure of trophoblastic invasion of spiral arteries leaving them vasoactive—properly invaded they cannot clamp down in response to vasoconstrictors and this protects placental flow. Increasing BP is a mechanism which partially compensates for this. Pre-eclampsia also affects hepatic, renal and coagulation systems. It develops after 20 weeks and usually resolves within 10 days of delivery. Eclampsia (1 in 2000 maternities) is a major cause of maternal death and fetal morbidity/mortality. Pre-eclampsia may be asymptomatic, so frequent screening is vital. It may recur in a subsequent pregnancy.

Risk factors: *Maternal:* Past or family history of pre-eclampsia; sexual union for <4 months (or primips, or IVF by ICSI, p 293—all ?from no sperm-mediated partner-specific immune tolerance[40]); <155cm tall; weight↑; age <20 or >35; past migraine; BP↑; renal disease. Incidence is lower in smokers.

Fetal: Hydatidiform mole (↑BP at 20 weeks); multiple pregnancy; placental hydrops (eg rhesus disease). Fetal causes all have increased placental bulk.

Effects of pre-eclampsia: Plasma volume↓; peripheral resistance↑; placental ischaemia. If the BP is >180/140mmHg microaneurysms develop in arteries. DIC may develop. Oedema may develop suddenly (eg weight↑ by 1kg suddenly). Proteinuria is a late sign, meaning renal involvement, which may be detected earlier by doing urate levels (>0.29mmol/L at 28 weeks, >0.34mmol/L at 32 weeks, and >0.39mmol/L at 36 weeks suggest pre-eclampsia). Initially glomerular filtration is normal and only serum urate is ↑, later urea *and* creatinine increase. The liver may be involved (contributing to DIC)—and HELLP syndrome (p 26) may be present with placental infarcts. Fetal asphyxia, abruption, and small babies (p 52 & p 47) may also occur.

Preventing eclampsia Antenatal BP checks/urinalysis; use of $MgSO_4$ if risk↑. Uterine artery Doppler scans can identify high-risk women in whom aspirin use results in a significant reduction in pre-eclampsia.[41]

Symptomatic pre-eclampsia may mimic 'flu, with *headache, chest* or *epigastric pain, vomiting*, and *pulse*↑—but also *visual disturbance, shaking, hyper-reflexia*, and *irritability*. The mother is now in danger of *generalized seizures* (eclampsia) and treatment must occur. Death may be imminent from *stroke* (commonest), *hepatic, renal*, or *cardiac failure*. ►Prophylactic magnesium sulfate halves risk of eclampsia, and may ↓maternal deaths; without substantive short-term side-effects (mother or baby).[1]

Management *Early phase:* Admit if BP rises by >30/20mmHg over booking BP; if BP ≥160/100; if ≥140/90 + proteinuria, or there is growth restriction. In hospital, measure BP 2–4-hourly, weigh daily, test all urine for protein; regularly monitor fluid balance, check U&E, LFT, urate, placental function, and platelets (beware falls to <110 × 10^9/L). Also do regular antenatal cardiotocography (p 44) with US scan to check growth and biophysical profiles. In asymptomatic pre-eclampsia, ↑BP may be treated with drugs, eg methyldopa 250mg to 1g/6h under supervision in hospital if BP rises to 170/110mmHg, in order to buy time for fetal maturation, and if all other variables are satisfactory. If signs worsen deliver the baby (liaise with paediatricians). Delivery is the only cure. Give all pre-eclamptic women H_2-blockers at onset of labour.

1 Further reading: *Pre-eclampsia community guideline* (PRECOG): how to screen for and detect onset of pre-eclampsia in the community *BMJ* 2005 **330** 576 & : The Magpie Trial 2002 *Lancet* **359** 1877

⏩Managing severe pre-eclampsia

Why mothers die: www.chemach.org.uk

This applies to those with BP >160/110 with proteinuria >0.5g/day ***or*** BP ≥ 140/90 with proteinuria plus one or more of:
- Seizures
- Headache or epigastric pain
- Platelets $<100 \times 10^9$/L
- Visual disturbance
- Creatinine >100μmol/L
- ALT >50iu/L
- Clonus (>3 beats)
- Creatinine clearance <80mL/min.

⏩Continuously monitor maternal oxygen saturation, and BP every 15min.
⏩'Magpie' regimen of prophylactic magnesium sulfate: 4g (8mL of 50% solution) IVI over 15min in 100mL 0.9% saline; then maintenance as below.
⏩Catheterize for urine output; hourly T°; FBC, U&E, LFTs, creatinine every 12h.
⏩Monitor fetal heart rate; assess liquor volume and fetal growth by scan; umbilical cord doppler if possible.
⏩*Delivery is the only cure for these women.* When a decision is made to deliver, contact on-call consultant, anaesthetist, and senior labour ward midwife.

Treatment of hypertension Beware: automated BP devices underestimate BP.
⏩If BP >160/110mmHg or mean arterial pressure (MAP) >125mmHg, use hydralazine 5mg IV slowly unless pulse >120bpm, repeating every 20mins until 20mg total given; if needed. Alternative: labetalol 20mg IV increasing after 10min intervals to 40mg then 80mg until 200mg total is given.
⏩Give prophylactic H_2 blockers until normal postnatal care starts.
⏩Restrict fluids to 85mL/h. Hourly urine output: if oliguria <100mL/4h consider giving 500mL human albumin solution (HAS) IVI. Consider HAS also prior to hydralazine use, caesarean section, or use of regional anaesthesia. If HAS is used, consider inserting central venous pressure (CVP) line: if further oliguria, one is recommended. If CVP >10mmHg, give 20mg furosemide (or if there is persistent oliguria). If central venous pressure is <10mmHg consider giving 500mL of human albumin solution by IVI.

Treatment of seizures (eclampsia):
⏩Treat a first seizure with 4g magnesium sulfate in 100mL 0.9% saline IVI over 5min + maintenance IVI of 1g/h for 24h. Beware ↓ respiration.
⏩If there are recurrent seizures give 2g IVI magnesium sulfate as a bolus.
⏩Check tendon reflexes and respiratory rate every 15min.
⏩Stop magnesium sulfate IVI if respiratory rate <14/min or SaO_2 <95%.
⏩Monitor Mg^{2+} levels (*therapeutic range:* 2–4mmol/L) if recurrent fits or renal compromise; have IV calcium gluconate ready in case of $MgSO_4$ toxicity.
⏩Use diazepam if fits continue at consultant's discretion (eg 5–10mg slowly IV). If seizures continue consider other causes (consider CT scan).

Pitfalls in the management of eclampsia and pre-eclampsia
- Belief that the disease behaves predictably, and that BP is a good marker.
- Ignoring mild proteinuria; even if 1+, the patient may be dead within 24h.
- Believing antihypertensives stop pre-eclampsia (they may stop stroke). They don't. Only delivery cures. Diuretics deplete the already reduced plasma volume, and are especially contraindicated (except in the rare left ventricular failure or laryngeal oedema complicating pre-eclampsia).
- Believing that delivery removes risk. In the UK, half of eclamptic fits are postpartum: half of these are >48h postpartum. Continue vigilance until clinically and biochemically normal. Avoid early discharge.
- Ergometrine should not be used for the third stage (oxytocin may be used). Ergometrine further increases BP so would risk stroke.
- Not replacing significant blood loss *meticulously*. Risks are hypovolaemia or fatal fluid over-load ± acute respiratory distress syndrome. Have one person (the most experienced) in charge of all the IVIs.
- Failure to inform anaesthetists early and use intensive care facilities.

Prematurity

►This is a leading cause of perinatal mortality and morbidity.

Premature infants are those born before 37 weeks' gestation. Prevalence: ~6% singletons, 46% of twin, 79% of triplet or higher order deliveries. About 2% are before 32 weeks—when neonatal problems are greatest. In 25%, delivery is elective (p 62). 10% are due to multiple pregnancy; 25% are due to APH, cervical incompetence, amnionitis, uterine abnormalities, diabetes, polyhydramnios, pyelonephritis, or other infections. In 40% the cause is unknown, but abnormal genital tract colonization (bacterial vaginosis) with ureaplasma and *Mycoplasma hominis* is implicated, either as a risk factor or risk marker. We also know that consumption of fish oil in pregnancy can ↑birth weight by ↓risk of recurrence of preterm delivery.[1]

Managing preterm rupture of membranes (PROM) Admit; do T° MSU, and HVS—using a sterile bivalve speculum. Assess for causes/associations: eg abruption, twins, and polyhydramnios. If liquor is not obvious its presence is suggested if nitrazine sticks (pH-sensitive) turn black (false +ve with infected vaginal discharge, semen, blood, and urine). In 80%, membrane rupture initiates labour. The problem with the 20% who do not go into labour is balancing advantages of remaining *in utero* (maturity and surfactant↑) against the threat of infection (causes 20% of neonatal deaths after PROM). Intrauterine infection supervenes after membranes have ruptured in 10% by 48h, 26% by 72h, 40% by >72h. Prophylactic antibiotics may allow labour to be delayed. If infection develops, do blood culture and give IV antibiotics (eg ampicillin 500mg/6h IV + netilmicin 150mg/12h IV) and expedite labour (p 62). Antibiotics for ~24h pre-labour, ↓rates of intraventricular haemorrhage and periventricular malacia (below) in the baby. If labour supervenes, allow it to progress. If liquor stops draining for >48h (rare) slowly mobilize the mother.[42]

Management of preterm labour In 50% contractions cease spontaneously. Treating the cause (eg pyelonephritis) may make it cease. Attempts to suppress contractions (tocolysis) are unlikely to succeed if membranes are ruptured or the cervix >4cm dilated. The rationale for tocolytic use was that delay of preterm labour would improve fetal outcome without causing harm to mother or fetus. Trials have shown them to be of almost no clinical benefit, and only nifedipine is associated with improvement of fetal outcome. It is quite reasonable not to use tocolytic drugs; though they may be considered desirable in certain circumstances eg to give time for corticosteroids to work; or for *in utero* transfer.[2] Use only between 24–33 weeks. Consider transfer to hospital with SCBU facilities. Call paediatrician to attend to the baby at birth. See cord-cutting recommendations p 58.

Tocolytic drugs Absolute CI: chorioamnionitis, fetal death or lethal abnormality, condition (fetal or maternal) needing immediate delivery. Relative CI: fetal growth restriction or distress, pre-eclampsia, placenta praevia, abruption, cervix >4cm. β-sympathomimetics, associated with maternal fluid overload and pulmonary oedema are not recommended. Atosiban (licensed in Europe) has less maternal effects, has not been shown to benefit the fetus, and is expensive. Nifedipine is as effective, and associated with less newborn respiratory distress and admission to intensive care. Regimen: nifedipine 20mg PO then 10–20mg/6–8h PO according to uterine activity (unlicensed indication). SE: ↓BP; headache; flushing; pulse↑ (transient); myocardial infarction (very rare).[43]

1 S Olsen 2002 *BMJ* i447 If fish oil intake is low, small amounts of n-3 fatty acids provided as fish or fish oil *may* protect against prematurity & low birth weight.

2 K Groom 2004 The Obstetrician and Gynaecologist **6** 4

Glucocorticoids Betametasone 12mg IM followed by a second dose 12 hours later, (or, less favoured dexamethasone 6mg/12h × 4 doses) promote fetal surfactant production, lowering mortality and complications of RDS (p 118) by 40–50%. They also help close patent ductuses and protect against periventricular malacia, a cause of cerebral palsy. Use between 24 and 34 weeks. Avoid if maternal systemic infection eg TB.

If diabetic, monitor glucose. Benefit is maximal after 24h; effects last a week.

Prematurity, survival, and disability—the figures

►One major, landmark question is: *Is the baby over 28 weeks' gestation?*

- The disability rate is 25% if gestation is <28 weeks—but half this if gestation is 28–29 weeks.
- 10% of those who survive at gestations <28 weeks will never be independently mobile, or communicate intelligibly with others.
- Only 4% of babies born before 24 weeks will survive, and of survivors, >50% will be severely disabled.
- Use of surfactant (p 118) has not reduced the viability threshold, or rates of severe disability in babies born at <28 weeks' gestation.
- Of babies born >30 weeks' gestation, in the absence of deformity, ~100% now survive.

Small for gestational age (SGA)

►When talking to parents, avoid the term *growth retardation* as this may imply to them the inevitability of mental handicap—which is not the case. Distinguish premature babies from those who are small-for-gestational age (SGA): they are at risk from different problems after birth.

Causes of growth restriction (IUGR) Growth restricted neonates are those weighing < the 10th centile for their gestational age (*Tables*, p 129).

Maternal factors: Multiple pregnancy, malformation, infection, smoking, diabetes, BP↑, Hb↓, pre-eclampsia, heart or renal disease, asthma.[MET 44] Those having intensive shared-care with an expert have less hypoxia, and less intra-uterine growth restriction (IUGR).[45]

~10% are to mothers who only ever produce small babies.

Asymmetric growth restriction: Where placental insufficiency was the cause, head circumference is relatively spared (the baby has been starved).

Antenatal diagnosis 50% are undetected before birth, and many babies suspected of IUGR do not have it. Measuring fundal height progress from the symphysis pubis is a reasonable method of measuring growth, especially if used with centile charts. Oligohydramnios and poor fetal movements are other indications of placental insufficiency. If growth restriction is suspected, growth *in utero* can be monitored by serial ultrasounds of head circumference and abdominal circumference. If umbilical cord Doppler blood flows are normal the outcome of growth restricted pregnancies is better (fewer premature births and stillbirths). Those with abnormal Dopplers may benefit from maternal low-dose aspirin (p 47), eg 75mg/24h PO. Biophysical profile monitoring (p 46) and antenatal cardiotocography (p 44) are used to try to detect those babies who are becoming hypoxic *in utero* and who would benefit from delivery. Advise the mother to stop smoking, and to take plenty of rest.

Labour and aftercare Growth restricted fetuses are more susceptible to hypoxia, so monitor in labour (p 44). After birth, temperature regulation may be a problem, so ensure a warm welcome; nurse those <2kg in an incubator. After being relatively hypoxic *in utero* the Hb at birth is high, so jaundice is more common. They have little stored glycogen so are prone to hypoglycaemia. Feed within 2h of birth and measure blood glucose before each 3-hourly feed. If hypoglycaemic despite regular feeds, transfer to a special care unit. They are more susceptible to infection. Birth reveals those for whom abnormality was the cause of growth restriction.

Distinguishing growth restriction from prematurity Before 34 weeks' gestation there is no breast bud tissue, from then it develops at 1mm diameter/week. Ear cartilage develops between 35 and 39 weeks so premature babies' ears do not spring back when folded. Testes lie in the inguinal canal at 35 weeks, in the scrotum from 37. Labia minora are exposed in premature girls. Skin creases on the anterior ⅓ of the foot appear by 35 weeks (on anterior ⅔ by 39, and all over from 39). 'Prems' have red, hairy skin. Vernix is made from 28 weeks and is maximal at 36 weeks. Prems do not lie with legs flexed until 32 weeks. All limbs are flexed from 36 weeks.

Effects of IUGR in adult life Many studies have confirmed ↑risk from:
- Hypertension
- Coronary artery disease
- Non-insulin-dependent diabetes mellitus
- Autoimmune thyroid disease

So fetal malnutrition casts a long shadow. Specific early deficiencies are important too (eg iodine, iron).

Large for gestational age

These are babies above the 90th centile in weight for gestation.

Causes: Constitutionally large (usually familial—the largest 10% of the population); maternal diabetes (p 24); hyperinsulinism; Beckwith-Wiedemann syndrome (p 638).

Labour and aftercare: Large babies are at risk of birth injury (see impacted shoulder p 72). Large babies are prone to immaturity of suckling and swallowing and may need temporary tube feeding. They are prone to hypoglycaemia and hypocalcaemia. Polycythaemia may result in jaundice. They are also prone to left colon syndrome: a self-limiting condition clinically mimicking Hirschsprung's disease (p 130) whereby temporary bowel obstruction (possibly also with meconium plug) occurs. Rarely, there is risk of renal vein thrombosis.

Postmaturity (prolonged pregnancy)

Prolonged pregnancy is defined as that exceeding 42 completed weeks or more from the LMP. Affecting 5–10% of pregnancies it is associated with increased perinatal mortality (5/1000 if 37–42 weeks, 9.7/1000 if >42 weeks). The dangers are placental insufficiency, and problems during labour due to the fetus being larger (25% are >4000g), the fetal skull more ossified and less easily moulded, the passage of meconium more common (25–42% labours), and fetal distress more common. Stillbirth rate is ↑ × 4, neonatal deaths ↑ × 3, and neonatal seizures ↑ × 10 in pregnancies going beyond 42 weeks compared with birth between 37 and 42 weeks.

Antepartum monitoring with use of cardiotocography (p 44), and biophysical profiles (p 46) can be used to try to detect fetuses who may be becoming hypoxic. Doppler studies of cord blood flow may be used to look for absent end diastolic flow as a predictor of fetal compromise. Without evidence to suggest problems, induction should be recommended from 41+ weeks after which time there are higher rates of caesarean section for those managed 'conservatively'. Use ultrasound dates not LMP for calculating gestation. 'Membrane sweeps' remain a valid non-pharmacological prelude to induction; more women go into spontaneous labour if as much membrane as possible is swept from the lower segment at examination between 41–42 weeks than if examined unswept. 6 women will be membrane swept for 1 formal induction avoided.[MET 46] Induction with vaginal prostaglandins may be associated with lower rates of instrumental delivery than induction with oxytocin. It is estimated that 500 inductions are needed to prevent 1 perinatal death. Vaginal misoprostol eg 50μg/4h to a maximum of 5 doses appears to be a good induction agent, although not yet routinely used as there are worries about uterine hyperstimulation. After induction, monitor the fetus in labour (p 44).

Postnatal signs of postmaturity: Dry, cracked, peeling, loose skin; decreased subcutaneous tissue; meconium staining of nails and cord.

▸▸Fetal distress

Fetal distress signifies hypoxia. Prolonged or repeated hypoxia causes fetal acidosis. An early sign may be the passage of meconium in labour (p 72). Other signs that the fetus may be hypoxic are a fetal tachycardia persisting above 160 beats per minute (tachycardia may also occur if the mother has a high temperature or is dehydrated). Hypoxia may also be reflected by loss of variability of the baseline in the fetal heart rate trace and slowing and irregularity of the heart rate (especially late decelerations—p 45). ▸▸If the heart rate falls below 100 beats per minute urgent assessment is required. Hypoxia may be confirmed by the use of fetal blood sampling (p 44). When significant hypoxia appears to be present (eg pH <7.24), deliver promptly (by the quickest route available, eg caesarean section or vaginal extraction). In complete anoxia the pH falls by 0.1 unit per minute.

▸▸Obstetric shock

Most obstetric shock is associated with severe haemorrhage. It should be remembered that with placental abruption, actual bleeding may be far in excess of that revealed *per vaginam* (p 56). Other causes of shock may be: ruptured uterus (p 80), inverted uterus (p 86); amniotic fluid embolus (p 89), pulmonary embolism, adrenal haemorrhage, and septicaemia.

Vomiting, diarrhoea and abdominal pain may be signs of genital sepsis. There may be rash. Fever may be absent. Persistent tachycardia, peripheral vascular shut down, increased respiratory rate, oliguria, metabolic acidosis, and reduced oxygen saturation indicate critical illness needing urgent management. Check blood gases to detect metabolic acidosis. Unfortunately young women can maintain blood pressure, appearing deceptively well and talking until sudden cardiovascular decompensation occurs. Septicaemia may lack classical signs (eg pyrexia) and must be considered where profound persisting shock is present, be appropriately investigated (eg blood cultures), and treated promptly, eg amoxicillin/clavulanic acid 1g/6h IV + metronidazole 500mg/8h IVI (+ gentamicin 1.5mg/kg/8h IV given over >3min; do levels, but not needed acutely, see *OHCM* p 547), whilst awaiting results.

Prompt resuscitation is required (see individual pages for management). Renal function and urine output should always be measured after shock has occurred (p 28). A late complication can be Sheehan's syndrome (also called Simmonds' disease) whereby pituitary necrosis leads to lack of thyroid-stimulating hormone, adrenocorticotrophic hormone, and the gonadotrophic hormones, hence leading to hypothyroidism, Addisonian symptoms and genital atrophy.

▸▸Antepartum haemorrhage (APH)

Traditionally this has been defined as bleeding at >24 (formerly 28) weeks' gestation. Any bleeding in pregnancy is associated with increased perinatal mortality. Severe bleeds can cause maternal death.[47]

▸Avoid vaginal examination: placenta praevias may bleed catastrophically.

Dangerous causes Abruption, placenta praevia, vasa praevia (here the baby may bleed to death).

Other uterine sources: Circumvallate placenta, placental sinuses.

Lower genital tract sources: Cervical polyps, erosions and carcinoma, cervicitis, vaginitis, vulval varicosities.

Placental abruption ('accidental haemorrhage') Part of the placenta becomes detached from the uterus. The outcome depends on the amount of blood loss and degree of separation. The cause is unknown but it is associated with pre-eclampsia, may recur in a subsequent pregnancy (6%), is commoner in smokers, and may complicate external cephalic version. Bleeding may be well localized to one placental area and there may be delay before bleeding is revealed.

Consequences: Placental insufficiency may cause fetal anoxia or death. Compression of uterine muscles by blood causes tenderness, and may prevent good contraction at all stages of labour, so beware a PPH (which occurs in ~25%). Posterior abruptions may present with backache. There may be uterine hypercontractility (>7 contractions per 15min). Thromboplastin release may cause DIC (10%). Concealed loss may cause maternal shock after which beware renal failure and Sheehan's syndrome (p 55).

Placenta praevia (For terminology and complications see p 14). The placenta lies in the lower uterine segment. Bleeding is always revealed.

Distinguishing ***abruption*** ⟶	From ***placenta praevia:***
Shock out of keeping with the visible loss	Shock in proportion to the visible loss
Pain constant	No pain
Tender, tense uterus	Uterus not tender
Normal lie and presentation	Both may be abnormal
Fetal heart: absent/distressed	Fetal heart usually normal
Coagulation problems	Coagulation problems rare
Beware pre-eclampsia, DIC, anuria	Small bleeds before large

Note: the risk of PPH is increased in both conditions. The lower segment may not contract well after a placenta praevia.

Management of APH *Always admit* ▸▸If bleeding is severe call emergency ambulance, put up IVI, take bloods, and raise legs. Give O_2 at 15L/min via mask with reservoir. On admission, if shocked give fresh ABO Rh compatible or O Rh-ve blood (eg 6U, 2 IVIs) fast until systolic BP >100mmHg. Send blood for clotting screen. Catheterize bladder; keep urine output >30mL/h. Call anaesthetist to monitor fluids (CVP lines help). ***Summon expert help urgently***. If bleeding is severe, ***deliver***—caesarean section for placenta praevia (sometimes for abruption, or induction). Beware PPH.

For milder bleeding, set up IVI, do Hb, crossmatch, coagulation studies, and U&E. Check pulse, BP, and loss regularly. Establish diagnosis (ultrasound of placenta, speculum examination). If placenta praevia is the diagnosis, keep in hospital until delivery (usually by caesarean section at 37–38 weeks). If pain and bleeding from a small abruption settles and the fetus is not compromised the woman may go home (after anti-D, if indicated), but treat as 'high-risk' pregnancy thereafter. Arrange follow-up.

Normal labour

From the 1st trimester, the uterus has Braxton Hicks contractions (ie non-painful/irregular contractions, eg to a 15mmHg pressure; in labour pressure is ~60mmHg). They are commoner after 36 weeks.

Normal labour is that occurring after 37 weeks' gestation. It should result in the spontaneous vaginal delivery of the baby within 24h of the onset of regular spontaneous contractions. It is often heralded by a 'show', ie a plug of cervical mucus and a little blood as the membranes strip from the os. The membranes may then rupture.

The first stage of labour is the time from the onset of regular contractions until the cervix is fully dilated (no cervix felt around the head). The cervix initially *effaces* (becomes shorter and softer) before it dilates. A satisfactory rate of dilatation from 3cm dilated is 1cm/h. The first stage generally takes up to 12h in a primip, and 7.5h in a multip. During the first stage check maternal pulse, BP, and T° half-hourly; assess the contractions every 15min, their strength (you should not be able to indent the uterus with the fingers during a contraction) and their frequency (ideally 3–4 per 10min, lasting up to 1min). Carry out vaginal examinations, eg every 4h to assess the degree of cervical dilatation, the position and the station of the head (measured in cm above the ischial spines) and note the degree of moulding (p 42). Note the state of the liquor (see p 72). Test maternal urine 4-hourly for ketones and protein. If the mother becomes ketotic set up an IVI and give her 10% dextrose.[1] Measure the fetal heart rate (if not being continuously monitored) every 15min. Note the rate before, during, and immediately after a contraction.

The second stage is the time from complete cervical dilatation until the baby is born (see *Movement of head in labour*, p 42).

The mother has an urge to push and uses abdominal muscles and the Valsalva manoeuvre to help move the baby. As the head descends, the perineum stretches and the anus gapes. Normal time for second stage is 45–120min in a primip, and 15–45min in a multip. Prevent a precipitate delivery (and so intracranial bleeding) by pressure over the perineum.

Delay in clamping the cord for 30sec and holding the baby 20cm below the introitus results in higher haematocrit levels, so reducing transfusion and oxygen supplement requirements in premature babies.

The third stage is delivery of the placenta. As the uterus contracts to a <24-week size after the baby is born, the placenta separates from the uterus through the spongy layer of the decidua basalis. It then buckles and a small amount of retroplacental haemorrhage aids its removal.

Signs of separation: Cord lengthening + rush of blood (retroplacental haemorrhage) per vaginam + uterus rises + uterine contracts in the abdomen (felt with hand as a globular mass).

Routine use of Syntometrine (ergometrine maleate 500µg im + oxytocin 5U im) as the anterior shoulder is born has decreased third stage time (to ~5min) and decreased the incidence of PPH but may cause problems for undiagnosed twins. It can precipitate myocardial infarction and is contraindicated in those with pre-eclampsia, severe hypertension, severe liver or renal impairment, severe heart disease and familial hypercholesterolaemia.

Examine the placenta to check it is complete.

Is thromboprophylaxis needed? (p 15)

1 Beware giving large volumes of dextrose in labour without sodium—may cause hyponatraemia and other neonatal problems.

Normal labour

From the 1st trimester, the uterus has Braxton-Hicks contractions[48] (ie non-painful 'practice' contractions, eg to ≤15mmHg pressure; in labour pressure is ~60mmHg). They are commonest after 36 weeks.

Normal labour is that occurring after 37 weeks' gestation. It should result in the spontaneous vaginal delivery of the baby within 24h of the onset of regular spontaneous contractions. It is often heralded by a 'show', ie a plug of cervical mucus and a little blood as the membranes strip from the os. The membranes may then rupture.

The first stage of labour is the time from the onset of regular contractions until the cervix is fully dilated (no cervix felt around the head). The cervix initially *effaces* (becomes shorter and softer) before it dilates. A satisfactory rate of dilatation from 3cm dilated is 1cm/h. The first stage generally takes up to 12h in a primip, and 7.5h in a multip. During the first stage check maternal pulse, BP, and T° half-hourly; assess the contractions every 15min, their strength (you should not be able to indent the uterus with the fingers during a contraction) and their frequency (ideally 3–4 per 10min, lasting up to 1min). Carry out vaginal examination eg every 4h to assess the degree of cervical dilatation, the position and the station of the head (measured in cm above the ischial spines) and note the degree of moulding (p 42). Note the state of the liquor (see p 72). Test maternal urine 4-hourly for ketones and protein. If the mother becomes ketotic set up an IVI and give her 10% dextrose.[1] Measure the fetal heart rate (if not being continuously monitored) every 15min. Note the rate before, during, and immediately after a contraction.

The second stage is the time from complete cervical dilatation until the baby is born (see *Movement of head in labour*, p 42).

The mother has an urge to push and uses abdominal muscles and the Valsalva manoeuvre to help move the baby. As the head descends, the perineum stretches and the anus gapes. Normal time for second stage is 45–120min in a primip, and 15–45min in a multip. Prevent a precipitate delivery (and so intracranial bleeding) by pressure over the perineum.

Delay in clamping the cord for 30sec and holding the baby 20cm below the introitus results in higher haematocrit levels, so reducing transfusion and oxygen supplement requirements in premature babies.

The third stage is delivery of the placenta. As the uterus contracts to a <24-week size after the baby is born, the placenta separates from the uterus through the spongy layer of the decidua basalis. It then buckles and a small amount of retroplacental haemorrhage aids its removal.

Signs of separation: Cord lengthening → rush of blood (retroplacental haemorrhage) *per vaginam* → uterus rises → uterine contracts in the abdomen (felt with hand as a globular mass).

Routine use of syntometrine (ergometrine maleate 500μg IM + oxytocin 5U IM) as the anterior shoulder is born has decreased third stage time (to ~5min), and decreased the incidence of PPH, but may cause problems for undiagnosed twins. It can precipitate myocardial infarction and is contraindicated in those with pre-eclampsia, severe hypertension, severe liver or renal impairment, severe heart disease and familial hypercholesterolaemia.[49] Examine the placenta to check it is complete.

►Is thromboprophylaxis needed? (p 16)

1 Beware giving large amounts of dextrose in IVIs with no sodium—may cause hyponatraemia and other neonatal problems.

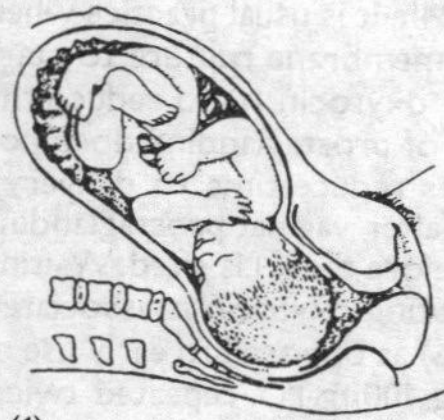

(1)
1st stage of labour. The cervix dilates. After full dilatation the head flexes further and descends further into the pelvis.

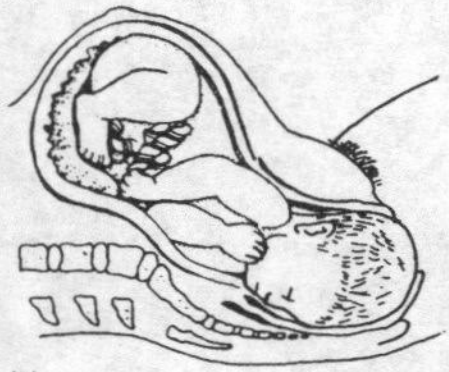

(2)
During the early second stage the head rotates at the levels of the ischial spine so the occiput lies in the anterior part of pelvis.
In late second stage the head broaches the vulval ring (crowning) and the perineum stretches over the head.

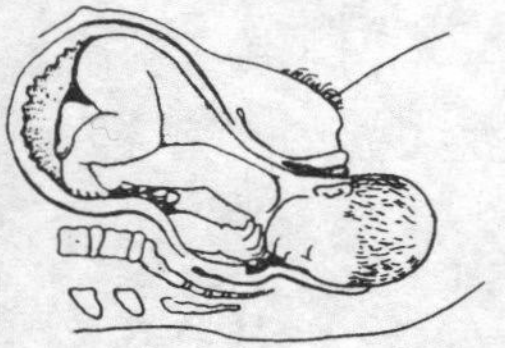

(3)
The head is born. The shoulders still lie transversely in the midpelvis.

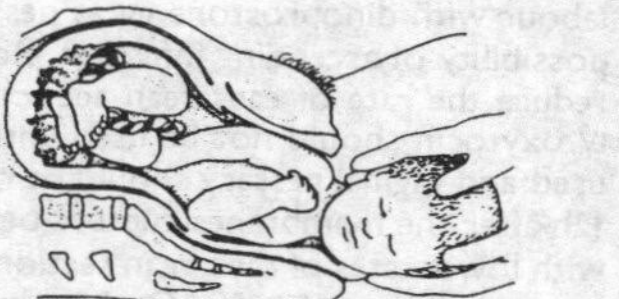

(4)
Birth of the anterior shoulder. The shoulders rotate to lie in the anteroposterior diameter of the pelvic outlet. The head rotates externally, 'restitutes', to its direction at onset of labour. Downward and backward traction of the head by the birth attendant aids delivery of the anterior shoulder.

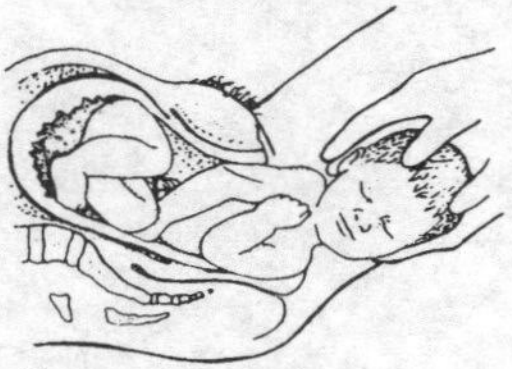

(5)
Birth of the posterior shoulder is aided by lifting the head upwards whilst maintaining traction.

Prelabour rupture of membranes at term

2–4% of term births are complicated by prelabour rupture of membranes without labour spontaneously starting within 24h. It is usual practice when labour does not ensue within a few hours of membrane rupture to start labour with dinoprostone eg as pessary or an oxytocin IVI to reduce the possibility of ascending infection. Routine use of prostaglandins does not reduce the rate of caesarean section (but does reduce time to delivery). IV oxytocin should not be used until after 6h after vaginal prostaglandins used: and vaginal pessary should be removed before the IVI is sited. Waiting 12h after the membranes rupture before instituting oxytocin is associated with lower rates of caesarean section (rate ~11%) as opposed to early use of oxytocin (rate ~15–20%). Oral misoprostol, eg 100μg PO, repeated twice, 4 hourly if needed, is as effective as oxytocin for inducing labour and reduces time to delivery in nulliparous women. 50

When delay is intended maternal temperature must be monitored and oxytocin started should pyrexia develop.

Induction of labour[1]

5–20% of UK labours are induced artificially, usually because it has been decided that to remain in utero is relatively more risky for the fetus than to be born, but in some it is because of risk to the mother. 70% of inductions are for hypertension, pre-eclampsia, prolonged pregnancy or rhesus disease. Other indications are diabetes, previous stillbirth, abruption, fetal death in utero, and placental insufficiency.

Inducing mothers at [illegible] weeks reduces stillbirth rates.

Contraindications Cephalopelvic disproportion which is absolute; malpresentations other than breech or face presentation; fetal distress; placenta praevia; cord presentation; vasa praevia; pelvic tumour; previous repair to cervix. [illegible] requires caution.

Cervical ripeness When an induction is being planned the state of the cervix will be assessed. In 95% of women at term the cervix is ripe. If primips are induced with an unripe cervix (Bishop's score [illegible]—see below) the rates of prolonged labour, fetal distress, and caesarean section are increased. This is less marked in multips.

Modified Bishop score	0	1	2
Cervical dilatation (cm)	0	1–2	3–4
Length of cervix (cm)	3	2	1
Station of head (cm above ischial spines)	−3	−2	−1/0
Cervical consistency	firm	medium	soft
Position of cervix	posterior	middle	anterior

A score of [illegible] an unripe cervix may be ripened using prostaglandin (eg vaginal gel (PGE2)) the commonest method of ripening & induction, [illegible] in the latter case fetal heart rate monitoring is indicated; this should commence before prostaglandin insertion. If this fails to induce labour, further PGE2 may be given [illegible] later. If the cervix still remains unripe, consider caesarean section. PGE2 may stimulate uterine contractions or precipitate labour.

Once the cervix is ripe, rupture the membranes (amniotomy) and start intrapartum fetal heart rate monitoring using a scalp clip or pulse oximetry (less invasive, see OHCM p [illegible]). Oxytocin is given IV in 5% dextrose using a pump system (eg ivac). Infusions start at 1 milliunit/min, doubling every 30min until effective uterine contractions are produced (usually at a rate of 4–12mU/min; occasionally [illegible] may be necessary). Beware water retention: oxytocin has an antidiuretic effect and the use of large volumes of IV fluid may result in water intoxication—ie confusion, convulsions, and coma. Use standard strength solutions as per BNF. When the cervix is [illegible] dilated the uterus is more sensitive to oxytocin and half dose may be sufficient to maintain contractions. Note: the Dublin regimes (p 64) results in most women going into spontaneous labour.

Misoprostol (a prostaglandin E1 analogue) orally is as effective at cervical ripening and inducing labour as PGE2 and oxytocin. Vaginal route shortens time to delivery but possibly results in more caesarean sections.

Problems of induction • Iatrogenic prematurity • Infection (use antibiotic cover (p 20) in women with heart lesions at risk of endocarditis) • Bleeding (vasa praevia) • Cord prolapse (eg with a high head at amniotomy) • Caesarean section ([illegible]) and instrumental delivery ([illegible]) rates are higher than when it is not for induction ([illegible] and [illegible] respectively).

1 [illegible]

[illegible]

Induction of labour

5-20% of UK labours are induced artificially, usually because it has been decided that to remain *in utero* is relatively more risky for the fetus than to be born, but in some it is because of risk to the mother. 75% of inductions are for hypertension, pre-eclampsia, prolonged pregnancy or rhesus disease. Other indications are diabetes, previous stillbirth, abruption, fetal death *in utero*, and placental insufficiency.

►Inducing mothers at 41+ weeks reduces stillbirth rates.

Contraindications Cephalopelvic disproportion which is absolute, malpresentations other than breech or face presentation, fetal distress, placenta praevia, cord presentation, vasa praevia, pelvic tumour, previous repair to cervix. Cone biopsy requires caution.

Cervical ripeness When an induction is being planned the state of the cervix will be assessed. In 95% of women at term the cervix is ripe. If primips are induced with an unripe cervix (Bishop's score ≤3, see below) the rates of prolonged labour, fetal distress, and caesarean section are increased. This is less marked in multips.

Modified Bishop score	0	1	2
Cervical dilatation (cm)	0	1-2	3-4
Length of cervix (cm)	>2	1-2	<1
Station of head (cm above ischial spines)	-3	-2	-1
Cervical consistency	firm	medium	soft
Position of cervix	posterior	middle	anterior

A score of >5 is 'ripe'. An unripe cervix may be ripened using prostaglandin (PGE2) vaginal gel (1mg) the evening before or the morning of induction (use 2mg for unfavourable primip cervix). If antenatal fetal heart rate monitoring is indicated, this should commence before prostaglandin insertion. If there is failure to ripen (occurs in 12%) PGE2 may be repeated 6-8h later. If the cervix still remains unripe consider caesarean section. PGE2 may stimulate uterine contractions or precipitate labour.

Once the cervix is ripe, rupture the membranes (amniotomy) and start intrapartum fetal heart rate monitoring using a scalp clip or pulse oximetry (less invasive, see *OHCM* p 168). Oxytocin is given IV in 5% dextrose using a pump system (eg Ivac®). Infusions start at 2 milliunits (MU) per min, doubling every 30min until effective uterine contractions are produced (usually at a rate of 4-12MU/min: occasionally 32MU/min may be necessary). Beware uterine hyperstimulation and the use of large volumes of IV fluid (if >4 litres, there is risk of water intoxication—ie confusion, convulsions, and coma). Use standard strength solutions as per *BNF*. When the cervix is 5cm dilated the uterus is more sensitive to oxytocin and 8MU/min may be sufficient to maintain contractions. Note: the Dublin regimen (p 64) results in most women going into spontaneous labour.

Misoprostol (a prostaglandin E1 analogue) PO or PV is as effective at cervical ripening and inducing labour as PGE2 and oxytocin. Vaginal route shortens time to delivery but possibly results in more caesarean sections.[1]

Problems of induction • Iatrogenic prematurity • Infection (use antibiotic cover (p 20) in women with heart lesions as risk of endocarditis). • Bleeding (vasa praevia). • Cord prolapse (eg with a high head at amniotomy). • Caesarean section (19%) and instrumental delivery (14%) rates are higher than when drugs not for induction (11%, and 11% respectively).[2]

1 J Kwon 2001 *BJOG* **108** 23
2 *NHS Maternity Statistics, England*: 2003-4 available at www.dh.gov.uk

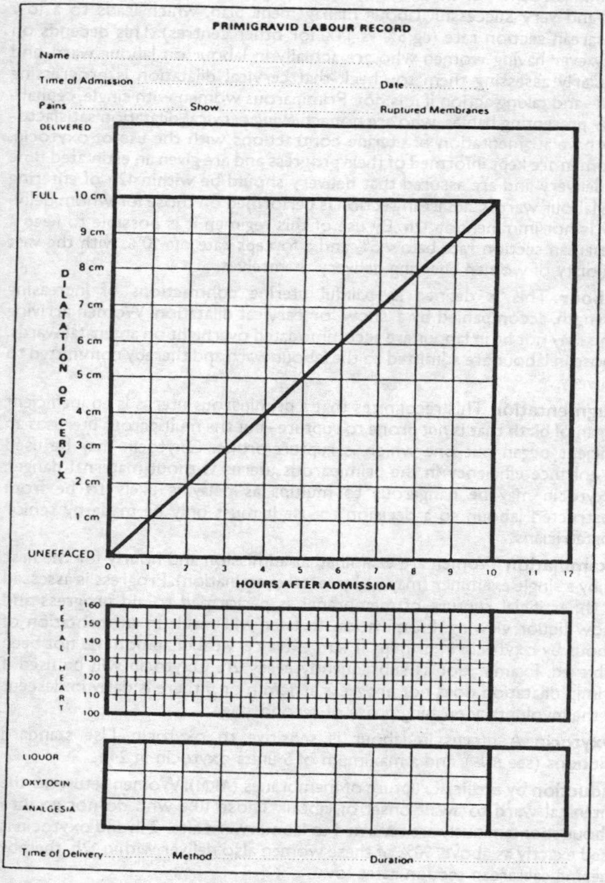

This graph shows the simple Dublin partogram ('simple' because it does not show 'latent' phase of labour). It has a steep *x/y* gradient of ratio 1:1. Less steep ratios (eg 2:1) may predispose to premature intervention, as does inclusion of the 'latent' phase on the partogram.

The active management of labour

Dublin is a centre of excellence for labouring mothers because of its coherent and very successful labour management plan, which leads to a low caesarean section rate (eg 5% *vs* 14% for other centres). This depends on only ever having women who are actually in labour on labour ward, and regularly assessing them to check that cervical dilatation is progressing well—and taking action if it is not. Primiparous women with single, cephalically presenting babies, who are not achieving cervical dilatation satisfactorily have augmentation of uterine contractions with the use of oxytocin. Women are kept informed of their progress and are given an estimated time of delivery and are assured that delivery should be within 12h of entering the labour ward. Caesarean section is performed on those for whom delivery is not imminent at 12h. By use of this regimen it is possible to keep a caesarean section rate below 5% and a forceps rate of ~10%, with the vast majority of women effecting delivery themselves.

Labour This is defined as painful uterine contractions of increasing strength, accompanied by a 'show' or cervical dilatation. Women arriving who may not be in labour are accommodated overnight on antenatal wards. Those in labour are admitted to the labour ward and thereby committed to delivery.

Augmentation This recognizes that a primiparous uterus is an inefficient organ of birth that is *not* prone to rupture—but the multiparous uterus is an efficient organ but one which *is* rupture-prone. Oxytocin may be used to enhance efficiency in the primiparous uterus without maternal danger. Oxytocin may be dangerous to multips as delay is likely to be from obstructed labour, so a decision to use it must only be made by senior obstetricians.

Examination Women are examined at admission and hourly for the first 3h by a single examiner (may be by rectal examination). Progress is assessed at 1h; artificial rupture of membranes is performed to aid progress and allow liquor viewing. Examination 1h later will result in augmentation of labour by oxytocin in primips if 1cm extra cervical dilatation has not been achieved. Examination is subsequently every 2h. Oxytocin will be used if primip dilatation does not progress at 1cm/h or if there is delay in descent in the involuntary pushing phase of second stage.

Oxytocin A uterus in labour is sensitive to oxytocin. Use standard dilutions (see *BNF*), and a maximum of 5 units oxytocin in 24h.

Induction by artificial rupture of membranes (ARM). Women return to the antenatal ward to await onset of labour. Those 10% who do not go into labour spontaneously are returned to labour ward after 24h and oxytocin is used exactly as above. 90% of these women also deliver within 12h, thereby keeping caesarean section rates low.

The partogram This graphs labour's progress (p 63). Dublin uses a simple partogram with time plotted against cervical dilatation, and records fetal heart rate, state of liquor, analgesia, and oxytocin use.

Meconium in liquor At ARM this suggests placental insufficiency. Meconium other than light staining in good liquor volume prompts fetal blood sampling and scalp clip electronic monitoring—or prompt caesarean section (fetal blood pH low, or very thick meconium).

The opposite page depicts Dublin practice for primiparous mothers with term babies of vertex presentation with a normal head. Its authors stress the benefit of their policies both to mothers and also from the financial management point of view as it allows them to have a personal midwife for each mother throughout the time that she is in labour, but with unit costs per delivery of only one-third of costs of UK hospitals.

Midwife monitoring is normally every 15min using a Pinard scope; electronic monitoring is used if there is meconium staining of liquor. Membranes are ruptured so that the liquor can be regularly inspected.

Other UK units have different policies. Some argue that artificially rupturing membranes may not be entirely beneficial as the liquor cannot cushion the fetal head and there is evidence that artificial rupture of membranes is associated with more fetal heart rate decelerations. ARM may also facilitate spread of HIV from mother to baby (p 23). A review of current knowledge suggests that of early amniotomy, early use of oxytocin, and the provision of professional support throughout first labours, it is the last that is the most important for reducing rates of operative delivery. *Support* may be the key, as shown by shorter labours, fewer forceps and caesarean section deliveries, and reduced analgesia requirements of women supported by doulas (trained female companions) during labour—an effect not seen when the expectant father is the companion. 51

One large randomized USA trial found active management of labour had no benefits, and did not reduce rates of caesarean section. 52

Whether to institute or abandon active management is being overtaken by women's views: many reject intervention, even if it is offered.

Pain relief in labour

►Adequate pain relief in labour is the obstetrician's greatest gift to womankind. Not everyone wants natural birth—and do not make people feel guilty about requesting pain relief. A good anaesthetic agent in labour must be harmless to mother and baby, allow maintenance of maternal cooperation, and must not affect uterine contractility.

Education That given by the National Childbirth Trust meets all these criteria. Education about labour reduces fear; breathing exercises and relaxation techniques teach the mother ways to combat pain herself.

In the first stage, **narcotic injections** are often tried, eg pethidine 50–150mg IM (not if birth expected in <2-3h as neonatal respiratory depression may occur, reversible with naloxone 0.1–0.2mg as a single dose IM). Expect analgesia by 20min and to last 3h. NB: doses in the lower range frequently produce vomiting, but no relief of pain. Other SE: disorientation, ↓gastric emptying, neonatal respiratory depression. CI: mother on MAOIs (p 368). In Scandinavia **sterile water injections** are used for 1st stage low back pain. Four 0.1–0.25mL injections of sterile water are given intracutaneously adjacent to Michaelis' rhomboid (in the lumbosacral area). Initially causing pain, the injections produce a wide papule with red circumference. Pain reduction by 50% has been reported lasting 90min. Pain of injection can be reduced by use of nitrous oxide simultaneously or by giving them subcutaneously. 53

Nitrous oxide (50% in O_2 = Entonox®) can be inhaled throughout labour and is self-administered using a demand valve. CI: pneumothorax.

Pudendal block (sacral nerve roots 2, 3, and 4) uses 8–10mL of 1% lidocaine (= lignocaine) injected 1cm beyond a point just below and medial to the ischial spine on each side. It is used with perineal infiltration for instrumental delivery, but analgesia is insufficient for rotational forceps.

Spinal block See p 634; used for rotational delivery or caesarean section.

Epidural anaesthesia See p 67. Pain relief is by anaesthetizing pain fibres carried by T11–S5. Epidurals must only be set up once labour is established (cervix >3cm). Set up IVI first, give 500mL Hartmann's solution to prevent ↓BP. Check pulse, BP, respirations, contractions, and fetal heart every 15min after the epidural is set up. Top-ups are required ~2-hourly. Epidurals may be very helpful for the following: OP position (p 71), breech, multiple pregnancy, preterm delivery, pre-eclampsia, forceps delivery, inco-ordinate uterine contractions. ***Problems:*** For those due to technique, see p 635. There may be postural hypotension (put up IVI, nurse 15° to left side), urinary retention (catheterize regularly), paralysis (pelvic floor muscle paralysis reduces rotation and voluntary effort in 2nd stage, perhaps increasing need for forceps). But note that when compared with systemic pain-relief labour is shorter and there is no increased risk of recourse to caesarean section.[1]

After delivery: urinary retention and headache (esp. after dural puncture).

Epidural anaesthesia for those having heparin thromboprophylaxis: 54
►Understand what type of heparin the patient is using. With low dose subcutaneous heparin, wait 4h after heparin given before siting the block or removing catheter. After giving block allow ≥2h before giving next dose of heparin. Where *low molecular weight heparin* LMWH is used, wait 12h after heparin dose before inserting block or removing catheter; wait at least 6h after block siting before next dose of LMWH. Aim to give LMWH at 18.00h each day. Beware use of other anticoagulants or nonsteroidal anti-inflammatory drugs. All patients must be extremely vigilantly monitored to detect new numbness; weakness; bowel or bladder dysfunction. Any neurological problem must be investigated as an emergency.

1 Wong C 2005 *N Engl J Med* **352** 655

Combined spinal epidural (CSE) anaesthesia gives quicker pain relief, with little or no motor blockade in most mothers, allowing standing, walking, sitting, and voiding urine. Using the intrathecal route (27G Whiteace needle) apparently does not cause a significant rise in the incidence of headache (only ~0.13%). The patient can control the dose, and this leads to a dose reduction of 35%, and reduces motor blockade. Women should inform their midwife if they notice light-headedness, nausea, or weak legs. Spontaneous delivery rates are not better than with traditional epidural. ►Skilled anaesthetic help is vital.

Transcutaneous electrical nerve stimulation (TENS) Electrodes placed on the back, give pulses stimulating large nerve fibres to the brain, aiming to block pain impulses. It needs careful instruction but is under the mother's control. In 1 meta-analysis, 6 out of 9 trials showed no effect; those that did, showed only weak effects, eg ↑time before epidural use.

Multiple pregnancy

Incidence[uk] Twins: 3/200 pregnancies; triplets: 1/10,000.

Predisposing factors Previous twins; family history of twins (dizygotic only); increasing maternal age (<20yrs 6.4/1000, >25yrs 16.8/1000); induced ovulation and *in vitro* fertilization (1% of all UK pregnancies); race origin (1/150 pregnancies for Japanese, 1/36 in Nigerian Igbo women). The worldwide rate for monozygotic (monochorionic) twins is constant at 3-5/1000.

Features Early pregnancy: uterus too large for dates; hyperemesis. Later there may be polyhydramnios. The signs are that >2 poles may be felt; there is a multiplicity of fetal parts; 2 fetal heart rates may be heard (reliable if heart rates differ by >10 beats/min). Ultrasound confirms diagnosis (and at 10–14 weeks, can distinguish monochorionic from dichorionic twins).[1]

Complications during pregnancy Polyhydramnios; pre-eclampsia is more common (10% in singleton pregnancies; 30% in twins); anaemia is more common (iron and folate requirements are increased). There is an increased incidence of APH (6% for twins, *vs* 4.7% for singletons) due to both abruption and placenta praevia (large placenta).

Fetal complications Perinatal mortality for twins is 36.7/1000 (8/1000 if single; 73/1000 for triplets; and 204 for higher multiples). The main problem is prematurity. Mean gestation for twins is 37 weeks, for triplets 33 weeks. Growth restricted babies (p 52) are more common (growth the same as singletons up to 24 weeks but may be slower thereafter). Malformation rates are increased 2–4 times, especially in monozygotic twins. Severe disability rate 1.5% for singletons, 3.4% for twins. Ultrasound is the main diagnostic test. Selective fetocide (eg with intracardiac potassium chloride) is best used before 20 weeks if indicated. With monozygotic twins, intermingling blood supply may result in disparate twin size and one being born plethoric (hence jaundiced later), the other anaemic. If one fetus dies *in utero* it may become a fetus papyraceous which may be aborted later or delivered prematurely.

Complications of labour PPH is more common (4–6% in singletons, 10% in twins). Malpresentation is common (cephalic/cephalic 40%, cephalic/breech 40%, breech/breech 10%, cephalic/transverse (Tv) 5%, breech/Tv 4%, Tv/Tv 1%). Rupturing of vasa praevia, increased rates of cord prolapse (0.6% singleton, 2.3% twins), premature separation of the placenta and cord entanglement (especially monozygous) may all present difficulties at labour. Despite modern technology some twins remain undiagnosed, staff are unprepared, and syntometrine may be used inappropriately, so delaying delivery of the second twin. Epidural anaesthesia is helpful for versions.

Management

- Ensure adequate rest (need not entail admission).
- Use ultrasound for diagnosis and monthly checks on fetal growth.
- Give additional iron and folate to the mother during pregnancy.
- More antenatal visits, eg weekly from 30 weeks (risk of eclampsia ↑).
- Tell the mother how to identify preterm labour, and what to do.
- Consider induction at 40 weeks. Have an IVI running in labour and an anaesthetist available at delivery. Paediatricians (preferably one for each baby) should be present at delivery for resuscitation should this be necessary (second twins have a higher risk of asphyxia).

Monozygous or dizygous? Monozygous twins are always same-sex and the membrane consists of 2 amnions and 1 chorion (if in doubt send for histology).

1 S Carroll 2002 *BJOG* **109** 182

Triplets are difficult ... more than simply difficult

Bringing up one child is difficult: bringing up twins is often very very difficult—but bringing up triplets is more than very very very difficult: it is frequently a source of significant psychopathology. During infertility consultations, eager couples may say in one breath: "We wouldn't worry about twins ... delighted—even triplets would be OK..." But how do they know, and would they find the following information chastening?

Even 4 years after their birth, all mothers in one study[55] suffered from exhaustion and emotional distress. The relationships with the children was often difficult (aggression and conflicts). One-third of mothers had sufficient depression to require psychotropic medication, and one-third spontaneously expressed regrets about having triplets. But do not conclude from this that it will necessarily be right to offer mothers selective termination. After triplets have been reduced to twins *in utero*, subsequently one-third of mothers will suffer emotional problems (persistent sadness and guilt) up to one year. However, adjustment had occurred in ~90% by 2 postnatal years.[56]

Legislation in most developed countries is trying to limit the numbers of embryos that may be implanted at in vitro fertilization in order to reduce higher order pregnancies (already there has been a reduction by 25% since 1998). In the UK current practice is to implant only 2 embryos in mothers <40y; though 3 may be implanted if she is >40 years.[1]

1 R Simmons 2004 *BJOG* **111** 856

Breech (ie buttock) presentations

Breech presentation is the commonest malpresentation. Although 40% of babies are breech at 20 weeks, 20% will be at 28 weeks, and only 3% by term. It is normal in pregnancy for the buttocks to come to lie in the fundus. Conditions predisposing towards breech presentation: contracted pelvis, bicornuate uterus, fibroid uterus, placenta praevia, oligohydramnios, spina bifida, or a hydrocephalic fetus. Ultrasound may show the cause and influence the management.

Extended breech presentation is commonest—ie flexed at the hips but extended at the knees. **Flexed breeches** sit with hips and knees both flexed so that the presenting part is a mixture of buttocks, external genitalia, and feet. **Footling breeches** are the least common. The feet are the presenting part and this type has the greatest risk (5-20%) of cord prolapse.

Diagnosis of breech presentation should be made antenatally. The mother may complain of pain under the ribs. On palpation the lie is longitudinal, no head is felt in the pelvis, and in the fundus there is a smooth round mass (the head) which can be ballotted, a sensation akin to quickly sinking an apple in a bowl of water.

External cephalic version (ECV)—turning the breech by manoeuvring it through a (usually forward), somersault. Turn the baby only if vaginal delivery planned. Version at 36 weeks is recommended by NICE. It can be used from 37 weeks using tocolysis. Success rate ~53%. Version contraindications: placenta praevia, multiple pregnancy, APH, small-for-dates babies, and in mothers with uterine scars or uterine abnormality, pre-eclampsia, or hypertension (the risk of abruption is increased), who have a bad obstetric history, unstable lie. Monitor CTG (p 44). Give anti-D (500U) to rhesus-negative patients and take Kleihauer test (p 9) to detect the 1% who may need additional anti-D. ECV results in emergency caesarean in 0.43%.[1]

Mode of delivery Planned caesarean section provides better outcome for the fetus *vs* vaginal delivery. A large multicentre trial ($n = 2088$) using experienced breech deliverers found that 1 baby avoided death or serious morbidity for every 14 extra caesarean sections done. Serious maternal complications were similar in both groups,[2] and death and abnormal neurodevelopment levels of the babies at 2 years are similar.[3] That randomized trials may be inappropriate for evaluation of complex issues such as breech delivery is argued.[4] Evidence is less clear for pre-term singletons and twins. If vaginal delivery occurs attendants experienced at breech delivery should be present.

Assisted breech delivery The breech engages in the pelvis with the bitrochanteric diameter (9.5cm) transverse. With further descent through the pelvis, rotation occurs so the bitrochanteric diameter lies anteroposteriorly as it emerges from the birth canal, being born by lateral flexion of the trunk. External rotation then occurs so that this diameter is again transverse. The shoulders enter the pelvis with the bisacromial diameter transverse, rotate through 90° emerging in the AP diameter. The head enters the pelvis with the sagittal suture transverse and rotates 90°. When the body is completely born it is allowed to hang for about 1-2 minutes until the nape of the neck is well seen. The body is then lifted above the vulva by an assistant, the head being delivered with forceps.

►Check baby for hip dislocation (↑incidence): also, if vaginal delivery, for Klumpke's paralysis (p 766) and signs of CNS injury.

1 R Collaris 2004 *Acta Obstet Gynecol Scand* **83** 511
2 M Hannah 2000 *Lancet* **356** 1375
3 H Whyte 2003 *Am J Obstet Gynecol 2003 suppl* **189** (6) *Abstract* 7
4 A Kotasha 2004 *BMJ* **329** 1039

Other malpresentations

Occipitoposterior presentation (OP) In 50% of patients the mothers have a long 'anthropoid' pelvis. Diagnosis may be made antenatally by palpation (p 40). On vaginal examination the posterior fontanelle will be found to lie in the posterior quadrant of the pelvis. Labour tends to be prolonged because of the degree of rotation needed, so adequate hydration and analgesia (consider epidural) are important. During labour 65% rotate 130° so that the head is occipitoanterior at the time of birth, 20% rotate to the transverse and then arrest ('deep transverse arrest'), 15% rotate so that the occiput lies truly posterior and birth is by flexion of the head from the perineum. Although in 73% delivery will be a spontaneous vaginal delivery, 22% will require forceps and 5% a caesarean section.

Face presentation Incidence 1:994. 15% are due to congenital abnormality such as anencephaly, tumour of or shortened fetal neck muscles. Most occur by chance as the head extends rather than flexes as it engages. Antenatal diagnosis: the fetal spine feels S-shaped, the uterus is ovoid without fullness in the flanks and there is a deep groove between the occiput and the back. On early vaginal examination, the nose and eyes may be felt but later this will not be possible because of oedema. Most engage in the transverse (mentobregmatic diameter ≈9.5cm). 90% rotate so that the chin lies behind the symphysis (mentoanterior) and the head can be born by flexion. If the chin rotates to the sacrum (mentoposterior), caesarean section is indicated.

Brow presentation This occurs in 1:755 deliveries and is often associated with a contracted pelvis or a very large fetus. Antenatal diagnosis: the head does not engage (mentovertical diameter ≈13cm) and a sulcus may be felt between the occiput and the back. On vaginal examination the anterior fontanelle and supraorbital ridges may be felt. Deliver by caesarean section.

Transverse lie (compound shoulder presentation) This occurs in 1 in 400 deliveries and is usually in multiparous women. Other predisposing factors: multiple pregnancy; polyhydramnios; in primips: arcuate or septate uterus, placenta praevia, contracted pelvis. Antenatal diagnosis: ovoid uterus wider at the sides, the lower pole is empty, the head lies in one flank, the fetal heart is heard in variable positions. On vaginal examination with membranes intact no distinguishing features may be felt, but if ruptured and the cervix dilated, ribs, shoulder, or a prolapsed hand may be felt. The risk of cord prolapse is high. External cephalic version (p 70) may be attempted from 32 weeks. If malpresentation persists or recurs caesarean section will be necessary. Those with persistent instability of lie need hospital admission from 37 weeks (to prevent cord prolapse at home when the membranes rupture) and decision as to elective caesarean section.

▸▸Prolapsed cord

Cord prolapse is an emergency because of the risk of cord compression causing fetal asphyxia. There is an increased incidence at twin deliveries, footling breech delivery, and with shoulder presentations. If a cord presentation is noted prior to membrane rupture, carry out caesarean section. Always be aware when artificially rupturing membranes, when the presenting part is poorly applied, that cord prolapse is a possible risk.

Management The aim is to prevent the presenting part from occluding the cord. ▸▸This may be effected by:

- Displacing the presenting part by putting a hand in the vagina; push it back up (towards mother's head) during contractions.
- Using gravity, either place the woman head down or get her into knee–elbow position (kneeling so rump higher than head).
- Infuse 500mL saline into bladder through size 16 catheter.
- Keep cord in vagina: do not handle it (to prevent spasm).

If the cervix is fully dilated and the presenting part is sufficiently low in pelvis, deliver by forceps (if cephalic) or by breech extraction (by a suitably experienced obstetrician). Otherwise arrange immediate caesarean section, if the fetus is still alive. There are few other emergencies where speed is so vital.

▸▸Impacted shoulders (shoulder dystocia)

This is inability to deliver the shoulders after the head has been delivered.

Associations: Large/postmature fetus; malformation; short cord.[57]

Management The danger is death from asphyxia ▸▸Speed is vital as the cord is usually squashed at the pelvic inlet. Make a large episiotomy, then:

- Use the McRoberts' (this is hyperflexed lithotomy) position.[58] [59] Abduct, rotate outwards, and flex maternal femora so each thigh touches the abdomen (1 assistant to hold each leg). This straightens the sacrum relative to the lumbar spine and rotates the symphysis superiorly helping the impacted shoulder to enter the pelvis without manipulating the fetus.
- Apply suprapubic pressure: with flat of hand laterally in the direction baby is facing, and towards mother's sacrum. Apply steady traction to the fetal head towards the floor. This aims to displace the anterior shoulder allowing it to enter the pelvis. If this fails, check anterior shoulder is under the symphysis (here the diameter of the outlet is widest); if not rotate it to be so and repeat traction. If this fails, rotation by 180° (so posterior shoulder now lies anteriorly) may work, as may delivery of the posterior arm. If all else fails replacement of the fetal head by firm pressure of the hand to reverse the movements of labour and return the head to the flexed occipito-anterior position and caesarean delivery can be very successful. If the baby dies prior to delivery, cutting through both clavicles (cleidotomy) with strong scissors assists delivery.
- Check the baby for damage, eg Erb's palsy or fractured clavicle.

Meconium-stained liquor

In late pregnancy, it is normal for some babies to pass meconium (bowel contents), which stains the amniotic fluid a dull green. This is not significant. During labour, fresh meconium, which is dark green, sticky, and lumpy, may be passed. This may be a response to the stress of a normal labour, or a sign of distress, so transfer to a consultant unit (if in a GP unit) and commence continuous fetal heart rate monitoring (p 44). Aspiration of fresh meconium can cause severe pneumonitis. As the head is born, suck out the oropharynx and nose. Have a paediatrician in attendance (p 120) to suck out pharynx and trachea under direct vision using a laryngoscope.

Dystocia

Dystocia is difficulty in labour. There may be problems with the passenger (large baby, see impacted shoulders—shoulder dystocia p 72, or an abnormal presentation), the passages (for ideal pelvis see p 42; note that cervical dystocia may be a problem after biopsy of the cervix, or as consequences of female genital mutilation p 246) or of propulsion (the uterine powers). Cephalopelvic disproportion results if diameters are unfavourable (p 42).

The pelvis The ideal pelvis has a round brim (ie gynaecoid), but 15% of women have a long oval brim (anthropoid). A very flat brim is less favourable (platypeloid) occurring in 5% of women (<a 13cm (5%). It occurs in 20% of women <13.2cm. Spinal scoliosis, kyphosis, sacralization of the L5 vertebra, spondylolisthesis and pelvic fractures may all affect pelvic anatomy. Rickets and polio were formerly important causes of pelvic problems. Suspect pelvic contraction if the head is not engaged by 37 weeks in a Caucasian primip (after excluding placenta praevia).

The presentation Cephalic presentations are less favourable, the less flexed the head. Transverse lie and brow presentations will always need caesarean section. Face and OP (p 73) presentations may deliver vaginally but are more likely to fail to progress. Breech presentation is particularly unfavourable if the fetus >3.5kg.

The uterine powers Contractions start in the fundus and propagate downwards. The intensity and duration of contractions are greatest at the fundus, but the contraction reaches its peak in all parts of the uterus simultaneously. Normal contractions occur at a rate of 1 per 10min, they should last up to 75sec, the contraction peak usually measures 30–60mmHg, and the resting uterine tone between them should be 10–15mmHg. Uterine muscle has the property of retraction. The shortening of the muscle fibres encourages cervical dilatation.

Uterine dysfunction Contractions may be hypotonic (low resting tone, low contraction peaks) or they may be normotonic but occur too infrequently. These dysfunctions can be corrected by augmentation with oxytocin (p 64). Whenever oxytocin is used discuss with a senior obstetrician. Pain and fear cause release of catecholamines which can inhibit uterine activity. Thus adequate analgesia is needed (p 56) and may speed the progress of labour.

Cervical dystocia Failure of cervical dilatation may be due to previous trauma, repair, cone biopsy and cauterization. It is difficult to distinguish from failure to dilate due to uterine dysfunction though the latter should respond to oxytocin (note the important difference between primips and multips, p 64). The treatment for cervical dystocia is delivery by caesarean section.

Consequences of prolonged labour Neonatal mortality rises with prolonged labour, as does maternal morbidity (especially infection). With modern management of labour careful monitoring of progress in labour (p 64) takes place to diagnose delay early and treat it as necessary to prevent prolonged labour occurring.

- When there is dystocia, ask 'is safe vaginal delivery possible?'

Dystocia

Dystocia is difficulty in labour. There may be problems with *the passenger* (large baby, see impacted shoulders = shoulder dystocia p 72, or an abnormal presentation), *the passages* (for ideal pelvis, see p 42—note that cervical dystocia may be a problem after biopsy of the cervix, or a consequence of female genital mutilation p 246) or of *propulsion* (the uterine powers). Cephalopelvic disproportion results if diameters are unfavourable (p 42).

The pelvis The ideal pelvis has a round brim (ie gynaecoid), but 15% of women have a long oval brim (anthropoid). A very flat brim is less favourable (platypoid); occurring in 5% of women over 152cm (5ft), it occurs in 30% of women <152cm. Spinal scoliosis, kyphosis, sacralization of the L5 vertebra, spondylolisthesis and pelvic fractures may all affect pelvic anatomy. Rickets and polio were formerly important causes of pelvic problems. Suspect pelvic contraction if the head is not engaged by 37 weeks in a Caucasian primip (after excluding placenta praevia).

The presentation Cephalic presentations are less favourable, the less flexed the head. Transverse lie and brow presentations will always need caesarean section: face and OP (p 71) presentations may deliver vaginally but are more likely to fail to progress. Breech presentation is particularly unfavourable if the fetus >3.5kg.

The uterine powers Contractions start in the fundus and propagate downwards. The intensity and duration of contractions are greatest at the fundus, but the contraction reaches its peak in all parts of the uterus simultaneously. Normal contractions occur at a rate of 3 per 10min, they should last up to 75sec, the contraction peak usually measures 30-60mmHg, and the resting uterine tone between them should be 10-15mmHg. Uterine muscle has the property of retraction. The shortening of the muscle fibres encourages cervical dilatation.

Uterine dysfunction Contractions may be hypotonic (low resting tone, low contraction peaks) or they may be normotonic but occur too infrequently. These dysfunctions can be corrected by augmentation with oxytocin (p 64). Whenever oxytocin is used discuss with a senior obstetrician. Pain and fear cause release of catecholamines which can inhibit uterine activity. Thus adequate analgesia is needed (p 66) and may speed the progress of labour.

Cervical dystocia Failure of cervical dilatation may be due to previous trauma, repair, cone biopsy, and cauterization. It is difficult to distinguish from failure to dilate due to uterine dysfunction though the latter should respond to oxytocin (note the important difference between primips and multips, p 64). The treatment for cervical dystocia is delivery by caesarean section.

Consequences of prolonged labour Neonatal mortality rises with prolonged labour as does maternal morbidity (especially infection). With modern management of labour, careful monitoring of progress in labour (p 64) takes place to diagnose delay early, and treat it as necessary, to prevent prolonged labour occurring.

►When there is dystocia, ask 'is safe vaginal delivery possible?'

Forceps

Forceps are designed with a cephalic curve which fits around the fetal head and a pelvic curve which fits the pelvis. Short-shanked (eg Wrigley's) forceps are used for 'lift out' deliveries when the head is on the perineum. Long-shanked (eg Neville Barnes) for higher deliveries when the sagittal suture lies in the AP diameter. Kielland's forceps have a reduced pelvic curve, making them suitable for rotation (only in experienced hands).

Conditions of use The head must be engaged; the membranes ruptured; the position of the head known and the presentation suitable (ie vertex or face (mentoanterior)); there must be no cephalopelvic disproportion (moulding not excessive); the cervix must be fully dilated and the uterus contracting, and analgesia adequate (perineal infiltration for episiotomy; pudendal blocks may be sufficient for midcavity forceps and ventouse deliveries but not for Kielland's). The bladder must be empty.

Indications for use Forceps may be used when there is delay in the second stage; this is frequently due to failure of maternal effort (uterine inertia or just tiredness/epidural analgesia) or malposition of the fetal head. They may be used when there is fetal distress or a prolapsed cord, or eclampsia, all occurring only in the second stage. They are also used to prevent undue maternal effort (eg in cardiac disease, respiratory disease, pre-eclampsia). They are used for the aftercoming head in breech deliveries.

Technique Learn from demonstration. The following is an aide-memoire for non-rotational forceps. Place the mother in lithotomy position with her bottom just over the edge of the delivery bed. Use antiseptic fluid to clean the vulva and perineum; catheterize; check the position of the head. Insert pudendal block and infiltrate the area of the episiotomy (not necessary if she has an epidural). Assemble the blades to check they fit, with the pelvic curve pointing upwards. The handle which lies in the left hand is inserted to the mother's left side and then the right; the handles should lock easily. Traction must not be excessive (the end of the bed is not for extra leverage). Synchronize traction with contractions, guiding the head downwards initially. Do a large episiotomy when the head is at the vulva. Change the direction of traction to up and out as the head passes out of the vulva. If baby needs resuscitation, [illegible] vitamin K (p 120). [illegible] See p 10.

Forceps complications Maternal trauma (commoner than with ventouse). Fetal facial bruising, VII paralysis (usually resolves), brachial plexus injury.

Ventouse The ventouse, or vacuum extractor, is associated with less maternal trauma than forceps. It is used worldwide, but not in the UK. It may be used in preference to rotational forceps because, as traction is applied with the cup over the occiput, rotation normally occurs during delivery. It can be used [illegible] dilated cervix [illegible] should be fully dilated. The ventouse should not be used if the head is above the ischial spines; it is contraindicated in face presentation and for premature babies. A cup is applied with a suction force of 0.8kg/cm². The baby's scalp is drawn up to form a 'chignon' which resolves in 2 days. There is increased rate of cephalhaematoma and neonatal jaundice so give vitamin K (p 120). Maternal trauma still occurs (eg [illegible]).

If ventouse/low forceps do not succeed, [illegible] delivery by Caesarean section. [illegible] delivery are [illegible] of indication or management. Women having assisted delivery are more [illegible] with birth, less anxious about the baby and more likely to breast feed. Only about a third will have vaginal delivery after previous Caesarean section.

Forceps

Forceps are designed with a cephalic curve, which fits around the fetal head, and a pelvic curve which fits the pelvis. Short-shanked (eg Wrigley's) forceps are used for 'lift out' deliveries, when the head is on the perineum; long-shanked (eg Neville Barnes) for higher deliveries, when the sagittal suture lies in the AP diameter. Kielland's forceps have a reduced pelvic curve, making them suitable for rotation (only in experienced hands).

Conditions of use The head must be engaged; the membranes ruptured; the position of the head known and the presentation suitable, ie vertex or face (mentoanterior); there must not be cephalo-pelvic disproportion (moulding not excessive); the cervix must be fully dilated and the uterus contracting, and analgesia adequate (perineal infiltration for the episiotomy; pudendal blocks may be sufficient for mid-cavity forceps and ventouse deliveries but not for Kielland's). The bladder must be empty.

Indications for use Forceps may be used when there is delay in the second stage: this is frequently due to failure of maternal effort (uterine inertia or just tiredness), epidural analgesia, or malpositions of the fetal head. They may be used when there is fetal distress or a prolapsed cord, or eclampsia—all occurring only in the second stage. They are also used to prevent undue maternal effort, eg in cardiac disease, respiratory disease, pre-eclampsia. They are used for the after-coming head in breech deliveries.

Technique Learn from demonstration. The following is an *aide-mémoire* for non-rotational forceps. Place the mother in lithotomy position with her bottom just over the edge of the delivery bed. Use sterilizing fluid to clean the vulva and perineum; catheterize; check the position of the head. Insert pudendal block and infiltrate the site of the episiotomy (not necessary if she has an epidural). Assemble the blades to check they fit, with the pelvic curve pointing upwards. The handle which lies in the left hand is the left blade and is inserted first (to the mother's left side) and then the right: the handles should lock easily. Traction must not be excessive (the end of bed is not for extra leverage!). Synchronize traction with contractions, guiding the head downwards initially. Do a large episiotomy when the head is at the vulva. Change the direction of traction to up and out as the head passes out of the vulva. If baby needs resuscitation, give to paediatrician. Give vitamin K (p 120). Is thromboprophylaxis needed? See p 16.

Forceps complications: *Maternal:* Trauma (commoner than with ventouse). *Fetal:* facial bruising, VII paralysis (usually resolves); brachial plexus injury.

Ventouse The ventouse, or vacuum extractor, associated with less maternal trauma than forceps is preferred worldwide, but not in the UK. It may be used in preference to rotational forceps because, as traction is applied, with the cup over the posterior fontanelle, rotation during delivery will occur. It can be used through a partially dilated cervix (primips should be almost fully dilated, multips >6cm), but should not be used if the head is above the ischial spines. It is contraindicated for face presentations and for premature babies. A cup is applied with a suction force of 0.8kg/cm^2. The baby's scalp is sucked up to form a 'chignon', which resolves in 2 days. There is increased rate of fetal cephalhaematoma (p 90) and neonatal jaundice so give vitamin K (p 120). Maternal trauma still occurs in ~11%.

If ventouse, low forceps, or mid forceps are needed for 1st delivery, spontaneous rates for 2nd delivery are 91%, 88%, 82% respectively in the absence of induction or augmentation.[60] Women having vaginal delivery are more satisfied with the birth, less anxious about the baby, and more likely to breast feed. Only about a third will have vaginal delivery after previous Caesarean Section.

Indications for forceps delivery[1]

Relative indications (ventouse or Caesarean an alternative)
- Delay or maternal exhaustion in second stage.
- Dense epidural block with diminished urge to push.
- Rotational instrumental delivery for malposition of head.
- Suspected fetal distress.

Specific indications for forceps (forceps delivery is usually superior to ventouse or Caesarean in these circumstances)
- Assisted breech delivery, forceps to deliver head.
- Assisted delivery of preterm infant <34 weeks gestation.
- Controlled delivery of head at Caesarean section.
- Assisted delivery with face presentation.
- Assisted delivery with suspected coagulopathy or thrombocytopenia in fetus.
- Instrumental delivery where maternal condition precludes pushing (eg cardiac disease, respiratory disease).
- Cord prolapse in second stage of labour.
- Instrumental delivery under GA.

Obstetric brachial plexus palsy (OBPI)

OBPI complicates <0.5% of live births.

Risk factors: Large birth weight; shoulder dystocia with prolonged 2nd stage of labour; forceps delivery; vacuum extraction; diabetes mellitus; breech presentation. Formerly, the cause of OBPI was excessive lateral traction applied to the fetal head at delivery, in association with anterior shoulder dystocia.

Instrumental-associated OBPI may arise because of nerve stretch injuries after rotations of >90° or from direct compression of the forceps blade in the fetal neck.[61] Not all cases of brachial plexus palsy are attributable to traction. Intrauterine factors may play some role.[62]

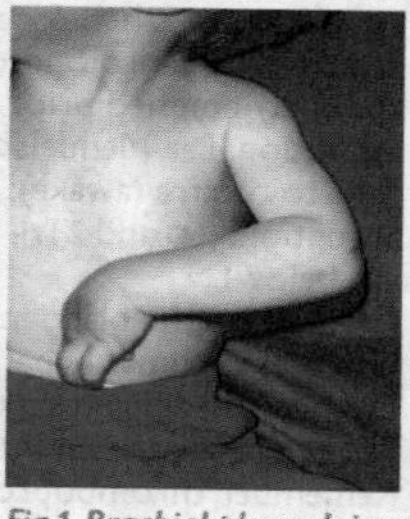

Fig 1. Brachial plexus Injury

Management: 10–20% require surgical intervention for optimal results.[63] Some injuries will be permanent.[64] See p 766 for orthopaedic insights.

1 R Patel 2004 *BMJ* 328 1303

Caesarean section

Incidence 23% of UK labours in 2002; (9% pre-labour). *Maternal mortality:* 1 per 100,000 (2000–2). *Morbidity* is higher—from infection, ileus, and thromboembolism. For 1st operations 25% are due to failure to progress, 28% for fetal distress, 14% for breech; of 2nd caesareans 44% have had previous section. Use of support (eg doualas p 65) in labour, induction at 41 weeks, consultant involvement is decision to section, fetal blood sampling when fetal monitoring is used, and use of a 4 hour partogram with action line all help reduce incidence of caesarean sections. 9:1000 will require ITU care.

Lower uterine segment incision Joel Cohen incision (straight incision 3cm above symphysis pubis) with blunt dissection thereafter is recommended (reduces blood loss). Fetal laceration rate is 2%.

Classical caesarean section (vertical incision) Rarely used. Indications: • Very premature fetus, lower segment poorly formed • Fetus lies transverse, with ruptured membranes and liquor draining • Structural abnormality makes lower segment use impossible • Constriction ring present • Fibroids (some) • Some anterior placenta praevia when lower segment abnormally vascular • Mother dead and rapid birth desired.

Before an emergency section ►*Explain to the mother what is to happen.*
- Activate the anaesthetist, theatre staff, porters, and paediatrician.
- Have the mother breathe 100% O_2 if there is fetal distress.
- Neutralize gastric contents with 20mL of 0.3 molar sodium citrate, and promote gastric emptying with metoclopramide 10mg IV. (NB: there is no time for H_2 agonists to work; ranitidine is kept for elective sections, eg 150mg PO 2h before surgery.) Consider pre-operative emptying of stomach (eg if prolonged labour or opiate given). The stomach should be routinely emptied prior to extubation to minimize risk of postoperative aspiration. See Mendelson's syndrome, p 80.
- Take to theatre (awake); set up IVI. Take blood for crossmatch, eg 2U; if for abruption, (6U and 2 IVIs if previous section and anterior placenta praevia—see below).
- Catheterize the bladder. Tilt 15° to her left side on operating table.
- Use pulse oximetry peri- and post-operatively in those with dark skins (cyanosis is difficult to detect).
- Tell the paediatrician if the mother has had opiates in the last 4h.
- Remember thromboprophylaxis (see OPPOSITE).

Halothane should not be used for obstetric procedures because uterine muscle relaxation increases bleeding. Other anaesthetic problems include vomiting on induction (use rapid sequence induction, p 626), and light anaesthesia (out of consideration for the baby) causing paralysed awareness. ►In reducing maternal mortality, the importance of having an experienced anaesthetist cannot be overemphasized. When appropriate offer regional anaesthesia. Document indication for and urgency of operation. Note: in 2002-3 only 8% of Caesarean sections were under GA.

Indications for *elective* caesarean sections Known cephalo-pelvic disproportion; placenta praevia; breech presentation (but offer version at 36 weeks) and twins where 1st twin not cephalic; some malpresentations (p 71); after vaginal surgery (suburethral repair; vesico-vaginal fistula repair); or with some maternal infections, eg 3rd trimester herpes, HIV (p 34). If a repeat section is planned, arrange ultrasound placental localization to exclude placenta praevia as this is more common and more likely to be complicated by placenta accreta (hence risk of massive haemorrhage) in the presence of a uterine scar.

Emergency section may be needed because of antenatal complications, eg severe pre-eclampsia, abruptio placentae (baby still alive). In others, the need becomes apparent during labour: fetal distress; prolapsed cord (if fetus alive); after failed induction; or failure to progress.

Trial of scar in labour: See p 80. Beware oxytocin. ***Antibiotic prophylaxis*** is recommended. Infection (wound, endometritis, and UTI) is reduced by IV antibiotics (eg 2g cefradine at induction, 1g at 6h and 12h post-op) for both emergency and elective sections. Longer courses do not appear to be superior, nor do more expensive second generation cefalosporins.

Management of women already on thromboprophylaxis[1] If on high dose or therapeutic dose prophylaxis (see p 16) halve to same dose/24h as was previously being given/12h, on the day before planned caesarean. For all on prophylaxis omit dose on morning of caesarean and give 3h post-op unless epidural used: see p 66. 2% of women will get a wound haematoma.

At caesarean section Remove placenta by controlled cord traction (less endometritis than manual removal). In Rh-ve mothers, remove all excess blood from peritoneal cavity. Use a Kleihauer test (p 9) to determine dose of anti-D.

After caesarean section[2] Give 1:1 support in recovery unit. Check pulse, respiration rate (RR), BP and sedation levels half hourly for 1st 2h, then hourly until stable (and all but BP until 12h if intrathecal diamorphine given, 24h if intrathecal morphine and until 2h after epidural or patient controlled opiate analgesia discontinued). After epidural remove urinary catheters when mobile or 12h after last top-up dose (whichever later). After general anaesthesia, give extra midwife support to help establish breast feeding. Mobilize the mother early. Remove wound dressing at 24h. Give analgesia (ibuprofen + co-codamol if pain severe, co-codamol if moderate, paracetamol if mild). Average hospital stay is 3–4 days but mothers can be discharged after 24 hours if they wish and are well.

Prophylaxis against thromboembolism ***Low-risk:*** Women with no risk factors undergoing elective caesarean section in an uncomplicated pregnancy require only early mobilization and good hydration.

Moderate risk:

- Age >35 years
- Obesity (>80kg)
- Para 4+
- Pre-eclampsia
- Emergency section in labour
- Gross varicose veins
- Current infection
- ≥4 days prior immobility
- Major current illness
- Labour ≥12 hours

These women require heparin prophylaxis or mechanical methods.

High risk: These women should all receive heparin until 5 days post-operatively or until fully mobilized if longer. Leg stockings confer additional benefit.

- Any woman with ≥3 risk factors above
- Extended pelvic or abdominal surgery, eg caesarean hysterectomy
- FH or past history of thromboembolism or thrombophilia
- Paralysed lower limbs
- Women with antiphospholipid antibody (cardiolipin antibody or lupus anticoagulant)

Women who have had thromboembolism in pregnancy should receive thromboprophylaxis for 6 weeks postpartum. See p 16.

1 RCOG Clinical Guideline **37** 2004 *Thomboprophylaxis*
2 NICE Clinical Guideline 2004 *Caesarean section*

⇛Uterine rupture

Ruptured uterus is rare in the UK (1:1500 deliveries—but 1:100 in parts of Africa). Associated maternal mortality is 5%, and the fetal mortality 30%. ~70% of UK ruptures are due to dehiscence of caesarean section scars. Lower segment scars are far less likely to rupture (1.4%) than the classical scars (6.4%)—see p 78. Other risk factors: • Obstructed labour in the multiparous, especially if oxytocin is used • Previous cervical surgery • High forceps delivery • Internal version • Breech extraction. Rupture is usually during the third trimester or in labour. ***Trial of scar:*** In general, a trial of labour is safer than automatic repeat caesars—particularly if the thickness of the lower uterine segment is >3.5mm on ultrasound at 36–38 weeks. Risk of subsequent rupture after caesarean is: 1.2/1000 if repeat caesarean without labour; 3.5/1000 for vaginal delivery with spontaneous labour; 8/1000 when labour induced by non-prostaglandins and 24/1000 if labour is induced using prostaglandins.[1] 20–40% undergo repeat emergency section.

Signs and symptoms Rupture is usually in labour. In a few (usually a caesarean scar dehiscence) rupture precedes labour. Pain is variable, some only having slight pain and tenderness over the uterus. In others pain is severe. Vaginal bleeding is variable and may be slight (bleeding is intraperitoneal). Unexplained maternal tachycardia, sudden maternal shock, cessation of contractions, disappearance of the presenting part from the pelvis, and fetal distress are other presentations. Postpartum indicators of rupture: continuous PPH with a well-contracted uterus; if bleeding continues postpartum after cervical repair; and whenever shock is present.

Management If suspected in labour, perform laparotomy, deliver the baby by caesarean section, and explore the uterus. ⇛• Give O_2 at 15L/min via a tight-fitting mask with reservoir • Set up IVI • Crossmatch 6u of blood and correct shock by fast transfusion. • Arrange laparotomy. The type of operation performed should be decided by a senior obstetrician; if the rupture is small, repair may be carried out (possibly with tubal ligation); if the cervix or vagina are involved in the tear, hysterectomy may be necessary. Care is needed to identify the ureters and exclude them from sutures. Give post-operative antibiotic cover, eg ampicillin 500mg/6h IV and netilmicin 150mg/12h IV (unless there is renal impairment). 85% of spontaneous ruptures require hysterectomy, but >66% of ruptured scars are repairable.

⇛Mendelson's syndrome

This is the name given to the cyanosis, bronchospasm, pulmonary oedema, and tachycardia that develop due to inhalation of acid gastric contents during general anaesthesia. Clinically it may be difficult to distinguish from cardiac failure or amniotic fluid embolus. Pre-operative H_2 antagonists, sodium citrate, gastric emptying, cricoid pressure (p 626), the use of cuffed endotracheal tubes during anaesthesia, and pre-extubation emptying of stomach aim to prevent it (p 78).

Management ⇛Tilt the patient head down. Turn her to one side and aspirate the pharynx. Give 100% oxygen. Give aminophylline 5mg/kg by slow IVI and hydrocortisone 1000mg IV stat. The bronchial tree should be sucked out using a bronchoscope under general anaesthesia. Antibiotics, eg ampicillin and netilmicin (as above), should be given to prevent secondary pneumonia. Ventilation conducted on intensive care may be needed. Physiotherapy should be given during convalescence.

1 NICE *Clinical Guideline* **11** 2004 Fertility: assessment and treatment for people with fertility problem

Stillbirth

Stillbirths are those babies born dead after 24 weeks' completed gestation. Rate: 5.7/1000 total births (2003). Death in utero may take place at any stage in pregnancy or in labour. Delivery is an emotional strain for both mother and attendant staff (as the pain and process of labour may seem so futile and mothers may feel guilty and that it is a punishment).

Some hours after a fetus has died in utero the skin begins to peel. On delivery such fetuses are described as macerated, as opposed to fresh stillbirths. If left, spontaneous labour usually occurs (80% within 2 weeks, 90% within 3 weeks), but it is common practice to induce labour once death is diagnosed, to prevent a long wait for labour for the mother and minimize risk of coagulopathy. DIC (p 88) is rare unless a dead fetus of more than 20 weeks' gestation has been retained for >3 weeks. If tests indicate a clotting disorder is present, some authorities recommend heparin (1000u/h for up to 48h prior to onset of labour—but get expert advice. Stop any heparin prior to labour), or if it is severe ensure excellent supply of freshest possible blood and fresh frozen plasma at delivery.

Causes of stillbirth Pre-eclampsia, chronic hypertension, renal disease, diabetes, infection, hyperpyrexia (T° >39.4°C), malformation (17% of macerated stillbirths and 4% of fresh have chromosomal anomalies), haemolytic disease, postmaturity. Abruption and knots in the cord may cause death in labour. In 20% no cause is found. Multiple pregnancy ↑ risk (15/1000).

Diagnosis The mother usually reports absent fetal movements. No heart sounds (using Pinard's stethoscope, Doppler, or cardiotocography). There is no fetal movement (eg heart beat) on ultrasound. It may help the mother to see lack of heart beat.

Management If mother Rh-ve do anti-D (p 9). Do Kleihauer to determine dose. The mother may want to go home after diagnosis to reflect, collect things and make arrangements. Check maternal Hb, urine for protein, and blood clotting screen if fetus not thought recently deceased. Labour is induced using prostaglandin vaginally or extra-amniotically (dose varied with uterine response). Oxytocin used concomitantly risks uterine or cervical trauma, so use after prostaglandin and in extra-amniotic infusion cases. Oxytocin infusion alone (p 42) may be used for induction if the cervix is ripe (Bishop's score ≥4, gestation ≥35 weeks). Amniotomy is traditionally contraindicated as it risks infection. Some use mifepristone orally before using prostaglandins to induce abortion.

Ensure good pain relief in labour (if epidural: check clotting tests are normal). Do not leave the mother unattended. When the baby is born wrap it (as with any other baby) and offer to the mother to see and to hold—if the mother so desires. A photograph may be taken for her to take home. A lock of the baby's hair and palm print given (keep in notes for later if she does not want them then). Unseen babies are difficult to grieve for. Naming the baby and holding a funeral service may help with grief.

Labour ward procedure (to try to establish cause) Thorough examination of the stillbirth; clinical photographs. Take time to talk to parents about how helpful a post-mortem may be to them in understanding what happened and planning further pregnancies. (If consent is refused, MRI (may miss significant pathology) and cytogenetics (eg small samples of tissue for metabolic studies) may be acceptable but are less informative.) Do placental histology, high vaginal swab for bacteriology; maternal & fetal blood for TORCH screen (p 34) and mother's blood for Kleihauer test (this detects fetomaternal transfusion—a cause of unexplained stillbirth), and lupus anticoagulant, and chromosome analysis of fetal blood and skin.

Stillbirth

Stillbirths are those babies born dead after 24 weeks completed gestation. Rate: 5.7/1000 total births (2003). Death *in utero* may take place at any stage in pregnancy or in labour. Delivery is an emotional strain for both mother and attendant staff as the pain and process of labour may seem so futile and mothers may feel guilty—and that it is a punishment.

Some hours after a fetus has died *in utero* the skin begins to peel. On delivery such fetuses are described as *macerated*, as opposed to *fresh* stillbirths. If left, spontaneous labour usually occurs (80% within 2 weeks, 90% within 3 weeks), but it is common practice to induce labour once death is diagnosed, to prevent a long wait for labour for the mother, and minimize risk of coagulopathy. DIC (p 88) is rare unless a dead fetus of more than 20 weeks' gestation has been retained for >3 weeks. If tests indicate a clotting disorder is present, some authorities recommend heparin (1000U IV/h for up to 48h prior to onset of labour)—but get expert advice. Stop any heparin prior to labour, or if it supervenes. Ensure excellent supply of freshest possible blood and fresh frozen plasma at delivery.

Causes of stillbirth Pre-eclampsia, chronic hypertension, renal disease, diabetes, infection, hyperpyrexia (T° >39.4°C), malformation (11% of macerated stillbirths and 4% of fresh have chromosomal anomalies), haemolytic disease, postmaturity. Abruption and knots in the cord may cause death in labour. In 20% no cause is found. Multiple pregnancy ↑ risk (16.6:1000).

Diagnosis The mother usually reports absent fetal movements. No heart sounds (using Pinard's stethoscope, Doppler, or cardiotocography). There is no fetal movement (eg heart beat) on ultrasound. It may help the mother to see lack of heart beat.

Management ►If mother Rh-ve give anti-D (p 9). Do Kleihauer to determine dose. The mother may want to go home after diagnosis to reflect, collect things and make arrangements. Check maternal T°, BP, urine for protein, and blood clotting screen if fetus not thought recently demised. Labour is induced using prostaglandin vaginally; or extra-amniotically (dose varied with uterine response). Oxytocin IV used concomitantly risks uterine or cervical trauma so use *after* prostaglandin extra-amniotic infusion ceases. Oxytocin infusion alone (p 62) may be used for induction if the cervix is ripe (Bishop's score ≥4, gestation ≥35 weeks). Amniotomy is traditionally contraindicated as it risks infection. Some use mifepristone orally before using prostaglandins to induce abortion.

Ensure good pain relief in labour (if epidural, check clotting tests all normal). Do not leave the mother unattended. When the baby is born wrap it (as with any other baby) and offer to the mother to see and to hold—if the mother so desires. A photograph may be taken for her to take home, a lock of the baby's hair and palm-print given (keep in notes for later if she does not want them then). Unseen babies are difficult to grieve for. Naming the baby and holding a funeral service may help with grief.

Labour ward procedure (to try to establish cause) Thorough examination of the stillbirth, clinical photographs. Take time to talk to parents about how helpful a post-mortem may be to them, in understanding what happened, and planning further pregnancies. If consent is refused, MRI (may miss significant pathology) and cytogenetics (± small volumes of tissue for metabolic studies) may be acceptable but are less informative. Do placental histology, high vaginal swab for bacteriology, maternal & fetal blood for TORCH^{etc} screen (p 34), and mother's blood for Kleihauer test, p 9 (detects fetomaternal transfusion—a cause of unexplained stillbirth), and lupus anticoagulant, and chromosome analysis of fetal blood and skin.

Helping parents after stillbirth

- Give parents a follow-up appointment to discuss causes found by the above tests. Consider a domiciliary visit if parents prefer. Refer for genetic counselling if appropriate.
- In England, a *Certificate of Stillbirth* is required (issued by an obstetrician), that the parents are required to take to the Registrar of Births and Deaths within 42 days of birth. The father's name only appears in the register if the parents are married, or if both parents make the registration.
- The Registrar then issues a Certificate of Burial or Cremation which the parents then give to the undertaker (if they have chosen a private funeral—in which case they bear the cost of the funeral), or to the hospital administrators if they have chosen a hospital funeral—for which the hospital bears the cost. Parents are issued with a Certificate of Registration to keep which has the name of the stillborn baby (if named), the name of the informant who made the registration, and the date of stillbirth.
- UK hospitals are directed by the Department of Social Security to offer 'hospital' funerals for stillbirths (arranged through an undertaker). If the parents offer to pay for this, the hospital may accept. The hospital should notify the parents of the time of the funeral so that they may attend, if they wish. With hospital funerals a coffin is provided and burial is often in a multiple-occupancy grave in a part of the graveyard set aside for babies. The hospital should inform parents of the site of the grave. Graves are unmarked, so should the parents not attend the funeral and wish to visit later it is recommended that they contact the graveyard attendants for the grave to be temporarily marked. Parents may buy a single occupancy grave, if they wish, on which they can later erect a headstone. Hospitals can arrange cremations, but the parents pay for this and parents should be told that there are unlikely to be any ashes after cremation.[1]
- In addition to arranging a follow-up appointment with the obstetrician to discuss implications for future pregnancy, and the cause (if known) of the stillbirth, it is helpful to give parents the address of a local branch of an organization for bereavement counselling, eg SANDS.[2] Grief may take a long time to resolve (p 498) and parents may find it difficult to contact ordinary medical staff without the 'excuse' provided by asking about the baby's ailments.

Each maternity unit should have a bereavement counsellor to support the mother and father, and help guide them through the formalities.

In the UK statutory maternity pay and the maternity allowance and social fund maternity payments are payable after stillbirth.

Note: stillbirth affects ~1:730 singleton pregnancies by 38 weeks: it is 4 times as common as sudden infant death syndrome p 148.

1 *Guidelines for professionals on pregnancy loss and the death of a baby.* (RCOG)
2 SANDS *Stillbirth & Neonatal Death* Soc, 28 Portland Place, London W1. 020 7436 5881 www.uk-sands.org

▸▸Postpartum haemorrhage (PPH)

Primary PPH is the loss of greater than 500mL (definitions vary) in the first 24h after delivery. This occurs after ~6% of deliveries; major PPH (>1 litre) in 1.3%. Causes: uterine atony (90%), genital tract trauma (7%), clotting disorders—p 88 (3%). Death rate: 2/yr in the UK; 125,000/yr worldwide.

Factors predisposing to poor uterine contractions •Past history of atony with PPH. •Retained placenta or cotyledon. •Ether or halothane anaesthesia. •A large placental site (twins, severe rhesus disease, large baby), low placenta, overdistended uterus (polyhydramnios, twins). •Extravasated blood in the myometrium (abruption). •Uterine malformation or fibroids. •Prolonged labour. •Poor second stage uterine contractions. •Trauma to uterus or cervix. •Older mothers.

Management •Give oxytocin 5U slowly IV. •Call emergency ambulance unit (p 4)—if not in hospital. Give high-flow O_2 as soon as available. •Set up IVI (2 large-bore cannulae). •Call anaesthetist (a CVP line may help guide fluid replacement, but not if it causes delay). •If shocked give Haemaccel® or fresh blood of the patient's ABO and Rh group (uncrossmatched in emergency) *fast* until systolic BP >100mmHg and urine flows at >30mL/h (catheterize the bladder). •Is the placenta delivered? If it is, is it complete? If not, explore the uterus. •If the placenta is complete, put the patient in the lithotomy position with adequate analgesia and good lighting. Check for and repair trauma. •If the placenta has not been delivered but has separated, attempt to deliver it by controlled cord traction after rubbing up a uterine contraction. If this fails, ask an experienced obstetrician to remove it under general anaesthesia. Beware renal shut-down.

If bleeding continues despite all the above, give 10 units of oxytocin in 500mL dextrose saline, eg at a rate of 15 drops/min. Bimanual pressure on the uterus may decrease immediate loss. Inform consultant. Check that blood is clotting (5mL should clot in a plain round-bottomed glass tube in <6min); formal tests: platelets, prothrombin ratio, kaolin-cephalin clotting time, fibrin degradation products. Involve consultant haematologist if coagulopathy. Explore the uterus for possible rupture. If uterine atony is the cause, and the circulation is still compromised, give carboprost 250μg (15-methyl prostaglandin F2α) eg as Hemabate® 1mL deep IM (max 8 doses, each >15min (usually 90min) apart). SE: nausea, vomiting, diarrhoea, T°↑; (less commonly—asthma, BP↑, pulmonary oedema). It controls bleeding in ~88%. If atony persists despite drugs a B-Lynch brace uterine suture[1] may well stop bleeding (can be used in conjunction with vessel ligations). Rarely, uterine packing, internal iliac artery or uterine vessel ligation or embolization, or hysterectomy is needed to stop bleeding. Ask a haematologist's advice on clotting factor replacement (fresh frozen plasma contains all of them; the cryoprecipitate has more fibrinogen, but lacks antithrombin III).

Secondary PPH This is excessive blood loss from the genital tract after 24h from delivery. It usually occurs between 5 and 12 days and is due to retained placental tissue or clot. Secondary infection is common. Uterine involution may be incomplete. If bleeding is slight and there is no sign of infection it may be managed conservatively—but heavier loss, the suggestion of retained products on ultrasound, or a tender uterus with an open os, requires exploration. Crossmatch 2 units of blood pre-operatively. Give antibiotics (eg ampicillin 500mg/6h IV, metronidazole 1g/12h PR) if there are signs of infection. Carefully curette the uterus (it is easily perforated at this stage). Send curettings for histology (excludes choriocarcinoma).

1 H Holtsema 2004 *Eur J Obstet Gynaecol Reprod Biol* **115** 39

Managing those refusing blood transfusion in pregnancy

- Know maternal attitude to transfusion at booking.
- Give oral iron and folate to mother to maximize haemoglobin stores.
- Book for delivery where there are good facilities to deal with haemorrhage promptly (including facilities for hysterectomy, balloon angioplasty to stabilize loss and interventional radiology techniques such as uterine embolization).
- Arrange ultrasound to know placental site.
- Inform consultant when admitted in labour. Ensure experienced staff conduct labour. Give oxytocin as soon as the baby is delivered. Do not leave the mother alone for first hour post-delivery.
- Consultants should perform caesarean section if required.
- Cell savers which wash the woman's own blood so that it may be returned may be acceptable to some women (suitable for intra-abdominal blood not contaminated by amniotic fluid).[1]
- Haemorrhage should be dealt with promptly, and clotting disorders excluded early. Involve a consultant obstetrician early (to decide if intervention may be needed eg embolization of uterine arteries, B-Lynch suture, internal iliac ligation or hysterectomy), and a consultant anaesthetist (for help with fluid replacement and for use of intensive care facilities). Liaise with a consultant haematologist. Avoid dextran (adversely affects haemostasis), but Haemacel® is useful.
- Ensure the woman does not want to change her mind and receive a transfusion.
- Should the woman die of exsanguination both bereaved relatives and distressed staff should be offered support.

1 M Hall 2004 Ch 4 in Why Mothers Die; *Confidential Enquiry into Maternal and Child Health 2000-2*

Retained placenta

Physiological third stage takes 30min. With the use of oxytocic drugs at delivery and controlled cord traction, ie active management, the third stage is complete in 10min in 97% of labours, and a placenta not delivered in 30min will probably not be expelled spontaneously. The danger with retained placenta is haemorrhage. *Associations:* Previous retained placenta; previous uterine surgery; preterm delivery; maternal age >35 years; placental weight <600g; pethidine use in labour; induced labour; parity >5.

Management If the placenta does not separate readily, avoid excessive cord traction—the cord may snap or the uterus invert. Check that the placenta is not in the vagina. Palpate the abdomen. If the uterus is well contracted, the placenta is probably separated but trapped by the cervix. Wait for the cervix to relax and release it. If the uterus is bulky, the placenta may have failed to separate. Rub up a contraction, put the baby to the breast (stimulates oxytocin production) or give more Syntometrine®, and empty the bladder (a full bladder causes atony). If the placenta still will not deliver, prepare to remove it manually (delay may precipitate a PPH).

Manual removal Set up IVI and crossmatch blood (eg 2U). Call the anaesthetist. The procedure can be done under epidural if *in situ*: Obtain consent. With the mother in lithotomy position, using aseptic technique, place one hand on the abdomen to stabilize the uterus. Insert the other hand through the cervix into the uterus. Following the cord assists finding the placenta. Gently work round the placenta, separating it from the uterus using the ulnar border of the hand. When separated it should be possible to remove it by cord traction. Check that it is complete. Give oxytocic drugs and start antibiotics, eg doxycycline 200mg stat, 100mg/24h and metronidazole 500mg/8h IV.

Rarely, the placenta will not separate (placenta accreta) and hysterectomy may be necessary—by a senior obstetrician.

▸▸Uterine inversion

Inversion of the uterus is rare. It may be due to mismanagement of the third stage, eg with cord traction in an atonic uterus (between contractions) and a fundal insertion of the placenta. It may be completely revealed, or partial when the uterus remains within the vagina. Even without haemorrhage the mother may become profoundly shocked.

Management The ease with which the uterus is replaced depends on the amount of time elapsed since inversion, as a tight ring forms at the neck of the inversion. With an inversion noted early before shock sets in, replacement by hand may be possible. If shock has ensued, set up a fast IVI and infuse colloid or blood. Summon expert help. Under halothane anaesthesia to relax the uterus, hold the uterus in the vagina with one hand. Run two litres of warm 0.9% saline fast into the vagina through cystoscopy tubing (or with a funnel and tube) with an assistant holding the labia encircled tightly around the operator's arm to prevent the fluid running away. Running the fluid through a silastic ventouse cap held in the vagina improves the 'vaginal seal'. The hydrostatic pressure of the water should reduce the uterus. Once the inversion has been corrected, give ergometrine to contract the uterus and prevent recurrence. Prophylactic antibiotics are advisable.

DIC and coagulation defects

DIC in pregnancy is always secondary to stimulation of coagulation by procoagulant substances released into the maternal circulation. Known triggers are: retention of a dead fetus (of greater than 20 weeks' gestation which has been dead for >3 weeks), pre-eclampsia, placental abruption, endotoxic shock, amniotic fluid embolism, placenta accreta, hydatidiform mole, prolonged shock from any cause, acute fatty liver of pregnancy (p26). **Pathogenesis:** Thromboplastins are released into the circulation, fibrin and platelets are consumed as intravascular clotting occurs. Tests for coagulation: clotting times; factors II, V, VIII, fibrinogen; their degradation products. In situations where DIC is a possibility send blood for crossmatch, platelets, and thrombin time or activated partial thromboplastin time (for more accurate estimation), and fibrin degradation products. Preliminary results should be available in 30mins. **Management:** Prevention: DIC may lead to massive bleeding and shock, and the first measure must be the correction of shock. Have O Rh-ve blood on hand ... preferably 2 wide-gauge IVs. Give blood as above and give blood fast. Fresh frozen plasma: 3–4 units. Stored blood is deficient in clotting factors. Give fresh frozen plasma to correct clotting factors and the prothrombin time. Platelets are indicated with prolonged bleeding and low platelet count. Calcium gluconate sometimes needed to counteract the citrate in stored blood (eg 10mL of 10% calcium gluconate IV after 6U of blood). Seek expert help from a haematologist. The coagulopathy is usually self-limiting if the stimulus can be removed. In the case of abruption, the fetus and delivery of the uterine contents is the way to remove the stimulus and this should be done as promptly as possible. **Mortality:** (in placental abruption) 50–80% (endotoxic shock).

Autoimmune thrombocytopenic purpura (AITP) Incidence: 1–2/10,000 pregnancies. IgG antibodies cause thrombocytopenia (associated with increased bone marrow megakaryocytes). If these antibodies (being able to) cross the placenta, they cause thrombocytopenia in 10% of fetuses. Exclude systemic lupus and thrombosis in the mother (thrombocytopenia may be an early presentation: do DNA binding, OHCM p423). Consider maternal therapy if maternal platelets fall below 50×10^9/L, or 50×10^9/L near delivery; give steroids (rarely splenectomy is necessary during pregnancy: ideally in the second trimester). Immunoglobulin IgG 0.4g/kg IV for 5 days is sometimes used near expected date of delivery, inducing maternal and fetal remission for up to 3 weeks, but it is extremely expensive. Aim for non-traumatic delivery for both mother and baby. Neonatal platelet counts may fall further in the first days of life, then gradually rise to normal over two weeks. Treatment is not needed unless the baby is compromised. Maternal mortality due to AITP is now negligible, but fetal mortality remains (due to intracranial bleeding). Take cord blood at delivery. If platelets $<20 \times 10^9$/L give baby IgG. If platelets low at birth observe baby for 3–4 days as further fall likely.

Thrombocytopenia in pregnancy 1 Spurious (clotting in the bottle).
2 Pregnancy-associated thrombocytopenia (benign gestational thrombocytopenia)—mild and self-limiting (platelets usually above 100×10^9/L).
3 Autoimmune thrombocytopenia.
4 Pre-eclampsia (platelets may fall early, preceding clotting abnormality).
5 DIC (above) and haemolytic uraemic syndrome (p??)/thrombotic thrombocytopenic purpura (parts of a microangiopathic spectrum, OHCM p323).
6 Folate deficiency.
7 Congenital (May–Hegglin anomaly, hereditary macrothrombocytopenia).
8 Marrow disease; hypersplenism.

⏩DIC and coagulation defects

DIC in pregnancy is always secondary to stimulation of coagulation by procoagulant substance release in the maternal circulation. Known triggers are: retention of a dead fetus (of greater than 20 weeks' gestation which has been dead for >3 weeks); pre-eclampsia; placental abruption; endotoxic shock; amniotic fluid embolism; placenta accreta; hydatidiform mole; prolonged shock from any cause; acute fatty liver of pregnancy (p 26). ***Pathogenesis:*** Thromboplastins are released into the circulation, fibrin and platelets are consumed as intravascular clotting occurs. ***Tests:*** Kaolin–cephalin clotting time↑ (↓ factors II, V, VII), fibrinogen↓, fibrin degradation products↑. In situations where DIC is a possibility send blood for crossmatch, platelets, partial thromboplastin time or accelerated whole blood clotting time, prothrombin time, fibrinogen estimation, and fibrin degradation products. Preliminary results should be available in 30min. ***Management:*** Presentation may be as heavy bleeding and shock, and the first measures must be the correction of shock. ⏩Give O_2 at 15 litres/min via a tight fitting mask with reservoir. Set up at least 1, preferably 2, wide-gauge IVIs, take bloods as above, and give blood fast (group-compatible blood—available in 5–10min or O Rh–ve blood if desperate). Stored blood is deficient in clotting factors. Give fresh frozen plasma to normalize the kaolin–cephalin clotting time and the prothrombin time. Platelets are indicated with prolonged bleeding and low platelet count. Calcium is sometimes needed to counteract citrate in stored blood (eg 10mL of 10% calcium gluconate IVI, eg after 6U of blood). Seek expert help from a haematologist. The condition is usually self-limiting if the stimulus can be removed. In the case of intrauterine death and abruption (p 56) removal of the uterine contents is the way to correct the stimulus, and this should be done as promptly as possible. ***Mortality:*** <1% if placental abruption; 50–80% if infection/shock.

Autoimmune thrombocytopenic purpura (AiTP) Incidence 1–2; 10,000 pregnancies. IgG antibodies cause thrombocytopenia (associated with increased bone marrow megakaryocytes) in the mother, and being able to cross the placenta, they cause thrombocytopenia in ~10% of fetuses. Exclude systemic lupus erythematosus in the mother (thrombocytopenia may be an early presentation; do DNA binding, *OHCM* p 422). Consider maternal HIV. If maternal platelets fall below 20×10^9/L or 50×10^9/L near delivery, give steroids. Rarely, splenectomy is necessary during pregnancy (ideally in the second trimester). Immunoglobulin IgG 0.4g/kg IV for 5 days is sometimes used near expected date of delivery, inducing maternal and fetal remission for up to 3 weeks but it is extremely expensive. Aim for non-traumatic delivery for both mother and baby. Neonatal platelet count may fall further in the first days of life, then gradually rise to normal over 4–16 weeks. Treatment is not needed unless surgery is contemplated. Maternal mortality due to AiTP is now negligible, but fetal mortality remains (due to intracranial bleeding). Take cord blood at delivery. If platelets $<20 \times 10^9$/L give baby IgG 1g/kg IVI at birth. If platelets low at birth observe baby for 2–5 days as further falls likely.

Thrombocytopenia in pregnancy **1** Spurious (try citrated bottle).
2 Pregnancy-associated thrombocytopenia (benign gestational thrombocytopenia)—mild and self-limiting (platelets stay above 100×10^9/L).
3 Autoimmune thrombocytopenia.
4 Pre-eclampsia (platelets may fall early, preceding clotting abnormality).
5 DIC (above) and haemolytic uraemic syndrome (p 176)/thrombotic thrombocytopenic purpura (2 ends of a microangiopathic spectrum, *OHCM* p 282).
6 Folate deficiency.
7 Congenital (May–Heggin anomaly, hereditary macrothrombocytopenia).
8 Marrow disease; hypersplenism.

Amniotic fluid embolism

This condition, with a mortality up to 26.4–61% presents with sudden dyspnoea and hypotension, heralded, in 20%, by seizures. 40% also develop DIC, and of those who survive the initial collapse 70% go on to develop pulmonary oedema (acute respiratory distress syndrome, ARDS, *OHCM* p 190). An anaphylactic type of response occurs to (possibly abnormal) amniotic fluid in the maternal circulation. ***Presentation*** is often at the end of the first stage of labour or shortly after delivery but can complicate amniocentesis, or termination of pregnancy, abruption, trauma, Caesarean section, and has even occurred up to 48h postpartum. Previously it was said to be related to uterine hyperstimulation (multiparous short labour and use of oxytocin). This may be anecdotal. Risk increases with increasing maternal age.

Management

- ▸▸The first priority is to prevent death from respiratory failure. Give mask oxygen and call an anaesthetist urgently. Endotracheal intubation and ventilation may be necessary. Set up IVI in case DIC should supervene. Cardiovascular collapse is due to left ventricular failure. DIC and haemorrhage then usually follow. Treatment is essentially supportive—important steps are detailed below. Diagnosis may be difficult: exclude other causes of obstetric shock (p 55).
- ▸▸Cardiopulmonary resuscitation if indicated.
- ▸▸Give highest available O_2 concentration. If unconscious, ventilate and use 100% inspired O_2.
- ▸▸Monitor for fetal distress.
- ▸▸If hypotensive, give fluids rapidly IVI to increase preload. If still hypotensive consider inotropes: dobutamine (a better inotrope than dopamine), eg in a dose range of 2.5–10μg/kg/min IVI may help.
- ▸▸Pulmonary artery catheterization (Swan-Ganz catheter if available) helps guide haemodynamic management.
- ▸▸After initial hypotension is corrected, give only maintenance requirements of fluid to avoid pulmonary oedema from acute respiratory distress syndrome. Transfer to intensive care unit as soon as possible.
- ▸▸Treat DIC with fresh whole blood or packed cells and fresh frozen plasma. Use of heparin is controversial, there is insufficient data to warrant routine heparinization.

Most mortality occurs in the first few hours. Mortality rates reported 26.4–61%. (Between 2000-2 there were 19 reported UK cases reported; and 5 deaths). Report suspected cases to National Amniotic Fluid Embolism Register.[1] Should the woman die, specifically request that the lungs be examined for the presence of amniotic squames (to confirm the diagnosis).

1 R Vlies 2004 Ch 5 in Why Mothers Die; *Confidential Enquiry into Maternal & Child Health 2000-2*

Birth injuries

►Give all babies with signs of trauma vitamin K 1mg IM at birth (unless already given as part of routine measures).

To the baby—*Moulding:* This is a natural phenomenon rather than an injury. The skull bones are able to override each other (p 42) to reduce the diameter of the head. Moulding is assessed by the degree of overlap of the overriding at the sutures. If moulding is absent, the cranial bones are felt separately. With slight moulding, the bones just touch, then they override but can be reduced; finally they override so much that they cannot be reduced. Excessive moulding during labour indicates cephalo-pelvic disproportion, and can result in intracranial damage.

Cephalhaematoma: This is a *subperiostial* swelling on the fetal head, and its boundaries are therefore limited by the individual bone margins (commonest over parietal bones). It is fluctuant. Spontaneous absorption occurs but may take weeks and may cause or contribute to jaundice.

Caput succedaneum: This is an oedematous swelling of the scalp, superficial to the cranial periosteum (which does not, therefore, limit its extent) and is the result of venous congestion and exuded serum caused by pressure against the cervix and lower segment during labour. The presenting part of the head therefore has the swelling over it. It gradually disappears in the first days after birth. When ventouse extraction is used in labour a particularly large caput (called a chignon) is formed under the ventouse cup.

Erb's palsy: See Fig 1, p 77. This may result from a difficult assisted delivery, eg shoulder dystocia. The baby's arm is flaccid and the hand is in the 'porter's tip' posture (p 766). Exclude a fractured clavicle and arrange physiotherapy. If it has not resolved by 6 months, the outlook is poor.

Subaponeurotic haematoma: Blood lies between the aponeurosis and the periosteum. As haematoma is not confined to the boundaries of one bone, collections of blood may be large enough to result in anaemia or jaundice. They are associated with vacuum extractions.

Skull fractures: These are associated with difficult forceps extractions. They are commonest over parietal or frontal bones. If depressed fractures are associated with neurological signs, ask a neurosurgeon if the bone should be elevated.

Intracranial injuries: Intracranial haemorrhage is especially associated with difficult or fast labour, instrumental labour, and breech delivery. Premature babies are especially vulnerable. Normally a degree of motility of intracranial contents is buffered by cerebrospinal fluid. Excessive moulding and sudden changes in pressure reduce this effect and are associated with trauma. In all cases of intracranial haemorrhage check babies' platelets. If low, check mother's blood for platelet alloantibodies (PLA1 system). Subsequent babies are at equal risk. IV maternal immunoglobulin treatment is being evaluated.

Anoxia may cause intraventricular haemorrhage (p 108). Asphyxia causes intracerebral haemorrhage (often petechial) and may result in cerebral palsy. Extradural, subdural, and subarachnoid haemorrhages can all occur. Babies affected may have convulsions, apnoea, cyanosis, abnormal pallor, low heart rate, alterations in muscle tone, restlessness, somnolence, or abnormal movements. Treatment is supportive and expectant. See p 108 & p 110.

Birth injuries to the mother: anal sphincter injury

This injury is common, and is not completely preventable by episiotomy (p 93). Of the 1% who suffer anal sphincter injury with vaginal delivery ~30% have problems with flatus incontinence, 8% problems with liquid stool incontinence and 4% with solid stool (though usually less than once a week). Faecal incontinence is a source of misery, and requires expert attention.

Risk of mechanical injury is greatest after the first vaginal delivery. Traumatic stretching of the pudendal nerves occurs in >30% of primips, but is mostly asymptomatic, or mildly/transiently so. These patients are at ↑risk in subsequent deliveries (cumulative pudendal nerve injury is well-recognized). Other risk factors: baby >4kg, persistent occipito-posterior position, induced labour, 2nd stage >1h, episiotomy, forceps.

If rectal incontinence occurs, and especially if there is a recto-vaginal fistula, get expert surgical help.[66] If symptomatic or abnormal anorectal manometry or abnormality on endoanal ultrasound after previous repair, consider elective caesarean for subsequent delivery, as 17–24% develop worsening faecal symptoms after subsequent vaginal delivery.[1]

1 RCOG Clinical Guideline 29 2001 *Management of 3rd & 4th degree perineal tears following vaginal delivery*

Episiotomy and tears

Perineal tears These are classified by the degree of damage caused. Tears are most likely to occur with big babies, precipitant labours, babies with poorly flexed heads, shoulder dystocia, when forceps are used, or if there is a narrow suprapubic arch. Perineal massage in pregnancy helps prevent perineal trauma but may be uncomfortable at first.

Labial tears Common, these heal quickly and suturing is rarely helpful.

First degree tears These tears are superficial and do not damage muscle. They may not need suturing unless blood loss is marked.

Second degree tears These lacerations involve perineal muscle. They are repaired in a similar fashion to repair of episiotomy (see below).

Third degree tears Damage involves the anal sphincter. If rectal mucosa is involved it is a **fourth degree tear**. See p 91. Repair by an experienced surgeon, under epidural or GA in theatre with intra-operative antibiotic cover. Rectal mucosa is repaired first using absorbable suture from above the tear's apex to the mucocutaneous junction. Muscle is interposed. Vaginal mucosa is then sutured. Severed ends of the anal sphincter are apposed using figure-of-eight stitches. Finally skin is repaired. Avoid constipation post-operatively by using a high-fibre diet and faecal softeners for 10 days.

Episiotomy This is performed to enlarge the outlet, eg to hasten birth of a distressed baby, for instrumental or breech delivery, to protect a premature head, and to try to prevent 3° tears (but anal tears are not reduced by more episiotomies in normal deliveries). Rates: 8% Holland, 12% England, 50% USA.

The tissues which are incised are vaginal epithelium, perineal skin, bulbocavernous muscle, superficial, and deep transverse perineal muscles. With large episiotomies, the external anal sphincter or levator ani may be partially cut, and ischiorectal fat exposed.[1]

Technique: Hold the perineal skin away from the presenting part of the fetus (2 fingers in vagina). Infiltrate area to be cut with local anaesthetic, eg 1% lidocaine (=lignocaine). Still keeping the fingers in the introitus, cut mediolaterally towards the ischial tuberosity, starting medially (6 o'clock), so avoiding the Bartholin's glands. (Midline episiotomy is ineffective at protecting perineum and sphincters and may impair anal continence).[2]

Repair: (See diagrams.) NB: use resorbable suture—polyglactin 910 recommended.[3] In lithotomy, and using good illumination, repair the vaginal mucosa first. Traditional method: start above the apex using interlocking stitches 1cm apart, 1cm from wound edges. Tie off at mucocutaneous junction of fourchette. Then repair muscles with interrupted stitches to obliterate any dead spaces. Finally close the skin (subcutaneous stitch is more comfortable than interrupted stitches). A loose continuous non-locking suturing technique to appose each layer is associated with less short-term pain compared with traditional interrupted method.

Problems with episiotomy: Bleeding (so may increase chance of spread of HIV from mother to baby); infection and breakdown; haematoma formation. For comfort some suggest ice packs, salt baths, hair dryer to dry perineum. 60% of women suffer perineal damage (episiotomy or tear) with spontaneous vaginal delivery; rectal diclofenac can provide effective analgesia. Superficial dyspareunia: see p 310. If labia minora are involved in the skin bridge, the introitus is left too small. If the deep layers are inadequately sutured, the introitus becomes rather rounded exposing the bladder to coital thrusts.

1 J Vifllar 2002 *BMJ* **i** 928
2 L Sigorello 2000 *BMJ* **320** 86
3 RCOG *Clinical Guideline* **23** 2003 Methods and materials used in perineal repair

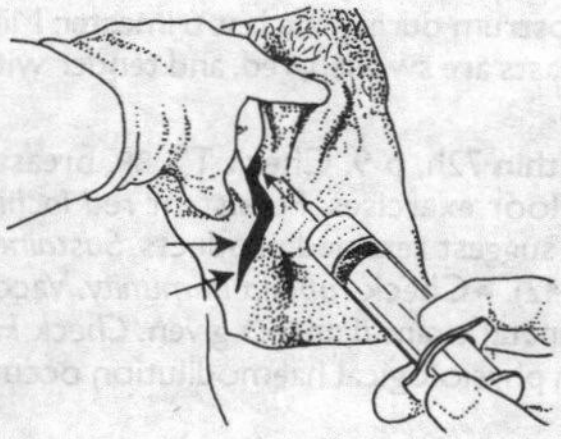

(1)
Swab the vulva towards the perineum. Infiltrate with 1% lignocaine → (*arrows*).

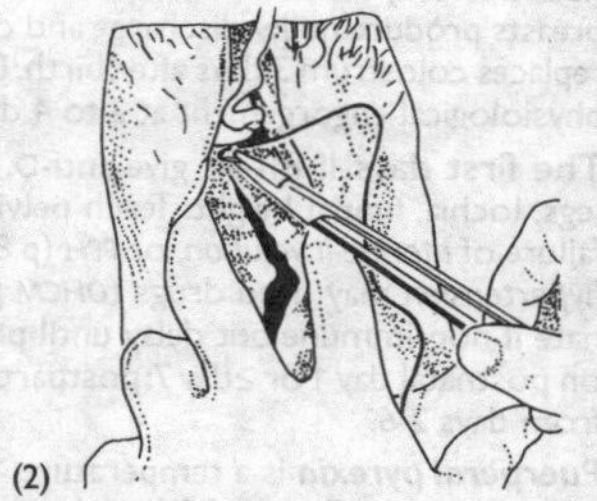

(2)
Place tampon with attached tape in upper vagina. Insert 1st suture above apex of vaginal cut (not too deep as underlying rectal mucosa nearby).

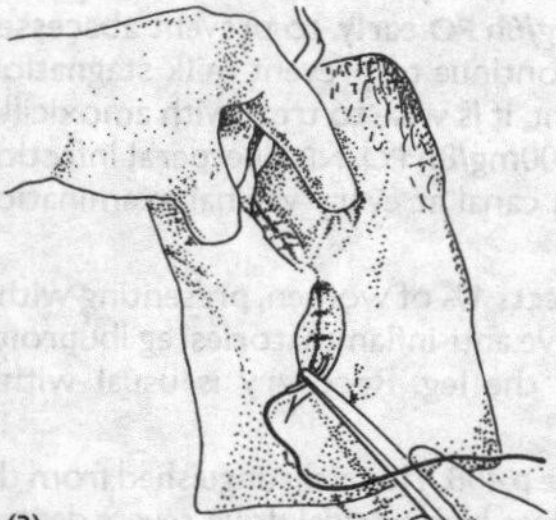

(3)
Bring together vaginal edges with continuous stitches placed 1cm apart. Knot at introitus under the skin. Appose divided levator ani muscles with 2 or 3 interrrupted sutures.

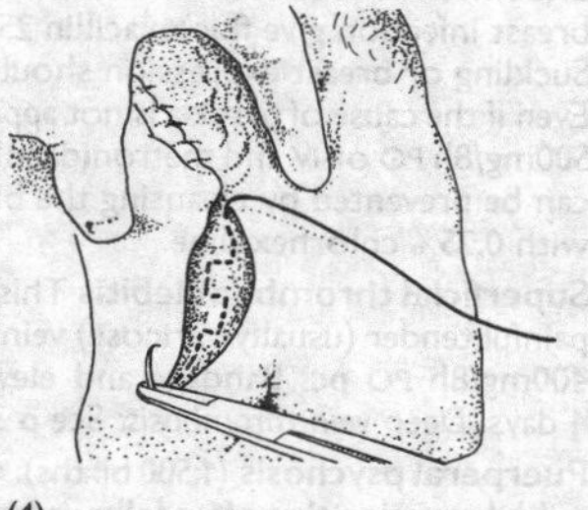

(4)
Close perineal skin (subcuticular continuous stitch is shown here).

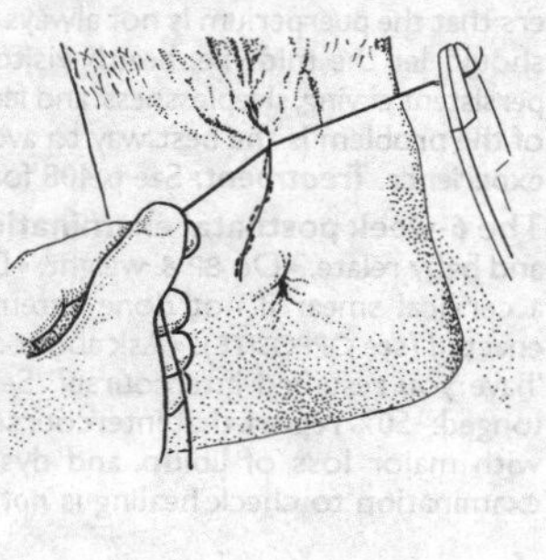

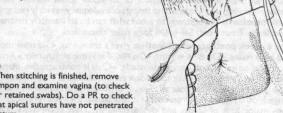

(5)
When stitching is finished, remove tampon and examine vagina (to check for retained swabs). Do a PR to check that apical sutures have not penetrated rectum.

The puerperium

The puerperium is the 6 weeks after delivery. The uterus involutes, from 1kg weight at delivery to 100g. Felt at the umbilicus after delivery, it is a pelvic organ at 10 days. Afterpains are felt (especially while suckling) as it contracts. The cervix becomes firm over 3 days. The internal os closes by 3 days, the external os by 3 weeks. Lochia (endometrial slough, red cells, and white cells) is passed *per vaginam*. It is red (*lochia rubra*) for the 1st 3 days, then becomes yellow (*lochia serosa*) then white over the next 10 days (*lochia alba*), until 6 weeks. The breasts produce milky discharge and colostrum during the last trimester. Milk replaces colostrum 3 days after birth. Breasts are swollen, red, and tender with physiological engorgement at 3 to 4 days.

The first days If Rh-ve, give anti-D, within 72h, p 9. Check T°, BP, breasts, legs, lochia, fundal height. Teach pelvic floor exercises. Persistent *red lochia*, failure of *uterine involution*, or *PPH* (p 84) suggest retained products. *Sustained hypertension* may need drugs (*OHCM* p 142). ►Check *rubella immunity*. Vaccinate if non-immune but delay until postnatal exam if anti-D given. *Check Hb* on postnatal day 1 or ≥day 7: postpartum physiological haemodilution occurs from days 2–6.

Puerperal pyrexia is a temperature >38°C in the first 14 days after delivery or miscarriage. Examine fully (chest, breasts, legs, lochia, and bimanual vaginal examination). Culture MSU, high vaginal swabs, blood, and sputum. 90% of infections will be urinary or of the genital tract. Superficial perineal infections occur around the second day. ***Endometritis*** gives lower abdominal pain, offensive lochia, and a tender uterus (on bimanual vaginal exam). Endometritis requires IV antibiotics (see below) and uterine curettage. For breast infection give flucloxacillin 250mg/6h PO early, to prevent abscesses. Suckling or breast expression should continue to prevent milk stagnation. Even if the cause of pyrexia is not apparent, it is wise to treat with amoxicillin 500mg/8h PO or IV and metronidazole 500mg/8h PO. NB: puerperal infection can be prevented by cleansing the birth canal at every vaginal examination with 0.25% chlorhexidine.

Superficial thrombophlebitis This affects 1% of women, presenting with a painful tender (usually varicose) vein. Give anti-inflammatories, eg ibuprofen 400mg/8h PO pc. Bandage and elevate the leg. Recovery is usual within 4 days. *Deep vein thrombosis:* See p 32.

Puerperal psychosis (1:500 births): ►See p 408. This is distinguished from the mild depression that often follows birth by a high suicidal drive, severe depression (p 336), mania, and more rarely schizophrenic symptoms (p 358) with delusions that the child is malformed. If an acute organic reaction (p 350) is present, suspect puerperal infection. It may be worthwhile explaining to mothers that the puerperium is not always a time of joy, and they may feel low—and should let the midwife, health visitor or GP know about negative feelings, persistent crying, sleeplessness, and feelings of inadequacy—as early recognition of the problem is the best way to avoid what can be an intensely destructive experience. ***Treatment:*** See p 408 for a fuller discussion.

The 6-week postnatal examination gives a chance to: • See how mother and baby relate. • Do BP & weight. • Do FBC if anaemic postnatally. • Arrange a cervical smear if not done antenatally. • Check contraceptive plans are enacted (see OPPOSITE). • Ask about depression, backache, incontinence. Ask 'have you resumed intercourse?' Sexual problems are common, and prolonged: ~50% report that intercourse is less satisfactory than pre-pregnancy, with major loss of libido, and dyspareunia the chief complaints. Vaginal examination to check healing is *not* usually needed.

Contraception after a baby

Lactational amenorrhoea (LAM)[1] This is Nature's contraception. Breastfeeding delays return of ovulation (suckling disrupts frequency and amplitude of gonadotrophin surges so that although there is gonadotrophin rise in response to falling placental sex steroids after delivery, ovulation does not occur). Women who are fully breastfeeding day and night (ie breast milk is baby's sole nutrient), are less than 6 months postpartum, and amenorrhoeic can expect this method to be 98% effective. Average 1st menstruation in a breast feeding mother is at 28.4 weeks (range 15–48). Contraceptive efficacy of LAM is decreased after 6 months, if periods return, if breastfeeding frequency reduces, night feeding stops, there is separation from the baby (eg return to work), if the baby receives supplements, or if mother or baby become ill or stressed. In the UK although 69% of mothers initiate breastfeeding only 21% still feed at 6 months. Aim for additional contraception once decreased efficacy is anticipated.

Progesterone only Pill (PoP, p 302) These may be started any time postpartum but if started after day 21 additional precautions are needed for 2 days. They do not affect breast milk production. Low doses (<1%) of hormone are secreted in the milk but have not been shown to affect babies.

Combined Pills Start at 3 weeks if not breastfeeding. They affect early milk production and are not recommended if breastfeeding until 6 months (but *can* be used from 6 weeks if other methods unacceptable). Levels of hormone in breast milk are similar to that of ovulatory cycles.

Emergency contraception Use of progesterone method is suitable for all. It is not needed before 21 days postpartum.

Depot injections These are not recommended until 6 weeks in those breast feeding (theoretical risk of sex steroid to baby's immature nervous system and liver). *Medroxyprogesterone acetate* (Depo-Provera®) 150mg given deep IM 12-weekly can given 5 days postpartum if bottle feeding, or *norethisterone enanthate* (Noristerat®) 200mg into gluteus maximus 8-weekly (licensed for short-term use only, but can be given immediately postpartum when Depo-Provera® use can cause heavy bleeding).

Progesterone implants Insertion is not recommended until 6 weeks in those who are breast feeding. 0.2% of daily dose of etornorgestrel is excreted in breast milk. Implant at 21–28 days in those bottle feeding.

Intrauterine contraceptive devices (IUCD) These should be inserted within the first 48h postpartum or delayed until 4 weeks. This is to minimize risk of uterine perforation at insertion. Levornogestrel releasing intrauterine devices are also inserted at 4 weeks.

Diaphragms and cervical caps The woman needs to be fitted at 6 weeks as different sizes may be required from previously. Alternative contraception is needed from day 21 until the new ones are confidently handled.

Sterilization Unless sterilization highly advisable at Caesarean section (eg repeated sections, family complete), it is best to wait an appropriate interval as immediate postpartum tubal ligation has possible increased failure rate and are more likely to be regretted.

1 Contraceptive choices for breastfeeding women 2004 *Br J Fam Plan and Reprod* **30** 181

Maternal mortality

Ideas, beliefs, art, work: none of these are worth sacrificing your life for; the only thing worth sacrificing life for is life itself. All mothers sacrifice themselves here to some degree: some pay the highest price, and it is to them that this page is dedicated.

Maternal mortality is defined in the UK as the death of a mother while pregnant or within 42 days of termination of pregnancy, from any cause related to or aggravated by the pregnancy or its management, but not from accidental or incidental causes (called *coincidental* deaths). Deaths are subdivided into those from '*direct causes*'—those in which the cause of death is directly attributable to pregnancy (eg abortion, eclampsia, haemorrhage)—and *indirect deaths*—those resulting from previous existing disease or disease developed during pregnancy, and which were not due to direct obstetric causes but were aggravated by pregnancy (eg heart disease). *Late deaths* are those occurring between 42 days and 1 year after termination, miscarriage, or delivery that are due to direct or indirect maternal causes.

History Since 1952 there have been 3-yearly confidential enquiries into maternal deaths. Prior to 1979, as many deaths were considered to have had 'avoidable factors' (this term was used to denote departures from acceptable standards of care by individuals, including patients) but since 1979 the wider term of 'substandard care' has been used to cover failures in clinical care and other factors, such as shortage of resources and back-up facilities.

Maternal mortality has almost halved every decade since reports have been issued (deaths per 100,000 maternities have been 67.1 in 1955–7, 33.3 in 1964–6, 11 in 1973–5, but 13.1 in 2000–2 of which direct deaths were 5.3 per 100,000).[1] Rates are lowest for women aged 20–24 years rising markedly in the over-35s. Mortality was highest for first pregnancies. Risk of dying in pregnancy, childbirth or from abortion is 1:65 in developing countries (1:16 in some) as opposed to 1:9000 in the United Kingdom. Note: pregnancy is very protective as all-cause mortality in 15–45 year old women is 58.4:100,000/year (ie rates of death 4 × *lower* in pregnancy and 1y after).

In 2000–2, 391 UK deaths were recorded including 94 late deaths. Of these 106 were direct obstetric deaths; 155 were indirect and 36 were coincidental (in no way related to pregnancy, eg car accident). Death was increased in non-affluent areas (×1.45); in non-whites (×3—but ×7 if black African or asylum seeker); if both parents unemployed (×20) or single mother (×3) and in those booking late or missing ≥4 antenatal appointments. Of those dying 14% had reported domestic violence; 35% were obese; 8% were substance abusers.

In 2000–2 thromboembolism was the chief cause of direct death in the UK (28% of deaths). Other direct causes: early pregnancy (14.1%)—(mainly ectopic pregnancy at 10.3%); hypertensive disorders (13.2%); genital tract sepsis (12%); amniotic fluid embolism (4.7%); haemorrhage (16.%); fatty liver of pregnancy (2.8%), anaesthetic deaths (5.6%). 33% died before delivery. When unreported deaths were also investigated, suicide was the commonest cause of (indirect) death overall; the mothers tending to be white, older, comfortably off, with other children, and dying by violent means.

The death rate from caesarean section for the 2000–2 period was 1 per 100 thousand operations. 4 direct deaths and 1 later were due to bowel perforation—3 due to Ogilvie's syndrome (pseudo-obstruction leading to perforation; not direct perforation), all in women who had had caesareans.

The maternal mortality rate was higher than in the previous triennium for direct deaths (5.3 *vs* 5:100,000), and again there were more indirect than direct deaths. Care was considered substandard in 67% of cases of direct death in 2000–2, in 47% this was 'major' ie might have affected outcome. 'Substandardness' includes pregnant women who refuse medical advice.

1 2004 Why Mothers Die; *Confidential Enquiry into Maternal and Child Health* 2000–2

Perinatal mortality

This is the number of stillbirths and deaths in the first week of life/1000 total births. Stillbirths only include those fetuses of >24 weeks' gestation, but if a fetus of <24 weeks' gestation is born and shows signs of life, and then dies, it is counted as a perinatal death in the UK (if dying within the first 7 days). Neonatal deaths are those infants dying up to and including the 28th day after birth. Other countries use different criteria—including stillbirths from 20 weeks and neonatal deaths up to 28 days after birth, so it is not always easy to compare statistics.

Perinatal mortality is affected by many factors. Rates are high for *small* (61% of deaths are in babies <2500g) and *preterm* babies (70% of deaths occur in the 5% who are preterm). See p 50 & p 128. *Regional variation* in the UK is quite marked. There is a *social class variation* with rates being less for social classes 1 and 2 than for classes 4 and 5. *Teenage mothers* have higher rates than mothers aged 20–29. From 35yrs rates rise until they are 1.5-fold higher than the low-risk group (25–35 years) by the age of >40. *Second babies* have the lowest mortality rates. Mortality rates are doubled for fourth and fifth children, trebled by sixth and seventh (this effect is not independent of social class as more lower social class women have many children). Rates are lower for *singleton births* than for multiple. Rates are higher for the offspring of mothers of Pakistani (14.6:1000) and Caribbean (15.5:1000) extraction living in the UK, as opposed to those of UK extraction (7.8:1000).

Perinatal mortality rates in the UK have fallen over the years from rates of 62.5/1000 in 1930–5 to 8.3/1000 in the 2002 for England and Wales.[67] Declining mortality reflects improvement in standards of living, improved maternal health, and declining parity, as well as improvements in medical care. The main causes of death were congenital abnormalities (21%), unclassified hypoxia (asphyxia) (18%) in 2002. Previously placental conditions (16%), birth problems including cord problems (11%), and maternal conditions (8%) have been other major causes.

Of neonatal deaths the main causes are prematurity (59%) and malformation (33%).

Examples of how changed medical care may reduce mortality:

- Worldwide, treatment of syphilis, antitetanus vaccination (of mother during pregnancy), and clean delivery (especially cord techniques), have the greatest influence in reducing perinatal mortality.
- Antenatal detection and termination of malformed fetuses.
- Reduction of mid-cavity procedures and vaginal breech delivery.
- Detection of placenta praevia antenatally.
- Prevention of rhesus incompatibility.
- Preventing progression of preterm labour.
- Better control of diabetes mellitus in affected mothers.
- Antenatal monitoring of 'at risk' pregnancies.

While we must try to reduce morbidity and mortality still further, this must not blind us to other problems that remain, such as the 'over-medicalization' of birth; the problem of reconciling maternal wishes to be in charge of her own delivery with the immediate needs of the baby; and the problem of explaining risks and benefits in terms that both parents understand, so that they can join in the decision-making process.

2 Paediatrics

who are you, little i
(5 or 6 years old)
peering from some high window
e e cummings

Other relevant pages: Orthopaedics (ch 11); Infectious disease (*OHCM* p 536–p 620); perinatal infection p 36; child psychiatry p 389; play therapy p 377; squint p 422; retinoblastoma p 421; pain (p 718); syndromes: p 638–p 655.

We thank Dr Patrick Davies—our Specialist Reader for this chapter.

Childhood: a time to become yourself

Manufacturing organs is the point of embryology…growth and development is the essence of childhood…and protection from a cynical world is the raison d'être of the family—that cardinal unit which prevents children cascading down the loveless spiral of truancy, illiteracy, street crime, violence, drug and solvent abuse, prostitution, and adolescent pregnancy. The abandoning of thousands and thousands of street children worldwide illustrates in a terrible way how paediatrics can never be done in a clinical vacuum—and that solutions to paediatric problems entail social issues and politics as much as medicine. This cascade of urban poverty contrasts with the sane and ordered world of our paediatric clinics. But always remember there is another world or two out there. Beyond the window, the child is on tiptoes, peering out, and before he flits through it and is lost forever, weigh him, measure him, feed him, clothe him, immunize him—and above all educate *him* (him or *her*, of course). Look after the body, and the soul will look after itself *provided the family is intact*. You will see the immense pressure illness puts on families: don't just observe. Help in any way you can: flexible clinics, home instead of hospital treatment, education going hand-in-hand with ward events, hospital-at-home, home-at-hospital facilities, and home-based nursing visits to help with complex cancer or HIV regimens.[1]

We cannot hope to enable children to realize their full potential—for potential is only ever lost. The egg has more potential than the embryo (its sex, for example is yet to be determined). The child has more potential than the medical student who is forever closing off lines of enquiry to concentrate on one thing. So if potential can only be lost we must aim for potential to be lost in the least harmful way.

The essence of paediatrics is aligning embryology, growth-and-development, family interactions, and preventive and therapeutic measures to achieve a person who is capable of making choices. Happy or free? Creative or reasonable? Self-destructive and isolated, or participatory and social? We cannot hand down the answers—we just peddle our wares down this one-way street. Ask children what childhood is for, and they will tell you 'Preparation. Learning. A time to become yourself…'[2] This is why Paediatrics must be holistic—otherwise it will not contribute to these aims. It is against this background of enabling children to become themselves that paediatricians practice their art and their science. We note with great interest that most patients between the ages of 15 and 20 who have acute leukaemia treated by paediatricians are cured—up to 63%, whereas <50% of this group survive if treated in adult units.[3] This chapter aims to explain how this difference might arise—and to encourage the reader to extend the skills learned in paediatrics to *all* medical practice.

Eliciting the history

There are 3 aims. 1 To establish a good relationship with the parents and the child, so that if there is nothing the matter with the child, the parents feel able to accept this. 2 Reaching a diagnosis or differential diagnosis. 3 Placing the diagnosis in the context of the child and family. There is no one treatment for pneumonia, or diabetes, or anything else (same disease, but different contexts require different treatments). If there is serious or untreatable illness, the aim is to build up trust, so that the parents are able to accept the best advice, and the child feels that he or she feels in safe, friendly hands. So if possible, avoid any hurry or distractions. Introduce yourself; explain your role in the ward or consulting room. Take a history from as many sources as possible, the child, mother, father, and any significant other—but beware allowing the child to feel marginalized, so address yourself to the child first, and last.

Presenting complaints Record the child's and parents' own words.

The present illness When and how did it start? Was he/she well before? How did it develop? What aggravates or alleviates it? Has there been contact with infections? Has the child been overseas recently?

Especially in infants, enquire about feeding, excretion, alertness, and weight gain. After ascertaining the presenting complaint, further questioning is to test the various hypotheses of differential diagnosis.

Past ***In utero:*** Any problems (eg PET, rubella, Rh disease); drug exposure?

At birth: Gestation, duration of labour, mode of delivery, birth weight, resuscitation required, birth injury, malformations.

As a neonate: Jaundice, fits, fevers, bleeding, feeding problems.

Ask about later illnesses, operations, accidents, screening tests, drugs, allergies, immunization, travel, and drug or solvent abuse.

Development (p 220) Does the mother remember milestones reliably?

Drugs Prescribed, recreational, *in utero*, and over-the-counter. Drug intolerances, adverse drug reactions, and true allergies (ie rashes; anaphylaxis).

Family history Stillbirths, TB, diabetes mellitus, renal disease, seizures, jaundice, malformations, others. Are siblings and parents alive and well? Find out about late-onset diseases with a genetic component.[1]

Consanguinity is common in some cultures and may be relevant to disease.

Social history It may be vital to know who the father is, but damaging to ask the mother directly. Asking about the 'family unit', or drawing a family tree (*OHCM* p 35) may be one way forward. Be prepared to allow information to surface slowly, after chats with friendly nurses. Ask about play, eating, sleeping (excessively wrapped or liable to cold?), schooling and pets. Who looks after the child if the parents work? What work do they do? Ask about their hopes, fears, and expectations about the child's illness and his stay in hospital.

Privacy, dignity, and confidentiality These are easy to pay lip-service to, but very hard to ensure in busy paediatric wards, where space is at a premium. During an average stay in hospital most patients and their relatives will overhear confidential exchanges, and only a few will ever recall being offered a screen to preserve privacy during examinations.[4]

►*If the family does not speak your language, find an interpreter.*

1 For example, if a parent has had a myocardial infarction before 40 years old, do serum lipids (>40% of these children will turn out to have hyperlipidaemia: the sooner it is treated, the better, p 156).

Systems review: questions coming to the fore depend on age:

	Neonate	Toddler	Older child
Cardio-respiratory	Tachypnoea, grunts Wheeze, cyanosis, cold sweats (heart failure)	Cough, exertional dyspnoea	Cough, wheeze sputum, chest pain
Gut	Appetite, D&V, feeding problems; stool frequency Jaundice	Appetite, D&V, stool frequency	Appetite, D&V, abdominal pain, stool frequency
Genito-urinary	Wet nappies (how often?)	Wet nappies (how often?)	Haematuria, dysuria, sexual development
Neuro-muscular	Seizures; attacks; jitters	Fits, drowsiness hyperactivity hearing, vision gait	Headaches, fits, odd sensations, drowsiness, academic ability, vision hearing, co-ordination
ENT; teeth	Noisy breathing	Ear discharge	Earache, discharge, sore throat

General questions: weight, *a*ppetite, *f*evers, *f*atigue, *l*umps, everything else OK?

'He went white, then red, then blue' If it's hard to ask the right questions, it can be harder still to interpret the answers. Each time a story is told (first to the grandmother, then to the GP, then to the house officer, then to the consultant) a new layer of colour, meaning, or ambiguity is revealed like layers of colour around a gobstopper—depending from whose mouth the story is currently issuing. Don't be impatient to get at the truth: suck it and see: the flavour may be as important as all the objectively verifiable facts. Often there are *no* verifiable facts: just 5 stories which interrelate but which do not mesh (yet). Wait on events; learn who you can trust, and accept that your conclusions are, at best, provisional—as is the case with any professional historian who juggles his disparate sources.

Paediatric encounters are one of the best places to start to become an expert in this generic skill of balancing different sources. In adult medicine we typically pay 100% attention to what the patient says about his or her symptoms, and 0% to what anyone else says. With preverbal infants the reverse is true—underlying the point that we should not assume that patients have the most privileged access to their symptoms.

Physical examination: a method

A single routine will not work for all children. If the child is very ill, examination is limited (p 103). Also, points in the examination assume varying importance depending on age (for neonates, see p 114). But it is helpful to have some sort of standard: here we look at a boy of 3 years who is being seen because of vomiting. Not everything on even this slimmed-down page will need to be done. The more experienced you are, the better you will be able to judge when and how to take short cuts. Do not mistake taking short cuts for being lazy. Use the time saved to be available to answer questions, and to address the fears and hopes of the parents and child. NB: there is no correct order: be opportunistic, eg with younger children on a lap.

1. Wash and warm your hands. Encourage both parents to be present.
2. Regard the child (eg while feeding). Is he ill or well?[1] Restless, still, or playing? If crying, is it high pitched or normal? Is he behaving normally? Any jaundice, cyanosis, rashes, anaemia, or dehydration (p 234)?
3. Talk to the child. Explain what you are doing. This helps you both relax, and enjoy the occasion (*not* a trivial point: a happy doctor is an engaged doctor, and an engaged doctor is amenable to receiving subtle signs and covert communications). If he seems anxious, examine his teddy in a playful way, to allow him to build up trust.
4. If the child is quiet or asleep, now is the time to get any listening done, so examine his heart, lungs, and abdomen. Use a warm stethoscope. Undress in stages.
5. Examine finger nails, then the hands, radial pulse, BP, axillary and neck nodes, neck lumps. Is there neck stiffness? (a 'useless' sign in infants)
6. Size and shape of head (p 224). Facial symmetry. Does the anterior fontanelle (between the parietal and frontal bones) feel tense (intracranial pressure ↑), or sunken (dehydration)?
7. Is there mucus in the nose? Leave ears and throat alone at this stage.
8. Count the respirations. Is there intercostal recession (inspiratory indrawing of the lower costal area, signifying ↑work of breathing?)
9. Percuss the chest if >2yrs old (not very reliable even then), and palpate the abdomen. Is it distended, eg by spleen, liver, fluid, flatus, faeces?
10. Undo the nappy, if worn. Have an MSU pot to hand. If urine is passed, make a clean catch (p 174). Inspect the nappy's contents. Examine the genitalia/anus. Find the testes. Rectal examination is rarely needed.
11. Note large inguinal nodes. Feel femoral pulses.

Neurological examination After completing the above, much will have been learned about the nervous system; if in doubt, check:
Tone: Passively flex and extend the limbs (provided this will not hurt).
Power and co-ordination: Watch him walk, run, and pick up a small toy and play with it, with each hand in turn. ***Reflexes:*** Look for symmetry.
Sensation: Light touch and pain testing are rarely rewarding. Fundi.

Ears/throat Leave to the end, as there may be a struggle. Mother holds the child on her lap laterally, one hand on the forehead, holding his head against her chest, and the other round his arms. Examine ear drums (p 536) first (less invasive). Then holding the child outwards, introduce a spatula and get one good look at mouth and tonsils. Inspect the teeth.

Growth Chart height, weight, and head circumference (p 224).

TPR charts Pulse and respiratory rate; T° (rectal T°: normally <37.8°C).

Finally ask child and mother if there is anything else you should look at.

1 In the mood of *la belle époque*, get the *whole* picture as a gestalt flash, and mirror the genius of photography, Jaques Lartigue: 'I open my eyes, then I close them, then open them again, wide, and hey presto! I capture the image with everything…and what I hold onto is something living, that moves and feels.'

Is this child seriously ill?[APLS]

Typical causes
• Sepsis, meningitis[et al]
• D&V/gastroenteritis
• Obstruction, eg volvulus
• Arrhythmias
• Hypoglycaemia
• U&E↑
• Metabolic errors
• Myocarditis
• Congenital heart dis.
• Cardiomyopathies
• Intussusception (p 172)
• DIC (p 120 & *OHCM* p 650)
• Haemolytic uraemic syn
• Reye's syndrome (p 652)

Recognizing the need of prompt help is a central skill of paediatrics. It can be uncanny to watch the moment of transformation that this recognition brings to a normally reflective, easy-going doctor who is now galvanized into an efficient, relentless device for delivering urgent care—*'omitting nothing necessary and adding nothing superfluous'*: a frame of mind recommended by Graham Greene for murder, but equally well suited to curing disease. If you are new to paediatrics, take every opportunity to observe such events, and, later, closely question the doctor about what made him act in the way he did, using this page to prepare your mind to receive and remember his or her answers.

Serious signs[1] • Consciousness↓ (not engaging you; apathy; agitation; coma).
- Hyperventilation or using alae nasae/sternomastoids; wheeze; stridor; apnoea.
- Ashen, cyanosed, or mottled—or signs of dehydration. [n > 1000]
- Grunting ± chest retractions or head-nodding in time with respirations.
- Weak/absent pulses, poor capillary refill. To elicit this, press on a digit for 5sec: capillary refill normally takes <2sec. *Don't rely on BP and pulse rate.*
- High core T°, but cold peripheries.
- Unreactive or unequal pupils; or decorticate (flexed arms, extended legs); or decerebrate (arms + legs extended); or rigid posture.
- Weak/high-pitched cry and no spontaneous movement during examination.
- 'I'm having a bad feeling about this': learn to trust your judgment[2]

Age	Reference interval for: Breathing rate	Pulse	Systolic BP mmHg
<1yr	30–40/min	110–160/min	70–90
2–5yr	20–30/min	95–140/min	80–100
5–12yr	15–20/min	80–120/min	90–110
>12yr	12–16/min	60–100/min	100–120

Rapid assessment of the seriously ill child (Should take <1 minute.)

Airway: • Patency.

Breathing: • Work of breathing *Look:* Rate; recession; accessory muscle use; cyanosis *Listen:* Stridor; grunting; wheeze.

Circulation: • Pulse rate and volume; capillary refill; skin colour; T°.

Response level: • ***A*** = ***a***lert • ***V*** = responds to ***v***oice • ***P*** = responds to ***p***ain; • ***U*** = ***u***nresponsive (ie '*AVPU*'); also assess pupils & posture.

Action—if very ill ▸▸100% O_2 by tight-fitting mask with reservoir, then:
- Immediate IV access. Go intraosseous if access cannot be found (p 236).
- Colloid: 20mL/kg bolus IV; repeat if no better. ≥40mL/kg; call PICU.
- Do blood glucose (lab and ward test); U&E (ask specifically for HCO_3^-, and, if vomiting, Cl^-); FBC; thick film if tropical travel possible or unknown.
- Crossmatch blood if trauma is possible, or patient looks anaemic.
- Consider the need for CXR, MSU, and lumbar puncture.
- Do swabs, blood culture (+suprapubic urine aspirate if <1yr, before starting blind treatment with IV antibiotics, eg ceftriaxone or cefotaxime, p 202).
- If worsening, insert CVP. Get expert help; do blood gases ± clotting screen.
- Ventilation may be needed if very sick, to offload the heart.
- If perfusion is still poor (despite 60mL/kg colloid), or CVP >10cmH_2O, inotropes may be needed (p 203).

1 See DoH[uk] free DVD *Spotting the Sick Child* (cat no. 40630): tel 08701 555455 or dh@prolog.uk.com
2 This is a reason to spend hours and hours on the wards: to gain the experience that validates 'bad feels'. We once asked an obstetrician how he had recognized placenta praevia during a vaginal exam in labour: "It was easy" he said "I felt sick and started to sweat as soon as my finger entered the os".

Common symptoms in infancy

Crying Crying peaks at 8 weeks old (~3h/day, especially in the evenings). The cries of hunger and thirst are indistinguishable. Feeding at adult-dictated intervals may cause crying in many babies, so demand feeding is preferred (but in some babies strict routines may pay dividends). Any thwarting of a baby's wishes may lead to crying, with bouts of screaming. No doubt there are good survival reasons for Nature making babies cry, but in the 21st century this provision may be counterproductive: prolonged crying (as well as lack of parental support) can provoke child abuse in vulnerable families. Crying may be the last straw for a parent with few reserves. Aim to offer help *before* this stage (eg CRY-SIS self-help group, UK tel. 020 7404 5011). The key skills are not to make parents feel inadequate, and to foster a spirit of practical optimism with parents taking it in turns to sleep.

3-month colic Paroxysmal crying with pulling up of the legs, for >3h on ≥3days/wk comprise a defining *rule of 3s*. Cow's milk protein allergy, and parental discord and disappointment with pregnancy are implicated—but it may be that such stressed parents may report more colic. There is an association with feeding difficulties,[6]—also, blunted rhythm in cortisol production is reported, suggesting delay in establishing circadian activity of the hypothalamic-pituitary-adrenocortical axis and associated sleep–wake activity.[7] ***Treatment:*** Nothing helps for long. Try movement (eg carry-cot on wheels, or go for a drive). Trials favour dimeticone (simethicone) drops (40mg/mL; 0.5mL PO before feeds; avoid if <1 month). Few other drugs are licensed for use at this age. Rarely, chloral is used. In breastfed babies, a cow's-milk-free diet for mother is unlikely to help, and a change to soya milk (p 127) in bottle fed babies is often tried, pointlessly, in desperation. Reassure strongly, consider encouraging grandparent involvement. Remember: a crying baby may be a sign of major family relationship problems.

Vomiting Effortless regurgitation of milk is very common during feeds ('posseting'). Vomiting between feeds is also common. >1 forceful vomit per day usually indicates some pathology, eg over-feeding, gastroenteritis; pyloric stenosis; hiatus hernia/reflux (p 170, eg with mucus ± blood in vomit, which is usually effortless); pharyngeal pouch; or duodenal obstruction (there is green bile in the vomit). Observing feeding is helpful in deciding if the vomiting is projectile (eg over the end of the cot), suggesting pyloric stenosis.

Nappy rash or diaper dermatitis 4 types:

1. The common 'ammonia dermatitis'—red, desquamating rash, sparing skin folds is due to moisture retention, not ammonia. It often responds to frequent changes of nappy, or nappy-free periods, careful drying, and emollient creams (Drapolene®=benzalkonium chloride+cetrimide). Avoid tight-fitting rubber pants. 'One way' nappies may be helpful at night (eg Snugglers®).[8]
2. Candida/thrush is isolatable from ~½ of all nappy rashes. Its hallmark is satellite spots beyond the main rash. Mycology: see p 598. Treatment: as above, + clotrimazole (± 1% hydrocortisone cream, eg as Canesten HC®). One trial favours thrice-daily mupirocin ointment.[9] [N=20]
3. Seborrhoeic eczematous dermatitis: a diffuse, red, shiny rash extends into skin folds, often associated with other signs of a seborrhoeic skin, eg on occiput (cradle cap). Treatment: as for 1.[10]
4. Isolated, psoriasis-like scaly plaques (p 594), which can be hard to treat.

Agents to avoid: Boric acid and fluorinated steroids (systemic absorption); oral antifungals (hepatotoxic); gentian violet (staining is unpopular).

Sleep problems See p 392.

Chronic childhood illness, and family support

Diseases such as severe asthma, CNS disease, and neoplasia may cause disintegration of even the most apparently secure families: ►*consequent strife and marital breakdown may be more severe and have more far-reaching consequences than the illness itself.*

Remember that illness makes families poor, and movement down the social scale may lead to unpredictable consequences in the fields of housing and (un)employment.

Marital disharmony may seem to be beyond the scope of paediatrics, but any holistic view of child health *must* put the family at the centre of *all* attempts to foster child health and wellbeing.

We see many families coping admirably with severe, prolonged illness in a child. But do not presume that because things are OK in clinic today, you can afford to neglect the fostering of family life. Given a certain amount of stress almost *all* families will show psychopathology, in time. Your job is to prevent this if possible. Counselling skills are frequently needed (p 380)—but do they work? Various tools are helpful in answering this question:[11]

- Communication is vital in any family, and this can be measured by scales such as the Communication Skills Test (CST).[1]
- The Dyadic Adjustment Scale (DAS) looks at the emotional interaction within a marriage or any other pairing.[12]
- The Miller Social Intimacy Scale (MSIS) looks at intimacy in relationships, and intimacy is, beyond doubt, a source of strength within a family experiencing illness in a child.
- Specific therapies validated in randomized trials in families coping with severe chronic illness in a child include Emotionally Focused Marital Therapy (EMT), with these benefits:[13]
  - Higher overall levels of marital adjustment (on the DAS scale). None of the couples receiving the active therapy deteriorated by >7 points, whereas one-third of couples in the control group had such a deterioration (which shows the stress these families were under, and supports the notion that family psychopathology in the face of chronic childhood illness is an evolving phenomenon—*the stress is reversible if you take certain steps*).
  - Better levels of intimacy as measured on MSIS scale, with effects persisting for at least 5 months.
  - Lower rates of negative communication (on the CST score).
  - NNT = 2 (2 couples need treating for one to improve).

E-BM 2 46

GMC GOOD DOCTOR TOPIC: FAMILY-CENTRED CARE

1 Full Instruments available in: K Corcoran *Measures for clinical practice: A sourcebook*. New York

▸▸The ill and feverish child

Two questions to ask: *How severe are the symptoms* and *How appropriate is the child's response to the illness?* The symptom may be severe (eg 'terrible diarrhoea all over the cot') without being biologically serious (if the baby is alert, drinking, wetting many nappies, and behaving as usual); but ANY apparently mild symptom should set your internal alarm bell ringing if:[14,15]

- Less than half the usual amount of feed has been taken in the last day.
- There is breathing difficulty, or high-pitched continuous moans or cries.
- There is a history of being pale, mottled, cyanosed, and hot.
- Dull expression; apathetic; uninterested in you; drowsy; dehydrated.
- A significant reduction in the number of wet nappies in the last 24h.
- Blood in diarrhoea.
- Seizures
- Tachycardia not explained by pain or fever.

Observe the limbs: pain causes ***pseudoparalysis***, eg with legs in a 'frog position' (hips & knees semiflexed; feet rotated outward), eg in osteomyelitis, septic arthritis, syphilis, CMV, or scurvy.[16,17,18]

NB: to recognize and treat severe illness, see p 103. The above carry extra weight in the immunocompromised (eg neonates; post measles; AIDS; cystic fibrosis; leukaemia; chemotherapy/malignancy; absent spleen; B/T cell dysfunction); congenital anomaly or foreign body, eg an indwelling IVI line (bacteria may be unusual and of low virulence).[19]

Fever (Meningitis, p 202; pneumonia, p 160; UTI, p 174.) Fever is the major acute presentation in paediatrics, eg from viruses, otitis media, or pharyngitis (p 564), and prognosis is good. Here, fever *may* be beneficial (aids neutrophil migration; ↑bioactivity of cytokines, increased production and activity of interferon and increased T-cell proliferation).[20]

The challenge is to identify serious bacterial infection; see above & below.

Bacteraemia This occurs in ~4% of febrile children, sometimes without an obvious focus of infection; this is made more likely if the child is between 3 and 24 months of age with fevers of ≥40°C, and a WCC >15 × 10^9/L (but using these criteria alone, 50% of those with bacteraemia will be missed). ESR >30mm/h and ↑C-reactive protein also indicate bacterial infection. Examples of organisms: *Strep pneumoniae*, *N. meningitidis*. If blind antibiotics are started (eg shocked), they must cover these organisms (p 202 & p 204). ***Cefotaxime:*** 50mg/kg/8h IV over 20min or ***ceftriaxone*** 20–45mg/kg once daily IM or IV; use IVI route over 30min for top dose (50–80mg/kg/day; max 4g daily); avoid in babies as can cause biliary sludging.

Finding a focus of infection entails a good history and examination, CXR ± LP (if the child is ill, see above). Rapid virology is becoming available—eg PCR and direct fluorescent assay (for adenoviruses).[21] If ill and no focus of infection is found, it may be appropriate to start blind antibiotics, or to observe. UTI is a common cause of occult infection.

▸▸Neonatal life support (NLS) after delivery

Most neonates are perfectly healthy, and the best plan is to return these babies to the mother with no interference, to augment bonding. Mother-and-baby skin-to-skin contact is ideal, rather than swaddling or nursery cots, and is the best way to maintain temperature.[22] A paediatrician or nurse trained in advanced neonatal resuscitation should attend the following births: emergency Caesars, breeches, twins, forceps for fetal distress, intrapartum bleeding, prematurity, hydrops fetalis, and eclampsia.

Before birth Check the equipment. Get a warm blanket. Heat the crib.

At birth If pulse <100, poor colour or respiratory effort, set a clock in motion, and see OPPOSITE. Be alert to:

- Hypothermia (use heat lamp).
- Hypoglycaemia: dextrose 10%, 5mL/kg IV.
- Pethidine toxicity: naloxone eg 200μg IM. Contraindicated in opioid abuse.
- Anaemia (heavy fetal blood loss?)—give 20mL/kg blood + 4.5% albumin.
- Is there lung disease or congenital cyanotic heart disease (p 136)? Transfer to NICU/SCBU for monitoring.
- Suck out the oropharynx only if meconium aspiration suspected.
- 21% O_2 (air) is better than 100% O_2.[MET 23]

Endotracheal intubation is a key skill: use 3.5mm uncuffed, unshouldered tubes on term infants; 3 if 1.25–2.5kg (2.5 if smaller). Learn from experts. Have many sizes to hand. Practice on models.

Prognosis Mortality for *prems* is 315/1000 if 5-min Apgar score 0–3, *vs* 5/1000 if score is ≥7. Corresponding figures *at term* are 244/1000 & 0.2/1000. If a term infant with Apgar score ≤3 has a low arterial pH (≤7), risk of neonatal death increases 8-fold.[24] Survival in those needing CPR (cardiac resus) is 63% for infants of 0.5–1.5kg, compared with 88% in these weight groups if CPR is not needed. Severe intraventricular haemorrhage is seen in 15% of those needing CPR *vs* 5% in those who don't.[25]

Dry the baby; remove any wet cloths and cover.

↓

Initial assessment; set a clock in motion; assess ***colour, tone, breathing*** and ***pulse***
If not breathing…

↓

Control the airway (head in the neutral position)

↓

Support breathing: 5 inflation breaths, each 2–3sec long. Confirm response: visible chest movements or increased heart rate.

↓

If no response, check ***head position*** and try a ***jaw thrust***; then 5 inflation breaths. Confirm response: visible chest movements or ↑ heart rate.

↓

If still no response, get a 2nd person to help with airway control and repeat inflation breaths.
- Direct vision of oro-pharynx
- Repeat 5 inflation breaths
- Insert an oro-pharyngeal airway
- Repeat inflation breaths

Consider intubation. Confirm response: visible chest movements or increased heart rate.

↓

When chest is moving, continue with ventilation breaths if no spontaneous breathing.

↓

Check heart rate; if undetectable or <60 (and not rising) ***start chest compressions***. Do 3 chest compressions to 1 breath, for 30sec

↓

Reassess pulse: if improving, stop chest compressions. If not breathing, continue ventilation. If heart rate still slow, continue ventilation and chest compressions.

↓

Consider ***IV or umbilical access*** and ***drugs***, eg adrenaline (epinephrine): 10μg/kg (0.1mL 1:10,000/kg) IV or 100μg/kg via endotracheal tube.

▸At all stages ask: ***Do I need help?***

Apgar	*Pulse*	*Respirations*	*Muscle tone*	*Colour*	*On suction*
2	>100	strong cry	active	pink	coughs well
1	<100	slow, irregular	limb flexion	blue limbs	depressed cough
0	0	nil	absent	all blue or white	no response

The neonatal intensive care unit (NICU)

Neonatal intensive care is a technological development of the basic creed of first aid—ABC; A for *a*irway, B for *b*reathing, and C for *c*irculation. Success depends on mastering this trinity, and designing the best *milieu intérieur* to encourage healing and growth without risking neurodevelopmental sequelae, (eg spasticity). Monitor temperature, pulse, BP (intra-arterial if critical), respirations (continuous read-out device), blood gases—transcutaneous oximetry (S_AO_2, *OHCM* p 168) and CO_2 monitoring, or via intra-arterial electrode, U&E, bilirubin, FBC, daily weight, and weekly head circumference.

The patient is usually a premature baby. His mortal enemies are: cold, hypoxia, hypoglycaemia (p 112), respiratory distress syndrome (p 118), infection (p 112); intraventricular haemorrhage; apnoea; necrotizing enterocolitis (p 120).[1] *You* may become the problem: overzealous investigation/handling is damaging,[26] as is under-intervention.[27] Getting the balance right is vital.

Cold With their small volume and relatively large surface area, this is a major problem for the premature and light-for-dates baby. The problem is circumvented by using incubators which allow temperature (as well as humidity and F_iO_2) to be controlled, and also afford some protection against infection. F_iO_2 is the fraction of O_2 in inspired air, ie 0.6 = 60% O_2.

Apnoeic attacks ***Prevalence:*** 25% of neonates <2.5kg; 90% if <1kg. ***Causes:*** Respiratory centre immaturity; aspiration; heart failure; infection; $P_aO_2\downarrow$; glucose↓; $Ca^{2+}\downarrow$; seizures; patent ductus (PDA); T°↑ or ↓; exhaustion; airway obstruction. If stimulating the baby doesn't restore breathing, suck out the pharynx and use bag and mask ventilation. Avoid wild P_aO_2 fluctuations to prevent RoP (below). ***Tests:*** CXR; U&E; infection screen; glucose; Ca^{2+}; Mg^{2+}. ***Treatment:*** If aspiration is the problem, give small frequent feeds, or continuous tube feeds. Monitor S_AO_2 continuously; if hypoxic despite an ambient O_2 of 40%, CPAP or IPPV is needed. Caffeine citrate 10mg/kg (caffeine base) IV, then 2.5mg/kg/day PO/IVI helps and has fewer SEs than theophyllines.[28] [N=85]

Nasal CPAP ± doxapram *may* prevent hypoventilation. If apnoea is seizure-related, see p 112. ***Weaning:*** Try 4–5 days after apnoea has stopped. ***Prevention:*** Betamethasone intrauterine maturation (p 51).[29]

RoP (retinopathy of prematurity) Retinal vessels in prems react badly to fluctuating P_aO_2, eg during resuscitations→retinal fibrosis→detachment→visual loss. ***Prevalence (lower limits):*** <1000g: 53%; ≤1250g: 43%; ≤1500g: 35%.[30] ***Classification:*** There are 5 stages, depending on site involved, the degree of retinal detachment, and extent (measured as clock hours in each eye). ***Treatment:*** Diode laser therapy causes less myopia than cryotherapy. ***Screening:*** If <1500g or ≤31 weeks' gestation. If ≤25 weeks, screen ophthalmoscopically under 0.5% cyclopentolate pupil dilatation at 6 weeks old, and 2-weekly until 36 postmenstrual weeks. Often one examination is enough if 26–31 weeks' gestation. It must be done by an experienced ophthalmologist.

IVH (intraventricular haemorrhage) occurs in 40% if birth wt ≲ 1500g. *Risk factors:* $P_aO_2\downarrow$, $P_aCO_2\uparrow$, BP↓, bleeding disorder (p 120), birth trauma, Caesarean section, Apgar <4 at 1min or <8 at 5mins, low birth weight, respiratory distress, PDA, anaemia, and umbilical arterial catheterization.[31]

Suspect in any neonate who deteriorates rapidly (esp. in 1st week of life). Opisthotonus, cerebral irritability, shock, ↓feeding skills, a bulging fontanelle with a rapidly expanding head, an exaggerated Moro reflex, fits, and somnolence are telling signs, but ~50% may be silent. ***Tests:*** Ultrasound; CT. ***Complications:*** IQ↓, cerebral palsy, hydrocephalus. Many survive unscathed. It is uncertain if late learning and behavioural problems occur. ***Treatment:*** Supportive or preventative: Rest, head elevation, seizure control (p 112).

1 *UK perinatal death trends:* Deaths from congenital defects and hypoxia are 50% of 1980s rates, but death rates for infection are similar. Rates of multiple births and their problems are rising.

The first breath and the road to pulmonary hypertension

With our first breath pulmonary vascular resistance falls, and there is a rush of blood to our lungs.[32] This is partly mediated by endogenous nitric oxide (NO). This breath initiates changes from fetal to adult circulation—a process which may be interrupted in various conditions, eg meconium aspiration, pneumonia, respiratory distress syndrome, diaphragmatic hernia, group B strep infection, and pulmonary hypoplasia.[33]

Pulmonary hypertension arises as a consequence of these adverse events. It may also be due to hypertrophy of the muscular layer in the pulmonary arteries (primary pulmonary hypertension).

The chief diagnostic features are a background (such as meconium aspiration) and persisting desaturation despite intensive O_2 therapy. When it is suspected, arrange immediate echocardiography, and get help. Echo will show right-to-left shunting at the ductus arteriosus or foramen ovale in the absence of structural heart disease.

Inhaled nitric oxide (iNO) helps promote adult circulation—and decreases the need for dramatic interventions such as extracorporeal membrane oxygenation (below). iNO relaxes smooth muscle by ↑production cyclic guanosine monophosphate. (NB: sildenafil inhibits its degradation—and may have a role[34][35]). Alternatives are adenosine, tolazoline, and inhaled prostacyclin (epoprostenol).[36] While arranging ECMO, ventilate (p 110), and correct reversible contributory factors (hypothermia, polycythaemia, hypocalcaemia, hypoglycaemia). There may be a role for hyperventilation.[37] Give surfactant as indicated (p 118).

Extracorporeal membrane oxygenation (*ECMO*) ECMO is a complex procedure (done in specialized units) providing life-support for respiratory failure, which obviates the need for lung gas exchange.

One trial showed that ECMO done after referral to one of 5 UK ECMO centres ↓deaths from respiratory failure (oxygenation index ≥40).[1] The trial was stopped early because the scrutineers found the results so strongly favoured ECMO over traditional measures: 30 out of 93 died in the ECMO group, compared with 54 out of 92 in the control group. The advantage was upheld irrespective of the primary diagnosis, or the type of referring centre. The number of infants suffering severe disability at follow-up at 1yr was 1 in each group.[RCT 38] [N=185]

Criteria which may make ECMO cost-effective: weight >2kg; no major congenital malformations or CNS abnormality on ultrasound; gestation >34 weeks; oxygen index (OI) >40 (unresponsive to NO inhalation).

NB: more premature babies *may* benefit, eg when problems with circuitry and heparinization are solved. Need for ECMO may be ~1/4000 live births. It is thought to be economically worthwhile.[RCT 39][40]

1 What is the oxygen index (OI)? In the equation, MAP is the mean airway pressure in cmH_2O. F_iO_2 is the partial pressure of inspired O_2.

$$OI = \frac{F_iO_2 \times MAP}{P_aO_2}$$

Ventilatory support for neonates

This is a skill to be learned at the cot side. Nurses and specialist respiratory therapists will help you. Needs of apparently similar babies vary, so what follows is only a guide to prepare your mind before teaching. Continuous refinement in the light of transcutaneous and blood gas analysis is needed.

PTCCF (pressure-limited, time-cycled continuous flow ventilation) Continuous flows of heated & humidified gas pass via an endotracheal tube. Nasotracheal siting is best (fewer tube displacements), but insertion needs skill.[41] ***Variables:*** F_iO_2 mix; peak inspiratory pressure (PIP); positive end-expiratory pressure (PEEP); inspiratory (T_I) and expiratory (T_E) times. The infant can make respiratory efforts between ventilator breaths (intermittent mandatory ventilation, IMV). Aim for a T_I of 0.3–0.45sec.

Initial settings: Choose to give good chest inflation and air entry on auscultation and adequate transcutaneous O_2 readings. Typical settings might be T_I 0.32sec, 40cycles/min, inspiratory pressure 14-16cmH_2O, and PEEP 5cmH_2O. Adjust in the light of blood gas analysis.

PEEP (positive end-expiratory pressure) A loaded valve is fitted to the expiratory limb of the ventilator, so airways pressure stays ≥atmosphere. Levels >10cmH_2O are rarely used (venous return to the thorax ↓).

CPAP (continuous positive airways pressure) Pressure is raised throughout the respiratory cycle, so assisting spontaneous inspiration. With skill, this method has few complications, and is useful as a first stage in ventilating a baby before it is known whether he or she will need IMV.

PTV (patient-triggered ventilation), including SIMV and SIPPV. Babies tend to fight ventilators, trying to expire during inflations, which requires either paralysis (making them dependent on the ventilator, retain fluid, and limb contractures may develop—also air-trapping, ↓gas-exchange, pneumothorax and bronchopulmonary dysplasia) or PTV. Paralysis helps by ↓rate of pneumothorax and IVH (p 108). Another option is PTV: here inspiratory and end-expiratory pressure is set by the operator, but the rate set by the baby. PTV is associated with a shorter duration of ventilation.[42,43] Hiccups cause problems if abdominal movement is used to detect inspiration. ***HFOV*** (high frequency oscillatory ventilation) is still non-standard.[44] HFOV is probably no better than conventional ventilation as primary mode of ventilation in preterm infants with respiratory distress syndrome for prevention of chronic lung disease or mortality at 36 weeks.[45]

Paralysis Pancuronium (eg 30μg/kg IV; then 10μg/kg every 1.5–4h to maintain paralysis) prevents pneumothorax ± IVH (p 108) in asynchronous respiratory efforts (eg needing unexpectedly high P_I).[46]

Other factors ***Pain relief/sedation:*** Consider 5% dextrose IVI with morphine 100–200μg/kg over 30min, then 5-20μg/kg/h. This is thought safe, and lowers catecholamine concentrations (an objective correlate of pain and stress which helps form valid pain assessment tools; see Royal College guidelines).[47]

Air leak: Air ruptures alveoli tracking along vessels and bronchioles (pulmonary interstitial emphysema), and may extend intrapleurally (pneumothorax + lung collapse), or into the mediastinum or peritoneum. Associated with high PIP, it is less common with HFOV. ***Signs:*** Tachypnoea, cyanosis, chest asymmetry. The lateral decubitus CXR is often diagnostic if you have time. Prompt 'blind' needle aspiration of a pneumothorax may be needed. Aspirate through the second intercostal space in the midclavicular line with a 25G 'butterfly' needle and a 50mL syringe on a 3-way tap. If the leak is continuous, use underwater seal drainage.

Weaning from the ventilator

Decrease the rate of IMV and lower P_I by $2cmH_2O$ at a time; try extubating if blood gas OK with ~$4cmH_2O$ PEEP and a PIP of 12–14 with spontaneous breaths over a backup rate of 5.

Racemic adrenaline doesn't stop intubation-associated ↑upper airways resistance.[48]

Nasal intermittent positive pressure ventilation (NIPPV) delivers ventilator breaths via nasal prongs. It is possible to synchronise delivery of NIPPV with the infant's own breathing efforts—and this may prevent the need for re-intubation.[49]

▸▸The ill neonate

Sepsis Common (1-10/1000 births), and commonly overwhelming (mortality 15-50%). Here, signs may be minimal, or as opposite (BOX).

Action: ABC (p 108). Clear the airway; intubate and ventilate if necessary. This should correct acidosis, so bicarbonate is rarely needed. Set up a colloid IVI (20mL/kg initially). Exclude hypoglycaemia; do blood gases.

Infection screen: •Blood-culture, virology, FBC, platelets, glucose, CXR. •Lumbar puncture: CSF (p 202) for urgent Gram stain, cell count, protein & glucose level, culture, and virology. •Stool: for virology. •Urine: microscopy, culture, and virology. •ENT swabs: for culture.

Antibiotics: In infections at <48h old, group B streps and *E. coli* (+ any organism prevalent in your NICU) are common. *Benzylpenicillin* 25mg/kg/12h IV (per 8h if >7 days old; per 6h if >1 month) + *netilmicin* 6mg/kg/24h IV (5mg/kg in prems <35 weeks' gestation—or gentamicin, see p 175).

Note on dilutions Dilute 600mg of benzylpenicillin in 1.6mL of water; 600mg of the powder displaces 0.4mL, so final concentration is 300mg/mL.

In late-onset infection (ie neonates over 48h old), coagulase -ve staphs are a likely cause, so regimens include *vancomycin* or *teicoplanin* (p 195). *Staph aureus* is rarer—*flucloxacillin dose:* 50-100mg per 12h IV over 3min (per 8h if 7-21 days old; per 6h if >21 days old). If creatinine clearance <10mL/min/1.73m^2, increase the dosage interval. Alternative: cefotaxime, p 202.

If the CSF suggests meningitis, see p 202.

Neonatal seizures (~4/1000 births) *Causes:* P_aO_2↓; infection; glucose↓, CNS damage (haemorrhage, hydrocephalus, CNS cysts); Ca^{2+} <1.7mmol/L; Na^+↑↓; Mg^{2+}↓ (eg <0.4mmol/L, see below).[50]

Treatment: Turn on the side. Ask an experienced nurse to help.

- Rule out, or treat hypoglycaemia: 5mL/kg 10% dextrose IV over 5min, then 100mL/kg/day IVI + hourly feeds, ↓IVI rate as plasma glucose allows.
- Phenobarbital 15mg/kg IV over 5mins + 5mg/kg at 1h if needed. Maintenance: reduce slowly from 2mg/kg/12h IV/PO. Monitor blood levels. Aim for 30-40μg/mL >4h after a PO dose; $t_{½}$=3 days at first, so once daily doses are used; $t_{½}$ halves after 10 days as liver enzymes are induced.
- If seizures continue, give phenytoin 20mg/kg IVI in 0.9% saline (≤3mg/kg/min; aim for a plasma level of 10-20μg/mL >1h post dose). Other agents: clonazepam; lorazepam; paraldehyde. Monitor EEG.[51]
- If fits continue: pyridoxine 50-100mg IV + 10-200mg/day PO (?for *all* <2yrs old with undiagnosed seizures: in case of pyridoxine deficiency). Autosomal recessive [52]

Hypocalcaemia: Use low PO_4^{3-} milk + Ca gluconate 10%, 4.4mL/kg/day PO (IV: 0.3mL/kg diluted in 4.8mL/kg of saline over 10min). Monitor ECG. NB: some favour higher IV emergency doses, eg 2mL/kg of the 10% solution.

Hypomagnesaemia: Give $MgSO_4$ 10% (100mg/mL), eg 100mg/kg IV.[53]

Shock *Causes:* Blood loss (placental haemorrhage, twin-twin transfusion; intraventricular haemorrhage; lung haemorrhage); capillary plasma leaks (sepsis, hypoxia, acidosis, necrotizing enterocolitis); fluid loss (D&V; ↑insensible loss; inappropriate diuresis); cardiac causes (hypoxia, hypoglycaemia, L to R shunts, valve disease, coarctation). *Signs:* Pulse ↑; BP ↓; urine output ↓; coma.

Management: ABC. Ventilate as needed. Treat causes. Aim for a CVP of 5-8cmH_2O. Give colloid 10-20mL/kg IV over 30-60min. Inotropes may be used, eg dopamine 5-20μg/kg per min ± dobutamine 5-20μg/kg/min as needed[54] (*may* act synergistically; detailed dosing: p 203). There is scant experimental evidence for this regimen, and there may be side-effects (blunting of respiratory drive; endocrine/immunological impairment; GI function↓).[55]

If the pH is <7.2, sodium bicarbonate, eg 1-2mmol/kg IV as a 4.2% solution, may be indicated (if adequate ventilation; don't mix with inotropes).

Problems with neonatal sepsis

Diagnosis is often hard, as signs may be non-specific, and cultures take time—and time is never on your side. ►Sepsis is always in the differential diagnosis of any unwell neonate.

Nonspecific and probably unreliable tests: C-reactive protein, FBC & film: looking at the ratio of immature to total neutrophils *may* help.

NB: it's possible that looking for soluble immunological mediators may help: ideal ones may be interleukin-1 receptor antagonist (IL-1ra), and interleukin-6 (IL-6). Specificity: 92% and 83%, respectively. Circulating intercellular adhesion molecule-1 (ciCAM-1) is less reliable.[56]

Blood and other cultures are definitive, but take ~48–72h.

Typical features:
- Unusual crying
- Sleepy or listlessness
- Feeding difficulty
- Grunting ± tachypnoea
- Cyanosis
- Cool peripheries; T° ↑↓
- ↑Use of respiratory muscles; flared nostrils
- Tachy- or bradycardias
- Poor capillary return/BP↓
- Hypotonia
- Vomiting ± rashes
- Fits or apnoeic episodes
- Omphalitis/abdo wall red

Normal values are often hard to define—eg a CSF WCC of up to 30/mm³ with 60% polymorphs may be normal in neonates.

Changing patterns of antibiotic resistance For example, resistance to netilmicin varies from 36% to 11% of isolates.[57,58]

In hospital-acquired infections, amikacin may be needed.[59]

Drug pharmacokinetic problems These are only partly obviated by doing levels. Creatinine, sex, and birthweight influence what is an acceptable level in complex ways. With netilmicin, adjust dose as indicated in the *Data sheet* if renal function is poor. Aim for a 1h post-dose (peak) level of 12mg/L, and ≤2mg/L before the next dose. If doing levels is problematic, cefotaxime is a good alternative (p 202).[60] Gentamicin: see p 175.

Subtle manifestations of neonatal seizures

Unless you have a high index of suspicion, you may miss seizures referable to the brainstem, eg nystagmus, conjugate eye movements, posturing, sucking movements, lip smacking, etc. Grand mal is rare. EEGs are helpful in diagnosing when unsure. Always look for metabolic abnormalities (these are treated with metabolic approaches; don't rely on conventional anticonvulsants).[61]

Examination of the neonate[1]

The aim is to screen for abnormality, and to see if the mother has any questions or difficulties with her baby. The following is a recommended routine before the baby leaves hospital—or during the first week of life for home deliveries. Before the examination find out if the birth weight was normal. Was the birth and pregnancy normal? Is mother Rhesus -ve? Find a quiet, warm, well-lit room. Enlist the mother's help. Explain your aims. Does she look angry or depressed? Listen if she talks. Examine systematically, eg from head to toes. Wash your hands meticulously before each examination.

The head Circumference (50th centile=35cm, p 224), shape (odd shapes from a difficult labour soon resolve), fontanelles (tense if crying or intracranial pressure↑; sunken if dehydrated). ***Eyes:*** Red reflex (absent in cataract and retinoblastoma); corneal opacities; conjunctivitis. ***Ears:*** Shape; position. Are they low set (ie below eyes)? The tip of the nose, when pressed, is an indicator of jaundice in white children. Breathing out of the nose (shut the mouth) tests for choanal atresia. Ensure that oto-acoustic screening is done (p 548). Are follow-up brainstem evoked responses needed? 62

The complexion: Cyanosed, pale, jaundiced, or ruddy (polycythaemia)? *Mouth:* Look inside. Insert a finger—is the palate intact? Is suck good?

Arms & hands Single palmar creases (normal or Down's). Waiter's (porter's) tip sign of Erb's palsy of C5 & 6 trunks (p 76). Number of fingers. Clinodactyly (5th finger is curved towards the ring finger, eg in Down's).

The thorax Watch respirations; note grunting and intercostal recession (respiratory distress). Palpate the precordium and apex beat. Listen to the heart and lungs. Inspect the vertebral column for neural tube defects.

The abdomen Expect to feel the liver and spleen. Are there any other masses? Next inspect the umbilicus. Is it healthy? Surrounding flare suggests sepsis. Next, lift the skin to assess skin turgor. Inspect the genitalia and anus. Are the orifices patent? Ensure in the 1st 24 hours the baby passes urine (consider posterior urethral valves in boys if not) and stool (consider Hirschprung's, cystic fibrosis, hypothyroidism). Is the urinary meatus misplaced (hypospadias), and are both testes descended? The neonatal clitoris often looks rather large, but if very large, consider CAH, p 134. Bleeding PV may be a normal variant following maternal oestrogen withdrawal.

The lower limbs Test for congenital dislocation of the hip (p 684). Avoid repeated tests as it hurts—and may induce dislocation. Can you feel the femoral pulses (to exclude coarctation)? Note talipes (p 684). Are the toes: too many, too few, or too blue?

Buttocks/sacrum Is there an anus? Are there 'mongolian spots'? (blue—and harmless). Tufts of hair ± dimples suggest bifida occulta? Any pilonidal sinus?

CNS Assess posture and handle the baby. Intuition can be most helpful in deciding whether the baby is ill or well. Is he jittery (hypoxia/ischaemia, encephalopathy, hypoglycaemia, infection, hypocalcaemia)? There should be some degree of control of the head. Do the limbs move normally, and is the tone floppy or spastic? Are responses absent on one side (hemiplegia)? The Moro reflex rarely adds important information (and is uncomfortable for the baby). It is performed by sitting the baby at 45°, supporting the head. On momentarily removing the support the arms will abduct, the hands open and then the arms adduct. Stroke the palm to elicit a grasp reflex. Is the baby post-mature, light-for-dates, or premature (p 128)?

►Discuss any abnormality with the parents *after liaising with a senior doctor.*

1 The neonatal period is the 1st 28 days of life; if prem, 44 completed weeks of the infant's conceptional age (=the chronological age plus gestational age at birth).

Neonatal jaundice

By allowing the early management of jaundice, transcutaneous bilirubin levels measured by midwives in homes may prevent kernicterus in babies discharged early. In non-Caucasians, the device needs recalibration: don't rely on tests such as pressing the nose.[63]

Hyperbilirubinaemia (<200μmol/L) after the 1st day of life is common and usually 'physiological' (eg in binding free radicals). Mechanisms:

1 Hepatic immaturity in bilirubin conjugation ± ↑removal and destruction of fetal RBCs. If albumin↓ unconjugated bilirubin is left unbound.
2 Absence of gut flora impedes elimination of bile pigment.
3 ↓Fluid intake; breastfeeding (not *usually* a reason to stop).[64] [N=116]

Jaundice within 24h of birth is always abnormal. ***Causes:*** ►Sepsis or:

- *Rhesus haemolytic disease:* +ve direct Coombs' test (DCT, p 117).
- *ABO incompatibility:* (mother O; baby A or B, or mother A and baby B, or vice versa) DCT +ve in 4%; indirect Coombs +ve in 8%. Maternal IgG anti-A or anti-B haemolysin is 'always' present.[65] High-dose IV immunoglobulin is one therapy to consider.[66] [N=116]
- *Red cell anomalies:* congenital spherocytosis (fragility tests/EMA binding, p 196); glucose-6-phosphate dehydrogenase deficiency (do enzyme test).[67]

Tests: FBC; film; blood groups (eg rare group incompatibility.); Coombs' test; urine for reducing agents; syphilis/TORCH*et al* screen, p 34.[68]

Prolonged jaundice (not fading after 14 days) *Causes:* breastfeeding; sepsis (UTI & TORCH, p 34); hypothyroidism; cystic fibrosis; biliary atresia if conjugated and pale stools. *Galactosaemia:* urine tests for reducing agents (eg Clinitest®) are +ve, but specific tests (Clinistix®) for glycosuria are –ve (an insensitive test; galactose-1-phosphate uradyl transferase levels diagnostic).

Kernicterus May occur if bilirubin is >360μmol/L (lower in prems). *Signs:* sleepy ± poor suck (stage I), through to 'setting sun' lid retraction, odd movements, cerebral palsy, deafness and IQ↓ (later, and stage IV). Lesser levels (170–323μmol/L) are unlikely to cause permanent problems, and have little effect on IQ unless preterm or light-for-dates. It is prevented by phototherapy (below) ± exchange transfusion.[69]

Starting phototherapy *A plasma bilirubin guide:* (use your unit's protocol): *Term baby at age 48h:* 230μmol/L. (*At 72h* 250μmol/L; *at 4 days* 275μmol/L; *at 5 days* 300μmol/L.) If prem (but >25 weeks) or low-birth-weight, ↓thresholds by ≥25μmol/L. Stop when levels fall (eg by >25μmol/L) below these thresholds. SE: T°↑↓; eye damage; diarrhoea; separation from mother; fluid loss (give 30mL/kg/day extra water). Ensure the baby is naked (no nappy, no hat). *Intense phototherapy* is an adjunct to exchange transfusion.[70] [71] [72]

Exchange transfusion Uses warmed blood (37°C), crossmatched *vs* maternal serum, given ideally via umbilical vein IVI. Aim to exchange 160mL/kg over ~2h (≈blood volume ×2). IV Ca^{2+} isn't needed if citrate phosphate dextrose blood is used. Monitor ECG, U&E, Ca^{2+}, bilirubin, clotting, FBC, & glucose. Consider more exchanges if bilirubin goes on rising. ***Stop*** if the pulse rate fluctuates by >20 beats/min. ►*Ensure the volumes exchanged always balance.* If anaemic, consider a simple fresh blood transfusion (20mL/kg). *Complications:* Pulse↓, apnoea, platelets↓, glucose↓, Na^+↓,[73] O_2 Hb saturation↓ (as fetal Hb↓).[74]

Bilirubins needing exchange transfusion: *Term baby* at **birth**, 50μmol/L; at **12h**, 125μmol/L; *at* **24h**, 200μmol/L; *at* **36h**, 250μmol/L; *at* **48h**, 325μmol/L; *at* **72h**, 350μmol/L; *at* **4 days**, 375μmol/L; *at* **5 days**, 400μmol/L.

If prem or weight <2.5kg ↓these thresholds (eg by 50μmol/L, after age 48h).

Rhesus haemolytic disease

Physiology When a RhD-ve mother delivers a RhD+ve baby a leak of fetal red cells into her circulation may stimulate her to produce anti-D IgG antibodies (isoimmunization). In later pregnancies these can cross the placenta, causing worsening rhesus haemolytic disease (*erythroblastosis fetalis*) with each successive Rh+ve pregnancy. First pregnancies may be affected due to leaks, eg: •Threatened miscarriage •APH •Mild trauma •Amniocentesis •Chorionic villous sampling •External cephalic version.

An affected oedematous fetus (with stiff, oedematous lungs) is called a *hydrops fetalis*. Anaemia-associated CCF causes oedema, as does hypoalbuminaemia (the liver is preoccupied by producing new RBCs). *ΔΔ:* Thalassaemia; infection (eg toxoplasmosis, CMV, p 34); maternal diabetes.

Clinical Rh disease ►*Test for D antibodies in all Rh-ve mothers, at booking, 28 & 34 weeks' gestation.* Anti-D titres <4U/mL (<1:16) are very unlikely to cause serious disease; it is wise to check maternal blood every 2 weeks. If >10U/mL, get the advice of a referral centre: fetal blood sampling ± intraperitoneal (or, with fetoscopy, intravascular via the cord) transfusion may be needed.

Signs
• Jaundice—eg on day 1
• Yellow vernix
• CCF (oedema, ascites)
• Hepatosplenomegaly
• Progressive anaemia
• Bleeding
• CNS signs
• Kernicterus (p 115)

Expect fetal Hb to be <7g/dL in 10% of those with titres of 10–100U/mL (75% if titres >100U/mL).[75] [n=14]

Do regular ultrasound (+amniocentesis if anti-D titre >4U/mL). Timing is vital. Do it 10 weeks before a Rh-related event in the last pregnancy (eg if last baby needed delivery at 36 weeks, expect to do amniocentesis at 26 weeks). Fetuses tolerating high bilirubins may be saved risky transfusions (fatality 2–30%) if monitored by serial measurements of fetal Hb (by fetoscopy or non-invasive middle cerebral artery peak velocity) and daily ultrasound, to detect oedema, cardiomegaly, pericardial effusion, hepatosplenomegaly, or ascites.[76]

Anti-D is the chief antibody. Others: Rh C, E, c, e, Kell, Kidd, Duffy (all are IgG). Low concentrations sometimes produce severe disease.

Prognosis is improving. Mortality is <20% even for hydropic babies. Note that maternal antibodies persist for some months, and continue to cause haemolysis during early life.[77]

Exchange transfusion ***Indications/technique:*** If Hb <7g/dL, give 1st volume of the exchange transfusion (80mL/kg) as packed cells, and subsequent exact exchanges according to response. ►*Keep the baby warm.*

Ultraviolet photodegradation of bilirubin (with phototherapy lamp) may be all that is needed in less-than-severe disease. Give extra water (30mL/kg/24h PO). Avoid heat loss. Protect the eyes. Keep the baby naked.

Giving Rh-ve mothers anti-D immunoglobulin (p 9) This strategy has markedly reduced need for exchange transfusion.[78]

ABO incompatibility 1 in 45 of group A or B babies born to group O mothers will have haemolysis from maternal antibodies. Exchange transfusion may be needed, even in first-borns.

Hydrops fetalis: management

- Get expert help.
- At birth, take cord blood for Hb, PCV, bilirubin (conjugated and unconjugated), blood group, Coombs' test,[1] serum protein, LFT, and infection screen (p 112) to find the cause—eg isoimmunization; thalassaemia; infection (eg toxoplasmosis, syphilis, parvoviruses, CMV, p 34); maternal diabetes; twin-twin transfusion; or hypoproteinaemia.
- Expect to need to ventilate with high inspiratory peak pressure and positive end pressure. HFOV may have a role, p 110.
- Monitor plasma glucose 2–4 hourly, treating any hypoglycaemia.
- Drain ascites and pleural effusions if severe.
- Correct anaemia.
- Vitamin K 1mg IM, to reduce risk of haemorrhage.
- If CCF is present, furosemide may be needed, eg 1–2mg/kg/12h IV.
- Limit IV fluids to 60mL/kg/24h (crystalloid); if exchange transfusing, aim for a deficit of 10–20mL/kg. Monitor urine output.
- Prognosis: 90% of those with non-immune hydrops die *in utero*; 50% die postnatally. Babies with non-immune hydrops not secondary to infection have a good neurological outcome.

1 The direct Coombs' test (DCT) identifies red cells coated with antibody or complement and a positive result usually indicates an immune cause of haemolysis (*OHCM* p 638).

Respiratory distress syndrome (RDS)

Insufficient surfactant is made so that the lungs are unable to stay expanded; re-inflation between breaths exhausts the baby, and respiratory failure follows. It is the major cause of death from prematurity.

Infants at risk: 100% if 24–28 weeks' gestation; 50% if 32 weeks. Also: maternal diabetes, male sex, second twin, Caesarean birth.

Prevention Betamethasone or dexamethasone helps prenatally (p 51—but postnatal benefits may be outweighed by GI bleeding, intestinal perforation, hyperglycaemia, BP↑, hypertrophic cardiomyopathy, and poor growth).[80]

Signs Worsening tachypnoea (>60/min) in the first 4 hours after birth. Increased inspiratory effort, with grunting, flaring of the nasal alae, intercostal recession and cyanosis. CXR: diffuse granular patterns, with air bronchograms. Mild signs subside after ~36h.

Differential diagnosis ***Transient tachypnoea of the newborn, TTN*** is due to excess lung fluid. It usually resolves after 24h. ***Meconium aspiration*** (p 120); congenital pneumonia (group B strep); tracheo-oesophageal fistula (suspect if respiratory problems after feeds); congenital lung abnormality.

Treatment Learn at the cot side. If gestation ≤28wks, intubate at birth; give surfactant by ET tube, eg bovine Beractant® 4mL/kg within 8h of birth ± 3 further doses 6h apart. Rock gently (but beware extubation) to aid spread in the bronchial tree. Monitor O_2, as needs may suddenly↓.[RCT 81]

- Some centres give a dose of surfactant then extubate pending developments, others keep the baby intubated and extubate as tolerated.
- Wrap up warmly and take to NICU/SCBU incubator.
- Monitor blood gases. Aim for a P_aO_2 of 6–10kPa, enhancing the ambient O_2 if not intubated. *Giving O_2:* There are many methods: all need supervision to detect complications—eg P_aCO_2↑ with headbox and facemask O_2; dislodgement with nasal cannulae—and obstruction of the catheter or upper airway, as well as gastric distension, with nasopharyngeal catheters.[82]
- If blood gases worsen, intubate and support ventilation (p 110), *before* exhaustion sets in. ↑P_aCO_2 may indicate either that CPAP is too high, or that further ventilation is needed.
- ***Traditional ventilator settings:*** (p 110). Inspiratory pressure 20cmH_2O with 60% O_2; positive end-expiratory pressure 5cmH_2O; 40breaths/min, with an inspiratory duration of 0.32s. On connecting the endotracheal tube check chest movement is adequate and symmetrical. Listen for breath sounds. P_aO_2 is increased by ↑mean pressure (not too high). P_aCO_2 is decreased by ↑minute volume (↑ breath frequency) by lessening inspiratory time. One option is ***high-frequency oscillatory ventilation***. Its role is uncertain; get help.[83,84]
- ►If any deterioration, consider: blocked or dislodged tube (a common occurrence), infection, faulty ventilator, or pneumothorax.

Fluids: Avoid milk for 24–28h. Give 10% dextrose IVI (p 122). *Nutrition:* Get help. Inositol is an essential nutrient promoting surfactant maturation and plays a vital role in neonatal life. Supplementing nutrition of prems with inositol reduces complications (IVH, p 108; bronchopulmonary dysplasia, p 119).[85]

Signs of a poor prognosis Persistent pulmonary hypertension, large right to left shunt via the ductus; ↑dead-space fraction in lungs.[86]

If, despite everything, hypoxia worsens, the baby is dying. Confer with your senior. Explain what is happening to the parents, and that the baby will feel no pain. Encourage christening, or what is congruent with parents' beliefs. Relieve pain (p 172); keep the baby comfortable. In the light of dialogue with parents and nurses it may be appropriate to disconnect the tubes, so allowing the parents to hold the baby, and, in so doing, to aid their grief. NB: contact your Trust's head and defence organization if legal issues beckon.[87]

Communicating with parents

Take time to explain to parents exactly what is happening to their baby—not just for the respiratory distress syndrome, but for *any* serious diseases. Structured, tested interviews yield these guidelines:[88]

- Ask both parents to be present (plus a nurse whom they trust).
- Hand your bleep to a colleague. Allow time. Call the parents by name.
- Look at the parents (mutual gaze promotes trust).
- Name the illness concerned with its complications. Write it down.
- Give details of support groups available. (Phone 020 7240 0671 for a list.)
- Elicit what the parents now know. Clarify or repeat as needed.
- Answer any questions. Arrange follow-up (<50% may be remembered).

Doctors decisions are increasingly being questioned by parents. If you and your team are sure your actions are in the child's best interests, and the parents take a different view, take any steps you can to resolve the issue in a non-confrontational way. Violent fights between doctors and parents endanger other children (some UK units have had to be evacuated while police are called). You should know emergency procedures for contacting the High Court to settle the issue (or go through the on call manager: your Trust can make applications day or night). Failure to get Court approval will leave you open to criticism from the European Court of Human Rights, which is likely to take the view that 'do not resuscitate' notices fail to guarantee respect for the child's 'physical and moral integrity'—guaranteed by Article 8 of the Convention on Human rights—see Glass vs United Kingdom, 2004 (61827/00).[89]

Bronchopulmonary dysplasia (BPD)

This is a big complication of ventilation for respiratory distress syndrome. There is persistent hypoxaemia ± difficult ventilator weaning. Classically, BPD is mainly from barotrauma and oxygen toxicity, whereas surfactant-related BPD is multifactorial with airway infections triggering inflammatory cascades. (Without surfactant, many would not survive to get BPD.)[90] Oxidative processes may also play a key role, but antioxidants are unproven.[91]

Tests: CXR: hyperinflation, rounded, radiolucent areas, alternating with thin denser lines. *Histology:* necrotizing bronchiolitis+alveolar fibrosis.

Mortality: Variable, ∵ complex interaction with surfactant use.[92]

Early sequelae: ↓IQ; cerebral palsy; feeding problems. O_2 desaturation during feeds is not uncommon. Visuo-spatial abilities at aged 5½yrs are only reduced in those with the severest forms of chronic lung disease.[93]

Late sequelae: By adolescence/early adulthood the main changes remaining are airways obstruction, airways hyper-reactivity, and hyperinflation.

Prevention: Steroids (antenatal & postnatal); surfactant treatment and 'suitably high' calorie feeding.[94]

Pulmonary hypoplasia

Suspect this in all infants with persisting neonatal tachypnoea ± feeding difficulties, particularly if prenatal oligohydramnios. Hypoplasia may be a consequence of oligohydramnios, eg in Potter's syndrome or premature rupture of the membranes. In diaphragmatic hernia it is a consequence of the 'space-occupying lesion'. Cystic adenomatoid malformations are another cause. CXR is likely to be misleadingly reported as normal. The condition need not be fatal: postnatal catch-up growth occurs.

Differential: RDS, meconium aspiration, sepsis, or primary pulmonary hypertension.[95] Some degree of pulmonary hypoplasia is the price of adopting an expectant plan for early spontaneous rupture of the membranes, but despite this, expectant management leads to fewer deaths.[96]

Other neonatal problems

Necrotizing enterocolitis (NEC) This is necrosis of bowel mucosa. Typically it occurs at the end of the first week of life in a prem infant on NICU/SCBU (it affects 1-2% of admissions to NICU). If mild, a little blood and mucus may be passed per rectum. At worst, there is sudden abdominal distension, tenderness (± perforation), shock, DIC, and sloughing of the rectal mucosa. It may be sporadic or epidemic. ***Treatment:*** Stop oral feeding; barrier nurse; culture faeces; do abdominal x-rays ± lateral shoot through, to look for oedematous loops of bowel with intramural gas and perforation. Crossmatch blood (to correct anaemia); give antibiotics—metronidazole 7.5mg/kg/12h IV over 20min with penicillin and netilmicin (p 112; or gentamicin, p 175) and regimens of cefotaxime with vancomycin have been used.[97]

Liaise early with a surgeon. Do repeated imaging and girth measurement. Platelets mirror disease activity; <100 × 10^9/L is 'severe'.[98] [n=58]

Laparotomy indications: Progressive distension, perforation. ***Prophylaxis:*** Oral antibiotics may (perhaps) reduce incidence of NEC (NNT≈10).[99]

Meconium aspiration syndrome Only thick meconium is important (aspiration pneumonitis). Suck out pharynx & trachea with oral mucus extractor after delivery of the head, but before the body is born. If meconium is present, intubate the trachea (large tube) for suction. The obstetrician may try compressing the thorax as he passes the baby to the paediatrician, so minimizing inspiratory effort until the airway is clear (this doesn't stop diaphragm effort). Observe closely, postnatally. Ventilation may be needed (p 110). Try a PEEP of 6cmH_2O and an inspiratory time of 0.5–0.75sec. Give penicillin + netilmicin (p 112; or gentamicin, p 175). Use of anti-inflammatories, high-frequency ventilation, exogenous surfactant, inhaled nitric oxide and liquid ventilation are unsupported by randomized evidence.[100]

Vitamin K deficiency bleeding (VKDB=haemorrhagic disease of the newborn) occurs from days 2-7 postpartum. ***Cause:*** no enteric bacteria to make vit K. The baby is usually well, apart from bruising/bleeding. Prothrombin & partial thromboplastin times (PT & PTT)↑; platelets ↔. ***Prevention:*** (many regimens) vit K eg 1mg IM (if at ↑risk)—or give 2 doses of a colloidal (mixed micelle) phytomenadione 2mg in the 1st week; if breast-fed, give a 3rd dose at 1 month old; not needed if bottle-fed (already fortified). NB: a weak correlation[101] with childhood cancer caused a scare, but there is no hard evidence. ***℞:*** Plasma, 10mL/kg IV & vit K (eg 1mg IV) for active bleeding (monitor coagulation).[102]

Disseminated intravascular coagulation (DIC) ***Signs:*** Septic signs (ill); petechiae; venepuncture oozings; GI bleeding. ***Tests:*** Platelets↓; schistocytes (fragmented RBCs); INR↑; fibrinogen↓; partial thromboplastin time↑; D-dimer↑ (hard to interpret if birthweight very low).[103] [104]

Treatment: Get help; treat cause (NEC, p 120; sepsis[etc]); give vit K 1mg IV then:

- Platelet transfusion, to keep platelets >30×10^9/L.
- Fresh plasma ± cryoprecipitate, 10mL/kg IVI ± heparin IV ± protein C.[105]
- If bleeding still continues, consider exchange transfusion.

Autoimmune thrombocytopenia (ITP) <10% of babies of women with ITP get thrombocytopenic (p 88). ***Alloimmune thrombocytopenia:*** (1:2000 births; via fetomaternal incompatibility of platelet antigens). It develops *in utero*. 50% are 1st born (it recurs in ~80% of later pregnancies with same or ↑severity). If affected *in utero* 25% have CNS problems; 10% an intracerebral bleed *in utero*. Platelets continue to fall for 48h post-delivery. Treat severe thrombocytopenia with *compatible platelets* or *irradiated maternal platelets*. IV Ig 400mg/kg/day for 48h may help. *Platelet transfusion via cordocentesis* from 24wks may be needed in later pregnancies. Diagnose by detecting *maternal platelet alloantibody* against father's platelets. Do *neuroimaging* on all patients.[106]

Minor neonatal problems

Most neonates will have a few insignificant lesions; the more you examine neonates the better you will become at reassuring mothers.[107]

Milia: These tiny cream sebaceous cysts on the nose or palate (Epstein's pearls) are self-limiting. Differential: pyogenic granuloma.[108]

Erythema toxicum (neonatal urticaria): These are harmless red blotches, often with a central white pustule which come and go in crops. They last ~24h (try ringing them), in contrast to septic spots which are smaller and not mobile. If in doubt take a swab. Ask for a Wright's stain: neutrophils indicate sepsis; eosinophils suggest erythema toxicum.[109]

Miliaria/heat rash: This itchy red rash fades rapidly when the baby is unwrapped. It is found in >8% of babies in some populations.[110]

Stork mark: These are areas of capillary dilatation on the eyelids, central forehead and back of the neck—where the baby is deemed to have been held in the stork's beak. They blanch on pressure and fade with time.

Harlequin colour change: One side of the face or body suddenly flushes for a few minutes. It is a shortlived vasomotor event.

Peeling skin: Common in postmature babies, it does not denote future skin problems. Olive oil prevents skin folds from cracking.

Petechial haemorrhages, facial cyanosis, subconjunctival haemorrhages: These temporary features generally reflect suffusion of the face during delivery (sometimes inaccurately referred to as 'traumatic asphyxia').

Swollen breasts: These occur in both sexes and occasionally lactate (witch's milk). They are due to maternal hormones and gradually subside if left alone, but if infected need antibiotics. Witch's milk may persist until 2 months old.[111]

The umbilicus: It dries and separates through a moist base at about day 7. Signs of infection: odour, pus, periumbilical red flare, malaise. Isolate the baby, take swabs and blood cultures, give antibiotics. Granuloma: exclude a patent urachus and cauterize with a silver nitrate stick.

Sticky eye: (Common; usually from an unopened tear duct, p 418.) Swab to exclude *ophthalmia neonatorum* (p 36)/chlamydia (special swab). Whenever vertically transmitted sexual infections occur, use direct fax referrals which promptly co-ordinate your microbiology department and your local genito-urinary medicine (GUM) clinic.[112]

Feeding anxieties: Healthy term babies require little milk for the first few days and early poor feeding is not an indication for investigation or bottle top-ups. The exceptions are babies of diabetic mothers, and light-for-dates babies, because of their risk of hypoglycaemia.

New babies may have difficulty co-ordinating feeding and breathing and briefly choke, gag, or turn blue. Exclude disease, check feeding technique (too much? too fast?) and reassure.

Regurgitation is often due to overfilling a tiny stomach with milk and air. Check feeding technique; if bottle fed, is the teat too big for the mouth or the hole too small or the amount too great?

Winding during feeds may help but is not essential to health.

Red-stained nappy: This is usually due to urinary urates but may be blood from the cord or baby's vagina (oestrogen withdrawal bleed).

Sneezing: Neonates sneeze to clear amniotic fluid from the nose. Sneezing is occasionally a sign of drug withdrawal.

Enteral and parenteral nutrition

Breastfeeding (p 124–6) is the ideal way to feed babies, but not all neonates can do this (and we must respect mothers who choose not to breastfeed). Here, formula milk is a viable alternative (p 127), as is expressed breast milk (EBM—technique). EBM is often inadequate to supply the increased demands of preterm infants. If <2kg, powder sachets of Breast Milk Fortifiers® (Cow & Gate) have a role.

Gavage tube feeding *Indications:* Any sick infant who is too ill or too young to feed normally (eg respiratory distress syndrome). Expressed breast milk or formula milk is fed via a naso- or oro-gastric tube either as a bolus or as a continuous infusion. If gastro-oesophageal reflux or aspiration is a problem, then a silastic naso-jejunal tube can be used. After entering the stomach, the tube enters the jejunum by peristalsis: confirm its position on x-ray. When the baby improves, start giving some feeds by mouth (PO), eg 1 PO per day, progressing to PO every 3rd feed. Then try alternating PO and gavage; then gavage every 3rd feed; finally try all PO. If during PO feeds, cyanosis, bradycardia or vomiting supervene, you may be trying too soon.

Trophic feeding *Synonyms:* Minimal enteral feeding; gut priming; hypocaloric feeding. Rationale: If prems go for weeks with no oral nutrition, normal GI structure and function are lost despite an anabolic body state. Villi shorten, mucosal DNA is lost, and enzyme activity is less. Feeding a small volume of milk may prevent this.

Technique: Typically, milk volumes of ~1mL/kg/h are given by tube starting on day 2–3. The milk employed is ideally expressed breast milk or a preterm formula (eg Nutriprem®).

Effects: Studies show that weight gain and head growth is improved, and that there are fewer episodes of neonatal sepsis, fewer days of parenteral nutrition are needed, and time to full oral feeding is less.

Eligibility: Experience shows that almost all prems with non-surgical illness tolerate at least some milk as trophic feeds. RCT 113

Parenteral nutrition (PN) This is given into a central vein. Indications: post-op; trauma; burns; if oral nutrition is poor (eg in ill, low-birth-weight babies) and necrotizing enterocolitis (when the gut must be 'rested'). *Day-by-day guide:* see BOX. ►*Sterility is vital*; prepare using laminar flow units. Monitoring needs to be meticulous.[1]

Daily checks: Weight; fluid balance; U&E; blood glucose; Ca^{2+}. Test for glycosuria. Change IVI sets/filters; culture filters, Vamin® & Intralipid® samples.

Weekly: Length and head circumference; skin fold thickness. LFT; Mg^{2+}; PO_4^{3-}; alk phos; ammonia; triglycerides; FBC; ESR or CRP (helps determine if sepsis is present).

Complications: Infection; acidosis; metabolic imbalances; thrombophlebitis; hepatobiliary stenosis; cholelithiasis; osteopenia. 114 If plasma $PO_4^{3-}\downarrow$, consider giving PO_4^{3-} (0.25–0.5mmol/kg/day) as the potassium salt. Mix with dextrose, but not Vamin® or trace element mixtures. PN is complex: get expert help. In addition, some precipitation errors are preventable by using computer-based decision support. 115

Stopping IV nutrition Do in stages to prevent hypoglycaemia.

1 See Brit. Assoc for Parenteral and Enteral Nutrition Guidelines ISBN 1-899-467-408

Parenteral nutrition: day-by-day guide. ►*All values are per kg/day.*

Type of baby	Day of PN	Age days	PROTEIN Vaminon®; mL	CARBOHYDRATE Dextrose 10%; mL	FAT Intralipid 20%; mL	IONS (mmol) Na	K	Ca	PO_4	FLUID PN volume; mL[1]
Neonates & low birth Weight babies	1	3	20	97.5	2.5	3	3	1	0.4–1	120
	2	4	30	115	5	3	3	1	0.4–1	150
	3	5	40	115	10	3	3	1	0.4–1	165
	M	>5	50	100	15	3	3	1	0.4–1	165
Infants >1 month[1] & <10kg	1		20	95–125	5	2.5	2.5	0.6	0.4	120–150*
	2		30	80–110	10	2.5	2.5	0.6	0.4	120–150*
	M		40	65–125	15	2.5	2.5	0.6	0.4	120–150*
10–30kg	1&2		14	23.5–78.5	7.5	2	2	0.2	0.1	45–100*
	M		28	7–57	10–15	2	2	0.2	0.1	45–100*
>30kg	1&2		14	26–56	5	1.5–2	1.5–2	0.2	0.1	45–75*
	M		21	14–51.5	10–12.5	1.5–2	1.5–2	0.2	0.1	45–75*

Note: M = maintenance. *See p 234 for 24h fluid requirement.

Trace elements: Peditrace® eg 1mL/kg (max 10mL) if renal function OK—caution if prolonged treatment, eg >1 month, or if ↓biliary excretion (stop if cholestasis); checking Mn^+ may be needed. ***Vitamins:*** Solivito N®: add 1mL/kg/day (max 10mL) to Vaminolact® (protect from light). Cater for A, D, & K with Vitalip N® 1–4ml/kg/day (max 10mL/kg/day) to Intralipid®. ►These values are a guide only. *Individual needs vary greatly.* Supplementing very preterm infants with selenium is controversial. It may help reduce sepsis; data are dominated by one large trial from areas with low selenium levels and may not be readily translated elsewhere.[116] Get expert help.

1 This is the total volume of fluid required (60 & 90mL/kg for days 1 & 2).

Learning to breast feed

It is better to be apprenticed antenatally to a breastfeeding mother than to rely on simple encouragement and leaflets. [117]

Reflexes Rooting (searching, with wide-open mouth)→suckling (jaw goes up and down while the tongue compresses the areola against the palate)→swallowing reflex (as milk hits the oropharynx, the soft palate rises and shuts off the nasopharynx; the larynx rises, and the epiglottis falls, closing the trachea).

Skill Don't assume this comes naturally; commonly, learning to breast feed is as hard as learning to drive—and as anxiety-provoking. The best way to learn is from an experienced person in comfortable surroundings—eg sitting in an upright chair, rather than inadequately propped-up in bed. Reassure that a few problematic feeds do not mean that the baby will starve, and that bottle feeding is needed. *Most term babies have plenty of fuel reserves* (earthquake infant-victims may survive for >1 week)—and perseverance will almost always be rewarded. Furthermore, 'top-up' bottle feeds may undermine confidence, and, by altering the GI milieu, diminish the benefits of breastfeeding.

A good time to start breastfeeding is just after birth (good bonding; PPH risk↓), but labour procedures may make this hard, eg intrapartum pethidine ± instrumental delivery, T° and BP measurements, washing, weighing, going to a postnatal ward. ►*It is never too late to put to the breast, provided lactation has been maintained.*

Beware of intervening too quickly without observing the mother's efforts. Rather than saying 'that's completely wrong: do it like this…' try 'good: you and your baby are going to get on fine. One extra tip might be…'

From the baby's viewpoint, breastfeeding entails taking a large mouthful of breast-with-nipple, which he or she gets to work on with tongue and jaw. Ensure the baby is close to the mother with the shoulders as well as the head facing the breast—which, if large, may need supporting (mother's fingers placed flat on the chest wall at the base of the breast: avoid the 'scissors' grip which stops the baby from drawing the lactiferous sinuses into his mouth).

- Avoid forcing the nipple into the mouth; so do not place a hand over his occiput and press forwards. Cradle the head in the crook of the arm.
- Explain the signs of correct attachment:
  - Mouth wide open, and chin touching the breast (nose hardly touching).
  - The baby should be seen to be drawing in breast, not just nipple.
  - Lower lip curled back, maximally gobbling the areola (so angle between lips >100°). (Don't worry about how much areola can be seen above the top lip: this gives little indication of where the tongue and lower jaw are.)
  - Slow, rhythmic, and deep jaw movements, as well as sucking movements. The 1st few sucks may be fast, shallow, and non-nutritive: here the baby is inducing the 'let-down' reflex, which promotes flow.
- When helping with placing, it is quite appropriate to 'tease' the baby by brushing his lip over the nipple, and then away. This may induce a nice big gape. With one movement bring to the breast, aiming his tongue and lower jaw as far as possible from the base of the nipple—so his tongue can scoop in the nipple and a good mouthful of breast.
- Keeping on the postnatal ward for a few days, and having the mother learn with an experienced, friendly midwife is very helpful, but this is rare in the UK, as cost and other pressures make admissions shorter.

How to express breast milk

It is good for every breastfeeding mother to learn this skill (access to teaching is *required* before the accolade of 'baby-friendly' can be granted to UK hospitals). There are at least 4 times when expressing is valuable:

- To relieve (sometimes very) painful breast engorgement between feeds.
- To keep milk production going when it is necessary to give nipples a rest owing to soreness—which is quite a common problem.
- To aid nutrition if sucking is reduced for any reason (eg prematurity or cleft lip).
- If the mother is going to be separated from her baby for a few feeds, eg going out to work.

The best way to learn is from a midwife, and by watching a mother who is already successfully expressing milk. Pumps are available from any chemist. If not, wash hands, and dry on a clean towel, then, try to start flow by:

- Briefly rolling the nipple: this may induce a let-down reflex, especially if the baby is nearby.
- Stroke the breast gently towards the nipple.
- With circular movements, massage the breast gently with the 3 middle fingers.

Applying warm flannels, or expressing in the bath may aid flow, eg while the mother is learning, and only a few drops are being expressed.

Teach the mother to find the 15 or so ampullae beneath the areola: they feel knotty once the milk comes in. Now with the thumb above the areola and the index finger below, and whole hand pressing the breast back on the chest wall, exert gentle pressure on the ampullae. With rhythmic pressure and release, milk should flow. Use a sterile container.

Take care that the fingers do not slip down on to the nipple, and damage the narrowing ducts. Fingers tire easily: practice is the key. Concentration is also needed to be sure to catch oddly angled jets.

If kept in a fridge, the milk lasts 24–48h. Frozen milk should be used within 3 months. It is thawed by standing it in a jug of warm water. Any unused milk should be discarded after 24 hours, not refrozen. NB: it is known that the antioxidant level of stored breast milk falls, but it is not known if this matters. Refrigeration is better than freezing and thawing.[118]

Breastfeeding and social/biological influences

Factors which make starting breastfeeding harder • Family pressures, including partner's hostility (10% breast feed *vs* ~70% if he approves).
- If mother and baby are separated at night in hospital.
- Urbanization/unfriendly working environments.
- Cultural reframing of breasts as sex objects; no non-sexual role models.
- Don't underestimate the commitment a breastfeeding mother makes. This is a 24/7 commitment for many months, which no one can help her with.

Breastfeeding advantages ►Mutual gaze ↑emotional input from mother.
- Sucking promotes uterine contractions, so avoiding some PPHs.
- Less insulin resistance, BP↑ & obesity (growth is less rapid, p 181)[119] due to ↑breast milk Long-Chain PolyUnsaturated Fatty Acids.[120] ►LCPUFAs *may* also ↑IQ.[121]
- Breast milk is cheap and clean, and gives babies an attractive smell.
- Colostrum has endorphins: good for birth-associated stress?[122]
- IgA, macrophages, lymphocytes (with interferon) and lysozyme protect from infection. Acids in breast milk promote growth of friendly lactobacillus in the baby's bowel. Gastro-enteritis may be less severe if the mother makes and transfers antibodies (an 'immune dialogue'). NB: one meta-analysis casts doubt vis à vis prems and infection.[123]
- Infant mortality, otitis media, pneumonia & diarrhoea are less if breast fed.[124]
- Breast milk contains less Na^+, K^+ & Cl^- than other milk, so aiding homeostasis. If dehydration occurs, risk of fatal hypernatraemia is low.
- Breastfeeding reduces the risk of juvenile-onset diabetes mellitus, rheumatoid arthritis, inflammatory bowel disease, and food allergies.
- Breastfeeding protects against atopic eczema and other allergies.[125] To aid this, the USA Pediatric Academy[126] says to delay weaning till 6 months old,[127] and cows' milk to 1yr, egg to 2yrs; and peanuts, tree nuts & fish to 3yrs old. This may be valuable in prems;[128] evidence is conflicting in term babies.[129]
- Breastfeeding helps mothers lose weight, and is contraceptive (unreliable!).
- Some protection in premenopausal years against maternal breast cancer.

Why is feeding on demand to be encouraged?
- It keeps the baby happy, and enhances milk production.
- Fewer breast problems (engorgement, abscesses).
- Feeding by routine is possible with a structured plan (see the *New contented little baby book*), which may help to promote a diurnal sleep cycle.

NB: sleep may be less disturbed if baby is kept in bed with mother provided there are no nearby solid objects (eg a wall) against which a baby might be crushed, but there remains a risk of inadvertent smothering (p 148).

Contraindications to breastfeeding • An HIV +ve mother in developed countries • Amiodarone • Antimetabolites • Antithyroid drugs • Opiates.

Problems These include breast engorgement and breast abscess. Treat by using the breast more effectively (better latching-on); aim to keep breasts empty, eg by hourly feeds or milk expression.

If a breast abscess forms, discard the milk if it is pus-like. Give the mother flucloxacillin 250mg/6h PO (it is safe for her baby). Surgery may be needed.

Treat sore nipples by ensuring optimal attachment (p 124), and moist wound healing (eg Jelonet® dressing) not by resting, except in emergency.

Preterm breast milk is the best food for prems. Give unheated, via a tube (p 122). Add vitamins D 1000U/day & K (p 122). Phosphate supplements may be needed. Even term babies may (rarely) develop rickets ± hypocalcaemia (eg fits, recurrent 'colds' lethargy, or stridor), if exclusively breast fed, unless vitamin supplements are used (p 150).

Bottle feeding

There are few contraindications to breastfeeding but many pressures not to (p 124). In many communities >50% mothers are breastfeeding at 2 weeks but this reduces to ≤40% at 6 weeks. Most change to bottle because of lack of knowledge or no encouragement. Advertising also has a role. The WHO/UNICEF *International Code of Marketing of Breastmilk Substitutes* bans promotion of bottle feeding and sets out requirements for labelling and information on feeding. www.babymilkaction.org/regs/thecode.html

Advantages of bottle feeding Fathers and others can help. Some mothers value the reassurance of knowing how much milk the baby is taking.

Standard infant formulas (Cow's milk 'humanized' by reducing the solute load and modifying fat, protein, and vitamin content.) As with breast milk, the protein component is whey-based. Many brands are available, eg SMA Gold Cap®. Brands are similar so shopping around for a brand which 'suits better' is unlikely to be an answer to feeding problems.

Follow-on formula milks are like standard formulas, but the protein component is casein-based (∴ delays stomach emptying and allows less frequent feeds). These are marketed to satisfy hungrier babies before they start weaning. Typical age of use: 6–24 months. SMA White® is an example.

Soya milks These contain corn syrup or sucrose, but no lactose, and are indicated in secondary lactose intolerance, galactosaemia, primary hypolactasia, and in vegan families, as they ban all cow's milk. Wysoy® is *not* the solution for infants with eczema—p 597. Because of their high aluminium content, avoid soya if preterm, and in renal disease. Soya milk is *not* indicated in re-establishing feeding (regrading) after gastroenteritis.[1]

Hydrolized formula is a cow's milk formula where protein is hydrolized into short peptides (eg Nutramigen®). Indications: *cow's milk allergy* (seen in 1% of babies, eg with bloody diarrhoea ± perioral rash) or *soya allergy*; prevention of atopy (eg in babies with a strong family history). Cow's milk can be reintroduced eg at 1 year (can be risky: so do so in hospital).

Specialist milks Many types exist (eg for gastro-oesophageal reflux, malabsorption, metabolic diseases, etc. Get help from a paediatric dietician.

Preparing feeds Hands must be clean, equipment sterilized, and boiled water used—infective gastro-enteritis causes many deaths in poor countries and considerable morbidity in the UK. Powder must be accurately measured. Understrength feeds lead to poor growth and overstrength feeds have, in the past, caused dangerous hypernatraemia, constipation, and obesity.

Feeding Babies need ~150mL/kg/24h (30mL=1oz) over 4–6 feeds depending on age and temperament. If small-for-dates up to 200mL/kg/day is needed; if large-for-dates, <100mL/kg. Feeds are often warmed, but there is no evidence that cold milk is bad. Flow should almost form a stream; check before each feed as teats silt up. The hole can be enlarged with a hot needle. Bottles are best angled so that air is not sucked in with milk.

Weaning Introduce solids at 4–6 months by offering cereal or puréed food on a spoon. Don't add cereals to bottles. After ~6 months follow-on formula may be tried; lumpy food is started so that the baby can learn to chew. Normal supermarket cow's milk *may* be used from when the baby is ~1 year old, but it may still be too rich in protein, Na^+, K^+, phosphorus—and is poor in iron, trace elements, linoleic and alpha-linolenic acids,[1] and vitamins C & B complex. Infants must be able to cope with its higher solute load. 130

1 Docosahexaenoic acid (DHA) is the main lipid in our brain; it is derived endogenously via α-linolenic acid (ALA). Several studies have tried to improve blood DHA concentrations of formula-fed infants by ↑ ALA in feeds and measuring changes in growth & development. Results are far from clear-cut.

Preterm and light-for-dates babies

A neonate whose calculated gestational age from the last menstrual period is <37 completed weeks is preterm[1] (ie premature).

Low-birth-weight babies fall into 3 groups:

1 <2500g but appropriate for gestational age.

2 <2500g term infants who are *small* for gestational age (SGA, ie weight <10th centile for gestation; see BOX).

3 Low-birth-weight preterm babies (weight is small for gestational age).

NB: *small* can mean low birth length and low birth weight (SGA^{L+W}) or just low birth weight—or just short (SGA^{L}). SGA^{L} children have normal body proportions except for head circumference (HC), which is *relatively* larger in many of these children. SGA^{L+W} babies still have a smaller HC at the age of ~6 years compared with SGA^{L} children. ***Are SGA effects reversible?*** In one randomized study, 3yrs of growth hormone (33μg/kg/day) induced a proportionate growth resulting in a normalization of height and head circumference.[131]

6% of UK infants are <2500g at birth, and 50% of these are preterm. 10% of pregnancies end in spontaneous preterm delivery, and 70% of all perinatal deaths occur in preterm infants (particularly if also growth-retarded).

Causes of prematurity are mostly unknown; smoking tobacco, poverty, and malnutrition play a part. Others: past history of prematurity; genitourinary infection/chorioamnionitis (eg *Ureaplasma*)[2]; pre-eclampsia; polyhydramnios; closely separated pregnancies; twins; uterine malformation; placenta praevia; abruption; premature rupture of the membranes. Labour may be induced early on purpose or accidentally (p 62).

Estimating the gestational age Use the Dubowitz score (p 228).

Small for gestational age babies ***Chief causes:*** ►Poverty/poor social support may account for 30% of variance in birth weights.[132] Constitutional/familial factors are also important. ***Other causes:*** Malformation; twins; placental insufficiency (maternal heart disease, BP↑, smoking, diabetes, sickle-cell disease, pre-eclampsia).[133] The incidence of live-born, very-low-birth-weight infants <1500g is ~0.6%. Neonatal mortality (within 28 days of birth) is ~25%. If the weight is 500–600g only about 10% survive, at best.

Gestational age (based on LMP and ultrasound) is more important for predicting survival than the birth weight alone.

Management If 32 weeks or less, transfer *in utero* to a special centre, if possible. Once born, ensure airway/breathing is optimal; protect from cold. Take to NICU/SCBU. Plan supplemental breast milk or low-birth-weight formula if <2kg. Measure blood glucose before each 3-hourly feed. Tube feed if oral feeds are not tolerated. If oral feeding is contraindicated (eg respiratory distress) IV feeding is needed (p 122).

Survival if very premature The 'EPICure' study survival figures (UK): ***23 weeks' gestation:*** 12% of live births survived ***24 weeks' gestation:*** 26% of live births survived. ***25 weeks' gestation:*** 45% of live births survived.

In other studies, 19% survived at 23wks, 40% at 24wks, and 54% at 25 wks.[134] Mortality is associated with intracranial abnormalities seen ultrasonically.

Disability *As a percentage of live births:* if 23 weeks' gestation: 5% had no or minor subsequent disability (24 weeks = 12%; 25 weeks = 23%). Morbidity relates to cerebral palsy, squint, and retinopathy (p 108).[135] [n>150]

Disability may be subtle but specific: one pattern is ↓numeracy if gestation is <30/40, from ↓grey matter in the left parietal lobe.[136] ADD risk↑ (p 211).

1 Premature is now used as a synonym for preterm; beware older books, as premature once meant birth weight <5lbs (2.5kg), before the difference between light-for-dates and preterm was recognized.

2 Kiss H *BMJ* 2004. Ureaplasma also causes neonatal sepsis, resp. distress & intraventricular haemorrhage. Screening mothers in pregnancy can ↓rates of prem birth (3% vs 5.3% in the control group).

Is this baby small for gestational age?

Use centile charts which take into account that first-borns are lighter than subsequent births: the table below gives sample data.

Weeks gestation	*Tenth centile weight (grams)* First born: boy	*girl*	*Subsequent births: boy*	*girl*
32	1220	1260	1470	1340
33	1540	1540	1750	1620
34	1830	1790	2000	1880
35	2080	2020	2230	2100
36	2310	2210	2430	2310
37	2500	2380	2600	2480
38	2660	2530	2740	2620
39	2780	2640	2860	2730
40	2870	2730	2950	2810

Preventing neonatal deaths—worldwide[1]

Each year, of the 130 million babies who are born, ~4 million die in the 1st 4 weeks of life (the neonatal period)—most from preventable causes. Two-thirds occur in India, China, Pakistan, Nigeria, Bangladesh, Ethiopia, the Democratic Republic of the Congo, Indonesia, Afghanistan, and Tanzania. Most of the deaths are caused by preterm births, infections, respiratory problems, and tetanus. (Malaria and some diarrhoeal diseases are less important in the neonatal period except in those areas of the highest neonatal mortality.) Prevention depends on:

- Tetanus vaccination.
- Access to antibiotics.
- Breastfeeding advice.
- Sanitary delivery rooms.
- Basic emergency services (caesarean sections and blood transfusion; obstructed labour is a major problem).
- Preventing and managing low-birthweight. Low birthweight affects 14% of births worldwide, but accounts for ~70% of neonatal deaths. Managing low-birthweight babies need not require expensive technology. Much could be achieved by application of known primary care principles of warmth, feeding, and the prevention and early treatment of infection.
- Preventing maternal mortality (0.5 million maternal deaths/yr) is a prerequisite for preventing many neonatal deaths. In one small but harrowing study from Gambia ***all*** the children born to mothers who died from pregnancy-related causes were themselves dead at one year. 137

MDG-4 *Millennium Development Goals* are internationally 'agreed' commitments to reduce poverty and ill-health. The 4th goal aims to reduce mortality in under-5s by two-thirds before 2015. The developing world spends ~$2 billion annually on this issue. It is estimated that another $4 billion is needed to do the job.

1 Lawn J 2005 *Lancet* **365** 891

Some GI malformations

Meckel's diverticulum: see **p 650**.

Tracheo-oesophageal fistula (± oesophageal atresia) ***Prenatal signs:*** Polyhydramnios; small stomach. ***Postnatal:*** Cough, airway obstruction, ↑secretions, 'blowing bubbles', distended abdomen, cyanosis, recurrent pneumonias. ***Diagnosis:*** Inability to pass a catheter into the stomach; x-rays show it coiled in the oesophagus. Avoid contrast radiology. ***Treatment:*** Correction of fistulae, using a cervical incision.[138]

Diaphragmatic hernia ***Signs:*** Difficult resuscitation at birth; respiratory distress; bowel sounds in one hemithorax (usually left so heart is best heard on the right). Cyanosis augers badly (∵ lung hypoplasia). Associations: other malformations (neural tube in 50%); trisomy 18; chromosome deletions eg at 15q2, Pierre Robin (p 138).[139] ***Incidence:*** 1:2200. ***Diagnosis:*** Prenatal: ultrasound; postnatal: CXR. ***Treatment:*** • *Prenatal:* Fetal surgery is not usually practical or available (tracheal obstruction may be tried: it encourages lung growth, so pushing out other viscera)—but premature birth may be caused. • *Postnatal:* Insert a large bore nasogastric tube when diagnosis suspected: at birth if prenatal diagnosis. The aim is to keep all air out of the gut. Face mask ventilation is contraindicated (so immediately intubate, ventilate, and paralyze, with minimal pressures). Get surgery in an appropriate centre.

Hirschsprung's disease Congenital absence of ganglia in a segment of colon (or in the rare 'long-segment' disease, all the way up to the stomach) leading to infrequent, narrow stools, GI obstruction, and megacolon. Faeces may be felt *per abdomen*, and PR exam may disclose only a few pellet-like faeces. ♂/♀ ≈3:1. *Complications:* GI perforation, bleeding, ulcers, enterocolitis (may be life-threatening). Short gut syndrome after surgery. ***Tests:*** Barium enema or sigmoidoscopy/biopsy of the aganglionic section, staining for acetylcholinesterase-positive nerve excess. Excision of the aganglionic segment is needed ±colostomy. This does not always lead to immediate recovery.

Hydroceles in infancy A processus vaginalis patent at birth, and allowing *only fluid* from the peritoneal cavity to pass down it, generally closes during the first year of life—so no action is usually needed. If the fluid-filled sac is adjacent to the spermatic cord, it is called an encysted hydrocele or a spermatic cord cyst. If the proximal opening of the processus vaginalis is wide, a true inguinal hernia is formed, and action is always required.[140]

Inguinal hernias These are due to a patent processus vaginalis (the passage which ushers the descending testicle into the scrotum). They present as a bulge lateral to the pubic tubercle. They may be intermittent, appearing during crying. In 25% there are bilateral hernias. The aim is to repair these promptly as there is risk of incarceration. Note: there is often an associated hydrocele, and this may be difficult to distinguish from an incarcerated hernia—exploration is required if there is doubt.

Imperforate anus Most girls have a posterior fourchette fistula, boys having a posterior urethral fistula (may pass meconium in urine). Absence of perineal fistula in boys indicates communication with the urethra (so colostomy may be required). Do GU imaging to show commonly associated GU abnormalities. Posterior sagittal anorectoplasty is possible.[141]

Mid-gut malrotations ►Bilious neonatal vomiting merits immediate surgical referral (pass NGT).[142] Absent attachment of the small intestine mesentery can cause mid-gut volvulus or obstruction of the third part of the duodenum by fibrotic bands. Presentation may be late; passage of blood per rectum heralds mid-gut necrosis—and is an indication for emergency surgical decompression. See *OHCM* p 488 for acute gastric volvulus.

Anterior abdominal wall defects

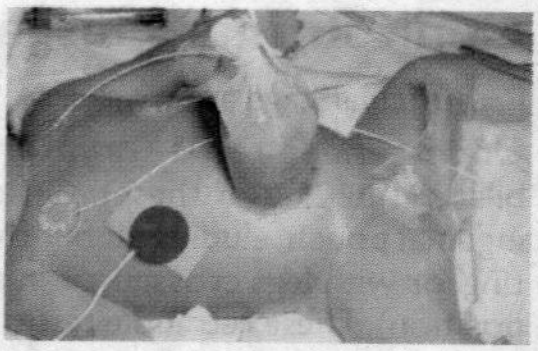

Fig 1. Gastroschisis

Gastroschisis: A paraumbilical defect with evisceration (extrusion of viscera) of abdominal contents. *Incidence:* ~1.6/10,000; rising, and possibly caused by a vascular event associated with cocaine use. The typical pregnancy is in a young, socially disadvantaged primip. There is usually *no* other defect, and corrective surgery has a good outcome in 90% (so deliver where there are good paediatric surgical facilities, if diagnosed prenatally—aim to diagnose at ultrasound).[143] [144] Manage as per diaphragmatic hernia: aim to have no air in the gut, so intubate and paralyze at birth.

Exomphalos: This is a ventral defect with herniation of abdominal contents into the base of the umbilical cord. There is a covering with peritoneum. *Incidence:* ~4.3/10,000. Other abnormalities are often present. Manage as above.[145]

Genitourinary diseases

Preauricular tags are markers of GU problems; consider GU ultrasound.[146]

Undescended testis—cryptorchidism (2-3% of neonates, 15-30% of prems; bilateral in 25% of these). On cold days retractile testes may hide in the inguinal pouch, eluding all but the most careful examination (eg while squatting, or with legs crossed, or in a warm bath they may be 'milked' down into position). These retractile testes need no surgery. If truly undescended it will lie along the path of descent from the abdominal cavity. Early (eg at 1 year) fixing within the scrotum (orchidopexy) may prevent infertility and reduces later neoplasia (untreated, risk is ↑ >5-fold). Intranasal gonadotrophin-releasing hormone is unreliable. NB: biopsy may cause later malignancy.[147]

Posterior urethral valves present with oligohydramnios or absent or feeble voiding (± uraemia and a palpable bladder). *Micturating cystogram:* posterior urethral dilatation. Laser resection is possible. *Antenatal diagnosis:* ultrasound scan (USS) shows GU dilatation.

Hypospadias (Narrow meatus on ventral penis). Avoid circumcision: use foreskin for preschool repair; attend to aesthetic considerations.[148]

Epispadias (Meatus on dorsum of penis). May occur with bladder extrophy.

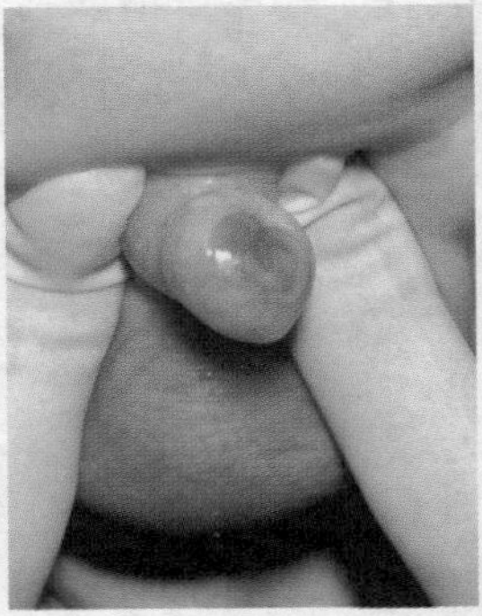

Fig 1. Epispadias

Some congenital/genetic disorders

Horseshoe kidney (crossed-fused kidney): *Symptoms:* Silent or obstructive uropathy ± renal infections. USS diagnosis: kidneys 'too medial'; lower pole 'too long'; anterior-rotated pelvis; poorly defined inferior border; isthmus often invisible.[149] [n=34]

Infantile polycystic kidneys may cause obstructed labour and respiratory difficulties, with later uraemia and BP↑. Radiology: collecting tubule cysts (<5mm across). The histology of the liver is always abnormal. Survivors risk UTIs and portal hypertension with haematemesis. *Inheritance:* Recessive (dominant in adult polycystic disease, *OHCM* p 286).[150]

Ectopic kidney: May be seen on US scan (eg pelvic mass) or renal scintigraphy. Associations: anorectal abnormalities, UTIs; calculi.[151]

Renal agenesis causes oligohydramnios, Potter's facies + death if bilateral. VACTERL association (vertebral, anal, cardiac, tracheoesophageal, renal and limb anomalies). *Diagnosis:* prenatal US scan.[152]

Patent urachus: Urine leaks from the umbilicus. *Image:* excretory urogram.

Bladder extrophy: Pubic separation with bladder exposure.[153]

Double ureter: *Associations:* ureterocele, UTI, pyelonephritis; may be symptomless.

Renal tubular defects: (eg renal glycosuria, cystinuria, or diabetes insipidus). In *renal tubular acidosis* conservation of fixed base is impaired, causing metabolic acidosis + alkaline urine. ***Symptoms:*** Failure to thrive; polyuria; polydipsia.[154]

Wilms' nephroblastoma This is the commonest intra-abdominal tumour of childhood (20% of all malignancies). It is an undifferentiated mesodermal tumour of the intermediate cell mass. It may be sporadic, or familial (2%), or associated with Beckwith–Wiedemann syndrome (BWS, p 638), *a*niridia, *G*U malformations, and *r*etardation (WAGR). One of the Wilms' tumour genes (WT1 on chromosome 11) encodes a protein which is a transcriptional repressor downregulating IGF-II, an insulin-like growth factor. [155]
Median age at presentation: 3.5yrs. 95% are unilateral. Staging:

I Tumour confined to the kidney	*IV* Distant metastases
II Extrarenal spread, but resectable	*V* Bilateral disease
III Extensive abdominal disease	

The patient: Features include fever, flank pain, an abdominal mass. Haematuria is not common. Ultrasound: renal pelvis distortion; hydronephrosis.
Management: Avoid biopsy; nephrectomy + vicristine & actinomycin 4 weeks pre-op can cure. Radiotherapy may help. Genetic & biological factors guide risk categorization and help individualize care. [156] [157] [N=382]

Ambiguous genitalia (intersexuality)

This is rare: *refer promptly.* ►Distinguish genetic, gonadal, phenotypic (affected by sex hormone secretion etc), psychological, and social-role sexualities. Male sex differentiation depends on SRY genes (on Y chromosomes) transforming an indifferent gonad into a testis; its products (testosterone & Mullerian inhibiting substance) control fetal sex differentiation.[1] [158]

Ask about Exposure to progesterone, testosterone, phenytoin, aminoglutethamide? Past neonatal deaths (adrenogenital synd. recessive). Note phallic size and urethral position. Are the labia fused? Have the gonads descended? Undescended impalpable testes are more likely to signify intersexuality than palpable maldescended testes—likewise with severity of hypospadias. [159]

Tests Buccal smear (Barr body suggests ♀); WBC mustard stains make Y chromosomes fluoresce; these take <24h *vs* 5 days for chromosome analysis. If there is a phallus and buccal smear is '♀', diagnose adrenogenital syndrome or maternal androgens (drugs, tumours) or true hermaphroditism, ie ovary and testis coexist (1 on each side) 46,XY, 46,XX, 45,XO/46,XY or 45,X/47,XYY mosaic). [160] If a phallus & buccal smear is ♂, tell mother the baby is a boy.

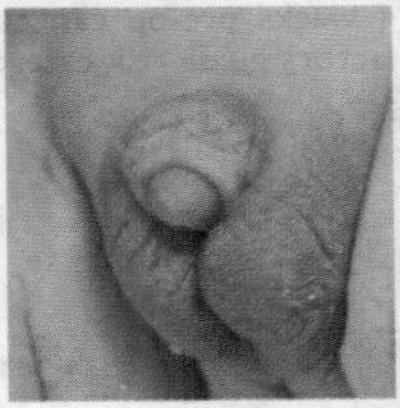

Fig 1. Ambiguous genitalia

Don't rely on appearances whenever babies have: bilateral cryptorchidism (at term), even if a phallus is present; unilateral cryptorchidism with hypospadias; penoscrotal or perineoscrotal hypospadias. These patients need examination by a paediatric endocrinologist to exclude androgen resistance (eg testicular feminization).[1] Genetic tests are also vital: eg terminal deletion of 10q deletes genes essential for normal male genital development. [161]

NB: if the stretched phallus is <25mm long, normal procreation is unlikely. If there is uncertainty due to a short penis, a paediatric endocrinologist may try 3 days' treatment with human chorionic gonadotrophin. If the baby is a boy, the penis will grow (possibly even to normal length) after 5 days. [162]

Aromatase deficiency CYP19 genes are needed for normal oestrogenization: recessive mutations cause ambiguous genitalia in 46,XX individuals; at puberty there is hypergonadotropic hypogonadism, with no secondary sexual characteristics, except for progressive virilization. Boys have normal male sexual differentiation but are tall with brittle bones. Oestrogen receptor gene mutations are similar. [163] Note that sexual differentiation of the brain is mostly dependent on prenatal exposure to testosterone, and congenital aromatase deficiency is thought not to disturb the maleness of brain development in men. But it is not known if this is true for sexually dimorphic brain areas possibly related to sexual orientation and gender-identity, [164] [165] eg the bed nucleus of the stria terminalis (BSTc is bigger in men but not in some ♂ transsexuals). [166]

Congenital adrenal hyperplasia CAH is due to excess secretion of androgenic hormones because of deficiencies of 21-hydroxylase, 11-hydroxylase, or 3-β-hydroxysteroid dehydrogenase. Cortisol is inadequately produced, and the consequent rise in adrenocorticotrophic hormone leads to adrenal hyperplasia, and overproduction of androgenic cortisol precursors. CAH is a leading cause of male pseudohermaphroditism. *Incidence:* 1:14000. [167]

Clinical & chemical features: Vomiting, dehydration, and ambiguous genitalia. Boys may seem normal at birth, but will exhibit precocious puberty, or may have ambiguous genitalia (↓androgens in 17-hydroxylase deficiency), or incomplete masculinization (hypospadias with cryptorchidism from ↓3β-hydroxysteroid dehydrogenase). Hyponatraemia, (with paradoxically ↑urine Na^+) and hyperkalaemia are common. ↑Plasma 17-hydroxyprogesterone in 90%; urinary 17-ketosteroids↑ (not in 17-hydroxylase deficit).

1

Emergency treatment of adrenocortical crisis

Babies may present with an adrenocortical crisis (circulatory collapse) in early life. Other presentations include hyponatraemic seizures in infancy (often misdiagnosed as a febrile convulsion). ➡Urgent treatment is required with 0.9% saline IVI (3-5g Na^+/day), glucose, and hydrocortisone 100mg/2-6h IV (all ages). Give fludrocortisone 0.1mg/day PO.

Assigning sex and gender

►There are two pieces of information every new parent is asked: the weight and the sex. It is traumatic for them not to be able to tell. However, don't shy away from telling patients that you do not know whether their baby is a boy or girl, and that tests must be done (it may be wise to await results before naming the child). This is unsatisfactory, but much better than having to reassign gender. This is why a neonate with ambiguous genitalia is a sexual emergency. Choice of gender must take into account chromosomal and gonadal sex, the hormonal milieu during fetal life, surgical aspects, internal anatomy, fertility issues, psychosexual development, and adult sexual function. NB: ♀ karyotype does not guarantee absence of intra-abdominal testes—so future risks of malignancy have to be assessed too.[168]

Your job may be to assemble an optimum team: ie a paediatric endocrinologist with psychological expertise, and a laparoscopic surgeon skilled in neonatal cystoscopy and genitography as well as in reconstruction.

Prenatal preparation entails comparing prenatal karyotype with US genital scans to formulate an intersex differential diagnosis—but US scans are unreliable in >50% of ♀ pseudohermaphroditism.[169] [170] NB: it is common to assign ♀ gender when in doubt,[171] but while some favour a gender compatible with the chromosomal sex, if possible, others point out that this is a simplification as we don't fully understand determinants of gender role (social sex).[172] [173] It is important not to think simply in terms of what promotes the greatest efficiency in the act of sexual intercourse.[174]

Advise against registering the birth until a definite treatment plan is in place. Once registered, legal sex cannot be changed in most countries.

Screening for congenital adrenal hyperplasia

The common cause of adrenal hyperplasia is one of ~10 gene defects (6p21.3; the gene is called *CYP21*) that cause deficiency of 21-hydroxylase (which mediates the penultimate step in cortisol biosynthesis). Corticotrophin-induced accumulation of 17OH-progesterone leads to ↑levels of testosterone (via hepatic conversion). Most affected infants are also salt losers, as 21-hydroxylase is needed for aldosterone biosynthesis, and in boys this is usually the sole early manifestation (excess virilization may be early or delayed to adulthood). Biochemical screening is rarely universal, but some centres use it in boys, aiming for diagnosis before life-threatening adrenal hyperplasia. (Girls are generally detected by finding virilization at neonatal examination providing the baby is not misdiagnosed as a boy—also prenatal diagnosis is possible, and treatable by giving the mother dexamethasone from early in pregnancy.)

One difficulty is the diversity in time of onset and clinical presentation despite identical *CYP21* mutations, making adrenal hyperplasia a continuum of disorders. Treatment is medical and surgical (clitoral reduction and vaginoplasty). Growth and fertility are also impaired.[175]

1 Androgens cause maleness in 46, XY individuals, provided no mutations in the X-linked androgen receptor occur. Mutations cause more or less complete androgen insensitivity and female phenotype, with normal levels of testosterone and dihydrotestosterone (DHT). If there is partial insensitivity, topical (periscrotal) DHT (Andractim®) has been used to augment maleness; but if *in vitro* functional assays show this is impossible, babies are usually brought up as girls.

Congenital heart disease

Incidence 8/1000 births. 2 questions: *Is the defect compensated?* (unobtrusive); if not, *Is there cyanosis? Signs of decompensation:* Poor feeding, dyspnoea, hepatomegaly, engorged neck veins, pulse↑. (or ↓, premorbidly)

Physiological types: • Left to right shunt (ASD; VSD; AVM) • ↓Systemic perfusion: weak pulse ± acidosis (hypoplastic L heart; aortic stenosis; coarcation; any left outflow obstructions) • Pulmonary venous congestion (mitral stenosis) • Transposition streaming (of caval return→aorta) • ↓Pulmonary blood flow (eg Fallot's) • Intracardiac mixing of 'blue' and 'red' blood (truncus arteriosus).

Acyanotic causes of uncompensated defects (left to right shunt) Atrio-septal defects (ASD), VSD, aortopulmonary window, patent ductus (PDA). Later pulmonary hypertension causes shunt reversal + cyanosis (Eisenmenger, p 642).

Cyanotic causes (R to L shunt) Fallot's (p 642), transposition of great arteries; shunt-associated tricuspid or pulmonary atresia.

Tests FBC, CXR, P_aO_2 (in air & 100% O_2), ECG, 3D echo, cardiac catheter.

VSD: (25% of cases) Symptoms: usually mild. Signs: harsh, loud, pansystolic 'blowing' murmur ± thrill; ± a diastolic apical inflow murmur. ECG: Normal at birth. Later left (or combined) ventricular hypertrophy. CXR: pulmonary engorgement. Course: 20% close spontaneously by 9 months (*maladie de Roger*). Large defects are closed by 6 months.

ASD: (7% of cases) Symptoms: Usually none. Signs: widely split, fixed S_2 + systolic murmur due to L to R shunt a pulmonary flow murmur (upper left sternal edge). The ASD itself does not cause a murmur. CXR: cardiomegaly, globular heart (primum defect). ECG: RVH ± incomplete R bundle branch block.

Patent ductus: Signs: failure to thrive, pneumonias, CCF, SBE, collapsing pulse, thrill, S_2↑, systolic pulmonary area murmur, or continuous 'machinery hum'. CXR: vascular markings↑, big aorta. ECG: LVH. Dexamethasone in preterm labour helps close PDAs, as does ibuprofen lysine 10mg/kg, then 5mg/kg after 24 & 48h is similar to IV indometacin 0.2mg/kg/12h (3 doses).[176] Meta-analyses favour indometacin.[MET 177] If aged 2-7 days, see *BNF*. Beware oliguria, renal failure, and ↓platelets.[178]

Coarctation: Aortic constriction makes feeling femoral pulses hard; BP↑ in the arms (± epistaxis) and ↓ in legs, absent foot pulses, ± systolic murmur at the left back, heart failure. Think of this whenever there is shock, eg on days 3-10, when the ductus closes. CXR: rib notching (very late). ECG: LVH.

Transposition of great arteries (TGA): Cyanosis, CCF, ± systolic murmur. CXR: egg-shaped heart. ECG: RVH. Balloon atrial septostomy allows oxygenated blood to reach the aorta via ASD. Correction is possible.[179]

Pulmonary stenosis: Pulmonary thrill and systolic murmur. See *OHCM* p 150.

Treatment • Treat heart failure in babies with nasogastric feeds, sitting upright, O_2, furosemide eg 1mg/kg/24h slow IV ± spironolactone; digoxin 4-5μg/kg/12h PO is rarely used. • You may be advised to keep the ductus open in duct-dependent cyanotic conditions with prostaglandin E_1 (≤0.05–0.1μg/kg/min IV); intubate and ventilate if needed before transfer to specialists; during transfer be alert to: T°↓; Ca^{2+}↓; glucose↓; hypovolaemia. • Prevent SBE/IE (p 166). Open-heart surgery using hypothermia and circulatory arrest is possible at any age, eg for: Fallot's, VSD, TGA, total anomalous pulmonary venous drainage (in which pulmonary veins drain, eg into the portal system, causing CCF). Balloon valvuloplasty decreases need for open surgery in pulmonary stenosis (there is more of a problem with restenosis and residual incompetence with aortic valvuloplasty). It is also employed in coarctation. Examples of palliative surgery: pulmonary artery banding to restrict blood flow; systemic to pulmonary shunts to enlarge an under developed pulmonary arterial tree, before inserting a valve-bearing conduit.

Prenatal screening echocardiography Sensitivity: 88%; specificity and +ve predictive value: 100%. Intrauterine cardiac intervention is possible.[180]

Murmurs and heart sounds in children

We hear benign flow murmurs (eg parasternal low-frequency 'twangs', in early systole) in ~80% of children, at some time (eg with fever, anxiety, exercise). ***Still's murmur*** is an example, and may be abolished by hyperextension of the back, and neck. Lack of other features distinguishes these from malformations: ***no*** clubbing; ***no*** cyanosis; ***no*** thrills; ***no*** rib recession; ***no*** clicks; ***no*** arrhythmias; normal pulses & apex; ***no*** failure to thrive. When in doubt, get a skilled echocardiogram. CXR & ECG often mislead.[181] Another (validated) option is to use an electronic stethoscope and e-mail the sounds to a cardiologist.[182]

Questions to ask yourself while listening to the 2nd heart sound (S_2)
- Is it a double sound in inspiration, and single in expiration? (Normal)
- Is S_2 split all the time? (ASD—atrial septal defects)
- Is S_2 never split, ie single? Fallot's; pulmonary atresia; severe pulmonary stenosis; common arterial trunk; transposition of the great arteries (the *a*nterior *a*orta masks sounds from the *p*osterior *p*ulmonary trunk).
- Is the pulmonary component (2nd part) too loud? (Pulmonary stenosis)

NB: the 2nd heart sound is more useful diagnostically than the first.

Points to note on hearing murmurs If you have an ear for detail! ***Timing:***
- *Ejection systolic* (innocent, or semilunar valve or peripheral arterial stenosis).
- *Pansystolic* with no crescendo-decrescendo (VSD, mitral incompetence).
- *Late systolic*, no crescendo-decrescendo (mitral prolapse, *OHCM* p 146).
- *Early diastolic* decrescendo (aortic or pulmonary incompetence).
- *Mid-diastolic* crescendo-decrescendo (↑atrio-ventricular valve flow, eg VSD, ASD; or tricuspid or mitral valve stenosis). An opening snap (*OHCM* p 146) and presystolic accentuation suggest the latter.
- *Continuous murmurs* (PDA, venous hum, or arterio-venous fistula).

Loudness: The 6 grades for systolic murmurs: (Thrills mean pathology.)

1 Just audible with a quiet child in a quiet room. *2* Quiet, but easily audible.
3 Loud, but no thrill. *4* Loud with thrill.
5 Audible even if the stethoscope only makes partial contact with skin.
6 Audible without a stethoscope.

Place:

AS=aortic stenosis; PS=pulmonary stenosis

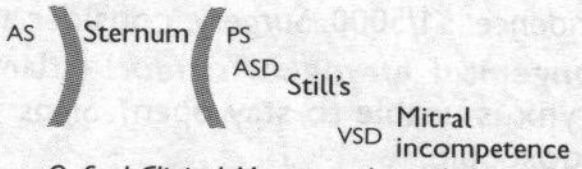

(Use our *Oxford Clinical Mentor* to hear the sounds)

Accentuating/diminishing manoeuvres: Inspiration augments systemic venous return ('negative' pressure draws blood from abdomen into the thorax), and therefore the murmurs of pulmonary stenosis and tricuspid regurgitation.

Expiration augments pulmonary venous return and decreases systemic return, and therefore VSD, mitral incompetence, and aortic stenosis too. In (mild) pulmonary stenosis, the ejection click is augmented by expiration.

Valsalva manoeuvre ↓ systemic venous return and benign flow murmurs, but ↑ murmurs from mitral incompetence and subaortic obstruction.

- Sitting or standing (*vs* lying) ↓ innocent flow murmurs, but ↑ murmurs from subaortic obstruction or from a venous hum (places to listen: right base; below left clavicle; neck—it is abolished by gently pressing the ipsilateral jugular; PDA murmurs are similar, but no change with posture).

Catheter findings Images: www.kumc.edu/kumcpeds/cardiology/pedcardiodiagrams.html

Pulmonary stenosis	RV pressure↑; pulmonary artery pressure↓
+ foramen ovale	as above with right atrial pressure↑ and P_aO_2↓
VSD	RV pressure↑; RV O_2 >R atrial O_2
ASD	right atrial pressure & oxygenation↑ compared to IVC
Patent ductus	RV pressure↑; pulmonary artery O_2 >RV O_2
Fallot's tetrad	see p 642; RV O_2 & P_aO_2↓

Orofacial clefts (cleft lip and palate)

This is the commonest facial malformation. It results from failure of fusion of maxillary and premaxillary processes (during week 5). The defect runs from lip to nostril. It may be bilateral, when there is often a cleft in the palate as well, with the premaxillary process displaced anteriorly. Palate clefts may be large or small (eg of uvula alone). ***Incidence:*** ~1/1000. ***Causes:*** Genes, benzodiazepines, antiepileptics, rubella. Other malformations are common, eg trisomy 18, 13–15, or Pierre Robin short mandible (causing cyanotic attacks). ***Prevention:*** Folic acid ≥6mg/day periconceptually ± multivitamins.[183] ***Treatment:*** A long-term team approach is best (orthodontist, plastic surgeon, oral surgeon, GP, paediatrician & speech therapist). Feeding with special teats may be needed before plastic surgery (usually, lip repair is at 3 months, and the palate at 1yr; some surgeons do the lip at 1 week old). Repair of unilateral complete or incomplete lesions often gives good cosmesis. Refer to expert centres. If bilateral, there is always some residual deformity. ***Complications:*** Otitis media, aspiration pneumonia, post-op palatal fistulae, speech defects (get speech therapy help). Avoid taking to NICU/SCBU (?hinders bonding).

Other malformations in the head and neck

Eyes Anophthalmos: there are no eyes; rare; part of trisomy 13–15.
Ectopia lentis: presents as glaucoma with poor vision. The lens margin is visible; seen in Marfan's (*OHCM* p 730), Ehlers-Danlos (p 642), homocystinuria; incidence: <1/5000; autosomal-dominant (a-Dom) or recessive (a-R).
Cataract: rubella, Down's, others: recessive or sex-linked.

Coloboma: notched iris with a displaced pupil; incidence: 2/10,000; (a-R).
Microphthalmos: small eyes; 1/1000; due to rubella—or genetic (a-Dom).

Ears Accessory auricles: seen in front of the ear; incidence: 15/1000.
Deformed ears: Treacher-Collins' syndrome (p 656).
Low-set ears: associations—Down's syndrome; congenital heart disease.

Nose/throat ***Choanal atresia:*** *Signs:* postnatal cyanotic attacks; nasal catheter doesn't go into the pharynx because of nasal malformation. *Incidence:* ≤1/5000. *Surgery:* consider a micro-endoscopic nasal approach.[184]

Congenital laryngeal stridor: (∵ laryngeal webs or laryngomalacia: the larynx is unable to stay open). *Signs:* shrill inspirations; dyspnoea. *Surgery:* endoscopic.

Laryngeal atresia: Breaths don't expand the lungs, which are hypoplastic. Look for co-existing anomalies.[185] *Branchial fistula:* These open at the front of sternomastoid (a remnant of the 2nd or 3rd branchial pouch). *Incidence:* <1/5000. Branchial and thyroglossal cysts: p 576.

Skull & spine ***Brachycephaly:*** Short, broad skull from early closure (craniostenosis) of the coronal suture; incidence: <1/1000; Down's-associated or a-Dom.

Cleidocranial dysostosis: No clavicles (so shoulders meet). Slow skull ossification, no sinuses, high-arched palate; incidence <1/5000; a-Dom.

Craniofacial dysostosis: Tower skull, beaked nose, exophthalmos. Δ: spiral CT.
Klippel-Feil syndrome (p 648): fused cervical vertebra (so the neck is short).

CNS Hydrocephalus: incidence 0.3–2/1000. Ante- or neo-neonatal injury, infection, or genes (sex-linked) may cause aqueduct stenosis. Dandy-Walker syndrome (p 640); Arnold-Chiari malformation (*OHCM* p 718).

Microcephaly: *Causes:* genetic,[186] intrauterine viruses (eg rubella), hypoxia, x-rays, maternal alcohol. *Incidence:* 1/1000. Recurrence risk: 1/50.

Spina bifida and ***anencephaly*** See p 140.

Fetal alcohol syndrome Severity depends on how much alcohol the mother has had in pregnancy. Features: microcephaly, short palpebral fissure, hypoplastic upper lip, absent philtrum, small eyes, IQ↓, cardiac malformations.

Some words about the head and neck

www.icomm.ca/geneinfo/cephaly.htm

Acrocephaly: This term may be applied to tower headed conditions.

Arhinencephaly: Congenital absence of the rhinencephalon.

Arthrogryposis: This term implies contracture of a joint.

Brachycephaly: The head is too short, with a flat occiput.

Cebocephaly: A small, flat nose with a single nostril below close-set eyes.

Cephalocele: Intracranial contents protrude. 'Kélé' means hernia in Greek.

Craniostenosis=craniosynostosis=premature closure of skull sutures.

Cyclopia: A single eye in the area normally occupied by the root of the nose, which is missing, or present in the form of a proboscis (a tubular appendage) located above the eye. In some, it can be viewed as an extreme form of hypotelorism. It may be part of trisomy 13 (Patau's syndrome).

Dolicephalic: The head is elongated, eg as in Marfan's, or El-Greco portraits.

Dystopia canthorum: Intercanthal distance is increased, but not the interpupillary or (bony) interorbital distances.

Holoprosencephaly: (a whole, ie single-sphered, brain) Hypotelorism with cleft palate ± premaxillary agenesis ± cyclopia ± cebocephaly (see above)—follows failure of the lateral ventricles to separate (defective cleavage of the prosencephalon), eg with fusion of the basal ganglia. 3 types: alobar (often fatal in infancy), semilobar, and lobar, reflecting degree of the cleavage abnormality. Deletions of chromosomes 7q and 3p or trisomy 13, 18, and 21 may be causal (sometimes). There may be mental retardation, epilepsy, quadriplegia, neuroendocrine anomalies, and poor growth.

Lissencephaly: Smooth cortex with no convolutions (agyria), with 4 layers instead of the usual 6. Signs: failure to thrive, microcephaly, developmental delay, seizures, optic nerve hypoplasia, and microphthalmia. In some, it is associated with the Miller–Dieker syndrome (prominent forehead, bitemporal hollowing, anteverted nostrils, prominent upper lip, and micrognathia). The gene LIS-1 gene at 17p13.3 may be deleted. www.isabel.org.uk/

Metopic suture: This is the same as the frontal suture.

Micrognathia: The mandible is too small.

Neurocranium: That part of the skull holding the brain.

Obelion: The point on the saggital suture crossed by a line joining the parietal foramina.

Oxycephalic (=*turricephaly*=*acrocephaly*) The top of the head is pointed.

Plagiocephaly: If fully expressed, synostosis affects coronal (rarely lambdoidal) sutures (±palpable bony ridge) with a flat forehead and elevation of the orbit on the one side. Minor (unfused) plagiocephalic asymmetry is common in infants sleeping on their backs, improves with time, and is of no significance. Associations: scoliosis and pelvic obliquity.

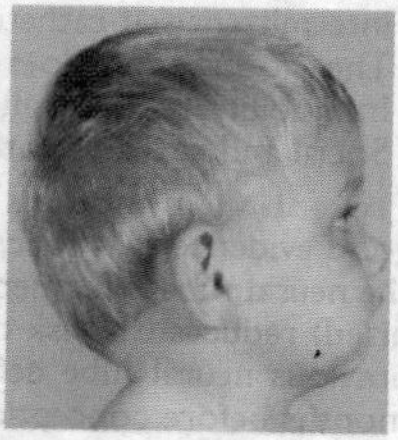

Fig 1. Plagiocephaly

Rachischisis: Congenital fissure of spinal column.

Sinciput: The anterior, upper part of the head.

Viscerocranium: Facial skeleton.

Wormian bones: Supernumerary bones in the sutures of the skull.

Neural tube defects

Myelodysplasia: Any neuroectoderm defect, eg of the cord, either multiple anterior horns, several central canals, failure of cord fusion so that there is a flat neural plaque, not a fused tube (*myelocele*), or a double neural tube (*diplomyelia*), or herniation through a bony defect as a *meningocele* (contains dura & arachnoid) or meningomyelocele (the cord is involved too). *Spina bifida* implies an incomplete vertebral arch (*spina bifida occulta* if covered by skin). *Anencephaly* implies absent skull vault and cerebral cortex. *Encephalocele* means that part of the brain protrudes through the skull.

UK prevalence 5.6/10,000 (half of what it was in 1990).[187] [n=934]
Risk increases with young primips, lower social class—and homozygosity for a point mutation (C677→T; prevalence ≈ 10%, interfering with folate metabolism). *Recurrence risk* rises 10-fold if one pregnancy is affected, 20-fold if 2, 40-fold if 3 pregnancies affected; and 30-fold if a parent is affected. See below for risk reduction.

Neurological deficit is very variable, depending on the level of the lesion, and the degree to which the lower cord functions independently from the upper cord. The defect may progress after birth (and after subsequent operations); subsequent hydrocephalus gradually worsens mental performance. A child who learns to walk during his 2nd year may outgrow his ability to support himself during the next years (weight increases as the cube of surface area, power only as its square). Those with lumbosacral myelomeningoceles usually learn to walk with callipers by the age of 3, but ≤20% with higher lesions ever walk. An unstable condition exists when there is paralysis below L3, as unopposed hip flexors and adductors are likely to dislocate the hips. Only 5-13% retain their ability to walk.[188] [n=173]

Postnatal surgery Firm guidelines on whom to treat often prove simplistic in individual infants. The final outcome of early closure of the defect depends on the state of the kidneys after multiple UTIs, and the extent of delayed hydrocephalus (requiring ventriculoperitoneal CSF shunts). Early post-operative mortality may account for ~25% of deaths. Many operations may be needed for spinal deformity (often severe and very hard to treat).

Intrauterine diagnosis A maternal serum α-fetoprotein >90U/mL at 18 weeks detects ~80% of open spina bifidas, and 90% of anencephalics, but also 3% of normal singleton fetuses, twins, and some with exomphalos, congenital nephrosis, urethral valves, Turner's syndrome, trisomy 13, and oligohydramnios. Amniocentesis and skilled ultrasound ↑pick-up rates further.

Intrauterine surgery (*eg at 23 weeks' gestation*) This is very controversial.

Hurdles for the developing child

- Urinary and faecal incontinence. Penile appliances, urinary diversions or intermittent self-catheterization save laundry and bed sores.
- The mother who 'does it all' can prevent maturity developing.
- Immobility. Mobility allowances are small and of little help.
- Social and sexual isolation, if a special school is needed.[189]

Prevention In mothers who have already had an affected baby, there is good evidence that folic acid (5mg/day) given from before conception (as the neural tube is formed by 28 days, before pregnancy may even be recognized) reduces the risk of recurrence of neural tube defects by 72%. If no previous neural tube defects, 0.4mg of folic acid is recommended in the months before conception and for 13 weeks after. See p 2.[190]

Many mothers don't take folate pre-conception, hence the call for folate-fortification of bread etc. This is adopted in the USA, but is not ideal, as pernicious anaemia may be masked.[191] [192] [193]

Measles, rubella, mumps, and erythroviruses

Measles Cause: RNA paramyxovirus. *Spread:* Droplets. *Incubation:* 7–21 days. *Infective:* from prodrome (catarrh, fever, conjunctivitis, cough) until 5 days after rash starts. Conjunctivae look glassy, then the periorbital folds swell. There's a light Koplik spots are pathognomonic (grain-of-salt-like spots on buccal mucosa). They are often faded as the rash appears (eg behind ears), spreading down the body, becoming confluent.

Complications: Febrile fits, otitis media, meningitis, D&V, keratoconjunctivitis, immunosuppression, subacute sclerosing panencephalitis, if immunosuppressed giant cell pneumonitis, intussusception, malformations. The worst complication is the encephalitis which starts [illegible] 15% mortality; 25% develop fits, deafness or ↓cognition. In the developing world, the death rate is 1:2000.

Treatment: Isolate—if hospitalized. The patient is it ordinarily compromised or malnourished, or has pneumonitis, CNS signs, or dehydration, treat:
- Ensure adequate nutrition. Each item is [illegible] high [illegible] including breastfeeding even during diarrhoea. [illegible] feeding is a [illegible] intake is poor.
- Frequent mouth washes with water [illegible] to prevent mouth lesions.
- In the developing world, dose for vitamin A: [illegible] consider 2 doses, a 1 more at 6 weeks later (to 4000 [illegible] prognosis [illegible] not to go deficient).
- Treat secondary bacterial infection, antibiotics such as amoxicillin for otitis media and pneumonia. Prophylactic antibiotics are used [illegible] note.

Immunization (p151). *Prognosis:* Mostly excellent in the rich world, but in poor areas death rate is ~10%; 0.9 million/yr, mostly in Africa.

Rubella (=German measles, german was a pathetic leucopenic virus (to) Cause: RNA virus. Incubation: 14–21 days. Infectivity: 5 days before to 5 days after the rash starts. Signs: Usually mild macular rash, suboccipital lymphadenopathy (*Treatment*): Symptomatic. Immunization: live virus, p151. Congenital defects: Small joint arthritis. Malformations in infants (p 35). Infection during the 1st 4 weeks: eye abnormalities in 70%; during weeks 5–8: cardiac abnormalities in 40%; weeks 9–12: deafness in 30%.

Mumps (RNA paramyxovirus) Spread: Droplets/saliva. *Incubation:* 14–21 days. *Immunity:* Lifelong once infected. *Infectivity:* 7 days before and 9 days after parotid swelling starts. Symptoms: Abdominal malaise, fever, pain. Parotid swelling, becoming bilateral in 70%. Differential: streptococcal, dengue, herpes virus, EBV, HIV, sarcoidosis, pneumococcal, haemophilus, stones, anaphylaxis, blowing glass or trumpets. *Complications:* Usually none; orchitis (→ infertility?), arthritis, meningitis, pancreatitis, myocarditis, deafness, myelitis. ℞: Rest. MMR vaccine p151 (not if immunocompromised or child [illegible]).

Erythrovirus (=parvovirus B19) This causes 'slapped cheek' syndrome, also known as fifth disease and erythema infectiosum. This is usually a mild, acute childhood infection, with malar erythema (a raised, red rash on the cheeks) and a rash mainly on the limbs. Constitutional upset is mild. Arthralgia is commoner in adults—who may present with a glandular fever-like illness and a false +ve Paul–Bunnell test. Spread is rapid in closed communities. It is also the cause of aplastic crises in sickle-cell disease. It is uncommon in pregnancy but risks fetal death in ~10% (esp. mid-trimester). It is also a cause of hydrops (results by inhibition of multiplication and lysis of erythroid progenitor cells) (monitor Hb for several weeks if it rises abnormally, do ultrasound). Fetal/neonatal problems do occur: hydrops (occurs in ~3% ?) treat by intrauterine transfusion if severe), growth retardation, meconium peritonitis, myocarditis/infarction, glomerulonephritis, hepatomegaly, splenomegaly, oedema, rashes, anaemia, platelets, WCC. Respiratory insufficiency and deaths are rare, 1:10 of those affected before 20 weeks will miscarry; in the rest, the overall risk of congenital abnormality is <1%.

Measles, rubella, mumps, and erythroviruses

Measles *Cause:* RNA paramyxovirus. *Spread:* Droplets. *Incubation:* 7-21 days. Infective from prodrome (catarrh, wretchedness, conjunctivitis, fever) until 5 days after rash starts. Conjunctivae look glassy; then the semilunar fold swells (Meyer's sign). *Koplik spots* are pathognomonic (grain-of-salt-like spots on buccal mucosa). They are often fading as the rash appears (eg behind ears, eg on days 3-5, spreading down the body, becoming confluent).

Complications: Febrile fits, otitis media, meningitis, D&V, keratoconjunctivitis; immunosuppression; subacute sclerosing panencephalitis, if immunosuppressed, giant cell pneumonitis. Intrauterine infection: malformations. The worst complication is the encephalitis (headache, lassitude, fits, coma)—up to 15% may die; 25% develop fits, deafness, or ↓cognition. In the under 2 year olds, the death rate is 1:7000.

Treatment: Isolate—in hospital, if the patient is ill or immunocompromised or malnourished, or has pneumonitis, CNS signs, or dehydration, then:
- Ensure adequate nutrition (catabolism is very high). Continue breastfeeding, even during diarrhoea. Pass a nasogastric feeding tube if intake is poor.
- Frequent mouth washes with water + 1% gentian violet to mouth lesions.
- In the developing world, need for vitamin A arises; consider 2 doses, + 1 more at 6 weeks later (p 450). CI: pregnancy; known not to be deficient.
- Treat secondary bacterial infection, antibiotics such as amoxicillin for otitis media and pneumonia. Prophylactic antibiotics have no clear role.[194]

Immunization: p 151. *Prognosis:* Mostly excellent in rich countries—but in poor areas death rate is ~10% (0.9 million/yr, mostly in Africa).[195]

Rubella (=german measles, german being *germane* ie closely akin to) *Cause:* RNA virus. *Incubation:* 14-21 days. *Infectivity:* 5 days before & 5 days after the rash starts. *Signs:* Usually mild; macular rash; suboccipital lymphadenopathy. *Treatment:* Symptomatic. *Immunization:* Live virus, p 151.[196] *Complications:* Small joint arthritis. Malformations *in utero* (p 34). Infection during the 1st 4 weeks: eye abnormalities in 70%; during weeks 4-8: cardiac abnormalities in 40%; weeks 8-12: deafness in 30%.

Mumps (RNA paramyxovirus) *Spread:* Droplets/saliva. *Incubation:* 14-21d. *Immunity:* Lifelong, once infected. *Infectivity:* 7 days before and 9 days after parotid swelling starts. *Symptoms:* Prodromal malaise; fever; painful parotid swelling, becoming bilateral in 70% (ΔΔ: Sjögren's; leukaemia; dengue; herpesvirus; EBV; HIV; sarcoidosis; pneumococci; haemophilus; staphs; anaphylaxis; blowing glass or trumpets; drugs).[197] [198] *Complications:* Usually none; orchitis (± infertility), arthritis, meningitis, pancreatitis, myocarditis, deafness, myelitis.[199] *℞:* Rest. *MMR vaccine:* p 151, for *any* non-immune adult or child.

Erythrovirus (=parvovirus) Type B19 causes 'slapped cheek' syndrome, also known as 'fifth disease' and erythema infectiosum. This is usually a mild, acute childhood infection, with malar erythema (a raised, fiery flush on the cheeks) and a rash mainly on the limbs. Constitutional upset is mild. Arthralgia is commoner in adults—who may present with a glandular fever-like illness and a false +ve Paul-Bunnell test.[200] Spread is rapid in closed communities. It is also the cause of aplastic crises in sickle-cell disease. It is uncommon in pregnancy but risks fetal death in ~10% (esp. midtrimester),[201] [n=136] and is a cause of hydrops fetalis by inhibition of multiplication and lysis of erythroid progenitor cells (monitor AFP, for several weeks; if it rises abnormally, do ultrasound). Fetal/neonatal problems *do* occur: hydrops (occurs in ~3%; treat by intrauterine transfusion if severe), growth retardation, meconium peritonitis, myocarditis/infarction, glomerulonephritis, placentomegaly, hepatomegaly, oedema, rashes, anaemia, platelets/WCC↓. Respiratory insufficiency and deaths are rare. ~1:10 of those affected before 20 weeks will miscarry; in the rest, the overall risk of congenital abnormality is ~1%.[202]

Hand, foot & mouth disease The child is mildly unwell; develops vesicles on palms, soles, and mouth. They may cause discomfort until they heal, without crusting. ***Incubation:*** 5–7 days. ***Treatment*** is symptomatic. ***Cause:*** Coxsackievirus A16 or enterovirus 71 (suspect in outbreaks with herpangina, meningitis, flaccid paralysis ± pulmonary oedema). Herpangina entails fever + sore throat + vesicles or macerated ulcers (on palate or uvula, which heal over 2 days) ± abdominal pain and nausea.[203]

Herpes infections See *OHCM* p 568.

Roseola infantum This is a common, mild, self-limiting illness in infants (usually <1yr old), causing fever and then a maculopapular rash on subsidence of fever at the end of the 4th febrile day. Uvulo-palatoglossal junctional (UPJ) ulcers may be a useful early sign.[204,205]

Cause: Herpes virus 6 (HHV6), a double-stranded DNA virus. It is morphogenetically related to other herpes viruses (HSV 1 & 2, varicella zoster virus, EBV & CMV). Interaction between host immunities and other viruses may lead to cellular immunodeficiency and fatal illness. *Synonyms:* exanthem subitum, fourth disease, 3-day fever. It is neurotropic (a rare cause of encephalitis/focal gliosis on MRI—maybe accounting for why the not uncommon roseola 'febrile' seizures tend to occur *after* the fever).[206,207]

Other causes of rashes in children See also *skin diseases* section (p 582).

- A transient maculopapular rash is a feature of many trivial viral illnesses (but a few macules may be a sign of early meningococcaemia).
- Purpuric rashes: meningococcaemia (p 202); Henoch-Schönlein purpura (p 197); idiopathic thrombocytopenic purpura (check FBC and film).
- Drug eruptions: maculopapular rashes in response to penicillins and to phenytoin are particularly common.
- Scabies (p 608); insect bites.
- Eczema (p 596); urticaria (p 584); psoriasis—guttate psoriasis may follow a respiratory tract infection in children (p 594); pityriasis rosea (p 602).
- Still's disease: transient maculopapular rash, fever, and polyarthritis.

Managing fever in viral illnesses

Paracetamol (acetaminophen) syrup (120mg/5mL) is for *high* fever or *pain*. ***6-hrly dose:*** <3 months: 5–10mg/kg (a loading dose of up to 30–40mg/kg PR may be tried); 3 months–1yr: 60–120mg; 1–5yrs: 120–250mg; 6–12yrs: 250–500mg. Ibuprofen 5mg/kg is also a good antipyretic (beware in asthma, cellulitis, or chicken pox).

Paracetamol suppositories are available (60mg). Also unwrap the child and rehydrate (this avoids vasoconstriction).

Do not assume that paracetamol is necessarily helpful. Meta-analyses are equivocal.[208] Usually antipyretics are *not* required, and there is evidence of increased mortality if used in severe sepsis.[209,210] Tepid sponging is a validated alternative or additional measure[211] (but cold water is unwise).

NB: Measles, rubella, and mumps are notifiable diseases in the UK. MMR vaccine: see p 151.

Varicella (herpes) zoster virus (VZV)

Chickenpox is a primary infection with varicella-zoster virus. Shingles (*OHCM* p 568) is a reactivation of dormant virus in posterior root ganglia.

Chickenpox ***Presentation:*** Crops of vesicles of different ages on the skin, typically starting on back. ***Incubation:*** 11–21 days. ***Infectivity:*** 4 days before the rash, until all lesions have scabbed (~1 week). ***Spread:*** Droplets. It can be caught from someone with shingles. It is one of the most infectious diseases known. 95% of adults have been infected; immunity is life-long.

Tests: Fluorescent antibody tests and Tzanck smears are rarely needed.

Differential: Hand, foot, and mouth disease; insect bites; scabies; rickettsia.

Course: Starts as fever. Rash starts 2 days later, often starting on the back: macule→papule→vesicle with a red-surround→ulcers (eg oral, vaginal) →crusting. 2–4 crops of lesions occur during the illness. Lesions cluster round areas of pressure or hyperaemia. ***Dangerous contexts:*** Immunosuppression; cystic fibrosis; severe eczema; neonates. ***Treatment:*** Keeping cool may reduce lesion numbers. Trim nails to lessen damage from scratching. Daily antiseptic for spots may be tried (chlorhexidine). Flucloxacillin 125–250mg/6h PO if bacterial superinfection—treat for septicaemia if deteriorating. Antivaricella-zoster immunoglobulin (12.5U/kg IM max 625U) + aciclovir if immunosuppressed or on steroids and within 10 days of exposure (as soon as possible). Aciclovir is licensed as a 7-day course in chickenpox; begin within 24h of the rash. *Aciclovir dose:* (20mg/kg/6h PO), eg <2yrs: 200mg/6h PO; 2–5yrs: 400mg/6h PO. ≥6yrs: 800mg/6h. Tablets are 200, 400, or 800mg; suspension: 200mg/5mL or 400mg/5mL. In renal failure, ↓ dose. There is *no* clear evidence on aciclovir ↓complications if immunocompetent, but it may help severe symptoms, eg in older patients, or 2nd or 3rd family contacts. If used, use at the first sign of infection—or as a 7-day *attenuating dose* of 10mg/kg/6h starting 1wk post-exposure. Famciclovir is less well studied.[212]

Complications: If spots are blackish (*purpura fulminans*) or are coalescing and bluish (necrotizing fasciitis), get urgent help on ITU.[213] Be alert to pneumonia, meningitis, myelitis, CNS thrombi, DIC, LFT↑, Guillain-Barré, Henoch-Schönlein, nephritis, pancreatitis, myositis, myocarditis, orchitis, and ataxia. If susceptible, ***live attenuated vaccine*** pre-cytotoxics/steroids may be wise.

Shingles ***Treatment:*** Oral analgesia. Ophthalmic shingles: p 420. Aciclovir may reduce progression of zoster in the immunocompromised (may be rampant, with pneumonitis, hepatitis, and meningoencephalitis). Aciclovir IVI dose: 10mg/kg/8h (over 1h), with concentration <10mg/mL.

Varicella in pregnancy Pneumonitis and encephalitis are no commoner in pregnancy, despite pregnancy being an immunocompromised state (1 in 400 and 1 in 1000, respectively). Infection in the 1st 20 weeks (esp. 13–20 weeks) causes varicella zoster virus (VZV) fetopathy 2%.[214] ***Signs of VZV fetopathy*** are variable, eg cerebral cortical atrophy and cerebellar hypoplasia, manifested by microcephaly, convulsions and IQ↓; limb hypoplasia; rudimentary digits ± pigmented scars. Maternal shingles is *not* a cause. If the mother is affected from 1 week before to 4 weeks after birth, babies may suffer severe chickenpox. Give the baby zoster immune globulin 250mg IM at birth; if affected, isolate from other babies, and give aciclovir.

Infection is preventable by pre-pregnancy vaccination with live varicella vaccine,[215] but testing for antibodies pre-conceptually is expensive, and cost-effectiveness depends on local rates of seronegativity. ~80% of those who cannot recall any previous chickenpox are, in fact, immune.[216]

Varicella zoster globulin prevents infection in 50% of susceptible contacts, eg 1000mg IM (adults). Infection in pregnancy merits aciclovir (it's probably OK for the fetus). Chickenpox at birth is a problem. Barrier nursing mothers causes distress and is of unproven value; infant mortality: up to 20%.[217]

Vertical HIV infection

Prenatal/labour: p 34/p 23, adult HIV: OHCM p 578

Worldwide 3 million children are living with HIV of whom ~600 live in the UK. 5 million infected children have died, and >13 million have been orphaned. In many sub-Saharan countries, ~40% of all under-5 mortality is a result of AIDS. If an HIV +ve mother breast feeds, this ↑risk of vertical transmission by ~50%. Risks and benefits of breastfeeding need explaining to mothers.[218] If reliable water is on tap, with sufficient formula feed (eg in the UK), then this may be preferable. Infection can occur from the 1st trimester; ~50% of infections occur around the time of delivery, and are more likely if mothers have symptomatic HIV infection or a high viral load. Transmission rates with full intervention (ie antiretrovirals around birth, Caesarean section, no breast-feeding) are <5%. In a cohort of 330 HIV +ve mothers, those with the p24 antigen had a 3-fold risk of transmission compared with those who were p24 –ve. For Caesarean section and zidovudine in preventing vertical transmission, see p 34. PCP (below) and CMV are potentially fatal in infants whose mother's HIV status wasn't recognized in pregnancy.[219]

Diagnosing vertically acquired HIV-1 *Don't use standard tests* (placentally transferred IgG lasts for ≤18 months). Virus culture & PCR are reliable, and more sensitive than finding p23 antigen in blood. HIV-specific IgA doesn't cross the placenta, but only occurs in 50% of infected infants <6 months old. Discuss with lab. ►*Aim to diagnose 95% of infected infants before the age of 1 month.* Monitoring CD4 counts (*OHCM* p 578) helps in staging HIV. The all clear can only be given if all tests are negative at 6 months.

Consider HIV in children with: PUO; lymphadenopathy; hepatosplenomegaly; persistent diarrhoea; parotid enlargement; shingles; rife molluscum; thrombocytopenia; recurrent slow-to-clear infections; failure to thrive; clubbing, unexplained organ disease;[220]—or known TB; pneumocystosis; toxoplasmosis; cryptococcosis; histoplasmosis; CMV; or LIP (below).

Lymphoid interstitial pneumonitis (LIP): Signs: tachypnoea; hypoxia; clubbing; diffuse reticulonodular infiltrates on CXR; bilateral hilar lymphadenopathy. It is not an AIDS-defining illness. It is 5-fold less serious than pneumocystosis.

Prognosis By 3yrs old, up to half with early-onset opportunistic infection have died, *vs* 3% of those with no such infection. Children with slow progression of HIV have persistent neutralizing antibodies. Transplacental passage of maternal neutralizing antibody may also have a role.

Guidelines for preventing *pneumocystosis* (PCP) with co-trimoxazole

Age/HIV status	*PCP prophylaxis*	*Do CD4 cell counts at:*
0–5wks, HIV exposed	No	1 month
5wks–4 months, HIV exposed	No	3 months
4–12 months: –HIV infected	Yes	6, 9, and 12 months
–Status unknown	Yes	6, 9, and 12 months
–No HIV infection	No	No monitoring needed
1–5yrs, HIV infected	Yes, if CD4 <500 per µL or CD4 percentage <15%	At least 3–4 monthly
6–12yrs, HIV infected	Yes, if CD4 <200 Per µL or CD4 percentage <15%	At least every 3–4 months

Ensure full course of vaccines (+*Pneumococcus*; avoid live vaccines if very immunocompromised, and BCG if symptomatic & TB prevalence is low).[221,222]

Highly active antiretroviral therapy[HAART] Use PENTA régime.[Pediatric European Network for the Treatment of AIDS] ([223] *OHCM* p 584) Those with AIDS defining conditions or CD4 <15% (esp. if falling) should start HAART at once. If few symptoms and CD4 stable at >20% consider deferring HAART.[224] ***Obstacles:*** Poor adherence (unpleasant tasting Pills); SE (lipids↑, glucose↑, bone metabolism↓); lack of family routines.[225] Teach HIV+ve children about safe sex and other HIV issues before puberty.

Non-accidental injury (NAI)

►Involve a consultant sooner rather than later when issues of abuse arise. This page should be read with your local child protection guidelines and the relevant legislation in your country, eg in England, the *Children's Act* (which states that *the child's welfare is paramount*). Abuse may be physical, sexual, emotional, or by neglect. (In ***Munchausen's by proxy***, a parent fabricates alarming symptoms in their child to gain attention via dangerous interventions.) ***Risk factors:*** Birth weight <2500g; mother <30yrs; unwanted pregnancy; stress; social class IV & V. ***Suspect abuse if:*** Disclosure by child, or:

- Odd story, lacking congruence with injuries
- Odd mode of injury[1]
- Late presentation, to an unknown doctor
- Odd constellation of signs
- The accompanying adult may not be a parent
- Parental financial problems
- History inconsistent with the child's development. Can the baby really walk?
- Efforts to avoid full examination, eg after an immersion burn.
- Psychological sequelae (stress; depression) from sexual or emotion abuse.
- Unexplained fractures; injury to buttocks, perineum or face; intracranial haemorrhage; torn lingual frenulum; vitreous/retinal bleeds, hyphaema (p 452), lens dislocation, bulging fontanelle, head circumference↑ ± xanthochromia; ►if in doubt, do CT. ***Other signs:*** Cigarette burns; linear whip marks (look for outline of a belt buckle, or the loop of a double electric flex); bruised *non-mobile* baby; signs of suffocation or finger-mark bruising.

Dangerous questions Although non-medical, these need addressing because we are not simply technicians following protocols, and they influence what we do, how we react to child abuse, and how society perceives our role.

- Could *proving* of abuse be more destructive than the abuse itself?[2] Note that even if the answer is yes, society places a duty on us to report abuse.
- Is it better for him to be loved and battered than neither?
- Is help from the extended family more desirable than the law? Is it possible that the parents can grow through crisis, as abuse is discussed, and help given?

Remember that the first aim is to prevent organ damage, murder, and other significant harm. If this is a real danger ►*contact the duty social worker today*—eg for an emergency protection order. Offer help to the parents. Learn to listen, leaving blame and punishment to judges. Find out about local policies and referral routes. Remember that often our duty is not to diagnose child abuse, but to recognize *possible* abuse, and then to get help.

Sexual abuse This may be prevented by teaching about 'personal safety' and how to say 'No'. Know your local guidelines. Follow them. Inform Social Services. If you do not, ask yourself with whom you are colluding. Forensic specimens (eg pubic hair, vaginal swabs) are to be taken by an expert who knows to be gentle, and to avoid a 'second rape'. Prepubertal venereal disease means abuse until proven otherwise. Does abuse cause psychological harm? Yes, usually, but the position is complex. See p 323.

Repertoire of actions in primary care ►After informing Social Services, liaise with health visitor (may be a very helpful source of information) or NSPCC (National Society for the Prevention of Cruelty to Children).

- Admission to a place of safety (eg hospital or foster home).
- Continuing support for parents and protection for siblings.
- Prevention: encourage impulses to be shared, and not acted on.
- Attend a case conference (social worker, health visitor, paediatrician; police).[3]

1 Look for injuries inconsistent with child's level of development. UK phone no. for adolescents in distress: ChildLine: 0800 884 444 validated in *Arch Dis Chi* 2000 **82** 283

2 K Hulme 1984 *Bone People*, Spiral. This novel tests Samuel Johnson's aphorism that 'it is better that a man should be abused than be forgotten'. Read it before making quick judgments about families.

3 Lord Laming's ***Climbié report*** recommends: • Always follow local guidelines. • At each contact record basic information such as school etc. • Know whom to contact as soon as abuse is suspected. • Confirm social services referrals in writing. • Question other's opinions if you disagree. • Document all phone-calls. • Record discussions if there is disagreement over risk of deliberate harm.

A possible sequence of events might be:

Unexplained signs (or disclosure, or allegations), eg odd bruising

↓

'Testing of professional hypotheses' ≈ weighing it up in your own mind

↓

'Clarification by discussion with an experienced colleague' ≈ tell your boss

↓

'Reach a critical threshold of professional concern' ≈ you're both worried

↓

'Weigh the pros and cons of breaking confidentiality' ≈ you must breach confidentiality if doing so prevents a serious crime against a child.

↓

'Sharing concerns with statutory agencies' ≈ phone Social Services/police

↓

'Act within a timeframe not detrimental to the child' ≈ aim to do it now

↓

'Contemporaneous records detailing all your sources',≈ write it down now

↓

'Preliminary consultation with all concerned': don't promise to keep secrets

↓

'Strategic multidisciplinary discussion' ≈ is an abuse investigation needed?

↓

'If so, 'Instigation of child abuse investigation'' ≈ plan case conference

↓

'Must parents/child be present?' ≈ bend the ear of the conference chairman

↓

Tell parents & child (if appropriate) what your report to conference will be

↓

Case conference timed to let doctors fulfil their major role ≈ ?get a locum

↓

Register your dissent (if any) to the conference conclusions in its minutes

↓

Child is placed on a Register indicating that questions of abuse are unresolved and that the child remains at risk

↓

'Establish networks for information exchange, discussion & advice' ≈ follow up by social services, or a national society protecting children from cruelty (NSPCC)

↓

Second (review) conference to weigh new evidence

↓

Death of a child

↓

Agencies must issue reports to the Area Child Protection Committee[UK]

↓

Judge issues life sentence (♂ breadwinner removed from family for ≥10yrs)

↓

No ♂ role model for siblings ≈ perpetuation of cycles of poverty and abuse

↓

Unexplained bruising in a member of the next generation

↓

*Man hands on misery to man**

Man hands on misery to man.
It deepens like a coastal shelf.
Get out as early as you can,
And don't have any kids yourself.

*Philip Larkin, *This Be The Verse*

Not all our efforts to protect children end thus. Successes are frequent. And of course this sequence oversimplifies...the sign ≈ is not meant flippantly: it is intended as a short-hand, denoting the exercise of reflection, good judgment, action, and following agreed procedures.

Sudden infant death syndrome (SIDS)

This page should be read with the 2005 Royal College of Paediatrics guidance.[226]

Definition 'Sudden death of an infant under 1 year of age, which is unexpected after a thorough case investigation, including a complete autopsy, examination of the death scene, and review of the clinical history.' ►SIDS is the leading 'cause' of death in infants aged over 1 week old.

Epidemiology ***Peak incidence:*** 1–4 months; ***Risk:*** Lower socio-economic classes, passive smokers, males, premature babies, winter, previous sibling affected by SIDS; co-existing minor upper respiratory infection is common, co-sleeping. There are many theories as to the cause.[227, 228]

> **Putative causes:**
>
> ***Obstructive apnoea:***
> - Inhalation of milk
> - Airways oedema
> - Passive smoking
>
> ***Central apnoea:***
> - Faulty CO_2 drive
> - Prematurity
> - Brainstem gliosis
>
> ***Others:***
> - Long Q–T interval[1]
> - Staph infection[2]
> - Overheating
> - ↑Vagal tone or Mg^{2+}↑
> - Immature diaphragm
> - Genetic & viral causes

Sleeping supine ('back to sleep'), preventing overheating, and cigarette smoke exposure are the main areas for intervention/prevention: risk from passive smoking is dose-dependent, and often at least doubles risk.[229]

The face is an important platform for heat loss—and it is known that the incidence of SIDS is ~5–10-fold higher among infants usually sleeping prone (17-fold higher if sleeping in a room separated from parents): ►so always recommend sleeping supine. Advise as follows:

- Do not overheat the baby's bedroom. Aim for a temperature of 16–20°C.
- Do not use too much bedding, and avoid duvets if less than 1 year of age.
- If ill or feverish, consult a GP—do not increase the amount of bedding.
- Have feet come down to the cot's end to avoid under-blankets migration.
- While sleeping, avoid heaters, hot water bottles, electric blankets, and hats. Do wrap up if going out in winter, but remember to unwrap once back indoors, even if this means disturbing the baby.
- Babies >1 month do not need to be kept as warm as in hospital nurseries.
- Avoid co-sleeping if possible and never, ever if very tired (new parents!), if parents are deep sleepers, or if they have had any alcohol or drugs.

Autopsy is unrevealing; minor changes are common; petechial haemorrhages over pleura, pericardium, or thymus, and vomit in the trachea may be agonal events. *Causes to exclude:* sepsis, metabolic defects (eg MCAD deficiency; medium-chain acyl-CoA dehydrogenase↓); heart defects; and always bear in mind the possibility of murder.

Action after failed resuscitation in the Emergency Department

- Document all interventions, venepuncture sites, and any marks on the baby. You don't have to keep all tubes *in situ*, but ensure that someone who did not intubate confirms endotracheal placement of the tube before extubation.
- Take samples of blood for culture, CSF for culture/PCR, urine, and stool.
- Keep all clothing and the nappy.
- Explain clearly to parents that despite your best efforts, the baby has died.
- Unless the cause is obvious, be non-committal about cause of death. Explain the baby *must* have a post mortem (this is a coroner's case).
- Contact the consultant on call, the police child protection team, and the coroner at once; also GP, health visitor, and any other involved professions.

How the GP can help the family on the first day

- A prompt visit to express sympathy emphasizing that no one is to blame.
- Explain about the legal requirement for an autopsy and coroner's inquest. The parents may be called upon to identify the body.
- Bedding may be needed to help find the cause of death.

1 Risk↑ if Q-T corrected for rate (QT^c) ≥440msec; NB: $QT^c = (Q\text{-}T)/(\sqrt{R\text{-}R})$
2 Staphs in mattress foam are implicated (∴ do not reuse); Jenkins 2005

Subsequent help[1]

Don't *automatically* suppress lactation, but if this becomes necessary cabergoline (250μg/12h PO for 48h) is preferred to bromocriptine. NB: continued lactation may be an important way of grieving for some mothers. Many parents will not want anxiolytics, but may want hypnotics.
Admit a twin sibling to hospital (their risk is increased).
Advise the parents of likely grief reactions (guilt, anger, loss of appetite, hearing the baby cry). Make sure that the coroner informs you of the autopsy result; take some trouble to explain these to the parents. They should already have a routine appointment with a consultant paediatrician. This can provide helpful reinforcement and encouragement to the parents and yourself. The parents may find an electronic apnoea alarm reassuring in caring for later infants. Ask if they would like to join a self-help group. Programmes exist to prevent a future SID—eg the CONI programme (care of next infant).

1 UK Cot Death Helpline (24h) 0845 601 0234; 14 Halkin St, London SW1

Screening and child health promotion

The main aims: • Encouraging breastfeeding (p 124) • Monitoring development • Immunization • Overseeing growth (p 180) • Parental support • Education and reassurance about normal childhood events. • Talking to the child, and building up a good relationship to be used in later illnesses.

Monitoring The most cost-effective times to screen are unknown. A *best buy* might be checks after birth (p 114), at 4–6 weeks; arrange vaccinations and DoH vitamin drops (A, D & C, unless sure that diet/sunlight is adequate), then:

6–9 months: Hips, testes descent, CVS examination.
18–24 months: *Educate* on diet, dental care, accidents; *walking* (look for waddling), social and linguistic *milestones*; Hb if *iron deficiency* likely—it may well be. *Any parental depression?*
4 years: Testes descent, CVS examination. Nutrition, dental care.

At each visit: • Encourage airing of queries • Ask about, and test for, squint, vision and deafness • Chart centiles. *Beware reading too much into a single test.* See Denver developmental test, p 218. Remember to correct age for prematurity. Note the milestones below. There is much individual variation.

1 month: Lifts head when prone; responds to bell; regards face.
2 months: Holds head at 45° when prone; vocalizes; smiles.
4 months: Uses arm support when prone; holds head steady when supported while sitting; reaches out; spontaneous smiling.
6 months: Bears some weight on legs; on pulling to sitting, there is no head lag; reaching out; transfers things from hand to hand.
≥1 year: Just stands; walks using a table's support; clashes cubes; pincer grip; can say 'Mummy' ± 'Daddy'. Plays 'pat a cake'.

18 months: Can walk backwards; scribbles; 2-cube tower. 2–4 words. Recognizes/shows interest in TV images, eg of a dog. NB: drooling ± throwing items on the floor is abnormal by now.
2 years: Kicks a ball; overarm 'bowling'; gets undressed.
3 years: Jumps; can stand on one foot; copies; can build an 8-cube tower; knows his first and last name; dressing needs help.
4 years: Stands on 1 foot for >4sec; picks the longer of 2 lines.

Health promotion in refugee children/asylum-seekers Unaccompanied children may request asylum explicitly or implicitly. Our job is to look after them not to interpret laws. Tell immigration officers/police that such children cannot be detained even if there is doubt about a child's age. UK immigration officers must abide by the UN convention on the Rights of the Child (1989). This stipulates that each State must ensure the rights of each child within its jurisdiction *without discrimination of any kind*. Any child who has been tortured has the right to physical and psychological recovery and social integration. (Prison is not a form of social integration.) Take any opportunity to promote children's health. If from areas of chronic conflict, do not assume the child has been vaccinated. Start from scratch. Test for TB (skin test) and give BCG, or refer to a chest clinic if needed. See Home Office[230] & Royal College Guidelines.[231] Paediatricians and GPs can promote refugee health by:

- Documenting development, ensuring nutrition and treating physical illness.
- Easing access to antenatal and all other preventive care activities.
- Identifying depression/anxiety, and picking up clues that torture may have taken place: nightmares; hallucinations; panic attacks; sexual problems; phobias; difficulties with relationships. These may also be signs that the child has been recruited to fight other people's wars. Treating childhood depression is controversial (SSRI, p 390) *but not treating it may be worse*.[232]
- Recognizing and treating TB and HIV (eg if vertically transmitted, look for persistent oral candida, caries, UTIs, widespread lymphadenopathy, hepatosplenomegaly; failure to thrive; developmental delay). See p 145.
- Liaising with social services to ensure housing and schooling.

Vaccination schedules

►An acute febrile illness is a contraindication to any vaccine. Note: Give live vaccines either together, or separated by ≥3 weeks.
Don't give live vaccines if primary immunodeficiency, or if on steroids (≥2mg/kg/day of prednisolone); but if HIV+ve, give all immunizations (including live) except for BCG, in areas where TB prevalence is low.

Age:	*Immunization:* L=live; MCC=meningititis C conjugate vaccine
3 days	*BCG*[L] (if TB in family in last 6 months or the family comes from area of high TB prevalence); avoid in some immunodeficiencies.
2, 3, & 4 months	*MCC* (meningitis C) + 5-in-1 *DTaP/IPV/HIB* as Pediacel®, ie diphtheria+tetanus+acellular pertussis+inactivated polio+haemophilus b (*HIB*); if prem, still give at 2 mths; can give if ≤10 yrs if missed vacs.
~13 mths	*MMR* 1st dose (Measles/Mumps/Rubella[L] 0.5mL SC).
3¼–5yrs	*DTAP/IPV* Diphtheria, tetanus acellular pertussis, inactivated polio eg as Repevax®; *MMR* dose 2.
10–14yrs	*BCG*[L] (if skin test shows that it is needed, ie tuberculin –ve)
13–18+yrs	*Td/IPV* (low-dose diphtheria, tetanus, inactivated polio eg as Revaxis®); can also be used for primary vaccination if >10yrs. *MCC* if unvaccinated and aged between 15 and ~24yrs.
Any age	One-off ***23-valent pnueumococcal vaccine*** + yearly ***'flu vaccine*** if chronic heart, chest, or renal disease; DM; immunosuppression (eg HIV +ve, cirrhosis, on chemotherapy, or spleen function↓, eg related to coeliac or sickle cell diseases). Consider a 2nd pneumococcal vaccine if at ↑risk after >5yrs.[233] Some recommend 3 doses of pneumococcal *conjugate* vaccine if HIV+ve (separated by 2mths, if <2yrs old).[234] [235]
Adults	*Td/IPV* boosters (see above). Travellers: *OHCM* p 558.

***Hepatitis B** (Engerix B®):* Give at birth, 1 & 2 months, if mother is HBsAg +ve 0.5mL IM via anterolateral thigh (adult dose: 1mL via deltoid; 1st dose with 200U hepatitis B immunoglobulin at a different IM site, eg if high risk or e antibody –ve or e status unknown). *Other risk groups: OHCM* p 242.

Chickenpox vaccination: In the USA this is routine. Whether it is worth doing depends on local rates of transmission—declining in the UK (2004 data);[236] also, there is a high-ish level of population immunity. So the benefits of universal vaccination might not be great.

Immunization in immunodeficiencies: See Royal College Guidelines.

Can the pain of the injection be reduced? Topical lidocaine-prilocaine 5% cream (EMLA®) and oral glucose at the time of vaccination does decrease the latency to 1st cry, and other objective markers of pain.[237]

MMR is not just for children: In the UK, in 2005, mumps rates briefly rose 10-fold (to 5000/month), eg among students who were too old to have had full vaccination. Any non-immune adult is eligible for MMR (exclude pregnancy). If >18 months, the 2 doses of MMR should be seperated by 3 months. MMR vaccine may also be offered to unimmunized or measles-only immunized, or seronegative post-partum women. ***Does MMR vaccine cause autism?*** Since 1997 when a study found 12 children who had both autism and measles virus in the gut, this has been a controversy. Large-scale studies find no link. The original research is discredited (monetary conflict of interest, and a skewed sample base). The *Lancet* has withdrawn the paper. Some parents prefer single M, M, and R injections, but the rationale is unclear.

Genetic disease and prevention

►It is more important to be able to love the handicapped and to respect their carers than it is to prevent the handicap; in doing the first we become more human. In the second, do we risk our own inappropriate deification?

Gene probes use recombinant DNA technology to link genetic diseases of unknown cause to DNA markers scattered throughout our genome. Using fetal DNA from amniotic fluid cells (amniocentesis) in the 2nd trimester, or from chorionic villus sampling in the 1st, it is possible to screen for many genetic diseases (OPPOSITE)—eg Huntington's chorea; muscular dystrophy; polycystic kidneys; cystic fibrosis; thalassaemias.

Enzyme defects Many of the inborn errors of metabolism can be diagnosed by incubation of fetal tissue with a specific substrate.

Chromosomal studies can be undertaken on cultured cells or on direct villus preparations. The most important abnormalities are aneuploidies (abnormalities in chromosome number)—eg trisomy 21, 18, and 13. Screening for chromosomal abnormalities (eg the fragile X syndrome, p 648) may be performed on at-risk mothers who may be carriers.

Nondisjunction After meiosis one gamete contains two number 21 (say) chromosomes[1] and the other gamete has no 21 chromosome. After union of the first gamete with a normal gamete the conceptus has trisomy 21, and develops Down's syndrome (but 50% of these will spontaneously abort). This is the cause in ≥88% of Down's babies, and is related to maternal age (the mechanism is unknown). ***Risk at 20yrs:*** 1 in 2000; ***30yrs:*** 1 in 900; ***35yrs:*** 1 in 365; ***40yrs:*** 1 in 110; ***45yrs:*** 1 in 30; ***47yrs:*** 1 in 20.[238, 239]

Swapping chromosomal fragments Cells contain the correct amount of genetic material (a balanced translocation); but any gamete cell may have one intact chromosome (say number 21), and another mixed chromosome (say number 14), which, because of the swap, contains material from chromosome 21. After union with a normal gamete, cells have 3 parts of chromosome 21. This translocation trisomy 21 is the cause in 4% of Down's syndrome (unrelated to maternal age). If the father carries the translocation, risk of Down's is 10%; if it is the mother, the risk is 50%. 0.3% of mothers have this translocation.

Mosaicism A trisomy may develop during early divisions of a normal conceptus. If the proportion of trisomy 21 cells is low (eg 4%) cognitive development may be normal. It accounts for ≤8% of Down's babies.[240]

Other chromosomal abnormalities Turner's (p 655), Klinefelter's (p 646), Edward's (p 642), and Patau's (p 650) syndromes. In the *cri-du-chat* syndrome there is deletion of the short arm of chromosome 5, causing a high-pitched cry, CVS abnormalities, microcephaly, widely spaced eyes, and a 'moon' face.

Down's syndrome ***Causes:*** See above. ***Recognition at birth:*** Flat facial profile, abundant neck skin, dysplastic ears, muscle hypotonia, and x-ray evidence of a dysplastic pelvis are the most constant features. Other features: a round head, protruding tongue, peripheral silver iris spots (Brushfield's), blunt inner eye angle, short, broad hands (eg with a single palmar crease), and an incurving 5th digit. Widely spaced 1st & 2nd toes and a high-arched palate are more visible later. If uncertain, it is best to ask an expert's help, rather than baffle the mother by taking karyotype tests "just in case it's Down's".[2] ***Associated problems:*** Duodenal atresia; VSD; patent ductus; AVSD (foramen primum defects, p 136); and, later, a low IQ and a small stature. Helping the mother accept her (often very lovable) child may be aided by introducing her to a friendly mother of a baby with Down's syndrome. ***Prenatal diagnosis:*** p 10–12.

1 Chromosome 21 contains only 225 genes: most of its DNA is apparently meaningless.
2 Even in good hands, accuracy of suspicion is only 64%, so at some stage karyotyping is needed.

Ways of looking at genetic diseases such as Down's syndrome

The swot's approach: Learn the clinical manifestations—it might be asked in an exam. In the case of Down's syndrome, this person will focus on features such as a simian palmar crease, hypotonia, flat face, upward slanted palpebral fissures and epicanthic folds, speckled irises (Brushfield spots); mental and growth retardation; pelvic dysplasia, cardiac malformations, short, broad hands, hypoplasia of middle phalanx of 5th finger, intestinal atresia, and high arched palate. Associations learned about: 241

- Lung problems (lung capacity is reduced in almost 100%)
- Hearing loss (60%)
- Congenital heart disease (40%)
- Digestive problems 6%
- Leukaemia

44% survive to age 60 yrs. 50% of adult survivors develop Alzheimer's.

The problem with this approach is that it does not make us good doctors because it is not much help to people and their families.

The dangerous young idealist: Down's syndrome is preventable. The focus should be on prenatal diagnosis and termination of affected fetuses. Down's cases are unfortunate. These patients are a burden to the State (someone might argue). Their claims on scarce health resources are burdensome. Normal people should take priority. The problem with this approach is that there are no genetically normal people. This purist has engaged in too much abstract thought: and as Dostoyevsky has taught us: 'too much abstract thought makes men cruel'. (Crime & Punishment)

The health needs approach: This approach starts by asking: How can I help? Health maintenance for Down's children is more important, not less, compared with the needs of other children—because their families are vulnerable, and many conditions are more likely in those with Down's. Examples are: otitis media, thyroid disease, congenital cataracts, leukaemoid reactions, dental problems, and feeding difficulties. 242

The patient-centred approach: Let's go down to the farm and milk the cow. Let's see how muddy we can get…

Different approaches are needed at different times: a key skill in becoming a good doctor is to be able to move seamlessly from one approach to another—and knowing when to adopt which approach.

The American College of Medical Genetics screens for:

Organic acid disorders:
β-ketohiolase deficiency
Glutaric acidaemia type 1
Hydroxymethylglutaric acidaemia
Isovaleric acidaemia
3-methylcrotonyl-CoA carboxylase deficiency
Methylymelonic acidaemia
Multiple carboxylate deficiency
Propionic acidaemia

Fatty acid disorders:
Carnite untake defect
Long-chain hydroxyacyl-CoA dehydrogenase lack
Medium-chain acyl-CoA dehydrogenase deficiency
Trifunctional protein deficiency
Very-long-chain acyl-CoA dehydrogenase deficiency

Haemoglobin disorders
Hb S/b-thalassaemia
Hb S/C disease
Sickle-cell anaemia

Amino acid disorders:
Arginosuccinic adidaemia
Citrullaemia
Homocysteinuria
Maple syrup urine disease
Phenylketonuria
Tyrosinaemia type 1

Other congenital diseases:
Biotinidase deficiency
Adrenal hyperplasia
Hypothyroidism
Cystic fibrosis
Galactosaemia
Hearing disorders

The great question is: just because a disease can be screened for, should it be screened for? Answer: only if the Wilson criteria are met: see p 487.

Genetic counselling

Goal To provide accurate, up-to-date information on genetic conditions to enable families and patients to make informed decisions.

►Genetic counselling is best done in regional centres to which you should refer families. (nearest centre: UK tel.:020 7794 0500) *Don't do blood tests on children lightly which might have long-term consequences, unless some form of treatment is available. The child may never forgive you for labelling him or her.*

In order to receive most benefit from referral:

- The affected person (proband) ideally comes with family (spouse, parents, children, siblings); individuals can of course be seen alone as well.
- The family should be informed that a detailed pedigree (family tree) will be made, and medical details of distant relatives may be asked for.
- Irrational emotions (guilt, blame, anger) are common. Deal with these sensitively, and do not ignore. *Remember:* you do not choose your ancestors, and you cannot control what you pass on to your descendants.
- Warn patients that most tests give no absolute 'yes' or 'no' but merely 'likely' or 'unlikely'. In gene tracking, where a molecular fragment near the gene is followed through successive family members, the degree of certainty of the answer will depend on the distance between the marker and the gene (as crossing-over in meiosis may separate them).
- Accept that some people will not want testing, eg the offspring of a Huntington's chorea sufferer—or a mother of a boy who might have fragile X syndrome, but who understandably does not want her offspring labelled (employment, insurance, and social reasons). Offer a genetic referral to ensure that her decision is fully informed (but remember: 'being fully informed' may itself be deleterious to health and wellbeing).

Naming chromosomes Autosomes are numbered 1 to 22 roughly in order of size, 1 being the largest. The arms on each side of the centromere are named 'p' (petite) for the short arm, and 'q' for the long arm (there's always a long Q for a short P). Thus 'the long arm of chromosome 6' is written '6q'.

Chromosomal disorders include Down's (trisomy 21, p 152), Turner's (45,X0, p 655) and Klinefelter's (47,XXY, p 646) syndromes. Many genes are involved when the defect is large enough to be seen microscopically.

Autosomal-dominants Adult polycystic kidney (16p), Huntington's chorea, (4p). A single copy of a defective gene causes damage. Some people inheriting the defective gene are phenotypically normal (=*reduced penetrance*).

Autosomal recessives Infantile polycystic kidney; cystic fibrosis (7q), β-thalassaemia, sickle cell (11p), most metabolic conditions, and almost all which are fatal in childhood. In general, both genes must be defective before damage is seen, so carriers are common. Both parents must be carriers for offspring to be affected, so consanguinity (marrying relatives) increases risk.

X-linked Duchenne muscular dystrophy, p 642; Haemophilia A & B; fragile X (p 648). In female (XX) carriers a normal gene on the 2nd X chromosome prevents bad effects manifesting. Males (XY) have no such protection.

NB: being pregnant and unwilling to consider termination does *not* exclude one from undergoing useful genetic counselling.

'Couple screening' A big problem with counselling is the unnecessary alarm caused by false +ve tests. In cystic fibrosis screening (analysis of cells in mouthwash samples) this is reducible by 97% (0.08% *vs* 3.2%) by screening mother and father together—who need only get alarmed if they *both* turn out to be screen-positive. The trouble with this is false reassurance. Many forget that they will need future tests if they have a different partner, and those who do not are left with some lingering anxieties.

Genetic counsellors to try to influence pregnancy out-come?

Three contrasting principles:

1) The parents must decide: counselling must be nondirective.
2) Every newborn child has the right to be born healthy, if possible.
3) Every child has a right to be born.

Nondirective counselling is something of a mantra among counsellors, partly as a reaction to Nazi eugenic excesses, and partly because of an unwillingness to promulgate a single view of what is right in what can be a very complex area. Public health doctors are questioning this obedience to the nondirective ethic because, from their point of view, it makes attainment of their chief goal more difficult—namely to improve the health and well-being of all residents, including newborns. For example, we should tell pregnant women not to drink much alcohol, public health doctors assert, because this is necessary to prevent the fetal alcohol syndrome. The same goes for other syndromes. When we know what to do we should state clearly and unequivocally what the mother should do. This is our duty to her and her unborn child.

Let us examine the public health doctor's stand point more closely. He wants to improve health. To do this, it is necessary to define health. We have done this elsewhere (p 470) and have argued that health entails more than just soundness of body and mind. It is not clear that an autocratic society in which patients were told what to do would be more healthy than a society of autonomous individuals each addressing the great questions of health and existence from his or her own view point.

Another problem for the public health doctors is that, in the case above, it is not clear whether the directive 'don't drink if you are pregnant' would lead to fewer children with the fetal alcohol syndrome. It might lead to more orphans (a mother knows she is doing wrong, feels guilty, avoids health professionals, and dies of some unforeseen consequence of pregnancy, or from guilt-borne suicide).[243]

As ever, the way forward is not by abstract thought but by getting to know our patients better. There may be rare occasions when we know our patients well enough to risk 'You are mad not to follow this advice...' But mostly we cannot be sure that this injunction will work, and it is wiser to explore the patient's world view and their expectations, and then use this knowledge to reframe the benefits of our proposed action in a way that makes sense to the individual concerned taking into account his or her culture and system of beliefs.

In the UK, the Children's Act states that the welfare of the child is paramount. What this means in the context of a family is open to interpretation.

GMC GOOD DOCTOR TOPIC: PATIENT-CENTRED CARE

Preventing adult diseases—*starting in childhood*

Childhood obesity is rising fast in the West[1]: half the children born in the UK will soon be obese—by the time they are 10[244]—with inevitable consequences for heart disease and cancer. It is known for example that there is a higher prevalence of colorectal cancer in men who were overweight during adolescence. Similar effects are seen for cancers of the endometrium, kidney, gall-bladder, and breast.[245] *Consequences vis à vis insulin resistance:* >30% of obese children have insulin resistance (detailed on p 252),[2] and ~25% of *all* adolescents have 3 or more features of the metabolic syndrome X: obesity, hypertension, dyslipidaemia, and poor glycaemic control.[246] ►Risk factors for adult heart disease and DM begin to cluster in 'normal' children.[247] Primary prevention needs to start in childhood. Hence the importance of recognizing small differences from normal in apparently health children. See BP table below, and p 226 for centile BMI charts defining obesity by age. But do not focus exclusively on weight. Insulin resistance starts before the teenage years—and may occur in children of near-normal weight.[248] ***UK incidence of type 2 DM in children:*** 0.2/100,000[249] (↑×13 if Asian). ***When to start prevention?*** It is never too early (obesity can start with bottle-feeding)[250]—and it's often too late. Re-educate parents, teachers, and children; encourage exercise—and less: • Fast foods[251] • Soft drinks[252] • TV[253] • Sun-bathing (melanoma).[254]

We assume that growth and development somewhere in the middle of our centile charts is optimal. But these charts are not goals—they are statements of heights and weights for particular historical populations. Now population weights are moving up, what appears normal to parents (and us) may in fact be detrimental. For example, in Plymouth, in the UK, mean weights of toddlers are now 460g heavier than the historic reference population.[255]

Age	*Significant hypertension*		*Severe hypertension*	
(*Years*)	*Systolic* mmHg	*Diastolic* mmHg	*Systolic* mmHg	*Diastolic* mmHg
At birth	≥96mmHg[3]		≥106mmHg[3]	
<2	≥112	≥74 k4	≥118	≥82 k4
3–5	≥116	≥76 k4	≥124	≥84 k4
6–9	≥122	≥78 k4	≥130	≥86 k4
10–12	≥126	≥82 k4	≥134	≥90 k4
13–15	≥136	≥86 k5	≥144	≥92 k5
16–18	≥142	≥92 k5	≥150	≥98 k5

Take ≥3 BPs (snugly fitted cuff of bladder-width >75% of upper arm length) >1 week apart (in general) before diagnosing hypertension. As the 5th Korotkoff sound (*k5*) is inaudible, use ***k4*** for diastolic BPs, until adolescence. Some BP standards break populations by age, sex, and height, but this doesn't greatly change hypertension prevalence.[256,257]

Ambulatory BPs can show that white coat hypertension is about as common in children as in adults.[258,259] But beware automated devices: mercury sphygmomanometers are more accurate, and are of negligible risk to health.

Causes of ↑BP—neonates: Renal artery stenosis (or thrombosis), congenital renal malformations, coarctation of the aorta, bronchopulmonary dysplasia.
Infants: Renal parenchymal disease, coarctation, renal artery stenosis.
6–10yrs olds: Renal artery stenosis, renal diseases, primary hypertension.
Adolescence: Primary hypertension, renal diseases, syndrome X.

1 Health Survey 2005; >25% are currently overweight/obese. **2** Viner R 2005 *Arch Dis Child* **90** 10
Correlates of 'normal children' in the top quintile of postprandial glucose (7.4–11.4mmol/L):
- Lower vasodilatation to acetylcholine (Ach, P <0.005) and sodium nitroprusside (SNP, P <0.02) than those in the lower quintile (3.9–4.9mmol/L).
- ↑Waist-to-hip ratio and ↑fasting insulin resistance.
- ↑Fasting triglycerides & cholesterol (r=0.4, P <0.05). **MODY**=maturity onset diabetes of the young.

3 Doppler may be needed. Often only systolic BPs are recordable. Values need adjusting if taller or shorter than expected for age (tables are available); compared with a 50th height-centile the reference interval is 1–4mmHg lower for a child on the 5th height-centile (1–4mmHg higher if on 95th centile).

Upper respiratory infection

Stridor and epiglottitis Acute stridor may be a terrifying experience for children; this fear may lead to hyperventilation, which worsens symptoms. Causes: p 565. The leading causes to be distinguished are viral croup and epiglottitis (rare in the UK since haemophilus vaccination; see BOX).

Investigations This is a clinical diagnosis. Lateral neck x-ray may show an enlarged epiglottis, but this wastes time at a dangerous and critical time.

Croup (Acute laryngotracheobronchitis) Epidemics: Autumn and spring. Causes: Parainfluenza virus (types 1, 2, 3), respiratory syncytial virus, measles (rare). Pathology: Subglottic oedema, inflammation, and exudate.

Management of croup Mostly at home; ask parents to watch for respiratory rate, fatigue, and restlessness. Anecdotal (but not observed) evidence says that a warm, humid environment is helpful, but mist tents have lost favour as they frighten children, and subsequent hyperventilation worsens distress. In hospital, aim for minimal interference and careful observation (TPR, SaO_2) by experienced nurses. Watch for restlessness, rising pulse and respiratory rate. Pulse oximetry will indicate fatigue/drowsiness. Remember that the volume of the stridor is a factor of flow, lessening as the disease progresses. This will prompt intubation under general anaesthesia. Other nebulized drugs: adrenaline 1:1000 (one dose of 5mL). Nebulized budesonide also helps: loading dose 2mg, then 1mg/12h eg as Pulmicort Respules®. Dexamethasone 0.15mg/kg (orally or injected) is equally effective and cheaper.

Management of suspected epiglottitis Avoid examining the throat. This may precipitate obstruction. Do not distress the patient or upset him. Once in hospital, summon the most experienced anaesthetist. Ask him to make the diagnosis by laryngoscopy. If the appearances are those of epiglottitis (a cherry-red, swollen epiglottis), electively intubate before obstruction occurs. (A smaller diameter endotracheal tube than normal for that age may be needed—so don't present as routine.) Then do blood cultures. The cause is usually Haemophilus influenzae type b, and strains resistant to ampicillin (and less so chloramphenicol) are prevalent, so the only safe initial treatment is a 3rd generation cephalosporin eg cefotaxime 25-50mg/kg/6h IV (the adult dose is 1-2g/8h IV). Hydrocortisone (1-2mg/kg/6h IV) is often given, but is not of proven value. Expect to extubate after about 24h (longer if the diagnosis turns out to be a staph laryngotracheobronchitis, much more common), when rifampicin 20mg/kg/24h PO should also be given.

Diphtheria is caused by the toxin of *Corynebacterium diphtheriae*. It usually starts with tonsillitis ± a false membrane over the fauces. The toxin may cause polyneuritis, often starting with cranial nerves. Shock may occur from myocarditis, toxaemia, or involvement of the heart's conducting system. Other signs: dysphagia; muffled voice; bloody nasal discharge; airway obstruction preceded by a brassy cough (laryngotracheal diphtheria); nasal discharge with an excoriated upper lip (nasal diphtheria). If there is tachycardia out of proportion to fever, suspect a toxin-induced myocarditis. Monitor with frequent ECGs. Motor palatal paralysis also occurs.

Diagnosis: Swab; culture of material below pseudomembrane; PCR.

Treatment: Diphtheria antitoxin 10,000–30,000U IM (any age; more if severe) and erythromycin; give contacts 7 days' erythromycin syrup (>2yrs old 125mg/6h PO) before the swab results are known.

Prevention: Isolate until 3 −ve cultures separated by 48h. Vaccinate (p151). There is a resurgence of diphtheria in the former USSR, especially among those born in the lull before 1947 when vaccination started.

Upper respiratory infection (URTI: *OHCM* p 545; sore throat: p 564)

Stridor and epiglottitis ►►Acute stridor may be a terrifying experience for children; this fear may lead to hyperventilation, which worsens symptoms. Causes: p 566. The leading causes to be distinguished are viral croup and epiglottitis (rare in the UK since haemophilus vaccination): see BOX.

Investigations: This is a clinical diagnosis. Lateral neck x-ray may show an enlarged epiglottis, but this wastes time at a dangerous and critical time.

Croup (Acute laryngotracheobronchitis) *Epidemics:* Autumn and spring. *Causes:* Parainfluenza virus (types 1, 2, 3), respiratory syncytial virus, measles (rare). Pathology: subglottic oedema, inflammation, and exudate.

Management of croup: Mostly at home; ask parents to watch for respiratory rate, fatigue, and restlessness. Anecdotal (but not research) evidence says that a warm, humid environment is helpful, but mist tents have lost favour as they frighten children, and subsequent hyperventilation worsens distress. In hospital, aim for minimal interference and careful observation (TPR; S_AO_2) by experienced nurses. Watch for restlessness, rising pulse and respiratory rate, ↑ chest-wall indrawing, fatigue/drowsiness. Remember that the volume of the stridor is a factor of flow: in severe disease, the stridor will be very soft. This will prompt intubation under general anaesthesia. Other nebulized drugs: adrenaline 1:1000 (one dose of 1mL). Nebulized budesonide also helps—loading dose: 2mg, then 1mg/12h eg as Pulmicort Respules®. Dexamethasone, 0.15mg/kg (orally or injected) is equally effective, and cheaper.

►►***Management of suspected epiglottitis*** ►*Avoid examining the throat.* This may precipitate obstruction. Do not bleed the patient or upset him. Once in hospital, summon the most experienced anaesthetist. Ask her to make the diagnosis by laryngoscopy. If the appearances are those of epiglottitis (a cherry-red, swollen epiglottis), electively intubate, *before* obstruction occurs. (A smaller diameter endotracheal tube than normal for that age may be needed—so don't precut all your tubes!) Then do blood tests. The cause is usually *Haemophilus influenzae* type b, and strains resistant to ampicillin (and less so chloramphenicol) are prevalent, so the only safe initial treatment is a 3rd generation cefalosporin (eg cefotaxime, 25–50mg/kg/8h IV; the adult dose is 1–2g/8h IV). Hydrocortisone (1–2mg/kg/6h IV) is often given, but is not of proven value. Expect to extubate after about 24h (longer if the diagnosis turns out to be a staph laryngotracheobronchitis (much more common), when flucloxacillin 50mg/kg/6h IV should also be given.

Diphtheria is caused by the toxin of *Corynebacterium diphtheriae*. It usually starts with tonsillitis ± a false membrane over the fauces. The toxin may cause polyneuritis, often starting with cranial nerves. Shock may occur from myocarditis, toxaemia, or involvement of the heart's conducting system. Other signs: dysphagia; muffled voice; bronchopneumonia; airway obstruction preceded by a brassy cough (laryngotracheal diphtheria); nasal discharge with an excoriated upper lip (nasal diphtheria). If there is tachycardia out of proportion to fever, suspect a toxin-induced myocarditis. Monitor with frequent ECGs. Motor palatal paralysis also occurs.

Diagnosis: Swab culture of material below pseudomembrane; PCR. [260]

Treatment: ►►Diphtheria antitoxin: 10,000–30,000U IM (any age; more if severe, see *BNF*) and erythromycin; give contacts 7 days' erythromycin syrup: <2yrs old 125mg/6h PO (500mg per 6h if >8yrs) *before swab results are known.*

Prevention: Isolate until 3 -ve cultures separated by 48h. Routine vaccination: p 151. There is a resurgence of diphtheria in the former USSR, especially relevant to those born in the UK before 1942, when vaccination started.

Croup … distinguished from …	… Epiglottitis
Onset over a few days	▸▸Sudden onset
Stridor only when upset	▸▸Continuous stridor
Stridor sounds harsh	▸▸Stridor softer, snoring
Can swallow oral secretions	▸▸Drooling of secretions
Voice hoarse	▸▸Voice muffled/whispering
Likely to be apyrexial	▸▸Toxic and feverish (eg T° >39°C)
Barking cough	Cough not prominent

NB: *the distinction may not be clear cut; if in doubt, admit to hospital.*

Lower respiratory infections

Each year ~3 million infants die from these infections.

►If severely ill, think of staphs, streps, TB, and HIV (pneumocystosis, *OHCM* p 174). *In chronic cough think of:* •Pertussis •TB •Foreign body •Asthma.

Acute bronchiolitis is *the* big lung infection in infants; coryza precedes cough, low fever, tachypnoea, wheeze, apnoea, intercostal recession ± cyanosis. ***Typical cause:*** Winter epidemic of respiratory syncytial virus (RSV; diagnosis: immunofluorescence of nasopharyngeal aspirates; PCR). ***Others:*** Mycoplasma, parainfluenza, adenoviruses. Those <6 months old are most at risk. ***Signs prompting admission:*** Poor feeding, >50 breaths/min, apnoea, dehydration, rib recession, patient or parental exhaustion. ***Tests:*** Usually none. If severe; CXR (hyperinflation); blood gases/oximetry; FBC; virology, eg direct fluorescent assay (rapid DFA).[261] ***R:*** O_2; nasogastric feeds. 5% need ventilating (mortality≈1%; 33% if symptomatic congenital heart disease). Evidence supports nebulized salbutamol (0.15mg/kg) and, 15min later, dexamethasone 0.6mg/kg IM, but this is non-standard.[262] Ribavirin's role is unclear.[263]

Pneumonia Signs: fever, malaise, poor feeding, tachypnoea, and cyanosis. Older children may have typical lobar pneumonia, with toxaemia and pleural pain. Auscultation: creps; bronchial breathing (easy to miss). CXR: consolidation. Cavitation suggests TB or staphs. Take samples (blood; MSU) before starting 'blind' antibiotics, eg penicillin G 25mg/kg/4h IV + erythromycin eg as sugar-free solution (250mg/5mL)—2.5mL/6h PO for babies ≤2yrs, 5mL/6h from 2 to 8yrs. Alternative: amoxicillin, cephalosporin. High-flow O_2 may be needed. If compliance/concordance is a problem, once daily azithromycin may be the answer: 10mg/kg, ie 200mg (5mL) if 15-25kg, PO for 3 days. ***Causes:*** *Pneumococcus, Haemophilus, Staphylococcus, Mycoplasma* (hence choice of erythromycin), TB, viruses.

TB Suspect if: overseas contacts, HIV+ve; odd CXR ***Signs:*** Anorexia, low fever, failure to thrive, malaise. Cough is common, but may be absent. ***Diagnosis:*** Tuberculin tests (*OHCM* p 566); culture and Ziehl-Neelsen stain of sputa (×3) and gastric aspirate. CXR: consolidation, cavities. Miliary spread (fine white dots on CXR) is rare but grave. ***R:*** Get expert help. 6-month supervised plan: isoniazid 15mg/kg PO 3 times a week + rifampicin 15mg/kg/PO ac 3 times a week + pyrazinamide (1st 2 months only) 50mg/kg PO 3 times a week. Monitor U&E & LFT before and during treatment. Stop rifampicin if bilirubin↑ (hepatitis). Isoniazid may cause neuropathy (give concurrent pyridoxine). ►Explain the need for prolonged treatment. Multiple drug resistance: *OHCM* p 565.

Whooping cough (*Bordetella pertussis*) ***Signs:*** Apnoea; bouts of coughing ending with vomiting (± cyanosis), which are worse at night, and after feeding. The whoop (not always present) is caused by inspiration against a closed glottis. Differentiation from pneumonia, asthma, bronchitis, and bronchiolitis is aided by the (usual) absence of a fever >38.4°C and wheeze. Co-infection with RSV (above) is common. ***Peak age:*** 3yrs. In the UK, the illness is often mild, with ~1% needing admission (eg with secondary pneumonia); but severe in the very young where it may be fatal.[264] ***Diagnosis:*** PCR; culture is unsatisfactory: organisms often die on the way to the lab. Fluorescent antibody testing of nasopharyngeal aspirates is specific but insensitive. Absolute lymphocytosis is common (sometimes very high). ***Incubation:*** 10-14 days. ***Complications:*** Prolonged illness (the 100 day cough). Coughing bouts may cause petechiae (eg on cheek), conjunctival, retinal & CNS haemorrhage, apnoea, inguinal hernias, and lingual frenulum tears. Deaths may occur (esp. in infants), as may late bronchiectasis. ***Treatment/prevention:*** Salbutamol and steroids don't help much. Erythromycin is often used in those likely to expose infants to the disease (benefit unproven). Admit if <6 months old (risk of apnoea). May need ventilating and even ECMO (p 110). ***Vaccine:*** p 151—not always effective. ~30% of severe infections are via a fully vaccinated sibling.[265]

'Chesty' infants and virally induced lower airways disease

Many children with cough and wheeze do not fit into the categories opposite, and are too young for a diagnosis of asthma to be made with confidence. These infants often end up being treated with escalating bronchodilator therapy with frequent courses of antibiotics against uncultured organisms. While it is true that asthma can begin in infancy, most of these chesty infants do not have asthma—but we tend to prescribe 'just in case'. As the natural history of symptoms is to vary from hour to hour, sometimes we *appear* to be successful. NB: ***viral wheeze/virally induced respiratory distress*** or ***virally induced lower airways disease (VILAD)*** may be the appropriate label here: it is a non-atopic disorder; *respiratory syncytial virus* is more often the culprit rather than *haemophilus*.[266] An alternative diagnosis is ***altered awareness of minor symptoms***.[267]

The role of passive smoking is under investigation. 'Happy wheezers' (ie undistressed) probably need no treatment, but if chest symptoms start very early in life, a sweat test is needed to rule out cystic fibrosis. Between these ends of the spectrum of 'chestiness' lie those who clearly need some help. These may benefit from relatively high-dose inhaled steroids, given regularly for 8 weeks or so.[268] If ill enough to consider admission, 3 days oral prednisolone 2mg/kg/day can ↓ length of hospital stay, and duration of symptoms in children 6–35 months old with VILAD.[269] Assess benefit by reference to reduction in sleep disturbance.

Aim to engage in a constructive dialogue with parents so that they understand that treatment is often unsuccessful, but that their child is unlikely to come to harm, while he or she is 'growing out of it'.

If cough is a chronic problem, exclude serious causes (eg TB; foreign body; asthma) and reassure. There is no good evidence that brand name cough medicines are better than placebo—but they may help the parents.

Alternative therapies: Prevention of winter chestiness may be possible with vitamin C + herbal remedies, and parents will ask about this. Chizukit®, for example, contains 50mg of echinacea (*E. purpurea* + *E. angustifolia* roots) plus 50mg of propolis, and 10mg of vitamin C per mL. Echincea is considered to be an immune stimulant (animal studies show effects on cytokines, macrophages, and natural killer cells). Propolis is found in beehives and is said to be anti-infective. Vitamin C is possibly immunomodulatory. In one randomized study, reductions of >50% were seen in diagnoses of upper respiratory tract infection, otitis media, pneumonia, and tonsillo-pharyngitis. Follow-up was poor because of its unpleasant taste.[270] (Do not assume that herbs and vitamins are harmless: apoptosis may be affected, and ↑risk of neoplasia in adults has been suggested).[271]

DIALOGUE IS THE KEY ...

Cystic fibrosis

This is one of the commonest autosomal recessive diseases (~1/2000; ~1/22 of Caucasians are carriers); it reflects mutations in the cystic fibrosis transmembrane conductance regulator gene (CFTR) on chromosome 7, which codes for a cyclic AMP-regulated sodium/chloride channel. There is a broad range of severity of exocrine gland function, leading to meconium ileus in neonates (and its equivalent in children), lung disease akin to bronchiectasis, pancreatic exocrine insufficiency and a raised Na^+ sweat level—depending in part on the type of mutation (often ΔF_{508}; but other mutations, eg in intron 19 of CFTR, cause lung disease but no increased sweat Na^+).

Antenatal (p 152) carrier-status testing is possible, as is pre-implantation analysis after *in vitro* fertilization: at the 8 cell stage, 1 cell is removed from the embryo, and its DNA analysed; only embryos without the cystic fibrosis gene are reimplanted. This may be more acceptable than fetal terminations.

Diagnosis 10% present with *meconium ileus* as neonates. Most present later with *recurrent pneumonia* (±*clubbing*), steatorrhoea (if >7g/day/100g of undigested fat), or *slow growth*. ***Sweat test***[1]: Sweat Cl^- <40mmol/L is normal (CF probability is low); >60mmol/L supports the diagnosis. Intermediate results are suggestive but not diagnostic of cystic fibrosis.[272] The test is capricious, so find an experienced worker (false +ves in dehydration, endocrine diseases, if on certain antibiotics, and in eczema). Sweat is collected on to filter paper fixed to the forearm.[273] ***Other tests:*** IRT/DNA (below)[2]; CXR: shadowing suggestive of bronchiectasis, especially in upper lobes; malabsorption screen; glucose tolerance test; lung function tests; sputum culture. Mycobacterial colonization affects up to 20%; consider if rapid deterioration.

Neonatal screening using immunoreactive trypsin (IRT): Dried blood samples at 3 days old, after consent (the French regimen). If IRT↑, DNA analysis is done on the same sample—looking for ≥30 mutations (gives 85% coverage).[274] This is routine on the Guthrie card in certain areas in the UK.

Treatment ►*Genetic counselling* (p 154). Long survival depends on antibiotics and good nutrition. ***Respiratory problems (neutrophilic airway inflammation):*** Start physiotherapy (×3/day) at diagnosis. Teach parents percussion + postural drainage. Older children learn forced expiration techniques. Organisms are usually *Staph aureus*, *H. influenzae* (rarer), and *Strep pneumoniae* in younger children. Eventually >90% are chronically infected with *Pseudomonas aeruginosa*. *Berkholderia cepacia* (*Ps cepacia*) is associated with rapid progression of lung disease (prompt diagnosis using PCR may be available: isolate the patient). Treat acute infection after sputum culture using higher doses, and for longer than normal. If very ill, ticarcillin (50–60 mg/kg/6h IV) + netilmicin (p 112; or gentamicin, p 176), or ceftazidime (50mg/kg/8h IV) alone may be needed 'blind'. Nebulizing ticarcillin and tobramycin at home *does* prevent admissions. Colistin and meropenem are reserved for panresistant *P. aeruginosa*.[275] In reversible airway obstruction, give inhaled salbutamol. Look for *Aspergillus* in sputum. Ensure full vaccination (+pneumococcal). Methicillin-resistant *Staph aureus* is unlikely to do great harm to the lungs.[276]

Gastrointestinal problems & nutrition: Energy needs rise by ~130% (∵ chronic lung inflammation. Most have steatorrhoea from pancreatic malabsorption and need enzymes: Pancrex V® powder mixed with tepid food for infants—and Pancrex V Forte® for older children, ≤10 tabs/meal—to give regular, formed, non-greasy bowel actions. Most older children have enzymes in microspheres (eg Pancrease®, Creon®) so fewer tablets are needed. Omeprazole (or cimetidine, or ranitidine) helps absorption by ↑duodenal pH.[277] If all this controls steatorrhoea, a low-fat diet is not needed, but vitamins are still needed (A & D, eg as Abidec® 0.6mL/24h PO for infants or as multivitamin capsules 2/24h PO for older children). Diet should be high calorie/high protein.

Fine-bore nasogastric feeding is needed only if weight cannot otherwise be maintained.

Complications of CF

- Haemoptysis
- Pneumonia
- Pneumothorax
- Pulmonary osteo-arthropathy
- Diabetes mellitus
- Cirrhosis
- Cholesterol gallstones
- Fibrosing colonopathy
- Male infertility

GI obstruction if Pancrex® is omitted: admit urgently to a specialist centre for medical treatment (avoid laparotomy unless perforation imminent).

Impaired glucose tolerance: Risk rises with age and is higher if homozygous for ΔF_{508} mutations. Insulin may be needed; optimize diet, then optimize dose, not vice versa. Only try oral hypoglycaemics if nutrition is satisfactory.[278]

Psychological help: Parents and children need expert counselling. The Cystic Fibrosis Research Trust and regional centres may help here.

Meconium ileus Presents with failure to pass stool or vomiting in the 1st 2 days of life. Distended loops of bowel are seen through the abdominal wall. A plug of meconium may show as a firm mass in one such loop. In causes other than CF, lateral decubitus films show fluid levels. Tiny bubbles may be seen in the meconium ('inspissated'). ***Options:*** • Nasogastric tube drainage • Washout enemas • Excision of the gut containing most meconium.

Prognosis Death may be from pneumonia or cor pulmonale. Most survive to adulthood (median survival is >30yrs). 5-year survivorship models take account of forced expiratory volume in 1sec (% of expected), gender, weight-for-age z score, pancreatic function, plasma glucose, *Staph aureus* and *Burkerholderia cepacia* infection, and number of acute lung exacerbations/yr.[279]

New options ***Recombinant human deoxyribonuclease (rhDNase)*** has been shown to improve lung function and reduce the number of pulmonary exacerbations—and, over the long term, the natural (untreated) increase in elastase activities and interleukin-8 concentrations can be curtailed.[280]

Lung transplantation (heart + lung, or double lung) is getting safer; consider in those who are deteriorating (FEV_1 <30% of expected) despite maximum therapy, provided nutrition is good, and there is no TB or aspergillus. Good results are limited by donor availability (avoid raising hopes).

Gene therapy aims to deliver normal copies of the cystic fibrosis gene into patients, so allowing them to make CFTR protein. Viral vectors and liposomes have been used to get the gene into cells.[281]

1 Explain the test and the reason for doing it. Give written information sheet. Other rules:
- Sweat tests can be done at 2wks old in infants >3kg who are normally hydrated and without significant systemic illness. In term infants, sweat sodium and chloride can be high in the first 7 days.
- Delay sweat tests if oedematous or if on systemic steroids. (Flucloxacillin is OK.)
- For safety, do not do if on O_2 by an open delivery system (headbox & nasal prong O_2 are OK).
- Stimulation, collection, storage, and analysis of sweat must be done according to written standards. Sweat should be collected for <30mins and ≥20mins.

2 Having 2 mutations is associated with severe disease (ΔF508, W1282X, G542X, N1303K, 1717-1G→A). Carrying one mutation may not be so bad (3849 + 10 kb → A T).

▸▸Asthma in schoolchildren[APLS]

BTS 2004 guidelines[282]

Asthma implies reversible airways obstruction (peak flow varies by >20%), with wheeze, dyspnoea, or cough. >20% wheeze at some time; prevalence↑ if: ♂, birth weight↓, +ve family history; bottle-fed, atopy, or past lung disease.
Genetics: Asthma susceptibility genes are being identified (eg ADAM33).
Triggers: Pollen; dust; feathers; fur; exercise; viruses; chemicals; smoke.
Differential: Foreign body; pertussis; croup; pneumonia; TB; hyperventilation; aspiration; cystic fibrosis (wet cough, starting at birth, failure to thrive).
Signs of severe asthma: (Patients may not be distressed). Too breathless to speak or feed; respirations >30 breaths/min (>50 if <5yrs old); pulse ≥120 (or >130 if <5yrs old); peak flow ≤50% predicted.
Life-threatening if: Peak flow <33% of predicted •Cyanosis •Silent chest •Fatigue or exhaustion •Agitation/reduced level of consciousness.

Treatment •Avoid triggers •Check inhaler technique •Address fears •Have self management plan •Check compliance •Give a peak flow meter •Rescue prednisolone may be needed, 1–2mg/kg/day PO for 2–5 days. Titrate inhaled steroid to the lowest dose which controls the asthma.

Step 1: Occasional β-agonists via pMDI.[1] If needed ≥3×/wk, add step 2, (or if many exacerbations, or asthma wakes from sleep >once weekly).

Step 2: Add inhaled steroid, eg fluticasone 50–100μg/12h. Beware growth retardation, but fluticasone may be least problematic in this regard.[283] 100μg fluticasone=200μg beclometasone, so it's high-potency; its dose-response appears to plateau between 100 and 200μg per day.[284]

Step 3: Review diagnosis; recheck inhaler technique/concordance; eliminate triggers; monitor height; add inhaled salmeterol, eg 50μg/12h.

Step 4: If poor control persists, get help; ?do CXR; add 1 of: •Theophylline, eg Slo-Phyllin® eg 6mg/kg/12h PO •↑Inhaled fluticasone, ≤200μg/12h. •Leukotriene receptor antagonist, eg 1 evening dose of montelukast as a mouth-dissolving capsule (<5yrs, 4mg; 6–14yrs, 5mg); use is non-standard, but evidence is mounting that it is good as a steroid sparing agent in children.[285] [286] [287] (Cromoglicate is controversial.)

Step 5: Add oral prednisolone at lowest possible dose, eg 5–10mg/24h PO (alternate-day unverified). Check: growth; glucose; eyes (cataract).

Dose examples: β-agonists: Avoid oral salbutamol: it has poor efficacy. Inhalers are far more preferable: salbutamol 100μg as needed, terbutaline 250μg per 4–6h (1 puff)—eg always with spacer until 8yrs old; ipratropium.
Xanthines: Uniphyllin Continuous® tablets 9mg/kg/12h or Slo-Phyllin® above; capsules are 60, 125, or 250mg. Their enclosed granules may be spread on soft food. Try to monitor levels; bioavailability varies between brands.

Treating severe asthma Calmness helps. **Give these treatments if the above life-threatening signs are present, or if not improving 15–30min after ℞ starts.*

1 Sit the child up; high-flow 100% O_2.[288]
2 Salbutamol: 5mg O_2-nebulized in 4mL saline (2.5mg if <2yrs) ± 5μg/kg slow IV.
3 Prednisolone 1–2mg/kg PO (max 40mg) ± hydrocortisone 5mg/kg IV over 3min.
4* Aminophylline 5mg/kg IV over 20min (omit if already on a xanthine); then IVI aminophylline (BOX); do levels.
5* Hydrocortisone 100mg IV/6h; add ipratropium 0.125–0.25mg to nebulizer.
6 Oximetry & CXR if S_AO_2 ≤92%.
7 Treat any pneumonia.
8 Chart peak flow before & after each nebulizer treatment; for normal values, see BOX.
9 Repeat nebulizers as needed, eg at 30min, 1h, 2h, 3h, & 4h
10 Take to ITU if exhaustion, confusion, feeble respirations, or coma.

NB: there may be a role for IV magnesium sulfate, but its use is not universal.[MET 289]

Before discharge ensure: •Good inhaler technique •Is stable on the discharge regimen •Taking inhaled steroids *and* oral soluble prednisolone. •Written management plan •Follow-up by GP in 1wk & in clinic in <4wks.

Prevention Avoid triggers; (yearly flu vaccinations offer ?no benefit).[290] [n=800]

Peak flow (litres/min) in normal boys and girls (5–18 years)

Height cm	Mean	3rd centile	Height cm	Mean	3rd centile
100	110		150	360	300
113	160	100	155	400	320
120	210	140	160	420	350
125	240	160	165	450	370
130	260	190	170	470	400
135	290	220	175	500	430
140	310	240	180	520	450
145	350	270	185	550	470
			190	570	500

Lung function measurements cannot reliably guide management in those <5 years of age.

Which inhaler device is best if <5yrs old? *EBM* guidelines

- Pressurized metered dose inhalers (pMDI)[1] with spacer system[2] are best for routine use in stable asthma for both steroids and bronchodilators.
- If this is inadequate, nebulizers may be considered if 3–5yrs old. A dry powder inhaler may also be considered.
- Choice of devices should be governed by specific individual need and the likelihood of good compliance. www.nice.org.uk

Are there better alternative to nebulizers? (bulky and need servicing): Evidence supports use of valved holding chambers (eg AeroChamber Plus®)—highly responsive inspiratory valves allow opening on minimal effort to allow aerosol inhalation—and closes, at the end of inhalation, to prevent disturbing the aerosol inside the chamber during exhalation. MET 291

Dose of continuous IVI aminophylline *(mg/kg/h, after loading dose[3] of 5mg/kg IV (multiply by 0.85 for the dose of theophylline)*

Only use after consulting with an expert. Aim for a plasma level of 10–20mg/L. SE: BP↓, arrhythmias, cardiac arrest (if ≥25mg/L). Monitor ECG.

	Aminophylline (mg/kg/h)
Infants[4]	0.47
6 months–9 years	1.0
Children 10–16yrs	0.8

Pitfalls in managing asthma

- Reluctance to diagnose until a serious attack occurs. Formerly, 50% of diagnoses were made after >15 visits to the GP. Things are better now.
- Faulty inhaler technique. Watch the patient operate the device.
- Inadequate perception of, and planning for, the severe attack.
- Unnoticed, marked diurnal variation in airways obstruction. Always ask about nocturnal waking: it is a sign of dangerous asthma.
- Being satisfied with less than total symptom control.
- Forgetting to start prophylaxis—and not using oral prednisolone early.
- Giving *too much* inhaled steroid[5]: consider adrenal insufficiency if ↓consciousness; check blood glucose. ⇛IM hydrocortisone may be needed. NB: you cannot screen for risk of adrenal suppression (defined as peak cortisol ≤500nmol/L) simply by monitoring growth. 292

1 pMDI=press-and-breathe pressurized meter dose inhaler—as recommended by NICE.
2 *Spacers:* Static charge is a problem. Clean monthly (manufacturers say weekly; this is too much). Wash in detergent. Dry in air. Wipe mouthpiece clean of detergent before use. Replaced yearly.
3 Omit loading dose if previous theophyllines have been taken. If the plasma theophylline concentration is known and is subtherapeutic, an additional loading dose may be given. Increasing the dose by 1mg/kg causes an increase in serum theophylline of ~2μg/mL).
Erythromycin ↑aminophylline's half-life—also ciprofloxacin, propranolol, and the Pill. Drugs which ↓t½: phenytoin, carbamazepine, barbiturates, and rifampicin. Do plasma concentrations.
4 Infants do not usually get asthma—think of alternative diagnoses.
5 Anti-IgE agents may ↓ need for steroids. Omalizumab is a recombinant humanized monoclonal antibody directed against IgE and can inhibit the immune system's response to allergen exposure. It prevents IgE from attaching to mast cells, reducing IgE mediated inflammation. Cochrane

Infective endocarditis (IE)

OHCM p 152

Signs Fever, splenomegaly, clubbing, splinter haemorrhages, anaemia, rash, heart failure, microscopic haematuria, new murmur (eg with known congenital heart lesion or IV line *in situ*). *Typical cause:* Streps; staphs.[293]

Tests Blood cultures (different times and different sites), echocardiograms.

Blind treatment After 3 blood cultures: benzylpenicillin 25mg/kg/4h IV + netilmicin 2mg/kg/8h IV (p 112 or gentamicin, p 175); get microbiological help.

Preventing IE in those with heart lesions *Dental procedure example* (aged 5–10yrs): Amoxicillin 1.5g PO 4h pre-op, repeated as soon as possible after the procedure. If allergic or if at ↑ risk, try teicoplanin 6mg/kg IV and gentamicin 2mg/kg by slow IV 15min pre-op. ►See *BNF* & *OHCM* p 154.

Rheumatic fever

This is a systemic febrile illness caused by a cross-sensitivity reaction to Group A β-haemolytic streptococcus, which, in the 2% of the population that is susceptible, may result in permanent damage to heart valves. It is common in developing countries, but is rare in the West, although pockets of resurgence have been noted in the USA sometimes in overcrowded areas (favours streptococcal spread). Some specific Group A streptococcal serotypes are known to be particularly rheumatogenic—eg type 5 of the M-protein serotypes. Other ubiquitous serotypes appear to be non-rheumatogenic (eg type 12).[294] Prevalence 500,000/yr (worldwide).

Diagnosis 2 of Jones' major criteria or 1 major and 2 minor ***plus*** evidence of preceding strep infection: scarlet fever, a throat swab with β-haemolytic streptococci or a serum ASO titre >333U/L (reference intervals vary).[295]

Major criteria (revised 2001)	***Minor criteria***
Carditis, ie 1 of: changed murmur; CCF; cardiomegaly; friction rub; +ve echo	Fever
Polyarthritis (often migratory)	ESR >20mm or C-reactive protein↑
Erythema marginatum, *OHCM* p 428	Arthralgia, ie pain but no swelling
Subcutaneous nodules	ECG: PR interval >0.2sec
Sydenham's chorea (p 654)	Previous rheumatic fever or rheumatic heart disease

Don't count arthralgia if polyarthritis is a major criterion; likewise for long P–R if carditis is used. ***Joints:*** Knees, ankles, elbows & wrists may be *very* tender, but no permanent sequelae. ***Echo criteria:*** Mitral regurgitant jet is: >1cm; holosystolic (throughout systole); visible in 2 planes; mosaic pattern (ie chaotic flow).

The MacCullum plaque is at the base of the posterior mitral leaflet.[1] Aortic, pulmonary and tricuspid valves are affected in descending order of frequency.

Treatment of rheumatic fever Rest/immobilization helps joints & heart.
- Aspirin (eg 80mg/kg/day; but get advice *re* Reye's syndrome, p 652).
- If severe, get expert help. Prednisolone 2mg/kg/24h *may* help.[296]
- Penicillin for pharyngitis (~125mg/6h PO) preceded by one dose of benzylpenicillin (25mg/kg IM or IV).

Prophylaxis Symptoms are likely to be worse on recurrence of rheumatic fever. In one study, recurrence happened in 2.6%.[297] Prevent this by giving phenoxymethylpenicillin 250mg PO once or twice daily (eg if 6–12yrs old). Cover surgery/dentistry with antibiotics (see above and Carapetis, R, 2005 ***Lancet*** 366 155).

PANDAS *(paediatric autoimmune neuropsychiatric disorders associated with strep infections).* Suspect this in those with tics (or Tourette's syndrome, *OHCM* p 724) and obsessive compulsive disorder. Anorexia nervosa *may* also be a feature. Antibiotics and risperidone have been tried.[298][299][300] See p 654

1 MaCcullum's plaque is due to subendocardial Aschoff bodies: these are a classic histological feature of rheumatic fever. They are perivascular with a necrotic core set in a layer of lymphocytes. Nodules are found in joints, tendons, heart, and blood vessels. They heal with extensive myocardial fibrosis.

Diarrhoea

Faeces are sometimes so liquid they are mistaken for urine. NB: it is normal for breast-fed babies to have liquid stools. Some cows' milk causes harmless green stools. Diarrhoea may be an early sign of any septic illness.

Gastroenteritis The big danger from small intestine infection is dehydration ± fluid imbalance (p 234) from d&v. Rotavirus causes 30% of deaths.[illegible] There is often associated otitis media ± coryza. Other enteric viruses: Astrovirus; small round-structured viruses (eg Norwalk agent), calicivirus.

Treatment: If dehydrated, see p 234. Weigh, to monitor progress and quantify the dehydration, if a recent previous weight is available. Stop bottle milk (but if breastfeeding, continue) and solids; start oral rehydration mixture, eg Dioralyte®, which is 60mmol Na+/L with an osmolarity of 240mmol/L, and is better in non-cholera diarrhoea than standard WHO solution (90mmol & 311mmol/L respectively)—and vomiting is less of a concern. Milk is re-introduced after 24h (avoid regrading, even if <6 months) or sooner if the child recovers and is hungry, starving delays recovery. Breastfeeding supplies antibodies & helps milk production, but in poor places breast milk is likely to be Zn-deficient, and Zn supplements + vit A help stop diarrhoea getting chronic (10mg Zn/day PO for 14d).

Complications: Dehydration; malnutrition; temporary sugar intolerance after D&V with explosive watery acid stools (Rx: return to a lactose-free diet); post-gastroenteritis enteropathy resolves spontaneously after 2wks.

Tests: Stool: look for bacteria, ova, cysts, parasites. **Prevention:** Hygiene, good water & food, education, fly control. Rotavirus vaccines are being assessed.

Secretory diarrhoea Causes: Bacteria (Campylobacter, enterotoxic E coli, and if sanitation is poor, salmonella, shigella and Vibrio cholerae), giardiasis, rotavirus, amoebiasis, cryptosporidium, inflammatory bowel disease.

Toddler peas & carrots diarrhoea, from intestinal hurry, resolves by 4yrs.

Other causes: Food intolerance (coeliac disease, cows' milk or wheat), galactose, glucose, sorbitol, or lactose intolerance (to find reducing substances, mix 1 drop of stool with 10 drops H₂O and 1 Clinitest® tablet), antibiotics, deficiencies (zinc, copper, niacin), vitamin A, kwashiorkor.

Causes of bloody diarrhoea Campylobacter, shigella, necrotizing enterocolitis (neonates), intussusception (eg 6mths old), pseudomembranous colitis, haemolytic uraemic syndrome (p 177), inflammatory bowel disease (rare even in older children; look for weight ↓, anaemia, ↑WCC, ↑platelets, ↑ESR).

Malnutrition

Being a major cause of death and misery, this is a global issue for us all.

Kwashiorkor is due to ↓intake of protein & essential amino acids.

Signs: Poor growth, diarrhoea, apathy, anorexia, oedema, skin/hair depigmentation, abdominal distension, glucose ↓, K⁺ ↓, Mg²⁺ ↓, ↓cholesterol, ↓albumin. **Treatment:** Re-educate child, family, and politicians. Offer gradually increasing high-protein diet + vitamins. **Prevention:** Give to charity.

Marasmus is deficiency of calories + discrepancy between height & weight. It is [illegible]. **Signs:** Abdominal distension, diarrhoea, constipation, infection, ↓serum albumin. Mid arm circumference <9.9cm (children any age) predicts severe malnutrition better than being <60% of median weight for age or <85% of median height for age and <70% of median weight for height. Treatment: Parenteral feeding may be needed to restore hydration and renal function. Next offer a balanced diet with vitamins. Despite this, stature and head circumference may remain poor. Kwashiorkor and marasmus may occur together (protein-energy malnutrition). See Culberto H 2003 [illegible]

Diarrhoea

Deaths/yr=3×10⁶ children, worldwide

Faeces are sometimes so liquid they are mistaken for urine. NB: it is *normal* for breast-fed babies to have liquid stools. Some cow's milk causes harmless green stools. Diarrhoea may be an early sign of *any* septic illness.

Gastroenteritis The big danger from small intestine infection is dehydration ±U&E imbalance (p 234) from D&V. Rotavirus causes 30% of deaths.[301] There is often associated otitis media ± coryza. *Other enteric viruses:* Astrovirus; small round-structured viruses (eg Norwalk agent), calicivirus.

Treatment: ►If dehydrated, see p 234. Weigh, to monitor progress and quantify the dehydration, if a recent previous weight is available. Stop bottle milk (but if breastfeeding, continue) and solids; start oral rehydration mixture, eg Dioralyte®, which is 60mmol Na^+/L with an osmolarity of 240mmol/L, and is better in non-cholera diarrhoea than standard WHO solutions (90mmol & 311mmol/L respectively)—and vomiting is less.[302 303 304] [N=447]

Milk is re-introduced after 24h (avoid regrading, even if <6 months), or sooner if he/she recovers and is hungry: starving delays recovery.[305] [N=159] Breastfeeding supplies antibodies & helps milk production, but in poor places breast milk is likely to be Zn-deficient, and Zn supplements + vit A help stop diarrhoea getting chronic (~20mg Zn/24h PO for 14d).[RCT 306] [N=800]

Complications: Dehydration; malnutrition; temporary sugar intolerance after D&V with explosive watery acid stools. (Rare; manage with a lactose-free diet.) Post-enteritis enteropathy resolves spontaneously after ~7wks.

Tests: Stool: look for bacteria, ova, cysts, parasites. ***Prevention:*** Hygiene, good water & food, education, fly control. Rotavirus vaccines are being assessed.

Secretory diarrhoea *Causes:* Bacteria (campylobacter, staphs, *E. coli*, and, if sanitation is poor, salmonella, shigella, and *Vibrio cholerae*); giardiasis; rotavirus; amoebiasis; cryptosporidium. Inflammatory bowel disease.

Toddler 'pea & carrot' diarrhoea from intestinal hurry resolves by 4yrs.

Other causes Food intolerance (coeliac disease; cows' milk or wheat, galactose, glucose, sorbitol, or lactose intolerance): to find reducing substances, mix 5 drops of stool with 10 drops H_2O and 1 Clinitest® tablet; antibiotics; deficiencies (zinc, copper, Mg^{2+}, vitamins); kwashiorkor.[307]

Causes of bloody diarrhoea Campylobacter; shigella; necrotizing enterocolitis (neonates); intussusception (eg <4yrs old); pseudomembranous colitis; haemolytic uraemic syndrome (p 176); inflammatory bowel disease (rare, even in older children: look for weight↓; anaemia; WBC↑; platelets↑; ESR↑).

Malnutrition

►Being a major cause of death and misery, this is a global issue for us all.

Kwashiorkor is due to ↓intake of protein & essential amino acids.
Signs: Poor growth; diarrhoea; apathy; anorexia; oedema; skin/hair depigmentation; abdominal distension; glucose↓; K^+↓; Mg^{2+}↓; Hb↓; cholesterol↓; albumin↓. ***Treatment:*** Re-educate child, family, and politicians. Offer a gradually increasing, high-protein diet + vitamins. ***Prevention:*** Give to charity.

Marasmus is deficiency of calories + discrepancy between height & weight. It is HIV-associated.[308] *Signs:* Abdominal distension, diarrhoea, constipation, infection; serum albumin↓. Mid-arm circumference <9.9cm (child of any age) predicts severe malnutrition better than being <60% of median weight for age, or 85% of median height for age and 70% of median weight for height. *Treatment:* Parenteral feeding may be needed to restore hydration and renal function. Next offer a balanced diet with vitamins. Despite this, stature and head circumference may remain poor. Kwashiorkor and marasmus may occur together (***protein-energy malnutrition***). See Ciliberto H 2005 *BMJ* 330 1109

Southern diarrhoea is only an excuse for Northern amnesia

As you read this page two events unfold: in the Northern hemisphere a child is born with a silver spoon in his mouth—his future assured thanks to incubators, ventilators, wealth, and family planning; and, diametrically opposed to this birth another occurs in the Southern hemisphere where the silver was mined for that silver spoon. This child, according to our stereotype must 'Wait for his future like a horse that's gone lame *To lie in the gutter and die with no name*.'[309] We assume that this death is from diarrhoeal diseases that we are all working, more or less efficiently, towards controlling—and we are pleased to blame non-human agencies for these deaths. This model of our imperfect world does not stand up to scrutiny for two reasons: one is easy to understand (the diarrhoea was the mode of dying not the cause of death, which was poverty) and the other is impossible to understand—we didn't just let him die. We wanted him to die: in fact we killed him: in some cases, literally. Follow this well-documented thought sequence: There are too many homeless children living in my back yard→This threatens health and hygiene→How do we deal with this?→Other threats to health and hygiene are vermin→Street children are a sort of vermin→Vermin need eradicating→Let's shoot the vermin→Extrajudicial shooting of children—as occurred in Rio de Janeiro in 1994 and Sao Paulo in 2004.[310] In the former case, most 'ordinary decent folk' approved of the killings when they phoned a local radio station, as the events unfolded… '*I killed you because you had no future.*'[311] The point of all this is to illustrate that if we want to do something for children it is no good just doing something about the big killers, such as diarrhoea, and it's no good simply attacking poverty, for there is something dark in our human heart which needs addressing before purely statistical or biological interventions have a chance of success. There is only one way of influencing human nature, and that is through dialogue. So in this sense, the treatment of diarrhoea is dialogue.

Abdominal pain

Acute abdominal pain Children often have difficulty in localizing pain, and other factors in the history may be more important. Pointers may be:
- Hard faeces suggest that constipation is the cause (p 210).
- In those of African or Mediterranean origin, suspect sickle-cell disease.
- Do tuberculin test (*OHCM* p 566) if travel or other factors suggest TB risk.
- In children with pica (p 210), do a blood lead level.
- Abdominal migraine is suggested by periodic abdominal pain with vomiting especially if there is a positive family history.
- If any past UTI, suspect GU disease (eg renal colic or hydronephrosis).

Common physical causes Gastro-enteritis, UTI, viral illnesses (eg tonsillitis associated with mesenteric adenitis), and appendicitis.

Some rarer causes Mumps pancreatitis; diabetes mellitus; volvulus; intussusception; Meckel's diverticulum; peptic ulcer; Crohn's/ulcerative colitis, Hirschsprung's disease; Henoch-Schönlein purpura and hydronephrosis. Consider menstruation or salpingitis in older girls. ►In boys always check for a torted testis.

Tests ►Always microscope and culture the urine. Others: consider plain abdominal x-ray; ultrasound; FBC; ESR; renal imaging, barium studies.

Appendicitis (*OHCM* p 476) is rare if <5yrs, but perforation rates are high in this group (nearing 90%). Think: how can I tell this from other causes of abdominal pain? • Clues in the history: increasing pain in right lower quadrant, no previous episodes, anorexia, slight vomiting, absence of cough and polyuria. • Examination hint: fever and pulse↑ are likely; if the child appears well and can sit forward unsupported, and hop, appendicitis is unlikely. • Tests have very low positive and negative predictive values.

Gastro-oesophageal reflux/oesophagitis Presents with regurgitation, distress after feeds, apnoea, pneumonia, failure to thrive, and anaemia. ***Tests:*** Endoscopy and evaluation with an oesophageal pH probe is more reliable than barium studies. Ultrasound is not much help. ***Treatment:*** Reassurance; avoid over feeding (a common cause). Drugs may be needed, eg an antacid + sodium/magnesium alginate, eg for term infants, Infant Gaviscon® dual dose sachets, 1 dose mixed with 15mL boiled (cooled) water. This paste is given by spoon after each breast feed. If bottle fed, give the dose dissolved in feeds. Children >4.5kg may have a whole dual dose sachet. Carobel® thickens the feeds. If this fails, some experts use domperidone ± omeprazole (or similar). Most resolve by 6-9 months; if not, consider fundoplication, eg if there is failure to thrive, severe oesophagitis, apnoea, or bleeding.

Abdominal distension

Always remember acute GI obstruction as a cause; also consider:

Air:	*Ascites:*	*Solid masses:*	*Cysts:*
Faecal impaction	Nephrosis	Wilms' tumour	Polycystic kidney
Air swallowing	Hypoproteinaemia	Neuroblastoma	Hepatic; dermoid
Malabsorption	Cirrhosis; CCF	Adrenal tumour	Pancreatic

Hepatomegaly Infections: many, eg infectious mononucleosis, CMV.
Malignancy: leukaemia, lymphoma, neuroblastoma (see below).
Metabolic: Gaucher's and Hurler's diseases, cystinosis; galactosaemia.
Others: sickle-cell disease, and other haemolytic anaemias, porphyria.

Splenomegaly All the above causes of hepatomegaly (not neuroblastoma).

Neuroblastoma This is the most common extracranial solid tumour that occurs in early childhood: it is highly malignant and derived from sympathetic neuroblasts. It is thought to be an embryonal neoplasm, presenting with decreasing frequency from birth to 5yrs of age. ***Prevalence:*** 1:6000–1:10,000. It is the most common solid tumour in the under-5s. ***The Patient:*** can present with abdominal swelling. ***Metastatic sites:*** Lymph nodes, scalp, bone (causing pancytopenia and osteolytic lesions). In 92%, urinary excretion of catecholamines (vanillylmandelic and homovanillic acids) will be raised. ***Treatment:*** Refer to special centre. Excision (if possible) and chemotherapy (eg cyclophosphamide and doxorubicin). ***Prognosis:*** Worse if certain genotypes (pseudodiploid karyotypes, chromosome 1p deletions, N-*myc* gene amplifications), less mature catecholamine synthesis, and if >12 months old. Those <1yr do best, and if stage I and II disease, spontaneous remission may occur in 25%. If older, the disease is often disseminated by the time of presentation. ***Prevention:*** Pre-morbid screening by looking for excretion of catecholamines in the urine detects disease early, but appears not to save lives.[312]

Recurrent abdominal pain ≥10% of children >5yrs suffer recurrent abdominal pains interfering with normal activity. Is there organic disease? No cause is found in most, but this should neither encourage complacency (you may delay a diagnosis of ***Crohn's*** (*OHCM* p 246) or ***peptic ulcer***) or lead to an over-zealous diagnosis of underlying psychological problems (now thought to be less important—but do consider it: who is present when the pain starts; what, or who, makes the pain better?). NB: long-term follow-up indicates a 4-fold ↑risk of psychological problems manifesting in adult life. Consider: gastro-oesophageal reflux, small bowel dysmotility, gastritis, duodenitis, carbohydrate malabsorption (eg lactose, sorbitol), abdominal migraine.

Who to investigate: There are no hard rules. Be suspicious if the pain is unusual in terms of localization, character, frequency, or severity. Whenever symptoms are present for more than a few months recheck for associated features—eg in inflammatory bowel disease (Crohn's) there may be no diarrhoea in 50%, according to one careful study,[313] but poor growth is often the clue that prompts further investigations.

Coeliac disease: an example of malabsorption

Malabsorption typically presents with diarrhoea, failure to thrive ± anaemia (folate↓; ferritin↓), possibly with abdominal protrusion, everted umbilicus and wasted buttocks (if late-presenting). As subclinical/latent forms exist, investigate any unexplained anaemia, fatigue, 'irritable bowel' symptoms, diarrhoea, weight↓, arthralgia, eczema, and short stature. Patients may present at *any* age. Coeliac disease may cause short stature without overt gastrointestinal signs or symptoms. There may be a deceleration on the growth chart after introduction to gluten at weaning (4–6 months).

Cause: Enteropathy induced by gluten (in wheat, barley, rye, and oats).

Diagnosis: Screen with IgA gliadin, anti-reticulin, & anti-endomysium antibodies; specificity ≈100%, if there is no IgA deficiency (coeliacs are at ↑risk of this, so measure this too, + CRP & ferritin[314]). Confirm by finding villous atrophy on small bowel biopsy (endoscopic under GA is better than Crosby capsule). Villi return to normal on the special diet; avoid a gluten challenge test, unless diagnosis is in doubt.[315]

Treatment: *Gluten-free diet*: no wheat, barley, rye, or oats (hence no bread, cake, pasta, pizza, or pies). Rice, maize, soya, potato, and jam are OK. Gluten-free biscuits, flour, bread, and pasta are prescribable. Minor dietary lapses may matter. *After 5yrs:* cautious reintroduction of gluten may be tried.

Other causes of malabsorption: Cystic fibrosis; post-enteritis enteropathy; giardia; rotaviruses; bacterial overgrowth; milk sensitivity; worms; short bowel syndrome. ***Coeliac associations:*** Diabetes mellitus (type I).

Some acute surgical problems

Congenital hypertrophic pyloric stenosis This does not (contrary to its name) present at birth, but presents at 6–8 weeks (♂/♀ ≈4:1).

Presentation: Vomiting which occurs after feeds, and becomes projectile (eg vomiting over far end of cot). Congenital pyloric stenosis is distinguished from other causes of vomiting (eg gastric reflux) by the following:

- The vomit does not contain bile, as the obstruction is so high.
- No diarrhoea: constipation is likely (occasionally 'starvation stools').
- Even though the patient is ill, he is rarely obtunded: he is alert, anxious, and always hungry—and possibly malnourished, dehydrated.
- The vomiting is extremely large volume and within minutes of a feed.

Observe left-to-right LUQ (left upper quadrant) peristalsis during a feed (seen in late-presenting babies). Try to palpate the olive-sized pyloric mass: stand on the baby's left side, palpating with the *left* hand at the lateral border of the right rectus in the RUQ, during a feed, from a bottle or the left breast. There may be *severe* water & NaCl deficit, making urine output & plasma Cl^- (also K^+ & pH) vital tests to guide resuscitation, and determine when surgery is safe (Cl^- should be >90mmol/L). The picture is of hypochloraemic, hypokalaemic metabolic alkalosis. NB: don't rush to theatre. 316 [n=84]

Ultrasound detects early, hard-to-feel pyloric tumours, but is only needed if examination is -ve. 317 Barium studies are 'never' needed. ***Management:*** Before surgery (Ramstedt's pyloromyotomy) pass a wide-bore nasogastric tube.

Intussusception The small bowel telescopes, as if it were swallowing itself by invagination. Patients may be any age (eg 5–12 months; ♂:♀ ≈ 3:1) presenting with *episodic* intermittent inconsolable crying, with drawing the legs up (colic) ± vomiting. He may pass blood PR (like red-currant jam or merely flecks—late sign). A sausage-shaped abdominal mass may be felt. He may become shocked, and moribund.

Tests/Management: The least invasive approach is ultrasound with reduction by air enema (preferred to barium). CT may be problematic, and is less available. There may be a right lower quadrant opacity ± perforation on plain abdominal film. Doppler studies to show bowel viability have been used but are non-standard. If reduction by enema fails, reduction at laparoscopy or laparotomy is needed. Any necrotic bowel should be resected.

Pre-op care: ▶▶Resuscitate, crossmatch blood, pass nasogastric tube.

NB: children over 4 years old present differently: rectal bleeding is less common, and they have a long history (eg >3 weeks) ± contributing pathology (cystic fibrosis, Henoch-Schönlein or Peutz-Jeghers' syndromes; ascariasis, nephrosis or tumours such as lymphomas—in the latter obstructive symptoms caused by intussusception are the most frequent mode of presentation). Recurrence rate: ~5% (especially in adults, eg after gastrojejunostomy). 318

Post-operative pain relief Morphine IVI: child's loading dose: 100μg/kg in 30min, then 10–50μg/kg/h (prem neonates 50μg/kg, then 5μg/kg/h)—or diclofenac 0.5–1.5mg/kg/8–12h if over 1yr (eg a 12.5mg suppository every 8–12h if ~1yr old). Ibuprofen dose: 5mg/kg/6h PO (syrup is 100mg/5mL). Pre-op (pre-emptive) tramadol also has a few advocates (~0.5–1mg/kg). 319 [N=45]

Phimosis (The foreskin is too tight, eg due to circumferential scarring, so that retraction over the glans is impossible, eg with foreskin ballooning on micturition ± balanitis.) *It is normal to have a simple non-retractile foreskin up to the age of 4yrs.* Time, or a wait-and-see policy will usually obviate the need for circumcision. *Forced* retraction may be causative, not therapeutic. 0.05% betamethasone cream is also said to be effective. 320 [n=25]

Other surgical problems: ***appendicitis, hernias, volvulus, torsion of the testis, acute abdomen***: p 170, p 130, *OHCM* p 494 and p 474.

Childhood urinary tract infection (UTI)

Presentation: Often the child may be non-specifically ill. **Infants** may present with collapse and septicaemia, and toddlers as abdominal pain, vomiting, gastroenteritis, failure to thrive, colic, or PUO. Many with dysuria and frequency have no identifiable UTI, and often have vulvitis. The urinary tract is normal in most with UTI, but 35% have a structural abnormality (eg reflux); 4% have renal scars (most have reflux too); ~10% of these may develop hypertension. Each year in the UK, 10–20 children enter end-stage renal failure programmes because of complications from reflux and chronic pyelonephritis.

Definitions: Bacteriuria: Bacteria in urine uncontaminated by urethral flora. It may be covert (no symptoms), and can lead to renal scarring, 80% at <1yr, rarely chronic renal failure. **UTI** denotes symptomatic bacteriuria that may involve different GU sites (eg loin/suprapubic tenderness; fever; dysuria). **Chronic pyelonephritis** is a histological/radiological diagnosis (juxtaposition of cortex scar and a dilated calyx is the key feature); it is a big cause of hypertension and can result in renal failure, eg if the kidneys are congenitally dysplastic. **Grading micturition:** urine reflux up the ureters, seen on a micturating cystogram (requires catheterization) or MAG3 scan (catheterization not needed)—I: ureter only, incomplete filling of upper urinary tract without dilatation. II: Complete filling ± slight dilatation. III: Ballooned calyces. IV: Megaureter. V: Megaureter + hydronephrosis.

Incidence Boys: 0.2%/yr; girls: 0.3–1%; all are more likely in neonates. **Recurrence:** 15% if <2yrs old. **Prevalence** of covert bacteriuria in schoolgirls: ~2%. Prevalence of urological abnormalities: 40% (vs 4% have reflux, scars, malformations, obstruction, hydronephrosis). Renal scars: 1 in 4 of those aged <4yrs, and 1 in 5 aged ≥1yr; so used to concentrate on the babies early, thinking new scars were rare after 4yrs old, but prospective ⁹⁹ᵐTc dimercaptosuccinate (DMSA) scintigraphy (the best test) shows new scars appearing on repeat scans in 10% of those <1yr old, 14% of those aged 1–5, and 20% of those >5yrs old.

Tests: Dipstick all ward urines. In infants or when wet, get a clean catch (or a suprapubic aspirate, bag urines have many false positives from vulvitis or balanitis). Wash the genitals gently with water and tap repeatedly in cycles of 1min with 2 fingers just above the pubis, 1h after a feed, and wait for a clean voided urine (void) sample, avoiding the perineum (1st catch). Do prompt microscopy & culture: >10⁵ organisms/mL of a pure growth signifies UTI. For suprapubic aspiration, ward ultrasound helps identify a full bladder. Method: clean skin over the bladder. Insert a 21G needle in the midline 2.5cm above symphysis pubis. Aspirate on advancing (any organisms found are significant). **Ultrasound (us):** us is cheap, non-invasive, getting more accurate, and occasionally worthwhile even in 1st UTI: sensitivity, specificity, positive predictive value, and negative predictive value for detecting reflux are 18%, 89%, 25%, and 83% respectively. Reserve renography for • Infants • Recurrent UTI • +ve family history of urinary abnormality. If these are present and us is normal, proceed not to MCU (an MCU is radiation-rich and unreliable) but for ⁹⁹ᵐTc-mercaptoacetyltriglycine—a scan for scarring. ⁹⁹ᵐTc DMSA scan: dynamic for obstructive uropathy ± reflux. MCU (micturating cystourethrogram) by conventional MCU is still the best way of excluding reflux. In general, it is not needed if initial tests are normal, pyelonephritis is unlikely, there is no family history of reflux, and there are no recurrent UTIs. It is invasive and unpleasant, but careful preparation with play therapy (p 177) mitigates this. If it is done ill-advisedly on an uncomprehending and angry toddler it may constitute assault. NB: operating on reflux is unlikely to improve renal function.

Childhood urinary tract infection (UTI)

Presentation ►Often the child may be *non-specifically* ill. Infants may present with collapse and septicaemia, and toddlers as vomiting, 'gastro-enteritis', failure to thrive, colic, or PUO. Many with dysuria and frequency have *no* identifiable UTI, and often have vulvitis. The urinary tract is normal in most with UTI, but ~35% have vesico-ureteric reflux (VUR), ~14% have renal scars (most have reflux too), ~5% have stones, ~3% develop hypertension. Each year in the UK, 10–20 children enter endstage renal failure programmes because of complications from reflux and chronic pyelonephritis.

Definitions *Bacteriuria:* Bacteria in urine uncontaminated by urethral flora. It may be *covert* ('no' symptoms), and can lead to renal scarring, BP↑, and, rarely, chronic renal failure. *UTI* denotes symptomatic bacteriuria, that may involve different GU sites (∴ loin/suprapubic tenderness; fever; dysuria). *Chronic pyelonephritis* is a histological/radiological diagnosis. Juxtaposition of a cortex scar and a dilated calyx is the key feature. It is a big cause of hypertension and can result in renal failure, eg if the kidneys are congenitally dysplastic. During micturition, urine may *reflux* up ureters, seen on a micturating cystogram (requires catheterization) or MAG3 scan (catheterization not needed)—grading: *I* Incomplete filling of upper urinary tract, without dilatation. *II* Complete filling ± slight dilatation. *III* Ballooned calyces. *IV* Megaureter. *V* Megaureter + hydronephrosis.

UTI incidence Boys: ≤0.23%/yr; girls: 0.31–1%; ratios are reversed in neonates. ***Recurrence:*** 35% if >2yrs old. ***Prevalence of covert bacteriuria*** in schoolgirls: ~3%. ***Prevalence of associated GU anomalies:*** 40% (½ have reflux; others: malpositions, duplications, megaureter, hydronephrosis). ***Renal scars and age:*** We used to concentrate on treating babies early, thinking new scars were rare after 4yrs old, but prospective ^{99m}Tc dimercaptosuccinate (DMSA) scintigraphy (the best test) shows new scars appearing on repeat scans in 43% of those <1yr old, 84% of those aged 1–5, and 80% of those >5yrs old.

Tests Dipstick all ward urines. If nitrites or WCC +ve, get a clean catch (or a suprapubic aspirate; bag urines have many false positives from vulvitis or balanitis). Wash the genitals gently with water, and tap repeatedly in cycles of 1min with 2 fingers just above the pubis, 1h after a feed, and wait for a *clean voided urine (CVU) sample*, avoiding the stream's 1st part. Do prompt microscopy[1] & culture. >10^8 organisms/L of a pure growth signifies UTI. For suprapubic aspiration, ward ultrasound helps identify a full bladder. Method: clean skin over the bladder; insert a 21G needle in the midline 2½cm above symphysis pubis. Aspirate on advancing (any organism found are significant). ***Ultrasound (US):*** US is cheap, non-invasive, getting more accurate, and is occasionally worthwhile even in 1st UTIs; *sensitivity, specificity, positive predictive value, and negative predictive value* for detecting reflux are 18%, 88%, 23%, and 83% respectively.[321] Reserve renography for: •Infants •*Recurrent* UTI •+ve family history of GU abnormality. If these are present and US is normal, proceed not to IVU, (IV urography is radiation-rich and unreliable), but to: ***^{99}Technetium renography***—static for scarring (^{99m}Tc DMSA scan, dynamic for obstructive uropathy) ± ***isotope cystography. Micturating cystourethrography (MCU)*** is still the best way of excluding reflux. In general, it is *not* needed if initial tests are normal, pyelonephritis is unlikely, there is no family history of reflux, and there are no *recurrent* UTIs; it is invasive and unpleasant, but careful preparation with play therapy (p 377) mitigates this. If it is done ill-advisedly on an uncomprehending and angry toddler, it may constitute assault. NB: operating on reflux is unlikely to improve renal function.[RCT 322] [N=52]

1 Microscopy is more reliable than stix tests for nitrites & leucocytes: *Effective Health Care* 2004 8.6

Treatment and prevention of urinary infections

Antibiotics ***Trimethoprim***[1] 50mg/5mL, 4mg/kg/12h PO for 7 days then prophylaxis (see below), ***nalidixic acid***, or ***co-amoxiclav*** • Avoid constipation • ↑Oral fluids • Encourage full voiding • Repeat MSU.

If the child or infant is ill (pyelonephritis ± septicaemia) and blind parenteral therapy is needed, ➤➤***gentamicin*** may be given in a once-a-day regimen (IM if IV access fails). In one study, children and infants were randomly assigned to once-daily gentamicin 5mg/kg/day[2] or 2mg/kg/8h slowly IV. There was no difference in efficacy, nephrotoxicity, ototoxicity, or renal scarring.[323] If <2wks old, *BNF* recommends 3mg/kg/12h IV, slowly: consider a longer course if premature (gestation <34 weeks).[324] Do levels.[3]

Treating reflux If prophylactic antibiotics fail, ureteric reimplantation can reduce reflux, but scarring remains. Keep on antibiotic prophylaxis.

Prevention Just one episode of reflux of infected urine may initiate renal scarring, so *screening* for bacteriuria is useless: damage is too quick. But once a UTI is suggested (eg by stix) treat it *at once*, before you know culture sensitivities, as renal damage may be about to happen. Obtain 2 high-quality urine samples for analysis. Give trimethoprim prophylaxis (1-2mg/kg/ at night), while awaiting imaging—and sometimes indefinitely (optimum duration is unknown, but may be after 2 -ve cystograms, if the indication is reflux). Consider screening siblings for reflux. Prophylaxis can be stopped after reflux has been ruled out if there is no scarring. Surgical correction of moderate reflux is 'unlikely to be beneficial', and in minor reflux is 'likely to be harmful' (carefully made EBM phrases!)

1 Trimethoprim every 12h, if aged 6 weeks-5 months 25mg; 6 months-5yrs 50mg, 6-12yrs 100mg.
2 Assumes normal renal function; give lower dose if the patient is obese. See *OHCM* p 712.
3 Levels may not be needed if gentamicin is given for <72h (usually the case). One-hour post-dose (peak) serum gentamicin concentration should be 5-10mg/L (3-5mg/L for streptococcal or enterococcal endocarditis); pre-dose ('trough') concentration should be <2mg/L (<1mg/L for streptococcal or enterococcal endocarditis—*BNF* advice). In neonates phlebotomy is difficult and causes anaemia—so an example of monitoring advice from one NICU is: No levels before 48h of therapy unless proven infection requiring gentamicin and one of: • Perinatal asphyxia • Congenital renal defects • Renal insufficiency (creatinine >133μmol/L, ie >1.5mg/dL). www.cop.ufl.edu/wppd/research/sample7.pdf

Renal failure and some renal diseases

Acute renal failure (ARF) Essence: an acute severe fall in glomerular filtration rate (GFR) leading to a rapidly rising K^+ and urea often with anuria (<100mL/day) or oliguria (<200mL/m^2/day) and ↑BP. ***Causes:*** Acute tubular necrosis (ATN); GU obstruction; toxins (eg sulfonamides); glomerulonephritis (GN, *OHCM* p 268); haemoglobinuria; myoglobinuria (*OHCM* p 281). ***ATN causes:*** •Crush injury •Burns •Dehydration •Shock •Septicaemia •Malaria.

Plasma biochemistry: K^+↑, creatinine↑, urea↑, PO_4^{3-}↓; Ca^{2+}↓, Na^+↓, Cl^-↓.

MSU: Are there red cell casts (=GN)? If no RBCs seen but Labstix +ve for RBCs, consider haemo/myoglobinuria (*OHCM* p 281).

Other tests: ECG, serum and urine osmolality, creatinine, acid–base state, PCV, platelets, clotting studies (DIC), C_3, ASO titre, ANA (antinuclear antibody).

Radiology: ►Arrange prompt abdominal ultrasound. Are the ureters dilated (eg stones: 90% radio-opaque)? If so, urgent surgery may be required.

Treatment: Remove or reduce the cause, promptly.

- Treat shock and dehydration (p 234)—then:
- If the urine/plasma (U/P) osmolality ratio is >5 the kidneys concentrate well; the oliguria should respond to rehydration. If the U/P ratio is low, try for a diuresis: furosemide 1.5mg/kg IV slowly, maximum 20mg/day.
- Monitor BP. If BP↑↑: nitroprusside (p 177).
- 24h fluid requirement: Avoid overhydration. Replace losses + insensible loss (12–15mL/kg). Aim for weight loss (0.5%/day).
- Give no K^+. Monitor ECG. Tall T-waves and QRS slurring prompt urgent lowering of K^+, with IV salbutamol 4μg/kg or 5mg nebulized (2.5mg if <25kg). A less easy to use alternative is glucose (4g/kg) with soluble insulin (1U/4g of glucose) IVI over 2h.[325] Also consider Resonium A® 0.5g/kg PO and calcium gluconate (10%, 0.5mL/kg IV over 10min; monitor ECG: stop IVI if heart rate↓) to counteract electrophysiological effect of hyperkalaemia. Albumin IVI can reverse pre-renal ARF in nephritic children.[326]
- High energy, protein limited diet to slow catabolism.
- Dialysis indications (a guide, only): K^+ >7mmol/L; urea >40mmol/L; HCO_3^- <13mmol/L; severe hypertension; overhydration. Peritoneal dialysis requires minimal equipment and infrastructure is easy to do and remains the favoured method of replacement therapy in children. But continuous haemofiltration has a role especially in ARF and severe fluid overload.[327]

►Improvement is ushered in with a diuretic phase.

Haemolytic uraemic syndrome *Essence:* Microangiopathic haemolytic anaemia, thrombocytopenia, renal failure, and endothelial damage to glomerular capillaries. ***Typical age:*** 3 months to 3yrs. Epidemics may occur from *E. coli* Verocytotoxin. Diarrhoea is usual but not *always* present.

Other causes: Shigella, HIV, SLE, drugs, tumour, scleroderma, BP↑.

Clinical features: Colitis→haemoglobinuria→oliguria ± CNS signs→encephalopathy→coma. LDH↑. WCC↑. Coombs' -ve. PCV↓. Fragmented RBCs.

Mortality: 5–30%. A few have many relapses—to form a condition rather like thrombotic thrombocytopenic purpura (TTP).

Treatment: Seek expert advice. Treat renal failure (above). There is no evidence that fibrinolytic agents or anticoagulation help. Relapses in TTP may be preventable by steroids, splenectomy, or vincristine.

Chronic renal failure *Causes:* Congenital dysplastic kidneys, pyelonephritis, glomerulonephritis; chronic infection, reflux nephropathy; acute renal failure leading to cortical necrosis. ►Monitor growth, BP, U&E, Ca^{2+}, PO_4^{3-}.

The Child: Weakness, tiredness, vomiting, headache, restlessness, twitches, BP↑, hypertensive retinopathy, anaemia, failure to thrive, seizures, and coma.

Treatment: (See BOX). Talk with experts about haemodialysis & transplants.

Chronic renal failure: metabolic and other issues

Get a dietician's help. Calorie needs may not be met if vomiting is a problem. Eggs & milk may be appropriate (high biological protein value). Provide protein at a level of 2.5g/kg/24h. Vitamin drops may be needed. Nasogastric or gastrostomy tube feedings has a role. Growth hormone therapy combined with optimal dialysis improves growth: see *BNF*.

Acidosis is common needing no treatment if serum bicarb is ≥20mmol/L.[1]

Renal osteodystrophy: A bone disease resulting from poor mineralization due to renal failure, causing poor growth, muscle weakness, bone pain, bone deformities, and slipped epiphyses. It is like rickets and osteomalacia (↓parathormone [PTH] release causes ↓bone turnover). If glomerular filtration rate falls to ≤25% of normal, compensatory mechanisms to enhance phosphate excretion fail; the resulting hyperphosphataemia promotes hypocalcaemia, so PTH rises, which enhances bone resorption to release calcium in an attempt to correct hypocalcaemia. PTH↑ leads to marrow fibrosis (osteitis fibrosis cystica). Also, the failing kidneys cannot convert adequate amounts of 25-hydroxycholecalciferol to active 1,25-dihydroxycholecalciferol, so GI calcium absorption falls, so worsening hypocalcaemia. *Management:* Aim to normalize calcium and reduce the associated hyperphosphataemia, eg with PTH of 200–400pg/mL.

Hyperphosphataemia is treated with calcium carbonate taken immediately before food, which binds phosphate. Typical dose: 11-16mg/6h PO eg before meals. This combines with dietary phosphate to form calcium phosphate, which is expelled in faeces.

If Ca^{2+} is low despite correcting serum phosphate, give 1,25-dihydroxycholecalciferol (calcitriol), eg 15 nanograms/kg/24h PO. The dose may be increased in increments of 5ng/kg until Ca^{2+} and alk phos are normal, PTH level is reduced to 200–400pg/mL. X-ray evidence of healing rickets may also exist. Then reduce the dose. SE: ↓renal function, hypercalcaemia, and hyperphosphataemia. Because normal bone requires adequate levels of PTH to promote bone modelling, oversuppression of PTH must be avoided to avoid adynamic osteodystrophy.

Anaemia is common, and is the result of inadequate renal production of erythropoietin (± poor iron and folic acid intake). A typical Hb is 6-9g/dL. Do not transfuse, as this suppresses erythropoietin production. Subcutaneous erythropoietin may be indicated in pre-dialysis and peritoneal dialysis patients, and intravenously to patients on haemodialysis.

▶▶Hypertensive emergencies

Get expert help. While awaiting this, use ***sodium nitroprusside*** 0.5-1μg/kg IV then 0.5-8μg/kg/min IVI by pump to allow precise control of IVI rate. Protect from light. Monitor BP continuously; ↑dose slowly to the required level. CI: severe hepatic impairment. Withdraw over ≥20min to prevent rebound hypertension. If used for >1 day, do blood and plasma cyanide levels (keep to <38μmol/L & <3μmol/L, respectively). ***Labetalol*** is an easy to use alternative, eg 0.25mg/kg/dose IV, doubled every 10min (as needed) up to 2mg/kg/h IV; CI: phaeochromocytoma. 328 329

1 If pH ≤7.2, bicarbonate may be needed (by IVI if arrhythmias): get help as response is unpredictable, and dosing is difficult. Typical oral dose: 1-3mmol/kg/day in divided doses; bicarbonate 500mg capsules have ~6mmol of HCO_3^- (& Na^+). Infant HCO_3^- deficit in mmol ≈ 0.3 × weight (kg) × base deficit (mmol/L) *or* 0.5 × weight (kg) × (20—serum HCO_3^-). In children it is 0.5 × weight (kg) × (24—serum HCO_3^-). Ask the expert what proportion of this deficit should be given IVI and over how long.

Acute nephritis and nephrosis

Causes of nephritis:
• β-haemolytic strep via a preceding sore throat • Henoch–Schönlein purpura • Toxins or heavy metals • Berger's dis. (*OHCM* p 718) • Malignancies • Viruses • Bacteria (IE/SBE; syphilis) • Renal vein thrombosis

Acute nephritis ***Essence:*** Haematuria & oliguria (± BP↑, ± uraemia) produced by an immune glomerulonephritis (GN) in the kidney. ***Peak age:*** 7yrs.

Uncomplicated presentation: Haematuria; oliguria; BP↑ (50%); periorbital oedema; fever; GI disturbance; loin pain.

Complicated presentations:

- *Hypertensive encephalopathy:* Restless; drowsy; bad headache; fits; vision↓; vomiting; coma.
- *Uraemia:* Acidosis, twitching, stupor, coma.
- *Cardiac:* Gallop rhythm, cardiac failure ± enlargement, pulmonary oedema.

Blood tests: Urea↑ in ⅔; ESR↑; acidosis. Complement (C_3) often ↓ 2–8 weeks after onset (not in Henoch–Schönlein purpura). Find the cause: do ASO titre, antinuclear factor, syphilis serology, blood cultures, virology.

MSU: Count RBCs, WBCs, hyaline, granular casts; red cell casts mean glomerular bleeding. Skilled phase-contrast microscopy detects odd-shaped red cells, signifying glomerular bleeding. This change may not be present at first. 24h urine for protein and creatinine clearance. Check urine culture, and specific gravity (normal range: infants 1.002–1.006; child/adult 1.001–1.035).

Other tests: Renal ultrasound; renal biopsy, check platelets & clotting pre-op.

Treatment: Restrict protein when in oliguric phase. Give penicillin 10mg/kg/4h IV for the first few days, then PO for 3 months to prevent further streptococcal infection. Measure BP often. Treat severe hypertension. If encephalopathy, give nitroprusside (p 177).

Nephrotic syndrome (nephrosis; NS) *Essence:* Oedema, proteinuria (eg 4g/24h), hypoproteinaemia ± hypercholesterolaemia. In 90% the cause is unknown, but any of the causes of nephritis (above) can cause nephrosis too. *Histology:* Usually minimal change GN (often associated with allergy and IgE production).[1] *Symptoms:* Anorexia, GI disturbance, infections, irritability; then oedema (periorbital, genital), ascites, oliguria.

Urine: Frothy; albuminous ± casts; Na^+↓ (secondary hyperaldosteronism).

Blood: Albumin↓ (so total Ca^{2+}↓); urea and creatinine usually normal.

Renal biopsy: Reserve this for older children with any of: haematuria, BP↑, urea↑, if protein loss is unselective (ie large molecular weights as well as small), and treatment 'failures'. SE: haematuria; haematoma. 330 [n=111]

Complications: Pneumococcal peritonitis or other spontaneous infections. Consider pneumococcal vaccination if >2yrs.

Treatment: Get help. Limit oedema with protein-controlled (3g/kg/24h), low Na^+ diet (<50mmol/24h). Consider furosemide 1–2mg/kg/24h slow IV/PO + spironolactone (1.2mg/kg/12h PO). Prednisolone 60mg/m²/day for 6 weeks, then 40mg/m²/48h for ≥6 weeks. 90% respond in 8 weeks. If steroid toxicity and relapsing NS, consider cyclophosphamide 2mg/kg/day for ≥8 weeks (SE: haemorrhagic cystitis; WCC↓). If still relapsing, levamisole may help. Steroid-dependent NS may be treated with ciclosporin. RCT 331 Ciclosporin is nephrotoxic, *OHCM* p 674. 332

►Monitor BP. Meticulous control -minimizes progression to renal failure.

1 Acharya B 2005 *Am J Nephrol* **1** 30. Genetic variations in the IL-4 and IL-13 genes may be associated with predisposition to nephritic syndrome with minimal change glomerulonephritis.

Steroids in nephrotic syndrome

In nephrotic syndrome, protein leaks from blood to urine through glomeruli, causing hypoproteinaemia and oedema. Before steroids (and antibiotics), many died from infections. Most children with nephrotic syndrome respond to corticosteroids, but many experience a relapsing course with recurrent oedema and proteinuria. Corticosteroids reduce mortality to ~3%, with infection remaining the most important cause of death. NB: steroids cause obesity, poor growth, BP↑, diabetes, osteoporosis, avascular necrosis (hip), and adrenal suppression.[333]

Steroid-resistant proteinuria and *ACE-i*

Enalapril has been used in courses of >2yrs (0.2–0.6mg/kg/24h PO). In one study, urine protein electrophoresis showed a reduction of 80% and 70% in the total protein and albumin, respectively, after enalapril. Some patients become free of proteinuria. ACE-i are discontinued if renal failure occurs, eg during infections.[334,335]

Growth, failure to thrive, and short stature

Is growth normal? is a key question in determining the health of a child. Take any opportunity to weigh and measure a child. A series of plots on centile charts (p 224) shows if growth is slow (growth curve crosses the centiles). NB: the growth rate in mid-childhood is 5-6cm/yr; this accelerates at puberty (peak height velocity), before epiphyses start to fuse.

Failure to thrive means poor weight gain in infancy (falling across centile lines). Head circumference is preserved relative to height, which is preserved relative to weight. In 95% this is due to not enough food being offered, or taken. Worldwide, poverty is the main cause; in the UK it is difficulty at home, neglect, unskilled feeding, or not enough breast milk (top-up bottles *may* be needed). *Idiosyncratic growth pattern* is one cause, or normal child of short stature (↓birth weight, short siblings or parents)—likely if he is a contented child. Be sceptical about reliability of data. Was the child clothed during weighings? Length measurements are particularly prone to error: growth velocity is more useful than measurements taken at a single time.

Features to note:
- Signs of abuse (p 146)
- Feeding patterns
- Behaviour
- Activity level
- Family finances
- Health and happiness
- Chart family heights
- Any parental illnesses?
- Dysmorphic face

Issues to address: Feeding and maternal interaction are most important. Is the child anorectic or ravenous—'hyperphagic short stature'?[336] Also:
- If breastfeeding, does he get a good mouthful of breast? (p 124)
- If bottle feeding, does the teat's hole allow milk to flow through?
- Does weight gain return if the child is removed from the family?
- Is there evidence relevant to child protection proceedings?

Tests: Check feeding technique. It is a great skill to know *when* to investigate. It's better from the child's point of view to ask a trusted colleague's advice *before* painful tests. In one study only 39 of 4880 tests were helpful.[337]

MSU (expect false +ves if bags are used; but avoid routine suprapubic aspirations); U&E/glucose, LFT, Ca^{2+}, proteins, immunoglobulins, CRP, TSH; FBC; sweat test; urinary amino ± organic acid chromatography; stools (MC&S ± sugar detection); CXR, renal or CNS ultrasound, skeletal survey for dwarfism and abuse; jejunal biopsy; ECG/echo. In ***non-organic failure to thrive***, studies favour weekly visits from trained lay visitors.[RCT 338]

Short stature is a height <3rd centile (p 224). Use the method shown on the charts to correct for mid-parental height (short stature may represent 'regression towards the mean' of their heights. ►*Any chronic disease can cause short stature.* Hypopituitarism (an important cause of short stature) usually manifests after age 2yrs: look for relative obesity, without any other explanation for low growth velocity (ie <25th centile; measure for ≥1yr, see p 226). Deficiency of growth hormone (GH) is shown by an impaired rise (peak GH <15mU/L) after a stimulus (eg sleep or hypoglycaemia, induced by IV insulin, *OHCM* p 318). Preschool screening for short stature is the aim. To be effective, start synthetic GH early. Somatotropin example: 23-39μg/kg/day SC; expect growth velocity to ↑ by ≥50% from baseline in year 1 of treatment. Other pituitary hormones may also be deficient (*OHCM* p 318).

Typical causes:
- Constitutional(~80%)—if both parents short
- Psychological neglect
- Poverty; physical abuse
- Drugs: eg steroids
- Genetic:, eg Turner's or cystic fibrosis
- Ineffective diet (coeliac)
- Inflammatory bowel dis.
- Hypothyroidism
- Infection (eg UTI; TB)
- GH↓ (as above)
- Rarities, eg Noonan, p 650

Causes of height↑: Thyrotoxic; precocious puberty; Marfan's; homocystinuria.

Ethnospecific growth charts[339]

It is clear that some populations are inherently shorter than others, and this poses problems when using growth charts. Consider these facts:

- The Dutch are the tallest *nation* on earth (mean ♂ height = 1.84m): the tallest *population group* is the Masai people (eg in Tanzania and Kenya).
- African and Afro-Caribbean 5–11yr-olds height is ~0.6 standard deviations scores (SDs) greater than white children living in England.
- Gujarati children and those from the Indian subcontinent (except those from Urdu- or Punjabi-speaking homes) have heights ~0.5 SDs less than white children living in England.
- Gujarati children's weight-for-height is ~0.9 SDs less than expected for Afro-Caribbeans, or white children in England—so Gujarati children's weight is ~1.5 SDs less than for white children living in England.
- Urdu and Punjabi weight is ~0.5 SDs < expected for white UK children.
- Published charts have centile lines 0.67 SDs apart; for height and weight shift the centile lines up by 1 centile line division for Afro-Caribbeans.
- Re-label Gujarati children's weight charts, so the 0.4th centile becomes the ~15th centile, and the 2nd weight centile becomes the ~30th centile.
- For most other Indian subcontinent groups, height & weight need shifting down, eg relabel the 0.4th & 2nd centile lines 1.5th & 6th respectively. NB: Sikh children are taller and heavier than Caucasians.[340]
- Body-mass index centiles are said to be appropriate for Afro-Caribbeans, but recalculate as above for Indian subcontinent children, except for Gujarati speaking children (0.4th & 2nd centiles→4th & 14th).

Trends towards tallness with each generation occur at varying rates in all groups, so 3rd generation immigrants are taller than expected using 2nd generation data. Intermarriage adds further uncertainty. NB: to print the ***new CDC charts***, see www.cdc.gov/nchs/about/major/nhanes/growthcharts/clinical_charts.htm

NB: obesity (± diabetes) in school children is a big public health issue. See p 156 for preventing 'adult' diseases by measures starting in childhood.

Breast-fed babies need different charts

One of the most important limitations of current centile charts based on North American data is that they relate to predominantly formula-fed infants whose pattern of growth deviates substantially from that of healthy breast-fed infants.[341] This means that breast-fed babies may be deemed 'underweight and in need of formula top-ups' when this is not the case—and may lead to obesity. The acceptable range for weight of a 1-year-old formula fed baby is 10.2kg to 13kg (22.5 to 28.5lbs); for a breast-fed baby corresponding figure is 9.5kg to 11.8kg (21 to 26lbs—2005 data).[342] [343] New charts reflecting this divergence are awaited.

Some endocrine and metabolic diseases

Hypothyroidism *Congenital:* Thyroid scans divide these into 3 groups: athyreosis; thyroid dysgenesis; and dyshormonogenesis. Also remember maternal antithyroid drugs (p 25, eg propylthiouracil). *Acquired:* Prematurity; Hashimoto's thyroiditis; hypopituitarism; x-rays; Down's syndrome.

Signs: May be none at birth—or prolonged neonatal jaundice, widely opened posterior fontanelle, poor feeding, hypotonia, and dry skin are common. Inactivity, sleepiness, slow feeding, little crying, and constipation may occur. Look for coarse dry hair, a flat nasal bridge, a protruding tongue, hypotonia, umbilical hernia, slowly relaxing reflexes, pulse↓, and poor growth and mental development if it has not been picked up. Other later signs: IQ↓, delayed puberty (occasionally precocious), short stature, delayed dentition.[344]

Universal neonatal screening: Cord blood or filter paper spots (at ~7 days, from heel prick) allow early diagnosis (the 'Guthrie card'). They *do* prevent serious sequelae. Act on high *and* low TSHs (may indicate pituitary failure).[345]

Tests: T_4↓, TSH↑ (but undetectable in secondary hypothyroidism), ^{131}I uptake↓, Hb↓. Bone age is less than chronological age. As it is unwise to x-ray the *whole* skeleton, the left wrist and hand are most commonly used. There are a large number of ossification centres. Each passes through a number of morphological stages, and using comparisons with key diagrams from 'normal' populations, a rough bone age may be determined. There is no hard-and-fast answer to the question of how much discrepancy (eg 2yrs) between skeletal and chronological years is significant.

Using levothyroxine (LT4): Infants need ~10µg/kg/day; this rises to ~100µg daily by 5yrs (adult doses by 12yrs). There is debate about the best starting dose in neonates. ***Standard dose:*** 6-8µg/kg/day; 2 studies find up to 12µg/kg/day may prevent loss of IQ.[346][347] We await further studies. Adjust according to growth and clinical state. *Avoid high TSH levels.* Those with athyreosis need the highest doses of T_4 and the closest monitoring early on. Those with dysgenesis and dyshormonogenesis need more attention later.

Hyperthyroidism ***Typical child:*** Girl at puberty. ***Signs & lab features:*** OHCM p 304. Fine-needle cytology of goitres may show *juvenile autoimmune thyroiditis.* *Carbimazole* starting dose: ~250µg/kg/8h. Adjust according to response.[348] *Propylthiouracil:* 2-3mg/kg/8h PO; expect remission in ~67%.[349] Higher doses may be needed. Typical maintenance dose: ⅓-⅔ of remission-inducing dose.

Thyroid disease in pregnancy and neonates See p 25.

The glycogenoses result from defects in synthesis and degradation of glycogen. Abnormal stores are deposited in liver, muscle, heart, or kidney. Most types (there are >7) are autosomal recessives. Types include: von Gierke disease (type I, p 655), Pompe's disease (type II, p 652), Cori disease (type III—hypoglycaemia, hepatomegaly, with failure to thrive), Anderson disease (type IV), McArdle disease (type V), Hers disease (type VI) and Tauri disease (type VII—phosphofructokinase↓—like McArdle's, but with haemolysis and gout: diagnose by muscle enzyme assay).

In McArdle's, the cause is myophosphorylase deficiency (do muscle biopsy). Inheritance: autosomal recessive. Stiffness and myalgia follow exercise (with electrically silent muscle contractions). During exercise, as circulating fatty acids become available, there may be some recovery ('2nd wind'). There may also be cardiomyopathy.[1] Venous blood from exercised muscle shows ↓levels of lactate & pyruvate. Lack of phosphorylase staining in muscle biopsy confirms diagnosis. There may be myoglobinuria (red urine ± renal failure). ***Treatment:*** No extreme exercise. Oral glucose and fructose may help.

1 Arad M 2005 *N Engl J Med* **52** 362 Glycogen-storage cardiomyopathy produced by LAMP2 or PRKAG2 mutations resembles hypertrophic cardiomyopathy (but distinguishable by electrophysiology).

Inborn errors of metabolism and phenylketonuria (PKU)

These are often diagnosed by a urine metabolic screen (eg amino acids, organic acids, carbohydrates, mucopolysaccharides—in deciding which tests to perform, get help; interest the lab in your problem).[350] Typical signs: diarrhoea, lethargy, respiratory distress, metabolic acidosis (± odd body smells), jaundice, hypoglycaemia, U&E imbalance, fits, and coma. Features may be intermittent, and provoked by crises (eg infection; dehydration). In addition, look for:

Urine amino acids ↑ in:

- Alkaptonuria
- Canavan leukodystrophy
- Cystinosis
- Cystathioninuria
- Fructose intolerance
- Galactosemia
- Hartnup disease
- Homocystinuria
- Hyperammonaemia

Physical sign:	*Possible significance:*
Hepatosplenomegaly	eg amino acid and organic acid disorders, lysosomal storage diseases (Anderson-Fabry disease[1]).
Coarse facies	Mucopolysaccharidoses, eg Hurler's syndrome, p 646, gangliosidoses, mannosidoses.
WCC↓, platelets↓	Organic acidurias.
Mental retardation	See p 216.
Failure to thrive	Aminoacidurias, organic aciduria, cystinuria, lactic acidosis, storage diseases.

PKU (Phenylalanine ketonuria)—***Cause*** Absent or reduced activity of phenylalanine hydroxylase—inherited as an autosomal recessive (the gene—on chromosome 12—often mutates, and there is a full range of clinical manifestation from nearly symptom-free to severe mental impairment). The defect leads to ↓CNS dopamine, reduced protein synthesis, and demyelination.[351]

Clinical features Fair hair, fits, eczema, musty urine. The chief manifestations is ↓IQ (eg dyscalculia ± poor spelling ± ↓cognition).[352]

Tests Hyperphenylalaninaemia (reference interval: 50-120μmol/L). 'Benign' phenylketonuria may be indicated by levels <1000μmol/L.

Treatment See check-list on p 216. Get expert help. *Diet:* protein substitute that lacks phenylalanine but is enriched in tyrosine. Aim to keep phenylalanine to <600μmol/L—by prescribing artificial food-substitutes (amino acid drinks) to give <300mg–8g of natural protein/day (depending on age and severity of phenylalanine hydroxylase deficiency).[353]

Hypomyelination may be proportional to degree of phenylketonaemia, but some studies fail to show stricter diets are associated with higher IQs. Despite treatment, children are more prone to depression, anxiety, phobic tendencies, isolation, and a less 'masculine' self image.[354]
Adherence to the diet may be poor (it's unpalatable).[355]
Also, the diet may cause changes of questionable significance in levels of selenium, zinc, iron, retinol, and polyunsaturated fatty acids.[356]

Prevention of manifestations Screen blood at 1 week (using a heel-prick and filter paper impregnation—the Guthrie test).

Maternal phenylketonuria ►Pre-conception counselling is vital. Effects on the baby: facial dysmorphism, microcephaly, growth retardation, IQ↓.[2]

1 Anderson-Fabry disease may present with torturing, lancinating pains in the extremities (± abdomen) made worse by cold, heat, or exercise. It is a neuritis (vasculitis of the vasa nervorum). By adolescence, angiokeratomata appear (clusters of dark, nonblanching, petechiae) in the 'bathing trunk' area (esp. umbilicus & scrotum). Also: paraesthesiae, corneal opacities, hypohidrosis, proteinuria and renal failure. It may respond to enzyme ℞ (α-galacotosidase is ↓). Carbamazepine may help the pain.
2 Lee P 2005 *Arch Dis Child* **90** 143

Precocious puberty

Puberty may start as early as 8yrs of age in girls and 9yrs of age in boys. Refer to a paediatric endocrinologist if onset is before this. ♀/♂ ≈4:1.[357]

Biology Each of the physical signs of puberty may be thought of as a bioassay for a separate endocrine event. Enlargement of the testes is the first sign of puberty in boys, and is due to pulses of pituitary gonadotrophin. Breast enlargement in girls and penis enlargement in boys is due to gonadal sex steroid secretion. Pubic hair is a manifestation of adrenal androgen production. Growth in boys accelerates when testis volume reaches 10–12mL (if measured by comparison with orchidometer beads rather than ultrasound, expect overestimates by up to 60%).[358] Girls start to grow more quickly once their breasts have started to develop. Stage 4 breast development is a prerequisite for menarche (in most girls). The best sign that precosity is pathological is when this *consonance of puberty* goes awry: in Cushing's syndrome, pubic hair is 'too much' for the testicular volume; in hypothyroidism, the testes are large (FSH↑ as TSH↑↑) in the presence of a low growth velocity.[359]

Signs of precocious puberty (variable) boys: rapid growth of penis and testes, increasing frequency of erections, masturbation, appearance of pubic hair, changing body odour, and acne. There will be corresponding changes in the secondary sexual characteristics of girls. The chief consequence is short stature caused by early fusion of epiphyses. Premature adrenal maturity (adrenarche) may presage insulin resistance and syndrome X.[360]

Enquire about symptoms of more general hypothalamic dysfunction: polyuria, polydipsia, obesity, sleep, and temperature regulation. There may also be manifestations of raised intracranial pressure and visual disturbance.

In girls, often no cause is found, but in 8% of boys a cause is found. If onset is before 2yrs, the cause may well be a hypothalamic hamartoma (do MRI/CT). LH receptor gene mutations are the cause of sporadic or familial male gonadotrophin-independent precocious puberty.[361] Genetic mechanisms include substitution of T for C at nucleotide 1103, resulting in substitution of leucine at position 368 by proline. *Other causes:*

- CNS tumours/hydrocephalus/craniopharyngioma
- Post encephalitis, meningitis, or cranial irradiation
- McCune–Albright syn. (↑oestrogen ∵ ovarian cysts)[1]
- Primary empty sella syndrome[362]
- Tuberous sclerosis
- Hepatoblastoma
- Choriocarcinoma
- Hypothyroidism

Tests Cranial CT and MRI; bone age by skeletal x-ray; urinary 17-ketosteroids; karyotype analysis; pelvic ultrasound (girls), T_4; TSH.[363][364]

Management: a physiological approach Initiation of puberty depends on release from inhibition of neurones in the medial basal hypothalamus that secrete gonadotrophin-releasing hormone (GnRH), and on decreasing hypothalamic-pituitary sensitivity to –ve feedback from gonadal steroids. These changes are accompanied by a marked increase in frequency and magnitude of 'pulses' of luteinizing hormone (LH), and, to a lesser extent, follicle stimulating hormone (FSH). It is the ability to secrete GnRH pulses at a fast rate which leads to normal gonadal function. Continuous high levels of GnRH paradoxically suppress the secretion of pituitary gonadotrophins, and this forms the basis for treatment of precocious puberty with synthetic analogues of GnRH. After subcutaneous or nasal insufflation there is a reversal of gonadal maturation and all the clinical correlates of puberty (not for pubic hair, as there is no change in the secretion of androgens by the adrenal cortex). There is deceleration in skeletal maturation. Treatment is continued eg up to 11yrs. Families need reassurance that the child will develop normally.

Endogenous oestrogen accelerates growth (♂ & ♀), as well as mediating ♀ sexual characteristics: testolactone can help by ↓its biosynthesis. Antiandrogens (eg flutamide) and spironolactone also have a role.[365]

1 Zacharin M 2005 *Pediatr* End *Met* **18** 33 ℞ example with octreotide, flutamide, and testolactone.

Diabetes mellitus: patient-centred care in action

Type 1 diabetes is the (joint) most common chronic disease in childhood [illegible]

[illegible] **Diagnostic criteria** [illegible] **Typical insulin starting doses** [illegible] **Diet** [illegible]

Type 2 DM [illegible]

What should the family of a newly diagnosed diabetic child know?

- Insulin doses [illegible]
- Diet [illegible] What does the child do if the child is hungry?
- [illegible]
- What does the carer do if the blood sugar is not well controlled?
- [illegible]
- [illegible] (Hypoglycaemia [illegible])
- What should happen if the child [illegible]
- What happens to insulin requirements during fever and other illnesses?
- [illegible]
- [illegible] follow-up arrangements?
- Encourage [illegible] a Diabetes Association [illegible]

What are the aims of routine follow-up in the diabetic clinic?

- To achieve [illegible]
- To prevent complications [illegible]
- [illegible]

[illegible]

Diabetes mellitus: patient-centred care in action

Type 1 diabetes is the third most common chronic disease in UK children (after asthma and cerebral palsy).

Presentation: Infection (eg UTI), poor growth; ketosis.[1] *Typical age:* 4–12yrs.[2] *Diagnostic criteria: OHCM* p 294. *℞:* If non-ketotic, IV fluids are rarely needed. *Typical insulin starting dose:* 0.2U/kg SC followed by 0.35–0.5U/kg/12h SC, 30min before breakfast and tea. ~70% of the dose should be long-acting. With help from the pancreas a period may follow in which insulin needs fall. *Diet:* Ask a paediatric dietician. Energy needs≈1500kcal/m² or 1000kcal + 100–200 kcal for each year of age: ►understand and respect your patient's lifestyle: don't be prescriptive. Aiming for 30% of this with each major meal, and 10% as a bedtime snack may suit some children. *Fit the insulin regimen to the lifestyle*, not the other way round. Giving ~20% of calories as protein, ~50% as unrefined carbohydrate, and ≤30% as fat is a rule of thumb. If the child is mildly to moderately symptomatic and clinically well, subcutaneous insulin and oral diet and fluids may be begun at diagnosis, avoiding hospital admission. 366

Type 2 DM is rare in children (0.2/100,000; 367 ↑×13 if of Asian extraction); but insulin resistance/pre-syndrome X is burgeoning: ►see p 156 for prevention.

What should the family of a newly diagnosed diabetic child know?

- Insulin: doses (eg during illness); practice self-injecting skills on oranges.
- Diet: What is it? Why is it important? What does the carer/parent do if the child is hungry?
- Can blood sugar be monitored accurately? Watch the carer's technique.
- What does the carer do if the blood sugar is not well controlled?
- Does the parent or carer know what 'well controlled' means?
- Too much insulin? How does hypoglycaemia evolve? (Weakness, hunger, irritability, faintness, sweating, abdominal pain, vomiting, fits, and coma). What should be done? Some units practise inducing hypoglycaemia (glucose <2mmol/L) on the ward, by omitting breakfast after morning insulin. Explain symptoms as they happen, and their reversal with oral drinks (or Hypostop® oral jelly).
- What should happen if the child misses a meal, or is sick afterwards?
- What happens to insulin requirements during 'flu and other illnesses?
- Who does mother contact in emergency? Give written advice.
- Is the GP informed of discharge and follow-up arrangements?
- Encourage membership of a *Diabetic Association* (UK tel: 0207 323 1531).

'What are the aims of routine follow-up in the diabetic clinic?'

- To achieve normoglycaemia through education/motivation. Groups provide better shared learning opportunities than didactic doctor-sermons.
- To prevent complications. So check growth and fundi (dilate pupils; NB: retinopathy usually takes 10yrs to develop). Blood: glucose, Hb_{A1c}.
- If normoglycaemia is unachievable, choose the best compromise with the child's way of life and strict glucose control. Insulin-storing pen-shaped injectors allow great flexibility in the timing and dose of insulin, delivering a variable dose (2U/push) of drawing up insulin at inconvenient times (eg during a party). Introduce to a friendly local diabetic nurse-teacher.

1 Mean duration of symptoms pre-diagnosis is 30 days. Feeding with cows' milk, and infant exposure to enteroviruses, may ↑incidence. 10% have mild coeliac disease, so screening these patients is wise.
2 *Genes & environment:* DM was a disease of the over-5s, but in the UK, incidence is rising in infancy from ~1:10,000 in 1985-90 to >1.6/10,000. Islet cell antibodies are found in HLAB8 (but not HLA-B15) children. ≥4 genes are important (6q partly determines islet sensitivity to damage), but most susceptibility to is environmentally acquired. Most with type 1 DM have antibodies to cows' milk albumin which react with β-cell surface proteins. Also, mumps, rubella, coxsackie & CMV have the potential to injure β-cells—but their exact role is unclear. If one child in a family has DM, risk to siblings is >5%.

Hypoglycaemic coma

- ▸▸Get IV access. Get help.
- ▸▸Give glucose 0.5g/kg as a 25% IVI, or by rectal tube if no IV access, with glucagon 0.5-1mg IM or slowly IV. Then give 10% dextrose, 5mL/kg/h. *Expect quick return to consciousness*. If not, recheck glucose; if low, give IV dexamethasone (p 200); if normal, ask yourself *is this is a post-ictal state after a hypoglycaemic fit?* Here, giving more glucose worsens cerebral oedema.

Childhood diabetic ketoacidosis (DKA)[1]

The Patient Listlessness; confusion, vomiting; polyuria; polydipsia; weight loss; abdominal pain. *Look for:* Dehydration; deep and rapid (Kussmaul) respirations; ketotic (fruity-smelling) breath; shock; drowsiness; coma.

Diagnosis Usually straightforward, based on the combination of hyperglycaemia (may be mild as capillary blood glucose may be falsely low if the patient is vasoconstricted), acidosis and ketones in urine. Where there is a severe metabolic acidosis without hyperglycaemia (or other obvious causes of acidosis, eg renal failure); consider these other causes: lactic acidosis (including glycogen storage disease Type I), alcoholic ketoacidosis, salicylate overdose, other inborn errors of metabolism (propionic acidaemia, methylmalonic acidaemia) and septicaemia (eg Gram -ve).

Resuscitation Do coma score (p 722; p 201 if <4yrs). True coma is rare (<10%) in DKA: exclude other causes of coma and remember DKA may have been precipitated secondarily. Very rarely cerebral oedema may occur *before* IV treatment.[1] If consciousness↓, nurse semi-prone, or consider intubation.

Take the following action if shocked, consciousness↓, coma, or vomiting[1]:

- *ABC:* Oro-pharyngeal airway 100% O_2. ± NGT. Give up to 3 IV boluses of 10mL/kg of 0.9% saline or 4.5% albumin if BP↓; beware over-enthusiastic fluid resuscitation. Take to ITU if BP↓, or very young, or ward staff busy.
- Weigh; FBC; U&E; glucose; Ca^{2+}; PO_4^{3-}; blood gas; ECG monitoring.
- Use clinical signs to assess dehydration (capillary refill time >3sec ≈ >10% dehydration). Calculate the volume of fluid to be replaced (fluid requirement): ie maintenance fluid (basal 24 hour requirement—eg 100mL/kg/day) + the water deficit. It should be given at a constant steady rate over the first 24–48 hours. Ongoing losses (eg vomiting) should be replaced if excessive and balance remains negative. Use a maximum of 10% dehydration for the initial calculations (10% dehydrated = water deficit of 100mL/kg).
- If child is <5% dehydrated and tolerating oral fluids, it may be appropriate to start with oral fluids and sc insulin rather than IV regime below.
- Aim to complete rehydration over 24h (longer if very young or plasma glucose ↑↑—rapid infusions of large volumes risks cerebral oedema).[2]
- 0.9% saline + 20mmol KCl/500mL at the start of IV therapy until blood glucose falls to ~12mmol/L: then change to 0.45% saline + dextrose 5% + KCl.
- Insulin (eg Actrapid®). If >5yrs: 0.1U/kg/h IVI by pump in 0.9% saline. If no pump, give 0.25U/kg IM stat, then 0.1U/kg/h IM. Halve dose to 0.05U/kg/h if glucose falls by >5mmol/L/h. If <5yrs, consider using a lower dose (0.05U/kg/h)—but this may be insufficient to switch off ketogenesis. Don't switch off the insulin IVI if the blood glucose falls; add more dextrose to the IVI; insulin is needed to reverse ketosis.
- Add IVI K^+, 20mmol for every 500mL of IVI fluid,[3] as guided by U&E. The danger is hypokalaemia; aim for plasma K^+ of 4–5mmol/L. Even if K^+ is normal there will be a total body depletion due to urinary losses.

Avoid bicarbonate in DKA: it can increase the risk of cerebral oedema. If acidosis persists, consider giving further colloid, or ↑dose of insulin (more glucose may be needed in the IV fluids). Ask yourself: is this child septic?

Ongoing monitoring • Hourly blood glucose • CNS status ≥half-hourly. • Nurses must tell you of headache or behaviour change promptly as these may indicate cerebral oedema (BOX) • Hourly fluid input/output • U&E + blood gases (acid/base balance) 2h after starting IVI, then 4-hourly. It is useful to have either a dedicated IV cannula for drawing blood or an arterial line. • If a central venous catheter (CVC) is used to aid monitoring, consider DVT prophylaxis. 368 • Weigh twice daily • Monitor ECG for T-wave changes • CXR • Infection screen. When drinking well and tolerating food (urine ketones may still be +ve), start subcut insulin, stopping intravenous insulin 1h later.

Pitfalls in diabetic ketoacidosis

CNS deterioration

If warning signs (irritable, headache, rising ICP, or falling consciousness):
- ➡Call your senior
- ➡Exclude hypoglycaemia
- ➡Give mannitol 0.5g/kg IVI or NaCl 5% 3mL/kg
- ➡Restrict IV fluids by ⅔
- ➡Move to ITU and do CT
- ➡Treat sepsis vigorously

- Cerebral oedema (BOX) is a big threat, and is almost exclusively a condition of childhood. Pathophysiology is poorly understood: it usually occurs 4-12h from the start of treatment, but it may be present at onset of DKA or up to 24h afterwards, presenting as a sudden CNS deterioration after an initial improvement. It is the major cause of death in diabetic children, not the much-feared hypoglycaemia.
- A high white cell count (even a leukaemoid reaction) may occur without any infection.
- Infection: (there may be no fever). Do MSU, blood cultures, and CXR. Start broad spectrum antibiotics (p 202) if infection suspected.
- Creatinine: some assays for creatinine crossreact with ketone bodies, so plasma creatinine may not reflect true renal function.
- Hyponatraemia (from osmotic effects of glucose): if <120mmol/L, search for other causes, eg triglycerides ↑↑. Hypernatraemia >150mmol/L may be treated with of 0.45% saline to start with (0.9% saline thereafter).
- Ketonuria does not equate with ketoacidosis. Normal individuals may have ketonuria after an overnight fast. Not all ketones are due to diabetes—consider alcohol, if glucose normal. Test plasma with Ketostix® or Acetest® to demonstrate ketonaemia.
- Acidosis without gross elevation of glucose may occur, but consider poisoning, eg with aspirin.

Serum amylase is often raised (up to 10-fold), and nonspecific abdominal pain is common even in the absence of pancreatitis.

1 Guidelines for the management of DKA in children, Diabetes UK. www.diabetes.org.uk
2 Because thrombotic complications are rare, heparin is not usually required and is not recommended as part of standard therapy, but see www.brighton-healthcare.nhs.uk/diabetes/newpage17.htm SE: thrombotic thrombocytopoenia.
3 Note that pooling of KCl and insulin may cause uneven delivery in some IVI containers, so repeated mixing may be needed.

▸▸Poisoning: general management

- Find the name and quantity of the poison ingested; the number of tablets dispensed is often given on the bottle. The dispenser may also have a record and be able to name the tablets; or try *MIMS* or the *BNF*. www.emims.net
- When was the poison ingested? Has he or she vomited since? If the child is *comatose*, enlist expert help. Proceed thus:
- Place in the *semi-prone recovery position*. Note the pupil size.
- Have *suction*, O_2, *a laryngoscope* and *endotracheal tube* to hand.
- APLS/ABC. If there is respiratory failure (clinically or on blood gases), summon expert help. Intubate and ventilate. Treat shock (eg with plasma). Note: the mean systolic BP in mmHg (±1 standard deviation) is 85 (±15) at birth, 95 (±15) at 1yr, 100 (±10) at 4yrs and 110 (±8) at 10yrs.
- Do ward test for *blood glucose*. Treat hypoglycaemia (p 186).
- Record *level of consciousness* (coma scale p 722; p 201 if <4yrs). Record *time*.
- If narcotic poisoning is possible, give *naloxone* 10μg/kg IV, then 100μg/kg if no response (SC or IM is OK, but slower). Frequent doses may be needed.
- Send blood and urine for a *drug screen*—and blood alcohol if indicated (give 10% dextrose IVI: the danger is hypoglycaemia).
- A gastric lavage is rarely indicated: typically for iron ingestion or salicylates. Intubation may be necessary to protect the airway. Have the child held with his head lower than his trunk. The length of orogastric tube required is estimated by the length from the mouth to the ear lobe and thence to the xiphisternum. Pass the tube and keep the initial aspirate for analysis. Use gravity to drain 50mL of 1.4% sodium bicarbonate solution or saline into the stomach. Aspirate after a few mins and repeat eg 10 times. Do not lavage if volatile or corrosive materials have been ingested.
- Monitor TPR, BP, urine output, and blood glucose frequently.

The alert child It is possible to induce vomiting by ipecacuanha 10–15mL mixed with 200mL juice, but this is of uncertain value and risks aspiration.[369]

Activated charcoal (p 192) does reduce absorption. This may have to be given by NG tube.

Specific poisons Always *get poisons unit help*. Aspirin & paracetamol, see p 192.

- *Atropine poisoning* (eg from deadly nightshade) causes dilated pupils, dry skin and mouth, tachycardia, excitement ± psychosis.[370] With Lomotil® (atropine & diphenoxylate) the pupils may be constricted.
- *Iron poisoning:* get help. Expect GI symptoms if >20mg/kg elemental iron is ingested (a 200mg $FeSO_4$ tablet ≈ 60mg iron). Plain abdominal films may help to identify tablets in the stomach. Systemic symptoms, including respiratory distress, occur if >60mg/kg ingested.[371,372] After gastric emptying, give 60mL milk. If >50mg/kg ingested, do iron levels (serum) urgently. If >90μmol/L, give desferrioxamine 15mg/kg/h IVI; max 80mg/kg/24h. Leave 5g in 50mL water in the stomach after gastric lavage. Beware hypotension. Whole bowel irrigation is tried.[373]
- *Tricyclic signs:* seizures, coma, cyanosis, arrhythmias (eg if >10mg/kg of amitriptyline is taken); death. Lowest toxic dose: 6.7mg/kg. Monitor ECG (tachycardia + wide QRS). Bretylium may be needed.[374,375]
- *Paraffin or petrol (kerosene, gasoline):* ►Avoid gastric lavage and emetics. Inhalation may cause lung collapse and consolidation. Do CXR. Lung complications may be delayed 12h. Leaded petrol abuse causes encephalopathy, cerebellar plus corticospinal signs, dementia, and psychosis.[376]
- *Toxic alcohols/ethylene glycol:* ?Try fomepizole.[377,378]
- *Sulfonylureas:* ?Try octreotide.[379] *Other antidotes: OHCM* p 830.

►Contact a National Poisons Information Service (eg 0207 635 9191 UK).

Principles of management

- As always: ABC is your priority. Also check blood glucose.
- Support homeostasis by supporting respiration; protect the airway; maintain BP; correct hypoglycaemia; monitor urine output.
- Remove the poison—eg gastric lavage.
- Stop further absorption from the gut—eg charcoal.
- Get help in determining if a specific antidote is available, or if a specific treatment regimen is indicated—eg in aspirin, paracetamol, iron poisoning, and ingestion of corrosives. (The latter requires especial care of the airway, and gastric lavage is contraindicated—see above.)

Salicylate poisoning

Most children can tolerate ingesting 100mg/kg aspirin, and if there is no doubt that a smaller quantity has been ingested and the patient is well, he need not be admitted. Those who have ingested more than this may show deep respiratory movements, causing a respiratory alkalosis, but this is an early sign, before the dangerous metabolic acidosis sets in.

If the child is unconscious, the first step is to place him in the semi-prone recovery position and do a ward test for blood glucose so any hypoglycaemia can be corrected. Protect the airway with an endotracheal tube and perform a gastric lavage (p 190), even if 24h have elapsed since ingestion. Do an urgent plasma salicylate level with blood gases, U&E, and bicarbonate. Blood samples taken within 6h of ingestion may be misleadingly low.

Serious poisoning is indicated by levels >2.5mmol/L—consider alkaline diuresis (under expert guidance in ITU, as there is significant morbidity) or activated charcoal, which is a much safer means of enhancing the elimination of salicylates. NB: charcoal tastes gritty—and patients may be vomiting after salicylate poisoning, so consider giving by wide-bore nasogastric tube, providing you are happy the airway is protected (±intubation). A good regimen is 25–50g (or 1g/kg body weight) of activated charcoal on admission, or after gastric lavage, then 25g/2–4h, until recovery or until plasma drug concentrations have fallen to safe levels. The dose of charcoal is more related to the quantity of poison ingested than to the size of the child, although the quantity of fluid with which it is mixed may need to be reduced. Charcoal is *not* contraindicated if the child is pregnant. Adding an emetic (ipecacuanha) to this regimen is of no benefit.

An alternative is urinary alkalinization in ITU, with small boluses of sodium bicarbonate 1.2% IV; do catheter urine pH every 15min—aim for ~8. If none of these are practicable, try haemodialysis or charcoal haemoperfusion (esp. if plasma salicylate is ↑↑, eg >5.2mmol/L). *Seek expert help.*

Paracetamol (acetaminophen) poisoning

This is rare in infants as a 100mL bottle of paediatric paracetamol mixture typically contains only 2.4g of paracetamol. Serious hepatotoxicity is likely to occur if ≥150mg/kg is ingested. The initial features are nausea and pallor. Jaundice and an enlarged, tender liver occur after 48h.

Other features: Hypotension, arrhythmias, excitement, delirium, coma.

Management:

- Empty the stomach if within 2h of ingestion.
- If you are sure the ingested paracetamol is <150 mg/kg and ipecac-induced emesis occurs within 1h, management may be safely done at home.[380]
- Patients ingesting >200 mg/kg or an unknown amount should be referred for a serum acetaminophen concentration.
- Give acetylcysteine if plasma paracetamol level is above the line on the graph OPPOSITE (take sample ≥4h after ingestion). The initial dose is 150mg/kg in up to 200mL (depending on the child's size; see *BNF*) of 5% dextrose infused over 15min, followed by 50mg/kg IVI over the next 4h, and 100mg/kg IVI over next 16h. It is very effective in preventing liver damage.
- All patients with a delayed presentation (>8hrs) should have acetylcysteine started immediately.
- Consider the cause: typically teenage girls seeking attention. All need psychiatric evaluation. Causes may be extremely complex and deep-seated: although the patient may claim a seemingly superficial cause this may be hiding deep social or psychiatric pathology.

Late presentations: Seek expert advice. Check often for hypoglycaemia.

Graph for use in deciding who should receive acetylcysteine. 381

One tablet of paracetamol (acetaminophen) = 500mg; 150mg = 1mmol.

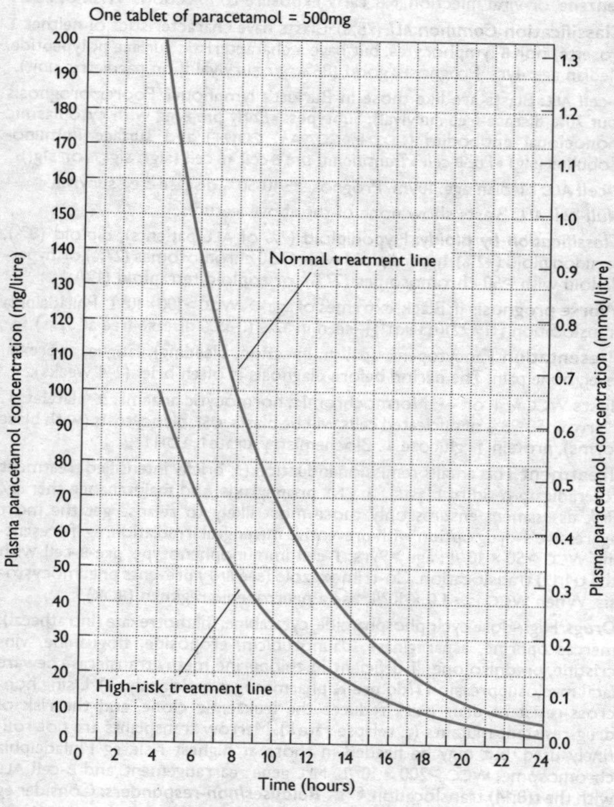

Patients whose plasma paracetamol concentrations are above the 'normal treatment line' should be treated with acetylcysteine by IVI or, provided the overdose has been taken within 10–12h and there is no vomiting, with methionine by mouth. Patients who are on enzyme-inducers (eg carbamazepine, phenobarbital, phenytoin, rifampicin, alcohol, and St John's wort) or who are malnourished (eg anorexia, alcoholism, HIV +ve) should be treated if their plasma paracetamol level is above the 'high-risk treatment line'.

Acute lymphoblastic leukaemia (ALL)

ALL is the commonest childhood leukaemia (~500 cases/yr^{uk}); other forms: *OHCM* p 654. **Causes:** Prenatal mutations with later exposure to a trigger, eg benzene, or viral infection. NB: early exposure to infections ↓risk of ALL.

Classification ***Common ALL*** (75%): Blasts have characteristics of neither T (rosette) nor B lymphocytes, but have a characteristic surface polypeptide. Median age: 4yrs. Prognosis: good (86% 5yr survival if on paediatric unit).

B-cell ALL: Blasts are like those in Burkitt's lymphoma. Poorer prognosis (but 70% disease-free survival). Subtypes: •*Early pre-B*, eg with cytoplasmic monoclonal antibodies (CD22+, CD79A+, CD19+) and surface immunoglobulins (sIg) •*Pre-B-cell* •*Transitional pre-B-cell* •*B-cell* (sIg^+, sIg_κ^+, or sIg_λ).

T-cell ALL: Median age: 10yrs. Prognosis: ~40–50% disease-free survival.

Null-cell ALL: Blasts show none of the above features.

Classification by ploidy: Hypodiploid (7% of ALL patients), diploid (8%), pseudodiploid (42%), hyperdiploid with 47–50 chromosomes (27%) or hyperdiploid with >50 chromosomes (27%), or triploid/tetraploid (1%).

Worse prognosis if: Black, extremes of age, ♂, WCC >100×10^9/L; Philadelphia translocation [t(9;22)(q34:q11)]—seen in 12% (0–15% disease-free at 5yrs).

Presentation Pancytopenia (pallor, infection, bleeding), fatigue, anorexia, fever, bone pain. The period before diagnosis is often brief (2–4 weeks).

Tests WCC↑, ↓ or ↔. Normochromic, normocytic anaemia ± platelets↓. Marrow: 50–98% of nucleated cells will be blasts. CSF: pleocytosis (with blast forms), protein ↑, glucose ↓. Biochemistry: urate↑, LDH↑.

Treatment This entails remission induction (± briefly intensified treatment to eradicate residual blasts[382]), CNS prophylaxis, and maintenance therapy. *Risk assessment* ensures only those most likely to relapse get the most aggressive 4-drug option with preventive meningeal irradiation, eg if presenting WCC >50 × 10^9/L; age >9yrs; T-cell immunophenotype; pre-B-cell with the t(1;19) translocation. Co-trimoxazole (see *BNF*) prevents pneumocystosis. When WCC is <1.0 × 10^9/L use a neutropenic regimen (BOX).

Drugs: High-dose cyclophosphamide, cytarabine, methotrexate (intrathecal), mercaptopurine, asparaginase, daunorubicin, etoposide, tioguanine, vincristine, prednisolone. If deficient in thiopurine methyltransferase beware fatal myelosuppression (?do pre-℞ pharmacogenomic analysis). Using non-cross-resistant drug pairs reduces the leukaemic clone, and the risk of drug-resistant mutants (∴ relapse rate↓). Marrow transplants are not routinely used, but *may* be needed in those at highest risk, eg Philadelphia chromosome, WCC >200 × 10^9/L, MLL gene rearrangement, and B-cell ALL with the t(8;14) translocation.[383] ***Relapses/non-responders:*** Consider eg FLAG[1] or clofarabine (a nucleoside analogue that damages tumour DNA).[384]

Prognosis 75% 5yr event-free survival. ***Treatment related deaths:*** <2%; eg from bacteria, CMV, or fungi—or *pneumocystis carinii* when in remission.[385]

Pitfalls ►For management serious sepsis, see BOX (and p 106).

- Hyperuricaemia at induction after massive cell destruction. Prevent by pre-treating with ↑ fluid intake + allopurinol 10–20mg/kg/24h max 400mg/day.
- Ignoring quality of life issues; eg most cytotoxics may be given at home.
- Omitting to examine the testes (a common site for recurrence).
- Inappropriate transfusion (leukostasis if WCC >100 × 10^9/L).[386]
- Failing to treat side-effects of chemotherapy optimally—eg 5-HT_3 receptor antagonists such as ondansetron are better than other anti-emetics.
- Drug-induced delayed cancer elsewhere (risk of CNS tumours or a 2nd acute leukaemia is ~3–4%). Risk assessment allows lower doses.
- Vincristine must ***only ever be given IV***. It is universally fatal if given intrathecally. ►All cytotoxics should only ever be given by fully trained staff.

▸▸Febrile neutropenic patients who may be septicaemic (eg from an infected venous catheter)

Suspect infection when untoward events happen in a neutropenic patient (WCC <2 × 10^9/L, or neutrophils <1 × 10^9/L). Do T° often; brief rises to ≤38°C *may* be ignored if lasting for <6h only if the child is well. Emphasize to the parents and child the importance of swift routes to hospital.

Do blood cultures and MSU; swab all orifices. Do FBC, CRP & serology. Get help from your senior and a microbiologist; follow local protocols.

Blind treatment will depend on local protocols, and may include imipenem, the broadest spectrum beta-lactam[2] antibiotic, which may have advantages over cefalosporins if an anaerobe such as *Bacteroides* is suspected (NB: imipenem is not indicated in CNS infections).[387]

Imipenem—Dose in children <40kg: 15mg/kg/6h max 2g/24h. Heavier children have the adult dose: 12.4mg/kg/6h IVI; max dose, eg 1g/6h. Do U&E. If creatinine clearance <70mL/min, ↓dose frequency (see *Data sheet*). NB: do not use IM formulations IV, and the IM formulation is not to be used in children. If blood culture *does* prove +ve, either change imipenem after microbiological advice, or continue it for 5 days, provided he or she has been afebrile for >24h. If blood cultures are –ve, give for a few days and send home when well and afebrile for >24h.

Imipenem SEs: (It is usually well-tolerated.) Thrombophlebitis, anuria, polyuria, seizures (eg in ~2%), confusion, psychic disturbance, encephalopathy, vertigo, tinnitus, transient hearing loss, BP↓, pruritus, taste perversion, pseudomembranous colitis; arthralgia; eosinophilia; WCC↓; Hb↓; LFT↑. There are no clinically important drug interactions.[388]

Meropenem is preferred in some units. It is more active against most Gram –ve pathogens than imipenem but is less active against most Gram +ve ones.[389] Dose: 3 months to 12 years: 10–20mg/kg/8h IVI over 5mins; over 50kg weight: adult dose (eg 1g/8h IVI). ***SE:*** D&V (eg antibiotic-associated colitis); abdominal pain; LFT↑; platelets↓; partial thromboplastin time↓; +ve Coombs' test; eosinophilia; neutropenia; headache; paraesthesiae; rash; pruritus; convulsions (rare).[390]

Teicoplanin For blind treatment of the worst infections, consider adding this to imipenem. Dose: 6–10mg/kg/12h IV for 3 doses, then daily (neonates: 16mg/kg on day 1, then 8mg/kg/day). ***SE:*** (few): dizziness; headache; WCC↓; platelets ↓/↑; LFT↑; allergy (rare). No major interactions.[391]

If fever persists and blood cultures remain –ve ask: Is ***aciclovir*** indicated? Is a fungus possible; for ***amphotericin*** see *data sheet* & *OHCM* p 180.

1 FLAG = Fludarabine, cytarabine (Ara-C), and G-CSF (recombinant human granulocyte-colony stimulating factor); clofarabine is not yet available in UK.

2 Named for the beta-lactam ring in their structure. Examples: penicillins, cefalosporins, etc.

Anaemia

The clinical problem You have the results of a full blood count, showing anaemia (Hb <11g/dL, p 222, the WHO criterion). *How should you proceed?*

1 Take a history (include travel, diet, ethnic origin); examine the child.
2 MCV <70fl: suspect iron deficiency (IDA) or thalassaemia (*IDA* esp. if poor diet, low socio-economic class, bleeding, stomatitis, koilonychia; *thalassaemia* if from Mediterranean or SE Asia areas, short stature, muddy complexion, icteric sclerae, distended abdomen ∵ hepatosplenomegaly, bossed skull, and prominent maxillae, from marrow hyperplasia).
3 MCV >100fl: suspect ↓folate (malabsorption, p 171; phenytoin), ↓ B_{12} (breast milk from a vegetarian, ↓intrinsic factor, malabsorption), or haemolysis.
4 MCV 81–97fl (normocytic), suspect haemolysis, or marrow failure (transient, after infections, or chronic, eg thyroid, kidney, or liver failure, or malignancy). Causes of aplasia: chloramphenicol; Diamond–Blackfan syndrome (p 640); Fanconi's anaemia (p 644).
5 Is the WCC or differential abnormal? As an example, eosinophilia (>400 × 10^9/L) + anaemia = hookworms until proved otherwise, in the Tropics.
6 Next look at the ESR and CRP. This may indicate some chronic disease.
7 Do a film + reticulocyte count ± thick films for malaria. Hypochromic microcytic RBCs≈IDA; target cells≈liver disease or thalassaemia; ferritin for IDA; sickling tests + Hb electrophoresis for thalassaemia & sickle-cell anaemia (do eg in Afro-Caribbeans); B_{12}; red cell folate.
8 Prevention: no cows' milk if <1yr; if formula-fed, use iron-fortified; wean at 4–6 months. Adequate vitamin C intake; iron supplements if premature.

Iron deficiency (20% of the world's population). Despite fortification of breakfast cereals, this is common (12% of white children and 28% of Asian children admitted to hospital). The chief behavioural effect is that iron deficient babies are less happy than others. Dietary causes are the most common—eg poverty, lack of education, or coeliac disease. In recurrent IDA, suspect bleeding (eg Meckel's diverticulum or oesophagitis). Treat with ferrous fumarate syrup (140mg/5mL), 2.5–5mL/12h PO (if <6yrs old; for prems: 0.6mL/kg/day), or Plesmet®/Sytron®. Warn of the dangers of overdosage. Aim for a rise in Hb of >1g/month (do reticulocyte count after 2 months).

Haemolysis Is malaria or sickle-cell disease possible? Get help, and try to provide the expert with sufficient information to answer these 4 questions:
- Any evidence of ↑RBC production (polychromasia, reticulocytosis)?
- Is there decreased RBC survival? (Bilirubin ↑, haptoglobins ↓.)
- Is there intravascular haemolysis? (Haemoglobinuria.)
- Is there an inborn error of metabolism (eg G6PD deficiency), spherocytosis, or is the defect acquired (usually with +ve Coombs' test)?

Hereditary spherocytosis is the chief cause of haemolysis in north Europe. Mostly it is mild. Presentation with parvovirus B19 infection causing transient severe anaemia can occur. Flow cytometric analysis of eosin-5-maleimide (EMA) binding to red cells is replacing nonspecific osmotic fragility tests.[392] Splenectomy leads to ↑red cell survival and is indicated for severe and ?moderate disease; gallstones may occur in the 1st decade, and if symptomatic are an indication for cholecystectomy and splenectomy.[393]

Sickle-cell disease: *OHCM* p 640. Hydrate and give O_2. ***Pain relief:*** Warmth, hydration, ibuprofen 10mg/kg/8h PO, ± Oramorph®, load with 0.4mg/kg PO, then 0.3mg/kg/3h + MST® 1–1.5mg/kg/12h for background analgesia; this *may* be preferred to IVI morphine, eg 0.1mg/kg (give lactulose 2.5–10mL/12h PO ± senna). ***Patient-controlled analgesia:*** Morphine 1mg/kg in 50mL 5% dextrose at 1mL/h with self-delivered extra boluses of 1mL as needed; do respiration & sedation score every ¼h + S_AO_2 if chest or abdominal pain.[394]

Iron deficiency without anaemia

►Don't think that if a child is not anaemic he's not iron deficient. CNS iron levels fall *before* RBC mass. If in doubt, check ferritin. Treating low ferritins may improve: •Memory •Lassitude •Developmental delay •Mood •Cognition—in toddlers and adolescent girls, facing demands of puberty and menstruation. NB: pica is a sign of iron deficiency.

Purpura in children

►►If a child is ill with purpura presume meningococcaemia (give penicillin, p 202), leukaemia or disseminated intravascular coagulation (investigate initially with a visual non-automated blood film and WCC). If the child is well, and there is no history of trauma, Henoch–Schönlein purpura or idiopathic thrombocytopenic purpura, are likely—the former if platelets are normal). (Aplastic anaemia is very rare.) Vomiting or coughing can cause petechiae in a superior vena cava-distribution.

Henoch–Schönlein (anaphylactoid) purpura (HSP) presents with purpura (purple spots/nodules which don't disappear on pressure ∵ intradermal bleeding) eg over buttocks and extensor surfaces (± urticaria. ♂/♀ >1:1. ***Other features:*** •Nephritis (with crescents, in ⅓ of patients—an IgA nephropathy—we could think of HSP as being a systemic version of Berger's syndrome, *OHCM* p 718) •Joint involvement (common) •Abdominal pain (as if 'acute abdomen') •Intussusception.

The fault lies in the vasculature (platelets are normal). It may follow respiratory infection, and is typically self-limiting after a few months. Complications (worse in adults): big GI bleeds, ileus, haemoptysis (rare), and renal failure (rare). One option in HSP nephritis (not usually needed) is high-dose steroids + cyclophosphamide; this ↓proteinuria (a risk factor for renal insufficiency in HSP).[395] Chronic renal failure occurs in 5%.

Idiopathic thrombocytopenic purpura ***Presentation:*** Acute bruising, purpura, and petechiae. Less commonly there is bleeding from gums, nose or rectum. If this is present to any large extent, or there is lymphadenopathy, hepatosplenomegaly, or pancytopenia, another diagnosis is likely. *Tests:* The peripheral blood film usually shows only simple thrombocytopenia. ITP may be a response to a virus, and it is worth looking for congenital CMV if the patient is <1yr old. Also look for Epstein–Barr virus and erythrovirus (formerly called parvovirus B19). There may also be a lymphocytosis. It is not necessary to do a marrow biopsy, unless:
- Unusual features are present, eg equivocal or abnormal cells on a film.
- Platelet count is not rising after ~2 weeks.
- Treatment is contemplated with steroids or immunoglobulins.
- Platelet antibody tests are unhelpful. If SLE possible, do DNA binding.
- CT to exclude cerebral bleed, eg if there is headache or CNS signs.

Natural history: Eg gradual resolution over ~3 months, or more chronic (>6 months in 10–20%; the chronic form is compatible with normal longevity, and normal activities, provided contact sports are avoided).

Management: Admit eg if: •Unusual features, eg excessive bleeding. •Social circumstances. •There are rowdy siblings at home who might engage in physical badinage (the risk of intracranial haemorrhage is <1%).

Splenectomy may benefit ⅔ of those with chronic ITP if >6yrs old, and have had ITP for >1yr. NB: Platelet transfusion is only indicated if very severe haemorrhage (or during splenectomy). Steroids and immunoglobulin are now not used (unfavourable risk/benefit ratio). Follow-up of 92 children with chronic ITP revealed only one death from bleeding, and this was associated with a major physical assault.

Primary antibody deficiency

Typical features:
- Frequent infections
- Bronchiectasis
- Chronic sinusitis
- Failure to thrive
- Nodular lymphoid hyperplasia (gut)
- Absent tonsils
- Enteropathy
- Hepatosplenomegaly
- Anaemia
- Arthropathy
- Hepatosplenomegaly
- Lymphopenia
- Serum total protein↓ (albumin ↔; immunoglbulins are missing). 396

Synonyms: *primary hypogammaglobulinaemia* (not secondary to protein-losing enteropathy, chronic lymphatic leukaemia, or myeloma). Prevalence: ~4/100,000. Most diagnoses are in those >6yrs old (but some will be adults). When the signs in the box are unexplained, refer to an immunologist, to assess antibody responses to protein and carbohydrate antigens, measure IgG subclasses, and count lymphocytes involved in antibody production (CD4, CD8, CD19, CD23 +ve lymphocytes). Immunoglobulin levels are interpreted by age. There is a role for watching responses to test vaccinations.

Types of primary immunodeficiency IgA deficiency (39%); common variable immunodeficiency (14%; IgG↓, IgA↓, IgM variable), severe combined immunodeficiency/T-cell defects (13%), complement deficiency (10%), X-linked agammaglobulinaemia (4%; often ♂; B cells may be abnormal), IgG subclass deficiency (3%), chronic granulomatous disease (3%). 397 [n=2050]

Management Aim to include the patient and the family in the process. Ensure prompt treatment of intercurrent infections. This may include postural physiotherapy, and bronchodilators as well as antibiotics.

Immunoglobulin replacement obviates most complications and is best delivered by an immunologist, after detailed assessment. Many patients can join a self-infusion programme. Before infusions, exclude active infection (to minimize risk of adverse reactions), and a baseline check of transaminase enzymes, creatinine, and anti-IgA antibody titres should be done.

The dose of IV immunoglobulin is determined by the severity and frequency of infections, and the plasma level of IgG. Most receive ~400mg/kg/month, usually as 2 doses, 2 weeks apart. 398 Have hydrocortisone and an antihistamine at the ready. *SE:* headaches, abdominal pain, anaphylaxis, transmission of hepatitis. 399 IM immunoglobulins are not favoured, but the subcutaneous route is being investigated and appears satisfactory. 400 [N=40]

Complications
- *Chest:* Bronchiectasis, granulomas, lymphoma.
- *Gut:* Malabsorption, giardia, cholangitis, atrophic gastritis, colitis.
- *Liver:* Acquired hepatitis, chronic active hepatitis, biliary cirrhosis.
- *Blood:* Autoimmune haemolysis, ITP (p 197), anaemia of chronic disease, aplasia.
- *Eyes/CNS:* Keratoconjunctivitis, uveitis, granulomas, encephalitis.
- *Others:* Septic arthropathy, arthralgia, splenomegaly.

Gene therapy[1] Autologous haematopoietic stem cells transduced with the γc gene can restore immune system in boys with severe combined immunodeficiency. A harmless retrovirus carries the replacement gene, and infects the stem cells *in vitro*. When these are replaced in the marrow an immune system develops within a few months[2]—obviating the need for intrusive anti-infection isolation measures and IV immunoglobulin. It is an alternative to marrow transplants (eg if no HLA match can be found). There is likely to be a limitation to initiation of normal thymopoiesis, so do it promptly.

1 Blood 2005 Feb 1 & C Hue 2002 *NEJM* **346** 1185 n=5.
2 T cells & repertoires of T-cell receptors were ~normal up to 2yrs post-op; thymopoiesis is shown by naive T cells. Antibody production is adequate.

▶▶Rising intracranial pressure[APLS]

Causes: Meningoencephalitis; head injury; subdural/extradural bleeds (eg abuse); hypoxia, eg near-drowning; ketoacidosis; Reye's syndrome (p 662) may all cause sudden rises in ICP; the rise with brain tumours is slower.

Presentations: Irritability; drowsy; headache; diplopia; vomiting; tense fontanelle; ↓level of responsiveness (assess by children's Coma Scale, or by Glasgow Coma Scale if >4yrs (p 722)); pupil changes (ipsilateral dilatation); ↑BP and ↓ pulse (Cushing reflex); intermittent respiration. Later (ie chronic): papilloedema and hydrocephalus.

Management: Aim to prevent secondary damage. Help venous drainage by keeping head in the midline, elevated at 20°. Give O_2; ↓fluid intake. Check for hypoglycaemia. Control seizures (p 208). Get help:
- Intubate and hyperventilate to aim for $PaCO_2$ 4–4.5kPa if Coma Scale is ≤8.
- Give mannitol 20% (check it is dry, ie crystal-free), eg 2.5mL/kg IV over 15min if the child is deteriorating—but discuss with an intensivist if you have time.
- Dexamethasone 0.1mg/kg IV stat, then 0.05–0.1mg/kg/6h IV.
- Fluid restriction and diuretics, but avoid hypovolaemia (keep Na 145–150mmol/L, osmolality ≤300, and CVP 2–5cm H_2O).
- Measure pulse and BP continuously (check that cuff fits well).
- Remember the possibility of nonaccidental injury.
- Do not do an LP: this risks coning.

Herpes simplex encephalitis (HSE) is the most treatable encephalitis.
- Think of it in any febrile child with focal or general fits and CNS signs, temporal lobe signs ± ↓consciousness. Neck signs are often nonspecific. Prodromal illness is often absent; CNS deficits may be mild or gross (eg hemiparesis).

Tests: Urgent CT and CSF examination: focal abnormality (unless polymerase chain reaction is available). Early EEG may show focal changes and periodic complexes. Herpes simplex antibodies are produced too late to guide management. Brain biopsy is rarely justified.

Treatment: Start aciclovir as soon as HSE is suspected. Give by slow IV infusion over 1h (250–500mg/m^2/8h for 2 weeks—20mg/kg/8h in neonates). Monitor U&E & urine output; adjust dose according to Data sheet.

Mortality: ~70% → 30% survive without CNS sequelae. There may be Klüver–Bucy syndrome: hypersexuality + episodic rage ± visual agnosia.

Brain tumours: ⅔ are in the posterior fossa. Key features in their diagnosis are: raised ICP with focal signs (below) ± false localizing signs (eg VI nerve palsy, due to its long intracranial course). Space-time clustering suggests a viral cause of astrocytomas and ependymomas.

Medulloblastoma: Radiosensitive midline cerebellar embryonal tumour (inferior vermis) causing ↑ICP, speech difficulty, truncal ataxia ± falls. ♂/♀ ≈ 2; peak age of occurrence: 7 years. Seedlings along CSF pathways.

Brainstem astrocytoma: Cranial nerve palsies, pyramidal tract signs (eg hemiparesis), cerebellar ataxia. Signs of ↑ICP are rare.

Midbrain and third ventricle: Tumours may cause hydrocephalus; pinealomas or pineal cysts (cause posture-dependent drowsiness). Signs: behaviour change (early); pyramidal tract and cerebellar signs; upward gaze defect.

Suprasellar gliomas: Visual field defects, optic atrophy, pituitary disorders (growth arrest, hypopituitarism, delayed puberty), diabetes insipidus (DI). Cranial DI is caused by ↓ADH, so that there is polyuria and low urine osmolality (always <300mmol/L) despite dehydration.

Cerebral hemispheres: Usually gliomas. Headache and raised ICP are rare. Fits may be the presenting sign. Signs depend on the lobe involved (OHCM p 387).

Tests: eg Skull x-ray; CT scan; magnetic resonance imaging.

▸▸Rising intracranial pressure[APLS]

Causes Meningoencephalitis; head injury; subdural/extra-dural bleeds (eg abuse); hypoxia (eg near-drowning); ketoacidosis; Reye's syndrome (p 652) may all cause sudden rises in ICP. The rise with brain tumours is slower.

Presentation Listless; irritable; drowsy; headache; diplopia; vomiting; tense fontanelle; ↓level of responsiveness—assess by Children's Coma Scale if <4yrs (see OPPOSITE), or by Glasgow Coma Scale if >4yrs (p 722); pupil changes (ipsilateral dilatation); rising BP and falling pulse (Cushing reflex); intermittent respiration. Later (ie chronic): papilloedema and hydrocephalus.

Management Aim to prevent secondary damage. Help venous drainage by keeping head in the midline, elevated at ~20°. Give O_2. Fan/sponge (tepid water) if T° >40°C. Check for hypoglycaemia. Control seizures (p 208). Get help.

- ▸▸Intubate and hyperventilate: aim for P_aCO_2 of ~3.68kPa if *Coma Scale* is <8.
- ▸▸Give mannitol 20% (check it is crystal-free), eg 2.5mL/kg IVI over 15min if the child is deteriorating—but discuss with an intensivist if you have time.
- ▸▸Dexamethasone 0.1mg/kg IV stat, then 0.05–0.1mg/kg/6h IV.
- ▸▸Fluid restriction and diuresis, but avoid hypovolaemia (keep Na^+ 145–150mmol/L, osmolarity to 300–310, and CVP to 2–5cmH_2O).
- ▸▸Measure pulse and BP continuously (check that cuff fits well).
- ▸▸Remember the possibility of non-accidental injury.
- ▸▸Do not do LP: this risks coning.

Herpes simplex encephalitis (HSE) is the most treatable encephalitis ▸*Think of it in any febrile child with focal or general fits and* CNS *(esp. temporal lobe) signs ± ↓consciousness.* NB: signs are often nonspecific. Nasolabial

herpes is often absent. CNS deficits may be mild or gross (eg hemiparesis).

Tests such as CT and CSF examination are often nonspecific (unless polymerase chain reaction is available). MRI is better. EEG may show focal changes and periodic complexes. Herpes simplex antibodies are produced too late to guide management. Brain biopsy is rarely used.

Treatment: ▸▸Start aciclovir as soon as HSE is suspected. Give 10mg/kg[IBW]/8h by IVI over 1h (250–500mg/m^2) eg for 2 weeks—20mg/kg/8h in neonates.[401] Monitor U&E & urine output; adjust dose according to *Datasheet*.

Mortality: ~7%. 60% survive without CNS sequelae. There may be Kluver-Bucy syndrome: hypersexuality + episodic rage + visual agnosia.

Brain tumours ⅔ are in the posterior fossa. Key features in their diagnosis are a raised ICP with focal signs (below), ± false localizing signs (eg VI nerve palsy, due to its long intracranial course). Space-time clustering suggests a viral cause of astrocytomas and ependymoma.[402]

Medulloblastoma: Radiosensitive midline cerebellar embryonal tumour (inferior vermis) causing ICP↑, speech difficulty, truncal ataxia ± falls. ♂/♀ ≈4:1. Peak age of occurrence: 7 years. Seeding is along CSF pathways.

Brainstem astrocytoma: Cranial nerve palsies; pyramidal tract signs (eg hemiparesis); cerebellar ataxia; signs of ICP↑ are rare.

Midbrain and third ventricle tumours may be astrocytomas, pinealomas or colloid cysts (cause posture-dependent drowsiness). Signs: behaviour change (early); pyramidal tract and cerebellar signs; upward gaze defect.

Suprasellar gliomas: Visual field defects; optic atrophy; pituitary disorders (growth arrest, hypothyroidism, delayed puberty); diabetes insipidus (DI). Cranial DI is caused by ADH↓, so that there is polyuria and low urine osmolality (always <800mosmol/L) despite dehydration.

Cerebral hemispheres: Usually gliomas. Meningiomas are rare. Fits may be the presenting sign. Signs depend on the lobe involved (*OHCM* p 387).

Tests: EEG, skull x-ray, CT scans ± magnetic resonance imaging.

Treatment options: Excision, CSF shunting, radio- and/or chemotherapy (eg 3 post-op cycles of cyclophosphamide, vincristine, methotrexate, carboplatin & etoposide + intraventricular methotrexate for medulloblastoma). 403

Other space-occupying lesions Aneurysms; haematomas; granulomas; tuberculomas; cysts (cysticercosis); ▶abscess—suspect whenever signs of ICP ↑, fever and a leukocytosis occur together; arrange urgent referral.

Other causes of headache Viruses; meningitis; sinusitis (frontal sinus not developed until >10yrs); hypertension (always do BP), stress, behavioural.

Migraine (*OHCM* p 342) is common (~10% of children). It is associated with stress.[1] Good data on prophylaxis are scarce. Only one study of propranolol and one of flunarizine show clear benefits. In one meta-analysis, nimodipine, timolol, papaverine, pizotifen, trazodone, clonidine, metoclopramide, and domperidone were ineffective. 404 Signs to prompt referral:

- Headaches of increasing frequency or severity, or if aged <6yrs.
- Headache unrelieved by paracetamol.
- Irritable; loss of interest/skills; slowing of physical or cognitive development.
- Head circumference above the 97th centile, or greatly out of line.

Children's coma scale (use if <4yrs)APLS

There is an objective scale to record the level of coma, and to help answer questions such as: *is she getting better or worse; what is the prognosis?*

Best motor response (6 grades)

6 Carrying out a request ('obeying command'): The child moves spontaneously, or to your request.

5 Localizing response to pain: Put pressure on the patient's finger nail bed with a pencil then try supraorbital and sternal pressure: purposeful movements towards changing painful stimuli is a 'localizing' response.

4 Withdraws to pain: Pulls limb away from painful stimulus.

3 Flexor response to pain: Pressure on the nail bed causes abnormal flexion of limbs—decorticate posture.

2 Extensor posturing to pain: The stimulus causes limb extension (adduction, internal rotation of shoulder, forearm pronation; decerebrate posture).

1 No response to pain. Score best response of any limb.

Best verbal response (5 grades) If intubated *can the patient grimace?*

5 Orientated: Smiles, is orientated to sounds, fixes and follows objects.

Crying	*Interaction score the highest out of either column*
4 Consolable	Inappropriate
3 Inconsistently consolable	Moaning
2 Inconsolable	Irritable
1 No response	No response

Eye opening (4 grades)

4 Spontaneous eye opening.

3 Eye opening in response to speech: Any speech, or shout, not necessarily request to open eyes.

2 Eye opening to response to pain: Pain to limbs as above.

1 No eye opening.

An overall score is made by summing the score in the 3 areas assessed. Eg: no response to pain + no verbalization + no eye opening = 3. ▶If >4 yrs, see *Glasgow Coma Scale*, p 722. Scores may be hard to interpret. As a rule of thumb, a score of <8 means intubation may be needed; 4–8 means intermediate prognosis; 3 means a bad prognosis.

1 El-Metwally A 2005 *Headache* 45 98

Encephalitis

Signs Consciousness↓; odd behaviour; vomiting; fits; T°↑; meningism. Consider: herpes simplex (▸▸aciclovir, p 200); zoster; mumps; rubella; influenza; measles; rickettsia; toxoplasmosis; TB; mycoplasma; Murray Valley encephalitis; dengue; rabies. Do CSF PCR; test stool, urine, and blood.

Non-infective encephalopathies: kernicterus (p 115), hepatic failure (eg Reye's syndrome), lead or other poisoning, lupus. 405 **Treatment** p 200.

▸***Consider malaria*** if a malarious area is visited (even for a 'stop-over'). Don't wait to see how the illness unfolds: do a thick blood film at once, and enlist expert help (assume chloroquine resistance, *OHCM* p 562).

▸***Prolonged fevers***—consider: endocarditis; Still's (p 654); malignancy.

▸▸Meningitis[APLS]

Suspect this in any ill baby or child. The only signs may be unusual crying, poor feeding, or vomiting. Pay great attention to the fontanelle: in GI vomiting it becomes sunken; with meningitis it may be tense. ▸*Get expert help from your senior and a microbiologist.* If there is any hint of meningococcal disease, the GP should give penicillin at once if involved (dose below). If you do a lumbar puncture, start a broad-spectrum IV agent (eg ceftriaxone below) at once, while awaiting microscopy and further advice.

Meningeal signs: Stiff neck (unable to kiss knee; often absent if <18 months); photophobia (late; unreliable); Kernig's sign (resistance to extending knee with hip flexed); Brudzinski's sign (hips flex on bending head forward); opisthotonus.

ICP↑: Irritable; high-pitched cry; drowsy; vomiting; fontanelle tense (late).

Septic signs: T°↑; odd behaviour; rash (don't *expect* petechiae with meningococcus); cyanosis; DIC; pulse↑; BP↓; tachypnoea; arthritis/limb pain; WCC↑.

Other causes of stiff neck: Tonsillitis, pneumonia, subarachnoid bleed.

Lumbar puncture: Often inappropriate ∵ focal signs; DIC; purpura (top priority is penicillin, p 205); or *brain herniation* is near (odd posture or breathing; coma scale <13, p 201; dilated pupils, doll's eye reflexes, BP↑, pulse↓, papilloedema). Preliminary CT is incapable of showing that LP would be safe. ***Technique:*** Learn from an expert; a common error is aiming too low. • Explain everything to mother. • Get IV access first: acute deterioration is possible. Ask an experienced nurse to help, by positioning child fully flexed (knees to chin) on the side of a bed, with his back exactly at right angles with it. • Mark a point just above (cranial to) a line joining the spinous processes between the iliac crests. • Drape & sterilize the area; put on gloves. • Infiltrate 1mL of 1% lidocaine superficially if required. • Insert LP needle aiming towards umbilicus. • Catch 4 CSF drops in each of 3 bottles for: *urgent Gram stain, culture, virology, glucose, protein* (do blood glucose too). • Request frequent CNS observations. • Report to mother. ***After LP:*** FBC, U&E, culture blood, urine, nose swabs, stool virology. CRP: is it >20mg/L? CXR. Fluid balance, TPR & BP hourly. Is CSF lactate >3mg/L? (a more sensitive means of distinguishing bacterial from aseptic meningitis than the blood/CSF glucose ratio.)

Treating pyogenic meningitis before the organism is known

- Protect airway; give high flow O_2; set up IVI: colloid in 10–20mL/kg boluses.
- If meningococcaemia likely use antibiotics as detailed on p 204.
- ***Ceftriaxone*** 80mg/kg/day IV over ½h (50mg/kg if <7 days old, over 1h)—or ***cefotaxime*** ≤50mg/kg/6h IV over 15min + ***benzylpenicillin*** 50mg/kg/8h slowly IV if 1 week to 1 month old; 50mg/kg/4h if older. ***Netilmicin*** slowly IV may be used in neonates, eg 3mg/kg/12h (2.5mg/kg/8h if older than 1 week); do plasma levels & creatinine, ↓dose as needed; see *Data sheet*; see p 175 for gentamicin); add ***ampicillin*** (p 204) for listeria. In general, the intrathecal route is not required for antibiotic therapy.
- If pre-hernia signs, treat for ICP↑ (p 200), eg mannitol 20%, 2.5–5mL/kg IVI.

Treat for cryptococcus if HIV+ve. After culture, check the minimum inhibitory concentration (MIC) of the antibiotics used to the organism *in vitro*.

Complications Disseminated sepsis, subdural effusion, hydrocephalus, ataxia, paralysis, deafness, mental retardation, epilepsy, brain abscess.

CSF in meningitis	*Pyogenic:*	*Tubercular:*	*Aseptic:*
Appearance	often turbid	may be fibrin web	usually clear
Predominant cell	polymorphs eg 1000/mm³	mononuclear 10–350/mm³	mononuclear 50–1500/mm³
Glucose level	<⅔ of blood	<⅔ of blood	>⅔ of blood
Protein (mg/dL)[406]	↑ (mean≈300)	↑ >40 (mean≈200)[407]	≥40 and <1500

Bacterial antigen detection for *N. meningitidis, H. influenzae* & streps helps in partially treated meningitis. *CSF* lactate typically rises before the CSF glucose falls in pyogenic meningitis.

Preventing deaths from meningococcal disease

- Because death is so swift, this can seem a hopeless task—as even when we doctors contract meningococcal disease, we simply think we have 'flu', and our families are surprised to find us dead in bed just hours after reporting sick. Nevertheless, good practice (and luck) *can* save lives, and the meningococcus is not always *that* fast.
- Rapid skilled assessment of all febrile children. Nurse triage is unreliable.
- Don't expect meningeal signs; septicaemic signs feature in fatal illness.
- Any rash (or none) will do for the meningococcus. If you wait for purpura, you may be waiting until the disease is untreatable.
- In primary care, for any acutely unwell child *leave your consulting room door ajar.* Explain that a doctor can be contacted *at any time* if:

–He seems to be worsening	–He seems to be unrousable
–A rash develops	–He starts crying in an odd way
–Poor response to antipyretics	–Odd features eg limb/joint pain

- Beware fever + lethargy + vomiting even if no headache or photophobia.
- Give parenteral penicillin *early*, before admission to hospital.
- Monitor pulse, BP, respiratory rate, pupil size/reactivity, level of consciousness (AVPU, p 103); WCC and platelets (both may be ↓).
- Urgent activation of and transfer to paediatric intensive care unit (PICU). Do blood gases to assess degree of acidosis. Get fresh frozen plasma to the bedside NOW to deal with coagulopathy. Intubation, ventilation and vigorous IV fluid resuscitation must be prompt. Monitor catheter urine output. Crossmatch blood. Continuously monitor ECG.
- Inotropes may be needed: dopamine or dobutamine (same dose) eg at 10μg/kg/min (put 15mg/kg in 50mL of 5% dextrose and infuse at 2mL/h).[408] This is OK by peripheral vein, but if adrenaline is needed, use a central line (0.1μg/kg/min, ie 300μg/kg in 50mL of 0.9% saline at 1mL/h).[409]
- If plasma glucose <3, give 10% dextrose 5mL/kg as a bolus, then as needed.

Heroic, non-standard ideas (*OHCM* p 739): Extracorporeal membrane oxygenation; terminal fragment of human bactericidal/permeability-increasing protein (rBPI21) to ↓cytokines; heparin with protein C concentrate to reverse coagulopathy; plasmapheresis to remove cytokines, and correct acidosis, and thrombolysis (rTPA) for limb re-perfusion.[410]

Case histories www.rcpch.ac.uk/publications/recent_publications/Junior_Doctor_Handbook.pdf

Other issues Ensure immunization (Protein-polysaccharide conjugate vaccine prevents type C but not the common type which is B; p 151). Inform your local CDC (consultant in communicable diseases).

Meningococcal prophylaxis for household contacts & those in contact with secretions.[411] *Rifampicin*—12hrly for 4 doses: if <1yr, 5mg/kg; 1–12yrs: 10mg/kg; >12yrs: 600mg. It interacts with the contraceptive Pill, can stain contact lenses, and turns urine red. *Ceftriaxone* single IM dose: 125mg if <12yr; 250mg if >12yrs. If >15yrs a single dose of *ciprofloxacin* 250mg is an option.

Meningitis: the organisms

The meningococcus, the pneumococcus, and, in the unvaccinated, *Haemophilus influenzae* are the great killers. In the former, the interval between seeming wellbeing and coma may be counted in hours. If you suspect meningitis, give benzylpenicillin (BOX) before hospital admission (don't worry about ruining the chance of a +ve blood culture later).

Neisseria meningitidis Abrupt onset ± rash (purpuric or not, eg starting as pink macules on legs in 20%); septicaemia may occur with no meningitis (Waterhouse–Friderichsen, *OHCM* p 738), so early LPs may be normal, giving false reassurance. Arthritis, conjunctivitis, myocarditis & DIC may coexist. ***Typical age:*** Any. ***Film:*** Gram –ve cocci in pairs (long axes parallel), often within polymorphs. Drug of choice: benzylpenicillin (G) 50mg/kg/4h IV. If penicillin-allergic, give cefotaxime (p 202) or chloramphenicol (below). Treat shock with colloid (± inotropes, p 203). ***Prevention:*** p 202. Observe closely.

Haemophilus influenzae (Rare if immunized). *Typical age:* <4yrs. *CSF:* Gram –ve rods. The lower the CSF glucose, the worse the infection. ***Drugs:*** Ceftriaxone (p 202) or, where resistance is not a problem, chloramphenicol 12–25mg/kg/6h IVI (neonates: see *BNF*) with IV ampicillin (neonate 50mg/kg/6h; 1–3 months old 50–100mg/kg/6h; 3 months–12yrs 100mg/kg/6h; max 12/day). Rifampicin (below) may also be needed. If chloramphenicol is used, monitor peak levels; aim for 20–25μg/mL; usual doses may be far exceeded to achieve this. (Trough level: <15μg/mL.) As soon as you can, switch to PO (more effective). Dexamethasone (0.15mg/kg/6h IV for 4 days) can ↓post-meningitis deafness. Some units give it as soon as possible, if the CSF shows Gram –ve rods.[412]

Strep pneumoniae (eg via respiratory infections, skull fracture, meningocele). ***Typical age:*** Any. ***Risk factors:*** HIV.[413] ***Film:*** Gram +ve cocci in pairs. ℞: Benzylpenicillin 25–50mg/kg/4h slow IV—or, if resistance likely (eg parts of Europe, USA), vancomycin (if >1 month old: 10mg/kg/6h IVI over 1h) with a 3rd-generation cefalosporin (ceftriaxone, p 202) is advised. Monitor U&E.

E. coli This is a cause of meningitis in the neonate (in whom the signs may consist of feeding difficulties, apnoea, fits & shock). Drug of choice: cefotaxime (p 202) or netilmicin (p 112; see p 175 for gentamicin).

Group B haemolytic streptococci eg *via* mother's vagina (so swab mothers whose infant suddenly fall ill at ~24h-old). Infection may be delayed a month. Drug of choice: benzylpenicillin 25–50mg/kg/8–12h slow IV.

Perinatal listeriosis (*Listeria monocytogenes*) presents soon after birth with meningitis and septicaemia (± pneumonia). Microabscesses form in many organs (granulomatosis infantiseptica). ***Diagnosis:*** Culture blood, placenta, amniotic fluid, CSF. ***Treatment:*** IV ampicillin (above) + gentamicin (p 175).

TB can cause CNS infarcts, demyelination with cranial nerve lesions and tuberculomas ± meningitis (long prodrome: lethargy, malaise, anorexia). Photophobia/neck stiffness are likely to be absent. The 1st few CSFs may be normal, or show visible fibrin webs, and widely fluctuating cell counts. ***Dose examples:*** Isoniazid 10mg/kg/24h IV (? with vit B_6) + rifampicin 10mg/kg/24h (≤600mg/day) for 1yr + (for 2 months) pyrazinamide 35mg/kg/day with eg streptomycin 15mg/kg/day IM adjusted to give a peak plasma level <40μg/mL and a trough of <3μg/mL; alternative: ethambutol 15mg/kg/day PO if old enough to report visual problems.[414] Adding dexamethasone improves survival (at least in those >14yrs old) but probably doesn't prevent disability.[415]

Other bacteria Leptospiral species (canicola); Brucella; Salmonella.

Causes of 'aseptic' meningitis Viruses (eg mumps, echo, herpes, polio), partially treated bacterial infections, cryptococcus (use ink stains).

Giving IM benzylpenicillin before hospital admission

- 300mg IM up to 1 year old.
- 600mg if 1–9yrs.
- 1.2g if >10yrs.
- When in doubt, give it: it may be negligent not to do so.
- If penicillin-allergic, cefotaxime may be used tried (50mg/kg IM). 416

Epilepsy and febrile convulsions

EPILEPSY is a tendency to intermittent abnormal electrical brain activity. Classification depends on whether signs are referable to one part of a hemisphere (partial epilepsy) or not (generalized), and on whether consciousness is affected (complex) or not (simple). The 4 kinds of ***generalized epilepsy***:

- ***Tonic/clonic (grand mal):*** Limbs stiffen (the tonic phase) and then jerk forcefully (clonic phase), with loss of consciousness.
- ***Absences:*** Brief (eg 10sec) pauses ('he stops in midsentence, and carries on where he left off'); eyes may roll up; he/she is *unaware of the attack*.
- ***Infantile spasms:*** Eg at 5 months. Jerks forwards with arms flexed, and hands extended ('Salaam attack'). Repeated every 2-3sec, up to 50 times. Here the EEG is characteristic (hypsarrythmia). Treat with valproate or vigabatrin.
- ***Myoclonic fits:*** 1-7-year-olds; eg 'thrown' suddenly to the ground.

Partial epilepsy Signs are referable to part of one hemisphere. Complex phenomena: (temporal lobe fits) consciousness↓; automatisms (lip smacking, rubbing face, running); fits of pure pleasure. [417] [418]

Causes Often none is found. Infection (eg meningitis); U&E↑, glucose↓, Ca^{2+}↓, Mg^{2+}↓; Na^{+}↑↓; toxins; trauma; metabolic defects; tuberous sclerosis; CNS tumour (<2%) or malformation; flickering lights, eg TV; exercise. [419]

ΔΔ: Arrhythmias, migraine, narcolepsy, night terrors, faints (reflex anoxic seizures, p 207), tics, Münchausen's (eg by proxy, *OHCM* p 730).

Tests Expert EEG; CT eg in infantile spasms, unusual seizures, CNS signs, or partial or intractable epilepsy. MRI is more sensitive but may require anaesthesia or sedation—but there is no exposure to radiation.

A SIMPLE FEBRILE CONVULSION is diagnosed if the following occur together:

- A tonic/clonic, symmetrical generalized seizure with no focal features
- Occurring as the temperature rises rapidly in a febrile illness
- In a normally developing child between 6 months and 5yrs of age
- With no signs of CNS infection or previous history of epilepsy

ΔΔ: Meningoencephalitis, CNS lesion, trauma, glucose↓, Ca^{2+}↓; Mg^{2+}↓.

Lifetime prevalence: ~3% of children have at least one febrile convulsion.

Examination: Find any infection; any neck stiffness should prompt LP.

Tests: FBC, MSU, CXR, ENT swabs, LP (only if clinically indicated). [420] Get help in deciding if an LP is needed. If it is not, review this decision in ~2h. If LP *is* indicated, be sure to exclude signs of ICP↑ (p 202).

Management: Lie prone; lorazepam IV (p 208) or diazepam PR. Tepid sponging if hot; 15mg/kg/6h paracetamol syrup, 120mg/5mL. ***Parental education:*** Allay fear (a child is *not* dying during a fit). Febrile convulsions don't usually mean risk of epilepsy. For the 30% having recurrences, try teaching carer to use rectal diazepam 0.5mg/kg, eg with a 5mg tube (Stesolid®) if 1-3yrs,[1] or a 10mg tube if older. This dose may also be used at home *during* seizures before help comes.

Further prevention: Prophylactic anticonvulsants are almost never needed.

Follow-up: Explain that fever due to any cause (eg vaccinations) should prompt oral antipyretics (p 142)—with rectal diazepam to hand if indicated.

Prognosis: If no focal signs, and the seizure lasts <30min, and is single only, 1% develop epilepsy. <1% have all these adverse signs: their risk of epilepsy is much higher (50%, eg if coupled with pre-existing CNS abnormality).

Treatment and prevention of epilepsy See p 208 and p 209.

1 If <3yrs insert PR half way to nozzle mark. ~2.5mL is expellable; don't worry about the bit left behind; it's allowed for by the manufacturer). Alternative: ***diazepam Rectubes®***: its licence is for a 0.5mg/kg ***single*** dose (adults & children >10kg, a typical weight for a 1yr-old), ***which shouldn't be repeated until after 12h***; very few reports of respiratory problems at this dose: all survived.

Are these paroxysmal/episodic 'spells' epilepsy?

This is often a true dilemma, and it matters as epilepsy treatment can be toxic. Also, if it is also harmful to label any child—it is doubly so to mislabel a child. So always get help with the diagnosis. Watching and waiting, repeat EEGs, and home videos of attacks may be needed.

In one study of 22 babies <1yr old referred for '?epilepsy', 9 *did* have epilepsy. The other 13 showed one of five patterns of non-epileptic paroxysmal events (NEPE)—(1) blinking; (2) head-shaking movements; (3) body posturing with head and arm jerks; (4) rhythmic masturbation movements ('gratification disorder', eg with grunts, leg-crossing, flushing etc—in the presence of a normal EEG); and (5) myoclonic head flexion. NEPE may be clinically indistinguishable from epilepsy. In the infants described above, ≥4 interictal EEGs were normal, the spells completely resolved after a fairly short period without anticonvulsants, and the infants continued to develop normally with no evidence of epilepsy at follow up.[421]

Some specific types of seizure

Reflex anoxic seizures Paroxysmal, self-limited brief (eg 15sec) asystole triggered by pain, fear (eg at venepuncture) or anxiety, or an overwhelming confrontation with reality, perhaps in the form of a bath which is unexpectedly hot or cold. During this time the child is deathly pale—± hypotonia, rigidity, upward eye deviation, clonic movements, and urinary incontinence. Typical age: 6 months to 2 years (but may be much older). ***Prevalence:*** ~0.8% of preschool children. *ΔΔ:* Epilepsy is often misdiagnosed, as the trigger aspect to the history is ignored or unwitnessed. When in difficulty, refer to a specialist for vagal excitation tests under continuous EEG & ECG monitoring (ocular compression induces the oculo-cardiac reflex; do not do this test if there is glaucoma, or known arrhythmia, or if you lack experience: it is uncomfortable). NB: tongue-biting is not described in reflex anoxic seizures. ***Management:*** Drugs are rarely, if ever, needed. Atropine has been tried, to reduce sensitivity to vagal influences. Anticonvulsants are not needed. Inserting a pacemaker is one option under review. ***What to tell parents:*** Avoid the term 'seizure', as this is all that is likely to be remembered, *however* careful your explanation. *Pallid syncopal attack*, or *white breath-holding attacks* are useful synonyms. Emphasize its benign nature, and that the child usually grows out of it (but it may occur later in life, and in older siblings).[422]

Panayiotopoulos syndrome (eg 6% of those with seizures—peak age: 5yrs). It occurs mainly at night, with vomiting and eye deviation with impaired consciousness before the convulsion starts. Many seizures last for 30mins (some may last hours)—but there is no permanent brain damage. ***Diagnosis:*** EEG. ***Treatment:*** As remission often occurs within 2 years, antiepileptic medication is often not needed. Reassure.[423]

Age-dependent epileptic encephalopathy Ohtahara syndrome: tonic spasms ± clustering. EEG: suppression-burst.[424] Chloral hydrate may help.[425] This transforms over time into West syndrome, and thence to Lennox-Gastaut syndrome. Think of these as age-specific epileptic reactions to non-specific exogenous CNS insults, acting at specific developmental stages.[426]

Rolandic epilepsy (benign epilepsy with centrotemporal spikes, BECTS) 15% of all childhood epilepsy. Infrequent, brief partial fits with unilateral facial or oropharyngeal sensory-motor symptoms, speech arrest ± hypersalivation. Sulthiame may be used in some units.[RCT 427 428]

Mozart's sonata for 2 pianos, K448, has been found to reduce interictal epileptiform EEG discharges (compared with Beethoven's *Für Elise*) in a randomized, single-blind, crossover, placebo-controlled trial.[RCT 429]

MOZART THERAPY?

Epilepsy: management[APLS] (Neonates: see p 112)

Stepwise ℞ of status epilepticus *Supportive therapy:* • Secure airway; give O_2. Set a clock in motion. • Check T°; if ↑, give rectal paracetamol (it may be a febrile convulsion) • Do BP, pulse, glucose, Ca^{2+} ($\pm Mg^{2+}$). ►If hypoglycaemic, give glucose 0.5g/kg IV as a 25% solution, then 5–10mg/kg/min as 10% dextrose IVI.

»*Seizure control:* Proceed to the next step only if fits continue.

0min	Estimate child's weight: kg = 2 × [age in yrs + 4]. Gain IV access
at once	»***Lorazepam*** 0.1mg/kg IV (slow bolus via a large vein).
10min	***Repeat lorazepam***
20min	»***Paraldehyde*** 0.3mL/kg PR in olive oil: max 10mL PR; avoid contact with plastics/rubber. For diazepam PR, see p 206.
30min	»***Phenytoin*** 15mg/kg IVI; max rate 1mg/kg/min. Monitor ECG.
50min	***Call PICU & your anaesthetist.*** Locate thiopental, ET tube,[etc] p 627.
60min	Paralyze & ventilate on PICU: use »***thiopental*** (=thiopentone) IV.

►These times refer to elapsed time on the clock from the 1st drug, *not* gaps between each drug. Some authorities recommend starting ventilation earlier, and always be ready to do this to protect the airway.

Tests S_AO_2, ECG monitor, glucose, U&E, Ca^{2+}, Mg^{2+}, arterial gases, FBC, platelets, ECG. Consider anticonvulsant levels, toxicology screen, blood ammonia, lumbar puncture, culture blood and urine, virology, EEG, MRI, CT, carbon monoxide level, lead level, amino acid levels, metabolic screen.

Once the crisis is over, start prophylaxis, eg with sodium valproate or carbamazepine, guided by regimen on p 209. Aim to use one drug only. Increase dose until fits stop, or toxic levels reached. *Out of the context of status, it is not known when to start prophylaxis;* after 2–3 fits is a rule of thumb.

Carbamazepine *SE:* Rash (± exfoliation); platelets↓, agranulocytosis, aplasia (all rare). It induces its own enzymes, so increasing doses may be needed.

Sodium valproate The sugar-free liquid is 200mg/5mL. ***SE:*** vomiting, appetite↑, drowsiness, thrombocytopenia (do FBC pre-treatment). Rare hepatotoxicity can be fatal (eg if co-existing unsuspected metabolic disorder). Routine LFT monitoring is needed, eg only in 1st 6 months of use.

Ethosuximide The syrup is 250mg/5mL. ***SE:*** D&V, rashes, erythema multiforme, lupus syndromes, agitation, headache. Indication: absence epilepsy.

Newer anticonvulsants NICE reserves gabapentin, lamotrigine, oxcarbazepine, tiagabine, topiramate, and vigabatrin (as an adjunctive therapy for partial seizures) for children not benefiting from older drugs (above) ***or*** older drugs have contraindications/interactions (the Pill) ***or*** they are already known to be poorly tolerated—***or*** the child is currently of childbearing potential ***or*** is likely to need treatment into her childbearing years. 430

Lamotrigine Uses: absences & intractable epilepsy as an add-on. *Dose when given with valproate if aged 2–12yrs:* 0.15mg/kg/day PO for 2wks, then 0.3mg/kg daily for 2wks, then ↑ by up to 0.5mg/kg every week. Usual maintenance: 1–5mg/kg/day (higher if with non-valproate anticonvulsants: ~2.5–7mg/kg/12h).

Vigabatrin (May be 1st choice in infantile spasms and tuberous sclerosis fits.) This blocks GABA transaminase. Consider adding it to regimens if partial seizures are uncontrolled. Vigabatrin starting dose: 40mg/kg/day PO (sachets and tabs are 500mg). Max: 100mg/kg/day. Blood levels do not help (but monitor concurrent phenytoin: it may fall by ~20%). ***SE:*** Drowsiness, depression, psychosis, amnesia, diplopia, and field defects (test every year).

Education If fits are few, educate teachers on lifting bans on supervised swimming, and cycling etc. Showers are safer than baths. Emphasize compliance/concordance (one seizure *may* ↓the threshold for the next, ie *kindling*).

Drug	Starting dose mg/kg/24h	Target dose for initial assessment of effect mg/kg/24h	Dose increement		Usually effective dose mg/kg/24h	Doses per day	Target trough drug level in plasma	
			Size mg/kg/24h	Interval in days			mg/L	µmol/L
Carbamazepine	5	12.5	2.5	7	10–25	2-3	4-10	
Valproate	10	20	10.0	10	15–40	1-2	Not helpful	
Phenytoin	5	7	1.0	10	4-8	1-2	10-20	40-80
Phenobarbital	4	6	2.0	10	4-9	1	15-40	60-180
Ethosuximide	10	15	5.0	5	15-40	1	40-99	280-700
Clonazepam	0.025	0.05	0.025	7	0.025-0.1	2-3	Not helpful	

Which drug? Tonic/clonic fits: first try sodium valproate or carbamazepine or lamotrigine (p 208).
Absences: first choice, ethosuximide; second, sodium valproate.
Myoclonic or akinetic fits: sodium valproate or benzodiazepines.
Infantile spasms: prednisolone or vigabatrin. See Riikonen R. *Curr Opin Neurol* 2005 **18** 91
Partial fits: first try carbamazepine; then sodium valproate.

If drugs fail Do not use ever more toxic combinations: ►refer for neurosurgical advice and specialist imaging.[431]

Stopping anticonvulsants See *OHCM* p 381. The risk of seizure recurrence during the tapering down process is no greater if the tapering period is 6 weeks compared with 9 months.

Behavioural problems

►*Only enter battles you can win.* If the child can win, be more subtle, eg consistent rewards, not inconsistent punishments. Get a health visitor's advice; ensure everyone is encouraging the same response from the child.

Entrances ***Food refusal*** and ***food fads*** are common. Reducing pressure on the child, discouraging parental over-reaction, and gradual enlarging of tiny portions of attractive food is usually all that is needed. Check Hb. ***Overeating:*** Eating comforts, and if the child is short on comfort, or if mother feels inadequate, the scene is set for overeating and life-long patterns are begun. Diets may fail until the child is hospitalized (p 348). If obese (p 226, 530), remember hypothalamic syndromes (eg Prader–Willi, p 652).

Pica is eating of things which are not food; all will do this at some time; if it is persistent, there may be other signs of disturbed behaviour, or ↓IQ. *Causes:* Iron deficiency; obsessive-compulsive disorder. *Complications:* lead poisoning; worm infestations.[432]

Exits ***Soiling*** is the escape of stool into the underclothing.

Encopresis is the repeated passage of solid faeces in the wrong place in those >4yrs old. Faecal retention is the central event. ***Constipation*** is difficulty in defecation; it may lead to distress, abdominal pain, rectal bleeding, abdominal masses, overflow soiling ± 'lavatory-blocking' enormous stools (megarectum), and anorexia. Causes: often poor food, fluid, or fibre intake—or fear, eg as a result of a fissure. Rarely Hirschprung's disease (think of this in infants if there is an explosive gush of faeces on withdrawing the finger after rectal exam, or if there is alternating diarrhoea with constipation and abdominal distension, and failure to thrive). *Action:* • Find out about pot refusal • Does defecation hurt?• Is there parental coercion? Break the vicious cycle of: large faeces→pain/fissure→fear of the pot→rectum overstretched call-to-stool sensation dulled→soiling→parental exasperation→coercion. Exonerate the child to boost confidence for the main task of obeying calls-to-stool to keep the rectum empty, aided by *docusate sodium* (a softener *and* a stimulant), then a dose of *sodium picosulfate* elixir or *polyethylene glycol*, followed by maintenance *lactulose* or *methyl cellulose tablets* ± prolonged alternate-day *senna*). NB: biofeedback methods have not proved efficacious.[MET 433] Clinics run by nurse specialists can be more effective than those run by consultants.[RCT 434] Aim to give the family time to air feelings which encopresis engenders (anger, shame, ridicule). Treat perianal cellulitis co-amoxiclav (for example).

Enuresis: Bedwetting occurs on most nights in 15% of 5-yr-olds, and is still a problem in up to 3% of 15-yr-olds—usually from delayed maturation of bladder control (family history often +ve). Tests for diabetes, UTI and GU abnormality (p 174) can occasionally yield surprises. The term 'secondary enuresis' implies wetness after >6 months' dryness. ***Treatment:*** Avoid blame, restrict fluid before bed, and allow time to pass. Reassure the child that he is neither infantile nor dirty. A system of rewards for dry nights as documented on a star chart above the child's bed may be effective. Alarms (± vibrations) triggered by urine in the bed can make 56% dry at 1yr; relapses are preventable by continuing use after dryness. They are cheap or loanable from Community Health/Child Guidance Services (or equivalent)—eg Drinite®. www.bedwetting.co.uk Imipramine 25–50mg/24h PO should not be used for >3 months, has side-effects, and high relapse rates on discontinuation. Desmopressin (DDAPV) 20–40μg (2–4 nasal puffs/night) is a better option.[435] Oral dose (if >5yrs): 0.2mg at bedtime; fluid overload (Na^+↓) is rare, eg after gulping in swimming pool water, or going to rave parties. Have 1 week 3-monthly with no drugs. CI: cystic fibrosis, uraemia, BP↑. Oxybutynin 2.5–5mg PO at night (if ≥7yrs old) helps bladder irritability (unreliably).[MET 436 437]

Hyperactivity/ADD The spectrum ranges from a level of activity more than parents are happy with, to serious lack of concentration, impulsivity, and scholastic failure—known as ***attention deficit disorder* (ADD)** or ***minimal brain dysfunction***. ADD is commoner in learning-disabled children, and if there has been prenatal cannabis exposure.[438,439] Not *all* those with ADD are hyperactive. *There is no diagnostic test* (but positron emission tomography may show ↓function of frontal lobes and near-by connections). Most parents first note hyperactivity at the toddler stage, but most locomotor hyperactivity at this stage abates with time, so the diagnosis is usually delayed until school entry or later. Signs often attenuate during adolescence, but may persist into mid-adulthood. There is a familial tendency, and families with ADD are more likely to have other diagnoses too, such as learning difficulties, mood, anxiety, and psychosocial disorders (DSM IV, p 312). Associations: conduct disorder or other disruptive behaviour disorders (oppositional defiant disorder).[440] Children and adolescents with ADD are at risk of being victims of assaults, as well as suicide and self harm.[1]

Typical features:

- 'On the go all the time'
- Squirming/fidgeting
- Inconsiderate of others
- Blurts out answers
- Sustained attention↓
- Interrupts continually
- Behind with school
- Speech↑
- Requests not obeyed
- Butts in during games

Treatment: Take time to explain the condition. Offer a booklet. Cognitive therapy may increase parental tolerance. Hypoallergenic diets (eg no tartrazine) are controversial and may cause obsessions in parents. Get help.

Psychostimulants (not depressants) can help; get expert help: methylphenidate (Ritalin®) is said to offer the best benefit-to-hazard ratio. *SE:* insomnia, slowing of growth; monitor growth, BP, pulse. Some side-effects associated with stimulant use may respond to dosing or timing adjustments. Be cautious of exceeding 0.3mg/kg/day in divided doses. In one randomized study, increasing to 0.6mg/kg yielded little incremental improvement in social behaviour and academic performance.[441] Multiple domains of functioning must be assessed by an expert to determine the best dose. Evidence in long-term use is uncertain.[MET 442, MET 443] Parental training programmes and behavioural modification techniques such as prolonged eye-contact between parent and child should also be considered.[444] Alternative treatments such as Yoga have been tried with mixed results.[445]

Other drugs (don't use without deep reflection; side-effects may be serious): haloperidol 0.01–0.04mg/kg/12h PO; imipramine 0.2–0.5mg/kg/8h, especially if co-existing anxiety/depression; clonidine (3–5μg/kg/day PO in divided doses,[446,447,448] eg if tic disorder is present; Gilles de la Tourette syn. *OHCM* p 724).[449]

School refusal ***Setting:*** Emotional overprotection; high social class; neurotic parents; schoolwork of high standard. In truancy, the reverse is true. ***Treatment:*** Confer with headteacher, parents, and an educational psychologist. Escort by an education welfare officer aids the prompt return to school. Often anxiety and/or depression will also need treatment.[450]

1 Lam L 2005 *J Adolesc Health* **36** 19

Dyslexia

Reading ability usually goes hand-in-hand with intelligence, but when this is not the case, and someone with, say, an IQ of 130, finds reading difficult, the term dyslexia is often used. The term 'specific learning difficulty' is preferred by some people, as 'dyslexia' is often a term used by parents to help them cope with having a child whose general intellectual skills, including reading, are less than hoped for. Dyslexia can be seen with other speech and language disorders: consider referral to speech and language therapists (SALT).

Essence There is a problem with appreciating phonemes, eg that 'cat' comprises /c/, /a/, and /t/. Breaking up unfamiliar words into phonemes and having a go at stringing them together is the central act of learning to read. This is what needs to be taught, educationalists say, and children should not be made to rely on unstructured guesswork (the 'look and say' approach) which is discredited as the sole means of equipping children for reading.

Quite often, distortion/jumbling of text during reading is reported. Visual aids have been used with some success to improve reading. RCT 451

Children with dyslexia also have difficulty in telling how many syllables there are in a word (don't we all?—'How many syllables are there in *strength?*' analytical dyslexics are prone to ask). They also have difficulty with verbal short-term memory—eg for meaningless strings such as telephone numbers. There is also a problem with telling if two words rhyme or not, and in distinguishing phonemes which sound similar (eg /k/ and /g/). There may also be left/right muddle. ***Genetics:*** Boys are more afflicted than girls, and show stronger genetic effects (up to 50% of boys are dyslexic if their fathers are). Genes on chromosomes 1, 2, and 15 are implicated, and linkage on chromosome 6 near the human leukocyte complex may explain associations between dyslexia and autoimmune diseases. 452

Neurobiology Rarely, CNS examination reveals a left-sided cerebral lesion. Usually changes are only seen at *postmortem*, eg in perisylvian regions ± unusual asymmetry of the plenum temporale (Wernicke's area), with cortical dysplasia and scarring. *In vivo* correlates of this asymmetry are described. 453

Perhaps dyslexia reflects weak connectivity between anterior and posterior parts of the language areas of the brain, and the angular gyrus. Positron emission tomography shows that when dyslexic adults perform rhyme judgments and verbal short-term memory tasks they activate less than the full set of centres normally involved with these tasks.

Going along-side these theories is the functional MRI observation of specific involvement of one subsystem of the visual pathways which prevents rapid processing of brief stimuli presented in quick temporal succession. This is the so-called ***magnosystem hypothesis***. 454

Management Make sure the 'dyslexia' is not from lack of teaching. The person may gain insight by discussing his or her problem with fellow sufferers, and by finding out about past dyslexics such as Leonardo da Vinci. Special educational programmes are available for addressing dyslexic problems, as the phonetic approach to learning to read usually presents problems. NB: 'wait-and-see' is not wise—studies tend to find best results if identification is pre-school. Then exercises in sound categorization using rhyme and alliteration, with special teaching of letter sounds can be started early. 455

Doctors may be asked about dietary supplements with long-chain fatty acids (eg Efalex®). These do play a role in neurodevelopment and one small randomized study (N=41) over 12 weeks had good-ish results, and few SEs. RCT 456

Delay in walking

Babies usually learn to walk at ~14 months old. If this has not occurred by 20 months, ask yourself 2 questions: is the child physically normal? is development delayed in other areas too? The commonest causes reflect chronic illness, global delay, benign immaturity, and generalized joint hypermobility. In boys consider Duchenne muscular dystrophy early (genetic counselling before mother's next pregnancy). Congenital hip dislocation may present as walking delay if the fact of limping is overlooked. The main reason for identifying late walkers is to exclude cerebral palsy.

Typical causes

Prenatal factors
- APH (with hypoxia)
- X-rays
- Alcohol
- CMV, rubella, HIV
- Toxoplasmosis
- Rhesus disease

Perinatal factors
- Birth trauma
- Fetal distress
- Hypoglycaemia
- Hyperbilirubinaemia

Postnatal factors
- Trauma/intraventricular haemorrhage
- Hypoxia
- Meningoencephalitis
- Sagittal sinus thrombosis from dehydration

Cerebral palsy comprises chronic disorders of posture and movement caused by non-progressive CNS lesions sustained before 2yrs old, resulting in delayed motor development, evolving CNS signs, learning disability (25%), and epilepsy. Most are due to antenatal events unrelated to birth trauma.

Prevalence: 2/1000 (50% are of low birth weight).

Typical survival: 20yrs if quadriplegic (much longer if less affected).

Clinical picture: Weakness, paralysis, delayed milestones, seizures, language and speech problems. Spasticity suggests a pyramidal lesion; slow, writhing, involuntary movements and postures (dystonias) suggest basal ganglia involvement. Most children have either a hemiparesis or a spastic diplegia—eg both legs affected worse than the arms, so that the child looks normal until he is picked up, when the legs 'scissor' (hip flexion, adduction, and internal rotation, with knee extension and feet plantar-flexed).

Type 1 Ataxic palsies (page 210)	Type 2 Ataxic diplegia
Hypotonia (floppy baby)	Hypertonia
Other defects rare	Other defects common
Flexor plantars	Extensor plantars
Associations: deafness, strabismus, IQ↓ (its rare)	Associations: hydrocephalus, spina bifida
Normal developmental milestones	

Dyskinetic cerebral palsy: Unwanted actions, poor movement flow/posture control, ataxia, athetosis, imbalance, hypotonia, hearing↓, dysarthria. Associated with kernicterus.

Management teams (physio- and occupational therapists, orthopaedic surgeons, and orthoses experts) aid holistic assessment: can he roll over (both ways)? Sit? Grasp? Transfer objects from hand to hand? Good head righting? Ability to shift weight (when prone) with forearm support (is getting possible)? Can he hold a pen or a spoon? Treat epilepsy (p 208). Callipers may prevent deformity (equinovarus/equinovalgus, hip dislocation from excessive flexion/adduction). Attempts to show benefits of neurodevelopmental physiotherapy (to improve equilibrium and righting) don't show benefit over simple stimulation of motor activity. Some parents try the Hungarian Petö approach: here the 'conductor' devotes herself to the child and uses interaction with peers to motivate success, eg manipulation, handwriting, fine movement, and social skills.

Botulinum toxin (p 460) has an uncertain role. [illegible] Epidural cord electrostimulation and intrathecal baclofen [illegible]. Their role is uncertain.

Prognosis by 6yrs, 55% with quadriplegia (90% if hemiplegic or diplegic) gain urinary continence spontaneously ([illegible]); [illegible] are dry at the [illegible]

Delay in walking

Babies usually learn to walk at ~14 months old. If this has not occurred by 20 months, ask yourself 2 questions: Is the child physically normal? Is development delayed in other areas too? The commonest causes reflect chronic illness, global delay, benign immaturity, and generalized joint hypermobility. In boys consider Duchenne muscular dystrophy early (genetic counselling *before* mother's next pregnancy). Congenital hip dislocation may present as 'walking delay' if the fact of limping is overlooked. The major reason for identifying late walkers is to exclude cerebral palsy.

Typical causes:

Prenatal factors
- APH (with hypoxia)
- X-rays
- Alcohol
- CMV; rubella; HIV
- Toxoplasmosis
- Rhesus disease

Perinatal factors:
- Birth trauma
- Fetal distress
- Hypoglycaemia
- Hyperbilirubinaemia

Postnatal factors:
- Trauma/intraventricular haemorrhage
- Hypoxia
- Meningoencephalitis
- Cerebral vein thrombosis, from dehydration

Cerebral palsy comprises chronic disorders of posture and movement caused by non-progressive CNS lesions sustained before 2yrs old, resulting in delayed motor development, evolving CNS signs, learning disability (35%), and epilepsy. Most are due to antenatal events unrelated to birth trauma.

Prevalence: 2/1000 (50% are of low birth weight).

Typical survival: 20yrs if quadriplegic (much longer if less affected). ♀:♂ ≈1:1.

Clinical picture: Weakness, paralysis, delayed milestones, seizures, language and speech problems. Spasticity suggests a pyramidal lesion; unco-ordinated, involuntary movements and postures (dystonias) suggest basal ganglia involvement. Most children have either a hemiparesis or a spastic diplegia—eg both legs affected worse than the arms, so that the child looks normal until he is picked up, when the legs 'scissor' (hip flexion, adduction and internal rotation; with knee extension and feet plantar-flexed).

Type 1 Ataxic palsies (pure ataxia):	*Type 2 Ataxic diplegia:*
Hypotonia ('floppy baby')	Hypertonia
Other defects rare	Other defects common
Flexor plantars	Extensor plantars
Associations: deafness; strabismus; IQ↓ (fits rare)	Associations: hydrocephalus; spina bifida
Normal developmental milestones	

Dyskinetic cerebral palsy: Unwanted actions, poor movement flow/posture control, agonist/antagonist imbalance, hypotonia, hearing↓, dysarthria. Associated with Kernicterus.

Management teams (Physio- and occupational therapists, orthopaedic surgeons, and orthoses experts) aid holistic assessment: can he roll over (both ways)? Sit? Grasp? Transfer objects from hand to hand? Good head righting? Ability to shift weight (when prone) with forearm support. IQ. Is toileting possible? Can he hold a pen or a spoon? Treat epilepsy (p 208). Callipers may prevent deformity (equinovarus, equinovalgus, hip dislocation from excessive flexion/adduction). Attempts to show benefits of neurodevelopmental physiotherapy (to improve equilibrium and righting) don't show benefit over simple stimulation of motor activity. Some parents try the Hungarian *Petö approach:* here the 'conductor' devotes herself to the child and uses interaction with peers to reinforce successes: eg manipulation, art, writing, fine movement, and social skills.[457]

Botulinum toxin (p 460) has an uncertain role.[458] [459] [RCT 460] *Epidural cord electrostimulation* and *intrathecal or oral baclofen:* Their role is uncertain.[461] [462]

Prognosis By 6yrs, 54% with quadriplegia (80% if hemiplegic or diplegic) gain urinary continence spontaneously. If IQ↓, 38% are dry at this age.[463] [n=601]

Delay in talking

(For autism, see p 394.)

►When in doubt, ask the mother what she thinks is wrong.
►Always test the hearing. *Ensure the result is as reliable as possible.*

Speech development After the first few months of life, language differentiation is already occurring. Chinese babbling babies can be distinguished from European ones. Before the first year babbling gives way to jargon—plausible-sounding 'words' which have little by way of fixed meaning.

- *At ~1 year* a few words may be used meaningfully.
- *At 1½yrs old* 2-word utterances ("Daddy come").
- *At 2 years old*…subject-verb-object sentences appear ("I want a pudding").
- *At 3½yrs old*… the child has mastered thought, language, abstraction, and the elements of reason, having a 1000-word vocabulary at his or her disposal, enabling sentences such as: "I give her cake' cos she's hungry".

Words exist to give ideas currency, and so often that currency proves counterfeit—a process which so often starts with *if*, eg "*If I hadn't thrown the cup on the ground, I might have got a pudding*". The uttering of "If…", linked with an emotional response, is the most human of all constructions, opening up worlds divorced from reality, providing for the exercise of imagination, the validation of dreams, the understanding of motives, and the control of events. The rest of life holds nothing to match the intellectual and linguistic pace of these first years. Further linguistic development is devoted to seemingly conceptually minor tasks, such as expanding vocabulary.

There is much variation in speech timing: *what is 'clearly abnormal'?*

Vocabulary size: If <50 words at 3yrs old, suspect deafness—or:

- Expressive dysphasia or speech dyspraxia (eg if there is a telegraphic quality to speech, poor clarity, and deteriorating behaviour, eg frustration).
- Audio-premotor syndrome (APM). The child cannot reflect sounds correctly heard into motor control of larynx and respiration. Instead of babbling, the child is quiet, unable to hum or sing.
- Respiro-laryngeal (RL) dysfunction (dysphonia from incorrect vocal fold vibration/air flow regulation). The voice is loud and rough.
- Congenital aphonia (thin effortful voice; it's rare).

Other causes of delayed talking:
Congenital:
• Klinefelter's syn.
• Galactosaemia
• Histidinaemia
• Auditory agnosia
• Floating-harbor syn.
Acquired (with or after):
• Meningoencephalitis
• Head injury
• Landau-Kleffner syn. (epilepsy + progressive loss of language)

Speech clarity: By 2½yrs, parents should understand most speech. If not, suspect deafness—or:

- Articulatory dyspraxia (easy consonants are *b* and *m* with the lips, and *d* with the tongue—the phonetic components of babbling). ♂:♀ ≈3:1. Tongue-tie is a possible cause (∴ poor sounds needing tongue elevation— *d* and *s*)—surgery to the frenum may be needed (+speech therapy). Distinguish from phonological causes (disordered *sound for speech processing*—may present as *sound awareness problems* (difficulty in analysing sound structure of words). Both are common.
- APM or RL dysfunction, as described above.

Understanding: By 2½ years a child should understand "Get your shoes" (if he has any), if not suspect: • Deafness—if the hearing is impaired (eg 25–40dB loss) secretory otitis media is likely to be the cause. Worse hearing loss is probably sensorineural • Cognitive impairment • Deprivation.

Speech therapy Refer early, before school starts. NB: randomized trials have not shown any clear benefits from this strategy. RCT 464 [N=159]

Impairment, disability, and handicap

WHO definitions *Impairment* entails a pathological process, eg spina bifida, which may cause certain *disabilities*, eg walking difficulty. Handicap is their social consequence (eg cannot walk to school).

Learning delay (mental handicap) *The mother often makes the first diagnosis.* An IQ <35 constitutes a severe learning disability (mental handicap, p 314).

►Beware conflating IQ with intellect: the latter implies more than problem-solving and memory: intellect entails the ability to speculate, to learn from mistakes, to have a view of oneself and others, to see relationships between events in different domains of experience—as well as the ability to use language either to map the world, or to weave ironic webs of truth and deceit (and, on a good day, to do both simultaneously).

Causes: Severe mental impairment usually has a definable cause, whereas mild retardation is often familial, with no well-defined cause. Be prepared to refer to an expert. *Congenital disorders* are legion: chromosomal (eg Down's; fragile X, p 648); metabolic (eg PKU p 183). *Acquired:* Perinatal infection p 34–37, birth injury and cerebral palsy, trauma, meningitis.

Lead exposure: This is a leading preventable cause of mildly impaired IQ. For example in 2-yr-olds for each 0.48μmol/L plasma increment there is an associated 5–8 point fall in IQ as measured on the Wechsler Intelligence Scale for children (revised). This defect is long-lasting.

Chemical defects associated with mental retardation—eg: *Homocystinuria:* Paraplegia, fits, friable hair, emboli, cataracts; homocystine is found in the urine. Treat with a low methionine, cystine-supplemented diet, with large doses of pyridoxine. *Maple syrup urine disease:* Hypoglycaemia, acidosis, fits, death. Urine smells of maple syrup, due to defective metabolism of branched chain keto acids. Treatment: high calorie amino acid controlled diet. Thiamine has been tried. *Tryptophanuria:* Rough, pigmented skin. Treat with nicotinic acid.

Management: Refer to an expert, so that no treatable cause is missed. Would the family like help from group, such as MENCAP? Other members of the family may need special support (eg normal siblings, who now feel neglected). If the IQ is >35, life in the community is the aim.

Physical handicap *Sensory:* Deafness, see p 548. Blindness: congenital defects are described on p 454. Principal acquired causes of blindness are: retinopathy of prematurity, vitamin A deficiency, onchocerciasis (p 450), eye injuries, cataract (eg Down's syndrome).

CNS & musculoskeletal problems: (Congenital or acquired) Causes: accidents (eg near-drowning), cerebral palsy (p 214), spina bifida (p 140), after meningitis, polio, congenital infections (above), tumours, syndromes (p 638).

Wheelchairs:[1] For indoors or outdoors? Patient-operated, motorized or pushed? What sort of restraints to prevent falling out? If collapsible, how small must it be to get into the car? Are the sides removable to aid transfer from chair to bed? Can the child control the brakes? Are there adjustable elevated leg rests? Liaise with the physio and occupational therapist.

Callipers will allow some patients to stand and walk. Long-leg callipers are required for those with complete leg paralysis. The top should be constructed so that it does not induce pressure sores. A knee lock supports the knee in the standing position. An internal coil spring prevents foot drop.

1 Disabled Living Foundation, www.dlf.org.uk UK tel. 0845 130 9177 (local rate).

Check-list to guide management of handicap

Whether based in hospital or in the community the doctor should address each of these points:

- Screening and its documentation on local handicap registers.
- Communication with parents.
- Refer to and liaise with district handicap team and community paediatrician.
- Ensuring access to specialist services, including physiotherapy, orthopaedic surgery.
- Assessing special needs for schooling and housing.
- Co-ordinating neuropsychological/neurodevelopmental assessments.
- Co-ordinating measures of severity (eg electrophysiology ± CT/MRI).
- Liaison with dietician on special foods.
- Promotion of long-term concordance/compliance with treatment or education programmes.
- Education about the consequences of the illness.
- Encourage contact with family support groups.
- Offering family planning *before* patients become unintentionally pregnant.
- Pre-conception counselling (p 2, with specialist in molecular genetics).
- Co-ordinating prenatal diagnostic tests and fetal assessment.

Denver developmental screening test

This is a detailed test to consider if results of simple tests are equivocal (p 150). Begin with observation, as children often spontaneously demonstrate many of the milestones. Then do the specific tests, and then question the parents about what words the child can say. Younger children may be examined while sitting on their mother's lap. Explain to her that the child is not expected to pass every test. Begin with a few very easy tests. Go slowly.

Test materials Ball of red wool, box of raisins, rattle with handle, small bottle, bell, tennis ball, 8 blocks (one inch cubes).

Administering the test Draw a vertical line at the child's chronological age on the charts on p 220-1. If premature, subtract the months premature from the chronological age. Note that:

- Items to be administered are those through which the line passes. A parent may administer a test if the child wishes.
- Failure to pass an item passed by ≤90% of children may or may not be abnormal. Note how the child behaves during the test.

Test footnotes (See top corner of test boxes on p 220-1.)

1 When prone lifts head up, using forearm support (± hands).
2 No head lag as you pull by the hand from supine to sitting.
3 Child may use a wall or rail for help (but not a person).
4 Throws ball overhand 3 feet to within your reach.
5 Jumps over a distance (eg over an A4 piece of paper).
6 Walk forward, heel within one inch of toe.
7 Bounce a ball. He must catch it. Allow up to 3 trials.
8 Walk backwards, toe within 1 inch of heel.
9 Wave wool slowly before eyes: do eyes move 90° to midline?
10 Grasps rattle when it touches his finger tips.
11 Looks for ball of wool dropped out of sight over table's edge.
12 Child grasps raisin between thumb and index finger.
13 Overhand grasp of raisin between thumb and index finger.
14 'Copy this' (circle). Do not name or demonstrate.
15 'Which line is longer?'; turn upside down and repeat.
16 'Copy this' (cross). Pass crossing lines at any angle.
17 'Copy this' (square). You may demonstrate if he fails.
18 Two arms or two eyes or two legs only count as one part.
19 Name the pictures at the bottom of the chart.
20 'Give the block to Mum'. 'Put it on the table'. No gestures.
21 Answer $^2/_3$ of: 'What do you do if you are cold/hungry/tired?'
22 Put this on/under/in front of/behind the chair. No gestures.
23 Answer $^2/_3$: 'Fire is hot, ice is—'. 'Mum is a woman, Dad is a—'. 'A horse is big, a mouse is—'.
24 Define $^6/_8$ of ball, lake, desk, house, banana, curtain, hedge, pavement. An verbal indication of understanding is passed.
25 Answer $^3/_3$ of: 'What is a spoon/shoe/door made of?' (No others).
26 Smile, talk or wave, to elicit smile (3 tries). Do not touch.
27 While he plays with a toy, pull it away. Pass if he resists.
28 Child need not be able to tie shoes or button at the back.

►This test is poor at picking up articulatory or mild linguistic deficits—if this is suspected, liaise with speech experts. ***NB:*** an alternative version of this test (***Denver II***), contains more language items, new age scales, new categories of item interpretation and a behaviour rating scale. ***Parents' Evaluation of Developmental Status (PEDS):*** Parents complete a 10 item questionnaire which is interpreted according to an algorithm. It is simple and quick, and unlike the Denver test, special items do not need purchasing. www.pedstest.com 465

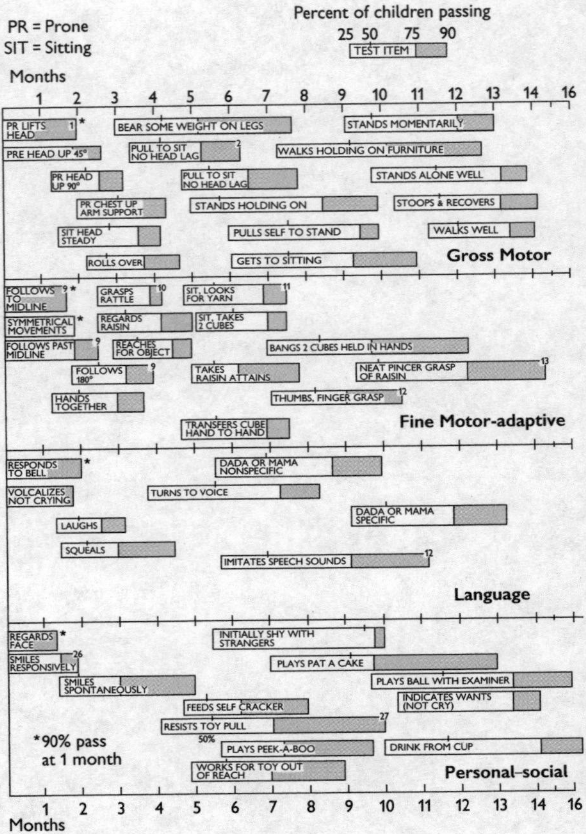

PR = Prone
SIT = Sitting
Percent of children passing
25 50 75 90
TEST ITEM
Months
1 2 3 4 5 6 7 8 9 10 11 12 13 14 16
PR LIFTS HEAD
BEAR SOME WEIGHT ON LEGS
STANDS MOMENTARILY
PRE HEAD UP 45°
PULL TO SIT NO HEAD LAG
WALKS HOLDING ON FURNITURE
PR HEAD UP 90°
PULL TO SIT NO HEAD LAG
STANDS ALONE WELL
PR CHEST UP ARM SUPPORT
STANDS HOLDING ON
STOOPS & RECOVERS
SIT HEAD STEADY
PULLS SELF TO STAND
WALKS WELL
ROLLS OVER
GETS TO SITTING
Gross Motor
FOLLOWS TO MIDLINE
GRASPS RATTLE
SIT, LOOKS FOR YARN
SYMMETRICAL MOVEMENTS
REGARDS RAISIN
SIT, TAKES 2 CUBES
FOLLOWS PAST MIDLINE
REACHES FOR OBJECT
BANGS 2 CUBES HELD IN HANDS
FOLLOWS 180°
TAKES RAISIN ATTAINS
NEAT PINCER GRASP OF RAISIN
HANDS TOGETHER
THUMBS, FINGER GRASP
TRANSFERS CUBE HAND TO HAND
Fine Motor-adaptive
RESPONDS TO BELL
DADA OR MAMA NONSPECIFIC
VOLCALIZES NOT CRYING
TURNS TO VOICE
DADA OR MAMA SPECIFIC
LAUGHS
SQUEALS
IMITATES SPEECH SOUNDS
Language
REGARDS FACE
INITIALLY SHY WITH STRANGERS
SMILES RESPONSIVELY
PLAYS PAT A CAKE
SMILES SPONTANEOUSLY
PLAYS BALL WITH EXAMINER
INDICATES WANTS (NOT CRY)
FEEDS SELF CRACKER
RESISTS TOY PULL
50%
PLAYS PEEK-A-BOO
DRINK FROM CUP
WORKS FOR TOY OUT OF REACH
*90% pass at 1 month
Personal–social
1 2 3 4 5 6 7 8 9 10 11 12 13 14 16
Months

Denver developmental screening test (after H Silver *Handbook of Paediatrics*, Lange).

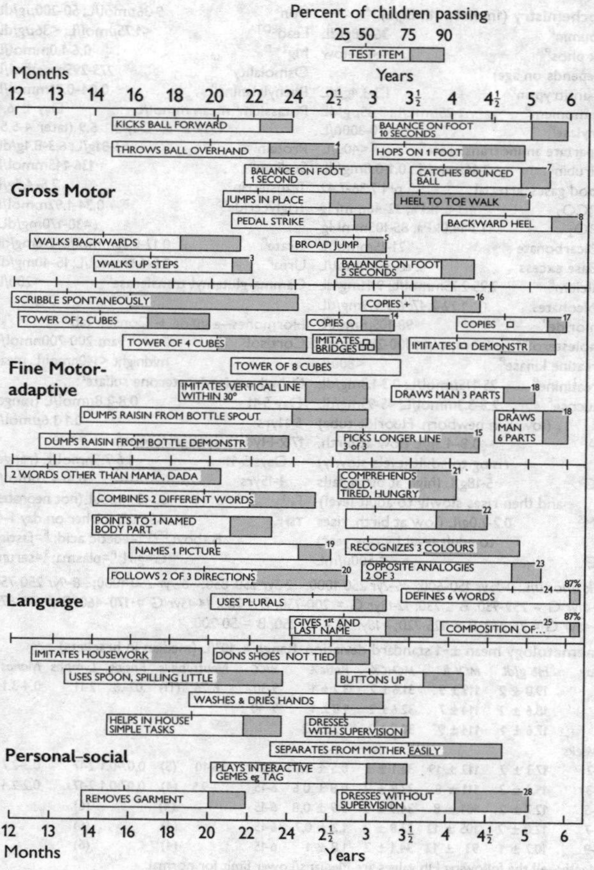
Percent of children passing
25 50 75 90
TEST ITEM
Months
12 13 14 16 18 20 22 24
Years
2½ 3 3½ 4 4½ 5 6
Gross Motor
KICKS BALL FORWARD
THROWS BALL OVERHAND
BALANCE ON FOOT 1 SECOND
JUMPS IN PLACE
PEDAL STRIKE
WALKS BACKWARDS
WALKS UP STEPS
BROAD JUMP
BALANCE ON FOOT 5 SECONDS
BALANCE ON FOOT 10 SECONDS
HOPS ON 1 FOOT
CATCHES BOUNCED BALL
HEEL TO TOE WALK
BACKWARD HEEL
Fine Motor-adaptive
SCRIBBLE SPONTANEOUSLY
TOWER OF 2 CUBES
TOWER OF 4 CUBES
TOWER OF 8 CUBES
IMITATES VERTICAL LINE WITHIN 30°
DUMPS RAISIN FROM BOTTLE SPOUT
DUMPS RAISIN FROM BOTTLE DEMONSTR
COPIES +
COPIES O
IMITATES BRIDGES
COPIES □
IMITATES □ DEMONSTR
DRAWS MAN 3 PARTS
DRAWS MAN 6 PARTS
PICKS LONGER LINE 3 of 3
Language
2 WORDS OTHER THAN MAMA, DADA
COMBINES 2 DIFFERENT WORDS
POINTS TO 1 NAMED BODY PART
NAMES 1 PICTURE
FOLLOWS 2 OF 3 DIRECTIONS
USES PLURALS
GIVES 1st AND LAST NAME
COMPREHENDS COLD, TIRED, HUNGRY
RECOGNIZES 3 COLOURS
OPPOSITE ANALOGIES 2 OF 3
DEFINES 6 WORDS
COMPOSITION OF...
87%
Personal–social
IMITATES HOUSEWORK
USES SPOON, SPILLING LITTLE
WASHES & DRIES HANDS
HELPS IN HOUSE SIMPLE TASKS
REMOVES GARMENT
PLAYS INTERACTIVE GEMES eg TAG
DONS SHOES NOT TIED
BUTTONS UP
DRESSES WITH SUPERVISION
SEPARATES FROM MOTHER EASILY
DRESSES WITHOUT SUPERVISION
Months
Years

Paediatric reference intervals

P=plasma; S=serum; F=fasting

Biochemistry (1mmol = 1mEq/L)

Albumin^{P}	36–48g/dL
Alk phos^{P} (depends on age)	see below
α1-antitrypsin^{P}	1.3-3.4g/dL
Ammonium^{P}	2-25μmL/L; 3-35μg/dL
Amylase^{P}	70-300u/L
Aspartate aminotransferase^{P}	<40u/L
Bilirubin^{P}	2-16μmol/L; 0.1–0.8mg/dL
Blood gases, arterial	pH 7.36-7.42
P_aCO_2	4.3-6.1kPa; 32–46mmHg
P_aO_2	11.3-14.0kPa; 85-105mmHg
Bicarbonate	21-25mmol/L
Base excess	-2 to +2mmol/L
Calcium^{P}	2.25-2.75mmol/L; 9-11mg/dL
Neonates:	1.72-2.47; 6.9-9.9mg/dL
Chloride^{P}	98-105mmol/L
Cholesterol^{P,F}	≤5.7mmol/L; 100-200mg/dL
Creatine kinase^{P}	<80u/L
Creatinine^{P}	25-115μmol/L; 0.3-1.3mg/dL
Glucose^{F}	2.5-5.3mmol/L; 45-95mg/dL (lower in newborn. Fluoride tube)
IgA^{S}	0.8–4.5g/L (low at birth, rising to adult levels slowly)
IgG^{S}	5-18g/L (high at birth, falls and then rises slowly to adult level)
IgM^{S}	0.2-2.0g/L (low at birth, rises to adult level by one year)
IgE^{S}	< 500u/mL

Iron^{S}	9-36μmol/L; 50-200μg/dL
Lead^{EDTA}	<1.75μmol/L; <36μg/dL
Mg^{2+} ^{P}	0.6-1.0mmol/L
Osmolality^{P}	275-295mosmol/L
Phenylalanine^{P}	0.04–0.21mmol/L
Potassium^{P} mean mmol/L	Day 1: 6.4; Day 2: 6; Day 3: 5.9 (later 4-5.5)
Protein^{P}	63-81g/L; 6.3-8.1g/dL
Sodium^{P}	136-145mmol/L
Transferrin^{S}	2.5-4.5g/L
Triglyceride^{F,S}	0.34-1.92mmol/L (=30-170mg/dL)
Urate^{P}	0.12-0.36mmol/L; 2-6mg/dL
Urea^{P}	2.5-6.6mmol/L; 15-40mg/dL
Gamma-glutamyl transferase^{P}	<20u/L

Hormones—a guide. ► Consult lab

Cortisol^{P}	9am 200-700nmol/L; midnight <140nmol/L, mean
Dehydroepiandrosterone sulfate^{P}:	
Day 5-11	0.8-2.8μmol/L (range)
5-11yrs	0.1-3.6μmol/L
17α-Hydroxyprogesterone^{P}:	
Days 5-11	1.6-7.5nmol/L (range)
4-15yrs	0.4-4.2nmol/L
T_4 ^{P}	60-135nmol/L (not neonates)
TSH^{P}	<5mu/L (higher on day 1-4)

B=boy; ^{EDTA}=edetic acid; ^{F}=fasting
G=girl; ^{P}=plasma; ^{S}=serum.

Alk phos u/L: *0–½yr* 150–600; *½–2yr* 250–1000; *2–5yr* 250–850; *6–7yr* 250–1000; *8–9yr* 250–750; *10–11yr* G = 259–950, B ≤ 730; *12–13yr* G = 200–750, B ≤ 785; *14–15yr* G = 170–460, B = 170–970; *16–18yr* G = 75–270, B = 125–720; *>18yr* G = 60–250, B = 50-200.

Haematology mean ±~1 standard deviation. Range × 10^9/L (median in brackets)

Day	*Hb g/dL*	*MCV fl*	*MCHC%*	*Retic%*	*WCC*	*Neutrophils*	*Eosins*	*Lymphs*	*Monos*
1	19.0 ± 2	119 ± 9	31.6 ± 2	3.2 ± 1	9-30	6-26 (11)	.02-.8	2-11	0.4-3.1
4	18.6 ± 2	114 ± 7	32.6 ± 2	1.8 ± 1	9–40				
5	17.6 ± 1	114 ± 9	30.9 ± 2	1.2 ± 0.2					
Weeks									
1-2	17.3 ± 2	112 ± 19	32.1 ± 3	0.5 ± 0.03	5-21	1.5-10 (5)	0.07-0.1	2-17	0.3-2.7
2-3	15.6 ± 3	111 ± 8	33.9 ± 2	0.8 ± 0.6	6-15	1-9.5 (4)	0.07-0.1	2-17	0.2-2.4
4-5	12.7 ± 2	101 ± 8	34.9 ± 2	0.9 ± 0.8	6-15	(4)		(6)	
6-7	12.0 ± 2	105 ± 12	33.8 ± 2	1.2 ± 0.7	6-15	(4)		(6)	
8-9	10.7 ± 1	93 ± 12	34.1 ± 2	1.8 ± 1	6-15	(4)		(6)	
Months—all the following Hb values are Medians/Lower limit for normal									
3	11.5/9	88/88			6-15	(3)		(6)	
6	11.5/9	77/70			6-15	(3)		(6)	
12	11.5/9	78/72			6-15	(3)		(5)	
Year									
2	11.5/9	78/74			6-15	(3)		(5)	
4	12.2/10	80/75			6-15	(4)		(4)	
6	13/10.4	82/75			5-15	(4.2)		(3.8)	
12	13.8/11	83/76			4-13	(4.9)		(3.1)	
14B	14.2/12	84/77			4-13	(5)		(3)	
14G	14/11.5								
16B	14.8/12	85/78	30-36	0.8-2	4-13	2-7.5 (5)	0.04-.4	1.3-3.5	0.2-.8
16G	14/11.5								
18B	15/13								

Note *Basophil range:* 0–0.1 × 10^9/L; B_{12}^{S}; ≥150ng/L.
Red cell folate ^{EDTA} 100–640ng/mL. B = boys; G = girls.

Platelet counts do not vary with age; range: 150–400 × 10^9/L.

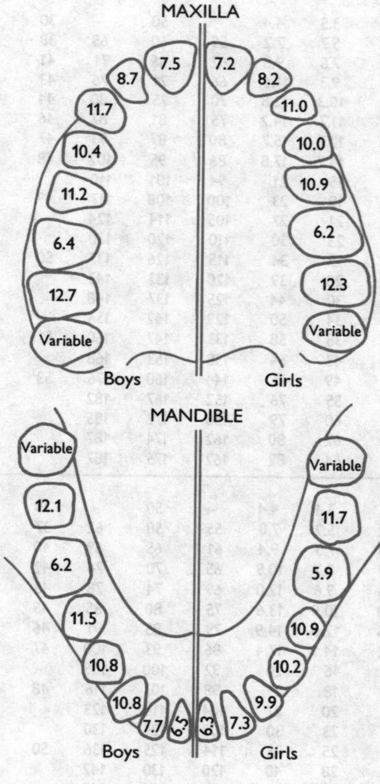

Mean times of eruption (in years) of the permanent teeth.

Deciduous teeth	Months		Months
Lower central incisors	5-9	First molars	10-16
Upper central incisors	8-12	Canines	16-20
Upper lateral incisors	10-12	Second molars	20-30
Lower lateral incisors	12-15		

A 1-year-old has ~6 teeth; 1½yrs ~12 teeth; 2yrs ~16 teeth; 2¼yrs ~20.

Centile tables

Age	Weight (kg)			Height (cm)			Skull circumference (cm)		
Centile	3	50	97	3	50	97	3	50	97
Boys									
Birth term	2.5	3.5	4.4	-	50	-	30	35	38
3 months	4.4	5.7	7.2	55	60	65	38	41	43
6 months	6.2	7.8	9.8	62	66	71	41	44	46
9 months	7.6	9.3	11.6	66	71	76	43	46	47
12 months	8.4	10.3	12.8	70	75	80	44	47	49
18 months	9.4	11.7	14.2	75	81	87	46	49	51
2 years	10.2	12.7	15.7	80	87	93	47	50	52
3 years	11.6	14.7	17.8	86	95	102	48	50	53
4 years	13	15	21	94	101	110			
5 years	14	19	23	100	108	117	49	51	54
6 years	16	21	27	105	114	124			
7 years	17	23	30	110	120	130			
8 years	19	25	34	115	126	137	50	52	55
9 years	21	28	39	120	132	143			
10 years	23	30	44	125	137	148			
11 years	25	34	50	129	142	154			
12 years	27	38	58	133	147	160	51	54	56
13 years	30	43	64	138	153	168			
14 years	33	49	71	144	160	176	53	56	58
15 years	39	55	76	152	167	182			
16 years	46	60	79	158	172	185			
17 years	49	62	80	162	174	187			
18 years	50	64	82	162	175	187			
Girls									
Birth term	2.5	3.4	4.4	-	50	-	30	35	39
3 months	4.2	5.2	7.0	55	58	62	37	40	43
6 months	5.9	7.3	9.4	61	65	69	40	43	45
9 months	7.0	8.7	10.9	65	70	74	42	44	47
12 months	7.6	9.6	12.0	69	74	78	43	46	48
18 months	8.8	10.9	13.6	75	80	85	45	47	50
2 years	9.6	12.0	14.9	79	85	91	46	48	51
3 years	11.2	14.1	17.4	86	93	100	47	49	52
4 years	13	16	20	92	100	109			
5 years	15	18	23	98	107	116	48	50	53
6 years	16	20	27	104	114	123			
7 years	18	23	30	109	120	130			
8 years	19	25	35	114	125	136	50	52	54
9 years	21	28	40	120	130	142			
10 years	23	31	48	125	136	148			
11 years	25	35	56	130	143	155			
12 years	28	40	64	135	149	164	51	53	56
13 years	32	46	70	142	156	168			
14 years	37	51	73	148	160	172	52	54	57
15 years	42	54	74	150	162	173			
16 years	45	56	75	115	162	174			
18 years	46	57	75	-	-	-			

Measure height 'exactly': • Feet together • Straight legs; loose arms • Buttocks, shoulders & heels touching wall • Hair firmly compressed • Ear canal level with infraorbital margin • Take reading in expiration.

More up-to-date charts are being designed to take into account new growth data, and to amalgamate American, WHO, and European centile divisions.[1]

►Breast-fed and some Indian babies need different charts: see p 181 [466]

1 'UK90' reference charts: Harlow Publishing, Maxwell St, South Shields, NE33 4PU. 0191 427 0195. Freeman 1995 *Arch Dis Child* 73 17 **NB:** the 1995 Castlemead charts have not met with 100% approval as the upper centile on the weight chart is too low, classifying too many children as obese; but these charts have the (unproven) advantage of being based on serial measurements, not cross-sectional data.

BOYS BMI CHART

(BIRTH - 20 YEARS): United Kingdom cross-sectional reference: 2002/1

Name ....

D.O.B. [DDMMYY] ☐☐/☐☐/☐☐☐☐

NHS No. ☐☐☐ ☐☐☐ ☐☐☐☐

Body Mass Index (BMI)

BMI is used in growth monitoring to assess fatness. Although highly correlated with fatness, BMI is not a direct measure of body fat and must be interpreted with caution; rapid changes in BMI can occur during normal childhood growth. Intervention/referral shouldn't be based on BMI alone.

The standard 9 centile lines for BMI from UK data. The International Obesity Task Force (IOTF) has proposed paediatric cut-offs for obesity and overweight that correspond to the adult cut-offs at age 18, of BMI ≥30 for obesity & BMI ≥25 for overweight (the lines composed of dots & dashes).

BMI = the child's weight in kg divided by (the height in metres, squared)

Further information: www.heightmatters.org.uk; www.healthforallchildren.co.uk & Royal College of Paediatrics & Child Health & National Obesity Forum *An approach to weight management in children and adolescents (2–18 years) in primary care.*

►These charts are reproduced for illustrative purposes only, by kind permission. ©Child growth foundation. They may not be reproduced in any form whatsoever.

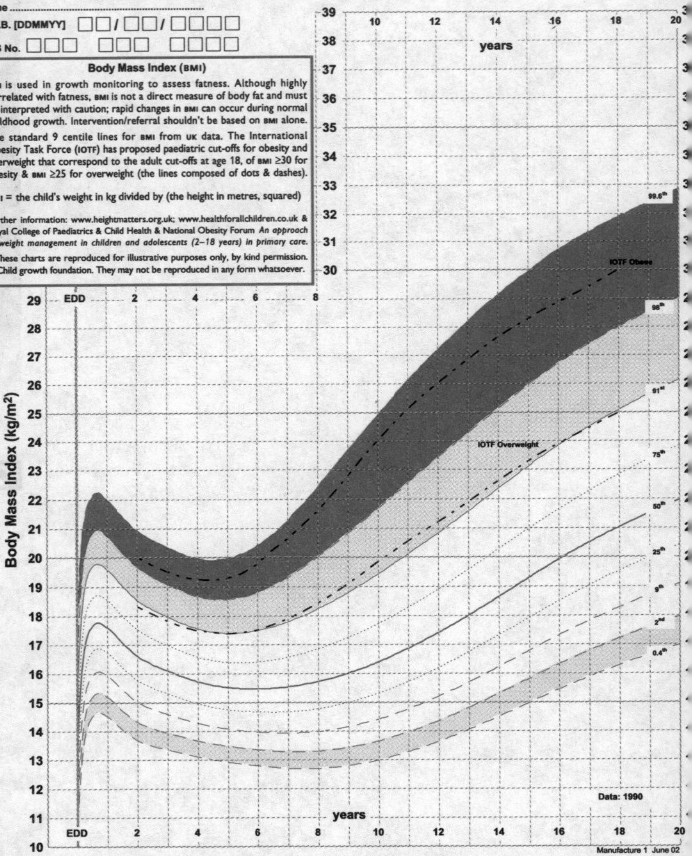

Manufacture 1 June 02

Reference

Body Mass Index reference curves for the UK, 1990 (TJ Cole, JV Freeman, MA Preece) *Arch Dis Child* 1995; **73**: 25-29

Establishing a standard definition for child overweight and obesity: international survey, (Cole TJ, Bellizi MC, Flegal KM, Dietz WH) *BMJ* 2000; **320**: 1240-3

Designed and Published by

© CHILD GROWTH FOUNDATION 1997/1
(Charity Reg. No 274325)
2 Mayfield Avenue,
London W4 1PW

Printed and Supplied by

HARLOW PRINTING LIMITED
Maxwell Street ¹ South Shields
Tyne & Wear ¹ NE33 4PU

GIRLS BMI CHART

(BIRTH - 20 YEARS): United Kingdom cross-sectional reference: 2002/1

Name ....

D.O.B. [DDMMYY] ☐☐ / ☐☐ / ☐☐☐☐

NHS No. ☐☐☐ ☐☐☐ ☐☐☐☐

Body Mass Index (BMI)

BMI is used in growth monitoring to assess fatness. Although highly correlated with fatness, BMI is not a direct measure of body fat and must be interpreted with caution; rapid changes in BMI can occur during normal childhood growth. Intervention/referral shouldn't be based on BMI alone.

The standard 9 centile lines for BMI from UK data. The International Obesity Task Force (IOTF) has proposed paediatric cut-offs for obesity and overweight that correspond to the adult cut-offs at age 18, of BMI ≥30 for obesity & BMI ≥25 for overweight (the lines composed of dots & dashes).

BMI = the child's weight in kg divided by (the height in metres, squared)

Further information: www.heightmatters.org.uk; www.healthforallchildren.co.uk & Royal College of Paediatrics & Child Health & National Obesity Forum *An approach to weight management in children and adolescents (2–18 years) in primary care.*

►These charts are reproduced for illustrative purposes only, by kind permission. ©Child growth foundation. They may not be reproduced in any form whatsoever.

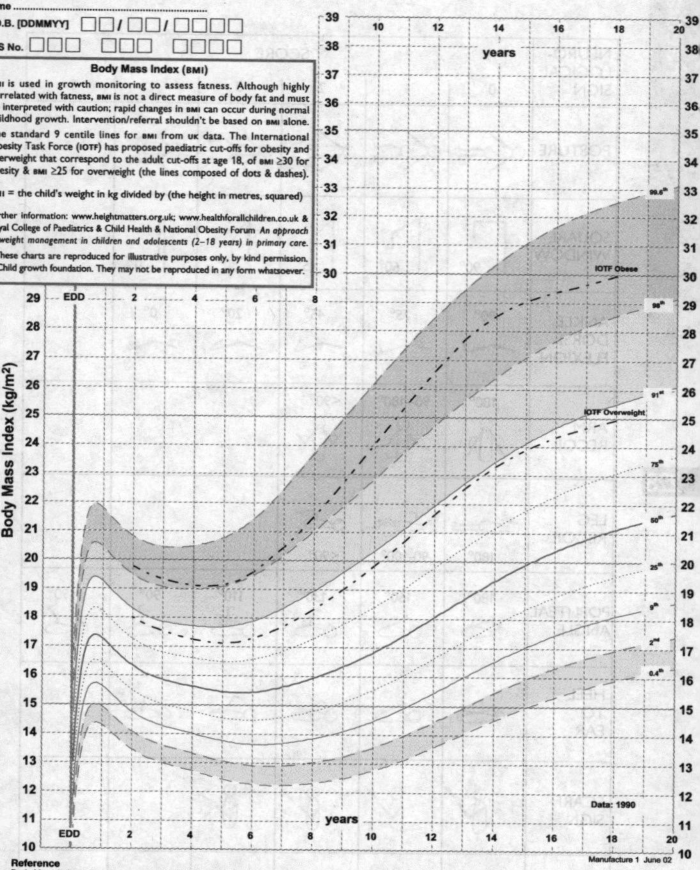

Manufacture 1 June 02

Reference

Body Mass Index reference curves for the UK, 1990 (TJ Cole, JV Freeman, MA Preece) *Arch Dis Child* 1995; **73**: 25-29

Establishing a standard definition for child overweight and obesity: international survey (Cole TJ, Bellizi MC Flegal KM, Dietz WH) *BMJ* 2000; **320**: 1240-3

Designed and Published by

© CHILD GROWTH FOUNDATION 1997/1
(Charity Reg. No 274325)
2 Mayfield Avenue,
London W4 1PW

Printed and Supplied by

HARLOW PRINTING LIMITED
Maxwell Street ¹ South Shields
Tyne & Wear ¹ NE33 4PU

Dubowitz system for assessing gestational age

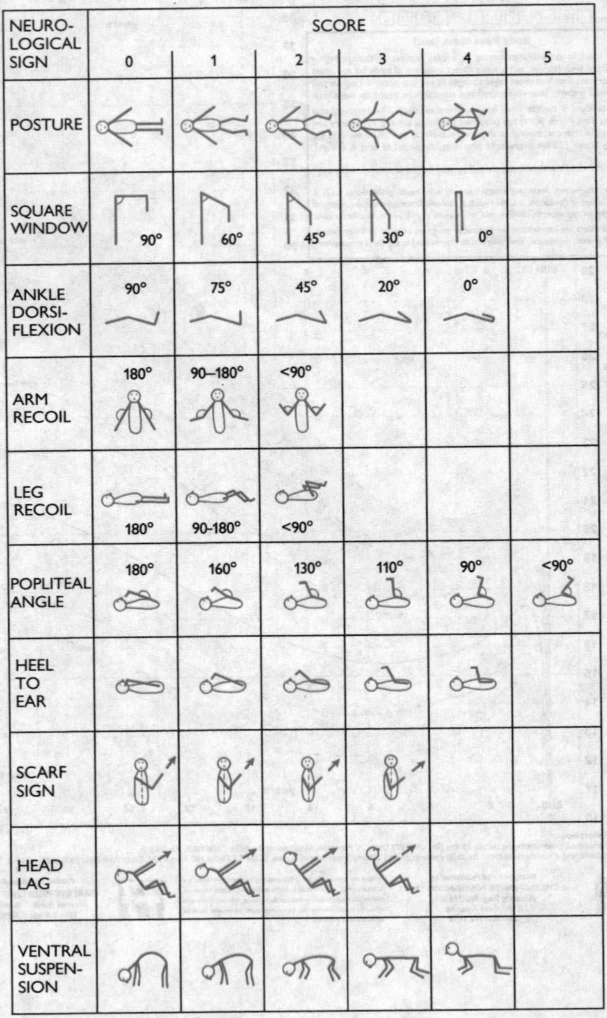

NEUROLOGICAL SIGN	SCORE 0	1	2	3	4	5
POSTURE						
SQUARE WINDOW	90°	60°	45°	30°	0°	
ANKLE DORSIFLEXION	90°	75°	45°	20°	0°	
ARM RECOIL	180°	90–180°	<90°			
LEG RECOIL	180°	90-180°	<90°			
POPLITEAL ANGLE	180°	160°	130°	110°	90°	<90°
HEEL TO EAR						
SCARF SIGN						
HEAD LAG						
VENTRAL SUSPENSION						

Neurological criteria. 467

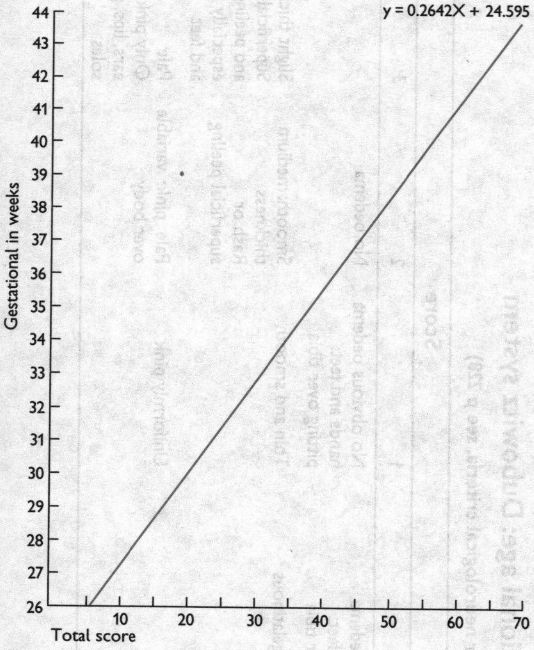

Assessment of gestational age: Dubowitz system. Graph for reading gestational age from total score. 468

Assessment of gestational age: Dubowitz system

Physical (external) criteria (for neurological criteria, see p 228)

	Score				
External sign	0	1	2	3	4
Oedema	Obvious oedema hands and feet: pitting over tibia	No obvious oedema hands and feet: pitting over tibia	No oedema		
Skin texture	Very thin, gelatinous	Thin and smooth	Smooth: medium thickness Rash or superficial peeling	Slight thickening Superficial cracking and peeling, especially hands and feet	Thick and parchment-like: superficial or deep cracking
Skin colour (infant not crying)	Dark red	Uniformly pink	Pale pink: variable over body	Pale Only pink over ears, lips, palms, or soles	

Skin opacity (trunk)	Numerous veins and venules clearly seen, especially over abdomen	Veins and tributaries seen	A few large vessels clearly seen over abdomen	A few large vessels seen indistinctly over abdomen	No blood vessels seen
Lanugo (over back)	No lanugo	Abundant long and thick over whole back	Hair thinning especially over lower back	Small amount of lanugo and bald areas	At least half of back devoid of lanugo
Plantar creases	No skin creases	Faint red marks over anterior half of sole	Definite red marks over more than anterior half: indentations over less than anterior third	Indentations over more than anterior third	Definite deep indentations over more than anterior third
Nipple formation	Nipple barely visible: no areola	Nipple well defined: areola smooth and flat diameter <0.75cm	Areola stippled, edge not raised: diameter <0.75cm	Areola stippled, edge raised diameter >0.75cm	
Breast size	No breast tissue palpable	Breast tissue on one or both sides <0.5cm diameter	Breast tissue both sides: one or both 0.5–1.0cm	Breast tissue both sides: one or both >1cm	

Assessment of gestational age: Dubowitz system

Physical (external) criteria (for neurological criteria, see p 228)

External sign	Score				
	0	1	2	3	4
Ear form	Pinna flat and shapeless, little or no incurving of edge	Incurving of part of edge of pinna	Partial incurving whole of upper pinna	Well-defined incurving whole of upper pinna	
Ear firmness	Pinna soft, easily folded, no recoil	Pinna, soft, easily folded, slow recoil places, ready recoil	Cartilage to edge of pinna, but soft in places, ready recoil	Pinna firm, cartilage to edge, instant recoil	
Genitalia • Male	Neither testis in scrotum	At least one testis high in scrotum	At least one testis right down		
• Female (with hips half abducted)	Labia majora widely separated, labia minora protruding	Labia majora almost cover labia minora	Labia majora completely cover labia minora		

Nomogram for calculating the body surface area of children

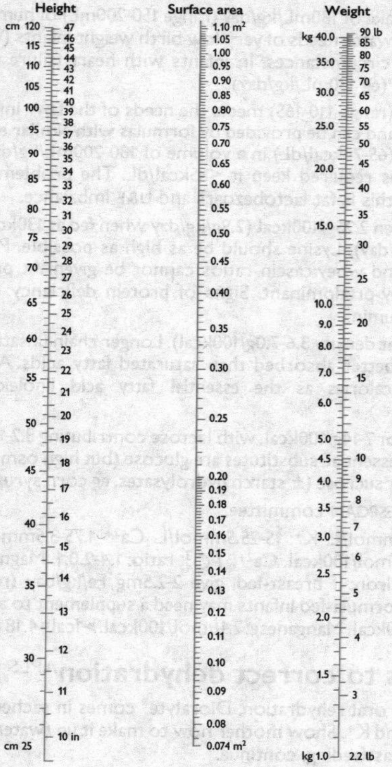

Reference intervals: nutritional requirements for preterm babies

Water See p 235. An intake of 180mL/kg/day (range 150–200mL) of human or formula milk meets the water needs of very low birth weight infants (VLBW; <1500g) under normal circumstances. In infants with heart failure water restriction is necessary (eg 130mL/kg/day).

Energy 130kcal/kg/day (range 110–165) meets the needs of the LBW infant in normal circumstances, and can be provided by formulas with similar energy density to human milk (65–70kcal/dL) in a volume of 180–200mL/kg/day. If a higher energy density is required keep it <85kcal/dL. The problem with energy densities above this is fat lactobezoars and U&E imbalance.

Protein Aim for between 2.25g/100kcal (2.9g/kg/day when fed at 130kcal/kg) and 3.1g/100kcal (4g/kg/day). Lysine should be as high as possible. Precise guidelines on taurine and whey:casein ratios cannot be given. At present LBW formulas are whey-predominant. Signs of protein deficiency: a low plasma urea and prealbumin.

Fat Aim for 4.7–9g/kg (fat density 3.6–7.0g/100kcal). Longer chain unsaturated fatty acids (>C12) are better absorbed than saturated fatty acids. Aim to have ≥4.5% of total calories as the essential fatty acid linoleic acid (500mg/100kcal).[469]

Carbohydrates Aim for 7–14g/100kcal, with lactose contributing 3.2–12g per 100kcal. Lactose is not essential; substitutes are glucose (but high osmolality may cause diarrhoea) or sucrose (± starch hydrolysates, eg corn syrup oils).

Vitamins See p 123 & ESPGAN committee.[470]

Elements Na^+: 6.5–15mmol/L. K^+: 15–25.5mmol/L. Ca^{2+} 1.75–3.5mmol per 100kcal. PO_4^{3-}: 1.6–2.9mmol/100kcal. Ca^{2+}: PO_4^{3-} ratio: 1.4–2.0:1. Magnesium: 0.25–0.5mmol/100kcal. Iron: if breast-fed, give 2–2.5mg Fe/kg/day (recommended total intake). Formula-fed infants may need a supplement to achieve this. Iodine: 10–45μg/100kcal. Manganese: 2.1μmol/100kcal. ►1cal=4.18 joules.

Fluid regimens to correct dehydration[APLS]

If tolerated, always use oral rehydration. Dioralyte® comes in sachets, and contain glucose, Na^+ and K^+. Show mother how to make it up (water is the vital ingredient!). If breastfeeding, continue.

Daily IV water, Na, and K (mmol/kg/day) MAINTENANCE needs

Age (yr)	*Weight (kg)*	*Water (mL/kg/day)*	*Na^+*	*K^+*
<0.5	<5	150	3	3
0.5–1	5–10	120	2.5	2.5
1–3	10–15	100	2.5	2.5
3–5	15–20	80	2	2
>5	>20	45–75	1.5–2	1.5–2

Use "Half Normal Saline with 5% Dextrose" for these needs (contains few calories, but prevents ketosis). Pre-existing deficits and continuing loss must also be made good. Reliable input-output fluid balance charts are essential.

Calculating pre-existing deficit mL ≈ % dehydration × weight (kg) × 10; give eg as 0.45% saline over 24h (eg 750mL for a 10kg child who is 7.5% dehydrated). Add in K^+ (20mmol/500mL) once the child has passed urine.

Estimating dehydration ***Mild dehydration:*** Decreased urine output.

5% dehydration: Dry mucous membranes; decreased urine output.

10% dehydration: The above + sunken fontanelle (but if crying, pressure↑), eyeball pressure↓ (hard to assess if young); pulse↑; hoarse cry; skin turgor↓.

>10%: The above, but worse, with: shock; drowsiness; hypotension. If a recent weight is known, this is useful in quantifying dehydration.

Fluids for the first 24h in MILD dehydration You will rarely have to start IV fluids for this. However, if the child will not drink, try little and often (ie 5mL every 5 min by syringe), nasogastric fluids, or otherwise IV maintenance only (above), and start oral fluids when possible.

IV fluids for the first 24h in 5–10% dehydration

- Give maintenance water requirement (above) + the deficit. Keep the rate <25mL/kg/h. 'Rapid rehydration' involves 4 hours of 10mL/kg/h 0.45% NaCl/5% dextrose (= "½ normal saline with dextrose") then maintenance after. Ensure the nurses are aware to drop the fluid rate after 4 hours.
- Measure and replace ongoing losses (eg from the bowel).
- Monitor U&E on admission, and at 2, 12, and 24h. Also do PCV.

▸▸IV fluid replacement in the first 24h in >10% dehydration NB: Fluids should be given orally if possible—or by nasogastric tube. Reserve IVI for those who are shocked (if IV access fails, use the intraosseous route, p 236).

- 0.9% saline (or plasma, if desperate) 20mL/kg IVI bolus, while calculations are performed. Continuously monitor pulse, BP, ECG.
- Continue until BP rises, pulses are felt, and urine flows (catheterize).
- Then give the daily requirement + fluid deficit as above, making good continuing loss with 0.45% or 0.9% saline depending on type of dehydration.
- Measure plasma and urine creatinine and osmolality (p 176), and plasma bicarbonate. Metabolic acidosis usually corrects itself.

Guidelines for success: Above all *be simple*. Complex regimens cause errors.

1. Stay at the bedside; use clinical state + lab results to adapt IVI.
2. Beware sudden changes in Na^+ (↑ or ↓); may cause seizures or central pontine myelinolysis.
3. Beware hidden loss (oedema, ascites, GI pools), and shifts of fluid from the intravascular space to the interstitial space ('third-spacing').
4. Measure U&E and urine electrolytes often.
5. Give potassium once you know that urine is flowing. Using the ready-prepared fluid "0.45% Saline With 5% Dextrose With Potassium Chloride 20mmol/L" is usually a good choice. Be guided by serum K^+.[471]

Hypernatraemic dehydration: (greater water loss than salt, eg from wrongly made feeds, or rarely, if breast-fed.) It causes intracellular dehydration (± fits, CNS thrombosis/haemorrhages on MRI).[472] Treatment: rehydrate slowly with 0.45% or 0.9% saline (which is hypotonic for a hypernatraemic patient): replace deficit over 48h, lowering Na^+ by <12mmol/L/24h, and giving only 60% of maintenance volume, to avoid CNS oedema (p 200). A big danger is too rapid rehydration. Hyperglycaemia is common, but self-correcting.[473] [474]

Water balance in the preterm infant Water comprises 50–70% of weight gain (eg of 15g/day) in preterm babies.

Insensible water loss (IWL) falls with increasing body weight, gestational age, and postnatal age; it increases with ↑T° (ambient & body) and low humidity. In a single-walled, thermoneutral incubator with a humidity of 50–80% IWL≈30–60mL/kg/day (may double in infants on phototherapy under a radiant heater).

Faecal water loss ≈ 5–10mL/kg/day (except during diarrhoea).

Urine loss: If ~90mL/kg/day, there is no excessive renal stress.

▸▸APLS procedures—intraosseus transfusion

(APLS=advanced paediatric life support.)

Immediate vascular access is required in paediatric and neonatal practice in the following circumstances: cardiopulmonary arrest, severe burns, prolonged status epilepticus, hypovolaemic and septic shock. In many cases rapid intravenous access is not easily obtained, and intraosseous infusion is a relatively safe, easy, and effective means of obtaining vascular access, and is recommended for life-threatening paediatric emergencies in which other methods of access have failed. 475

Contra-indications Osteoporosis, osteogenesis imperfecta, and infection or fracture at the site of insertion.

Technical aspects *Learn from an expert.* The following is one technique.

Preparation: Set trolley: Dressing pack, Betadine®, needles, 10mL syringe, lidocaine (=lignocaine) 1% (5mL), scalpel, intraosseous needle, paediatric infusion set, 10mL 0.9% saline, adhesive tape.

Choosing the site of insertion: The proximal tibia is the best site. Other sites are the distal tibia, or distal femur. Choose a point in the midline on the flat anteromedial surface of the tibia, 2 finger-breadths below the tibial tuberosity. The patient's leg should be restrained, with a small support placed behind the knee.

Procedure:

- Sterilize the skin with antiseptic, infiltrate with lidocaine as necessary. (Puncturing the skin with the scalpel is not usually necessary.)
- Insert the intraosseous needle at an angle of 60–90 degrees away from the growth plate, and advance with a boring or screwing motion into the marrow cavity. Correct location of the needle is signified by a decrease in resistance on entering the marrow cavity.
- Stabilize the needle and verify the position by aspirating marrow, or by the easy flushing of 5–10mL of 0.9% saline, without any infiltration of surrounding tissue. The needle should stand upright without support, but should be secured with tape.
- Take samples for culture, U&E, FBC. Do not do blood gas (will clog machine). Warn haematology lab they will see blasts!
- Flushing with heparinized saline (0.9%) may prevent clotting.
- Connect to IV infusion—but better flow rates are often achieved by syringing in boluses of fluid (standard bolus is 20mL/kg of crystalloid or colloid).
- Any drugs or fluids can be infused except brettylium and strong $NaHCO_3$.

Complications These are infrequent, but there may be extravasation of fluid, or cellulitis, fractures, osteomyelitis, pain, and fat or bone microemboli. These are more common with prolonged use—so intraosseous infusion should be discontinued as soon as conventional IV access is attained.

NB: Intraosseous delivery may also be used in adults (if you are strong enough!). 476

▸▸Anaphylaxis

(Adrenaline=epinephrine)

Doses of IM adrenaline ► *Note the ampoule strength! (1:1000 or 1:10,000).*

Age	mL of 1:1000
<6 months	0.05mL
6 months–6yrs	0.12mL
6–12yrs	0.25mL
Adolescent	0.5mL

Use suitable syringe for measuring small volumes; absolute accuracy isn't essential. 477

Doses may need repeating every 5–15min, until improvement occurs. Also: • O_2 (± IPPV) • Hydrocortisone (4mg/kg IV) • Chlorpheniramine (0.2mg/kg) • Colloid (20mL/kg IVI). *NB:* weight (kg)≈2(age in yrs+4). OK if 1–10yrs.

IVI route for adrenaline: If the circulation is so compromised that the IM route is no good, try IV adrenaline in a strength of 1:10,000, at a dose of 0.1mL/kg (10μg/kg) over several minutes.

Adrenaline dose by endotracheal tube: 100μg/kg.

If bronchospasm is a feature, give salbutamol 2mg nebulized too. After the emergency, take blood at 1–5h for mast cell tryptase; refer to an allergist. Self-use of pre-loaded pen injections may be needed (eg EpiPen®). 478

EpiPen® contains 0.3mg of adrenaline (=epinephrine, 1:1000). This is suitable if weight is more than 30kg. If 15–30kg, use Anapen Junior® or EpiPen Junior®, which both contain 0.15mg of adrenaline. Epipen Junior (1:2000) delivers 0.15mg of adrenaline (1.7mL remains after using the autoinjector). This is suitable for a 15kg child—ie aged about 4yrs.

List of drugs in this chapter which are not detailed in the *BNF*.

[Link]	Address	P
[1]	http://www.resus.org.uk/pages/pals.htm. UK resusc council accessed 2005. Give tracheal dose quickly down a narrow bore suction catheter beyond the tracheal end of the tube and then flushed in with 1 or 2 mls of normal saline.	107
[2]	http://pubmedhh.nlm.nih.gov/cgi-bin/abstract.cgi?id =12881619& from=cqsr Epileptic seizure discharges subside within 2–6 minutes after the intravenous injection of 50–100 mg of pyridaoxine.	112
[3]	http://www.ucsfhealth.org/childrens/health_professionals/ manuals/48_Seizures.pdf UCSF Intensive Care Nursery House Staff Manual [Accessed 2005].	112
[4]	http://www.paclac.org/Manuals_Guidelines/Hypotension_and_ Shock_Final_5.30.98.pdf. If dopamine fails to improve BP dobutamine is recommended. Both doses are 5–20mcg/kg/min. Perinatal advisory council paclac.org.	112
[5]	http://www.paclac.org/Manuals_Guidelines/Hypotension_and_ Shock_Final_5.30.98.pdf. If dopamine fails to improve BP dobutamine is recommended. Both doses are 5–20mcg/kg/min. Perinatal advisory council paclac.org.	112
[6]	http://medind.nic.in/maa/t04/i4/maat04i4p333.pdf Neonatal Immune Thrombocytopenia (Col Uma Raju; Lt Gen Punita Arora).	120
[7]	http://medind.nic.in/maa/t03/i3/maat03i3p228.pdf this paper also gives a loading dose of digoxin.	136
[8]	http://www.emedicine.com/med/topic1097.htm Dose of calcium carbonate from eMedicine (specific paediatric dose).	177
[9]	http://128.196.82.74/artman/publish/flaped_a97.pdf This dose of labetolol comes from Division of Pediatric Critical Care, University of Florida (hypertensive emergencies in tetanus).	177

►►European paediatric basic life-support algorithm[1]

This algorithm assumes no equipment and that only one rescuer is present.

►► Remove yourself and the child from danger

↓

Check responsiveness — stimulate and shout

↓

Open the airway — remove obstructions; upward head tilt; chin lift

↓

Check breathing — look, listen, feel; if breathing, place in recovery position

↓

Give 2 breaths — have up to 5 goes at giving 2 rescue breaths sufficient to raise the chest

↓

Assess for signs of life (10sec only) — signs of circulation: pulse, coughing, movement etc; phone for help at once

↙ ↘

Circulation present: Continue rescue breathing

No circulation: compress chest give breaths — 100 compressions/min 5 strokes to 1 ventilation; check circulation every min

Compress sternum to ⅓ of the chest's depth; use the heel of one hand (or, in babies, with both your thumbs, with your hands encircling the thorax) If >8yrs, the adult 2-handed method is OK. For an infant, 2 fingers are sufficient, positioned in the middle of a line joining the nipples. Perform resuscitation for ~1min before going for help. Remove the cause, if possible. Causes are: drowning; pulmonary embolism; trauma; electrocution; shock; hypoxia; hypercapnia; hypothermia; U&E imbalance; drugs/toxins, eg adrenaline (=epinephrine), digoxin, and blue-ringed octopi. 479

How to give the rescue breaths *to a child* Ensure head tilt and chin lift. Pinch the soft part of his nose. Open his mouth a little, but maintain chin up. Take a breath, and place your lips around his mouth (good seal). Blow steadily into his mouth over 1-1.5sec. Does his chest rise? Take your mouth away, and watch for the chest to fall. Take another breath, and repeat this sequence up to 5 times. ***With an infant*** Do as above, but cover the nasal apertures and the mouth with your lips. If the chest does not move, respiratory obstruction may exist ►►move on to '***Removing foreign body' sequence*** for obstructed airway—ie:

- Remove any obvious obstructions. Recheck that there is adequate head tilt and chin lift, but do not overextend the neck.
- Do up to 5 back blows between the scapulae to dislodge hidden obstructions (hold prone, positioning the head lower than chest).
- If this fails, do 5 chest thrusts: turn to supine; over 12sec, give 5 sternal thrusts (same position as for compressions, but be sharper and more vigorous). Remove any foreign bodies which have become visible.
- Tilt head upwards; lift chin to reopen the airway, and assess breathing.
- If not breathing; do 5 more rescue breaths: does the chest move now?
- If not, for a child, give 5 abdominal thrusts (directed towards diaphragm); use the upright position if the child is conscious; supine if not.
- Repeat these sequences until breathing is OK, alternating chest and abdominal thrusts. *Do not give abdominal thrusts to infants.*

When breathing place in the recovery position—as near to the true lateral position as possible, with mouth dependent to aid draining of secretions. The position must be stable (eg use pillows placed behind back). The degree of movement is determined by risk of spinal injury.

1 www.resus.org.uk/SiteIndx.htm—medical & www.ncems.org/pdf/emsc/manual.pdf

Cardiac arrest: *paediatric advanced life-support*[1]

Each step assumes the previous one has been unsuccessful

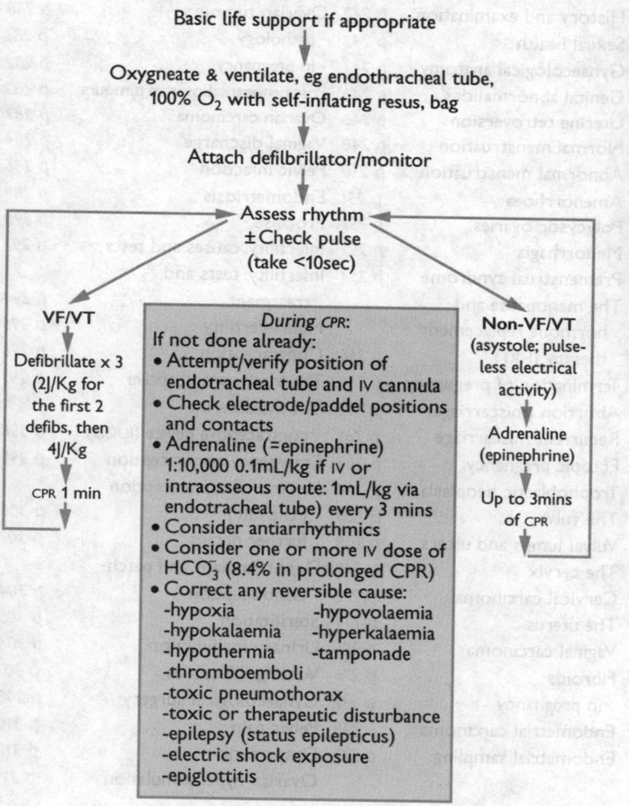

Basic life support if appropriate
Oxygneate & ventilate, eg endothracheal tube, 100% O2 with self-inflating resus, bag
Attach defilbrillator/monitor
Assess rhythm
± Check pulse
(take <10sec)
VF/VT
Defibrillate x 3 (2J/Kg for the first 2 defibs, then 4J/Kg
CPR 1 min
During CPR:
If not done already:
• Attempt/verify position of endotracheal tube and IV cannula
• Check electrode/paddel positions and contacts
• Adrenaline (=epinephrine) 1:10,000 0.1mL/kg if IV or intraosseous route: 1mL/kg via endotracheal tube) every 3 mins
• Consider antiarrhythmics
• Consider one or more IV dose of HCO3 (8.4% in prolonged CPR)
• Correct any reversible cause:
-hypoxia
-hypovolaemia
-hypokalaemia
-hyperkalaemia
-hypothermia
-tamponade
-thromboemboli
-toxic pneumothorax
-toxic or therapeutic disturbance
-epilepsy (status epilepticus)
-electric shock exposure
-epiglottitis
Non-VF/VT
(asystole; pulse-less electrical activity)
Adrenaline (epinephrine)
Up to 3mins of CPR

Treat acidosis with good ventilation. Sodium bicarbonate may worsen intracellular acidosis and precipitate arrhythmias, so use it only in severe acidosis (eg 1mmol/kg, by slow IV bolus). NB: in adults bicarbonate is normally recommended only after prolonged resuscitation. In children, particularly neonates, the heart is often the last thing to stop—so when it does, severe acidosis may *already* be present.

1 After http://www.resus.org.uk/pages/palsalgo.pdf

3 Gynaecology

A holistic approach to gynaecology: Parry's dictum

It is more important to know what sort of patient has the disease than what kind of disease the patient has.

Caleb Parry (1755–1822) was a doctor in Bath who was fascinated by the events in his patients' lives, and their connection with their diseases—some of which he described for the first time. These early descriptions are remarkable for their effortless intertwining of psychological and physical phenomena.[1,2]

All this suggests a serious, one-sided doctor, but this is wrong. To get away from it all, he became a keen balloonist, lending ideas and materials to Edward Jenner (who dedicated his magnum opus on smallpox to him). From the Royal Crescent in Bath, he launched his great hydrogen balloon, which, like his bedside manner, was made of varnished silk.

His aphorism is particularly relevant to this chapter because many of its diseases are chronic, and the choices of treatment are many. Take endometriosis (p 288), for example. If an examiner were to ask you 'what is the treatment for endometriosis'—you might well look at him thoughtfully, before replying that it all depends on who has got it—where they are in their lives, how much the pain matters, what the plans are for future pregnancies, how these plans may be ambiguous and change, according to work, relationships, and the onset of friendships. What does the patient feel about long-term medication with agents which can change her sexuality, and hence the person who is suffering the disease? Some may tolerate doctor-induced hypoestrogenism (flushes, decreased libido, loss of bone density) thinking the price well worth paying for relief of endometriosis symptoms; others will take the opposite view; in a few, their ability to take a decision will be influenced by the drugs they are already taking.[3]

Sometimes rational choice is the hardest thing 'How can you expect me to make a rational choice until you sort out these dreadful periods of mine: I cannot even think…'[4]

Be optimistic; discourage passive dependency; let the patient do the driving.
►take time ►understand your patient ►offer all options, ***then let her choose.***

GMC GOOD DOCTOR TOPIC: PATIENT-CENTRED CARE: LET THE PATIENT DO THE DRIVING!

History and examination

History Let her tell the story. Note down her exact words. She may be reluctant to admit some problems, particularly if you are a man, so make sure to cover them in your questions. A frustration for the medical student is that the story you are told is different to the one elicited by the consultant or the GP. But sometimes the first telling is the most valid. ►It is also true that none of us (doctors and patients) can tell the same story twice.[1]

Menstrual history: ►Date of last menstrual period (LMP; 1st day of bleeding) or menopause. Was the last period normal? Cycles: number of days bleeding/number of days from day 1 of one period to day 1 of next (eg 5/26). Are they regular? If heavy, are there clots or floods? How many pads/tampons are needed (an unreliable guide)? Are periods painful? Any bleeding between periods, postcoitally, or since the menopause? Age at menarche?

1 ***Obstetric history:*** How many children? For each pregnancy: antenatal problems, delivery, gestation, outcome; weights of babies; puerperium? Terminations/miscarriages—at *what* stage, *why*, and (terminations) *how*?

2 ***Symptoms:*** If she has *pain* what is it like? Uterine pain may be colicky and felt in the sacrum and groins. Ovarian pain tends to be felt in the *iliac fossa* and radiates down front of the thigh to the knee. Ask about *dyspareunia* (painful intercourse). Is it superficial (round the outside) or deep inside? If she has *vaginal discharge* what is it like (amount, colour, smell, itch); when does she get it? Ask about *prolapse* and *incontinence*. When? How bad? Worse whilst standing? Ask about bowel symptoms (irritable bowel can cause pelvic pain), and faecal incontinence.

3 ***Sex and contraception:*** Is she sexually active? Are there physical or emotional problems with sex? What contraception is she using and is she happy with it? What has she tried previously? Has she had problems conceiving? If so, has she had treatment for infertility? What about sexually transmitted infections? Date and result of last cervical smear?

4 ***Other:*** General health, smoking. Previous gynaecological treatment.

Examination ►Many women find pelvic examination painful, undignified, and embarrassing: especially if you are male. Explain what you are going to do. Be gentle. Use a chaperone. (Royal Colleges recommend chaperone use for all intimate examinations; the General Medical Council recommends offering them; use is increasing but not universal in General Practice).[2]

General: Is she well or ill? Is she shocked? If so, treat it.

Abdomen: Look for tenderness and peritonism. If there is a mass, could it be a pregnancy? Listen for a fetal heart (p 40).

Vaginal examination: (p 246). Use your eyes to inspect the vulva, a *speculum* to examine the vagina and cervix and your *fingers* to assess the uterus and adnexae bimanually. Examination is usually done with the patient on her back or in the left lateral position (preferable for detecting prolapse). ***Sims' speculum*** has 2 right-angle bends, and is used for inspecting the vaginal walls, eg for prolapse and incontinence.

Cusco's (bivalve) speculum is used for inspecting the cervix with the aid of a light. Insert the speculum closed (warmed under a tap) with the blades parallel to the labia; use lubricating jelly. When it is in, rotate it and open it. The speculum should achieve its full length before opening and usually the cervix will pop into view. If it does not, do a bimanual to check the position of the cervix and try again. Do swabs (p 284) and a cervical smear (p 270) if indicated. Close the speculum gradually, under direct vision, as you withdraw it, to avoid trapping the cervix.

1 The first telling awakes memories which colour or transform the next telling, which itself influences the next telling in an infinite regression in which one telling becomes the audience for the next.

2 S Conway 2005 *Brit Med J* **330** 235

Sexual health

Sexual health is the enjoyment of sexual activity of one's choice, without causing or suffering physical or mental harm.[5] Of course there is more to sex than enjoyment. 'Perhaps the sexual life is the great test. If we can survive it with charity to those we love, and affection to those we have betrayed, we needn't worry so much about the good and the bad in us. But jealousy, distrust, cruelty, revenge, recrimination... then we fail. The wrong is in that failure even if we are the victims and not the executioners. Virtue is no excuse...'[1]

Once one understands that human sexuality is infinitely complex, it is easier to appreciate statistics such as 'sexual dysfunction is a big health problem, affecting 43% of women and 31% of men'.[6]

Enemies of sexual health include:

- Disharmony in personal relationships, or simply *too many* relationships.
- Pain, or any medical, or gynaecological condition.
- Anxiety (whether or not related to fear of failure); depression; fatigue.
- Drugs (eg tamoxifen; the Pill; cyproterone; antidepressants; narcotics).
- A multiplicity of irreconcilable roles (if your patient is trying to achieve ascendency in her work, as well as being chief shopper, cook, housewife, mother, and friend, then the role of lover may be eclipsed—all the more if she also finds herself in the role of being chief person to blame if things go wrong—if the fridge is empty, if the money runs out, if the children do not get to school on time, or if her partner loses his job).
- Myths about sexual performance (eg that all physical contact must lead to sex, that sex equals intercourse, and that sexual relations should come naturally and easily).[7]

1 G Greene 1965 *The Comedians*, Penguin, page 139, ISBN 0-14-018494-5.

Gynaecological anatomy

The vulva comprises the entrances to the vagina and urethra, the structures which surround them (clitoris, labia minora, and fourchette), and the encircling labia majora and perineum. The hymen, when broken (by tampons, or intercourse) leaves tags at the mouth of the vagina (*carunculae myrtiformes*).

Look for: Rashes; atrophy; ulcers; lumps (p 266 & p 268); deficient perineum (you can see the back wall of the vagina); incontinence.

The vagina is a potential space with distensible folded muscular walls. The contents of the rectum, which runs behind the posterior wall, are palpable through the vagina. The cervix projects into the vault at the top which forms a moat around it, deepest posteriorly, conventionally divided into anterior, posterior, and 2 lateral fornices. From puberty until the menopause lactobacilli in the vagina keep it acidic (pH 3.8–4.4), discouraging infection.

Look for: Inflammation; discharge (p 284); prolapse (p 290).

The cervix is mostly connective tissue. It feels firm, and has a dent in the centre (the opening, or os, of the cervical canal). Mucin-secreting glands of the endocervix lubricate the vagina. The os is circular in nulliparous women, but is a slit in the parous.

Look for: Pain on moving the cervix (excitation—p 262 and p 286); ectopy; cervicitis and discharge; polyps, carcinoma (p 272).

The uterus has a thick muscular-walled *body* lined internally with columnar epithelium (the endometrium) connected to the cervix or neck. It is supported by the uterosacral ligaments. The peritoneum is draped over the uterus. The valley so formed between it and the rectum is the rectovaginal pouch (of Douglas), and the fold of peritoneum in which the Fallopian tubes lie is known as the broad ligament. The *size* of the uterus is by convention described by comparison with its size at different stages of pregnancy. Since that is variable, estimates are approximate, but the following is a guide: nonpregnant—plum-sized; 6 weeks—egg; 8 weeks—small orange; 10 weeks—large orange; 14 weeks—fills pelvis.

In most women the uterus is *anteverted*, ie its long axis is directed forward and the cervix points backwards. The body then flops forwards on the cervix—*anteflexed*. An anteverted uterus can be palpated between the two hands on bimanual examination (unless the woman is obese or tense or the bladder is full.)

In 20% it is *retroverted and retroflexed* (p 246).

Look for: Position (important to know for practical procedures); mobility (especially if retroverted); size; tenderness (p 262 & p 286).

Adnexae These are the *Fallopian tubes, ovaries*, and associated connective tissue (parametria). They are palpated bimanually in the lateral fornices, and if normal cannot be felt. The ovaries are the size of a large grape and may lie in the rectovaginal pouch.

Look for: Masses (p 280) and tenderness (p 286).

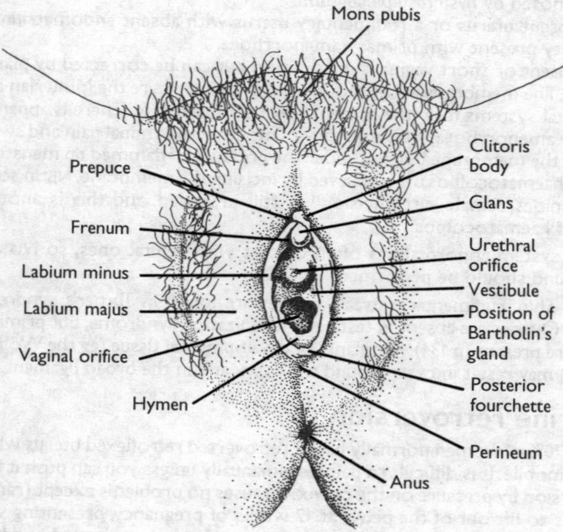
Mons pubis
Clitoris body
Prepuce
Glans
Frenum
Urethral orifice
Labium minus
Vestibule
Labium majus
Position of Bartholin's gland
Vaginal orifice
Posterior fourchette
Hymen
Perineum
Anus

Genital abnormalities

Vagina and uterus These are derived from the Müllerian duct system and formed by fusion of the right and left parts. Different degrees of failure to fuse lead to duplication of any or all parts of the system.

Vaginal septae are quite common (and often missed on examination).

Duplication of the cervix and/or uterus may also be missed, eg until the woman becomes pregnant in the uterus without the IUCD!

A partially divided (*bicornuate*) uterus or a uterus where one side has failed to develop (*unicornuate*) may present as recurrent miscarriage, particularly in the second trimester, or as difficulties in labour. Such abnormalities are diagnosed by *hysterosalpingogram*.

An absent uterus or a rudimentary uterus with absent endometrium is rare. They present with primary amenorrhoea.

An absent or short vagina is uncommon but can be corrected by plastic surgery. The membrane at the mouth of the vagina where the Müllerian and urogenital systems fuse (the hymen) may be imperforate. There is apparent primary amenorrhoea, with a history of monthly abdominal pain and swelling, and the membrane bulging under the pressure of dammed up menstrual blood (haematocolpos). It is relieved by incising the membrane. NB: in some communities, female 'circumcision'[1] is still practised, and this is another cause of haematocolpos.

►Renal system abnormalities often coexist with genital ones, so IVU and ultrasound should be performed.

Ovary Thin, rudimentary 'streak' ovaries are found in Turner's syndrome (p 655). Ovaries are absent in testicular feminization syndrome, but primitive testes are present (p 134). Remnants of developmental tissue (eg the Wolffian system) may result in cysts around the ovary and in the broad ligament.

Uterine retroversion

About 20% of women normally have a retroverted retroflexed uterus which is fully mobile. It is difficult to palpate bimanually unless you can push it into anteversion by pressure on the cervix. It causes no problems except (rarely) if it fails to lift out of the pelvis at 12 weeks of pregnancy, presenting with discomfort and retention of urine, eg at 14 weeks; catheterization and lying prone may relieve it.

Inflammation in the pelvis (due to infection or endometriosis) can cause adhesions which tether the uterus in a retroverted position. The patient may present with dysmenorrhoea, dyspareunia, or infertility—problems which can only be relieved by treatment of the underlying disease.

1 Circumcision is a misnomer, as it implies a parallel with male circumcision, which is incorrect. Another term is female genital mutilation. 140 million women are believed to be affected. The female 'operation' is carried out later (at 5-7yrs) and may be much more damaging and extensive, eg as practised in Somalia. In the UK most affected women come from Somalia, Eritrea, Ethiopia and the Yemen. It is common in Mali, Guinea and Egypt. Procedures include clitoridectomy ± infundibulation (removal of the clitoris, labia minora and labia majora, with oversewing or aposition by thorns). Even the milder Sunna entails removal of part of the clitoris, and more may be removed than intended. At betrothal, an attendant cuts the scar tissue to allow intercourse. Long-term problems include very slow urination, urinary tract infections, haematocolpos, dyspareunia or non-consummation, obstructed labour, increased susceptibility to HIV and other blood-borne diseases as well as emotional trauma. Defibulation may be performed before marriage; ideally electively at 20 weeks gestation, or in 1st stage of labour.
See H Gordon 1998 *Diplomate* **5** 86 and RCOG *Statement no. 3* 2003 Female Genital Mutilation

Normal menstruation

Puberty is the development of adult sexual characteristics. The sequence: breast buds develop, then growth of pubic hair, then axillary hair. Then menses begin (menarche) from age 10½ years (mean 12.8yrs). The age was falling in the UK, but no longer. It is earlier if short and overweight. Investigate if no periods by 16yrs (p 250). A growth spurt (p 161) is the first change in puberty and is usually completed 2yrs after menarche when the epiphyses fuse.

The menstrual cycle The cycle is controlled by the hypothalamic–pituitary–ovarian (HPO) axis. Pulsatile production of gonadotrophin-releasing hormones by the hypothalamus stimulates the pituitary to produce the gonadotrophins: follicle stimulating hormone (FSH) and luteinizing hormone (LH). These stimulate the ovary to produce oestrogen and progesterone. The ovarian hormones modulate the production of gonadotrophins by feeding back on the hypothalamus and pituitary.

Day 1 of the cycle is the first day of menstruation. Cycle lengths vary greatly; only 12% are 28 days. Cycles soon after menarche and before the menopause are most likely to be irregular and anovulatory. In the first ½ days of the cycle, FSH levels are high, stimulating the development of a primary follicle in the ovary. The follicle produces oestrogen, which stimulates the development of a glandular proliferative endometrium and of cervical mucus which is receptive to sperm. The mucus becomes clear and stringy (like raw egg white) and if allowed to dry on a slide produces ferning patterns due to its high salt content. Oestrogen also controls FSH and LH output by positive and negative feedback.

14 days before the onset of menstruation (on the 14th day of the cycle of a 28-day cycle) the oestrogen level becomes high enough to stimulate a surge of LH. This stimulates ovulation. Having released the ovum, the primary follicle then forms a corpus luteum and starts to produce progesterone. Under this influence, the endometrial lining is prepared for implantation: glands become convoluted ('secretory phase'). The cervical mucus becomes viscid and hostile to sperm and no longer ferns. If the ovum is not fertilized the corpus luteum breaks down, so hormone levels fall. This causes the spiral arteries in the uterine endometrial lining to constrict and the lining sloughs—hence menstruation.

Menstruation This is the loss of blood and uterine epithelial slough. It lasts 2–7 days and is usually heaviest at the beginning. Normal loss is 20–80mL, median 28mL.

Climacteric The ovaries fail to develop follicles. Without hormonal feedback from the ovary, gonadotrophin levels rise. Periods cease (menopause), usually at ~50 years of age (p 256).

Postponing menstruation (eg on holiday) Try norethisterone 5mg/8h PO from 3 days before the period is due until bleeding is acceptable, or take 2 packets of combined contraceptive Pills without a break.

Normal menstruation

Puberty is the development of adult sexual characteristics. The sequence: breast buds develop, then growth of pubic hair, then axillary hair. Then menses begin (**menarche**) from 10½ years onwards (mean ~13yrs; age was falling in the UK, but no longer); it is earlier if short and overweight; investigate if no periods by 16yrs (p 250). A growth spurt (p 184) is the first change in puberty and is usually completed 2yrs after menarche when the epiphyses fuse.

The menstrual cycle The cycle is controlled by the 'hypothalamic-pituitary-ovarian (HPO) axis'. Pulsatile production of gonadotrophin-releasing hormones by the hypothalamus stimulates the pituitary to produce the gonadotrophins: follicle stimulating hormone (FSH) and luteinizing hormone (LH). These stimulate the ovary to produce oestrogen and progesterone. The ovarian hormones modulate the production of gonadotrophins by feeding back on the hypothalamus and pituitary.

Day 1 of the cycle is the first day of menstruation. Cycle lengths vary greatly; only 12% are 28 days. Cycles soon after menarche and before the menopause are most likely to be irregular and anovulatory. In the first 4 days of the cycle, FSH levels are high, stimulating the development of a primary follicle in the ovary. The follicle produces oestrogen, which stimulates the development of a glandular 'proliferative' endometrium and of cervical mucus which is receptive to sperm. The mucus becomes clear and stringy (like raw egg white) and if allowed to dry on a slide produces 'ferning patterns' due to its high salt content. Oestrogen also controls FSH and LH output by positive and negative feedback.

14 days before the onset of menstruation (on the 16th day of the cycle of a 30-day cycle) the oestrogen level becomes high enough to stimulate a surge of LH. This stimulates ovulation. Having released the ovum, the primary follicle then forms a corpus luteum and starts to produce progesterone. Under this influence, the endometrial lining is prepared for implantation: glands become convoluted ('secretory phase'). The cervical mucus becomes viscid and hostile to sperm and no longer ferns. If the ovum is not fertilized the corpus luteum breaks down, so hormone levels fall. This causes the spiral arteries in the uterine endothelial lining to constrict and the lining sloughs—hence menstruation.

Menstruation This is the loss of blood and uterine epithelial slough. It lasts 2-7 days and is usually heaviest at the beginning. Normal loss is 20-80mL, median 28mL.

Climacteric The ovaries fail to develop follicles. Without hormonal feedback from the ovary, gonadotrophin levels rise. Periods cease (menopause), usually at ~50 years of age (p 256).

Postponing menstruation (eg on holiday) Try norethisterone 5mg/8h PO from 3 days before the period is due until bleeding is acceptable, or take 2 packets of combined contraceptive Pills without a break.

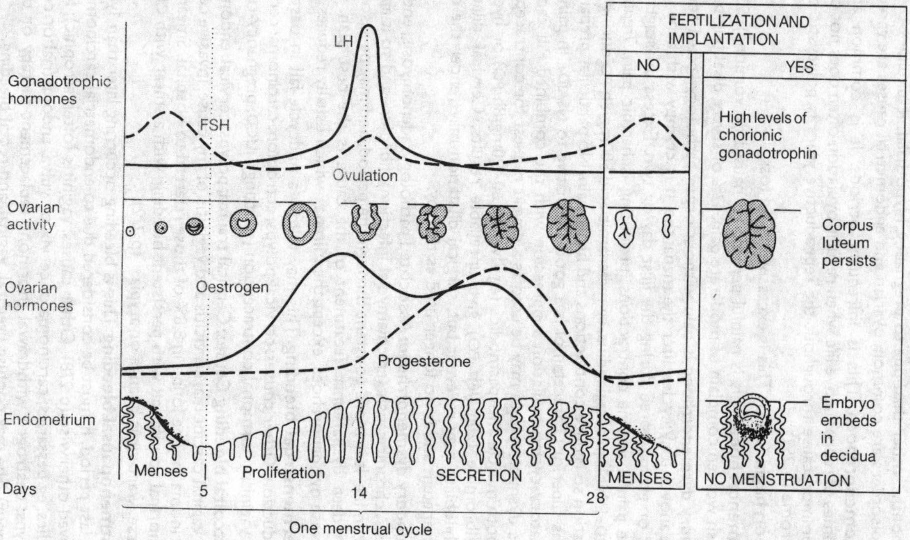
Gonadotrophic hormones
FSH
LH
Ovulation
Ovarian activity
Ovarian hormones
Oestrogen
Progesterone
Endometrium
Days
Menses
Proliferation
SECRETION
5
14
28
One menstrual cycle
FERTILIZATION AND IMPLANTATION
NO
YES
High levels of chorionic gonadotrophin
Corpus luteum persists
Embryo embeds in decidua
MENSES
NO MENSTRUATION

Abnormal menstruation

Primary amenorrhoea (see p 251) This is failure to start menstruating. It needs investigation in a 16-year-old, or in a 14-year-old who has no breast development. For normal menstruation to occur she must be structurally normal with a functioning control mechanism (hypothalamic-pituitary-ovarian axis).

Secondary amenorrhoea (see p 251) This is when periods stop for >6 months, other than due to pregnancy. Hypothalamic-pituitary-ovarian axis disorders are common, ovarian and endometrial causes are rare.

Oligomenorrhoea This is infrequent periods. It is common at the extremes of reproductive life when regular ovulation often does not occur. A common cause throughout the reproductive years is polycystic ovary syndrome (p 252).

Menorrhagia (p 253) This is excessive blood loss.

Dysmenorrhoea This is painful periods (± nausea or vomiting). 50% of British women complain of moderate pain, 12% of severe disabling pain.

Primary dysmenorrhoea is pain without organ pathology—often starting with anovulatory cycles after the menarche. It is crampy with ache in the back or groin, worse during the first day or two. Excess prostaglandins cause painful uterine contractions, producing ischaemic pain. *Treatment:* NSAIDs inhibit prostaglandins, eg mefenamic acid 500mg/8h PO during menstruation so reduce contractions and hence pain. No particular preparation seems superior.[1] Paracetamol is a good alternative to NSAIDs. In pain with ovulatory cycles, ovulation suppression with the combined Pill can help (thus dysmenorrhoea may be used as a covert request for contraception). Smooth muscle antispasmodics (eg alverine 60-120mg/8h PO) or hyoscine butylbromide (20mg/6h PO) give unreliable results. Cervical dilatation in childbirth may relieve it but, surgical dilatation may render the cervix incompetent and is no longer used as therapy.

Secondary dysmenorrhoea: Associated pathology: adenomyosis, endometriosis, chronic sepsis (eg chlamydial infection), fibroids—and so it appears later in life. It is more constant through the period, and may be associated with deep dyspareunia. Treatment of the cause is the best plan. IUCDs increase dysmenorrhoea, except the Mirena® which usually reduces it.

Intermenstrual bleeding This may follow a midcycle fall in oestrogen production. ***Other causes***: cervical polyps; ectropion; carcinoma; cervicitis and vaginitis; hormonal contraception (spotting); IUCD; pregnancy-related.

Postcoital bleeding *Causes:* Cervical trauma; polyps; cervical, endometrial and vaginal carcinoma; cervicitis and vaginitis of any cause. Invasive cervical carcinoma may be found in 3.8% of those referred to hospital. Smears may be normal so refer all with persistent bleeding, with a smear with CIN I or worse, wart virus change or atypia[8] (p 272).

Postmenopausal bleeding This is bleeding occurring later than 1yr after the last period. It must be considered due to endometrial carcinoma until proved otherwise (p 278). Other causes: vaginitis (often atrophic); foreign bodies, eg pessaries; carcinoma of cervix or vulva; endometrial or cervical polyps; oestrogen withdrawal (hormone replacement therapy or ovarian tumour). She may confuse urethral, vaginal, and rectal bleeding.

1 Marjoribanks J 2003 Cochrane database systemic review (4) CD001751

Amenorrhoea

►*Always ask yourself 'Could she be pregnant?'*

Primary amenorrhoea (see also p 250). This may cause great anxiety. In most patients puberty is just late (often familial), and reassurance is all that is needed. In some, the cause is structural or genetic, so check:

- Has she got normal external secondary sexual characteristics? If so, are the internal genitalia normal (p 246)?
- If she is not developing normally, examination and karyotyping may reveal Turner's syndrome (p 655) or testicular feminization (p 134). The aim of treatment is to help the patient to look normal, to function sexually, and, if possible, to enable her to reproduce if she wishes.

Causes of secondary amenorrhoea

- Hypothalamic-pituitary-ovarian causes are very common as control of the menstrual cycle is easily upset, eg by emotions, exams, weight loss, excess prolactin (30% have galactorrhoea), other hormonal imbalances, and severe systemic disease, eg renal failure. Pituitary tumours and necrosis (Sheehan's syndrome) are rare.
- Ovarian causes: polycystic ovary syndrome (p 252), tumours, ovarian failure (premature menopause), are uncommon.
- Uterine causes: pregnancy-related, Asherman's syndrome (uterine adhesions after a D&C). 'Post-Pill amenorrhoea' is generally oligomenorrhoea masked by regular withdrawal bleeds.

Tests Serum LH and testosterone (↑in polycystic ovary syndrome), FSH (very high in premature menopause), prolactin (↑by stress, prolactinomas and drugs, eg phenothiazines) and TFT are the most useful blood tests. 40% of those with hyperprolactinaemia have a tumour so do MRI scan (p 294).

Treatment is related to cause. Premature ovarian failure cannot be reversed but hormone replacement (p 256) is necessary to control symptoms of oestrogen deficiency and protect against osteoporosis. Pregnancy can be achieved with oocyte donation and *in vitro* fertilization techniques.

Hypothalamic-pituitary axis malfunction: If mild (eg stress, moderate weight loss): there is sufficient activity to stimulate enough ovarian oestrogen to produce an endometrium (which will be shed after a progesterone challenge, eg norethisterone 5mg/8h for 7 days), but the timing is disordered so cycles are not initiated. If the disorder is more severe the axis shuts down (eg in severe weight loss). FSH and LH and hence oestrogen levels are low. Reassurance and advice on diet or stress management, or psychiatric help if appropriate (p 348), and time may solve the problem. She should be advised to use contraception as ovulation may occur at any time. If she wants fertility restored now, or the reassurance of seeing a period, mild dysfunction will respond to clomifene but a shut-down axis will need stimulation by gonadotrophin-releasing hormone (see p 294 for both).

Polycystic ovarian syndrome (PCOS)

This would be better named polyfollicular ovary syndrome. It comprises hyperandrogenism, oligo-ovulation, and polycystic ovaries on ultrasound in the absence of other causes of polycystic ovaries, eg as seen with later onset adrenal hyperplasia and Cushing's. The cause is unknown. It is common (5–20% of premenopausal women). Acne, male pattern baldness and hirsutism can all be features. Darkened skin (acanthosis nigricans) on neck and skin flexures may reflect hyperinsulinaemia. LH is raised in 40%, testosterone in 30%. Infertility may be a problem. The result appears to be a vicious circle of ovarian, hypothalamic-pituitary, and adrenal dysfunction.

Insulin resistance and hyperinsulinaemia are features. There may be diabetes (40% of women with the syndrome have impaired glucose tolerance or diabetes by age 40, the obese are at greatest risk, but those of lean habitus are also at risk). Insulin resistance/metabolic syndrome is likely to be a problem in those with obesity—eg waist >80cm (♂, p 530)[9] + any 2 of: triglycerides >1.7mmol/L; HDL cholesterol <1.1mmol/L (<0.9 if ♂); BP >130/85; fasting glucose >5.6mmol/L. MI, stroke and transient ischaemic attack rate is ↑ (eg ×3).

Hypertension may also be a problem; especially affecting older postmenopausal women. Hormonal cycling is disrupted and the ovaries become enlarged by follicles which have failed to rupture. Ovarian cancer risk is increased, as is endometrial cancer.

Stein-Leventhal syndrome eponymizes the subset of obese hirsute women with polycystic ovaries.

Diagnosis Increased LH:FSH ratio (eg between days 5 and 8 of cycle). Look for a reversed LH:FSH ratio of about 3:1 with ↑testosterone ± ↑prolactin with US scan showing 5 or more small follicles all <5mm along the periphery of the ovary. Laparoscopy shows enlarged ovaries.

Management Advise smoking avoidance. Detect and treat diabetes, hypertension, and hyperlipidaemia. Encourage weight loss and increased exercise to increase insulin sensitivity. Metformin may also improve insulin sensitivity, menstrual disturbance, and ovulatory function, and is recommended by NICE for those of body mass index >25 trying to conceive.

Clomifene usually induces ovulation (50–60% conceive in 1st 6 months of treatment; so offer before using to other methods; use on specialist advice). Warn of risk of multiple pregnancy and ovarian cancer (p 280). Monitor response by ultrasound in at least 1st cycle. Those not ovulating in response to clomifene are at ↑ risk of ovarian hyperstimulation (p 311) with assisted conception. Ovarian drilling (creating holes in ovaries by diathermy with the intent of reducing steroid production) is recommended by NICE[1] for those who not responding to clomifene (though it may be as useful primary treatment).[10] 65% conceive. It does not increase risk of multiple pregnancy.

The combined Pill will control bleeding and reduce risk of unopposed oestrogen on the endometrium (risk of endometrial carcinoma). Some recommend annual ultrasound to look for endometrial thickening and need for endometrial biopsy. Recommend regular withdrawal bleeds[2] eg 3-monthly eg induced with dydrogesterone 10mg/12h PO on days 11–25 in those in whom oestrogen use is not wanted or is contraindicated.

Hirsutes may be treated cosmetically, or with an anti-androgen, eg cyproterone 2mg/day, as in Dianette® (avoid pregnancy). Spironolactone 25–200mg/24h/PO is also antiandrogenic (avoid pregnancy as teratogenic). Finasteride 5mg/24h/PO has also been used for hirsutism, again avoid pregnancy. Neither spironolactone nor finasteride is licensed for this use.

1 NICE *Clinical Guideline* **11** 2004 Fertility: assessment & treatment for people with fertility problems
2 RCOG *Guideline* **33** 2003 Long term consequences of polycystic ovarian syndrome

Menorrhagia

This is increased menstrual blood loss (defined as >80mL/cycle); in reality loss is rarely measured, so management deals with those whose significant menstrual loss interferes with life. What makes a woman consult may be a change in volume (clots; floods, etc), or a change in life (eg job change, or depression). Ask about both. Is she hypothyroid (eg constipation; weight↑; *OHCM* p 306) or anaemic? Examine with these in mind.

Causes In *girls*, pregnancy and dysfunctional uterine bleeding are likely. With increasing age, think also of IUCD, fibroids, endometriosis and adenomyosis, pelvic infection, polyps. Also hypothyroidism. In *perimenopausal women*, consider endometrial carcinoma. Ask about general bleeding problems as she may have a blood dyscrasia, eg von Willebrand's. Do abdominal and pelvic examination[1]—which may reveal polyps, fibroids, or endometriosis.

Tests[1] Do FBC; TFT if seems hypothyroid; consider clotting studies; ultrasound or laparoscopy if pelvic pathology suspected; ultrasound and endometrial sampling, or hysteroscopy and directed biopsy if irregular bleeding or suspected cancer.

Dysfunctional uterine bleeding (DUB) This is heavy and/or irregular bleeding in the absence of recognizable pelvic pathology. It is associated with anovulatory cycles, so is common at the extremes of reproductive life or it may be ovulatory (eg with inadequate luteal phase). If PV is normal and organic pathology is ruled out, this is the diagnosis, by exclusion.

Treatment of menorrhagia Treat any underlying condition. For dysfunctional uterine bleeding, treatment depends on age. Reassurance helps. Teenage menorrhagia generally settles without interference as cycles become ovulatory. Those with unacceptable loss should be offered treatment. Refer those with irregular bleeding or bulky uterus (>10 week size).

Drugs *Antifibrinolytics* Taken during bleeding these reduce loss (by 49%)—eg *tranexamic acid* 1g/6-8h PO (for up to 4 days). CI: thromboembolic disease—but this is no more common in those on tranexamic acid. ***Antiprostaglandins***, eg *mefenamic acid* 500mg/8h PO pc (CI: peptic ulceration) taken during days of bleeding particularly help if there is also dysmenorrhoea. They reduce bleeding by 29%. ***Hormones*** The *combined Pill* is effective but may be contraindicated in older women—(eg smokers >35 years). *Danazol* 100mg/6-24h PO is effective, and expensive. Use only on special advice. It inhibits ovulation (unreliably, so advise condoms as it masculinizes the ♀ fetus). Oral cyclical low dose *progestogens* are not effective. Norethisterone 5-10mg/8h is useful to stop heavy bleeding.

Progesterone-containing IUCDs, eg the Mirena® are good for those wishing to avoid pregnancy and to reduce bleeding (by up to 86% at 3 months, 97% at 1yr). They are effective in dysfunctional uterine bleeding and should possibly be considered for first-line management of menorrhagia. They have also been shown to reduce fibroid volume after 6-18 months use. 5-year follow up gives satisfaction levels similar to hysterectomy (in the 58% continuing with this method).[1]

For those women who have completed their families consider endometrial resection or hysterectomy (p 308). Endometrial resection removes the first few millimetre thickness of endometrium; eg by rollerball or laser or by heating (microwave, balloon). Ablation is more effective if the endometrium is thin, and pre-treatment with goserelin or leuproprelin (p 288) may be better than using a progestogen or danazol. About 30% become amenorrhoeic and a further 50% have reduced flow after any method of ablation. Contraception is still required and treat as with uterus for HRT (p 256).

1 Hurskainen R 2004 *JAMA* **291** 1456

The premenstrual syndrome (PMS)

Most women notice that their mood or physical state may be worse premenstrually. Symptoms may be mild one month and severe the next, eg depending on external events and tend to be worse in the 30s and 40s and improve on the combined Pill. 3% of women regularly have cyclical symptoms so severe that they cause major disruption to their lives: premenstrual syndrome (PMS) or tension (PMT). Causes: See BOX.

Symptoms Commonest symptom patterns are tension and irritability; depression; bloating and breast tenderness; carbohydrate craving and headache; clumsiness; libido↓. Almost any symptom may feature.

Diagnosis Suggest symptom diary. If she has PMS her symptoms are worst before periods, are relieved by menstruation, and there is at least one symptom-free week afterwards. Diaries may also reveal psychiatric disorders (which may be worse premenstrually) or menstrual disorders.

Treatment Simply to acknowledge her problem, listen, and reassure may be all that is needed to enable her to cope. Are her partner and children understanding? Can she rearrange work schedules to reduce stress premenstrually? Some women find self-help groups supportive. Health measures, eg improved diet, reducing smoking and drinking, increased exercise and relaxation, often help. Herbal remedies are not scientifically tested but some find them helpful, eg sage and fennel for irritability. Any drug evokes a big placebo effect, improving 90% in some studies. Pyridoxine (vit B_6) 10mg/24h PO for the symptomatic period or continuously, may help low mood and headache (DoH says higher, more effective, doses cause neuropathy). For severe ***cyclical mastalgia*** consider:

1 Reduce saturated fats eaten: these increase the affinity of oestrogen-receptors for oestrogen.
2 Gamolenic acid 160mg/12h PO. 1 capsule=40mg in evening primrose oil. A contraindication is a past history of seizures.
3 Bromocriptine 2.5mg/12h PO days 10–26, even if prolactin normal.
4 Danazol 100–200mg/12h PO for 7 days before menstruation (see below).

Some benefit from suppression of ovulation with the combined Pill (Yasmin® may be especially suitable),[1] oestrogen patches or implants, with cyclical progesterone, or danazol 200mg/24h (SE nausea, weight gain, masculinization of the ♀ fetus, so advise barrier contraception). Avoid diuretics unless fluid retention is severe (when spironolactone 25mg/6h PO days 18–26 of the cycle is the drug of choice).

SSRIs, eg fluoxetine 20mg/day PO help,[2] with ~30% experiencing remission (but license for use in PMS in UK withdrawn), and can be used just in the luteal phase.[3] Alprazolam (0.25mg/day PO during the luteal phase) also helps, with apparently low risk of dependence. Other treatments for PMS include mefenamic acid (250–500mg/8h PO from day 16 until 3 days into period). This may help fatigue, headache, pains, and mood. Agnus castrus fruit extract helped these symptoms in 50% of women in a placebo controlled trial. RCT 11 Goserelin (*OHCM* p 498) may help severe PMS but symptoms return when ovarian activity recommences and after 6 months' use bone thinning can be detected. It is better used to predict the severely affected women who may benefit from hysterectomy with oophorectomy (results in 96% satisfaction rates[4]—these women can then have oestrogen replacement).

Follow-up: it is not 'cheating' to ensure that her next appointment will *not* be in the premenstrual phase—more objectivity may be forthcoming.

1 Rapkin A 2003 *Psychoneuroendocrinology* **28** 39
2 Wyatt K 2002 *Cochrane Database Review* Pub Med 12519554
3 Freeman E 2004 *CNS Drugs* **18** 453
4 Cronje W 2004 *Hum Reprod* 2004 **19** 2152

The Rapkin hypothesis and putative pathways in PMS[1]

Some physiological and pharmacological observations:

- There is no evidence that ovarian events cause premenstrual syndrome: models presupposing progesterone deficiency have not been confirmed (and progesterone suppositories are no panacea for the condition).
- Artificially altering circulating progesterone and oestradiol (estradiol) does not induce premenstrual symptoms in previously well women—only in those already prone to PMS.
- Studies with psychoactive compounds suggest that the key events are occurring in the brain, not the ovary—eg an abnormal CNS response to normal progesterone excursions occurring in the luteal phase.
- Allopregnanolone and pregnenolone (metabolites of progesterone) are psychoactive, interacting with γ-aminobutyric acid A (GABA-A) receptors.
- Allopregnanolone is anxiolytic, so low levels may cause anxiety.

Putative conclusion: Neurones or glia in those with PMS preferentially metabolize progesterone to pregnenolone (which heightens anxiety) rather than allopregnanolone (which is anxiolytic and up-regulates serotonin receptors, so ameliorating depression). On this view, alprazolam, by augmenting GABA-A-receptor function, is a substitute for allopregnanolone.

1 A Rapkin 1997 *Obstet Gynaecol* **90** 709-14 & S Berga 1998 *Lancet* **351** 465

The menopause and HRT

The climacteric is the time of waning fertility leading up to the last period (menopause). The menopause enables grandmothering—a unique institution, in humans (and whales).[12] Problems are related to falling oestrogen levels:

- Menstrual irregularity as cycles become anovulatory, before stopping.
- Vasomotor disturbance—sweats, palpitations, and flushes (brief, nasty, and may occur every few minutes for >10yrs, disrupting life and sleep).
- Atrophy of oestrogen-dependent tissues (genitalia, breasts) and skin. Vaginal dryness can lead to vaginal and urinary infection, dyspareunia, traumatic bleeding, stress incontinence, and prolapse.
- Osteoporosis. The menopause accelerates bone loss which predisposes to fracture of femur neck, radius, and vertebrae in later life.
- Attitudes to the menopause vary widely, and partly depend on irritability, depression, 'empty nest syndrome'—all exacerbated by the menopause.

Management ≥20% of women seek medical help.

- Is it the menopause? Thyroid and psychiatric problems may present similarly. Measure FSH if diagnosis in doubt (very high in menopause).
- Counselling helps psychosocial *and* physical symptoms. Enlist family's support.
- Menorrhagia may respond to treatment (p 253). A D&C is required if irregular bleeding is abnormal (it may be difficult to decide).
- Continue contraception for 1yr after the last period, eg POP, IUCD, condoms.
- Hot flushes may respond to clonidine 50–75μg/12h PO, HRT, or tibolone (NB: one cohort study associates tibolone with an excess risk of endometrial cancer—54% more likely compared with other hormonal HRT).[1]
- Vaginal dryness responds to oestrogen (can be used locally).

Hormone replacement therapy (HRT) Oestrogen is not a panacea for all problems, but may help flushes and atrophic vaginitis. It postpones menopausal bone loss but is no longer recommended just for osteoporosis prevention. Trials show no cardiovascular benefits, no protection against dementia in the over 65s, and increased stroke and thromboembolism in users.[1] HRT ↑breast cancer risk (below), endometrial cancer (↑risk with unopposed oestrogen or sequential progesterone, possible ↓risk with continuous combined), and those using for >10yrs have double the risk of ovarian cancer of non-users.[13]

Women with a uterus should also receive cyclical progestogens to reduce incidence of endometrial carcinoma—or use tibolone 2.5mg/day PO, a preparation which aims not to cause bleeds—or continuous combined oestrogen/progestogen combinations, eg Kliofem®, estradiol (=oestradiol) 2mg and norethisterone 1mg. For both these, start if >1yr after the last period, or, if changing from cyclical HRT, wait until after 54yrs of age; bleeding is common, in the 1st 4 months of use—reassure; if after 8 months, do an endometrial biopsy. Kliofem® may be useful if cyclical HRT causes 'premenstrual' symptoms. There *may* be advantages in using 'lipid-friendly' progestogen, dydrogesterone (no androgenic, mineralocorticoid, or oestrogenic action), eg Femoston 2/10® or (2/20 tabs, ie 2mg 17β oestradiol tabs, with added 20mg dydrogesterone after day 14), but see p 302 for possible SE (DVT). Raloxifene, a selective oestrogen receptor modulator (SERM) protects bones while *reducing* breast and endometrial cancer risk. It is ineffective for flushes.

HRT contraindications: • Oestrogen-dependent cancer • Undiagnosed PV bleeding • LFT↑ • Pregnancy • Breastfeeding • Phlebitis • Past pulmonary embolus. Avoid or monitor closely in Dubin-Johnson/Rotor syndromes (*OHCM* p 722). If past spontaneous DVT/PE: *is there thrombophilia* (*OHCM* p 678)?

Side-effects: Weight↑; 'premenstrual' syndrome; cholestasis; vomiting.

Alternative therapies eg black cohosh[2] (role uncertain)—see p 515.

1 *Drug Safety* 2005 **28** 241 &: Review in 2004 *Current Trends in Pharmacovigilance* **30** 4
2 Black cohosh can cause hepatotoxicity see 2004 *Current Trends in Pharmacovigilance* **30** 10

Annual check-up: Breasts; BP (stop if BP >160/100 pending investigation and treatment). Weight; any abnormal bleeding?

Creams, pessaries, and rings are useful for vaginal symptoms, eg Ovestin®, ie oestriol 0.1%, 1 applicator-full PV daily for 3 weeks, then twice weekly. They are absorbed but, if used intermittently, progestogens are probably unnecessary. If creams are unacceptable, consider an oestrogen-containing vaginal ring (eg Estring®) replaced every 3 months, for up to 2yrs. Vagifem® is an estradiol (=oestradiol) 25μg vaginal tablet daily for 2 weeks, and then twice weekly, with reassessment every 3 months.

Transdermal patches are less 'medical' but are expensive and women with a uterus still need progestogen, eg as tablets or Estracombi® patches. Estradiol (=oestradiol) patches supply 25-100μg/24h for 3-4 days. SE: dermatitis.

18-Oestradiol implants (Surgical) 25mg lasts ~36 weeks. They give as good symptom control as 50mg. [14] Aim for serum oestradiol levels 300-500pmol/L (300 is sufficient to maintain bone), as levels >500pmol/L may be associated with dependence.

Oestradiol gel 2 measures are applied daily to arms, shoulders, or inner thighs. Women with a uterus using gel or implants also require progestogens for 12 days per cycle.

HRT and breast cancer The Women's Health Initiative[RCT 15] confirmed ↑breast cancer risk (and showed excess stroke and heart attack risk, and 2-fold increase in dementia[RCT 16] in users: the Million Women Study[1] showed that there is greater risk when combined oestrogen/progesterone preparations are used (relative risk = RR 2) compared to oestrogen alone (RR 1.3) or tibolone (RR 1.45). Risk increases with length of use. For this reason our policy on HRT is:

- To discuss the risk of breast cancer with each patient considering HRT.
- To document this discussion in the patient's notes.
- Encourage breast awareness and to report breast change. Formal breast examination by nurses may give false reassurance (advice of the UK's chief medical officer). Mammographic screening may be less effective in current users.[2] It is difficult if aged 40-50yrs (breast density↑).
- To use for symptomatic treatment (warn symptoms often return on stopping therapy however long it has been used for), at the lowest dose needed to control symptoms, for the shortest time possible.
- To be wary about HRT in those with a family history of breast cancer.
- To consider stopping HRT before 5 completed years of therapy.

For those wanting HRT only for their bones consider raloxifene (which ↓risk of breast cancer: it is related to tamoxifen),[3] or bisphosphonates.

HRT and venous thromboembolism Overall HRT doubles risk (which ↑ with age). Consider other predisposing factors, such as prolonged immobility, surgery, obesity, *severe* varicose veins (others see p 16). Before starting, elicit personal and family history of venous thromboembolism (VTE), discuss thrombophilia screen if positive history. Thrombophilia ↑ risk ×3 overall (×8 if Factor V Leiden or prothrombin 20210A mutation). If thrombophilia present seek expert advice. Transdermal use may have less risk,[4] and oral HRT should be avoided if past history of VTE.[5] SERM therapy (OPPOSITE) carries same VTE risk as HRT. Surgery does not require HRT to be routinely stopped but use thromboprophylactic measures.

1 V Beral Million Women Study Collaborators 2003 *Lancet* **362** 419
2 E Banks 2004 *BMJ* **329** 477 3 M Sporn 2004 *Clin Ther* **26** 830
4 P Scarabin 2003 *Lancet* **362** 428
5 RCOG *Clinical Guideline* **19** 2004 Hormone replacement therapy and venous thromboembolism

Termination of pregnancy (ToP)

►Under UK law, no one *has* to have an abortion, and no one *has* to do one. Worldwide, 30% of pregnancies are terminated and in the UK 1/3 of women have had a ToP by age 45. ***Incidence:*** ~197,500 ToPs/yr in Great Britain.

Legal (UK) constraints The 1967 Abortion (amended 2002) and 1990 Human Fertilization and Embryology acts allow termination on grounds:

A Risk to mothers life if pregnancy continues.
B Termination necessary to prevent grave injury to physical/mental health of the woman.
C Continuance risks injury to physical/mental health of the woman greater than if terminated (and fetus not >24 weeks).
D Continuance risks injury to physical/mental health of existing children of the woman greater than if terminated (and fetus not >24 weeks).
E There is substantial risk that if the child were born he/she would suffer such physical or mental abnormalities as to be seriously handicapped.

Two doctors must sign certificate A. If <16y try to get patient's consent to involve her parents or other adult.[1] 94% are for ground C; 4% for D. <1% of ToPs are done after 20 weeks, usually after amniocentesis, or when very young or menopausal mothers have concealed, or not recognized, pregnancy. ToPs after 24 weeks may only be carried out in NHS hospitals.

Before ToP ►She has to live with the decision for the rest of her life.
- Counselling to help her reach the decision she will least regret.
- Is she definitely pregnant? Is ToP what she really wants? Why? Has she considered alternatives? What about her partner? Ideally give her time to consider. Do a VE or scan to confirm dates. If she chooses ToP:
- Screen for chlamydia. Untreated, 25% get post-op salpingitis, p 286.
- Routine antibiotic prophylaxis ↓post-op infections (from 10% to 6%) eg metronidazole 1g PR at operation and azithromycin 1g PO same day.
- Discuss contraception (IUCD or sterilization at operation need plans).
- If RhD-ve she needs anti-D (all gestations, whatever method see p 9). Bloods for Hb, ABO+RhD group and antibodies; ±HIV, hepatitis B & C, and haemoglobinopathies if relevant.

Methods ***Medical abortion*** refers to use of an antigestagen eg mifepristone to disimplant the fetus followed by a prostaglandin eg gemeprost or misoprostol to complete abortion. It is highly effective from ≥6 weeks use (98% effective at ≤7 weeks, 95% weeks 7-9) and is also used for second trimester abortions. Misoprostol can be used orally or vaginally (sometimes both) and is much cheaper than vaginal gemeprost. Gemeprost is more effective when used between 7 and 9 weeks. For early abortions arrange follow up (and scan) 2 weeks after procedure unless complete abortion confirmed on the day of abortion. 5% will need surgical evacuation.

Suction termination Used from 7 to 15 weeks, women <18 years of age or with gestations >10 weeks require cervical priming pre-operatively. Local anaesthesia is safer but uncommon in UK. Medical termination is preferable if <7 weeks as gestational sacs may be missed so early. Mortality is low (1:100,000), as is infection risk.

Dilatation and evacuation using surgical forceps may be used between 15 and 18 weeks. Experienced operators are required. Real time ultrasound use reduces uterine perforation rates. Morbidity and mortality ↑ with gestation.

Complications The physical ones are listed opposite but what of other imponderables such as coarsening of attitudes to life and death when ToP is done lightly. We all dream[2] of a time when no one needs our services, but for those who do, today, we must show a willingness to help and console.

Some regimens[3]

Early medical terminations ≤9 weeks:

Mifepristone 600mg PO + gemeprost 1mg PV 36–48h later. Observe for 6h post gemeprost as risk of ↓BP: or

*Mifepristone 200mg PO + misoprostol 800μg (4×200μg tablets) vaginally 24–72h later. For ♀ 49–63d gestation if no abortion 4h after misoprostol give a further 400μg PO/PV. NB: the same regime can be used for pregnancies 9–13 weeks with the further 400μg misoprostol PO/PV being given 3-hourly to a maximum of 4 doses depending on the preference and amount of bleeding. (*Unlicensed regimen from guidelines of Royal College of Obstetricians and Gynaecologists (RCOG).)

Cervical priming prior to surgical termination:

*Misoprostol 400μg (2×200μg tablets) PV 3h before surgery. (*Unlicensed regimen but given in the guidelines of the RCOG.) or:

- Gemeprost® 1mg PV 3h before surgery: or
- Mifepristone 600mg PO 36–48h before surgery

In terminations later than 21 weeks and 6 days (eg for abnormality) it is essential that the fetus is born dead. This may be achieved by use of intracardiac potassium chloride (± anaesthetic and/or muscle relaxant instillation beforehand to abolish fetal movement). Confirm asystole with ultrasound. If born after 24 weeks the dead fetus is a stillbirth and will need to be registered (p 83). If there are signs of life then a death certificate will be required.[4]

Mid-trimester medical termination:

Mifepristone 600mg PO followed 36–48h later by gemeprost 1mg PV every 3h to a maximum of 5 pessaries: or

*Mifepristone 200mg PO followed 36–48h later by misoprostol 800μg PV: then misoprostol 400μg PO every 3h to a maximum of 4 oral doses depending on the amount of bleeding. (*Unlicensed regimen but given in the guidelines of the RCOG.)

Complications of termination:

- Failure to abort (1–14:1000 for medical ToP, 2.3:1000 if surgical).
- Infection post-abortion (10%); see screening and antibiotics opposite.
- Haemorrhage (1:1000)
- Uterine perforation (1:1000)
- Uterine rupture (mid-trimester, especially if uterine scar): 1:1000
- Cervical trauma (1:100)
- Small risk of miscarriage and premature labour in future pregnancies.

After termination Has she had anti-D (p 9)? Is contraception arranged? (Can start Pill same day). Follow up at 2 weeks.

1 If the girl is a ward of Court, the Court has to approve abortion.

2 *'You dream', he said, 'because of the child*
Asleep in the nest of your body, who dreams ...' Stephen Spender, *The Dream*

3 RCOG *Evidence-based clinical guideline* No 7 2004 The care of women requesting induced abortion

4 See RCOG publication 2001 *Further Issues relating to late abortion, fetal viability and registration of births and deaths.*

Abortion (miscarriage)

Abortion is the loss of a pregnancy before 24 weeks' gestation. 20–40% of pregnancies miscarry, mostly in the first trimester. Most present with bleeding PV. Diagnosis may not be straightforward (consider ectopics p 262): have a low threshold for doing an ultrasound scan. Pregnancy tests remain +ve for several days after fetal death.

Management of early pregnancy bleeding Consider the following:
- ►Is she shocked? There may be blood loss, or products of conception in the cervical canal (remove them with sponge forceps).
- Has pain and bleeding been worse than a period? Have products of conception been seen? (Clots may be mistaken for products.)
- Is the os open? The external os of a multigravida usually admits a fingertip.
- Is uterine size appropriate for dates?
- Is she bleeding from a cervical lesion and not from the uterus?
- What is her blood group? If RhD-ve does she need anti-D (p 9)?

If symptoms are mild and the cervical os is closed it is a *threatened abortion*. Rest is advised but probably does not help. 75% will settle. Threatened abortion (especially second trimester) is associated with risk of subsequent preterm rupture of membranes and preterm delivery—so book mother at a hospital with good neonatal facilities.

If symptoms are severe and the os is open it is an *inevitable abortion* or, if most of the products have already been passed, an *incomplete abortion*. If bleeding is profuse, consider ergometrine 0.5mg IM. If there is unacceptable pain or bleeding, or much retained tissue on ultrasound, arrange evacuation of retained products of conception (ERPC). Expectant management is used when the volume of retained products is small eg <15mm across on transvaginal scan; when 15–50mm, medical management eg with mifepristone may be offered (benefit may not be conclusive).[17]

Missed abortion: The fetus dies but is retained. There has usually been bleeding and the uterus is small for dates. Confirm with ultrasound. Mifepristone and misoprostol may be used to induce uterine evacuation if the uterus is small but 50% will require surgical evacuation if uterine products are >5cm² in the transverse plane; >6cm² in the sagittal plane.[1] Surgical evacuation is required for larger uteruses.

Mid-trimester abortion This is usually due to mechanical causes, eg cervical incompetence (rapid, painless delivery of a live fetus), uterine abnormalities; or chronic maternal disease (eg DM, SLE). An incompetent cervix can be strengthened by a cervical encirclage suture at ~16 weeks of pregnancy. It is removed prior to labour.

After a miscarriage ►Miscarriage may be a bereavement. Give the parents space to grieve, and to ask why it happened and if it will happen again. Fetal products should be incinerated but if the mother requests alternative disposal (eg to bury herself) her wishes should be respected.[1]

Most early pregnancy losses are due to aneuploidy and abnormal fetal development; 10% to maternal illness, eg pyrexia. 2nd trimester loss may be due to infection, eg CMV (p 34). Bacterial vaginosis has been implicated. Most subsequent pregnancies are normal although at increased risk.

Recurrent miscarriage See OPPOSITE.

Septic/'backstreet' abortion Presents as acute salpingitis (p 286) and is treated similarly. Start broad-spectrum antibiotics 1h prior to uterine curettage, eg co-amoxiclav (ampoules are 1.2g; 1g is amoxicillin and 200mg clavulanic acid; give 1.2g/6h IV) + metronidazole (eg 1g by suppository/8h).

1 RCOG *Clinical guideline* no 7 2004 The care of women requesting induced abortion

Causes of recurrent spontaneous miscarriage (RSM)

This is loss of 3 or more consecutive pregnancies. It affects 1% of women. Prognosis for future successful pregnancy is affected by the previous number of miscarriages, and maternal age.

Possible causes

Endocrine: Polycystic ovaries (found in 41% on ultrasound), but polycystic morphology does not predict ↑ risk of pregnancy loss in ovulating women with RSM who conceive spontaneously.

Infection: Bacterial vaginosis (p 284) is associated with 2nd trimester loss. Screening (and treatment) is recommended for those with previous mid-trimester miscarriage or pre-term birth.

Parental chromosome abnormality: ~4% of those with RSM. It is usually a balanced reciprocal or Robertsonian translocation. Refer to a clinical geneticist. Genetic counselling offers prognosis for future pregnancy, familial chromosome studies, and appropriate advice for subsequent pregnancy where there may be 5–10% chance of a pregnancy with unbalanced translocation.[1]

Uterine abnormality: It is uncertain how much abnormality is associated with RSM or if hysteroscopic correction of abnormality contributes to successful pregnancy outcome. It is known that open uterine surgery increases chance of uterine rupture in pregnancy.

Antiphospholipid antibodies: (lupus anticoagulant, phospholipid and anticardiolipin antibodies) These are present in 15% of women with RSM. Most women with antibodies miscarry in the first trimester. If they are present, giving aspirin eg 75mg/24h PO from the day of positive pregnancy test + heparin (unfractionated self-administered Calciparine®) 5000U/12h SC as soon as the fetal heart is seen (eg at 5 weeks on vaginal ultrasound) until 34 weeks' gestation helps.[2] Get expert advice. Resulting pregnancies are at high risk of repeated miscarriage, pre-eclampsia, fetal growth restriction, and pre-term birth so need special surveillance.

Alloimmune causes: The theory is that these women share human leukocyte alleles (HLA) with their partners and do not mount the satisfactory protective response to the fetus. Immunotherapy has not been found to increase live birth rate, is potentially dangerous and should not be offered.

Recommended investigations[3]

- Karyotyping peripheral blood of both parents
- Karyotyping fetal products
- Pelvic ultrasound to assess ovaries and uterus
- Tests for antiphospholipid antibodies twice, taken 6 weeks apart with a third test taken if discordant results.

1 RCOG *Clinical Guideline* **17** 2003 Investigation and treatment of couples with recurrent miscarriage.
2 R Rai 1997 *BMJ* **314** 253 Live births with aspirin alone were 42%; with aspirin and heparin 71%. This study is criticized because of the unexpectedly high rate of fetal loss overall; also no cytogenic analysis was done. NB: heparin has serious side-effects; osteoporosis and thrombocytopenia.
3 http://www.rcog.org.uk/guidelines/recurrent.html

Ectopic pregnancy

The fertilized ovum implants outside the uterine cavity. The UK incidence is 11.1:1000 pregnancies and rising; worldwide rates are higher. ~7% of maternal deaths are due to ectopics (1.8 deaths/1000 ectopic pregnancies).

Predisposing factors Anything slowing the ovum's passage to the uterus increases risk: damage to the tubes (salpingitis; previous surgery); previous ectopic; endometriosis; the presence of an older IUCD; the PoP (p 302), GIFT (p 294).

Site of implantation 97% are tubal. Most implant in the ampulla, 25% in the narrow inextensible isthmus (so tend to present early and to rupture). 3% implant on the ovary, cervix, or peritoneum.

Natural history The trophoblast invades the tubal wall, weakening it and producing haemorrhage which dislodges the embryo. If the tube does not rupture, the blood and embryo are shed or converted into a tubal mole and absorbed. Rupture can be sudden and catastrophic, or gradual, giving increasing pain and blood loss. Peritoneal pregnancies may survive into the third trimester, and may present with failure to induce labour.

Clinical presentation ►Always think of an ectopic in a sexually active woman with abdominal pain or bleeding.

There is generally ~8 weeks' *amenorrhoea* but an ectopic may present before a period is missed. Tubal colic causes *abdominal pain* which may precede *vaginal bleeding*. Blood loss may be dark ('prune juice', as the decidua is lost from the uterus) or fresh. The ectopic may rupture the tube with sudden severe pain, peritonism, and shock. More often there is gradually increasing vaginal bleeding, and bleeding into the peritoneum producing shoulder-tip pain (diaphragmatic irritation) and pain on defecation and passing water (due to pelvic blood). The patient may be faint, with a tender abdomen (95%), enlarged uterus (30%), cervical excitation (50%), adnexal mass (63%). Presentation may just be as diarrhoea and vomiting; or nausea and dizziness. Classical features may be absent. Examine gently, to reduce risk of rupture; preferably with an IVI *in situ*.

Management ►Remember to give anti-D prophylaxis (p 9), if needed. Early diagnosis is vital. Dipstix testing for βHCG (human chorionic gonadotrophin) is sensitive to values of 25iu/L. Quantitate βHCG (blood); do ultrasound. If βHCG >6000iu/L and an intrauterine gestational sac is not seen, ectopic pregnancy is very likely, as is the case if βHCG 1000–1500iu/L and no sac is seen on *transvaginal* ultrasound. The higher the index of suspicion, the quicker the diagnosis. Unless urgent laparotomy required consider type of treatment required in the light of the woman's future desires for pregnancy.

Immediate laparotomy ►►Shock from a ruptured ectopic can be fatal. Immediate laparotomy is necessary as only clamping the bleeding artery will relieve it. If you suspect an ectopic, put up an IVI; if already shocked put up 2 (14 or 16G). Give colloid as fast as possible (use pressure bag to ↑flow), followed by blood—O-ve if desperate, but usually better to wait for group compatible. Inform your consultant. Take immediately to theatre.

Laparoscopy versus laparotomy Laparoscopy is preferred to laparotomy as recovery time is reduced. Rates of subsequent intrauterine pregnancy are similar but persisting trophoblast is more of a problem (12% *vs* 1.2%). Persistent trophoblast can cause later rupture and will need further treatment (surgical or methotrexate). See OPPOSITE. Repeat ectopic is slightly less common after laparoscopy.

Salpingotomy versus salpingectomy In the presence of a healthy contralateral tube RCOG guidelines state there is no clear evidence that salpingotomy should be used in preference to salpingectomy. Subsequent intrauterine pregnancy rates are higher after salpingotomy but so are rates of persisting trophoblast (8% *vs* 4%), and subsequent ectopic pregnancy (18% *vs* 8%). Salpingotomy should be primary treatment if the other tube is not healthy[1] to preserve chance of future intrauterine pregnancy (49%) but warn of risk of future ectopic pregnancy.

Methotrexate Methotrexate (eg 50mg/m^2 IM or intratubal injection into the gestation sac) is sometimes used for small early ectopics (eg <3.5cm in greatest diameter; βHCG level <3000iu/L, minimal symptoms. Visualization of a fetal heart is a contraindication to treatment). ≥15% will require more than 1 dose, and 10% surgical intervention (rupture rate 7% despite methotrexate treatment. 75% of women will get some abdominal pain with treatment and admission for observation and ultrasound may be required to distinguish rupture from the pain of separation with tubal abortion). Advise avoidance of intercourse during treatment and use of effective contraception for the next 3 months. Subsequent fertility rates seem higher after methotrexate treatment. 18 19 Multiple ovarian cysts, life-threatening neutropenia, pneumonitis, and late pelvic collections of blood have been reported with methotrexate treatment.

Expectant management Some tubal pregnancies end themselves without any problem so conservative treatment *may* be an option in those without acute symptoms and with falling βHCG levels that are <1000iu/L initially. 88% successfully resolve if initial βHCG <1000iu/L. There should be no evidence of blood, and <100ml fluid in the pouch of Douglas. Follow up twice weekly. Ideally βHCG drops by 50% and the adnexal mass is seen to be reducing in size by day 7. Follow up until βHCG <20iu/L (as tubal rupture has been known to occur at low levels of βHCG). Expectant management may also be used for women with pregnancy of unknown origin (ie no ultrasound evidence of uterine or ectopic pregnancy). It may be used if initial βHCG 1000-1500iu/L. Actively intervene if symptoms develop, or βHCG levels plateau or rise at 48–72h (23–29%).

Management of persistent trophoblast This occurs in 8.2% having laparoscopic salpingotomy; 4% after open salpingectomy. Diagnosis is by finding that βHCG does not drop according to the expected curve. Surveillance regimes vary: eg suspect if not fallen to <65% of pre-op value by 48h post-op, or to <10% by 10 days post-op. Treatment is with methotrexate IM as above.

Measures to reduce missing ectopic pregnancies

- Always send uterine curettings at ERPC (p 308) for histology.
- If histology does not confirm uterine failed pregnancy, recall the patient. (Ensure rapid return of histology results.)
- When ultrasound reports suggest an incomplete abortion but the fetus has not been seen—think: could this be an ectopic?

1 RCOG *Clinical Guideline* **21** 2004 The management of tubal pregnancy

Gestational trophoblastic neoplasia (GTN)

This comprises hydatidiform mole and choriocarcinoma. A fertilized ovum forms abnormal trophoblast tissue, but, usually, no fetus. The growth may appear 'benign' (mole) or 'malignant' (choriocarcinoma)—but these terms are confusing because *normal* trophoblast shows some features of malignancy (invasion and metastasis: in most normal pregnancies trophoblastic tissue ends up, for example, in the mothers lungs—so it may be better to think of the tissue as a failed pregnancy rather than a true neoplasia).

In GTN the trophoblast is usually genetically paternal but has a 46XX karyotype. Rarely, a triploid, partial mole is found with a fetus (usually abnormal). Partial moles do not seem to develop into choriocarcinoma.

Hydatidiform mole The tumour consists of proliferative chorionic villi which have swollen up and degenerated. Since it derives from chorion, it produces human chorionic gonadotrophin (HCG) in large quantities. This gives rise to exaggerated pregnancy symptoms and a strongly +ve pregnancy test. Incidence is 1.54:1000 births (UK). It is more common at extremes of maternal age, after a previous mole, and in non-Caucasians. A woman who has had a previous mole is at increased risk for future pregnancies; 0.8–2.9% after one mole, 15–28% after 2 moles.

Presentation Most present with early pregnancy failure, eg failed miscarriage or an embryonic pregnancy is seen on ultrasound. Bleeding may be heavy and molar tissue aborted may look like frogspawn. Ultrasound may show 'snowstorm effect' in a uterus that is 'large for dates'. Severe morning sickness or 1st trimester pre-eclampsia are rarer presentations. If accompanying twin pregnancy, proceed, if wished, (40% viable baby outcome) without ↑ persisting neoplasia or adverse treatment results.[1]

Abdominal pain may be due to huge theca-lutein cysts in both ovaries. These may rupture or tort. They take ~4 months to resolve after molar evacuation. HCG resembles TSH, and may cause hyperthyroidism. ►Tell the anaesthetist as thyrotoxic storm can occur at evacuation.

Treatment of moles: Molar tissue is removed from the soft, easily perforated uterus by gentle suction. Pregnancy should be avoided for a year while HCG levels are monitored. Register the woman at specialist centre (see below) for HCG monitoring. Levels should return to normal within 6 months. If levels drop rapidly to normal, oral contraceptive steroids may be used after 6 months. If they do not, either the mole was invasive (myometrium penetrated) or has given rise to choriocarcinoma (10%). Invasive mole may metastasize, eg to lung, vagina, brain, liver, and skin. Both conditions respond to chemotherapy.

Choriocarcinoma This highly malignant tumour occurs in 1:40000 deliveries. 50% follow a benign mole, 20% follow abortions and 10% follow normal pregnancy. ***Presentation:*** May be many years after pregnancy, with general malaise (due to 'malignancy' and to raised HCG); or uterine bleeding; or with signs and symptoms from metastases, which may be very haemorrhagic, eg haematoperitoneum, or nodules on CXR. Pulmonary artery obstruction via tumour emboli may lead to pulmonary artery hypertension (haemoptysis and dyspnoea).

Treatment: Choriocarcinoma in the UK is treated at 3 specialist centres and is extremely responsive to combination chemotherapy based on methotrexate. Outlook is good if non-metastatic and fertility is usually retained.

►Persistent vaginal bleeding after a pregnancy requires investigation to exclude choriocarcinoma.

1 RCOG *Clinical Guideline* **38** 2004 The management of gestational trophoblastic neoplasia

The vulva

Pruritus vulvae Vaginal itch is distressing and embarrassing. Causes: There may be a disorder causing general pruritus (p 588; consider diabetes (for thirst & other complaints). The cause may be local: infection and vaginal discharge (eg candida); infestation (eg scabies, pubic lice, threadworms); or vulval dystrophy (lichen sclerosus, leukoplakia, carcinoma). Symptoms may be psychosomatic in origin. Obesity and incontinence exacerbate symptoms. Postmenopausal atrophy does not cause itch.

The history may suggest the cause. Examine general health and look for widespread skin conditions. Examine the vulva and genital tract, under magnification if possible, and take a cervical smear. Take vaginal and vulval swabs and test for glycosuria. Biopsy if in doubt about diagnosis. Scratching and self-medication may have changed the appearance.

Treatment: This is often unsatisfactory. Treat the cause if possible. Reassurance can be very important. Advise her to avoid nylon underwear, chemicals and soap (use aqueous cream) and dry with a hair dryer. A short course of topical steroids may be helpful. Some patients find lidocaine cream 0.5% may help. Avoid antihistamine preparations which may sensitize the skin, so give antihistamines orally if needed, eg promethazine 25–50mg/24h.

Lichen sclerosus Due to elastic tissue turning to collagen after middle age (occasionally before puberty; the reddened and purpuric signs may lead to the mistaken suggestion of sexual abuse), there are bullae, erosions and ulcerations. The vulva gradually becomes white, flat and shiny. There may be an hourglass shape around the vulva and anus. It is intensely itchy. It may be pre-malignant and long-term surveillance is advisable (due to ~4% risk of carcinoma). Treatment: Clobetasol dipropionate cream daily for 28 days then alternate days for 2 weeks, twice weekly, then as needed. Vulval ablation may be needed (or allow skin to heal). 30% resolve by menarche.

Leucoplakia White vulval patches due to skin thickening and hypertrophy. Itch is likely. It should be biopsied as it may be a pre-malignant lesion. Treatment: Topical corticosteroids and emollients; other options: laser ablation with ultraviolet photodynamic therapy, methotrexate, ciclosporin.

Carcinoma of the vulva 95% are squamous. They are rare and occur mostly in the elderly.

Vulval malignancy has a preinvasive phase, vulval intra-epithelial neoplasia (VIN, see fig 1) which may be slow to progress to invasive carcinoma. VIN is associated with human papilloma virus (HPV) infection. There may not be visible warts but 5% acetic acid stains affected areas white. If VIN is found on biopsy, examine the cervix and anal canal within 15cm, and because 20% have coexistent neoplasia elsewhere, most commonly cervical. Treatment for VIN is aimed at symptom control by wide local excision or laser ablation. Avoid topical steroids. Recurrence is common so follow up regularly.

Any indurated ulcer with an everted edge suggests carcinoma. Tumour may be unnoticed unless it causes pain and bleeding, so is often presents late (30% already have inguinal lymph node involvement).

Treatment of stage 1 and 2 disease (tumour <2cm, no node involvement) may be treated by triple incision surgery. Radical vulvectomy (wide excision of the vulva + removal of inguinal glands) is used if more extensive disease. Chemoradiation if unsuitable for surgery. Skin grafts may be needed. 5-year survival is 75% for lesions <2cm, no node involvement; otherwise <50%.

1 [illegible]
2 Neill 2002 Br J Dermatol 147 640
3 [illegible]

The vulva

Pruritus vulvae Vaginal itch is distressing and embarrassing. ***Causes:*** There may be a disorder causing general pruritus (p 586) or skin disease (eg psoriasis, lichen planus). The cause may be local: infection and vaginal discharge (eg candida); infestation (eg scabies, pubic lice, threadworms); or vulval dystrophy (lichen sclerosis, leukoplakia, carcinoma). Symptoms may be psychogenic in origin. Obesity and incontinence exacerbate symptoms. Postmenopausal atrophy does not cause itch.

The history may suggest the cause. Examine general health and look for widespread skin conditions. Examine the vulva and genital tract, under magnification if possible, and take a cervical smear. Take vaginal and vulval swabs and test for diabetes. Biopsy if in doubt about diagnosis.
►Scratching and self-medication may have changed the appearance.

Treatment: This is often unsatisfactory.[1] Treat the cause if possible. Reassurance can be very important. Advise her to avoid nylon underwear, chemicals, and soap (use aqueous cream) and dry with a hair dryer. A short course of topical steroids, eg betamethasone valerate cream 0.1% may help. Avoid any topical preparation which may sensitize the skin, so give antipruritics orally if needed, eg promethazine 25-50mg/24h.

Lichen sclerosis Due to elastic tissue turning to collagen after middle age—or, occasionally, before puberty, the 'bruised' red, purpuric signs may appear, to the ignorant, to suggest abuse—particularly if there are bullae, erosions, and ulcerations. The vulva gradually becomes white, flat, and shiny. There may be an hourglass shape around the vulva and anus. It is intensely itchy. It may be pre-malignant and long-term surveillance is desirable if unresponsive to treatment. ***Treatment:*** Clobetasol diproprionate cream daily for 28 days, alternate days × 14, twice weekly × 8, then as needed;[2] vulval ablation may be needed to relieve itch. In children, 50% resolve by menarche.

Leukoplakia (White vulval patches due to skin thickening and hypertrophy). It is itchy. It should be biopsied as it may be a pre-malignant lesion. ***Treatment:*** Topical corticosteroids (problems: mucosal thinning, absorption); psoralens with ultraviolet phototherapy; methotrexate; ciclosporin.

Carcinoma of the vulva 95% are squamous. They are rare and occur mostly in the elderly.

Vulval malignancy has a pre-invasive phase, vulval intra-epithelial neoplasia (VIN—see fig 1), which may be itchy. ~6% progress to invasive carcinoma. VIN is associated with human papilloma virus (HPV) infection. There may not be visible warts but 5% acetic acid stains affected areas white. If VIN is found on biopsy, examine the cervix, anal canal if within 1.5cm,[3] and breasts (>10% have coexistent neoplasia elsewhere, most commonly cervical). ***Treatment for VIN*** is aimed at symptom control by wide local excision or laser ablation. Avoid topical steroids. Recurrence is common so follow up regularly.

An indurated ulcer with an everted edge suggests carcinoma. It may not be noticed unless it causes pain and bleeding, so it often presents late (50% already have inguinal lymph node involvement).

Treatment of stage 1 and 2 disease (tumour <2cm, no node involvement) may be treated by 'triple incision surgery'. Radical vulvectomy (wide excision of the vulva + removal of inguinal glands) is used if more extensive disease; chemoradiation if unsuitable for surgery. Skin grafts may be needed. 5-yr survival is 75% for lesions <2cm, no node involvement; otherwise <50%.

1 As chronic vulval itch and chronic vulval pain are often recalcitrant (often ignored, or inappropriately diagnosed as candida)—and because of its effects on mood and sexuality, a patients' group (with professional input) has been set up in the UK (www.vul-pain.dircon.co.uk)
2 J Neill 2002 *B J Dermatol* **147** 640
3 RCOG *Lower Genital Tract Neoplasia Study Group recommendations* 2003

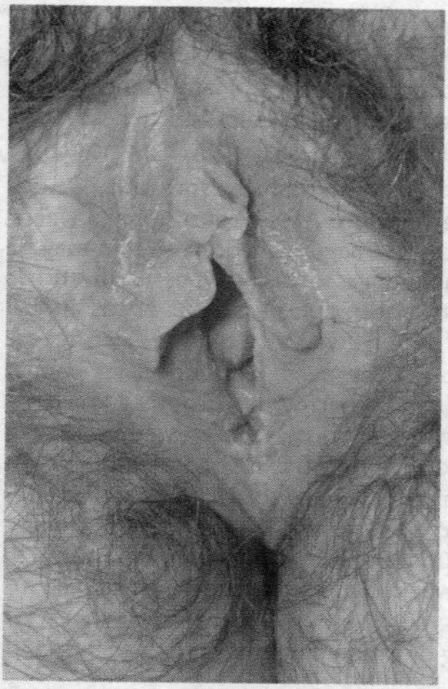

Fig 1. VIN: vulval intra-epithelial neoplasia

Vulval lumps and ulcers

Causes of vulval lumps Local va…
keratoacanthomata (rare); viral warts (c…
lata (syphilis); primary chancre; mollus…
abscess; uterine prolapse or polyp; …

Vulval warts Human papilloma virus…
contact. Incubation: weeks. Her partner…
The vulva, perineum, anus, vagina, or c…
very florid in the pregnant and immun…
can cause vulval and cervical intra-epi…
cervical smears and observation o…
anal carcinoma (OHCM p 530). Treat b…
infections. Warts may be destroyed …
Vulval and anal warts (condylomata …
surgeries and GU clinics with 15% podo…
(CI: pregnancy). Other treatments …
application with 0.5% podophyllotox…
enough for 4 treatment courses …
for 3 days, repeated up to 4 times …
excision. Relapse is common; …
respiratory papillomas in the …
50% are about 67% effective…

Exclude other genital infections; treat sexual partners.

Urethral caruncle This is a small red swelling at the urethral orifice. It is caused by meatal prolapse. It may be tender and cause pain on micturition. **Treatment:** Excision or diathermy.

Bartholin's cyst and abscess The Bartholin's glands and their ducts lie under the labia minora. They secrete thin lubricating mucus during sexual excitation. If the duct becomes blocked, a painless cyst forms; if this becomes infected the resulting abscess is extremely painful (she cannot sit down) and a hugely swollen, hot red labium is seen. **Treatment:** The abscess should be incised and permanent drainage ensured by marsupialization, ie the inner cyst wall is folded back and stitched to the skin. **Tests:** Exclude gonococcal infection.

Vulvitis Vulval inflammation may be due to infections (eg candida (p 284), herpes simplex), chemicals (bubble-baths, detergents). It is often associated with, or may be due to, vaginal discharge.

Causes of vulval ulcers Always consider syphilis. Herpes simplex is common in the young. Others: carcinoma; chancroid; lymphogranuloma venereum; granuloma inguinale; TB; Behçet's syndrome; aphthous ulcers; Crohn's.

Herpes simplex Herpes type II, sexually acquired, classically causes genital infection but type I transferred from cold sores can be the cause. The vulva is ulcerated and exquisitely painful. Urinary retention may occur. **Treatment:** Strong analgesia, lidocaine gel 2%, salt baths (and micturating in the bath) help. Exclude coexistent infections. Aciclovir topically and 200mg 5 times daily PO for 5 days shortens symptoms and infectivity. Reassure that subsequent attacks are shorter and less painful. Prescribe aciclovir cream for use when symptoms start. For herpes in pregnancy, see p 35.

Vulval lumps and ulcers

Causes of vulval lumps Local varicose veins; boils; sebaceous cysts; keratoacanthomata (rare); viral warts (condylomata acuminata); condylomata lata (syphilis); primary chancre; molluscum contagiosum; Bartholin's cyst or abscess; uterine prolapse or polyp; inguinal hernia; varicocele; carcinoma.

Vulval warts Human papilloma virus (HPV)—is usually spread by sexual contact. Incubation: weeks. Her partner may not have obvious penile warts. The vulva, perineum, anus, vagina, or cervix may be affected. Warts may be very florid in the pregnant and immunosuppressed. HPV types 16, 18, and 33 can cause vulval and cervical intra-epithelial neoplasia, so she needs annual cervical smears and observation of the vulva. Warts may also cause anal carcinoma (*OHCM* p 520). Treat both partners. Exclude other genital infections. Warts may be destroyed by diathermy, cryocautery or laser. Vulval and anal warts (condylomata acuminata) may be treated weekly in surgeries and GU clinics with 15% podophyllin paint, washed off after 30min (CI: pregnancy). Only treat a few warts at once, to avoid toxicity. Self-application with 0.15% podophyllotoxin cream (Warticon® 5g tubes—enough for 4 treatment courses—is supplied with a mirror): use every 12h for 3 days, repeated up to 4 times at weekly intervals if the area covered is <4cm^2. Relapse is common. NB: HPV types 6 and 11 may cause laryngeal or respiratory papillomas in the offspring of affected mothers (risk 1:50–1:1500; 50% present at <5yrs old).

Exclude other genital infections. Treat both partners.

Urethral caruncle This is a small red swelling at the urethral orifice. It is caused by meatal prolapse. It may be tender and give pain on micturition. ***Treatment:*** Excision or diathermy.

Bartholin's cyst and abscess The Bartholin's glands and their ducts lie under the labia minora. They secrete thin lubricating mucus during sexual excitation. If the duct becomes blocked a painless cyst forms; if this becomes infected the resulting abscess is extremely painful (she cannot sit down) and a hugely swollen, hot red labium is seen. ***Treatment:*** The abscess should be incised, and permanent drainage ensured by marsupialization, ie the inner cyst wall is folded back and stitched to the skin. ***Tests:*** Exclude gonococcal infection.

Vulvitis Vulval inflammation may be due to infections, eg candida (p 284), herpes simplex; chemicals (bubble-baths, detergents). It is often associated with, or may be due to, vaginal discharge.

Causes of vulval ulcers: Always consider syphilis. *Herpes simplex* is common in the young. Others: carcinoma; chancroid; lymphogranuloma venereum; granuloma inguinale; TB; Behçet's syndrome; aphthous ulcers; Crohn's.

Herpes simplex Herpes type II, sexually acquired, classically causes genital infection, but type I transferred from cold sores can be the cause. The vulva is ulcerated and exquisitely painful. Urinary retention may occur. ***Treatment:*** Strong analgesia, lidocaine gel 2%, salt baths (and micturating in the bath) help. Exclude coexistent infections. Aciclovir topically and 200mg 5 times daily PO for 5 days shortens symptoms and infectivity. Reassure that subsequent attacks are shorter and less painful. Prescribe aciclovir cream for use when symptoms start. For herpes in pregnancy, see p 36.

Gynaecology

The cervix

It is the part of the uterus below the internal os. The endocervical canal is lined with mucus-secreting columnar epithelium, the vaginal cervix with squamous epithelium. The transformation zone provides the squamo-columnar junction. It is the area which is exposed to potential malignant change.

Cervical ectropion This is often called erosion, a misleading term for a normal phenomenon. There is a red ring around the os because the endocervical epithelium has extended its territory over the paler epithelium of ectocervix. Ectropions extend temporarily under hormonal influence during pregnancy, with the combined Pill, and during puberty. The columnar epithelium is soft and vulnerable. Ectropion is prone to bleeding, to excess mucus production, and to infection. *Treatment:* Cryocautery will treat these if they are a nuisance, otherwise no treatment is required.

Nabothian cysts These mucus retention cysts found on the cervix are harmless. *Treatment:* cryocautery if they are discharging.

Cervical polyps These pedunculated benign tumours of endocervical epithelium may cause increased mucus discharge or postcoital bleeding. *Treatment:* in young women they may be simply avulsed, but in older women treatment usually includes D&C to exclude intrauterine pathology.

Cervicitis This may be follicular or mucopurulent presenting with discharge. *Causes:* Chlamydia (up to 50%), gonococci, or herpes (look for vesicles). Chronic cervicitis is usually a mixed infection and can respond to antibacterial cream. Cervicitis may mimic neoplasia and vice versa.

Cervical screening Cervical cancer has a pre-invasive phase: cervical intraepithelial neoplasia (CIN—not to be pronounced 'sin'). Exfoliative cytology smears collect cervical cells for microscopy for dyskaryosis (dyskaryotic nuclei which reflect CIN). A smear therefore identifies women who need cervical biopsy. The degree of dyskaryosis approximates to the severity of CIN (Box, p 273). 50% of CIN I lesions return to normal but most CIN III lesions progress to invasive carcinoma. This may take ~10 yrs, but may happen much faster in young women.

In the UK from 2003 it is recommended that 1st smear be taken at aged 25, then 3-yearly until 49 years, 5-yearly from 50–64 years and only to screen after 65 years if one of the last 3 included an abnormal result. Those most at risk are the hardest to trace and persuade to have screening, eg older women, smokers, and those in inner cities. 85% of the eligible UK population is screened and mortality rates are starting to fall:[1] this depends critically on being able to maintain skilled lab staff.

Taking a smear Explain the nature and purpose of the test and how results will be conveyed. Warn that results are not always unequivocal.

The cervix is visualized with a speculum (p 242). Are there any suspicious areas? If so, carry on with the smear and indicate this on the referral form but do not wait for the results before arranging further care.

Cells are scraped from the squamo-columnar transformation zone with a special spatula or brush then transferred to a slide and fixed at once. Liquid based cytology (LBC) involves rinsing the sampler or detaching its head into a vial of liquid creating a cell suspension from which slides are prepared which are quicker and easier to screen than conventional 'smears'. The suspensions can also be tested for herpes virus and chlamydia. Inadequate smear rates are reduced with LBC. Good technique is needed (make sure that all 4 quadrants of the cervix are sampled): it is best to learn by instruction from an expert at the bedside.

1 [illegible] 2004 [illegible]

The cervix

This is the part of the uterus below the internal os. The endocervical canal is lined with mucous columnar epithelium, the vaginal cervix with squamous epithelium. The transition zone between them—the squamo-columnar junction—is the area which is predisposed to malignant change.

Cervical ectropion This is often called erosion, an alarming term for a normal phenomenon. There is a red ring around the os because the endocervical epithelium has extended its territory over the paler epithelium of the ectocervix. Ectropions extend temporarily under hormonal influence during puberty, with the combined Pill, and during pregnancy. As columnar epithelium is soft and glandular, ectropion is prone to bleeding, to excess mucus production, and to infection. ***Treatment:*** Cryocautery will treat these if they are a nuisance; otherwise no treatment is required.

Nabothian cysts These mucus retention cysts found on the cervix are harmless. ***Treatment:*** Cryocautery if they are discharging.

Cervical polyps These pedunculated benign tumours of endocervical epithelium may cause increased mucus discharge or postcoital bleeding. ***Treatment:*** In young women they may be simply avulsed, but in older women treatment usually includes D&C to exclude intrauterine pathology.

Cervicitis This may be follicular or mucopurulent, presenting with discharge. ***Causes:*** Chlamydia (up to 50%), gonococci, or herpes (look for vesicles). Chronic cervicitis is usually a mixed infection and may respond to antibacterial cream. Cervicitis may mask neoplasia on a smear.

Cervical screening Cervical cancer has a pre-invasive phase: cervical intraepithelial neoplasia (CIN—not to be pronounced 'sin'). Papanicolaou smears collect cervical cells for microscopy for dyskaryosis (abnormalities which reflect CIN). A smear therefore identifies women who need cervical biopsy. The degree of dyskaryosis approximates to the severity of CIN (*Table*, p 273). ~50% of CIN I lesions return to normal but most CIN III lesions progress to invasive carcinoma. This may take ~10yrs, but may happen much faster in young women.

In the UK from 2005 it is recommended that 1st smear be taken at aged 25, then 3 yearly until 49 years, 5 yearly from 50 to 64 years and only to screen after 65 years if one of the last 3 included an abnormal result. Those most at risk are the hardest to trace and persuade to have screening, eg older women, smokers, and those in inner cities. 83% of the eligible UK population is now screened, and mortality here is starting to fall; this depends critically on being able to retain skilled lab staff.

Taking a smear Explain the nature and purpose of the test, and how results will be conveyed. Warn that results are not always unequivocal.

The cervix is visualized with a speculum (p 242). Are there any suspicious areas? If so, carry on with the smear and indicate this on the referral form, but do not wait for its results before arranging further care.

Cells are scraped from the squamo-columnar transformation zone with a special spatula or brush, then transferred to a slide and fixed at once. Liquid based cytology (LBC)[1] involves rinsing the sampler or detaching its head into a vial of liquid creating a cell suspension from which slides are prepared which are quicker and easier to screen than conventional smears. The suspensions can also be tested for herpes virus and chlamydia. Inadequate smear rates are reduced with LBC. Good technique is needed (make sure that all 4 quadrants of the cervix are sampled); it is best to learn by instruction from an expert at the bedside.

1 E McGoogan 2004 *J Fam Plan and Reprod Health Care* **30** 123

Cervical carcinoma

Easy to detect, pre-invasive disease, ~1400 women die yearly of cervical cancer in the UK. Many have had no smear but this is changing: see p 270. Causes: The main cause is human papilloma virus (eg serotypes 16 and 18). Type 16 is associated with squamous carcinoma, type 18 with adenocarcinoma. Vaccines are effective (if combined with screening this is a cost-effective preventive strategy).[1] [illegible] also if given locally to the uterus, eg by [illegible] ingress).[2] Prolonged Pill use is thought to be an important co-factor (the risk [illegible] 4-fold in those [illegible] for HPV DNA).[3] Other risk factors: high parity, many (≥4) sexual partners or a partner with many other partners (especially if the male is uncircumcised), early first coitus, HIV, other STDs, smoking.

Management of abnormal smears (See p 270: the histology of cervical intra-epithelial neoplasia (CIN) is explained there.) Either a repeat smear or colposcopy and biopsy are needed, depending on likelihood of the smear reflecting CIN III or small volume invasive disease (<5mm).

• Abnormal smears cause anxiety and guilt. Explain. Give support.

Treatment of pre-invasive carcinoma Examine the cervix by colposcope (×10 binocular microscope). Abnormal epithelium has characteristic blood vessel patterns and stains white with acetic acid. Take punch biopsies for histology. CIN is destroyed by cryotherapy, laser, cold coagulation, or large loop excision of transformation zone (LLETZ). These give ~90% cure rates with one treatment. She needs annual smears for at least 10 years. If the squamo-columnar junction cannot be seen, or if small volume invasive carcinoma is found on histology, the abnormal tissue is removed by cone biopsy, which may be curative. Colposcopy does not detect adenocarcinoma (it usually lies within the endocervical canal).

Invasive disease Most are squamous cancers; 15–20% are adenocarcinomas (from endocervical epithelium, with unknown risk factors) especially affecting women under 40. Spread is local and lymphatic.

Stage I tumours are confined to the cervix.
Stage II have extended locally to upper ⅔ vagina (IIa) or to parametria (IIb).
Stage III have spread to lower ⅓ of vagina (IIIa) or pelvic wall (IIIb).
Stage IV have spread to bladder or rectum (IVa) or spread to distant organs.
Most present in stages I or II.

Diagnosis Overt carcinoma is rarely detected on a smear. Non-menstrual bleeding is the classic symptom. The early tumour is firm. It grows as a friable mass which bleeds on contact.

Treating invasive cancer Stage Ia1 (microscopic lesions, invasion <3mm) may be treated by cervical cone biopsy in those wishing to preserve fertility, extrafascial hysterectomy for those with completed families. Radical hysterectomy with pelvic lymphadenectomy or radiotherapy is used for stage Ia2 (microscopic invasion 3–5mm depth, <7mm horizontally) disease and some stage Ib1 (macroscopic tumour <4cm). Chemoradiation is the gold standard for most stage Ib, II or bulky stage II disease—it is also used for stage III and IV disease. Use of chemotherapy in advanced and recurrent disease is palliative. The main chemotherapy agent is cisplatin. Pelvic exenteration (p 309) is sometimes used in stage IVa disease. Cure rates for stages I (80% 5yr survival) and II (60%). Radiotherapy causes vaginal stenosis, so encourage intercourse within 2 months of treatment (±lubricant). Follow-up annual smears: smears are of no value after radical radiotherapy. Terminal problems are pain, fistulae, and GI/GU obstruction.

1 D Harper 2004 Lancet 364 1757
2 IARC multicentric cervical cancer study group 2002 Lancet 359 1085 and 1080 [editorial]
3 X Bosch 2003 NEJM 348 1055 [illegible] HPV infection is common
4 S Waggoner 2003 Lancet 361 2217

Cervical carcinoma

►*Aim to detect pre-invasive disease.* ~1600 women die yearly of cervical cancer in the UK. Many have had no smear, but this is changing: see p 270.

Causes The main cause is human papilloma virus (eg HPV 16, 18, and 33). Type 16 is associated with squamous carcinoma, type 18 with adenocarcinoma.[1] Vaccines are effective (if combined with screening this is a cost-effective preventive strategy; also, if given locally to the uterus, CIN 1, 2 & 3 can regress). Prolonged Pill use is thought to be an important co-factor (*may* ↑risk 4-fold in those +ve for HPV DNA).[2] Other risk factors: high parity; many (>4) sexual partners or a partner with many other partners (especially if that male is uncircumcized);[3] early first coitus; HIV; other STDs; smoking.

Management of abnormal smears (See p 273: the histology of cervical intra-epithelial neoplasia (CIN) is explained there.) Either a repeat smear or colposcopy and biopsy are needed, depending on likelihood of the smear reflecting CIN III or small volume invasive disease (<3mm).

►Abnormal smears cause anxiety and guilt. Explain. Give support.

Treatment of pre-invasive carcinoma Examine the cervix by colposcope (×10 binocular microscope). Abnormal epithelium has characteristic blood vessel patterns and stains white with acetic acid. Take punch biopsies for histology. CIN is destroyed by cryotherapy, laser, cold coagulation, or large loop excision of transformation zone (LLETZ). These give ~90% cure rates with one treatment. She needs annual smears for at least 10 years. If the squamo-columnar junction cannot be seen, or if small volume invasive carcinoma is found on histology, the abnormal tissue is removed by cone biopsy, which may be curative. Colposcopy does not detect adenocarcinoma (it usually lies within endocervical canal).

Invasive disease Most are squamous cancers. 15–30% are adenocarcinomas (from endocervical epithelium, with unknown risk factors), especially affecting women under 40. Spread is local and lymphatic.

Stage I tumours are confined to the cervix.
Stage II have extended locally to upper 2/3 vagina; ***IIb*** if to parametria.
Stage III have spread to lower ⅓ of vagina ***IIIa***; or pelvic wall ***IIIb***.
Stage IV have spread to bladder or rectum. ***IVb*** if spread to distant organs.
Most present in stages I or II.

Diagnosis ►Overt carcinoma is rarely detected on a smear. Non-menstrual bleeding is the classic symptom. The early tumour is firm. It grows as a friable mass which bleeds on contact.

Treating invasive cancers[4] Stage Ia1 (microscopic lesions, invasion <3mm) may be treated by cervical conization in those wishing to preserve fertility, extrafascial hysterectomy for those with completed families. Radical hysterectomy with pelvic lymphadenectomy or radiotherapy is used for stage Ia2 (microscopic, invasion 3–5mm depth <7mm horizontally) disease and some stage Ib1 (macroscopic, tumour <4cm). Chemoradiation is the 'gold standard' for most stage Ib, II or bulky stage II disease. It is also used for stage III and IV disease. Use of chemotherapy in advanced and recurrent disease is palliative. The main chemotherapy agent is cisplatin. Pelvic exenteration (p 309) is sometimes used in stage IVa disease. Cure rates for stages I (80% 5-yr survival) and II (60%). Radiotherapy causes vaginal stenosis: so encourage intercourse within 2 months of treatment (+lubricant). Follow-up: annual smears. Smears are of no value after radical radiotherapy. Terminal problems are pain, fistulae, and GI/GU obstruction.

1 D Harper 2004 *Lancet* **364** 1757
2 IARC multicentric cervical cancer study group 2002 *Lancet* **359** 1085 and 1080 (editorial)
3 X Bosch 2002 *NEJM* **346** 1005; n= 1913; occult ♂ HPV infection is common
4 S Waggoner 2004 *Lancet* **361** 2217

Histology of cervical pre-malignant disease (CIN = cervical intra-epithelial neoplasia)

	Papanicolaou class	*Action*	*Histology*
I	Normal	Repeat in 3 years (Unless clinical suspicion)	0.1% CIN II–III
II	Inflammatory	Take swab; treat infection Repeat in 6 months (Colposcopy after 3 abnormal)	6% CIN II–III
	Mild atypia	Repeat in 4 months (Colposcopy after 2 abnormal)	20–37% CIN II–III
III	Mild dyskaryosis	Colposcopy	20–30% CIN II–III
	Moderate dyskaryosis	Colposcopy	50–75% CIN II–III
IV	Severe dyskaryosis 'Positive' 'Malignant cells'	Colposcopy	80–90% CIN II–III 5% Invasion
V	Invasion suspected	Urgent colposcopy	50% Invasion
	Abnormal glandular cells	Urgent colposcopy	?Adenoca cervix or endometrial ca

CIN I = mild dysplasia; CIN II = moderate dysplasia; CIN III = Severe dysplasia/ *carcinoma-in-situ*

The table above shows comparative terms and the recommended action. The third column, headed histology, shows the percentage of smears in each Papanicolaou (cytological) class which have more serious lesions (CIN II or III) on histology. With inflammatory smears, swabs should be taken and any infection treated. 6% of inflammatory smears have serious pathology, hence the recommendation for colposcopy if inflammation persists.

Borderline nuclear abnormality **(BNA)** implies doubt as to the neoplastic nature of any change. Re-smearing (eg at 3–6 months), or colposcopy (eg after 2 smears with BNA, if numbers of affected cells are static over time). Such colposcopy should be seen as part of the screening process, and need not prompt treatment. This goes part of the way to avoid false negatives, as well as to avoid the problems of overtreatment.

In the UK, 6×10^6 smears are done per year on women up to 65yrs old, and cervical cancer deaths have fallen by 15% in recent years to <1900/yr. The incidence of cervical cancer in England and Wales fell by 42% between 1988 and 1997. Cervical screening is thought to prevent 5000 deaths/year in the UK.[1] 2.4% of smears show mild dyskaryosis, and 2.2% have BNA. As most of these will eventually need colposcopy because of further smear results and 48% can be expected to have CIN II or III, and as a significant proportion may be lost to follow-up, it is suggested that *immediate* colposcopy with directed biopsy is indicated. However, this would be very expensive, and anxiety-provoking. The cost in the USA of adopting this policy is ~$1 billion, and the benefits are uncertain as no randomized trials have been done.

Terminology used in reporting smears changed in the 1980s, and different countries use different nomenclature—eg the Bethesda system.

1 J Peto 2004 *The Lancet* **364** 249

The uterus

Endometritis Uterine infection is uncommon unless the barrier to ascending infection (acid vaginal pH and cervical mucus) is broken, eg after abortion and childbirth, IUCD insertion, or surgery. Infection may involve Fallopian tubes and ovaries.

Presentation: Lower abdominal pain and fever; uterine tenderness on bimanual palpation. Low-grade infection is often due to chlamydia. ***Tests:*** Do cervical swabs and blood cultures. ***Treatment:*** Give antibiotics (eg doxycyline 100mg/12h PO with metronidazole 500mg/8h PO, eg for 7 days).

Endometrial proliferation Oestrogen stimulates endometrial proliferation in the first half of the menstrual cycle; it is then influenced by progesterone and is shed at menstruation. A particularly exuberant proliferation is associated with heavy menstrual bleeding and polyps.

Continuous high oestrogen levels (eg anovulatory cycles) make the endometrium hyperplastic ('cystic glandular hyperplasia'—a histological diagnosis after D&C). It eventually breaks down, causing irregular bleeding (dysfunctional uterine bleeding). ***Treatment:*** Cyclical progestogens (p 253).

In older women proliferation may contain foci of atypical cells which may lead to endometrial carcinoma (p 278).

Pyometra This is a uterus distended by pus eg associated with salpingitis or secondary to outflow blockage. ***Treatment:*** Drain the uterus, treat the cause.

Haematometra This is a uterus filled with blood due to outflow obstruction. It is rare. The blockage may be an imperforate hymen in the young (p 246); carcinoma; or iatrogenic cervical stenosis, eg after cone biopsy.

Endometrial tuberculosis Genital tract tuberculosis is rare in Britain, except among high-risk groups (eg immigrants). It is blood-borne and usually affects first the Fallopian tubes, then the endometrium.

It may present with acute salpingitis if disease is very active, or with infertility, pelvic pain, and menstrual disorders (40%) eg amenorrhoea, oligomenorrhoea. There may be pyosalpinx. Exclude lung disease by CXR.

Treatment is medical with antituberculous therapy (*OHCM* p 564–7). Repeat endometrial histology after one year. Total abdominal hysterectomy with bilateral salpingo-oophorectomy is treatment of choice if there are adnexal masses and the woman is >40yrs.[1]

Uterine ultrasound[2] Transvaginal ultrasound gives better resolution than transabdominal (as the probe is closer to the target and a higher frequency transducer can be used). Homogeneity, echoes of low intensity and presence of a linear central shadow are associated with absence of endometrial abnormality. Endometrial carcinoma is suggested by endometrial thickness >20mm (>5mm if postmenopausal not on hormones), heterogeneous appearance, and hypoechoic areas. Polyps have cystic appearance (also with hyperechoic endometrium).

If postmenopausal and not on HRT, double-layer endometrial thickness should be <5mm (if perimenopausal <5mm on day 5 of cycle). Sequential hormone replacement ↑endometrial thickness (average 5–8.5mm); if on continuous combined replacement HRT thicknesses are ~4.5–7mm; tibolone treated endometrium <5mm; but tamoxifen thickens it to ~13mm. It thins down by 6 months after stopping tamoxifen, then stays thin.[22]

Ultrasound is useful for detecting fibroids; and assessing cystic change in rapidly growing fibroids to assess risk of malignant change.

1 P Sinha 2000 *BJOG* **107** 139

2 K Davidson 2003 *Radiol Clin North Am* **41** 769

Vaginal carcinoma

These tumours are usually squamous. They are commonest in the upper third of the vagina. Presentation is usually with bleeding. Clear cell adenocarcinoma is associated with intrauterine exposure to diethylstilboestrol before 18 weeks gestation but risk is low (0.1–1:1000). (Note, risk of invasive cervical carcinoma is also increased 3-fold, and structural abnormalities of the genital tract-uterine 69% and cervical 44% are after problems with past exposure).[1] Spread is local and by lymphatics. Treatment is usually radiotherapy.

1 RCOG Statement no. 2 *Fetal and Maternal risks of diethylstilboestrol exposure in pregnancy* 2002

Fibroids (uterine leiomyomata)

Fibroids are benign smooth muscle tumours of the uterus (leiomyomas). They are often multiple, and vary in size from seedling size to tumours occupying a large part of the abdomen. They start as lumps in the wall of the uterus but may grow to bulge out of the wall so that they lie under the peritoneum (subserosal, 20%) or under the endometrium (submucosal, 5%), or become pedunculated. Fibroids are common (20% of women have fibroids), increasing in frequency with age, and in non-Caucasians.

Associations Mutation in the gene for fumarate hydratase can cause fibroids and a rare association with skin & uterine leiomyomata, and renal cell cancer.[1]

Natural history Fibroids are oestrogen-dependent. Consequently they enlarge in pregnancy and on the combined Pill and atrophy after the menopause. They may degenerate gradually or suddenly (red degeneration). Occasionally they calcify ('womb stones'). Rarely, they undergo sarcomatous change—usually causing pain, malaise, bleeding, and increase in size in a postmenopausal woman.

Presentation Many are asymptomatic.
- ***Menorrhagia:*** Fibroids often produce heavy and prolonged periods. They do not generally cause intermenstrual or postmenopausal bleeding.
- ***Fertility problems:*** Submucosal fibroids may interfere with implantation ('natural IUCD'). Large or multiple tumours which distort the uterine cavity may cause abortion should pregnancy occur.
- ***Pain:*** This may be due to torsion of a pedunculated fibroid, producing symptoms similar to that of a torted ovarian cyst. 'Red degeneration' following thrombosis of the fibroid blood supply: see page 39.
- ***Mass:*** Large fibroids may be felt abdominally. They may press on the bladder, causing frequency, or on the veins, causing oedematous legs and varicose veins. Pelvic fibroids may obstruct labour or cause retention of urine.

Treatment In many women, no treatment is needed.

Menorrhagia due to fibroids tend to respond poorly to anti-prostaglandins, progestogens, or danazol. Women who have completed their families may opt for *hysterectomy*. In younger women, a reversible menopausal state may be induced with analogues of LHRH (leutinizing hormone releasing hormone), eg *goserelin* (better than buserelin[2]). A single dose of 10.8mg SC reduces bulk by ≥50%.[3] Bone demineralization can occur, but is ameliorated by concurrent raloxifene,[4] which helps shrink fibroids further.[5] They may be used pre-op to reduce fibroid bulk; in those unfit for surgery; or those desiring later pregnancy. Side-effects are menopausal symptoms. Fertility (and fibroids) return when drugs are stopped.

Alternatively, fibroids may be surgically shelled out (*myomectomy*). *Complications:* torrential bleeding needing hysterectomy; post-op adhesions. Pregnancy rates may increase markedly post-op.[6] Laparoscopic surgery ± laser use is possible but needs much patience. *Embolizing fibroids* (interventional radiology) can shrink them, so resolving menorrhagia. This involves only a short hospital stay, but it is not widely available. It can be very painful.

Red degeneration requires only analgesia until symptoms settle.

Torsion may resemble an acute abdomen, requiring urgent surgery.

1 Tomlinson I 2002 *Nat Genet* 2.25 Gene location: 1q42.3—q43
2 Buserelin nasal spray 100µg/4h is expensive and intermittent use may cause fibroid size to *increase*.
3 Bozzini N 2004 *J Am As Gyn Lap* **11** 462 RCT; N=45; size ↓by 54% vs 43% with 3 4-weekly 3.6mg doses
4 Palomba S 2002 *J Clin Endocrinol Metab* **67** 4476
5 Palomba S 2002 *Hum Reprod* **17** 3213
6 Marchioni M 2004 *Fertil Steril* **82** 154

Fibroids in pregnancy

5/1000 Caucasian women have fibroids in pregnancy. They are commoner in Afro-Caribbean women. They may cause abortion. They increase in size in pregnancy—especially in the 2nd trimester. Ultrasound aids diagnosis. If pedunculated they may tort. Red degeneration is when thrombosis of capsular vessels is followed by venous engorgement and inflammation, causing abdominal pain (± vomiting and low grade fever), and localized peritoneal tenderness—usually in the last half of pregnancy or the puerperium. 'Here, a certain feverishness leads them to their final degeneration', and imitating the course of all grand passions, 'they grow big and tender, and then die' (DH Lawrence, *Sons & Lovers*, JPS, 324).

Treatment is expectant (bed rest, analgesia) with resolution over 4–7 days. Most fibroids arise from the body of the uterus and do not therefore obstruct labour, as they tend to rise away from the pelvis throughout pregnancy. If large pelvic masses of fibroids are noted prior to labour Caesarean section should be planned. Obstruction of labour also needs Caesarean section.

Endometrial carcinoma

►Postmenopausal vaginal bleeding must be investigated as the cause may be endometrial carcinoma.

Carcinoma of the uterine body is less common than carcinoma of the cervix. It usually presents after the menopause. Most tumours are adenocarcinomas and are related to excessive exposure to oestrogen unopposed by progesterone. There is marked geographical variation: North American: Chinese ratio = 7:1.

Risk factors •Obesity •Nulliparity •Diabetes •Unopposed oestrogen therapy •Late menopause •Pelvic irradiation •Functioning ovarian tumour •Tamoxifen[1] •FH of breast, ovary, colon cancer •Polycystic ovaries 23

Presentation This is usually as postmenopausal bleeding (PMB). Any woman with a history of PMB has a 10–20% risk of genital cancer. It is initially scanty and occasional, perhaps with a watery discharge. Over time, bleeding becomes heavier and more frequent. Pre-menopausal women may have intermenstrual bleeding, but 30% have only menorrhagia.

Diagnosis Postmenopausal bleeding is an early sign, and generally leads a woman to see her doctor, but examination is usually normal. Endometrial carcinoma can sometimes be seen on a smear. Uterine ultrasound may be suggestive (p 274). The diagnosis is made by uterine sampling (p 279) or curettage. All parts of the uterine cavity must be sampled; send *all* material for histology. Hysteroscopy enables visualization of abnormal endometrium to improve accuracy of sampling. Sceptics claim it may cause spread through the Fallopian tubes to the peritoneum.

Pathology Most tumours start in the fundus of the uterine cavity. The tumour spreads slowly to the uterine muscle. With time, it may reach the cervix or peritoneum and may metastasize to the vagina (5%), ovary (5%), and any of the pelvic lymph nodes (7%).

Staging

I: Tumour is confined to the body of the uterus.
II: As for I but with cervical involvement.
III: Tumour has extended beyond the uterus but not beyond the pelvis.
IV: Extension outside the pelvis. Bowel and bladder may be affected.

Treatment Stages I and II may be cured by total hysterectomy with bilateral salpingo-oophorectomy and/or radiotherapy if unfit for surgery (5-yr survival: stage I = 72%, stage II = 56%). Post-operative vault irradiation reduces vault recurrence. In advanced disease consider radiotherapy and/or high-dose progestogens, eg medroxyprogesterone acetate 250mg/24h PO, which shrinks the tumour (SE: fluid retention). Radiotherapy may either be given pre-operatively (caesium or radium rods inserted into the uterus and upper vagina) or post-operatively (external radiation).

Recurrent disease usually presents in the first 2-3yrs. Common sites are pelvic (in nonirradiated patients), lung, bone, inguinal, and supraclavicular nodes, vagina, liver, peritoneal cavity. Surgical exenteration, radiotherapy, and medroxyprogesterone may all be of use. Cytotoxics may be used for those who fail to respond to the above.

1 Note: tamoxifen 20mg daily reduces annual risk of breast cancer recurrence by 27%. Risk of endometrial carcinoma from taking tamoxifen is 1.2 per 1000 person-years. Counsel to report abnormal vaginal bleeding.

Endometrial sampling in outpatients

This bedside investigation is used for postmenopausal bleeding, perimenopausal irregular bleeding, and unexpected bleeding patterns in women on hormone replacement therapy because it is cheap, reliable, and gives quick results without the need for anaesthesia. If transvaginal uterine ultrasound precedes the procedure, sample if endometrium >5mm thick. It is less useful in menorrhagia in women with regular cycles, as pathology is less common. It is not indicated if <35 years old.

A sample is obtained using a side-opening plastic cannula in which a vacuum is created by withdrawal of a stopped central plunger mechanism. As the cannula is then withdrawn and rotated within each quadrant of the uterine cavity, endometrial tissue is sucked into its interior, through the hole in the side of the cannula. Successful insertion is possible in 90–99% of women (D&C possible in 99%). Adequate samples will be obtained in 91% of these, and in 84% of those for whom postmenopausal bleeding (PMB) was the indication. Abandon the procedure if it is impossible to enter the uterus, or if it causes too much pain.

Technique

1 Bimanual examination to assess size and position of uterus (p 242).
2 Bend cervical cannula to follow the curve of the uterus.
3 Insert device, watching the centimetre scale on the side; observe resistance on entering the internal os (at 3–4cm) and then as the tip reaches the fundus (eg at 6cm if postmenopausal or 8cm in an oestrogenized uterus).
4 When the tip is in the fundus, create a vacuum by withdrawing plunger until the stopper prevents further withdrawal. Then move sampler up and down in the uterus, rotate and repeat to sample whole cavity.
5 Remove cannula, and expel tissue into formalin. Send for histology. Vabra vacuum aspiration samples a greater area of tissue, has higher cancer detection rates, but is more uncomfortable. [24]

Management Reassure those in whom the results show normal or atrophic endometrium and those in whom tissue was sufficient for diagnosis. If those with PMB re-bleed refer for hysteroscopy (polyps or a fibroid will be present in 20%). Those with simple hyperplasia on histology can be treated with cyclical progesterones (but refer if >55yrs to search for exogenous oestrogen source). Refer those with polyps or necrotic tissue on histology for hysteroscopy and curettage; and those with atypical hyperplasia or carcinoma for hysterectomy and bilateral salpingo-oophorectomy. If transvaginal uterine ultrasound not already done, perform in those on whom the procedure was impossible or abandoned to establish endometrial thickness (<5mm normal in the postmenopausal; refer if >5mm thick or if polyps seen, for hysteroscopy and curettage).

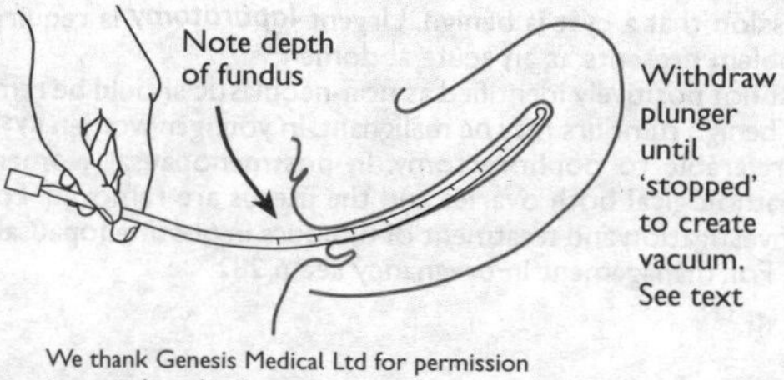
Note depth of fundus
Withdraw plunger until 'stopped' to create vacuum. See text

We thank Genesis Medical Ltd for permission to reproduce the diagram

Ovarian tumours

Any of the ovary's many tissue types may become neoplastic.

Benign tumours (94%). They are usually cystic. 24% of all ovarian tumours are functional cysts. Others: endometriotic cysts (5%—p 288); theca-lutein cysts (p 264); epithelial cell tumours (serous and mucinous cystadenomas—40%); mature teratomas (from germ cells—20%); fibromas (solid—5%).

Malignant tumours (6%). 5% are cystadenomas which have become malignant. 0.5% are a group of rare germ cell or sex cord malignancies (p 281). 0.5% are secondaries, eg from the uterus, or the stomach (Krukenberg tumours—in which spread is transcoelomic, ie, in the case of the abdomen, via the peritoneum).

Risk markers of ovarian malignancy: Nulliparity (risk↑ × 1.5); infertility; early menarche; +ve family history (p 283); no past use of the Pill; high total fat intake (associated with a 24% ↑risk).[MET 25] [n=6,689]

Presentations are varied, depending on size, form, and histological type:

Asymptomatic—chance finding (eg on doing a bimanual for a smear test).

Swollen abdomen—with palpable mass arising out of the pelvis which is dull to percussion (and does not disappear if the bladder is catheterized).

Pressure effects (eg on bladder, causing urinary frequency).

Infarction/haemorrhage—this mimics torsion (see below).

Rupture ± local peritonism. Rupture of a large cyst may cause peritonitis and shock. Rupture of a malignant cyst may disseminate malignant cells throughout the abdomen. Rupture of mucinous cystadenomas may disseminate cells which continue to secrete mucin and cause death by binding up the viscera (pseudomyxoma peritonei). See p 281. Pseudomyxoma peritonei is treated by surgical debulking. 10-year survival is 30–50%.

Ascites—shifting dullness suggests malignancy or Meigs' syndrome (p 281). If tense, ascites may be hard to distinguish from a mass.

Torsion—to twist, a tumour must be small, and free on a pedicle. Twisting occludes the venous return but the arterial supply continues to engorge the tumour, and cause great pain (with a high WBC). Tumours may twist and untwist, giving a history of intermittent pain. If the pain is not too severe, a firm tender adnexal swelling may be felt.

Endocrine or metastatic effects—Hormone-secreting tumours may cause virilization, menstrual irregularities, or postmenopausal bleeding.

Management *Ultrasound* may confirm the presence of a mass and may show whether it is cystic or solid.

Laparoscopy may distinguish a cyst from an ectopic pregnancy or appendicitis. Note: laparoscopy is not advised if malignancy is possible, due to seeding along the surgical tract. ***Fine needle aspiration*** may be used to confirm the impression that a cyst is benign. Urgent ***laparotomy*** is required when a cyst problem presents as an acute abdomen.

Any cyst not positively identified as non-neoplastic should be removed, as seemingly benign tumours may be malignant. In younger women ***cystectomy*** may be preferable to oophorectomy. In postmenopausal women, if one ovary is pathological both ovaries and the uterus are removed. For guidelines for investigation and treatment of tumours in postmenopausal women see p 282. For management in pregnancy see p 282.

Ovarian tumours: pathology

Functional cysts These are enlarged or persistent follicular or corpus luteum cysts. They are so common that they may be considered normal if they are small (<5cm). They may cause pain by rupture, failing to rupture at ovulation, or bleeding.

Serous cystadenomas These develop papillary growths that may be so prolific that the cyst appears solid. They are commonest in women aged 30–40 years. About 30% are bilateral and about 30% are malignant.

Mucinous cystadenomas The commonest large ovarian tumours; these may become enormous. They are filled with mucinous material and rupture may rarely cause pseudomyxoma peritonei (p 280). They may be multilocular. They are commonest in the 30–50 age group. About 5% will be malignant. Remove the appendix at operation in those with suspected mucinous cystadenoma and send for histology. (Interestingly men can get pseudomyxoma from intestinal or appendicular neoplasms; most women with pseudomyxoma peritonei do not have overt rupture of ovarian tumours and 90% have concurrent intestinal or appendicular tumours and it is now thought that the ovarian tumours may be secondary to GI ones).

Fibromas These are small, solid, benign, fibrous tissue tumours. They are associated with Meigs' syndrome (pleural effusion + benign ovarian fibroma or thecoma ± ascites) and ascites.

Teratomas These arise from primitive germ cells. A benign mature teratoma (dermoid cyst) may contain well differentiated tissue, eg hair, teeth. 20% are bilateral. They are most common in young women. Poorly differentiated malignant teratomas are rare.

Other germ cell tumours (all malignant and all rare) Nongestational choriocarcinomas (secrete HCG); ectodermal sinus tumours (yolk sac tumours—secrete α-fetoprotein); dysgerminomas.

Sex-cord tumours (rare; usually of low-grade malignancy) These arise from cortical mesenchyme. Granulosa-cell and theca-cell tumours produce oestrogen and may present with precocious puberty, menstrual problems, or postmenopausal bleeding. Arrhenoblastomas secrete androgens.

Ovarian tumours in pregnancy

These are found in ~1/1000 pregnancies. It is easier to distinguish them (lying as they do in the rectovaginal pouch) with an anteverted uterus than with a gravid retroverted uterus. Suspicion of presence of a tumour can be confirmed by ultrasound. Torsion of ovarian cysts is more common in pregnancy and the puerperium than at other times. Cyst rupture and haemorrhage into cysts may also occur, but are not more common than at other times. Torsion may present with abdominal pain, nausea, vomiting, shock, local tenderness (usually at 8–16 weeks). 2-5% of tumours are malignant. Suspect malignancy with ruptures (then biopsy other ovary). ~25% of malignant tumours will be dysgerminomas.

Tumours can become necrotic due to pressure on them in labour. Tumours lying in the pelvis can obstruct labour so Caesarean section will be needed unless they are cysts which can be aspirated under ultrasound control before labour.

Asymptomatic simple cysts <5cm across can be left until after delivery if watched by ultrasound. Those 5-10cm may be aspirated under ultrasound control (and the aspirate examined cytologically). Other tumours (those that are complex multilocular or with solid portions on ultrasound) should be removed at about 16 weeks' gestation (by which time the pregnancy is not dependent on the corpus luteum and miscarriage is less likely) to exclude carcinoma and prevent complications developing. If the diagnosis is made late in pregnancy and the tumour is not obstructing the pelvis, it is usual to let labour progress normally, and to remove the tumour in the early puerperium because of the risk of torsion then.

Postmenopausal ovarian tumours

The aim is to identify those with high risk of cancer and treat those at special cancer centres. 21% of post-menopausal women have cysts on screening ultrasound. Ultrasound is 89% sensitive and 73% specific for detecting cancer. CA-125 (p 283) estimations 81% and 75% respectively. A CA-125 >30u/mL is +ve in 80% malignancy (but in only 50% stage I). Risk of malignancy (RMI) can be calculated with the formula below. RMI < 25 has a cancer risk <3%, risk is 75% if RMI > 250 (manage these high-risk women at a cancer centre).

RMI=U × M × CA-125 (M=3; CA-125 is the number for U/mL; U is 1 if ultrasound score=1, and 3 if ultrasound score 2-5.) To calculate ultrasound score add 1 for each of the following ultrasound features: multilocular cyst; solid area in cyst; bilateral lesions; evidence of metastases; ascites present.[1]

Unilocular cysts <5cm with a normal CA-125 can be managed conservatively (ultrasound every 4 months for 1 year). Low-risk cysts may be removed at bilateral laparoscopic oophorectomy (if suitable for laparoscopic treatment). Postmenopausal cysts should not be aspirated. High-risk cysts need total abdominal hysterectomy + bilateral salpingo-oophorectomy + infracolic omentectomy at a cancer centre with cytology of ascites and washings; biopsy of suspicious areas/adhesions; ± selective pelvic/para-aortic lymphadenectomy.

1 RCOG *Clinical Guideline* **34** 2003 Ovarian cysts in postmenopausal women

Ovarian carcinoma

This is rare, but more women die from it (it is the fourth commonest cause of cancer-related death in Western women) than from carcinoma of the cervix and uterine body combined because in ~80% it causes few symptoms until it has metastasized, often to the pelvis with omental and peritoneal seedlings (± lymphatic spread via the para-aortic nodes).

Incidence 1 in 2500 women >55yrs; 1 in 3800 if >25yrs. If *2 close relatives* affected lifetime ovarian cancer risk is 40% (liaise with a gynaecologist; see below). 10% of affected North American women carry mutations in *BRCA1* or *BRCA2* genes. Carrier risk of developing carcinoma is 40% for women with *BRCA1* mutation, 25% if *BRCA2*. It is commoner in those with many ovulations (*early menarche, nullipara*) and, possibly, after infertility treatment (p 294). Combined oral contraceptive Pill use reduces risk.

Presentation Symptoms are often vague and insidious and include abdominal pain, discomfort, and distension.

Screening There is really no good screening test. Transvaginal ultrasound with tumour blood flow measurement can differentiate between benign and malignant neoplasms at an early stage but does not seem to reduce mortality in high-risk women.[1] Plasma levels of cancer associated antigen (CA-125) lack sufficient sensitivity or specificity for population screening.[2]

Consider prophylactic oophorectomy when older women have hysterectomy. It is used for those with *BRCA1* & *2* mutations. The combined oral contraceptive Pill reduces the risk (up to 40%). Tubal ligation also reduces risk in those with *BRCA1* mutation.

Diagnosis Histology. Ascites, ultrasound/CT, and CA-125↑ suggestive.

Staging at laparotomy

Stage I: Disease limited to 1 or both ovaries.
Stage II: Growth extends beyond the ovaries but confined to the pelvis.
Stage III: Growth involving ovary and peritoneal implants outside pelvis (eg superficial liver), or +ve retroperitoneal or inguinal nodes.
Stage IV: Those with distant metastases (including liver parenchyma).

80% present with stage III or IV disease. 5-yr survival: Stage I, 67%; Stage II, 42%; Stage III and IV, 14.4%.

Treatment This depends on tumour type. Cystadenocarcinomas (80%) are treated with surgery and chemotherapy, which aims for cure. Surgery removes as much tumour as possible: the less left, the more effective is chemotherapy and the better the prognosis. In a young woman with early disease, the uterus and other ovary may be left, for fertility; if the tumour involves both ovaries, uterus and omentum are removed.

Chemotherapy for ~6 months post-op is usual. Carboplatin with paclitaxel (from Pacific yew trees) produces higher response rates and longer survival both when used for initial treatment and for treatment of recurrences compared to use of carboplatin alone.[3] Radiotherapy may be tried.

Further treatment may involve a 'second look' laparotomy, further chemotherapy, or radiotherapy. Colloidal gold may control ascites.

Advanced or relapsed ovarian cancer: see NICE. Options include paclitaxel, pegylated liposomal doxorubicin, and topotecan. Palliative care involves relief of symptoms, which are generally due to extensive peritoneal disease.

1 R Hogg 2004 *J Clin Oncol* **22** 1315 2 M Fung 2004 *J Obstet Gynaecol Can* **26** 717
3 D Dizon 2003 *Gynecol Oncol* **91** 584

Vaginal discharge[1]

Discharge may be physiological (eg pregnancy; sexual arousal; puberty; Pill). Most discharges are smelly, itchy, and due to infection. Foul discharge may be due to a foreign body (eg forgotten tampons, or beads in children).

Note the details of the discharge. Has she a sexually transmitted disease (STD)? See *OHCM* p 586. If so, refer to a genito-urinary clinic.

Do a speculum examination and take swabs: urine and endocervical samples for chlamydia (BOX); cervical swabs for gonorrhoea (*OHCM* p 586).

►Discharges rarely resemble their classical descriptions.

Thrush (*Candida*) The 2nd commonest cause of discharge (commonest is bacterial vaginosis), 95% is due to *C. albicans*, 5% *C. glabrata* (harder to treat).[2] Vulva and vagina may be red, fissured, and sore, especially if allergic component; discharge is non-offensive, classically white curds. Her partner may be asymptomatic. Pregnancy, contraceptive and other steroids, immunodeficiencies, antibiotics, and diabetes are risk factors—check for glycosuria. Candida elsewhere (eg mouth, natal cleft) of both partners may cause re-infection. Thrush is not necessarily sexually transmitted.

Diagnosis: Microscopy (shows mycelia or spores) and culture.

Treatment: Topical treatment (eg clotrimazole 500mg pessary + cream for the vulva) gives similar cure rates to oral fluconazole 150mg PO as a single dose. *C. glabrata* may require topical nystatin or 7-14 day course of imidazole. Use topical regimen alone if pregnant or breastfeeding. Very recurrent infection may be treated by weekly maintenance doses of treatment (unlicensed).

Trichomonas vaginalis (TV) This produces vaginitis and a thin, bubbly, fishy smelling discharge. It is sexually transmitted. Exclude gonorrhoea, which often coexists. The motile flagellate may be seen on a wet film (×400 magnification), or cultured. ***Treatment:*** Metronidazole 400mg/12h PO for 5 days or 2g PO stat; treat the partner; if pregnant, use the 5-day regimen.

Bacterial vaginosis Prevalence ~10% (UK), most are asymptomatic. If discharge, it has fishy odour, from cadaverine and putrescine. Vaginal pH is >4.5. The vagina is not inflamed and pruritus is uncommon. Mixed with 10% potassium hydroxide on a slide, a whiff of ammonia may be detected. Stippled vaginal epithelial 'clue cells' may be seen on wet microscopy. There is altered bacterial flora—overgrowth, eg of *Gardnerella vaginalis*, *Mycoplasma hominis*, peptostreptococci, *Mobiluncus* and anaerobes, eg *Bacteroides* species—with too few lactobacillae. There is increased risk of preterm labour, intra-amniotic infection in pregnancy, susceptibility to HIV-1, 27 and post-termination sepsis. ***Diagnosis:*** By culture.

Treatment: Metronidazole 2g PO once, gel PV, or clindamycin 2% vaginal cream, 1 applicatorful/night PV 7 times. If recurrent, treating the partner may help. If pregnant, use metronidazole 400mg/12h PO for 5 days.

Discharge in children may reflect infection from *faecal flora*, associated with alkalinity from lack of vaginal oestrogen (prepubertal atrophic vaginitis). *Staphs* and *streps* may cause pus. *Threadworms* cause pruritus. Always consider *sexual abuse*. Gentle rectal examination may exclude a *foreign body*.

Tests: Vulval ± vaginal swab (hard to know if result is normal flora).[3] MSU: *is there glycosuria?* For prolonged or bloody discharge, examine under anaesthesia (paediatric laryngoscopes can serve as specula) ± ultrasound or x-rays.

Management: Discuss hygiene. If an antibiotic is needed, erythromycin is a good choice. An oestrogen cream may be tried (≤1cm strip).

1 Melville C 2005 *J Fam Plann Reprod Health Care* **31** 26 (RTC) Discharge can be well-managed in primary care, despite no access to near-patient wet microscopy (compared with genito-urinary clinics).
2 An update on vulvovaginal candidiasis (thrush) MeReC 2003-4
3 Joishy M 2005 *BMJ* **330** 187

Testing for chlamydia

Special swabs/kits exist for chlamydia transport to the lab and conventional enzyme immunoassay assay—but may be unreliable (sensitivity ~79%).[28] An example is the *IDEIA chlamydia specimen collection kit*® with a Dacron® tip supplied by some labs.

First-void (early morning) urine may be the single best diagnostic specimen (for *M. genitalium* and *C. trachomatis*) detection by PCR. An additional ***endocervical specimen*** may also be needed.[29] In one study, sensitivities for LCR (ligase chain reaction), PCR (polymerase chain reaction), gene probe, and EIA (enzyme immuno-assay) on urine were 96, 86, 92, and 38%, respectively, while on cervical swabs the corresponding sensitivities of PCR, gene probe, and EIA were 89, 84, and 65%. DNA amplification methods may work best for urine and swabs in low-prevalence populations.[30]

Pelvic infection

Pelvic infection affects the Fallopian tubes (salpingitis) and may involve ovaries and parametra. 90% are sexually acquired, mostly chlamydia: 60% of these are asymptomatic (♀/♂=1:1) but infertility or ectopic pregnancy may be the result, *which is why screening has been proposed*—eg by a urine ligase chain reaction DNA: see BOX. Other causes, eg the gonococcus are rarer (14%—if found, retest after treatment). Organisms cultured from infected tubes are commonly different from those cultured from ectocervix, and are usually multiple. 10% follow childbirth or instrumentation (insertion of IUCD, ToP) and may be streptococcal. Infection can spread from the intestinal tract during appendicitis (Gram -ve and anaerobic organisms) or be blood-borne (tuberculosis).

Salpingitis Patients with ***acute salpingitis*** may be most unwell, with pain, fever, spasm of lower abdominal muscles (she may be most comfortable lying on her back with legs flexed) and cervicitis with profuse, purulent, or bloody vaginal discharge. Heavy menstrual loss suggests endometritis. Nausea and vomiting suggest peritonitis. Look for suprapubic tenderness or peritonism, cervical excitation, and tenderness in the fornices. It is usually bilateral, but may be worse on one side. ***Subacute infection*** can be easily missed, and laparoscopy may be needed to make either diagnosis.

Management ►Prompt treatment and contact-tracing minimizes complications. Take endocervical and urethral swabs if practicable. Remember to check for chlamydia. Admit for blood cultures and IV antibiotics if very unwell (eg ceftriaxone 2g/24h slow IV with doxycycline 100mg/12h PO) initially, then doxycycline 100mg/12h PO and metronidazole 400mg/12h PO until 14 days treated. Seek advice from microbiologist if gonorrhoea isolated.

If less unwell give ofloxacin 400mg/12h PO and metronidazole 400mg/12h PO for 14 days. If infection is severe remove intrauterine contraceptive device (not needed if mild).[1] Trace contacts (from within last 6 months and ensure they seek treatment—seek help of the genito-urinary clinic). Advise avoidance of intercourse until patient and partner treatments complete.

Complications If response to antibiotics is slow, consider laparoscopy. She may have an abscess (draining via the posterior fornix prevents perforation, peritonitis, and septicaemia—but laparotomy may be needed). Inadequate or delayed treatment leads to chronic infection and to long-term tubal blockage (8% are infertile after 1 episode, 19.5% after 2, 40% after 3). Advise that barrier contraception protects against infection. Ectopic pregnancy rate is increased 10-fold in those who do conceive.

Chronic salpingitis Unresolved, unrecognized, or inadequately treated infection may become chronic. Inflammation leads to fibrosis, so adhesions develop between pelvic organs. The tubes may be distended with pus (pyosalpinx) or fluid (hydrosalpinx).

Pelvic pain, menorrhagia, secondary dysmenorrhoea, discharge, and deep dyspareunia are some of the symptoms. She may be depressed. Look for tubal masses, tenderness, and fixed retroverted uterus. Laparoscopy differentiates infection from endometriosis.

Treatment is unsatisfactory. Consider long-term broad-spectrum antibiotics (eg tetracycline 250mg/6h PO 1h before food for 3 months), short-wave diathermy and analgesia for pain, and counselling. The only cures are the menopause or surgical removal of infected tissue.

1 RCOG *Guideline* 32 2003 *Management of acute pelvic inflammatory disease*

Screening tests to prevent chlamydial pelvic infection

Opportunistic screening in family planning and ToP contexts, and routine GP appointments for all sexually active women aged up to 25yrs has been suggested. This might miss up to 20% of infections (increasing the age limit to 30 might miss just 7%). It is not clear how this screening is to be woven into routine appointments (which are already overfull), and whether patients will find screening acceptable. What is clear is that chlamydia is common in the young, with rates of 8.1% prevalence in under 20s reported as having infection from general practice settings, and 17.3% from genitourinary settings.[1] In Scotland prevalence was found to be 12.1% in under 20s at antenatal clinics, 12.7% at abortion clinics and cost effectiveness studies suggest screening younger women attending these clinics and all attending colposcopy clinics as being the most cost effective.[2]

In the UK, some pharmacies (eg Boots) offer free chlamydia tests funded by the NHS—for those aged 16–24yrs (eg in London, and if +ve to their partners, whatever the age). There is also a national screening program that operates in colleges, prisons, and the armed forces.

Treatment of uncomplicated genital chlamydial infection is with azithromycin 1g PO as a single dose.

1 E Adams 2004 *lsfsnT* **80** 354

2 J Norman 2004 *BJOG* **111** 1261

Endometriosis

Foci of endometrial glandular tissue, looking like the head of a burnt match, occur beyond the uterine cavity, eg on an ovary (*chocolate cyst*), in the rectovaginal pouch, uterosacral ligaments, on pelvic peritoneum, and rarely in the umbilicus (fig 1), lower abdominal scars, and distant organs, eg lungs. If foci are found in uterine wall muscle, the term *adenomyosis* is used. Prevalence: ~10% of all women; 35-50% of those with infertility.

Cause Possibly cell rests, or retrograde menstruation (Sampson's theory, explaining its association with age—typically 40-44yrs, long duration of IUCD and tampon use, its negative association with pregnancy and the Pill, and its pelvic distribution, but not its appearance elsewhere). There are genetic components, autoantibody associations, and environmental factors.[31] Endometriotic foci are under hormonal influence with waning in pregnancy and (usually but not always[32]) at the menopause—and bleeding during menstruation. Free blood irritates, provoking fibrosis, adhesions and infertility.

Presentation Asymptomatic (even in extensive disease)—or pelvic pain (classically cyclical, at the time of periods). It may be constant, eg if due to adhesions. Secondary dysmenorrhoea and deep dyspareunia are common. Thigh pain and pain on defecation may occur. ►*Always think of endometriosis as an alternative to diagnosing irritable bowel syndrome.* Periods are often heavy and frequent, especially with adenomyosis. Patients may present with infertility. Extra-pelvic endometriosis causes pain or bleeding at the time of menstruation at the site of the pathology, eg haematuria or haemothorax.

Diagnosis *Per vaginam:* fixed retroverted uterus or uterosacral ligament nodules and general tenderness suggest endometriosis. An enlarged, boggy, tender uterus is typical of adenomyosis. MRI may help. Laparoscopy reveals cysts and peritoneal deposits, and differentiates it from chronic infection.

Treatment See p 241. If asymptomatic, don't treat. Join an endometriosis society,[1] as treatment can be long and difficult: ►*mutual support helps*. If analgesia/NSAIDs fail, consider the options below. Stress is a key exacerbating factor; address this too (p 386).[33] Don't forget other pain management methods.[2]

Hormonal therapy aims to suppress ovulation for 6-12 months during which some (non-GI) lesions atrophy. Don't use if pregnant or lactating. The *combined Pill* helps some (low dose monophasic, continuously). If insufficient, or contraindicated, or has bad side effects, consider *progestogens*—oral (eg continuous norethisterone), injected, or by IUCD (eg Mirena®, p 298—eg if adenomyosis) or *gonadotrophin releasing hormone* (GnRH) agonists.[34] Systematic reviews suggest GnRH agonists (eg leuproprelin) are most effective[35] but they are expensive, and long-term treatment is not possible because of loss of bone density. Side-effects are of those of premature menopause (oestrogen add back can alleviate side-effects but may make it less effective).

Surgery/laparoscopy Excision of endometriotic tissue is believed to be more effective, but less safe than ablation by bipolar diathermy/laser.[36] Alternative: total hysterectomy + bilateral salpingo-oophorectomy, depending on lesion site and wishes for fertility. Surgery may be best if symptoms seriously impinge on a patient's life, but relapse is common, and repeat surgery is often needed.

Complications Obstruction (GI; ureteric; fallopian); low-grade malignancy (rare; genes coding β-catenin implicated);[37] site of origin is often ovary (63%); *others:* vagina; fallopian tube; mesosalpinx; pelvic wall; colon; parametrium.[38]

Prognosis Endometriosis is chronic or relapsing, being progressive in 50%. Surgery minimally helps fertility, but is recommended by NICE. www.nice.org.uk

1 In the UK, 50 Artillery Road, London, tel. 0207 222 2776 www.endo.org.uk
2 ►Encourage optimism; discourage passive-dependency. Biofeed may ↓endometriosis pain.

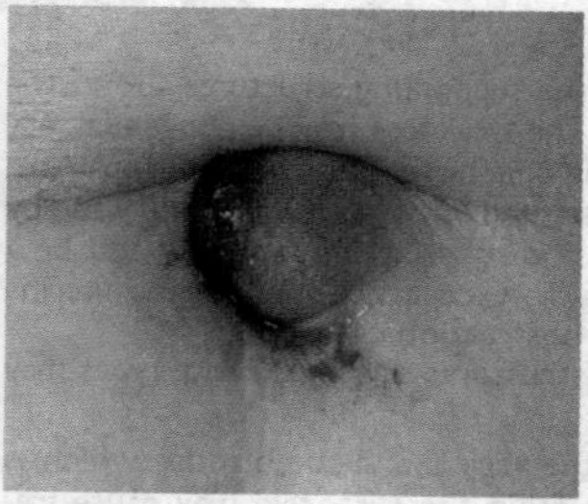

Fig 1. Endometriotic nodule in the umbilicus seen at menstruation.

Prolapse

A prolapse occurs when weakness of the supporting structures allows the pelvic organs to sag within the vagina. The weakness may be congenital, but it usually results from stretching during childbirth. Poor perineal repair reduces support (p 92). Weakness is exacerbated by menopausal atrophy and by coughing and straining. They may cause distressing incontinence and be a nuisance but are not a danger to health—except for third degree uterine prolapse with cystocele when ureteric obstruction can occur.

Types of prolapse are named by the structures sagging. Several types may coexist in the same patient.

Cystocele The upper front wall of the vagina, and the bladder which is attached to it, bulge. Residual urine within the cystocele may cause frequency and dysuria.

Urethrocele If the lower anterior vaginal wall bulges, this will displace the urethra and impair the sphincter mechanisms (p 306), so leading to stress incontinence. Does she leak when she laughs?

Rectocele The middle posterior wall, which is attached to rectum, may bulge through weak levator ani. It is often symptomless, but she may have to reduce herniation prior to defecation by putting a finger in the vagina.

Enterocele Bulges of the upper posterior vaginal wall may contain loops of intestine from the pouch of Douglas.

Uterine prolapse With *first degree prolapse* the cervix stays in the vagina. In *second degree prolapse* it protrudes from the introitus when standing or straining. With *third degree prolapse* (procidentia) the uterus lies outside the vagina. The vagina becomes keratinized and the cervix may ulcerate.

Symptoms: 'Dragging' or 'something coming down' is worse by day. Cystitis, frequency, stress incontinence, and difficulty in defecation may occur depending on the type of prolapse. Examine vaginal walls in left lateral position with a Sims' speculum, and ask the patient to bear down to demonstrate the prolapse. Do urodynamic studies (p 307) to exclude detrusor overactivity and to assess voiding.

Prevention: Lower parity; better obstetric practices, pelvic floor exercises.

Treatment: Mild disease may improve with reduction in intra-abdominal pressure, so encourage her to lose weight, stop smoking, and stop straining. Improve muscle tone with exercises or physiotherapy, and, if postmenopausal, topical oestrogens, eg estriol cream 0.1% as often as required (try twice weekly).

Severe symptomatic prolapse is best treated surgically. Incontinence needs to have the cause treated (so arrange urodynamic studies to plan the best type of surgery). Repair operations (p 308) excise redundant tissue and strengthen supports, but reduce vaginal width. Is she sexually active? If so, surgery must compromise between reducing prolapse and maintaining width. Marked uterine prolapse is best treated by hysterectomy.

Ring pessaries may be tried as a temporary measure or for the very frail. Select size by diameter of vagina at level of the fornices; it will only stay in if the vagina narrows nearer the introitus. Insert into the posterior fornix and tuck above the pubic bone (easier if the ring has been softened in hot water first). Problems: discomfort, infection, ulceration (change 6–12 monthly). For those in whom they keep falling out, try a shelf pessary.

Infertility: causes and tests

Infertility can be devastating to both partners. Its investigation is a tremendous strain, so sympathetic management is crucial. 84% of young couples having regular intercourse conceive within a year (92% by 2 years). Offer investigation after 1 year of trying (earlier if ♀ aged >35 years, amenorrhoea, oligomenorrhoea, past pelvic inflammatory disease, undescended testes or cancer treatments which may affect fertility). Arrange counselling throughout: fertility decreases with age. In the 10% of subfertile couples consider:
- Is she producing ova? (Anovulation causes 21%.)
- Is he producing enough healthy sperm? (Male factors cause 24%.)
- Are ova and sperm meeting? (Tubal cause 14%; coital problems ~6%, sexual dysfunction 6%.) Aim for intercourse 2–3 times/week throughout the cycle.
- Is the embryo implanting?

Endometriosis is thought to be the cause in 6%. The cause is unexplained in 27% of couples. With unexplained infertility 60–70% of women will achieve conception within 3 years.

Initial management It takes two to be infertile, see both partners. Advise both to stop smoking and for her to take 0.4mg folic acid daily whilst trying to conceive. If her body mass index is >29 encourage weight loss. Ask her about: Menstrual history, previous pregnancies and contraception, history of pelvic infections or abdominal surgery, drugs. Ask him about: puberty, previous fatherhood, previous surgery (hernias, orchidopexy, bladder neck surgery), illnesses (venereal disease and adult mumps), drugs, alcohol intake, job (is he home when ovulation occurs?). Ask both about: Technique, frequency, and timing of intercourse (nonconsummation is a rare problem); feelings about infertility and parenthood; previous tests.

Examination Check the woman's general health and sexual development and examine the abdomen and pelvis. If the sperm count is abnormal, examine the man for endocrine abnormalities, penile abnormalities, varicoceles; confirm there are 2 normal testes.

Tests for ovulation If cycles are regular ovulation is likely. Basal body temperature rises midcycle (but charting is difficult and may raise anxieties).

Blood tests Check rubella status: immunize if nonimmune. If you suspect anovulation check: • Serum progesterone 7 days before expected period (>30 nmol/L is indicative of ovulation). • FSH (>10U/L indicates a poor response to ovarian stimulation; it may indicate primary ovarian failure—but FSH is pulsatile in release and one may get a high reading depending on the stage of the cycle). • LH (for polycystic ovary syndrome) • TFT if symptomatic. • Blood prolactin if anovulation or galactorrhoea (if high, may be due to prolactinoma: MRI of brain and pituitary gland).

Semen analysis for: • Volume >2mL (mean 2.75mL now, formerly 3.4mL in the 1940s) • sperm count/morphology • infection. Normal count >20 million sperm/mL, ≥50% motile within 1h of ejaculate production (the ejaculation also within 1h) and ≥30% normal forms (WHO: ≥15 million/mL). Mean sperm count ~66 million/mL (113 million/mL in the 1940s; this change is falling—which may be due to environmental influences—or more frequent ejaculations). Examine 2 specimens (ideally 3 months apart so spermatozoa cycle completed) but also, if sperm severely deficient, karyotyping may be considered. Transport sample fresh to lab (masturbated into a wide-topped container). Avoid temperatures <15°C or >38°C. Reduced counts require specialist referral.

Infertility: causes and tests

►*Infertility can be devastating to both partners:* its investigation a tremendous strain. Sympathetic management is crucial. 84% of young couples having regular intercourse conceive within a year (92% by 2 years). Offer investigation after 1 year of trying (earlier if ♀ aged ≥35 years, amenorrhoea, oligomenorrhoea, or past pelvic inflammatory disease, undescended testes or cancer treatments which may affect fertility). Arrange counselling throughout. Fertility decreases with age. In the 10% of subfertile couples consider:

- Is she producing ova? (Anovulation causes 21%.)
- Is he producing enough, healthy sperm? (Male factors cause 24%.)
- Are ova and sperm meeting? (Tubal cause 14%, hostile mucus 3%, sexual dysfunction 6%.) Aim for intercourse 3 times/week throughout the cycle.
- Is the embryo implanting?

Endometriosis is thought to be the cause in 6%. The cause is 'unexplained' in 27% of couples. With 'unexplained' infertility 60–70% of women will achieve conception within 3 years.

Initial management It takes two to be infertile. See both partners. Advise both to stop smoking and for her to take 0.4mg folic acid daily whilst trying to conceive. If her body mass index is >29 encourage weight loss. ***Ask her about:*** Menstrual history, previous pregnancies and contraception, history of pelvic infections or abdominal surgery, drugs. ***Ask him about:*** Puberty, previous fatherhood, previous surgery (hernias, orchidopexy, bladder neck surgery), illnesses (venereal disease and adult mumps), drugs, alcohol intake, job (is he home when ovulation occurs?). ***Ask both about:*** Technique, frequency, and timing of intercourse (nonconsummation is a rare problem); feelings about infertility and parenthood; previous tests.

Examination Check the woman's general health and sexual development and examine the abdomen and pelvis. If the sperm count is abnormal, examine the man for endocrine abnormalities, penile abnormalities, varicoceles; confirm there are 2 normal testes.

Tests for ovulation If cycles are regular ovulation is likely. Basal body temperature rises midcycle (but charting is difficult and may raise anxieties).

Blood tests Check rubella status; immunize if nonimmune. If you suspect anovulation check: • Serum progesterone 7 days before expected period (>30nmol/L is indicative of ovulation) • FSH (>10U/L indicates a poor response to ovarian stimulation; it may indicate primary ovarian failure—but FSH is pulsatile in release and one may get a high reading depending on the stage of the cycle) • LH (for polycystic ovary syndrome) • TFT if symptomatic; • Blood prolactin if anovulation or galactorrhoea (if high may be due to prolactinoma; MRI of brain and pituitary gland).

Semen analysis for: • Volume >2mL (mean 2.75mL now, formerly 3.4mL in the 1940s) • Sperm count/morphology. • Infection. Normal count >20 million sperm/mL, >50% motile within 1h of ejaculate production (liquefaction also within 1h), and >30% normal form; WBC < 1 million/mL; mean sperm count = 66 million/mL (113 million/mL in the 1940s; this average is falling—which may be due to an environmental influence—or more frequent ejaculations). Examine 2 specimens (ideally 3 months apart so spermatozoa cycle completed but soon if sperm severely deficient) as variation may be considerable. Transport sample fresh to lab (masturbated into a wide topped container). Avoid temperatures <15°C or >38°C. Reduced counts require specialist referral.

Subfertility options: abbreviations, problems, and ethics[1]

DI	Donor insemination (In some countries, children have no rights to information about their father: this can lead to problems—eg most children want their fathers to be proud of them, and with DI this is impossible.)[2] The great metaphysical questions such as *where do I come from* become more opaque than ever. In the UK, legislation is due in 2006 to enable tracing of fathers.
FEC	Fetal egg child (offspring from an egg taken from the ovary of an aborted fetus).
ICSI	Intracytoplasmic sperm injection (directly into an egg). If necessary, the sperm may be obtained surgically from the testis or epidydimis. Such patients, with no exposure to their partner's sperm, are at increased risk of pre-eclampsia (p 48): this supports a model of pre-eclampsia postulating absence of partner-specific immune tolerance as a causative factor.[3]
IUI	Intrauterine insemination with superovulation: a USA favourite. In 20%, this causes twins (in 10%, higher order pregnancies when pregnancy is achieved; a possibly unacceptable disadvantage).[4]
IVF	*In vitro* fertilization
GIFT	Gamete intrafallopian transfer
MESA	Microepididymal sperm aspiration from testis, post-vasectomy
OT/NT(P)	Ooplasmic transfer/nuclear transfer procedure: the baby has 2 mothers: one (too old to conceive normally) provides a nucleus; the other provides fresher cytoplasm (+mitochondrial DNA) for the ovum. This is an example of human germline modification which is legal in the USA, but illegal in the UK.[5]
PESA	Percutaneous epididymal sperm aspiration (rather like MESA, but using a 22G butterfly needle inserted into the epididymis—so scrotal exploration is not required).
PHC	Pregnancy by human cloning (illegal in many countries partly because of concern about premature ageing—but achieved by Italian doctors, up to 8 weeks gestation, in April 2002).
POST	Peritoneal oocyte sperm transfer
POT	Pregnancy by ovary transplantation (China leads the field in ovarian transplantation).
SUZI	Subzonal sperm injection (directly into an egg)
TET	Tubal embryo transfer
TUFT	Transuterine fallopian transfer
ZIFT	Zygote intrafallopian transfer

Ethical issues

Various national embryology authorities exist and pronounce on the ethical dimensions of fertility treatments—and their edicts can appear to be set in stone (although being mutually contradictory with those from other countries); one problem with this approach is that fertility treatments are constantly changing, as is society's views on what is acceptable—and it is not clear whether these views should lead, or simply be taken into account (an opaque phrase) or be trumped by appeal to some higher authority (God, or the conscience of a quango).

1 E Velde 1999 *NEJM* **340** 224
2 Anon 2002 *BMJ* **i** 797
3 S Bhattacharya 2000 *NEJM* **343** 58
4 J Wang 2002 *Lancet* **359** 673
5 A Ferriman 2001 *BMJ* **i** 1144

Infertility: tests and treatment

Tests of tubal patency (Screen for chlamydia first).

Unless damaged tubes are expected do hysterosalpingogram (or hysterosalpingo-contrast ultrasonography) first.

1 A hysterosalpingogram (contrast x-ray) demonstrates uterine anatomy and tubal 'fill and spill'. Unpleasant, it may require premedication. False positives may occur with tubal spasm. Give antibiotics, eg cefradine 500mg/8h PO with metronidazole 1g/12h PR for 24h before and eg 400mg/12h PO for 5 days after procedure, to prevent pelvic infection.

2 Laparoscopy with dye. Pelvic organs are visualized and methylene blue dye injected through the cervix: if tubes are blocked proximally they do not fill with dye; with distal block there is no 'spill' into the peritoneal cavity.

Treatment of infertility Treatment is directed at the cause.

Azoospermia is unresponsive to treatment. A low sperm count may be improved by avoiding tobacco and alcohol. Avoiding tight pants does not change testis T° or semen parameters. Will they consider donor insemination (AID=artificial insemination by donor)? If so check ♀ ovulating, if tubal damage suspected, investigate. Give 3 cycles of intrauterine insemination (IUI) post ovulation, if unsuccessful do tubal investigations, then further 3 cycles. If still unsuccessful offer other treatment.

Problems of sperm deposition (eg erectile dysfunction) can be circumvented by artificial insemination using the partner's sperm.

Hyperprolactinaemia (*OHCM* p 322) Remove the cause if one is found (pituitary macro-adenoma, drugs); if not, give bromocriptine 2.5mg/24h PO, increasing slowly until blood prolactin is normal. (Side effect: nausea.)

Anovulation World Health Organization classification: • Class 1 is hypothalamic pituitary failure (this responds to pulsed gonadotrophin releasing hormone or gonadotrophins with luteinizing hormone activity): • Class 2 is hypothalamic pituitary dysfunction (usually polycystic ovary syndrome, see p 252): Class 2 is managed by stimulating follicle development using clomifene 50-150mg/24h PO on days 2-6 inclusive. SE: flushes (10%), visual disturbance (1.5%), abdominal pain (5.5%—see p 311); warn about risk of multiple pregnancy ± excess risk of ovarian cancer (p 280). Monitor response to clomifene with luteal phase progesterone (+ ultrasound in at least 1st cycle). If clomifene does not induce ovulation, try gonadotrophins. After 6 months ovulating offer clomifene assisted IUI if not pregnant. • Class 3 is ovarian failure (treatment is IVF, see *below* using donated ova).

Tubal problems may respond to surgery but results are poor. Proximal blocks may respond to tubal catheterisation or hysteroscopic cannulation. For ***endometriosis*** see p 288. If amenorrhoeic with ***intrauterine adhesions*** use hysteroscopic adhesiolysis.

Assisted fertilization Screen couple for HIV, hepatitis B & C. Women with hydrosalpinges should have salpingectomy prior to IVF to ↑chance of live birth. Psychological stability is required in the UK (some non-UK clinics are happy to give IVF eg to single women >65yrs old).[1] Chance of live birth per treatment cycle is age dependent: 20% if ♀ aged ≤35; 15% if 36-38; 10% if 39; 6% if ≥40. *In vitro* fertilization (IVF) is used for tubal (and other) problems. The ovaries are stimulated (see *hyperstimulation* p 311), and ova are collected (by transvaginal aspiration under transvaginal ultrasound guidance), fertilized, and 2 embryos returned under ultrasound guidance to the uterus as an outpatient procedure.

The possibility of adoption should not be forgotten. Those who remain childless may value counselling or a self-help group.

1 In 2005 the world's oldest mother gave birth to her first child when aged 66 years—via IVF.

Male infertility

Spermatogenesis takes place in the seminiferous tubules. Undifferentiated diploid germ cells (spermatogonia) multiply and are then transformed into haploid spermatozoa, a process taking 74 days. FSH and LH are both important for initiation of spermatogenesis at puberty. LH stimulates Leydig cells to produce testosterone. Testosterone and FSH stimulate Sertoli cells to produce essential substances for metabolic support of germ cells and spermatogenesis.

Spermatozoa A spermatozoon has a dense oval head (containing the haploid chromosome complement), capped by an acrosome granule (contains enzymes essential for fertilization) and is propelled by the motile tail. Seminal fluid forms 90% of ejaculate volume and is alkaline to buffer vaginal acidity. Only about 200 sperm from any ejaculate reach the middle third of the Fallopian tube, the site of fertilization.

Male infertility Male factors are the cause of infertility in ~24% of infertile couples. In reality, most are subfertile. Only a small number of men have an identifiable cause. Causes include (% cited in one study):

- Idiopathic oligo/azoospermia (16%): Testes are usually small and FSH ↑.
- Asthenozoospermia/teratozoospermia (17%): In asthenozoospermia sperm motility is reduced due to structural problems with the tails. Teratozoospermia indicates an excess of abnormal forms.
- Varicocele (17%): this is controversial for varicocele is found in 15% of males, most of whom have normal fertility.
- Genital tract infection (4%): gonococci, chlamydia, & Gram -ve enterococci cause adnexal infection (± painful ejaculation, urethral discharge, haematospermia, dysuria, tender epididymes, tender boggy prostate). Confirm by semen culture, urethral swab or finding $>10^6$ peroxidase +ve polymorphs/mL semen. Treatment has not been shown to restore fertility.
- Sperm autoimmunity (1.6%): *Risk factors for antibodies:* vasectomy, testis injury, genital tract obstruction, family history of autoimmunity. Most are on sperm membranes or in seminal fluid, but may occur in the woman.
- Congenital (cryptorchidism, chromosome disorders—2%): Klinefelter's account for 50% chromosome disorders. For optimal fertility undescended testes should be fixed in the scrotum before 2yrs of age.
- Obstructive azoospermia (1.8%): Azoospermia, normal sized testes with normal or high FSH suggests this. It may follow infection, vasectomy, or be congenital (as in cystic fibrosis). It may be amenable to surgery, eg epididymovasostomy to bypass epididymal obstruction.
- Systemic—eg iatrogenic, or from drugs, eg cannabis (1.3%). 39
- Coital disorders (1%).
- Gonadotrophin deficiency (0.6%): this is the only cause of testicular failure consistently treatable by hormone replacement.

Examination Look at body form and secondary sexual characteristics. Any gynaecomastia? Normal testicular volume is 15-35mL (compare with Prader orchidometer). Rectal examination may reveal prostatitis.

Tests *Semen analysis* (p 292). *Plasma FSH* distinguishes primary from secondary testicular failure. *Testosterone and LH* levels are indicated if you suspect androgen deficiency. *Agglutination tests* to detect antibodies.

Treatment Intracytoplasmic sperm injection (direct into egg) is the main tool for most male infertility. The source of sperm is the epididymis or testis in men with obstructive azoospermia; even if the problem is non-obstructive, sperm can be retrieved in ~50%.

Contraception

►*Any method, even coitus interruptus, is better than none.* Without contraception about 85 of every 100 premenopausal sexually active women will become pregnant each year. Properly used, contraception reduces this rate (see OPPOSITE). When dealing with under-16s use Fraser Guidelines (BOX).

Barrier methods ►The main reason for failure is not using them. Sheaths (condoms) reduce transmission of most STDs but not those affecting the perineum. Caps give some protection against gonorrhoea and chlamydia but not syphilis or herpes. Some spermicides inactivate HIV *in vitro*. When failure is anticipated (eg 'split sheath'), remember post-coital emergency contraception (p 299).

- **Sheaths** are effective when properly used and with spermicides. Unroll onto the erect penis with the teat or end (if teatless) pinched to expel air. This prevents bursting at ejaculation.
- **Caps** come in several forms. Diaphragms stretch from pubic bone to posterior fornix. She must check after insertion that the cervix is covered. Cervical caps fit over the cervix (so need a prominent cervix). Insert <2h before intercourse (keep in place >6h after sex). Use with a spermicide. Some find them unaesthetic. Problems: UTIs, rubber sensitivity.
- **Cervical sponges** These are simple but often fail.
- **The female condom** (eg Femidom®) Prescription and fitting are not needed. It has not proved popular. One reason for failure is that the penis goes alongside it, rather than in it; another, that it gets pushed up in the vagina or may fall out. They can be noisy.
- **Spermicides** This is unreliable unless used with a barrier.

Natural (mucothermal) methods involve monitoring physiological phenomena to find fertile times (6 days prior to ovulation; the life of a sperm) to 2 days afterwards (the life of the ovum). Cervical mucus becomes clear and sticky at the beginning of the fertile time and dry at ovulation (but is altered by semen and vaginal infections). Basal body temperature ↑~0.3°C after ovulation (affected by fevers, drugs, recent food, or drink). Additional observations (mittelschmerz, p 310 ± cervix changes) improve accuracy. Success is common if: •Regular cycles •Dedication •Self-control. UK teachers are available (tel. 01222 754628).

High-technology natural methods Devices such as Persona® use solid-state urine chemistry on sticks for dual measurements of the oestrogen oestrone-3-glucuronide (E3G—peaks 24h pre-ovulation) and luteinizing hormone (LH—ovulation occurs within 36h of LH surge and sperm penetration through cervical mucus drops after the surge). Microtechnology builds up a database of the woman's natural variability over time, and this is used to give her either a green light (almost infertile), a red light (fertile—typically days 6-10) or an orange light (do an early-morning urine test for E3G and LH). Usually, only 8 urine tests are needed per cycle. She needs to purchase sticks and one monitor (this houses a button to press the morning her period starts: she needs to check the lights on the monitor before passing urine each morning, in case a test is needed). ***Reliability:*** 93-95% (manufacturer's data, in motivated patients: it may be much less in practice; results must be regarded as only preliminary: explain uncertainty to your patient). *CI:* Cycle <23 or >35 days or variation >10 days; breastfeeding; if already on hormones or tetracycline (minocycline is OK); menopausal; liver or kidney disease; polycystic ovary disease, or if pregnancy is definitely unwanted.

Further information: UK Family Planning Assocn, 2 Pentonville Rd, London NI 0207 837 4044

The ideal contraceptive—and the realities

An ideal contraceptive is: 100% *effective*, with only *desirable side-effects* (eg protection from sexually transmitted disease)—and it must be *readily reversible*, and be usable *unsupervised by professionals*. Try to find the best compromise for each person depending on age, health, and beliefs. Methods available:

- 'Natural methods' (no intercourse near time of ovulation)—acceptable to Catholic Church; also, the simplest are free, requiring no 'pollution of the body' with drugs—see OPPOSITE.
- Barrier methods (low health risk but need high user motivation—with some protection to HIV). See OPPOSITE.
- Hormonal (complex health risks but highly effective, p 300–3).
- IUCD (convenient and effective—if not contraindicated—p 298).
- Sterilization (very effective but effectively irreversible, p 305).

Failure rates are described per 100 women/yrs ie the number of women per 100 using the method who may become pregnant each year.

They are: for no method 85; cervical cap 30; spermicides 21; female condom 21; withdrawal 20; male condom 12; progesterone only Pill 3; copper coil 0.22 (for T-Safe® Cu380A); depot injection 0.3; tubal ligation 0.17; combined Pill 0.08; vasectomy 0.04.

'Is she pregnant already?'

This is a frequent question in family planning and other clinics. If a pregnancy test is not available, women who may be pregnant already will often be denied the contraception they need. Here, consider using this check list to see if the patient may be pregnant. If she answers Yes to ***any*** of these questions, and she is free from signs or symptoms of pregnancy, then pregnancy is very unlikely (negative predictive value >99%).

- Have you given birth in the past 4 weeks?
- Are you <6 months postpartum **and** fully breastfeeding, **and** free from menstrual bleeding since you had your child?
- Did your last menstrual period start within the last 7 days?
- Have you been using a reliable contraceptive consistently and correctly?
- Have you not had sex since your last period?[40]

Fraser guidelines (Gillick competence)

A young person (<16y) may be prescribed contraception in the absence of parental consent if:

- They understand the doctor's advice.
- The young person cannot be persuaded to inform their parents that they are seeking contraceptive advice.
- They are likely to begin or continue intercourse with or without contraceptive treatment.
- Unless the young person receives contraceptive treatment their physical or mental health is likely to suffer.
- The young person's best interests require that the doctor gives advice and/or treatment without parental consent.

The intrauterine contraceptive device (IUCD)

IUCDs (coils) are plastic shapes ~3cm long with copper wire wound around, and a plastic thread from the tail. They inhibit implantation and may impair sperm migration. Most need changing every 2–8 years. The larger, noncopper-bearing 'inert' types (eg Lippes loop®), caused more complications but did not need changing (still sometimes found *in situ*). Use those with ≥300mm² eg T-Safe® Cu380A,[1] for which pregnancy rate is 2.2 per 100 ♀ years. Most of those who choose the IUCD (5%) are older, parous women in stable relationships, in whom the problem rate is low.

Problems with IUCDs **1** They tend to be expelled (5%) by a uterus which is nulliparous or distorted (eg by fibroids). **2** They are associated with pelvic infection and infertility, following sexually transmitted disease—or sometimes introduced during insertion. **3** They tend to produce heavy, painful periods. ***Contraindications:*** Pregnancy; current pelvic infection (including TB); current STD; trophoblastic disease; ca ovary, endometrium or cervix, distorted uterine cavity. If prosthetic heart valve or previous IE insert and remove under IV antibiotic cover. Screen high-risk ♀ (eg age <25y) for STD prior to insertion or use prophylactic antibiotics.

Insertion Skilled insertion minimizes complications. Each device has its own technique, so read the instructions carefully and practise beforehand.

An IUCD can be inserted any time (and as postcoital contraception), as long as she's not pregnant. Insert <48h or 4 weeks after birth. Determine the position of the uterus. Then insert a uterine sound to assess the cavity length. Then insert the IUCD, placing it in the fundus. This may cause cramps. Uterine perforation rate is <1:1000. Once the coil is in place, cut threads to leave 3cm visible in the vagina. Teach her to feel the threads: ask her to check after each period. ►Insertion of IUCDs may provoke 'cervical shock' (from increased vagal tone). Have IV atropine and resuscitation equipment to hand.

Follow-up Most expulsions (5%) are in the first 3 months. Follow up after 1st period. Threads after may be easier to feel than to see.

Lost threads The IUCD may have been expelled, so advise extra contraception and exclude pregnancy. Seek coil on ultrasound; if missing arrange x-ray to exclude extra-uterine coils (surgical retrieval advised).

Infection Treat with the device in place, but if removed do not replace for 3 months. With symptomatic Actinomyces, remove coil, cut off threads and send for culture. If positive, seek expert advice on treatment.

Pregnancy >90% are intrauterine. Remove coil, if you can as soon as pregnancy is diagnosed to reduce risk of miscarriage (20% if removed early, 50% if left), and to prevent late septic abortion. Exclude ectopic.

Removal Alternative contraception should be started (if desired) prior to removal, or a fertilized ovum may be in the tubes. At the menopause, remove after 2y amenorrhoea if age <50y; 1y amenorrhoea if age >50y.

IUCDs carrying hormones—eg Mirena® (carries levonorgestrel). Local effects make implantation less likely, and periods lighter; perhaps 20% may experience reversible amenorrhoea (reliability matches that of sterilization, see p 305). It lasts ~5 years. There may be less risk of ectopic pregnancy. Risk of some sexually transmitted infections is reduced. Warn about spotting ± heavy bleeding (NB: bleeding may become *scanty* or *absent* after a few cycles).

1 *J Fam Plan and Reprod Health Care* 2004 **30** 29

Emergency contraception

This is for use after isolated episodes of unprotected intercourse (UPSI), eg 'the split sheath' and should not be used regularly.

Management History of LMP; normal cycle; number of hours since unprotected intercourse; history of personal thromboembolism or focal migraine. Check BP. Explain that teratogenicity has not been demonstrated. Discuss future contraception. Give supply of oral contraceptives if day 1 start at next period is planned. Arrange follow-up at 3–4 weeks.

Levonorgestrel This is with progesterone-only Pills initiated within 72 hours of unprotected intercourse. It is suitable for those with focal migraine and past thromboembolism. It is not suitable for those with acute active porphyria. Dose of levonorgestrel: 1.5mg (1 Levonelle-1500® tablet) preferably within 12h and no later than 72h after unprotected intercourse. If vomiting occurs within 3h of taking the tablet, take another immediately. The failure rate is about 1.1%. The earlier it is taken after unprotected intercourse, the fewer the pregnancies which occur. In fact 1.5mg levonorgestrel has some protective effect up to 120 hours. If on enzyme inducers (p 300) take also further 0.75mg 12h later.

When prescribing post-coital hormonal contraception warn that the first period may be early or late; that barrier contraception should be used until the next period; and that she should return if she suffers any lower abdominal pain or the next period is abnormal.

Recent UK initiatives: Levonelle® may now be bought 'over the counter'—and lessons on its use are being conducted in schools, particularly emphasizing the 72h time limit, rather than just 'the morning after'. Although it is usually given after UPSI advance issue does not increase use and may be sensible to 'be prepared'. ('Carrying an umbrella in the British climate is considered sensible not a wish for rain.')[1]

The emergency IUCD More effective than hormonal contraception, a copper IUCD can be inserted within 120 hours of unprotected intercourse. If exposure was more than 5 days previously it can be inserted up to 5 days after likely ovulation, so is useful in women who present later. Failure rates are extremely low. Infection is a risk (eg after sexual assault) and should be screened for, if suspected. It is possible to insert under antibiotic cover. It inhibits implantation.

1 A Webb 2004 *J Fam Plann Reprod Health Care* **30** 7

Hormonal contraception (the Pill)

3 million women in the UK take the combined oral contraceptive (COC). COCs contain oestrogen (eg ethinylestradiol) with a progestogen, either in fixed ratio or varying through the month (phased). Low-dose Pills (≤30μg oestrogen) are the norm. The combined Pill is taken daily for 3 weeks followed by a week's break. This inhibits ovulation, giving a withdrawal bleed in the Pill-free week. When prescribing COCs, pay attention to these areas:

History Why does she want the Pill? Does she know about risks? These must be explained. Has she considered the alternatives? Are there contraindications? Ask about smoking (see below) and drugs, and about contact lenses (Pill use may cause dry eyes). Does she have any anxieties, eg weight-gain? Can she be helped to stop smoking? If 1st degree relative with thromboembolism <45y do thrombophilia screen.

Contraindications These are legion; check *BNF*. Obesity (body mass index BMI >39kg/m^2); diabetes with complications; BP consistently >140/90; smoking >40/day; age >50yrs; migraine as described on p 301; past history of venous or arterial thrombosis; thrombophilia p 33; heart disease with pulmonary hypertension or embolus risk; transient ischaemic attacks; liver disorders, eg adenoma, gallstones, Dubin-Johnson and Rotor syndromes (*OHCM* p 734), pre-recovered hepatitis; porphyria; systemic lupus erythematosus; past haemolytic uraemic syndrome, pruritus or cholestatic jaundice of pregnancy, pemphigoid gestationis, hydatidiform mole (until experts advise safe); chorea; deteriorating otosclerosis; breast or genital tract tumours; breastfeeding (<6months, not weaning off), undiagnosed vaginal bleeding; immobility (in bed/leg in plaster cast).

Cautions See *BNF*. Hyperprolactinaemia (unless specialist advice); sickle-cell disease; inflammatory bowel disease (eg Crohn's); severe depression.

Venous risk factors: Prescribe with caution if one of the following (avoid if ≥2 risk factors are present): obesity (BMI >30kg/m^2); varicose veins (avoid during sclerotherapy); immobility (wheelchair).

Arterial risk factors: Prescribe with caution if one of the following (avoid if 2 or more): smoker; age >35yrs; migraine without aura; obesity (BMI >30kg/m^2); diabetes mellitus, family history of first degree relative arterial disease <45yrs (avoid if known atherogenic lipid profile).

Drugs interfering with the Pill ***Liver enzyme inducers***, eg some anticonvulsants,[1] griseofulvin, and rifampicin reduce efficacy by ↓ circulating oestrogen. If short-term use, take extra precautions (p 302) whilst used and for 28 days after. With long-term use consider using 50μg oestrogen Pills with higher doses of progesterone, eg Norinyl-1®. Use another type of contraceptive if on long-term rifampicin. ***Antibiotics:*** p 302.

Benefits of the Pill Very effective contraception; lighter, less painful 'periods'. In long-term users, reduced risk of ovarian tumours (carcinoma ↓ 40%) and endometrial carcinoma (↓ 50%).

Serious disadvantages Risks of arterial and venous disease are increased, eg DVT and myocardial infarction. Risk of death from the Pill increases sharply in those >40yrs: 1:2500 for nonsmokers; 1:500 for smokers. *Breast cancer:* In one large retrospective study (n=9257)[41] in women aged 35–64yrs, current or former Pill use was not associated with a significantly increased risk of breast cancer. But in younger women, rates may rise from ~0.2% to ~0.3%. The Pill acts as a co-factor with human papilloma virus to increase risk of invasive cervical cancer.[42]

1 Enzyme inducers: carbamazepine, oxcarbazepine, phenobarbital, phenytoin, primidone, topiramate.

Migraine, ischaemic stroke, and the Pill

The problem is ischaemic stroke. The background annual incidence is 2 per 100,000 women aged 20, and 20 per 100,000 for those aged 40. Migraine itself is a risk factor. For those with migraine and CoC use, incidence of ischaemic stroke becomes 8:100,000 if aged 20; and 80:100,000 in those aged 40. Low-dose CoCs only should be used. Those with migraine with aura are known to be at special risk precluding use of combined Pills in these women (however, there is no problem with them using progesterone only or non-hormonal contraception). Other risk factors for ischaemic stroke include smoking, age >35yrs, raised BP, obesity (body mass index >30), diabetes mellitus, hyperlipidaemia and family history of arterial disease <45yrs. Women known to have migraine should be warned to stop Pills immediately if they develop aura or worsening of migraine. If a woman has 1st migraine attack on CoC, stop it, observe closely: restart cautiously only if there are no sequelae and if migraine attack was without aura and there are no other risk factors (above).[43]

Diagnosing migraine with aura (Formerly called *classical/focal migraine*.)

- Slow evolution of symptoms (see below) over several minutes.
- Duration of aura usually 10–30min, resolving within 1h, and typically before onset of headache.
- Visual symptoms (99% of auras), eg:
  - Bilateral homonymous hemianopia.
  - Teichopsia and fortification spectra, eg a gradually enlarging C  with scintillating edges.
  - Positive (bright) scotomata.
- Sensory disturbance (31% of auras).
  - Usually associated with visual symptoms.
  - Usually in one arm spreading from fingers to face (leg rarely affected).
- Speech disturbance (18% of auras):
  - Dysphasia; dysarthria; paraphasia.
- Motor disturbances (6% of auras).

Both motor and speech disturbances are usually accompanied by visual and/or sensory disturbances.

Migraine without aura: (Formerly called *simple* or *common* migraine) includes symptoms of blurred vision, photophobia, phonophobia, generalized flashing lights affecting the whole visual field in both eyes, associated with headache.

Absolute contraindications to CoC use

- Migraine with aura.
- Migraine without aura in women with >1 risk factor for stroke.
- Severe migraine or status migrainosus (>72h).
- Migraine treated with ergot derivatives.

Hormonal contraception: further details

Do BP 6-monthly. Do a cervical smear if due (p 270). Adverse effects are dose-related: aim for lowest dose Pill that gives good cycle control (ie no breakthrough bleeding). ►If breakthrough bleeds screen for chlamydia.

Progesterone issues Norethisterone and levonorgestrel-containing CoCs may cause breakthrough bleeding, acne, headaches, weight↑, so prompting a search for newer progesterones, eg gestodene or desogestrel (Femodene®, Marvelon®, Minulet®, Mercilon®, Triadene®, Triminulet®), but see problems with thrombosis (p 303). These *may* have a role in those without risk factors for thrombosis (p 300), in those with arterial risk factors (p 300), or bad acne. Overall, risk of death with newer Pills from PE *is* higher than expected (eg ≥1/100,000/yr).

Drospirenone (DRSP; Yasmin®) is a spironolactone-like progesterone with antiandrogenic/antimineralocorticoid action (said not to ↑weight; useful in those with acne or polycystic ovaries); clotting may still be a problem.[44]

Switching from PoP: *If to a CoC*, start on day 1 of period. Use condoms for 7 days. *If to a progesterone-only Pill (PoP)*, start as the old pack finishes.

Switching from CoC: *If to a CoC*, start immediately with no Pill-free interval. *If to a PoP*, start immediately the *CoC* packet is finished.

Starting CoCs and PoPs Day 1 of cycle, or on the day of ToP, or 3 weeks postpartum or 2 weeks after full mobilization after major surgery. With day 1-3 CoC starting regimen, contraceptive cover is immediate; use other precautions for 7 days with PoP and if CoC started day 4 or 5 of period.

Stopping the Pill Tell to stop at once if she develops: •Sudden severe chest pain •Sudden breathlessness (or cough with bloody sputum) •Severe calf pain •Severe stomach pain •Unusual severe prolonged headache. See cautions on p 300; low-risk nonsmokers may continue into their 40s. On stopping, 66% menstruate by 6 weeks, 98% by 6 months; women who are amenorrhoeic after the Pill were usually so before.

Missed Pills (or diarrhoea): Encourage users to know and understand package inserts, as advice varies. Recent WHO advice that backup condoms are not required until ≥3 30–35μg Pills or ≥2 20μg Pills are missed is probably too lax.[45] In general, if the delay is >24h, continue Pills but use condoms too for 7 days (+ days of diarrhoea); if this includes Pill-free days, start next pack *with no break* (omitting inactive Pills in 'ED' formulations). Use condoms during and for 7 days after antibiotics. If Pill from 1st 7 days in pack is forgotten, consider postcoital contraception. ***Vomiting <3h post-Pill:*** Take another. ***Postcoital options:*** p 299.

Progestogen-only Pills (PoP=mini-Pill) Low-dose progestogen renders cervical mucus hostile to sperm. Cerazette® (desogestrel 75μg) is, according to some authorities (Guillebaud)[46] *the* PoP of choice for new users, as it also inhibits ovulation in 97%. This also means it isn't contraindicated if past ectopic—older PoPs are—and they also need to be taken at the same time (±3h *vs* ?±12h for Cerazette®; further data needed). PoPs can be used in most women with problems contraindicating combined Pills (also if lactating). Avoid if on enzyme inducers (p 300). Extra precautions are needed for 48h for late Pills. Older PoPs still have a role, eg in less fertile women (≥45yrs old or lactating).

Postnatal Start 21 days after birth: eg CoC if not breastfeeding; PoP, Depo-Provera® (or ?Implanon®) if breastfeeding. IUCD: fit ~4 weeks postpartum.

At the menopause Stop PoP if >50yrs old with >1 year's amenorrhoea (2yrs if <50yrs old)—as a rough guide. A spermicide and sponge may then be adequate in view of declining fertility. As CoC masks the menopause, aim to stop at 50yrs, and replace with a nonhormonal method.

Buying the Pill over the counter This might be safe for non-smokers with no hypertension who are having regular cervical smears.

Terminology

1st generation Pills are the original Pills containing 50μg oestrogen. *2nd generation Pills* are those containing ≤ 35μg oestrogen and levonorgestrel, norethisterone, norgestimate, or cyproterone acetate. *3rd generation Pills* contain desogestrel, or gestodene as the progesterone. Although designed to be more lipid friendly 3rd generation Pills have not been proven to be better in those with cardiac risk factors and are more thrombogenic.[1]

Risk of thrombosis[1]

Not on Pill	5:100,000
2nd generation Pill	15:100,000
3rd generation Pill	25:100,000
Pregnancy	60:100,000

Carriage of factor V Leiden mutation particularly increases risk of thrombosis to 285 per 100,000 on the Pill. 3rd generation Pills particularly increase resistance to our natural anticoagulant (activated protein C, APC), so increasing thrombosis. Counsel those starting the Pill that it does increase the risk of thrombosis, but it is still a rare event.

The Pill and travel: If immobile for >5h, the *BNF* recommends mid journey exercises ± support stockings.[2]

1 See Mansour D 2005 *Lancet* **365** 1670 & 1588 & *Drug Ther Bul* 2000 **38**
2 *BNF* 2005 i 7.3.1

Depot, implant and patch contraception

Depot progestogen ('the injection') Simple, safe and effective, two preparations are available: *medroxyprogesterone acetate* (Depo-Provera®) 150mg given deep IM 12-weekly; start during the first 5 days of a cycle (post-partum see p 95) or *norethisterone enanthate* (Noristerat®) 200mg into gluteus maximus 8-weekly—licensed for short-term use only, but can be used immediately postpartum (p 95). Exclude pregnancy biochemically and use condoms for 14 days after late injections (eg if she turns up one week late). They inhibit ovulation and thicken cervical mucus. ***CI:*** Pregnancy; abnormal undiagnosed vaginal bleeding; acute liver disease; severe cardiac disease.

Advantages of progesterone injections:

- No oestrogen content
- Fewer ovarian cysts
- Reduces PMS (p 254)
- No compliance problems
- Reduced endometriosis
- Secret
- Good when GI disease
- Abolishes menorrhagia eventually
- Protects against ectopics
- Reduces PID (p 286)
- Useful when breastfeeding
- No thrombosis risk
- 5-fold protective effect against endometrial carcinoma.

Problems: Irregular vaginal bleeding usually settles with time with amenorrhoea then supervening so encourage perseverance: eg 33% amenorrhoeic after 6-months use; 50% for 1 year, and 60% for 18 months (14%, 27%, and 33% respectively for Noristerat®). If very heavy bleeding occurs, exclude pregnancy; give injection early (but >4 weeks from previous dose) and give oestrogen if not *CI:* (eg Premarin® 1.25mg/24h PO for 21 days or a combined contraceptive Pill). Fears of osteoporosis in users have prompted the Committee of Safety of Medicines to recommend review of use after 2 years in all users and avoidance in adolescents unless the only acceptable method. Other problems include weight gain (up to 2kg in 70% of women) and acne.

Special uses: Depot injections may be particularly useful:

- To cover major surgery. If given when stopping combined Pill 4 weeks before surgery it gives contraceptive cover for the next 8 or 12 weeks.
- Sickle-cell disease (reduces incidence of sickle-cell crises).
- Epileptics if on liver enzyme inducers (p 300); give Depo-Provera® injection every 10 weeks.47
- After vasectomy while awaiting partner's 'sperm-free' ejaculates.
- Where bowel disease may affect oral absorption.

There may be some delay in return of ovulation on stopping injections (median delay 10 months) but long-term fertility is not reduced.

Implants Progesterone implants give up to 3 years' contraception with one implantation. Implanon® is a flexible rod containing etonogestrel 68mg which is implanted subdermally into the lower surface of the upper arm. It inhibits ovulation and thickens mucus. Contraceptive effect stops when the implant is removed. <23% of users become amenorrhoeic after 12 months use. Infrequent bleeding occurs in 50% in the first 3 months use; 30% at six months. Prolonged bleeding affects up to 33% in first 3 months; frequent bleeding affects <10%. Effective contraception may not occur in overweight women in the 3rd year, so consider earlier changing of implant in these women. Liver enzyme inducers (p 300) reduce efficacy, so use other, eg barrier contraception if they are started.

Patches Containing oestrogen and progesterone eg Evra® are similar to the combined Pill but breast discomfort and breakthrough bleeding is commoner in first 2 cycles. They are relatively expensive, twice as many women discontinue due to side-effects,[1] but compliance may be better.[2]

1 DTB 2003 vol **41** (12) 89 2 New Product Review 2004 *J Fam Plann Reprod Health Care* **30** 43

Sterilization

Sterilization is popular. Each year ~47,000 women and ~64,000 men are sterilized (UK). ~25% of women rely on sterilization for contraception.

Ideally see both partners and consider the following:

- Alternative methods. Do they know about depot progesterone injections, coils, and implants? Give written information (in relevant language) about alternative contraception and ♂ and ♀ sterilization.
- Consent. Is it the wish of both partners? Legally only the consent of the partner to be sterilized is required but the agreement of both is desirable. Those lacking mental capacity to consent require High Court judgement.
- Who should be sterilized? Does she fear loss of femininity? Does he see it as being neutered? Does the ♀ really want or need hysterectomy? Examine the one to be sterilized.
- Irreversibility. Reversal is only 50% successful in either sex. Tubal surgery increases the risk of subsequent ectopics. Sterilization should be seen as an irreversible step. Sterilizations most regretted (3–10%) are those in the young (<30y), childless, at times of stress (especially relationship problems), or immediately after pregnancy (termination or delivery). Explain reversal or subsequent fertility treatment is rarely funded by the NHS.
- For sterilization at Caesarean section, explain that it will only be done if the baby is normal and healthy. Counsel and agree ≥1 week pre-op.
- ***Warn of failure rates***—10-year follow-up of 10,863 USA women gave pregnancy rates of 18.5/1000 procedures,[48] no better than new IUCDs (Copper T 380s®, Mirena®, GyneFIX®). Advise seeking medical confirmation if future pregnancy suspected or abnormal vaginal bleeding or abdominal pain. If pregnancy occurs there is ↑ risk of ectopic (4.3–76%).
- Side-effects. A women who has been on the Pill for many years may find her periods unacceptably heavy after sterilization.

►Record in the notes: *Knows it's irreversible; lifetime failure rate discussed*, eg 1:2000 for vasectomy, and 1:200 for ♀ sterilization: see above.

Female sterilization The more the tubes are damaged, the lower the failure rate and the more difficult reversal becomes. In the UK, most sterilizations are carried out laparoscopically with general anaesthesia. Filshie clip occlusion is recommended[1] with local anaesthetic applied to tubes (or modified Pomeroy operation at minilaparotomy if post-partum or at caesarean). Do pregnancy test pre-op. Advise use of effective contraception until the operation and next period. Remove IUCD after the next period in case an already fertilized ovum is present. NB: early reports of post-sterilization excessive menstrual blood loss have not been confirmed.[1]

Vasectomy This simpler procedure than female sterilization can be performed as an outpatient. The vas deferens is identified at the top of the scrotum. Lumenal cautery with fascial interposition is more effective than ligation and excision with fascial interposition.[2] Bruising and haematoma are complications. Late pain affects 3% from sperm granulomata, which are less common if thermal cautery (rather than electrical cautery) is used. Warn of risk of chronic testicular pain.

The major disadvantage of vasectomy is that it takes up to 3 months before sperm stores are used up. Obtain 2 ejaculates 'negative' for sperm (the first 8 weeks post-op; 2nd 2–4 weeks later) before stopping other methods of contraception. Reversal is most successful if within 10 years of initial operation. SE: Evidence of ↑risk of prostate cancer post-vasectomy. Meta-analysis suggests a small risk which may be due to bias rather than causal.[MET 49]

1 RCOG *Evidence-based Clinical Guideline No 4* 2004 Male and Female Sterilization
2 K Wright 2005 *BMJ* 330 296

Urinary malfunction

Control of bladder function Continence in women is maintained in the urethra by the external sphincter and pelvic floor muscles maintaining a urethral pressure higher than bladder pressure. Micturition occurs when these muscles relax and the bladder detrusor muscle contracts.

Incontinence or the threat of incontinence dominates many people's lives. Ask about incontinence impact, role limitations, physical and social limitations, personal relationships, emotions, sleep/energy, and symptom severity.

Urge incontinence 'If I've got to go, I've got to go *now*'. The bladder is 'unstable' with high detrusor muscle activity. It occurs in nulliparous and parous women. Usually no organic cause is found (rarely it is neurogenic).

Stress incontinence Small quantities of urine escape as intra-abdominal pressure rises, eg during sneezing. It is commoner in parous women (pregnancy, not mode of delivery is the risk factor).[50] Examination may reveal prolapse (p 290) or incontinence (ask her to cough).

Detrusor overactivity usually presents with *urge* incontinence, but in 25% presents as *stress* symptoms. It is a common cause of incontinence (33% of women; 50% of men, of the UK 3.5 million incontinent population).[51]

Management

- Exclude UTI and diabetes. Do cystometry if stress incontinence (cannot be diagnosed reliably from even the best urological history). Without cystometry, incontinence from detrusor instability is missed in 5-10%.[52]
- Mild stress incontinence responds well to pelvic floor exercises and physiotherapy, eg with weighted vaginal cones—insert the heaviest that can be retained (base up) for 15 minutes twice daily, graduating to heavier cones (up to 100g) as tone improves, to improve muscle tone. A vaginal tampon supports the bladder neck, stopping leaks, eg while playing sport.
- Surgery for severe stress symptoms aims to increase intraurethral pressure (by bringing the upper urethra into the zone of abdominal pressure when previously it was below the pelvic floor) and to reduce prolapse. Options include: urethroplasty, transabdominal colposuspension. For some, periurethral tension free tape inserted under local anaesthetic, will cure. Others may be helped by periurethral bulking, but effects may wear off after 1-2yrs. Colposuspension eg Burch colposuspension and tapes are most effective.[53]
- Duloxetine (Yentreve®, a serotonin/norepinephrine uptake inhibitor) 40mg/12h PO can reduce stress incontinence.[1] It is licensed for use in moderate to severe stress incontinence in the UK.
- In some postmenopausal women urgency, increased frequency, and nocturia may be helped by topical estriol 0.1% cream PV used long term.
- In those mixed stress/urge incontinence treat the detrusor overactivity first as this can be made worse by operations for stress incontinence.

True incontinence Continuous leakage may be due to congenital abnormality, eg ectopic ureters, or to acquired problems, eg vesicovaginal fistula due to trauma (eg post-abdominal hysterectomy in developed countries, after long labours with vertex presentation elsewhere), malignancy, or radiotherapy. If surgery is impossible, seek the help of the continence adviser.

Interstitial cystitis Pathogenesis may involve loss of the bladder's glycosaminoglycan protective layer and a high number of activated bladder mast cells.[2] ***Symptoms:*** Frequency, urgency, bladder pain, and dyspareunia for >6 months. Symptoms are exacerbated by stress, ovulatory hormones, and certain foods. ***Rx:*** Dietary modification, bladder training, biofeedback, antidepressants, anticholinergics, NSAIDs), and bladder hydrodistension may be tried.

1 Millard R 2004 *BJU Int* **93** 311 **2** Theoharides T 2005 *Int J Immunopathol Pharmacol* **18** 183

Managing detrusor overactivity

- Refer if any neuropathy, prolapse, pelvic masses, or haematuria.
- Avoid caffeine (it is a mild diuretic and stimulates detrusor activity).
- Bladder training to increase time between voiding. Keep a bladder diary.
- Pelvic floor muscle physiotherapy if stress incontinence symptoms.
- Antimuscarinic drugs may be effective,[54] eg oxybutynin, starting with 2.5mg/12h, increasing slowly up to 5mg/6h (12 hourly if elderly; SE: dry mouth, blurred vision, nausea, headache, constipation, diarrhoea, abdo pain—SEs are less if modified-release once daily tablets are used—30mg/day of Lyrinel XL® may be tolerated; approach this by weekly 5mg jumps). Tolterodine eg 2mg/12h is also effective; with lower side-effect profile. Solifenacin (=Vesicare® 5mg PO daily; up to 10mg as needed) is an alternative which may ↑ bladder capacity and ↓episodes of incontinence by 50%.[RCT 55] Quality of life improves during long-term therapy.[1]
- Nocturia may respond to *desmopressin* (unlicensed use).[56]

Voiding difficulty

Voiding difficulty is rarer in women than detrusor overactivity.

Symptoms
- Poor flow
- Straining to void
- Incontinence, eg overflow
- Intermittent stream
- Retention (acute/chronic)
- Incomplete emptying
- Hesitancy
- UTI from residual urine

►*Remember faecal impaction as a cause of retention with overflow.*

Causes ***CNS:*** These may be suprapontine (eg stroke); due to cord lesions (cord injury, multiple sclerosis); peripheral nerve (prolapsed disc, diabetic or other neuropathy); or reflex, due to pain (eg with herpes infections).

Obstructive: Early oedema after bladder neck repair is a common cause. Others: Uterine prolapse, retroverted gravid uterus, fibroids, ovarian cysts, urethral foreign body, ectopic ureterocele, bladder polyp, or cancer.

Bladder overdistension—eg after epidural for childbirth.

Detrusor weakness or myopathy causes incomplete emptying + dribbling overflow incontinence. *Diagnosis:* cystometry; electromyography.[57] *Causes:* neurological conditions and interstitial cystitis. It may lead to a contracted bladder, eg requiring substitution enterocystoplasty.[58]

Drugs: Especially epidural anaesthesia; also tricyclics, anticholinergics.

Tests
- MSU (?UTI) plus ultrasound for residual urine and bladder wall thickness: >6mm on transvaginal scan is associated with detrusor overactivity.[59]
- Cystourethroscopy.
- Urodynamic studies: uroflowmetry (a rate of <15mL/sec for a volume of >150mL is abnormal). Do this before any surgery is contemplated.
- Subtraction cystometry is a subtraction of intra-abdominal pressure from measured intravesical pressure to give detrusor pressure (intravesical measure is a mix of bladder pressure and intra-abdominal pressure).

Treatment ***Acute retention*** may require catheterization (suprapubic if needed for several days). For persistent conditions (eg CNS conditions) self-catheterization may be learned, eg with a Lofric® gel coated catheter.

Detrusor weakness may respond to drugs to relax the urethral sphincter or stimulating detrusor: α-blockers, eg *tamsulosin* 400μg/24h, relax the bladder neck; *diazepam* relaxes the sphincter. Surgery may overcome obstructive causes, eg *urethrotomy* for distal urethral stenosis (uncommon).

1 Cardozo L 2005 *BJU* **95** 81 *n*=*1637*. SE: headache; somnolence. Solifenacin's role is still uncertain.

Gynaecological surgery

Hysterectomy *Abdominal hysterectomy* is usually total (uterine body + cervix removed), but may be *Wertheim's* (extended to include local lymph nodes and a cuff of vagina)—used for malignancy. At *vaginal hysterectomy* the uterus is brought down through the vagina. Hospital stay is shorter but difficulties may arise at operation if the uterus is very bulky. Lower segment Caesarean section and nulliparity may also impede operation. Healthy ovaries are usually conserved, especially in young women, whichever route the uterus is removed by, unless the hysterectomy is for an oestrogen-dependent tumour. Complication: residual ovary syndrome (pain, deep dyspareunia, ovarian failure). *Laparoscopic hysterectomy* was developed for patients in whom problems with open surgery are anticipated (eg extensive adhesions with endometriosis), but most of these patients can have a vaginal hysterectomy—which is much quicker (77min *vs* 131min), with a similar complication rate. Hospital stays are shorter, but total recovery not quicker.

75,000 hysterectomies are performed in the UK NHS annually, the majority for menorrhagia or fibroids, and rates vary widely. Femininity and sexuality are bound up with the uterus. *Subtotal hysterectomy* leaves the cervix behind so remember to go on smearing these cervices. The cervix is left in the belief that orgasm is less disrupted (controversial, and not borne out in randomized studies)[60] but late cervical problems (including bleeding) are relatively common (11%). ►Women who are counselled, and make their own decision about surgery, are less likely to have regrets. Operative mortality: ~0.06%. Severe complications occur in 3% and are commoner in younger women and with laparoscopically assisted surgery.[1] Hysterectomy does not cause ↑ psychological/sexual morbidity when compared with ablation (below) at 1 year post-op.

Manchester repair (Fothergill's operation) Pregnancy is still possible after this operation for uterine prolapse. The cervix is amputated and the uterus is supported by shortening the ligaments.

Dilatation and curettage (D&C) The cervix is dilated sufficiently to admit a curette to scrape out a sample of endometrium for histology. D&C is a procedure for diagnosing abnormal bleeding (but outpatient endometrial sampling (p 279) may make D&C unnecessary). Adequate sampling occurs in 75% but in 10% abnormal pathology may be missed. Evacuation of retained products of conception from the uterus after miscarriage (ERPC), or termination of early pregnancy, are carried out by **dilatation and suction**.

Hysteroscopy As an outpatient alternative to D&C, a hysteroscope can be inserted through the cervix into the uterus to visualize the endometrium. 'Blind' samples may then be taken using a sampler.

Hysteroscopic endometrial ablation by laser, diathermy, microwave, or other ablative method (under GA or spinal ± paracervical block) reduces bleeding by achieving a deliberate Asherman's syndrome (p 251); as an alternative to hysterectomy, it has fewer complications. Endometrium may be thinned pre-op by leuprorelin or danazol. By 4 months 10% have menorrhagia again. Complications: (major in 4% requiring further operation in 1%) haemorrhage; infection (eg late necrotizing granulomatous endometritis); uterine perforation; haematometra, vesicovaginal fistula, fluid overload from irrigation fluid can cause ↑BP, ↓Na^+, pulmonary oedema, CNS symptoms, and haemolysis. Some endometrium remains in the majority (so give progesterone containing HRT later, if needed). Pregnancy and endometrial cancer can still occur after ablation. See p 253. Microwave endometrial ablation (MEA) is a better long-term option for heavy menstrual bleeding than transcervical resection of the endometrium (TCRE) eg with wire loops.[2]

1 McPherson K 2004 *BJOG* **111** 688 2 Cooper K 2005 *BJOG* **112** 470 RCT; N=239, followed for 5yrs.

Laparoscopy The laparoscope is inserted sub-umbilically. Instruments are inserted through ports in the *iliac fossae*. Occasionally a Verres needle is placed suprapubically to insufflate and aid manipulation of organs. This procedure allows visualization of the pelvic organs and is used for diagnosis of pelvic pain and ectopic pregnancy. The patient is spared a full laparotomy unless needed for treatment. A 'lap and dye' demonstrates tubal patency. Sterilization and hysterectomy may be laparoscopically carried out, and ectopic pregnancies treated.

Colporrhaphy or 'repair' The lack of support from the vaginal wall in cases of prolapse is rectified by excising redundant mucosa and doing a fascial repair. It is *not* an operation to correct urinary incontinence. The operation may be combined with Manchester repair or vaginal hysterectomy. The more mucosa is removed, the tighter the vagina. Enquire before surgery if she is sexually active. Catheterization circumvents post-operative retention of urine.

Cone biopsy A cone of tissue (point inwards) is cut out around the external cervical os, using knife or laser. This removes neoplastic tissue for histology, and may be curative. Complications: (immediate) bleeding, (long-term) cervical stenosis or incompetence.

Pelvic exenteration Consider this option when initial surgery fails to control neoplasia of the cervix, vulva, or vagina. It involves removal of the pelvic organs—ie ultra-radical surgery, which should only be contemplated if there is a chance of cure. Do your best to establish whether disease has spread to the pelvic sidewall or nodes, eg with MRI or CT scans and intra-operative biopsy with frozen section: if so, exenteration is probably not worthwhile. Only ~20% of possible candidates for surgery meet this criterion: in addition the patient should be quite fit, and ideally have a supportive partner. We know that palliative exenteration in those with unresectable disease is not worthwhile. 5-yr survival: ~50%. Operative mortality: ~5%. Complications: GI obstruction/fistulae; urinary fistulae. Remember to give full pre-operative counselling about colostomies, and sexual function (refashioning of the vagina *may* be possible).

Chronic pelvic pain

This can be a cause of much misery to women of reproductive age. The history is usually of longstanding pelvic pain with secondary dysmenorrhoea and deep dyspareunia. The pain may cause, or be exacerbated by, emotional problems. She may be depressed.

Laparoscopy may reveal a likely cause: chronic pelvic infection, endometriosis, adenomyosis, adhesions, or congested pelvic veins. If it does not (or if all gynaecological causes have been surgically removed) the cause may be gastrointestinal: consider irritable bowel syndrome (*OHCM* p 248).

Pelvic congestion Lax pelvic veins become painfully congested with blood. The pain is worse when she is standing, walking (gravity fills the veins), and premenstrually. It is typically variable in site and intensity and there is unpleasant postcoital ache. She is maximally tender to deep palpation over the ovaries. The vagina and cervix may appear blue due to congestion and there may be associated posterior leg varicosities. The dilated veins may be demonstrated by venography or laparoscopically.

Relief may be difficult, though explanation helps ('pelvic migraine'). Medroxyprogesterone 50mg/24h PO for 3 months reduces pain (SE: amenorrhoea, weight gain, bloating); migraine remedies (*OHCM* p 342) and relaxation may be tried. When symptoms are very severe bilateral ovarian vein ligation, or embolization radiologically, may cure, as may hysterectomy with bilateral salpingo-oophorectomy with hormone replacement therapy post-operatively.

Mittelschmerz This is mid-cycle menstrual pain which may occur in teenagers and older women around the time of ovulation—from the German 'mittel' (=middle) and 'Schmerz' (=pain).

Dyspareunia

This means pain during intercourse. There may be a vicious circle in which anticipation of pain leads to tense muscles and lack of lubrication, and so to further pain. ►*The patient may not volunteer the problem so ask about intercourse.* Her attitude to pelvic examination may tell you as much as the examination itself. Ask her to show you where the problem is. If the problem is actually vaginismus do not insist on examination and consider counselling and sex therapy (p 384). Was there 'female circumcision' (p 246)?

Dyspareunia may be superficial (introital)—eg from infection so look for ulceration and discharge. Is she dry? If so is the problem oestrogen deficiency (p 256) or lack of sexual stimulation? Has she had a recent postpartum perineal repair? A suture or scar can cause well-localized pain which is cured by removing the suture and injection of local anaesthetic. If the introitus has been rendered too narrow, she may need surgery.

Deep dyspareunia is felt internally (deep inside). It is associated with endometriosis and pelvic sepsis; treat the cause if possible. Ovaries lying in the rectovaginal pouch (or after hysterectomy), may be subject to coital thrusts; try other positions or ventrosuspension if a 'cure' can be obtained with trial use of a Hodge pessary.

Dermatographism is a rare cause of dyspareunia: look for itchy vulval wheals some minutes after calibrated dermatographometer application. It can occur on any surface. It is the commonest physical cause of urticaria, and the clue to its presence is linear wheals with a surrounding bright red flare (but no angio-oedema) elsewhere on the skin, in response to a firm stroke. Cause is unknown. Relief of dyspareunia in these cases has been achieved by 2% epinephrine (adrenaline) cream, and cetirizine 10mg/24h PO.

Ovarian hyperstimulation

Sudden multiplication of follicles in response to drugs, especially when gonadotrophins are used in assisted reproduction, gives diffuse lower abdominal pain and cystic ovarian enlargement on palpation. The incidence for severe cases is 0.5–2% in women having ovarian stimulation (mild cases occur in 22–33% of treatment cycles).[1] It is commoner in conception cycles. Women with polycystic ovarian syndrome are at particular risk.[1] Associated complications are ascites, reduced intravascular volume, pulmonary effusions and (rare) pericardial effusions. Thromboembolic complications may ensue (especially in upper limb and cerebral vessels).

Presentation Abdominal discomfort, nausea, vomiting, and abdominal distension ± dyspnoea. Presentation is usually 3–7 days after HCG administration, or 12–17 days, if pregnancy has ensued.

Prevention In those in whom hyperstimulation is suspected (peak serum oestradiol >6000pg/mL and >30 follicles stimulated), the surest way to avoid hyperstimulation is to avoid administration of human chorionic gonadotrophin (HCG) so the stimulated follicles do not ovulate, thereby cancelling the cycle of treatment (or discontinue gonadotrophins and delay HCG injections until the serum oestradiol returns to 'safe' levels). Some selectively cryopreserve embryos for later transfer.

Risk factors

- Age <35yrs
- Asthenic habitus
- Pregnancy
- Luteal phase hCG stimulation
- Polycystic ovarian syndrome
- Serum oestradiol >4000pg/mL
- Multiple follicles (>35)

Management Admit to hospital. Give adequate analgesia (opiates if necessary). Check FBC, U&E, creatinine, LFT, and coagulation profile. Do CXR if chest pathology suspected; blood gases if tachypnoeic or dyspnoeic. Chart urine output (if oliguria suspected catheterize and measure fluid output hourly). Ovarian size is a guide to severity unless oocytes have been harvested.

Hyperstimulation is *severe* if haematocrit is >45%, WCC $>15\times10^9$/L, there is massive ascites, oliguria, mild renal, or liver dysfunction. Put up IVI, and consider CVP monitoring. Fluid replacement may be required, eg 500mL albumin over 2 hours. Paracentesis of ascites can improve renal function. To avoid thromboembolism use antiembolic stockings, encourage leg mobility, and use heparin (p 16) during inpatient stay.[2]

The situation is *critical* if the haematocrit is >55% and WCC $>25\times10^9$/L, there is tense ascites and renal failure, thromboembolic phenomena, and acute respiratory distress syndrome (*OHCM* p 190). Admit to ITU. Symptomatic pleural effusions may need drainage. Use antiembolic measures as above. Pay meticulous attention to fluid balance. Aim to maintain intake at 3L/24h using alternating normal and dextrose saline (but beware hyponatraemia).

The severity of effusions determines the time to recovery. In non-conception cycles with little ascites there will be resolution with menstruation. In conception cycles cysts may persist for weeks. Resolution usually occurs, but exceptionally termination of pregnancy may be needed. Deaths have been reported but are extremely rare (~1:500,000 stimulated cycles).[1]

1 B McElhinney 2000 *Clin Obs Gyn* **14** 103
2 RCOG *Guideline* **37** 2004 Thromboprophylaxis during pregnancy, labour and after vaginal delivery

4 Psychiatry

Sources: EBM sources include *BMJ*, Cochrane, *EBM*, etc, but note that 'too great an emphasis on EBM oversimplifies the complex and interpersonal nature of care'. ►In psychiatry it is better to think of each encounter with a patient as an opportunity for creative thought and intimate dialogue, not as an opportunity to apply a previously agreed set of rules.

Other pages elsewhere: Puerperal psychosis, p 94; consultations, p 478; social/ethnic matters, p 522 & p 492; prescribing & compliance, p 519; children, p 210.

*This chapter should be read with the ***Diagnostic and Statistical Manual of Mental Disorders (DSM IV)***; note that *DSM IV* is mainly for research purposes, and its definitions are too rigid for general psychiatric purposes—ie its specificity is excellent, but its sensitivity is questionable.

This chapter was masterminded by Dr Anish Patel, assisted by Dr Danilo Arnone & Dr Giles Tan

International classification of diseases: *major adult diagnoses*

Affective (mood) disorders:
- Depressive disorders p 336
- Mania p 354

The neuroses
- Anxiety neurosis p 344
- Obsessional neurosis p 346
- Depersonalization p 346; phobias p 346
- Hysteria p 334
- Sexual disorders p 384

Organic reactions
- Acute p 350
- Chronic (dementia) p 350–2

Schizophrenia p 356–61
Paranoia & other psychoses p 354
Mental retardation p 364
Personality disorders p 366
Alcoholism p 363
Drug problems and addiction p 362

Problems with classificatory systems:** No system can be equally successful in guiding treatment ***and in illustrating basic biological distinctions. For example, depression spans the neurosis/psychosis division, and mania has both affective (mood) and psychotic components.

- There is no such thing as a correct classification, only more or less useful ones. Bear in mind that in ancient times (as reported by Borges) one approved classification of animals had as its first 6 categories: **1** Animals that belong to the Emperor. **2** Embalmed ones. **3** Those that are trained. **4** Suckling pigs. **5** Mermaids. **6** Fabulous ones. We do not know how many mermaids and other fabulous beings are included in the above classificatory system.
- Not all the diagnostic categories have the same value. If a patient with features of schizophrenia (eg hallucinations) is later found to have an organic psychosis (eg from a brain tumour) the schizophrenic element is usually subsumed under the more powerful diagnostic category of organic illness. This is an example of the 'hierarchy of diagnosis', in which organic illness 'trumps' schizophrenia and affective disorders, which in turn trump neurosis, but this does preclude multiple diagnoses, eg schizophrenia with depression and substance abuse disorder.

No one is *just* a member of a class, and it is a common error to abandon patients, once they have been categorized. Because of its tragic essence, it is possible for mental illness to be a humanizing experience for those affected (patient, family, and friends)—as well as being a destructive one, and there is much to be said for the idea that we should embrace our patients, rather than analyse them. But being holistic must sometimes give ground to reductionism, for diagnosis is the best tool we have to help our patients.

Introduction to psychiatry

Doctors have never been very important because nothing that happens to our bodies ever really matters. In historical terms, the importance of what happens to our bodies rarely outlives our own times. Even the exceptions to this prove a different rule: for example, we recall forever the human images burnt on to stone at their moment of immolation in Nagasaki and Hiroshima. Surely what happened to them was important, and transcended the times in which they lived? True. But it is all the more true that it isn't the way they lived, but the way they died that is important, and it is not the body nor its image on stone which is important, but the image left on our minds. And so it is with psychiatrists, psychologists, and psychiatric nurses who play such a role in determining whether we live and die in hope or despair, who mitigate our madness giving meaning, purpose, and dignity to the mental sufferings of so many of us. So when we think of these men and women going about their work, we think of them burnishing humanizing images not on stone, but on the mind itself. How they do it is the subject of this chapter.

Mental health and mental illness

The essence of mental health Ideally, healthy humans have:

- An ability to love and be loved. Without this cardinal asset, human beings, more than all other mammals, fail to thrive.
- The power to embrace change and uncertainty without fear—and to face fear rationally and in a spirit of practical optimism.
- A gift for risk-taking free from endless worst-case-scenario-gazing.
- Stores of spontaneous *joie de vivre*, and a wide range of emotional responses (including negative emotions, such as anger; these may be important for motivation, as well as being a natural antidote to pain).
- Efficient contact with reality: not too little; not too much. (As T S Eliot said, humankind cannot bear very much reality.)
- A rich fantasy world enabling hope and creativity to flourish.
- A degree of self-knowledge to encourage the humane exercising of the skill of repairing the self and others following harm.
- The strength to say 'I am wrong', and to learn from experience.
- An adequate feeling of security and status within society.
- The ability to satisfy the requirements of the group, combined with a freedom to choose whether to exercise this ability.
- Freedom of self-expression in whatever way he or she wants.
- The ability to risk enchantment and to feel a sense of awe.
- The ability to gratify his own and others' bodily desires.
- A sense of humour to compensate should the foregoing be unavailable.

Happiness need not be an ingredient of mental health; indeed the merely happy may be supremely vulnerable. All that is needed is for their happiness to be removed. The above are important as they are what a person needs should this misfortune befall him. The above may also be seen as a sort of blueprint for our species' survival.

The essence of mental illness ***Whenever a person's abnormal thoughts, feelings, or sensory impressions cause him objective or subjective harm that is more than transitory, a mental illness may be said to be present.*** Very often the harm is to society, but this should not be part of the definition of mental illness, as to include it would open the door to saying that, for example, all rapists or all those opposing the society's aims are mentally ill. If a person is manic (p 354), and not complaining of anything, this only becomes a mental illness (on the above definition) if it causes him harm as judged by his peers (in the widest sense of the term). One feature of mental illness is that one cannot always rely on the patient's judgment, and one has to bring in the judgment of others, eg family, GP, or psychiatrist. If there is disparity of judgment, there is much to be said for adopting the principle of 'one person one vote', provided it can be shown that the voters are acting solely in the interests of the person concerned. The psychiatrist has no special voting rights here—otherwise the concepts of mental health and illness become dangerously medicalized. Just because the psychiatrist or GP is not allowed more than one vote, this does not stop them from trans-illuminating the debate by virtue of his or her special knowledge.

For convenience, English law saves others from the bother of specifying who has a mental illness by authorizing doctors to act for them. This is a healthy state of affairs only in so far as doctors remember that they have only a small duty to society, but a larger duty to their patient (not, we grant, an overriding duty in all instances—eg when murder is in prospect).

Learning disabilities (mental impairment/retardation) This is a condition of arrested or incomplete development of mind which is especially characterized by subnormality of intelligence.

Dignity on psychiatric wards

Apart from showing sympathy, nothing is more to be desired than giving our patients dignity—not the dignity that they deserve (who among us would merit an ounce of dignity on this measure?) but the dignity that confirms to our patients that, mad, bad, or rambling, they are, root and branch, body and mind, just as human as their doctors—perhaps more so, because they are suffering.[1] *Let patients:*

- Decide on mode of address, 'Miss Hudson' may be preferred to 'Agatha, dear'. Dignity entails giving choices, and then respecting them.
- Know who we are (eg wear name badges).
- Wear their own clothes—and clothe them decently if they have none.
- Choose whether to take part in research—and whether to see students.
- Have personal space—both to stow their belongings, and to walk in, in private, whether alone, or with visitors.
- Participate in their treatment plans; explain about common side-effects.
- Know what to do if a crisis develops. It's a great help to know that you will be seen in 4h rather than be left to moulder all weekend.

These 7 points underpin the UK *patient's charter* in mental health, and are congruent with UK Human Rights law which lays out the right to life, freedom from inhuman (degrading) treatment and torture, respect for privacy, the right to a fair hearing and freedom of expression. Some of these rights are inalienable, and unrevokable, even in time of war (on British soil). So defences such as '*the ward was busy on that day*' or '*there was no money to purchase this service*' are unlikely to impress judges.

Our patients' other needs: Maslow's hierarchy

Maslow states that a healthy personality (ie fully functioning and self-actualizing) entails the meeting of a hierarchy of needs:

1. Biological needs (eg oxygen, food, water, warmth).
2. Safety needs (no present threats to safety).
3. Love, affection, and 'belongingness' needs.
4. Esteem needs (self-respect, and need for respect from others: *see above*).
5. Self-actualization needs (our need to *be* and *do* that which we feel born to do—his or her calling). If such needs are unmet, restlessness and anxiety result. To meet this need we might teach ourselves and others:
   - To be aware of the inner self and to understand our inner nature. To transcend cultural conditioning.
   - To transcend the trifling and to grapple with life's serious problems.
   - To refresh consciousness by appreciating beauty and all good things.
   - To feel joy and the worth of living. www.connect.net/georgen/maslow.htm

Violation of rights to a fair hearing and to privacy can be defended (usually by tyrants) on grounds of public interest, protection of health or morals and, perhaps, economics. See www.coe.fr/eng/legaltxt/e-dh.htm

1 Do our sufferings make us more human? Only if we can breath meaning into them. Toothache doesn't make us more human because it has no meaning; but there is a kind of suffering 'which is a more effective key, a more rewarding principle for exploring the world in thought and action than personal good fortune'. [Deitrich Bonhoeffer]. This suffering makes our souls. Not all our patients regret their psychological illnesses: sometimes, in retrospect, these patients refer to their break*through*, not their break*down*. It is this power to grow and to transform experience which is human and humanizing. This is also why, paradoxically, illness is not the opposite of health. For humans, the true opposite to health is being stuck ***In Status Quo***—that state which brooks no development. So if you find yourself writing ***ISQ*** (in status quo) in patients' notes you are invoking a kind of death.

Odd ideas

It is important to decide whether a patient has delusions, hallucinations, or a major thought disorder (see below), because if these are present the diagnosis must be: schizophrenia, affective disorder, an organic disorder, or a paranoid state—and it is *not* a neurosis or a personality disorder.

Patients may be reluctant to reveal odd ideas. Ask gently: 'Have you ever had any thoughts which now seem odd; perhaps that there is a conspiracy against you, or that you are controlled by outside voices or the radio?'

Hallucinations are auditory, visual, gustatory, or tactile sensations experienced in the absence of a stimulus. Often-encountered pre- or post-sleep (hypnagogic/hypnopompic) hallucinations don't indicate pathology. A pseudohallucination is one in which the patient knows the stimulus is in the mind (eg a voice heard within him- or herself, rather than over the left shoulder). They are more common, and needn't indicate mental illness, but they may be a sign that a genuine hallucination is being internalized before being disbanded (ie the person hears a voice but no longer believes it represents an outside agent). Tactile or visual hallucinations (without auditory hallucinations) suggest an organic disorder (eg alcohol withdrawal, or Charles Bonnet syndrome, p 438). NB: 2–4% of the general population experience auditory hallucinations, but only ~30% of these have a mental illness.

Delusions are beliefs which are held unshakably, irrespective of counter-argument, and which are unexpected, given the patient's cultural background. If the belief arrives fully formed, and with no antecedent events or experiences to account for it, it is said to be *primary*, and is suggestive of schizophrenia (or genius[1]). Such delusions form around a 'delusional perception', as illustrated by the patient who, on seeing the traffic lights go green (the delusional perception) knew that he had been sent to rid his home town of materialism. Careful history-taking will reveal that delusions are often *secondary*—for example, a person who is psychotically depressed may come to think of himself as being literally worthless.

Ideas of reference The patient cannot help feeling that other people are taking notice of the very thing he feels ashamed of. What distinguishes this from a delusion is that he knows the thoughts come from within himself, and are excessive. It is important to distinguish delusions and hallucinations from obsessional thoughts. With any odd idea, get a clear description:

- Hearing the thought as a voice (a hallucination, eg from a psychosis).
- The voice is 'put into my head'—thought insertion (hallucination + delusion).
- The voice is 'my own voice' but intrusively persistent (obsessional neurosis).

Major thought disorder This is a bizarre or incongruent transition from one idea to another. (*Mania*—flight of ideas, p 354; *schizophrenia*, p 358).

If hallucinations or delusions are present, ask yourself: **1** What other evidence there is of psychopathology. Hearing the voice of one's dead spouse is common, and does not indicate mental illness. **2** Could the odd ideas be adaptive—and the patient be better off 'ill'? A woman once believed she saw planes flying over her home, and that this data was taken from her head by the British Ministry of Defence. She 'knew' she was playing a key role in the defence of Britain. When she was cured of these delusions she committed suicide. An odd story—or is it so odd? According to the great poets, everything we cherish is an illusion, especially our sense of distinctive self-hood, and without this primordial delusion, madness beckons.

1 'At the moment I put my foot on the step the idea came to me without anything in my former thoughts seeming to have paved the way for it, that the transformations I had used to define the Fuchsian functions were identical with those of non-Euclidean geometry…the idea came to me with…brevity, suddenness, and immediate certainty.' A Koestler *The Act of Creation* **115**

Some causes of odd ideas

A typical problem is trying to diagnose a young man presenting with hallucinations and or delusions. The question often is: *Are these odd ideas due to schizophrenia, drug abuse, or physical illness?*

- Most auditory hallucinations not associated with falling asleep or waking up are caused by schizophrenia or depression.
- In 90% of those with non-auditory hallucinations (eg seeing things), the cause is substance abuse, drug withdrawal, or physical disease.
- Evidence that substance abuse is to blame includes:
  - *The history:* Ask the patient, the family, and friends about abuse. Be precise about timing. If ≥4 weeks elapse between abuse and starting of odd ideas, intoxication from substance abuse is an unlikely cause (but substance abuse may be an enabling factor promoting later psychosis).[1]
  - *Severity of symptoms:* If symptoms are severe, and the quantity of drug ingested is trivial, the drug is unlikely to be causative.
  - *Drug-seeking behaviour:* Be on the lookout for this.
  - *Physical examination:* This may reveal signs of drug abuse (eg injection marks ± cellulitis), chronic alcohol abuse (eg spider naevi, liver palms, atrophic testes), or a physical medical illness (eg brain tumour).
  - *Blood or urine tests* may disclose the substance abused or give a hint of abuse (MCV↑ and gamma GT↑ in alcohol abuse).
  - *Imaging:* Consider CNS imaging if the patient is elderly with nothing to suggest substance abuse, or if there are CNS signs.
- NB: middle-age is not a typical time for schizophrenia to present: alcohol abuse or a primary CNS condition is more likely.
- Diagnosing a *substance-induced psychotic disorder* implies that the patient responds to the hallucinations or delusions as if they were real. If the patient recognizes the hallucinatory nature of the experience, then consider diagnosing *substance intoxication, substance withdrawal* or, if there is past but no current exposure to hallucinogens, the diagnosis may be 'flashbacks'—ie *hallucinogen persisting perception disorder*. This condition presents episodically up to 5yrs after exposure to an hallucinogen, with flashback hallucinations, any visual hallucinations or phenomenon such as: geometric visual hallucinations, seeing flashes of colour, or intensified colours, seeing dots, spots, or flashes, seeing trailing images or after-images, seeing complementary coloured images of objects gone from view, seeing halos, seeing things too small (micropsia), or seeing things too big (macropsia). These phenomena may be self-induced or triggered by darkness, stress, or fatigue.

(See DSM-IV 313.)

1 *BMJ* 2005 330 11 'Cannabis use moderately increases the risk of psychotic symptoms in young people but has a much stronger effect in those with evidence of predisposition for psychosis.'

Introduction to psychiatric skills

Only people can change people: 'Alyosha's arrival seemed to have a sobering effect on him…as though something had awakened in this prematurely aged man that had long been smothered in his soul…"For you see, my dear boy, I feel that you are the only man in the world who has not condemned me".'

(Father speaking to his son in *The Brothers Karamazov*, 25, Dostoevsky.)

On beginning psychiatry you are likely to feel unskilled. A 'medical' problem will come as a relief—you know what to do. Do not be discouraged: you already have plenty of skills (which you will take for granted). The aim of this chapter is to build on these. No one can live in the world very long without observing or feeling mood swings, and without devising ways to minimize what is uncomfortable, and maximize what is desirable. Anyone who has ever sat an important exam knows what anxiety is like, and anyone who has ever passed one knows how to master anxiety, at least to some extent. We have all survived periods of being 'down', and it is interesting to ask how we have done this. The first element is time. Simply waiting for time to go by is an important psychotherapeutic principle. Much of what passes as successful treatment in psychiatry is little more than protecting the patient, while time goes by, and his (and his family's) natural processes of recovery and regeneration bring about improvement. Of course, there are instances when, to wait for time to go by could lead to fatal consequences. But this does not prevent the principle from being a useful one.

Another skill with which we are all more or less adept is *listening*. One of the central tenets of psychiatry is that it helps our patients just to be listened to. Just as we all are helped by talking and sharing our problems, so this may in itself be of immense help to our patients, especially if they have been isolated, and feel alone—which is a very common experience.

Just as spontaneous regeneration and improvement are common occurrences in psychiatry, so is relapse. Looking through the admissions register of any acute psychiatric ward is likely to show that the same people keep on being re-admitted. In one sense this is a failure of the processes of psychiatry, but in another sense each (carefully planned) discharge is a success, and a complex infrastructure often exists for maintaining the patient in the community. These include group support meetings, group therapy sessions, and social trips out of the hospital. We all have skills in the simple aspects of daily living, and in re-teaching these skills to our patients we may enable them to take the first steps in rebuilding their lives after a serious mental illness.

So *time*, *listening*, and the *skills of daily living* are our chief tools, and with these simple devices much can be done to rebuild the bridges between the patient and his outside world. These skills are simple compared with some of the highly elaborate skills such as psychoanalysis and hypnosis for which psychiatry is famous. The point of bringing them to the fore is so that the newcomer to psychiatry need not feel that there is a great weight of theoretical work to get through before he starts doing psychiatry. On the contrary, you can engage in the central process of psychiatry from your first day on the wards—using the knowledge and experience gained as a foundation on which to build the constructs required for the more specific and effective forms of psychotherapy.

Suspending judgment

In judging others, we expend energy to no purpose…But if we judge ourselves, our labour is always to our profit. *Thomas à Kempis*

If we knew more about ourselves, we would understand more about our fellow patients, bearing in mind that 'all gods and devils that have ever existed are within us as possibilities, desires, as solutions'. (Hermann Hesse, *Reflections*). What we want our patients to achieve is insight—and judging our fellows does not help this process. Judgment turns our patients away from us. We cannot expect our patients to be honest with us if they know that we are judging them.

- The good listener is *not* silent—but reflective. We hold a mirror up to our patients so they may get insight into themselves. Mirrors do not judge but they can enable self-judgment. Unless some criminal act is underway, it really does not matter what we think about our patients. What matters is how the patient thinks about him- or herself and his or her near-ones—and how these thoughts can be transformed.
- If we judge people they will not trust us. No trust ≈ no healing.
- If we judge, patients will leave us for others less well-qualified.
- There is no evidence that judging improves outcomes. Worse outcomes are likely if the patient feels alienated.
- If patients detect that we feel bad about them, they may internalize this, and assume that things will always be bad because *they* are bad.

Notwithstanding these bullets, there is a problem that will not go away. If we find ourselves talking to perpetrators rather than victims, we may not be wise to suspend judgment forever. If a crime is afoot putting others at risk, you may need to break confidentiality. Discuss this with a colleague. Ask yourself whether Nazi and Rwandan doctors were *too* nonjudgmental with their officer-patients. If '*tout comprendre c'est tout pardonner*', then to pardon *all* actions is to abdicate our moral selves. What is the consequence of this—for us, and for our patients? Unless we exercise judgment, it might be thought, we may be condoning evil. 'For evil to flourish in the world, all that is required is for the good to remain silent'. If we remain silent long enough, then will our own moral sense sicken, and die? What human duties do doctors have which trump *anything* that goes on in the consulting room? Whenever you think the time may have come to judge, check with yourself that it is not from outrage, or disgust, or through the exercise of pride, or from a position of power that you are judging—but reluctantly, and from *duty*. The dreadful history of some doctors in the twentieth century teaches that we must be human first, and physician-scientists second.

Listening (and swallowing)

Some time ago, a child said *"To understand me you must swallow a world."*[3] Taking this quest for "truthfulness about the inner life" further, one of our most rigorous therapists has said that he must perform "the essential Jonah act of allowing himself to be swallowed, remaining passive, accepting..."[4] The sign that we are listening properly, from *within* the whale, so to speak, is that we are *immersed* in our patient and that what we are hearing could, perhaps, *change* us. Patients intuitively understand and respond to this level of listening. It takes great concentration. *Doing* something is always easier—hence Anthony Storr's aphorism: *Don't just do something—Listen!*[1]

Once we had the good luck to work on a psychiatric ward with a would-be surgeon, who, before he accustomed himself to psychiatry, would pace restlessly up and down the ward after clerking his patients, wondering when the main action would start, impatient to get his teeth into the business of curing people. What he was expecting was some sort of equivalent to an operating list, and not knowing where to find one he was at a loss, until he gradually realized that taking a history from a psychiatric patient is not a 'pre-op assessment', but the start of the operation itself. Even advanced textbooks of psychiatry appear to have missed the belated insight of this surgeon, describing psychotherapy as something which should only happen after 'a full psychiatric history'.[5] There is no such thing as a full psychiatric history. In describing the salient psychological events of a single day even the best authors (eg James Joyce in *Ulysses*) need substantial volumes. This is why this chapter is starting so slowly: to give time for these notions of listening to take root. So swallow hard. Calm your restlessness. Stop. Reflect.

Taking a history sounds like an active, inquisitorial process, with lists of questions, and the tone of our page on this process (p 322 & *mental state examination*, p 324) seems to perpetuate this error. It isn't a question of *taking* anything. It's more about *receiving* the history, and *allowing* it to unfold. ►If you only ask questions, you will get only answers as replies.

As the history unfolds, sit back and listen. This sounds easy, but during a busy or difficult day you will find your mind wandering (or galloping away)—over the last patient, the next patient, or some aspect of your own life. You may find yourself worrying about having to 'section' this patient or see the relatives afterwards. By an act of Zen, banish extraneous thought, and concentrate totally on the person in front of you—as if your life depended on it. Concentrate on the whole person—the language, the words, the nonverbal cues, and get drawn into their world. Initially don't even think of applying diagnostic labels. Open your mind and let everything flood in. Listening is hard. We wish we did it better. We all need to practice it more.

Avoid interruptions and seeming too purposeful, at least for the first few minutes. Expect periods of silence. If prompts are needed try 'and then how did you feel?' or just 'and then...'; or repeat the last words the patient spoke. Don't be anxious if the patient is not to be covering major areas in the history. Lead on to these later, as the interview unfolds. At first you will have to ask the relevant questions (p 322) in a rather bald way (if the information is not forthcoming during the initial unstructured minutes), but it is important to go through this stage as a prelude to gaining information by less intrusive methods. Always keep in mind the chief aims of *making a diagnosis, defining problems,* and *establishing a therapeutic relationship.*

1 The converse of this aphorism is the Parris dictum: "***When people are anxious it isn't clever to make a virtue of listening. Sometimes our patients simply need to be told.***" Sometimes they need space for self-expression. Which approach is right—when? We only know this by knowing our patients: this entails listening, which is why, 9 times out of 10, Storr is right: but 9 out of 10 is not always.

What is the point of all this listening?

Listening enables patients to start to *trust* us. Depressed patients often believe they will never get better. To believe that they *can* get better, patients need to trust us, and this trust is often the start of the therapeutic process. In general, the more we listen, the more we are trusted. Our patients' trust in us can be one of our chief motivations, at best inspiring us to pursue their benefit with all vigour. A story bears this out. One day, in 334 BC, Alexander the Great fell ill with fever. He saw his doctor, who gave him a medicine. Later he received a letter saying his doctor was poisoning him as part of a plot (it was an age of frequently fatal intrigues). Alexander went to his doctor and drank the medicine—then gave him the letter. His confidence was rewarded by a speedy recovery. We think it is unreasonable to expect *quite* this much trust from our patients, and one wonders what can have led Alexander to such undying trust in his doctor. We suspect that his doctor, above all else, must have been a good listener.

Lifeworlds, and how to keep them intact

Even if we all listen the same way, what we will hear will depend on our own expectations, anxieties, and past experience. Take this dialogue.[6]

Doctor:	'How long have you been drinking that heavily?'
Patient:	'Since I've been married'
Doctor: [impatiently]	'How long is that?'
Patient: [giggling]	'For years'. Perhaps the doctor hears '4 years'.

The doctor may be worrying about the length of time her liver has been exposed to alcohol, or perhaps he wants his notes to look complete. He needs facts in historical 'linear' time, but the patient chooses to answer in event-time, or personal time. This is Mishler's great distinction between the *voice of medicine* and the *voice of the lifeworld*.[7] The doctor has forced his patient to submit to his world. Sometimes this may seem unavoidable: the chief thing is to recognize when this is happening, and to be preemptive by biting your tongue. What would this patient have gone on to say if her doctor had swallowed her world? What did those giggles signify? We will never know, but they might have explained her coming death.

To understand me you must swallow a world

Eliciting the history

Introduce yourself, explain how long the interview will take, and describe its purpose. Find out how the patient came to be referred, and what his expectations are (eg about treatment). If the patient denies having any problems or is reluctant to start talking about himself, do not hurry him. Try asking 'How are you?' or 'What has been happening to you?' or 'What are the most important things?' Another approach for hospital patients is to indicate why the GP referred the patient and then ask what the patient thinks about this. Sit back and listen, without interrupting, noting exact examples of what he is saying. Take more control after ~3min, to cover the following topics.

Presenting symptoms Agree a problem list with the patient early on, and be sure it is comprehensive, eg by asking 'If we were able to deal with all these, would things then be all right?' or 'If I were able to help you, how would things be different?' Then take each problem in turn and find out about onset, duration, effects on life and family; events coinciding with onset; solutions tried; reasons why they failed. The next step is to enquire about mood and beliefs during the last weeks (this is different from the mental state examination, p 324, which refers to the mental state at the time of interview). Specifically check for: suicidal thoughts, plans, or actions—the more specific these are, the greater the danger. Discussing suicide does not increase the danger. Questions to consider: 'Have you ever felt so low that you have considered harming yourself?' 'Have you ever actually harmed yourself?' 'What stopped you harming yourself any more than this?' 'Have you made any detailed suicide plans?' 'Have you bought tablets for that purpose?' Depression—ie low mood, anhedonia (unable to feel pleasure), self-denigration ('I am worthless'; 'Oh that I had not been born!'), guilt ('It's all my fault'), lack of interest in hobbies and friends plus biological markers of depression (early morning waking, decreased appetite and sexual activity, weight loss); mania (p 354); symptoms of psychosis (persecutory beliefs, delusions, hallucinations, p 316); drug and alcohol use; obsessional thoughts; anxiety; eating disorders (eg in young women; often not volunteered, and important). Note compulsive behaviour (eg excessive hand-washing).

Present circumstances Housing, finance, work, marriage, friends.

Family history Physical and mental health, job, and personality of members. Who is closest to whom? Any stillbirths, abortions?

Birth, growth, and development How has he spent his life? Ask about school, play (alone? with friends?) hobbies, further education, religion, job, sex, marriage. Has he always been shy and lonely, or does he make friends easily? Has he been in trouble with the law? What stress has he had and how has he coped with it? NB: noting early neurotic traits—nail-biting, thumb-sucking, food fads, stammering (not really a neurotic feature)—rarely helps.

Premorbid personality Before all this happened, how were you? Happy-go-lucky, tense, often depressed? Impulsive, selfish, shy, fussy, irritable, rigid, insecure? ►Talk to whoever accompanies him (eg wife), to shed light on premorbid personality and current problems. But don't let her speak for the patient (at least make sure that the patient has the first and last word).

Next examine the mental state (p 324 & p 353). You may now make a diagnosis. Ensure that the areas above have been covered in the light of this diagnosis so that the questions '***Why did he get ill in this way at this time?***' and '***What are the consequences of the illness?***' are answered.

Discussing childhood sexual abuse (CSA) with an adult who is currently experiencing psychological difficulties

A frequent question to arise is 'how far does past CSA account for current problems, and how much should this issue be explored now?' Each person is different: try to learn to use whatever your patient gives you, for their benefit. See p 328 for how to talk about sexual issues. Sometimes it is possible to be optimistic, despite the fact that many patients and professionals believe that CSA causes intense harm pervasively in the general population, regardless of gender. This issue has been examined in careful meta-analyses looking at 59 studies based on college data. These show that students with CSA were, on average, only slightly less well adjusted than controls. But this poorer adjustment cannot be attributed to CSA: family environment is consistently confounded with CSA and explains much more adjustment-variance than CSA. Self-reported reactions to and effects from CSA indicate that negative effects are neither pervasive nor often intense. Also, men react much less negatively than women. Even though this college data is consistent with data from national samples, this optimistic meta-analysis should not blind you to the possibility that the patient sitting in front of you might be *very* damaged by CSA—but do not *assume* that CSA is the underlying reason for everything.[MET 8]

►When in doubt, get further help.

The mental state examination

This assesses the state of mind at the time of interview. Take notes under the following headings.

- ***Appearance and behaviour:*** Eg signs of self-neglect; slowness, anxiety, or suspiciousness.
- ***Mode of speech:*** Speech rate, eg gabbling (pressure of speech), or slow/retarded. Note content.
- ***Mood:*** Note thoughts about harming self or others. Gauge your own responses to the patient. The laughter and grandiose ideas of manic patients are contagious, as to a lesser extent is the expression of thoughts from a depressed person.

Beliefs: Eg about himself, his own body, about other people and the future. Note abnormal beliefs (delusions) eg that thoughts are overheard, and ideas (eg persecutory, grandiose). See p 316.

- ***Unusual experiences or hallucinations:*** 'Sometimes when people are low they have unusual experiences; have you heard anything unusual recently?' Note modality, eg visual. See BOX.
- ***Orientation:*** In time, place, and person. What year? What season? What month/day of week? What time of day is it? What is your name?
- ***Short-term memory:*** Give a name & address; test recall after 5min. Ensure he has the address clear in his head before waiting for the 5min to elapse.
- ***Long-term memory:*** Current affairs recall. Who is the Monarch? (This tests many other CNS functions, not just memory.)
- ***Concentration:*** Months of the year backwards.
- Note the patient's ***insight*** and the degree of your ***rapport***.

Direct questions to try:

- Any odd thoughts?
- Might your thoughts be being interfered with?
- Do you feel anyone is controlling you?
- Is anyone putting thoughts into your head?
- Do other people access or hear your thoughts?
- Is anyone harming you?
- Any plots against you?
- Do you hear voices when there's no-one nearby? What do they say? Echoing you? Telling you off?
- Do you see things that others cannot see?
- Are you low/depressed?
- Is life worth living?
- Can anything give you pleasure?
- Sleep and appetite OK?
- Energy levels ↑ or ↓?
- Can you concentrate OK?
- Are you feeling guilty?
- Is your confidence low?
- Are you wanting to harm anyone? Yourself?
- Any worries/anxieties?

Non-verbal behaviour *Why are we annoyed when we blush, yet love it when our friends do so?* Part of the answer to this question is that non-verbal communication is less well controlled than verbal behaviour. This is why its study can yield valuable insights into our patients' minds, particularly when analysis of their spoken words has been unrevealing. For example, if a patient who consistently denies being depressed sits hugging himself in an attitude of self-pity, remaining in a glum silence for long periods of the interview, and when he does speak, uses a monotonous slow whisper unadorned even by a flicker of a gesticulation or eye contact—we are likely to believe what we see and not what our patient would seem to be telling us.

Items of non-verbal behaviour:
- Gaze and mutual gaze
- Facial expression
- Smiling, blushing
- Body attitude (eg 'defensive')

Dress:
'The apparel oft proclaims the man'[9]
- Hairstyle
- Make-up
- Body ornament (ear-rings, tattoos)

Signs of auditory hallucinations:
- Inexplicable laughter
- Silent and distracted while listening to 'voices' (but could be an 'absence' seizure, p 206)
- Random, meaningless gestures

Anxious behaviour:
- Fidgeting, trembling
- Nail-biting
- Shuffling feet
- Squirming in the chair
- Sits on edge of chair

Signs of a depressed mood:
- Hunched, self-hugging posture
- Little eye contact
- Downcast eyes; tears
- Slow thought, speech, and movement

What is a mental state?

A true description of a mental state entails valid knowledge about a person's current emotions plus his or her reactions to those emotions. These reactions are themselves emotional (eg being annoyed or dumbfounded at finding oneself in love again)—as well as being the bedrock out of which beliefs and attitudes are formed. These interactions make a picture to an external observer which is complex, paradoxical, subjective, error-prone, contradictory—and fascinating.

Describing and communicating mental states is the central puzzle that confronts not just psychiatrists and their patients, but also all artists. All the great poets and songwriters can summon up and make sense of diverse mental states (herein lies their genius)—but none can control them or their infinite progeny (what happens next). This might be said to be the proper province of psychiatry. If doctors could control mental states at will, then it is not necessarily the case that the job of psychiatry is done (there remains the problem of the will)—but at least the job would be half done (and, no doubt, there would be some unfortunate side-effects). Drugs, psychotherapy, and behavioural methods are the chief tools available for this task, and they all, crucially, impinge on mental state. You cannot tell if these modalities are helping if you cannot access your patient's mental state, which is why the page opposite is *so* important. But if you think you can access mental states *just* by applying the formulaic regimen opposite, you will often fail, because any trip into the mind of another is not just a voyage without maps, it is ultimately a creative and metaphysical enterprise.

On this view, knowledge of mental states is difficult and doubtful—but often this is not so: take the mental state of a baby being put to the breast after separation from his or her mother, or of an audience giving a standing ovation, or screaming fans waving at an idol, and we know *without doubt* that these mental states comprise unalloyed satisfaction, pleasure, and adulation. Note that so often it is non-verbal behaviour that allows valid judgment about mental states: don't rely on words alone—those capricious (but indispensable) tokens of disguise and deception.

Helping patients avoid doctor-dependency

A patient may become over-dependent on his or her doctor in many spheres of medicine. This is a particular danger in psychiatry because of the intimate and intense rather one-sided or asymmetrical relationship which may be built up between the patient and his psychiatrist—who is likely to come to know far more about the patient's innermost hopes and fears than many of his close friends. This encourages the patient to transfer to the therapist thoughts and attitudes that would more naturally be directed to a parent-figure. This process (known as transference) powerfully stimulates doctor-dependency, sometimes with serious consequences.

Signs of non-therapeutic dependency Repeated telephonings for advice, the inability to initiate any plan without help from the therapist, and the patient's disallowing of attempts by the therapist to terminate treatment (eg by threatening relapse).

Assessing whether dependency is a problem Clearly, in the examples above, the patient's dependency on his doctor is non-therapeutic. At other times, for example, early on in treatment, doctor-dependency may be quite helpful. In these circumstances the danger is that the doctor will be flattered by his patient's dependency on him. Most therapists either want to be loved by their patients or want to dominate them (or both), and it is important to know, in each session with each patient, just where you lie within the space marked out by these axes. Ask yourself 'Why do I look forward to seeing this patient?' 'Why do I dread seeing Mr X?' 'Why do I mind if this patient likes me?'

►When you feel good after seeing a patient always ask yourself why (it is so often because he is becoming dependent on you).

Avoiding dependency Planning and agreeing specific, limited goals with patients is one way of limiting dependency. If the patient agrees from the outset that it is not your job to provide him with a new job, wife, or family, the patient is more likely to have realistic expectations about therapy.

Planning discharge from the beginning of therapy is another important step in limiting doctor-dependency. Discharge is easy to arrange from the hospital outpatient department, but for the general practitioner the concept of discharge is diluted by the fact of his contractual obligation to the patient—who is perfectly within his rights to turn up the day after being 'discharged' and demand that therapy be started all over again. He must have more subtle methods at his disposal to encourage the patient to discharge himself. For example, he can learn to appear completely ineffective, so that the dependency cycle (patient presents problem→doctor presents solution→patient sabotages solution→doctor presents new solution) is never started. Another approach is to bore your patient by endlessly going over the same ground, so that the patient seizes control and walks out as if to say 'I've had enough of this!'

The foregoing makes patients out to be perpetual seekers after succour and emotional support—and so it can seem at times; but a great mystery of clinical medicine is that, spontaneously and miraculously, many apparently irremediably dependent patients *can* change, and start leading mature and independent lives. So do not be downcast when you are looking after these poor people: there is much to be said for simply offering a sympathetic ear, staying with your patient through thick and thin, and waiting for time to go by, and for the wind to change. Of course, the wind may change back again, but, if it does, you will not be back at square one, for you will be able to inject the proceedings with the most powerful psychotherapeutic agent of all: namely hope.

How to talk about sex with young people

Sexual issues are as [illegible] (contraception, [illegible] sexual assault). More [illegible] [illegible] problems. [illegible] sex [illegible] with [illegible] and [illegible] consequences [illegible] [illegible] by [illegible] [illegible] [illegible] [illegible]
• [illegible] is important as they are [illegible] socially acceptable (eg [illegible] sex). [illegible] people think you are trying to be [illegible] but [illegible] and may [illegible] [illegible] the patient's words [illegible] Ask if these words are [illegible]
• Avoid ambiguity. Make sure that you [illegible] know what is being talked about. For instance, some young people [illegible] oral sex [illegible] asked [illegible] [illegible] though they had [illegible] [illegible] part family [illegible]
• Do not assume sexual knowledge. [illegible] young people know [illegible] but when we were younger, sex [illegible] confusing and [illegible] There are still many [illegible] for young people to admit that they don't know something. Sex education at schools is [illegible]
• Don't assume a sexual orientation [illegible] young [illegible] feelings they are confused or [illegible] by their [illegible] [illegible] sexuality [illegible] outside [illegible] your [illegible] [illegible] one [illegible] people may include [illegible] in the future. [illegible] The issue of sexuality [illegible] can be [illegible] until you're [illegible] [illegible] do you know you're [illegible] issues with your brothers and sisters? [illegible] your parents? Do you [illegible] outside the home?
• Don't appear embarrassed [illegible] think that you aren't able to cope [illegible] Don't [illegible] shocked and don't [illegible] and they will stop being honest with you [illegible] further discussion of [illegible] Ask if you have plenty of time [illegible] in the world.
• The more you [illegible] in [illegible] problem to you [illegible] techniques of sexual [illegible] self-esteem [illegible] negotiation [illegible] partners [illegible] Also [illegible] the foundation for [illegible]

Asking about sexual abuse: [illegible] you feel uncomfortable [illegible] touched you in a way that made you feel [illegible] I don't know [illegible] if anyone has hurt you in a sexual way.

Young people need to know that you may have to discuss [illegible] with someone else if they (or someone else) [illegible] danger.

[illegible]

How to talk about sex with young people

Sexual issues are easier when an overt part of consultations (contraception, fertility, and sexual diseases). More commonly they are a covert part of other emotional or behavioural problems. We may find sexual dialogue embarrassing and avoid it—with unpredictable or fatal consequences, eg for those made suicidal by abuse[1] or by confusing emotions relating to sexuality.

Language is important. it may be ***medical*** (eg 'coitus'); ***slang*** (eg 'fucking'); or ***socially acceptable*** (eg 'having sex'). It is not advisable to use slang as people think you are trying to be hip. Most will expect socially acceptable language; slang may shock and may put up barriers. But occasional mirroring of the patient's words can gain rapport. Ask if your words are acceptable.

- Avoid ambiguity. Make sure that you both know what the other is talking about. For instance, some young people do not count oral sex as sex. So if asked 'have you had any sexual relations with her?' he may say no even though they had oral sex. If a new phrase crops up (slang changes all the time), ask for an explanation right away (a little gentle helping on your part usually overcomes any embarrassment here).
- Do not assume sexual knowledge. Not all young people know everything. Just as when we were younger, sex can seem confusing and mysterious. There are still many behind-the-bike-sheds myths, and it is just as hard as it ever was for young people to admit that they don't know something. Sex education in schools is uneven, and is sometimes useless.
- Don't *assume* a sexual orientation. It may be best to let these issues surface gradually rather than asking directly early on. Imply that it is safe to reveal feelings that are confused or non-standard. Your patient may be boxed in by societal, religious, or family views of what sexuality should be, so that suicide can seem to only way out.[10] Through your dialogue you may be able to show that there are other options, and that 'there no straight way through this world for any of us'.[11] If orientation is causing distress, point out that there is more to a personhood than sexuality—roles they may be good at may include being a friend, colleague, brother, daughter, or son—as well as lover, now or in the future. 'You don't need not have sex just to settle the issue of sexuality; feelings can be explored without sex acts, which can be left until you feel ready'. In helping gay people decide when to 'come out' eg to parents, explain that reactions can be unpredictable.[12] 'How well do you know your parents? How have they dealt with religious or sexual issues with your brothers and sisters? Are you economically dependant on your parents? Do you have a social support outside the home?'[13]
- Don't appear embarrassed. It is easier for people to open up if they think that you aren't going to blush, tell them off, or, worst of all, laugh. Don't act shocked and don't judge; give the wrong impression and they will stop being honest with you—see p 319 for further discussion of this vital point.
- Act as if you have plenty of time to listen—all the time in the world.
- The more you practice sexual dialogue, the easier it gets. If you shy away from it, it will remain a problem to you. Also, your patients may learn techniques of sexual dialogue, helpful in their lives as a whole, augmenting self-esteem, enabling sexual negotiation (useful in negotiating safer sexual practices with partners).[14] Also, you may lay the foundation for honest sexual dialogue between this teenager and his or her offspring, 15 years from now.

Asking about sexual abuse Have you been in any relationships that made you feel uncomfortable? Has anyone touched you in a way that made you feel embarrassed? I am wondering if anyone has hurt you in a sexual way.

Young people need to know that you may have to discuss your conversation with someone else if they (or someone else) is in mortal danger.[15] [16]

1 McFarlane J 2005 *Obstet Gynecol* **105** 99 Those who feel they can approach doctors after rape have a rate of repeat attack which is reduced by 32% compared with those who feel unable to so confidea.

How to identify and use the full range of psychiatric services

Any good psychiatric service will have much more to it than out-patient clinics and hospital wards. The latter are very important, but many significant psychiatric interventions go on in the community. Alternatives to the cycle of outpatient/inpatient treatments include:

- Assertive outreach teams
- Home treatment teams
- On-call community psychiatric nurses (CPNs)
- Crisis intervention teams
- Substance abuse teams
- Drop-in services during weekends and unsocial hours
- Telephone helplines
- Self-help groups
- Mental illness hostels
- Occupation centres (voluntary or statutory)
- Sheltered work
- Supervised living quarters so patients are not alone
- Intermediate care (p 472)
- EMI homes (for the elderly mentally infirm)[17]
- Self-running group homes
- Voluntary bodies, eg multidenominational charities for the homeless which provide meals, direct access hostels—and 'one stop' help with addictions.[18]

These components of any comprehensive service are not only important in keeping patients out of hospital (a prime aim of those who are purchasing care—as well as of patients and doctors); they are also important in gradually normalizing the patient's relationship with his environment.

Integrated care has theoretical advantages—eg for a schizophrenic patient who is a substance abuser, integrating psychiatric and substance abuse therapy leads to better outcome than either alone.[19]

In a way, the benefits of integrative care seem obvious (which is why it is puzzling that earlier meta-analyses have not found it to be advantageous, perhaps because the wrong questions were asked).[20]

How to help patients not to be manipulative

Fireships on the lagoon We have all been manipulated by our patients, and it is wrong to encourage in ourselves such stiffness of character and inflexibility of mind that all attempts by our patients to manipulate us inevitably fail. Nevertheless, a patient's manipulative behaviour is often counterproductive, and reinforces maladaptive behaviour. A small minority of patients are *very* manipulative, and take a disproportionate toll on your resources, and those of their family, friends, and colleagues. We are all familiar with these patients who Ford Madox Ford describes as being like fireships on a crowded lagoon, causing conflagration in their wake.[1] After destroying their family and their home we watch these people cruise down the ward or into our surgeries with some trepidation. Can we stop them losing control, and causing melt-down of our own and our staff's equanimity? The first thing to appreciate is that, unlike an unmanned ship, these people *can* be communicated with, and you *can* help them without resorting to hosing them down with cold water.

Setting limits One way of avoiding becoming caught up in this web of maladaptive behaviour is to set limits, as soon as this behaviour starts. In a small minority of patients, the therapist may recognize that their needs for time, attention, sedation, and protection are, for all practical purposes, insatiable. Whatever the therapist gives, such patients come back for more and more, and yet in spite of all this 'input' they do not appear to get any better. The next step is to realize that if inappropriate demands are not met, the patient will not become sicker (although there may be vociferous complaints). This realization paves the way for setting limits on the patients' behaviour, specifying exactly what is and is not acceptable.

Take for example the patient who demands sedation, threatening to 'lose control' if it is not given immediately, stating that he cannot bear living another day without sedation, and that the therapist will be responsible for any damage which ensues. If it is decided that drugs do not have a part to play in treatment, and that the long-term aim is for the patient to learn to be responsible for himself, then it can be simply stated to the patient that medication will not be given, and that he is free to engage in destructive acts, and that if he does so this is his responsibility.

The therapist explains that in demanding instant sedation he usurps her professional role, which is to decide these matters according to her own expert judgment, and that such usurpation will not be tolerated. If there is serious risk of real harm, admission to hospital may be indicated, where further limits may be set. If necessary, he is told that if he insists on 'going crazy' he will be put in a seclusion room, to protect others.

1 Ford Madox Ford 1915 *The Good Soldier*, Penguin. J Holmes 2002 *Mental Health in Primary Care*, OUP

How to help patients be less lonely

***Being unwanted is the worst disease that any human being can experience.*[1]**

***Loneliness does not come from having no people about one, but from being unable to communicate the things that seem important to one.*[2]**

Loneliness is not a condition you will find in many psychiatric classifications—yet it is the root of much psychopathology. It is also frequently the result of psychopathology. Some people, of course, *like* to avoid their fellows. For them, intrusion into their private world may cause despair; but, for most of us, these intrusions are welcome, and necessary for health. Loneliness seriously affects 1 in 10 older people, and can contribute to alcoholism, depression, and suicide. Suspect that loneliness is important whenever you find your hand being gripped for comfort after one would have thought that a social encounter was over—also whenever there is a verbal outpouring and a 'defeated demeanour'.[3]

Do not assume that loneliness means social isolation. Someone who has brief visits 3 times a day, from, say, a nurse, a care assistant, and a 'meals on wheels lady' is not socially isolated, but may be very lonely. But if he or she gets on well with just one of these visitors, this can be enough to banish loneliness. So this is the first lesson: *be nice to people, and take trouble to find out their hopes and fears*. But more is possible: in general, it is depressing waiting for the doorbell to ring, so tailor your suggestions in the light of your patient's mobility. This needs initiative on your patient's part: but do not think you must treat your patient's depression *before* you tackle a lonely lifestyle: tackling this may be the route out of depression. Areas to think about include:

- What facilities already exist? Is there a local pub, day centre, or lunch club available? 'God, I wouldn't be seen dead in one of those places!' we so often hear. But take time to point out that it does not matter initially whether they get anything out of a social interaction. After all, they may meet someone of like mind, so enabling these artificial crutches to be thrown away.
- Is the person religious? There may be activities and outings to plan and talk about, and reminisce over, even if not actually enjoyed at the time.
- Housing: if the person is planning a move, will they be near family, and other people who speak their own language (metaphorically and literally)?
- Alternative therapies, eg massage and aromatherapy, can relieve loneliness.
- Adult education classes are a good (but often expensive) way to meet like-minded people—and with the acquisition of new skills, confidence improves and social interaction becomes more pleasurable.
- Involvement with community action groups may be a source of friends (and a source of frustration and disappointment—but do not expect your interventions to be without side-effects: the thing is to plan for them).
- Details of local community activities can be found in the UK at the local *Council for Voluntary Services*. Other organizations advertise at local libraries.
- While at the library, ask about joining a book club.
- Befriending schemes can be very helpful to those who are housebound.
- Technology forums such as the Internet may provide relief from boredom and loneliness—and for some this will offer the best chance of meeting with a kindred spirit, unlimited by the constraints of time and space.
- Befriending others, and offering phone support is an option, whether or not one is housebound. Some local authorities give help to get phones.

1 Mother Teresa **2** Carl Jung **3** A Forbes 1996 *BMJ ii* 352.

Useful UK addresses:

University of the Third Age, 26 Harrison St, London WC1, tel. 020 7837 8838

Names of leaders of local religious groups: 15 Henrietta St, London WC2E 8QH, tel. 020 7240 0630

Age Concern: 1268 London Road, London SW16 4EJ, tel. 020 8679 8000

Cruse: Bereavement line: 020 8939 9530

Saga Holidays: Bouverie House, Middelburg Square, Folkstone, Kent CT20 1AZ

How to recognize and treat your own mental illnesses

Doctors have a higher than average incidence of suicide and alcoholism, and we must all be prepared to face (and try to prevent) these and other health risks of our professional and private lives. Our skill at looking after ourselves has never been as good as our skill at looking after others, but when the healer himself is wounded, is it clear that his ability to help others will be correspondingly reduced? Our own illnesses are invaluable in allowing us to understand our patients, what makes people go to the doctor (or avoid going to the doctor), and the barriers we may erect to resist his advice. But the idea of an ailing physician remains a paradox to the average mind, so that we may ask: ►Can true spiritual mastery over a power ever be won by someone who is counted among her slaves?[1] If the time comes when our mental state seriously reduces our ability to work, we must be able to recognize this and take appropriate action. The following may indicate that this point is approaching:

- Drinking alcohol before ward rounds or surgeries.
- The minimizing of every contact with patients, so that the doctor does the bare minimum which will suffice.
- Inability to concentrate on the matter in hand. Your thoughts are entirely taken up with the workload ahead.
- Irritability (defined as disagreeing with >1 nurse/24h).
- Inability to take time off without feeling guilty.
- Feelings of excessive shame or anger when reviewing past débâcles. To avoid mistakes it would be necessary for us all to give up medicine.
- Emotional exhaustion (defined as knowing that you should be feeling pleased or cross with yourself or others, but on summoning up the affairs of your heart, you draw a blank).
- Prospective studies suggest that introversion, masochism, and isolation are important risk factors for doctors' impairment.

The first step in countering these unfavourable states of mind is to recognize that one is present. The next step is to confide in someone you trust. Give your mind time to rejuvenate itself.

If these steps fail, various psychotherapeutic interventions may be relevant, eg cognitive behavioural therapy (p 372), or you might try prescribing the symptom. For example, if you are plagued by recurring thoughts about how inadequately you treated a patient, set time aside to deliberately ruminate on the affair, avoiding distractions. This is the first step in gaining control. You initiate the thought, rather than the thought initiating itself. The next step is to interpose some neutral topic, once the 'bad' series of thoughts is under way. After repeated practice, the mind will automatically flow into the neutral channel, once the bad thoughts begin, and the cycle of shame and rumination will be broken.

If no progress is made, the time has come to consult an expert, such as your general practitioner. Our own confidential self-help group for addiction and other problems is the British Doctors' and Dentists' Group and may be contacted via the Medical Council on Alcohol (UK tel. 020 7487 4445). If you are the expert that another doctor has approached, do not be deceived by this honour into thinking that you must treat your new patient in any special way. Special treatment leads to special mistakes, and it is far better for doctor-patients to tread well-worn paths of referral, investigation, and treatment than to try illusory short cuts.

1 Thomas Mann 1924 *The Magic Mountain*, page 132-3, Penguin

Burnout

Typical features:

- Stress and depression
- Exhaustion
- Motivation↓; apathy↑
- Libido↓ and insomnia
- Guilt or denial
- Feeling isolated
- Paranoia
- Amnesia
- Indecision
- Temper tantrums

Risk factors—for doctors Pressure of work, a less personal relationship with patients, overly formal hierarchies, and suboptimal income are put forward to explain the fact that some doctors (urologists, for example) in the public sector are more at risk of burnout compared with private-service urologists.[21] [n=75]

Management (Difficult) Some may respond to plans such as these:

- Diagnose and treat any depression (p 336–7).
- Allow time for the person to recognize that there is a problem.
- More hobbies, and more nice holidays.
- Advice from wise colleagues in the specialty (regular follow-up). Mentoring consists in forming a supportive relationship with an independent colleague for the sole purpose of support.
- Learn new professional skills.
- Set achievable goals in work and leisure (eg protected time with family).
- Early retirement.

Prevention Strategies such as career counselling are said to be effective but really do no more than point a lollipop at a furnace.[22] [n=171]

Patients in disgrace: the fat-folder syndrome

The sorrow that has no vent in tears may make other organs weep.[1]

One of the roles of the psychiatrist is to act as the terminus for patients who have been shunted from hospital department to hospital department. These patients offer their doctor an 'organ recital' of incapacitating physical symptoms for which no physical cause can be found (somatization). She knows that 'there must be something wrong'. In the end, the patient is sent in disgrace to the psychiatrist because the doctor declares that there is 'nothing wrong' and that the patient is 'just a hypochondriac'. The psychiatrist then has to do much work undoing the cycle of symptom-offering and investigation, by acknowledging that there *is* something wrong. The aim is to reframe symptom offering into problems which need to be solved, starting with the doctor accepting that the patient is distressed and looking for helpful responses from her carers which are yet to be defined. After establishing rapport, agree a contract with the patient, that we will give regular consultations for listening to how the patient feels and will try to offer help, if she acknowledges that past investigations have not helped, that psychological factors may play a part (somatization, p 640), and that she agrees not to consult other doctors until a specified number of sessions have elapsed.[2] Also, cognitive therapy (p 374) which examines the way that conscious thoughts and beliefs perpetuate disability, *can* lead to symptom reduction.[23]

Dissociation (formerly known as hysteria)

Our stream of consciousness does not progress from cradle to grave as a single line: there are separations (dissociations) and confluences—for example, when we day-dream, or drive to Porlock with no recollection of the scenery along the way—only of our inner landscape. Dissociation may be partially adaptive, eg in annihilating pain in near-death experiences. Another example is a patient who was homosexually raped, had no conscious memory of the event, but felt an irresistible urge to write insulting letters about the person who had raped him. Most instances subside spontaneously, but if they do not it is important to refer early to a psychiatrist, before associated behaviour becomes habitual.

Types of dissociation *Amnesia* is the commonest type: see BOX. *Depersonalization:* (Feeling of being detached from one's body or ideas, as if one were an outsider, observing the self; '*I am in a dream*' or '*I am an automaton*'—but unrelated to drugs/alcohol). This may be a response to stress.

Dissociative identity disorder: The patient has multiple personalities which interact in complex ways. It is present in 3% of acute psychiatric inpatients.

Fugue: Inability to recall one's past ± loss of identity or formation of a new identity—associated with unexpected, purposeful travel (lasts hours to months, and for which there is no recollection).

Prognosis Follow-up over ~6yrs shows that ~5% of those referred to a CNS hospital who had hysteria or dissociation diagnosed turned out to have organic illness. However, these patients may not be typical of those diagnosed with dissociation (diagnoses included spinocerebellar degeneration).

Treatment Exploring the stresses in the patient's life may help. In general, be ready to recognize the psychological components of physical illness, and get expert psychiatric help, while leaving the door open for reappraisal if new features develop.

1 Dr Francis J Braceland, 'Living with executive tensions' *The National Observer* Dec 28th 1964
2 Rosendal M 2005 *BMJ* **330** 4

Is this amnesia dissociative?

- Has a physical cause been carefully discounted? (Drugs, epilepsy, etc)
- Is the patient young? Beware making the first diagnosis if >40yrs old.
- Have the symptoms been provoked by stress? Ask the family.
- What is the pattern of amnesia? If for distant *and* near memories, then dissociation is more likely (as opposed to organic causes) than if the amnesia is for shorter term memory.
- Is there secondary gain?—ie is it worthwhile perpetuating symptoms? Many diseases have gain for the patient: this sign is most useful if *absent*.
- Do related symptoms 'make sense' (eg aphonia in a news-reader)?
- Indifference to what should constitute a major handicap (*la belle indifférence*) is of marginal diagnostic use.
- Is malingering likely? The answer is almost always 'No', except in prisons and the armed services (when secondary gain is easy to identify).
- Is there a dissociative personality? The dissociative experiences scale (DES) screens for this. It is a 28-item visual analogue scale on which patients indicate percentages of time during which they have different types of dissociative experiences (excluding those influenced by alcohol or drugs)—ranging from non-pathological experience of being so absorbed in TV that the person is unaware of what is happening in the room, to severe dissociations, eg of having no memory of important personal events, or feeling that his or her body belongs to another. Those with dissociative disorders typically have DES scores of 30 or higher; most others score nearer zero.[24]

Calibrating our sensitivity to psychosomatic events

Why do some doctors preferentially diagnose somatic illness? Why, when confronted by unexplained symptoms do we often subconsciously try to fit them to a physical ailment? The reason is usually that prescribing a pill is easier than changing, or regulating, intrapsychic events. The patient and the doctor may collude with this approach, and then get very frustrated when it yields nothing of value. Alternatively, some doctors are so used to diagnosing psychological problems that they are all too prone to launch into treating someone's depression and malaise, rather than their endocarditis or brucellosis. There is no single correct approach. We all make errors—but the point is to find out in which direction you tend to make errors, then allow for this in your interactions with patients.

Depression

NICE guidance[25]

Each year 40% of us have quite severe feelings of depression, unhappiness, and disappointment. Of these, 20% experience a clinical depression, in which low mood occurs with sleep difficulty, change in appetite, hopelessness, pessimism, or thoughts of suicide. *Diagnosis* of major depression:

- Loss of interest or pleasure—***anhedonia*** in daily life with dysphoric mood (ie 'down in the dumps') plus ≥4 of the following (the first 5 are 'biological' symptoms)—present nearly every day for at least 2 weeks:
- ***Poor appetite*** with ***weight loss*** (or, rarely, increased appetite).
- ***Early waking***—with ***diurnal mood variation*** (worse in mornings).
- ***Psychomotor retardation*** (ie a paucity of spontaneous movement, or sluggish thought processes), or ***psychomotor agitation***.
- Decrease in ***sexual drive*** and other appetites.
- Evidence of (or complaints of) reduced ***ability to concentrate***.
- Ideas of ***worthlessness***, inappropriate ***guilt*** or ***self-reproach***.
- Recurrent ***thoughts of death*** and ***suicide***, or ***suicide attempts***.

Why is depression so often missed? • Lack of knowledge. • Preoccupation with physical disease. • Psychiatric labels are hated (doctors and patients collude). • It's hard to spot depression coexisting with other illness.

Classification Classify as: • *Mild; moderate; severe.* • *With/without biological features.* • *With/without delusions or hallucinations.* • *With/without manic episodes* (ie bipolar not unipolar). These replace the old reactive/endogenous labels. ΔΔ: Cyclothymic disorder; substance-induced mood disorder; schizophrenia, dementia; mood disorder due to a general medical condition.

Why we get depressed: some ideas • Genetics: identical twins reared apart show 60% more concordance for depression than dizygotic twins (NB: these twin studies are suspect; see *PsychiatrQ* 2002 71[26] for the reasons why).

- Biochemistry: there are excess 5-hydroxytryptamine ($5HT_2$) receptors in the frontal cortex of brains taken from suicide victims. See *OHCM* p 334.
- Endocrinology: cortisol suppression (dexamethasone suppression test, *OHCM* p 311) is abnormal in ~30%. Melatonin is also implicated (p 404). Also, 17β-estradiol is known to help depression if perimenopausal. *EBM* 2002 **77** 21
- Stressful events (eg new births, job loss, divorce, illness): present in 60%.
- Freudian reasons: depression mirrors bereavement, but loss is of a valued 'object', not a person. There is ambivalence with hostility turned inwards.
- Learned helplessness: if punishment is unrelated to actions, but is perceived as random, the response is helplessness and depression.[27]
- Vulnerability factors: physical illness, pain, and lack of intimate relationships may allow depression to arise and be perpetuated.[MET 28]

Management There is no clear distinction between the low moods we all get and illness needing vigorous treatment, but the lower the mood and the more marked the slowness, the more vigorous the treatment needs to be.

- ***Psychological treatment*** (eg cognitive therapy, p 372) is part of the treatment of *all* depression; it may be all that is needed in milder depressions.
- Presence of biological features or stress predicts a good response to ***antidepressants*** (p 340) especially if symptoms are severe. Not everyone wants drugs. Discuss all options. Herbalism can work: hypericum (St John's wort) may be useful in mild to moderately severe depression.[MET 29]
- Delusions or hallucinations prompt a physical treatment, ie ***ECT*** (p 342) or ***drugs*** (antidepressants ± antipsychotic drugs, p 360).
- The depressive phase of bipolar illness is treated as above, but note:
  1 Be cautious with the physical treatments: they may induce mania.
  2 Lithium or valproate prophylaxis may be needed (p 354).[30]
- ***Reasons to admit:*** Social circumstances; high suicide drive; isolation.

Who is likely to benefit from antidepressant drugs? (p 340)

Those who have had low mood or loss of desire for pleasure (anhedonia) most of the day for at least the last 2 weeks who show 4 or more of the following 7 markers of severe depression:

- Suicide plans in existence, or ideas of self-harm.
- Unexplained or unbidden feelings of guilt or worthlessness.
- Inability to function—eg psychomotor retardation or agitation.
- Concentration impaired.
- Impaired appetite.
- Decreased sleep (especially early morning waking).
- Energy low, or unaccountable fatigue.

►Enquire about these phenomena *whenever* depression is possible. NB: treatment may still be needed if the above criteria are not met: listen to their story. Patients will often not accept that they could be depressed because 'there is nothing to *make* me depressed'. It helps to suggest that they could still be depressed, and that treatment could be very helpful. Give them time to go away and think about it, perhaps discussing it with someone they know (get consent). Try 'would your wife (or partner) say you were depressed? Please could you ask and let me know what they say?' Such patients often return enriched by dialogue and reflection, and are successfully treated. This may not be over-medicalizing a patient's symptoms: there is evidence that such patients are simply inexperienced in understanding their depression: when they *next* become depressed, their views much more nearly match those of their doctor.[31]

(a moon swims out of a cloud
a clock strikes midnight
a finger pulls a trigger
a bird flies into a mirror) e e cummings

Suicide and attempted suicide

NICE guidance[32]

Suicide needs to be distinguished from attempted suicide and self-harm. The latter is very common, but remember that every non-fatal event may be fatal next time,[1] which is why the subjects are treated together here. Men aged 15–30 are most at risk of completed suicide; incidence of self-harm is highest in teenage and older females (>1%/yr). Suicide rates are rising (now as common as road deaths)[33] being higher in island peoples and in eastern Europe, and rarer in Islamic peoples. Worldwide, 10^6 people/yr commit suicide; increasingly they are young.[34][35]

Understanding suicide Suicide may be a way of avoiding pain, or keeping honour and autonomy, and avoiding shame (the noble Roman in us prefers suicide to being forced to walk on our knees).[2] *Self-harm may be a way of:*
- Controlling change in families, eg when a member is about to leave.
- Communicating important messages in a not-to-be ignored way.
- Gaining power in family transactions, by escalating conflict.

Often an argument with a partner is an antecedent to self-harm. Immaturity, inability to cope with stress, weakening of religious ties, and availability of drugs (psychotropics & alcohol are popular poisons) are also important, as is 'copy-cat' behaviour: when celebrities try suicide, others follow. Antecedents of suicide: chronic disease, depression, bankruptcy, etc.[36] Reducing levels of psychiatric care are also important.[37] [n=149]

Bullying, intolerable stress to succeed, and 'falling behind in my homework' are also risk factors. If this mirrors your own state after trudging through too many handbook pages, shut this book, and have a good holiday.

After assessment, there are 5 stages in trying to help the survivors:
- Agreement of a contract offering help (p 339)—by negotiation.
- Discussion with the family as to how problems might be tackled.
- Problem-solving by facilitating the patient's understanding of her predicament, and by pointing out how she has coped with problems in the past. The aim is to engender a greater ability to cope in the future as well as helping immediate personal and social problems.
- Prevention: open-access, walk-in clinics or 24h phone service.
- Follow-up—either with family or with the patient alone.

Assessment Think of a target with 3 concentric rings. *The inner ring* is the circumstances of the attempt: what happened that day; were things normal to start with? When did the feelings and events leading up to the act start? Get descriptions of these in detail. Was there any last act (eg a suicide note)? What happened after the event? Was this what he/she expected? ***The middle ring*** is the background to the attempt: how things have been over the preceding months. Might the attempt have been made at any time over the last months? What relationships were important over this time? ***The outer ring*** is the family and personal history (p 322).
After the above, come to the *bulls-eye*—the intentions lying behind the attempt, and the present feelings and intentions. Does the attempt represent a wish to die (a grave, not-to-be-ignored sign); a wish to send a message to somebody; or a wish to change intolerable circumstances? Ask: 'If you were to leave hospital today, how would you cope?' Examine the mental state (p 324) to find out if there is any mental illness. *Summary:* •Any plan? What? When? Where? •Are the means available? •Ever tried before? How seriously? •Preparations (making a will, giving things away).
Before arranging hospital admission, ask what this is *for*. Is it only to make you feel happier?—or to gain something that cannot be gained outside hospital. Ask: *Why will discharge be safer in a few weeks rather than now?*

1 Harriss L 2005. The measurement of suicidal intent is valuable in the evaluation of future suicide among self-harm patients. *B J Psych* **186**.

How to cope with threats of suicide

Suicidal behaviour is powerful. *Boyfriend:* 'After last night, I think we should separate—we'd better just be good friends...' *Girlfriend* thinks: 'You are not going to treat me like that', but says: 'So we are not getting married after all?' 'Well not for a little while, maybe'. 'So you don't love me ... I knew you loved Amanda more than me'. Exit to bathroom, where she swallows handfuls of her mother's tranquillizers. Next day in hospital the boyfriend says 'I'm so sorry—I didn't know you loved me that much'. He thinks: 'No one has ever thought that much of me... Fancy wanting to kill herself because I wouldn't marry her! I feel guilty; I should not have led her to this...' Whereupon he proposes marriage. This disastrous ending may be complicated by threats of suicide from jilted Amanda.

The psychiatrist may become enmeshed in these webs of suicide threats, and may wrongly assume that because someone threatens suicide, they should be admitted to hospital (compulsorily if necessary) so that they can be kept under constant surveillance, and suicide prevented. This reasoning has 3 faults. The first is the idea that it is possible to prevent suicide by admission. There is no such thing as constant surveillance. Second, hospital admission may achieve nothing if it simply removes the patient from the circumstances which he must learn to cope with. Third, it is necessary to distinguish between suicide gestures, which have the object of influencing others' behaviour, and a genuine wish to die.[3]

Before death, many suicide victims see a GP, and it is wise to be alert to undercurrents of suicide which only sometimes surface during consultations. Ask *unambiguously* about suicide plans (p 322). On deciding that a threat is more manipulative than genuine, very experienced therapists may influence the person's use of suicide behaviour by forcing him to face the reality of his suicide talk, eg by asking: 'When will you kill yourself?' 'How will you do it?' 'Who will discover the corpse?' 'What sort of funeral do you want? Cremation, burial, with or without flowers?' 'Who will come?'

The standard pointers to risk of death from a suicide attempt are being male, older, unemployed, with prolonged psychiatric or painful illness, ± drug abuse. Recent attempts to validate this list have failed. It is better to think dynamically of risks and protective factors (such as family support), with suicide occurring after key events which accumulate risk. ►*Take all suicide threats seriously*—but the emphasis differs depending into which group the patient falls. Aim to form a *contract* with the patient, eg:

- The therapist will listen and help if the patient agrees to be frank, and to tell the therapist of any suicide thoughts or plans.
- Agreement about which problems are to be tackled is made explicit.
- The type of change to aim for is agreed.
- Specification of who else will be involved in treatment (eg other members of the family, friends, the patient's GP).
- An agreement about the timing and place of sessions.
- An agreement about the patient's responsibility to work effectively with the therapist, and to carry out any 'homework'.

2 If in doubt about the energy with which we may pursue our own destruction, let us call to mind a notable Japanese pilot who, during World War II, persistently volunteered to be a Kamikazi pilot to run a suicide mission against US ships, in the defence of Okinawa. The authorities just as persistently refused his request—he had a wife and 3 daughters. He kept on reapplying, determinedly. Not wanting to risk her husband's failure again, and not wanting to stand in Destiny's way, his wife killed their 3 daughters, and then herself, so removing the obstacle to her husband's mission—and on May 28, 1945, he finally took to the air, and achieved his end.

3 Nice says: 'the decision to discharge a person without follow-up after an act of self-harm shouldn't be based solely on the presence of low risk of repetition of self-harm and the absence of a mental illness, because many such people may have a range of other social and personal problems that may later increase risk. These problems may be amenable to interventions'.

Which antidepressant? Sample regimens (see NICE, 2004)

Drugs improve mood and ↑synaptic availability of noradrenaline or 5HT. Don't rely on drugs alone. Your own personal qualities ± psychotherapeutic interventions are just as important. See p 370 for more details. Specifically, encourage socializing, and the countering of negative thoughts (p 372).

- ***Uncomplicated depression in middle age: little or no risk suicide:*** If a cheap agent is essential, try dosulepin (a tricyclic) 50mg/8-24h PO. Start with 50-75mg at night. Explain side-effects (below). Warn about driving and using machinery. Explain that benefits take weeks to develop. Avoid if risk of arrhythmia (eg post myocardial infarction). We have never been persuaded that any other drug is, in general, *more* effective than dosulepin. If side-effects are tolerated, it is an excellent drug. Typical dose: ≤150mg at night. Maximum: 225mg/day (eg in hospital use).[38]
- ***Depression with retardation:*** Try SSRIs, eg fluoxetine, 20mg/24h PO. $t_{1/2}$ ≈ 3 days. In women, consider combining with 0.5mg/day folic acid: folate is low in major depression, and supplementation helped in one study.[RCT 39] [N=127]
- ***Past history of good response to tricyclics, now suicidal:*** Try lofepramine, 70mg/12h (less likely to be fatal in overdose; less risk of fatal arrhythmias).
- ***Depression in an adolescent:*** See p 390. Tricyclics/SSRI rarely help. Unlicenced indication
- ***Depression if elderly:*** May be less tolerant of SEs; halve doses (tricyclics).
- ***Depression + psychosis:*** ECT (p 342) ± neuroleptics (p 360) may be needed.
- ***Depression in those insisting on driving:*** Paroxetine (20mg each morning, increased by 10mg increments; max: 50mg/24h) is safer than tricyclics. It is the SSRI most associated with the unpleasant dystonias on withdrawal.
- ***Depression + disordered sleep pattern:*** Tricyclic, eg dosulepin, as above. If suicidal, nefazodone (SSRI, & blocks $5HT_2$ receptors) and mirtazapine (blocks 5HT2, H1, and 5HT3—15mg at bedtime, max 45mg) *may* have a role. Warn patients not to rely on the 'fact' that day time sleepiness usually wears off after a few weeks. NB: ordinary SSRIs can aggravate insomnia. Sleep is such a restorative for some patients, so give them the best chance.
- ***Depression not responding to SSRI:*** Venlafaxine (SNRI[1]) *may* have a role.[MET 40] [n=5562]
- ***Pregnancy/breastfeeding:*** Tricyclics may be best; p 408; get expert help.
- ***Depression with obsessive–compulsive features:*** Clomipramine or an SSRI.
- ***Depression with Parkinson's disease:*** SSRI. Nortriptyline has been found to be effective, and may not make the Parkinson's much worse.
- ***Post-stroke depression:*** Nortriptyline is ?better than fluoxetine.[41]
- ***Depression at menopause*** HRT may help but ↑ breast cancer risk, p 256.
- ***Depression + obesity:*** Fluoxetine sometimes leads to weight↓.[42]
- ***Worried about drug interactions:*** Citalopram and sertraline have lowest risk. Most SSRIs inhibit CYP450 enzymes so can ↑levels of many drugs.

Side-effects—*SSRI:* Citalopram & sertraline: • *Common:* Nausea, vomiting, dyspepsia, diarrhoea, abdominal pain. • *Others:* Rash, sweating, anxiety, agitation, headache, insomnia, tremor, sexual dysfunction, hyponatraemia, cutaneous bleeding disorders. Fluoxetine as for above except insomnia and agitation more frequent. Fluvoxamine as for citalopram but nausea more common. Paroxetine as for citalopram except more antimuscarinic effects and sedation, also extrapyramidal symptoms (but rare).

Tricyclics: Amitriptyline: • *Common:* Sedation, dry mouth, urine retention, blurred vision, postural hypotension, tachycardia, constipation. • *Other SE:* Arrhythmias; convulsions (dose-related). Clomipramine, dosulepin, doxepin as for amitriptyline. Imipramine and lofepramine less sedating than amitriptyline. Trimipramine more sedating than amitriptyline.

1 SNRI = serotinin and noradrenaline reuptake inhibitor. Avoid if BP↑, U&E↑↓, or heart disease. **Specialist use only**; monitor BP if on >200mg/day. Usually starting dose: 37.5mg/12h PO. **SE:** Constipation; nausea; dizziness; dry mouth; BP↑; ADH↑; Na↓; T°↑; dyspnoea, hallucinations, arthralgia etc: see *BNF*.

Suicide risk with taking SSRIs

This has received much attention. Research using the UK General Practice Research Database for 1993–9 found the risk of suicidal behaviour was not significantly greater with SSRIs than it is for tricyclics.[43]

A Patient-centred approach to depression

We can sometimes feel perplexed with the use of antidepressants; it can feel like trial and error when prescribing them. What works very well in one person may not help someone else. There also seems to be an ever increasing choice of drugs and conflicting information on their safety. It is often stated that all antidepressants are of equal efficacy,[44] but this does not mean they are all equally effective in all situations (suicide risk, side-effect profile, and perhaps cost, need to be considered).

Advice to give a patient when treating depression

- Discuss with the patient the choice of drug and non-pharmacological therapy. Cognitive therapy is proven to be as effective as antidepressants in mild to moderate depression.[45] Their combined use has been shown to be better than either treatment alone.[46,47]
- Inform patient of side-effects, not all side-effects are undesirable (SSRIs are effective in treatment of premature ejaculation). Warn patients that there may be an initial worsening of symptoms in the first 1–2 weeks so persevere before the delayed therapeutic effect is seen.
- Prescribe a dose at a known therapeutic level. Assess after 4–6 weeks. If effective continue for at least 4–6 months after recovery, if stopped too soon 50% relapse.[MET 48] If not effective increase dose and review in 2 weeks. If still no response increase dose (unless poorly tolerated), review again in 2 weeks. If no response with increasing titration or poor tolerability, switch to an alternative class of antidepressant (special method, p 369).
- Recurrent depression: of those who have one episode of major depression 50–85% will have further episodes. Continuing antidepressants lowers the odds of depressive relapse by around two-thirds which about equals half the absolute risk.[49]

Theories of antidepressant action At least 8 pharmacological actions are known, and over 20 antidepressants exist. How do all these different actions ultimately lead to a similar clinical response? and why is there a delay? Two theories predominate: The ***Neurotransmitter receptor hypothesis:*** Postulates that a change in receptor sensitivity by desensitization and down regulation of different receptors and not simply increasing neurotransmitter at the synapse leads to clinical effects which takes weeks. The ***monoamine hypothesis of antidepressant on gene expression:*** This suggests that the effect of increased neurotransmitter at the synapse initiates a sequence of events to give the antidepressant response. This includes the up and down regulation of various genes with subsequent varying expression of receptors and critical proteins.[50]

Have a non-pharmacological arm to *every* treatment plan

Exercise, social interaction, psychotherapy (p 370), counselling (p 380), Tai Chi, Yoga, reading clubs, meditation, poetry (reading *and* writing). Join a club, eg Ramblers, or pottery. Rest from work. Some people don't want drugs: does he think that drugs equate with moral failure? If still unconvinced, an alternative therapy, eg St John's wort, might be acceptable?[51]

Electroconvulsive therapy (ECT)

Indications *Depression* if: •Not responding to antidepressants, or •Psychotic features are present, or •Needing to be controlled fast (eg patient refusing to drink, high suicide risk, or postpartum): electroconvulsive therapy (ECT) is the fastest acting physical treatment. Emergency ECT is possible, eg in some elderly patients, but should rarely be necessary.

Schizoaffective depression: (depression with signs of schizophrenia).

Mania: If not responding to drugs. *Typical course length:* 6 sessions (2/week).

Contraindications Recent subdural/subarachnoid bleeding; lack of consent (p 402; involve relatives, but they cannot consent for another adult).

Cautions Recent stroke, myocardial infarct, arrhythmias. SE: anterograde amnesia; anaesthesia complications.

Technique Check the patient's identity and that 'nil by mouth' for >8h.

- Ensure a detailed medical history and physical examination has been done, and any illnesses investigated and treated as far as possible. High anaesthetic risk?—See p 614; seizure threshold ↑ if on concurrent benzodiazepines or anticonvulsants; also ↑risk of heart complications if on tricyclics. Liaise between psychiatric and anaesthetic staff. Do benefits outweigh risks?
- Give calm reassurance away from the site where ECT is going on. (It may be distressing to watch ECT actually happening.)
- Are the consent forms in order (p 402)? In the rare instances in the UK where ECT is given without consent, a second opinion from the Mental Health Commission must state that the treatment is necessary (p 402).
- Ensure that fully equipped resuscitation trolleys are present including a functioning defibrillator, suction apparatus, and pulse oximeter.
- Ensure that the anaesthetist (senior and ECT trained) knows about allergies or drugs interfering with anaesthesia. For countering ECT-induced vagal stimulation, she is most likely to use atropine or methscopolamine before using an ultra-short-acting anaesthetic agent (eg methohexital) with muscle relaxation (eg with suxamethonium) to minimize the seizure.
- The ECT machine: checked recently? Reserve machine to hand? What charge/energy is to be given? Which waveform will be used (bidirectional or modified sinusoidal, or unidirectional)? See manufacturer's information.
- In unilateral ECT,* position one electrode (A) 4cm above the midpoint between the auditory meatus and the lateral angle of the eye, and the other (B) 10cm away from A, above the ear (see diagram).
- Put electrode jelly on the chosen sites (not enough to allow shorting).
- When the anaesthetist gives the word, give the shock. Be prepared to restrain the patient if paralysis is incomplete. While the current passes, the muscles will contract. This will cease as the current ceases. After ~10sec, further clonic spasms occur, lasting about 1min. The only sign may be lid fluttering. Clonus is probably needed for ECT to be fully effective.
- Put the patient in the coma position. Check BP and pulse, etc until conscious. Ask the anaesthetist to consider IV midazolam for those (few) who become very agitated during the recovery process.

ECT may be frightening, partly from its bad press; so explain, step-by-step, what will happen; and patients should not witness others having ECT. The author also finds it helpful to tell patients that he would opt for ECT, if the right indications pertained, because it can be so effective—indeed life-saving.

*Right unilateral high-dose ECT is rarely used but is as effective as bilateral ECT, but produces less severe and persistent cognitive effects.[RCT 52] [N=80]

What is the correct 'dose' of unilateral ECT?

There is no universal answer, but there is evidence that therapeutic effects of ECT are proportional to seizure length. Be sure that you have adequate training on this issue by the consultant in charge of the session. Dose is better measured in millicoulombs (mC) than milliamps. It depends on *seizure threshold*, which varies 40-fold among patients. A moderately 'suprathreshold' dose (eg 200% above seizure threshold) usually gives seizures of adequate duration, while aiming to minimize cognitive side-effects—according to the Royal College of Psychiatrists *ECT Handbook*.

Doses need change depending on response, and dose of propofol [MET 53] in the anaesthetic: also, seizure threshold rises by ~80% as courses progress. NB: a 'good' seizure is one which is of adequate duration (~15sec during early sessions; duration is less important later), with both a tonic and a clonic phase. Some machines allow EEG monitoring—useful as anaesthesia renders seizure analysis difficult. If the seizure lasts >2min, tell the anaesthetist, who will provide a bolus of diazepam, or more of the GA agent.

The frequency and speed of response of ECT varies according to indication, eg bipolar depression patients show more rapid improvement and need fewer treatments than unipolar patients. [54] [N=228] One retrospective study has found that female patients respond better to ECT than male patients.[1]

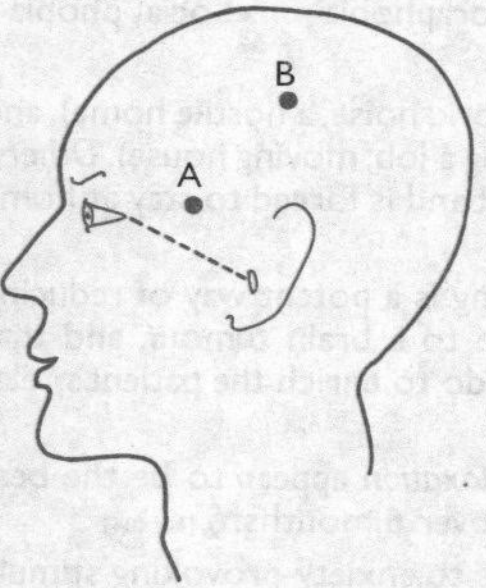

Electrode positions (see text)

1 Bloch Y 2005 *J Affect Disord* **84** 99

Anxiety neurosis/generalized anxiety disorder

Anxiety is a universal experience; it is, according to various reckonings, the chief factor limiting human potential; it causes much suffering, costing the UK ≳£5 billion/yr. *Neurosis* refers to ***maladaptive psychological symptoms not due to organic causes or psychosis, and usually precipitated by stress.*** Apart from free-floating anxiety and depression, such symptoms are: fatigue (27%), insomnia (25%), irritability (22%), worry (20%), obsessions, compulsions, and somatization (p 640). These are judged to be more intense than normal, ie out of proportion to the stress that precipitates them. Symptoms are not just part of a patient's normal personality, but they may be an exaggeration of personality: a generally anxious person may become even more so—ie develop an anxiety neurosis—as a result of job loss. The *type* of neurosis is defined by the chief symptom (eg anxiety, obsessional, depressive). Before diagnosing neurosis, consider carefully if there is underlying depression that needs treating with antidepressants.[55]

Symptoms of anxiety: Tension, agitation; feelings of impending doom, trembling; a sense of collapse; insomnia; poor concentration; 'goose flesh'; 'butterflies in the stomach'; hyperventilation (so tinnitus, tetany, tingling, chest pains); headaches; sweating; palpitations; poor appetite; nausea; 'lump in the throat' unrelated to swallowing (globus hystericus); difficulty in getting to sleep; excessive concern about self and bodily functions; repetitive thoughts and activities (p 346). *Children's symptoms:* Thumb-sucking; nail-biting; bedwetting; food-fads. The various types of anxiety:

- Generalized anxiety disorder (GAD)
- Panic disorder
- Simple phobia
- Post-traumatic stress disorder
- Agoraphobia
- Social phobia
- Obsessive-compulsive disorder

Causes Genetic predisposition; stress (eg work, noise, a hostile home), and life events (eg gaining or losing a spouse; losing a job; moving house). *Others: Faulty learning* or *secondary gain* (eg a husband is forced to stay at home with his agoraphobic wife).

Treatment *Symptom control:* Simple listening is a potent way of reducing anxiety. Explain that headaches are not due to a brain tumour, and that palpitations are harmless. Anything you can do to enrich the patient's relationship with others is likely to help.

Cognitive-behavioural therapy (p 372) and *relaxation* appear to be the best specific measures,[1] with 50–60% recovering over 6 months.[RCT 56] [N=404]

Behavioural therapy employs *graded exposure* to anxiety-provoking stimuli.

Anxiolytics may augment psychological methods, eg diazepam 5mg/8h PO for <6 weeks. Side-effects/withdrawal (p 368) severely limit their usefulness.

SSRI: Social anxiety with alcohol abuse syndrome: Paroxetine may help.[RCT 57] [N=9] Other *drugs:* Buspirone (5HT1A partial agonist; 5mg/8–12h[2]), hydroxyzine, and β-blockers may be tried (short-term) in generalized anxiety disorder.[58]

Progressive relaxation training: Teaching deep breathing using the diaphragm, and tensing and relaxation of muscle groups—eg starting with the toes and working up the body can ↓stress. Practice is essential. Tapes/CDs aid learning. NB: in some contexts, eg stress, relaxation is not as good as cognitive restructuring.[RCT 59] [N=87] *Hypnosis:* This is a powerful mechanism for reducing anxiety. Initially the therapist induces progressively deeper trances using such techniques as guided fantasy and concentration on various bodily sensations, such as breathing. Later, some patients will be able to induce their own trances. It may be very useful, eg medical contexts (eg post-op).[RCT 60] [N=32]

1 Linden M 2005 *Psychother Psychosom* **74** 36 If 25 sessions of CBT are given, effect lasts ≥8 months

2 SE: headache, nervousness, lightheaded/dizzy, excitement; *rare:* pulse↑, palpitations, dry mouth, fits.

Some remarks on the nature of anxiety

Anxiety is the engine in us, and also our steering wheel, weaving us in and out of the fast or slow lanes of our lives. Some of us deliberately seek out anxiety as a way of feeling alive (think of the tightrope walker, or the falconer who places the meat for his bird between his own eyes). The lives of others are dominated by the imperative of minimizing anxiety, to the extent that some of us never leave home, either physically or metaphorically. Anxiety implies heightened awareness, which is why it is one of the dominant colours in the artist's metaphysical palette. The artist makes us anxious so that we see familiar objects differently. Anxiety, up to a point, makes us sit up, and take note; beyond a certain level (different in all of us, and different at different times) anxiety is counter-productive: we become preoccupied with the feeling itself, which chokes our ability to act (*angere*, Latin for to choke, gives us both angina, and anxiety—*OED 1*^{e} i 378).

So anxiety is no more a disease or a symptom than the circulation of the blood is a disease or symptom: rather it is one aspect of our human condition: it's a part of the way we work. Just as our circulation can fail, so our ways of interacting with anxiety can fail. The most arresting manifestation of this phenomenon is panic (Pan is the god of groundless fear)—ie becoming petrified on being caught in the heart-stopping glare of events beyond our control. The strategies we adopt to recover our equilibrium are revealing: song, humour, camaraderie, and faith in God, gin, or our own genius. When these remedies fail, we turn to the psychiatrist and the strategies of cognitive therapy, hypnosis, and ritual relaxation. When these remedies fail in their turn (not always the case!), we are left on our own: this aloneness is another aspect of the human condition, and out of it grows our creativity and originality, born from the painful union of anxiety, fear, and hope.

Other neurotic disorders

Phobic disorders These involve symptoms of anxiety occurring in specific situations only, and leading to their avoidance. These are labelled according to specific circumstance: agoraphobia (*agora*, Greek for market place) is fear of crowds, travel, or situations away from home; social phobias (where we might be minutely observed, eg small dinner parties); simple phobias, eg to dentists, intercourse, Friday the 13th (triskaidecophobia), spiders (arachnophobia), beetles (paint them red, and put black spots on and they become charming ladybirds). There may also be free-floating 'fear of fear', or fear of disgracing oneself by uncontrollable screaming.

It is important to find out exactly what the phobic stimulus is. It may be very specific, eg travelling by car, not bicycle. Why are some situations avoided? If the patient is deluded that he is being followed or persecuted, paranoia rather than phobia is likely. Panic attacks are lessened by cognitive therapy (p 372) & paroxetine 20–50mg/day PO.[RCT 61] [N=290][62]

Obsessive–compulsive disorder Compulsions are senseless, repeated rituals. Obsessions are stereotyped, purposeless words, ideas, or phrases that come into the mind. They are perceived by the patient as nonsensical (unlike delusional beliefs), and, although out of character, as originating from themselves (unlike hallucinations or thought insertion). They are often resisted by the patient, but if longstanding, the patient may have given up resisting them. An example of non-verbal compulsive behaviour is the rambler who can never do a long walk because every few paces he wonders if he has really locked the car, and has to return repeatedly to ensure that this has, in fact, been done. Cleaning (eg hand-washing), counting, and dressing rituals are other examples.

Pathophysiology: CNS imaging implicates the orbitofrontal cortex[1] and the caudate nucleus. Successful treatment is reflected by some normalization of metabolism in these areas.[63]

Treatment: Behavioural (or cognitive) therapy (p 372). Clomipramine (start with 25mg/day PO) and SSRIs (eg fluoxetine, start with 20mg per day PO) really can help (even if patients are not depressed): see p 340.

Depersonalization This is an unpleasant state of disturbed perception in which people, or the self, or parts of the body are experienced as being changed ('as if made of cotton wool'), becoming unreal, remote, or automatized ('replaced by robots'). There is insight into its subjective nature, so it is not a psychosis, but the patient may think he is going mad. Depersonalization may be primary, or part of another neurosis. CNS imaging shows that it is associated with functional abnormalities in the sensory cortex in areas where visual, auditory, and somatosensory (cross-modal) data integrate.[64]

Derealization These are psychosensory feelings (akin to depersonalization) of detachment or estrangement from our surroundings. Objects appear altered: buildings may metamorphose in size and colour. The patient acknowledges the unreality of these ideas, but is made uneasy by them.

(Our isolation in an alien or unreal universe, and our estrangement from ourselves, are major themes of leading novelists such as Albert Camus.)[65]

Dissociation (formerly *hysteria*) *Clinical details:* p 334. *Example of mass hysteria spread by TV*—Pokeman induced 'seizures': see '*the Pokeman contagion*'.[66] [n=12,000]

Treatment: Consider behaviour therapy (p 372 ± antidepressants, p 340) if the patient really wants to change.

1 Ogai M Acta *Psychiatr Scand* 2005 **111** 74

Stress, post-traumatic stress disorder

'Razing out the written troubles of the brain and other rooted sorrows'

There are many biological consequences of stress, eg depression; ↑weight, ↑BP, ↑alcohol intake; peptic ulcer; irritable bowel syndrome; ↓wound healing (interleukin-1β mRNA↓); and migraine.

Relieving stress Smoking, alcohol, and chattering are the most popular methods. If drugs must be given, and there is no asthma, heart failure, or heart block, propranolol (eg 10mg/8h PO) may ↓autonomic symptoms, but side-effects are common. Some people try safer alternatives, eg exercise, singing, progressive relaxation (p 344), or counselling (p 380).

Post-traumatic stress disorder Suspect this if the symptoms in the box become chronic, eg after great psychological trauma (near-death, shellshock, earthquake, rape, crimes of passion, shipwreck). Symptoms may be delayed many months.

MRI implicates the anterior cingulate area, with a failure to inhibit amygdala activation ± ↓amygdala threshold to fearful stimuli. Hippocampal atrophy is thought to be from chronic hyperarousal symptoms mediated by amygdala activation.[69] [70]

Acute stress reactions to a bad event

- Fear, helplessness; horror
- Numb, detached, ↓emotional responsiveness
- In a daze
- Intrusive thoughts
- Derealization (p 346)
- Depersonalization
- Dissociative amnesia.
- Reliving of events
- Avoidance of stimuli[67]
- Hypervigilance
- Concentration↓
- Restlessness
- Autonomic arousal: pulse↑; BP↑, sweating↑
- Headaches; abdo pains

NB: if the event is minor, the term 'adjustment disorder' may apply.[68]

Treatment may focus on psychotherapeutic reliving of the emotional trauma, with skilled interpretation by the therapist, but success is elusive, and Macbeth's 'sweet oblivious antidote to cleanse the stuffed bosom of that perilous stuff which weighs upon the heart' has yet to be found. After wars the 'talking cures' of psychotherapy have sometimes been found to do more harm than good:[71] here the best advice may be to try to forget or ignore the past: Macbeth's doctor replied (*Act V*) that such a patient 'must minister to himself', when he had been unreasonably but royally requested to 'pluck from the memory a rooted sorrow' and 'raze out the written troubles of the brain'—and perhaps tragic literature *can* offer more than medicine here. In the wake of the 2004 tsunamis, psychological problems were as prevalent as physical problems—but one of the key recommendations of WHO workers is to use practical outreach approaches, and avoid using mental health labels.[1] This is not exactly congruent with NICE advice, which concentrates on 8-12 individual trauma-focused cognitive therapy sessions which should last 90mins. If symptoms have been present for >3 months, more sessions may be needed, according to NICE (esp if multiple traumatic events, traumatic bereavement, chronic disability caused by the trauma, and if there are co-existing co-morbidities or social problems). There is some evidence that paroxetine (and mirtazepine) and amitriptyline can help (warn about SEs, p 340). Cochrane CD002795 & NICE 2005

Prognosis: Predicting when a given trauma will cause acute, delayed, or chronic post-traumatic stress disorder, or whether it will be a stimulus to growth and have salutary effects on overall functioning (sometimes the case) is impossible. Presence of co-morbid disorders (eg depression) may be important, as well as age at exposure, and social networks.

Prevention: This may involve promoting teamwork, techniques of stress inoculation (by exposure), and desensitization by experience with real casualty management (eg when preparing for war). www.killology.com

1 Chatterjee P 2005 *Lancet* **365** 833

Eating disorders: *anorexia and bulimia nervosa*

Definition of anorexia nervosa: 4 criteria are typically used:[72] 1) Weight <85% of predicted taking into account height, sex, and population the patient belongs to (p 181), or BMI ≤17.5kg/m². 2) Fear of weight gain, even when underweight leading to dieting, induced vomiting, or excessive exercise. 3) Feeling fat when thin. 4) Amenorrhoea: 6 consecutive menstrual cycles absent unless they are on the Pill (in women), or ↓libido (in men).
Epidemiology: ♀:♂ ≈10:1 (but men are more likely to be undiagnosed). Typical age of onset is mid-adolescence. ***Prevalence:*** 0.7% in teenage girls and no restriction to a particular ethnic group.[73] The incidence in primary care has been stable over the 20yrs at 20/100,000 in ♀ aged 10-39.[74]

Cause: Multifactorial. 55% concordance in monozygotic twins.

Essence: There is a compulsive need is to control eating. An association with westernized societies which judge self-worth in terms of shape and weight is recognised.[75] Low self-worth is frequent and the patient attaches excessive importance to weight reduction (an over-valued idea) despite excessive weight loss. Weight control is achieved by overexercising, induced vomiting, laxative abuse, diuretics, and appetite suppressants. Many also have episodes of binge eating, followed by remorse, vomiting, and concealment.[76]

Co-morbidity/predisposing factors: Depression, anxiety, obsessive compulsive (=anankastic) features, personality disorders (anxious/avoidant, dependent), substance misuse.[77] [n=11315][78] Adverse life events and difficulties, most commonly in the area of close relationship with family or friends, low self-esteem, perfectionism, impulsivity, rarely dietary problems in early life, parental preoccupation with food, family relationships that leave the person without a sense of identity. There is scant evidence that the chief problem is psychosexual immaturity; also, antecedent sexual abuse is not a *specific* risk factor.[79, 80, 81]

Other features: Fatigue, cognition↓, altered sleep cycle, sensitivity to cold, dizziness, psychosexual problems, dental caries, constipation, fullness after eating, subfertility/amenorrhea, normochromic normocytic or macrocytic anaemia, ↓WCC, ↓platelets, glucose abnormalities, ↓K^+, ↓PO_4, ↑bicarbonate, ↑LFT, ↑amylase if binging/purging, ↑T_3/T_4, normal or ↓TSH, ↓LH, ↓oestrogen, ↑GH, ↑cortisol, ↑CCK, normal prolactin, ↓renal function, osteoporosis if prolonged poor nutrition, BP↓, prolonged QT interval, amorphous ovary.
The SCOFF questionnaire is a validated screening tool[1]: Do you ever make yourself **S**ick because you feel uncomfortably full? Do you worry you have lost **C**ontrol over how much you eat? Have you recently lost more than **O**ne stone in a 3 month period? Do you believe yourself to be **F**at when others say you are too thin? Would you say that **F**ood dominates your life?[82] ***ΔΔ:*** Depression, Crohn's/coeliac disease, hypothalamic tumours.

Treatment strategies[1]: Aim to restore nutritional balance (eg weight gain of 1.5kg/week; final BMI 20-25). Treat complications of starvation. Explore comorbidity. Involve the family/carers. Address factors that maintain the illness.[MET 83] [N=99][84] Severe anorexia (BMI <15kg/m², rapid weight loss and evidence of system failure) requires urgent referral to eating disorder unit (EDU), medical unit (MU) or paediatric medical wards (P). Re-feeding is considered 'treatment' under the Mental Health Act 1983/Children Act 1989, and it may be required if insight is lacking. In moderate anorexia (BMI 15-17.5 and no evidence of system failure) the patient can be routinely referred to the local community mental health team (CMHT)/adolescent unit or eating disorder unit (EDU) if available. Rapid weight loss is an indication for urgent referral. In mild anorexia (BMI >17.5) work is focused on building a trusting relationship with the patient, encourage use of self-help books and food diary.

1 See NICE 2004 Prevention: Screen those with low BMI; amenorrhoea; children from 8yrs with poor growth; unexplained vomiting; poorly-compliant type 1 diabetics.

If there is no response within 8 weeks, consider referral to secondary services. No drug treatments for anorexia nervosa are validated by good randomized trials. Fluoxetine (20–60mg/day) may prevent relapse in open trials. Monitor Q–T interval. There is wide variability in the availability of psychological therapies and no uniform approach. Cognitive therapies (p 372), analytic therapies, interpersonal therapy, supportive therapy, family therapy may be tried. In children and adolescents consider family therapy.[85]

Refeeding syndrome: This can happen on starting to eat after prolonged starvation, particularly if given rapid active interventions. Clinical features include: rhabdomyolysis, respiratory or cardiac failure, BP↓, arrhythmias, seizures, coma, sudden death. Refeeding syndrome is very rare when the patient is treated at home. Acute gastric dilatation can occur if a poorly nourished patient binges.[86]

Prognosis: 43% of anorectic patients recover completely, 36% improve and 20% develop a chronic eating disorder and 5% die. Most deaths result from suicide or direct medical complications (K^+↓ and prolonged Q–T interval predisposing to arrhythmias). The mortality rate is higher for people with lower weight loss during their illness, age between 20 and 29 at presentation, delayed access to treatment, bingeing and vomiting.[87]

Bulimia nervosa ***Definition:*** 1) Recurrent episodes of binge eating characterized by uncontrolled overeating; 2) Preoccupation with control of body weight 3) Regular use of mechanisms to overcome the fattening effects of binges, eg starvation, vomit-induction, laxatives, excessive exercise; 4) BMI >17.5.[88]

Prevalence: ?0.5–1.0% in young women with even social class distribution, 90% are ♀. Prevalence is increasing in developed countries.[89] In Britain, young Muslim Asian women may be at higher risk.[90]

Cause/associations: Mostly shared with anorexia. Also premorbid obesity.[91] Commoner in female relatives of anorexic suggesting a common familiar liability with anorexia. Genetic contribution of 54–83%.[92]

Natural history: *Age of onset:* ~18yrs. There may be a past history of anorexia. The disturbance is substantially similar to that of anorexia with dietary restriction interrupted by episodes of reactive binge eating. Compensatory behaviours follow in order to counteract the effect of binge eating with a resulting weight usually in the normal range.

Symptoms: Fatigue, lethargy, feeling bloated, constipation, abdominal pain, oesophagitis, gastric dilatation with risk of gastric rupture, heart conduction abnormalities, cardiomyopathy (if laxative use), tetany, occasional swelling of hands and feet, irregular menstruation, erosion of dental enamel, enlarged parotid glands, calluses on the back of the hands (Russell's sign, from tooth marks during induction of vomiting), oedema (use of laxatives and diuretics), metabolic alkalosis, hypochloraemia, hypokalaemia, metabolic acidosis (if laxative use), less commonly hyponatraemia, hypocalcaemia, hypophosphataemia, hypomagnesaemia, abnormal EEG, abnormal menstrual cycle, blunted response of TSH and growth hormone to thyroid releasing hormone.

Treatment: Mild symptoms: support, self-help books and food diary similarly to anorexia. Referral to CMHT or EDU (above) in case of no response, moderate or severe symptoms and MU if medical complications.[93] Antidepressants have the most robust evidence at usual doses but fluoxetine may be needed at 60mg/day.[94] Cognitive therapy can help (p 370–1).[95]

Prognosis: In 2–10 years 50% of patients improve with treatment, 20% show no change, and 30% show remissions and relapses. Impulsive behaviour and weight fluctuations are associated with worse outcome.[96]

Organic reactions

Acute organic reactions (Acute confusion, delirium) The key feature is impaired consciousness with onset over hours/days. It is difficult to describe; take any opportunity to be shown it. You have the sense when trying to communicate that your patient is not with you. He is likely to be disoriented in time (doesn't know day or year) and, with greater impairment, in place. Sometimes he is very quiet/drowsy; sometimes agitated, and you are called when he is disrupting the ward. On other occasions the patient appears deluded (for example, accusing staff of plotting against him/her) or to be hallucinating. If there is no past psychiatric history, and in the setting of a physical illness or post-surgery a confusional state is particularly likely—especially if symptoms are worse at the end of the day.

Differential diagnosis: If agitated, consider anxiety (usually readily distinguished on history-taking). If onset uncertain, consider dementia.

Causes: Infection; drugs (benzodiazepines, opiates, anticonvulsants, digoxin, L-dopa); U&E↑↓; hypoglycaemia; P_aO_2↓; P_aCO_2↑; epilepsy; alcohol withdrawal; trauma; surgery (esp. if pre-op Na^+↓ or visual or hearing loss).97

Investigations: U&E, FBC, blood gases, blood glucose, appropriate cultures, LFT, ECG, CXR. Consider LP and CT scan/MRI.

Management: Find the cause. Optimize surroundings and nursing care. Examine with above causes in mind; do tests; start relevant treatment, eg O_2.

1 If agitated or disruptive, sedation may be needed before examination and tests are possible. Try haloperidol 1–10mg IV/IM/PO. Use the smallest doses possible (esp. if elderly). Wait 20min to judge effect and need for further dose. In alcohol withdrawal, use diazepam (*OHCM* p 254).98
2 Nurse ideally in a *moderately lit* quiet room with same staff in attendance. Reassure and re-orientate often. A compromise between a quiet room and a place where staff can keep under close surveillance has to be made.

Chronic organic reactions (dementia) 6% of those ≥65yrs. ***Cardinal signs:*** Global intellectual deterioration without impairment of consciousness—plus memory loss. Get a history from friends/relatives. Exclude depression (may need a drug trial). Behaviour: restless; no initiative; repetitive, purposeless activity; sexual disinhibition; social gaffes; shoplifting; rigid routines.

- Speech: syntax errors; dysphasia; mutism.
- Thinking: slow, muddled; delusions. Poor memory. No insight.
- Perception: illusions, hallucinations (often visual).
- Mood: irritable, depressed; affect blunt; emotional incontinence (much crying).

Identifying treatable causes: • Haematology: FBC, B_{12}, red cell folate (macrocytosis suggests alcoholism, or B_{12} or folate deficiency). ESR (malignancy). • Biochemistry: U&E, LFT, γGT, Ca^{2+} (renal/hepatic failure, alcoholism, malignancy, endocrine causes leading to Ca^{2+}↑ or ↓). TSH (hypothyroidism). • Serology: for *syphilis* (*OHCM* p 584). After counselling carers, *test for HIV* if at risk. • Radiology: CXR (malignancy); CT (hydrocephalus, tumours, subdurals, CNS cysticercosis). As drugs for Alzheimer's become more available, CNS imaging becomes more important in ruling out other diagnoses.99

Management: Exclude treatable illness. Relatives may feel unable to look after the immobile, incontinent, aggressive patient. Good palliative care,[1] a walking frame, an indwelling catheter, day care, holiday admission, and an attendance allowance can transform this picture. If not, long-stay institutional care may be needed. Consider arranging power of attorney.

Protective agents (possibly): **Statins** (relative risk 0.29); **antioxidants.**100 [n=1364]

1 BMJ 2005 **330** 57 ***Palliative care entails:*** Symptom control; ↑quality of life; holistic approaches with the patient and the family involved in all decisions (ie ***patient-centred dementia care***).

Causes of organic reactions

	Acute organic reactions:	Chronic organic reactions:
Degenerative		*Alzheimer's; *Lewy-body dementia (eosinophilic intracytoplasmic neuronal inclusion bodies, *OHCM* p 374) Creutzfeldt-Jakob; Pick's; (p 650) or Huntington's diseases (*OHCM* p 726)
Other CNS	Cerebral tumour or abscess; subdural haematoma; epilepsy; acute post-trauma psychosis	Brain tumour; subdural haematoma; multiple sclerosis; Parkinson's; normal pressure hydrocephalus[101]
**Infective*	Many, eg meningoencephalitis; septicaemia; cerebral malaria; trypanosomiasis	Late syphilis; chronic or sub-acute encephalitis; CNS cysticercosis; cryptococcosis; HIV
Vascular	Stroke (or TIA); hypertensive encephalopathy; SLE	Thromboembolic multi-infarct (arteriosclerotic) dementia; hypertension; anaemia
Metabolic	*U&E imbalance; *hypoxia; *liver & kidney failure; nonmetastatic cancer; porphyria; *alcohol withdrawal	Liver and kidney failure non-metastatic or metastatic cancer
Endocrine	Addisonian or hyperthyroid crisis; diabetic precoma; hypoglycaemia; hypo/hyperparathyroidism	T_4↓; Addison's; hypoglycaemia hypopituitarism; hypo-/hyper-parathyroidism[102]
Toxic	*Alcohol; many drugs (check *Data sheet*); lead; arsenic; mercury	*'Alcoholic dementia'; barbiturate or bromide abuse; too much manganese or carbon disulfide
Deficiency	Thiamine↓; B_{12}↓; folate↓; nicotinic acid↓	Thiamine↓; B_{12}↓; folate↓; nicotinic acid↓ (pellagra)[103]

* = leading causes

Example of advice addressed to relatives of demented patients

- Alzheimer's disease is progressive; some problems, eg aggression, *may* improve in time. Both the rate of change and the length of life vary greatly. ***Should you try to explain to your relative what the diagnosis is?*** There is no easy answer. There is no evidence that knowing causes depression (but he may be depressed if he realizes his memory is fading). The advantage of frank talking is that he can participate in his care (so the vexed issue of stopping driving may be easier to handle). Also, during the early stages, he can give consent to future treatments. Most (71%) people *would* want to be informed if they got Alzheimer's.
- Take opportunities to talk of your predicament with other people in the same position. This is often just as useful as talking to doctors. The Alzheimer's Disease Society exists to put you in touch: UK *tel*: 020 7306 0606.
- Accept offers of help, eg with care-giver training programmes, and of daycare (you certainly deserve, and need, a break from time to time).
- Lock up any rooms in the house which you do not use. Your relative will not notice this restriction—and this may make your life much easier.
- Lock drawers which contain important papers or easily spoiled items to prevent him storing odd things in them, such as compost, or worse.
- Remove locks from the lavatory—so he/she cannot get locked in.
- Sexual activities may stop. Spouses should try not to fall into the trap of asking 'What's the matter with me?' NB: medroxyprogesterone acetate (eg 100–200mg/2 weeks IM) may help if hypersexuality becomes a problem.[104]
- Prepare yourself psychologically for the day when he/she no longer recognizes you. This can be a great blow, unless you prepare for it.
- In the UK, apply to social services for *attendance allowance* + *council tax rebate*.

Alzheimer's dementia (AD)

This is the major neuropsychiatric disorder of our times, dominating not just psychogeriatric wards, but the lives of many thousand sons, daughters, and spouses who have given up work, friends, and all their accustomed ways of life to support relatives through the last long years. The struggle of caring for loved ones through terminal illness always puts us on our mettle: never more so than when that loved one's personality disintegrates, and the person who is loved is gone long before their eventual death. *Suspect Alzheimer's disease* in any enduring, acquired deficit of memory and cognition, eg as revealed in the mental test score and other psychometric tests (p 353). Onset may be from 40yrs (earlier in Down's syndrome)—so the notions of 'senile' and 'pre-senile' dementia are blurred (and irrelevant). Chemically, there is a deficit of neurotransmitter acetylcholine.

Genetics This is complex (defective genes on chromosomes 1, 14, 19, 21; the apoE4 variant is a major risk-factor, also bringing forward age of onset).

Diagnosis *Psychometric tests* (BOX) show dementia is present; *blood tests* etc (p 350) rule out hypothyroidism, ↓ B_{12}, etc, but *histology* (plaques + neurofibillary tangles + cortical β-amyloid protein) is needed to tell apart vascular, frontal lobe, Lewy-body (*OHCM* p 374), and Pick's dementias (p 650). In the elderly, mixed dementias are very common, further complicating things. *MRI* is nonspecific, although serial MRIs (separated by >3 months) may show ↑loss in the medial temporal lobe (especially the hippocampus). *Blood-flow images* typically show hypoperfusion in the temporal-parietal areas, and more anteriorly in frontotemporal dementia. *ApoE genotyping* (E4 allele) *may* help, as may *CSF analysis* (β-amyloid↓; tau protein↑).[105] ***Presentation:*** In stage I of AD there is failing memory and spatial disorientation. In stage II (which follows after some years) personality disintegrates (eg with increased aggression and focal parietal signs, eg dysphasia, apraxia, agnosia, and acalculia). Parkinsonism may occur. She may use her mouth to examine objects (hyperorality). In stage III she is apathetic (or ceaselessly active—akathisia), wasted, bedridden, and incontinent, ± fits and spasticity.

Mean survival 7yrs from onset.

Drugs (often disappointing) Liaise with an expert about increasing CNS acetylcholine by inhibiting the enzyme causing its breakdown (***donepezil***; ***rivastigmine***; ***galantamine***) NICE had recommend treatment with MMSE >12 and continued if no deterioration in function but in 2005 NICE became less convinced about the cost-effectiveness of these agents. Get up-to-date advice. ***Memantine*** is a NMDA (N-methyl-D-aspartate) receptor antagonist may help moderate to severe AD. *Cautions:* creatinine↑; epilepsy. SE: confusion, headache, hallucinations, tiredness; less commonly, vomiting, anxiety, hypertonia, cystitis, ↑libido. *Dose:* initially, 5mg in the morning, increased in steps of 5mg at intervals of 1wk up to 10mg/12h. NICE has not approved this agent.

Antioxidants eg ginkgo biloba (EGB 761, 120mg/day PO) are endorsed by randomized trials. EGB may delay need for institutional care.[106]

Practical issues ►See *Help for relatives of the demented*, p 351. Exclude treatable dementias (B_{12}, folate, syphilis serology, T_4, HIV). Treat concurrent illnesses (they worsen dementia). In most, the dementia progresses. Involve relatives and relevant agencies.

Prevention Vitamins (and possibly fish oils (omega-3 and docosahexaenoic acid, ie DHA), but not NSAIDs)[1]; cognitively stimulating hobbies (a 1-point ↑in cognitive activity score can ↓risk of AD by 33%).[107] [n=801] A cohort study of 678 nuns shows that education and use of syntactically and imaginatively rich language at 18yrs old predicts subsequent onset of AD ~50y later.[108]

1 Mannila A 2005 *Eur J Pharm Sci* **24** 101. Brain to plasma ratio of ibuprofen is only ~0.02.

Hodgkinson's abbreviated mental test score (max score=10)[109]

Present year & your age	2	Name of your country's president, ruler or premier	1
Time to nearest hour	1	Memorize address (42 West St)	1
Recognition of people	1	Date of world war (I or II)	1
Name of place	1	Count backwards from 20 to 1	1
Birthday (day & month)	1		

Using a score of ≤6 to separate normal elderly persons from those who are confused or demented gives a correct assignment in ~80%.[110] Serial changes are more meaningful than a one-off value. Processes other than dementia may cause low scores (eg ↓cardiac output in CCF).[111]

Other *possibly* significant questions Increasingly, do you find that:

- You forget what you are saying or reading in mid-sentence?
- You have to rely on lists whereas previously this was not necessary?
- Thought is slow or imprecise, harmonizing poorly with motor control?
- Mental agility is lacking, with powers of concentration declining?
- Is there difficulty executing fast movements of eyes or limbs, or difficulty in walking?—eg with spastic ataxic gait or quadriparesis of *HIV-1-associated cognitive/motor complex*, or psychomotor retardation, ± release reflexes such as a snout response, or hyperactive deep tendon reflexes.

NB: Including an 'informant report questionnaire' improves the efficiency of the mental test score as a screening tool for dementia.[112]

Bedside tests of frontal lobe function (eg executive function).[113]

- *Verbal fluency and initiation:* Ask the patient to recall as many words as possible in 1 minute starting with 'S' ; fewer than 10 is abnormal.
- *Cognitive estimates:* Ask to give educated guesses to questions which they are unlikely to know the answer, eg 'How old is the oldest person in the country?' 'How many camels are there in Holland?'
- *Abstract thinking:* Proverb interpretation (however interpretation highly dependent on educational, cultural factors). Explain the linkage between pairs: eg poem & statue; praise & punishment; orange & banana.
- *Tests of 'response inhibition' and 'set shifting'*—eg a triangle and square test: Draw an alternating sequence of triangles and squares—and ask the patient to copy what you are doing. Only the grossly impaired will keep drawing just one of the shapes (perseveration).
- *Clock drawing test:* 'draw a large clock face, put the numbers in, put the hands in to show ten past five'. Useful screening for frontal (executive) and parietal (praxis) function, and an adjunct to mental test scores.

Mania and bipolar affective disorder

Mania is one of the earliest described diseases; its essence was captured by Aretaeus of Cappadocia in AD90 *'Some patients with mania are cheerful, they laugh, play, dance day and night, they stroll in the market, sometimes with a garland on the head, as if they had been winner in a game: these patients do not bring worries to their relatives. But others fly into rage… The manifestations of mania are countless. Some manics, who are intelligent and well educated, are dealing with astronomy, although they never studied it…'* [114]

Clinical features of mania

- *Mood symptoms:* Irritability (80%), euphoria (71%), lability (69%).
- *Cognitive symptoms*: Grandiosity (78%), flight of ideas, racing thoughts (71%), distractibility, poor concentration (71%), confusion (25%).
- *Activity and behavioural symptoms:* Hyperactivity (87%), decreased sleep (81%), rapid speech (98%), hypersexuality (57%), extravagance (55%).
- *Psychotic symptoms:* Delusions (48%), hallucinations (15%).

Less severe states are termed ***hypomania***. If depression alternates with manic features, the term ***bipolar affective disorder*** is used—particularly if there is a history of this in the close family. During mood swings, risk of suicide is high.[1] Cyclical mood swings without the more florid features (listed above) are termed ***cyclothymia***.

Causes of mania ***Drugs:*** Many, eg amphetamines, cocaine, antidepressants, cimetidine, captopril, corticosteroids, procyclidine, levodopa and baclofen.

Organic causes: *Typical age at onset:* >35yrs. Infections, hyperthyroidism; SLE; thrombotic thromocytopenic purpura; stroke; ECT.

Psychiatric disorder: *Typically part of bipolar disorder and age at onset* <25. In a 1st attack of mania, be sure to ask about recent infections, use of drugs, and past or family history of psychiatric disorders. Do a good medical examination, CT of the head, EEG, and screen for drugs and toxins. [115]

Treatment of acute mania Assess for the presence of psychotic symptoms (p 316), cycling frequency of mood and suicidal risk. The following is based on www.nice.org.uk advice (2003). For acute moderate to severe mania use olanzapine 10mg, adjusted to daily range 5-20mg, or valproate semisodium, eg 250mg/8h PO (=Depakote®; may be increased rapidly up to 1-2g/24h).

Prophylaxis Those who have bipolar affective disorder after successful treatment of the manic or depressive episode should be treated with a mood stabilizer for more long-term control. If compliance is good, and U&E, ECG, and T_4 normal, give lithium carbonate 125mg-1g/12h PO. Adjust dose to give a plasma level of ~0.6- 1mmol/L Li^+, measured on day 4-7, ~12h post-dose; intracellular levels take time to build up. A range of 0.4-1 may be equally valid; or 0.5-0.8 if elderly (greater sensitivity to neurotoxicity). [116]

- Check Li^+ levels weekly until the dose has been constant for 4 weeks; then monthly for 6 months, and then every 3 months, if stable. Do more often if on diuretic, NSAIDs, ACE inhibitors (all can increase level) or on a low salt diet or if pregnant (avoid Li^+ if possible).
- If Li^+ levels are progressively rising, suspect progressive nephrotoxicity.
- Do plasma creatinine and TSH every 6 months; Li^+ affects thyroid and kidney (hypothyroidism; nephrogenic diabetes insipidus).
- Avoid changing proprietary brands, as Li^+ bioavailability varies.
- Make sure you know how to contact the patient by phone if Li^+ levels are high (>1.4mmol/L prompts urgent contact with patient to adjust dose).

Toxic effects: Blurred vision, D&V, $K^+\downarrow$, drowsiness, ataxia, coarse tremor, dysarthria, hyperextension, seizures, psychosis, coma, and shock.

1 Mother to the memory of her manic daughter, after suicide: 'Perhaps you were too fine for us? The beat of the drum you danced to didn't fit in with our drab, calculating world.' D Schwarz.

When lithium does not give good control

Note abrupt cessation of lithium precipitates acute mania in up to 50% of patients. Discontinuation should be gradual over two to four weeks.

Anticonvulsants: Semisodium valproate (above) and carbamazepine (*OHCM* p 380; 400mg/8h PO) are next steps (swallow whole; do not chew).[117] [N=136] Some authorities say that semisodium valproate is better than lithium, but evidence is equivocal. Its most specific indication may be in 'rapid cyclers' (≥4 acute mood swings/yr). Olanzapine may also have a role here.[118] New anticonvulsants such as lamotrigine, gabapentin and topiramate are being increasingly investigated as potential mood stabilizers. Lamotrigine has the stronger evidence base for its efficacy in bipolar disorder.[RCT 119]

Combination treatments: The use of combination treatments is common. The anti-manic effects of lithium and carbamazepine has suggested synergistic action in trials.[120] Several studies report the use of add-on atypical antipsychotic drugs such as risperidone, olanzapine with lithium or valproate in those unresponsive to monotherapy.[121] [122]

Antidepressants and lithium Lithium (or an alternative mood stabilizer) reduces risk of mood fluctuations from mania to depression in people with bipolar affective disorder. For depression occurring during lithium treatment antidepressants can be used: selective serotonin reuptake inhibitors (SSRI) bupropion, and venlafaxine[♦] are said by expert committees to be best. Taper from 2 to 6 months after remission to minimize manic relapse.[123] Monoamine oxidase inhibitors should be considered for patients with anergic (=lacking in energy) bipolar depression.[124]

Non-drug methods ECT can help: consider if a manic episode responds poorly to drugs.[125] There is sparse evidence for transcranial magnetic stimulation (TMS) and vagal nerve stimulation.[126] Psychological treatments, eg cognitive therapy, may be used to target recognition of early warning signs (a relapse signature), but depends on the maintenance of insight.[RCT 127]

A little word on 'psychosis'

Beware labelling people; remember that even during the best of times, only a thin veil separates us from insanity. In its most florid form, psychosis is the archetype of the layman's 'madness', and it signifies a state of mind in which contact with reality is lost and the landmarks of our normal mental processes are suspended and turned awry, with an abandoning of constraints imposed by reason and morality. But, the *usual* picture is much less obvious: the patient may be sitting alone, quietly attending to his or her voices.

Key features suggesting psychosis are: hallucinations, delusions, and thought disorder—defined on p 316 & p 358. If one of these features is present, the diagnosis is limited to 3 entities: schizophrenia and related disorders (p 358), a disorder of affect (ie mania or depression or both p 336), or an organic, ie physical disease eg drug misuse, head injury. So the term psychosis is not in itself a diagnosis, but is a useful term to employ, while the underlying diagnosis is being formulated.

Schizophrenia: history and current concepts

Since Kraeplin wrote in 1919 'the causes of dementia praecox (ie schizophrenia) are at the present still mapped in impenetrable darkness'[128] the understanding of schizophrenia has progressed considerably. A number of causative factors are now known to be relevant, and the challenge now is to explore the mechanisms by which they interact and produce the clinical picture of schizophrenia. Schizophrenia is a common condition which typically presents in late teens or early twenties. It is characterized by psychotic symptoms (hallucinations, delusions, passivity experiences); disorganization symptoms (incongruous mood, abnormalities of speech and thought); negative symptoms (apathy, self-neglect, blunted mood, loss of motivation); and cognitive impairment [129] [130] ***Incidence*** ~0.15/1000/yr ***Prevalence*** ~3/1000. It is a disorder with major implications for patients and family.

Genes and environment Susceptibility genes include the neuregulin 1 gene (NRG1)[1] on chromosome 8 (the at risk haplotype is found in 15% of people with schizophrenia but only 7% of controls).[131] The dysbindin gene on chromosome 6 is another important locus.[132] There are ≥6 promising candidate genes for schizophrenia.[133] Evidence points to multiple susceptibility genes with environmental factors triggering schizophrenia; eg early use of cannabis can trigger schizophrenia in those with VV homozygosity of the catechol-O-methyltransferase gene (COMT; risk ↑ ×10 compared with MM variants).[134] The timing of triggers is important. Those starting cannabis at 18yrs are 1.6 × more likely to have a schizophreniform psychosis by 26yrs, but those who start by 15yrs are at least 4.5 × as likely to develop such psychosis.[135] [136]

Schizophrenia a neurodevelopmental disorder or not? The simple neurodevelopmental model suggests people with schizophrenia suffer deviant neurodevelopment either through inheriting genes and/or some insult to the brain that impairs brain development. This leads to subtle cognitive and behavioural effects in childhood[137] and then psychosis in adolescence or early adult life. Several prenatal and obstetric complications are associated with increased risk of developing schizophrenia (early rupture of membranes, gestational age <37 weeks, incubator use, winter births).[138]

Imaging studies show marked differences in the brains of people with schizophrenia: larger lateral ventricles, reduced frontal lobe and parahippocampal gyrus. Reduced (particularly on left) temporal lobe, hippocampus (memory function) and amygdala (involved in expression of emotion). MRI has shown diffuse reduction in cortical grey matter associated with poor premorbid function.[139] However schizophrenia also has an onset later in life particularly women >30yrs.[140] It has been estimated that about 40% of people who develop schizophrenia have a developmental problem, but the majority are not remarkably different from the general population and have no cognitive deficits. So what are the other pathways that lead to psychosis?

Social factors Being bought up in cities increases the risk of schizophrenia; (UK incidence is particularly high in London), and there are higher levels of schizophrenia in migrant groups such as Asians and African-Caribbeans (?mechanism through social adversity, racial discrimination, social isolation).[141] The associated 'stress' on the brain has been suggested to affect the morphology of the brain via hormonal influences as well as the stress of being psychotic resulting in high cortisol levels causing further brain changes.

1 NRG1 is expressed at CNS synapses and activates eg glutamate receptors. Mutant mice heterozygous for either NRG1 or its receptor, ErbB4, show a behavioural phenotype that overlaps with 'mouse schizophrenia' and which is partially reversible by clozapine (an antipsychotic drug).

Understanding the symptoms of schizophrenia

The way we think about psychosis is changing. How can we explain the symptoms? Professor Robin Murray[1] has given the following overview. 142

Auditory hallucinations One theory is that there is a misinterpretation of inner speech. If, for example, you think of your favourite poem, you can produce the words of the poem in your mind, but you know that you produced them. A person with schizophrenia produces words in their mind a similar way but then may misinterpret them as coming from an outside source. We know that during hallucinations muscle activity resembling phonation is detectable in the tongue. Sub-vocal speech can be picked up from the larynx, and this may correspond to what the hallucinations are telling the patient to do. We know that during inner speech Broca's area is activated, and SPET[2] scan studies show that auditory hallucinations activate Broca's area, indicating that they result from a misinterpretation of inner speech. But why do sufferers not realize it is their own inner speech? Shergill has shown that during auditory hallucinations there is *also* activation in the auditory cortex, temporal lobe and various subcortical areas. 143 This reflects the activation of a system used when we are listening to external speech but not to our internal speech. This is why the patient's mind is tricked into thinking the words are coming from outside.

Delusions The dopamine hypothesis of schizophrenia is now well established. Factors that increase dopamine worsen psychosis while blocking dopamine helps treat the psychosis. It is the dysregulation of mesolimbic dopamine that underlies the positive symptoms of psychosis. Dopamine mediates the attachments of salience or importance to ideas and objects, hence excess mesolimbic dopamine leads to a person attaching significance to all sorts of insignificant events, making meaningful connections between things that are not connected. Sufferers cannot have a rational explanation and instead create what seems to them to be a convincing explanation: it is this we call a delusion.

Antipsychotics reduce the underlying dopaminergic drive and this attenuates the abnormal attribution of salience. So people stop hallucinating or they stop thinking their neighbours are persecuting them, but they still believe last week there really were voices telling them to do things. Antipsychotics prevent new experiences but do not resolve previous psychotic experiences and beliefs because these are memories of experiences that have been integrated into an explanatory delusional system. However antipsychotics provide a platform for the re-evaluation of these experiences using cognitive behavioural therapies (see p 372).

1 2005 Psychosis Interdisciplinary Research Group. 2 SPET = single-photon emission tomography.

Schizophrenia: *diagnosis and prognosis*

Schizophrenia and related disorders (schizoaffective, schizotypal and delusional disorders) entail characteristic distortions of thinking and perception. These involve the functions that give a normal person a feeling of individuality, uniqueness, and self-direction. Although no pathognomonic symptom is identified, it is useful to see symptoms as part of groups that have special importance for the diagnosis and often occur together[1]. The ICD-10 classification of mental and behavioural disorders describes the following groups:

1 *Thought insertion*: 'Someone is putting thoughts into my head.' *Thought broadcasting*: 'People overhear my thoughts.' *Thought withdrawal*: 'Thoughts are being taken out of my head', or repeating of thoughts—*écho des pensées*.
2 Delusions of control, influence, or passivity, clearly referred to body or limb movements or thoughts, actions, sensations. Delusional perception.
3 Hallucinatory voices giving a running commentary on a patient's behaviour, or discussing the patient among themselves.
4 Persistent delusions of other kinds that are culturally inappropriate and completely impossible ('Rasputin has put a transmitter in my brain').
5 Persistent hallucinations in any modality (somatic, visual, tactile) which occur everyday for weeks on end.
6 Breaks or interpolations in the train of thought, resulting in incoherence or irrelevant speech—*knight's move thoughts* that change direction, flying off at tangents, with odd logic, or neologisms (made up words).
7 Catatonic behaviour, such as excitement, posturing, or waxy flexibility, negativism, mutism, echopraxia (involuntary imitation of the movements).
8 Negative symptoms (apathy, paucity of speech, blunting or incongruity of affect, eg laughing at bad news) usually resulting in social withdrawal.

(1–5 are co-extensive with Schneider's 1st rank symptoms of schizophrenia.)

Diagnostic guidelines for schizophrenia the normal requirement for the diagnosis is that a minimum of one very clear symptom (and usually two or more if less clear-cut) belonging to any of the groups 1–4 above, or symptoms form at least two of the groups 5–8. Symptoms should have been clearly present most of the time *during a period of 1 month or more*.

ICD-10 distinguishes the following subtypes of schizophrenia: *Paranoid* commonest subtype, where hallucinations and/or delusions are prominent. *Hebephrenic* age of onset 15–25yr, poor prognosis, changes in mood prominent with fleeting fragmented delusions and hallucinations. *Catatonic* characterised by stupor, excitement, posturing, waxy flexibility, negativism. *Simple* and *Residual* types where negative symptoms predominate.

The most frequent symptoms: Lack of insight 97%, auditory hallucinations 74%, ideas of reference 70%, paranoia 66%, flatness of affect 66%, persecutory delusions 62%. **The most frequent behaviours:** Social withdrawal 74%, apathy 56%, lack of conversation 54%, anhedonia (inability to gain pleasure from activities) 50%, psychomotor retardation 48%, overactivity 41%, self-neglect 30%, posturing ± odd movements 25%.

Better prognosis if: Sudden onset; no negative symptoms; supportive home. Also: low scores on measures of expressed emotion, premorbid psychosocial evolution, female sex, later onset of illness, no CNS ventricular enlargement, and -ve family history (data from WHO's *disability assessment schedule* [144]). Overall, only 10% ever have one episode. With treatment, ≤7% stay in hospital for >2yrs after 1st admission. 28% go at least 2yrs without needing further hospital admission. The lifetime risk of schizophrenia in the general population is ~1%. *Suicide rates:* 10% in acute phase; 4% in chronic sufferers.

1 Johnstone E 2005. Neuropsychological measures can predict with accuracy those who will develop schizophrenia in high risk groups years before onset. *B J Psych* **186**.

Managing violence (Maudsley *Prescribing Guidelines*, 2003)

A person may exhibit violent behaviour as a result of psychiatric illness, substance misuse, personality disorder, or physical illness.

- Recognize early warning signs: tachypnoea, clenched fists, shouting, chanting, restlessness, repetitive movements, pacing, gesticulations. Your own intuition may be helpful here. At the first hint of violence, get help. If alone, make sure you are nearer the door than the patient.
- Do not be alone with the patient; summon the police if needed.
- Try calming and talking with the patient. Do not touch him. Use your body language to reassure (sitting back, open palms, attentive).
- Get his consent. If he does not consent to treatment, emergency treatment can still be given to save life, or serious deterioration.
- Use minimum force to achieve his welfare. ***Rapid tranquillisation*** (RT) is the use of medication in controlling a person's behaviour. It should only be used as a last resort when non-pharmacological methods of behaviour control have failed.

De-escalation, time-out, placement, as appropriate

↓

Offer **oral treatment**. Haloperidol 5mg or olanzapine 10mg or risperidone 1–2mg. With or without lorazepam 1–2mg. Repeat every 45–60min. Go to step 3 if three doses fail.

↓

Consider **IM treatment**. Haloperidol 5mg or olanzapine 5–10mg. With or without lorazepam 1–2mg. Repeat up to 3 times at 30 min intervals.

↓

If insufficient effect promethazine 50mg IM is an alternative in benzodiazepine tolerant patients (maximum dose 100mg).

↓

After any parenteral administration of drugs, monitor temperature, pulse, BP, and respiratory rate every 5–10min for 1h, then half-hourly until ambulatory again. Do ECG and FBC if parenteral antipsychotics are given. Hypokalemia, stress, agitation place patients at risk of arrhythmias.

↓

Choice of antipsychotic depends on current treatment. If the patient is established on antipsychotics, lorazepam may be used alone.

- If the patient uses street drugs or is already receiving bezodiazepines regularly, an antipsychotic may be used alone.
- For the majority of patients the best response will be obtained with a combination of an antipsychotic and lorazepam.
- Ensure that parenteral anticholinergics are available. Procyclidine 5–10mg IM may be required to reverse acute dystonic reactions.
- In administration of IM medication review the patient's legal status. The requirement for enforced IM medication in informal patients should prompt the use of the Mental Helath Act (p 400).
- Mix lorazepam 1:1 with water for injections before injecting.
- Promethazine has a slow onset of action but is often an effective sedative. Dilution is not required before IM injection.
- Caution if very young or old, and those with pre-existing brain damage, or impulse control problems as disinhibition reactions are more likely.

Schizophrenia: *management*

Aims Antipsychotics in the short run have a much more dramatic effect on the symptoms of schizophrenia than any other therapeutic measure. However the management of schizophrenia is more than just medication and requires an individualized care plan that also includes appropriate psychological and social interventions.

Advice and monitoring all patients before starting an antipsychotic should be asked personal/family history of diabetes, hypertension and cardiovascular disease. They should be given appropriate advice on diet, weight control and exercise. Perform BP, weight, fasting blood glucose, lipid profile, FBC, ECG if on clozapine or zotepine. Additional 6-monthly monitoring of LFT, U&E, prolactin, weight, Hb_{A1c} is recommended.[145]

Typical or atypical? That is the question *Typical antipsychotics* (chlorpromazine, haloperidol) reduce symptoms in ~75% of patients with acute schizophrenia, but are less effective for negative symptoms. Blockade of D2 receptors is the major mechanism for the antipsychotic effect of these drugs—and the cause of unwanted effects that often affect concordance with therapy. ***Treating extrapyramidal side-effects (EPSE)*** • Parkinsonism: reduce dose, change to atypical or try procyclidine 2.5mg/8h PO; increase if necessary; max 30mg/24h • Acute dystonia can occur within hours of starting antipsychotics. ℞: Procyclidine 5–10mg IM or IV, repeat after 10min, max 30mg/24h • Akathisia— occurs within hours to weeks of starting antipsychotics, restlessness may be very distressing; so use lowest possible dose or change to atypical—treatment may be needed with propranolol ~20mg/8h PO ± cyproheptadine 4mg/6h PO • Tardive dyskinesia (chewing, grimaces, choreoathetosis) may be irreversible; but try tetrabenazine 12.5–50mg/6–24h PO.

Symptomatic hyperprolactinaemia: Galactorrhoea, amenorrhoea, oligomenorrhoea, female/male infertility. Reduce dose or switch to quetiapine. If not tolerated try amanatadine 100mg/24h PO; max 200–300mg/24h PO.

Atypical antipsychotics are those causing no or minimal EPSE. They differ from one another significantly in pharmacodynamic and unwanted effects, which influences choice. Atypical antipsychotics relieve psychotic symptoms as effectively as typical drugs,[146] [MET 147] and may lower relapse rates.[MET 148] NICE says to consider oral atypical antipsychotics 'in the choice of 1st-line treatments for individuals with newly diagnosed schizophrenia'.

Which antipsychotic? 8 atypical antipsychotics are available (UK): amisulpride, aripiprazole, clozapine, olanzapine, quetiapine, risperidone, sertindole, and zotepine. Clozapine is restricted to schizophrenics resistant to, or intolerant of, other antipsychotics (risk of agranulocytosis in ≤0.8% in 1st year of treatment—specialist monitoring is required). Sertindole is only available on a named patient basis due to significant QTc prolongation and fatal arrhythmias.[149] Except for clozapine which definitely causes less EPSE,[MET 150] there is no convincing advantage for any one atypical antipsychotic over another, therefore side-effect profile is important in tailoring the treatment for the individual patient. Most unwanted effects are dose-related, so 'start low increase slow'. All antipsychotics ↓seizure threshold (esp. zotepine & clozapine). ***Special patient groups*** Elderly, children and adolescents may be more susceptible to side-effects. In breastfeeding, most atypicals enter breast milk. Trials of use in pregnancy are few; weigh up potential benefits against harm to mother fetus/neonate. Avoid breastfeeding. ***Extrapyramidal side effects*** (EPSE) are rare with quetiapine[151] and clozapine, and uncommon with aripiprazole and zotepine. Can occur at high doses with amisulpride, olanzapine and risperidone. ***Hyperprolactinaemia:*** Aripiprazole, clozapine and quetiapine no, or minimal effect on serum prolactin, olanzapine does at higher doses.[152]

Sexual dysfunction: All atypicals can cause sexual dysfunction eg erectile dysfunction, ↓libido, ↓arousal, anorgasmia, eg from ↑prolactin (check level) and ↓semen volume/viscosity;[153] retrograde ejaculation (α_1-receptor antagonism, eg with risperidone).[154] In one study, ~30% had stopped their drugs at some point owing to sexual side effects.[155] So ask about sex (p 328; few will volunteer this information). If experiencing problems, adding cabergoline, bromocriptine, or amantadine, or switching to quetiapine may be appropriate.[156]
Weight gain is common, and ↓compliance and ↑risk of cardiovascular events and diabetes (greatest with olanzapine & clozapine, moderate with risperidone, sertindole & zotepine; least with amisulpride & aripiprazole).[157]
Diabetes mellitus: Prevalence in schizophrenics is twice the expected rate;[158] antipsychotics further increase risk (esp. clozapine & olanzapine).
Cardiovascular effects: Olanzapine and risperidone ↑risk of stroke in the elderly when used to treat behavioural symptoms of dementia.[159] Postural hypotension is common (α_1 adrenoreceptor blockade). Long QTc on ECG with zotepine, sertindole; fatal myocarditis and cardiomyopathy (clozapine).
Daytime drowsiness: ~40% of those on clozapine (30% if on olanzapine or risperidone; 15% if on amisulpride, quetiapine, or sertindole).

Managing acute episodes of schizophrenia •If acutely disturbed use the *rapid tranquilisation protocol* (p 359) •Approach patients with optimism and empathy •Provide comprehensive information and consult any advance directive •Discuss antipsychotic choice with the patient and start promptly if distressed and symptoms not tolerable, otherwise refer to specialist in the mental health service (MHS). ***Dose example:*** *Quetiapine* 25mg/12h on day 1; 50mg/12h on day 2; 100mg/12h on day 3; 150mg/12h on day 4; then adjust according to response (eg 300–450mg daily in 2 doses; max 750mg/24h).

Managing risk and psychosocial aspects[160] Risk can be divided into risk to self, others, and risk of self-neglect. Look at past psychiatric and forensic history. Is there past violence or suicidal, or self-harming behaviour? Ask yourself *where is the patient to be treated? Do they have insight? Can they be managed at home?* (via early intervention/home treatment teams), or *do they need to be an in-patient* (?via the mental health act). Risk assessments are an important component of the management of a person with mental health problems and close liaison with mental health services is essential.

Psychological interventions towards the end of an acute episode look at treating any residual symptoms eg difficult thoughts, voices, negative symptoms. Quicker recovery and relapse prevention is the aim through education, psychotherapy (CBT, p 372–4) and family interventions (reduce high expressed emotion); all have a substantial evidence base.[161][162]

Social support Just as physicians are concerned about how pollution impacts on respiratory function, psychiatrists must look at the effects of the social environment and how it impacts on brain function. It is possible that particular social circumstances may result in alterations in dopamine that make relapse more likely. Addressing issues with housing, employment, support groups, benefits and social skills training are all just as important as being concordant with medication. **Aftercare** Co-ordination of care (via an allocated key-worker) is via a multidisciplinary team approach looking at the biological, psychological, social and risk issues. It is performed through the Care Programme Approach (CPA). Involvement of carers/family is crucial. If concordance with medication is an issue depots are useful, risperidone is now available in a long acting injectable form which means less EPSE compared to the older 'typical' depot preparations.

Drug problems and addiction (See also *OHCM* p 550)

Epidemiology Cannabis is commonly used by young people (33% men and 22% women), ecstasy is the commonest class A drug (9% of men and 4% of women aged 16–24).163 Heroin users make up ~70% of Home Office notified addicts. For nicotine and alcohol addiction, see p 512 & p 363. *Other drugs of addiction*: hydrocarbons (glue sniffing), barbiturates, opiates, LSD, and ecstasy.

Causes Individual factors (age, gender, personality, family background) and interact with external factors such as surrounding culture, price, availability, setting, advertising.164 Inherited vulnerability is equally important.165

Suspect drug addiction if: •Arrests for larceny, to buy drugs •Odd behaviour, eg visual hallucinations, elation, mania •Unexplained nasal discharge (cocaine sniffing, p 558) •The results of injections: marked veins; abscesses; hepatitis; HIV •Repeated requests for analgesics, with only opiates acceptable.

Clinical presentation166 ***Acute intoxication:*** Follows administration of alcohol or other psychoactive substances resulting in disturbances of level of consciousness, cognition, perception, affect, or behaviour. ***Harmful use:*** A pattern of psychoactive substance use that is causing actual damage to the mental or physical health of the user ***Dependence syndrome:*** Three or more of the following: 1) Strong desire or sense of compulsion to take the substance (craving) 2) Difficulty in controlling substance taking behaviour in terms of onset, termination, level of use 3) A physiological withdrawal state when reducing or ceasing substance use 4) Tolerance: increased doses of the substance are required to produce the original effect 5) Progressive neglect of alternative pleasures or interests 6) Persisting use despite clear evidence of harmful consequences.

Opiate detoxification ideally as part of a regimen in which a contract is made with the patient (p 339), eg in a special clinic or in primary care, provided the GP has an interest and ongoing commitment (guidance available at www.rcgp.org.uk). Drugs used ***methadone***, eg 20–70mg/12h PO, reducing by 20% every 2 days. Cocaine use by patients on methadone is a big problem, and is associated with a poorer prognosis. Disulfiram has a role here.167 [N=67] A non-addictive alternative is ***lofexidine*** (α_2-noradrenergic agonist like clonidine)—eg 0.2mg/24h PO, increased by 0.2–0.4mg increments/day (max 2.4mg/day); a 5-day regimen may be better than 10-day ones. SE: drowsiness, BP↓, pulse↓, dry mouth, rebound hypertension on withdrawal.RCT 168 [N=5 trails] ***Buprenorphine*** is a synthetic opioid acting as a partial agonist at μ-opioid receptors. It is regarded safer then methadone[1]; t½ ≈35h. Start at 2–8mg/24h, titrate by 2–4mg increments (max 32mg/day, maintenance: 12–24mg/day usually reached within 1–2 weeks). *Cautions:* liver dysfunction; intoxication with other drugs (eg CNS depressants). ***Naltrexone*** 25mg/24h PO after suitable opioid free period interval. Warn patient of possible withdrawal reactions and monitor patient for 4h after first dose. Maintenance dose up to 50mg/24h. ***Psychological interventions*** usually tailored on individual's specific needs, can be offered as residential or out-patient programmes, in groups or an individual basis. Counselling, motivational enhancement therapy, cognitive therapy (p 372), alcoholics anonymous, '12 steps program', family therapy (p 386) are all valuable ways to address triggers, motivation to change, and relapse prevention.

Relapse prevention As strong cravings precede relapse, anti-craving drugs seem to be a promising but unvalidated approach.[2] See acamprosate, p 363.

Barbiturate withdrawal may cause seizures and death, and withdrawal should be as an inpatient, giving one-third of the previous daily dose as phenobarbital. Lower the dose over 14 days.

1 Simoens S 2005 *BJGP* **55** 139 Methadone can cause significant depression and death

2 Herzig V 2005—Anti-craving drugs acamprosate and naloxone do not reduce expression of morphine conditioned place preference in isolated and group-housed rats. *Neurosci Lett* **374** 119

Alcohol-related problems

See p 513 for prevention

Alcohol causes as much harm as smoking and hypertension. *Abuse* implies that repeated drinking harms a person's work or social life. *Addiction* implies:

- Difficulty or failure of abstinence
- Narrowing of drinking repertoire
- Increased tolerance to alcohol
- Often aware of compulsion to drink
- Priority is to maintain alcohol intake
- Sweats, nausea, or tremor on withdrawal

Ask about tolerance, worry about drinking, 'eye opener' drinks used in the mornings, amnesia from alcohol use, and attempts to cut down. 2 points is TWEAK +ve (?more sensitive than CAGE questions).[169, 170]

Alcohol & organ damage *Liver:* (normal in 50% of alcoholics). *Fatty liver:* Acute, reversible; hepatitis; 80% progress to cirrhosis (*liver failure* in 10%) *Cirrhosis:* 5yr survival 48% if alcohol intake continues (if it stops, 77%). *CNS:* Poor memory/cognition; cortical/cerebellar atrophy; retrobulbar neuropathy; fits; falls; accidents; neuropathy; Korsakoff's/Wernicke's encephalopathy (*OHCM* p 738; ⇒urgent parenteral vitamins are needed).
Gut: D&V; peptic ulcer; erosions; varices; pancreatitis. ***Marrow:*** Hb↓; MCV↑.
Heart: Arrhythmias; BP↑; cardiomyopathy; *fewer* MIs (?benefit only if ≥55yrs).
Skeleton: Heavy drinking disrupts calcium metabolism (osteoporosis risk↑).[1]
Malignancy: GI & breast. *Social:* Alcohol is related to violent crime & suicide.

Alcohol & drug levels Regular heavy drinking *induces* hepatic enzymes; binging *inhibits* enzymes; it's probably not a good idea to indulge in both and hope for the best. Be alert with phenytoin, warfarin, tolbutamide, etc. NB: paracetamol may cause ↑*N*-acetyl-*p*-benzoquinoneimine (it is hepatotoxic).

Withdrawal signs (Delirium tremens) Pulse↑; BP↓; tremor; fits; visual or tactile hallucinations, eg of crawling animals. *Treatment:* • Admit; monitor vital signs (beware BP↓). • For the 1st 3 days give diazepam generously, eg 10mg/6h PO or PR if vomiting—or IVI during fits, Chlordiazepoxide is an alternative. After a few days, ↓diazepam (eg 10mg/8h PO from day 4–6, then 5mg/12h PO for 2 more days). β-blockers, clonidine, carbamazepine, and neuroleptics (if no liver damage) are adjuncts (not advised as monotherapy).[MET 171]

Treatment Key determinants of success are the patient's commitment and willingness to undergo treatment—so it is worth taking time to explore concordance between your own ideas and those of your patient.

Treat co-existing depression (p 336). Refer to specialists. Group psychotherapy/self-help groups (*Alcoholics Anonymous*) may help, ± agents which produce an unpleasant reaction if alcohol is taken (eg disulfiram 800mg stat then ↓ to 100–200mg/24h PO over 5 days). Reducing the pleasure that alcohol brings (and craving on withdrawn) with *naltrexone* 25–50mg/24h PO (an opioid receptor antagonist) can halve relapse rates.[172] [N=111] SE: vomiting, drowsiness, dizziness, cramps, joint pain. CI: hepatitis; liver failure. Liaise with experts on its best use. *Acamprosate* (*OHCM* p 335) can treble abstinence rates. CI: pregnancy, severe liver failure, creatinine >120μmol/L; SE: D&V, libido fluctuation; dose example: 666mg/8h PO if >60kg and <65yrs old. Economic analysis supports its use, at least in some communities.[173] [N=448]

Non-drug, physician-based brief interventions for problem drinkers: (Education, counselling, goal-setting + monitoring of γGT in those who have social or physical problems from alcohol, but who do not exhibit full dependency.) 4 out of 8 randomized trials show that γGT falls in the intervention group, but none show convincing improvement in alcohol-related morbidity. More costly, specialized interventions fare no better.

Homelessness is common; help with housing, problem solving, communication, drink refusal, and goal setting *can* help this desperate problem.[174] [N=114]

1 Kogawa M 2005 *Clin Calcium* **15** 102. Mild use may help prevent osteoporosis

Mental retardation and learning disabilities[175]

Definition Below-average general intellectual functioning which originated during the development period and is associated with impairment in adaptive behaviour (Heber 1981). *People with learning difficulties are at ↑risk for mental illness.* Four Subtypes: ***Mild*** (IQ 50–70): Accounts for 80% of people with learning disabilities. There is useful development of language, and learning difficulty only emerges, as schooling gets under way. Most can lead an independent life ***Moderate*** (IQ 35–49) most can talk and find their way about ***Severe*** (IQ 20–34) limited social activity is possible ***Profound*** (IQ <20) simple speech may be unachievable. Special schooling and medical services are needed, as is adequate care and counselling for the families involved. In the UK, lack of resources and ambiguous community responsibilities are big problems.[176] *Further information:* ask MENCAP (tel.[uk] 020 7454 0454).[177]

Epidemiology 27 per 1000 (80% have IQ 50–70). People with learning difficulties are at ↑risk for mental illness compared to the general population.

The Patient *Physical:* Sensory and motor disabilities, epilepsy, incontinence. *Psychiatric:* All psychiatric disorders can occur but the *presentation* is modified by low intelligence. In the *diagnosis* of psychiatric disorder, emphasis is given to the behavioural manifestation of the disorder.

Causes *Physical causes* are found in 55–75% of severely learning disabled individuals. *Chromosomal abnormalities:* Down's syndrome, fragile X syndrome p 648. *Antenatal causes:* Infections, alcohol, hypoxia, nutritional growth retardation, hypothyroidism. *Perinatal causes:* Cerebral palsy. *Postnatal causes:* Injury, Infections, impoverished environment.

Forensic issues Arson and sexual offences (usually exhibitionism) are particularly common in those who offend. Special care is required in questioning a learning disabled person about an alleged offence due to their increased suggestibility and risk of making false confessions.

Assessing the Learning Disabled individual •Cause(s) of the learning disability •Associated medical conditions •Intellectual and social skills development •Psychological and social functioning.

Care of people with Learning Disability •Prevention and early detection •Regular assessment of attainments and disabilities •Advice, support, and practical help for families •Provision of education, training and occupation •Housing and social support to enable self-care •Medical, nursing, and other services, as outpatients, day patients, or inpatients •Psychiatric and psychological services usually from a community based multidisciplinary team.

Treatment of psychiatric disorders •Side effects of medication may not be apparent as the learning disabled patient may not be able to draw attention to them •Antipsychotics can lower seizure threshold and patients with learning disability are more likely to get seizures •Behavioural therapy is widely used.

Personality disorders and psychopathy

Personality comprises lasting characteristics which make us who we are: easy-going or anxious, optimistic or pessimistic, placid or histrionic, ambitious or stay-at-home, fearless or timid, self-deprecatory or narcissistic (self-love founded on a grandiose belief in ones unique superiority). Personality can change and develop, and it may even change quickly, eg after religious conversion, which a timid man is committed [illegible] (more or less actively). Personality is a spectrum lying between the above opposites. Factorial analysis reveals that all these distinctions may in fact overlap, and are describable in terms of two or three dimensions (eg introversion/psychoticism, introversion/extroversion). Those with abnormal personalities may then be defined as occupying the extremes of the spectrum. Abnormality of personality only matters if it is maladaptive, causing suffering either to its possessor or his associates. In general, psychological symptoms which are part of a personality disorder are harder to treat than those arising from other causes.

Psychopathy The defects showing his [illegible] adding [illegible] to [illegible] his real journey into words: [illegible] for [illegible] and [illegible] self. So says Dostoyevsky. Tests for psychologists dwell on recklessness, antisocial acts, impulsivity, lack of guilt ± non-conformity with social and legal codes. Dostoyevsky's definition [illegible] because of its breadth, and because of that telling word 'perhaps'. Can we change? What must change before psychopaths can [illegible]? This idea perhaps allows us to [illegible] from our 19th-century [illegible] passed down our 21st-century [illegible]; perhaps, all are psychopaths as we [illegible] to [illegible] to change. What needs to change? Read *Crime and Punishment* to find out. [illegible]

Psychotherapists are beginning to work in this area [illegible] success [illegible]; it may be easier to help older psychopaths than younger ones.

Causes Brain damage, genetic and cultural inheritance, parental psychopathy, illness or injury, have been suggested, but none is pre-eminent.

Treatment is problematic as patients are rarely in a frame of mind conducive to change. Peer group pressure (eg in group therapy, p 376) may be a motivating force. It is rarely wise to use drugs, but there is evidence that SSRIs (p 341) may be beneficial in aggressive personality disorder.

Other personalities *Obsessional personality:* The rigid, obstinate bigot who is preoccupied with unimportant (or only) detail. *Emotionally unstable personality:* Tendency to form intense relationships and rapid fluctuations in mood, with impulsivity. *Histrionic personality:* The self-centred, sexually provocative (but frigid) person who enjoys (but does not feel) angry scenes. *Schizoid personality:* Cold, aloof, introspective, misanthropic.

DSM-IV classification of personality disorders

Cluster	Description	Disorder
A	Odd or eccentric behaviour	Paranoid Schizoid Schizotypal
B	Dramatic or emotional behaviour	Antisocial (psychopathic)[1] Borderline Histrionic Narcissistic
C	Anxious or avoidant behaviour	Avoidant Dependent Obsessive-compulsive

1 Antisocial personality disorder. A key sign of psychopathy is knowing and articulating the [illegible] while meaning nothing. Is this [illegible] a word [illegible] or [illegible] the voice [illegible]. Acoustic analysis [illegible] psychopaths [illegible] more quietly than controls, with no tone change [illegible] emotionally charged words.

Personality disorders and psychopathy

Personality comprises lasting characteristics which make us who we are: easygoing or anxious; optimistic or pessimistic; placid or histrionic; ambitious or stay-at-home; fearless or timid; self-deprecatory or narcissistic (self-love, founded on a grandiose belief in ones unique superiority).[178] Personality *can* change and develop, and it may even change quickly, eg after religious conversion in which a timid man is remoulded into a fearless activist. Personality is a spectrum lying between the above opposites. Statistical analysis reveals that all these distinctions may in fact overlap, and are describable in terms of a few orthogonal dimensions (eg neuroticism/psychoticism; introvert/extrovert). Those with abnormal personalities may then be defined as occupying the extremes of the spectrum. Abnormal personality only matters if it is maladaptive, causing suffering either to its possessor or his associates. In general, psychological symptoms which are part of a personality disorder are harder to treat than those arising from other causes.

Psychopathy '*He dislikes showing his feelings, and he'd rather be cruel than put his real feelings into words…he doesn't care for anyone and perhaps never will*'. So says Dostoyevsky; lesser psychologists dwell[1] on reckless, antisocial acts, impulsivity, lack of guilt ± nonconformity with social and legal codes. Dostoyevsky's definition lasts because of its brevity and because of that telling word *perhaps*. Can we change? *What* must change before psychopaths can love? This little *perhaps* blowing to us on a wind from 19th-century Russia sends a shiver down our 21st-century spines: perhaps all the psychopaths we lock up *might* be able to change. *What* needs to be unlocked? Read *Crime and Punishment* to find out. www.readprint.com/chapter-3268/Fyodor-Dostoevsky

Psychotherapists are beginning to work in this area, not always successfully. It may be easier to help older psychopaths than younger ones.[RCT 179] [N=160][180]

Causes Brain damage, genetic and cultural inheritance, parental psychiatric illness or laxity have been suggested, but none is pre-eminent.

Treatment is problematic as patients are rarely in a frame of mind conducive to change. Peer group pressure (eg in *group therapy*, p 376) may be a motivating force. It is rarely wise to use drugs, but there is evidence that SSRIs (p 341) may be beneficial in aggressive personality disorder.

Other personalities *Obsessional personality:* The rigid, obstinate bigot who is preoccupied with unimportant (or vital) detail. *Emotionally unstable personality:* Tendency to form intense relationships and rapid fluctuations in mood, with impulsivity. *Histrionic personality:* The self-centred, sexually provocative (but frigid) person who enjoys (but does not feel) angry scenes. *Schizoid personality:* Cold, aloof, introspective, misanthropic.[181]

DSM–IV classification of personality disorders[182]

Cluster	*Description*	*Disorder*
A	Odd or eccentric behaviour	Paranoid Schizoid Schizotypal
B	Dramatic or emotional behaviour	Antisocial (psychopathic)[1] Borderline Histrionic Narcissistic
C	Anxious or avoidant behaviour	Avoidant Dependent Obsessive–compulsive

1 Antisocial personality disorder: A key sign of psychopathy is deceiving and manipulating the unwary, while seeming sincere. Is this achieved just via gesture & facial expression, or is the voice different? Acoustic analysis shows psychopaths speak more quietly than controls with no tone change related to emotionally-charged words.

Managing psychopathy: beyond medicine and the law

Psychiatrists are sometimes unfairly criticized for abandoning psychopaths—as if they were too much trouble. This easy criticism does not take into account civil liberties: patients must either want treatment, or they must have a *treatable* mental illness before they can be detained against their will (or admission must be likely to prevent deterioration). Preventive detention is problematic as the rule 'innocent until proven guilty of a crime' is central to the requirements of justice.

Renewable sentences and protective custody It is against this background that the suggestion has arisen that those with a history of psychopathic violence should receive care outside current penal and health set-ups. Such people, it is argued by the National Association for the Care and Resettlement of Offenders (NACRO), could be detained at the end of their sentences if they are still thought to be a risk to others. For this to take place, courts would need to have new powers, and there is also a need for new specialist services. However, this is no guarantee against injustice occurring: for example, a man without psychopathy who poisoned his wife might be free to marry again after 12 years in prison, but a man with psychopathy who had held hostages without harming them might never be free to rebuild his life.

The Lord Chief Justice Lord Woolf has endorsed sparing use of protective custody for 'a very small minority of people', while recognizing that this is a great infringement on the rights of the individual. But he has argued that this must be weighed against the rights of those who would be offended against in the future. It is estimated that there were ~1400 male prisoners, 400 male patients in special hospitals, and 300–600 people in the community who require this kind of protective custody. 183

Withdrawal of psychotropic drugs

Withdrawing benzodiazepines ►*The withdrawal syndrome may well be worse than the condition for which the drug was originally prescribed.* So try to avoid benzodiazepine use, eg relaxation techniques for anxiety, or, for insomnia, a dull book, sexual intercourse, and avoiding night-time coffee may facilitate sleep. If not, limit hypnotics to alternate nights.

One-third of those taking benzodiazepines for 6 months experience withdrawal symptoms if treatment is stopped, and some will do so after only a few weeks of treatment. Symptoms appear sooner with rapidly eliminated benzodiazepines (eg lorazepam compared to diazepam or chlordiazepoxide). It is not possible to predict which patients will become dependent, but having a 'passive dependent' or neurotic personality appear to be partially predictive. Symptoms often start with acute anxiety or psychotic symptoms 1-2 weeks after withdrawal, followed by many months of gradually decreasing symptoms, such as insomnia, hyperactivity, panic attacks, agoraphobia, and depression. Irritability, rage, feelings of unreality and depersonalization (p 334, p 346) are common, but hallucinations less so. Multiple sclerosis is sometimes misdiagnosed as these patients may report diplopia, paraesthesiae, fasciculation, and ataxia. Gut symptoms include D&V, abdominal pain, and dysphagia. There may also be palpitations, flushing, and hyperventilation symptoms. The problem is not so much how to stop benzodiazepine treatment, but how to avoid being manipulated into prescribing them unnecessarily. This issue is addressed on p 330.

Method of withdrawal: •Augment the patient's will to give up (elaborate disadvantages of continuous prescribing). •Withdrawal is harder for short-acting benzodiazepines, so change to diazepam. •Agree a contract that you will prescribe a weekly supply, but will not add to this if the patient uses up his supply early. •Withdraw slowly (eg by 2mg/week of diazepam). Warn to expect withdrawal symptoms, and not to be alarmed.

Withdrawing antidepressants All antidepressants have the potential to cause a 'discontinuation syndrome'. There is a distinction between this and 'withdrawal' symptoms as the latter implies addiction, and often patients worry that they may get hooked onto antidepressants which can affect compliance. Discontinuation symptoms are explained by the theory of *receptor rebound*, eg an antidepressant with potent anticholinergic side-effects may be associated with diarrhoea on discontinuation,[184] about a third of patients experience the syndrome and may mimic original symptoms of the illness.[185] Withdrawal should be over at least 4 weeks (not required with fluoxetine as this drug has long half life, so it is useful in patients with troublesome discontinuation symptoms).

Discontinuation symptoms •Onset is usually within 5 days of stopping treatment, sometimes after cross tapering or missing doses. Usually mild and self-limiting but occasionally can be prolonged and severe. Some symptoms are more likely with certain drugs. ***MAOIs:*** *Common:* •Agitation, irritability, ataxia, movement disorders, insomnia, cognition↓, slowed or pressured speech. *Occasionally:* •Hallucinations, paranoid delusions. The most troublesome are MAOIs: Tranylcypromine, when metabolised, has amphetamine like properties so can have true withdrawal syndrome. ***Tricyclics:*** *Common:* •'Flu-like symptoms, insomnia, excessive dreaming. *Rarer:* •Movement disorders, mania, cardiac arrhythmias. The most troublesome are amitriptyline, imipramine. ***SSRIs:*** *Common:* •'Flu-like symptoms, 'shock-like' sensations, dizziness, insomnia, tearfulness, irritability, vivid dreams. *Occasionally* •Movement disorders, impaired concentration and memory. The most troublesome SSRIs: paroxetine, venlafaxine (both have sort half lives).

Swapping antidepressants

When an antidepressant has failed to work at an adequate dose, or is poorly tolerated, changing drug is appropriate. Avoid abrupt withdrawal when swapping antidepressants, cross-tapering is preferred. Speed of cross-tapering is best judged on patient tolerability. Note co-administration of some antidepressants is absolutely contraindicated (see below). Potential dangers of simultaneous administration of two antidepressants include precipitating the serotonin syndrome.[186]

Serotonin syndrome: Symptoms: Restlessness, diaphoresis (excessive sweating), tremor, shivering, myoclonus, confusion, convulsions, death.

Example of cross-tapering based on the Maudsley regimen[187]

	Week 1	*Week 2*	*Week 3*	*Week 4*
Withdrawing amitriptyline from 150mg/24h	100mg/24h	50mg/24h	25mg/24h	Nil
Introducing sertraline	25mg/24h	50mg/24h	75mg/24h	100mg/24h

Specific cautions When swapping from MAOIs or tranylcypromine to any other antidepressant withdraw and wait for 2 weeks (this is the time taken for the monamine oxidase enzyme to be reproduced), for moclobemide wait 24h. Do not co-administer clomipramine and SSRIs or venlafaxine. Beware interactions with fluoxetine which may still occur for 5 weeks after stopping due to long half-life.

Introduction to the psychotherapies[1]

As usual, it was dialogue that combed out my muddle. Arthur Miller *Timebends* **88**

Medicine has three great branches: *prevention, curing by technical means*, and *healing*—and psychotherapy is the embodiment of healing: a holistic approach in which systematic human dialogue becomes a humanizing enterprise for the relief of suffering and the advancement of self-esteem. Questions such as 'what is the meaning of my life' and 'what is significant?' are answered in a different way after exposure to a gifted psychotherapist. Changes occur in cognition, feelings, and behaviour. This is why psychotherapy is dangerous and exciting: it changes people. Hence the need for supervision and ongoing training and self-awareness on the part of the therapist.

Psychotherapy stands in stark contrast to the increasingly questioned technical, machine-based realm of medicine, and we accord it great prominence here, in the hope that our explicit descriptions, and their reverberations throughout our books will produce corresponding reverberations in our minds and in our daily work in *any* branch of medicine, to remind us that we are not machines delivering care according to automated formulae, but humans dealing with other humans. So, taken in this way, psychotherapy is the *essence* of psychiatry—and the essence of all psychotherapy is communication. The first step in communication is to open a channel. The vital role that listening plays has already been emphasized (p 320).

It is not possible to teach the skills required for psychotherapy in a book, any more than it is possible to teach the art of painting in oils from a book. So what follows here (p 372–5) is a highly selective tour round the gallery of psychotherapy, in an attempt to show the range of skills needed, and to whet the reader's appetite. It is not envisaged that the reader will try out the more complicated techniques without appropriate supervision.

The psychotherapies may be classified first in terms of *who is involved* in the treatment sessions: an individual, a couple, a family, or a whole group; and secondly they may be classified by their *content and methods* used: analytic, interpersonal, cognitive, behavioural.

Behavioural therapies (more details: p 372) aim to change behaviour, eg if avoiding crowded shops (agoraphobia) is the issue, a behavioural approach focuses on the avoidance-behaviour. Such approaches will define behavioural tasks that the patient is expected to carry out between sessions.

Cognitive therapy (p 374) focuses on thoughts and assumptions, promulgating the idea that we respond to cognitive representations of events, not to raw events alone. If this is so, cognitive change may be required to produce emotional and behavioural change. So in the above example of agoraphobia, the therapist would encourage articulation of thoughts associated with entering crowds. The patient might report that she becomes anxious that she might be about to faint—fearing that everyone will think her a fool. These thoughts would be looked at using a Socratic approach: 'Have you in fact ever fainted? How likely would you be to faint? If someone fainted in front of you in a shop, what would you think? *Are they foolish?*'

Long-term psychoanalytical therapies (p 382) are concerned with the origin and meaning of symptoms. They are based on the view that vulnerability arises from early experiences and unresolved issues, eg from childhood. The therapist adopts a non-dominant stance, encouraging the patient to talk without inhibitions. The therapist encourages change by suggesting interpretations for the content of the patient's talk.

Which psychotherapy is most successful? This is tackled on p 388.

1 *Further reading:* I Levi *Basic Notes in Psychotherapy*, Petroc Press ISBN 1-900603-50-0

Definitions of psychotherapy

There are important differences in how people use the term psychotherapy. The first recorded definition states that

> ***Psychotherapy includes every description of therapeutics that cures by means of the intervention of the psychical functions of the sufferer.*** (F van Eeden 1892 *Med Mag* **I** 233)

This definition is worth bearing in mind because, uniquely, it focuses on the content of the intervention made by the patient, not on the specifics of the therapist's intervention. The most general modern definition, and the one employed in this section, is summarized thus:

> ***Psychotherapy denotes treatment of mental disorders and behavioural disturbances using such psychological techniques as support, suggestion, persuasion, re-education, reassurance, and insight in order to alter maladaptive patterns of coping, and to encourage personality growth.*** (Dorland's *Medical Dictionary*)

Some commentators draw a distinction between counselling and psychotherapy—but using the above definition (or *any* definition that recognizes the great heterogeneity of psychotherapy) no valid distinction can be made, unless it is between the various *types* of psychotherapy. The main issue to bear in mind is that psychotherapy can be more or less *specific*, and more or less involved in, and driven by, *theory*.

So is 'just being nice to patients' in the normal course of one's medical activities an example of psychotherapy at work? The answer is 'no'—not because being nice is therapeutically neutral, but because one's attention is not focused on planning change through the systematic use of interpersonal techniques.

The issue of training is very important, and here are some questions that might usefully be addressed to anyone offering psychotherapy:

1 Is there proof of efficacy? Ask for evidence of long-term results.
2 What qualifications does the therapist hold? Is he or she supervised?
3 Is the recommended regimen tailored to the patient's unique needs?
4 How will progress be monitored?
5 Is confidentiality assured?
6 Is there support and follow-up after the formal programme ends?

Behavioural therapy

Aims to change a person's behaviour, there are several techniques that can be employed individually or together depending on the nature of the condition. When used in conjunction with cognitive therapies (see p 374) the term cognitive behavioural therapy is used (CBT).

Exposure/flooding/implosion ***Technique:*** •Exposure involves patients being presented with anxiety provoking stimuli (objects or situations) in real life (*in vivo*) or in imagination. •Flooding involves prolonged exposure of patients in vivo to stimuli in a non-graded manner. •Implosion involves exposing patients in imagination to stimuli in a non-graded manner. •The patient then stays with the anxiety provoking stimuli until there is habituation ie becomes accustomed to the anxiety by frequent exposure, and the avoidance response is extinguished. ***Indication:*** Phobic disorders.

Relaxation training ***Technique*** •A system of exercises and regular breathing causing progressive relaxation of individual muscle groups. •Linking the relaxed state with a pleasant, imagined scene so that relaxation can be induced by recalling the imagined scene. ***Indication:*** Mild/moderate anxiety.

Systematic desensitisation ***Technique:*** •Patients are exposed to stimuli (objects or situations) that are anxiety provoking, starting with those that evoke little anxiety and progressing upwards through carefully planned stages (hierarchy) to stimuli that evoke more anxiety. •At each stage, anxiety is neutralised by relaxation training ***Indications:*** Phobic disorders.

Response prevention ***Technique:*** •Involves exposure to an anxiety provoking stimulus (eg toilet seat for patients fearing contamination). •The patient is subsequently prevented from carrying out the usual compulsive behaviour or ritual until the urge to do so has passed ***Indications:*** Obsessions.

Thought stopping ***Technique:*** The patient is asked to ruminate and then taught to interrupt the obsessional thoughts by arranging a sudden intrusion, eg snapping an elastic band on the wrist. ***Indications*** •Obsessional thoughts occurring without compulsive rituals. •Undesired sexually deviant thoughts.

Aversion therapy/Covert sensitization ***Technique:*** •Aversive therapy involves producing an unpleasant sensation in the patient in association with an aversive or noxious stimulus (eg electric shocks, chemically induced nausea, pain) with the aim of eliminating unwanted behaviour. •Covert sensitisation involves the use of aversive stimuli in imagination (eg the approach of a policeman to arrest him/her for his/her undesirable behaviour). ***Indications:*** •Alcohol dependence syndrome (disulfiram used to induce nausea if alcohol is consumed). •Sexual deviations. ***Cautions:*** •Punishment procedures are generally ineffective unless patients are taught more appropriate behaviours.

Modelling & role play ***Technique:*** The acquisition of new behaviours by the process of imitation. ***Indications:*** Lack of social skills and assertiveness.

Social skills training ***Technique:*** •Aims to modify a patient's social behaviour in order to help overcome difficulties in forming and/or maintaining relationships with other people. •Video recordings can be used to define and rate elements of the patient's behaviour in standard social encounters •The patient is then taught more appropriate behaviour by a combination of direct instruction, modelling, video-feedback and role play. ***Indications:*** Patients with social deficits due to a psychiatric disorder.

Token economy (positive reinforcement) ***Technique*** •Uses positive & negative reinforcement to alter behaviour. •A unit of exchange (the token) is specified and its gift is made contingent on the occurrence of the required behaviour. •An exchange system is devised so that the tokens can be exchanged for goods or privileges. ***Indications:*** •Children (p 210). •Learning disabled patients. •Addictive disorders. •Chronic psychiatric disorders.

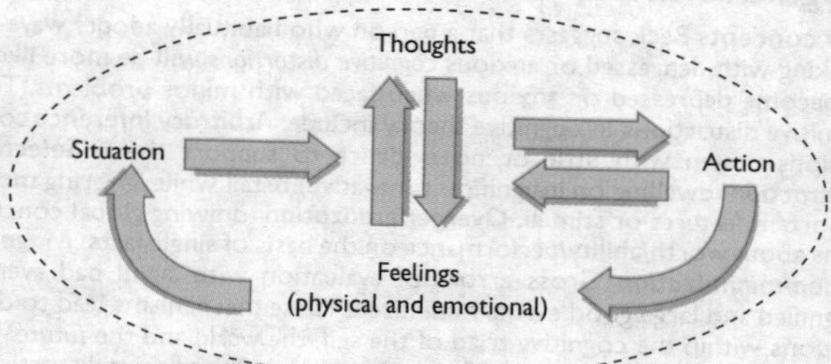

CBT (cognitive behaviour therapy) can help people to change how they and hence how they feel. The above diagram may be a vicious circle if the thoughts are negative and lead to hostile or negative actions. By defining these relationships CBT lets us see how thoughts and feelings interact—so by changing the thoughts, the cycle is either broken or turned into a virtuous cycle. www.rcpsych.ac.uk/info/factsheets/pfaccog.asp

Cognitive therapy

Key concepts Beck suggests that a person who habitually adopts ways of thinking with depressed or anxious *cognitive distortions* will be more likely to become depressed or anxious when faced with minor problems. The cognitive distortions in cognitive theory include: ***Arbitrary inference*** conclusions drawn with little or no evidence to support them. ***Selective abstraction***≈dwelling on insignificant (negative) detail while ignoring more important features or stimuli. ***Overgeneralization***≈drawing global conclusions about worth/ability/performance on the basis of single facts. ***Magnification/minimization***≈Gross errors of evaluation with small bad events magnified and large good events minimised. These mechanisms lead to distortions within the cognitive triad of the *self*, the *world* and the *future*.

- In cognitive therapy, the patient first learns to identify cognitive distortions from present or recent experiences with the use of daily records/diaries.
- The patient records such ideas and then learns to examine the evidence for and against them ie tests out beliefs in real life.
- The patient is encouraged to undertake the pleasurable activities that were given up at the onset of depression or anxiety.
- In this way, *cognitive restructuring* takes place when the patient is able to identify, evaluate and change the distorted thoughts and associated behaviour.

Techniques •Patients are evaluated to get a good history and background information to better understand the nature of the difficulties for which treatment is being sought. •Assessment tools or questionnaires may be used. •Treatment usually takes place on a weekly basis and focuses on current issues. •A *treatment plan* is formulated with clear goals and objectives and progress is monitored. •The number of sessions varies with the type of difficulties being treated. •Patient's participate actively in their own therapy.

Indications 188 ***General*** •The patient prefers to use psychological interventions, either alone or in addition to medication. •The target problems for CBT (extreme, unhelpful thinking; reduced activity; avoidant or unhelpful behaviours) are present. •No improvement or only partial improvement has occurred on medication. •Side-effects prevent a sufficient dose of medication from being taken over an adequate period. •Significant psychosocial problems (eg relationship problems, difficulties at work or unhelpful behaviours such as self-cutting or alcohol misuse) are present that will not be adequately addressed by medication alone.

Specific •Depressive disorder. •Generalised anxiety disorder. •Panic disorder. •Agoraphobia and other phobias. •Social phobia. •Obsessive compulsive disorder. •Post traumatic stress disorder. •Hypochondriasis. •Bulimia •Schizophrenia. •Bipolar affective disorder.

Cautions It is difficult to carry out therapy if the patient is feeling severely depressed and has very poor concentration. There is a need to pace sessions so as not to disappoint or overwhelm the patient. Patients may have difficulty talking about their feelings of depression, anxiety, shame or anger.

Applying cognitive therapy, using the example of depression

We respond to cognitive representations of events, not raw data. Mood and thoughts can form a vicious cycle. Using the example of depression: low mood leads to gloomy thoughts and memories (eg dwelling on exams you did badly in, rather than those in which you performed well). These gloomy thoughts make you feel more depressed (mood) and this lowering of mood makes your thoughts even more gloomy. Cognitive therapy tackles this circle by tackling the thoughts. Take, for example, the thought: 'I'm a failure, and all my friends are avoiding me'. In cognitive therapy the process is to: •Clarify exactly what the thought is (do not let it be just a vague negative belief) •Look for evidence for and against the proposition in the thought •Look for other perspectives •Come to a conclusion. 6 sessions are better than fewer. RCT 189 [N=104]

The therapist encourages the patient to find other explanations by challenging him, eg by examining what 'I'm a failure' really means. 'What are the important areas in your life?' 'What do you count as success or failure?' *Catastrophizing* denotes the tendency to see disasters in small mishaps, eg he didn't like my hat; he doesn't like me; nobody likes me. There are many kinds of biased thinking that cognitive therapy helps patients to recognize: eg *black and white thinking*, *over-generalizing* (as in the case of regarding one failure as a symbol of everything).

Evidence is increasingly available that CBT is as effective as pharmacological therapy for mild to moderate depression, with the added advantage that relapses are less likely.[1] Is it possible to apply these lessons in primary care? The answer is Yes—but only if extensive training is offered. Randomized trials of bringing CBT to primary care with less extensive training (4 half-days) and hence with more realistic costs have been disappointing. In one study, GPs knowledge of depression, and attitudes towards its treatment showed no major difference between intervention and control groups at 6 months—ie training had no discernible impact on patients' outcomes. RCT 190 One reason for this may be that skills were indeed learned, but that there was insufficient time to apply these skills in ordinary general practice, where depression may only be one of a series of problems presented to the GP in a single 10-minute consultation. The lesson is: if the benefits of CBT are to be brought to primary care, what is needed is *time*: time to learn a new skill, and, above all, time to exercise it.

One solution maybe **computerised cognitive behavioural therapy** (CCBT) which NICE supports (visit www.nice.org advice 2005). This is a generic term that is used to refer to a number of methods of delivering CBT via an interactive computer interface. It can be delivered on a personal computer, over the Internet or via the telephone using interactive voice response (IVR) systems. The availability of CCBT systems would increase access to CBT services and permit increased treatment flexibility, especially in individuals who do not want or who are not suitable for drug therapy. They may also be of benefit to individuals with social phobias as they can be accessed at home. It is vital that health professionals delivering the care are suitably trained and that potential users are screened for suitability. 191

1 Asarnow JR 2005 *JAMA* **293** 311

Group psychotherapy

The rationale underlying group psychotherapy is that the group provides an interactive microcosm in which the patient can be confronted by the effect his behaviour and beliefs have on others, and be protected during his first attempts to change.[1] This implies that group psychotherapy (as with all psychotherapies) is only practical for those who want to change.

General indications It has also been found that the most suitable patients are: **1** Those who enter into the group voluntarily, and not as a result of pressure from relatives or therapists; **2** Those who have a high expectation from the group, and do not view it as inferior to individual therapy; **3** Those who have adequate verbal and conceptual skills. See also psychodynamic psychotherapy p 382.

Specific Indications • Personality disorders • Addictions.[192] Drug and alcohol dependence • Victims of childhood sexual abuse • People with difficulties in socialization • Major medical illnesses—eg breast cancer.[193] [N=50]

Technique Clearly the selection procedure needs to be carried out by an experienced psychotherapist. He will aim for a group of, say, 6–8 members balanced for sex, and avoiding mixing the extremes of age. He will decide if the group is to be 'closed', or whether it will accept new patients during its life. He will usually take on a co-therapist of the opposite sex, and he will prepare the patients in detail before the group starts. The life of the group (eg 18 months) will develop through a number of phases ('*forming*'→'*norming*'→'*storming*'). First there is a settling-in period when members seem to be on their best behaviour, seeking to be loved by the therapist, and looking to him for directive counselling (which he rarely provides). Next is the stage of conflict, as the patient strives to find his place in the group other than through dependency on the leader. Frustration, anger, and other negative feelings are helpful in allowing the patient to test the group's trustworthiness. It is worth learning that expressing negative feelings need not lead to rejection—and this is a vital prelude to the next stage of intimacy, in which the group starts working together.

Various models of group therapy are used, and typically the therapist will need to steer the group away from outside crises and searches for antecedent causes towards the here and now—eg by asking 'Who do you feel closest to in the group?' or 'Who in the group is most like you?' 'Who would you say is as passive (or aggressive) as you are?' But the therapist must avoid sacrificing spontaneity. He learns to use what the group gives him, eg 'You seem very angry that John stormed out just now'. He avoids asking unanswerable questions, especially those beginning with 'Why?'. His task is to encourage interaction between members and to facilitate learning and observation by members. Special methods used to augment this process include written summaries of group activities, video, and psychodrama.

Cautions Patients who are unlikely to benefit include those with severe depression, acute schizophrenia, or extreme schizoid personality (the aloof, cold, hypersensitive introvert); hypochondriacs; narcissistic (very self-centred) or paranoid (suspicious and pessimistic about the role of others) patients; and sociopathic types (they have low thresholds for frustration and little sense of responsibility)—but sociopathy is notoriously difficult to treat by *any* means, and group therapy may be the least bad option, as other members of the group may provide the only valid mirror that can be held up to these people, and other people *may* provide the impetus for change. See also psychodynamic psychotherapy p 382.

1 Miriam was the threshing-floor on which he threshed out all his beliefs. While he trampled his ideas upon her soul, the truth came out for him...because of her, he gradually realized where he was wrong. And what he realized, she realized.' DH Laurence, *Sons and Lovers*, JPS, 227

Play therapy

The people who have most experience in psychotherapy with children are parents. They hold the key cards for influencing a child's behaviour. These comprise love, mutually understood channels of communication, systems of valid rewards, and a shared knowledge of right and wrong. It is the families without these, which are most likely to need the help of professionals.

The following guidelines are offered to help these children:

►Never underestimate a child's capacity for insight: if there is lack of insight, it may be your own: *do not expect children's methods of communicating insight to mesh with adult's*. Play, rather than talk, may be its medium.[194]

- Take time early on to make friends with the child. Don't rush
- Accept the child on his own terms—exactly as he is
- Avoid questioning, praising, or blaming. Be totally permissive
- Don't say 'Don't', and only restrain if about to harm himself
- Show the child that he is free to express any feeling openly
- The responsibility to make choices is the child's alone
- Follow where the child leads: avoid directing the conversation
- Use whatever he gives you. Reflect his feelings back to him
- Encourage the child to move from acting-out his feelings in the real world, to expressing them in words and play
- Prepare the parents for change in the child.

In play therapy the child and the therapist play together with toys which give the child an opportunity to verbalize his innermost fantasies. As Virginia Axline explained to one of her 5-year-olds[1] play therapy is 'a time when you can be the way you want to be. A time you can use any way you want to use it. A time when you can be you'.

Art therapy

Art therapy is the use of art materials for self-expression and reflection in the presence of a trained art therapist. Clients who are referred to an art therapist need not have previous experience or skill in art; the art therapist is not primarily concerned with making an aesthetic or diagnostic assessment of the client's image. The overall aim of its practitioners is to enable a client to effect change and growth on a personal level through the use of art materials in a safe and facilitating environment.

The relationship between the therapist and the client is of central importance, but art therapy differs from other psychological therapies in that it is a three way process between the client, the therapist and the image or artefact. Thus it offers the opportunity for expression and communication and can be particularly helpful to people who find it hard to express their thoughts and feelings verbally. Art therapists have a considerable understanding of art processes underpinned by a sound knowledge of therapeutic practice, and work with both individuals and groups in a variety of residential and community based settings, for example: adult mental health, learning disabilities, child and family centres, palliative care and the prison service. The diversity of these areas of work is reflected in the number of special interest groups that have developed in affiliation with the British Association of Art Therapists.[2]

In the UK, NICE recommends that serious consideration be given to non-drug treatments for depression—so what are the experiences of UK primary care? In one setting with 3 artists in residence in Dursley (a ceramicist, a poet, and a painter) there was a reduction in anxiety, an increase in self-esteem, and there were fewer consultations from 'heartsink' patients.[195]

1 Axline V *Play Therapy* Dibs: *in Search of Self*.

2 For further information visit www.baat.org

Crisis intervention

Occupying the interval between the spilling of our lives and their congealing into history, crisis intervention recognizes that moments of maximum change are times of greatest therapeutic opportunity.[1] The heroic policeman who intervenes between the blade and the self's autotarget is, by this action, in the prime position, if he only knew it, to cut through to the heart of the matter, by entering into *dialogue* (and this takes courage too, for there are no rules of engagement, and your only tools are those your patient gives you). During the rescue you may concentrate on these questions:

- What events have led to the person's difficulties? Concentrate on his thoughts and actions in the last few days.
- What is his mental state at the moment (p 324)? It is vital to know about depression, suicidal ideas, and psychosis.
- When his mental state allows, get to grips with methods he has used in the past to combat stress and resolve crises.
- Who are the significant people in the person's life?
- What help can the person rely on from family and friends?
- What solutions has the person (or his or her family, school, or employer) tried in the present crisis? How have they failed?

Subsequent therapeutic strategies

- If the person has been very severely affected by the crisis, it will be appropriate to offer, and sometimes insist upon, his abandoning of his normal obligations and responsibilities. Temporarily relieving the patient of his responsibilities is necessary to allow concentrated contact ('intensive care') within a therapeutic environment—eg a hospital or crisis unit.
- Ensure by taking practical steps that the patient's commitments are adequately looked after (eg arrange transport of children to foster parents).
- Decide on the best way of lowering arousal (time spent talking is often preferable to administering anxiolytics, which may only serve to delay the natural process of adaptation). If the patient is shocked, stunned, or mute, take time to establish the normal channels of communication.
- As soon as the person is receptive, promote a sense of hope about the outcome of the crisis. If there is no hope (a mother, consumed by grief, after losing all her children in a fire), then this too must be addressed.
- The next step is to encourage creative thinking about ways whereby the patient might solve the problems. Start by helping him think through the consequences of all options open to him. Then help compartmentalize his proposed solutions into small, easily executed items of behaviour.

As the immediate crisis passes, and the patient has reasonable psychological functioning, it will be necessary to put him back in charge of his own life. A period of counselling is likely to be appropriate. This is described on p 380. Making a contract about therapy is important in encouraging the patient to transfer from the 'sick role' to a self-dependent, adult role.

Crisis intervention often focuses on loss of face, loss of identity, or loss of faith—in oneself, in one's religion, one's goals, or one's roots.

Meta-analyses suggest that crisis intervention is a viable part of home-care, and can be used during the acute phase of any mental illness.[196]

►*All home-care packages for severe mental illness need crisis management plans.* Where implemented, this keeps the vulnerable in contact with staff (NNT≈13 over 1yr) *and* reduces family burden (NNT≈3), *and* is a more satisfying form of care for patients and families. It is also said to be cheaper.

1 See Sylvia Plath 1963 *A Birthday Present* in *Ariel*, Penguin, page 50

Community care with 24h-available crisis-resolution teams

- UK policy requires creation of crisis-resolution teams to help manage acute crises experienced by the severely mentally ill (including psychotic reactions).
- In one randomized trial (Johnson 2005),[RCT 197] availability of a crisis-resolution team reduced the admission rate from 59% to 22% at 8 weeks—and was highly cost-effective.
- In the year after randomization and the crisis-resolution team was involved in *all* decisions to admit, the rate of admission was reduced by about one-third.
- Patient satisfaction with crisis intervention is reasonable. There may be problems with follow up and continuity of care.

Counselling

Good novelists (and counsellors) are somehow large enough to embody the world—so their characters (clients) are not just recreated in their own image. *Nothing* human is alien to them. Such exercise of the imagination is what enables virgins to counsel prostitutes—which they *can*, if they are submerged in and are fully aware of human affairs outside themselves.

Indications

- Current problems and stresses (eg experiencing acute psychological distress in response to life events or relationship problems).
- Brief anxiety disorders, especially when anxiolytic drugs not required.

Technique • Focusing on helping the person clarify what it is they want to do, and what would be needed to achieve it • Listening, understanding, and reflecting • History-taking: note how previous stress has been coped with • Production of an agreed full inventory of problems • Redefining problems in terms of attainable goals • Use of therapeutic contracts to negotiate small behaviour changes • Aim for adult relationships between patient, family, and therapist, eg with a contract vis à vis duties, frequency, and duration of therapy, and what is expected of the patient (*homework*), eg learning anxiety-reducing techniques, and carrying out *rewards*, eg cooking an extra-nice meal with the family if the patient achieves an anxiety-provoking task such as shopping • *Talking* out (not *acting* out) anger in safe but cathartic ways • Reassurance. The therapist must not only give overt reassurance, but also by his demeanour he must reassure the patient that *whatever* he reveals (eg incest or baby battering), he will not be condemned, but accepted.

Note that not all counselling is nondirective. 'Problem-solving' models of counselling (BOX) are sometimes directive—and *may* be appropriate if the therapist knows the client well.

Caution • 'Giving expert advice': the patient may need advice of a medical, legal or financial nature. It is usually preferable for such advice to come from a specialist agency not involved in the counselling • Patients with personality disorder, where the problems are too deep seated to be changed by counselling. Here there must be an awareness of the need to refer such patients for more formal psychotherapy.

Supportive psychotherapy

There are many people who need continuous psychotherapy, as they find daily activities pose unending stress. The smallest decisions are insurmountable problems, and the patient, lacking even a glimmer of insight, seeks support at every turn. What can we offer here?

Indication Relevant to all forms of psychiatric disorder

Technique • Listening to what (s)he is saying, picking up verbal and nonverbal cues. Ensure a reasonably full account of the situation and problems • Reassurance: relieve fears, boost self-confidence and promote hope, • Explanation to a patient why they are experiencing certain symptoms • Guidance and suggestion with regards to a particular problem • Expression of feelings eg anger, frustration and despair within a supportive setting.

Caution Patients can become dependent on the therapist and not be able to cope when therapy comes to an end—see p 326 for how to deal with this.

Where tested against cognitive therapy, this less-sophisticated therapy sometimes comes out well, eg in long-term schizophrenia care,[198] and also in care of adolescents with major depression—but not in minor depression.[1]

1 Maina G 2005 *Psychother Psychosom* **74** 43. Randomized controlled trial comparing brief dynamic and supportive therapy with waiting list condition in minor depressive disorders.

Counselling in primary care

Counselling has long been a central activity in general practice. Don't think of this as the expert handing down treatment to poor, benighted patients. It's more of a joint exploration between two humans who know each other reasonably well. Indeed, on occasion, roles may be reversed—for example, following a medical disaster, a doctor, who may be blameless, may become so relentlessly and excoriatingly self-questioning that despair ensues. In these circumstances, it has been known for counselling and support from the original victim or one of his or her relatives to restore the doctor to health, and avert resignation.

Many UK general practices employ or have access to counsellors. This huge growth reflects the fact that people love to be listened to, and that GPs themselves may not have the time or inclination to satisfy this need. It is hard to prove the effectiveness of counselling, especially as skills and training vary markedly. But this does not mean it is ineffective.

There are 3 facets to counselling in general practice:

1 In some patients, problem-solving strategies are used, with the counsellor using a non-directive approach.

2 In fostering coping strategies, the therapist helps the patient to make the most of the position they are in (eg afflicted by a chronic disease).

3 In cognitive therapy, we concentrate on elucidating negative thinking processes, and help the patient learn how to intervene in negative cycles of thinking.

Randomized trial evidence: Counselling and cognitive-behaviour therapy carried out in primary care are both more effective in treating depression than usual GP care in the short term. However, in one recent study, after 1 year, there was no difference in outcome. RCT 199 [N=197] RCT 200

NB: 'no difference' may indicate that too few counselling sessions were offered—or, perhaps that GPs were already effective counsellors—or maybe more focused counselling would be more effective. 201

Psychodynamic psychotherapy

Key concepts: 1) *The unconscious:* Individual dynamic psychotherapy is based on the premise that a person's behaviour is influenced by unconscious factors (thoughts, feelings, fantasies). Evidence for the existence of unconscious activity include • Dreams • Artistic and scientific creativity • Hysterical symptoms • Abreaction • Parapraxes—'slips of the tongue'.

2) *Psychological defences:* Just as the immune system protects our physical integrity, so psychological vulnerability is shielded by psychological defences. As with the immune system, overactive defences can lead to trouble. They include: ***Psychotic defences:*** • Delusional projection • Denial • Distortion. ***Immature defences:*** • Projection • Schizoid fantasy • Dissociation • Acting out • Hypochondriasis • Passive aggression. ***Neurotic defences:*** • Repression • Displacement • Reaction formation • Intellectualization. ***Mature defences.*** • Altruism • Humour • Suppression • Anticipation • Sublimation. 202

3) *Transference and counter-transference:* The past patterns (transfers) our present reactions to people. If we have trusted our parents, we will be likely to trust our doctors, teachers, and friends. The intense psychotherapeutic relationship brings these assumptions to the fore where they can be examined, understood, and learned from. The doctor in turn has unconscious reactions to her patients based on the past, ie counter-transference. For example, if her mother was an alcoholic she may be oversolicitous, or rejecting, with alcoholic patients. The doctor's reactions are also a key to the patient's feelings: if a patient makes us feel rejected (as alcoholics often do), perhaps that person himself was rejected as a child and has turned to the bottle in compensation.

Assessment of suitability ***Psychological understandibility:*** The patient's difficulties must be understandable in psychological terms ***Psychological mindedness:*** The capacity to think about problems in psychological terms ***Motivation:*** The patient must have sufficient motivation for insight and change. ***Intelligence and verbal fluency:*** The ability to communicate thoughts and feelings through talking. ***Introspectiveness:*** The ability to reflect and think about their feelings. ***Dreams:*** The capacity to remember dreams. ***Ego strength:*** The ability to tolerate frustrating or distressful feelings without engaging in impulsive behaviour. ***Capacity to form relationships:*** There should be a history of at least one sustained relationship in the past or current life.

Specific indications • Dissociative/Conversion disorders • Depressive disorders • Psychosomatic disorders • Personality disorders • Relationship problems • Grief reactions.

Technique The therapist provides a secure *frame*—a regular time and place and her own consistency and acceptingness. The patient *narrates* vignettes about himself and his life—usually about three per session. The therapist *listens* carefully, both to the stories and to her reactions to them. She then makes *linking hypotheses*, or *interpretations* that offer *meaning* to the patient. Previously inexplicable behaviour begins to make sense. At the same time the patient forms a close relationship with the therapist based on *empathy*, *genuineness*, and *non-possessive warmth* (shown experimentally to be key therapeutic factors)—and, where necessary *challenge*. These may be novel experiences for the patient that can be *internalized*. The patient can *work through* his difficulties in the comparative safety of the therapeutic relationship, especially his reactions to *ending*, which will bring up previously unprocessed losses.

Psychodynamic therapy can be *time-limited* (brief dynamic psychotherapy)—suitable for circumscribed problems, eg unmourned grief, or *open ended*, which in the UK NHS is usually ~2 years, but in private practice may be longer, and is suitable for patients with severe personality disorders.

Cautions: when dynamic psychotherapy might not be right

1 Repeated hospital admissions, frequent suicide attempts, repeated risk-taking or serious somatization may suggest insufficient ego strength for psychotherapy.
2 A history of repeatedly dropping out of relationships or repeated failures to complete ventures makes sticking at therapy less likely.
3 In general, patients with acute psychotic disorders are not amenable to psychodynamic psychotherapy.
4 Severely depressed patients may be too slowed up and unresponsive to psychotherapy.
5 If on medication, over-sedation should be avoided as this may hinder the patient's capacity to access feelings.
6 Patients who are actively abusing alcohol or illicit drugs are not amenable to psychotherapy.
7 No real motivation to change or grossly unreal expectations of dynamic psychotherapy.
8 A lack of personal, social and family resources to cope with the demands of dynamic psychotherapy.

Sex therapy for couples

This is an example of *couple therapy*: often the problem is not specifically sexual, and sexual difficulties may recede once other aspects of the relationship improve. Here, specific sexual dysfunctions are considered in the light of a modernized *Masters & Johnson* approach using a model of sexual response entailing excitation, plateau, orgasm, and resolution.[203]

Start with a full (joint) description of the problem. This may be premature (or delayed) ejaculation, female frigidity (anorgasmia), erectile dysfunction, or dyspareunia (eg from spasm—vaginismus—or other physical causes). How did the problem start (eg after childbirth)? Was there ever a time when sex occurred as desired? Is the problem part of some wider problem? What does your partner expect from you? Are you self-conscious or anxious during sex? Are there medical problems, eg ischaemic heart disease,[204] or mastectomy; prosthesis use is discouraged at intercourse as it delays confrontation with and acceptance of mastectomy. Techniques of body imagery and sensate focus (below) have special roles here.[205] [206]

Sexual history Early experiences; present practices; any hints pointing towards transexualism, commercial sex work, or drug abuse? Orientation to either or both sexes. Difficulties with other partners? When did you meet? What attracted you to each other?

Drugs Alcohol, hypotensives (erectile dysfunction, ED); *SSRIs* (delayed ejaculation); β-blockers, finasteride, the Pill, and phenothiazines (loss of libido). ***Other causes of ED:*** (*OHCM* p 316): diabetes, cord pathology, prolactin↑, drugs.

Principles of behavioural therapy for sexual difficulties comprise:

1. Defining the task which the couple wishes to accomplish.
2. Reducing the task to a number of small, attainable steps.
3. Asking the couple to practise each small step in turn.
4. At the next session, discussing difficulties encountered.
5. Ameliorating maladaptive attitudes.
6. Setting the next task.

Example premature ejaculation and vaginismus: (Both relate to performance anxiety, and vaginismus may be part of a *generalized* anxiety-defence mechanism[207]). One sequence to agree with the couple might be:

1. A ban on attempted sexual intercourse (to remove fear of performance failure). Education and 'permission' giving (ie to talk about and engage in 'safe' sexual fantasies) is vital.
2. Touching without genital contact, 'for your own pleasure', initially, with any non-genital part of the body, to explore the range of what is pleasurable, and then to concentrate on whatever erogenous zones are discovered ('sensate focus').
3. Touching as above 'for your own and your partner's pleasure'.
4. 'Homework' using a vaginal dilator and lubricating jelly.
5. Touching with genital contact, first in turn, later together. Problems in taking the initiative may now surface. In premature ejaculation, the partner stimulates the penis, and as orgasm approaches the man signals to his partner, who inhibits the reflex by squeezing his penis at the frenulum.
6. Concentrate on playing down the distinction between foreplay and intercourse, so that anxiety at penetration is reduced.
7. Vaginal containment in the female superior position so that she can stop or withdraw whenever she wants. She concentrates on the sensation of the vagina being filled.
8. Periods of pelvic thrusting, eg with a 'stop/start' technique.

NB: drugs (eg sertraline) may also improve ejaculatory control.[208] [N=37]

Sexual universals

There is a great deal more to helping people with sexual difficulties than is outlined opposite, which is just one approach to a common problem. Alternative psychodynamic approaches are equally valid.

In any therapy the following universals need to be addressed:

- Never assume that your patient is too old or too ill for sexual issues to be relevant. Assume that everyone has a sex life, albeit sometimes in fantasy only. Whenever it is explored, fantasy is always found to be an important component of sexuality.209 [n=94]
- Treat sexual problems holistically—eg there may be relevant medical, drug, or other psychological factors at work (depression is common).[1]
- Psychological approaches are always important, whatever is offered by way of physical props or drugs such as sildenafil.
- Psychological events have physical sequelae, and physical events have psychological sequelae.
- All pleasure, including all erotic pleasure, is either purely sensory or arises from associations of ideas: this offers many points of intersection for negative operators, such as distraction, spectatoring, guilt, anxiety, fear of failure, pain, and inappropriate stimulation.
- All humans have a need to give as well as to take. Reawakening this instinct may be an important part of therapy.210 [n=1]

1 Wald M 2005 *J Urol* **173** 167.

Systemic practice (family therapy)

What used to be called *family therapy* is now better known as *systemic practice*, which is an evolving body of ideas and techniques focusing on a person's difficulties within the context of the people and culture that surround them. Therapy is based on the assumption that most people have the resources and potential for resolving life's difficulties. Therapists may work with individuals or families. Screening rooms may be used where co-therapists observe family interactions during therapy via a one-way screen.

Its origins began in *cybernetics*.[1] Behaviour maintains itself by feedback loops, eg disruptive behaviour in a son draws divorcing parents together. This led to *strategic therapy*—the paradoxical approach where the symptom is prescribed so interrupting the behaviour-problem cycle. *Structural therapy*[2,3] sought to be more objective. A family can be described in terms of dimensions. Research interviews have given rise to a measure of 'expressed emotion' (EE) which is associated with severity of chronic illness in many disorders (eg schizophrenia, anorexia nervosa, cystic fibrosis). Therapy includes prescribed exercises, eg parents may agree to go out for a meal at a secret location. In an over-involved family, this strengthens parental executive subsystems, providing opportunity for disengagement and management of concomitant anxiety. *Systemic family therapy* was pioneered by the Milan School, emphasizing family behaviour according to 'myths', 'scripts', and family secrets, which dominate the inter-generational transmission of repeating behaviours. Drawing a genogram (family tree) with the family is a good way to reveal these. Hypothesizing, maintaining a neutral stance and the use of circular questioning are important components.

Narrative therapies[4] consider that knowledge is developed by storytelling rather than through the logico-scientific method, working on the basis that there is no single truth about the reasons for problems but that 'truths' are constructed via conversations between therapist and therapee. People can be maintained in problem-saturated lives by 'viewing themselves in the context of a dominant knowledge'. By constructing an alternative knowledge, they can be liberated to challenge the problem. Narrative therapists help by restoring people's control over their problems via externalizing the problem. Faecal soiling is popularly viewed as an act committed by the child as a response to family dysfunction. But if it is viewed as a struggle between the family and the problem by identifying the 'sneaky poo' as the enemy, then the family can be engaged in a battle against it. The use of written letters is also considered a useful tool.

Brief solution focused therapy[5] makes use of a structured approach to draw on people's resilience, and motivate problem solving. It centres conversations on solutions, not problems. 'If it works, do more of it. If it doesn't work do something different. No problem happens all the time.'

Session 1	*Session 2 and beyond*
1 Why have you come?	1 What's better?
2 How may we be of help?	2a Elicit: Ask about positive changes
3 The miracle question	2b Amplify: Ask for details on +ve changes
4 Exception questions	2c Ensure he notices and values change
5 Spectograms	2d Start again. Ask what else is better.
6 Agreed achievable tasks	3 Ending. How can you get back on track?

'Miracle' question: 'If you woke up and a miracle had occurred in the night, how would you know? How would your life be different?' *Exception question:* Search with the client for possible exceptions.
Spectograms: 'On a scale of 0 to 10, how much would you like your miracle to happen?' 'What would have to happen/What would you have to do to make your score move from 3 to 4?'

Family structure and functioning

Family structure is viewed by Minuchin[3] as an invisible set of functional demands that organize family interactions. These transactional patterns are self-regulating in a way that attempts to return a family to its habitual mode and minimize anxiety.

Dimensions of family functioning[6] (McMaster model) The 6 dimensions allowing any practitioner to describe family functioning are:

- ***Problem solving:*** Can the family act together to solve everyday emotional and practical problems? Can they identify a problem, develop, agree, and enact solutions and evaluate their performance. Success may be dependent upon functioning in other dimensions.
- ***Congruence of verbal and non-verbal communications:*** Are communications clear and direct or are there hidden agendas or hidden meanings? Do people listen to one another?
- ***Roles:*** Who is in charge and how are executive decisions made? Who provides for the family? Who is concerned for the child's education and emotional development? Families may function most effectively when roles are appropriately allocated and responsibilities explicit.
- ***Affective involvement:*** Relationships in families tend to exist on a continuum between over-involved (enmeshed) to disinvolved (disengaged). Empathic involvement is ideal. This depends on development, as greater involvement is needed for babies than adolescents. Enmeshment may lead a child to be so anxious about a parent that they feel unable to leave them, and avoid school as a consequence.
- ***Affective responsiveness:*** How do individual family members respond emotionally to one another both by degree and quality? Welfare feelings would include love, tenderness, and sympathy. Emergency feelings would include fear, anger, and disappointment.
- ***Behavioural control:*** How is discipline maintained? Is there negotiation? Is it flexible? Chaotic? Absent? (depends on quality of communication).

Dysfunctional family patterns ***Triangulation:*** When parents are in conflict, each demands the child sides with them. When the child sides with one, they are automatically considered to be as attacking the other. The child is paralysed in a no-win situation where every movement is defined by one parent as an attack.

Scapegoating: When an individual is singled out by the family as the sole cause of the family troubles. This serves to temporarily bury conflicts that the family fear will overwhelm them.

↑***Expressed emotion:*** Derived from a family interview: reflects hostility, emotional over-involvement, critical comments, and contact time.

1 G Barnes *Family Therapy* 946, in M Rutter 1994 *Child and Adolescent Psychiatry* 3e, Blackwell
2 D Will 1985 *Integrated Family Therapy*, Tavistock, London
3 S Minuchin 1974 *Families and Family Therapy*, Tavistock, London
4 M White 1990 *Narrative Means to Therapeutic Ends*, Norton, New York
5 S De Shazer 1985 *Keys to Solution in Brief Therapy*, Norton, New York
6 N Epstein 1981 *Problem-centred Systems Therapy* in A Gurman *Handbook of Family Therapy*. New York, Brunner/Mazel and H Klar 1995 *Pediatr Clin North Am* **42** 31

Comparing the psychotherapies

212

Principal recommendations and levels of evidence[1]

- Psychological therapy should be routinely considered as an option when assessing mental health problems. B
- Patients who are adjusting to life events, illnesses, disabilities or losses may benefit from brief therapies such as counselling. B
- Post-traumatic stress symptoms may be helped by psychological therapy, with most evidence for cognitive behavioural methods. Routine debriefing following traumatic events is not recommended. A
- Depression may be treated effectively with cognitive therapy or interpersonal therapy. A number of other brief structured therapies for depression may be of benefit, such as psychodynamic therapy. A
- Anxiety disorders with marked symptomatic anxiety (panic disorder, agoraphobia, social phobia, obsessive compulsive disorders, generalized anxiety disorders) are likely to benefit from cognitive behaviour therapy. A
- Psychological intervention should be considered for somatic complaints with a psychological component with most evidence for cognitive-behaviour therapy (CBT) in the treatment of chronic pain and chronic fatigue. C
- Eating disorders can be treated with psychological therapy. Best evidence in bulimia nervosa is for CBT, interpersonal therapy (IPT) and family therapy for teenagers. Treatment usually includes psycho-educational methods. There is little strong evidence on the best therapy type for anorexia. B
- Structured psychological therapies delivered by skilled practitioners can contribute to the longer-term treatment of personality disorders. C

Evidence • Psychological therapy shows benefits over no treatment for a wide range of mental health difficulties • There is evidence of counselling effectiveness in mixed anxiety/depression, most effective when used with specified client groups, eg postnatal mothers, bereaved groups • CBT has been found helpful. Some evidence of efficacy has been shown for other forms of psychological therapy. Single session debriefing appears to be unhelpful in preventing later disorders • CBT and IPT (interpersonal psychotherapy) can effectively reduce symptoms of depression. Benefit has also been found for other forms of psychological therapy, including focal psychodynamic therapy, psychodynamic interpersonal therapy and counselling • CBT effectively reduces symptoms of panic and anxiety. Behaviour therapy and cognitive therapy both appear effective in treatment of obsessional problems • Psychological therapies have benefit in a range of somatic complaints including gastrointestinal and gynaecological problems. CBT has been found more effective than control in improving functioning in chronic fatigue and chronic pain • Efficacy of CBT and IPT in bulimia has been established. Individual therapies have shown some benefit in anorexia, with little to distinguish treatment types. Early onset of anorexia may indicate family therapy, and later onset, broadly based individual therapy • A number of therapy approaches have shown some success with personality disorders, including dialectical behaviour therapy, psychoanalytic day hospital programme and therapeutic communities.

1 A Based on a consistent finding in a majority of studies in high quality systematic reviews or evidence from high quality studies. B Based on at least one high quality trial, a weak or inconsistent finding in high quality reviews or a consistent finding in reviews that do not meet all the criteria of 'high quality'. C Based on evidence from individual studies that do not meet all the criteria of 'high quality'. D Based on evidence from structured expert consensus.

Index on child mental health problems

The next section (up to p 398) deals with some aspects of childhood mental health—but many issues in child psychiatry overlap with pages in the adult section of this chapter, and also with paediatric practice. The psychiatry of attempted suicide is a good example. Many of these patients will be in the last phases of childhood, and it is unclear which service will suit them best. As ever, take a holistic view of your patient, and design a care plan which takes these facets into account.

Depression in children and adolescents

Prevalence Depression affects at least 2% of children under 12 years, and 5% of teenagers, much going unrecognized.

Presentation is often with somatic symptoms ± anxiety. Sometimes presentation is simply as poor functioning at school, socially, or at home, even masquerading as bad behaviour (particularly in boys). Mood is characteristically much more variable and less pervasive than adults—rapid swings commonly occur. The fact that children are able to enjoy some aspects of their life shouldn't preclude the diagnosis of depression.

Features as seen in adults:	***Features common in childhood:***
Low mood	Running away from home
Loss of interest	Separation anxiety ± school refusal
Socially withdrawn	Complaints of boredom
Poor self-esteem	Poor school performance
Psychomotor retardation	Antisocial behaviour
Tearful; feelings of guilt	Insomnia (often initial, not early waking)
Anxiety	Hypersomnia
Lack of enjoyment in anything	Eating problems

Young children may present with sadness and helplessness; slightly older children with feelings of being unloved and unfairly treated; whilst guilt and despair may be more prominent in teenagers.[1]

Interviewing is usually best conducted one-to-one. Consider the possibility of concealed factors (eg past child abuse, bullying). Parents can be interviewed separately (ask the child's permission, and see the child alone, again, if appropriate, *after* seeing the parents, to report back: this helps avoid the impression that you are somehow colluding with the parents). NB: parents may not always be aware of depression in their children. Assessment is often difficult: questions may only be answered by silence or a shrug. If not getting anywhere, talk to the child—or just offer silences—but do not give up.

Always ask about suicidal ideas and thoughts of selfharm. Note any past attempts: ~15-20% make further attempts (excess risk if: male, conduct disorder, ↑alcohol use, hopelessness, and those in local authority care). Self harm can be regarded as a form of communication—a message in a bottle; not always 'picked up' and sometimes it is difficult to decipher the teenager's exact intentions.[1] Refer urgently if risk is considered significant. Adolescents with conduct disorders can be manipulative and extremely difficult to assess—an urgent second opinion is frequently of help.

Management Ideally this should be a combined approach:

- Social interventions—addressing any sources of distress (eg bullying) and removing opportunities for self-harm (eg paracetamol at home).
- Psychological interventions—encourage the patient to talk about their fears and anxieties. Counsellors, sympathetic teachers, and youth workers may be suitable resources. Cognitive behavioural therapy has been shown to be of help—but may not be freely available in primary care.
- Drugs: often disappointing (and dangerous); *fluoxetine* may be the least bad. Beware of behavioural problems. *Tricyclics* are less good.[213] [MET 214] Where there is a marked sleep disturbance, mirtazapine may be less stimulating, and effects on sleep start immediately.[1]

Specific drugs to avoid if <18yrs old *(BNF/CSM)*: SSRIs such as citalopram, escitalopram, paroxetine, sertraline. Also venlafaxine, and fluvoxamine.

1 Q Spender *et al. Child Mental Health in Primary Care*, Radcliffe Medical 2001 ISBN 1-85775-262-7 See also S Kingsbury; *Parasuicide in adolescence: a message in a bottle* ACPP *Rev Newsletter* **15**: 253-9

Psychosis-like symptoms in childhood

In many centres, early-onset schizophrenia is diagnosed with the same criteria as adults (p 358) as it appears to be continuous with later onset forms (with more males being affected).[215] This may be over-simplistic, as hearing voices and delusional beliefs are not uncommon in childhood and have a role in augmenting the worlds of play and makebelieve. They may also be culturally mediated, eg in some Jewish communities where demons are personified.[216] Another example is delusional erotomania (p 640) which is reported to be common in adolescents living in places such as China where expressing sexual interest has to be indirect. There are many other examples where to equate delusions and hallucinations with psychopathology would be wrong.[217]

If hallucinations *do* reflect psychopathology, the diagnosis may be obsessions rather than psychosis, as in the unwanted hearing of tunes.

Hallucinations are also more common in the isolated and withdrawn; here their importance may lie in alerting you to this fact.[218,219]

Some hallucinations should receive very serious attention:

- Those which are imperative ('kill so-and-so')
- Those heard as if outside the head
- Those exciting strong emotions
- Those referring to ideas that the person feels are not their own.
- Multiple voices talking at once, and especially voices talking to *each other*.

Sometimes hallucinations resist diagnosis. This is not in itself a problem as the diagnosis will sooner or later become clear. Meanwhile, ask yourself whether these odd ideas are likely to indicate that your patient is at increased risk of serious outcome, eg suicide.[220,221]

Causes of odd ideas Substance abuse; drugs; schizophrenia; anxiety/depression; hypomania; head injury; epileptic aura; migraine; Charles Bonnet syndrome (rare, p 438); SLE; encephalopathy (eg lead exposure); infections (herpes, EBV-associated Alice-In-Wonderland syndrome); stress; physical abuse.

Tests MRI/CT may be indicated, eg in olfactory hallucination.[222]

Management ►Early intervention helps, and may reduce chances of later chronic schizophrenia, so refer promptly.[223]

If you are the child's GP, ensure there is a treatment plan with a named worker, incorporating antipsychotics (if indicated, p 360) with psychoeducational, psychotherapeutic, and social components. New antipsychotics (p 361) are rarely *specifically* licensed for children, but their use in well-monitored environments is encouraging.[224] SEs are legion; they may not be as bad as older drugs see p 361.[225,226]

Prognosis Spontaneous improvement of psychotic-like symptoms occurs in the majority of children. In one follow-up study, many developed chronic mood disorders; <50% met diagnostic criteria for a major disorder (schizoaffective or bipolar disorder, depressive disorder, 'psychotic disorder not otherwise specified'). In those not developing a mood or psychotic disorder, disruptive behaviour disorders are very common.[227]

Sleep problems and the parasomnias

Waking at 3am ***(ready to play, or wanting entry to parent's bed)*** For those not appreciating these visitations from the pure of heart, the easiest thing is to refuse to play and buy ear plugs to lessen the impact of screaming—or to let the child into the bed. Or try extinguishing the behaviour by attending the child ever more distantly: cuddle in bed → cuddle on bed → sitting on child's bed → voice from doorway → distant voice. Try to avoid hypnotics. If essential, consider triclofos sodium. *Dose example:* if <1yr: 25–30mg/kg; 1–5 years 2.5–5mL of the 500mg/5mL solution.

Other sleep disturbances Hunger/colic (infants); poor routines (pre-school); worry (adolescence). Bedroom TV may be to blame.[228] Try behavioural therapy before hypnotics. Day-time sleepiness: Causes: night sleep↓; depression; sleep apnoea (*OHCM* p 204); narcolepsy (*OHCM* p 724); and encephalitis lethargicans (rare in children): suspect this whenever sleepiness occurs with extrapyramidal effects, oculogyric crises, myoclonus, inversion of diurnal rhythms, obsessions, and mood change. The cause is said to be viral (influenza, rarely measles), but Q fever and mycoplasma have also caused this syndrome, as has infiltration of the hypothalamus (eg by lymphoma). MRI: look for subcortical involvement.

Sleepwalking & parasomnias Of all our non-insane automatisms, somnambulism is the most familiar and striking, literally (rarely) as households may be endangered when the bloodiest dreams of junior somnambulists are enacted. The young are by far the best sleepwalkers (the old may emulate them if stressed, especially if this is associated with excess alcohol or caffeine use, and lack of stage IV sleep—our deepest sleep). Any psychic event associated with sleep may be termed a parasomnia.

Parasomnias comprise: • ***Arousal disorders*** (sleep walking; night terrors; & 'confusional arousal') • ***Sleep–wake transition disorders*** (rhythmic head-banging disorder) • ***REM sleep parasomnias*** (rapid eye movement sleep associated nightmares, sleep paralysis, hallucinations, and REM sleep behaviour disorders, involving motor enactment of dreams, rarely with injury to the self or others) • ***Miscellaneous disorders*** (sleep-talking; nocturnal enuresis; myoclonus nocturnus; nocturnal bruxism, ie teeth grinding).

Suffering from night terrors is often a familial problem. The child awakens frightened, hallucinated, and inaccessible—and is obviously alarmed.

It is common to observe movement in children during sleep: it is their *repetitive* nature which allows the diagnosis of rhythmic movement disorder. The movement may be body rocking, leg rolling, or head-banging (this 'jactatio capitis' may lead to subdurals, fractures, eye injuries, and false accusations of abuse). Tongue-biting may suggest epilepsy. But do not try to be too obsessive in differentiating parasomnias from nocturnal epilepsy, for three reasons: the first is that our definition of epilepsy is tested to destruction by the parasomnias ('epilepsy is intermittent abnormal brain activity manifesting as simple or complex seizures'). The second reason is that those with clearly defined parasomnias are at risk of developing tonic–clonic nocturnal seizures later in life. The third reason is that some parasomnias are signs of autosomal-dominant nocturnal frontal lobe epilepsy (ADNFLE). ADNFLE is associated with abnormalities in genes coding nicotinic acetylcholine receptor α_4-subunit (chromosome 20). In these individuals, correct diagnosis may be aided by EEG (rhythmic slow anterior activity) and video-polysomnography (shows sleep-related violent behaviour, sudden awakening and dyskinetic or dystonic movements, and complex behaviours ± enuresis).[229]

Antiparasomniacs: Bedtime clonazepam; amitriptyline; carbamazepine.[230] If these do not work, self-hypnosis may help, or the simple expedient of waking the patient half-an-hour before the expected parasomnia.

Sleep paralysis

When we sleep we trawl forbidden seas, arranging and being rearranged by the flotsam and jetsam of our waking lives. As our nets descend through the various stages of sleep, our Sovereign Reason or Will usually remains quietly on deck, but if by chance it descends with the nets then, like the tail wagging the dog, it adopts and propagates a life of its own, which may be full of danger. Because our vessel has been vacated, Marie-Celeste-style, we are judged, in Law, not to be responsible for our actions while asleep—be they theft, arson, or homicide. Without will or wind, our vessel, like Coleridge's *Mariner's*, is moved 'onward from beneath' by secret forces.* So here we have the model of Reason and Will residing, during sleep, either upstairs or downstairs: but in sleep paralysis, neither is the case—the tail cannot wag the dog, nor the dog wag his tail. Sleep paralysis may involve complete paralysis of all voluntary muscles, even the diaphragm. For anyone who has experienced it, it is frightening, unforgettable, and difficult to describe—like being aware during anaesthesia with total neuromuscular blockade.

Sleep paralysis was first described by Ishmael during a reverie on deck, sleeping between Queequeg, the cannibal whaler from the South Seas, and his harpoon, before Herman Melville embarks them on the *Pequod's* voyage to track down Moby Dick '… At last I must have fallen into a troubled nightmare of a doze; and slowly waking from it—half steeped in dreams—I opened my eyes, and the before sunlit room was now wrapped in outer darkness. Instantly I felt a shock running through all my frame; nothing was to be seen, and nothing was to be heard; but a supernatural hand seemed placed in mine. My arm hung over the counterpane … for what seemed like ages piled on ages, I lay there frozen with the most awful fears … thinking that if I could but stir it one single inch, the horrid spell would be broken…'

* ***Till noon we quietly sailed on,***
Yet never a breeze did breathe:
Slowly and smoothly went the ship,
Moved onward from beneath.
Under the keel nine fathom deep,
From the land of mist and snow,
The spirit slid: and it was he
That made the ship to go.

Samuel Taylor Coleridge Part V of the *Rime of the Ancient Mariner*

Autism

Autism is a chronic and lifelong pervasive developmental disorder and its management remains a major challenge for clinicians. Autism is a triad of:

1 Impaired reciprocal social interaction (A symptoms).
2 Impaired imagination, associated with abnormal verbal and non-verbal communication (B symptoms).
3 Restricted repertoires of activities & interests (C symptoms).[231]

Prevalence: 1:500 of those <16yrs; estimates vary. ♂:♀ ≈ 4:1.

Cause Unknown. Autism may be a kind of testosterone-mercury toxicity.[232] Severity correlates with testosterone level in amniotic fluid.◆ Blood glutathione levels are low and this may jeopardize CNS & GI antioxidant acitivity.[233] NB: any association with MMR vaccine is thought to be due to changing definition of autism at the time that MMR was introduced see p 151.[234]

Diagnosis Try to identify >8 of the following symptoms—and these should include at least 2 'A' symptoms; 1 'B' symptom and 1 'C' symptom. (Telling comments before the age of about 2 are: he does not respond to his own name; he hates his routine being changed; he is not interested in toys.)

Impaired reciprocal social interaction *(A symptoms)*

- Unawareness of the existence and feelings of others (treating people as a furniture; being oblivious to others' distress or need for privacy).[1]
- Abnormal response to being hurt (he does not come for comfort; or makes a stereotyped response, eg just saying 'Cheese, cheese, cheese').
- Impaired imitation (eg does not wave 'bye-bye').
- Abnormal play: eg solitary, or using others as mechanical aids.
- Bad at making peer friendships. If he tries at all, the effort will lack the social conventions, eg reading the phone directory to uninterested peers.

Impaired imagination *(B symptoms, associated with abnormal communication)*

- No babbling, facial expressions or gestures in infancy.
- Avoids mutual gaze; no smiles when making a social approach; does not greet his parents; stiffens when held.
- Does not act adult roles; no interest in stories; no fantasy.
- Odd speech production (eg echolalia, ie repetitions); odd use of words ('Go on green riding' for 'I want a go on the swing'); pronoun misuse ('You' instead of 'I'); irrelevances (odd interjections).
- Difficulty in initiating or sustaining conversations.

Poor range of activities and interests *(C symptoms)*

- Stereotyped movements (hand-flicking, spinning, head-banging).
- Preoccupation with parts of objects (sniffing or repetitive feeling of a textured object, spinning wheels of toys) or unusual attachments (eg to coal).
- Marked distress over changes in trivia (eg a vase's place).
- Insists on following routines in precise detail.
- Narrow fixations, eg lining up objects, or amassing facts about weather.

For the *CHAT screening test*, see: www.nas.org.uk/nas/jsp/polopoly.jsp?d=128&a=2226 CHAT sensitivity is 38% and its specificity is 98% if done at 18 months old.[235] [n=16,235]

Treatment: There is no cure. Behaviour therapy may be tried. ►*A good teacher is more helpful than a good doctor.* Special schooling may not be needed (but IQ may be ↓). Learning may be better by overhearing than by direct methods. Joining a self-help group is wise. UK phone: 020 81830 0999

Encourage parents to give more attention for 'good' behaviour, and to have rules for behaviour. 70% remain severely handicapped. 50% develop useful speech; 30% develop seizures by adulthood. 15% will lead an independent life. Apply for benefits (disability living allowance[uk]). Risperidone has some success.[236] Parents will ask about secretin; trials don't support its use.[237] [N=60]

1 For a moving account, see Mark Haddon, *The Curious Incident of the Dog in the Night Time*, Vintage.

Bullying

When individuals who have the power use it to cause depression and [illegible], intentional humiliation, [illegible] society [illegible]. Bullying is important not just because it is unacceptable to the child concerned, but also because it leads to depression, somatization, drug abuse, and suicide. Bullying is also [illegible] antisocial behaviour, persists into adulthood with [illegible] dysfunctional relationships [illegible].

Incidence: [illegible] of primary and [illegible] children report bullying each term, and [illegible] secondary pupils. In a study of adolescents, [illegible] were bullies, [illegible] bully-victims (both bully and victim), and [illegible] were victims. Bully-victims especially girls were more likely to have psychosomatic symptoms [illegible]. Bullies who were not victimized have the least physical or psychosomatic health problems.

Risk factors: Isolation; [illegible] being [illegible].

Signs of bullying: Stress, depression, [illegible] unexplained bruising or [illegible] accidents, hypervigilance, submissive behaviour, school refusal.

Management: Interventions that target bullying [illegible] may reduce the severity of [illegible] problems [illegible]. Psychotherapy has a role. Ensure the bully [illegible] does not get away with bullying [illegible] dominance over others [illegible].

The hardest task is to confront the culture among bystanders, which allows bullying to continue as if it were none of my business.

This implies that we all have a role in minimizing bullying. Bullying in the workplace is widespread [illegible], and we have probably all been affected [illegible] people [illegible] power [illegible] bullied people [illegible] a bad [illegible] our own humiliation is that important, it is easier to take a more [illegible] view when we see others being bullied. We simply must not allow it, and recognize that the bullier may not be able to stop the behaviour [illegible]. Help [illegible] is available [illegible].

School-based anti-bullying intervention programmes are a success in primary schools, but less so in secondary schools. [illegible] homophobic bullying: research suggests that teachers are aware of homophobic bullying but are confused, unable, or unwilling to address needs of these pupils. Citizenship education programmes may be important here. [illegible] teachers [illegible] Problems [illegible] bullying [illegible] the policy and [illegible] discussing [illegible].

Our more universal [illegible] is to recognize that we ourselves are potential bullies, and [illegible] confront [illegible] when we are stressed, frightened, overworked, and [illegible] by uncontrollable events [illegible]. [illegible]

[illegible] bullying [illegible]

Bullying

►*Every individual should have the right to be spared oppression and repeated, intentional humiliation, in school as in society at large.*[238] Bullying is important not just because it is unacceptable to the child concerned, but also because it leads to depression, somatization, drug abuse, and suicide.[239] Bullying is also bad for bullies: antisocial behaviour persists into adulthood with impaired reciprocal diadic relationships (≈poor love life).[240]

Incidence 27% of primary and middle school children report bullying each term, and 10% in secondary pupils. In a study of prevalence, 4% were direct bullies, 10% bully/victims (both bully and victim), and 40% victims. Pure victims, especially girls, were most likely to have physical health symptoms (eg repeated sore throats, colds, and coughs). Pure bullies (who never got victimized) have the least physical or psychosomatic health problems.[241]

Risk factors Isolation; being small; being gay or seeming gay.[242]

Signs of bullying Stress; depression; suicidal ideas; unexplained bruising or vomiting; accidents; hyperventilation; submissive behaviour; school refusal.

Management Interventions that target either bullying or emotional distress may reduce the severity of both problems.[243] Liaise with the school. Psychotherapy has a role. Ensure that the bully doesn't prosper from bullying, so learning to 'achieve dominance over others by the abuse of power'.[244]

The hardest task is to combat the ethos among bystanders, which allows bullying to continue as if it were 'none of my business'.[245]

This implies that we all have a role in minimizing bullying. Bullying in the health services is well-documented,[246] and we have probably all been affected by insecure people abusing their positions of power. We fear to act when we are bullied because we might get a bad reference or because we don't think our own humiliation is that important. It is easier to take a more rational view when we see others being bullied—we simply must not allow it, and recognize that the bullier may not be able to stop the behaviour without help. Help is available: see www.nhs-exposed.com.

School-based anti-bullying intervention programmes are successful in primary schools but less so in secondary schools.[247] Vis-à-vis homosexual bullying, research suggests that teachers are aware of homophobic bullying but are confused, unable, or unwilling to address needs of these pupils. Citizenship education programmes may be important here.[248] *When the teacher is the bully:* Problems may become very deep-rooted. Studies of bullying by teachers reveal the subtlety and complexity of teachers' strategies for distancing themselves from being held accountable for intimidation.[249]

On a more universal plain, the first step is to recognize that we ourselves are potential bullies, and these traits come to the fore when we are stressed, frightened, overworked, and threatened by uncontrollable events (such as patient demand). We stop ourselves from being bullies, more or less successfully, by intrapsychic appeals to our well-respected mentors who 'would never behave like that', and by communicating our feeling to our colleagues directly before they are forced underground only to resurface as bullying. Try: 'I'm feeling rather stressed at the moment: tell me if I seem bullying or hectoring—but we've got to get this job done, and I suggest doing it like this…'

False accusations of bullying *You are trying to bully me* is a phrase which may be used correctly, or it may be an attempt to stop someone in authority from persuing her proper role. The test is: 'is this action tyrannical, and is its purpose to belittle me, or is it that I am being asked to do something I don't want to do by someone who is honestly trying to make an institution work?' Professors of Organizational Behaviour emphasize that *everyone* suffers if dynamism and the promotion of change are mistaken for bullying.[250]

Dyslexia

Reading ability usually goes hand-in-hand with intelligence, but when this is not so, and someone with a normal IQ finds reading difficult, the term dyslexia is often used. The term 'specific learning difficulty' is preferred by some people, as dyslexia is often a term used by parents to help cope with having a child whose general intellectual skills (including reading) are less than hoped for. Dyslexia can be associated with other developmental language disorders: consider referral to a speech and language therapist (SALT). Causes: There is a problem with appreciating phonemes, eg the phonemes /b/, /a/, and /g/. Breaking up unfamiliar words into phonemes, and finding a way of splicing them together, is the central task of learning to read. These phonemes need to be taught, especially to dyslexics, and children should not be made to rely on unstructured osmosis. The 'look and say' approach (whole language) is now discredited as the sole means of supporting children in reading.

[illegible] and [illegible] have been used with [illegible] for [illegible].

Children with dyslexia also have difficulty in telling how many syllables there are in a word (donkey has 2—How many syllables are there in [illegible]—analytical dyslexics are prone to ask). They also have difficulty with verbal short-term memory—eg for meaningless strings such as telephone numbers. There is also a problem with telling if two words rhyme or not, or in distinguishing phonemes which sound similar (eg /p/ and /b/). They may also be left-right muddled. Genetics: Boys are more affected than girls, and show strong genetic effects (up to 50% of boys are dyslexic if their fathers are). Genes on chromosomes 1, 2, and 15 are implicated, and linkage to chromosome 6 near the human leukocyte complex may explain associations between dyslexia and autoimmune diseases.

Biology [illegible]: CNS examination shows [illegible] cerebral lesions [illegible] changes may be seen [illegible] with reduced [illegible] asymmetry of the planum temporale (Wernicke's area), with cortical dysplasia and scarring, in two characterizations of this asymmetry [illegible].

Perhaps dyslexia reflects weak connectivity between the anterior and posterior parts of the language areas of the brain, and the [illegible]. Positron emission images show that when dyslexic adults perform rhyme judgments and verbal short-term memory tasks, they activate less and [illegible] of regions normally involved with these tasks [illegible].

Going along side these theories is the [illegible] observation of specific involvement of one subsystem of the visual pathways which prevents rapid processing of brief stimuli presented in quick temporal succession. This is the so-called magnocellular system hypothesis.

Management: Make sure the 'dyslexia' is not from lack of teaching. The person may gain insight by discussing his or her problem with fellow sufferers, and by finding out about past dyslexics such as Leonardo da Vinci. Special educational programmes are available for addressing dyslexic problems, eg the phonetic approach, as learning to read usually presents problems. NB: [illegible]—studies tend to find best results if identification is pre-school. Then exercises in sound categorization using rhyme and alliteration with special teaching of letter sounds can be started early.

Doctors may be asked about dietary supplements with highly unsaturated fatty acids (HUFA, eg Efalex®). These do play a role in neurodevelopment, but evidence of benefit in dyslexia from large randomized trials is sparse. They appear to reduce dyslexic-associated delay in dark adaptation.

[illegible]

Dyslexia

Reading ability usually goes hand-in-hand with intelligence, but when this is not so, and someone with, say, an IQ of 130, finds reading difficult, the term dyslexia is often used. The term 'specific learning difficulty' is preferred by some people, as 'dyslexia' is often a term used by parents to help cope with having a child whose general intellectual skills, including reading, are less than hoped for. NB: dyslexia can be associated with other speech and language disorders: consider referral to a speech and language therapist (SALT).

Essence There is a problem with appreciating phonemes, eg that 'cat' comprises /c/, /a/, and /t/. Breaking up unfamiliar words into phonemes and having a go at stringing them together is the central act of learning to read. This is what needs to be taught, educationalists say, and children should not be made to rely on unstructured guesswork (the 'look and say' approach) which is now discredited as the sole means of equipping children for reading.

Quite often, distortion/jumbling of text during reading is reported. Visual aids have been used with some success to improve reading. [251] [N=47]

Children with dyslexia also have difficulty in telling how many syllables there are in a word (don't we all?—'How many syllables are there in *strength?*' analytical dyslexics are prone to ask). They also have difficulty with verbal short-term memory—eg for meaningless strings such as telephone numbers. There is also a problem with telling if two words rhyme or not, and in distinguishing phonemes which sound similar (eg /k/ and /g/). There may also be left/right muddle. *Genetics:* Boys are more afflicted than girls, and show stronger genetic effects (up to 50% of boys are dyslexic if their fathers are). Genes on chromosomes 1, 2, and 15 are implicated, and linkage on chromosome 6 near the human leukocyte complex may explain associations between dyslexia and autoimmune diseases. [252]

Biology ♂:♀ >1:1.[1] CNS examination shows left-sided cerebral lesions (rare) or changes may be seen *postmortem*, eg in perisylvian regions ± unusual asymmetry of the plenum temporale (Wernicke's area), with cortical dysplasia and scarring. *In vivo* characterization of this asymmetry is becoming possible. [253]

Perhaps dyslexia reflects weak connectivity between anterior and posterior parts of the language areas of the brain, and the angular gyrus. Positron emission images show that when dyslexic adults perform rhyme judgments and verbal short-term memory tasks they activate less than the full set of centres normally involved with these tasks. www.shianet.org/~reneenew/hist.html

Going along-side these theories is the functional MRI observation of specific involvement of one subsystem of the visual pathways which prevents rapid processing of brief stimuli presented in quick temporal succession. This is the so-called *magnosystem hypothesis*. [254]

Management Make sure the 'dyslexia' is not from lack of teaching. The person may gain insight by discussing his or her problem with fellow sufferers, and by finding out about past dyslexics such as Leonardo da Vinci. Special educational programmes are available for addressing dyslexic problems, as the phonetic approach to learning to read usually presents problems. NB: 'wait-and-see' is not wise—studies tend to find best results if identification is pre-school. Then exercises in sound categorization using rhyme and alliteration, with special teaching of letter sounds can be started early. [255]

Doctors may be asked about dietary supplements with highly unsaturated fatty acids (HUFA, eg Efalex®). These do play a role in neurodevelopment, but evidence of benefit in dyslexia from large randomized trials is sparse. [RCT 256] They appear to reduce dyslexia-associated delay in dark adaption. [257] [n=10]

1 Ptok M 2005 *Laryngorhinootologie* **84** 20. Boys acquire language skills later than girls, but there is no sex difference in the discrimination of phonemes

Compulsory hospitalization

- The patient must have a mental disorder (= mental illness (p. 718), mental impairment (p. 714) or psychopathy (p. 666)) and need detention for treatment or to protect himself or others before compulsion may be used. If voluntary means have failed.

Admission for assessment (mental health act 1983, section 2)
- The period of assessment (and treatment) lapses after 28 days.
- Patient's appeals must be sent within 14 days to the mental health tribunal (composed of a doctor, lay person, and lawyer).
- An approved social worker (or the nearest relative) makes the application on the recommendation of 2 doctors (not both the same hospital), one of whom is 'approved' under the Act (in practice a psychiatric consultant or senior registrar). The other doctor should ideally know the patient in a professional capacity. If this is not possible, the Code of Practice recommends that the second doctor should be an approved doctor.

Section 3: admission for treatment (for 6 months)
- The exact mental disorder must be stated.
- Detention is renewable for a further 6 months (annually thereafter).
- 2 doctors must sign the appropriate forms and know why treatment in the community is contraindicated. They must have seen the patient within 24h. They must state that treatment is likely to benefit the patient, or prevent deterioration, or that it is necessary for the health or safety of the patient or the protection of others.

Section 4: emergency treatment (for 72h)
- The admission to hospital must be an urgent necessity.
- May be used if admission under section 2 would cause undesirable delay (admission must follow the recommendation rapidly).
- An approved social worker or the nearest relative makes the application after recommendation from one doctor (eg the GP).
- The GP should keep a supply of the relevant forms, as the social worker may be unobtainable (eg with another emergency).
- It is usually converted to a section 2 on arrival in hospital, following the recommendation of the duty psychiatrist. If a second recommendation is not completed, the patient should be discharged as soon as the decision not to is made. The section should not be allowed to lapse.

Detention of a patient already in hospital: section 5(2) (72h)
- The doctor in charge (ie the consultant psychiatrist, his or her deputy, or a senior house officer) applies to the hospital administrator. Two or more:
- A patient in an A&E department is not in a ward and so cannot be detained under this section. Common law is all that is available to provide temporary restraint of a lunatic who has run amok and is a manifest danger either to himself or to others, while a warrant is obtained by a GP/doctor.
- Plan what the patient is to go before the 72h has elapsed, eg by talking with the doctor/GP/physician under section.

Nurses holding power: section 5(4) (for 6h)
- Any registered psychiatric nurse may forcibly detain a voluntary mental patient who is taking action to discharge against advice, if such a discharge would be likely to involve serious harm to the patient (eg suicide) or to others.
- During the 6h the duty doctor must be found and a decision made to sign a section 5 application (or discharge the patient) as appropriate.

[illegible]

Compulsory hospitalization

►The patient must have a mental disorder, ie mental illness (p 314), mental impairment (p 314) or psychopathy (p 366), and need detention for treatment of it, or to protect himself or others, before compulsion may be used (if voluntary means have failed).

Admission for assessment (mental health act[1] 1983, section 2)
- The period of assessment (and treatment) lapses after 28 days.
- Patient's appeals must be sent within 14 days to the mental health tribunal (composed of a doctor, lay person, and lawyer).
- An approved social worker (or the nearest relative) makes the application on the recommendation of 2 doctors (not from the same hospital), one of whom is 'approved' under the Act (in practice a psychiatric consultant or senior registrar). The other doctor should ideally know the patient in a professional capacity. If this is not possible, the Code of Practice recommends that the second doctor should be an 'approved' doctor.

Section 3: admission for treatment (for ≤6 months)
- The exact mental disorder must be stated.
- Detention is renewable for a further 6 months (annually thereafter).
- 2 doctors must sign the appropriate forms and know why treatment in the community is contraindicated. They must have seen the patient within 24h. They must state that treatment is likely to benefit the patient, or prevent deterioration; or that it is necessary for the health or safety of the patient or the protection of others.

Section 4: emergency treatment (for ≤72h)
- The admission to hospital must be an urgent necessity.
- May be used if admission under section 2 would cause undesirable delay (admission must follow the recommendation rapidly).
- An approved social worker or the nearest relative makes the application after recommendation from one doctor (eg the GP).
- The GP should keep a supply of the relevant forms, as the social worker may be unobtainable (eg with another emergency).
- It is usually converted to a section 2 on arrival in hospital, following the recommendation of the duty psychiatrist. If the second recommendation is not completed, the patient should be discharged as soon as the decision not to is made. The Section should not be allowed to lapse.

Detention of a patient already in hospital: section 5(2) (≤72h)
- The doctor in charge (or, if a consultant psychiatrist, his or her deputy, eg a senior house officer) applies to the hospital administrator, day or night.
- A patient in an A&E department is not in a ward, so cannot be detained under this section. Common law is all that is available, to provide temporary restraint 'on a lunatic who has run amok and is a manifest danger either to himself or to others'[2] while awaiting an assessment by a psychiatrist.[3]
- Plan where the patient is to go before the 72h has elapsed, eg by liaising with psychiatrists for admission under section 2.

Nurses' holding powers: section 5(4) (for ≤6h)
- Any authorized psychiatric nurse may forcibly detain a voluntary 'mental' patient who is taking his own discharge against advice, if such a discharge would be likely to involve serious harm to the patient (eg suicide) or others.
- During the 6h the nurse must find the necessary personnel to sign a section 5 application or allow the patient's discharge.

1 This Act operates in England; Scottish law is different. The situation in the UK is changing and these pages should be read along with current legislation in the area where you are working.
2 Lord Justice Keith, 1988 *The Times* May 28
3 R Jones 1991 *Mental Health Act Manual*, 3e, London, Sweet and Maxwell

Section 7: application for guardianship Enables patients to receive community care if it cannot be provided without using compulsory powers.

- Application is made by an 'approved social worker (ASP)' or 'nearest relative' and also needs two medical recommendations.
- The guardian, usually a social worker, can require the patient to live in a specified place, to attend at specified places for treatment and to allow authorized persons access.

Renewal of compulsory detention in hospital: section 20(4)

- The patient continues to suffer from a mental disorder and would benefit from continued hospital treatment.
- Further admission is needed for the health or safety of the patient—which cannot be achieved except by forced detention.

Section 25: supervised discharge This is as a result of The Mental Health (Patients in the Community) Act 1995, which has been incorporated within the 1983 Act.

- It allows formal supervision to ensure that a patient who has been detained for treatment under the Act receives follow up care.
- The application is made at the time of detention for treatment by the Resident Medical Officer. It is supported by an ASW and a doctor involved in the patients treatment in the community.
- A supervisor is appointed who can convey the patient to a place where treatment is given.

Section 117: Aftercare & the *Care Programme Approach* (CPA) Section 117 requires provision of after-care for patients who have been detained on the 'long sections' (3, 37, 47, or 48). The CPA is not part of the Act but stipulates that no patient should be discharged without planned after-care: the systematic assessment of health and social needs, an agreed care plan, the allocation of a keyworker, and regular reviews of progress.

Section 136 (for ≥72h) allows police to arrest a person 'in a place to which the public have access' and who is believed to be suffering from a mental disorder. The patient must be conveyed to a 'place of safety' (usually a designated A&E department or police station) for assessment by a doctor (usually a psychiatrist) and an approved social worker. The patient must be discharged after assessment or detained under section 2 or 3.

Section 135 This empowers an approved social worker who believes that someone is being ill-treated or is neglecting himself to apply to a magistrate to search for and admit such patients. The ASW or a registered medical practitioner must accompany the police.

Consent to treatment (Mental health act)

►Emergency treatment to save life or to prevent serious harm to the patient can (must) always be given, overriding all the safeguards below, if the patient is unable to consent to treatment (eg owing to drunkenness).

Background In general a patient must give consent for any procedure (any touching), otherwise the doctor is liable under the UK common law of battery. This means that a competent person can refuse any treatment, *however* dire the consequences. Within common law there are defences to battery other than consent: if a patient is not competent to give or withhold consent, and if treatment is in their best interests, then treatment may be undertaken under 'necessity'. The defence of 'emergency' is to allow restraint where you must act quickly to prevent the patient from harming themselves or others (or committing a crime). For example, you could restrain a patient running amok on a ward before you have a chance to assess the situation. The English mental health act enables treatment of someone suffering from a mental disorder *for that mental disorder* under certain circumstances (p 400) and sets down some conditions for consent for treating in certain circumstances, as follows.

Consent is required *and* a second opinion is needed (section 57) All forms of psychosurgery require this level of consent. If patients are incapable of giving informed consent or decline consent, no treatment can be given.

The Mental Health Act Commission must validate the informed consent. It does this by sending 3 members to interview the patient and review the notes. One member is a doctor (who decides if the treatment is appropriate); others are non-medical. The patient must understand the nature, purpose, and likely effects of the recommended treatment for the conditions of informed consent to hold. If the patient is confused, demented, or would consent to *any* treatment, consent is not informed. Signing of an ordinary consent form is needed as well as certificate from the mental health act commission. Although grades of informed consent are probably more realistic, the law is black and white: either the consent is informed, or it is not.

Consent is required or a second opinion (section 58)
Note: no treatment can be given to a voluntary patient without his informed consent. If the responsible medical officer (RMO) feels that electroconvulsive or drug treatment for ≥3 months is necessary, and the patient is incapable of giving informed consent, or withholds consent, these treatments may be given provided a second opinion from the mental health commission states that the treatment is necessary. Section 3 of the mental health act is then used. The advantage of doing this is that the patient then acquires well-defined rights for review and appeal. If informed consent is given, the RMO must sign Form 38 (as well as the ordinary consent form) stating that the patient understands the purpose, need for, and likely effects of the treatment.

Children under 16 require the same standard of informed consent from a parent or guardian for prolonged psychotropic treatment. If parents are unwilling or unable to consent, a Care Order may be necessary—under which the local authority social services department takes over responsibility for the child. It must be shown that the child's proper development or health is being avoidably prevented or neglected; or that he is exposed to a moral danger; or that he is beyond the control of his parent or guardian.

Withdrawal of consent Treatment must cease immediately, unless it is necessary to save life.

Medicolegal issues—use of Common Law in clinical situations

Common Law (England) Consists of principles identified by judges. It is separate from 'statute law' which comprises Acts of Parliament. It is used when statute law does not apply. Four aspects of common law apply to the management of medical patients with mental disturbance in a general hospital: Capacity, Best interests, Necessity, and Duty of Care.

Capacity: In order to give or refuse valid consent to treatment a patient must have the 'capacity' to reach such a decision. The patient lacks capacity if he or she lacks one of the following: • Comprehending and retaining treatment information • Believing such information • Weighing information balance… and arriving at a choice. Outside of the mental health act (MHA), the relationships between health care practitioners and their patients is governed by common law. Where consent cannot be given owing to a *lack* of capacity, the treating clinician (in consultation with a second clinician) must act in the person's ***best interests***—this includes considering medical, ethical, social and welfare aspects. The authority to give essential treatment depends on the ***necessity*** of that treatment—this principle allows the clinician to act without the consent of the patient. ***Duty of care*** is the principle imposed on all professionals within a hospital or primary care setting. Staff may be negligent by omission if eg no attempt is made to prevent a suicidal patient leaving hospital.

Clinical situations *Deliberate self harm* *Adapted from Feldman 2000:* 258 *'A 30 year old male is brought to A&E following an overdose of paracetamol. There is no history available and the patient refuses to say anything, other than he wants to be left alone to die. He refuses to give blood for a paracetamol level and is refusing any treatment.* What should we do?'

Should we assume that the patient has full capacity? If so, the patient may develop liver failure and possibly die—but ***autonomy*** is maintained. Or should the clinician act in the patient's best interests (the doctrine of ***necessity***) as part of their duty of care? Most people who self-harm are depressed—but this does not prove incapacity. However, in the acute setting, Feldman asserts that 'there are usually good grounds for reasonable doubt with respect to the patient's capacity to make a fully informed and reasoned choice, and to proceed with whatever action is necessary to save his life under the common law'.

Restraint The mental health act (MHA in England) is an *enabling act* in that it does not have to be used in all situations where it may apply. However application of the act gives certain legal safeguards for patients and staff. *'A 40 year old female with alcohol problems has been admitted to hospital following a head injury 2 days ago. She has shown fluctuating levels of confusion, agitation and is now trying to leave the ward'*

In this case due to the patient's lack of capacity to give meaningful consent or refusal, the transient nature of the disturbance and the need for intervention common law would be applicable. If stronger measures are needed or the situation persists, it may be advisable to use the MHA to detain a patient with delirium, however it is not commonly used.

Miscellaneous psychiatric conditions

Seasonal affective disorder (SAD)

Lying thus in the sun one is liberated from doubts and from misgivings; it is not that problems and difficulties are resolved, it is that they are banished. The sun's radiation penetrates the mind…anaesthetizing thought. AE Ellis 1958 *The Rack*

Some people find that symptoms of depression start in winter, and remit in spring or summer. It has been postulated that disordered secretion of the indole melatonin from the pineal gland is to blame in some of these patients with 'SAD'. Melatonin, the hormone of darkness, is secreted by the pineal only at night—eg at 30μg/night; evidence supporting the role of melatonin in depression includes the following:

Treatment choice: As a general rule, the more that the typical winter symptoms (such as hypersomnia, carbohydrate craving and weight gain) predominate, the more likely that light therapy should be the treatment of first choice. If, however, winter episodes are characterized by early morning wakening and weight loss, and especially when patients describe non-seasonal recurrences, antidepressants should be advised.

Light therapy

- The antidepressant effect of light is potentiated by early-morning administration in circadian time, optimally at ~8.5 hours after melatonin onset or 2.5 hours after a sleep's midpoint. 259 [n=42]
- A dose-response effect exists between the amount of light administered in phototherapy and the degree of improvement in depression (as measured on Hamilton ratings). 6h/day of increased light brought about a 53% decrease in scores, whereas treatments of 2h (or red-light treatment) produced only a 25% reduction. These effects were correlated with suppressed plasma melatonin concentrations at 23.00h. Variables of uncertain importance include: the type of light (device & spectrum); distance between patient and source; and the duration of treatment. MET 260
- Therapy should stimulate the nasal retina, as retinal ganglion cells projecting to suprachiasmatic nuclei are unequally distributed. 261 [n=8]
- However, evidence in this area is often contradictory, and it is probably unwise to rush into recommending light for all patients whose recurrent depressions start in the autumn or winter. This might have the undesirable effect of enticing such patients to book unaffordable winter holidays to exotic locations—with inevitable disappointments and recriminations.

Antidepressants

Sedative antidepressants are usually avoided and selective serotonin reuptake inhibitors (SSRI) are usually first choice. If unsuccessful try venlafaxine or reboxetine which can be more energizing. In patients with established winter recurrences, it is usual to instigate treatment as soon as symptoms re-emerge in the autumn and to phase out treatment in spring. For patients who also experience non-seasonal episodes, year-round prophylaxis may be deployed, sometimes regularly increasing the antidepressant dose during the winter months. 262

Community care

Since the early 1980s, most UK inpatients with psychosis have had the focus of their care moved from hospital to the community. The aim has been to save money and improve care: but, in the UK, this policy is now being partly reversed. Has community care failed, or have there been successes? Five questions keep recurring, each (ominously) prefixed by a 'Surely…'

1 ***Surely hospitals will always be needed for severely affected people?*** In general, the problem is not the severity of the mental illness, but the its social context which determines if community care is appropriate.

2 ***Surely community care, if it is done properly, will be more expensive than hospital care, where resources can be concentrated?*** Not so—at least not necessarily so. Some concentration of resources *can* take place in the community, for example, in day hospitals and mental illness hostels. It is also true that the 'bed and breakfast' element of inpatient care is likely to be expensive, if the running and maintenance costs associated with deploying inpatient psychiatric services are taken into account. In most studies, the cost of each type of service doesn't differ much, and sometimes good community care turns out cheaper.[MET 263, 264]

3 ***Surely there will be more homicides and suicides if disturbed patients are not kept in hospital?*** Offending by psychiatric patients is of great public concern. A recent cohort study however found the rate of violent offending is low and the strongest association with offending was previous offending. Psychiatric variables were less important, with diagnosis and number of previous admissions showing no significant association. Substance misuse and sexual abuse were associated with increased offending risk.[265]

4 ***Surely if inpatient psychiatric beds are not available, however good the daytime team is in the community, some patients will still need somewhere to go at night?*** The implication is that the skills available in bed-and-breakfast accommodation may be inadequate at times of day when there is no other support, other than the general practitioner. Studies that have looked at this have certainly found an increase in non-hospital residential care in those selected for community care, and this increase may be as much as 280% over 5yrs. In the UK, new proposals guarantee 24-hour open access to skilled help, but it is not known what pressures this will put services under.

5 ***Surely community care will involve a huge bureaucracy in pursuit of the unattainable goal of 100% safety?*** This will be so if every patient has a lengthy care plan, and repeated risk assessments. Concern for safety may also spawn a non-therapeutic custodial relationship.

Advantages reported for community care are: better social functioning, satisfaction with life, employment, and drug compliance—but in randomized studies in the UK these advantages are not always manifest. Furthermore, trends have been repeatedly found indicating that the longer studies go on for, the harder it is to maintain the initial advantages of community care. If it is hard for teams to keep up their enthusiasm during a trial, it will probably be even harder when the trial period has ended, or when team members are ill. These constraints may in part explain the observation that with inadequately funded and supervised community care, patients can fail to get essential services, and when hospitals are being run down, and a patient's condition worsens, so that 'sectioning' followed by admission becomes impossible, the patient is left in the community 'rotting with his rights on'. *Assertive community care & case management* is one way out of this impasse (here a key-worker has direct responsibility for care plans). This set-up helps ensure more people remain in contact with psychiatric services (NNT=15); this inevitably increases hospital admission rates.[266, 267] When combined with family therapy and social skills training results are good.[RCT 268]

Poverty and mental illness

Social deprivation is positively associated with premature mortality, and poverty makes almost *all* diseases more likely (but not Hodgkin's disease, eczema, bulimia, or melanoma).[269] See *Health and social class*, p 463. In the UK, the number of homeless people is 1-2 million. >30% suffer from mental illness (10% have schizophrenia), most do not know where to go for help, and most have no doctor. A 3-tier strategy may help. **1** Emergency shelters **2** Transitional accommodation **3** Long-term housing.

The cost in health terms to society and the individual is enormous. Diseases and symptoms such as diarrhoea, which may pass as a minor inconveniences to the well-housed, may be a major hurdle for the homeless, with severe social and psychological effects. Capture-recapture techniques show that the *unobserved* population of the homeless is about twice that observed. This method of enumeration collects samples (lists) and looks for tags (duplicates) in subsequent counts, and from this determines the degree of under-counting. If all in the subsequent count are duplicates, then there is no underestimate of the original count. Statistical techniques can allow for migration in and out of the population area.[270] These studies show that psychiatric morbidity is greatest in the observed homeless populations: the implication is that the psychiatric illness makes these people more 'visible'.

In the UK, as in many other Western countries, what started out as an enlightened policy of looking after people with mental health problems in the community (p 405) has resulted in large numbers of psychiatric patients living on the street in great poverty—relieved by occasional admissions to often overcrowded acute units. This 'revolving door' model of care has failed many patients, not least because continuity of care is compromised.

One way to tackle poverty is to pay people not to be poor: in the 1990s, in Singapore, poor families were paid SP$26,400 over 20yrs if they had $\leq$2 children. But economic success in Singapore evolved independently[271] from this idea which was perhaps *too* Quixotic (ie innocently impractical, see BOX).

Income support[uk] is an income-related (means-tested) benefit paid to those who do not have enough money to live on. Income is subtracted from a standard fixed income level (the 'applicable amount'), and the difference is the amount of income support payable. The person's capital is also taken into account. Income support is a non-contributory benefit. This means that a person does not have to have paid any national insurance contributions in order to qualify for income support. The rates of income support are fixed each year by government and are usually increased every April. Income support acts as a 'passport' to certain other help. A claimant and her/his partner will automatically qualify for: • Free school meals • Free prescriptions • Free dental care • Vouchers for spectacles • Free milk and vitamins for expectant mothers and children under 5 • Free vitamins for nursing mothers • Maximum housing benefit • Maximum council tax benefit.

Epidemiology There is no evidence that simply living in a deprived area makes a person more prone to illness and death. All the excess mortality and morbidity is explained by the person being poor.[272] Their immediate neighbours who are not poor do not share the same risk. So we need to target care at poor people wherever they live, not at poor areas.

Poverty, re-offending, and mentally ill offenders[1] *2 contrasting ideas:* **1** The economic arguments for keeping non-violent mentally ill criminals out of prison and rehabilitating them are self-evident. **2** Prison provides an ideal opportunity to treat people who are mentally ill who might otherwise be hard to reach. They should have optimum treatment to improve their quality of life, as well as to lessen the risk of reoffending.

1 *Lancet* editorial 2005 **365** 359

Nobility and mental illness: Don Quixote takes on all comers

'The innkeeper acquainted all in the inn with the lunacy of his guest (Don Quixote), about his standing vigil over his armour and the knighting he expected. They marvelled at so odd a form of madness and went to watch him at a distance, and saw that with a serene expression he sometimes pranced to and fro; at other times, leaning on his lance, he turned his eyes to his armour without turning them away for a long time. Night had fallen; but the moon shone with such a lustre as might almost vie with the sun who lent it; so that everything our new knight did was seen clearly by everyone. Just then it occurred to one of the mule-drivers in the inn to water his pack of mules, and for this it was necessary to move Don Quixote's armour, which was on the trough; our knight, seeing them approach, called in a booming voice:

"Oh thou, whosoever thou art, reckless knight, who would touch the armour of the most valiant knight whoever took up arms! Take heed what thou doest, and touch it not, unless thou wouldst pay for thy audacity with thy life."

The muleteer cared not a jot for this reasoning—it would have been better for him if he had, for it meant caring for his health. Instead, picking the armour up by the straps, he tossed it a good distance. And seeing this, Don Quixote lifted his gaze to the skies and, turning his thoughts (as it seemed) to his lady Dulcinea, he said:

"Help me, my lady, in this the first insult aimed at this thy servant's breast; in this my first crisis let not thy grace and protection fail me."

And, continuing this line of argument, and dropping his shield, he raised his lance in both hands and gave the mule-driver such a clout on the head as to demolish him; if this first blow had been followed by a second, he would have had no need for a doctor ('*maestro*') to cure him. Having done this, Don Quixote picked up his armour and began to pace again with the same gravity as before. A short time later, unaware of what had happened—for the first mule driver lay stunned—a second approached, also intending to water his mules, and when he began to remove the armour so as to get to the trough, without so much as a by-your-leave or even a word, Don Quixote let slip his shield and raised his lance, and without quite reducing the second mule-driver's head to smithereens, he thrice sliced it, fracturing the skull in four places. When they heard the noise, all the people in the inn hurried over, among them the innkeeper. When he saw this, Don Quixote took up his shield, placed his hand on his sword, saying:

"Oh queen of beauty, whose spark and fire warms the sickness in my heart (*debilitado corazón mío*)! From your greatness, it is time that you do bend your eye on this thy slavish knight, who expects so vast an exploit."

And with this he acquired, it seemed to him, so much courage, that if all the mule-drivers in the world charged him he would never retreat one step. The wounded men's comrades, seeing their two fallen friends, began to rain stones down on Don Quixote, and he did all he could to deflect them with his shield, not daring to move away from the trough and leave his armour unprotected. The innkeeper implored them to stop as he had already told them the knight was mad, and whatever the number of deaths no wind of blame could ever extinguish his innocence.' 273

Don Quijote de la Mancha 274 *by Miguel de Cervantes 1547–1616; see translations by Shelton (1605),* 275 *Grossman (2003, HarperCollins) & Jarvis (OUP) chapter 3 (p 33–5).*

WE PRESENT THE IDEALISTIC KNIGHT-ERRANT WHO TEACHES US TO VALUE THE VERY THINGS HE IS DELUDED BY: HEROISM AND VALOUR.

Postnatal depression

►*Suicide is a leading cause of maternal mortality.* The psychiatric and psychological phenomena of pregnancy and birth include the very common, and usually mild, 'blues'; puerperal psychosis; and major depression (the risk of developing this latter is 3-fold that of those with no recent pregnancy). There are many causes: individual and social circumstances; genetic; hormonal change (see below).

Natural history Reviews state that most postnatal depression resolves within 6 months, so we find ourselves thinking: 'Good! Those trusty psychiatric tools of "wait-and-see", and the passage of time will be my main tools in this illness: nothing depends critically on what I do now, to this poor depressed new mother with whom I am now confronted'. NOT SO!

Consider these facts ►For the patient, 6 months is a long, long time.

- For the infant, 6 months is more than a long time: it's literally an age.
- Suicide is a waste, but for a young family, a mother's suicide is especially destructive—unthinkable, indeed, for those who have not experienced it.
- There is impaired cognition and social functioning in the offspring of mothers with postnatal depression. MET 276 277

Our actions may spawn critical outcomes. The first step is to try not to be caught unawares by a major depression that apparently strikes like a bolt from the blue, but which, in reality, has been building up over time. Pregnancy and infant-motherhood is supposed to be a time of unclouded joy. We professionals often collude with this view. We are always hearing ourselves saying: 'Oh Mrs Salt, what a lovely baby! You must be so pleased—and you always wanted a little boy, didn't you? We are so delighted for you…' But what if *she* is not delighted? She hardly dares confess her traitorous thoughts that she is unaccountably sad, that she spends the nights crying, and that her exhausted days are filled with a sense of foreboding that she or some other agency will harm the child. The place to start to pre-empt these feelings is in the antenatal clinic. By addressing these issues, and, later, in the puerperium, by expressly asking after them, you give permission for the new mother to tell her woe. When this is revealed, counselling, and input from a health visitor and a psychiatrist is appropriate, as is particularly close follow-up. You may need to arrange emergency admission under the Mental Health Act: but the whole point of being prepared for postnatal depression is to avoid things getting this bad. Interventions for persistent depression need to address relationship difficulties as well as depressive symptoms.[1]

Pharmacology *Fluoxetine* is as effective as cognitive-behavioural counselling in the short-term. More trials with longer follow-up are needed to compare antidepressants and social interventions. 278 Although all antidepressants are excreted in breast milk, tricyclics and SSRIs are rarely detectable by standard tests. Observe babies for possible SEs; it may be best to stop breastfeeding if large doses are used.

Adding *lithium* (p 354) may help (ECT may also be needed). Trials show that *transdermal estrogen* is partly effective in severe postnatal depression. The Edinburgh Postnatal Depression Scale (EPDS, OPPOSITE) was used to assess outcome (along with other measures). In one study, the score started off at 21.8, falling within a month to 13.3—taking some patients out of the 'major depression' category. The control group also improved over time (from 21.3 to 16.5)—but still remained severely depressed. *Dose regimen:* 3 months of transdermal 17β-(o)estradiol (200μg/day) for 3 months on its own, then with added dydrogesterone 10mg/day for 12 days each month for 3 more months. CI: uterine, cervical, or breast neoplasia; past thromboembolism/thrombophlebitis; breastfeeding. 279

1 McMahon C 2005 *J Affect Disord* **84** 15

Edinburgh postnatal depression scale (EPDS) 280 [n=84]

Please underline what comes closest to how you have felt in the last 7 days.

1 *I've been able to laugh & see the funny side of things:* As much as always could / Not quite so much now / Definitely not so much / Now not at all

2 *I've looked forward with enjoyment to things:* As much as I ever did / Rather less than I used to / Definitely less than before / Hardly at all

3 **I've blamed myself unnecessarily when things went wrong:* Yes, most of the time / Yes, some of the time / Not very often / No, never

4 *I've been anxious or worried for no good reason:* No, not at all / Hardly ever / Yes, sometimes / Yes, very often

5 **I've felt scared or panicky for no very good reason:* Yes, quite a lot / Yes, sometimes / No, not much / No, not at all

6 **Things have been getting on top of me:* Yes, most of the time I haven't been able to cope at all / Yes, sometimes I haven't been coping as well as usual / No, most of the time I have coped quite well / No, I have been coping as well as ever

7 **I've been so unhappy that it is difficult to sleep:* Yes, most of the time / Yes, sometimes / Not very often / No, not at all

8 **I've felt sad or miserable:* Yes, most of the time / Yes, quite often / Not very often / No, not at all

9 **I've been so unhappy that I've been crying:* Yes, most of the time / Yes, quite often / Only occasionally / No, never

10 **Thoughts of harming myself have occurred to me:* Yes, quite often / Sometimes / Hardly ever / Never

Answers are scored 0, 1, 2, and 3 according to increased severity.
*Some are reverse scored (3, 2, 1, 0). Add scores for 1-10 for the total. Let her complete the scale herself, unless she has limited English or has difficulty with reading. EPDS may be used at 6–8 weeks to screen postnatal women, eg at the postnatal check-up. ►A score of 12/30 has a sensitivity of 77% and a specificity of 93 for postnatal depression.

The main point is that it's all too easy for doctors and midwives to go on thinking 'it's just postnatal blues' when in fact a serious depression is unfolding. The above tool is helpful in making this distinction.

5 Ophthalmology

What shall human optics know...?
my twentysix selves
bulging in immortal spring...
farthest becomes near
e e cummings

Sources: www.moorfields.org.uk (tel (uk) +44 (020 725 33411)) www.rnib.org.uk. www.rcophth.ac.uk (Royal College); www.meei.harvard.edu www.eri.harvard.edu (Schepens Eye Institute); www.bjophthalmol.com.

►*We especially thank Mr R Williams FRCS & Prof P Muthusamy FRCS Ed for their help.*

'We do not see the human eye as a receiver, it appears not to let anything in, but to send something out. The ear receives; the eye looks. (It casts glances, it flashes, radiates, gleams.) One can terrify with one's eyes, not with one's ear or nose. When you see the eye, you see something going out from it. You see the look in the eye. If you only shake free from your physiological prejudices, you will find nothing queer about the fact that the glance of the eye can be seen too. For I also say that I see the look that you cast at someone else.' ***Ludwig Wittgenstein*** (*Zettle*; 222-3). How is this 'giving a look' controlled? MRI shows that different parts of the medial frontal cortex become active when we choose to make an eye movement of our own free will, and when we face a difficult choice involving conflicting alternatives. Masud Husain 2005.

Accommodation Active changing of lens shape to focus near objects.
Acuity A measure of how well the eye sees a small or distant object.
Amblyopia ↓Acuity uncorrectable by lenses, with no anatomic defect.
Amsler grid Test chart of intersecting lines used for screening for macular disease. If present, lines may appear wavy and squares distorted.
Anisocoria Unequal pupil size.
Anisometropia Having different refractive errors in each eye.
Aphakia The state of having no lens (eg removed because of cataract).
Blepharitis Inflamed lids.
Canthus The medial or lateral angle made by the open lids.
Chemosis Oedema of the conjunctiva.
Choroid Vascular coat between the retina and the outer scleral coat.
Ciliary body Portion of uvea (uveal tract) between iris & choroid, containing ciliary processes & ciliary muscle (for accommodation).
Conjunctiva Mucous membrane on anterior sclera & posterior lid aspect.
Cycloplegia Ciliary muscle paralysis preventing accommodation.
Dacryocystitis Inflammation of the lacrimal sac.
Dioptre Units for measuring refractive power of lenses.
Ectropion The lids evert (especially lower lid).
Entropion The lids invert (so that the lashes may irritate the eyeball).
Epiphora Passive overflow of tears on to the cheek.
Fornix Where bulbar (scleral) and palpebral (lid) conjunctivae meet.
Fovea The tiny, vital, cone-rich area of retina capable of 6/6 vision.
Fundus That part of retina normally visible through the ophthalmoscope.
Keratoconus The cornea is shaped like a cone. See p 458.
Keratomalacia The cornea is softened.
Limbus The annular border between clear cornea and opaque sclera.
Macula Rim of avascular retina surrounding the fovea.
Miotic An agent causing pupil constriction (eg pilocarpine).
Mydriatic An agent causing pupil dilatation (eg tropicamide).
Near point Where the eye is looking when maximally accommodated.
Papillitis Inflammation of the optic nerve head.
Optic cup The cup like depression in the centre of the optic disc (p 441).
Optic disc That part of optic nerve seen ophthalmoscopically in the fundus.
Presbyopia Age-related reduced near-acuity from failing accommodation.
Pterygium Wing-shaped degenerative conjunctival condition (p 416).
Ptosis Drooping lids.
Refraction Ray deviation on passing through media of different density; or determining refractive errors and correcting them with lenses.
Retinal detachment The sensory retina separates from the pigmented epithelial layer of retina.
Sclera The whites of the eyes starting from the corneal perimeter.
Scotoma A defect causing a part of the field of view to go missing.
Slit lamp A device which illuminates and magnifies structures in the eye.
Strabismus (squint) Eyes deviate (they are not looking at the same thing).
Tarsorrhaphy A surgical procedure for uniting upper and lower lids.
Tonometer A device for measuring intraocular pressure.
Uvea Iris, ciliary body and choroid.
Vitreous Jelly like substance filling the globe behind the lens.
Vitrectomy Surgical removal of the vitreous.

Examining eyes

History indicates the part of the examination to focus on. Asking about trauma, symptoms of pain *vs* irritation, loss of vision, and pattern and speed of onset. Examination assesses the retina and optic nerve (nerve of vision), tests acuity, visual fields and colour vision (p 455).

Acuity is a measure of central (macular) vision; always test it carefully as any loss may be serious. Record it accurately, especially in a patient with eye injury. Examine the right eye first. Sit the patient 6 metres from the Snellen chart (p 415); to get 6 metres in a 4 metre room, place the chart just above the patient, pointing towards a mirror 3 metres away. Obscure the left eye with a lollipop-shaped 'eye paddle' or card, not *pressed* against the eye—simply enough to *occlude* the visual access (more reliable than peepable through fingers or a slipping palm). Ask the patient to read the chart from the top using the right eye, then the left. Use glasses if worn. The last line completed accurately indicates the acuity for distant vision.

The chart is designed so that the top line can be read by someone with normal vision at 60 metres, the next at 36 metres, the next at 24, the next at 18, the next at 12, the next at 9, and the next at 6 metres. Acuity is recorded as 6/60, 6/36, 6/24, 6/18, 6/12, 6/9, 6/6 to indicate the last line accurately read (6/6 vision is normal). For acuities <6/60 patients can be brought forward to 5, 4, 3, 2 and 1 metre from the chart to read the top line. If he can read it then acuity is expressed as that distance, eg 5/60, 4/60, 3/60, 2/60 or 1/60. If the vision is below 1/60 ask the patient to count your fingers at 50cm distance. This is recorded as CF (count fingers). If unable to count your fingers move your hand in front of the eye at a distance of 25cm. If the patient can appreciate that your hand moves, record HM (hand movement). If the patient cannot appreciate hand movement, dim the light in the examination room and shine a torch light into the eye. If the patient perceives light, record PL. If there is no perception, record 'no PL' (the eye is blind). NB: in practice, if nothing on the Snellen chart can be read, it is common to go straight to finger counting.

If the patient sees less than 6/6 with or without glasses, examine again with a pin-hole in front of the eye: a narrow beam removes the need for focus. In simple refractive errors, acuity will improve through the pin-hole. This is an important test as it eliminates ocular pathology as a cause of reduced acuity. (Make a pin-hole with a 22G needle in a 10 × 10cm opaque card; check that you can see through the hole before giving it to the patient.)

If patients >40 years old complain of near-vision blurring, the cause may be presbyopia (p 426). Test near vision using a near vision testing card (p 414). If the patient can read N5 at 30cm, near vision is normal.

Visual field This is the area that can be seen with both eyes without shifting gaze. The uni-ocular field is smaller than the binocular field. Questions to address: does the defect affect one eye or both? Are there any clear boundaries to the defect? Does the boundary lie in the vertical or horizontal meridians? Is acuity affected? ***Confrontation tests:*** p 428.

Extraocular movements It is vital to examine these in those with diplopia. Ask the patient to watch a pencil move diagonally: up left; up right; down left; down right; horizontally left; horizontally right. Ask which movement provokes most diplopia, and when looking in that direction, block each eye in turn and ask which one sees the *outer* image: that is the eye which is malfunctioning. NB: avoid extremes of movement as inability to maintain fixation stimulates nystagmus. For eye movements and squint see p 422.

Ophthalmoscopy This helps detect pathology in the lens, vitreous, and retina. Start with high + numbers (often marked in colour on the dial). To examine the lens and the vitreous focus the beam of the ophthalmoscope at the pupil at ~1 metre from the eye. In the normal eye there is a red glow from the choroid (the red reflex). Any lens opacity (cataract) will be seen as a black pattern obstructing the red reflex. Blood or loose floaters in the vitreous are seen as black floaters. To determine their position, move your head horizontally, to and fro, like a cobra waiting to strike. The opacity will either move in the same direction as you (so lies behind the lens), in the opposite direction (so lies in front of the lens) or will not move at all (so *in* the lens).

Red reflexes are absent with dense cataract and intraocular bleeding. When the retina is in focus, ask the patient to look at the Snellen chart or anything right ahead in the distance. This may bring the optic disc into the view. It should have precise boundaries and a central cup (p 440). Cupping means an excavated appearance (seen in glaucoma). A pale disc suggests optic atrophy (eg chronic glaucoma, multiple sclerosis, *et al.*, p 438). Examine radiating vessels and the macula (ask the patient to look at the light).

Aids to successful ophthalmoscopy: Ensure the batteries are fully charged.
- Darken the room; remove spectacles; dial up a lens to correct the resulting refractive error (- lenses correct myopia, + correct hypermetropia).
- If very myopic, try examining with spectacles on (discs appear small).
- If you find ophthalmoscopy difficult using your non-dominant eye, try using your dominant eye for examining *both* fundi—while standing behind the seated patient, whose neck is fully extended. ►Start looking for the disc by making the twinkle of the ophtlmoscope's light strike the pupil's margin at 9 o'clock for the right eye and 3 o'clock for the left. Then move the beam medially and you will find the disc somewhere along that line.
- Always check the lens for opacities before trying to examine the fundus.
- Get *close enough* to the patient, even if one of you has had garlic for lunch.
- Consider using a short-acting mydriatic to dilate the pupil (see p 456).
- Remember that most retinal tears are peripheral and are difficult to see. It isn't possible to see the margin of the retina with an ophthalmoscope.

The panoptic ophthalmoscope has a wide field of view (25° *vs* 5°). The patient's skull makes contact with its eyecup (so you don't have to get so close!). Good views even if the pupil is constricted. Magnification (×5) & ↑field width are achieved by focusing a beam on the cornea, which is then fanned out.[2]

Slit lamp examination This instrument has a bright light source and a horizontally mounted microscope to examine the structures of the living eye. The light source can be converted to a slit (hence the name). Tonometric attachments allow intraocular pressure measurement.

External eye ***Lids:*** Symmetrical? Normal retraction on upward gaze (abnormal in thyroid disease), ptosis (p 416), spasm, inflammation or swellings (p 416)? ***Conjunctiva:*** Look for inflammation (if circumcorneal, suspect anterior uveitis; injection of the bulbar, fornix, and the tarsal surfaces suggests conjunctivitis; focal injection adjacent to cornea means a problem on the cornea). Is there discharge, follicles, or upper lid cobblestone patterning, or any subconjunctival haemorrhage (p 432)?

Cornea: Use a torch. Any opacity, abrasion/ulcer (the latter stains green with 1% fluorescein), or oedema? ***Anterior chamber:*** Its clear aqueous humor can be cloudy in anterior uveitis (p 430), may have sterile pus (hypopyon) ***with*** corneal ulcer, or blood (hyphaema) after injury (fig 1).
Lens: With a normal lens a pupil is black; cataract may make it white. ***Pupils*** should be equal and react to light and accommodation (written 'PERLA'). They are small and irregular in anterior uveitis (dilated and fixed in acute glaucoma, p 430). For other pupil signs, see p 424.

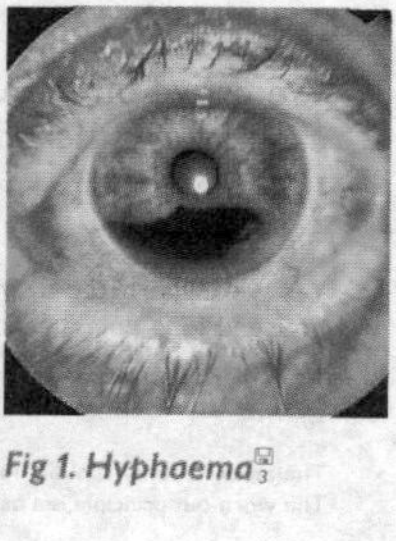

Fig 1. Hyphaema[3]

N. 48

He moved

N. 36

forward a few

N. 24

fine chattering gems.

N.18

He knew exactly who would

N. 14

now sneeze calmly through an open door. Had there been another year

N. 12

of peace the battalion would have made a floating system of perpetual drainage.

N. 10

A silent fall of immense snow came near oily remains of the purple-blue supper on the table.

N. 8

We drove on in our old sunless walnut. Presently classical eggs ticked in the new afternoon shadows.

N. 6

We were instructed by my cousin Jasper not to exercise by country house visiting unless accompanied by thirteen geese or gangsters.

N. 5

The modern American did not prevail over the pair of redundant bronze puppies. The worn-out principle is a bad omen which I am never glad to ransom on purpose.

H
A L
T N C
O L H A
E C T N O
C L O H N A
A E N L O M C T
I S Q W E N L D E P O

Read these test types at 30cm—with reading glasses if used.

H

T

O Y

H U V

A T Y M

X O W U H

Y U V T X O

A W I M H Y T

Test types (N. 48–N. 5 opposite) should be read at 30cm.

Lines on the Snellen chart are as follows Use distance glasses

6	Able to read at 6m what can normally be read at *6*m	*'6/6'*
9	Able to read at 6m what can normally be read at *9*m	*'6/9'*
12	Able to read at 6m what can normally be read at *12*m	*'6/12'*
18	Able to read at 6m what can normally be read at *18*m	*'6/18'*
24	Able to read at 6m what can normally be read at *24*m	*'6/24'*
36	Able to read at 6m what can normally be read at *36*m	*'6/36'*
60	Able to read at 6m what can normally be read at *60*m	*'6/60'*
Counts *f*ingers; counts fingers held ½m distance		*'cf'*
*H*and *m*ovement; perceives hand moving ¼m distance		*'hm'*
*P*erceives *l*ight; can see a torchlight when shone into eye		*'pl'*
*N*o light *p*erception, abbreviated to 'no PL', ie blind		*'no pl'*

m=metres

The external eye

Entropion Lid inturning is typically due to degeneration of lower (rarely upper) lid fascial attachments and their muscles. It is rare if <40yrs old. The inturned eyelashes irritate the cornea. Taping the (lower) eyelids to the cheek gives temporary relief; more lasting relief needs surgery. [4] [N=41]

Ectropion Lower lid eversion causes eye irritation, watering (drainage punctum malaligned) ± exposure keratitis. ***Associations:*** Old age; facial palsy. Plastic surgery may correct the deformity. If facial palsy is the cause, consider eg a modified temporalis muscle transfer. [5]

Upper lid malposition may result from the globe's hypotropic position or excess tissue in the lid—***pseudoptosis***, or intrinsic levator weakness,—true ptosis from: •Congenital (absent nerve to levator muscle; poorly developed levator); •Mechanical (oedema, xanthelasma or upper lid tumour); •Myogenic (muscular dystrophy, myasthenia); •CNS (III nerve palsy, p 422; Horner's, p 424). Congenital ptosis is corrected surgically early if the pupils are covered or if it is unilateral (risk of amblyopia ex anopsia, p 422).

Lagophthalmos This is difficulty in lid closure over the eyeball. ***Causes:*** Exophthalmos; mechanical impairment of lid movements (eg injury or lid burns); leprosy; paralysed orbicularis oculi giving sagging lower lid; infective keratitis. [6] Corneal ulceration and keratitis may follow. Lubricate eyes with liquid paraffin ointment. If corneal ulceration develops, temporary tarsorrhaphy (stitching lids together) may be needed.

Styes The word stye is used more by patients than by ophthalmologists for referring to inflammatory lid swellings. ***Hordeolum externum*** is an abscess or infection, usually staphylococcal, in a lash follicle; these may also involve the glands of Moll (sweat glands) and of Zeis (sebum-producing glands attached directly to lash follicles). They 'point' outwards and may cause much inflammation. Treatment is with local antibiotics—eg fusidic acid. (The word 'stye' implies infection: if this is not present, the term ***marginal cyst***—of Zeis or Moll—may be used.) Less common is the ***hordeolum internum***, an abscess of the Meibomiam glands (hordeolum is Latin for *barleycorn)*. These 'point' inwards, opening on to conjunctiva, cause less local reaction but leave a residual swelling called a ***chalazion*** or a ***Meibomian cyst*** (tarsal cyst) when they subside. Vision may be ↓ if corneal flattening occurs (rare). [7] Treatment for residual swellings is incision & curettage (+ eg fusidic acid applied for some days pre-op). Lidocaine-prilocaine cream can obviate need for GA. [8]

Blepharitis (Lid inflammation eg from staphs, seborrhoeic dermatitis, or rosacea). Eyes have 'burning' itching red margins, with scales on the lashes. ***Treatment:*** Cleaning crusts off the lashes is essential (use cotton-wool buds) ± Tears Naturale®, fusidic acid, or steroid drops (or creams). In children with blepharokeratitis, consider oral erythromycin too. [9]

Pinguecula Degenerative vascular yellow nodules on the conjunctiva either side of the cornea (usually the nasal side). ***Typical patient:*** Adult male. ***Associations:*** ↑Hair & skin pigment; sun-related skin damage. [10] [n = 3564] If inflamed (pingueculitis) topical steroids are tried. If encroaching on to the cornea, as it may in dusty, [11] wind-blown life-styles, the word **pterygium** is used; surgery may be needed. [12] images

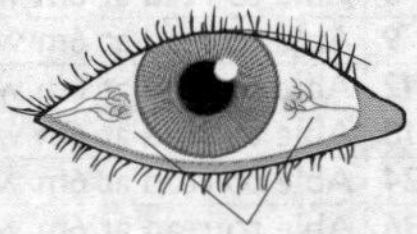

Pinguecula

Fig 1. Pinguecula

Dendritic ulcer (*Herpes simplex* corneal ulcer) ***Signs:*** Photophobia & watering. If steroid drops are used, corneal invasion and scarring may occur, risking blindness. 1% fluorescein drops stain the lesion. ***℞:*** Aciclovir 3% eye ointment 5× daily for ≥3 days after healing. Get help if aciclovir resistance possible. MET [13] [14]

Tears and lacrimation

The lacrimal gland is in the superior temporal side of the orbits. The tear film is spread over the eye during blinking and drains via the lacrimal puncta (found at the medial side of the upper and lower eyelid) through the lacrimal sac, lacrimal duct, and inferior meatus (just lateral to the inferior turbinate) into the nasal passages. Dry eyes may be due to insufficient tear formation, and watering eyes may be due to blockage of the drainage system.

Acute dacryocystitis This is acute inflammation of the tear sac which is located medial to the medial canthus. This may spread to surrounding tissues and result in systemic upset. Immediate antibiotic therapy may resolve the infection; it also leads to local abscess formation.

Nasolacrimal duct non-canalization The nasolacrimal duct may not be canalized at birth and may not open fully until 1 month old. Tear sacs tend to get infected and a sticky discharge is produced. Ask an ophthalmologist to teach the mother to massage the sac to empty the contents four times daily and then apply antibiotic (eg chloramphenicol) eye drops. Should this fail after 9 months, probing of the duct under anaesthesia is an option.

Chronic dacryocystitis This typically occurs in the middle-aged and elderly. There is lacrimal sac distension, discharge of mucopus into the eye, ± nasolacrimal duct block. Syringing the lacrimal drainage system is done so as to clear the system (may need repeating). If the nasolacrimal duct is permanently blocked, dacryocystorhinostomy establishes communication between the lacrimal sac and the nasal cavity. Squamous cell cancer of the lacrimal drainage system is rare: do CT or MRI of all masses arising at the medial canthus.

Dacroadenitis Lacrimal gland inflammation causes pain and swelling on the temporal side of the upper eyelid, which may become S-shaped. Cause: viral (mumps, measles, influenza) or gonococcal. Chronic swelling can occur in sarcoid, TB, lymphatic leukaemia, or lymphosarcoma.

Tear production The volume of tears normally in the eye is 6μL; the turnover rate being 1.2μL/min. Tears are similar in electrolyte concentration to plasma, but rich in proteins, especially IgA. They also contain lysozyme and β-lysin which have antibacterial properties.

Dry eye syndrome (keratoconjunctivitis sicca) This may be due to ↓**tear production** by the lacrimal gland in old age or is seen commonly in Sjögren's syndrome associated with connective tissue disorders (especially RA) and sarcoidosis, amyloid, lymphoma, leukaemia, haemochromatosis. Other causes: **excess evaporation of tears** (post-exposure keratitis), or **mucin deficiency in the tears** (avitaminosis A, Stevens–Johnson syndrome, pemphigoid, chemical burns). Schirmer's test (strip of filter paper put over lower lid: tears should soak >15mm in 5min) reveals insufficient production. Artificial tears may be used for symptomatic relief.

Excess lacrimation Causes: emotional (joy, or sorrow),[1] corneal abrasions or foreign body, conjunctivitis, iritis, acute glaucoma.

Epiphora is normal lacrimal volume abnormally drained to the inferior meatus of the nose. **Causes:** ectropion, entropion, drainage system blockage (idiopathic, or rarely from head and neck tumours).[2] **Treatment:** Dacryocystorhinostomy (eg endoscopic) for nasolacrimal duct obstruction; surgery for other causes.

1 [illegible]

2 [illegible]

Tears and lacrimation

The lacrimal glands are on the superior temporal side of the orbits. The tear film excreted over the eye drains via the lacrimal puncta (found at the medial side of the upper and lower eyelid) through the lacrimal sac, lacrimal duct and inferior meatus (just lateral to the inferior turbinate) into the nasal passages. Dry eyes may be due to insufficient tear secretion, and watering eyes may be due to blockage of the drainage system.

Acute dacryocystitis This is acute inflammation of the tear sac which is located medial to the medial canthus. This may spread to surrounding tissues and result in systemic upset. Immediate antibiotic therapy may resolve the infection. Failure leads to local abscess formation.

Nasolacrimal duct non-canalization The nasolacrimal duct may not be canalized at birth and may not open fully until 3 months old. Tear sacs tend to get infected and a sticky discharge is produced. Ask an ophthalmologist to teach the mother to massage the sac to empty the contents four times daily and then apply antibiotic (eg gentamicin) eye drops. Should this fail after several months, probing of the duct under anaesthesia is an option.

Chronic dacryocystitis This typically occurs in the middle-aged and elderly. There is lacrimal sac distension, discharge of mucopus into the eye ± nasolacrimal duct block. Syringing the lacrimal drainage system is done early to clear the system (may need repeating). If the nasolacrimal duct is permanently blocked, dacryocystorhinostomy establishes communication between the lacrimal sac and the nasal cavity. *ΔΔ:* Squamous cell cancer of the lacrimal drainage system: do CT or MRI of all masses arising in the medial canthus.[15]

Dacroadenitis Lacrimal gland inflammation causes pain and swelling on the temporal side of the upper eyelid, which may become S-shaped. ***Cause:*** Viral (mumps, measles, influenza) or gonococcal. Chronic swelling can occur in sarcoid, TB, lymphatic leukaemia, or lymphosarcoma.

Tear production The volume of tears normally *in* the eye is 6μL, the turnover *rate* being 1.2μL/min. Tears are similar in electrolyte concentration to plasma, but rich in proteins, especially IgA. They also contain lysozyme and β-lysin which have antibacterial properties.

Dry eye syndrome (keratoconjunctivitis sicca) This may be due to ***↓tear production*** by the lacrimal glands in old age, or, less commonly, in: Sjögren's syndrome associated with connective tissue disorders (especially RA); mumps; sarcoidosis; amyloid; lymphoma; leukaemia; haemochromatosis. Other causes: ***excess evaporation of tears*** (post-exposure keratitis); or ***mucin deficiency in the tears*** (avitaminosis A, Stevens-Johnson syndrome, pemphigoid, chemical burns). Schirmer's test (strip of filter paper put overlapping lower lid; tears should soak >15mm in 5min) reveals insufficient production. Artificial tears may be used for symptomatic relief.

Excess lacrimation *Causes:* Emotion (joy or sorrow),[1] corneal abrasions or foreign body, conjunctivitis, iritis, acute glaucoma.

Epiphora ie normal volume, but not normally drained to the inferior meatus of the nose. ***Causes:*** Ectropion, entropion, drainage system blockage (idiopathic, or rarely from head and neck tumours).[2] ***Treatment:*** Dacryocystorhinostomy (eg endoscopic) for nasolacrimal duct obstruction; surgery for other causes.[16]

1 Some sceptics argue that tears of joy don't exist. Sandor Feldman claims they are really tears of anticipated loss (T Lutz, 1999, *Crying, the Natural and Cultural History of Tears*, ISBN 0393047563). In support of this, the 'fact' is cited that children do not cry with tears of joy. Were such psychoanalysts too absorbed to have noticed infant tears of joy at family reunions?

2 Diba R 2005 *Head Neck* **27** 72.

Anatomy of the lacrimal drains

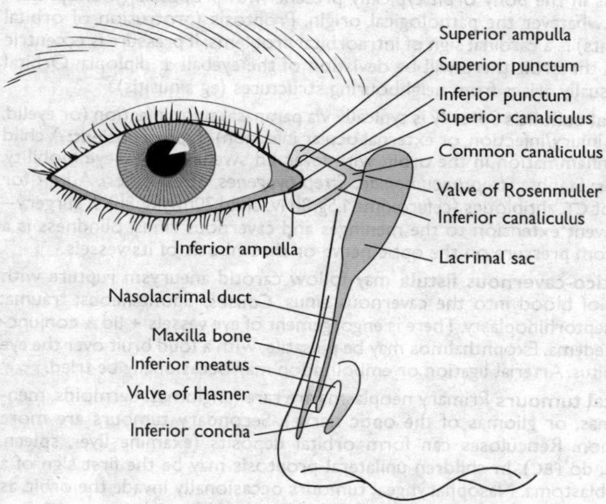

Orbital swellings

Lesions in the bony orbit typically present with proptosis (ie exophthalmos), whatever the pathological origin. Proptosis (protrusion of orbital contents) is a cardinal sign of intraorbital problems. If pressure is eccentric within the orbit there will be deviation of the eyeball ± diplopia. Orbital pain usually arises from neighbouring structures (eg sinusitis).

Orbital cellulitis Spready is typically via paranasal sinus infection (or eyelid, dental injury/infection, or external ocular infection). ***Typical patient:*** A child with inflammation in the orbit, with fever, lid swelling, and ↓eye mobility. ***Causes:*** Staphs, *Strep pneumoniae*, *Strep pyogenes*, *Strep milleri*. Admit for prompt CT, antibiotics (cefuroxime 1.5g/8h IV; child 20mg/kg/8h) ± surgery—to prevent extension to the meninges and cavernous sinus. Blindness is a risk from pressure on the optic nerve or thrombosis of its vessels.[18,19]

Carotico-cavernous fistula may follow carotid aneurysm rupture with reflux of blood into the cavernous sinus. ***Causes:*** Spontaneous; trauma; post-septorhinoplasty. There is engorgement of eye vessels + lid & conjunctival oedema. Exophthalmos may be pulsatile, with a loud bruit over the eye ± tinnitus. Arterial ligation or embolization may occasionally be tried.[20,21,22]

Orbital tumours Primary neoplasms are rare (angiomas, dermoids, meningiomas, or gliomas of the optic nerve). Secondary tumours are more common. Reticuloses can form orbital deposits (examine liver, spleen, nodes; do FBC). In children unilateral proptosis may be the first sign of a neuroblastoma. Nasopharyngeal tumours occasionally invade the orbit, as may mucocoeles and pyocoeles of the ethmoid and frontal sinuses. CT scan pictures give a clear representation of the orbit.

Hyperthyroidism may cause exophthalmos (*OHCM* p 305).

Ophthalmic shingles (herpes zoster ophthalmicus, HZO)

This is zoster of the 1st (ophthalmic) branch of the trigeminal nerve and accounts for 20% of all shingles. Only thoracic nerves are more affected (55%). Pain, tingling or numbness around the eye may precede a blistering rash which is accompanied by much inflammation. In 50% of those with HZO the globe is affected (corneal signs ± iritis in >40%—rarely sectoral iris atrophy). Nose-tip involvement—Hutchison's sign—means involvement of the nasociliary branch of the trigeminal nerve which also supplies the globe and makes it likely that the eye will be affected. The eye can be afflicted with little rash elsewhere. Beware dissemination if immunocompromised.[23] Varicella zoster virus (VZV) may persist in the cornea and retina. The different patterns of retinal disease caused by VZV relate to immune status.

Presentation:
- Mucopurulent conjunctivitis
- Limbal lesions
- Preauricular node tenderness
- Episcleritis
- Visual loss
- V nerve palsy
- Keratitis
- Iritis (± atrophy)
- Pupillary distortion
- Optic atrophy
- Scleritis

Treatment: Systemic antivirals improve the early quality of life but cannot be relied on to prevent post-herpetic neuralgia.[1] Famciclovir offers the best dosing schedule (750mg once daily PO for 7d; SE vomiting; headache) but is much more expensive than aciclovir (800mg 5 times daily PO for 7 days—it has more serious SE such as hepatitis and renal failure). Start within 4 days of onset. It is wise for all with ophthalmic shingles to see a specialist if the nose-tip is involved or the eye turns red within 3 days to exclude anterior uveitis with a slit lamp. Prolonged steroid eyedrops may be needed.

1 Wassilew S 2005 *J Eur Acad Dermatol Venereol* **19** 47. Incidence of neuralgia is 16% if aged >65yrs (also risk↑ if rash is extensive). It causes insomnia, fatigue, depression, interference with daily living—even suicide. Amitriptyline 25mg at night may help, as may gabapentin (max 3.6g/day, but see *BNF*).

Retinoblastoma

This is the most common primary intraocular tumour in children.

Incidence 1 in 15,000 live births.

Signs Strabismus and leukocoria (ie a white pupil). Always suspect retinoblastoma when the red reflex is absent (the mother may come with a photo showing only one eye reddened during flash photography); NB: multiple tumours may be present.[24]

Inheritance Hereditary retinoblastoma is different from the non-hereditary type: there is a mutation of the RB gene located at 13q14. Inheritance is autosomal dominant with 80% penetrance. The RB gene is present in everyone, and is normally a suppressor gene or anti-oncogene. Those with hereditable retinoblastomas typically have one altered allele in every cell. If a developing retinal cell undergoes mutation in the other allele, a retinoblastoma results. The retinoblastoma gene is the best characterized tumour suppressor gene. Its product is a nuclear phosphoprotein which helps regulate DNA synthesis.

Associations 5% occur with a pineal or other tumour (=trilateral retinoblastoma). Secondary malignancies such as osteosarcoma and rhabdomyosarcoma are more frequent, and they are the main causes of death of patients with hereditary retinoblastoma.[25]

Treatment There is a trend away from enucleation (eye removal) + radiotherapy towards focal procedures to preserve eye and sight, if possible.

Enucleation may be needed with large tumours, long-standing retinal detachments, and optic nerve invasion or extrascleral extension.

External beam radiotherapy has a role (may *cause* secondary non-ocular cancers in the radiation field, esp. if carrying the RB-1 germline mutation).

Ophthalmic plaque brachytherapy has a more focal and shielded radiation field, and may carry less risk, but is limited to small-medium retinoblastomas in accessible locations.

Cryotherapy and transpupillary thermotherapy (TTT) can give control of selected small tumours. 'Chemoreduction' is achieved by IV or subconjunctival chemotherapy to allow TTT, cryotherapy, and radiotherapy.

Haemopoietic stem cell rescue This may ↑survival if distant metastasis—but CNS involvement means poorer prognosis.[26]

Screening parents and siblings This is needed for accurate genetic counselling and to allow presymptomatic treatment. ***Germ-line mosaicism*** must be considered as a genetic transmission pattern. If a parent is germline mosaic, the possibility of bearing more babies with retinoblastoma is higher than conventionally believed.[27]

Eye movements and squint

To maintain single vision, fine co-ordination of eye movement of both eyes is necessary. Abnormality of the co-ordinated movement is called squint. *Other names for squint:* strabismus; tropia. Exotropia is divergent (one eye turned out) squint: esotropia is (one eye turned in) convergent squint. Prominent epicanthic folds (diagram) may produce pseudosquint.

Non-paralytic squints These usually start in childhood. The range of eye movements is full. Squints may be constant or not. All squints need ophthalmological assessment as vision may be damaged if not treated.

Diagnosis: Difficult, eg in uncooperative children. Screening tests:

1 Corneal reflection: reflection from a bright light falls centrally and symmetrically on each cornea if no squint, asymmetrically if squint present.

2 Cover test: movement of the uncovered eye to take up fixation as the other eye is covered demonstrates manifest squint; latent squint is revealed by movement of the covered eye as the cover is removed.

Convergent squint (esotropia) This is the commonest type in children. There may be no cause, or it may be due to hypermetropia (p 426). In ***strabismic amblyopia*** the brain suppresses the deviated image, and the visual pathway does not develop normally—and the eye may be blind in later life.[1]

Divergent squint (exotropia) These tend to occur in older children and are often intermittent. Amblyopia is less commonly a problem.

Management Remember 3 *'O's*: ***Optical; Orthoptic; Operation***. Treatment starts as soon as the squint is noticed. ***Optical:*** Assess the refractive state after cyclopentolate 1% drops; the cycloplegia allows objective determination of the refractive state; the mydriasis allows a good view into the eye to exclude abnormality, eg cataract, macular scarring, retinoblastoma, optic atrophy. Spectacles are then provided to correct refractive errors.

Orthoptic: Patching the good eye encourages use of the one which squints.

Operations (*eg resection and recession of rectus muscles*): These help alignment and give good cosmetic results. NB: use of botulinum toxin has helped some patients with esotropia (see p 460).[28, 29]

Paralytic squint Diplopia is most on looking in the direction of pull of the paralysed muscle. When the separation between the two images is greatest the image from the paralysed eye is furthest from the midline and faintest.

Third nerve palsy (oculomotor) Ptosis, proptosis (as recti tone ↓), fixed pupil dilatation, with the eye looking down and out. Causes: p 424.

Fourth nerve palsy (trochlear) There is diplopia and the patient may hold his head tilted (ocular torticollis). The eye looks upward, in adduction and cannot look down and in (superior oblique paralysed).[2] Causes: trauma 30%, diabetes 30%, tumour, idiopathic.

Sixth nerve palsy (abducens) There is diplopia in the horizontal plane. The eye is medially deviated and cannot move *laterally* from midline, as the *lateral* rectus is paralysed. ***Causes:*** Tumour causing ↑intracranial pressure (compresses the nerve on the edge of the petrous temporal bone), trauma to base of skull, vascular, or multiple sclerosis.[30] ***R:*** Botulinum toxin can eliminate need for strabismus surgery in selected VI palsies.[31] [n=19]

1 With ***anisometropic amblyopia***, each eye has different refractive powers. The brain favours the eye with the clearer image, ignoring the other. Other causes of amblyopia: congenital cataract; uncorrected myopia or hypermetropia in one or both eyes; severe ptosis. The term ***amblyopia ex anopsia*** means ↓acuity from failure of development of the visual pathways due to lack of a sharp image on the macula at a critical stage of development.

2 Superior oblique and inferior oblique aid eye abduction (ie lateral rotation), while the superior and the inferior rectus adduct the eye. The superior oblique also lowers the gaze while the inferior oblique elevates it—S Ali *BMJ* 2002 i 962.

Medial rectus: 'Look at your nose' (adduction).
Lateral rectus: 'Look away from your nose'.[32]
Superior rectus (fig 1) primarily moves the gaze upward and secondarily rotates the *top* of the eye towards the nose (intorsion). Note its eccentric attachment.
Inferior rectus primarily moves the gaze down (Secondary action: rotation of the *bottom* of the globe towards the nose.)
Superior oblique primarily rotates the top of the globe towards the nose; it secondarily depresses gaze.[1] Note its eccentric attachment.
Inferior oblique primarily rotates the bottom of the globe towards the nose[1] and secondarily moves gaze upward. Tertiary action of each obique: abduction.[33]

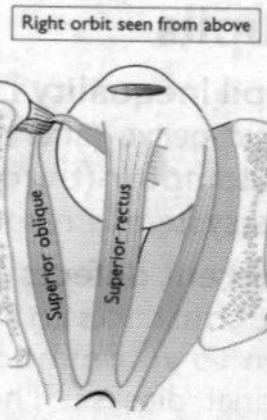

Fig 1. Superior oblique

Best results are achieved in childhood strabismus by:

- Early detection of amblyopia. If >7yrs old, amblyopia may be permanent.[34]
- Conscientious and disciplined amblyopia treatment.
- Optimal glasses (especially full plus in esotropia).
- Having the child see as straight as possible as soon as possible after amblyopia treatment is optimized.[35]

Gobin's principles: Evaluate *all* aspects of the strabismus (horizontal, vertical and oblique); search for the obstacles to ocular movements which cause alteration of binocular vision; remove them.[36] [n=449]

The cover test[2]

PSEUDOSQUINT Wide epicanthic folds give the appearance of squint in the eye looking towards the nose. That the eyes are correctly aligned is confirmed by the corneal reflection.

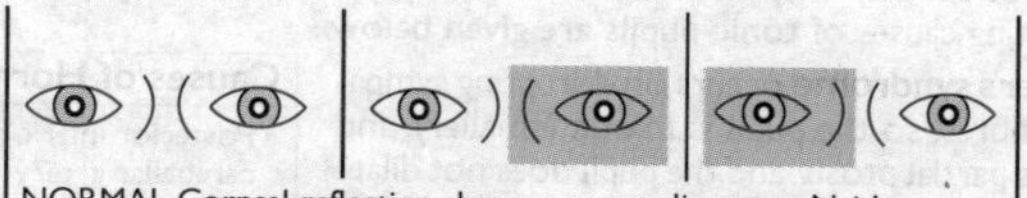

NORMAL Corneal reflection shows correct alignment. Neither eye moves as they are alternately covered.

LEFT CONVERGENT SQUINT Corneal reflection shows malalignment. As the right eye is covered the left moves out to take up fixation.

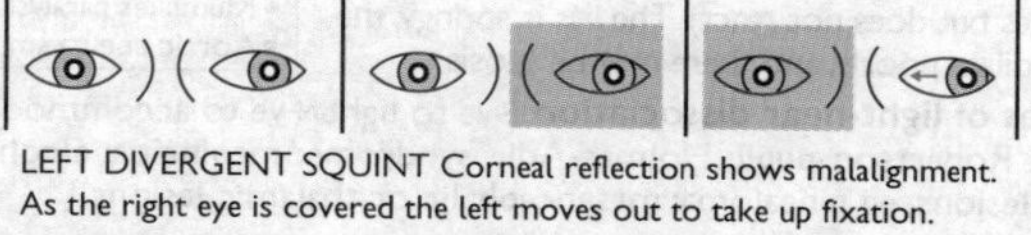

LEFT DIVERGENT SQUINT Corneal reflection shows malalignment. As the right eye is covered the left moves out to take up fixation.

1 The primary muscle moving an eye in a given direction is the *agonist*. A muscle in that eye that moves it in the same direction as the agonist is a *synergist*—eg in abducting the left eye, the left lateral rectus is the agonist, the left superior and inferior obliques are synergists; the left medial, superior, and inferior recti are *antagonists*. Superior & inferior obliques are the primary muscles of torsion.
2 **NB:** The cover test relies on the ability to fixate. If there is *eccentric fixation* (ie foveal vision is so poor that it is not used for fixation), the deviating eye will not move to take up fixation. Corneal reflection shows that malalignment is present.

Pupils

Pupil inequality Light detection by the retina is passed to the brain via the optic nerve (afferent pathway) and pupil constriction is mediated by the oculomotor (third) cranial nerve (efferent pathway). The sympathetic nervous system is responsible for pupil dilatation via the ciliary nerves.

Afferent defects (absent direct response) The pupil won't respond to light, but constricts to a beam in the other eye (consensual response). Constriction to accommodation still occurs. Causes: optic neuritis, optic atrophy, retinal disease. The pupils are the same size (consensual response unaffected). ***Marcus Gunn swinging flashlight test:*** On beaming light to the normal eye, both pupils constrict (direct & consensual reaction); if swinging the light to the affected eye, the pupil *dilates* it is a Marcus Gunn pupil.

Efferent defects The third nerve also mediates eye movement and eyelid retraction. With complete third nerve palsy there is complete ptosis, a fixed dilated pupil, and the eye looks down (superior oblique still acts) and out (lateral rectus acting). Causes: cavernous sinus lesions, superior orbital fissure syndrome, diabetes mellitus, posterior communicating artery aneurysm. The pupil is often spared in vascular causes, eg with diabetes and hypertension. Pupillary fibres run in the periphery, and are the first to be involved in compressive lesions by tumour or aneurysm.

Other causes of a fixed dilated pupil Mydriatics, trauma (blow to iris), acute glaucoma, coning ie uncal herniation (*OHCM* p 816).

Holmes–Adie pupil Initially monolateral, then bilateral, pupil dilatation with delayed responses to the near vision effort, with delayed redilation. ***Typical patient:*** A young woman, with sudden blurring of near vision, and one dilated pupil, with slow responses to accommodation, and, especially, to light (looks unreactive, unless an intense light is used for >15min), ie a ***tonic pupil***. *Slit lamp exam:* Iris shows spontaneous wormy movements (***iris streaming***). ***Holmes–Adie syndrome:*** Tonic pupil, absent knee/ankle jerks and BP↓.[1]

The pupil's size may fluctuate, and get smaller than its brother (if both pupils are involved they may be confused with Argyll Robertson pupils). Other interesting causes of tonic pupils are given below.[2]

Horner's syndrome occurs on disrupting sympathetic fibres, so the pupil is miotic (smaller), and there is partial ptosis, and the pupil does not dilate in the dark. Unilateral facial anhydrosis (sweating↓) may indicate a lesion proximal to the carotid plexus—if distal, the sudomotor (*sudor* = sweat) fibres will have separated, so sweating is intact.

Argyll Robertson pupil occurs in neurosyphilis and diabetes. There is bilateral miosis, pupil irregularity, and no response to light, but there is response to accommodation (the prostitute's pupil accommodates but does not react). The iris is spongy, the pupils dilate poorly, and there may be ptosis.

Causes of Horner's

- Posterior inferior cerebellar artery or basilar artery occlusion
- Multiple sclerosis
- Cavernous sinus thrombosis
- Pancoast's tumour
- Hypothalamic lesions
- Cervical adenopathy
- Mediastinal masses
- Pontine syringomyelia
- Klumpke's paralysis, p 766
- Aortic aneurysm

Causes of light-near dissociation (-ve to light +ve to accommodation): Argyll Robertson pupil; Holmes-Adie syndrome; meningitis; alcoholism; tectal lesions, eg pinealoma; mesencephalic or thalamic lesions.[3]

1 Selective impairment of monosynaptic connections of 1a afferents ± ↑presynaptic inhibition on afferent 1a input to ventral horn motor neurones; ∴ absent deep reflexes persist despite cord pathology. There is autonomic dysfunction too with disturbed vasomotor and sweating functions—and cough.
2 Migraine; syphilis; diabetes; chickenpox; arteritis; sarcoid; myasthenia; hamartoma; anti-Hu autoantibodies to neural nuclei; Sjögren's; Meige's synd.; botulism; dermatomyositis; amyloid; paraneoplasia.
3 The path from the optic tract to the Edinger–Westphal nucleus is disrupted but deeper cortical connections remain intact, so accommodation is spared.

Refraction

Refractive errors arise from mismatching of the size and shape of the eye. Correct refraction depends upon the distance between the cornea and the retina, and the curvatures of the lens and cornea.

Myopia (short-sightedness) The eyeball is too long. In any eye, the nearer an object comes to the eye the further back the image falls. With a myopic eye a close object will focus on the retina (short-sightedness). In order to form the image from more distant objects (which focus too far forward), concave spectacle (or contact) lenses are needed. *Causes:* Genetic (chromosome map: 2q); and extensive close work in the early decades (not just at school) may lead to changes in the synthesis of DNA and the concentration of matrix metalloproteinase, resulting in myopia. Note: when traditional people are exposed to western education, rates of myopia rise from 0% to Western levels (ie 30%). Animal models suggest altering the balance of retinal and scleral growth—eg acetylcholine, dopamine, and glucagon.

In normal growth, changes in axial and lens curvature compensate for the eye getting longer as it grows, but in myopic children, such compensations may not be perfect, and so myopia worsens with age. Most children become myopic around the age of 8yrs (a few are born myopic). Myopia will then usually continue to worsen until the late teens, when changes stop (below 5 dioptres in most people). So it is important, therefore, for children with myopia to have their eyes regularly checked, as spectacle changes are to be expected (perhaps every 6 months). Avoid over-correction as this can make myopia worse. In later life, increasing myopia may indicate developing cataract.

Pathological myopia: Rarely (≤2%) myopia progresses above 6 dioptres (sometimes up to ~20 dioptres). This has serious consequences later in life because secondary degeneration of the choroid and retina can lead to retinal detachment, chorioretinal atrophy and macular bleeding.

Management: Spectacles, contact lenses or laser (p 454). Bifocals prevent near-blur and accommodative lag (which promotes myopia). Don't insist on spectacles when reading; ensure good lighting, and advocate a balance of physical activity and reading.

Astigmatism This is present if cornea or lens do not have the same degree of curvature in horizontal and vertical planes, so that the image of objects is distorted either longitudinally or vertically. Correcting lenses compensate accordingly. It can occur alone, or with myopia or hypermetropia.

Hypermetropia (long-sightedness) This is due to too short an eye. Distant objects (when the eye is at rest (ie accommodation not active)) are focused behind the retina. The ciliary muscles contract and the lens gets more convex to focus the object on the retina. This can produce tiredness of gaze, and sometimes convergent squint in children. Hypermetropia is corrected by convex lenses to bring the image forward to focus on the retina.

Presbyopia The eye is provided by nature with a convex lens for focusing near objects (when the lens is at rest, the focus is on distant objects; ciliary muscle action reduces tension in the lens, allowing it to get more convex—increase focusing). With age, the natural lens of the eye becomes stiffer and less easy to deform, so that focusing on close objects becomes less possible. Hence the development of long-sightedness with age (presbyopia) and the need for glasses for reading. These changes usually start in the lens at about 40 years, and are complete by 60 years.

Refraction

Refractive errors arise from disorders of the size and shape of the eye. Correct refraction depends upon the distance between the cornea and the retina, and the curvatures of the lens and cornea.

Myopia (short sightedness) The eyeball is too long. In any eye, the nearer an object comes to the eye, the further back the image falls. With myopic eyes a close object will focus on the retina (short sightedness). In order to focus the image from more distant objects (which focus too far forward), concave spectacle (or contact) lenses are needed. ***Causes:*** Genetic (chromosome 18P & 12Q)[37]—also excessive close work in the early decades (not just at school) may lead to changes in the synthesis of mRNA and the concentration of matrix metalloproteinase, resulting in myopia. NB: when aboriginal people are exposed to western education, rates of myopia rise from ~0 to Western levels (eg 50%). Animal models are characterizing the triggers of retinal and scleral growth—eg acetylcholine, dopamine, and glucagon.[38]

In normal growth, changes in eyeball and lens curvature compensate for the eye getting longer as it grows, but in myopic children, such compensations may not be occurring, so myopia worsens with age. Most do not become myopic until the age of ~6yrs (a few are born myopic). Myopia will then usually continue to worsen until the late teens, when changes stop below 6 dioptres in most people. So is important, therefore, for children with myopia to have their eyes regularly checked, as spectacle changes are to be expected, perhaps every 6 months. Avoid over-correction as this can make myopia worse.[39]

In later life, increasing myopia may indicate developing cataracts.

Pathological myopia: Rarely (≤3%), myopia progresses above 6 dioptres (sometimes up to >20 dioptres). This has serious consequences later in life because secondary degeneration of the vitreous and retina can lead to retinal detachment, choroidoretinal atrophy and macular bleeding.

Management: Spectacles, contact lenses, or LASIK, p 464. Bifocals prevent retinal blur if accommodative lag (blur promotes myopia). Don't just think: 'spectacles': when reading, ensure good lighting, and advocate a balance of physical activity and reading.[40][41]

Astigmatism This is present if cornea or lens don't have the same degree of curvature in horizontal and vertical planes, so that the image of objects is distorted either longitudinally or vertically. Correcting lenses compensate accordingly. It can occur alone, or with myopia or hypermetropia.

Hypermetropia (long sightedness) This is due to too short an eye. Distant objects, when the eye is at rest (not accommodating) are focused behind the retina. The ciliary muscles contract, and the lens gets more convex to focus the object on the retina. This can produce tiredness of gaze, and sometimes, convergent squint in children. Hypermetropia is corrected by convex lenses to bring the image forward to focus on the retina.

Presbyopia The eye is provided by nature with a convex lens for focusing near objects (when the lens is in its resting state, focus is on distant objects; ciliary muscle action reduces tension in the lens, allowing it to get more convex—for close focusing). With age, the natural lens of the eye becomes stiffer and less easy to deform, so that focusing for close objects becomes less possible—hence the development of long sightedness with age (presbyopia) and the need for glasses for reading. These changes usually start in the lens at about 40 years and are complete by 60 years.

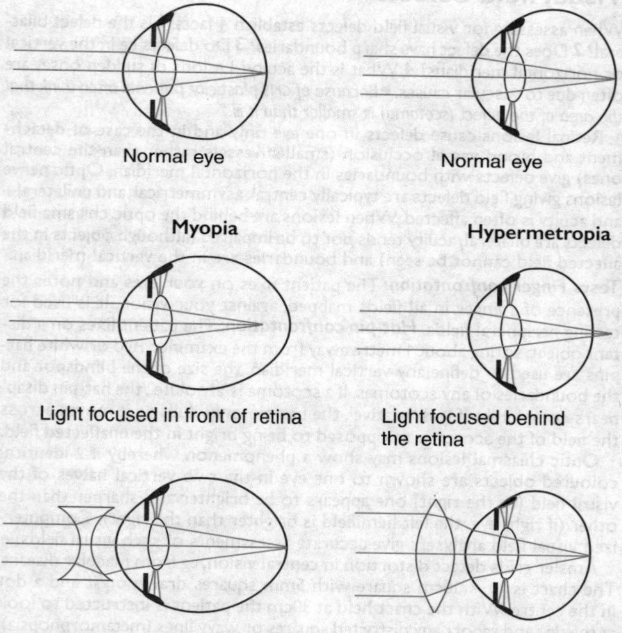
Normal eye
Normal eye
Myopia
Hypermetropia
Light focused in front of retina
Light focused behind the retina
Corrected with concave lens
Corrected with convex lens

Visual field defects

When assessing for visual field defects establish 4 facts: **1** Is the defect bilateral? **2** Does the defect have sharp boundaries? **3** Do defects lie in the vertical or horizontal meridians? **4** What is the acuity? Lesions of sudden onset are often due to vascular causes. ►*Because of CNS plasticity, patients often think that the area of the defect (scotoma) is smaller than it is.* 42

Retinal lesions cause defects in one eye only and in the case of detachment and blood vessel occlusion (smaller vessels rather than the central ones) give defects with boundaries in the horizontal meridian. Optic nerve lesions giving field defects are typically central, asymmetrical, and unilateral—and acuity is often affected. When lesions are behind the optic chiasma field defects are bilateral, acuity tends not to be impaired (although objects in the affected field cannot be seen) and boundaries are in the vertical meridian.

Tests ***Finger confrontation:*** The patient fixes on your eyes and notes the presence of a finger in all fields mapped, against your vision. It is used for testing peripheral fields. ***Hat-pin confrontation:*** The patient fixes on a distant object, sitting about 1 metre away from the examiner. Red or white hat-pins are used to define any vertical meridian, the size of the blindspot and the boundaries of any scotomas. If a scotoma is 'absolute', the hat-pin disappears completely. If it is 'relative', the hat-pin only dulls as it moves across the field of the scotoma, as opposed to being bright in the unaffected field.

Optic chiasmal lesions may show a phenomenon whereby if 2 identical coloured objects are shown to one eye in the two vertical halves of the visual field (eg the right) one appears to be brighter and sharper than the other (if right eye, the left hemifield is brighter than the right). Computerized visual field analysers give accurate assessments of such visual fields.

Amsler grids detect distortion in central vision, eg from macular disease. The chart is 10 × 10cm square with 5mm squares drawn on it and a dot in the centre. With the chart held at 30cm the patient is instructed to look at the dot and report any distorted squares or wavy lines (metamorphopsia).

Diagnosing the lesion's site Superior parts of the visual field fall inferiorly on the retina, temporal fields on the nasal retina and vice versa. Fibres from the nasal retina of both eyes cross in the optic chiasma to join uncrossed temporal retinal fibres. A pituitary tumour may disrupt the chiasma, affecting fibres crossing from nasal retinas, so causing bitemporal field defects. If it grows more to one side than the other, it can superimpose a central optic nerve defect as well. As fibres cross they maintain position (superior fibres stay superior). From the optic chiasma fibres pass in the optic tract to the lateral geniculate body, then as the optic radiation to the visual cortex.

A contralateral upper homonymous quadrantanopia may be caused by temporal lobe tumours. Posterior visual cortex lesions cause non-peripheral homonymous hemianopic scotomas (anterior visual cortex deals with peripheral vision)—with macular sparing, if the cause is posterior cerebral artery ischaemia (central areas have overlap flow via the middle cerebral artery, which is why acuity may be preserved). MRI is the best aid to diagnosis.

Causes of visual cortex field defects: • Ischaemia (TIA, migraine, stroke) • Glioma • Meningioma • Abscess • AV malformation • Drugs, eg ciclosporin. 43

NB: cortical visual defects may be fundamentally capricious—in that when an object is presented to the affected field of view, the patient announces that he cannot see it—yet 'guesses' correctly that it is there (non-cortical visual pathways): there are some things we know we can see; other things we see without knowing (blindsight[1]) and others that we know without seeing (for example that a table has 4 legs when we can only see 3 at any one time).

1 Liddell B 2005 *Neuroimage* **24** 235. Blindsight lesion patients respond to visual fear signals independently from conscious experience—ie these signals reach the amygdala bypassing the visual cortex.

Scotomata

Arcuate scotoma—
moderate glaucoma

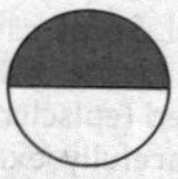

Unilateral defect
found with:
arterial occlusion
branch retinal vein
thrombosis
inferior retinal
detachment

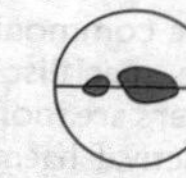

Central scotoma
macular
degeneration or
macular oedema

The visual pathways

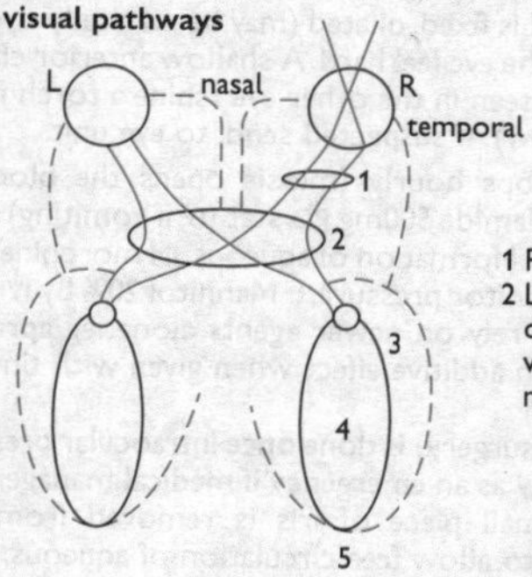

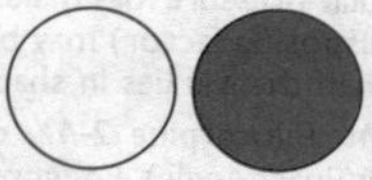

1 R optic nerve lesion
2 Lesion of chiasm—complicated defects depending upon which of the fibres are most affected

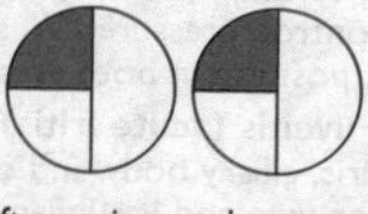

3 Left superior quadrantanopia due to R temporal lobe lesion

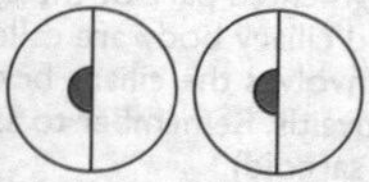

5 L homonymous scotoma due to lesion at tip of R occipital lobe

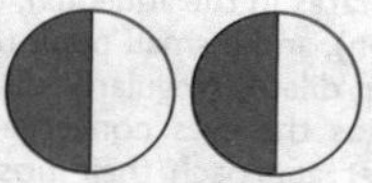

4 Homonymous hemianopia from lesions affecting all R optic radiation or visual cortex

Confrontation depends on mutual fixation, and it is necessary to concentrate hard to work out what is going on, but, for one second, allow yourself to reflect on what your patient will be thinking and feeling, most eloquently expressed by John Donne on accomplishing this manoeuvre:

I fix mine eye on thine, and there
Pity my picture burning in thine eye…

Towards the end of your professional life you will have engaged in mutual fixation many, many times, and as you continue to do so, ask yourself if these images of suffering are falling on your retina like so many layers of snow on a barren land, or whether, just sometimes, you might allow your eye to thaw and resolve itself into perhaps just one true tear.

The red eye

Red eyes are commonly also painful. Some causes are dangerous to vision and require specialist supervision (acute glaucoma, acute iritis, corneal ulcers); others are more easily treated (episcleritis, conjunctivitis, spontaneous conjunctival haemorrhage). Carefully examine all red eyes to assess acuity, cornea (use fluorescein drops p 432), and pupillary reflexes.

Acute closed angle glaucoma This is a disease of middle years or later life. The acute uniocular attack is commonly preceded by blurred vision or haloes around lights—particularly at night-time. It is caused by blockage of drainage of aqueous from the anterior chamber via the canal of Schlemm. Dilatation of pupils at night exacerbates drainage block. Intraocular pressure then rises from the normal 15–20mmHg to 60 or 70mmHg.

Pain may be severe with nausea/vomiting; vision↓; corneal oedema (haze); redness (circumcorneal); the pupil is fixed, dilated (may be vertically ovoid). ↑Intraocular pressure may make the eye feel hard. A shallow anterior chamber (predisposing factor) may be seen in the other eye (shine a torch from the side, half the iris lies in shadow). If suspected send, to eye unit.

Treatment: Pilocarpine 2–4% drops hourly (miosis opens the blocked, 'closed' drainage angle) + acetazolamide 500mg PO stat (IV if vomiting) then 250mg/8h PO or IV. Acetazolamide ↓formation of aqueous. IM morphine may be needed for pain. Admit, and monitor pressure. ▸▸Mannitol 20% by IVI may be needed (up to 500mL). Don't rely on newer agents alone, eg apraclonidine drops but they may have an additive effect when given with timolol and pilocarpine.[44 45]

Peripheral iridectomy (laser or surgery) is done once intraocular pressure has been medically reduced (rarely as an emergency if medical management fails to control pressure). A small piece of iris is removed from the 12 o'clock position in both eyes to allow free circulation of aqueous.

Anterior uveitis (acute iritis) The uvea is the pigmented part of the eye including iris, ciliary body, and choroid. The iris and ciliary body are called the anterior uvea and iris inflammation invariably involves the ciliary body too, so inflammation is best referred to as anterior uveitis. Remember to ask about systemic diseases (eg ankylosing spondylitis, sarcoid).[1]

Presentation is with pain of acute onset, photophobia, blurred vision (due to precipitates in the aqueous), lacrimation, circumcorneal redness (ciliary congestion), and a small pupil (initially from iris spasm; later it may be irregular or dilate irregularly due to adhesions). ***Talbot's test*** is +ve: pain increases as the eyes converge (and pupils constrict) as patients watch their finger approach their nose.[46] A slit lamp reveals white precipitates on the back of the cornea and cells in the anterior chamber. Sometimes sterile anterior chamber pus (hypopyon) may be seen.

It tends to afflict the young or middle-aged. There are many causes. Associations: joint problems (eg ankylosing spondylitis, Still's). It may relapse.

Treatment: Refer to an ophthalmologist for treatment and follow-up. The aim is to prevent damage from prolonged inflammation (this can cause disruption of flow of aqueous inside the eye, with glaucoma occurring ± adhesions forming between iris and lens). Treatment is with steroids, eg prednisolone 0.5% drops every 2h, to reduce inflammation (hence pain, redness, and exudate). To prevent adhesions between lens and iris (synechiae) keep pupil dilated with cyclopentolate 0.5% 1–2 drops/6h, unless the iritis is very mild. Use the slit lamp to monitor inflammation.

1 This is one of the few occasions when the Sherlock Holmes's among us can properly ask *Have you been handling tarantulas recently?* (their hairs cause uveitis).

Identifying dangerous red eyes

Ask yourself the following questions:

1 Is acuity affected? A quick but sensitive test is the ability to read newsprint with refractive errors corrected with glasses or a pin-hole. Reduced acuity suggests dangerous pathology.

2 Is the globe painful? Pain is potentially sinister, foreign body sensation may be so, irritation rarely is.

3 Does the pupil respond to light? Absent or sluggish response is sinister.

4 Is the cornea intact? Use fluorescein eyedrops, p 432. Corneal damage may be due to trauma or ulcers.

Enquire also about trauma and discharge, general health and drugs, and remember to check for raised pressure.

►If in doubt, obtain a specialist opinion today.

	Conjunctivitis	*Anterior uveitis*	*Acute glaucoma*
Pain	±	++	++ to +++
Photophobia	+	++	–
Acuity	Normal	↓	↓
Cornea	Normal	normal	steamy or hazy
Pupil	Normal	Small	large
Intraocular pressure	Normal	normal	↑

★★★CRITICAL BEDSIDE SKILL★★★

More red eyes—cornea and conjunctiva

Corneal problems *Keratitis* is corneal inflammation (identified by a white spot on the cornea—indicating a collection of white cells in corneal tissue).

Corneal ulceration is an epithelial breach; it may occur without keratitis, eg in trauma, when prophylactic antibiotic ointment (eg chloramphenicol) may be used. Ulceration with keratitis is called ulcerative keratitis and must be treated as an emergency—see below. There is pain, photophobia, and sometimes blurred vision. Non-infective corneal ulceration may result from a scratch from a contact lens, trauma, or previous corneal disease.

Ulcerative keratitis: Use fluorescein drops & a (blue) bright light (shone tangentially across the globe) to aid diagnosis. Corneal lesions stain green (drops are orange and become more yellow on contact with the eye). Ulcers may be bacterial (beware pseudomonas: may progress rapidly), herpetic (simplex; zoster), fungal (candida; aspergillus), protozoal (acanthamoeba) or from vasculitis, eg in rheumatoid arthritis. Except for a simple abrasion, which can be treated with chloramphenical ointment ± an eye pad, get expert help. Don't try treating ulcerative keratitis on your own: scarring and visual loss may occur. ►Refer the same day, as treatment depends upon the cause; delay may cause acuity↓. Anyone with corneal ulceration or stromal suppuration must have an urgent diagnostic smear/Gram stain and scrape by a specialist. Liaise with microbiologist. ℞: p 433. In early stages of ophthalmic shingles, use oral aciclovir (p 420). *H simplex* dendritic ulcers: p 416. Cycloplegics (p 456) may prevent iris adhesions.

Episcleritis Inflammation below the conjunctiva in the episclera is often seen with an inflammatory nodule. The sclera may look blue below engorged vessels, which can be moved over the area, unlike in scleritis, where the engorged vessels are deeper. The eye aches dully and is tender, especially over the inflamed area. Acuity is usually OK. Usually no cause is found, but it may complicate PAN/SLE and rheumatic fever. It responds to steroid drops. 47 48

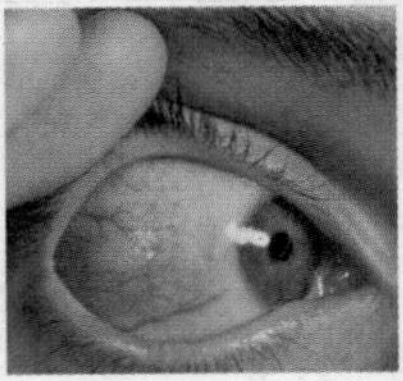

Fig 1. Episcleritis

Scleritis (Vasculitis of the sclera[1]) Rarely, the sclera itself is inflamed. There is more generalized inflammation with oedema of the conjunctiva and thinning of the sclera (if severe, globe perforation is a risk). Association: connective tissue disorders. Refer to a specialist. Most will need oral corticosteroids or immunosuppressives to control the disease. 49

Conjunctivitis ►Conjunctivitis is usually bilateral, if unilateral consider other diagnoses (p 431), eg acute glaucoma. The conjunctiva is red and inflamed, and the hyperaemic vessels may be moved over the sclera, by gentle pressure on the globe. Acuity, pupillary responses, and corneal lustre are unaffected. Eyes itch, burn, and lacrimate. There may be photophobia. Purulent discharge may stick the eyelids together. The cause may be viral (highly infectious adenovirus)—small lymphoid aggregates appear as follicles on conjunctiva, bacterial (purulent discharge more prominent), or allergic. The affliction is usually self-limiting (although allergic responses may be more prolonged). In prolonged conjunctivitis, especially in young adults or those with venereal disease consider chlamydial infection—see ophthalmia neonatorum, p 36. ℞: Usually with eg chloramphenicol ointment at night. For chlamydia, get expert help.

For allergic conditions, try antihistamine drops, eg emedastine; refer if not settling in a few days. Sodium cromoglycate and steroid drops (after advice from an ophthalmologist) may help. 50

Subconjunctival haemorrhage This self-limiting but alarming-looking collection of blood behind the conjunctiva from a small bleed. Check BP.

1 Ocular vasculitis: a multidisciplinary approach. *Curr Opin Rheumatol* 2005 **17** 25.

Management of corneal ulcers

Refer to a specialist. What appears below is more so that one can have an intelligent conversation with a specialist, and should not be regarded as a blueprint for therapy by the inexperienced.

Smears and cultures Liaise with microbiologist. Specialists may take:

1 Smear for Gram stain—if chronic ulcer Giemsa, PAS (periodic acid Schiff) for fungi, ZN (Ziehl-Neelsen) or auromine for TB.
2 Conjunctival swab to blood agar for tear film contaminants.
3 Corneal scrape (by experienced person) from multiple areas of ulcer edge with needle for direct innoculation.
4 Request the cultures detailed below.

Acute history: Presume bacterial, so culture with blood agar (grows most organisms), chocolate agar (for *Haemophilus* and *Neisseria*), nutrient broth (anaerobes), cooked meat broth (aerobes/anaerobes). ***Chronic history:*** Consider rarities; culture as above + BHI (brain heart infusion broth for fastidious organisms and fungi), Sabouraud's plate for fungi, anaerobic blood agar (peptococcus, proprionobacteria) + thioglycollate (anaerobes).

Unusual features: Use also viral transport medium, Lowenstein-Jensen agar slope for TB, *E. coli* seeded agar for acanthamoeba.

Management: Do smears & culture. Get help. Until cultures are known, alternate chloramphenicol drops (for Gram +ve organisms) with ciprofloxacin drops (for Gram -ve organisms) or cefuroxime 0.3% drops with gentamicin drops. Adapt these in the light of culture results.[1] Hospital admission may be needed, especially if there is diabetes or immunosuppression, or you doubt that the patient will manage his or her drops. Ciprofloxacin may be given up to 2 drops every 15min for 6h; then every 30mins for the next 18h; reducing to 2 drops hourly for day 2; then 2 drops 4-hourly for ≤12 days (maximum duration of therapy: 21 days).

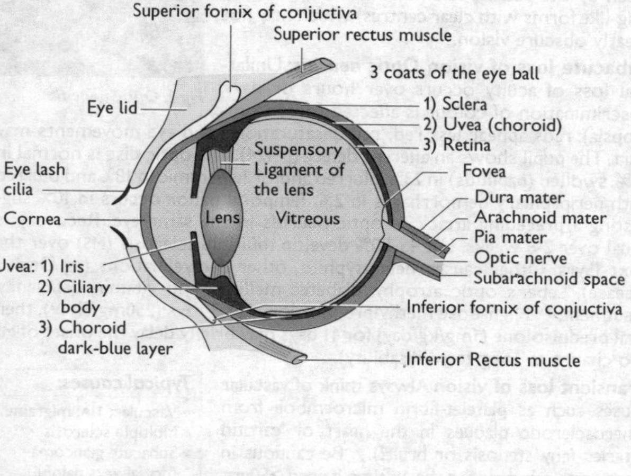

1 In one study, the chief Gram +ve organisms were coagulase negative staphs (19%) & corynebacteria (16%). The chief Gram -ve organisms were *Moraxella* (19%) and *Pseudomonas aeruginosa* (3%).

Sudden painless loss of vision

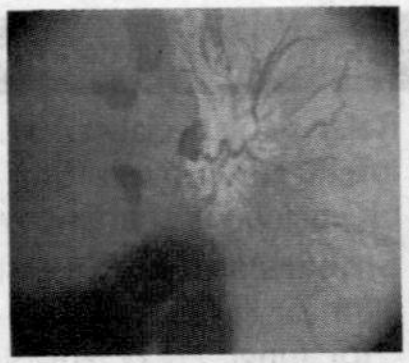

Fig 1. Vitreous haemorrhage (bottom left) from new vessels (top right).

▸▸Urgent help is needed in: retinal artery occlusion of <6h; any sudden visual loss of <6h if the cause cannot be established—or giant cell arteritis (GCA).

5 questions: •*H*eadache associated? (GCA, aged ≥50yrs; ESR↑); •*E*ye movements hurt? (optic neuritis); •*L*ights or flashes preceding visual loss (detached retina); •*L*ike a curtain descending? amaurosis fugax may precede permanent visual loss, eg from emboli or GCA). •*P*oorly controlled DM: fig 1 shows vitreous haemorrhage from new vessels.

Check: Acuity, pupil reaction, fundi. Then refer.

Ischaemic optic neuropathy The optic nerve is damaged if posterior ciliary arteries are blocked by inflammation or atheroma. *Fundoscopy:* pale, swollen optic disc. ***Giant cell arteritis:*** *The other eye is at risk* until steroids are given. *Symptoms:* malaise, jaw claudication (chewing pain) ± tender scalp/temporal arteries (±absent pulses). *Tests:* ESR >40; temporal artery biopsy may miss affected sections of artery. Transcranial Doppler: look for microemboli.[52] *Retinal changes:* ▸▸Start prednisolone 80mg/24h PO promptly (some advocate higher IV doses if visual failure is occurring). Tailing off steroids as ESR and symptoms settle may take >1yr. ***Arteriosclerotic ischaemic optic neuropathy:*** Associations: BP↑; lipids↑; DM. Treating these protects vision in the other eye. Histology: necrosis and apoptosis at the photoreceptor level.[53]

Vitreous haemorrhage See fig 1: this bleed from new vessels is a commoner cause than bleeding disorders, retinal detachment, or central retinal vein or branch vein occlusion. With a large enough bleed to obscure vision, there is no red reflex and the retina may not be seen. They undergo spontaneous absorption, and treatment is expectant for the haemorrhage itself, as well as being directed to the cause (eg photocoagulation of new vessels). If unresolved at 3 months, vitrectomy may be done to remove the blood in the vitreous. Small extravasations of blood produce vitreous floaters, (seen by the patient as small black dots or tiny ring-like forms with clear centres) which may not greatly obscure vision.

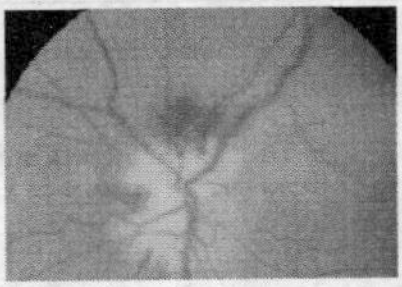

Fig 2. Optic neuritis

Subacute loss of vision ***Optic neuritis:*** Unilateral loss of acuity occurs over hours or days. Discrimination of colour is affected (dyschromatopsia): reds appear less red, 'red desaturation'—and eye movements may hurt. The pupil shows an afferent defect (p 424). The optic disc is normal in 64%, swollen (papillitis) in 23%, blurred and/or hyperemic in 18% and blurred with peripapillary hemorrhages in 2%. Temporal pallor occurs in 10% suggesting a preceding attack of optic neuritis in the same eye. Recovery is usual over 2–6 weeks, but 45–80% develop multiple sclerosis (MS) over the next 15yrs. Other causes: neurosyphilis, other demyelinations (eg Devic's disease), Leber's optic atrophy, diabetes mellitus, and vitamin deficiency. *Treatment:* High-dose methylprednisolone for 3 days (250mg/6h IV), then oral prednisolone (1mg/kg/day) for 11 days may briefly delay the onset of MS (no change to long-term disability).[54]

Transient loss of vision Always think of vascular causes such as platelet-fibrin microemboli from atherosclerotic plaques in the heart or carotid arteries (any stenosis or bruit?).[55] Be cautious in diagnosing migraine for the 1st time if aged >50yrs. Rainbow haloes around lights suggest glaucoma.

Typical causes:

- Vascular; TIA; migraine
- Multiple sclerosis
- Subacute glaucoma (not always painful)
- Papilloedema

Central retinal artery occlusion

There is dramatic visual loss within seconds of occlusion. In 90% acuity is finger counting or worse. An afferent pupil defect (p 424) appears within seconds and may precede retinal changes by 1h. The retina appears white, with a cherry red spot at the macula. Exclude temporal arteritis. Occlusion is often thromboembolic. Look for signs of atherosclerosis (bruits; BP↑), heart valve disease, diabetes, smoking, or lipids↑[56] ▸▸If seen within 1h of onset apply firm pressure on the globe, increasing until pain supervenes; then suddenly release. This may dislodge an embolus, and propel it down a branch. There is no *reliable* treatment; if occlusion lasts ≥1h, the optic nerve will atrophy, causing blindness.

If a single branch of the retinal artery is occluded, the retinal and visual changes relate only to the part of the retina supplied.

Retinal vein occlusions: central or branch vein?

Central retinal vein occlusion Incidence increases with age. It is commoner than arterial occlusion. Causes: chronic simple glaucoma, arteriosclerosis, BP↑, and polycythaemia. If the whole central retinal vein is thrombosed, there is sudden visual loss (eg acuity reduced to finger counting). The fundus is like a 'stormy sunset' (the angry-looking red clouds are haemorrhages, beside engorged veins). There is also hyperaemia.

Long-term outcome is variable, with possible improvement for 6 months to one year; peripheral vision tends to improve most, leaving macular vision impaired. The main problems are macular oedema and neovascular glaucoma secondary to iris neovascularization. ~⅓ of eyes show significant non-perfusion on fluorescein angiography, of which one-half would develop neovascular glaucoma (called '100 days glaucoma' as it develops about this time after the occlusion). There is no validated treatment for post-occlusion macular oedema.[57,58] Argon laser grid photocoagulation is used, but has yet to be fully validated.[59]

Branch retinal vein occlusion ***Signs:*** Unilateral visual loss and fundal appearances in the corresponding area. Retinal capillary non-perfusion can lead to retinal new vessel formation. Treatment of neovascularization (confirmed by fluorescein angiography) with laser photocoagulation, ↓risk of intraocular haemorrhage by 50%. Macular oedema persisting for months without improvement may receive grid pattern argon laser photocoagulation (± arterial crimping).[60] [n=72]

Diagnosis and differential diagnosis Doppler has a role in diagnosis.[61] Other causes of sudden loss of vision: • Retinal detachment (p 444) • Acute glaucoma (painful, p 430) • Migraine.

Stroke patients may complain of monocular blindness but visual field testing will usually reveal a homonymous hemianopia. Sudden bilateral visual loss is unusual (may be CMV infection in HIV patients, p 448).

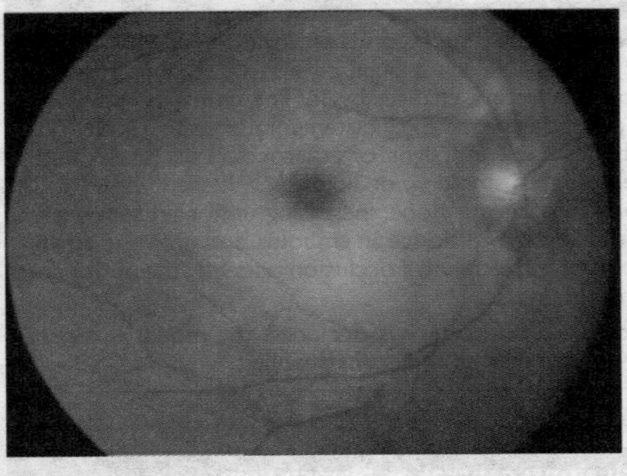

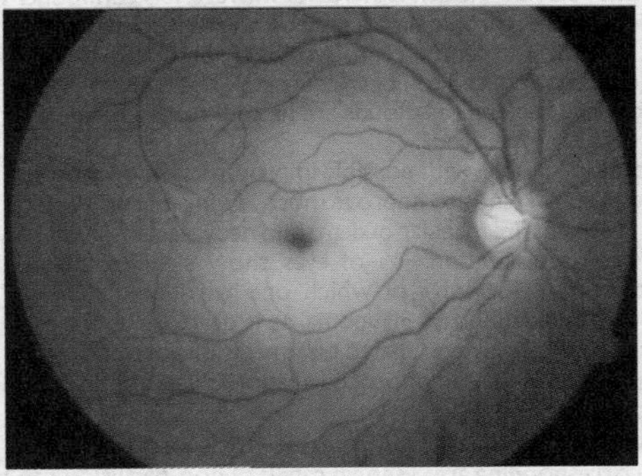

***Retinal artery occlusion (above) and central retinal vein occlusion (right).*[1]**
With arterial occlusion note retinal pallor and the cherry-red macula.
With central retinal vein occlusion note hyperaemia and haemorrhages.

1 Images kindly supplied by Dr Rajeev K Reddy, Dr Badrinath, and Dr Ravishankar—Sankara Nethralya, Chennai, India.

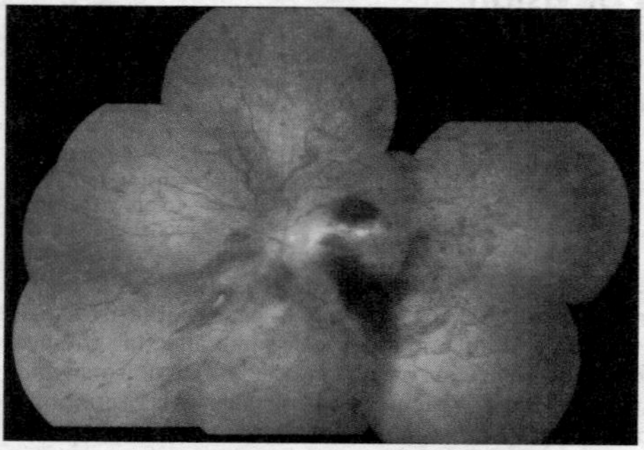

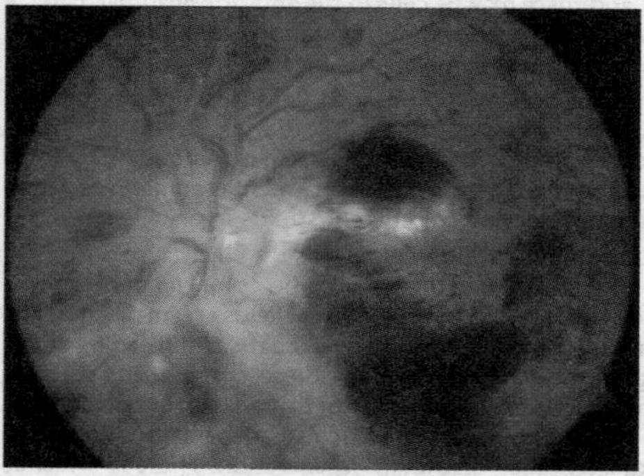

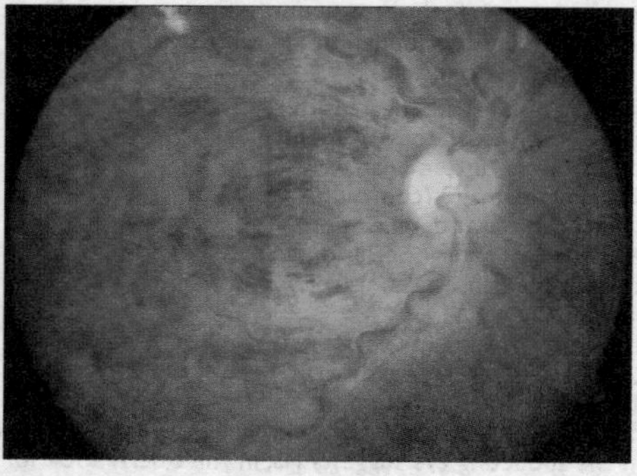

Gradual loss of vision

Be aware that for many, the chief question is likely to be 'will I go blind': be optimistic where possible. Patients may *not* tell you that they also fear they are going mad—having complex visual hallucinations, typically of faces. These occur without psychiatric signs and are often related to failing vision in the elderly: the Charles Bonnet syndrome.[62] The hallucinations arise as a complex cortical compensatory mechanism to evolving blindness.

Typical causes

- Cataract
- Macular degeneration
- Glaucoma (p 440)
- Diabetic retinopathy
- Hypertension (p 448)
- Optic atrophy (below)
- Slow retinal detachment
- Choroidal melanoma

Choroiditis (choroidoretinitis) The choroid is part of the uvea (iris, ciliary body and choroid), and inflammatory disorders affecting the uvea may also affect the choroid. The retina may be invaded by organisms which set up a granulomatous reaction (which can be mistaken for a retinoblastoma). Toxoplasmosis and toxocara are now more common than TB. Sarcoidosis is another cause. ***Tests:*** CXR; Mantoux; serology. In the acute phase, vision may be blurred, a grey-white raised patch is seen on the retina, vitreous opacities occur, and there may be cells in the anterior chamber. Later, a choroidoretinal scar (white patch with pigmentation around) will be seen, these being symptomless unless involving the macula. Treat the cause.

Choroid melanomas are the commonest malignant tumour of the eye. Appearing as mottled grey/black on the fundus, they cause retinal detachment immediately over the growth. Spread is haematogenous or by local orbit invasion. ***Treatment:*** Enucleation; local treatment is sometimes possible, eg sight- and globe-preserving stereotactic radiosurgery.[63]

Age-related macular degeneration (ARMD) is the chief cause of registrable blindness in the UK. It occurs in the elderly who complain of deterioration of central vision. There is loss of acuity; visual fields are unaffected. The disc appears normal but there is pigment, fine exudate, and bleeding at the macula. Drusen (fig 1 on p 439) may precede these changes, and as early treatment (BOX) may save vision, observation of drusen is an important (but rather difficult) art to acquire. Rarely, the macula is oedematous and lifted by a big mass of exudate, called disciform degeneration. There is evidence that use of statins (*OHCM* p 706) ***may*** cause a 10-fold ↓ in risk of ARMD.[64]

Tobacco-alcohol amblyopia This is the result of toxic effects of cyanide radicals when heavy smoking and alcohol consumption are combined. Signs: optic atrophy; loss of red/green discrimination (an early sign); scotomata. Vitamins *may* help (B_1, B_2, B_6, B_{12}, folic acid).[65,66,67,68]

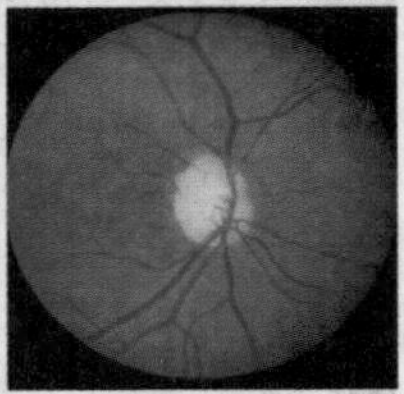

Fig 1. Optic atrophy

Optic atrophy The optic disc is pale (degrees of pallor don't correlate with visual loss). Optic atrophy may be secondary to ↑intraocular pressure (glaucoma), or retinal damage (choroiditis, retinitis pigmentosa, cerebromacular degeneration), or be due to ischaemia (retinal artery occlusion). ***Causative toxins:*** Tobacco methanol; lead; arsenic; quinine; carbon bisulfide.
Other causes: Leber's optic atrophy (p 648), multiple sclerosis (MS), syphilis, external pressure on the nerve (intraorbital or intracranial tumours, Paget's disease affecting the skull). Examine the cerebellum and eye movements: nystagmus in the abducting eye suggests MS; in the elderly look for temporal artery pulselessness (or a scar from a previous biopsy).

Use of services by older patients with failing vision

There is good evidence in the UK of under-use of services. Population-based cross-sectional studies in primary care show that prevalence of bilateral visual impairment (acuity <6/12) is ~30%. Most of these are not in touch with ophthalmic services. ►*Three-quarters of these have remediable problems.* In one study, 20% had acuity in one or both eyes of <6/60 ('blind'). Typical causes were found to be cataract (30%), macular degeneration (8%), and undiagnosed chronic glaucoma.[69] [n=1547]

Optic nerve drusen

Drusen signify optic nervehead axonal degeneration. Abnormal axonal metabolism leads to intracellular mitochondrial calcification. Some axons rupture and mitochondria are extruded into the extracellular space.[70] Calcium is deposited here, and drusen form. The optic disc edge is made irregular by the lumpy, yellowish mater. The optic cup is absent and the blood vessels show abnormal branching patterns.[71]

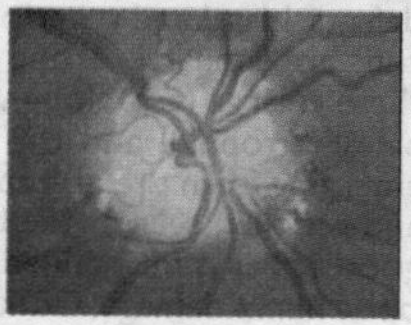

Fig 1. Optic drusen[72]

Managing age-related macular degeneration

Laser photocoagulation can halt progression, eg if choroidal neovascular lesions don't extend under the centre of the retina (photocoagulation destroys photoreceptors overlying abnormal vessels). Here ***photodynamic laser therapy*** (*OHCM* p 718) using the drug verteporfin may reduce vision loss.[73]

Screening: Once drusen are seen, screening needs to be one eye at a time, and very frequent, for signs of developing neovascularization: a simple method is to see if straight lines (on graph paper) appear straight? Sudden blank spots or distortions merit prompt referral.[74]

As getting neovascularization in one eye is associated with a 50% chance of developing it in the other, it is vital to save vision in either eye since one doesn't know which eye will end up being better.[75]

If these measures are inapplicable, most must rely on visual aids (eg to read). Zinc and β-carotene replacement are advocated by some. The best advice may be to take a diet rich in fruit and leafy green vegetables, with supplements if this diet causes problems. [MET 76]

Chronic simple (open angle) glaucoma

►Simple glaucoma is asymptomatic until visual fields are severely impaired; hence the need for screening—but most people found to have ↑intraocular pressures (IOP↑), eg on 10% of routine NHS sight tests if >40yrs old do not have glaucoma when their fundi and peripheral fields are charted (this can be a lengthy and tricky business). Once IOP↑ is found, life-long follow-up is needed (≥yearly, and much more often in the early stages)—which is why glaucoma accounts for 25% of ophthalmic workload, and why highstreet optometrists are being encouraged to take over at least part of this monitoring burden. Glaucoma accounts for 7% of new blind registrations.

Pathogenesis Intraocular pressure (IOP) ≥21mmHg causes optic disc cupping ± capillary closure, hence nerve damage, with sausage-shaped field defects (scotomata) near the blind spot, which may coalesce to form big defects. Nasal and superior fields are lost first (temporal last). Normal optic cups are similar in shape and occupy <50% of the optic disc. In glaucoma these enlarge (esp. along vertical axis). As damage progresses the optic disc pales (atrophy), and the cup widens and deepens, so the blood vessels emerging from the disc appear to have breaks as they disappear into the cup and are then seen at the base again (p 441). Since the central field is intact, good acuity is maintained, so presentation is often delayed until irreversible optic nerve damage. Control of IOP *does* stop visual field loss.[77] [N=738] Some get glaucoma with *normal* IOP (eg if retrobulbar blood flow↓).[78]

High-risk Screen if high-risk: >35yrs old, +ve family history (esp. siblings); Afro-Caribbean; myopia; diabetic or thyroid eye disease. NB: you may be asked about use of computer screens. This is only associated with myopia and heavy use—and employers may be wise of offer screening.[79] Technology is making primary prevention practical and cost-effective. *Tests must be combined*, as follows, in order of effectiveness: • Multiple stimulus static visual field screening • Optic disc cupping • IOPs↑.[80] [81]

Treatment Reduce IOP to <21mmHg. Surgery is used if drugs fail. ***Betaxolol*** 0.5% drops (or ***timolol*** 0.25–0.5%): use twice daily (/24h for Timoptol LA®) to ↓production of aqueous. They are β-blockers. (∴ caution in asthma or heart failure; systemic absorption occurs with no 1st-pass liver metabolism.) SE: dry eyes, corneal anaesthesia, allergy, ↓exercise tolerance.[82] [N=80] Betaxolol may cause stinging (less if Betoptic-S® is used—expensive).[83] ***Pilocarpine*** 0.5–4% drops ↓resistance to aqueous outflow. It causes miosis, acuity↓, and brow ache due to ciliary muscle spasm. Rarely, retinal detachment occurs. Presbyopes tolerate it better than the young and short sighted. Use 4 times daily. Because of these problems, and with improving surgical options, some would say that it is not even 2nd-line. ***Pilocarpine gel*** (Pilogel®) reduces blurred vision as it is applied at night. ***Dipivefrine*** 0.1% drops: this sympathomimetic probably acts to ↑ outflow via the trabecular meshwork and uveosclera. Caution if heart disease or BP↑; avoid in closed angle glaucoma. SE: sore, smarting, red eyes; blurred vision. Use once or twice daily. Carbonic anhydrase inhibitors, eg ***acetazolamide*** 250mg/24h–500mg/12h PO or topical ***dorzolamide*** (2%/8h) ↓production of aqueous. (Cosopt® = dorzolamide with timolol; use twice daily.)[RCT 84] [N=253] SE of acetazolamide: lassitude, dyspepsia, K^+↓, paraesthesia, so dorzolamide is preferred (but its SE are bitter taste, vision↓, epiphora). Avoid both if pregnant. ***Prostaglandin drops*** (*Latanoprost; travoprost*)[1] ↑uveoscleral outflow. *Dose:* once daily (evenings). Said to be better than timolol.[MET 85] ***Surgery:*** Flap-valve trabeculectomy is common; it probably acts as a drainage operation. Problems include early failure, and worsening of cataract (normal healing mitigates its effect, but this can be delayed by topical cytotoxics, eg fluorouracil). Effects of ***argon laser trabeculoplasty*** are often short-term: its role may be in the elderly.

1 Lee Y 2005 *Am J Ophthalmol* **139** 202. SE: hyperaemia; lash-length↑; 'flu-like symptoms; cramps.

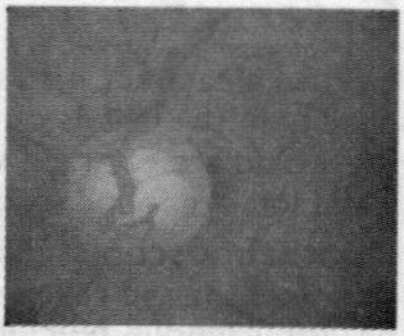

Fig 1. Cupped optic disc.[88]

Optic disc cupping is characterized by loss of disc substance—hence enlargement of the cup. Normal Cup:disc ratio 0.4-0.7.[86] This depends on the size of the disc: ►*a large cup in a small disc is probably pathological.*[1] As cupping develops, the disc vessels are displaced nasally. Asymmetric cupping suggests glaucoma. The cup:disc ratio is increased to >0.4 (fig 1). If the cup:disc ratio is >0.9, cupping is said to be severe.[87] Notching at the neuroretinal rim is usually inferior, and best seen where the vessels enter the disc. The sharp turning of the vessels is described as bayoneting.[89] Progression is more related to the size of the neuroretinal rim than to lack of disc size.[90] Glaucoma affects the anterior visual pathway at least up to the optic chiasm, to an extent that correlates with glaucomatous optic nerve damage. MRI of the anterior visual pathway can evaluate glaucomatous damage objectively.[91]

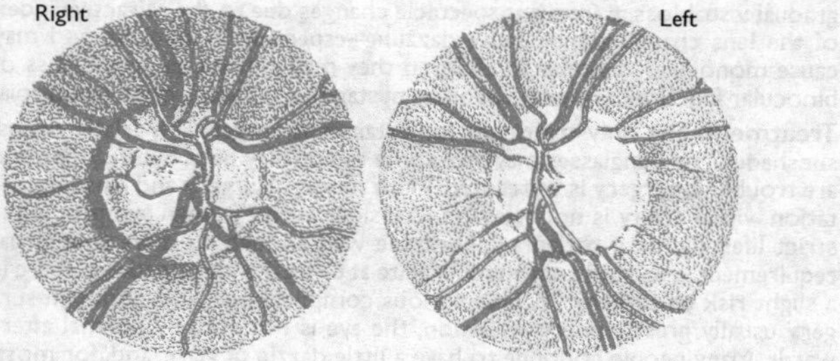

The two optic discs of a patient with open angle glaucoma which has not yet damaged the right optic disc. The left optic disc is grossly cupped and atrophic.[92]

1 Normal small discs have small cups and normal large discs have large cups, so large normal discs may be misdiagnosed as glaucomatous. The average disc diameter is 1.5mm; discs 1.0-1.3mm are classified as small, 1.4-1.7mm are medium, and >1.8 is large. Mean cup: disc ratio is about 0.35, 0.45, & 0.55 for these respective categories (95th centiles for upper limit of normal are 0.59, 0.66, & 0.74).

Cataract

►When a cataract is found, measure blood glucose (to exclude DM). ►Any opacity in the lens is called a cataract. ►The 4 major causes of blindness in the world are cataract, vitamin A deficiency, trachoma, and onchocerciasis. Cataracts are found in 75% of over 65s but in only 20% of 45–65-year-olds.

Ophthalmoscopic classification is by lens appearance. With immature cataracts the red reflex still occurs; if dense cataract there is no red reflex, or visible fundus. ***Nuclear*** cataracts change the lens refractive index and are common in old age, as are the cortical spoke-like wedge-shaped opacities. Anterior and posterior ***polar*** cataracts are localized, are commonly inherited, and lie in the visual axis. ***Subcapsular*** opacities from steroid use are just deep to the lens capsule—in the visual axis. ***Dot opacities*** are common in normal lenses but are also seen in fast-developing cataracts in diabetes or dystrophia myotonica.

Presentation Blurred vision; unilateral cataracts are often unnoticed, but loss of stereopsis may affect distance judgment. Bilateral cataracts may cause gradual visual loss ± frequent spectacle changes due to the refractive index of the lens changing, may cause dazzling—especially in sunlight, and may cause monocular diplopia. In children they may present as squint, loss of binocular function, as a white pupil, as nystagmus (infants), or as amblyopia.

Treatment The only treatment for cataract is surgery. Mydriatic drops, sunshades, and sunglasses may give some temporary help, but if symptoms are troubling, surgery is warranted. With modern surgery and lens implantation, visual acuity is not relevant. Consider surgery when symptoms restrict lifestyle, or if patients cannot see well enough to drive (the visual requirement is to read a car numberplate at 67 feet). Advise patients there is a slight risk to surgery: 2% have serious complications, and, although surgery usually greatly improves vision, the eye is not entirely normal afterwards. Many people continue to have a little dazzle of glare, and, for most, there is no effective near vision without spectacles. Distant spectacles are often required too. Remember one-third of people have co-existing ocular diseases, often macular degeneration, which may limit the outcome.

The ideal treatment is day-case surgery using local anaesthesia with small incision surgery and phacoemulsion with lens inplantation. This is applicable to the vast majority of patients. Younger people, high myopes, and the squeamish may prefer general anaesthesia. An incision of ~3mm is made, and the lens is removed by phacoemulsion (ultrasound breaks up the lens which is then aspirated into a cannula). The incision is then fractionally enlarged and an artificial lens (eg of perspex, acrylic, or silicon) implanted. Some lenses are foldable so they can be put through a smaller incision. The patient can usually return home immediately afterwards. A dressing may be needed for a few hours. With phacoemulsification, full activities can be resumed next day. With complicated surgery or extracapsular extraction, a larger incision is needed and there may be more limitations. Patients need to use antibiotic and anti-inflammatory eye drops for 3–6 weeks post-operatively. Then they need to change spectacles to get the full benefit of surgery.

Post-op complications: A very common event after surgery is posterior capsule thickening. This posterior membrane of the lens is deliberately left at surgery to make surgery safer. In 5–30%, over a few months to a few years post-operatively it opacifies. To the patient it seems as if the cataract is returning. It is easily treated by making a hole in the capsule (capsulotomy) with a Yag laser as an outpatient. People often have a little eye irritation requiring additional or altered drops postoperatively. Some may have anterior uveitis requiring alternative medication. Rarely, there may be vitreous haemorrhage, retinal detachment, or glaucoma which may lead to permanent visual loss. Endophthalmitis is very rare (<3 per 10,000).[1]

1 Olsen R 2005 *Am J Ophthalmol* **139** 141; ofloxacin drops are a better prophylactic than ciprofloxacin.

Cataract risk factors

Most cataracts are age related. Eating vegetables rich in the xanthophylls, lutein and zeaxanthin (broccoli, spinach) ↓risk of age-related cataract.[94]

In children, many are genetic (?some genetic influence in adults too). Cataracts may occur in diabetes mellitus; with topical, oral, or inhaled steroid use; with high myopia; dystrophia myotonica. In developing countries it may follow severe diarrhoea and there may be a racial element.

Pre- and post-operative care

Prior to surgery ocular biometry should be undertaken. This is a measurement of the curvature of the cornea and the length of the eye which enables prediction of the suitable intraocular lens implant for the patient. In most cases it is aimed to leave the patient emmetropic (in focus for distance), or just slightly myopic, but this may vary considerably depending on patient preference and pre-existing refraction. It is not an exact science as the clinical measurements vary and many people do continue to wear spectacles post-operatively for a remaining refractive error. On obtaining new spectacles many will experience symptoms of imbalance; these should settle in 2-3 weeks. If they do not, recommend return to the optometrist to check the correct spectacles have been dispensed. If there is still a continuing problem they should return to the ophthalmologist.

If patients develop a painful red eye or loss of vision post-operatively they should be referred back to the ophthalmologist urgently to deal with possible complications. Many experience awareness of the eye or dry, or gritty sensations and lubricants such as Viscotears® may help. If vision deteriorates with time they should initially visit the optometrist to see if they need a new prescription change; and thereafter the ophthalmologist to consider Yag laser capsulotomy or exclusion of other problems.

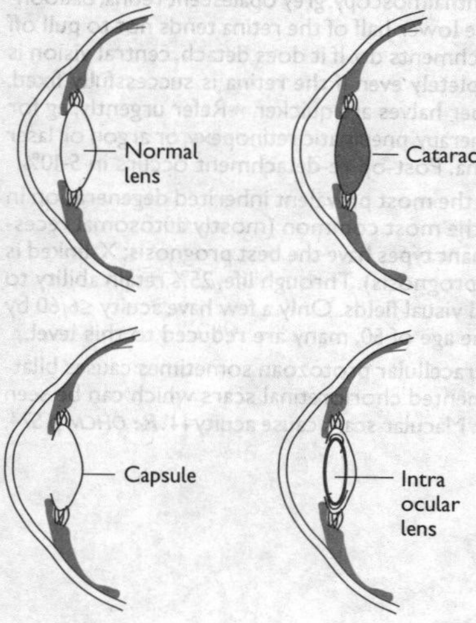

The retina

Retinoblastoma: see p 421.

Anatomy The retina consists of an outer pigmented layer (in contact with the choroid), and an inner sensory layer (in contact with the vitreous). At the centre of the posterior part lies the macula (the centre of which is termed the fovea), appearing yellowish and slightly oval. This has many cones, so acuity is greatest here. ~3mm medial to the fovea is the optic disc, which contains no rods or cones (the visual field's blind spot).

Optic disc Think *colour; contour; cup. Colour* should be a pale pink. It is more pallid in optic atrophy (p 438). *Contour:* the disc may appear oval in astigmatic eyes, and appear abnormally large in myopic eyes. Disc margins are blurred in papilloedema (eg from raised intracranial pressure, malignant hypertension, cavernous sinus thrombosis), and with optic neuritis. Blood vessels radiate away from the disc. The normal arterial/venous width ratio is 2:3. Venous engorgement appears in retinal vein thrombosis; abnormal retinal pallor with artery occlusion; and haemorrhages with exudates in hypertension and DM. *Cup:* the disc has a physiological cup which lies centrally and should occupy ~⅓ of the diameter of the disc. Cup widening and deepening occurs in glaucoma (p 440).

Retinal detachment[95] This may be 'simple', idiopathic, secondary to some intraocular problem (eg melanoma, or fibrous bands in the vitreous in diabetes), occur after cataract surgery, or result from trauma. Myopic eyes are more prone to detachment, the higher the myopia, the greater the risk—and lens surgery for myopia carries ↑risk of detachment.[1]

In simple detachment, holes in the retina allow fluid to separate the sensory retina from the retinal pigment epithelium.[96]

Detachment presents with 4 'f's: floaters, flashes (eg in 50%), field loss, and fall in acuity—painless and may be as a curtain falling over the vision (the curtain falls down as the lower half of the retina detaches upwards). Field defects indicate position and extent of the detachment (in superior detachments field loss is inferior). Ophthalmoscopy: grey opalescent retina, ballooning forward. Detachment of the lower half of the retina tends not to pull off the macula, but upper half detachments do. If it does detach, central vision is lost and doesn't recover completely even if the retina is successfully fixed. Rate of detachment varies: upper halves are quicker. ►►Refer urgently, eg for scleral silicone implants, cryotherapy, pneumatic retinopexy, or argon or laser coagulation to secure the retina. Post-op re-detachment occurs in 5-10%.

Retinitis pigmentosa This is the most prevalent inherited degeneration in the retina. Sporadic types are the most common (mostly autosomal recessive—but the autosomal dominant types have the best prognosis; X-linked is the rarest form, with poorest prognosis). Through life, 25% retain ability to read, albeit with much reduced visual fields. Only a few have acuity ≤6/60 by the time they are 20; but by the age of 50, many are reduced to this level.[97]

Toxoplasma This obligate intracellular protozoan sometimes causes bilateral 'punched-out' heavily pigmented chorioretinal scars which can be seen on routine fundal examination. Macular scars cause acuity↓↓. ℞: *OHCM* p 574.

1 Packard R 2005 *Curr Opin Ophthalmol* **16** 53 Risk is less with modern methods of lens implantation.

Macular holes

Synonyms Macular cyst, retinal hole, retinal tear, retinal perforation.

A macular hole is a full-thickness defect of retinal tissue (from the internal limiting membrane to the outer segment of the photoreceptor layer). It involves the fovea (visual acuity↓). Prevalence: eg 3.3/1000 in persons >55yrs. There is a 12% chance of a similar hole developing in the other eye.

Presentation Distorted vision with visual loss. Look for a tiny punched-out area in the centre of the macula: there may be yellow-white deposits at the base. Slit lamp exam (with an examination contact lens) shows a round excavation with well-defined borders interrupting the beam of the slit lamp. Often there is an overlying semitranslucent tissue suspended over the hole—typically surrounded by a grey halo of detached retina.

►Refer for urgent ophthalmological assessment in eye casualty.

Cause Idiopathic (typically ♀ >60yrs old); trauma; solar burn; after cystoid macular oedema; retinopathy of prematurity; post vitreoretinal surgery.[1] There may be age-related focal shrinkage of the prefoveal vitreous cortex, causing tangential traction on the fovea, hence detachment and macular holes.

Stage 1a Yellow spot (presumably intraretinal xanthophyll pigment, which has become more visible due to the foveolar detachment). This is not specific for macular hole: it can be associated with central serous chorio-retinopathy, cystoid macular oedema, and solar maculopathy.

Stage 1b Occult hole: donut-shaped yellow ring (~200–300μm) centred on the foveola. ~50% of holes progress to stage 2—when treatment is needed.

Stage 2 Full thickness macular hole (<400μm). Prefoveolar cortex usually separates eccentrically creating a semitransparent opacity, often larger than the hole, and the yellow ring disappears. These generally progress to stage 3.

Fig 1. Macular hole

Stage 3 Holes >400μm associated with partial vitreomacular separation (image).

Stage 4 Complete vitreous separation from the entire macula and disc.

Tests Fluorescein angiography (FA) is useful for differentiating macular holes from cystoid macular oedema and choroidal neovascularization (CNV). This typically shows a window defect early in the angiogram that does not expand with time, and there is no leakage or accumulation of dye. There may be Amsler grid abnormalities. Plotting small central scotomas is hard.

Treatment In stage 1, see what happens: no treatment is needed if there is spontaneous resolution or no progression. Surgery: the anterior and middle vitreous and internal limiting membrane are removed, an air bubble is introduced to nudge (tamponade) the macula back into position, which may work provided the patient spends 1–2 post-op weeks face down (a great part of success is dependent on this). Vitrectomy with fluid-gas exchange for stage 2, 3, and 4 holes improves vision (compared with conservative treatment). Series of patients have been variously reported, with hole closure rates of ≤95% (~67% improve by 2 or more lines on visual acuity). Success is also possible if the hole is long-standing (>6 months) or if aged >80.

However, in some cases more than one operation is required to close the hole, and adverse effects may occur: macular retinal pigment epithelium changes, retinal detachments, iatrogenic retinal tears, enlargement of the hole, macular light toxicity, postoperative intraocular pressure spikes. Many patients develop cataracts (76% of cases requiring extraction within 2 years). Patients not suitable or not wishing for this need visual aids (eg to read).

1 Ahmad O 2005 *Arch Ophthalmol* **123** 54

The eye in diabetes mellitus

►Keep BP <150/85 and all the major diabetic retinopathies are less common.[1]

Diabetes can be bloody and blinding—the leading cause of blindness in those aged 20-65 (UK). Almost any part of the eye can be affected: cataract and retinopathy are the chief pathologies. 30% of adults have ocular problems when diabetes presents. At presentation, the lens may have a higher refractive index (possibly due to dehydration) producing relative myopia. On treatment, the refractive index reduces, and vision is more hypermetropic—so do not correct refractive errors until diabetes is controlled.

Structural changes Diabetes accelerates formation and progress of age-related cataract. Typically this is premature senile cataract, but young diabetics can also be affected at presentation; here the lens has taken up a lot of glucose which is converted by the aldolase reductase to sorbitol. Rarely, diabetes affects the iris, with new blood vessel forming on it (rubeosis), and, if these block the drainage of aqueous fluid, glaucoma may result.

Retinopathy ***Pathogenesis:*** Microangiopathy in capillaries, precapillary arterioles and venules causes occlusion ± leakage. ***Vascular occlusion:*** causes ischaemia which leads to new vessels in the retina, optic disc, and iris, ie ***proliferative retinopathy***. New vessels can bleed (vitreous haemorrhage). As new vessels carry along with them fibrous tissue, retraction of this tissue increases risk of retinal detachment. Occlusion also causes ***cotton wool spots***, (ischaemic nerve fibres). ***Vascular leakage:*** As pericytes are lost, capillaries bulge (microaneurysms) and there is oedema & hard exudates (made up of lipoprotein & lipid filled macrophages). Rupture of microaneurysms, at the nerve fibre level causes flame shaped haemorrhages; when deep in the retina, ***blot haemorrhages*** form.

►Pre-symptomatic screening enables laser photocoagulation. Screen by regular eye exam or retinal photography. In rural areas, mobile screening has a role. 98 [n=2186] Lesions are mostly at the posterior pole and can be easily seen by ophthalmoscope. ***Background retinopathy*** comprises microaneurysms (seen as 'dots'), haemorrhages (flame shaped or 'blots') and hard exudates (yellow patches). Vision is normal. Background retinopathy can progress to sight-threatening maculopathy ± proliferative retinopathy. ***Maculopathy:*** Leakage from the vessels close to the macula cause oedema & maculopathy. ***Proliferative retinopathy:*** Fine new vessels appear on the retina. Engorged tortuous veins, cotton wool spots, large blot haemorrhages & vitreous haemorrhage.

►Refer those with maculopathy or proliferative retinopathy urgently to an ophthalmologist for treatment (eg photocoagulation) to protect vision.

Treatment Good control of diabetes can prevent new vessel formation. Concurrent diseases may accelerate retinopathy (eg hypertension, renal disease, pregnancy, and anaemia). Treat these (as appropriate), and hyperlipidaemia. Photocoagulation by laser is used to treat both maculopathy and proliferative retinopathy. Definite indications for photocoagulation are new vessels on the optic disc and vitreous haemorrhage. If vitreous haemorrhage is massive and does not clear, vitrectomy may be needed.

CNS effects Ocular palsies may occur, typically nerves III and VI. In diabetic third nerve palsy the pupil may be spared as fibres to the pupil run peripherally in the nerve, receiving blood supply from the pial vessels. Argyll Robertson pupils and Horner's syndrome may also occur (p 424).

1 UKPDS 69 data (2004); *N* = 1148. Absolute risks for blindness was 3.1 per 1000 patient-years if control was tight vs 4.1 for others. There was no difference if the BP was lowered by ACE-i or β-blockers.

Proliferative diabetic retinopathy may be treated with panretinal (scatter) laser photocoagulation (PRP). This type involves treating the peripheral retina which is not receiving adequate blood flow. By treating these areas it is thought that the stimulus driving the neovascular process may be halted. As this treatment involves many laser applications (eg >1000) it may be divided into ≥2 sessions. NB: panretinal photocoagulation does not improve vision. It is intended to help prevent blindness. It may cause some loss of peripheral, colour, and night vision. Some patients get generalized blurring of vision which is usually transient but may persist indefinitely.

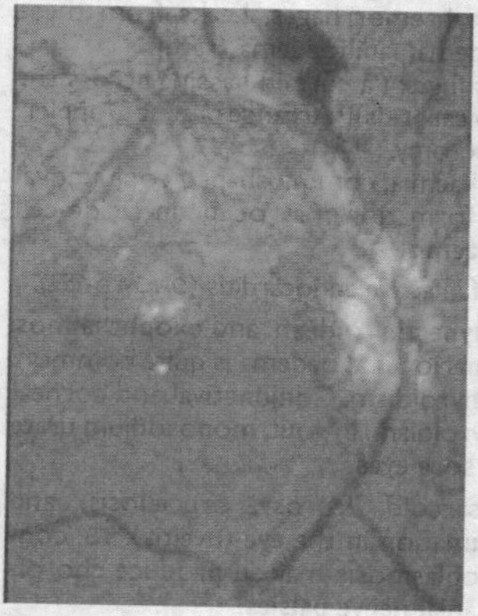

Fig 1. Retinopathy before the laser

Fig 2. After the laser

The eye in systemic disease

Systemic disease often manifests itself in the eye and, in some cases, eye examination will first suggest the diagnosis.

Vascular retinopathy This may be *arteriopathic* (arteriovenous ***nipping***: arteries nip veins where they cross—they share the same connective tissue sheath) or *hypertensive*—arteriolar vasoconstriction and leakage—producing ***hard exudates, macular oedema, haemorrhages***, and, rarely, ***papilloedema***. Thick, shiny arterial walls appear like wiring (called 'silver' or 'copper'). Narrowing of arterioles leads to localized infarction of the superficial retina seen as cotton wool spots and flame haemorrhages. Leaks from these appear as hard exudates ± macular oedema/papilloedema (rare).

Emboli to the retina cause *amaurosis fugax* ('a curtain passing across the eyes'). *Typical cause:* atheroma (listen to carotids).[1] Arrange urgent Doppler; treat eg by aspirin ± carotid endarterectomy.

Retinal haemorrhages are seen in leukaemia; comma-shaped conjunctival haemorrhages and retinal new vessel formation may occur in sickle-cell disease; optic atrophy in pernicious anaemia.

Note also Roth spots (retinal infarcts) of infective endocarditis (*OHCM* p 152).

Metabolic disease Diabetes: p 446. Hyperthyroidism, and exophthalmos: *OHCM* p 305. In myxoedema, eyelid and periorbital oedema is quite common. Lens opacities may occur in hypoparathyroidism. Conjunctival and corneal calcification may occur in hyperparathyroidism. In gout, monosodium urate deposited in the conjunctiva may give sore eyes.

Granulomatous disorders (TB, sarcoid, leprosy, brucellosis, and toxoplasmosis) can all produce inflammation in the eye (uveitis). TB, congenital syphilis, sarcoid, CMV, and toxoplasmosis may all produce choroidoretinitis. In sarcoid there may be cranial nerve palsies.

Collagen and vasculitic diseases These also cause inflammation. Conjunctivitis is found in SLE and Reiter's syndrome; episcleritis in polyarteritis nodosa and SLE; scleritis in rheumatoid arthritis; and uveitis in ankylosing spondylitis and Reiter's syndrome (*OHCM* p 418). In dermatomyositis there is orbital oedema with retinal haemorrhages. Behçet's syndrome and temporal arteritis may cause retinopathies.

Keratoconjunctivitis sicca Sjögren's syndrome, (*OHCM* p 734). There is reduced tear formation (Schirmer filter paper test), producing a gritty feeling in the eyes. Decreased salivation also gives a dry mouth (xerostomia). It occurs in association with collagen diseases. Treatment is with artificial tears ('tears naturale', or hypromellose drops).

AIDS Those who are HIV +ve may get CMV retinitis, with retinal spots ('pizza pie' fundus, signifying superficial retinal infarction) + flame haemorrhages involving more and more of the retina. This may be asymptomatic or cause blindness; it implies AIDS & ↓CD4 count. IV ganciclovir or its prodrug (oral valganciclovir) are used.[RCT 99]

Cotton wool spots may indicate HIV retinopathy (may present before the full picture of AIDS); it is a microvasculopathy, not a retinitis. Candidiasis of the aqueous and vitreous is hard to treat. Kaposi's sarcoma may affect the lids or conjunctiva.

Other causes of retinopathy (*haemorrhages, microaneurysms, hard exudates*)[100] radiation; carotid artery disease; central or branch retinal vein occlusion; retinal telangiectasia/Coats' disease; Leber's miliary aneurysms.

1 Causes of amaurosis fugax: giant cell arteritis, orbital schwannomas, meningiomas, ocular small vessel disease, Churg-Strauss vasculitis, antiphospholipid syndrome, arrhythmias, dysfibrinogenemia, uveitis-glaucoma-hyphaema syndrome post-cataract extraction.

Papilloedema In fig 1 & 2, the discs are swollen forwards and also outwards into the surrounding retina. Disc margins are hidden and in places retinal vessels are concealed, because oedema has impaired the translucency of the disc tissues. The retinal veins are congested and there are a few haemorrhages at 9 o'clock in fig 1. ►Whenever you see these appearances, get help. Measure the BP, and look in the other eye. Any hypertensive changes or haemorrhages? Or signs of central retinal vein occlusion? (p 435). ***Bilateral disc changes*** suggest intracranial hypertension. Is there *headache*—worse in the mornings, centred in the frontal region, and are aggravated by bending down? In young obese women, think of benign intracranial hypertension.

Pseudopapilloedema (=pseudo-neuritis=pseudo-papillitis, see fig 3) is usually associated with hypermetropia ± astigmatism or tilted discs, as in this patient below (from a 12yr-old boy referred for '?brain tumour'). The disc margins are blurred and the disc appears elevated. Its cup may be absent but there is no true oedema and veins are of normal size and pulsate (transmitted from a nearby artery). It is usually bilateral and symmetrical and does not change over time. Fluorescence angiography (FA) distinguishes it from papilloedema or optic neuritis (papillitis) by the absence of contrast leakage.

Opaque nerve fibres may be confused with papilloedema (fig 4).

Other causes of swollen discs include *optic neuritis* (p 434) and disorders of the nerve sheath (eg a *meningioma*, as seen in the MRI image, fig 5).

Optic nerve head drusen (fig 6) are multiple hyaline bodies which extend beyond the disc margins, and an abnormal branching of the retinal vessels is often present. The nerve head is usually small (bilateral 'crowded disc'). If the hyaline material is buried within the disc substance, diagnosis is confusing, especially if a field defect is also present. *NB:* Optic atrophy in the contralateral eye is the Foster-Kennedy syndrome (eg from meningioma of the optic canal in the eye with optic atrophy; in practice, the usual cause is consequential ischaemic optic neuropathy).[106]

Nystagmus suggests a lesion in the posterior fossa, and a ***sixth nerve palsy*** may be a false localizing sign. A ***homonymous field defect*** may accompany compression of the supra-geniculate or posterior visual pathway by a glioma, meningioma, or AV malformation.

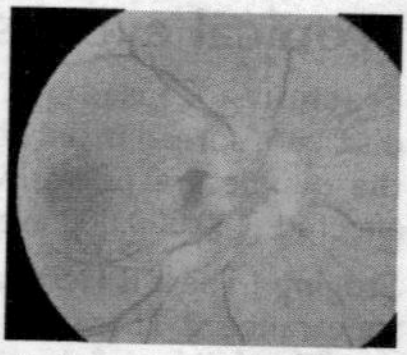

Fig 1. Papilloedema[101]

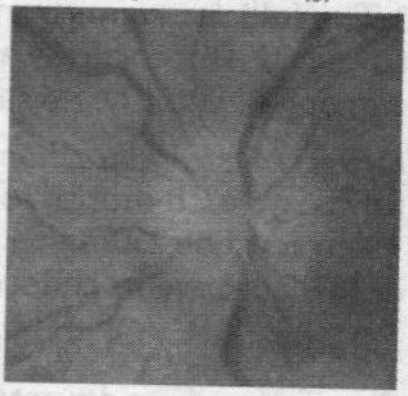

Fig 2. Papilloedema[102]

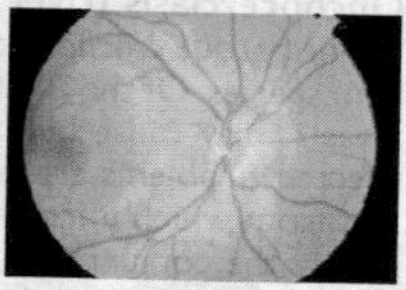

Fig 3. Pseudopapilloedema[103]

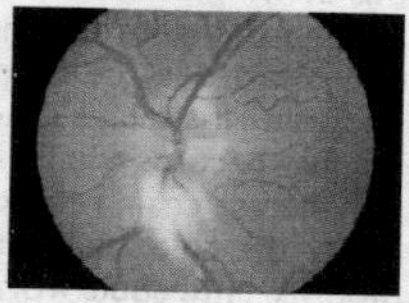

Fig 4. Nerve fibres mimicking papilloedema[104]

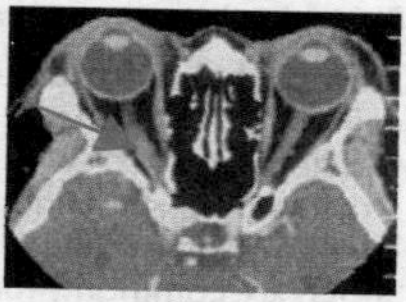

Fig 5. Meningioma of left optic nerve sheath (arrow)[105]

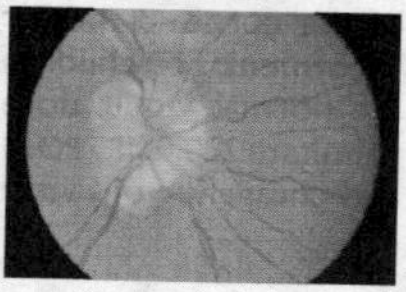

Fig 6. Optic drusen[107]

Tropical eye disease

Trachoma Caused by *Chlamydia trachomatis* (serotypes A, B, and C), this disease is spread mainly by flies—typically where it is hot, dry, and dusty and the people are poor, living near to their cattle. 400 million people are affected (100,000,000 are children).

Staging 1 There is lacrimation. Follicles under the upper lid give a fine granular appearance. 2 There is intense erythema. The follicles are larger and underneath both lids. A fine pannus and capillaries grow down towards the cornea. 3 The follicles rupture and are replaced by scar tissue. The pannus is more advanced. The cornea may ulcerate. 4 Scar tissue distorts the lids and causes entropion. Eyelashes scratch the cornea, which ulcerates.

Drugs: *Mass anti-trachoma treatment:* tetracycline 1% eye ointment 12-hrly for 5 days each month for 6 months. In active disease use 8-hrly for 6 weeks + tetracycline 250mg/6h PO for 14 days. Single-dose azithromycin (20mg/kg) is 78% effective in children. 108

Lid surgery: Eg lid margin splitting + tarsal plate fracture + everting sutures.

Prevention: Good water/sanitation. Regular washing of faces. 109

Onchocerciasis (river blindness) This is caused by the microfilariae of the nematode *Onchocerca volvulus*, transmitted by black flies of the Simulium species. Of the 20–50 million people affected, 95% live in Africa. In some areas it may cause blindness in 40% of the population. Unless the eye is affected, problems are mostly confined to the skin. Fly bites result in nodules from which microfilariae are released. These eventually invade the eye, mainly the conjunctiva, cornea, ciliary body, and iris, but occasionally the retina or optic nerve. Sometimes they may be seen swimming in the aqueous or lying dead in the anterior chamber. The microfilariae initially excite inflammation; fibrosis then occurs around them. Reaction around the dead microfilariae in the cornea causes corneal opacities (nummular keratitis). Chronic iritis causes synechiae formation and may precipitate cataracts. The iris may become totally fixed. ***Tests:*** Skin snip tests, triple-antigen serology; polymerase chain reaction. ***Treatment:*** Get expert help. Ivermectin is currently the chief microfilaricide, ~150μg/kg PO as a single dose every 6–12 months, until adult worms die (*OHCM* p 615). In lightly infected expatriates, the first 3 doses are recommended to be monthly, with observation in hospital after the first dose (reactions are common in expatriates). Macrofilaricidal drugs are currently being developed for human use. 110

Xerophthalmia and keratomalacia These are manifestations of vitamin A deficiency, eg if weaned early on to vitamin A deficient milk products, or toddlers who eat few vegetables. Peak incidence: 2–5yrs; 40 million children worldwide. Night blindness and dry conjunctivae (xerosis) occur early. The cornea is unwettable and loses transparency. Small grey plaques (Bitot's spots) are commonly found raised from interpalpebral conjunctiva. Vitamin A reverses these changes. Early corneal xerosis is reversible. Corneal ulceration and perforation can occur. In keratomalacia there is massive softening of the cornea ± perforation and extrusion of the intraocular contents. ***Treatment:*** For children: retinol palmitate 50,000U IM monthly until the eyes are normal (adult dose 100,000U, weekly to start with); or oral retinyl palmitate 200,000U PO. β-carotene (a provitamin) 1.2×10^6U PO, is as effective, and cheaper. Avoid vitamin A in pregnancy (vitamin A embryopathy).

Eye trauma

Prevention is the key, eg wearing goggles, or plastic glasses when near small moving objects or using tools (avoids splinters, fish-hooks, and squash-ball injuries). *Always record acuity* (both eyes: if the uninjured one is blind take all injuries very seriously). Take a detailed history of the event.

If unable to open the injured eye, instill a few drops of local anaesthetic (tetracaine 1%): after a few mins, comfortable opening may be possible. Examine lids, conjunctiva, cornea, sclera, anterior chamber, pupil, iris, lens, vitreous, fundus, and eye movement. An irregular pupil may mean globe rupture. Afferent pupil defects (p 424) do not augur well for sight recovery. Note pain, discharge, or squint. CT may be very useful (foreign bodies may be magnetic, so avoid MRI).

Penetrating trauma Refer urgently: delays risk of ocular extrusion or infection. With uveal injury there is risk of sympathetic ophthalmia in the other eye. ► A history of flying objects (eg work with lathes, hammers, and chisels) should prompt careful examination and x-ray to exclude intraocular foreign bodies. ► Don't try to remove a large foreign body (knife; dart). Support the object with padding. Transport supine. Pad the *unaffected* eye to prevent damage from conjugate movement. Consider skull x-ray or CT to exclude intracranial involvement.

Foreign bodies (FB) *Have a low threshold for getting help*; FBs often hide, so examine all the eye; for lid eversion see www.medinfo.ufl.edu/year1/bcs/clist/index.html FBs cause chemosis, subconjunctival bleeds, irregular pupils, iris prolapse, hyphaema, vitreous haemorrhage, and retinal tears. If you suspect a metal FB, x-ray the orbit. With high-velocity FBs, consider orbital ultrasound: pick-up rate is 90% vs 40% for x-rays—but skill is needed (not always available in busy A&E departments). Removal of superficial foreign bodies may be possible using a triangle of clean card. Use gentamicin 0.3% drops afterwards to prevent infection.

Corneal abrasions (Often from small fast-moving objects, eg children's finger-nails; twigs.) They may cause intense pain. Apply a drop of local anaesthetic, eg 1% tetracaine before examination. They stain with fluorescein and should heal within 48h. Apply gentamicin eye ointment, and pad the eye. Send the patient home with analgesics. Re-examine after 24h. If still having a foreign body sensation after removing the pad, stain again with fluorescein. If the cornea stains, repeat the procedure for another 24h. If it still stains after 48h, refer. NB: meta-analyses of small corneal abrasions do not favour using pads.

Burns Treat chemical burns promptly: instill anaesthetic drops (tetracaine) every 2min till the patient is comfortable. Then hold lids open and bathe the eyes in copious clean water while the specific antidote is sought. Often the patient will not hold the eye open due to excruciating pain. All burns may have late serious sequelae, eg corneal scarring, opacification, and lid damage. Alkali burns are more serious than acid.

Arc eye Welders and sunbed users who don't wear protection against UV light may damage corneal epithelium. There is a *foreign body sensation*, watering, and blepharospasm. Instill local anaesthetic drops every 2min. After the second application, excruciating pain can disappear like magic. Apply an antibiotic ointment, pad the eye, and it will recover in 24h. It's a very painful condition so be generous with analgesia.

Finally, remember to think of fat emboli in trauma patients who suddenly complain of visual problems.

Eye trauma[111]

►Prevention is the key, eg wearing goggles, or plastic glasses when near small moving objects or using tools (avoids splinters, fish-hooks, and squash-ball injuries). *Always record acuity* (both eyes; if the uninjured one is blind take all injuries *very* seriously). Take a detailed history of the event.

If unable to open the injured eye, instill a few drops of local anaesthetic (tetracaine 1%): after a few mins, comfortable opening may be possible. Examine lids, conjunctiva, cornea, sclera, anterior chamber, pupil, iris, lens, vitreous, fundus, and eye movement. An irregular pupil may mean globe rupture. Afferent pupil defects (p 424) do not augur well for sight recovery. Note pain, discharge, or squint. CT may be very useful (foreign bodies may be magnetic, so avoid MRI).

Penetrating trauma Refer urgently: delays risk of ocular extrusion or infection. With uveal injury there is risk of sympathetic ophthalmia in the other eye. ►A history of flying objects (eg work with lathes, hammers, and chisels) should prompt careful examination and x-ray to exclude intraocular foreign bodies. ►►*Don't* try to remove a large foreign body (knife; dart). Support the object with padding. Transport supine. Pad the *unaffected* eye to prevent damage from conjugate movement. Consider skull x-ray or CT to exclude intracranial involvement.

Foreign bodies (FB) *Have a low threshold for getting help*; FBs often hide, so examine *all* the eye; for lid eversion see www.medinfo.ufl.edu/year1/bcs/clist/index.html FBs cause chemosis, subconjunctival bleeds, irregular pupils, iris prolapse, hyphaema, vitreous haemorrhage, and retinal tears. If you suspect a metal FB, x-ray the orbit. With high-velocity FBs, consider orbital ultrasound: pick-up rate is 90% *vs* 40% for x-rays—but skill is needed (not always available in busy A&E departments). Removal of superficial foreign bodies may be possible using a triangle of clean card. Use gentamicin 0.3% drops afterwards to prevent infection.

Corneal abrasions (Often from small fast-moving objects, eg children's finger-nails; twigs.) They may cause intense pain. Apply a drop of local anaesthetic, eg 1% tetracaine before examination. They stain with fluorescein and should heal within 48h. Apply gentamicin eye ointment, and pad the eye. Send the patient home with analgesics. Re-examine after 24h. If still having a foreign body sensation after removing the pad, stain again with fluorescein. If the cornea stains, repeat the procedure for another 24h. If it still stains after 48h, refer. NB: meta-analyses of small corneal abrasions do not favour using pads.[MET 112, 113, 114]

Burns Treat chemical burns promptly: instill anaesthetic drops (tetracaine) every 2min till the patient is comfortable. Then hold lids open and bathe the eyes in copious clean water while the specific antidote is sought. Often the patient will not hold the eye open due to excruciating pain. All burns may have late serious sequelae, eg corneal scarring, opacification, and lid damage. Alkali burns are more serious than acid.

Arc eye Welders and sunbed users who don't wear protection against UV light may damage corneal epithelium. There is a foreign body sensation, watering, and blepharospasm. Instill local anaesthetic drops every 2min. After the second application, excruciating pain can disappear like magic. Apply an antibiotic ointment, pad the eye, and it will recover in 24h. It is a very painful condition so be generous with analgesia.

Finally, remember to think of ***fat embolus*** in trauma patients who suddenly complain of visual problems.

Contusions and intraocular haemorrhage

Our eyes are protected by our bony orbital ridges. Severe contusions from large objects may damage the eye, but smaller objects such as champagne corks, squash balls, and airgun pellets (p 720) cause local contusion, eg resulting in lid bruises and subconjunctival haemorrhage (if the posterior limit of such a haemorrhage cannot be seen, consider fracture of the orbit). Both usually settle in 2 weeks. ►*Any injury penetrating the eyeball should receive immediate specialist treatment.*

Intraocular haemorrhage: This usually affects acuity and should receive specialist attention. Blood is often found in the anterior chamber (hyphaema, fig 1, p 413): small amounts clear spontaneously but if filling the anterior chamber, evacuation may be needed. It is often recognizable by pen-torch examination. Even small hyphaemas must be carefully evaluated (∴ refer): it may signify serious injury. *Late complications:* Glaucoma; corneal staining. Pain suggests glaucoma or re-bleeding.

Secondary haemorrhage: This may occur within 5 days and may produce sight-threatening secondary glaucoma. Sometimes the iris is paralysed and dilated due to injury (called traumatic mydriasis). This usually recovers in a few days but sometimes it is permanent. Vitreous haemorrhage will cause dramatic fall in acuity. There will be no red reflex on ophthalmoscopy. Lens dislocation, tearing of the iris root, splitting of the choroid, detachment of the retina, and damage to the optic nerve may be other sequelae; they are more common if contusion is caused by smaller objects rather than large.

Blows to the orbit: Blunt injury (eg from a football) can cause a sudden increase in the pressure within the orbit, and may cause blowout fractures with the orbital contents herniating into the maxillary sinus. Tethering of the inferior rectus and inferior oblique muscles causes diplopia. Test the sensation over the skin of the lower lid. Loss of sensation indicates infraorbital nerve injury, confirming a blowout fracture. CT may show the depressed fracture of the posterior orbital floor. Fracture reduction and muscle release is necessary.[115]

Blindness and partial sight

The pattern of blindness around the world differs considerably, depending on local nutrition and economic factors. 90% of the world's blind live in developing countries—and 80% would not be blind if trained eye personnel, medicines, ophthalmic equipment, and patient referral systems were optimized. The diseases responsible for most of the blindness in the world are trachoma, cataract (50% of the world's blindness), glaucoma, keratomalacia, onchocerciasis, and diabetic retinopathy. In the past smallpox, gonorrhoea, syphilis, and leprosy (10% of those affected were blind) were also common causes of blindness.

Rates of blindness are higher than 10/1000 in some parts of Africa and Asia, but in the UK and the USA rates are 2/1000. Blindness may be voluntarily registered in England, registration making one eligible for certain concessions. Although the word blind suggests inability to perceive light, a person is eligible for registration if their acuity is less than 3/60, or if >3/60 but with substantial visual field loss (as in glaucoma). There are ~350,000 people registered blind in the UK. *Criteria for partial sighted registration:* acuity is <6/60 (or >6/60 with visual field restrictions).

Causes of blindness These have changed considerably in the UK over the last 70 years. Whereas in the 1920s ophthalmia neonatorum (p 36) was responsible for 30% of blindness in English blind schools, this is now a rare but treatable disease. Retrolental fibroplasia was common in the 1950s, mostly affecting premature infants: monitoring of intra-arterial oxygen in premature babies tries to prevent this. With an ever-aging population, the diseases particularly afflicting this population are the common causes of blindness. Nearly two-thirds of the blind population are over 65 years of age, and nearly half over 75. Macular degeneration, cataract, and glaucoma are the three commonest causes of blindness.

Registration In England, responsibility for blind registration lies with the local authority. Application is made by a consultant ophthalmologist and is voluntary, not statutory. Registration as blind entitles one to extra tax allowances, reduced TV licence fees, some travel concessions, and access to talking books. Special certification from an ophthalmologist is necessary for the partially sighted to receive talking books. At one time it was statutory that the registered blind should receive a visit from a social worker but this is no longer the case, although the social services employ social workers who specialize in care of the blind. The Royal National Institute for the Blind[1] will advise on aids, such as guide dogs (available if required for employment). It sells talking mobile phones and other helpful gadgets in its website. [116]

Special educational facilities These provide for visually handicapped children. Special schools have a higher staff/pupil ratio, specialized equipment, and many have a visiting ophthalmologist. The disadvantage is that the children may not mix much with other children—especially if they board.

1 Royal National Institute for the Blind, 224 Great Portland St, London W1N 6AA (UK 0845 766 9999)

Common causes of blindness in the world

1 Trachoma
2 Cataract
3 Glaucoma
4 Keratomalacia
5 Onchocerciasis
6 Diabetic retinopathy

The most common cause of irreversible blindness and partial sight in developed countries is age-related macular degeneration. In patients of working age, diabetic retinopathy is the leading cause in the West.

Colour vision and colour blindness

For normal colour vision we require cone photopigments sensitive to blue, green, and red light. The commonest hereditary colour vision defect is X-linked failure of red-green discrimination (8% ♂ and 0.5% ♀ affected—so those with Turner's syndrome have ♂ incidence and those with Klinefelter's have ♀ incidence). Blue-yellow discriminatory failure is more commonly acquired and sexes are affected equally.

Diagnosis: This is by use of coloured pattern discrimination charts (eg Ishihara plates).

Depressed colour vision may be a sensitive indicator of acquired macular or optic nerve disease.

Monochromatism This may be due to being born without cones (resulting in low visual acuity, absent colour vision, photophobia, and nystagmus), or, very rarely, due to cone monochromacy where all cones contain the same visual pigment, when there is only failure to distinguish colour.

Drugs and the eye

The eye does not retain drops for as long as ointments and 2-hourly applications may be needed. Eye ointments are particularly suitable for use at night and in conditions where crusting and sticking of the lid margins occurs. Allow 5min between doses of drops to prevent overspill.

The antibiotics most used are not those generally used systemically, eg fusidic acid, chloramphenicol, neomycin, gentamicin, and framycetin. All eye preparations have warnings not to use for more than one month.

Mydriatics (=cycloplegics) These drugs dilate the pupil. They also cause cycloplegia and hence blur vision (warn not to drive). Pupil dilatation prior to examination is best achieved using 0.5% or 1% tropicamide which lasts for 3h. 1% cyclopentolate has an action of 24h and is preferred for producing cycloplegia for refraction of children. These drugs may be used to prevent synechiae formation in iritis. ►Over-60s with shallow anterior chambers (especially if a family history of glaucoma) may have acute glaucoma triggered, so only use on ophthalmological advice.

Miotics These constrict the pupil and increase drainage of aqueous. They are used in the treatment of glaucoma (p 440).

Local anaesthetic Tetracaine (0.5% drops) is an example. This may be used to permit examination of a painful eye where reflex blepharospasm is a problem, and to facilitate removal of a foreign body. ►It abolishes the corneal reflex so use to treat pain is to risk corneal damage. To relieve pain, give an eye pad, and be generous with oral analgesia. In children use proxymetacaine as it stings less.

Steroid and NSAID drops ►Steroids are potentially dangerous as they may induce catastrophic progression of dendritic ulcers (p 416). Ophthalmoscopy may miss dendritic ulcers, and slit lamp inspection is essential if steroid drops are being considered, eg for allergy, episcleritis, scleritis, or iritis. Steroid drops ↑intraocular pressure (newer drops less so: eg rimexolone has a low IOP-elevating potential, comparable to fluorometholone and < dexamethasone & prednisolone acetate).[117] NSAID drops, eg ketorolac, may obviate the need for some steroid drops.[118]

Iatrogenic eye disease Glaucoma may be precipitated by steroid drops (above) or by mydriatics—also tablets with anticholinergic effects (some antiparkinson drugs and tricyclic antidepressants).

A few drugs affect the retina if used chronically. Those taking ethambutol should be warned to report *any* visual side-effects (loss of acuity, colour blindness). Chloroquine and other antimalarials are also implicated and damage may occur with long-term use, especially if high doses are used.

Obtaining and preparing antibiotic eyedrops

Fortified guttate gentamicin is 15mg/mL—(the normal commercial gentamicin is 3mg/mL); penicillin 5000U/mL, methicillin 20mg/mL, and antifungals can be obtained from the Chief Pharmacist, Moorfields Eye Hospital (tel. 020 725 33411). Antibiotics can be home-made as follows: ***Gentamicin forte:*** Add 2mL of 40mg/mL IV gentamicin to a 5mL bottle of commercial guttate gentamicin (3mg/mL).[1]

Other antibiotics can be made up using IV preparations to the required concentration using water or normal saline. These are stable for the time recommended for IV solutions in the manufacturers *Data sheets*. Penicillin G can be used up to 500,000U/mL.

1 From Mr JKG Dart FRCS, Moorfields Eye Hospital, City Rd, London EC1V 2PD

Eyedrops as a cause of systemic symptoms

Drugs applied to the eye may be absorbed through the cornea and produce systemic side-effects—eg bronchospasm or bradycardia in susceptible individuals using antiglaucoma β-blocking drops, eg **timolol** (Timoptol®), **carteolol** (Teoptic®), **betaxolol** (Betoptic®—which is cardio-selective). ►Symptoms may be subtle and insidious—eg gradually decreasing excercise tolerance, or falls from arrhythmias. Serious problems are more likely if there is co-morbidity (eg respiratory infection).

Other anti-glaucoma drops (p 440) cause headaches, and a bitter taste in the mouth; urolithiasis is reported with **dorzolamide** (Trusopt®).

Pilocarpine (eg Isopto Carpine®, Sno Pilo®) may cause parasympathetic sweating. Accommodation spasm may lead to brow-ache (worse if <40 years old, or just starting treatment). Other SE: 'flu-like syndrome, sweating, urinary frequency; more rarely: urinary urgency, D&V (or constipation ±flatulence), dyspepsia, flushes, BP↑, palpitations, rhinitis, dizziness, lacrimation, conjunctivitis, visual disturbances, ocular pain, rash, pruritus.

Even highly selective α_2-receptor agonists used in glaucoma, eg **brimonidine** (Alphagan®), can cause effects such as dry mouth (in 33% of patients), headache, fatigue, and drowsiness.[RCT 119]

Contact lenses

80% of contact lenses are worn for cosmetic reasons. Only 20% are worn because lenses are more suitable for the eye condition than spectacles. Among this 20% a minority wear the lenses to hide disfiguring inoperable eye conditions, a greater proportion have them for very high refractive errors. Myopia above -12 dioptres and hypermetropia above +10 dioptres are indications for lenses because equivalent spectacles produce quite distorted visual fields. Lenses are used for ocular reasons, eg after corneal ulceration or trauma when a new front surface of the cornea is needed to see through, and in keratoconus. Keratoconus is a rare degenerative, slowly progressive corneal condition with thinning and anterior protrusion of the central cornea. Blurred vision is the only symptom. Contact lens use may compensate for corneal distortion early, but later corneal grafting may be needed.

Types of lens Hard lenses are 8.5–9mm in diameter and are made of polymethylmethacrylate (PMMA). Gas-permeable hard lenses are about 0.5cm larger and are designed to allow gas to permeate through to the underlying cornea. They can only be made to cope with a limited degree of astigmatism and do not wet as well as standard hard lenses, so may mist up in the day. With the advent of the larger (13–15mm diameter) soft contact lenses it was hoped that many of the problems with hard lenses could be circumvented. Soft disposable lenses can be worn for 2–4 weeks and then disposed of. Special contact lenses called toric lenses can be used to correct astigmatism of up to 2 diopters. With more astigmatism, correction is not achieved because the lens fits the astigmatic cornea taking on its shape. They are more delicate than hard lenses and need meticulous cleaning. Extended wear-lenses can be worn for up to 4 months. Sometimes coloured lenses are used simply to change eye colour. Disposable contact lenses are becoming more common.

Patients may suffer from keratoconjunctivitis or giant papillary change in the upper tarsal conjunctiva, possibly due to sensitization to the cleansing materials used or to the mucus which forms on the lens.

Cleaning lenses Different cleaning solutions made by different manufacturers should not be mixed. With hard lenses 2 solutions are usually used, one for rinsing and cleaning, and one for storage. The storage solution should be washed off before the lens is inserted. Soft contact lenses, being permeable, tend to absorb the chemicals, so weaker solutions for cleaning are used. In addition, the lenses are usually intermittently cleaned with another system (eg enzyme tablets) to remove mucoprotein on their surface. Sensitivity to cleaning agents usually presents as redness, stinging, increased lens movement, increased mucus production, and thickened eyelids. It may be necessary to stop wearing lenses for several months. When restarting use a preservative-free cleansing system.

Complications

1. Despite a shift to using of frequent-replacement daily-wear contact lenses, corneal ulcer is still a real problem, eg from *Pseudomonas aeruginosa*.[1]
2. Corneal abrasion is common early while adjusting to wear. Pain ± lacrimation occurs some hours after removing the lens.
3. Sensitization to cleaning agents ±staining, eg by rifampicin or fluorescein. Eye ointments must no be used, nor eye-drying drugs. See *BNF*.
4. Losing the lens within the eye. Hard lenses may be lost in any fornix, soft lenses are usually in upper outer fornix.
5. Keratitis and risk of acanthamoeba infection.

1 Mah-Sadorra JH 2005 *Cornea* **24** 51.

Hygiene tips

- ►Pay attention to contact lens containers, as well as lenses.
- ►Do not assume that because a person uses disposable lenses there can be no nasty acanthamoebae infections. These free-living protozoa (found in soil and water, including bathroom tap water) may cause devastating keratitis even with disposable lenses.[120]
    - Scrub container's inside with cotton wool bud moistened with lens fluid.
    - Disinfect the container with hot water (≥80°C); leave to dry in open air.
    - Wash your hands before handling the contact lens container.
    - Replace the container at least every year.
    - Protozoa may survive new '1-step' solutions of 3% hydrogen peroxide. Amoebae are difficult to treat, and there is current interest in salicylate's potential to reduce microbial attachment when used in contact lens care solutions.[121]

Blepharospasm

Blepharospasm is involuntary contraction of orbicularis oculi. It commonly occurs in response to ocular pain. Repetitive blepharospasm, which may have a serious impact on quality of life,[1] or make the patient effectively blind, is a focal dystonia (*OHCM* p 342). If the condition is not recognized, it is all too easy to dismiss the patient as hysterical and to think that screwing up of the eyes is deliberate—especially, the more the sceptical doctor questions and probes the afflicted patient, the worse the blepharospasm may become (stress is an important exacerbating factor). It is important to understand that it may have a serious negative impact on patients' lives. 122

Presentation ♀:♂ ≈1.8:1. Blepharospasm is often preceded by exaggerated blinking. Other dystonias may be present (eg oro-mandibular). It usually starts unilaterally, becoming bilateral. Patients may develop various tricks to reduce blepharospasm such as touching or pulling the eyelids—a variation of *geste antagoniste* seen in other forms of dystonia.

Causes Mostly unknown. Recognized antecedent events are: neuroleptic drugs, Parkinson's disease, progressive supranuclear palsy.

Treatment ***Drugs:*** Response is variable; good effects may wear off. Try anticholinergics (trihexyphenidyl, eg 1mg/day PO, max 5mg/6h; tablets are 2mg or 5mg). Dopamine agonists (L-dopa, bromocriptine) may help. ***Botulinum neurotoxin:*** Palliation is achieved with nanogram doses given to orbicularis oculi, in which it produces a temporary flaccid paralysis. It can help some people recover effective vision. It binds to peripheral nerve terminals and inhibits the release of acetylcholine. Treatment may need to be repeated, eg 3-monthly. ***Supportive treatment:*** If the cause is compensation for apraxia of lid opening, wearing goggles may help. 123

Support is available from the UK Dystonia Society. tel: 0207 329 0797

Allergic eye disease

Allergic conjunctivitis is common, causing itch and eye watering with mild conjunctival congestion (red) and swelling (chemosis). Cold compresses may help. *Prescription drops:* levocabastine (/12h) may be better than nedocromil (/12h). 124 *Alternative:* azelastine. RCT 125

Over-the-counter drops: cromoglicate 2% (/6h). 126 [N=185]

Vernal keratoconjunctivitis (spring catarrh; seasonal conjunctivitis) This is an uncommon allergic bilateral conjunctivitis, usually appearing before puberty, and lasting ≥5yrs. ♂/♀>1. There is often a family history of atopy. It is almost non-existent in cold areas. ***Presentation:***

- Itching eye ± photophobia
- 'Cobblestones' under upper lid
- Pseudomembrane (Maxwell-Lyon)
- Milky conjunctiva and ropy discharge
- Papillae in lower tarsal conjunctiva
- Corneal arcus (± ulcer) near limbus

Management: If this is a very difficult problem to manage. Refer. In severe conditions, ophthalmologists will use steroid drops and taper it off. Cromoglicate (mast cell stabilizing agent) drops 2%(/6h) will be prescribed concomitantly and maintained till spring is over.

Delayed hypersensitivity: phlyctenular keratoconjunctivitis This may be a delayed response to mycobacteria, staphs, yeasts, or chlamydia. The conjunctival phlyctenule begins as a hard, red, 1-3mm diameter papule surrounded by hyperaemia. At the limbus, it is triangular (apex points to cornea). It ulcerates, and then subsides within 12 days. Corneal phlyctenules develop as an amorphous grey infiltrate, and leave a scar. They may cause intense photophobia. ***Management:*** Seek expert help. Steroid drops may help. Treat any bacterial cause. 127

1 Reimer J 2005 *Acta Neurol Scand* **111** 64.

Floaters, flashes, and haloes

When patients complain of flashes and floaters think of retinal detachment. When patients mention their haloes they may not be referring to their own saintliness. Halo = a circle of light, sometimes white or coloured, seen around any luminous body, eg [illegible] of saints. Also [illegible] cataracts (a cause of halo)—this not to imply that the great impressionist paintings are [illegible] in light (another definition of halo).

[illegible] there are no haloes [illegible] caused by old age on an [illegible] [illegible] in Paris [illegible] [illegible] and [illegible] the vision of gas lamps or streets [illegible] Monet reflects [illegible] how difficult [illegible] doctors and artists see the world. So before we recommend surgery it might be as well to get to know our patient's eyes as well as [illegible] poster!)

Floaters These are small dark spots in the visual field, particularly noticeable against a bright background. The cause is often degenerative: opacities in the vitreous (synchysis); here each floater is a shadow of a mobile vitreous opacity cast on the retina. After the eye comes to rest, they [illegible] more. They are common in myopes, after cataract operations, or after trauma. Mostly they are just annoying (if central), but [illegible] settle with time [illegible] the vitreous and retina before [illegible].

Sudden showers of floaters appearing in one eye (which may be accompanied by flashing lights) are due to [illegible]: refer immediately, as the cause may be retinal detachment (p [illegible]). Other causes:

- Diabetic retinopathy
- Old retinal branch vein occlusion
- Posterior vitreous bleeding
- Hypertension
- Endocarditis
- Sickle cell [illegible]
- Leukaemia
- [illegible]
- [illegible]

Flashing lights (photopsia) These may be from [illegible] or migraine—is there headache [illegible] or [illegible]? Detachment of the vitreous from the retina [illegible] gives flashes and floaters [illegible] retinal detachment. [illegible] is usually peripheral [illegible] immediately [illegible].

[illegible] **retinal detachment** [illegible] (it [illegible] concern) [illegible] is [illegible] field loss [illegible]. [illegible] are due to pulling on the retina, and [illegible] with eye movements. Field loss [illegible] [illegible] of vision [illegible] retinal detachment and [illegible] Falling acuity [illegible] detachments [illegible] the macula is affected, [illegible] vision [illegible] remains poor even after successful surgery.

Floaters [illegible] [illegible] field defects [illegible].

Haloes may be from acute [illegible] glaucoma [illegible] coloured [illegible] around lights are [illegible] seen when a white light [illegible] lights have haloes when seen through [illegible] or through [illegible] may also be the cause [illegible] corneal [illegible].

In acute glaucoma [illegible] haloes [illegible] intraocular pressure [illegible] with pupillary dilatation [illegible] by [illegible] consider this diagnosis and [illegible].

[illegible] haloes which [illegible] due to migraine [illegible] haloes [illegible] migraine [illegible] have not previously suffered from migraine.

[illegible]

Floaters, flashes, and haloes

►*When patients complain of flashes and floaters think of retinal detachment.* When patients mention their haloes they may not be referring to their own saintliness. *Halo* refers to a circle of light, either white or coloured, seen around *any* luminous body: not just those of saints. Also call to mind Monet and his cataracts (a cause of haloes). It is not simply that his great impressionist paintings are investments in light (another definition of *halo*)...

Doctor, you say there are no haloes
around the streetlights in Paris
and what I see is an aberration
caused by old age, an affliction.[1]
I tell you it has taken me all my life
to arrive at the vision of gas lamps as angels

Here, Monet refuses surgery for his cataracts (how differently doctors and artists see the world!). So before we recommend surgery it might be as well to get to know our patients a bit, as well as keeping a weather-eye on posterity.

Floaters These are small dark spots in the visual field, particularly noticeable against a bright background. The cause is often degenerative opacities in the vitreous (syneresis), here, each floater is a shadow of a mobile vitreous opacity cast on the retina. After the eye comes to rest, they continue to move. They are common in myopes, after cataract operations or after trauma. Mostly, they are just annoying (if central), but harmless, and may settle with time. Examine the vitreous and retina before reassuring.

Sudden showers of floaters appearing in one eye (which may be accompanied by flashing lights) are due to blood. ►*Refer immediately*, as the cause may be retinal detachment (p 444). Other causes:

- Diabetic retinopathy
- Old retinal branch vein occlusion
- Recurrent vitreous bleeding
- Hypertension
- Endocarditis
- Sickle-cell dis.
- Leukaemia
- Sarcoid
- TB; SLE

Flashing lights (photopsia) These may be from intraocular pathology or migraine. Is there headache, nausea, or previous migraine? Detachment of a shrinking vitreous from the retina (commoner in myopes) gives flashes and floaters. 5% go on to retinal tears and detachment. Retinal damage is usually peripheral and hard to see—refer immediately for specialist help.

4 'F's of retinal detachment • Floaters (numerous, acute onset, constant, and described as 'spider's web' • Flashes • Field loss (acute, progressive) • Falling acuity. Flashes are due to pulling on the retina, and may increase with eye movement. Field loss may be seen as a dark cloud covering a field of vision (superior field loss indicates inferior retinal detachment and vice versa). Falling acuity indicates a grave situation. Superior detachments may be fast so that the macula is affected, resulting in 6/60 vision. In this situation vision remains poor even after successful surgery.

Floaters in vitreous separation *(∵ Aggregates of collagen fibres)* • Gradual onset • Vision unaffected • Few in number • No field defects • Non-urgent.

Haloes may be from acute angle closure glaucoma. Smooth, coloured haloes around lights are diffractive phenomena, being seen when a white light is inside a steamed-up window (street lights have haloes when seen through misted windscreens), or through scratched spectacles. Hazy ocular media may also be the cause (cataract; corneal oedema).

In acute glaucoma it is corneal oedema that causes them as intraocular pressure rises with pupillary dilatation. If haloes are accompanied by eye pain consider this diagnosis and refer immediately.

Jagged haloes which change shape are usually due to migraine. Beware labelling haloes as being migrainous in patients over 50 years who have not previously suffered from migraine.

1 Lisel Mueller 1986 *Monet Refuses the Operation* in *Second Language*. See M Faith McLellan 1996 (*Lancet* 1996 **348** 1641)—to whom this page owes much—for a critique of this poem.

Refractive procedures

Refractive procedures are now increasingly undertaken as an alternative to wearing spectacles, mostly for cosmetic reasons. Occasionally, they are undertaken for anisometropia (imbalance of prescriptions) for astigmatism after surgery, or for intolerance of spectacles or contact lenses. A variation of PRK (photorefractive keratotomy) may be undertaken for some corneal diseases. Lasik (see below) is now the commonest procedure. It is well researched and in terms of surgical procedures is extremely safe but there are possible complications. It should be noted that the majority of ophthalmologists wear spectacles!

Radial keratotomy This is historical and should no longer be done. It involved surgical incisions of the peripheral cornea to alter the curvature.

Photorefractive keratotomy (PRK) This is an entirely laser treatment where the curved front of the cornea is altered by laser ablation. It is only done for low degrees of myopia and is less predictable than Lasik, with some people having under-correction and others over-correction. Occasionally some people develop corneal haze with reduced vision, glare, and haloes afterwards. In the majority of low myopes it gives good outcome but it is very painful for a few days.

Lasik (laser-assisted in situ keratomileusis) This is a combination of minor surgery where the cornea is incised and an extremely thin trapdoor shaped flap hinged away and then laser is applied to the bare corneal stroma underneath. Thereafter the flap is pushed back into position and adheres naturally. It is, surprisingly, virtually painless, settles very quickly and is fairly predictable in its outcome. Corneal sensitivity recovers after ~6 months. A thin flap with a nasally placed hinge is associated with the most rapid recovery of corneal sensitivity.[1] It is possible to undertake surgery on much greater degrees of refractive error, with up to 5 diopters of hypermetropia, 5 diopters of astigmatism and 15 diopters of myopia. Serious complications are rare but trauma to or infection of the flap may result in permanent corneal scarring.

Other procedures These are much less commonly undertaken. They include insertion of perspex rings into the cornea, other laser techniques to alter corneal curvature, and surgery to the sclera to attempt to correct presbyopia. They are much less certain in outcome and are best regarded as experimental.

1 Nassaralla B 2005 Am J Ophthalmol 139 18

Refractive procedures

Refractive procedures are now increasingly undertaken as an alternative to wearing spectacles; mostly for cosmetic reasons. Occasionally they are undertaken for anisometropia (imbalance of prescriptions); for astigmatism after surgery; or for intolerance of spectacles or contact lenses. A variation of PRK (photorefractive keratotomy) may be undertaken for some corneal diseases. Lasik (see below) is now the commonest procedure. It is well researched and in terms of surgical procedures is extremely safe but there are possible complications. It should be noted that the majority of ophthalmologists wear spectacles!

Radial keratotomy This is historical and should no longer be done. It involved surgical incisions of the peripheral cornea to alter the curvature.

Photorefractive keratotomy (PRK) This is an entirely laser treatment where the curved front of the cornea is altered by laser ablation. It is only done for low degrees of myopia and is less predictable than Lasik with some people having under-correction and others over-correction. Occasionally some people develop corneal haze with reduced vision, glare, and haloes afterwards. In the majority of low myopes it gives good outcome but it is very painful for a few days.

Lasik (laser assisted *in situ* keratomileusis) This is a combination of minor surgery where the cornea is incised and an extremely thin trapdoor shaped flap hinged away and then laser is applied to the bare corneal stroma underneath. Thereafter the flap is pushed back into position and adheres naturally. It is, surprisingly, virtually painless, settles very quickly, and is fairly predictable in its outcome. Corneal sensitivity recovers after ~6 months. A thin flap with a nasally placed hinge is associated with the most rapid recovery of corneal sensitivity.[1] It is possible to undertake surgery on much greater degrees of refractive error; with up to 5 diopters of hypermetropia; 5 diopters of astigmatism; and 15 diopters of myopia. Serious complications are rare but trauma to or infection of the flap may result in permanent corneal scarring.

Other procedures These are much less commonly undertaken. They include insertion of perspex rings into the cornea; other laser techniques to alter corneal curvature; and surgery to the sclera to attempt to correct presbyopia. They are much less certain in outcome and are best regarded as experimental.

1 Nassaralla B 2005 *Am J Ophthalmol* **139** 18.

6 Primary care

Relevant pages elsewhere: ►*Every page in all chapters.* All diseases are relevant. This is a key feature of primary care which is the axis around which all medical events revolve, every day drawing millions of patients to it before scattering a few to every corner of the medical world. Only in primary care is the full gamut of what can go wrong with people's lives made manifest. Because of the huge and undefined range of general practice, it has been said (not just by GPs) that the general practitioner 'needs to be the most comprehensively educated of any kind of doctor'.

Primary care is not a specialty in the usual sense, and GPs make much of being the only remaining generalists (they were also the first). They are specialists in their patients, rather than in diseases—having no special and unique knowledge of disease (except for disease in its earliest stage), and having no unique treatments. They can answer questions like '*Why doesn't Miss Phelps ever attend the antenatal clinic? What would have to change for her to do so?*' There are few medical instances in which GPs are in a position to offer more skill and expertise than all other doctors—but there are many circumstances when the GP's understanding of his patient is what counts, and for which no amount of expertise can be a substitute. So when, for example, Miss Phelps's baby dies, to whom does she turn in her distress? She is not a medical problem; she is not an obstetric problem; she is not even a psychiatric problem—she is Miss Phelps. And the doctor who specializes in Miss Phelps is (or ought to be) her GP. He is the one who knows what to do and what to say; when to be quiet and when to explain; and when to appear and when to disappear, humbled as he is by having witnessed a wealth of such grief.

With *knowledge of the patient*, and *knowledge of disease in its earliest phase*, there is a third skill which is vital: the *ability to diagnose health* taking into account all the definitions of health on p 470. If a patient is asking 'Am I well, or could I have cancer' the doctor who is always responding by saying '... Well, I'm not sure ... let's do one more test ...' is sometimes a bad doctor, and always an expensive one. Some doctors have the gift of appraising a patient, and knowing almost instinctively whether to treat now, or investigate, or refer, or reassure. Nowhere is this skill more apparent than in general practice—and this instinctive skill is born of countless contacts with patients from all walks of life, with diseases affecting any organ of the body or mind. A chest physician may tell you that your lungs are healthy, but if, on your way out, you say 'Oh, and I've also got this pain in my leg ...'—then he may feel out of his territory. He thought he was sending his patient away rejoicing in his health, but then one new symptom undermines this, and he is likely to end up saying 'Go and see your GP'. It is then up to the GP to reassure, treat, or to orchestrate the deployment of all the many sophistications of technological medicine.

Even if all our scientists had unlimited abilities and facilities, there would still be a limit to technological medicine. Even if we could turn the whole world into a hospital so skilled as to be able to manipulate the totality of the *milieu intérieur* there would still be a vast abyss between the possibility of health and its attainment. On the other side of the abyss is the patient, surrounded by unknown (but not unknowable) myths, hopes, fears, ideas, expectations, and fantasies directing him away from the very things that could help him most. It is the GP's role to bridge this abyss, not so much to haul the patient to safety, but rather to be the platform on which the patient crosses of his own (enlightened) free will. In bridging this gap, the GP needs sure foundations on both of its sides, and this is the great challenge of general practice—to foster in oneself an equal love of, and an excellence in, both the technological and the personal realm.

Although primary care is not a specialty in the usual sense, it *is* a discipline, as it creates and publishes original material about its sphere of activity in peer-reviewed journals (eg *British Journal of General Practice*; *Journal of Family Practice*). As such journals are the lifeblood at the scientific heart of the discipline, they are often hard to read, but they repay careful study.

Giving yourself to the highest bidder?

A healthy man is, above all, a man of this earth, and he must, therefore, only live the life of this earth for the sake of order and completeness. But as soon as he falls ill, as soon as the normal earthly order of his organism is disturbed, the possibility of another world begins to become more apparent, and the more ill he is, the more closely does he come into touch with the other world.[1]

We do not always understand the worlds inhabited by our patients but because of this, do not assume that our patients must travel these worlds alone. Taking time to find out what it's like for our patients is the first step in forging an enduring doctor-patient relationship. When our patients know that we are travelling with them, and that we will not abandon them, they will accept our foibles, even our errors. But how can we cope with this big commitment—big enough for one person, let alone a few thousand of our dependent patients? How can we do all this without destroying ourselves? Do we give in to the highest bidder? Here are some insights from a woman in a crisis with too many conflicting roles: daughter, mother, lover, and so on: 'There is a battle going on for my soul ... and I cannot just give it to the highest bidder. I have an interest in it too ... I have a duty to many people and somehow I will discharge it. I have a duty also to some continuing part of myself. I have ... ripped open my self-protective layers. I see now what I am. It's not a question of "happiness". I don't value my own more—or much less than anyone else's. It's something more lasting: it's a question of being faithful to an essence'.[2]

If we spend day after day in surgery without attending to our other roles we are not necessarily better than a person who leaves work on time, so enabling a visit to a grandparent, or a dialogue with a daughter, or time for recreation. The medical world encourages the dangerous delusion that we are somehow inadequate if we do not give our all. What gives rise to this is the delusion that the best unit of measurement of our medical lives is the single consultation. This is how we are assessed, as if there were no valid distractions during consultations—as if our own needs were non-existent, and 100% of the focus is placed on the patient sitting in front of us. But what if you should not really be seeing this patient at all, but should be out on a visit which might or might not be urgent? Or would it be better to be on the phone, talking to a possibly suicidal patient who has missed their appointment? Perhaps you need to do all three. Then you will do none of them well. If we are going to be successful in primary care, with its unending responsibilities, we have to recognize that the best doctors may not do anything *very* well. The best doctors just make the least bad decisions on how to spend their time, and themselves. As with the woman above, they do not simply give their soul to the highest bidder. Don't feel guilty about this. To give yourself to the highest bidder would be a betrayal: not even saints do this.

1 Dostoevsky *Crime And Punishment* Tr D Magashack, Penguin 305, www.bartleby.com/318/41.html
2 Sebastian Faulks 2001 *On Green Dolphin Street*, Hutchinson, 239

An English dictionary of primary care acronyms

►*If you speak the language, you may eventually come to understand it.*

ACBS Advisory committee on borderline substances; prescriptions thus endorsed reclassify special foods (eg without gluten) as a free drug
AGMS Alternative general medical services (non-NHS, purchased by PCTs)
CHI Commission for health improvement—aims to improve standards by: assessing NHS organizations and publicly investigating failure—and checking that the NHS is following national guidelines. It advises on best practice
CPN Community psychiatric nurse
DES Directed enhanced services (see LES and NES)
DoH/DSS Government department of health/department of social services
DNA Did not attend (for a booked appointment ≈ waste of NHS resources)
EBM Evidence-based medicine, or the journal of the same name
ECR Extracontractual referral; ie no existing contract exists (∴ costly)
EHR Electronic health record accessible anywhere in the NHS; doesn't exist
FMed 3 & 5 Forms for sick pay, p 522
FP10 The form on which NHS prescriptions are written—ie scrip(t)s
GMC General medical council
HIMP Health improvement & modernization program, eg ↓ smoking rates
IM&T Information management and technology
LES Locally agreed enhanced service (see NES and DES)
LIS Local implementation strategy, eg for IM&T
LMC Local medical committee (which approves or withholds approval for various centrally promulgated non-statutory health policies)
MASTA Medical advisory service for travellers abroad www.masta.org/
MCP Male chauvinist pig; medical care practitioner, ½-way between nurse & GP
MDU/MPS Medical defence union and the medical protection society
MeSH Medical subheadings used in medline searches, see p 504
NELH National electronic library for health www.nelh.nhs.uk/
NES National enhanced service eg GPs monitoring patients response to disease-modifying drugs in rheumatology (liaising with the consultant)
NHS National health service: a system for providing health services universally free at the point of use, funded out of general taxation
NICE National institute of clinical excellence
NMC Nursing and midwifery council (replaces UKCC)
NPSA National patient safety agency for reporting critical incidents
NSF National service framework (eg for diabetes, heart disease etc, p 523)
OTC Over the counter medicine
PACT® Trademark of the prescription pricing authority (PPA)
PCO Primary care organization (usually a Trust—PCT)
PDP Personal development plan (see *appraisals*, p 508) & emisPDP.com
POM Prescription-only medicine
PRODIGY Prescribing advice triggered by entering Read codes
QMAS Quality management analysis system (nationally agreed way of extracting data from GP computer systems to quantify quality points for QOF)
QOF Quality and outcomes framework (in the UK, getting paid by results, eg if 74% of diabetics have an Hb_{A1c} <7.4% and BP <145/85)
RCT Randomized controlled trial
SaFF Service and financial framework—a financial plan
SFE Statement of financial entitlement (NHS)
SLS Selected list scheme; written on an FP10, this makes Viagra etc free, eg if DM, MS, parkinsonism, prostate ca, spina bifida, cord injury or polio
SMR Standardized mortality ratios
SPN Supplementary prescribing nurse (p 474)
TQM Total quality management www.eiro.eurofound.ie/1997/05/Feature/UK9705113F.html
DVLA Driving vehicle licensing authority www.dvla.gov.uk/at_a_glance/content.htm

Some definitions and measures of health

Primary care and distributive justice There is a famous WHO Alma-Ata statement which declares that primary care should 'be made universally accessible to individuals and families in the community, by means acceptable to them, through their full participation, and at the cost that the community and country can afford to maintain in the spirit of self-reliance … [and] addresses the main health problems in the community, providing promotive, preventative, curative and rehabilitative services accordingly'. Factors affecting access to health include finance, ideology, and education.

Six GP job descriptions (Compare triage clinics with 'normal surgery'.)

- To clear the waiting room *efficiently* (*kindly* if possible) only spending yourself *et al* to gain specified worthwhile health gains. (*No time wasters, please!*)
- 'Get me better, so that I can go on doing the things that made me ill …'
- To do whatever the patient wants, within the law, usually. (*I'm a nice guy.*)
- To deal with local realities (loneliness, addiction, poverty, and mental illness) rather than hoping for diagnostic wonders to test your brilliance.
- To be skilled in: prioritization; delegation; health-need measurement; rationing; purchasing/delivery of healthcare; time- and staff-management.
- To care for people irrespective of age, sex, sexual orientation, race, illness, or social status. To make early diagnoses, framed in physical, psychological, and social terms. To make initial decisions about all problems presented or unearthed. To arrange continuing care of chronic, recurrent, or terminal illness. To practise in co-operation with colleagues, medical and nonmedical. To treat, prevent, and educate to promote health of patients and families, while reconciling professional responsibility to the community.

Health Five definitions to compare: **1** Health is the absence of disease—or:
2 A state of complete physical, mental, and social wellbeing. WHO definition [1]
3 A process of adaptation, to changing environments, to growing up and ageing, to healing when damaged, to suffering, and death. Health embraces the future so includes anguish and the inner resources to live with it. I Illisch, 1976
4 Any process enabling the giving or promoting of life.
5 'Health is whatever works, and for as long'. J Stone, 1980, *In All This Rain* [2]

All the above have limitations, but 1 and 4 seem least counter-intuitive. Consider the following: • Was Charles I healthy as he laid his head on the executioner's block? • What about a priest in the act of losing his celibacy? • Can a heart with a prosthetic valve which is gradually wearing out be healthy? • Was Gandhi healthy at the end of a hunger strike? • Can animals or babies be healthy? • What about death in childbirth? 'Answers' below:

	Healthy according to definition:				
	1	2	3	4	5
King Charles on the scaffold	yes	no	yes	yes	no
Fasting Ghandi	yes	no	yes	yes	yes
Babies and animals	yes	yes	no	yes	yes
Heart with failing valve	no	no	no	yes	yes
Priest losing his celibacy	yes	no	yes	yes	yes
Death in childbirth	no	no	yes	yes	yes

Measuring health Scores on the health survey Short Form 36 (SF36) are reproducible and quantifiable, related to patients' clinical state, the GP's decision to refer, and GP's views on severity. It is valid when combined with a patient-generated index of quality of life ('name the 5 chief activities/areas affected by your condition … and rank importance of improvements to them') and a daily time trade-off calculation (how much time would you give up to be in perfect health?). By combining instruments, defects in one can be mitigated (eg the SF36 asks if health limits your ability to walk a mile—irrelevant if you do not need or want to walk much). ***Health need*** is the difference between the state now and a goal. Needs may be ranked by the distances between states and goals.

What are the determinants of health?

One answer is ***wealth***. With wealth comes more stable political systems, and these are what are necessary for literacy and education to flourish, which in turn leads to easy access to clean water (the key issue, as more than 1 billion people have no such access), and the possibility of developing equitable health delivery systems. After clean water, the next steps focus on better nutrition, smaller families, more self-help, and anti-HIV strategies.

►*How do you move a Western post-industrial population from a low level of health to a higher level of health?* It's no good relying on the altruism of doctors to introduce public health measures into every consultation. A more systematic method is needed. Since 2004, UK NHS primary care has been a vast multi-million pound test-bed of a payment-by-results system. Over 25% doctors' income can now depend on meeting very specific targets, eg: '70% of hypertensives to have BP ≤150/90'; '60% of those with ischaemic heart disease to have cholesterol ≤5mmol/L'. For diabetics: '50% to have an Hb_{A1c} ≤7.4% and 55% to have BP ≤145/85'—etc. How successful are these targets? It is too early to quantify this, but most practices worked very hard and met most targets (*far* more than were expected). So the conclusion is that you need money *and* altruism to improve population heath. For the down-side of payment-by-results, see p 490.

Future determinants of health are thought to rest on:

- Reducing inequalities in access to health care, and in its content.
- Decline in tobacco consumption in all age groups.
- Better health services with more effective, more acceptable treatments.
- Fewer underdoctored areas (currently defined as populations where there are fewer than 52.695 GPs per 100,000—ie a list size of >1898 per whole-time GP)—and more GPs in deprived areas. Funding more GPs has been calculated as one of the most efficient ways of reducing mortality.
- Education capable of influencing behaviour to ↓exposure to risk factors.
- Better protection of the environment and better housing.
- More patient-centred health care, so that patients are not passive recipients of care, but well-educated partners in the struggle against disease.

Core competencies European academy of teachers in general practice EURACT

1 Dealing with unselected problems covering *all* health issues, co-ordinating care with other professionals in primary care and with other specialists.
2 Adopting a person-centred approach—seeing patients in the context of social realities; using the consultation to bring about an effective doctor-patient relationship, with respect for the patient's autonomy; to communicate, set priorities, and act in partnership; to provide longitudinal continuity of care as determined by the needs of the patient.
3 To adopt appropriate working principles, such as incremental investigation, using time as a tool, and to tolerate uncertainty.
4 Being able to manage many simultaneous complaints and pathologies—acute and chronic—at the same time as promoting health and well being—by applying health promotion and disease prevention strategies.
5 Community orientation includes the ability to reconcile health needs of individual patients and those of the community in which they live.
6 Holistic modelling[1]: the ability to use a bio-psycho-social model taking into account cultural and existential[2] dimensions in non-reductionist thinking.

1 ***Holism:*** (holon is Greek for *entity*) the tendency in nature to form wholes, that are greater than the sum of the parts, through creative evolution—Jan Smuts 1926. This process is called 'emergence'.
2 ***Existential*** here implies more than just spiritual—it means that 'everything affects health' See Joshua Freeman 2005 *BJBP* 55 154. Existential need not always mean wearing black jeans and black polo-neck jerseys and singing about one's angst. "The song is sung, not after it has come to be, but rather: in the singing the song begins to be a song."—an example of ***non-reductionist thinking***; see Heidegger.

Primary health care

Primary care core activities:
• Ensuring freedom from want: safe food, water[etc]
• Basic illness treatment
• Provision of drugs
• Preventive care (p 482)
• Enabling Maslow's hierarchy (p 315)

Primary care is the care we access as our first contact with health services. Where needed, referrals are made (in ~10% of UK patients) to secondary care, eg district hospitals. Tertiary referral to regional centres may then occur. This seductively simple model misses out entirely on the cornerstone of primary health care: the responsibility that individuals and families have for their own physical and mental wellbeing. ►*90% of health problems are taken care of outside official health care systems.* Unless individuals and families act on their own initiative to promote their health, no amount of medical care is going to make them healthy; coronary artery bypass grafting may be helpful, but it is no substitute for families taking the initiative in promoting their own health by trying to live sensibly (diet, smoking, etc). In fostering and enlightening this sense of initiative, many groups are involved: doctors, teachers, health educators, politicians and, above all, families. In assessing how good a community is at primary health care, one needs to look not just at medical care, but also at social, political, and cultural aspects. Ask questions such as: *Is society making it easy for individuals to choose a healthy lifestyle?* and *How is society targeting health education?* and *Is this 'education' in fact indoctrination?* 'What you are being taught is an amalgam of current prejudice and the choices of this particular culture. The slightest look at history will show how impermanent these must be.' Doris Lessing *The Golden Notebook*

Primary health care defined as a strategy No country in the world is rich enough to provide its citizens with everything that medical care can offer. This fact pinpoints the need for the efficient use of limited resources—and this presupposes an effective system of primary health care. To be effective, this must be accessible; relevant to the population's needs; properly integrated; have full community participation; be cost-effective, and characterized by collaboration between sectors of society.

Some UK-based facts • GP services are <10% of total NHS *costs*.
• 90% of illness known to the NHS are handled in general practice.
• The number of principals (unrestricted) in England is ~31,200[4] with ~2400 GP registrars, and ≥900 retainers.[5] Supporting staff: ≥2 per whole-time GP.

Intermediate care[6]

This newly named type of care lies between traditional primary care and secondary care. It integrates facilities from many areas to address complex health needs which do not require use of district general hospital services. Examples include pre-admission assessment units; early and supported discharge schemes; community (cottage) hospitals; domiciliary stroke units; hospitals-at-home schemes; rehabilitation units. It is one of the mechanisms by which health and social services mesh to allow patients to receive the most appropriate care. Its main advantages are that it is said to allow:
1 Care close to home. 2 Best use of new technology, eg information technology, near-patient testing, and phone-activated devices to summon help. 3 Cost-effective use of resources. 4 Less rigidly demarcated professional roles. 5 Creative integration of working practices. Don't think of it simply as reducing bed-blocking, but it can.[7] It may also be more expensive than traditional care.[1] NB: intermediate care also offers GPs a route to developing a special interest (GPSI). This option needs careful economic scrutiny: it's not obvious that such care will be cheaper, as someone else has to do the work of the GP while she is doing the special interest.[8]

1 Nurse-led intermediate care for those recovering from acute illness is a costly option. *BMJ* 2005.

Self-care and empowered self-care

Simple self-care constitutes the health activities which we do on our own and within families—such as brushing our teeth, or going to bed with aspirins during 'flu. Empowered self-care is what can happen when primary, secondary (district general hospital), and tertiary care (eg regional burns units and cancer specialisms) work together with social services within the context of the family life cycle. Crucially, it uses the principles of intermediate care (see OPPOSITE). ►*Of any health care system, ask how rich and deep are its community roots?* How many options are there for the care of this sick old lady who has a bad chest and is temporarily off her feet? If your health care system lacks depth, and if ties of religion and family are loose, the only option may be an emergency admission to a high-technology hospital. Emergency admissions in the UK and many other areas have been climbing inexorably—for many reasons. One important reason is lack of options at the primary care level.

Whenever you think of admitting a patient to hospital, ask ►***What are the other options?*** Do this not just to save the hospital work, but to force you to find out what your patient really wants, and to ensure that the most appropriate level of care is found.

Options not entailing admission:

- Neighbourly help
- Hospice
- Sheltered housing
- Hospital at home
- Nursing/rest home
- Social services home
- Twilight home nurses
- Domiciliary physio
- Occupational therapy
- Fast-response nursing

When you think of these options, don't think ***doctors or nurses?***—think ***universal health worker***. Universal health workers have various skills: find out about them, and judge them not according to historic professional codes but according to how good they are at empowering self-care. No health service can look after most patients most of the time. Empowered self-care in the context of interdependent social and medical services is not some new option that may or may not be used: it is the *only* option for health services which aim to look after more than one patient. Without this idea of empowered self-care hospitals become places of passive dependency, they get too full, and you cannot get people in, and you cannot get people out. NB: if you think that empowered self-care is a cliché, try doing your diabetic clinic without it: you will always fail.

Empowered self-care entails choice (p 99 & p 315), dialogue (p 370 & p 517), knowledge of mental states (p 324) informed consent (p 614 & p 12), literacy/education (p 494), participation in planning and respect by professionals for lifeworlds other than their own (p 321). We have to harmonize our care-plans with the patient's belief system. So if, for example, a man takes strength from meditation, this should feed into the dialogues which inform his empowered self-care. This yields more patient satisfaction ***and*** improved outcomes: see p 517.[9,10,11]

Barriers to this type of care

- People who are rendered helpless and hopeless by unemployment, poverty, and family strife. Others who have difficulty accessing care include: the homeless, refugees, drug abusers, ethnic minority groups, and patients living in rural areas without public transport.
- Professionals who want to monopolize and medicalize health.
- Nations which are keener to take up arms than to vaccinate them.
- A world which behaves as if it does not know the meaning of social justice and equality, and in which rich and poor fail to share common objectives—or simply fail to share anything.

Primary health care teams

Whenever a task can be successfully delegated, delegate it. The antithesis is: *If you want a job done properly, do it yourself.* Nature favours the first maxim: when we die all our tasks are either forgotten or delegated, often by default. So the question is not *whether* to delegate, but *when*, and *to whom*. The principle of team work is: ***No member is indispensable; all can contribute.*** Teams may be small and close-knit, or large—for example the NHS 'super surgery', with doctors, dentists, opticians, a pharmacy, and heart clinics.[et al]

Doctors ***Principals/partners:*** Some may specialize (eg diabetes, endoscopy), or have a role in the Primary Care Organization (PCO), eg in commissioning hospital care; ***GP non-principals/locums***; ***registrars***; ***pre-registration house physicians***. Medical and other students may also be present.

A good question for any partnership to ask is 'what is our range of skills, and is postgraduate training being arranged to fill in any lacunae?' GPs with a special interests need not undermine the central role of being a generalist.

Community nurses (Employed in England by Primary Care Trusts.) Activities: post-op visits for dressings and the removal of sutures, dressing leg ulcers, and giving 'all care' to the elderly housebound, giving injections (eg to blind diabetic patients), and supplying incontinence and other aids ± catheterizations. ***Nurse prescribers*** have additional training (≥37 days) and are termed ***Independent*** or ***Supplementary Nurse Prescribers*** (SNP). SNPs only prescribe according to protocols once a diagnosis has been made.[12]

Midwives They do antenatal classes, clinics, home visits, and home deliveries. They have a statutory obligation to visit in the puerperium for the 1st 10 days (she has right of access). At 10 days the health visitor takes over.

Health visitors have nursing and midwifery backgrounds, plus health visiting qualifications. Roles: developmental testing of children; immunization advice; breast feeding; minor illness in children; handicap; advice to adults about diet & smoking; implementing health education officer (p 494) strategies; screening of the elderly in their homes; bereavement visits.

Practice nurses activities include: • ***Tests:*** Urine; blood (best delegated to a phlebotomy-trained receptionist, with a 'health assistant' role); audiometry; ECGs; peak flow. • ***Advice:*** Diet; travel. • ***Treatment:*** Ear syringing; injections. • ***Prevention & audit:*** Vaccinations; BP; cervical smears; family planning/IUCDs (eg holding an English national board certificate). • ***Chronic disease:*** Diabetes, asthma, COPD, heart disease, etc. • ***Chaperoning:*** Usually she is too busy.

Nurse practitioners diagnose and initiate treatment. Patient satisfaction is high. No increase in adverse outcomes has been found; consultations are longer by 3–4 minutes, and more tests are done.[13] [RCT 14] **Community matrons** are a new and controversial idea—each has a case-load of ~60 vulnerable patients—eg with multiple pathologies such as CCF and a tendency to fall. She gives home care (*active case management*) aiming to ↓emergency admissions (which might fall by up to 6% on the most optimistic forecasts).[15]

Counsellors 30% of GP patients have psychological conditions, and to help with these, counsellors may be employed; their role is uncertain (p 381).[16]

Receptionists and secretaries Receptionists may take on a ***health assistant role*** taking blood, testing urines, doing BPs, capillary glucose, ECGs, or audits. Encourage hepatitis B vaccination. With the advent of e-mail referrals direct from the GP's desk, the role of secretaries is being re-defined.

Practice managers lead on: finance; employment law; tax; risk assessment/reduction; health & safety; finance; audit; commissioning care contracts.

Others Social worker, psychologist, physiotherapist. ***Beyond the surgery:*** NHS direct; NHS walk-in services; nurse-led personal medical services; community pharmacists, health education officers (p 494), community physicians.

Single-handed and small practices

In the UK, much of the progress in general practice over the recent past has evolved in the context of group practice and the primary health care team—the credo of modern-day doctoring. Single-handedness puts a question mark over the primacy and validity of these ideas. The benefits of highly ordered, management-led, high-investment, team-based general practice are real and not to be gainsaid; larger practices may also have easier rotas, with possible benefits to the mental health of GPs. But at what price have these benefits been bought? Can small be beautiful?—and what does this concept mean for health care the world over? Let us start with the observation that general practice is about people. Their illnesses are the incidental accidents, and their deaths the only certainties which mark the impingement of these individuals on our general practice nights and days. These emergency contacts are, for the larger practices, usually boring or worse. There is no before or after: just a job to be done. For the single-handed GP doing more of his or her own visiting, these occasions may also be boring—initially. But the utility and the interest inherent in these visits can, with continuity of care, stretch over the decades, as this example illustrates. One of us (JML) was called to an unrousable, sweating 60-year-old man, whom we admitted to hospital with suspected septicaemia—which, years later, turned out to be the presenting symptom of an occult, indolent malignancy. We looked after him until his death at home. The continuity of care made the job interesting for us, not the clinical details. But the continuity does not stop at the end of one life. Now, whenever we see his wife, on however trivial or grave a problem, we have this shared bond. Recently she refused hospital admission for pneumonia, and the doctor could use this shared bond to induce her, over a a day or so, to change her mind. Of course, doctors in large groups will be able to tell of similar instances. Our point here is simply that these stories are more common, the more personal your care. Small practices may be best placed to counter the rising tides of paperwork, targets and guidelines now engulfing general practice.

The dangers of exhaustion and isolation in single-handed practice are real, but they are usually pointed out by people who are thinking about isolation from one's colleagues. (How many partnerships are only partnerships on paper, and conceal or exemplify worse things than isolation?) The single-handed doctor is more likely to compensate for isolation from colleagues by identifying more with his or her patients.

As one GP has commented '... I am now about to start a day of single-handed general practice as my partner is away. The day is unplanned, the appointments book empty. People just turn up, bringing their infarcts, their sorrows, their trivia, and their life events to me. Some of the people who will come have not yet even fallen ill. There are the coronary artery plaques on the point of rupturing, the dizziness before the fall, the hallucination before its enactment, and someone is now writing a note to explain the impending suicide or the fact that they are leaving home forever, and taking the kids with them. All this is in the future; but for now, none of this has happened yet. I am completely up to date, and I command my general practice sitting behind an empty desk. I saw the last person who wanted to see me yesterday. There is no waiting list. Just the unknown. And what of the concept of the primary health care team? Can it really be called a team when I own the premises, hire most of the staff, pay them their wages, draw up their job description, and stipulate the bounds of their practice? It is certainly not an *equal* partnership. But when the patient's dizziness *does* lead to the fall in the village shop, as it did yesterday, I will be on hand to patch up the old lady, and the receptionist will kindly finish off the patient's shopping for her, and escort her home. We think that the price of a personal service is well worth paying'.

Time and patient-centred care

As the number of tasks to accomplish in the consulations ever lengthens, patient's own agendas often get crowded out. Depressed patients, for example, frequently hold back information they would like to discuss, because the doctor seems too busy. Does this matter? It does if your aim is patient-centred care (p 478). One study shows that far from doctors having a patient-centred approach it's usually the other way around—the patient has a doctor-centred approach and is altruistically keen to conserve scarce resources.[17] This concern about 'not worrying the doctor' is likely to be counterproductive. So every so often try saying 'Take your time—I'm not in any hurry. Let's try to get to the bottom of what's going on … [pause]'.

Time and the consultation ►Does heavy demand produce short consultations, or do short consultations produce heavy demand by failing to meet patients' needs? GPs' average consultation time is ~7min (with some consultations lasting ~½h). This seems short, but remember that over a year the average time spent with each patient is nearer one hour. The consultation time influences the degree of patient satisfaction, and may influence the consultation rate (2.5–6/patient/yr), with lower return visit rates for longer consultations, (not shown in all studies), and lower rates of prescription issue (especially antibiotics), and more preventive activities occurring. Mean face-to-face consultation time is 8min for 10min appointments but only 9.2min for 15min appointments suggesting extra time may not be well used by doctors when booking interval exceeds 10min. Running late is stressful for doctors (and patients): it is easier keeping to time for 10min (rather than shorter) bookings. Other factors apart from time of year and social setting which increase (↑) or decrease (↓) consultation rates:

- List size (↑,↓), and having personal lists (↓ by 7%).
- Not prescribing for minor ailments—see p 517 (?↓).
- New patients (for their 1st yr with a new GP), and patients over 65yrs (↑).[1]
- If the GP is extrovert (↑) he or she recalls more, and his rate is higher than others (eg 6/yr *vs* 2/yr). GP age and sex also influences rates.
- High latitudes—within the UK (↑). The South-East has lowest rates.
- Social deprivation (↑) & morbidity (↑). Increasing requirements to monitor diseases (eg asthma) and drugs, eg shared-care of rheumatoid arthritis (↑).
- Preventive activities (↑); but this can reduce need to invite people to clinics.

There is good evidence for the Howie hypothesis that average time of consultations is a valid and measurable marker of quality of care;[18] see p 517.

1 In females, the UK consultation rate at 10yrs old is ~2.4/yr; at 20 it is ~5/yr, at 80 it is 7/yr. In males, the consultation rate at 10yrs is 2/yr, at 20 it is 1.7/yr, at 50yrs it is 2.7, at 70 it is 5.6, at 80 it is 6.7/yr. A GP with a list of 2000 with 300 patients >65yrs will have provided 210 more consultations to this age group in 1998 than in 1992. This trend has continued beyond 2003, it is believed. S Rowlands 2002 *BJGP* **658**

Phone consultations: saving time or creating problems?

Phone consultations/triage (p 797) may seem a tempting way to reduce the need for precious appointment slots, and hence to move towards the UK government's 48-hour access targets (ie 'next available apointment' ≤2 working days away). What is the evidence about this? First of all, during phone consultations, most non-verbal cues are missing. To explore this issue in a practical way, try consultations with friends or actors with whom you are sitting back-to-back. One way to improve these consultations is to do more 'explicit categorization', eg 'First I am going to find out more about how you are now, then I'll ask about your drugs, then I'll go over what I can do to help, then what to do if things get worse …'

Research shows that use of telephone consultations in place of same-day, face-to-face consultations does save time, but is often offset by higher re-consultation rates and less use of opportunistic health promotion.[RCT 19]

From medical certification to living wills: all the GP forms

Incapacity/sick pay We despatch the metaphysical job of deciding who is well and who is sick, and for how long with amazing (but spurious) precision: appendicectomy ≈ 2-3 weeks; open hysterectomy or CABG ≈ 6 weeks; MI ≈ 5 weeks; cholecystectomy ≈ 2 weeks (5 weeks if open); laparoscopic inguinal hernia ≤2 weeks (with driving; longer with older techniques).

In England, form ***SC1*** can be used for self-certification for 7 days (got from surgeries, post offices, or benefit offices). For longer periods, GPs fill out ***Med 3*** if seeing the patient to-day (or yesterday). If the patient has an illness that keeps them at home, don't feel you have to visit just for the sake of being able to say you've seen them for Med 3—use form ***Med 5***; a patient can come in *after* a period of illness, and it can be back-dated. It can also be used without you seeing the patient if the patient has had a period in hospital (name the consultant). ***Med 6*** can be used where there is a problem informing the employer of the exact nature of the illness. It can receive a vague diagnosis, and tells Social Services to send a separate form for the exact diagnosis. Social Services may also ask you to fill in a one-off form ***Med 4*** (personal capacity) for further details of an illness.

Form ***MatB1*** gives a pregnant woman time off work once she is 20 weeks before the expected date of delivery (signed by a GP or midwife).

Enduring power of attorney This legally passes authority over financial affairs to a named person, who can then sign cheques, for example, for another person. It holds good eg if the patient has a stroke or dementia—provided the patient was fully aware at the time it was drawn up.[20]

Living wills Practices may keep advance directives which limit care a patient will accept after a mentally incapacitating illness, eg stroke. They have clauses such as 'after a stroke from which there is no prospect of recovery, I decline to be tube fed with nutrition, even if this hastens my death. I understand what tube feeding entails; it has been explained to me by my GP, Dr… on [date], and it is my considered, enduring wish that …' These documents have (some) legal force, and we must record on the patient's record that one is in existence. Patients send copies to the family and solicitor.[21] Knowledge of a person's wishes makes it easier for relatives to make difficult decisions.

The consultation

The consultation is the central act of medicine: all else derives from it. When medical errors occur, the reason usually lies in a failure of some process of the consultation. We must acquire flair for telling which part of which model is vital at any time, so that in busy surgeries with urgent visits mounting up, both the doctor and his or her patients can survive.

Medical model History→examination→tests→diagnosis→treatment→review.

A patient-centred model[22] ≤10 stages (►*depending on the patient's wish*):

1 The GP encourages patient contributions and communication. Preconsultation leaflets encouraging questioning and airing of concerns help here.[RCT 23]
2 The GP elicits patient's desire for information; knowing this, the GP decides to be *brief* & *authoritative* or *reflective*. ►The patient leads this process.[24]
3 The GP may set the patient's complaint in social or psychological context.
4 The GP explores and tests patient's ideas, concerns, expectations, and health beliefs. These beliefs are used to explain diagnosis and treatment.
5 The GP gets sufficient information for no serious condition to be missed.
6 Physical exam either addresses patient's concerns, or confirms or refutes hypotheses generated by the history, leading to shared working diagnosis.
7 The patient participates in the planning of treatment in the light of EBM.
8 Concordance (p 519) discussions; patient sets his own target BP, HbA_{1c} etc.[25]
9 The medical record entry may be something the patient wants to agree.
10 Establish rapport with the patient at all stages—and arrange follow-up.

Stott & Davis model[26] (other models: *www.skillscascade.com/models.htm*)

Managing presenting problems	Modifying help-seeking behaviour
Managing continuing problems	Opportunistic health promotion

A hypothesis-testing model Information is collected and its validity is ascertained by generating and testing hypotheses.

Goal models (ie ends matter, not means) Aim to:

- Cure; comfort; calm; counsel; prevent; anticipate; explain.
- Enable the patient to put himself back in control of his life.
- Manipulate society to the patient's advantage.
- Facilitate change where change is what the patient desires.
- Increase patients' stature—by tapping the sources of richness in their lives, so freeing them from the shadow of insoluble problems.

The inner consultation (Roger Neighbour; ISBN 0-7462-0040-4)

1 *Connecting* is establishing rapport.
2 *Summarizing* is the point at which the patient's reasons for attending, his hopes, feelings, concerns, and expectations have been well enough explored and acknowledged for the consultation to progress.
3 *Handing over* follows the doctor's assessment and diagnosis of the presenting problems and explained negotiated and agreed management plan.
4 *Safety netting* allows the doctor the security of knowing that she has prepared, or could prepare for, contingency plans to deal with an unexpected event and some departures from the intended management plan.
5 *Housekeeping* allows the GP to deal with any internal stresses and strains.

In consultations that are going wrong, ask yourself:

'Am I granting as much space to the patient's agenda as to mine?' This is a particular problem with GP contracts which demand attention to background diseases—eg patient: 'I'm worried about my husband …'; GP: 'OK, I'm going to test your vibration sense and pulses …'

'Have I discovered his hopes and expectations—and his fears?'

'Am I negotiating openly with the patient over our clashing ideas?'

'What are my feelings, and how can they be used positively?'

Try saying: 'Things aren't going very well. Can we start again?'

Unconscious consultations and decision analysis

What we want to examine here is that mental set and 'perceptual filter' which determines the outcome of consultations. When decision-analysts started work observing consultations they were amazed at the number of decisions per minute, and the wide range of possible outcomes, such as 'no action; review next week' or 'blue-light ambulance direct to tertiary referral centre' or 'refer to nurse for ECG' or 'prescribe X, Y, and Z, and stop Q in a week if the blood-level is such-and-such'. The average decision-analyst is disorientated by the sheer pace and apparent effortlessness of these decisions—so much so that doctors were often suspected of choosing plans almost randomly, until the idea of a 'perceptual filter' was developed.

Perceptual filters[27] This is the internal architecture of our mind—unique to each doctor—into which we receive the patient's history. It comprises:
- Our unconscious mental set (*tired/uninterested to alert, engaged, responsive*).
- Our entire education, from school to last night's postgraduate lecture.
- The sum of all our encounters with patients. Ignore the fact that we can recall very few of these: this does not stop them influencing us strongly: does the rock recall each of those many, many waves which have sculpted it into extraordinary shapes, or which have entirely worn it away?
- Our past specific, personal experience with this particular patient.
- Our past specific, personal experience with the disease(s) in question.
- Non-personal *subjective* (eg 'endocarditis is the most dangerous and stealthy disease…') or *objective* ideas (eg evidence-based medicine, p 489).

The mind's working space (random access memory, RAM)[28] The perceptual filter achieves nothing on its own. What is needed is: interpretation, rearrangement, comparison, and planning of executive action. ►*The abilities of our mental working space are determined by the number of items of data that can be integrated into a decision.* There is evidence[29] that this vital number is, for us, 3 to 8 (this is the number of factors we can consider *simultaneously*: like a juggler, we may have forty balls, but we can only keep 6 in the air at once). So, in trying to decide whether to start antidepressants, I might weigh the depression's severity (eg early waking with poor appetite and concentration), the patient's past omnivorous attitude to her pills (3 past overdoses), her expectations about treatment, the disadvantages of remaining depressed (eg child abuse), and knowledge that beating depression is a UK 'Health of the Nation' target. There may be just room enough in my 'RAM' to take into account evidence-based medicine on whether SSRIs (p 341) are likely to lead to deaths from overdose. The interesting experimental point here is that if we overload our 'RAM' in the consultation by recourse to a drawer full of guidelines, or unfiltered information—eg looking things up in an unstructured textbook, performance may decline.[30] As one juggler said (with 6 balls in the air) "How do I do it? … If I did know what I'm doing I would not be able to do it."[31]

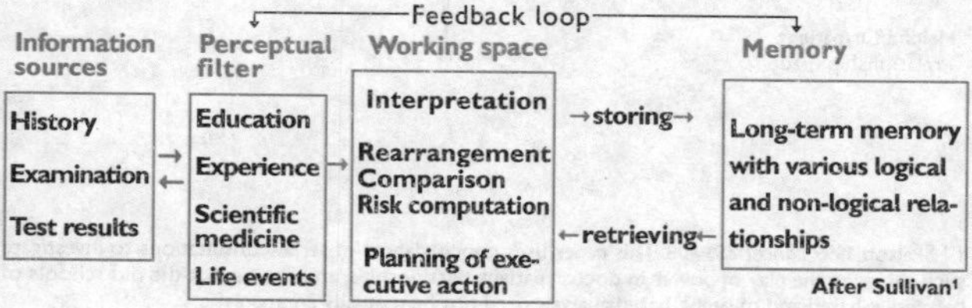

After Sullivan[1]

1 F Sullivan 1996 *Lancet* 348 941 [@8843817]

Consultation analysis

It is a sad fact that we lose some of our innate skills in communicating while at medical school. Consultation analysis aims to revive and extend this art, and we know it brings permanent improvement in those who participate. But do not conclude from this that research into the perceptible surface of behaviour can ever fully show us what is happening in the consultation.[1,2]

Methods The first step is to gain the patient's consent. The method which gives the most information and the most scope for learning employs an observer/director sitting behind a 2-way mirror, who can pass verbal instructions to the doctor through an earphone which is worn unobtrusively. The activity is videotaped for later analysis. By directing the verbal and nonverbal behaviour, the observer can demonstrate the potential of a consultation in ways that the doctor may not have imagined possible. Other methods include simple videotaping, audiotaping, and joint consultations, in which the second doctor either participates in or observes the first doctor's consultations.

Consultation analysis is likely to be a somewhat threatening activity, so rules have been evolved to minimize this.[3] For example, facts are discussed before opinions, the consulting doctor says what he did well, and then the group discusses what he did well. Then the consulting doctor says what he thinks he could have done better, and finally the group says what he could have done better. In practice, these constraints are occasionally stultifying, but it is better to be stultified than hurt.

Mapping the consultation and scoring its effectiveness In the consultation mapped below, the patient's inferior myocardial infarction (sudden chest pains on swallowing hot fluids) was mistaken by the doctor (JML) for indigestion, illustrating that there is no point in being a good communicator if you communicate the wrong message. It also shows how misleading it is to add the scores (50/84, but the patient nearly died).

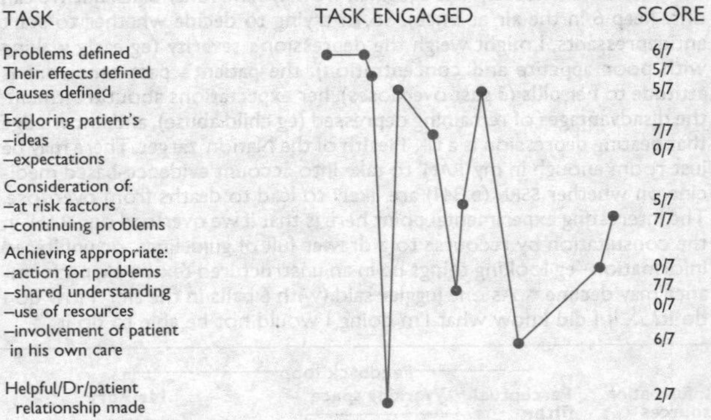

TASK
TASK ENGAGED
SCORE
Problems defined
6/7
Their effects defined
5/7
Causes defined
5/7
Exploring patient's
–ideas
7/7
–expectations
0/7
Consideration of:
–at risk factors
5/7
–continuing problems
7/7
Achieving appropriate:
–action for problems
0/7
–shared understanding
7/7
–use of resources
0/7
–involvement of patient in his own care
6/7
Helpful/Dr/patient relationship made
2/7

1 J Skelton 1999 *Lancet* **353** 108. This paper uses concordances of serial consultations to investigate such things as the play of power in doctor/patient relationships, and shows that the old schools of behaviour-based and meaning-based analysis need not be mutually antagonistic.
2 N Chomsky 1965 *Aspects of the Theory of Syntax*, Cambridge.
3 S Kurtz 1998 *Teaching and Learning Communication Skills in Medicine*. Radcliffe Medical Press.

On the impossibility of being a good doctor

Here is a list of some of the things pundits tell us we should be doing when we meet patients (don't get depressed yet: we promise there *is* a solution):

1. *Listen*—no interrupting or taking control of the agenda (how often are we guilty of implying: 'don't talk to me when I am interrupting you')?
2. Examine the patient thoroughly (a nonsensical idea, or at least, so it would seem to the average patient with sciatica when you ask them to name the parts of a clock, or to pronounce 'The British Constitution').
3. Arrange cost-effective investigation (via a trip to the library if needed).
4. Formulate a differential diagnosis in social, psychological, and physical terms (a famous triad, no doubt, but why exclude spiritual, allegorical, materialistic, metaphysical, and poetic dimensions of the consultation?).
5. Explain the diagnosis to the patient in simple terms (then re-explain it all to relatives waiting anxiously outside, and then try re-explaining it to the computer in terms *it* understands—ie 5-digit Read codes).
6. Consider additional problems and risk-factors for promoting health.
7. List all the treatment options, and seek out relevant systematic reviews, guidelines, clinical trials, etc. (evidence-based bedside medicine).
8. Incorporate the patient's view on the balance of risks and benefits, harmonizing his view of priorities, with your own assessment of urgency.
9. Arrange follow-up and communicate with all of the healthcare team.
10. Arrange for purchase of all necessary care, weighing up cost implications for your other patients and the community, welcoming accountability for all acts and omissions, and for the efficient use of resources—with justifications based on explicit criteria, transparency, and principles of autonomy, non-maleficence, beneficence, and distributive justice.

The alternative Look the patient in the eye. Look the disease in the eye, and then do your best.

The synthesis The alternative looks promising—even attractive, when compared to the ten impossibilities above. But note that the alternative only looks attractive because it is vague. 'Do your best' is not very helpful advice—and once we start unpacking this 'best' we start to get a list like the ten impossibilities. '***Professionalism***' sums up *part* of what being a good doctor entails—ie •Self-regulation •Self-actuating and self-monitoring of standards of care. •Altruism •Commitment to service •Specialist knowledge and technical skills reflecting but not determined by society's values •Consistently working to high standards of probity and quality (no bribes, no favouritism, but a dynamic concern for distributive justice). •Self-determination vis à vis the range and pattern of the kinds of problems it is right for it to attempt to solve. For a further discussion, see *On Being a Doctor: Redefining Medical Professionalism for Better Patient Care* (King's Fund).

Trying to achieve authenticity is a meta-goal, and may be a better mast to nail your colours to than the ten impossibilities above. Not because it is easier but because paying attention to authenticity may make you a better doctor, whereas striving for all ten of the ten impossibilities may make you perform less well (too many conflicting ideals). With ***inauthentic consultations*** you may be chasing remunerative activities, quality points, protocols, or simply be trying to clear the waiting room, at any cost, while the patient is trying to twist your arm into giving antibiotics, or a medical certificate. ***Authentic consultations*** are those where there are no barriers. There are simply two humans without status exploring and sharing hypotheses and beliefs and deciding what to do for the best (along the lines described in detail on p 531)—with no ulterior motives and no conflicts of interest. Authentic consultations know and tell the truth where possible, and where this is not possible, the truth is worked towards—diligently and fearlessly.

Prevention

►In all disease the goal is prevention. This is not to say that preventive activities are without side-effects. Classification: preventing a disease (eg by vaccination) is ***primary prevention.*** Controlling disease in an early form (eg carcinoma *in situ*) is ***secondary prevention.*** Preventing complications in those already symptomatic is ***tertiary prevention.***

Prevention through the human life cycle Pre-conception (p 2). Is she using folic acid supplements? Is she rubella immune? If not, vaccinate—ensure effective contraception for 1 month after vaccination. Is she diabetic? If so, optimize glycaemic control as early as possible (p 24).

The child: Vaccination (p 151); safety lessons; developmental tests (p 218).

Preventing myocardial infarction: See the UK National Service Framework for coronary heart disease.[33] Smoking trebles the risk above the rate for men who have never smoked. A systolic BP >148mmHg (40% of men) doubles risk,[1] and if serum cholesterol is in the top 20% of the observed range, the risk trebles. Help to stop smoking (p 512), and treating hypertension (*OHCM* p 142) and hyperlipidaemia (*OHCM* p 706) are the chief interventions. The UK government recommends reductions in total fat and saturated fat to 35% and 15%, respectively, of total energy. GPs and practice nurses have a central role in preventing cardiac deaths, eg by screening for hypertension, and encouraging less smoking—and prescribing statins (not based on a particular cholesterol level, but according to overall risk of MI and stroke).[2]

Preventing breast cancer deaths: Education and self-examination. Well-woman clinics. Mammography (using negligible radiation)—cancer pick-up rate: 5 per 1000 'healthy' women screened. Yearly 2-view mammograms in postmenopausal women might reduce mortality by 40%—but the price is the serious but needless alarm caused: there are ~10 false +ve results for each true +ve result. The UK national health service offers 3-yearly single views to those between 55 and 64 years old (older women may be screened too).

Prevention in the reproductive years (p 488): Safe sex education starting in adolescence (teaching to use condoms need not increase rates of sexual activity); family planning (p 296-7), antenatal/prenatal care (p 2, eg folic acid), screening for cervical cancer (p 272), blood pressure, rubella serology.

Preventing oxidative damage by free radicals: Antioxidants, eg vitamin E, C, carotenoids, flavenoids, and selenium (*OHCM* p 696) are found in diets rich in fruits, vegetables, grains, and nuts—and are thought to protect from various diseases (free radical action on LDL is central to atherogenesis), diabetes mellitus, cancer, and Alzheimer's (see p 352 for benefits of ginkgo biloba, extracted from the maidenhair tree).[34]

Old age and prevention: 'Keep fit', pre-retirement lessons, bereavement counselling visits from the health visitor may help in preventing disease. But the main aim is to adopt the measures outlined above to ensure that there *is* an old age in which to prevent disease.

Side-effects No intervention is without side-effects, and when carried out in large populations the problems may outweigh the benefits.

Smoking and prevention: p 512. Seat belts and prevention: p 791.

1 Reversible with antihypertensives and a statin (even if cholesterol 'normal or low'); ASCOT study.

2 The Heart Protection Study (HPS) indicates that if a patient has vascular risk factors, eg family history, obesity, sedentary life, smoking, ↑BP, DM) statins can be of benefit even if lipid levels are considered OK. In HPS (*N*=20,000) overall risk of MI & stroke was ↓ by 30% in those on simvastatin 40mg/24h. Statins also ↓risk of getting angina, the need for angioplasty/bypass, and amputations. Advantages hold good for women and men, and those over 70. The AFCAPS/TEXCAPS study shows that treatment can ↓ adverse coronary events even in the primary prevention of patients with normal cholesterol levels and no risk factors (past MI etc). www.chd-taskforce.de/pdf/sk_cost_02.pdf

Barriers to prevention

Biological and genetic barriers Not everyone responds to preventive measures. Some of us, because of our genes, are immune to the benefits of exercise, for example. Aerobic capacities depend on our maternal mtDNA; blanket advice of 'Take more exercise' is increasingly old fashioned. What we should really do is set to know our patients psychologically and genetically, and tailor advice such as 'for you, diet advice is more important than exercise'.

In one study, in the 8 volunteers showing the largest improvement in insulin sensitivity, 51 genes were expressed in muscles at double the levels of the 8 people who showed the least improvement after exercise.

Cognitive barriers (See p?) When, if ever, we contemplate catastrophic but preventable illness in ourselves, we may either believe that it will not happen to us, or we deliberately dare fate to make it happen to us. To some people, over-zealous and sanctimonious-sounding hectoring from bodies such as the UK Health Education Authority act as barriers to prevention, inciting anger and rejection by those who resent their lives being spent by some State Nanny who assumes that all her charges are backward 5-year-olds who cannot be trusted to think for themselves. So people are now proud to announce that 'I eat everything as much butter and fried foods as I can get', 'I smoke 40–60 cigarettes a day', 'Cornflakes? You've got to have sugar on them, and lots of cream, otherwise there is no point in eating them'... 'As long as you keep smoking cigarettes, and drink plenty of whisky you'll go on for ever'.

Psychological barriers All of us at times are prone to excuse our own destruction as keenly as we promote our own survival. Knowing that alcohol may bring about our own destruction gives the substance a certain appeal when we are in certain frames of mind—particularly if we do not know the sordid details of what death by alcohol entails. It provides an alluring means of escape without entailing too much trouble. Turning into the seductive arms of death, or taking any risks, is all part of this thrill.

Logistic barriers A general practice needs to be highly organized to be in a state of perpetual readiness to answer questions like 'Who has not had their blood pressure checked for 5 years?' or 'Who has not turned up to their recent appointment for screening?' or 'Who has stopped sending in for their repeat prescriptions for antihypertensives?' On a different front, providing a sequence of working fridges in the distribution of vaccines to rural tropical areas poses major logistic problems.

Political barriers It is not unknown for governments to back out of preventive obligations as if influenced by groups who would lose if prevention were successful. Some countries are keener to buy guns than vaccines.

Ethical barriers If child benefits were available only to those children who had had whooping cough immunization, much whooping cough would be prevented. This approach is not popular in the UK.

Financial barriers A practice may have to pay for extra staff to run an effective screening programme. Coronary artery bypass grafts may prevent some consequences of ischaemic heart disease, but they are too expensive to use on everybody whom they might benefit.

Motivation barriers As we walk out of morning surgery into the stress of the day, which might have been avoided, giving patients ... in the evening to screen or prevent the next one. Changing from a crisis-led work pattern to a strategic one is one way that prevention makes us less stressed, and may be particularly successful if the ... on which all good prevention depends.

Barriers to prevention

Biological and genetic barriers Not everyone responds to preventive measures. Some of us, because of our genes, are 'immune' to the benefits of exercise, for example. As genetic advances occur, our habitual blanket advice of 'take more exercise' looks increasingly old fashioned. What we should really do is get to know our patients psychologically and genetically, and tailor advice such as 'for you, diet advice is more important than exercise'.

In one study, in the 8 exercising volunteers showing the largest improvement in insulin sensitivity, 51 genes were expressed in muscles at double the levels of the 8 people who showed the least improvement after exercise.[35]

Cognitive barriers (See OPPOSITE.) When, if ever, we contemplate cataclysmic, but preventable, ill health in ourselves, we may either believe that '*It won't happen to me*' or we deliberately dare fate to *make* it happen to us. To some people, over-zealous and sanctimonious-sounding hectoring from bodies such as the UK Health Education Authority creates barriers to prevention, inciting anger and rejection by those who resent their taxes being spent by some State Nanny who assumes that all her charges are 'backward 5-year-olds' who cannot be trusted to think for themselves.[36] So people are now proud to announce that '... I eat everything, as much butter and fried foods as I can get ... I smoke 40–60 cigarettes a day ... To eat cornflakes, you've got to have sugar on them, and lots of cream, otherwise there is no point in eating them ... As long as you keep smoking cigarettes, and drink plenty of whisky, you'll go on for ever'.[37]

Psychological barriers All of us at times are prone to promote our own destruction as keenly as we promote our own survival. Knowing that alcohol may bring about our own destruction gives the substance a certain appeal, when we are in certain frames of mind—particularly if we do not know the sordid details of what death by alcohol entails. It provides an alluring means of escape without entailing too headlong a rush into the seductive arms of death. Gambling and taking risks is all part of this ethos.

Logistic barriers A general practice needs to be highly organized to be in a state of perpetual readiness to answer questions like 'Who has not had their blood pressure checked for 3 years'? or 'Who has not turned up to their request to attend for screening'? or 'Who has stopped sending in for their repeat prescriptions for antihypertensives?' On a different front, providing a sequence of working fridges in the distribution of vaccines to rural tropical areas poses major logistic problems.

Political barriers It is not unknown for governments to back out of preventive obligations as if influenced by groups who would lose if prevention were successful. Some countries are keener to buy tanks than vaccines.

Ethical barriers If child benefits were available only to those children who had had whooping cough vaccine, much whooping cough would be prevented. This approach is not popular in the UK.

Financial barriers A practice may have to pay for extra staff to run an effective screening programme. Coronary artery bypass grafts may prevent some consequences of ischaemic heart disease, but they are too expensive to use on everybody whom they might benefit.

Motivation barriers As we rush out of morning surgery to attend the latest vascular disaster we use up energy which might have been spent on studying patients' notes in the evening to screen to prevent the next one. Changing from a crisis-led work pattern to strategic prevention is one way that practice nurses can lead the way. They are particularly successful at the meticulous, repetitive tasks on which all good prevention depends.

Metaphysics at the bedside—and the world's worst patient

We often find ourselves sitting on beds trying to persuade wayward people to courses of preventive action which will clearly benefit them, usually at some distant time in the future. We think this very clarity should be enough to persuade the person to act. But, as we dismally stamp our feet on the bare boards of our impatience, we resign ourselves to the fact that action will not follow. Why is this so often the case?

The first person to know the answer to this question was the world's worst patient and our own greatest poet: great not because of his mastery of his world, but because, as the world used him, often cruelly, and as his London doctors gave him up as a hopeless addict, he took on all our petty confusions and made them human, compelling, and universal. Samuel Taylor Coleridge answers our question in this way:

> ***To love our future Self is almost as hard as to love our Neighbour—it is indeed only a difference of Space & Time. My Neighbour is my other Self, 'othered' by Space—my old age is to my youth and other Self, 'othered' by Time…*** See *Coleridge* ii 225 R Holmes

By being consumed by the fires of his addictions this poet becomes the burning wick in the lamp we now use to illuminate our patients' frailties—and hence our own.

Screening

This entails systematic testing of a population, or a sub-group for signs of illness—which may be of established disease (pre-symptomatic, eg small breast cancers), or symptomatic (eg unreported hearing loss in the elderly).

Modified Wilson criteria for screening (1–10 spells iatrogenic)[1]

1 The condition screened for should be an important one.
2 There should be an acceptable treatment for the disease.
3 Diagnostic and treatment facilities should be available.
4 A recognizable latent or early symptomatic stage is required.
5 Opinions on who to treat as patients must be agreed.
6 The test must be of *high discriminatory power* (below), *valid* (measuring what it purports to measure, not surrogate markers which might not correlate with reality) and be *reproducible*—with safety guaranteed.
7 The examination must be acceptable to the patient.
8 The untreated natural history of the disease must be known.
9 A simple inexpensive test should be all that is required.
10 Screening must be continuous (ie not a 'one-off' affair).

Summary: screening tests must be cost-effective.

Informed consent: Rees' rule Before offering screening, we have a duty to quantify for patients the chance of being disadvantaged by it—from anxiety (may be devastating, eg while waiting for a false +ve result to be sorted out) and the effects of subsequent tests (eg bleeding after biopsy following an abnormal cervical smear), as well as the chances of benefit. We are all guilty of exaggerating benefits and avoiding discussion of controversial areas with patients.[38]

Comparing a test with some 'gold standard'

		Patients with condition	Patients without condition
TEST RESULT	Subjects appear to have the condition	True +ve (a)	False +ve (b)
	Subjects appear not to have the condition	False -ve (c)	True -ve (d)

Sensitivity: How reliably is the test +ve in the disease? a/a+c
Specificity: How reliably is the test -ve in health? d/d+b

Partly effective screening
Cervical smears (if >25yrs, p 270)
Mammography (after menopause)[3]
Finding smokers (+quitting advice)
Looking for malignant hypertension (lesser hypertension is problematic)

Unproven/ineffective screening[2]
Mental test score (dementia, p 352)
Urine tests (diabetes; kidney disease)
Antenatal procedures (p 8)
Elderly visiting to detect disease[4]
Sigmoidoscopy for rectal cancer

Why screen in general practice? If screening is to be done at all, it makes economic sense to do it in general practice. In the UK ≥1 million people see GPs each weekday, providing great facilities for 'case-finding' (90% of patients consult over a 5-yr period). Provided the GP's records are adequate, the remaining 10% may then be sent appointments to attend for special screening sessions—eg at the well-woman clinic (p 488). Private clinics do limited work, eg in screening for cervical cancer, but there is no evidence that their multiphasic biochemical analyses are effective procedures.

1 ►For an excellent critique of the Wilson criteria, see Gray J 2004 *Br J Gen Pract* **501**:292-8. [@15113498]
2 There is evidence that some screening causes morbidity (mortality-awareness and hypochondriasis↑)—so why is screening promulgated? One reason is that it is easier for governments to be optimistic than to be rigorous
3 C White 2002 *BMJ* i 933
4 In one study (N=43,000 patients >75yrs old) neither in-depth assessment nor a targeted approach focused on those with ≥3 problems offered gains in survival or quality of life

Problems with screening

Take a healthy person, screen them, turn them into a patient, and then kill them. From a report on cervical screening: 'By offering screening to 250,000 we have helped a few, harmed thousands, disappointed many, used £1.5m each year, and kept a few lawyers in work.' Typical problems are:

1. Those most at risk do not present for screening, thus increasing the gap between the healthy and the unhealthy—the *inverse care law*.
2. The 'worried well' overload services by seeking repeat screening.
3. Services for investigating those testing positive are inadequate.
4. Those who are false positives suffer stress while awaiting investigation, and remain anxious about their health despite reassurance.
5. A negative result may be regarded as a licence to take risks.
6. True positives, though treated, may begin to see themselves as of lower worth than hitherto.

►Remember: with some screening programmes of dubious value, *it may be healthier not to know*.[39]

Primary care and shared-care clinics

Examples of mini-clinics which are conducted in primary care

- Well-woman/well-man clinic
- Elderly 'nonattending' patients
- Giving-up-smoking clinic (p 512)
- Joint outreach clinics with a consultant who shares care (eg orthopaedics)
- Antenatal clinic
- Cardiac[1] & hypertension clinic
- Citizen's advice clinic
- Diabetes clinic MET 40
- Asthma clinic

Advantages of mini-clinics

- Easy to keep to management protocol
- Check-lists prevent omissions
- Co-operation cards allow shared care
- Flow-charts to identify trends
- Help from specialist practice nurse
- Fewer outpatients referrals (↓by 20%)
- Better co-operation with hospitals
- GPs can improve clinical skills 41
- Improved dialogue with specialists 42

Disadvantages

- Extra time needed
- Extra training needed
- Not holistic
- Not flexible
- Value often unproven
- Access to hospital technology↓
- Travelling time by consultants to outreach clinics is wasteful

Activities in well-woman clinics

- Cervical smear and breast examination
- Breast examination/mammography
- Pre-conception counselling (p 2)
- Antenatal and postnatal care
- Rubella and tetanus* vaccination
- Smoking and alcohol advice*
- Safer sex advice for HIV*
- Family planning/sterilization*
- Diet and weight*
- Blood pressure*
- Discussion of HRT issues

Breast examination/teaching breast self-examination in nurse clinics There is disagreement about whether this is desirable, and, if so, whether we can delegate this to nurses. Some (but not all) studies report that cancers in those having this protocol are detected earlier, with improved survival, compared with mammography alone. But UK DoH advice is against breast palpation in asymptomatic women, even if on the Pill/HRT. The DoH advises against delegation to nurses, but in some practices it may *only* be nurses whom women find acceptable—so validating nurse training is a key issue.

Well-men Women live longer, so why should they get all the prevention? (it might be argued). Nurses can do all the well-woman activities *starred above in well-man clinics. One such clinic yielded ≥25% obese; 14% with diastolic BP ≥100mmHg; 66% needing tetanus vaccination; and 29% needing smoking advice. See the OXCHECK study, p 495 and the NHS National Service Framework for ischaemic heart disease (*OHCM* p 91). RCT 43 [N=874]

Diabetic clinic *Education and encouragement are the most important activities.* ►This is best conducted in group sessions where passive-dependency is minimized—and people (patients) help and motivate each other. Traditional one-to-one care *even when optimized*, is associated with progressive deterioration of knowledge, problem solving ability, and quality of life. Better cognitive and psychosocial results are associated with more favourable clinical outcomes—including falling BMI and Hb_{A1c}. RCT 44 [N=120]

Advantages over hospital clinics: patients see the same person each time; weekly appointments are possible during periods of difficult control; telephone advice is easily available. Mini-clinics are cheaper than outpatient clinics and outcome studies have 'proved' effectiveness. RCT 45

Even young insulin-dependent diabetics can be managed *wholly* in primary care from presentation provided there is no overt ketoacidosis. There are dangers in adhering too closely to protocols (p 490). However, the vital test is retinal photography or dilating the pupil for fundoscopy (p 412 & p 446). Other vital areas are diet, exercise & smoking advice, BP & lipid control, and round-the-clock blood glucose monitoring, with checks on U&E and Hb_{A1c}.

Liaison with community consultant-services: May prevent hospital admission.

1 Nurse-led clinics (eg to check if on β-blocker if post-MI etc) are cost-effective. Raftery J 2005 *BMJ* **707**

Evidence-based medicine (EBM)

This is the conscientious and judicious use of current best evidence from clinical care research in the management of individual patients—taking into account their values. *The problem* 2,000,000 papers are published each year. Patients may benefit from a tiny fraction of these. How do we find them?

A partial solution 50 journals are scanned not by experts in neonatal nephrology or the left nostril, but by searchers trained to spot papers which have a direct message for practice, and meet predefined criteria of rigour (below). Summaries are then published in *Evidence-based Medicine*.

Questions used to evaluate papers: 1 Are the results *valid*? (Randomized? Blinded? Were all patients accounted for who entered the trial? Was follow-up complete? Were the groups similar at the start? Were the groups treated equally, apart from the experimental intervention?) 2 What *are* the results? (How large was the treatment effect? How precise was the treatment effect?) 3 Will the results help *my* patients (cost-benefit sum).

Problems with the solution *The concept of scientific rigour is opaque*. What do we want? The science, the rigour, the truth, or what will be most useful to our patients? These may overlap, but they are not the same.

- Will the best be the enemy of the good? Are useful papers rejected due to some blemish? Answer: *all* evidence need appraising (often impossible!).
- By reformulating patients in terms of answerable questions, EBM risks missing the point of the patient's consultation. He might simply want to express his fears, rather than be used as a substrate for an intellectual exercise.
- Is the standard the same for the evidence for *all* changes to our practice? For example, we might want to avoid prescribing drug X for constipation if there is the slimmest chance that it might cause colon cancer. There are many other drugs to choose from. We might require far more robust evidence than a remote chance to persuade us to do something rather counter-intuitive, such as giving heparin in DIC. How robust does the data need to be? There is no science to tell us the answer to this: we decide off the top of our head (albeit a wise head, we hope).
- EBM is a lucky dip if gathering *all* the evidence on a topic proves impossible.
- What about letters columns? It may be years before fatal flaws are aired.
- There is a danger that by always asking 'What is the evidence ...' we divert resources from hard-to-prove activities (which may be very valuable—eg physiotherapy for cerebral palsy) to easy-to-prove services. The unique personal attributes of therapists are as important as the objective regimen. It is all too easy to transfer resources to some easy-to-quantify activity, eg neonatal screening for cystic fibrosis.
- Evidence-based medicine is rarely 100% up to date. Reworking meta-analyses in the light of new trials takes time—if it is ever done at all.
- EBM contributes to the problem of data-overload by churning out endless guidelines that don't quite apply to the patient sitting in front of you.

Advantages of evidence-based medicine
- It improves our reading habits.
- It leads us to ask questions, and then to be sceptical of the answers.
- As taxpayers, we should like it (wasteful practices can be abandoned).
- Evidence-based medicine presupposes that we keep up to date, and makes it worthwhile to take trips around the perimeter of our knowledge.
- Evidence-based medicine opens decision-making processes to patients.

Conclusion There is little doubt that, *where available*, EBM is better than what it is superseding. It may not have much impact, as gaining evidence is time-consuming and expensive. Despite these caveats, evidence-based medicine is one of the most rational recent medical developments. Let's all join in by subscribing to ideals and its journal.

Protocols, targets, and guidelines

- ►Freedom from only doing ordained tasks is essential for mental health.
- ►Beware accepting a protocol without knowing if it will affect your sympathy and time to communicate.
- ►Is the protocol independently validated. What is its *hidden objective*, eg cost-containment, conformity, self-advertisment, empire-building, or care?
- ►Reject protocols which don't specify conflicts of interests: most protocols (87%) are written by people with financial links to drug companies.[46 47 48]

Sympathy is a delicate flower which has often withered before the end of morning surgery. If a protocol says that you must do 10 things to Mrs James who happens to have diabetes, both of you may be irritated by item 5: the doctor is running out of time, and the patient is running out of goodwill. She is really worrying about her husband's dementia, having long-since stopped worrying about her own illnesses. She does not mind being assailed by lights, forks, stix, and lancets, if this is the price for a portion of her doctor's sympathy. But if she finds that this sympathy has withered, who knows what her feelings may be, and how she will view her doctor?

Guidelines are seen as friendly, if flexible and allow for the frailties of clinical science as it meets bedside reality; they can also be interactive, if instituted in a computerized record during the consultation. Protocols, particularly if they have been handed down from some supposedly higher authority, have a reputation for being strict, sinister, and stultifying instruments for thought-control. How well do these stereotypes stand up in practice? It is known that doctors working in highly regulated environments with strict protocols perform suboptimally.[49] It is also worth noting that very few laws are flexible: those which are, are dangerous because they invite abuse. (All men are equal, but …). But what laws *can* do is to state when they don't apply. This doesn't necessarily make them mere guidelines. You could say, that patients have a right to be asked if they want to participate in a protocol, and if they do, that it should be done properly. But what if it is the child's birthday today, and he really does not want to have his finger pricked for a glucose test, but he is most willing to go along with all other aspects of a protocol? If you are flexible, the price may be ketoacidosis after the party. Herein lies the paradox of protocols. They are designed to remove the many indefensible inconsistencies found in clinical medicine, yet the protocols depend on the individual doctor's own flair and instinctive judgment to be applied in the best way.

Perhaps the best approach is to welcome the good protocols, and develop some sort of meta-protocol which should be answered whenever (or almost whenever) such protocols are not adhered to. Why did you not adhere to the protocol? Please tick the appropriate box. ❒My own convenience. ❒The patient's stated wish. ❒The patient's stated wish after being given full information. ❒The protocol is contraindicated in this case because my instinctive flair and judgement tells me so.

Can we square guidelines & targets with patient-centred care? (p 478)
Answer: ***No***; discussing this issue with purveyors of guidelines is a good way reveal the hidden agendas described above. Point out that leading authorities[1] are now saying patients must decide their own target BP, HbA_{1c}, etc.

In conclusion, each protocol should come with a comment on the likely effect on the doctor's sympathy; how often, on average, one would expect the protocol not to be adhered to; and what resources and time will be needed, and how this will be funded.

1 Neil Campbell 2004 *BMJ* 329 523

The placebo effect

Placebo effects are very powerful and are important not just in research, but also in demonstrating to us how our demeanour may be just as important as the drugs we give. It is often said that if two obstetric units (for instance) do things quite differently (eg for or against artificial rupture of the membranes) then if one unit is vindicated by research, the other unit must be wrong. This need not follow—not just because the population served by the 'errant' unit may be different. The errant unit may believe it is a centre of excellence, and its staff may rupture membranes with joy in their hearts, knowing they are fulfilling their destiny as the best obstetric unit bar none. This feeling may communicate itself to labouring mothers, who, due to an interaction between communication, beliefs, cognition, and contractility, have their babies with few complications—so much so, that if the unit went over to the 'correct' method, their results might come to mirror their plummeting self-confidence. (This is an important reason for the failure of imposed protocols which look good on paper: see p 490.) Research in this area is very difficult to do, because you cannot easily control for 'joy in the heart'—but with care it can be systematically analysed: in a placebo-controlled study of antihypertensives the partners of the enthusiastic doctor broke the code, and told him that his experimental treatment appeared similar to existing treatments without telling him who was having the active drug, and who was having the placebo. ►From this point, there was an immediate, marked increase in BP in both groups, although the difference between the drug and the placebo was maintained.[50] [51]

►Our beliefs and our behaviour sometimes matter more than our drugs.

Speculative mechanisms ***Psychological:*** Expectancy, anxiety-reduction and Pavlovian conditioning may operate. ***Psychosomatic linkages:*** Endorphins, catecholamines, cortisol, and psychoneuroimmumunology.[52] NB: It is *not* the case that there is a 'placebo-responsive' personality.

Don't assume we should give placebos to all our patients, and be enthusiastic about their likely effects. Most of this book is founded on the precept that we should be honest and straightforward with our patients. Nevertheless, it may often be unwise to share too many of our doubts with our patients, as demonstrated by the GP who randomly assigned his consulting style in those with apparently minor illness to a 'positive encounter' or a 'negative encounter'. In the former, patients were given a diagnosis and told they would be better in a few days, the latter group were told that it was not certain what the matter was. Just over ⅓ of the patients having negative encounters got better in 2 weeks, but over ⅔ of the positive group did so.

Nocebo effects Pharmacists often 'leaflet' customers with long lists of their drugs' side-effects, which, like Voodoo death, may become self-fulfilling prophesies. When one of the authors (JML) gives diamorphine IV to patients having a myocardial infarction, he says in a loud voice 'Your pain will end now' (maximizes placebo effect)—and, in a very quiet voice to the spouse, 'Get a bowl: he may be sick.'—to avoid the reverse 'nocebo' effect. We tend not to tell patients about side-effects such as impotence, justifying this dishonesty on the grounds that in such a sensitive area, the mere mention of impotence will bring it about. Central to this debate is the question of how paternalistic we should be. We do not know the answer, but simply recommend getting to know individual patients well, and having a flexible approach: in doing so we may occasionally strike the right balance.

Bedside manners in a multicultural world

Eastern manners ►Do not expect an Afro-Asian to answer intimate questions, without first explaining about confidentiality.
- Avoid prolonged eye contact and loud speech (indicates lack of respect).
- Control your gesticulations (the 'thumbs up' sign is considered rude).
- A psychiatric referral may destroy eligibility for marriage.

Hindu First names (eg Lalita) are often male and female, but middle names (eg Devi) always denote sex and they are often written together (Lalitadevi).
- A Hindu is likely to give only his first 2 names, withholding his family name, to be polite. This can cause great confusion in registration.
- Some have dietary restrictions (no beef/veal); some are strict vegetarians.
- The cow is sacred to Hindus, so do not offer beef insulin.

Sikh names Some Sikhs have no family name. Singh and Kaur indicate only sex and religion, so that extra identification is needed on the notes.

Muslims (The largest non-christian UK sect). Sometimes the last name is not a family name, and the first name is not the personal name. There may be no shared family name. The first name is often religious (eg Mohammed). Common female second names (eg Banu, Begum, Bi, Bibi, and Sultana) are of as little help in identification as the title Ms is in UK names. Writing the father's name can give extra identification. See Mosby's *Guide to Physical Examination*.[53]
- Shoes are to be taken off before entering the house (for any purpose).
- Some Muslims do not shake hands with the opposite sex after puberty.
- Majority of Muslims do not drink alcohol (so do not offer tonics).
- Some Muslims may refuse to take their medication in Ramadan. If prescribing drugs once or twice daily (before sunrise; after sunset) is not OK, explain the disease: according to Islamic rules, ill people must not fast.
- Do not offer pork insulin to Muslims.

Muslims and death Religious observance requires prompt burial, not cremation. Washing and shrouding is an important ceremony traditionally done by elders of the same sex and only relatives and friends may do it
- The dead body is sacred and never abandoned by relatives; so it is rare for undertakers to be involved. Bereavement lasts for 3-7 days (prayers in the home may be said almost continuously).
- In some cultures, wives may stay at home for several weeks after death of a spouse and they cannot re-marry for up to 3-4 months.
- Some cultures have restrictions for transplantation or autopsy.

How to avoid offending Western manners This is not just a question of 'please', 'thank you', 'after you', and 'I'd love to …' rather than 'I don't mind if I do …' with feigned enthusiasm—Westerners are notoriously sensitive to gaze and mutual gaze: not enough, and they think you are shifty; too much, and you are making unwelcome advances; the same goes with interpersonal distance: if you get too close, invasion is threatened.

Clinical Centile charts are different (p 181). Bilateral cervical/inguinal lymphadenopathy may be normal in Asian & African children, or may indicate TB.
- A BMI of >23 in an Asian man carries a higher risk than for Caucasians (eg diabetes risk) and should trigger anti-obesity interventions.[54]
- Genetic diseases may be common, eg sickle-cell anaemia in Africans and West Indians; haemoglobin E disease in Chinese.
- Unusual malignancies (oesophagus in Japan, tongue from betel nuts).
- The length of gestation for Black infants averages 9 days shorter than that of White infants and they weigh 180-240g less than white infants at birth. However, at a similar gestational duration, Black infants are more mature than white infants and related to this increased maturity, premature Black infants also have a better survival rate than premature White infants.

Language, interpretation, and health

Dislocation, globalization, migration, refugee numbers, and war conspire to separate doctors and patients linguistically. 100 million people live outside their country of birth. All too often interpreters, if available, are only on hand during office hours. Friends and relatives may be available, but confidentiality issues are important. The interpreter's own cultural prejudices may distort your questions, and even make them vacuous.[55]

When a child interprets for his mother's or father's mortal illness, many other unknowable issues are raised.[56] Alternatives include telephone interpretation (eg with a hands-off conference telephone). Although nonverbal signs are lost, there may be advantages as some patients may say things to a telephone which they would be unhappy to say face-to-face.[57]

Whenever needed, ask for these services from Health Authorities/ Primary Care Trusts—and then the services are more likely to be in place, and the wheels well-oiled when the real emergency arises.

The Phelan–Parkman 'rules' for interviewing with an interpreter:
- Address patient in the second person; talk directly to your patient.
- Keep control of the consultation; make full use of written material.[58]
- Pause often, looking for nonverbal clues signalling misunderstanding.
- Be attentive when patient responds; check your patient's understanding.

Advice to consider before a Hajj journey to Mecca[1]

Hajj is a 5-day Muslim pilgrimage to Mecca to celebrate Abraham's readiness to sacrifice Ishmael. Its yearly date is unfixed. Pilgrims renew their faith shoulder-to-shoulder, as a sacred duty, with 2 million Muslims from all over the world. 20,000 travel from the UK, and another 29,000 also make a lesser pilgrimage to Mecca called Umrah. Hajj is physically taxing (but often exhilarating) involving walking and camping in the desert with basic sanitation. Hajj is not required for those in poor health, and your role may be to advise on poor health to enable religious dispensation.
- Meningococcal vaccination is mandatory (2 doses ACWY-Vax® conjugate meningitis vaccination, 3 months apart). Immunity is thought to last 3 years. Hepatitis A, and malaria prophylaxis are important. Consider also polio, typhoid and diphtheria vaccines and hepatitis B vaccines.
- Women should not menstruate during Hajj. Menstrual delay by norethisterone (p 248) or contraceptive pill may be requested.
- Sun stroke and heat exhaustion are major hazards. Advise acclimatization (so arrive 1 week before Hajj to enable sweating), 5L fluid with half teaspoonful salt/L intake daily; keep fluid bottle with one. Take an umbrella (preferably white) as sun shade. Avoid travel in middle of day and on open top buses. Use liberal sun block if fair skinned.
- Much walking is needed so advise comfortable shoes and carrying a shoe bag to carry them in when removed for prayers (so as not to lose them). Sand is so hot that bare foot walking may cause sole burns.
- Male head-shaving by shared razor blades risks blood-borne infections. Advise using new razor blades (hair trimming may be acceptable).
- Take an adequate supply of medications and a list of them in generic names. Also take simple analgesics.
- Most injuries are to feet. Being crushed by crowds will be best avoided by avoiding the most popular times (eg travel at night).
- Post-Hajj diagnoses to consider: meningitis, hepatitis, hydatid, TB, malaria.

1 Rashid A 2005 *BMJ* **350** 133

Health education

What is education?—four incomplete answers

- Education is the system used for passing down, from one generation to the next, society's values, attitudes, and culture. Thus are crime, duplicity and double standards (and, on a good day, idealism) perpetuated in a kind of cultural inheritance.
- Education is an activity carried out on ignoramuses by people who think they know better.
- Education is about changing people. It usually ends up implying 'change your ways…or else'. The most extreme form of education is prison.[1]
- Education performed on one mind by another, under duress, is indoctrination. Indoctrination has its uses. Its value is measured by its propensity to encourage *self-education*, through, for example, travel, reading, or dialogue. Self-education is the food of the mind: the procedure by which we can touch the great minds of the dead and know we are not alone in all our confusions and questionings. By standing on their shoulders we can find a new view of our world—sometimes, even, new worlds to view.

Health education messages These must be *specific* and *direct*. Eg in getting people to sign on for help for drinking problems, it is of little use saying 'If you don't stop drinking you'll get these diseases …' (~25% respond); saying 'Signing on is good for you because of these benefits …' (~50% respond); saying 'If you don't sign here, you've had it …' brings the biggest response. A certain amount of 'fear' in the message is not bad: in enlisting patients for a tetanus vaccine a 'low fear' message gets a 30% response, while a more fear gets a 60%. Optimum messages must be very specific about dates, times, and places of help. Too high a level of fear is counter-productive. A gruesome film about the worst effects of caries produces petrified immobility, not self-help or trips to dentists.

The messenger Peers may be better than authority-figures (eg in stop smoking messages). A message about breast feeding will come best from a mother. However, if the issues are not well understood, authority may be helpful (the BMJ is more effective than *Woman's Own* in suggesting to mothers that a new formulation of aspirin should not be taken).

Changing attitudes The following paradigm holds sway: **knowledge→attitudes→intentions→behaviour.** As Chinese thought reformers knew so well, attitude changes depend on a high level of emotional involvement. In questions of belief, as in so many other questions, emotion trumps reason '*people don't demand that a thing be reasonable if their emotions are touched. Lovers aren't reasonable, are they?…*'[2] Only resort to applying reason to attitudes if emotions are too hot to handle. NB: the arrows in the model above may be reversed: if our behaviour is inconsistent with our ideas (cognitive dissonance) it is often our ideas, not our behaviour which change.

Health education officers are likely to have a nursing, teaching, or health visiting background. They may have a postgraduate diploma in health education. There are ~300 in England and Wales. Teams comprise a technician and a graphic artist, as well as clerical staff. One role is to give information and Health Education Authority leaflets. They also liaise with health visitors and primary care trusts, as well as engaging in planning and research.

Examples of health education at work •Education about 'safer sex' and the prevention of AIDS. •Leaflets and tape/slide programmes can (slightly) increase knowledge of breast self-examination (which is associated with smaller tumours and less spread in those presenting with breast cancer). •Radio dramas with health issues reaching millions, eg *Soul City* in S Africa.[3]

1 P Theroux *Down the Yangtze*, Penguin ISBN 0-14-600032-3, page 35–6
2 Graham Greene 1951 *The End Of the Affair*, page 115, Heinemann
3 Its themes are social & medical: child care, empowerment of women, & HIV (Garth Japhet); evaluation shows a *huge* health impact, see www.comminit.com/idcc2001/sld-1765.html

Health promotion by nurses Nurses are the experts in this field—but even they are not very effective in reducing coronary risk. In the community-based OXCHECK randomized trial (N = 6124, aged 35–64) serum cholesterol fell by only 0.08–0.2mmol/L—and there was no significant difference in rates of giving up smoking, or in body mass index. Systolic (and diastolic) BP fell by ~2.5% in the intervention group receiving dietary and lifestyle advice. Blanket health promotion may not be a complete waste of resources, but it is certainly expensive for rather limited gains. Similar results have been obtained by the *Family Heart Study Group*. Depending on the assumed duration of risk reduction, the programme cost per discounted life year gained ranges from £34,800 if interventional benefits last for 1 year, compared with £1500 for 20-year duration. Corresponding OXCHECK figures are £29,300 and £900. These figures exclude broader long-term cost effects other than coronary mortality.[59]

The conclusion may be that energies are best spent on those with highest risk as determined in routine consultations by a few 'simple questions' about smoking, family history, etc. One trouble is that these questions are not always innocuous. It is not necessarily a good thing to bring up 'strokes and heart attacks in the family' in, for example, consultations about tension headaches. OXCHECK is not the last word—and there is evidence that if lipid-lowering drugs were used very much more extensively, cholesterol (and cardiac events) could fall by 30%.[60]

Novel ways of delivering health education messages

- For those who have difficulty in accessing health services, eg those in rural areas, videoconferencing and the internet may be a good way forward. Sustainability of these programmes depends upon the following issues: cost, delivery style, and availability of appropriate technology and patient-friendly internet sites.[61]
- Traditionally, health education has been given by experts, partly because they can answer questions authoritatively. But this authority is itself a problem. Risk-takers are unlikely to listen to the prim and proper. So peer-education has been developed as a tool to reach certain groups, and evidence suggests that this is a promising way forward.[62]

Patient groups

Mother-and-baby groups These are best set up in the first weeks after the birth of four or five babies. The health visitor encourages the group to form. A doctor may attend the group—regularly to start with, then less often as the group becomes self-sufficient. After a year or two a large practice will have a number of groups running. One aim is to increase motivation (through discussion) to enhance the uptake of health education and preventative medicine. Another aim is to ease the stresses involved in becoming a responsible parent by providing a social support network. A mother, noting for the first time her beautiful baby's ability to hate, to destroy, and to hurt, may find it a relief to know that other babies are much the same.

Patient participation groups ►Working *with* your patients is as important as working *for* them. The health care team meets with patients' representatives to discuss some of the following:

- Dealing with complaints (less adversarial than with formal methods).
- Harmonizing the 'consumer's' and the 'provider's' aims.
- Feedback to aid planning, implementation, and evaluation of services.
- Identifying unmet needs (eg among the isolated elderly).
- Improving links between the practice and other helpers.
- Health promotion in the light of local beliefs (p 472).
- Pressurizing government institutions over inadequate services.

Owing to lack of interest, or to there being no clear leader or task, up to 25% of groups have closed. The complaint that participation mechanisms lead to tokenism (ie the democratic ideal has been exercised, but what has been created is just a platform for validating the *status quo*) does not turn out to be true if a group has power over funds which it has raised. Here, our experience is that analysis may be penetrating and decision swift, in a way that makes even the best-run health authorities/Trusts look pedestrian.

The patients' association This group represents and furthers the interests of patients by giving assistance, advice, and information. It aims to promote understanding between patients and the medical world. Publications: Patient Voice and a directory of self-help organizations. See also the *Contact-a-Family* Directory. www.cafamily.org.uk/GAP.html

Self-help organizations Many thousands of these groups have been set up worldwide for sufferers of specific rare or common diseases. They offer information, companionship, comfort, and a life-line to patients and their families, eg for sharing techniques and self-remedies. A danger is that they share nightmares as well, for example, unnecessarily graphic descriptions of their children dying of cystic fibrosis may be spread, causing unneeded despondency. They raise funds for research, providing a 'welcome alternative to the expensive services of professionals'. Full directories exist (see above).

Groups as a way out of passive-dependency If people learn in groups they take more control of their lives, they are more optimistic about being able to change things in their lives (such as their weight); self esteem improves—and also objective measures of health (such as Hb_{A1c} in diabetics, as we have already mentioned). RCT [63] [N=120]

Advice for an NHS patient who wishes to complain…

Who should I complain to? Tell someone close to the cause of your complaint such as a doctor, nurse, receptionist, or practice manager *as soon as possible* (within 6 months of the incident, or within 6 months of discovering that you have a problem). It is often possible to sort out the problem at once. This is called Local Resolution.[1] You can telephone or write to the practice complaints officer or to the individual concerned. If Local Resolution fails, you may ask the Health Care Commission to consider the complaint. Such a request must be made within 2 months (or as soon as practicable) following any response provided by the practice. ***GP out-of-hours-service:*** Complain to your Primary Care Organization (PCO) or your own GP. If your complaint is about ***availability or organization of health care services***, contact the Complaints Officer of your local PCO.

How quickly will the complaint be dealt with? Within 2 working days is the aim. For written complaints and cases where more detailed investigation is required, your complaint will be acknowledged in writing within 3 working days and the aim is to respond fully in 20 working days.

What do I do if I am unhappy with the reply? You may request an Independent Review. You must ask for this within 28 calendar days from the date of the letter responding to your complaint. You will be asked to write a letter to The Convener of the NHS Trust responsible for the service saying why you are still dissatisfied. The convener is a specially trained member of the NHS Trust and, having taken advice, will decide whether to refer the complaint back for further Local Resolution, possibly suggesting Conciliation—or to set up an Independent Review panel to consider the complaint; (Complaints Officers can explain to you how these processes work). You will be advised of the Convener's decision within 20 working days of your request (10 working days if about GPs, Chemists, or Opticians).

Should an Independent Review Panel be set up, this will consist of the Convener, an Independent Lay Chairperson, and one other person nominated by the NHS Trust. The Panel will investigate the complaint and talk to everyone involved, seeking the specialist advice it needs. You will then be sent a report, including the Panel's conclusions.

What do I do if I am still unhappy? You may request an investigation by the Health Service Commissioner (ombudsman) who is independent of the NHS and the Government. NB: the General Medical Council can be involved with a complaint whether or not it relates to an NHS patient.

Clinical governance and continuous quality improvement Complaint systems are only a part of clinical governance, a system, which links continuing professional development, multidisciplinary learning, audit, risk management, and *critical incident reporting*. It is a 'framework through which the NHS is accountable for continuously improving the quality and safeguarding high standards of care by creating an environment in which excellence will flourish'. The sequence is: defining quality→assuring accountability→improving quality. 64

It is one mechanism by which the Commission for Health Improvement (CHI) operates. Its areas of priority are partly set by the National Institute of Clinical Excellence (NICE) and health improvement programmes (HImP).

1 It is the practice manager's duty to log each complaint with its outcome, to acknowledge written complaints within 3 days, and to send a copy of the Practice's Complaints Procedure leaflet. She ensures that the internal investigation takes ≤10 days (if longer, she must give reasons). She will take advice from any relevant medical defence organizations.

Dying at home

'Don't touch me! Don't question me! Don't speak to me! Stay with me!'[1]

Helping agencies
- Family
- Community nurse
- Hospice
- Friends/neighbours
- Night nurses
- GP/health visitor
- Pain clinic
- CRUSE (selfhelp group)

The UK death rate is ~12/1000/yr, or ~30 deaths/GP/yr. 65% die in hospital, 10% die in hospices, public places, or on the street, and 25% die at home. Of these deaths at home over half will be sudden. In the remainder, the GP has a central role to play in enabling the patient to die a dignified death in the way that he or she chooses. Pain relief and symptom control are the central preoccupations of death in hospices, where death has already been somewhat medicalized, but in those who choose to die at home there often runs a fierce streak of independence, so that their main aim is to carry on with the activities of normal living—come what may. This may cause distress to relatives who feel that the dying person is putting up with unnecessary pain. An open discussion is often helpful in harmonizing the family's aims. A key step is to find out what a patient wants—and then to enable him to do it, being aware that aims often change over time. The next step is to find out about his hopes and fears and how they interact with those of the family.

Pain ►See *OHCM* p 438 for the analgesic ladder. *Diagnose each pain.* Bone pain may need NSAIDs, eg naproxen 250mg/8h PO pc or prednisolone 5mg/8h PO; pain from constipation needs a laxative or enema. *Document each pain's response to treatment.* ***Morphine*** (oral) is given eg as 5-10mg/4h PO. Strength examples (/5mL): 10mg, 30mg, 100mg. Once the daily dose which controls pain is known, consider giving the same 24h dose as slow release tablets every 12h (eg MST® 5, 10, 15, 30, 60, 100, or 200mg). Take the 1st MST tablet 4h after the last dose of morphine solution. (Starting dose of MST in children: 200-800μg/kg/12h PO.) If pain breaks through, give extra morphine solution, and ↑ MST at the next dose (don't give more than twice daily to avoid pharmacodynamic confusion). If the patient cannot swallow, use diamorphine SC, at ½ the daily oral morphine dose, given eg divided into 4-hourly injections or via a pump. Laxatives ± antiemetics will be needed. Get help from a palliative-care nurse.

Fentanyl also has a role. One skin patch may last 72h. It may cause less sedation and constipation than morphine. Trans-mucosal lozenge forms exist.[2]

Bereavement is the process of adapting to a loss, which is causing sorrow. ***Mourning*** is the active evocation of that loss, which may take a formal, ritualistic, and dignified style, or be personal and idiosyncratic. ***Lamentation*** is the vocal outpouring of grief at its cusp, with wailing, lachrimation, or verbal expressions uttered from the depths of despair. ***Grief*** has components of all these, but its defining feature is the sense of irreversible personal loss.[3]

The normal grieving process: Numbness→denial→yearning→depression→guilt/aggression→reintegration. This process may take years. The process may become pathological if major depression (p 336) is precipitated. It is often tempting to try and 'do something' by giving psychotropics, but it is

1 Estragon in http://samuel-beckett.net/Waiting_for_Godot_Part2.html
2 2005 *Drug Ther Bul* 43 2
3 There is in this world in which everything wears out, everything perishes, one thing that crumbles into dust, that destroys itself still more completely, leaving behind still fewer traces of itself than Beauty: namely Grief. M Proust 1925 *Albertine Disparue.* NB: Proust's view is clear enough for grief surviving down generations—which it does not. But what of one person's grief? Surely this can last a lifetime, and Proust is wrong? No: we must assume that Proust had in mind an image from Gérard de Nerval (whom he rated very highly) who describes great grief as being carved into us, not like lettering on stone, which may be worn away by time, but like those initials we carve into the bark of a living tree. As the tree grows, the lettering sinks ever deeper, so that it seems to disappear, but really it has been embodied, internalized, and taken up into the inner life of the organism and distributed even to its fingertips (Richard Holmes on Gérard de Nerval in *Footsteps* 1996 HarperCollins, p 222).

known that most bereaved people do not want this, and there is no evidence that drugs reduce problems. Empathy and helping the patient to shed tears is probably the most valuable approach, especially when losses are covert or hard to acknowledge. Counselling after bereavement is effective.[65] After bereavement, risk of death in spouses rises in the 1st 6 months (men) or in the 2nd year (women). Men and younger bereaved are at greatest risk. It is not known whether this is due to shared unfavourable environments or to psychological causes (eg mediated by the immune system). The main causes of death are vascular, cancer, accidents, and suicide.[66]

Activities which we should try to avoid[67]

- Distancing tactics: 'Everyone feels upset when there is bad news, but you'll soon get used to it.'
- False reassurance: 'I am sure you will feel better; we have good antiemetics these days.'
- Selective attention: 'What is going to happen to me? I'm beginning to think I'm not going to get better this time. The pain in my hip is getting worse.' Doctor: 'Tell me more about your hip.'

Breaking bad news Bad news is any information that drastically alters a patient's view of their future for the worse. Patients have a right to such knowledge, but not a duty to receive it, so negotiation is needed to agree the type of information and the amount they want to hear at any moment. The advantage of patient's being aware of bad news are:

- It helps maintain trust in those caring for them. Trust is what the bedside manner is all about. 'Trust is necessary precisely where we cannot be certain. If we had certainty, we wouldn't need to trust.' Onora O'Neill, Reith lecture
- To reduce uncertainty
- To prevent inappropriate hope
- To allow appropriate adjustment
- To prevent a conspiracy of silence

The central activities in the breaking of bad news are:[68]

1. Preparation—choose a quiet place where you will not be disturbed.
2. Find out what the patient already knows or surmises.
3. Find out how much the person wants to know. You can be surprisingly direct about this. 'Are you the sort of person who, if anything were amiss, would want to know all the details?'
4. Fire a warning shot. 'I am afraid I have bad news.'
5. Allow denial.
6. Explain (if requested). Share information about diagnosis, treatments, prognosis, and specifically list supporting people (eg nurses) and institutions (eg hospices). Ask 'Is there anything else you want me to explain?'
7. Listen to concerns.
8. Recognize and encourage ventilation of the patient's feelings.
9. Summarize and make a plan.
10. Offer availability. The most important thing here is to leave the patient with the strong impression that, come what may, you are with him or her *whatever*, and that this unwritten contract will not be broken.

Useful agents in terminal care[1]

Pain *Remember that pain has physical, emotional, and spiritual components: all aspects need to be addressed. Diagnose and monitor each pain separately.* ***Opiates:*** Diamorphine PO: 2mg≈3mg morphine. SC: 1mg diamorphine≈1.5mg morphine. Sustained release morphine is available, eg MST-30® (30–100mg/12h PO) or MXL (lasts 24h). *Syringe drivers* or *suppositories* can be used when *dysphagia* or *vomiting* make oral drugs useless, eg oxycodone 30mg suppositories (eg 30mg/8h, ≈30mg morphine). If crystallization occurs with drugs mixed in syringe drivers, either increase the dilution, or use 2 syringe drivers. ***Transdermal patches*** are also useful, eg fentanyl (Durogesic® patches last 72h: typical starting dose for someone needing the equivalent of 90mg morphine/day would be one Durogesic-25® patch (the 25 means 25μg fentanyl/h; 50≈135–224mg MST, 75≈225–314mg MST and 100≈315–404mg MST). Use non-irritated, non-irradiated, non-hairy skin on trunk or upper arm; remove after 72h and replace by another patch at a different site. ***Non-opiate analgesia*** may especially help ***bone pain*** (ibuprofen 400mg/8h PO or diclofenac + misoprostol (Arthrotec®), 1 tablet/12h PO.) Pamidronate may also relieve pain from bony secondaries (*OHCM* p 696). ***Nerve destruction pain:*** Amitriptyline 25–50mg PO at night ± clonazepam 0.5–1mg/24h PO nocte, increased slowly to 1–2mg/8h. ***Resistant pain***—Nerve blocks are useful.

Gut symptoms ***Diarrhoea (post radiotherapy):*** Low residue diets.
Constipation: Co-danthramer capsules or liquid ± bisacodyl 5–10mg nocte.
Gastric irritation eg associated with gastric carcinoma—H_2 antagonists (eg cimetidine 400mg/12h PO or proton pump inhibitors (omeprazole).
Itch in jaundice—Cholestyramine 4g/6h PO (1h after other drugs).
Pain with dysphagia or ***vomiting:*** Buprenorphine sublingual 0.2–0.4mg/8h. Not a pure agonist. 'Ceiling' effects negate dose increases.
Foul rectal discharges—Betadine vaginal gel®.
Vomiting Cyclizine 50–150mg/4–8h PO, IM, SC. Haloperidol (p 360) 0.5–2mg PO. *If from inoperable GI obstruction*, try hyoscine hydrobromide 0.4–0.6mg SC/8h or 0.3mg sublingual. Octreotide, max 600μg/24h via a syringe driver may remove the need for palliative surgery, IVIs and NGTs. ***If from gastric stasis:*** Metoclopramide 10mg/8h PO or SC. If this fails, try domperidone 60mg/8h rectally.

Lung symptoms ***Pleural effusion:*** Thoracocentesis (bleomycin pleurodesis).
Air hunger: Chlorpromazine (eg 12.5mg IV).
Bronchial rattles: Hyoscine (as above) 0.4–0.6mg/8h SC or 0.3mg sublingual.
Dyspnoea: (hypoxic)—Table fans ± supplemental humidified oxygen.
Haemoptysis: Diamorphine, above, IV if massive.
Pleural pain: Intercostal nerve blocks may bring lasting relief.

Cardiovascular symptoms ***Distension from ascites*** often causes distressing symptoms. Try spironolactone 100mg/12h PO + bumetanide 1mg/24h PO.

Genitourinary symptoms ***Foul vaginal discharges:*** Betadine vaginal gel®.
Massive bladder bleeding—Alum irrigation (1%) by catheter (in hospital).

Others—***Coated tongues*** may be cleaned by 6% hydrogen peroxide, chewing pineapple chunks to release proteolytic enzmes, sucking on ice, or butter.
Superior vena cava or bronchial obstruction, or lymphangitis carcinomatosa—Steroids; dexamethasone is most useful: give 8mg IV stat. Tabs are 2mg (≈15mg prednisolone) NB: dexamethasone given at night can prevent sleep.

1 UK patients and relatives may get much support via *BACUP* (Brit Ass^n of Cancer United Patients, 3 Bath Place, Rivington St, London, EC2A 3JR, tel. 020 7613 2121). www.cancerbacup.org.uk/Home In the UK, ***Social Services*** can fast-track applications for financial help in the form of the ***Disability Living Allowance***, and the ***Attendance Allowance***, once the prognosis is <6 months. See p462-3. ***Sources:*** *Drug Ther Bul* 2005 **43** 9; *BNF* 2005 *Prescribing in Palliative Care* (ch 1)

Psychological symptoms

Agitation—Try diazepam 10mg suppositories (eg 10mg/8h), or haloperidol (p 360) 0.5–2mg PO (may help nightmares, hallucinations, and vomiting too). Or midazolam in syringe drivers (eg 5-100mg/24h)—or levomepromazine (Nozinan®) 12.5-50mg IM stat or 25-200mg/24h SC via a syringe driver.

Appetite low, or headache due to ↑ICP—Steroids; most useful is dexamethasone, eg 4mg/12-24h PO to stimulate appetite, reduce ICP, and in some patients induce a satisfactory sense of euphoria.

Records and computers

►We cannot make ourselves better people by using a system or a machine: reflection, dialogue, and action are more likely routes to self-improvement.

Problem-orientated records—*List problems as 'active' or 'inactive'* Eg 'breathlessness' (not '?bronchitis'—or 'Down's syndrome', which may be unproblematic to the individual, but a problem to us 'normals'. Use 'SOAP':

Subjective interpretation: How the patient and/or carer sees the problems.

Objective: Physical examination and results of tests (not always objective!).

Assessment: Social, psychological, and physical interpretation.

Plan: Do the following tests ...' or 'Wait on events'; treatment: eg 'Start psychotherapy' and explanation—note what the patient has been told.

Computers These enable faster communication with lab & hospital—also:

- Better and *more* preventive care in theory and in practice (eg 8–18% more vaccinations if a computer is on the GP's desk, more BP measurements, with a ~5mmHg fall in BP in hypertensives; the price is longer consultations—by 48–90sec). Computers now automatically scan patients' records so that we are alerted to missing data. A single keystroke (eg F12, or shift F5) prompts: 'No BP in last 3yr' or 'Has heart disease & chol >5 & not on statin' etc.[69] This single development (linked to payment by results/quality markers in the GP contract of 2004) is likely to be the mechanism by which the mortality of whole populations is *substantially* improved.[70]
- Audit is easier with electronic records of everyone's BP and vaccinations.
- Prescribing: computers save money (eg 8%) by making generic prescribing easy. They are more likely to be associated with complete records (95% *vs* 42%). The electronic *BNF* allows simultaneous viewing of various sections, and links to drug interactions. Computer-assisted prescribing linked to Read codes (eg PRODIGY) can aid prescribing, and aims to improve quality by automatically linking prescribing to practice-modifiable guidelines.[71]
- Can send letters to patients, eg in the light of new drug information.
- Integration of data from multiple sources—eg drug interactions.
- Quick exploration of hypotheses. (Do I see more depression in winter?)
- Assessing eligibility for social security benefits.
- Rule-based systems/neural networks—is this ECG/smear abnormal?
- Keeping up-to-date, decision support and evidence-based medicine, eg the Internet,* and the *Oxford Clinical Mentor*,[1] the latter uses this text, *OHCM*, and the *Oxford Handbook of Clinical Rarities*. This database is regularly updated and contains >25,000 key-worded facts connected by an intelligent index, linked to the medical record via Read codes to enable explanation of apparently unrelated or obscure signs, symptoms and results, eg chest pain, depression, MCV↑ and melaena are explained by alcoholism, with 'postulates' of related trauma (fractured ribs) or cardiomyopathy—both known associations of alcoholism—to account for the chest pain.
- Electronic health records are a goal, the basics of which are easy to see (communicating prescriptions, appointments, lab and clinic data seamlessly between hospitals, GPs, pharmacists and patients—eg in the UK NHS via the NHS net). Implementation on a large scale is proving difficult, and it's easy to criticize the NHS for delays—but note that the UK is the only country to have an overarching information-technology strategy agreed.
- Paperless care becomes possible with electronic booking of appointments (an unquantified benefit), no lost notes; more space; less staff time spent filing—but more dependency on having skilled staff in place and a working computer.

1 *Mentor*; EMIS, tel. +44 (0)1329 828533/1132 582454/01132 591122—see www.emisPDP.com

Medline

[illegible] www.ncbi.nlm.nih.gov/entrez/query.fcgi

We all need to know about Medline: this skill is as basic as taking blood, but easier. The **lucky-dip method** is good for finding information. For example, type [illegible] in the search box and press the go button. [illegible] If this is all you want and you want full text, [illegible].

This page aims to help if you want to be sure you are not missing something and want to cut down irrelevant [illegible] Medline [illegible] searches [illegible] in GREEN CAPITALS. [illegible] the go button, an automatic system [illegible] to match your search to MeSH headings (medical subheadings; [illegible]). To explore alternative therapies for angina, try ANGINA AND THERAPY, then [illegible] the 'details' button to show [illegible] ("angina pectoris"[MeSH Terms] OR angina[Text Word]) AND ("therapy"[Subheading] OR therapeutics[MeSH Terms] OR therapy[Text Word]) [illegible] hits. Adding AND [illegible] to your search phrase [illegible] ~5000; adding ALTERNATIVE before the word THERAPY gives ~40 hits.

Square brackets The contents of these limit or expand the search. Mostly, let Medline do this for you, as in the above example. But there are some square brackets to put in and do the search yourself; for example, ANGINA AND BMJ gives ("angina pectoris"[MeSH Terms] OR angina[Text Word]) AND (bmj[all fields]). There are [illegible]. Instead, try ANGINA AND BMJ [JOURNAL NAME] (exactly this) that automatically maps to ("angina pectoris"[MeSH Terms] OR angina[Text Word]) AND ("BMJ"[Journal Name] OR "Br Med J"[Journal Name] OR "Br Med J (Clin Res Ed)"[Journal Name]) OR BMJ [Journal Name]). This yields ~700 matches, [illegible] as well as fine-tunes your search.

Other useful things to put in square brackets relate to authors [AUTHOR], publication dates [PDAT] and publication types [PTYP]; eg entering ANGINA AND RANDOMIZED CONTROLLED TRIAL [PTYP] AND BLACK DM [AUTHOR] 1998:2006 [PDAT] gives a search which doesn't include articles using common words, such as black, and goes from 1998 to now. Using [illegible] may be more inclusive than using RANDOMIZED CONTROLLED TRIAL [PTYP], but will include sentences such as 'there are no randomized trials'.

Finding MeSH headings You can make search terms more certain by selecting them via the MeSH browser button—look carefully: it's in the left-hand blue margin, half way down. Typing into the search box yields [illegible] terms with ranked mapping. If no exact term is found, choose a likely one from the list offered, and press the browse terms button. Click the Add button to add this to your search. Try this with SMALL VESSEL ANGINA: this is not a MeSH term, but the MeSH browser offers Angina, microvascular among a host of other, less helpful possibilities. Confirm this for yourself.

Other ways of limiting searches Click the Limits button to explore this, or add a word such as HASABSTRACT (one word, no space, added to the search phrase) to retrieve only those articles which have abstracts (this will exclude editorials and correspondence items, for example). An example of **Boolean logic**: Try NIFEDIPINE AND (AMLODIPINE OR FELODIPINE) NOT [illegible] ANGINA [MESH]. This includes studies of [illegible] angina.

EBM try ANGINA AND COCHRANE NOT COCHRANE [AUTHOR], or ANGINA AND META-ANALYSIS, or try the **clinical queries** button. Choose 'sensitive' to avoid **missing** possible hits, or 'specific' if you are **getting** too many hits.

Exercises Now devise, for the idea, [illegible] patients, and find meta-analyses relevant to them. **Why are my searches going wrong?** • [illegible] • For using **capitals** [illegible] • Using the wrong search box

Medline

14 million abstracts & full texts free at www.ncbi.nlm.nih.gov/entrez/query.fcgi

We all need to know about Medline—it's a skill as basic as taking blood—but easier. The **lucky-dip method** is good, but undiscriminating: just enter anything in the search box, and press the 'go' button. A natural-language interface (AskMEDLINE) also exists at http://askmedline.nlm.nih.gov/ask/ask.php. If this is all you want and you want full-text, the best site is http://highwire.stanford.edu

This page aims to help if you want to be sure you are not missing something (and want to cut down irrelevant hits). If Medline is new to you, find an internet connection and an experienced friend and try the searches below in GREEN CAPITALS. When you click the 'go' button, the system tries to match your search to a nomenclature of medical subheadings (MeSH terms). To explore alternative therapies for angina: type ANGINA AND THERAPY (use capitals; ►check your spelling!); click 'go', then the 'details' button to show that this is mapped to (('angina pectoris'[MeSH Terms] OR angina[Text Word]) AND (('therapy'[Subheading] OR 'therapeutics'[MeSH Terms]) OR therapy[Text Word])). There are >23,000 hits. Adding AND RANDOM* to the search phrase (the star gets *randomized, randomised*, etc) narrows these to <3000; adding ALTERNATIVE before the word THERAPY gives <40 hits.

Square brackets The contents of these limit or expand the search. Mostly, let Medline do this for you, as in the above example. But there are some square brackets it's useful to add to the search yourself. For example, ANGINA AND BMJ gives (('angina pectoris'[MeSH Terms] OR angina[Text Word]) AND BMJ [All Fields]). There are <90 hits; but searching on ANGINA AND BMJ [JOURNAL NAME] (*exactly* like that) automatically maps to (('angina pectoris'[MeSH Terms] OR angina[Text Word]) AND ((("BMJ"[Journal Name] OR "Br Med J" [Journal Name]) OR 'Br Med J (Clin Res Ed)'[Journal Name]) OR 'BMJ'[Journal Name])) This yields >300 matches—ie MeSH can expand as well as limit your search.

Other useful things to put in square brackets relate to authors [AUTHOR], publication dates [PDAT] and publication types [PTYP]—eg entering ANGINA AND RANDOMIZED CONTROLLED TRIAL [PTYP] AND BLACK DM [AUTHOR] 1996:2005[PDAT] gives a search which doesn't include articles using common words such as black, and goes from 1996 to now. Using Random* may be more inclusive than using RANDOMIZED CONTROLLED TRIAL [PTYP], but will include sentences such as 'there are no randomized trials'.

Finding MeSH headings You can make search terms more certain by selecting them via the MeSH browser button—look carefully: it's in the left-hand blue margin, half way down. Typing into the search box yields MeSH terms which need no mapping. If no exact term is found, choose a likely one from the list offered, and press the 'browse term' button. Click the 'Add' button to add this to your search. Try this with SMALL VESSEL ANGINA. This is not a MeSH term, but the MeSH browser offers Angina, microvascular, among a host of other less helpful possibilities. Confirm this for yourself.

Other ways of limiting searches Click the 'Limits' button to explore this, or add a word such as HASABSTRACT (one word, no space, added to the search phrase) to retrieve only those articles which have abstracts (but this will exclude editorials and correspondence items for example). ***An example of Boolean logic:*** Try NIFEDIPINE AND (AMLODIPINE OR FELODIPINE) NOT PRINZMETAL ANGINA [MESH]. This excludes studies of Prinzmetal's angina.

EBM Try ANGINA AND COCHRANE NOT COCHRANE[AUTHOR] or ANGINA AND META-ANALYSIS, or try the **clinical queries button**. Choose 'sensitive' to avoid missing possible hits, or 'specific' if you are getting too many hits.

Exercises Now you've got the idea, recall your last 6 patients, and find meta-analyses relevant to them. ***Why are my searches going wrong?*** •Misspellings? •Not using capitals (AND, OR, NOT)? •Using the wrong search box?

Audit

Audit comes from the Latin audire—to hear, and the term was once used for formally presented verified financial accounts. Audit in clinical practice involves quality control by systematic review of (an aspect of) practice, implementing change, and verifying that the desired effect was produced. Its purpose is not exact so to achieve better quality clinical care. Audit means asking questions such as: Have we achieved aims in medical practice? and Are we falling short of these aims, and what can we do to improve? [illegible] Audit is a part of the summative assessment required for all GP registrars to pass before they can become principals. Since 2002 an 8 point audit is required. [See example]

1 **Title**: When selecting a topic think: is it a very common or important, or expensive area amenable to change? For a registrar audit is it simple? For other audits, is it worth the investment of time and money? e.g. why you chose the particular topic. [*Does exercise improve diabetic control?*]
2 **What criteria were chosen?** [illegible] [*HbA1c will be used as a marker of diabetic care*]
3 **Setting standards**: A standard is a statement of a criterion of good quality care. A target should be set (the degree to which the criterion will be met). Choose a realistic and obtainable target. Aim for standards to be evidence based. [*HbA1c <7.5% reflects adequate control. Target to have ≥50% patients with HbA1c <7.5%*]
4 **Planning and preparation**: What have you done. For example what literature has been consulted (essential) [*Consulted NICE, SIGN for evidence (literature); put all HbA1c results on computer at their clinic visit*]
5 **First Data Collection**: Gather the evidence. Observe current practice. Compare this to the standard. [*40% HbA1c <7.5%*]
6 **Implement change** [*Implement vigorous exercise programme*]
7 **Second Data Collection**: Compare with the standard and the first data collection. [*Check patients receiving intervention? 45% HbA1c <7.5%*]
8 **Conclusions** [*Exercise works, or is important to the cycle*] Use these to complete your next cycle to complete the audit cycle. [*Better exercise interventions*]

Other people's audits can seem boring: it is only when a practice engages in audit itself that interest is aroused, and it can be satisfying to watch ones practice develop through a series of audits. With computers, audits can be done on many aspects of care, to answer questions such as 'Is our care of diabetes adequate? Are all our fertile female patients rubella-immune?'

The practice manager can have a central role in running an audit exercise, e.g. by relieving doctors of the burden of data collection, and is able to communicate the results of the audit in a practice's annual report.

Possible dangers of audit (No intervention is without side-effects)

- It takes time away from eye-to-eye contact with patients.
- In becoming the province of professional enthusiasts, it can alienate some practice members who can then ignore the results of the audit.
- There is no guarantee that audit will improve outcomes.
- It may limit our horizons—from the consideration of the vast and ponderables of our patients' lives in a world of death, decay and rebirth to a pieced pattern with trainingly specific and very limited goals.
- Some doctors fear that in espousing audit, they risk transforming themselves from approachable [illegible] bureaucratic [illegible] who don't know exactly why they are going into complex administrative apoplexies, with too much of a gleam in their eyes and tails in their hearts.

Audit

Audit comes from the Latin audire—to hear; and the term was once used for verbally presented verified financial accounts. Audit in clinical practice involves quality control by systematic review of (an aspect of) practice, implementing change and verifying that the desired effect was produced. Its purpose is as a tool to achieve best quality clinical care. Audit means asking questions such as: 'Have we any agreed aims in medical practice?' and 'Are we falling short of these aims?' and 'What can we do to improve performance?' Audit is a part of the Summative Assessment required for all UK GP registrars to pass before they can become principals. As from 2002 an 8 point audit is required. *[See examples]*

1 *Title:* When selecting a topic think: is it relevant; common or important; measurable; amenable to change? For a registrar audit, is it simple? For other audits, is it worth the investment (of time and money)? Say why you chose the particular topic. *[Does exercise improve diabetic control?]*

2 *What criteria were chosen:* State why the criterion/criteria were chosen. *[Hb_{A1c} will be used as a marker of diabetic care]*

3 *Setting standards* A standard is a statement of a criterion of good quality care. A target should be set (the degree to which the criterion will be met). Choose a realistic and obtainable target. Aim for standards to be evidence based. *[Hb_{A1c} <7.5% reflects adequate control. Target to have >50% patients with Hb_{A1c} <7.5%]*

4 *Planning and preparation* What have you done? For example, what literature has been consulted (essential). *[Consulted NSF (p 523) for diabetes (literature): put all Hb_{A1c} results on computer as they came in]*

5 *First Data Collection* Gather the evidence. Observe current practice. Compare this to the standard. *[40% Hb_{A1c} <7.5%]*

6 *Implement changes* [Implement vigorous exercise programme]

7 *Second Data Collection* Compare with the standard and the first data collection. *[Check patients received intervention? 45% Hb_{A1c} <7.5%]*

8 *Conclusions [Exercise works; target not reached]* Use these to formulate your next title to complete the *audit cycle*. *[Better exercise intervention]*

Other people's audits can seem boring. It is only when a practice engages in audit itself that interest is aroused, and it can be satisfying to watch one's practice develop through a series of audits. With computers, audits can be done on many aspects of care, to answer questions such as—Is our care of diabetics adequate? Are all our fertile female patients rubella-immune?

The practice manager can have a central role in running an audit exercise—eg by relieving doctors of the burden of data collection, and is able to communicate the results of the audit in a practice's annual report.

Possible dangers of audit (No intervention is without side-effects.)

- It takes time away from eye-to-eye contact with patients.
- In becoming the province of professional enthusiasts, it can alienate some practice members, who can then ignore the results of the audit.
- There is no guarantee that audit will improve outcomes.
- It may limit our horizons—from the consideration of the vast imponderables of our patients' lives in a world of death, decay, and rebirth—to a preoccupation with attaining tiny, specific, and very limited goals.
- Some doctors fear that in espousing audit they risk transforming themselves from approachable but rather bumbling carers and curers who perhaps don't know *exactly* where they are going, into minor administrative prophets, with too much of a gleam in their eyes and zeal in their hearts.

Appraisal, assessment, and revalidation

Appraisal is not the same as assessment. For most UK GPs (for whom yearly appraisal is a contractual requirement) peer appraisal is less threatening—it is seen as a chat with a colleague about one's professional development.

What form does UK appraisal take? Log on to www.appraisals.nhs.uk and complete 2 administrative forms (Forms 1 & 2); then there is Form 3 which needs some thought and is an extensive (un)protected form, and a commentary on your work, an account of how it has developed since your last appraisal, your view of your development needs, and cataloguing of factors which constrain you in achieving your aims. Sample questions:

- What are the main strengths and weaknesses of your clinical practice?
- How has the clinical care you provide improved since your last appraisal?
- What do you think are the clinical care development needs for the future?
- What factors constrain you in achieving your aims for your clinical work?
- What steps have you taken to improve your knowledge and skills?
- What have you found particularly successful or otherwise about these steps?
- What professional or personal factors constrain you in maintaining and developing your skills and knowledge?
- How do you see your job and career developing over the next few years?
- What are your main strengths and weaknesses in your relationships with patients? How have these improved? What would you like to do better? What factors in the workplace (or more widely) constrain this?
- What are your main strengths and weaknesses in your relationships with colleagues? How have these improved? What would you like to do better? What factors in the workplace or more widely constrain this?
- Do you have any health-related issues which might put patients at risk?

Other areas: teaching, financial probity, research, management activities.

During the appraisal **Form 4** is completed and signed by the assessor and the assessee. In anonymized format, **Form 4** feeds through to Clinical Governance Leads, who identify trends and makes a report to the Chief Executive of his or her Primary Care Organization. **Form 5** is a non-obligatory form containing background ideas supporting Form 4 which may be used to inform subsequent appraisals. Finally there is a mechanism for supportive follow-up (eg a further visit or phone call).

In the words of the chief medical officer, appraisal is a positive and supportive developmental process, a constructive dialogue to ensure in such a way that those being appraised have the opportunity to reflect on their work and to consider any developmental needs. It gives individuals the chance to assess their career path and consider how they might gain more job satisfaction from their current role. And by giving feedback on performance, it provides the opportunity both to identify any factors that adversely affect performance, and to consider how to minimize or eliminate their effects. It is an important building block in a clinical governance culture that ensures high standards and the best possible patient care, [illegible]

There is a big question mark over assessment (see above). [illegible] appraisal in primary care [illegible] other opportunities for later reflection, [illegible] self-evaluation [illegible] work and career development in the wider medical world. [illegible] a catalyst for change and a safeguard against complacency.

Appraisal only makes sense assuming that GPs want to be good professionals, [illegible] performance [illegible] assessment will be [illegible]

Revalidation [illegible] gives authority to continue practising, and to [illegible] safety. [illegible] the process.

Appraisal, assessment, and revalidation

►*Appraisal is not the same as assessment.* For NHS UK GPs (for whom yearly appraisal is a contractual requirement) peer appraisal is least threatening when seen as a chat with a colleague about one's professional development.

What form does UK appraisal take? Log on to www.appraisals.nhs.uk and complete 2 administrative forms (***Forms 1 &2***); then there is ***Form 3*** which needs some thought and data gathering (in protected time)—with a commentary on your work, an account of how it has developed since your last appraisal, your view of your developmental needs, and cataloguing of factors which constrain you in achieving your aims. Sample questions:

- What are the main strengths and weaknesses of your clinical practice?
- How has the clinical care you provide improved since your last appraisal?
- What do you think are the clinical care development needs for the future?
- What factors constrain you in achieving your aims for your clinical work?
- What steps have you taken to improve your knowledge and skills?
- What have you found particularly successful or otherwise about these steps?
- What professional or personal factors constrain you in maintaining and developing your skills and knowledge?
- How do you see your job and career developing over the next few years?
- What are your main strengths and weaknesses in your relationships with patients? How have these improved? What would you like to do better? What factors in the workplace (or more widely) constrain this?
- What are your main strengths and weaknesses in your relationships with colleagues? How have these improved? What would you like to do better? What factors in the workplace or more widely constrain this?
- Do you have any health-related issues which might put patients at risk?

Other areas: Teaching; financial probity; research; management activities.

During the appraisal ***Form 4*** is completed and signed by the assessor and the assessee. In anonymized format, ***Form 4*** feeds through to Clinical Governance Leads, who identify trends, and makes a report to the Chief Executive of his or her Primary Care Organization. ***Form 5*** is a non-obligatory form containing background ideas supporting Form 4 which may be used to inform subsequent appraisals. Finally there is a mechanism for supportive follow-up (eg a further visit or phone call).

In the words of the chief medical officer, appraisal is 'a positive and supportive developmental process, a constructive dialogue structured in such a way that those being appraised have the opportunity to reflect on their work and consider any developmental needs. It gives individuals the chance to assess their career path and consider how they might gain more job satisfaction from their current role. And by giving feedback on performance it provides the opportunity both to identify any factors that adversely affect performance, and to consider how to minimize or eliminate their effects. It is an important building block in a clinical governance culture that *ensures* high standards and the best possible patient care.' www.doh.gov.uk/cmo/cmo0203.htm

There is a big question-mark over 'ensures', above. The effect of appraisal on patient care is unknown—but, appraisal, it is hoped (and it only is a hope) can offer opportunities, for interdependent support, self-education, self-motivation, and career development in the wider medical world. It may also be a catalyst for change and even a tonic against complacency.[73]

Appraisal only makes sense assuming that GPs want to be good, professional, life-long learners. If this is not the case, the less soft realms of revalidation, performance management/assessment will bite.

Revalidation (eg every 4-5yrs) gives authority to continue practicing, and to some extent guarantees public safety. Appraisals feed into this process.

Under- and over-performing doctors

It would be nice for the public and the 'leaders' of our profession if there were a small number of underperforming doctors who could be retrained or struck off. Things are rarely so simple, and we may have to accept that, for many reasons, including chance, training, and resilience, the performance of *all doctors* will, at times, be, or appear to be suboptimal. If all doctors were the same, and there was a valid yardstick for measuring quality (a big 'if'), then there would be, by chance, a large underperforming group, with a corresponding apparently 'over-performing' group. Anyone assessing performance data needs to take into account these questions:

What counts as data? Usually only what can be *quantified*; *quality* is different.
Is the data stratified for risk? Doctors' case-mixes can vary markedly.
Is our personal data's accuracy validated? Data entry is often unreliable.
Has the accuracy of the data we are being compared with been validated?
Could the differences between our data and others have arisen by chance? This is the most revealing question. Imagine a thought-experiment in which 4 equal doctors use different strategies for predicting whether a tossed coin will land heads or tails. One always chooses heads, one always chooses tails, and the other two alternate their choices out of synchrony with each other. When I did this experiment for a pre-decided 14 throws each (56 throws in total), the best doctor only had 2 errors, whereas the worse had 7 errors—over 3 times the rate for post-operative deaths (or whatever). The public would demand that this doctor be retrained or struck off, and the General Medical Council might feel obliged to comply, simply to keep public confidence (it is under great pressure to 'do something'). So must we all be prepared to be sacrificial lambs? The answer is *Yes*, but there are certain steps that can be taken to mitigate our own and our patients' risk-exposure.

- When we encounter doctors who are clearly underperforming (eg due to addictions) we must speak out. This will encourage belief in the system.
- For statistical reasons any series with <16 failures might be best ignored. Such series simply do not have enough power to detect real effects.
- We must strive to be both kind and honest with our patients. The best response to 'I'd like a home-delivery' might be to say 'I haven't done one for 5 years—and that one went wrong: are you sure you want my services?'—rather than 'the UK perinatal death-rate is the same for home and hospital'.
- It might be the case that, contrary to the GMC, we should *not* always be on the look-out for colleagues who might be underperforming so that we can report them to the proper authorities: rather we should be encouraging an atmosphere of mutual support and trust—the sort of environment in which doctors feel safe to say 'all my cases of X seem to be going wrong—can anyone think why?' To stop this trust turning into cronyism we must be prepared to engage in, or be subjected to, audit (p 506). The alternative is for clinicians to develop into secret police, informers, and counter-informers. No one would benefit from this. We note that malicious informing is not an isolated occurrence in the UK; 80% of those suspended for presumed underperformance are exonerated, but few return to their previous job owing to the stresses enquiries always engender.

Typical areas in which doctors are seen to be underperforming Local Medical Committees (LMCs), complaints bodies, and NHS commissioners have all been systematically questioned about doctors whose performance they are reviewing. In the case of LMCs, for example, clinical skills were the chief worry, followed, in order, by communication problems, management problems, prescribing problems, and record-keeping problems. NHS Trusts have more concern over referral patterns.

Patient satisfaction

►*The patient is the nearest thing we have to an infallible judge of what constitutes good medicine.* In summary, what patients mostly want is a *personal service* from a *sympathetic* doctor who is *nearby* and *easy to get to see.* Satisfaction is one of the few measures of *outcome* (not *process*) which is measurable, eg by questionnaire agreement with these 13 statements.[74]

Satisfaction[1]

1 I am totally satisfied with my visit to this doctor.
2 Some things about my visit to the doctor could have been better.
3 I am not completely satisfied with my visit to the doctor.

Professional care

4 This doctor examined me very thoroughly.
5 This doctor told me everything about my treatment.
6 I thought this doctor took notice of me as a person.
7 I will follow the doctor's advice because I think he/she is right.
8 I understand my illness much better after seeing this doctor.

Relationships

9 This doctor knows all about me.
10 I felt this doctor really knew what I was thinking.
11 I felt able to tell this doctor about very personal things.

Perceived time

12 The time I was allowed with the doctor was not long enough to deal with everything I wanted.
13 I wish I could have spent a bit longer with the doctor.

Why do patients change their doctor? The most common reasons are that either the patient has moved, or the doctor has retired or is perceived to be too far away. There are additional reasons:[75]

Patient needs:		*Organizational problems:*		*Problems with doctor:*	
One doctor for all the family	5%	Long waits	13%	Lost confidence in	21%
Wants woman doctor	4%	No continuity of care	6%	Uninterested/rude	20%
Wants alternative medicine	2%	Rude receptionist	6%	Prescriptions criticized	5%
Obstetric needs	1%	Wants appointments	1%	Doctor too hurried	4%
		Wants open surgeries	1%	Visits problematic	4%
		Other staff rude	1%	Communication poor	4%

A USA study found that a *participatory decision-making style* leads to patient satisfaction. Participation was found to depend, in part, on the *degree of autonomy* perceived to be enjoyed by the GP, and on the volume of work.[76]

Another approach to gaining satisfaction is to agree and publish standards of care patients can expect, with performance figures for how nearly these standards are met in practice. This is the philosophy behind the UK government-led *Patient's Charter*/British Standards kitemark BS5750, which aims to:

- Set standards, eg by agreement with patient participation groups (p 496).
- Monitor progress towards these standards, and publish progress locally.
- Provide information about how services are organized. Maximize choice.
- Let users know who is in charge of what, and what their roles are.
- Explain to users what is done when things go wrong, and how services are improved, and what the complaints procedure is.
- Show that taxpayers' money is being used efficiently.
- Demonstrate customer satisfaction.

This culture has proved alien to most GPs, perhaps owing to a very necessary preoccupation with illness and its curing, rather than service, and its glorification.

1 Other questionnaires (eg CFEP P3185(2)/10118-10120) ask about *the practice* (eg 48h access) and the *staff* (respect, conifentiality) as well as the *individual doctor.*

Stopping smoking tobacco

UK health improvement targets aim to decrease smoking from [illegible]% to [illegible]% by 2010. Current rate of progress is thought to be only 0.1–0.[illegible]%. Epidemiologists estimate that 50% of smokers will die of smoking if they do not give up, and [illegible] completely [illegible] survival [illegible] century's smokers lead to more [illegible] between the ages of 35 and [illegible]. Stopping smoking diminishes the excess risk from tobacco [illegible] after [illegible] years the risk of lung cancer [illegible] that of nonsmokers. A similar, but quicker, diminution of excess risk [illegible] in the first years is found for deaths from coronary heart disease and [illegible] (see [illegible] risk of stroke [illegible] of smokers [illegible].

Annual UK health costs of smoking [illegible] consultations [illegible] prescriptions [illegible] million [illegible] hospital episodes: [illegible] million

Advantages of stopping smoking [illegible]

- [illegible] babies (smokers' babies [illegible] less than expected [illegible] their physical and mental development may be less than optimal
- Less bronchitis [illegible] prescriptions [illegible] working days
- [illegible] risk from the [illegible] cigarettes [illegible]
- Less risk [illegible] smoking [illegible] lung cancer
- [illegible] and small [illegible]

Helping people quit [illegible] advise, assist [illegible] follow-up [illegible] at every possible consultation [illegible] those on smoking [illegible] keep up the patient['s] [illegible] you do not [illegible] standard.

- Advise [illegible] Explore [illegible] smokers [illegible] patients by getting them to [illegible] advantages of quitting [illegible]
- [illegible] practical [illegible] will [illegible] set a quit date [illegible] will be [illegible] (eg on [illegible] support [illegible]
- [illegible] nicotine [illegible] patches [illegible] chance of [illegible]
- [illegible] used [illegible] to [illegible] Starting [illegible] for [illegible] may be [illegible] in Wales [illegible] advice from [illegible] review [illegible] your [illegible] prescribing [illegible]
- Bupropion [illegible] quit rate [illegible] patients [illegible] if [illegible] above [illegible] within [illegible] the dose may be [illegible] for 7 weeks [illegible] is the [illegible] seizure [illegible] Warn of SEs [illegible] headache [illegible] [illegible] withdrawal [illegible]

Interactions: [illegible] antidepressants, [illegible] antipsychotics, [illegible]

For those who do not want to give up [illegible] better [illegible] and [illegible] harm [illegible] smokers [illegible] Education [illegible] of [illegible] smoking [illegible] cigarettes [illegible] children [illegible] [illegible] a fashion accessory.

Every health worker should [illegible] opportunity [illegible] primary health care teams, hospitals, midwives, [illegible] employers [illegible] also need to promote knowledge and training in this area.

Primary care

511

Stopping smoking tobacco

See www.nice.org.uk

NHS 'health inprovement targets' aim to decrease smoking from 26% to <21% by 2010—current rate of progress is thought to be only 0.1%-0.3%/yr.[1] Epidemiologists estimate that ~50% of smokers will die of smoking if they do not give up—and it is not the case that they only lose a few years: a quarter of a century is more likely for those dying between the ages of 35 and 69.[1] Stopping smoking diminishes the excess risk from tobacco, so that after 10-15yrs the risk of lung cancer effectively reverts to that of lifelong nonsmokers. A similar, but quicker diminution of excess risk (↓ by ~50% in the first year) is found for deaths from coronary artery disease and, to a lesser extent, risk of stroke.[77] ►*60% of smokers want to give up.*

Annual UK health costs of smoking
- GP consultations: >£89 million
- GP prescriptions: >£52 million
- Hospital episodes: >£470 million

Advantages of stopping smoking Saving of life (110,000/yr in UK).
- Larger babies (smokers' babies weigh on average 250g less than expected, and their physical and mental development may be less than optimal).
- Less bronchitis (accounts for millions of lost working days).
- Less risk from the Pill: cardiovascular risk↑ ×20 if uses >30 cigarettes/day.
- Less risk from passive smoking (cot deaths, bronchitis, lung cancers).
- Return of the sense of taste and smell—and relative wealth.

Helping people quit (AAAA=**a**sk, **a**dvise, **a**ssist, **a**rrange follow-up.)[RCT 78] Ask about smoking in all consultations, not just those on smoking-related diseases (be subtle; patients won't listen if you do not share agendas).
- Advise according to need. Ensure that advice is congruent with beliefs; motivate patients by getting *them* to list the advantages of quitting.
- Assist in practical ways, eg negotiate a commitment to a 'quit date' when there will be few stresses; agree on throwing away all smoking junk (cigarettes, ash trays, lighters, matches) in advance. Inform friends of new change.
  - *Nicotine gum*, chewed intermittently to limit nicotine release: ≥ten 2mg sticks may be needed/day. *Transdermal nicotine patches* may be easier. A dose increase at 1 week can help. Written advice offers no added benefit to advice from nurses/GPs. Review at 2 weeks; people sense (and act on) your committment. Only re-prescribe if abstinent.
  - *Bupropion* ups the quit rate to perhaps 30% at 1yr *vs* 16% with patches: consider if the above fails. *Dose:* 150mg/24h PO (while still smoking; quit within 2 weeks); the dose may be doubled from day 7; stop after 7 weeks. Give enough to last 3 weeks, then review; only re-prescribe if abstinent—ie the *abtsinent contingent treatment* (ACT) regimen. ***Warn of SEs:*** Seizures (risk <1:1000), insomnia, headache, ?arrhythmias. *CI:* Epilepsy; cirrhosis; pregnancy; lactation; bipolar depression; eating disorders; CNS tumours; alcohol/benzodiazepine withdrawal; ≤18yr old.

    Interactions: Antimalarials, antipsychotics, antidepressants, antihistamines, antiepileptics, quinolones, theophylline, tramadol, steroids.

For those who do not want to give up Give them a health education leaflet, record this fact in the record, and try again later.

►25% of school leavers smoke regularly. The Health Education Council has a smoking education project for schools. It has been commented that smoking rates may not be rising too fast in children owing to cost, and to mobile phones, which are cheaper, and just as good a fashion accessory.

Every health 'outlet' should have a policy on promoting nonsmoking, and offering practical advice: primary health care teams; hospitals; midwives; pharmacies—and also, perhaps, schools and employers. Health commissioners also needed to promote knowledge and training in this area.[79]

1 E Milne 2005 *BMJ* **330** 760

Reducing alcohol intake

With the toll that excess alcohol takes in terms of personal misery and the national purse (>£1600 million/yr in the UK), the need to reduce alcohol intake should rank as one of the leading aims of preventive care. The reason why alcohol is not at the top of the agenda is not just that doctors are so fond of it (the profession has three times the national rate of cirrhosis), but because there is a powerful and pervasive lobby which ensures that alcohol is cheaper (in relative terms) and more readily available than ever before—so that its use on an individually moderate scale arouses no comment. It is assumed to be safe, provided one is not actually an alcoholic. However, it is more helpful to view alcohol risks and benefits as a spectrum (see *OHCM* p 208 for the *benefits* of alcohol). Problems are listed on p 363. A strategy to reduce the bad effects of alcohol in your patients might comprise:

- If a symptom could be alcohol-related, ask *in detail* about consumption.
- Question any patient with 'alerting factors'—accidents, driving offences, child neglect, assault, attempted suicide, depression, obesity. Question others as they register, consult, or attend for any health check.

Helping people to cut down ►Time interventions for when motivation is maximal, eg as (or before) pregnancy starts. Small reductions *do* matter.[80]

- Take more non-alcoholic drinks; reduce the sip frequency, eg by shadowing a slow drinker in the group. Don't pick up your glass until he does (and don't hold your glass for long: put it down to avoid unconscious sipping).
- Limit your drinking to social occasions—and learn to sip, not gulp.
- Don't buy yourself a drink when it is your turn to buy a drinks' round.
- Go out to the pub later (may not work as some UK pubs, since 2005, are licensed, to be open all night). Take 'days of rest' when no alcohol is used.
- Learn graceful ways of refusing: 'No more for me please, I expect I'll have to drive Jack home' or 'I'm seeing what it's like to cut down.'

Maintaining reduced drinking • Agree goals with the patient.

- Suggest he keeps an alcohol diary in which he records all drinking.
- Teach him to estimate his alcohol intake (u/week, see below).
- Consider an 'Alcohol Card' in the notes to show: units/week; pattern of drinking; reasons for misuse; each alcohol-related problem (and whether a solution has been agreed and action implemented); job record; family events; biochemical markers (GGT, MCV); weight.
- Give feedback about how he is doing—eg if GGT (γ-glutamyl transpeptidase) falls are discussed at feedback, there is much lower mortality, morbidity and hospitalization compared with randomized control subjects.
- Enlist family support; agree a system of 'rewards' for sobriety.
- Group therapy, self-help groups, disulfiram, local councils on alcohol, community alcohol teams and treatment units may also help (p 363).

Setting limits for low-risk drinking eg ≤20U/week if ♂; ≤14U/week if ♀—there are no absolutes: risk is a continuum. NB: higher limits are proposed, on scant evidence (eg 4U/day; 3U for women). One unit is 9g ethanol, ie 1 measure of spirits, 1 glass of wine, or half a pint of ordinary-strength beer.[81] ►*Primary care is a good setting for prevention*: intervention leads to less alcohol consumption by ~15%, reducing the proportion of heavy drinkers by 20%—at one-twentieth the cost of specialist services.[82] There is no evidence that GP intervention has to include more time-consuming advice such as compressed cognitive/behavioural strategies.[83] Simple advice works fine as judged by falling GGT levels—at least for men. After interventions, women may report drinking less, but this is not reflected in a falling GTT.[84]

Does education work? A bit: as medical students, we drink less in the final year, compared with year 2; but, overall, 27% are problem drinkers.[85] Should we all write and implement a personal alcohol policy? ►'No doctor should practise after just 1 glass of wine.' *Lancet* 2005 *360*

Domestic and intimate partner violence

This is common and includes physical, sexual, emotional, and psychological abuse. It is rarely an isolated event, and often escalates in severity and frequency. ►Do not hesitate to ask directly about this in consultations. Distinguish between *generalized aggressors*, *family only aggressors*, and *non-family only aggressors*. Once violent always violent? This unfair generalization is less likely to be true for family-only aggressors.[86] This an important area because with each subsequent act of violence, guilt is less, at least when women are perpetrators.[87] Violence is not a male-only problem. 'To respond to violence only as a crime of a single party is a near-guarantee of failure to reduce future violence. Violence can be reduced only by treating each incident of violence as an opportunity for all parties ... the entire society—to explore their own involvement in and responsibilities for violence. Arbitrary 'punishment' of individuals for collective violence is, like most punishment, itself a form of violence. Arbitrary assignment of blame is an evasion of responsibility on the part of the blamer ... Most existing strategies on violence, which are primarily focussed on blame and criminalisation, are thus inherently counter-productive, resulting in the observed high rates of recidivism.'[88]

Epidemiology 35% women experience domestic violence at some time; ~1:10 in the last year. 30% of domestic violence starts in pregnancy.[89] Police record >1 million incidents of domestic violence/yr (1 in 4 of UK assaults). Of women murdered, 40% are killed by a current or ex-partner.

Those who are abused are: 5 times more likely to abuse alcohol; 9 times more likely to abuse drugs; 3 times more likely to be diagnosed psychotic or depressed; 5 times more likely to commit suicide; and 15 times more likely to suffer a miscarriage than non-abused women.

Those who work in the health service should be aware that abuse is common. Those who are abused may attend frequently with trivial or non-existent complaints; or conversely not attend for treatment because of lack of money. They may minimize signs of violence on the body; be evasive or reluctant to speak in front of partners, and partners may tend to be constantly present so that it may be difficult to talk to the woman alone. This can be particularly difficult if the partner is required for translation purposes: here another translator should be sought who is not from the family.

Social Services can help women disclose violence (eg after unexplained injury etc). Ask about abuse in antenatal clinics so that issues can be addressed *before* injury. Involve social services if children are involved (p 146).

Refuge The Women's Aid Federation (0345 023468[UK]) can provide legal advice, emotional support, and refuge. The police may also help.

Court orders are obtainable quickly, and may be the only way to prevent someone going near a previous victim.[90] They may also require someone to leave home, or let the victim return home. They are not a long-term solution, but are life savers in emergency. In the UK, Law Centres give access to legal protection: to find the nearest, phone 0207 387 8570. Alternatively, the patient's solicitor may be available. The police may also need calling.

Prevention Lack of full-time employment is a leading predictor of who is going to get abused[91]—but simply saying 'go out and get a job' may be unhelpful if child-care issues cannot be sorted out.

See also *Child abuse*, p 146. ***Parent–child interaction therapy*** (PCIT)[1] is one validated way of reducing family violence (compared with controls who simply have standard community-based interventions).[92] This offers practical help in recognizing antecedent events which tend to trigger violence.

1 Through a one-way mirror, the therapist watches the parent interact with the child. The parent wears an electric device in the ear to receive help & real-time feedback from the therapist next-door.

Alternative and holistic medicine

►We need to know about alternative medicine to understand our patients undeclared distress, which use of non-standard treatments is so often a sign of. We also need to be able to advise on the safety of various therapies.

'*Alternative*' describes therapies not included in conventional medical/paramedical training; many are being tested in blinded, randomized trials.

Some are the orthodoxies of a different time (eg *herbalism*) or place (the *Ayurvedic medicine* of India), some are mainly diagnostic techniques (*iridology*), some therapeutic (*aromatherapy*). Some doctors are suspicious of unorthodox medicine, and feel that its practitioners should not be 'let loose' on patients. But in many places the legal position is that, however unorthodox a practitioner's treatment may be, he or she cannot be convicted of unethical practice in the absence of clear harm to patients.

Many people (~5 million/yr in the UK) consult alternative practitioners, usually as a supplement to orthodox treatment and for a limited range of problems—predominantly musculoskeletal. Many will feel unable to tell their doctor about trips to alternative therapists, unless asked.

Modern medicine is criticized for sacrificing humanity to technology, and with little benefit for many people. In contrast to the orthodox doctor, alternative therapists is seen as taking time to listen, laying on hands rather than instruments, and giving medicines free (not always!) from side-effects.

Many alternative therapies seem implausible, and controlled trials are hard, if treatment is individualized and therapists' personality is a vital factor. But the same comments could be made of much orthodox care.

Acupuncture: Can treat many ailments; increasingly used in orthodox practice for pain relief, control of nausea and treatment of addiction. For these, endorphin release provides a scientific rationale.

Homeopathy: This is based on the principles that like cures like, and that remedies are made more efficacious ('potentiated') by infinite dilution. UK NHS GPs may prescribe homeopathic remedies on an FP10. Randomized trials are negative or suggest real (small) benefits, eg in asthma, but nobody knows if the reason *why* they are effective is 'like cures like'.

Manipulative therapies (osteopathy and chiropracty): These are widely used and of proven benefit in musculoskeletal problems, but some use them to treat more general conditions such as asthma.

Clinical ecology Starting from the fact that atmospheric pollutants, toxins, and xenobiotic chemicals (from other organisms) are known to be harmful, a system is built up around techniques (using intradermal injections) for provoking and neutralizing symptoms related to foods.

Holistic medicine Holism entails a broad view: of the patient as a whole person, of the role of the therapist, of the therapies used. The patient's autonomy is encouraged through involvement in decisions, and nurturing of self-reliance. ►*Specialism doesn't exclude holism:* nephrologists can be as holistic as naturopaths. As shown on p 478, most models of the GP consultation are based on a patient-centred approach which is essentially holistic. Compare the sequence 'bronchitis→antibiotic' with 'bronchitis→smoker →stressed→redundancy-counselling→?antibiotic'.

'Doctor, can I use alternative therapy for HRT?' One answer might be: 'Extracts from red clover (*Trifolium pratense*), soybean (*Glycine max*) and black cohosh (*Cimicifuga racemosa*; eg 8mg of standardized extract PO/24h) are often used. Unreplicated randomized trials support their use[93] [94]—but if these agents *are* active, they might have the same SEs as HRT. We do not know. Finding out would be a multi-million pound enterprise. You could try them, and you might well be lucky. ►Beware of being influenced by advertising.'[95]

Living dangerously

Some years ago a patient had a seminoma treated, apparently successfully, in a well-known London hospital, to which he had been referred from his distant Sussex village. In the year that follow-up stopped, the patient had a major myocardial infarction—again, followed by an apparently reasonable recovery. But the patient became morbid, self-centred, and depressed, perhaps because of the dawning appreciation of his mortality, his residual breathlessness, and his inability to carry out his hobby of carpentry. His GP tried hard to cheer him up, and rehabilitate him by encouraging exercise, sex, a positive self-image, and alternative hobbies. Rehabilitation was almost working when he began to develop headaches and kept asking forlornly whether these were a sign that his cancer had spread to his brain. There were no signs of recurrent tumour or raised intracranial pressure. His GP appreciated that there *was* a chance that the tumour was resurfacing, but judged that starting a pointless chain of investigations would be disastrous to the patient's mental health. So instead of arranging CT scans the GP interpreted the patient's forlorn question for him, saying that he was only asking questions like this because he was in a negative frame of mind, and the patient and his GP developed strategies to avoid negative cognitions, in co-operation with the local consultant who had helped to look after his myocardial infarction. The headaches improved, and the pressure to investigate was resisted.

Had a CT scan been done, it would by no means have achieved reassurance if it was negative—in the patient's frame of mind he would be all too willing to ask if the CT scan is 100% reliable, and then to request some other test in addition, and so on, until illness had become a major preoccupation. So in this case, it was rational for the doctor to live dangerously, take risks, and be prepared to take the blame if things had gone wrong.

How do we cope with and thrive on uncertainty? The first step is to get away from the idea that if you do not do all you can to reduce uncertainty, you are somehow being lazy. (The reverse may be true.) The next step is to share the uncertainty with a colleague—to see if he or she agrees with your judgment. From the medicolegal viewpoint it is wise to document your thought processes. Another caution is to follow in the steps of those adventurous but wise mountaineers who never plan a route without also planning an escape route: in the medical sense, this means the triad of follow-up, the taking of the family into one's confidence, and honest reflection on the chances of error and the chances of detecting it. This means that, as far as possible, you will get early warning of error, and then be able to adjust your therapeutic approach in line with the way the illness unfolds. In retrospect you may blame yourself if things go wrong: if you do, take time to purify your motives, and be comforted by Soren Kierkegaard's aphorism that ►*Life can only be understood **backwards**, but it must be lived **forwards**.*

Minor illness

Many people with apparently minor illnesses visit their GPs, although GPs do not have a sufficient monopoly of this to justify being called 'triviologists'. Most minor illnesses are dealt with from a disease point of view, in the relevant chapter in which they occur. Here, the concern is with the study of minor illness itself, and in this context much minor illness does not come to the general practitioner: only *people* come to general practitioners, and it may not be known for some time whether the symptoms are serious or minor (minor to whom?). A GP may not want to spend all his time on minor conditions, but this may become almost unavoidable if he issues a prescription for such complaints. This reinforces attendance at the surgery, as a proportion of patients will come to assume that a prescription is necessary. In current practice, GPs rate about 14% of their consultations as being for minor illness (mild gastroenteritis, upper respiratory problems, presumed viral infections, flu, and childhood exanthemata).[96] More than 80% are likely to receive a prescription, and >10% are asked to return for a further consultation. Why does this great investment of time and money occur? Desire to please, genuine concern, prescribing to end a consultation, and therapeutic uncertainty may all play a part. Positive correlations with low prescribing rates include a young doctor, practising in affluent areas and long consultation times. Patients in social classes I and II are more likely to get a home visit for minor ailments than those in other social classes. Membership of the Royal College of General Practitioners does not influence prescribing rates.[97] Not everyone wants to reduce prescribing, but advice is available for those who do:

- Using a self-care manual explaining about minor illness.[98]
- Using self-medication (eg paracetamol for fever).
- Using the larder (eg lemon and honey for sore throats).
- Using time (eg pink ear drums—follow-up).
- Using granny (a more experienced member of the family).
- Pre-empting the patient's request for antibiotics (eg for a sore throat), eg: 'I'll need to examine your throat to see if you need an antibiotic, but first let me ask you some questions … From what you say, it sounds as if you are going to get over this on your own, but let me have a look to see.' [GP inspects to exclude a quinsy.] 'Yes, I think you'll get over this on your own. Is that all right?'

Empowering patients Any illness, minor or otherwise, is an opportunity to empower patients. Use the time to enable patients to improve their ability to:

- Cope with life.
- Understand their illness.
- Cope with specific illnesses.
- Feel able to keep themselves healthy.
- Feel confident on handling health issues.
- Be confident about the ability to help themselves.

We know that time spent this way improves patient satisfaction and clinical outcome.[99] This may be better than delegating minor illness to nurse-led triage clinics—which may end up increasing demand and augment medicalization of human events.[1]

1 D Richards 2004 *Br J Gen Pract* **54** 207

Are you ready for emergencies and on call?

In your black bag (Keep in date!) *Contents depend on local needs, eg:*

IM/IV agents:	*Oral/topical agents*	*Administrative items:*
Netilmicin; ceftriaxone	Pain killers; antibiotics	Mental Health Act forms
Cyclimorph®; naloxone	Prednisolone (soluble)	Headed notepaper, etc.
Prochlorperazine	Lofepramine or SSRI	Phone N°: chemists, police
Furosemide	Ranitidine or similar	ambulance, hospitals, etc.
Atropine; adrenaline	Aspirin 75 & 300mg	Certificates; prescriptions
Chlorpheniramine	Paracetamol 'syrup'	inc. nursing for IV pumps
Benzylpenicillin	Rehydration sachets	Book to record batch
Diazepam	Inhalers; GTN spray	numbers for ampoules &
Glucagon	Enemas & suppositories	narcotic use
50% glucose	Fucithalmic ointment	Temporary resident and
Haloperidol	Hypostop® glucose gel	other forms
	Diazepam (pills + PR)	

The suppositories referred to include diclofenac 100mg (eg for renal colic) and paracetamol 60mg or 125mg for vomiting feverish children.

Equipment: Airway; stethoscope; auroscope; patella hammer; scalpel blade; BP wrist monitor or aneroid device; FeverScan® (or similar, for T°; no mercury); dipstix/capillary glucose; needles; syringes; gloves/KY jelly®; antiseptic fluid; sutures; specimen bottles & forms; sharps tin. ►This is just what is in the author's bag: it is not prescriptive.

In your pocket Bleep/phone (charged!). Try a ***palm-top device*** eg incorporating this book, *OHCM* (we declare an interest!) & *BNF*; see www.oup.co.uk/academic/medicine/handbooks/pda **NB:** the trouble with relying on books is that there is no room for more than one in a bag, and the danger is that if you keep them in your car, they are not to hand for easy reference. No-one wants to get to the top of a block of flats only to have to descend to see if x interacts with y or to find out the incubation time for scarlet fever. ***Permanently on internet access*** (eg with an XDA II® device[1]) means that as well as locally loaded books, everything else is available too in the way of decision support. For example, www.isabel.org can be very helpful—also www.emisPDP.com (we declare an interest). These devices will also be able to access patients records remotely.

In your car Maps, torches, nebulizer, spare batteries, speculum, defibrillator, ECG, dressings, giving sets for IVIs; peak flow meter; O_2.

In your mind We have a duty to be fully conscious and reasonably healthy. We have all been in the position of visiting patients who are less sick than we are—and we tend to carry on until we drop (see p 657). This is bad for us and bad for patients. If you are sick, and no locum is to hand, phone your local Primary Care Organization or out of hours co-operative.

1 This is an O_2-services integrated phone and handheld computer, using GPRS (general packet radio service) so e-mail is fast. http://forum.xda-developers.com/front_page.php. See also www.palm.com

Prescribing and compliance ('concordance')

On any day ~60% of people take drugs, only half of which are prescribed. The others are sold over the counter (OTC). The commonest OTCs are analgesics, cough medicines, and vitamins; for prescribed drugs the common groups are CNS and cardiovascular drugs, and antibiotics. On average, 6-7 NHS prescriptions are issued/person/year (21 in Italy and 11 in France).

GPs account for 75% of NHS annual prescribing costs (>£2000 million, or ~10% of the total cost of the NHS), although many of these 'GP drugs' will have been initiated in hospital. The cost of these prescriptions has risen by a factor of ~5 since 1949 (after allowance for inflation) and is ~£100,000–£300,000/GP/year. Positive correlations with low prescribing include a young doctor, practising in an affluent area, and longer consultation times. The reason may be that if extra time is spent with the patient, more explanation about minor ailments (p 517) may be given, so that a patient's expectation for a prescription is replaced by enlightened self-awareness.

Formularies aim is to reduce drug costs and to make prescribing more effective, by producing an agreed list of favoured drugs. This voluntary restriction can work in tandem with compulsory NHS restricted lists, and lead to substantial savings (eg 18%). The UK DoH recommends development at individual practice level but this time-consuming task may be better achieved by adapting an existing formulary. Unless you wish to reinvent the wheel, this would seem excellent advice. But beware: denying GPs drug choice may increase referral to secondary care, leading to *increased* costs.[101]

Dispensing doctors Where there is no chemist's shop (eg rural areas) GPs are paid to dispense to their patients. Their annual prescribing rate can be as low as 70% of their non-dispensing fellow GPs.

Compliance (Does the patient take the medicine?) ►*There is no point in being a brilliant diagnostician if nobody can be persuaded to take your treatments.* Even in life-threatening conditions, compliance is a major problem occurring in up to 56% of patients (eg adolescents with acute lymphatic leukaemia). The following are associated with increased compliance:

- Being able to identify with a personal doctor.
- Patient's overall satisfaction with the doctor.
- Simple therapeutic regimens.
- Written information (use short words—Flesch formula >70, *OHCM* p 3).
- Longer consultation times or prescribing on home visits.
- Prescribing in association with giving health education.
- Continuity of care, coupled with belief in efficacy of the treatment.
- Short waiting time for appointments.
- The encouragement of self-monitoring by the patient.

Monitoring compliance: Monitoring plasma drug levels is the most reliable way of doing this, but it is cheaper to ask patients to return with their tablets, so that you can count them—or, better still, establish a basis of trust so that the patient can check for him- or herself.

Compliance or concordance? *Compliance* suggests that you know best and patients who lapse are foolish. But it is known that patients who adapt advice to their needs get fewer side-effects, eg GI bleeding: your prescription may read 'ibuprofen 400mg/8h'—but the patient may, sensibly, only take the medicine when his joints are bad. Don't think of this as the patient failing to do something. It is you who have failed to reach a shared understanding of the pros and cons of medicine-taking with your patient. Concordance denotes even more than this: think of it as a liberating concept, promoting egalitarianism within medicine. ►There is no higher ideal.[102]

Healing

Since neolithic times, healing has had a central place in our culture, and has long been recognized as 'mor bettir and mor precious þan any medicyne' (*OED* V 152.1). Recently medicines have improved greatly, so that the role of doctors as the purveyor of medicines has eclipsed their more ancient roles. We all recognize the limits of our role as prescribers, and we would all like to heal more and engage in repetitive tasks less often. But what, we might ask, *is* healing? How is it different for from curing? Healing is, at one level, something mysterious that happens to wounds, involving inflammation→granulocyte, macrophage, and platelet activation→release of platelet-derived growth factor & transforming growth factors α and β→neovascular growth→fibroblast-mediated contraction→proteoglycans and collagen synthesis, lysis, and remodelling (see *Oxford Textbook of Surgery*).

On another level, healing involves transforming through communication—a kind of hands-on hypnosis. We can cure with scalpels and needles, but these are not instruments of communication. Here is an example of healing (an all too rare event in our own practice). On a rainy February evening, after a long surgery, I visited a stooped old man at the fag-end of life, with something the matter with his lung. 'I suppose it's rotting, like the rest of me—it's gradually dying.' I reply: 'Do you think you're dying?' 'Aren't we all?' 'Green and dying' I reply for some reason, half remembering a poem by Dylan Thomas (*Fern Hill*). The patient looks mystified: he thinks he misheard, and asks me to repeat. 'Green *and* dying' I say, feeling rather stupid. There is a pause, and then he rises to his full height, puffs out his chest, and completes, in a magnificent baritone, the lines: '… Time held me green and dying, though I sang in my chains like the sea.' www.bigeye.com/fernhill.htm By chance I had revealed a new meaning to a favourite poem of his which perhaps he thought was about childhood, not the rigours of his old age. Both our eyes shone more brightly as we passed to the more prosaic aspects of the visit. This illustrates the nature of healing: its unpredictability, its ability to allow us to rise to our full height, to sing, rather than mumble, and how externally nothing may be changed by healing, just our internal landscape, transformed and illuminated. It also shows how healing depends on communication, and how it is bound up with art. Healing may be mysterious, but it is not rare. We have so often kissed the grazed knees of our daughters that we expect the healing balm of kisses to wear out, but, while they are young, it never will, because children know how to receive but not how to doubt, and the kiss is the paradigm of healing: contact between two humans, wordless service of the lips.

Our central task of sifting of symptoms, deciding what is wrong, and prescribing treatment are all tasks which, according to the editor of the *Lancet* are destined for delegation to microchips.[103] This implies that our chief role will be as healers and teachers. Meta-analyses of randomized healing trials (prayer, mental/spiritual healing, therapeutic touching) bear this out to some extent: 57% of randomized trials show a positive effect.[RCT 104]

There will always be some way to go before healing, the central ideal of medicine, becomes its central activity. After all, the last thing any of us wants during appendicitis, is a poet or a healer—but last things will always retain their power to set us thinking. We should also be able to combine healing paradigms with mechanical neuropsychological approaches to consultations. This is the aim of spiritually orientated group therapy.[1]

1 S Sageman 2004 *J Am Acad Psychoanal Dyn Psychiatry* **32** 125. Group prayer, yoga breathing, and spiritual readings with severely ill women can improve mood, affect, motivation, interpersonal bonding, and sense of self, and can succeed in reaching patients and promoting recovery in new ways.

Social matters

Unemployment in families: UK data show an association between child deaths and unemployment (i.e. social class and poverty) [illegible] babies whose fathers [illegible] (by 150%). Unemployed fathers [illegible] greater [illegible] adjusting for other factors. Accidents and infection are more common among children of the unemployed compared with carefully matched controls, and their mothers may be more prone to depression. As unemployment rises, so does child abuse. Other factors associated with this are marital discord, debt, and parents' lack of self-esteem [illegible] (when he lost his job he went bonkers, [illegible] changed from [illegible] became depressed and angry. Frustrated [illegible]).

Marital breakdown heads the list of problems of women [illegible] (the employment difficulties) in men and is a leading factor in [illegible] of suicide attempts. In the USA, divorced males have the highest rates of mortality. The greater incidence of cardiac deaths is most marked in young divorced males. Being divorced and a nonsmoker is nearly as dangerous as smoking 1 pack a day and staying married. Marital harmony [illegible] progress from chronic [illegible], as shown in one prospective study of 10,000 Israeli men. Parental behaviours [illegible] among offspring include [illegible], getting angry easily, being [illegible].

Social security benefits For England [illegible]

Income support [illegible] applying for a pension is the only [illegible].

Help with care home fees The maximum help is [illegible] for residential homes and [illegible] for nursing homes. The type of care is [illegible] assessment.

Disability living allowance is available [illegible]. It is paid if [illegible] needs help looking after him/herself. It is paid at different rates depending on circumstances. For those [illegible] it is paid for a child with a physical or mental illness or disability if they need more help or looking after than other children of the same age because of their illness or disability—weekly amounts for care: higher rate = [illegible]; middle rate = [illegible]; lower rate = [illegible]; for mobility—higher rate = [illegible]; lower rate = [illegible].

The working person's tax credit is paid [illegible] to help working disabled people on a low income. Savings >£16,000 usually preclude payment. [illegible]

Council tax benefit is paid by local councils, irrespective of [illegible].

Attendance allowance (AA) [illegible] Tax-free weekly benefit for people aged [illegible] who need help with personal care owing to illness or disability. It is ignored as income for working out Income Support and Jobseekers Allowance. It is payable to the person needing attending to, and not the person attending. Depending on the disability, the weekly rate is either [illegible] or [illegible]. Special fast-track rules apply if terminally ill. AA stops 4 weeks after going into a home run by the local council or if social services help with the cost of an independent home.

Invalid care allowance (if aged [illegible]) is payable to a person who spends [illegible] looking after someone who is getting (or waiting to hear about) the Disability Living Allowance at the middle or highest rates, Industrial Injuries Disablement Benefit, Constant Attendance Allowance, or War Pensions Constant Attendance Allowance at the basic rate or above.

Finding out: Disability benefits [illegible]

Primary care

Social matters

Unemployment in families UK data show an association between child deaths and unemployment, lower social class and overcrowding. Babies whose fathers are employed are heavier at birth (by 150g) than unemployed fathers' babies, after adjusting for other factors. Accidents and infection are more rife among children of the unemployed compared with carefully selected controls, and their mothers may be more prone to depression. As unemployment rises, so does child abuse. Other factors identified with this rise are marital discord, debt, and parents' lack of self-esteem, as affected families reveal: 'When he lost his job he went bonkers. He changed completely. He became depressed and snappy. Frustrated.'

Marital breakdown heads the list of problems of women with neurosis, coming 2nd (to employment difficulties) in men, and is a leading factor in >60% of suicide attempts. In the USA, divorced males have the highest rates of mortality. The greater incidence of cardiac deaths is most marked in young divorced males. Being divorced and a nonsmoker is nearly as dangerous as smoking a pack a day and staying married. Marital harmony (eg cuddling) protects from cardiac death, as shown in one prospective study of 10,000 Israeli hearts. Parental behaviours predicting problematic marriages among offspring included jealousy, being domineering, getting angry easily, being critical, moody, or taciturn. [105]

Social security benefits For *England*, see www.dss.gov.uk/lifeevent/benefits

Income support: Worth applying for if a pension is the only income.

Help with care-home fees: The maximum help is £314/wk for residential homes and £387 for nursing homes. This type of care is free in Scotland.

Disability living allowance is available if 3 months to 65yrs old; [106] it is paid if a client needs help looking after himself. It is paid at different rates depending on circumstances. For those <16yrs, it is paid for a child with a physical or mental illness or disability if they need more help or looking after than other children of the same age because of their illness or disability—weekly amounts: *for care*: higher rate = £60.60; middle rate = £40.55; lower rate = £16.05; *for mobility*—higher rate = £42.30; lower rate = £16.05.

The working person's tax credit is paid eg to help working disabled people on a low income. Savings >£16,000 usually preclude payment. See tax credits on-line. http://www.taxcredits.inlandrevenue.gov.uk/HomeIR.aspx

Council tax benefit is paid by local councils, irrespective of other benefits.

Attendance allowance (AA): www.dwp.gov.uk/lifeevent/benefits/attendance_allowance.asp Tax-free weekly benefit for people aged 65 or over who need help with personal care owing to illness or disability. It is ignored as income for working out Income Support and Jobseeker's Allowance. It is payable to the person needing attending to, and not the person attending. Depending on the disability, the weekly rate is either £40.55 or £60.60. Special fast-track rules apply if terminally ill. The AA stops 4 weeks after going into a home run by the local council or if social services helps with the cost of an independent home.

Invalid care allowance (if aged 16–65yrs) is payable to a person who spends >35h/wk looking after someone who is getting (or waiting to hear about) AA, *Disability Living Allowance* at the middle or highest rates, Industrial Injuries *Disablement Benefit Constant Attendance Allowance*, or *War Pensions Constant Attendance Allowance* at the basic rate or above.

Finding nearby ***Disability benefits centres:*** www.dwp.gov.uk/localoffice/disability/index.asp

Health and social class

Throughout human history there have been inequalities in the health of classes and populations, caused by social factors. With the introduction of the British National Health Service, with its ideal of equal access to medical care for all groups in society it was assumed that differences in the health of different social (occupational) classes would be eliminated. We now know that this has not happened, and this has been amply documented in various reports such as the *Black Report (Inequalities in Health)* and the *Health Divide*. *National Service Frameworks* (NSFs) eg for care of those with ischaemic heart disease, diabetes, mental health problems and for older people who are designed to redress these inequalities.

Registrar General's scale of 5 social or occupational classes

Class I	Professional	eg lawyer, doctor, accountant
Class II	Intermediate	eg teacher, nurse, manager
Class III^{N}	Skilled non-manual	eg typist, shop assistant
Class III^{M}	Skilled manual	eg miner, bus-driver, cook
Class IV	Partly skilled (manual)	eg farmworker, bus-conductor
Class V	Unskilled manual	eg cleaner, labourer

There is a remarkable concurrence of evidence concerning the factor by which mortality rates are higher in social class V compared with those of social class I (with regular gradations between). For stillbirths, perinatal deaths, infant deaths, deaths in men aged 15–64 and women aged 20–59 this factor is respectively 1.8, 2, 2.1, 2, and 1.95. The same sort of factors hold true for specific diseases such as the standardized mortality ratios (SMR) from lung carcinoma (1.98), coronary heart disease (1.3) and cerebrovascular disease (1.9). Only malignant melanoma, anorexia/bulimia nervosa, eczema, and Hodgkin's disease in early adulthood show a reverse ('disease of affluence') trend. Note: the SMR is the ratio of mortality rates in one class compared with the average for the whole population. The whole population has an SMR of 1.00.

There is more emotional stress and chronic ill health in the 'lower' occupational classes. Furthermore, people who own their own homes have less ill health than private tenants, especially if they live in residential retirement areas.

Within occupations the effect of social class is seen in a 'purer' way than when groups of many occupations are compared: in a study of >17,000 Whitehall civil servants there was a greater than 3-fold difference in mortality from all causes of death (except genitourinary diseases) comparing those in high grades with those in low grades. Similarly in the army there is a 5-fold difference in mortality rates from heart disease between the highest and the lowest ranks.

It has been pointed out that being ill makes a person 'descend' the social scale, but it is estimated that this effect is not large enough to account for the observed differences between classes. It is much more likely that the differences are due to factors such as smoking behaviour, education, marital status, poverty, and overcrowding.

Purchasers and providers

2 sets of contrasting principles ►He who pays the piper, calls the tune. ►Priceless therapeutic assets cannot be bought or sold: compassion, continuity of care, and commitment. ►My job is to spend, spend, spend, until all my patients are healthy. ►The job of the Treasury is to squeeze, squeeze, squeeze, until all spending is within government targets. (The clarity of this dichotomy becomes turbid when the doctor is asked to do the squeezing.)

Never just ask how good a structure is without also asking how good it is at transforming itself: that which cannot transform, dies. The UK National Health Service is the largest employer in the Western world and for years the search has been on to find ways to control and transform this dear, mighty thing. The purchaser-provider split is the most powerful lever yet developed for this purpose. *Purchasers* commission care by drawing up contracts with competing *providers*, who deliver the care. In England, purchasers are chiefly Primary Care Trusts (which are run by a board comprising a minority of GPs). The better the provider delivers secondary care (do *not* pause to ask what 'better' means: speculation on this point might ruin the argument) the more likely they are to get the contract next year. The catch is that all the extra effort the provider makes to out-perform a contract this year will probably be taken for granted next year. The same may hold true if purchasing is used for the imposition of guidelines ('evidence-based purchasing'). What has been created is a treadmill which goes faster and faster, while taking less and less account of individual patients' and doctors' legitimate but varying needs. Unless the market is rigged, natural selection ensures that the fittest and fastest providers survive. Patients and taxpayers benefit—until the point where cynicism and exhaustion set in. There is no evidence that once the purchaser-provider path is chosen, then cynicism and exhaustion *inevitably* follow, and there is evidence at local level that benefits accrue, and services become more tuned to consumers' desires. (Consumers are not infallible judges of what constitutes health—but they are the best judges we have.) ►If the State runs both *supply* (money from general taxation) and *demand* (control of waiting lists etc), the rules of the market cannot operate and efficiency is hard to achieve—which is why some NHS trusts are being freed from central NHS control.

Controlling change from on top: *an historical example from maternity*

1 Government sets up an expert group (mothers, midwives, ministers, obstetricians, and general practitioners—these are jokers in the pack, because they are simultaneously consumers, purchasers *and* providers).

2 Issuing of objectives and indicators of success—eg by 5 years:
- Women should have a named midwife to ensure continuity of care.
- Women should be able to choose their place of delivery. Aim to achieve the outcome that she believes is best for her baby and herself.
- ≥75% of women should know the person who is to deliver them in labour.
- Midwives should have direct access to some beds in all maternity units.
- ≥30% of women should have a midwife as the lead professional.

3 The group's attractive-looking report is issued (using taxpayers' money) to all groups and personnel involved (except mothers).

4 Lack of finance is blamed when no improvements are detected at 5 years.

Anatomy of change Ideals (woman-centred care)→Specific policy objective (all women to have the chance to discuss their care)→Purchasers' action point (set up maternity services liaison committee with lay chairperson) → Providers' action point (provide link-workers, and advocacy schemes for women whose first language is not English). This type of activity may or may not lead to increased accountability and quality of services. 107

Referral statistics

There is great variability in individual GPs' referral statistics, which leads purveyors of government strategy to the error of saying 'Why is there a 4-fold difference in referral rates between GPs? Such variation is insupportable; some doctors must be referring too much ...' An advance is made when this issue is reframed as: 'there is *information* contained in this variability, and this information can guide service development'.[108]

Understanding the intricacies of purchasing health care depends on understanding referral patterns. If high-referring GPs refer unnecessarily, then the proportion of their referrals resulting in admission should be smaller than that of practices of similar size with low-referring GPs. Usually, this is not the case. Those with high-referral rates have high admission rates. How far does this relation hold? If I refer an ever-increasing number of my patients to a geriatric clinic, must a time come when admissions level off? The idea of a 'levelling-off effect' is important. If the consultant's actions are 'correct', and the GP's expectation as to the outcome of referral are uniform (probably never true) then when a levelling-off effect is observed, it may be true that the *average* referral rate is optimal, and that low-referrers are depriving patients, and high-referrers are wasting resources. In fact, levelling-off effects are rarely found—except in general surgery. What are we to conclude from most of the other specialties where no levelling-off effect is observed? Perhaps specialists admit a fixed proportion of patients referred to them. There is some evidence that this is true for ENT consultants and tonsillectomy. Another possibility is the Coulter-Seagroatt-McPherson hypothesis—that consultants have a threshold of severity for admission (eg a claudication distance of 50 metres) and even the majority of patients from the high-referrers fulfil this criterion. In this case (assuming the consultant is right), even the high-referrers are not referring enough. This may be true for all forms of angiography, for example. However, if the consultant is over-enthusiastic, and over-optimistic about the benefits of treatment, then the lower referrers are to be applauded for limiting the excesses of the consultant. ►*In general, only agree that a referral is inappropriate if the patient, the GP, and the consultant concur on its inutility.* Each of these parties have different motivations—eg reassurance/explanation, medico-legal, as well as getting necessary therapy.

Overall, referral rates are no more variable than admission rates, even among populations with similar morbidities. The reason is probably that there is still a great deal of uncertainty underlying very many clinical decisions. We don't know who should have knee replacements, coronary angiography, cholecystectomy, aneurysm surgery, transplants, or grommets.

►There is no known relationship between high or low referral rates and quality of care. Here are 3 cautions in interpreting referrals:

1. Individual list size should not be used as a denominator, as it takes no account of differing workloads within a practice. Consultations per year would be a better denominator.
2. If doctors within the practice have special interests, these must be taken into account in comparing referral patterns.
3. Years of data are needed to compare referrals to rarely used units.

Referral incentive schemes From 2005, PCOs have been setting aside funds to go the GP practices to incentivize GPs to 'streamline' our referrals—to get maximum value for money. The foregoing should demonstrate that this is a rather complex and uncertain enterprise at best.[109]

Fitness to drive,[UK] fly, & do sport

Ordinary UK driving licences issued by the DVLA (Driver & Vehicle Licensing Agency) are inscribed '*You are required by law to inform Drivers Medical Branch, DVLA, Swansea SA99 1AT at once if you have any disability (either physical or medical condition), which is, or may become likely to affect your fitness as a driver, unless you don't expect it to last >3 months.*' It is the responsibility of the driver to inform the DVLA. It is the responsibility of their doctors to advise patients that medical conditions (and drugs) may affect their ability to drive and for which conditions patients should inform the DVLA. Drivers should also inform their insurance company of any condition disclosed to the DVLA. ►If in doubt, ask your defence union.

Vascular disease *Uncomplicated MI:* don't drive for 4wks. *Angioplasty or pacemaker:* don't drive for 1st post-op week. *Angina:* stop driving if symptoms occur at the wheel; DVLA need not be informed. *Arrhythmias:* driving may be OK if the cause is found, and controlled for >1 month if risk of ↓consciousness & ↓motor power is sufficiently low. Syncope: OK to drive 1wk afterwards, if cause identified and treated. If no cause is found, stop for ≥6 months. *TIA/stroke:* stop for ≥1 month; no need to inform DVLA unless there is residual deficit for >1 month. *Abdominal aortic aneurysm >6.5cm:* Disqualification (if 6–6.4cm: inform DVLA; do annual review). www.dvla.gov.uk/at_a_glance/content.htm

Diabetes All on *oral hypoglycaemics* or *insulin* must inform DVLA (in general, stop driving for 1 month after starting insulin, to get stable; drivers must demonstrate satisfactory control, and must recognize hypoglycaemia). Check that vision conforms to required standard (BOX). Avoid driving if hypoglycaemic risk ↑ (eg meal delay; or after excess exercise). Carry rapidly absorbed sugar in vehicle and stop, turn off ignition and eat it if any warning signs. A card should be carried to say which medications they are using to aid with resuscitation if needed. If an accident is due to hypoglycaemia a diabetic driver may be charged with driving under the influence of drugs.

CNS disorders Disabling giddiness, vertigo, and problems with movements preclude driving. DVLA need to know about unexplained blackouts, multiple sclerosis, Parkinson's (any 'freezing' or on-off effects), motor neurone disease, recurrent TIAs and strokes. In the latter the licence is usually withheld for 3 months depending on an examination by an independent doctor, and sometimes a driving test. Those with dementia should only drive if the condition is very mild (do not rely on armchair judgments: on-the-road trials are better). Encourage relatives to contact DVLA if a dementing relative should not be driving. GPs may desire to breach confidentiality (the GMC approves) and inform DVLA of demented or psychotic patients (tel. 01792 783686[UK]). Many elderly drivers (~1 in 3) who die in accidents are found to have Alzheimer's.

For post-op driving in those with brain tumours, see below.[1]

Epilepsy and brain surgery: If a seizure while awake, he must not drive for 1yr. Attacks while asleep: stop driving for 1yr, unless the attack was while asleep and >3yrs ago and there have not been any awake fits since that asleep attack. *In any event, the driving of a vehicle by such a person should not be likely to cause danger to the public.* Provided a licence holder/applicant is able to satisfy the above, a 3yr licence will be normally issued. The 'till 70' licence may be restored if fit-free for 7yrs with medication if needed (if no other disqualifying condition).

Epileptic drug withdrawal risks a 40% seizure rate in year 1. Those wishing to withdraw from medication should cease driving from the beginning of withdrawal and not recommence until 6 months after treatment has ceased.

►*For the most recent advice, always consult:* www.dvla.gov.uk/at_a_glance/annex3.htm

1 H Binns 2002 *BMJ* i 927 & P Watkins 2000 *BMJ* i 1148

Driving is prohibited in certain general categories

- Severe mental disorder (including severe mental impairment).
- Severe behavioural disorders—or drug abuse/dependency.
- Alcohol dependency (including inability to refrain from drunken driving).
- Psychotic medication taken in quantities that impair driving ability.

Vision Acuity (± spectacles) should be sufficient to read a 79.4mm-high number plate at 20.5 metres (~6/10 on Snellen chart). Monocular vision is allowed only if the visual field is full. Binocular field of vision must be >120°. Diplopia is not allowable unless *mild* and *eye-patch correctable*.

Drugs Driving, or being in charge of a vehicle when under the influence (including side-effect) of a drug is an offence under the Road Traffic Act 1988. Many drugs affect alertness and driving ability (check *Data-sheets*), and many are potentiated by alcohol, so warn patients not to drive until they are sure of side-effects, not to drink and drive, not to drive if feeling unwell, and never to drive within 48h of a general anaesthetic.

Old age DVLA says: 'progressive loss of memory, impairment in concentration and reaction time with possible loss of confidence, suggest consideration be given to cease driving.' This is too vague to help, as when reapplying for a licence (every 3yrs after 70yrs old) a driver simply signs to say 'no medical disability is present'. 110

Fitness to fly: avoid hypobaric (high altitude) flights if…

- Climbing stairs causes troublesome dyspnoea (an easy screening test).
- Gas-filled dental caries (via putrifying bacteria): can cause severe odontalgia at altitude, and damage to the tooth.
- Within 48h after diving below 50 feet (the bends, p 814). Even at modest cabin altitudes death may occur. NB: barotrauma is worse on descent as the Eustachian tube is sucked flat by the low pressure in the middle ear, making the immediate equilibration of pressure more difficult.
- In uncontrolled cardiac failure. If O_2 supplementation is being used at sea-level, wean off before air travel, to help see if air travel is viable. All acute patients in this group should travel with enough supplementary O_2 to provide intermittent use eg at 2L/min.
- Confusional states and alcohol intoxication (synergistic with hypoxia).
- Pneumothorax; pneumomediastinum; or <10 days post-op to hollow organ.
- Neonates <3 days old, or women in the last 4 weeks of pregnancy (last 13 weeks if multiple pregnancy). See section on airlines, p 8.
- Anaemia (Hb <7.5g/dL); GI bleeding; any recent tissue infarctions.

►Encourage good hydration and mobility; use aspirin & compression stockings on long-haul flights—p 16. NB: the list above is not exhaustive. See International Air Transport Association advice. www.medinet.co.uk/crit.htm

Fitness to do sporting activities and cardiac rehabilitation

GPs often have to pronounce on this. Ensure that those involved know you do not have a crystal ball. Common sense, and attention to warm-up exercise is the key. If the patient is in an at-risk group, eg epileptics wanting to swim,[1] or personal or family history of hypertrophic obstructive cardiomyopathy, and wanting to do heavy exercise, get help. 111

NB: in CCF, mild work with hand weights need not be banned. 112

Is this drug on the 'banned' list? See *Sports Medicine* in *Mims Companion*.

1 OK if well-controlled; go with a friend, only to lifeguard supervised pools.

Chronic fatigue syndrome (CFS)

CFS entails severe, disabling fatigue for >6 months, affecting physical and mental functioning, and present for more than 50% of the time. Myalgia, sleep disorders, and mood disturbance are common.[113] ***Physical correlates of CFS:*** Abnormal gene expression in 16 genes related to mitochondrial function (Epstein-Barr or parvoviruses could switch on this abnormal expression—which *might* form the basis for a diagnostic blood test).[Kerr 2005] Neutrophil apoptosis is ↑.[114] Electrodermal responses are somewhat characteristic.

Work-up of a patient with 'query chronic fatigue syndrome' Exclude causes such as anaemia, TB, snoring, etc, with a history; physical examination; mental state (p 324), urinalysis, FBC, U&E, TSH, ESR, LFT, glucose ± autoantibody screen, plasma creatine kinase, blood culture, and CXR.

↓

Pursue abnormalities (eg ?TB/HIV if weight↓; ?depression if anhedonia, p 336)

↓

Does the pattern fit CFS?—ie persistent or relapsing fatigue, not relieved by rest, and leading to substantial reduction in previous levels of activity.

↓

Are any exclusion criteria present?—psychosis (p 316), bipolar depression (p 354), dementia, anorexia (p 348).

↓

Are 4 or more of the following present for >6 months?

- Impaired memory/concentration unrelated to drugs or alcohol use
- Unexplained muscle pain
- Polyarthralgia (but swelling suggests a joint diagnosis, p 430)
- Unrefreshing sleep
- Post-exertional malaise lasting over 24h
- Persisting sore throat not caused by glandular fever
- Unexplained tender cervical or axillary nodes

If criteria met, call it CFS; if not fully met, call it 'idiopathic chronic fatigue'.

↓

Co-morbid conditions are common, eg depression: consider diagnosing in a quantified way using formal diagnostic instruments (eg Beck inventory).

Treatment None is specific, and chronicity is common.[115] Aim for a therapeutic alliance with your patient. Some therapists aim to prevent somatic fixation: the strongest predictor of a poor prognosis is a fixed belief that symptoms are due only to physical causes. Allow non-threatening discussion about psychological issues, keeping an open mind on aetiology. Make it clear that psychological symptoms are not the same as malingering 'Perhaps what starts as an illness may not be what keeps it going'. Psychological factors affect the outcome of many illnesses: why should this be different? Cautious increases in levels of activity are best (not quite the same as 'take more exercise'), to maintain muscle function, and improve confidence.[RCT 116] [N=148]

Treat associated anxiety/depression (p 340). Address family and work problems. Talking with other patients sounds sensible, but there is a suggestion that this may prolong symptoms. Slow recovery is the norm.

Trials 3 trials support use of graded exercise programmes (not the same as 'pacing'[1]).[117] Relapses are triggered by over exercise. Cognitive therapy (p 374, via skilled therapists) can help. A trial found benefit from nicotinamide adenine dinucleotide (NADH) 10mg/24h (8/26 improved, compared with 2/26 on placebo; NADH helps generate ATP which may be depleted in CFS).[118]

When to get help: • Children with CFS • Unresponsive to the above measures • History of travel abroad • CNS signs • Walking difficulty • Fevers • Suicidal.

1 Pacing is setting a ***realistic*** exercise routine and sticking to it to avoid 'boom and bust' cycles that happen if someone tries to build too much on a small advance. Proper rest between exercise (eg relaxation/meditation) is said to be vital. Further reading: *DoH Working Party Report on CFS/ME.*

Managing obesity

Obesity (BMI >30) shortens life, aggravates diabetes, gout, osteoarthritis, hernia, DVT, oesophagitis, sleep apnoea, and IHD. Weight loss in the obese diminishes BP and cancer risk, and restores life expectancy to normal.

The hypothalamus, with its 40 neurotransmitters, regulates appetite and energy balance by integrating hormonal, neural, and peripheral messages (concerning gut distension). Neuropeptide Y is a transmitter, stimulating feeding, and suppressing the sympathetic nervous system (so energy expenditure↓). Other transmitters increase release of serotonin and noradrenaline from nerve terminals, mediating satiety, as does peripherally produced cholecystokinin. Leptin is thought to be a blood-borne signal from the adipose tissue that informs the brain about the size of the fat mass. Animal studies show that highly palatable foods lead to obesity, limited by futile thermogenesis, a metabolic cycling achieved by genetically controlled uncoupling oxidative phosphorylation in mitochondria. Genes for uncoupling proteins have been cloned, and may lead to novel treatments for obesity.

Desirable weight (BOX): A good guide to [illegible] normal fat (co-[illegible] with obesity's problems) is ≥94cm in men (≥80cm in women); [illegible] are overweight by this. In the UK, obesity has trebled in a decade; the more [illegible]. Waist girth has increased by 4 inches in the last 40yrs. Despite >31,000 publications on obesity and billions spent yearly there are no good, tried non-surgical pounding techniques for long-term maintained weight loss.

Prevention by education can work, eg at school. Another idea is to forget about weight loss, but concentrate on avoiding weight gain. For example eating one less biscuit/day may stop 7lbs weight gain per year.

Fat & fat measures (FFM): Excess weight is 75% fat and 25% FFM (worth [illegible], this being a useful value: 7000kcal/kg). With very low calorie diets (<800kcal/day) FFM loss is too high; exercise accounts for 20% of energy expenditure (so contributes much less to weight loss than diet). Simple lifestyle changes (eg 20min walks/day) are more likely than supervised exercise to produce long-term benefit, but don't rely on this for weight loss.

Very Low Calorie Diets (VLCDs) give 400kcal/day with adequate protein (≥40g for women, 500kcal/day and 50g protein/day for men; also women ≥[illegible]). 1 pint of skimmed milk with bran for bulk and unlimited calorie-free drinks gives the former; 1 pint is the latter. Also give 200mg ferrous sulfate and one multivitamin tablet/day. This is cheaper than commercial VLCDs. As [illegible] is lost, use for >4 weeks needs medical supervision.

Drugs for which there is randomized evidence of effectiveness:

Orlistat may be used for ≤2yrs in those with BMI ≥30 (≥28 if associated risk factors) who have lost weight on a diet (which must be continued). SE: malabsorption, steatorrhoea, flatus (± oily spotting), faecal incontinence/urgency; reduced by co-therapy with natural fibres (psyllium hydrophilic mucilloid). Dose: 120mg with a meal (up to 3/day); stop after 12 weeks if weight loss <5%.

Sibutramine inhibits serotonin & noradrenaline reuptake, promoting weight loss by enhancing postingestive satiety and increasing energy expenditure. Approved by NICE in those aged 18–65 if serious attempts at weight loss have failed, and BMI ≥27 with associated problems (eg DM, lipids↑), or BMI ≥30 and no associated problems. CI: [illegible].

Rimonabant blocks cannabinoid type 1 receptors (CB1), and ↓ cravings for alcohol, food and tobacco. Helps the metabolic syndrome. SE: depression.

Surgery is reserved for the morbidly obese (BMI >40 or >35 with a comorbidity, eg cardiovascular risk factors). Gastric bypass surgery in obesity results in sustained weight loss, ↓ dumping (OHCM p 530) and vitamin [illegible] deficiency.

Managing obesity

Obesity (BMI >30) shortens life, aggravates diabetes, gout, osteoarthrosis, heartburn, BP↑, lipids↑, sleep apnoea, and DVT. Weight loss in the obese diminishes BP and osteoarthrosis, and restores life expectancy to normal.

The hypothalamus with its 40 neurotransmitters regulates appetite and energy balance, by integrating hormonal, neural, and peripheral messages (concerning gut distension). Neuropeptide Y is a transmitter stimulating feeding, and suppressing the sympathetic nervous system (∴ ↓energy expenditure). Other transmitters increase release of serotonin and noradrenaline from nerve terminals, mediating satiety, as does peripherally produced cholecystokinin. Leptin is thought to be a bloodborne signal from the adipose tissue that informs the brain about the size of the fat mass. Animal models show that highly palatable foods lead to obesity, limited by 'futile thermogenesis', a metabolic cycling achieved by genetically controlled uncoupling oxidative phosphorylation in mitochondria. Genes for uncoupling proteins have been cloned, and may lead to novel treatments for obesity.

Desirable weight (BOX) A good guide to ↑intra-abdominal fat (correlates best with obesity's problems) is a waist >94cm in men (♀>80). ~⅓ are overweight by this criterion: *the richer a society, the more prevalent is obesity.* Mean girth has increased by ~6 inches in the last 50yrs. Despite >33,000 publications on obesity and billions spent yearly, there are no good, *well-tried* nonsurgical nondrug techniques for long-term *maintained* weight loss.

Prevention by education can work, eg in school. Another idea is to 'forget' about weight loss—but concentrate on avoiding weight gain. For example, eating one less biscuit/day may stop 2lbs weight gain per year.[119]

Fat & fat free mass (FFM) Excess weight is ~75% fat and 25% FFM, (water, protein & glycogen—energy value 1000kcal/kg). With very low calorie diets (<330kcal/24h) FFM loss is too high. Exercise accounts for 20% of energy expenditure (so contributes much less to weight loss than diet). Simple lifestyle changes (eg 2 brisk walks/day) are more likely than supervised exercise to produce long-term benefit; but don't rely on this to ↓weight. EBM 7 73[2002]

Very Low Calorie Diets (VLCDs) give 400kcal/24h with 40g protein/24h for women, 500kcal/24h and 50g protein/24h for men, and women >173cm. 2 pints of skimmed milk with bran for bulk and unlimited calorie-free drinks gives the former, 3 pints the latter. All should take 200mg ferrous sulfate and one multivitamin tablet/24h. This is cheaper than commercial VLCDs. As excess fat free mass is lost, use for >4 weeks needs medical supervision.

Drugs for which there is randomized evidence of effectiveness

Orlistat may be used for ≤2yrs in those with BMI >28kg/m² + associated risk factors who have shown weight↓ on a diet (which must be continued). CI: malabsorption. SE: (little is absorbed) faecal incontinence/urgency, reducible by co-therapy with natural fibres (psyllium hydrophilic mucilloid).[120] Dose: eg 120mg with a meal (up to 3/day); stop after 12 weeks if weight loss <5%.[MET 121]

Sibutramine inhibits serotonin & noradrenaline reuptake, promoting weight loss by enhancing postingestive satiety, and increasing calorie use. It's approved by NICE in those aged 18–65 if serious attempts at weight loss have failed, and BMI is >27 with associated problems (eg DM)—or if BMI >30 and no associated problems. **CI:** CCF/IHD; BP↑. **SE:** pulse↑; BP↑; dry mouth.[RCT 122] [*N*=485]

Rimonabant blocks cannabinoid type 1 receptors (CB1), and ↓cravings for alcohol, food, and tobacco. Helps the metabolic syndrome.[123] [*N*=3040]

Surgery is reserved for the morbidly obese (BMI >40; or >35 with associated cardiovascular risk factors). Gastric bypass and gastroplasty result in sustained weight loss. SE: dumping (*OHCM* p 530) and vitamin deficiency.

Weights and heights

Data from Fogarty

Men Height			Acceptable weight range						Overweight			Obese		
cm	*ft*	*in*	*kg*	*st*	*lb*	–	*st*	*lb*	*kg*	*st*	*lb*	*kg*	*st*	*lb*
158	5	2	44–64	6	13	–	10	1	70	11	0	77	12	2
160	5	3	44–65	6	13	–	10	3	72	11	5	78	12	4
162	5	4	46–66	7	3	–	10	6	73	11	7	79	12	6
164	5	4	47–67	7	6	–	10	8	74	11	9	80	12	8
166	5	5	48–69	7	8	–	10	12	76	12	0	83	13	1
168	5	6	49–71	7	10	–	11	3	78	12	4	85	13	5
170	5	7	51–73	8	0	–	11	7	80	12	8	88	13	12
172	5	8	52–74	8	3	–	11	9	81	12	11	89	14	0
174	5	9	53–75	8	5	–	11	11	83	13	1	90	14	2
176	5	9	54–77	8	7	–	12	2	85	13	5	92	14	7
178	5	10	55–79	8	9	–	12	6	87	13	10	95	14	13
180	5	11	58–80	9	2	–	12	8	88	13	12	96	15	2
182	6	0	59–82	9	4	–	12	13	90	14	2	98	15	6
184	6	0	60–84	9	6	–	13	3	92	14	7	101	15	13
186	6	1	62–86	9	11	–	13	8	95	14	13	103	16	3
188	6	2	64–88	10	1	–	13	12	97	15	4	106	16	10
190	6	3	66–90	10	6	–	14	2	99	15	8	108	17	0
192	6	3	68–93	10	10	–	14	9	102	16	1	112	17	9
Women			**Acceptable weight range**						**Overweight**			**Obese**		
cm	*ft*	*In*	*kg*	*st*	*lb*	–	*st*	*lb*	*kg*	*st*	*lb*	*kg*	*st*	*lb*
148	4	10	37–53	5	12	–	8	5	58	9	2	64	10	1
150	4	11	37–54	5	12	–	8	7	59	9	4	65	10	3
152	5	0	38–55	6	0	–	8	9	61	9	8	66	10	6
154	5	1	39–57	6	2	–	9	0	63	9	13	68	10	10
156	5	1	39–58	6	2	–	9	2	64	10	1	70	11	0
158	5	2	40–58	6	4	–	9	2	64	10	1	70	11	0
160	5	3	41–59	6	6	–	9	4	65	10	3	71	11	3
162	5	4	42–61	6	9	–	9	8	67	10	8	73	11	7
164	5	5	43–62	6	11	–	9	11	68	10	10	74	11	9
166	5	5	44–64	6	13	–	10	1	70	11	0	77	12	2
168	5	6	45–65	7	11	–	10	3	72	11	5	78	12	4
170	5	7	45–66	7	11	–	10	6	73	11	7	79	12	6
172	5	8	46–67	7	3	–	10	8	74	11	9	80	12	8
174	5	9	48–69	7	8	–	10	12	76	12	0	83	13	1
176	5	9½	49–70	7	10	–	11	0	77	12	2	84	13	3
178	5	10	51–72	8	0	–	11	5	79	12	6	86	13	8
180	5	11	52–72	8	3	–	11	9	81	12	11	89	14	0

Desirable weight relates to body mass index (BMI), W/H^2. W=weight (kg); H=height (metres). In many studies, a plot of relative risk of mortality against BMI is a U-shaped curve, with the minimum mortality close to a BMI of 25; mortality increases both as BMI increases above ~25 and as BMI decreases below 25. Some studies have found that being overweight is associated with a slightly increased risk of total mortality. Other studies (Flegal K, *JAMA* 2005, and others) suggest that a BMI of 25 to <30 is ***not*** associated with excess mortality.[124] ►So be sceptical of claims that 'the obesity epidemic will cause huge numbers of extra deaths'. NB: for a given weight, trunk (central) obesity is worse than devolved obesity (perhaps because omental fat causes insulin resistance via a molecule known as resistin).[125]

Dietary approaches Ask patients to keep a diary of foods eaten; then:
- Aim for realistic loss (eg <1kg/week for 1000kcal per day diet).
- Regular (weekly) weighing to watch trends.
- Consider weighing food to calculate calorie intake to prevent 'cheating'.
- Groups such as Weight Watchers can be very useful motivating forces.
- Aim to re-educate eating habits to maintain reduced weight.
- Ensure that the diet is nutritious. ►See the *Healthy Diet*, *OHCM* p 208.

Seven (Mayo Clinic) questions for weight-loss programmes to answer

1 Is there proof that it works (ask for evidence of long-term results)?
2 Any qualified dietician or specialist in behaviour modification employed?
3 Is the recommended intake nutritionally balanced?
4 Does the patient have to buy special products?
5 Will the patient receive advice on starting safe, moderate exercise?
6 How will the programme reward and monitor progress?
7 Is there support and follow-up for after the formal programme ends?

What to do for the best

Doctors are called on to make decisions about every patient they meet: few are curable at once, so making a plan for what to do for the best is the secret of success at the bedside. The aim here is to explain this secret, to enable you to flourish in the clinical world, and to keep you out of lawyers' offices.

Let us look at the steps of the history, physical, or mental examination, and investigations.

By the end of taking the **history**, you need to have acquired 3 things:

1 Rapport with the patient
2 A diagnosis or differential diagnosis
3 The placement of the diagnosis in the context of the patient's life

Rapport: Consultations are shorter when rapport is good.[126] [N=116] The patient is confident that he or she is getting the full attention of the doctor, and these patients are more understanding, and more forgiving when things go wrong. Doctors are far from infallible: so we need to have confidence that the patient will feel able to come back if things are not right, tell us what has happened, agree on an adjustment of the treatment, and, by giving feedback, improve our clinical acumen.

Diagnosis: Studies have shown that skilled physicians have made a provisional diagnosis soon after the consultation starts, and they spend the rest of the history in confirming or excluding it. What happens if you are not skilled, and you have no hint as to the diagnosis? You need to get more information:

- Pursue the main symptom: 'tell me more about the headache…'
- Elicit other symptoms—eg change of weight or appetitie, fevers, fatigue, unexplained lumps, itching, jaundice, or anything else odd?
- Get help from a colleague or even a diagnostic system—eg Mentor, p 502.
- Check you still have rapport with the patient. Are you searching for a physical diagnosis when a psychological diagnosis would be more appropriate? Here you might ask questions such as 'How is your mood?' 'What would your wife or partner say is wrong?' 'Would they say you are depressed?' 'What would have to change for you to feel better?'.

►Do not proceed to the physical examination until you have a working diagnosis: the answer is rarely found there (<10%).

Placing the diagnosis in the context of the patient's life: If you do not do this, you will not know what will count as a cure, and, more specifically, different patients need different treatments—see p 241. Some factors to focus on might be: the motivation of the patient to get better ('I've got to get my knee better so that I stay strong enough to lift my wife onto the commode'); their general health; social situation; drugs (not forgetting nicotine and alcohol); is help available at home; work (yes/no; type)?

At the end of the history, occasionally there is enough information to start treatment. Usually you may be only, say, 70% sure of the diagnosis, and more information is needed before treatment is commenced.

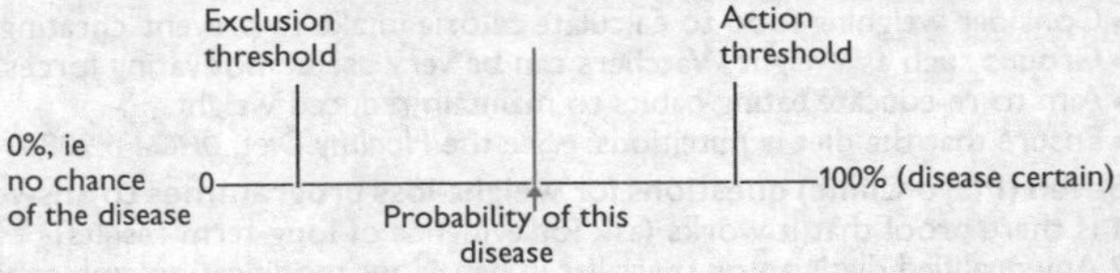

It is time for the physical **examination**. This aims to gain evidence to confirm or exclude the hypothesis, to define the extent of some process, or to assess the progress of known disease. At each step, ask 'what do I need to know?' Following the examination the diagram may look like this:

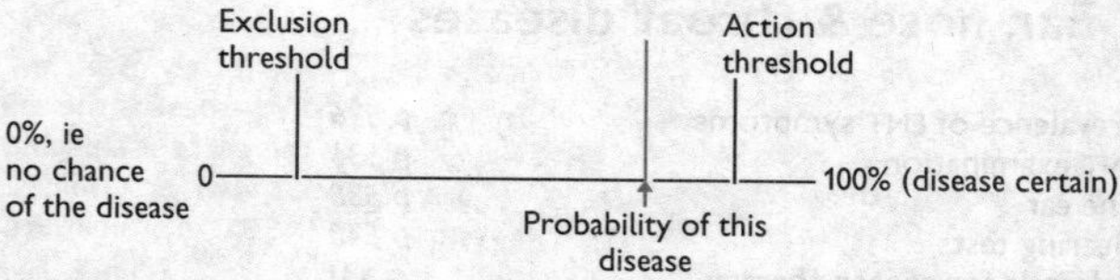

Investigations If the action threshold has not been crossed, further information is need. Action thresholds vary from doctor to doctor, and from disease to disease. When the treatment is dangerous, the action threshold will be high (eg leukaemia). In self-limiting illnesses, eg pharyngitis, the action threshold will be lower. Note that 'action' may be that, in agreement with such a patient, only symptomatic treatment is needed, and future episodes could be managed without medical input.

Similarly, it may be important to move the probability of a serious but unlikely disease beyond the exclusion threshold.

Once the probability of a disease passes the action threshold, treatment can commence, if the patient wishes.

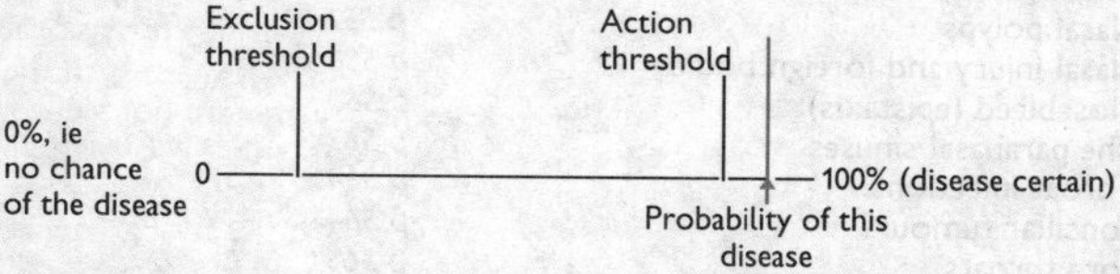

Supposing neither the action threshold, nor the exclusion threshold is exceeded, then more information is needed, eg from pathology, imaging, or from the passage of time. Time itself is an investigation: it may reveal sinister causes or the benign nature of the disease. To use time this way, you need to be reasonably sure that immediate treatment is not required.

If there is still not enough certainty to initiate management, get further information, eg from books, computers, colleagues, further tests—or you may feel it appropriate to refer the patient at this stage. Or go round the process again, starting with the history—from a different view point.

Once above the action threshold, it is time to decide what to do for the best. This is a decision shared by the doctor and the patient. It entails informed consent and consideration of: 127

- The probability of the diagnosis
- The likelihood of the different possible outcomes
- The costs and side-effects of treatment
- The hope and values of those affected, particularly the patient
- What is possible, considering the skills, resources, and time available

Finally, tell your patient how they will know if they are on the path to improvement or relapse, and if so, at what point to seek help (critical action threshold, below; record this in the notes)—eg if your peak flow falls by 40%, start this prescription for prednisolone, and come and see me.

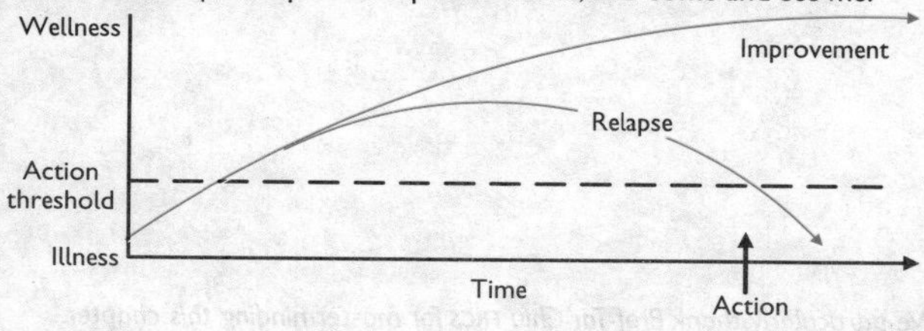

7 Ear, nose & throat diseases

▶Ideally, this chapter should be read with a ready supply of ENT patients and access to surgeons willing to teach about the various operative techniques employed. If this is impossible, Web-based guides to ENT examination are readily available, as are on-line free full text ENT journals:
www.ispub.com/ostia/index.php?xmlFilePath=journals/ijorl/current.xml

We particularly thank Prof Tor Chiu FRCS for masterminding this chapter.

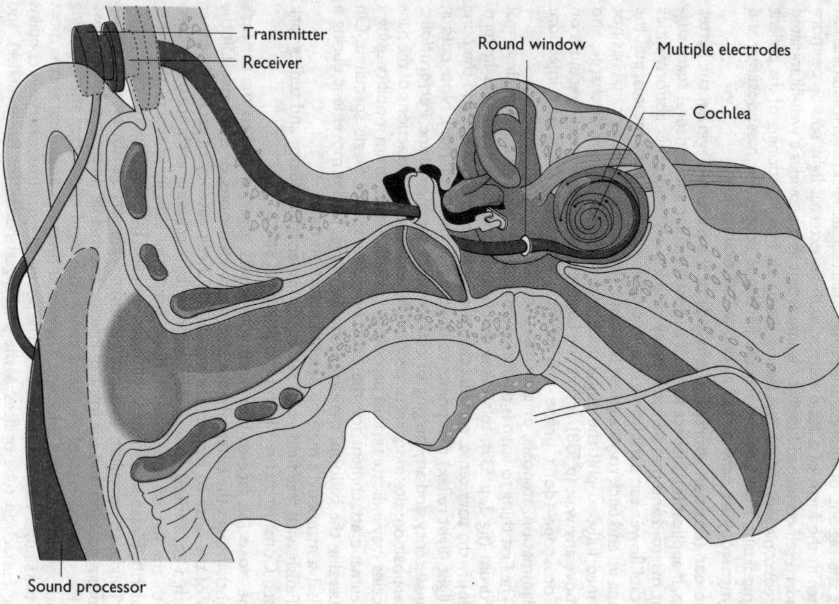

A cochlear implant. An electrode is inserted into the cochlea connected to a receiver implanted in the skull. The external audio processor is attached by a magnet to the overlying skin. After A. Richards and J. Bovosi *practitioner* 2000 **244** 12

Prevalence of ENT symptoms

In one UK community-based study in 2005 of 15,788 people >14yrs, ~20% reported current troublesome hearing difficulties, including difficulty with conversations when there is background noise (few wore a hearing aid regularly). 20% reported noises in head/ears (tinnitus) lasting over 5 minutes. ~15% reported hayfever[et al] in the last year, 7% sneezing or voice problems, and 31% had ≥1 severe sore throat/tonsillitis. ~21% reported ever having had dizziness in which things seemed to spin around the individual; 29% unsteadiness/light-headedness, and 13% reported dizziness in which the respondent seemed to move.[1] Nasal polyp symptoms (p 539): 2%.[2]

ENT examination

Examination in ENT is no different from other specialties, except for the fact that the regions of interest are rather inaccessible. Head worn illumination either in the form of a head mirror with an external light source or more modern self-contained headlight is important as it provides a well-illuminated stereoscopic view of cavities, leaving the hands free. Positioning of the patient is important. Rod lens and flexible fibreoptic scopes for nasendoscopy and laryngoscopy are now part of a routine ENT examination.

The ear (Position yourself to one side of the patient—begin on the better side, if applicable). Inspect for scars (postauricular and endaural scars suggest mastoid and middle ear surgery respectively) and other abnormalities eg cauliflower ear, perichondritis. To examine the auditory meatus, pull the pinna *up* and *back* to straighten the bend. (In infants, the bony canal has not formed fully, so pull the pinna *back* and *down*.) Swab any discharge, and remove any wax (p 538). Insert the largest comfortable aural speculum on an otoscope (don't probe too far—it's a sensitive area). Any infection/inflammation, stenosis, or exostoses (p 538)?

The first thing to learn is to distinguish between a normal and an abnormal eardrum (fig 3, p 539); this takes practice. Examine the quadrants in turn. Identify the pars tensa, pars flaccida, the handle of the malleus and the cone of light (light reflex) that points to the toes (ie anteroinferior). Note colour, translucency, and any bulging or retraction of the membrane. ***Perforations:*** Size; position; site: *marginal* or *central*? Perforations or retractions of the pars flaccida may indicate serious pathology (p 544). Assess drum mobility using a pneumatic attachment for the otoscope or a special Siegle speculum. On squeezing the balloon, the drum should move. Drum movement during a Valsalva manoeuvre means a patent Eustachian tube.

Finish with free field voice testing (whisper from 40cm) and tuning fork tests. Consider nerve VII and the postnasal space.

The nose (Sit face-to-face, with your knees together and to the patient's right). Inspect the external nose: size, shape, deviations, or deformity. Lift the tip of the nose to inspect the vestibule. Check patency of each side either with a cold metal tongue depressor or by occluding each nostril in turn with the flat of your thumb: don't press the side in (distorts the other nostril). 'Please sniff'. Test smell: often omitted, but often fascinating.[1]

Thudicum speculum (anterior rhinoscopy): insert gently; assess mucosa, septum position, and the front of inferior and middle turbinates. Any polyps?

Examine the rest of the nasal cavity with rigid endoscopy after spraying with xylometazoline & lidocaine. The middle meatus is a key nasal area as most of the sinuses ventilate via this cleft. The postnasal space (nasopharynx) contains the Eustachian tube orifices & the pharyngeal recess (of Rosenmuller), and may contain adenoids or nasopharyngeal cancer. A postnasal mirror can be used to examine the nasopharynx but is only produced during clinical exams! Examine the palate, as this forms the floor of the nose.

Examining the throat Position yourself as above; ask edentulous patients to remove dentures. Inspect the lips and perioral region. First ask him to open his mouth without protruding the tongue, then use a tongue depressor (with light) to retract the buccal mucosa on each side: inspect the buccal mucosa (including parotid duct opening opposite the upper 2nd molar), gums, teeth, floor of mouth, and in particular, the retromolar trigone.

Depress the tongue; say 'ah' and then 'aye' (check palate movement). Examine tonsils (prominent tonsils aren't necessarily enlarged; deep crypts with debris can be normal). Put on a glove for bimanual examination of the floor of mouth, checking the submandibular duct for stones or masses. Palpate the base of tongue for early tumours that are not easily visible.

Free field voice testing (other tests: p 540)

- Explain what you are about to do. Stand behind the patient.
- To test the right ear, use your left hand to rub the patient's left tragus to mask that ear, then 2ft (approximately arms length), whisper a simple polysyllable, eg 'forty-one' or 'chicken'.
- The patient should be able to repeat what is said at least 50% (or 2 out of 3) of the time; failure represents hearing impairment. This is clarified further by (a) coming closer to 6 inches and (b) raising the voice to conversational levels, it may even be necessary to shout!

Indirect laryngoscopy

- Explain what you are about to do to the patient; this is *very* important.
- Anaesthetize the throat with a topical 2% lidocaine spray; warn the patient not to eat anything hot for 1-2h after.
- The tongue is protruded and held with a swab with slight forward tension. With the other hand warm a mirror (check it is not too hot). Ask the patient to mouth breathe, and place the mirror up to the uvula/soft palate. Examine the epiglottis and the false cords (ventricular folds). As the patient says 'ee', vocal cords and their movement may be assessed.
- Flexible nasendoscopy (4mm) can be used in those who cannot tolerate indirect laryngoscopy.

1 Smells are as hard to name as emotions: we know we are feeling something—but we don't know precisely what it is. When we are told (by a novelist or a chef)—we say 'Yes of course—that's it!' Smells and emotions go hand in hand with memory. The engram is the brain's representation of a memorable event. Smells are encoded in engrams—and can be the means of their unlocking. We remember randomly paired associates (such as *butter* and *church*) better if the smells at their encoding are re-presented when we try to retrieve them. Functional MRI shows that the primary olfactory cortex and the anterior hippocampus mediate the olfactory route to hidden memory and the emotions which flow from them. ***So when we are testing the sense of smell we are really performing a test on consciousness itself—which is no more or less than the interaction of emotion, memory, and sensation***. When we re-smell the smells of our youth, or re-smell a perfume from a long-abandoned *affaire de coeur*, we are transported, de-realized, and moved back to, beyond, and beside our former selves. For a moment we re-inhabit lands of **lost content** or buried torment. This is how we come to grow and survive—by learning to smell and interpret the darkness which enfolds us.

This expanding of the sense of smell to encompass all things struck Kipling on re-entering Lahore: '*the heat and smell of oil and spices, and puffs of temple incense, and sweat and darkness, and dirt and lust and cruelty.*'

The ear

The external ear The auricle is fibroelastic cartilage, covered by skin. The ear drum is set obliquely, the external auditory canal is ~3cm anteriorly and ~2.5cm posteriorly. The canal's outer ⅓ is cartilage, having hairs and ceruminous (wax) glands in the skin; its inner ⅔ is bony and lined with sensitive skin.

Congenital anomalies The auricle develops from 6 hillocks derived from the 1st and 2nd branchial arches that appear at 4–6 weeks with the intervening 1st branchial groove forming the external auditory canal. Any malfusion may give rise to accessory tags/auricles or a preauricular pit, sinus, or fistula. An infected preauricular sinus can be mistaken for an infected sebaceous cyst, but there is often a deep tract that lies close to the facial nerve. It must be removed to avoid further infection.

Chondrodermatitis nodularis chronica helicis et antihelicis This latin mouthful describes an exquisitely tender cartilaginous inflamed nodule dwelling on the upper helix♂ or antihelix♀ (fig 2). A more convenient name is Winkler's disease.[3] It is commoner in men who work outdoors. Cause: ?poor blood flow (avascular chondritis) from pressure (eg phone addicts[4]) or vasoconstriction from cold. A pressure-relieving prosthesis may help.[5] If not, excise skin and underlying cartilage (eg 'wide excision' or 'deep shave').[6]

Pinna haematoma Blunt trauma may cause bleeding in the subperichondrial plane elevating the perichondrium to form a haematoma. Arrange formal, prompt evacuation. Aspiration is rarely adequate: firm packing conforming to the contours of the auricle *may* prevent reaccumulation.[7] Poor treatment leads to ischaemic necrosis, then fibrosis (a cauliflower ear).

Exostoses These are smooth multiple bilateral swellings of the bony canals and represent localized bony hypertrophy supposedly in response to cold exposure, such as in aquatic sports. Usually asymptomatic as long as the lumen is sufficient for sound conduction and thus often picked up incidentally. When they hinder migration of wax or debris, or when they occlude the canal so causing conductive deafness, surgical removal is then indicated. Osteomas are benign bony tumours that are usually solitary.

Wax (cerumen auris) Wax is secreted in the outer ⅓ of the canal, to protect against maceration. Due to epithelial migration, the ear is a self-cleaning organ; cotton buds are unnecessary and lead to deafness and discomfort if the wax impacts. Optimal treatment is suction under direct vision using a microscope—but syringing usually works well enough, using water at ~37°C, eg after softening with oil (olive or almond) or bicarbonate drops[8] daily for a week. NB: meta-analyses indicate that use of drops 30mins pre-syringing is just as good.[9] Or you can instil warm water 15min pre-op in un-oiled ears; this more than halves duration of syringing required.[10] [N=39] But as 40% of the time oiling is all that is needed, the longer regimen has advantages. At syringing, direct the jet back and up. *Give up after 3 attempts.*[11] Dry the ear afterwards. *Avoid syringing if the drum is perforated, or after mastoid surgery.* ***Complications:*** Pain; otitis externa; vertigo (0.2%); perforated drum (≤0.2%).[12][13]

Foreign bodies (FB) in the ear These are common in children (<5yrs) and adults with learning difficulty. Organic material may cause much inflammation. Syringing can be successful, particularly with small objects; take care with objects that almost fill the canal as these will impact and organic matter that may swell. Drown insects in oil before removal. For a tightly wedged smooth round FB, the hook and forceps are preferred in superficially and deep lying FBs respectively.[14] Suction methods prevent FBs penetrating ever deeper. Anaesthesia (GA) may be needed in children or anxious adults.

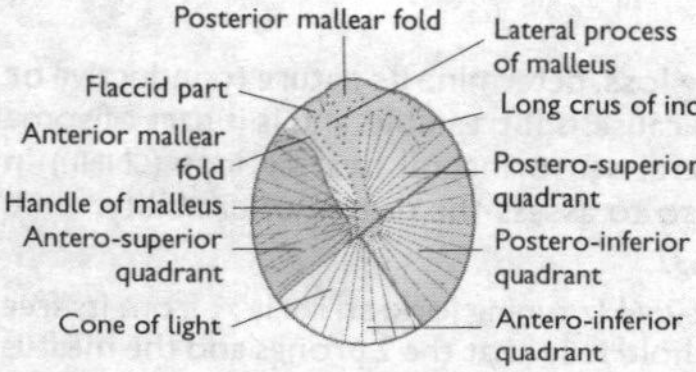

Fig 1. Left tympanic membrane from the lateral side. The 4 arbitrary quadrants are indicated by solid lines and by the handle of the malleus. [15]

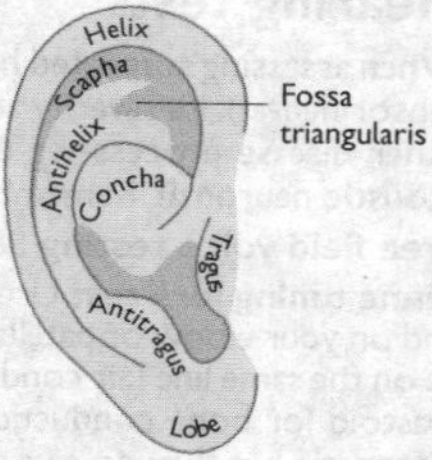

Fig 2. The external ear (pinna). [16]

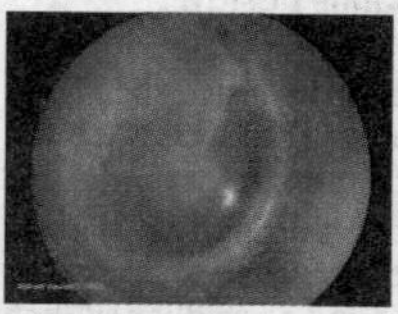

Fig 3. Normal right drum. [17]

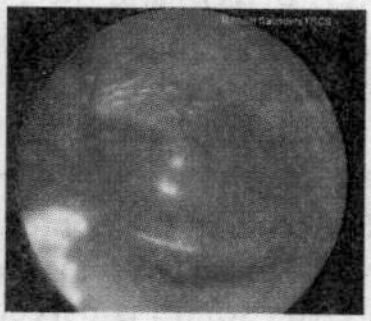

Fig 4. The left drum has retracted, along with the handle of the malleus (it appears shortened). The lateral process will also become much more prominent than normal. [18]

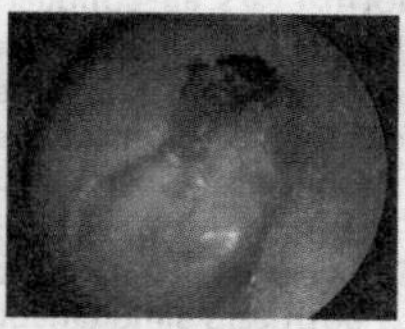

Fig 5. This crust in the attic represents a large underlying cholesteatoma. [19]

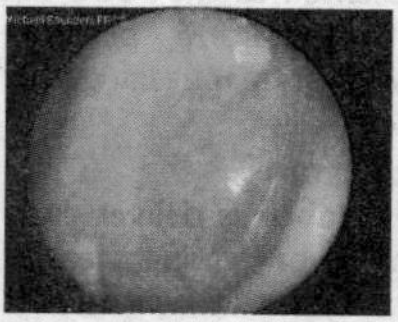

Fig 6. The drum is opaque. There is prominence of blood vessels suggesting a middle ear effusion. This is one of several appearances of glue ear. [20]

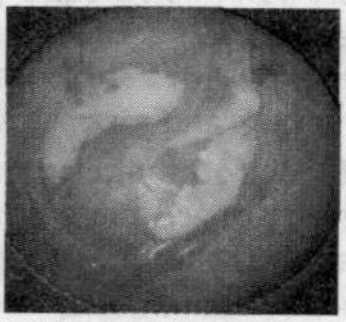

Fig 7. White patches are usually tympano-sclerosis (calcium deposition), eg after infection or trauma; they are usually of no significance, but if severe can cause mild conductive hearing loss. [21]

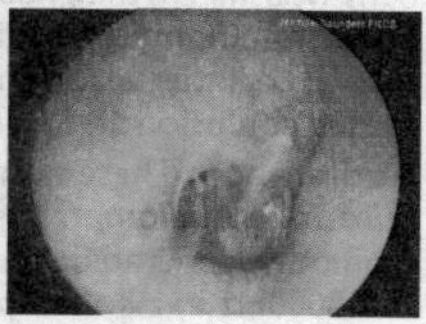

Fig 8. Posterior perforation. Although posterior perforations may be serious, this example is dry, and its posterior margin is defined. Traumatic perforations (eg barotrauma) are often posterior and linear, more like a tear rather than a round hole. [22]

We thank Michael Saunders FRCS *for the images (fig 3–8).*

Hearing tests

When assessing suspected hearing loss, determine its nature (conductive or sensorineural), its severity and its cause: is it treatable, and is it part of some other disease process—eg unilateral sensorineural hearing loss (SNHL) in acoustic neuroma? Remember also to assess the degree of disability.

Free field voice testing See p 537.

Rinne tuning fork test Use a 512-256Hz tuning fork; strike it ⅓ from its free end on your elbow or patella and hold it so that the 2 prongs and the meatus lie on the same line (air conduction, AC). Then place the vibrating stem on the mastoid for bone conduction (BC). Ask: which is louder? No single test is diagnostic but they do give useful information (also popular in exams).

Rinne negative: BC > AC. This occurs with conductive deafness >20dB (or with severe SNHL; ie a false -ve Rinne: the cochlea of the other ear picks up the sound by bone conduction—use of a Barany noise box to mask the other ear during the test, prevents this).

Rinne positive: AC > BC. Remember 'SNAC—rip': in sensorineural loss and normal ears, air conduction is better—and means Rinne positive.

Weber tuning fork test With the tuning fork on the vertex, forehead or upper incisors(!), ask the patient which ear the sound is heard in. Sound localizes to the affected ear with conductive deafness (>10dB loss), to the contralateral ear in SNHL, and to the midline if both ears are normal.

Factitious deafness Usually occurs in the context of compensation claims.

Stenger test: If 2 tuning forks of equal frequency and intensity are presented to both ears simultaneously, the sound is perceived in the midline. When one fork is brought closer the sound is heard only in that ear. If factitious deafness is suspected, ask him to close his eyes and so 'concentrate' on listening; the patient will confirm hearing a fork held 15cm away from the good ear but will deny hearing a fork held 5cm from the bad ear. Then both tuning forks, 15cm from the good ear and 5cm from the bad, are used simultaneously: with true deafness the noise is heard loudest in the good ear, but in factitious deafness it will actually be heard in the 'bad' ear but the patient will deny hearing anything, despite sound also being presented to the good ear.

Speech audiometry with feedback: As the subject reads aloud, speech is relayed back to the ear under test with a short delay. In normal hearing, this causes confusion and stammering, and a raised voice.

Audiometry These quantify loss and determine its nature.

Pure Tone Audiometry is the standard measure. Headphones deliver electronically generated tones at different strengths over frequencies of 250-8000Hz in a sound-proofed room. The patient registers when he first hears the sound (the threshold) and this intensity is recorded in decibels by the tester as the air conduction threshold. A bone conduction threshold is obtained by using a transducer over the mastoid process. Masking (presenting narrow band noise to the untested ear) is required in certain circumstances. Speech audiometry examines speech discrimination above the threshold by asking the patient to repeat the words presented through the headphones. It is useful in that it assesses disability, and can be used to predict whether a hearing aid would benefit a patient.

Both pure tone and speech audiometry are subjective tests, acoustic impedance audiometry (tympanometry) is objective. A probe with an airtight seal is introduced into the meatus; it measures the proportion of an acoustic signal reflected back at varying pressures and generates a graph of compliance. Tympanometry provides a useful measure of middle ear pressure. A normal ear shows a smooth bell-shaped compliance curve (type A). Fluid in the middle ear flattens the curve (type B). Negative middle ear pressure shifts the peak to the negative side or left (type C).

Referrals for speech therapy

For a full analysis of the problems of *delay in talking*, see p 215.

1 in 7 preschool children have transient speech/language problems. Many resolve spontaneously or with professional help but serious disorders affect 1 in 20 primary and 1 in 80 secondary school children. 110,000 UK children are so seriously affected that they cannot be understood outside the immediate family. **Consider speech therapy assessment if:**

0–18 months of age:
- Feeding difficulties from anatomical or neurological disorder, eg cleft lip or cerebral palsy.

2 years:
- If vocabulary is <30 words or no phrases (but not if good communication skills without speech, and he or she seems on the edge of talking).

3 years:
- Speech is unintelligible—eg oro-motor or verbal dyspraxia[1] (with a quiet voice, poor lip control, with mouth always open and dribbling).[24]
- Using sentences of 2 words only.
- No descriptive words or pronouns used.
- Limited comprehension (eg cannot identify scissors or pen by 'which do we draw with?').
- Parental anxiety, if the child is going through a stage of non-fluency.

4 years:
- Speech is not clear. (Problems with 'r', 'th', and lisps can be left until 5yrs.)
- Sentences used are less than 3 words; vocabulary is limited.
- Difficulty in carrying out simple commands.
- Stammering. The Lidcombe program is best started pre-school.[RCT 25] In this technique, parents provide verbal contingencies for periods of stutter-free conversation and moments of stuttering. Waiting for natural recovery is not acceptable because of negative social and cognitive consequences.

5 years:
- Persisting articulation difficulties.
- Difficulty understanding simple sentences.
- Difficulty in giving direct answers to simple questions.
- Difficulty with sentence structure; immature sentences; word order.

6 years and older:
- Persisting articulation problem.
- Difficulty understanding spoken language.
- Difficulty with verbal expression.
- Voice problems.

Children with voice problems, eg hoarseness or excessive nasality, are best referred at whatever age they present.

1 *Verbal dyspraxia* is a specific developmental language disorder with deficits at various levels of speech processing—phonological planning, phonetic planning, and implementation of motor speech.

Painful ears (otalgia)

The cause is often non-otological (in 50%); look for sources of referred pain, eg throat and teeth (does grinding/tapping hurt—see p 580).

Otitis externa Discharge, and tragal tenderness due to an acute inflammation of the skin of the meatus, eg caused by moisture (swimming), trauma eg fingernails (consequently conditions causing itch, eg eczema/psoriasis), high humidity, an *absence* of wax, a narrow ear canal, and hearing aids.[26] *Pseudomonas* is the chief organism involved. Aural toilet is the key to treatment.

If severe, the meatus is narrowed. A thin pope wick can be inserted and then hydrated with eardrops, eg Gentisone HC® (gentamicin with steroid), an alternative is using a strip of ribbon gauze soaked in glycerine-ichthammol (very soothing). After a few days, the meatus will open up enough for either microsuction or careful cleansing with cotton wool. Commercial Qtips® or cotton buds shouldn't be used: they are too large; instead either thin it out or make one yourself by wrapping a small piece of cotton wool gently around an orange stick. Non-specialists may syringe the ear. Use drops only short-term, as troublesome fungal infections can arise. Beware persistent unilateral otitis externa in diabetics/the elderly or immunosuppression: the risk is malignant/necrotizing otitis externa that is locally aggressive and can lead to pseudomonal skull infection, for example.

Furunculosis This is a very painful staphylococcal abscess arising in a hair follicle. Pathologically it is identical to a boil anywhere else; if there is cellulitis consider flucloxacillin. Diabetes is an important predisposing factor.

Bullous myringitis There are very painful haemorrhagic blisters on deep meatal skin and on the drum (± serosanginous fluid behind it). Classically associated with influenza infection, but *Mycoplasma pneumoniae* has also been implicated as having a variety of other organisms. It may simply represent a variant of acute otitis media. Sensorineural hearing loss is much more frequent than previously thought. Treatment is generally supportive only; oral antibiotics can be considered in cases with middle ear effusions.

Barotrauma (aerotitis) If the Eustachian tube is occluded, middle ear pressure cannot be equalized, during descent in an aircraft or diving so causing damage. Conditions inhibiting function of the eustachian tube eg inflammation/infection will predispose to barotrauma. There is severe pain as the drum becomes indrawn; transudation or frank bleeding into middle ear. Barotrauma to the inner ear causes vertigo, tinnitus, and deafness. ***Prevention:*** Not flying with a URTI; try decongestants (eg xylometazoline every 20min) into the nose or repeated yawns, swallows/jaw movements—and Valsalva manoeuvres during descent. In one study, Valsalvas normalized pressures in 46% of adults (33% of the children). Most of these with unsuccessful Valsalvas could improve middle ear pressure by inflating an Otovent® device, which is recommended to air passengers with problems clearing the ears during flight.[27]

With simple barotrauma, treatment is supportive; effusions usually clear spontaneously, and most perforations heal.

Temporomandibular joint dysfunction ***Symptoms:*** Earache, facial pain, and joint clicking/popping related to malocclusion, teeth-grinding (bruxism) or joint derangement, and, importantly, stress—making this a paradigm of a biopsychosocial disorder which may become a chronic pain syndrome (p 737).[28] ***Signs:*** Joint tenderness exacerbated by lateral movement of the open jaw, or trigger points in the pterygoids. ***Imaging:*** MRI. ***Associations:*** Depression;[29] Ehlers-Danlos, p 642.[30] ***Treatments:*** NSAIDs (PO or topically, eg as diclofenac topical solution 16mg/mL, where available, 10 drops/6h for 14 days[31]); stabilizing orthodontic occlusal prostheses;[32] cognitive therapy (p 374); physiotherapy; biofeedback; surgery (eg reconstruction).[MET 33]

Referred otalgia: when the cause is not in the ear

- Referred (secondary) pain can arise from disease processes in the territories of the sensory nerves supplying the ear.
- The great auricular nerve C2,3 (supplies lower half of the pinna) may refer pain from soft tissue injury in the neck and from cervical spondylosis/arthritis.
- The auriculotemporal nerve (trigeminal) (supplies lateral lower half of pinna) may refer pain from dental disease and TMJ dysfunction (temporomandibular joint dysfunction, OPPOSITE).
- The tympanic branch of the glossopharyngeal nerve and the auricular branch of the vagus (supplies medial surface of drum) refer pain from the carcinoma of the posterior third of the tongue, pyriform fossa, or larynx, or from the throat to the ear, eg in tonsillitis; quinsy. Otalgia is common post-tonsillectomy, particularly in adults. It is worth warning all patients.
- A sensory branch of the facial nerve (supplies lateral surface of drum) refers pain in geniculate herpes (Ramsay Hunt syndrome, p 652).
- Primary glossopharyngeal neuralgia is a rare cause of pain often induced by talking or swallowing.

Discharging ears

The character of the discharge provides clues to its source and cause:

- *External ear:* Inflammation, ie otitis externa (OE) produces a watery discharge as there are no mucinous glands. Blood can result from trauma to the canal. Liquid wax can sometimes 'leak' out. ►Beware persistent unilateral otitis externa in those with diabetes or immunosuppression: the risk is *necrotizing otitis externa* (eg with pseudomonal skull infection).
- *Middle ear:* Mucous discharges are almost always due to middle ear disease. Serosanguinous discharge suggests a granular mucosa of chronic otitis media (COM). An offensive discharge suggests cholesteatoma.
- *CSF otorrhoea:* CSF leaks may follow trauma or surgery. Clues to the identification of CSF include the halo sign on filter paper, or measuring glucose levels or by the presence of β_2-transferrin.

Common causes: otitis externa, acute otitis media (AOM)—but always be wary of cholesteatoma. NB: crust in the attic (pars flaccida/posterosuperior quadrant) often hides pathology, so remove it.

Otitis media is defined as inflammation in the middle ear and classification is mostly usefully based on the timing: acute, subacute, and chronic. Acute OM presents with rapid onset of pain and fever, and sometimes with irritability, anorexia, or vomiting, often after a viral upper respiratory infection. Chronic OM (serous, secretory, or glue ear) is inflammation with middle ear fluid of several months duration.

In AOM drum bulging causes pain, then purulent discharge if it perforates. (often settles in 48h). Give analgesia ± antibiotics (eg amoxicillin; common organisms are *Pneumococcus*, *Haemophilus*, other streps and staphs)—may not be needed if the child is well, *and ready access to follow-up is unproblematic*),[34] but see *Mastoiditis*, below. Decongestants are not much help.

Continuing discharge may indicate complications eg mastoiditis which is rare, and even rarer are petrositis; labyrinthitis; facial palsy; meningitis; intracranial abscesses. Mucopus may continue to drain when there is no mastoiditis, especially if grommets are in place. Treat with appropriate oral antibiotic according to swab results. Do aural toilet to remove infected material from meatus. If discharge continues get expert help.

Chronic suppurative otitis media This presents with discharge, hearing loss, but no pain. Central perforations indicate disease in the lower anterior part of the middle ear. ***Treatment:*** Aim to dry up the discharge (aural toilet, antibiotic with steroid eardrops, depending on culture) and surgery to correct ossicle discontinuities, and to close the drum.

Mastoiditis Middle ear inflammation leads to destruction of air cells in the mastoid bone. Beware intracranial extension. ***Risk factors:*** Withholding antibiotics in otitis media.[35] ***Signs:*** T°↑; tender mastoid; protruding auricle. ***Imaging:*** CT. ***Treatment:*** Myringotomy or definitive mastoidectomy.

Cholesteatoma is serious—and a serious misnomer as it is neither a tumour nor made of cholesterol. It is skin (stratified squamous epithelium) in the middle ear that is locally destructive, through a combination of cholesteatoma growth and collagenases. ***Classification:*** Congenital (classically with an intact drum) or acquired, which are much commoner and can be primary (accumulation within a retraction pocket) or secondary (ingrowth of skin through a perforation). It looks pearly white, with surrounding inflammation. ***Diagnosis:*** The patient may complain of foul-discharge or deafness, but often the patient does not present until later with headache, pain, facial paralysis, and vertigo, indicating impending intracranial complications such as meningitis and cerebral abscess. ***Treatment:*** Surgery is inevitable and aims to first provide a safe dry ear by removing the disease, improving or maintaining hearing is secondary.

Use of eardrops in otitis externa

►*Take a swab first, and perform aural toilet.*
- Betamethasone 0.1% (eg Betnesol®)—very cheap and good for non-infected, eczematous otitis externa.
- Betamethasone 0.1% + neomycin 0.5% (Betnesol-N®)—use if infected. NB: *prolonged use of steroid drops may cause fungal otitis.*
- Gentamicin 0.3% with hydrocortisone 1% (eg Gentisone HC® drops; 6 times the price of Betnesol® or Betnesol-N®) is good, but is recommended by some only as a 2nd-line agent, eg in *Pseudomonas* infections.
- Clioquinol 1% + flumethasone 0.02% (Locorten-Vioform®) or clotrimazole topical 1% solution are used in fungal infections.
- Sodium bicarbonate 5% drops are useful if wax is an additional problem.

Fluid in the middle ear

This is detected by otoscopy (fluid level or bubbles behind the drum) or indirectly, by tympanometry. 50% of 3yr-olds have ≥1 ear effusion/year.[36]

Glue ear Synonyms: otitis media with effusion (OME); serous otitis media.

►*Hearing impairment noticed by parents is the mode of presentation in 80%.* The fundamental problem lies with dysfunction of the Eustachian tubes (ET). Although the exact cause is unclear there are associations with upper respiratory tract infections, oversized adenoids and narrow nasopharygneal dimensions. Large adenoids themselves do not cause OME but are important because, if infected, they are a source of pathogenic bacteria.

Glue ear is the chief cause of hearing loss in young children, and can cause disastrous impairment in learning, though this is rare. Glue ear may cause no pain, and so its presence may not be suspected. It is commoner in: boys, atopics, Down's syndrome, and in those with cleft palates. It is also more prevalent in winter and in the children of smoking parents.

Signs: Variable. The drum can be retracted or bulging. It can look dull, grey, or yellow. There may be bubbles or a fluid level, there may be superficial radial vessels. Drum mobility when tested with a Siegle speculum or a pneumatic attachment is reduced.

Tests: *Audiograms* (look for conductive defects)
Impedance audiometry (look for flat tympanogram; type B); this helps distinguish glue ear from simple Eustachian tube dysfunction and otosclerosis.
Microbiology: In 33%, bacteria can be cultured from the middle ear.

Treatment: The natural history of the condition tends towards spontaneous resolution. Simple explanation and reassurance with a 3-monthly review may be enough. Drugs have little role: neither decongestants nor mucolytics improve glue ear. Tonsillectomy does not help either.[37] Some favour long-term low dose antibiotics but the data is questionable.[38]

If fluid persists and hearing is impaired, consider myringotomy with suction of fluid, and insertion of air-conducting grommets[1] ± adenoidectomy (so reducing recurrences but adding a small extra mortality risk). Grommets are preferred to T-tubes, which are associated with an unacceptably high rate of residual perforation (50%). The main complications of grommets are infections and tympanosclerosis. Treat infections with aural toilet and antibiotic/steroid ear drops, but removal of the grommet may be required. Autoinflation of the Eustachian tube using Otovent® balloon devices has been shown to be useful but are only effective during the period of use, and while they are less effective than grommets, they may be sufficient until time takes over.

90,000 operations/yr are done for glue ear in the UK (1 in 200 children).[2]
Aftercare: In some units, outpatient follow-up at one week occurs, but this does not prevent complications or ↓the GP consultation rate.[39]

It is all right to swim after grommet insertion, but avoid forcing water into the middle ear by diving. Though some form of ear plug is probably prudent especially when shampooing (because soap reduces the surface tension of the water). Grommets extrude after a variable period of 3-12 months, and a review is required to recheck the hearing. A significant proportion (25%) will require further subsequent grommet re-insertion.

►*In adults, exclude a postnasal space tumour as the cause of middle ear fluid.*

Prognosis: Language development sequelae, eg ↓reading skills & IQ↓, can persist into late childhood and the early teens.[40] [n > 1000]

1 Benefits will be greatest in those having an effusive ear for >90 days with a hearing loss of >20dB
2 F van Balen 1996 *Lancet* **348** 713

Who should be referred with glue ear?

Refer to community audiology service (if available) for:
- Determination of severity of hearing loss.
- Characterization of hearing loss. Is it conductive?
- Is the hearing loss leading to a disability?

Refer direct to an ENT consultant if:
- Deaf for over 3 months—or
- Difficulties with speech or learning—or
- Recurrent and persisting earache over a 3-month period—or
- Other disabilities making correction of deafness urgent.

►NB: *explain that immediate surgery is rarely justified.*

Possibilities while the patient is waiting to be seen:
- Discourage passive smoking. *What's it like at the childminder's?*
- Encourage drinking from a cup, not a bottle (better Eustachian function).
- Encourage interlocutors to sit at the child's level, and to keep instructions short and simple. Explain the problem to all.
- Turn off the TV (less background noise, and this makes it more likely that the patient will look at the person speaking to him).
- Tell the teacher which side hears best (for class seating plan).
- Nasal steroids for 1 month—or
- Co-amoxiclav for 14 days (may be of little real benefit)—or
- Oral steroids for 5 days (eg prednisolone 1mg/kg/day PO).

NB: *benefit may not be long-lasting, but medical treatment may diminish the need for surgery.*

Modified West Sussex protocol

Childhood deafness

Subdivisions • ***Hereditary** vs **acquired:*** Hereditary defects may be present at birth (congenital) or appear later. • ***Conductive*** or ***sensorineural hearing loss (SNHL)*** or ***mixed.*** • ***Isolated deafness** vs **syndrome complex**.*

Autosomal dominant syndromes Waardenburg's (SNHL, pigment abnormalities & telecanthus, ie ↑distance between medial canthi); Klippel-Feil (p 648); Treacher-Collins' (p 655); Pierre Robin (p 650); Alport's syndrome (p 638).

Autosomal recessive syndromes Pendred (SNHL with goitre); Usher's (SNHL, retinitis pigmentosa); Jewell-Lange-Nielson (SNHL, long QT interval).

Acquired *In utero:* Maternal infection (rubella, CMV, influenza, syphilis), ototoxic drugs and metabolic upset eg maternal diabetes.
Perinatal: Anoxia, birth trauma, cerebral palsy, kernicterus.
Postnatal: Meningitis, chiefly; also ototoxic drugs, lead, skull fracture.

Universal newborn hearing screening (UNHS) Screening within hours of birth is the best way to ensure that deafness is diagnosed and management implemented *before* 6 months of age. ►*The aim is to avoid language delay.* This is best achieved by detecting ***otoacoustic emissions*** (OAE; a microphone in the external meatus detects tiny cochlear sounds produced by movement in its basilar membrane). This is abnormal or equivocal in 3–8% of neonates.[41]

Most of these 'failures' (84%) have external ear canal obstruction (collapsed ear canal or debris).[42] In these patients ***audiological brainstem responses*** (ABR) should be measured.[43,44]

Prevalence of deafness found at UNHS: 0.9–3.24/1000 for permanent bilateral hearing loss of >35dB; 5.95/1000 when unilateral and moderate hearing loss infants are counted.[45] Note that no test performs perfectly.[46]

Subjective hearing tests in the older child

- 7 months: ***Distraction testing*** (suitable if aged 6–18 months): As the child is sat on parent's lap, an assistant in front attracts the child's attention while a tester attempts to distract by making noises behind and beside child, eg with a rattle, conversational voice.
- 2–4 years: ***Distraction testing*** or ***conditioned response audiometry*** (at 24–60 months): the child is trained to put pegs into holes or give toys to a parent, on a particular auditory cue. This method can also obtain PTAs (pure tone audiograms) in an older child. ***Speech discrimination:*** (24–60 months): the child touches selected objects cued by acoustically similar phrases, eg *key/tree*.
- 5 years: pure tone audiogram.

Treatment Once deafness is detected aim to provide as good hearing as possible to help speaking and education. Teachers of the deaf make arrangements for fitting hearing aids and help monitor progress. Children usually need higher gain from their hearing aids than adults. Ear moulds may need frequent changing to maintain a good fit. Encourage parents to talk as much as possible to their deaf children. Children may be educated at ordinary schools with visits from teachers of the deaf, or, for the partially hearing, in special units in ordinary schools, or in schools for the deaf, depending on need. For some, a cochlear implant may be suitable (p 550 & BOX). NB: The shorter the duration of deafness, the better the outcome: so funding decisions should not be delayed. ►Give pneumococcal vaccine ≥2wks before implant insertion (or vaccinate the unvaccinated if implant already in situ).

Issues with cochlear implants

For a diagram about cochlear implants, see p 535.

They may be damaged by direct trauma, MRI, surgical diathermy, dental pulp testers and 'therapeutic' (short wave and microwave) diathermy used in physiotherapy departments. See www.bcig.org tel.: 0207 915 1301

Ethical issues surrounding cochlear implants

These relate to adults and children, and revolve around cost, consent, and quality of life—and *who* should decide. The situation is complex as technical improvements ensure an ever-changing balance between benefits and risks (rejection of the device for difficult-to-predict psychological reasons, and post-op complications, eg VII palsy, and stimulator migration)—so beware simplistic statements coming from meta-analysists making statements such as 'cochlear implants are suitable for such-and-such a group (eg profoundly deaf adults) but not another group (eg congenital deafness)'. Also beware of statements such as 'after cochlear implant patients can lead normal lives' (this may only mean that *other people* don't notice the hearing problem). Post-op training is vital, and the user is by no means an inactive recipient. Remember that society is often biased in favour of technology (the black box that does everything), while all too often neglecting the human processes of communication.

The wealth of a society can be gauged by the level of deafness at which most cochlear implants are done. In the UK, cochlear implant candidates generally have no hearing (>110dB loss, ie 8000 candidates in the UK under the age of 70). If the criterion is 'relaxed' to 105dB, this number rises to 45,000. In the USA, the loss is generally >95dB (in the UK this would lead to 72,000 candidates and a bill of £2520 million).

For multichannel cochlear implants, average cost per QALY (quality-adjusted life-year) is ~£11,400/QALY[47] which is in the middle of quoted estimates for costed NHS therapies (for a list, see *OHCM* p 14). On this view, implantation of those at least up to 70 years old makes good economic sense. Furthermore, multiple disabilities are no bar to getting benefit from a device, but it is not clear that they merit *extra* consideration (they certainly merit very careful assessment).

Who should decide these issues is unclear (as usual!), but deaf people should have some input (in the USA, no deaf people helped decide the issue).

Cost per QALY *may* fall with further technical advances—eg beam-forming dual microphone systems to aid hearing in background noise, better speech processors, and new electrode arrays where more electrodes that lie close to the spiral ganglion cells. Difficulties in assessment are compounded by the need not simply to take into account hearing and language, but also learning, socialization, and cultural variables.

Does deafness always counts as a disability? Some deaf families particularly welcome the arrival of a deaf child, and some couples selecting donors for artificial insemination choose a deaf father with a 'good' pedigree of deafness.[48] (Such children will not grow up in a deaf world—so it is very debatable as to whether this is in the child's best interests, especially as in some areas sign language is dying out, owing to the absence of congenital rubella.)

It is not the actual sound itself that matters, but the reverberations that it makes as it travels through our mind. These are often to be found far away, strangely transformed; but it is only by gathering up and putting together these echoes and fragments that we arrive at the true nature of our experience.

Virginia Woolf *TLS 16.9.26*

Deafness in adults

10% of adults are hearing-impaired (UK). It can be a frustrating and isolating disability. A life without intonation can be humourless—but many cope well with some degree of hearing loss if given comprehensive rehabilitation.

Management Classify the deafness (OPPOSITE); find treatable causes. Exclude the dangerous (particularly the unilateral/asymmetric): acoustic neuroma, cholesteatoma, effusion from nasopharyngeal carcinoma. ►*Sudden sensorineural deafness demands immediate specialist referral.*

Definitive management may be required, eg surgery for perforations or otosclerosis—or simple fitting of the most suitable type of hearing aid.

Those with profound sensorineural deafness (>100-120dB) may benefit from a ***cochlear implant*** (diagram, p 535) to stimulate residual neural tissue; it takes ~2h to fit (under GA); an external device processes sound and transmits it across the skin to the subcutaneous receiver coil—to an electrode placed within the cochlea via the round window and directly stimulates the auditory nerve. The signal is not normal sound; rehabillitation is needed to understand the new sounds. Benefits include improved lip-reading and recognition of environmental sounds, and relieving isolation. Cost (UK) up to £35,000. Good pre-op assessment is vital. Give pneumococcal vaccine. Selection criteria include case (exclude central deafness), timing (most useful in postlingual patients), age (no limit) and health, commitment, etc.

Sudden hearing loss (SHL) ***Sensorineural:*** ►*Refer promptly.* Definition: loss of ≥30dB in 3 contiguous pure tone frequencies over ≤72h. Incidence: 5-20/100,000/yr. ♂:♀≈1. Partial or complete spontaneous recovery occurs in 30-65%. Detailed evaluation reveals underlying diseases (eg noise exposure; gentamicin toxicity; mumps; acoustic neuroma; MS; vasculopathy; TB; rarities[1]) in 10%. Do ESR; FBC; LFT; viral titres; audiology; evoked response audiometry ± CXR; Mantoux; MRI; pANCA; lymph node & nasopharyngeal biopsy for malignancy/TB culture. Start rehabilitation early. *Prognosis:* better if: early presentation; mild; unilateral; no vertigo.[49] There is evidence that idiopathic cases may respond to steroids ± hyperbaric O_2 therapy, only if given promptly.[50]

Conductive: A cause is 'always' found, eg infective, occlusive, trauma, fracture.

Otosclerosis Prevalence 0.5-2% clinically and 10% subclinically, although this is disputed. ***Cause:*** Autosomal dominant with incomplete penetrance; 50% have a family history. 85% are bilateral; ♀:♂ ≈ 2:1. ***Pathology:*** Vascular spongy bone replaces normal lamellar bone of otic capsule origin particularly around the oval window which fixes the stapes footplate. Symptoms usually appear in early adult life and are made worse by pregnancy, menstruation and the menopause. There is conductive deafness (hearing is often better with background noise), 75% have tinnitus and mild, transient vertigo is common too. 10% have Schwartz's sign—a pink tinge to the tympanic membrane; audiometry with masked bone conduction shows a dip at 2kHz (Cahart's notch). ***Treatment:*** Fluoride (controversial), hearing aid or surgery (stapedectomy/stapedotomy) replacing the adherent stapes with an implant helps 90%. Many prefer surgery to wearing a hearing aid and there is a 1-4% risk of a dead ear.

Presby(a)cusis (age-related hearing loss from accumulated environmental noise toxicity) Loss of high-frequency sounds starts before 30yrs; rate of loss is progressive thereafter. Deafness (loss of hair cells) is gradual and we do not usually notice it until hearing of speech is affected with loss of high-frequency sounds (consonants at ~3-4Hz are needed for speech discrimination). Hearing is most affected in the presence of background noise. Hearing aids are the usual treatment.

1 Stroke; sarcoidosis; Takayasu's arteritis; *Chlamydia pneumoniae*; immune complexes; autoantibodies to inner ear proteins; anticardiolipin (aCL) antibodies; cellular immune defects.

Classification of deafness

Conductive deafness: There is impaired sound transmission via the external canal and middle ear ossicles to the foot of the stapes through a variety of causes. External canal obstruction (impacted wax, discharge from otitis externa, foreign body, developmental abnormalities); drum perforation (trauma, barotrauma, infection); problems with the ossicular chain (otosclerosis, infection, trauma); and inadequate Eustachian tube ventilation of the middle ear with effusion present (eg secondary to nasopharyngeal carcinoma) all result in conductive deafness.

Sensorineural deafness: This results from defects central to the oval window in the cochlea (sensory), cochlear nerve (neural) or, rarely, more central pathways. Ototoxic drugs, eg streptomycin and aminoglycosides (esp. gentamicin), postinfective (meningitis, measles, mumps, flu, herpes, syphilis), cochlear vascular disease, Ménière's (p 554), trauma, and presbyacusis are all sensorineural. Rare causes: acoustic neuroma, B_{12} deficiency, multiple sclerosis, secondary carcinoma in the brain.

Tips on communicating with those who are hard of hearing

- Decrease background noise.
- Use short sentences.
- Place yourself on the same level as the person you are speaking with.

Ensure that light falls on your face.

▸▸Emergency treatment of unexplained sensorineural deafness

- Get expert ENT help.
- Look for causes: WR; ANA; INR; FBC; TSH; blood glucose; cholesterol.
- Imaging: MRI/CT.
- Audiometry and auditory brainstem evoked responses.
- High-dose steroids are no more effective when combined with antivirals. One starting regimen is prednisolone 80mg per day PO for 4 days tapered over 8 days.[51]
- Intratympanic dexamethasone may have a salvage role.

Tinnitus

Tinnitus (Latin *tinnire* meaning to ring) is a sensation of non-verbal sound not due to a stimulus outside the body. Peak age of onset is 50-60yrs. Ringing, hissing, or buzzing suggests inner ear or central pathology. Popping or clicking suggests problems in the external or middle ear, or the palate. Pulsatile sounds may reflect anxiety or acute inflammatory ear conditions—or vascular causes (glomus tumours, carotid body, carotid stenosis, arteriovenous malformations, intracranial aneurysms, and high cardiac output states).[1]

Mechanism of inner-ear/central tinnitus This is obscure. May be:
- Spontaneous otoacoustic emissions.
- Crosstalk between adjacent nerve fibres from myelin damage after trauma.
- Altered central processing. This is being recognized as more important and helps explain the psychological associations.

Causes Often unknown—but may be related to almost *any* ear disease. ***Specific:*** Hearing loss (20%); presbyacusis; noise-induced; head injury; otosclerosis/post-stapedectomy; Ménière's. ***General:*** *Cardiovascular:* BP$\uparrow$, Hb$\downarrow$, heart failure. *Drugs:* Aspirin; loop diuretics; aminoglycosides, quinine, alcohol excess. *Psychological associations:* Redundancy, divorce, retirement.

A holistic approach to tinnitus entails: time spent on the history; doing tests to exclude transmitted noise (eg glomus jugulare tumours); treating the treatable causes—and to offer support to help ameliorate symptoms.

History Site; character (constant? pulsatile?); alleviating and exacerbating factors; otalgia; otorrhoea; vertigo; head injury; family history of deafness or tinnitus; social surroundings (tinnitus is worse if isolated or depressed); drugs. Assess the disability, and, in particular, if it disturbs sleep.

Examination Otoscopy to detect tympanic membrane mobility (patulous Eustachian tube or myoclonus of tensor tympani) and middle ear disease; hearing tests including tuning fork. Check BP and pulse.

Tests Audiometry (with masking), tympanogram (including stapedial reflex thresholds). ►Investigate unilateral tinnitus fully (eg MRI or brainstem evoked response audiometry, ERA) to exclude an acoustic neuroma (p 570; 10% present this way). Others: Hb; syphilis serology, lipids.

Treatment Once serious disease is excluded, often simple reassurance alone is enough. A positive attitude is important; do not be dismissive and one should avoid terms such as 'untreatable' or 'you must learn to live with it'. Treat the person as a whole, not just as a malfunctioning ear.

Aids: If there is significant deafness (>35dB) a hearing aid that improves the perception of background noise makes tinnitus less apparent. A masking device generating white noise can be worn invisibly in the canal; a portable radio tuned 'off station' under the pillow can aid sleep.

Psychological support is central to helping tinnitus. Hearing therapists can employ tinnitus restraining therapy to make tinnitus less intrusive, partly by dealing with inappropriate beliefs and fears, and partly by devices that provide a low level of background sound, which may gradually decrease CNS oversensitivity to auditory neural signals. Cognitive therapy (p 374) also helps (meta-analyses support this), as do patient groups, below.

Drugs: Avoid tranquillizers, particularly if the patient is depressed (nortriptyline is best here), but hypnotics at night may help. Carbamazepine is disappointing; betahistine only helps if Ménière's is the cause. Randomized trials support use of melatonin (3mg at night)[52] and baclofen (10mg/12h PO increasing to 30mg/12h over 3 weeks). These latter two are non-standard.

1 Hannan A 2005 *BMJ* **330** 237 UK Tinnitus Assn www.tinnitus.org.uk 0800 018 0527. Sheffield S8 0TB

Vertigo

Typical causes

Peripheral:
- Ménière's disease
- Benign positional (postural) vertigo
- Vestibular neuronitis
- Labyrinthitis

Central:
- Multiple sclerosis
- Head injury
- Brainstem/cerebellar lesions
- Vertebrobasilar insufficiency

Vertigo (the illusion of movement) can be ghastly, esp if there are other features: driving unsafe, panic, loss of memory. Find out if it is acute, recurrent, usually benign positional vertigo if no other signs, focal (eg migraine), or due to dysfunction of a central cause, ie of nerve VIII, brainstem vestibular nuclei, medial longitudinal fasciculus, cerebellum, or vestibulospinal tracts.

Vestibular (peripheral) vertigo is often severe, and may be accompanied by nausea, vomiting, hearing loss, tinnitus, and nystagmus (usually horizontal). Hearing loss and tinnitus are less common in central vertigo (eg MS, CVA, tumours). Nystagmus may be horizontal or vertical (if central vertigo) and may be different in each eye, eg in the abducting eye. Drugs: Gentamicin, frusemide, co-trimoxazole, metronidazole; effects may be central or ototoxic. Miscellaneous: Cholesteatoma, trauma.

Is this symptom vestibular? Try to ask all in a story. Does this imply the illusion of movement? Try asking "Which way are things going?" The person with true vertigo usually has no hesitation in telling you—unlike others, who may look at you blankly—and there are lots of other causes: light-headed dizziness, a sense of collapse, can be cardiovascular, ocular, cervical, musculoskeletal, metabolic, or claustrophobic.

Examination and tests Assess CNS and ears (eg middle ear). Test cranial nerves (vestibular function and cerebellar signs; nystagmus). Watch gait, and Romberg's test (eyes closed: balance is kept as long as 2 of these 3 are normal: proprioceptive joint position sense or vestibular input and vision). Unterberger's (marching up and down on one spot with arms stretched out in front and eyes closed: veer of >45° right = ...). Provocation tests (Hallpike, below). Investigations: audiometry, electronystagmography, brainstem auditory evoked responses, calorimetry (the only way to test each labyrinth separately: irrigate each canal with water 7°C above and 7°C below body temperature—nystagmus is induced), CT, MRI, EEG, LP.

Ménière's disease Dilatation of the endolymphatic spaces of the membranous labyrinth causes vertigo for up to 12h, with prostration, nausea and vomiting. Uni- or bilateral tinnitus occurs ± progressive sensorineural deafness. Attacks occur in clusters. Treat acute vertigo symptomatically (cyclizine 50mg/8h po). Betahistine 16mg/8h po is unpredictable but is worth trying; diuretics (eg bendroflumethiazide) probably less so. Operative decompression of the saccus endolymphaticus may relieve vertigo and prevent progress of the disease, and preserve hearing. Vestibular neurectomy/labyrinthectomy may relieve vertigo but causes total ipsilateral deafness. Endolymphatic/transtympanic instillation of ototoxic drugs (gentamicin via a grommet) can help, and usually avoids deafness.

Vestibular neuronitis follows a febrile illness in adults, eg flu, and is probably viral. Sudden vertigo, vomiting, and prostration are exacerbated by head movement. Treatment: eg cyclizine 50mg/8h po. Improvement occurs in days, though full recovery occurs within 2–3 weeks. It is difficult to distinguish from viral labyrinthitis.

Vertigo

Typical causes
Peripheral:
• Ménière's disease
• Benign positional (postural) vertigo (BPV)
• Vestibular failure/ insufficiency
• Labyrinthitis
Central:
• Acoustic neuroma
• Multiple sclerosis
• Head injury
• Inner ear syphilis
• Vertebrobasilar insufficiency

Vertigo (the illusion of movement) can be *ghastly*. Are there other features: feeling unreal, panicky, loss of memory? Find out if it lasts seconds (usually benign positional vertigo, if no CNS signs), hours (eg migraine), or days (look for a central cause, ie of nerve VIII, brainstem vestibular nuclei, medial longitudinal fasciculus, cerebellum, or vestibulospinal tract).

Vestibular (peripheral) vertigo is often severe, and may be accompanied by nausea, vomiting, hearing loss, tinnitus, and nystagmus (usually horizontal). Hearing loss and tinnitus are less common in central vertigo (it is usually less severe). Nystagmus may be horizontal or vertical with central vertigo—and may be different in each eye (eg in the abducting eye).

Drugs: Gentamicin (neuronitis), diuretics, co-trimoxazole, metronidazole; effects may be central or ototoxic. ***Miscellaneous:*** Cholesteatoma; trauma.

Is this symptom vestibular? 'My head's all in a spin' is ambiguous. Does this imply the illusion of movement? Try asking 'Which *way* are things going?'. The person with true vertigo usually has no hesitation in telling you—but other patients may look at you blankly—and this a cue to pursue other causes (lightheaded dizziness ± a 'sense of collapse' can be cardiovascular, ocular, musculoskeletal, metabolic, or claustrophobic).

Examination and tests Assess CNS and ears (esp. middle ear). Test cranial nerves, cerebellar function, and reflexes. Assess nystagmus. Assess gait, and Romberg's test (+ve if balance is worse when eyes are shut—implying defective joint position sense or vestibular input) and Unterberger's (march up and down on the spot with arms stretched out in front and eyes closed; +ve if >45° turn in ≤50 steps[53]). Do provocation tests (Hallpike, below). If equivocal, do audiometry ± electronystagmography; brainstem auditory evoked responses; calorimetry (the only way to test each labyrinth separately; irrigate each canal with water 7°C above and 7°C below body temperature—is nystagmus induced?); CT; MRI; EEG; LP.

Ménière's disease Dilatation of the endolymphatic spaces of the membranous labyrinth causes vertigo for up to 12h with prostration, nausea and vomiting; uni- or bilateral tinnitus occurs ± progressive sensorineural deafness. Attacks occur in clusters. Treat acute vertigo symptomatically (cyclizine 50mg/8h PO). Betahistine 16mg/8h PO is unpredictable but is worth trying; diuretics (chlortalidone) probably less so. Operative decompression of the saccus endolymphaticus may relieve vertigo, prevent progress of the disease, and conserve hearing. Vestibular neurectomy/labyrinthectomy may relieve vertigo but causes total ipsilateral deafness. Day-case transtympanic instillation of ototoxic drugs (gentamicin via a grommet) can help, and usually avoids deafness.

Vestibular neuronitis follows a febrile illness in adults, eg in winter, and is probably viral. Sudden vertigo, vomiting, and prostration are exacerbated by head movement. Treatment: try cyclizine 50mg/8h PO. Improvement occurs in days, though full recovery occurs within 2-3 weeks. It is difficult to distinguish from 'viral labyrinthitis'.

Benign positional vertigo

There are attacks of sudden rotational vertigo lasting >30sec are provoked by head-turning. It is common after head injury. Other otological symptoms are rare. ***Pathogenesis:*** Displacement of otoconia in the semicircular canals. ***Causes:*** Head injury; spontaneous labyrinthine degeneration; postviral illness; stapes surgery (perilymph leak) 54; middle-ear disease. ***Diagnosis:*** *Hallpike test:* This manoeuvre rotates the posterior semicircular canal in the plane of gravity. Explain/reassure, and say 'Keep your eyes open and to look straight ahead'. While supine, the head is held between the examiner's hands, turned 30–40° to one side and then rapidly lowered 30° below the couch's level. Ask the patient if they feel dizzy and look for nystagmus. If +ve, the patient experiences vertigo and rotary nystagmus towards the undermost ear, after a latent period of 5-10sec. This lasts <1min (adaptation). On sitting, there is more vertigo (± nystagmus). If any of these features are absent (no latency, no symptoms, and persisting nystagmus), seek a central cause.

Treatment: Usually self-limiting within months; if persistent, try • *Physiotherapy* to teach vestibular habituation exercises (repeated adoption of the position causing vertigo). • *Reassurance* is most important. • ↓Alcohol intake may help. • *Drugs:* histamine analogues (betahistine); vestibular sedatives (prochlorperazine); antidepressants. • Otoconia repositioning with *Epley head manoeuvres.* 55 In this procedure the ENT doctor or physiotherapist procures 4 sequential head movements with rest in each position for ~30sec. The aim is to reposition otoconia away from the sensitive posterior canals. This works in ~80% (a 2nd treatment may help). • *Last resort:* posterior semicircular canal denervation and obliteration by transmastoid laser (deafness may follow).

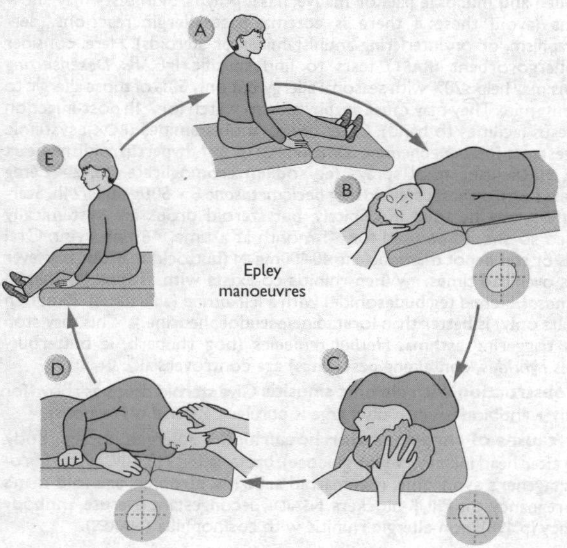

See Northwestern University www.dizziness-and-balance.com/disorders/bppv/bppv.html

Chronic nasal obstruction

Causes ***Child:*** Large adenoids, rhinitis, choanal atresia, postnasal space tumours (eg angiofibromata), foreign body (►refer same day—eg if ***unilateral*** obstruction ± foul or bloody discharge). ***Adult:*** Deflected nasal septum, rhinitis, polyps, sinusitis, granuloma (TB, syphilis, Wegener's, leprosy), topical vasoconstrictors, tricyclics. ►*Refer urgently if:* •Airway blocked by enlarged turbinate •Unilateral obstructing mass •A tumour may be present.

Diagnosis Ask about variability of symptoms, the pattern of obstruction, and effects on eating, speech, and sleep (snoring). Examine to assess any nasal deflection. Is either nostril *completely* blocked (hold a mirror under each nostril: does it steam up)? Examine the postnasal space with a mirror (in children imaging the postnasal space with lateral radiographs is easier).

Rhinitis medicamentosa Drops or sprays which decongest by vasoconstriction can damage the mucosa, due to hypoxia, with rebound engorgement and mucosal oedema encouraging further drug usage. The mucosa is swollen and red. Such decongestants should not be used for >one week.

Vasomotor rhinitis This causes ***variable***, ***bilateral*** obstruction ± rhinorrhoea. Swollen oedematous turbinates may be seen and there is excess mucus. ***Treatment:*** Measures as for allergic rhinitis are usually ineffective. Ipratropium nasal spray 2 × 20μg puffs/nostril/6h helps rhinorrhoea. Cautery or surgical reduction of inferior turbinates helps 'blocked nose'.

Deviated nasal septum Rare in children, this may affect 20% of adults. It may be secondary to injury. Surgical filleting of the bone and cartilage of the nasal septum—septoplasty repositions the septum into the midline.

Allergic rhinitis may be ***seasonal*** (hay fever, prevalence ≈2%, high risk at 5-14 yrs old) or ***perennial***. ***Cause:*** eg house dust mite; pollen. ***Symptoms:*** Sneezing; pruritus; rhinorrhoea (***bilateral*** & ***variable***). ***Signs:*** Turbinates may be swollen and mucosae pale or mauve; nasal polyps. Skin tests may show allergens (avoid these if there is eczema, past allergic reactions, dermatographism, or on interfering antihistamines or steroids). Here, consider radio-allergosorbent (RAST) tests to find specific IgE. ***℞:*** *Desensitizing injections may* help ≤70% with seasonal allergy, but only 50% of those allergic to house dust mite. They may cause anaphylaxis so watch for >1h post-injection (have resus facilities to hand). *Other drugs:* Antihistamines (BOX); systemic decongestants (*pseudoephedrine* 60mg/6h PO; CI: BP↑, hyperthyroidism, heart disease, MAOIs use), nasal sprays (eg sodium cromoglicate 2%, 2 × 2.6mg squeezes/4-6h), or nasal steroids, eg *beclometasone* 8 × 50μg puffs/24h. Steroid puffers may be used indefinitely, but steroid drops are systemically absorbed so should be used for <1 month at a time, <6 times/year. Oral steroids or stat depot *triamcinolone* 40-100mg IM (buttock) may tide hay fever patients over bad times. ►When rhinitis co-exists with asthma (it does in 60%) a *nasal steroid* (eg budesonide) with a *leukotrine* (zafirlukast 20mg/12h PO, adults only) is better than loratadine/pseudoephedrine.[RCT 56] This may stop rhinitis triggering asthma. *Herbal remedies* (bog rhubarb, ie butterbur/ *Petasites hybridus*, containing pestasines) are controversial.[RCT 57] [N=125]

Nasal obstruction with chronic sinusitis Give steroid drops as above for 1 month + antibiotics when discharge is purulent. Refer if no response.

Other causes of chronic rhinorrhoea/rhinitis Allergies, foreign body, CSF (eg after head injury; +ve for glucose), bacteria (eg TB), HIV, cystic fibrosis, Kartagener's syndrome, rheumatoid arthritis, atrophic, age (old man's drip), pregnancy, the Pill, β-blockers, NSAIDs, decongestant overuse, antibody deficiency (p 198), non-allergic rhinitis with eosinophilia (NARES).

Reducing mite load to help allergic rhinitis

Many strategies are tried; 3 have proved effective in (rather small) randomized trials. Their effect on symptoms is not guaranteed.

- Agents that destroy mites (acaricides)
- High-efficiency particulate air filters (HEPA)
- Bedroom-based environmental control programmes[58]

Which antihistamine is best?

Cetirizine, desloratadine, fexofenadine, and mizolastine are all similar at a one-tablet-a-day dose and choice may be according to patient preference, availability, interactions, and price. Typically, antihistamines interact eg with erythromycin and (other macrolides), grapefruit juice, fluoxetine, and systemic ketoconazole, but these effects are not seen with desloratadine. Antihistamines (except desloratadine) may cause ↑QT interval ± arrhythmias.[59]

When the above have been compared in pollen-induced rhinitis, they were all better than placebo, and had similar effects vis à vis nasal smears assessing eosinophilia, histamine/grass pollen skin tests, and grass pollen nasal provocation tests.[60]

Nasal polyps

Typical patient: a man >40yrs old; in children they are associated with cystic fibrosis. *Histology:* 90% are oedematous eosinophilic polyps. Typical sites: middle turbinates; middle meatus; ethmoids. Single, benign maxillary polyps may arise in the maxillary antrum, and prolapse into the nose to fill the nasopharynx (antro-choanal polyps). Prevalence: 2%.[61]

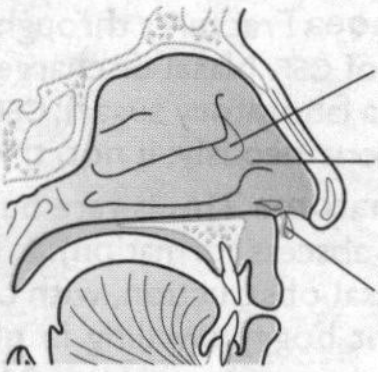

Fig 1. Nasal polyps

Associations: Allergic rhinitis, chronic ethmoid sinusitis, cystic fibrosis.

Symptoms: Watery anterior rhinorrhoea,[62] purulent postnasal drip, nasal obstruction, change in voice quality, anosmia and taste disturbance, mucocele (presents with a lump on the medial superior border of the orbit).

Signs: It can be hard to distinguish hypertrophied inferior turbinates from nasal polyps—but gentle palpation will show that the polyp, if that is what it is, is insensitive, pale, and mobile.

Drugs: Try 2 days of betamethasone sodium phosphate 0.1% nasal drops, instilled every 8h (longer courses may be safe). ►*Use of nose drops requires the correct posture:* bent double at the hips, with nostrils pointing at the sky—eg kneeling with the forehead on the floor. This may make polyps quickly diminish in size, and maintenance therapy with beclometasone spray may then be tried, eg 8 puffs/24h (50μg/puff).

Surgery: Polypectomy, eg by endoscopy. Local anaesthesia may have the advantage of a more bloodless field—and patient awareness, should the orbit or intracranial fossa be breeched. If more than simple polypectomy is planned, it is wise to do CT scans to show anatomical variations.

Post-op: Watch for bleeding. Douches may be given ± topical steroids.

Nasal injury and foreign bodies

Fractured nose The upper ⅓ of the nose has bony support; the lower ⅓ and septum are cartilaginous. Direct violence to the nose may fracture the nasal bones. Take a history as to the time of the injury, previous nasal injuries, epistaxis, nasal obstruction, and CSF rhinorrhoea. Ask about loss of consciousness. Consider other facial fractures: zygomaticomaxillary fractures may cause malocclusion of the teeth and impair normal jaw opening; there may be diplopia if there is fracture of the orbital floor. Carefully feel around the orbit to check no 'steps' in contour. Radiographs are not particularly helpful as there may be old injuries shown and cartilaginous injuries do not show up. They will not alter the acute management.

Soft tissue swelling at the initial examination may make deformity difficult to see, so re-examine after 7 days (especially children)—exclude a septal haematoma at initial examination. If present, refer to an ENT surgeon for evacuation (risk of septal necrosis if untreated). Fracture reduction (under GA) is best within the first 10-14 days (complete setting may have occurred by 3 weeks). Zygoma and maxilla fractures set faster and should be referred immediately to maxillofacial surgeons. Post-operatively patients are advised to apply ice for the first 12h; sleep with head elevated, sneeze through mouth, refrain from blowing the nose and taking vigorous exercise. Re-examine at two weeks and two months after operation. Septal deviation may require septoplasty several months later. Post-traumatic nasal deformity is common (seen in 14-50%); this is reducible to 9% by complete nasal assessment (bony and septum), and primary septal reconstruction if severe septal fracture-dislocation.[63] [n=110]

CSF rhinorrhoea Fractures through the roof of the ethmoid labyrinth may result in leak of CSF. Nasal discharge tests +ve for glucose (Clinistix® test, confirm with a laboratory sugar); CSF uniquely contains β_2-transferrin. Leaks often stop spontaneously; if not, try neurosurgical closure of the dura.

Septal haematoma This is rare but may be serious (beware rhinorrhoea; fever suggests abscess formation).[64] These may occur after injury and cause distressing nasal obstruction, with bilateral septal swellings. If you detect a large, fluctuant boggy swelling in place of the septum, refer immediately. Evacuate clots at once under GA. Suture and pack as needed. Give co-amoxiclav (or clindamicin) to prevent infection. If left untended there is risk of cartilage necrosis ± nasal collapse.[65] [n=20]

Foreign bodies Most are self-inserted by children. Organic material presents early with purulent discharge; inorganic bodies may remain inert for ages. If a child is co-operative it may be possible to grab the object with forceps. 2.5% cocaine spray may shrink the mucosa and allow extraction with a sucker. Foley catheters can also be useful. If general anaesthesia needed, protect the airway.[66] [n=60]

Causes of septal perforation After septal surgery (p 556); trauma; nose picking; body piercings; nasal prongs (O_2 delivery); sniffing chrome salts or cocaine (any odd behaviour, fever, or fits?); rodent ulcer or other malignancy; any chronic mucosal inflammation/granuloma—eg TB; syphilis; HIV, extra-GI Crohn's disease;[67] [n=1] sarcoidosis; SLE; Wegener's (*OHCM* p 738); leishmaniasis; cryoglobulinaemia; fungi; relapsing polychondritis (look for chondritis in auricles, nose and trachea ± non-erosive polyarthritis, eye inflammation, and vestibular or cochlear damage; it may be fatal).[68]

Perforations irritate, whistle, crust, and bleed. *Treatment:* symptomatic. Closure is hard (may be done with rhinoplasty; a one-stage procedure).[69] [n=20]

Nosebleed (epistaxis)

Nosebleeds are [illegible] as they can be fatal. Epistaxis is the commonest ENT emergency by far. It affects more than half the population at least once in their lifetime; while the vast majority will stop spontaneously or be easily controlled, in a minority it can be serious.

Causes In 85% the cause is unknown. The peaks in incidence occur in children, young adults, and those >50 or over. There is a seasonal variation: nosebleeds are more common in cold weather. Local trauma (nose picking, fractures) is a common cause; also haemorrhagic [illegible] (such as haemophilia, [illegible]). Hypertension is not regarded as a cause, but it can prolong bleeding. Ask about NSAIDs & anticoagulants (this makes things harder).

Conditions such as septal perforations and, rarely, neoplasms, can be the underlying cause. A search for the cause is often a secondary issue in the management; tests are only indicated for significant bleeds, and coagulation studies are not indicated. Don't waste too much time looking for rare causes, eg hepatic coagulopathy, Osler–Weber–Rendu syndrome, hereditary [illegible] and syphilis etc.

Management: first aid. Unless the patient is shocked, have them sitting up with the head tilted downwards to prevent blood trickling backwards. Firm pressure on the cartilaginous nose (not the bony) using finger and thumb is needed for 10–15min.

Protect yourself: it can be messy. Use protection: gloves, apron, and [illegible].

First, treat the patient. Assess for shock and resuscitate as needed.

Then treat the nose. Find the bleeding and stop it. Direct visualization is the key to treatment, but is often easier said than done. Bleeds are arbitrarily divided into anterior and posterior; anterior bleeds that can be easily seen with rhinoscopy are simpler to treat and are usually less severe. Always remember to check the oropharynx.

Anterior epistaxis: This is almost invariably septal. Little's area is used to describe this area, where anterior ethmoidal, sphenopalatine, and labial arteries anastomose to form an anterior anastomotic area.

1 Remove clots with suction, or by asking him to blow his nose. Clot obscures the view. As contains fibrinolytic factors, it hinders haemostasis.

2 Insert a cotton wool pledget, or a length of ribbon gauze soaked in a vasoconstrictor & local anaesthetic, eg xylometazoline 0.1% plus lidocaine 2% topical solution—into the nostril and leave for 5min. This will slow the bleeding and anaesthetize the area.

3 Obvious anterior bleeding can be cauterized with silver nitrate sticks. Warn that it stings. Apply it from outside in, and around the bleeding site, for 10sec. Be careful with the cleaning: it is corrosive.

4 Bleeding that persists can be treated with anterior packing with vaseline or BIPP (bismuth iodoform paraffin paste) impregnated ribbon gauze, or nasal tampons. Remember to attach a suture to the pack to facilitate its later removal.

If you cannot see the bleeding point, refer to an ENT or [illegible].

Nosebleed (epistaxis)

►*Never underestimate nosebleeds; they can be fatal.* Epistaxis is the commonest ENT emergency by far. It affects more than half the population at least once in their lifetime; while the vast majority will stop spontaneously or be easily controlled, in a minority it can be serious.

Causes In 80% the cause is unknown. The peaks in incidence occur in children, young adults, and those 50 or over. There is a seasonal variation: nosebleeds are more common in cold weather.[70] [n=1064] Trauma (nose-picking; fractures) is a common cause; also ↓haemostasis, eg blood dyscrasias, haemophilia, ↑alcohol intake.[71] [n=50] Hypertension is not regarded as a cause, but it can prolong bleeding. Ask about NSAIDs & anticoagulant use (makes things harder).[72]

Conditions such as septal perforations and, rarely, neoplasms can be the underlying cause. A search for the cause is often a secondary issue in the management; tests are only indicated for significant bleeds, and *routine* clotting studies are not indicated. Don't waste too much time looking for rare causes (hepatic coagulopathy, Osler-Weber-Rendu syndrome, leukaemia, malaria, and typhoid etc).[73] [n=140]

Management ***First aid:*** Unless the patient is shocked, have them sitting up with the head tilted downwards to prevent blood trickling backwards. Firm pressure on the cartilaginous nose (not the bridge) using finger and thumb is needed for 10–15min.

- Protect yourself. It can be messy. Eye protection, gloves, and an apron.
- First, treat the patient. Assess for shock and resuscitate as needed.
- Then treat the nose. Find the bleeding and stop it. Direct visualization is the key to treatment but is often easier said than done. Bleeds are arbitrarily divided into anterior and posterior; anterior bleeds that can be easily seen with rhinoscopy are simpler to treat and are usually less severe. Always remember to check the oropharynx.

Anterior epistaxis: This is almost invariably septal; Little's area is used to describe this area where anterior ethmoidal, sphenopalatine, and facial arteries anastomose to form an anterior anastomotic arcade.

1. Remove clots with suction, or by asking him to blow his nose. Clot obscures the view, & contains fibrinolytic factors hindering haemostasis.
2. Insert a cotton wool pledget or a length of ribbon gauze soaked in a vasoconstrictor ± local anaesthetic, eg xylometazoline (Otrivine®) with 2% topical lidocaine—into the nostril and leave for 5min. This will slow the bleeding and anaesthetize the area.
3. Obvious anterior bleeding can be cauterized with silver nitrate sticks. Warn that it stings. Apply firm pressure to, and around, the bleeding site for 10sec. Be careful with the clear fluid: it is corrosive.
4. Bleeding that persists can be treated with anterior packing with vaseline or BIPP (bismuth iodoform paraffin paste) impregnated ribbon gauze, or nasal tampons. Remember to attach a suture to the pack to secure it, and to aid removal.

If you cannot see the bleeding point, refer to an ENT unit.[74] [n=75]

Complicated epistaxis: (major or posterior epistaxis)

- Watch for shock especially in the elderly.
- Access is difficult and bleeding is usually more severe. Bleeding not localizable by anterior rhinoscopy, ie posterior epistaxis, can be treated by various methods depending on expertise and resources. The gold standard is visualizing the bleeding point eg with endoscopy, and then to directly treat, eg with bipolar cautery.
- If a bleeding site cannot be found, the nose may be packed with gauze. Bleeds arising more posteriorly require posterior packing: the simplest way is to pass a size 16G or 18G Foley catheter through the nose into the nasopharynx, inflate with 10-15mL water and then pull forward until it lodges to close off the posterior choanae. Place an anterior pack and remember to secure the catheter. Specialized balloon catheters such as Brighton balloons have an anterior and posterior balloon and are easier to use, but are less effective, as well as being more expensive. Inhalation of clot with respiratory obstruction has been reported with Brighton balloons.[75]
- Packing is generally left for 48h; the patient is admitted and monitored. There are well-recognized problems with infections and hypoxia: infarcts, strokes, and deaths have been reported. Oxygen and pulse oximetry are recommended, and prophylactic antibiotics should be considered especially if packs remain for more than 48h—toxic shock syndrome can occur (*OHCM* p 590).[76]

Persistent posterior epistaxis: Rebleeding after this can be treated by:

- ***Examination under anaesthesia:*** If a discrete bleeding point is found it can be treated directly, eg with diathermy otherwise repacking may be needed. Correction of septal deviation may improve access.
- ***Ligation:*** The emerging gold standard is endoscopic ligation of the maxillary/sphenopalatine artery around the sphenopalatine foramen. This is preferable to older techniques such as transantral arterial ligation of maxillary artery or ligation of the anterior ethmoidal artery. Embolization can be considered particularly for bleeding associated with tumours—but this can cause stroke.

The paranasal sinuses

These are air-filled cavities in the bones around the nose; their exact function is unclear. They are lined by ciliated mucosa; debris and mucus are swept towards and through ostia into the nasal cavity.

Viruses cause mucosal oedema and depression of cilia action, leading to mucus retention which may become secondarily infected. Polyps and septal deviation can lead to poor drainage and so to sinusitis. Current emphasis in the understanding and treatment of recurrent/chronic sinus disease concentrates on recognizing and correcting these drainage problems.

Sinusitis is generally divided into *acute* vs *chronic* types, distinguished primarily by their time characteristics but valid distinction is often impossible, and most features are common to both:

- Pain: maxillary (cheek; teeth) or ethmoidal (between eyes), or on bending.
- Discharge from nose, eg postnasal drip causing a foul taste in the mouth.
- Nasal obstruction/congestion
- Anosmia; ↓smell; cacosmia (bad smell sensation without external source)
- Systemic symptoms, eg fever

►Swelling is uncommon: exclude carcinoma or dental root infections.

Differential diagnoses (non-sinus pain): migraine, TMJ dysfunction (p 542), neuralgias, cervical spine disease, temporal arteritis, herpes zoster.

Causes Most are to secondary bacterial infection following viral infection. 5% are secondary to dental root infection.

- Diving/swimming in infected water.
- Anatomical susceptibility (septal deviation, prominent uncinate process, large ethmoidal bulla, and polyps).
- General causes: Kartagener's, immunodeficiency, or general debilitation.

Images Rigid endoscopy + CT is the most sensitive. The latter is generally reserved for planning surgery, identifying the underlying problem but also to avoid the anatomical pitfalls eg low cribiform plates, vulnerable carotid arteries. Plain radiographs (occipitomental, occipitofrontal, and lateral views typically) and ultrasound are of little use. Normal radiographs cannot exclude sinus disease and 30% of normal sinuses show mucosal thickening.[77] [78]

Treatment ***Acute/single episode:*** Most are self limiting and need little further investigation. Bedrest, decongestants (short course), and analgesia may be tried. There is little evidence to support the use of antibiotics but these are often given (amoxicillin ± clavulanic acid).[RCT 79] [N=214]
If there is no response then drainage with lavage may be required.

Chronic/recurrent episodes: More likely to be due to structural or drainage problems. Investigations should also consider general causes. The mainstay is ***FESS*** (functional endoscopic sinus surgery) tailored to the particular sinus(es) affected and related anatomical problems.[80] Post-op care varies. Post-op tamponade, packing, splinting, and stenting are of uncertain value.[81] Rinsing of the surgical cavity offers advantages in healing: high volume, low pressure is preferred. Suction cleaning may be tried weekly starting 1 week post-op and continues until secretions, blood, crusts disappear. Post-op antibiotics don't seem to help. Fluticasone nasal spray 200μg/12h starting 6 weeks post-op may have long-term advantages (fewer rescue courses of prednisolone and antibiotics needed at 5yrs).[RCT 82]

Complications Much less common than previously, probably related to improved state of the nation's health ± antibiotic use. *Mucocoeles* (esp. frontal sinus) may become infected pyocoeles. *Orbital cellulitis/abscess* (this is an emergency, p 420). *Osteomyelitis* (classically staph, eg frontal bone).

Intracranial infection: Meningitis, encephalitis, cerebral abscess, cavernous sinus thrombosis (fever, decreased conscious level and cerebral irritability).

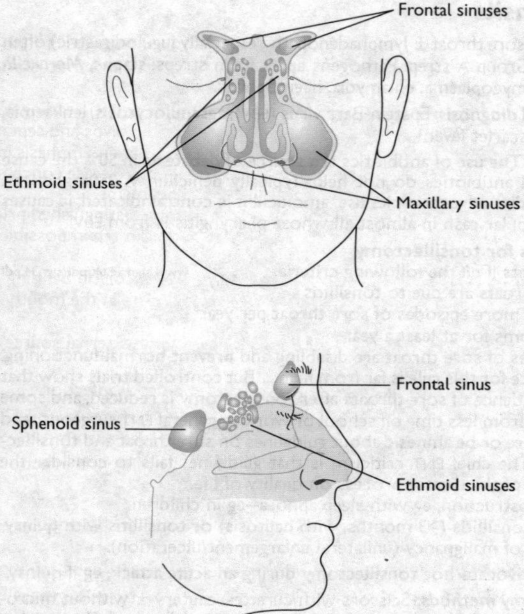

Fig 1. Sinus anatomy 83

The tonsils

Tonsillitis (sore throat ± lymphadenopathy, especially jugulodigastric) often caused by Group A strep. Pathogens apart from streps: staphs, *Moraxella catarrhalis*, mycoplasma, chlamydia, haemophilus.

Differential diagnosis: Epstein-Barr virus (EBV), agranulocytosis, leukaemia, diphtheria, scarlet fever.[1]

Treatment: The use of antibiotics is a source of debate as in 50% the cause is viral, and antibiotics do not help. Typically penicillin V, 250mg/6h PO. Despite studies advocating its use, amoxicillin is contraindicated: it causes a maculopapular rash in almost all whose pharyngitis is from EBV.

Indications for tonsillectomy

- Sore throats if *all* the following criteria: www.sign.ac.uk/pdf/sign34.pdf
  1. Sore throats are due to tonsillitis
  2. Five or more episodes of sore throat per year
  3. Symptoms for at least a year
  4. Episodes of sore throat are disabling and prevent normal functioning. Evidence for this rule is far from firm.[84] But controlled trials show that the incidence of sore throats after tonsillectomy is reduced, and some benefit from less time off school or work. In general ENT surgeons tend to ignore or be amnesic about guidelines on sore throat and tonsillectomy. The chief ENT criticism is that guidelines fails to consider the impact of the disease process on quality of life.[85]
- Airway obstruction, eg with sleep apnoea—eg in children.
- Chronic tonsillitis (>3 months, with halitosis) or tonsillitis with quinsy.
- Suspicion of malignancy (unilateral enlargement/ulceration).

NB: some advocate 'hot' tonsillectomy during an acute attack, eg if quinsy.

Tonsillectomy methods: Scissors with curettes; cautery ± without microscope. Lasers (CO_2; yttrium-aluminum-garnet, YAG) may offer quicker healing ± less blood loss.[86] Radiofrequency ablation can shrink tonsils.[87]

Local complications of tonsillitis: *Retropharyngeal abscess:* This is rare. Typical patient: an unwell child who fails to eat or drink. Lateral neck radiographs show soft tissue swelling. *Treatment:* Incision and drainage of pus under general anaesthesia in a head-down position to prevent aspiration.

Peritonsillar abscess (quinsy): Usually occurs in adults; odynophagia (pain on swallowing) and being unable to swallow saliva are cardinal symptoms. Trismus (lock-jaw)/swelling makes examination difficult. *Treatment:* incise/aspirate under local anaesthetic, or abscess tonsillectomy under GA; give antibiotics.

Complications: The worst is bleeding (rarely fatal): primary (<24h and often requires a return to theatre) and secondary (typically 5-10 days and usually due to infection—here repeat surgery is rarely needed: it often settles with rest and antibiotics; friable tissues make haemostasis difficult and the pillars may need to be sewn together). Use of the tonsillar gag may cause damage to teeth, the temporomandibular joint, and posterior pharyngeal wall.

Differential diagnosis of unilateral tonsillar enlargement

- True asymmetry. Do excision biopsy if malignancy possible.
- Apparent enlargement (shift ∵ peritonsillar abscess/parapharyngeal mass).
- Tumours: squamous ca (70%), reticulum cell sarcoma, lymphosarcoma. *Typical patient:* elderly, with sore throat, dysphagia, and otalgia. *Treatment:* Radiotherapy; surgery; cytotoxics. In one study, survival for stage III & stage IV squamous ca was 79% & 52%, respectively over 2-15yrs.[88][89]

1 *Scarlet fever:* The appearance of a rash after 48h on the neck and upper chest which spreads rapidly to abdomen and limbs suggests scarlet fever. It spares the mouth area, giving rise to contrasting circumoral pallor—and the tongue is covered with a white 'fur', which, when cleaned off, leaves prominent papillae ('strawberry' tongue). Cause: group A strep; treat with penicillin.

Sore throats[1]

In the past GPs readily gave antibiotics for sore throats in case the cause was a β-haemolytic streptococcal infection which may have resulted in rheumatic fever. Rheumatic fever is very rare in the West (p 166). We know that rheumatic fever patients had often had their sore throats treated, so antibiotics had not prevented the illness. GPs may not wish to give antibiotics for simple sore throats, as many are caused by viruses—in any case the proportion of those with sore throats consulting may be as low as 1 in 18.[1] Because sore throat is so common, treating everyone with penicillin is not only expensive, and encouraging of doctor dependency (p 326), but also risks more deaths from anaphylaxis than would be saved by any possible benefit. Evidence that penicillin relieves strep throat symptoms is scant. With this in mind, throat swabs only have a limited role (NB: sensitivity 30%; specificity 80%—they have a role in teaching patients about their sore throats, and in allowing time to go by while nature effects a cure[2]). Numerous antigen detection kits are available (specific, but not sensitive). When there is accompanying tonsillitis, there may be abdominal pain, fever, malaise, dysphagia, and painful neck lymph nodes.

A holistic approach to the person with a sore throat

►*Don't focus on the throat, the swab, or the microbiology: home in on people's health beliefs and work to harmonize these beliefs with your own.*

We often think patients expect antibiotics, and will be disappointed if they are not given. But frequently this is not the case. Does he attend with *every* sore throat? If not, why now? 'My nephew is coming to stay, and my wife told me come and get a prescription'—or symptoms may be worse than usual. If so, ibuprofen may help. But what may *really* help is a dialogue between you and your patient. Strangely enough, there is evidence that rich dialogue reduces symptoms rather than merely making them more acceptable.[90]

But improving symptoms is not the only aim: your dialogue may promote patients' trust in their own body. It may be a stepping stone to active health rather than passive disease. It may stop your patient being a patient at all.

1 ***SIGN guidelines for antibiotics:*** www.sign.ac.uk/pdf/sign34.pdf
- If you are concerned about the clinical condition of the patient, do not withhold antibiotics (don't give ampicillin/amoxicillin ∵ ↑risk of bad rashes during infectious mononucleosis).
- Antibiotics should not be used to secure symptomatic relief in sore throat.
- Sore throat should not be treated with antibiotics specifically to prevent the development of rheumatic fever or acute glomerulonephritis.
- Antibiotics may prevent cross-infection with group A beta-haemolytic streptococcus (GABHS) in closed institutions (such as barracks, boarding schools) but should not be used routinely to prevent cross infection in the general community. The prevention of suppurative complications is not a specific indication for antibiotic therapy in sore throat.; see www.sign.ac.uk/pdf/sign34.pdf. Also see: C Del Mar 2000 Cochrane Library Issue 3 & C Bradley 2000 *Br J Gen Pract* **50** 781

2 *The art of medicine consists of amusing the patient while nature cures the disease* (Voltaire).

▸▸Stridor

Stridor is noisy inspiration due to partial obstruction at the larynx or distal large airways. Children develop airways obstruction more commonly and more dramatically than adults due to their airways being narrower and more readily deformed. (Adults tend to develop hoarseness.)

Clinical features There may also be difficulty in swallowing, cyanosis, or pallor, use of accessory muscles of respiration, and downward plunging of the trachea with respiration (tracheal tug)—all of which are grave signs.

Causes ***Congenital:*** Laryngomalacia, web/stenosis, vascular rings.
- ***Inflammation:*** Laryngitis, epiglottitis, laryngotracheobronchitis, anaphylaxis.
- ***Tumours:*** Haemangiomas or papillomas (usually disappear with onset of immunity—but may require laser treatment before).
- ***Trauma:*** thermal/chemical—or from intubation.
- ***Miscellaneous:*** Airway or oesophageal foreign body; vocal cord paralysis.

Laryngotracheobronchitis (croup) is the commonest cause (much commoner than acute epiglottitis). 95% are viral—esp. parainfluenza (ribavirin can help, eg if immunodeficiency); bacteria include klebsiella & diphtheria; fungi are rare. Usually self-limiting, and treatable at home with humidification (steam) ± antibiotics. *Severity grading:* **1** Inspiratory stridor ± barking cough **2** Grade 1 + expiratory stridor **3** Grade 2 + pulsus paradoxus **4** Grade 3 + cyanosis or cognition↓. 91

Admit (eg to ITU) if severe. In children, CXR may show 'steeple sign' of a tapering trachea. Give antibiotics, humidified O_2, + nebulized adrenaline (5mL 1:1000, may buy time in severe disease needing ventilating), and dexamethasone 150μg/kg PO stat or budesonide 2mg nebulized.

▸▸Acute adult epiglottitis This is much rarer than croup—eg $9/10^6$/yr, but has a higher mortality (1.1%, but 17.6% if respiratory distress a presenting feature). ♂:♀≈3:1. It is an emergency as respiratory arrest can occur. Often the history is short, and the patient may become rapidly septicaemic. Other features: sore throat (100%), fever (88%), dyspnoea (78%), dysphagia (76%), anterior neck cellulitis or tenderness (27%), hoarseness (21%), pharyngitis (20%) and ↑anterior neck nodes (9%). 92 Also drooling with head forward and tongue out. Typical causes: *Haemophilus*; *Strep pyogenes*.

Managing epiglottitis
- ▸▸Don't examine throat (may cause resp. arrest)
- ▸▸Take to ITU
- ▸▸O_2 by mask till anaesthetist & ENT Dr arrive
- ▸▸Visual diagnosis at nasopharyngeal intubation
- ▸▸Blood/epiglottic culture
- ▸▸Find cricothyrotomy kit
- ▸▸IVI + penicillin G & ceftriaxone 2g/12h IV, p 204
- ▸▸Antipyretic (ibuprofen)

Laryngomalacia (congenital laryngeal stridor) may appear within hours of birth. Floppy aryepiglottic folds and glottis ↑tendency of the larynx to collapse in inspiration. Stridor may be most noticeable in certain positions, during sleep, or if excited/upset. In 85%, no treatment is needed and symptoms usually improve by 2yrs but problems may occur with concurrent laryngeal infections. Parents need supporting with 3 months' follow-up. 93 94

Laryngeal paralysis A congenital paralysis accounting for 25% of infants with stridor—often the cause is unknown (but thought to be from vagal stretching at delivery), which may cause feeding difficulties. Their cry is usually normal as adduction is not affected. Most recover by 2-3 years.

▸▸Acute airway obstruction This may be overcome by skilled intubation, but if this fails, do needle cricothyrotomy in children (*OHCM* p 756)—jet O_2 at 15L/min through a wide-bore cannula (14G) placed in cricothyroid membrane: allow O_2 in for 1sec and exhalation (through partially obstructed upper airway) for 4sec. Useful in adults too. Or surgical cricothyrotomy (not in children <12yrs)—see *OHCM* p 756. A tracheostomy in theatre is needed within 30min as jet insufflation oxygenates rather than ventilates, so CO_2 builds up.

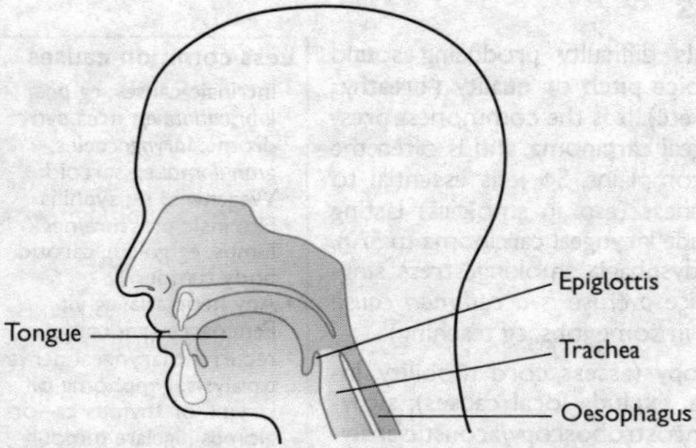

Fig 1. The epiglottis is a valve which occludes the airway when we swallow

Hoarseness

Hoarseness entails difficulty producing sound with change in voice pitch or quality ('breathy', 'scratchy', 'husky', etc). It is the commonest presentation of laryngeal carcinoma, and is often the only presenting complaint. So it is essential to investigate hoarseness (esp. in smokers) lasting >3 weeks to exclude laryngeal carcinoma (p 570). *Always ask about:* dysphagia, smoking, stress, singing & shouting: *voice overuse is a common cause* (prevalence >50% in some jobs, eg teaching).[97]

Tests Laryngoscopy (assess cord mobility, inspect the mucosa, exclude local causes); slow-motion videolaryngostroboscopy/acoustic analysis (causes have characteristic vibration patterns).

Notes on specific causes ***Laryngitis:*** This is often viral and self-limiting, but there may be secondary infection with streps or staphs. NB: in *chronic* laryngitis, any bacteria found are likely to be colonizers only.[98] ***Symptoms:*** Pain (hypopharyngeal, dysphagia; pain on phonation), hoarseness; fever. ***Treatment:*** Supportive. If necessary, give penicillin V 500mg/6h PO for 1 week. Steam inhalation may help. Chronic cord irritation from smoking ± chronic voice abuse may cause Reinke's oedema (a gelatinous fusiform enlargement of the cords, also associated with hypothyroidism—if conservative treatment fails, laser therapy may help).

Singer's nodules: Caused by vocal abuse (untrained singers in smoky atmospheres). These are fibrous nodules at the junction of the anterior ⅓ and posterior ⅔ of the cords. This is the middle of the membranous vocal folds (the posterior portion of the vocal fold is cartilage), and it may receive most contact-injury during speech. Nodules are often bilateral. ***Treatment:*** Speech therapy may help if used early, or they are excised.[99]

Functional disorders: Phonation yields no response in seemingly normal cord adductors, eg in young women at times of stress (but there are many functional voice disorders which may result in laryngeal oedema ± nodules.) The voice may vanish (aphonia) but is more often a whisper. A good differentiating test is to ask patients to cough (needs functional adductors). The best approach is speech therapy, with attention to the many emotional factors which may be present. It is a diagnosis by exclusion, eg allergic reactions may cause sudden aphonia, so don't assume a functional disorder without laryngoscopy.[100]

Laryngeal abscess: This is not uncommon in the immunocompromised (or post-trauma/intubation) and is difficult to diagnose (have a high index of suspicion, and remember TB). There is pain, fever, pain on swallowing (odynophagia), ± respiratory distress, and cervical lymphadenopathy. Lateral movement of the larynx is painful. Failure to respond to IV antibiotics (netilmicin with flucloxacillin to cover *pseudomonas*, staphs & *proteus*) or increasing respiratory distress warrants surgery.[101]

Less common causes

- Intrinsic causes, eg *poor lubrication*, eg sicca syndrome; *laryngocoeles*, *granuloma:* eg sarcoid; Wegener's; TB; syphilis
- Extrinsic pressure/neck lumps, eg goitre, carotid body tumour[96]
- Any neoplasia, eg via Pancoast's syndrome/recurrent laryngeal nerve paralysis; lymphoma or larynx, or thymus ca—or glomus jugulare tumour
- Endocrinopathies, eg: acromegaly, Addison's disease, myxoedema
- CNS causes: vagus lesion myasthenia gravis
- Injury causing arytenoid subluxation. CVP lines.
- Toxic, eg vomit; fumes[etc]
- Bacteria: epiglottitis; diphtheria; abscess; aortitis

Rarer causes

- Mycotic aneurysm
- Subclavian aneurysm
- Ortner's syndrome
- Malformations
- Mucormycosis/fungi in HIV
- Mucosal leishmaniasis
- Hamartoma/haemangioma
- Angioneurotic oedema
- Gouty cricoarytenoiditis
- Behçet's vasculitis of vasa nervorum of laryngeal nerve.
- Chondrosarcoma
- Relapsing polychondritis

Emergency presentations

- ▸▸Epiglottitis (p 566)
- ▸▸Aortic dissection
- ▸▸Anaphylaxis
- ▸▸Acid/alkali ingestion
- ▸▸Trauma

Get help to secure the airway.

Laryngeal nerve palsy

The recurrent laryngeal nerve is responsible for both abduction and adduction of the vocal fold. It originates from the vagus. Its course is complex (at one point under the ligamentum arteriosum it runs in a cephalic direction; in its passage between cricoid and thyroid cartilage it is vulnerable to compression from the cuff on an overinflated endotracheal tube). Symptoms suggesting vocal cord paralysis are:

- Hoarseness
- 'Breathy' voice with a weak cough.
- Repeated coughing due to aspiration from ↓ supraglottic sensation and weak sphincteric action
- Exertional dyspnoea (glottis is too narrow to allow maximal air flow). NB: while at rest the contralateral cord can compensate by increased abduction.

It is a common clinical finding that with partial paralysis cords are fixed in the midline, but in complete paralysis they are fixed mid-way (paramedian position). Proposed reasons for this include:

- Semon's Law: the nerve fibres supplying the adductors (posterior cricoarytenoid) are more susceptible to damage, and the midline position is due to unopposed adduction.
- Wagner-Grossman theory: the cricothyroid (adductor) is supplied by the superior laryngeal nerve (external branch of) that arises more proximally and is thus more likely to be spared. The Wagner-Grossman therory is not supported by recent studies: see www.informatics.sunysb.edu/anatomy/HBA531/clinical.html

Causes: 30% are cancers (larynx in ~40%; thyroid, oesophagus, hypopharynx, bronchus, or any malignant node).

25% are iatrogenic, ie after (para-)thyroidectomy, oesophageal, or pharyngeal pouch surgery. Paralysis after thyroid surgery is seen in ≤5%, and is reversible in about 35%.[102] [n=909]

Other causes: CNS disease (polio; syringomyelia); TB; aortic aneurysm; 15% are idiopathic and are often ascribed to a neurotropic virus.

Tests: CXR, barium swallow/meal, MRI, panendoscopy.

Treatment (nonmalignant causes): Unilateral cord palsies can be compensated for by movement of the contralateral cord, but may require formal medialization in the form of fat/Teflon® injections or a thyroplasty, eg Isshiki-type.[103]

Tracheostomy may be needed to protect the airway.

ENT (head and neck) tumours

Nasopharyngeal cancer (beware unilateral ear effusion in adults) 25% of all malignancy in China *vs* 1% in UK. ***Possible causes:*** • Genetics (abnormal HLA profiles) eg HLA A2 allele; there is ↓survival with B17 & BW46.[104] • Epstein-Barr (EBV) infection (there is increasing evidence).[105] • Weaning on to salted fish (?N-nitroso carcinogens). Its role may be overestimated—ingestion in quantity before age of 12 may be what is important. ***Histology:*** Squamous carcinomas (if keratinizing, risk factors are smoking and alcohol; if non-keratinizing, this is less of an association) and non-squamous: angiofibromas, lymphoepitheliomas, or lymphosarcomas. ***Lymphatic spread:*** Usually early to upper deep cervical nodes. Local spread may involve cranial nerves via the foramen lacerum or jugular foramen. ***Symptoms:*** Epistaxis, diplopia, conductive deafness (Eustachian tube affected), referred pain, cranial nerve palsy (not I, VII, VIII), nasal obstruction, or neck lumps. ***Diagnosis:*** Endoscopy & biopsy; PCR for EBV. NB: submucosal spread may mean the area *looks* normal. Stage by MRI, eg with STIR sequence (=short tau inversion recovery; better than CT).[106] ***Treatment:*** Radiotherapy is mainstay ± chemotherapy ± surgery (radical neck dissection). 3-yr survival for stage II: ~100% (93% for stage III; 69% for stage IV, in one study; worse if EBV +ve).[107, 108]

Acoustic neuroma These are slow growing, histologically benign lesions that cause problems by local pressure and then behave as a space-occupying lesion. It is a misnomer as it usually arises from the superior vestibular nerve schwann cell layer—hence the alternative name *vestibular schwannoma*. ***The patient:*** Progressive ipsilateral tinnitus ± sensorineural deafness, by compressing cochlear nerve. Big tumours may give ipsilateral cerebellar signs or ICP↑ signs. Giddiness is common; vertigo is rare. Trigeminal compression above the tumour may give a facial numbness. Nearby cranial nerves may be affected (esp. V, VI, VII). ***Tests:*** MRI is best. The main differential diagnosis is meningioma. There may be a role for screening patients with unilateral tinnitus/deafness. ***Treatment:*** Surgery is difficult; there are various approaches with different potentials for hearing preservation. Exercise judgment: not all acoustic neuromas need surgery.

Pharyngeal carcinoma are often advanced at presentation. ♂/♀ ≈ 5:1. Histologically, most (85%) are squamous. ***Typical patient:*** Elderly smoker with sore throat, sensation of a lump, referred otalgia, and local irritation by hot or cold foods, with risk factors: chewing or smoking tobacco (alcohol alone is not a risk factor but is synergistic with smoking). 30% of squamous pharyngeal tumours will have a 2nd primary within 10 years. 20% are lymph-node positive at presentation. Hypopharyngeal tumours may give dysphagia, voice alteration, otalgia, stridor, and throat pain; trismus is a late sign. Note any sign of premalignant conditions: leukoplakia and Patterson-Kelly-Brown syndrome (Plummer-Vinson)—in which a pharyngeal web is associated with iron deficiency, angular stomatitis, glossitis, and koilonychia: 2% risk postcricoid carcinoma. ***Imaging:*** MRI with STIR (above) contrast-enhanced CT.[109] ***Treatment:*** Surgery, eg with endoscopic stapling ± later radiotherapy; radiotherapy has a role as first-line therapy if the tumour is small, ie T1 (<2cm) and T2 (>2cm but <4cm). (T3 is >4cm and T4 beyond oropharynx.)

Sinus squamous cell cancer (~1% of all tumours) ***Typical patient:*** Middle-aged or elderly. Suspect when chronic sinusitis presents for the first time in later life. ***Early signs:*** Blood-stained nasal discharge and nasal obstruction. ***Later:*** Cheek swelling, swelling or ulcers of the buccoalveolar plate or palate, epiphora due to a blocked nasolacrimal duct, ptosis and diplopia as the floor of the orbit is involved, and pain in maxillary division of the trigeminal nerve. Local spread may be to cheek, palate, nasal cavity, orbit, and pterygopalantine fossa. Patients present late because epistaxis, obstruction and headache only occur with large tumours. ***Images:*** MRI/CT ± endoscopy (with biopsy) is best. NB: coronal CT is needed to show bone erosion (esp. around the cribriform plate).[110] ***Differential histology:*** Squamous cell (50%), lymphoma (10%), adenocarcinoma, adenoid cystic carcinoma, olfactory neuroblastoma, or chondrosarcoma, benign tumours.[1] *Treatment:* Radiotherapy ± radical surgical. 5yr and 10yr overall survival rates are 77%.[111]

Squamous cell laryngeal cancers ***Incidence:*** 2000/yr (UK). ***Typical patient:*** Male smoker with progressive hoarseness, then stridor, difficulty or pain on swallowing ± haemoptysis ± ear pain (if pharynx involved). Regular cannabis users are also at ↑risk.[112] [113] ***Sites:*** Supraglottic, glottic, or subglottic. Glottic tumours have the best prognosis as they cause hoarseness earlier and spread to nodes is late. ***Diagnosis:*** Laryngoscopy with biopsy. MRI staging.[114]

Treatment: *First-line options:* Radical radiotherapy—or total laryngectomy ± block dissection of neck glands. *If there is recurrence after radiotherapy:* Partial 'salvage' laryngectomy for *some* appears to be safe, effective, and results in reasonable preservation of laryngeal function.[115]

Emotional costs: Salvage laryngectomy's economic and personal costs are great, especially in stage III & IV recurrences. Careful studies showing strong correlation of noneconomic costs with advanced stage allow creation of *expectation profiles* that may be useful to patients faced with difficult decisions. ►This needs to be a personal choice made 'after honest and compassionate discussion' with the surgeon.[MET 116]

After total laryngectomy: Patients have a permanent tracheostomy, so need to learn oesophageal speech. If a voice prosthesis is fitted at surgery, reasonably normal speech is possible within weeks. Give pre-op counselling. Patients are usually discharged after ~10 days with a plastic stent or metal cannula to keep the tracheostomy open (discarded some weeks later). Excess secretions ± crusting around the stoma are common, needing meticulous attention—humidified stomal covers (eg Laryngofoam®) may get round this problem. Say to take care while having a bath, and to avoid fishing and deep water (unless expert training is to hand). ***Late complications:*** Stenosis; pneumonias; post-radiotherapy hypothyroidism (monitor TSH).[117]

Rehabilitation/self-help: Suggest a laryngectomy club. (UK: 0207 381 9993)

Hypopharyngeal tumours are rare and are usually a disease of the elderly. They can present as a lump in throat, dysphagia for solids then fluids, or as neck lumps. The anatomic limits of the hypopharynx are the hyoid bone to the lower edge of the cricoid cartilage: the 3 main sites are piriform fossa, postcricoid region, and the posterior pharyngeal wall. Males are more commonly affected except for postcricoid lesions. They are associated with smoking and alcohol, but not as clearly as laryngeal carcinoma. Treatment options are radiotherapy and surgery in various combinations. The prognosis is poor with 60% mortality at 1 year.

1 **Inverted papillomas (of Ringertz)** are the most important benign tumours of the sinuses. They are exophytic masses that show distinctive epithelial invagination of the stroma without destroying the basal lamina. Total excision can therefore be difficult without taking wide margins. Most significantly 2% show malignant change and 10% have a synchronous carcinoma.

Dysphagia

Malignant causes:
Oesophageal cancer
Pharyngeal cancer
Gastric cancer
Extrinsic pressure, eg from lung cancer or node enlargement
Neurological causes:
Bulbar palsy (*OHCM* p 394)
Lateral medullary syn.
Myasthenia gravis
Syringomyelia (*OHCM* p 404)
Other causes:
Benign strictures
Pharyngeal pouch
Achalasia[et al] (see below)
Systemic sclerosis
Oesophagitis
Iron-deficient anaemia

Dysphagia is difficulty in swallowing: unless it is associated with a transitory sore throat, it is a serious symptom: ►***Endoscopy is essential.***

Painful swallowing is termed 'odynophagia'.

Globus pharyngeus is a sensation of a lump in the throat, when not swallowing, with no *primary* swallowing difficulty. *Prevalence:* 6%♀ *Association:* Hoarseness; mood↓.[118] *Tests:* Endoscopy (?hypopharyngeal cancer; laryngeal cyst). *Cause:* Unclear. In a few there is cricopharyngeal overactivity[119] or ↑acid exposure at the laryngopharyngeal junction, with *normal* gastro-oesophageal pH.[120] *Treatment:* Reassure. NB: it is worsened by anxiety, and stress can form a vicious circle, but don't dismiss these patients as '*globus hystericus*'.[121] ►Make holistic biopsychosocial treatment plan.[122]

The patient As examination is typically normal (unless anaemic), the history is central. Dyspepsia? Weight loss? Lumps?

1 Can fluid be drunk as fast as usual, except if food is stuck?
Yes: Suspect a stricture (benign or malignant).
No: Think of motility disorders (achalasia, neurological causes).

2 Is it difficult to make the swallowing movement?
Yes: Suspect bulbar palsy, especially if he coughs on swallowing.

3 Is the dysphagia constant and painful?
Yes (either feature): Suspect a malignant stricture.

4 Does the neck bulge or gurgle on drinking?
Yes: Suspect a pharyngeal pouch (food may be regurgitated).

Tests FBC; ESR; barium swallow; rigid endoscopy with biopsy; oesophageal motility studies (this requires swallowing a catheter containing a pressure transducer). CXR. Ambulatory pH studies have no proven value.

Nutrition Dysphagia can cause malnutrition. Nutritional support may be needed pre- and post-treatment, eg via a percutaneous endoscopic gastrostomy (PEG) tube. Get expert (dietician's) help; see *OHCM* p 466.[123]

Oesophageal carcinoma This is associated with achalasia, Barrett's oesophagus (*OHCM* p 718), tylosis (a hereditary condition causing hyperkeratosis of the palms), Patterson-Brown-Kelly (Plummer-Vinson) syndrome, p 570. Post-resection 5yr survival is poor (*OHCM* p 508).

Benign oesophageal stricture *Causes:* oesophageal reflux; swallowing corrosives; foreign body; trauma. *Treatment:* Dilatation (endoscopic or with bougies under anaesthesia). **Barrett's oesophagus** See *OHCM* p 718.

Achalasia There is disordered oesophageal peristalsis and poor relaxation of its lower sphincter. Liquids *and* solids are swallowed *slowly*. It is an example of a *spastic disorder of the oesophagus* (others: diffuse oesophageal spasm; nutcracker oesophagus); these are associated with hypertrophy of circular and longitudinal muscle layers. Intraluminal ultrasound shows that a contraction of the longitudinal muscle of the oesophagus is temporally related to chest pain and heartburn and probably causes the symptoms.[1] CXR: Air/fluid level behind the heart, and double right heart border produced by an expanded oesophagus. Typical 'rat's tail' appearance. *Treatment:* Myomectomy cures ~75%. Pneumatic dilatation may help.

1 Mittal R 2005 *J Clin Gastroenterol* **39** S42

Facial palsy

Arising in the medulla, and emerging between pons and medulla, the facial nerve passes through the posterior fossa and runs through the middle ear before emerging from the stylomastoid foramen to pass into the parotid. Lesions may be at any part of its course. Branches in the temporal bone:

1 The greater superficial petrosal nerve (lacrimation).
2 Branch to stapedius (lesions above this cause hyperacusis).
3 The chorda tympani (supply taste to anterior ⅔ of the tongue).

Causes: Intracranial: Brainstem tumours; strokes; polio; multiple sclerosis; cerebellopontine angle lesions (acoustic neuroma, meningitis).
Intratemporal: Otitis media; Ramsay Hunt syndrome; cholesteatoma.
Infratemporal: Parotid tumours; trauma.
Others: Lyme disease; sarcoid; Guillain–Barré; herpes; diabetes; Bell's palsy.

Examination & tests: Lower motor neurone lesions can paralyse all of one side of the face but in upper motor neurone lesions, the facial muscles of the forehead may still work (they are bilaterally innervated). Brainstem lesions produce only muscle weakness and may be accompanied by sixth nerve palsies. Loss of lacrimation (Schirmer's test, p 418), stapedius reflex, taste (electrogustometry detects) and submandibular salive production (cannulate ducts) imply nerve lesions proximal to the origin of the relevant branches. Examine the ears (to exclude otitis media, zoster, and cholesteatoma) and parotid. Consider temporal bone radiography. Electromyography reveals completeness of the lesion.

Trauma: Examine the VII nerve in victims of head trauma. An incomplete palsy will probably recover; complete palsy demands surgical exploration.

Infection: In acute otitis media causing facial palsy myringotomy should be performed. When cholesteatoma is present emergency exploratory surgery should be performed. If rare acute necrotizing otitis externa is the cause, IV antibiotics (eg ticarcillin) and local toilet are needed.

Ramsay Hunt syndrome (herpes zoster oticus) See p 652.

Bell's palsy: At present the cause is unknown but many believe it part of a viral polyneuropathy (herpes simplex in some small studies) with demyelination, the V, X, and C2 nerves also being affected. Onset is abrupt and may be associated with pain. The mouth sags, and dribbling, taste impairment and watering (or dry) eyes may occur. The patient cannot wrinkle the forehead, blow forcefully, whistle, or blow out his cheek.

Treatment: Protect the eye with dark glasses, and tape closed during sleep. If recovery is expected to take months, consider lateral tarsorrhaphy. Instil artificial tears regularly at the slightest evidence of drying. There is good evidence that prednisolone helps, if given early (eg in the 1st 24h, eg 20mg/6h for 5 days, tail off over next 5 days).[1] Oral aciclovir (eg 400mg five times a day) appears to be a promising additional treatment.[2] Plastic and cheek implants may improve appearance. If electromyography reveals nerve degeneration, surgical exploration may be carried out to check nerve continuity, breaches of which may be grafted (eg with lateral cutaneous nerve of the thigh).

1 [illegible]
2 [illegible]

Facial palsy

Arising in the medulla, and emerging between pons and medulla, the facial nerve passes through the posterior fossa and runs through the middle-ear before emerging from the stylomastoid foramen to pass into the parotid. Lesions may be at any part of its course. Branches in the temporal bone:
1 The greater superficial petrosal nerve (lacrimation).
2 Branch to stapedius (lesions above this cause hyperacusis).
3 The chorda tympani (supply taste to anterior ⅔ of the tongue).

Causes ***Intracranial:*** Brainstem tumours; strokes; polio; multiple sclerosis; cerebellopontine angle lesions (acoustic neuroma, meningitis).
Intratemporal: Otitis media; Ramsay Hunt syndrome; cholesteatoma.
Infratemporal: Parotid tumours; trauma.
Others: Lyme disease; sarcoid; Guillain–Barré; herpes; diabetes; Bell's palsy.

Examination & tests Lower motor neurone lesions can paralyze all of one side of the face; but in upper motor neurone lesions, the facial muscles of the forehead may still work (they are bilaterally innervated). Brainstem lesions produce only muscle weakness and may be accompanied by sixth nerve palsies. Loss of lacrimation (Schirmer's test p 418), stapedius reflex, taste (electrogustometry detects) and ↓submandibular saliva production (cannulate ducts) imply nerve lesions proximal to the origin of the relevant branches. Examine the ears (to exclude otitis media, zoster, and cholesteatoma) and parotid. Consider temporal bone radiography. Electromyography reveals completeness of the lesion.

Trauma: Examine the VII nerve in victims of head trauma. An incomplete palsy will probably recover; complete palsy demands surgical exploration.

Infection In acute otitis media causing facial palsy myringotomy should be performed. When cholesteatoma is present emergency exploratory surgery should be performed. If rare acute necrotizing otitis externa is the cause, IV antibiotics (eg ticarcillin) and local toilet are needed.

Ramsay Hunt syndrome (herpes zoster oticus) See p 652.

Bell's palsy At present the cause is unknown but many believe it part of a viral polyneuropathy (Herpes simplex in some small studies) with demyelination, the V, X, and C2 nerves also being affected. Onset is abrupt and may be associated with pain. The mouth sags, and dribbling, taste impairment and watering (or dry) eyes may occur. The patient cannot wrinkle the forehead, blow forcefully, whistle, or pout out his cheek.

Treatment: Protect the eye with dark glasses, and tape closed during sleep. If recovery is expected to take months, consider lateral tarsorrhaphy. Instil artificial tears regularly at the slightest evidence of drying. There is good evidence that prednisolone helps, *if given early*[1] (eg in the 1st 24h, eg 20mg/6h for 5 days, tail off over next 5 days). Oral aciclovir (eg 400mg five times a day) appears to be a promising *additional* treatment.[2] Hooks and cheek plumpers may improve appearance. If electromyography reveals total degeneration, surgical exploration may be carried out to check nerve continuity, breaches of which may be grafted (eg with lateral cutaneous nerve of the thigh).

1 Many neurologists give steroids 'to reduce oedema' particularly to those seen within 6 days of onset. Helpful studies are those by Hat (2003) & Shafshak (1994 *J Laryng & Otology* **108** 940-3 & *Bandolier* 1995 2/11 3) showing that the extra benefit of steroids may be confined to those treated within 24h of onset. Spontaneous recovery is good in any case (85%). For every 3 persons treated with steroids within 24h, 1 extra had a good recovery compared with no treatment; for ethical reasons, this study was not randomized. Older randomized studies were inconclusive, but did not look specifically at early treatment. Meta-analyses support steroids.
2 Axelsson S 2003 *Ann Otol Rhinol* **112** 197 & Enting R 1998 *Ned Tijdschr Geneeskd* **142** 436

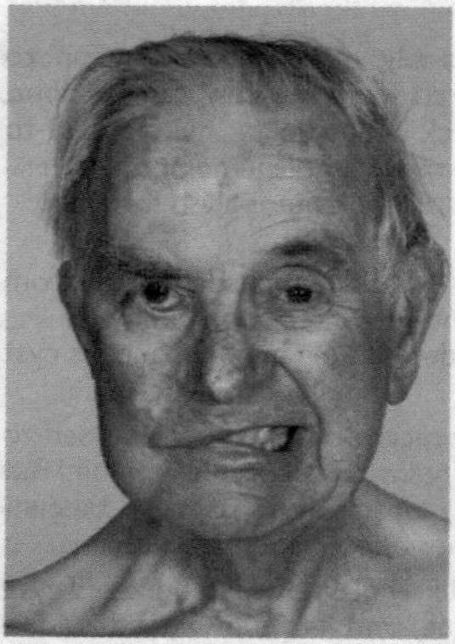

Fig 1. Bell's palsy: the patient is trying to smile, but, on his right side, the lower lid droops, the nasolabial fold is slack, and the lips do not move.

Lumps in the neck

►*Don't biopsy neck lumps!* Refer any possibly malignant neck lump to ENT, where thorough assessment and search for a primary can be done, eg in a dedicated fast-track '2-week rule' neck lump clinic,[124] with access to fine-needle aspiration (FNA for cytology—beware pulsatile lumps!) and CT/MRI (MRI is better). ►Culture any specimens for TB: don't put it all in formalin.

Diagnosis

- ***How long has the lump been present?*** If <3 weeks, lymphadenopathy from a self-limiting infection is likely, and extensive investigation is unwise.
- ***Which tissue layer is the lump?*** Is it intradermal? (eg from sebaceous cyst with a central punctum, or a lipoma.)

If the lump is not intradermal, and not of recent onset, allow yourself to feel the intoxicating pleasure of a hunt beginning over complex terrain. But remember—you are vastly outnumbered by a pack of diseases—so be cunning. *The first step in this process is a proper appreciation of anatomy.*

Midline lumps In patients <20yrs old, the likely diagnosis is a ***dermoid cyst***, or, if it moves on protruding the tongue, and is below the hyoid, a ***thyroglossal cyst*** (a fluctuant lump developing in cell rests in thyroid's migration path, treated by surgery). If over 20, it's probably a thyroid mass, unless it is bony hard, when the diagnosis may be a ***chondroma***.[125]

Submandibular triangle (Below jaw; above anterior belly of digastric.) If <20yrs, self-limiting lymphadenopathy is likely. If >20, exclude ***malignant lymphadenopathy*** (eg firm, and non-tender). ►Is TB likely? If it's not a node, think of ***submandibular salivary stone***, ***tumour***, or ***sialadenitis***.[126]

Anterior triangle (Below digastric and in front of sternomastoid.) Nodes are common (see above): remember to examine the areas which they drain (Is the spleen enlarged?—this may indicate lymphoma). Branchial cysts emerge under the anterior border of sternomastoid where the upper ⅓ meets the middle ⅓; age <20. The popular theory is that they are due to non-disappearance of the cervical sinus (where the 2nd branchial arch grows down over 3rd and 4th) but this is not universally accepted. Lined by squamous epithelium, their fluid contains cholesterol crystals. Treat by excision. ***Cystic hygromas*** arise from the jugular lymph sac and transilluminate brightly. Treat by surgery or hypertonic saline sclerosant. ***Carotid body tumours*** (***chemodectoma***) are very rare, move from side-to-side, but not up and down, and splay out the carotid bifurcation. They are firm (softness is rare) and pulsatile, and do not usually cause bruits. They may be bilateral, familial, and malignant (5%). This tumour should be suspected in tumours just anterior to the upper third of sternomastoid. Diagnose by digital computer angiography. Treatment: extirpation by vascular surgeon. If the lump is in the superoposterior area of the anterior triangle, is it a ***parotid tumour***? (more likely if >40yrs). A ***laryngocoele*** is an uncommon cause of a lump in the anterior triangle: it is painless, more common in males, and is made worse by blowing.[127]

Posterior triangle (Behind sternomastoid, in front of trapezius, and above the clavicle.) If there are many small lumps, think of ***nodes***—TB or viruses, eg HIV or EBV (infectious mononucleosis) or, if over 20yrs, consider lymphoma or metastases. The primary may be head and neck (eg tongue base, posterior nasal space, tonsils, etc) or bronchus, gut, breast, or gonad (in that order of likelihood). ***Cervical ribs*** may intrude here.[128]

Tests Ultrasound shows lump consistency. CT defines masses in relation to their anatomical neighbours. Do virology and Mantoux test. CXR may show malignancy or reveal bilateral hilar lymphadenopathy, when you should consider sarcoidosis. Consider fine-needle aspiration (FNA).

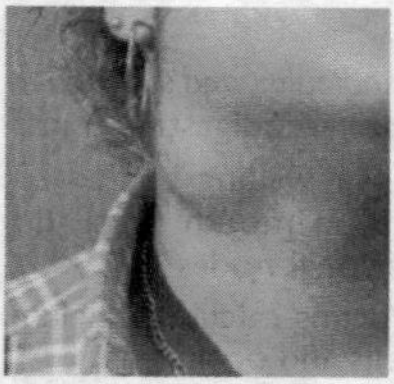
Fig 1. Branchial cyst[129]

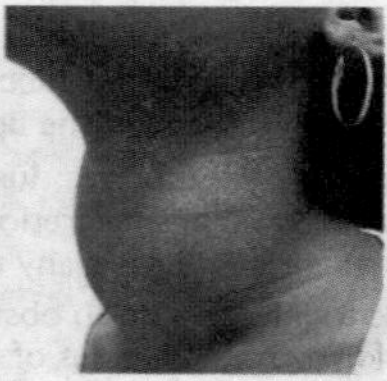
Fig 2. Goitre[130]

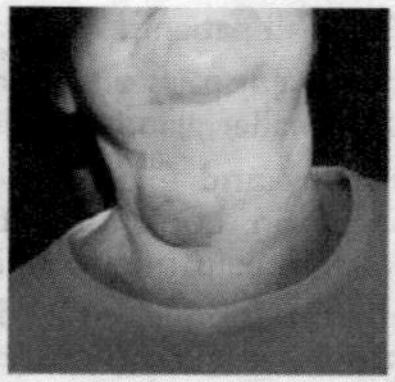
Fig 3. Infected cyst[131]

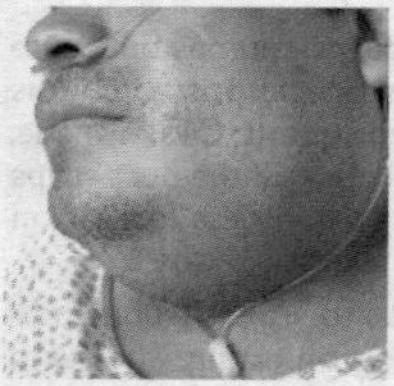
Fig 4. Deep cervical abscess[132]

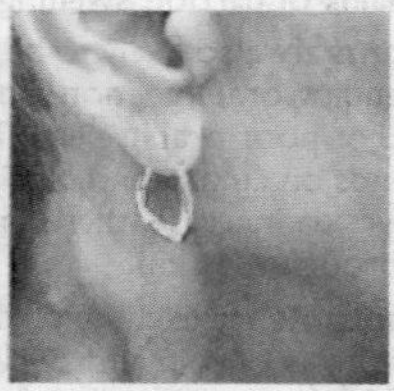
Fig 5. Lymph node metastases[133]

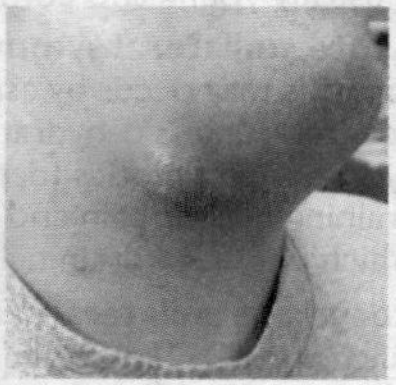
Fig 6. Submandibular abscess[134]

The salivary glands

►Refer all patients with salivary gland swelling.

The 3 major pairs of salivary glands are: *parotid, submandibular, and sublingual.* ~800 smaller glands are distributed through the upper aerodigestive tract.

History and examination Dry mouth/eyes; lumps; swelling related to food; pain. Look for external swellings, secretions (in mouth first), do bimanual palpation for stones, test VII nerve, any regional nodes?

Inflammation is usually due to infection or an obstructing calculus (calcium phosphates and carbonates form around a nidus of cells and organisms).

Classification Are symptoms unilateral, or bilateral? Acute or chronic?

Acute bilateral symptoms are usually due to mumps (p 142). The patient is usually young and complains of parotid swelling.

Acute, unilateral symptoms are also likely to be due to mumps but acute parotitis may occur by ascending oral infection. This occurs post-op but is now rare, unless dehydrated or poor oral hygiene. ***Treatment:*** Oral hygiene, hydration, antibiotics (depends on culture and sensitivities). If the duct stops draining pus, or pain and pyrexia increase, there may be abscess formation which will need draining through the skin.

Recurrent unilateral symptoms are likely to be due to stones (submandibular in 80%). The classic story is of pain and swelling on eating. The gland may be red, swollen, and tender (not necessarily infected). Stones may be seen on plain radiography or by sialography. ***Treatment:*** Distal stones are removed via the mouth but excise the gland if it contains the stone.

Chronic bilateral symptoms may be associated with dry eyes and mouth ± Sjögren's or Mikulicz's syndromes (*OHCM* p 730–4). ***Treatment*** is hard. If chronic infection is the cause, simple antibiotics will fail: what is needed is prolonged treatment with oxytetracycline 250mg/12h 1h ac PO.

Fixed swellings may be malignant, idiopathic or due to sarcoidosis.

Tumours '80% are in the parotid, 80% of these are benign pleomorphic adenomas, 80% of these are in the superficial lobe'. 10% are submandibular (50% are malignant here). ►*Remove any salivary gland swelling if present for >1 month* (or examine by fine needle aspiration for cytology: this does not lead to seeding along its track). VII nerve paresis suggests malignancy. As tumours grow by budding and have no capsule, lumpectomy leads to seedling deposits, so superficial parotidectomy is needed. NB: sialograms with CT (+bone filters) may be a useful pre-op test.

Classification ***Benign:***	***Intermediate:***	***Malignant:***
Pleomorphic (mixed parotid) adenoma	Mucoepidermoid tumour	Adenoid cystic cancer
Adenolymphoma (Warthin's tumour)	Acinic cell cancer	Adenocarcinoma
Haemangioma/lymphangioma (child)	Oncocytoma	Squamous cell cancer

Pleomorphic adenoma: Middle age; slow growth; must be removed by superficial parotidectomy or enucleation. Radiotherapy has a role if there was intra-operative spillage, or in residual disease, or recurrences (seen in ~1–2% at 12 years follow-up). Post-op complications: metastatic spread (rare); facial nerve palsy (with skill, risk is minimal); gustatory sweating (~7%).

Adenolymphoma: Usually elderly men; soft. *Treatment:* Enucleation.

Carcinomas: Rapid growth; hard fixed mass; pain & VIIth nerve palsy. Treat by combination of surgery and radiotherapy.

Complications of surgery: **1** VIIth nerve palsy—often transient.
2 Salivary fistula—often closes spontaneously.
3 *Frey's syndrome* (gustatory sweating); here tympanic neurectomy may help.

Assessing salivary lumps

- Note size, mobility, and extent of the mass, as well as fixity to surroundings. Any tenderness? Bimanually palpate the lateral pharyngeal wall for deep parotid tumours (any parapharyngeal space extension?).
- Also bimanually examine submandibular and sublingual masses.
- Assess surrounding skin as regional metastases from skin or mucosal malignancies may present as salivary gland masses.
- Cranial nerve examination may show neural infiltration.[135]

The dry mouth (xerostomia)

Signs

- Dry, atrophic, fissured oral mucosa
- Discomfort, causing difficulty eating, speaking, and wearing dentures.
- No saliva pooling in floor of mouth
- Difficulty in expressing saliva from the major ducts
- Check for salivary gland swelling.

Complications

- Dental caries
- Candida infection

Typical causes
• Hypnotics & tricyclics
• Antipsychotics
• β-blockers; diuretics
• Mouth breathing
• Dehydration
• ENT radiotherapy
• Sjögren's syndrome
• SLE and scleroderma
• Sarcoidosis
• HIV/AIDS
• Parotid sialoliths; 40% are radio-opaque *vs* >80% if submandibular

Management [136]

- Increase oral fluids; take frequent sips.
- Good dental hygiene; no acidic drinks and foods that demineralize teeth.
- Try a saliva substitute, eg SST® tablets (contains polyethylene and cottonseed oil). 'Allow a tablet to dissolve in the mouth—while moving it around with your tongue.' Up to 16 tablets per day may be needed.
- Chewing sugar-free gum or sweets may ↑salivary flow.[137]
- Pilocarpine (Salagen®) is rarely satisfactory. [138] [RCT 139] [*N*=60] Cholinergic SEs: sweating, lacrimation, rhinitis, amblyopia, diarrhoea, urinary frequency. Pilocarpine mouth washes may obviate these.[140] [*N*=40]
- *Irradiation xerostomia:* Acupuncture may help, eg as an 8-needle regimen of 3 weekly sessions followed by monthly sessions.[141] [n=50]

Dentistry for doctors

►Any oral ulcer which has not healed in 3 weeks should receive specialist assessment, for biopsy to exclude malignancy (*OHCM* p 210).

Causes of facial pain Tooth pathology, sinusitis, temporo-mandibular joint (TMJ) dysfunction, salivary pathology, migraine, trigeminal neuralgia, atypical facial pain (no clear cause), trauma, cluster headache (*OHCM* p 341), angina, frontal bone osteomyelitis (post sinusitis), ENT tumours.

►When helping a patient with a dental infection pay attention to these features—before consulting a maxillofacial surgeon, or a dentist (GDP).

1 *Is it the teeth?* History: ***Is the pain…***

- Worse with sugar and heat?
- Worse or better with cold?
- Intermittent?

} ► Tooth is alive (pulpitis)

Is the pain…

- Worse with percussion?
- Constant/uninterrupted?

} ► Tooth dead (osteitis/abscess)

Is the pain…

- Exacerbated by movement between finger and thumb

} ► Abscess

Radiography (usually helpful): Orthopantogram (OPT) is useful for imaging molars and pre-molars. If incisors are suspected, request periapical radiographs of the tooth in question. Interpretation of radiograph…

- **Abscess** (Tooth tender to percussion)
- **Periodontal disease** (Tooth mobile)

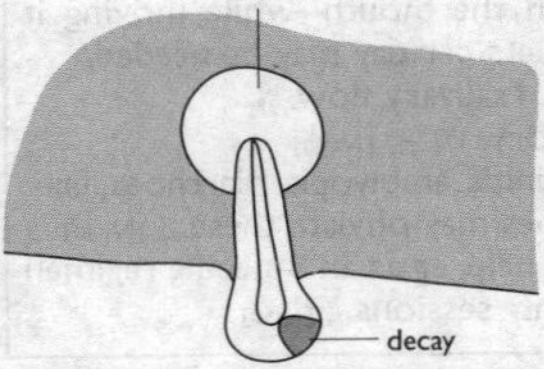

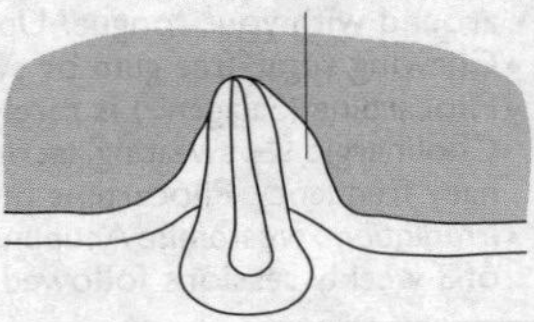

2 *Trismus:* (Opening mouth is difficult because of spasm or pain.) This is a sign of severe infection. Ask the patient to open mouth wide and measure how many fingers breadth between the incisor teeth. Trismus always requires maxillofacial advice. Other causes: tetanus; neoplasia.

3 *Facial swellings due to dental infection:* Usually subside with oral antibiotics. ►If swelling is related to the lower jaw, assess for airways obstruction; if spreading to the eye, assess the second cranial nerve. If in any doubt, refer to a maxillofacial surgeon.

4 *Bedside observations:* Temperature (very important), pulse and blood pressure. This information must be to hand *prior* to referral. Systemically unwell patients require maxillofacial advice/admission.

5 *Systemic disease complicating dental infection:* Any immunocompromise (eg HIV, leukaemia, diabetics, those on steroids); patients at risk of endocarditis; coagulopathy (eg haemophilia or warfarin). Seek specialist advice. In one HIV study, lesions included: candidiasis (29%), ulcers (15%), salivary gland disease (9%), necrotizing ulcerative gingivitis/periodontitis (5%), linear gingival erythema (4%), labial molluscum contagiosum (3%), oral warts (2%), hairy leukoplakia (2%), and herpes zoster (1%).[142]

Dental caries Although on the decline in the West due primarily to fluoride, this condition is increasing exponentially in developing countries. Causes: bacteria (esp. *S. mutans*), substrate (sugars) and susceptible tooth surface. In otherwise healthy individuals it is an entirely preventable disease.

Rampant caries is a variant found in children exposed to excessive sucrose in the forms of coated dummies, 'health' drinks, and prescribed medicines.

Radiation caries (eg post head & neck radiotherapy, eg with jaw osteoradionecrosis). *Treatment and complications:* Pain ± infection. Toothache pain responds best to NSAIDs, eg ibuprofen 200–400mg/8h PO pc (can buy it from pharmacists), and dental infection to penicillin and metronidazole, but drug treatment is never definitive, and a dental referral is required.

Periodontal disease 'Is one of the most widespread diseases of mankind' (WHO). Virtually the entire dentate adult population has gingivitis which is caused by bacterial and polysaccharide complexes at the tooth-gingival interface (=plaque). It is cured by good toothbrushing. Acute herpetic and rarely streptococcal infection can cause gingivitis.

Vincent's angina is a smoking or HIV associated, painful, foul-smelling, ulcerative gingivitis, caused by anaerobes (*Fusobacteria*) ± spirochetes (*Borellia vincentii*). ℞: penicillin 250mg/6h PO + metronidazole 200mg/8h PO.

Gingival swelling Fibrous hyperplasia may be congenital or via drugs (phenytoin, ciclosporin, nifedipine). Other causes: pregnancy, exacerbation of inflammation by immunodeficiency, scurvy, infiltration in leukaemia.

Periodontitis (pyorrhoea) is a progression of localized inflammation from the gums into the ligament supporting a tooth. It is associated with anaerobic bacteria, calcified bacterial deposits (calculi, tartar) and poor oral hygiene. It requires treatment by a dentist.

Juvenile periodontitis may be caused by lack of nutrients, an immune problem, neutropenia, or an intrinsic neutrophil disease—leukocyte adhesion deficiency, Chediak-Higashi or Papillon-Lefevre syndromes (with palmar keratosis), chronic granulomatous disease. 143 144 145

Malocclusion Inappropriate positioning of the teeth in the jaws or between the jaws themselves is common. Those with prominent upper teeth are particularly prone to trauma, and those children at risk (eg in epilepsy)—or those involved in contact sports should be referred to an orthodontist. Those with severe facial or jaw disharmony who may be unable to chew or have psychological difficulty with their appearance may be amenable to surgical correction by an oral or maxillofacial surgeon.

Wisdom teeth In the West, these can be considered, rather like the appendix, as a vestigial organ. They account for an enormous number of inpatient operations annually. If asymptomatic and not exposed to contamination by the mouth, they do not usually require removal. Complications are pain and infection and they may be involved in fractures of the mandible. Post-operative recovery is often complicated by pain and swelling, pain responds well to NSAIDs and poorly to opiates, particularly dihydrocodeine. Infection complicates up to 30% not receiving antibiotics. Penicillin and metronidazole (as above) are standbys.

Teething An acute sore mouth during tooth eruption is often caused by viral infections (eg herpetic). The onset of eruption of first deciduous teeth correlates with the fall off in transferred maternal antibody.

NB: Other oral mucosal diseases are described in *OHCM* p 210.

8 Dermatology

Acknowledgement: We particularly thank Dr Susannah Baron for her help with this chapter, and for supplying many of the images.

Dermatology on the web: www.freebooks4doctors.com/; images compendium: www.dermis.net/doia/mainmenu.asp?zugr=d&lang=e

MacKie Rona M. *Clinical Dermatology*, 4e 1997, OUP, ISBN 0-19-2627619, and Rook, Wilkinson/Ebling *Textbook of Dermatology* 5e OUP, ISBN 0-632-02396-1. ***Evidenced-based dermatology:*** see the Cochrane *Skin Group*.[1,2]

A holistic approach to dermatology

The skin is our largest organ and displays myriad clinical signs and reaction patterns. Recognizing these may allow diagnosis of previously unsuspected systemic diseases (listed on p 588). Primarily dermatological conditions such as eczema and psoriasis (p 594) are not only the domain of dermatologists but are likely to be encountered by us all, regardless of our field of practice. A practical knowledge and clinical confidence in the diagnosis of skin disease is thus a most valuable asset—and we all need to know how the dermatological aspects of our patients lives interact to form those complex social and biological matrices that are the lives of our patient with chronic skin conditions.

Dermatologists do not confine themselves to the skin. Skin symptoms are features of many medical (p 588) and psychiatric illness, eg body image problems, dermatitis artefacta, neurotic excoriations, and trichotillomania (neurotic pulling out of one's hair).[3]

Examples of psychocutaneous phenomena There is an association between major depression/social phobia and psoriasis, and between obsessive compulsive disorder, stress, and acne. Anyone who doubts the metaphysical relevance of psychocutaneous phenomena need look no further than Dennis Potter's *Singing Detective*, Philip Marlow.[1]

The psycho-physiology of acne is interesting. Sebaceous glands and their secretions appear to be involved in a pathway conceptually similar to the hypothalamic-pituitary-adrenal axis, so mediating a direct link between oily skin, and the stress hormone *CRH* (corticotrophin releasing hormone) which acts on sebaceous glands. So think of *CRH* as an autocrine hormone for human sebocytes that exerts homeostatic lipogenic activity, with testosterone and growth hormone inducing *CRH* negative feedback. These findings implicate *CRH* (hence stress) in mediating acne, seborrhoea, androgenic alopecia, skin ageing, and xerosis. Substance *P* is another route connecting stress, seborrhoea, and acne.[4][5]

Telemedicine, virtual outreach, and dermatology delivery

Traditionally, dermatologists see patients on wards and in central clinics: convenient for him or her, but less convenient for patients who live far away, and this paradigm does not allow for useful interaction between the referring doctor and the specialist. Also, urgency cannot be assessed until the patient presents (unless a photograph is sent with the referral letter; this simple idea requires e-mail, digital cameras, and technical commitment). Telemedicine uses high-quality video links and computer equipment to form a virtual consultation. Is the expense entailed worth it? Are there problems—even for this, the most visual of specialties?

Advantages	*Disadvantages*[6] RCT[7] [N=3170]
Travel times are less	Expense is not outweighed by ↓travel time
Fewer tests ordered	No proper sharing of a patients' problems
Teaching referring GPs	Technical problems can waste whole sessions
Patient satisfaction	Extra time needed from GPs and consultants
Fewer follow-ups	Important clinical cues are lost in telemedicine

A different way to address the problem of the referring doctor not knowing the degree of urgency (because he or she has 'no idea what's going on') is to use decision support (which additionally acts as a good teaching exercise) rather than to rely on sending images of dubious quality. This issue is discussed (with examples) on p 611.[8]

HOLISTIC MEDICINE UNDERSTANDS THAT THE SKIN AND THE BRAIN ARE A SINGLE ECTODERMAL SYSTEM

IF YOU HAVEN'T A CLUE…PHOTOS, TELEMEDICINE, OR DECISION SUPPORT?

1 http://bmj.com/cgi/content/full/315/7123/1709

History and examination

History Duration of rash; site of onset, spread, and distribution of lesions; symptoms (itch, pain); aggravating factors (sunlight, heat); previous treatments; medical conditions and medications; family history (psoriasis, atopy); occupation (industrial chemicals); pets.

Examination Examine all the skin; hair and nails where appropriate.

Distribution Symmetrical flexural (atopic eczema, fig 1 on p 596); contact with jewellery or cosmetics (allergic contact dermatitis); areas exposed to sun, eg backs of hands, face, neck (photosensitivity); grouped lesions (herpes virus); symmetrical extensor surfaces (psoriasis, p 594).

Pattern Ring (fungal—active edge with healing centre, p 598); linear (Köbner phenomenon, below), targetoid (erythema multiforme).

Terms used to describe lesions www.pediatrics.wisc.edu/derm/tutorials.html;images

Alopecia	Hair loss
Atopy/ atopic	Prone to allergic eczema, asthma, or rhinitis; *typical patient:* city-based child in a 1-child family of high socioeconomic class.[1]
Atrophy	Thinning and loss of skin substance
Bulla	Blister larger than a vesicle (see below, ie >0.5cm diameter)
Crust	Dried brownish exudate
Erosion	Superficial break in epidermal surface; heals without scarring
Erythema	Reddening of the skin which blanches on pressure
Excoriation	A scratch which has broken the surface of the skin
Filiform	Long, irregular projections, which may be threadlike, or broader, like close-packed tombstones on a mound (seen in warts)
Fissure	Crack, often through keratin
Induration	An area of cutaneous or subcutaneous hardening or thickening
Köbner phenomena	Skin lesions which develop at sites of injury—seen in psoriasis (p 594), lichen planus, plane warts, and vitiligo 9
Lichenification	Skin thickening with exaggerated skin markings, as a result of repeated trauma (eg in response to itch). See fig 1, p 585.
Macule	Defined, flat area of altered pigmentation; big macules are ***patches***.
Nodule	Solid lump >0.5cm in diameter; subcutaneous or intradermal
Papule	Raised well-defined lesion, usually less than 0.5cm in diameter
Plaque	Raised flat-topped lesion, usually over 2cm in diameter.
Purpura	Purplish lesion resulting from free red blood cells in the skin; it doesn't blanch on pressure, and may be nodular (vasculitis).
Pustule	Well-defined, pus-filled lesion
Scale	Fragment of dry skin
Scar	Permanent replacement of skin area with connective tissue
Ulcer	Loss of epidermis *and* dermis resulting in a scar (unlike *erosions*)
Vesicle	Blister less than 0.5cm in diameter 10
Weals/ urticaria	Transient pale papules with pink margins, eg '*nettle rash*' (=*hives*)

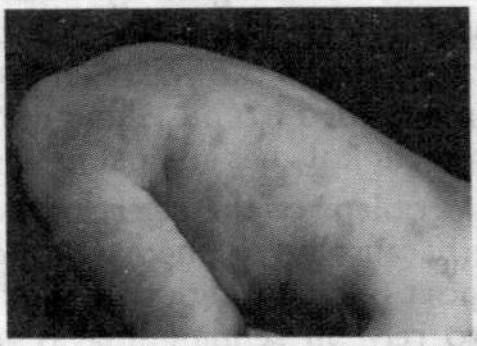

Fig 1. Urticaria 11

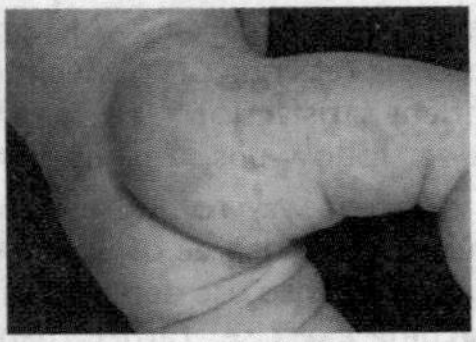

Fig 2. Urticaria in weal shapes

1 Pampura A 2005 *Med Hypotheses* **64** 575. Allergic conjunctivitis and urticaria are other features.

Creams, lotions, and ointments: 3 ends of a spectrum

In general, ointments are for dry areas, and creams are for moist areas. Any topical compound can be characterized as more or less like an idealized *ointment* (greasy as has no added water) *cream* (oil-in-water or water-in-oil emulsions) or *lotion* (water-based and typically made from powders). Lotions are less commonly used, but may be tried as a coolant—calamine lotion, for example. If a large area of skin is involved, a large volume of cream or ointment will be needed, eg 500g. Use clean procedures when getting creams out of pots, eg remove cream with a clean spoon first. Close tubs of ointment after each use. Pump dispensers are a good way around bacterial contamination.

Regimens may be complex, and you may get annoyed at the patient's 'poor compliance'—until you reframe this as loss of *concordance*: then you may get annoyed with yourself (just as bad). Avoid both by getting a nurse to help in planning treatment through dialogue, and understanding lifestyle constraints. ►Dermatology and practice nurses are invaluable in demonstrating topical therapies, and in optimizing concordance.

CONCORDANCE≈HARMONY≈SINGING THE SAME SONG

Latin[L] & Greek[G] for budding dermatologists

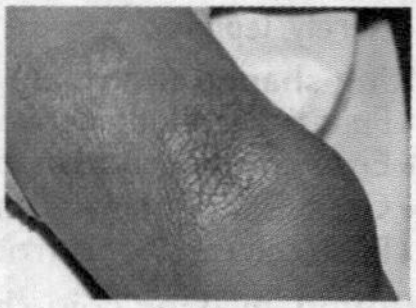
Fig 1. Lichenification

Alba[L]=white (as in albino).
Cutis[L]=skin (sub[L]=under—hence subcutaneous).
Derma[G] δερμα=skin (intra[L]=within, hence intradermal=within the skin).
Eczema[G], from ekzein, to break out, boil over: ek-, out; (zein=to boil).
Erythema=redness (eg of the skin).
Impetere[L]=to attack (as in impetigo).
Indurare[L]=to harden (as in induration).
Lichen[L]=tree moss; lichenification to a dermatologist means like Morocco leather—a condition brought on by scratching (fig 1).
Livedo[L] livid (furious, red/blue); reticulum[L]=NET[M]. Livedo reticularis, p 588.
Lupus[L]=wolf.

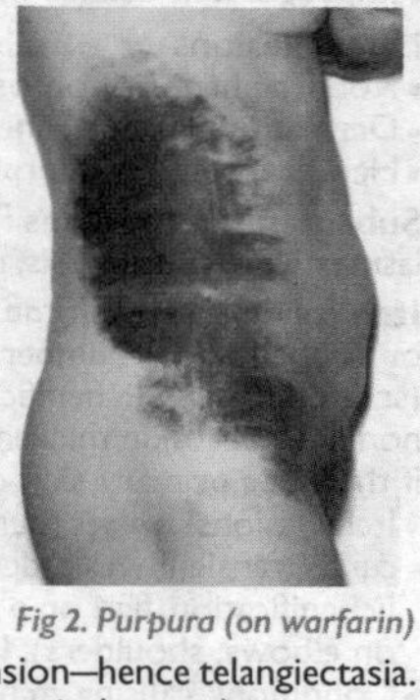
Fig 2. Purpura (on warfarin)

Macula[L]=stain (immaculate=without stain; macula peccati=the stain of original sin).
Mens/mentem[L]=mind; nature; temper; mentum=chin (submental=below the jaw).
Muto/mutat[L]=I (he) change(s); hence mutate.
Papilla [L]=nipple or teat (hence papule; papilloma).
Pilus/pili[L]=hair (hence fur coat; pelt)/hairs.
Pityriasis[G]=grain husk, scale; pityuron=bran.[12]
Psoriasis[G]=to have the itch (psora=itch; NB: psoriasis often does not itch).
Purpura[L]=purple, the imperial colour; porphyra[G]
Rosea[L]=pink; akmē[G]=acne (summit; acme; pimple);[13] so acne rosacea=pink pimples, p 600).
Seborrhoeic=making sebum[L] (tallow, suet, grease).
Senex[L]=old man.
Tel[G]...telos=end + angeion=vessel + ektasis=extension—hence telangiectasia.
Topicos[G]=surface (hence topography; creams are topical agents).
Vesica[L]=purse, football, bladder (hence fluid-filled blister).
Vitellus[L]=spotted calf (as in vitiligo).

Use the above to translate *lupus pilum mutat, non mentem*—the wolf changes his coat but not his nature (but it is unkind to think of dermatologists as wolves: think of them more as leopards who ***can*** change spots).

Possible causes of patterns of skin disease

Brown pigmented lesions Apart from sun-related freckles there are:
- Lentigos: persistent brown macules, often larger than freckles (fig 1).
- Café-au-lait spots: faint brown macules; if >5, consider neurofibromatosis.
- Seborrhoeic keratoses/warts: benign greasy-brown warty lesions usually on the back, chest, and face; very common in the elderly.
- Chloasma (melasma) are brown patches especially on the face, related to pregnancy or Pill use. The condition may respond to topical azelaic acid.
- Systemic diseases: Addison's (palmar creases, oral mucosa, scars); haemochromatosis; porphyria cutanea tarda (+ skin fragility and blisters).

White lesions
- Pityriasis versicolor: superficial slightly scaly infection with the yeast *Malassezia furfur*; appears depigmented on darker skins.
- Pityriasis alba: post-eczema hypopigmentation, often on children's faces.
- Vitiligo (*vitellus* is Latin for *spotted calf*: typically white patches ± hyperpigmented borders. Sunlight makes them itch. *Associations:* Autoimmunity: pernicious anaemia, thyroid or Addison's disease, diabetes, alopecia areata, hypoparathyroidism. *Treatment* (unsatisfactory): try cosmetic camouflage, narrowband UVB phototherapy/PUVA (p 595) 14 ± potent topical steroids.
- Rarely, leprosy. 15 1 image

Ring-shaped (annular) lesions www.geocities.com/NapaValley/4122/derm.html
- Fungal infections: active erythematous scaly edge with central healing.
- Erythema multiforme: target-like lesions, eg on extensor limb surfaces.
- Granuloma annulare: pinkish papules forming a ring.
- Basal cell carcinoma (rodent ulcer; p 590): pearly papule + central ulcer.

Round, oval, or coin-shaped (discoid) lesions
- Discoid eczema: well-defined, itchy, crusted/scaly eczema, worsened by heat.
- Psoriasis: well-defined scaly red/pink plaques (p 594). Distribution on extensor surfaces, scalp and natal cleft distinguishes it from discoid eczema (also, scales are thicker, get silvery on rubbing, and bleed on lifting).
- Pityriasis rosea: herald patch; oval red lesions with scaly edge, eg on trunk.
- Impetigo: well-defined red patches, covered with honey-coloured crust.

Linear lesions
- Köbner phenomenon: psoriasis, lichen planus.
- Dermatitis artefacta: linear or bizarre-shaped lesions, induced by patient.
- Herpes zoster: polymorphous vesicles/pustules in dermatomal distribution.

Subcutaneous nodules Rheumatoid nodules, rheumatic fever, PAN, xanthelasma, tuberous sclerosis, neurofibroma, sarcoid, granuloma annulare.

Itch (pruritus) ►*Itch can be very distressing.* Skin will usually be scratched or rubbed and a number of secondary skin signs are seen: excoriations (scratch marks); lichenification (skin thickening, fig 1 on p 585); papules or nodules (local skin thickening). ***Causes:*** (Dry skin tends to itch.) Determine if there is a primary skin disease or is itch due to a systemic disorder.
- Itchy lesions: *scabies* (burrows in finger-webs, wrists, groin, buttock); *urticaria* (transient weals, dermatographism); *atopic eczema* (flexural eruption, lichenification, fig 1 on p 596); dermatitis herpetiformis (very itchy blisters on elbows, shoulders); lichen planus (flat violet wrist papules). 16 44 images
- Conditions causing itch: *iron deficiency* (koilonychia, pale conjunctivae); *lymphoma* (lymphadenopathy, hepatosplenomegaly); *hypo/hyperthyroidism* (goitre); *chronic liver disease* (jaundice, spider naevi); *chronic renal failure* (dry sallow skin); malignancy (clubbing, masses); *adverse drug reactions*. Tests: *FBC, ESR*, ferritin, *LFT, U&E*, glucose, *TSH*, and *CXR*.

Treatment: Treat any primary disease; bland emollients (eg Diprobase®) to soothe dry skin; emollient bath oils; sedative antihistamines at night.

Lentigos are brown patches. Some are premalignant. Fig 1 shows a lentigo maligna (melanoma *in situ*)—the precursor to invasive lentigo maligna melanoma. It develops in chronically sun-damaged skin. Note that the lesion is flat, and has variable pigmentation, and an irregular edge. The darkly pigmented area is likely to become (or be) invasive. Not all lentigo maliginas show classic warning signs of malignancy (ABCDE).[1] Use of the dermoscope[2]/biopsy is advised in equivocal lesions. 17 Excision is the best option: if impossible, topical 5% imiquimod 5 times a week seems to work (*typical time to complete clearing:* 5–13 weeks). 18

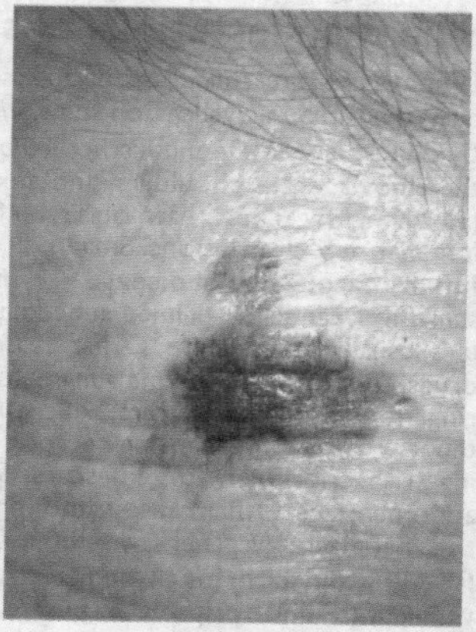

Fig 1. Lentigo maligna

1 *A* for asymmetry; *B* for border irregularity; *C* for colour (non-uniform browns, blacks, reds, whites, or blues); *D* for diameter >6mm; *E* for evolving over time.

2 The dermoscope is a battery-operated handheld microscope-like instrument using epiluminescence for evaluating pigmented skin lesions. It allows vision through the stratum corneum.

Skin manifestations of systemic disease

Diabetes *Flexural candidiasis; necrobiosis lipoidica* (waxy, shiny red/brown plaques, then atrophic/yellow, on shins, ♀/♂ ≈3; p 611); *folliculitis; skin infections.* [19]

Coeliac disease *Dermatitis herpetiformis* (very itchy/burning blisters on the elbows, scalp, shoulders, and ankles. It responds quickly to dapsone (50–200mg/day PO). *SE:* haemolysis, LFT↑, agranulocytosis. *CI : G6PD↓*. Gluten-free diet may clear lesions. Small risk of lymphoma with chronic disease.

Inflammatory bowel disease • *Erythema nodosum* (fig 1, tender ill-defined subcutaneous nodules, usually on the shins. Other causes: sarcoid, drugs, TB, streps) • *Pyoderma gangrenosum:* recurring nodulo-pustular ulcers, ~10cm wide, with tender red/blue overhanging necrotic edge, healing with cribriform (pitted) scars. *Site:* eg leg; abdomen; face. Other causes: autoimmune hepatitis; neoplasia; Wegener's; myeloma. ♀:♂ >1:1.

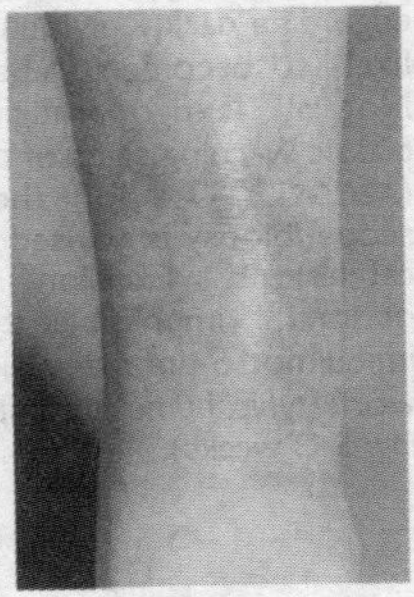

Fig 1. Erythema nodosum

Rheumatoid arthritis (RA) *Rheumatoid nodules; vasculitis* (nodular, palpable purpura, with ulcers).

Systemic lupus erythematosus (SLE) *Facial butterfly rash; photosensitivity* (face, dorsum of hands, V of neck); *red scaly rashes; diffuse alopecia.* Diagnosis: circulating autoantibodies; skin biopsy with immunofluorescence.

Erythema multiforme (fig 2) *Minor form:* Target lesions, usually on the extensor surfaces esp. of peripheries, palms, and soles. *Major form:* (Stevens-Johnson syndrome) associated with systemic upset, fever, severe mucosal involvement, including conjunctivae. **Cause:** Idiopathic; herpes simplex, mycoplasma, viruses (minor form); drugs esp. sulfonamides, penicillins (major form). **℞:** Treat the cause; give supportive management—steroids are controversial and may ↑mortality. [21]

Erythema chronicum migrans Early sign of Lyme disease (*Borrelia burgdorferi*). 50% give history of a tick bite. City-dwellers are now at similar risk to rural dwellers.[1] It presents as a small papule which develops into a spreading erythematous ring, persisting from weeks to months. **℞:** eg amoxicillin 500mg/8h PO, 3 weeks of doxycycline 100mg/12h PO. *Lyme disease: OHCM* p 600. [22]

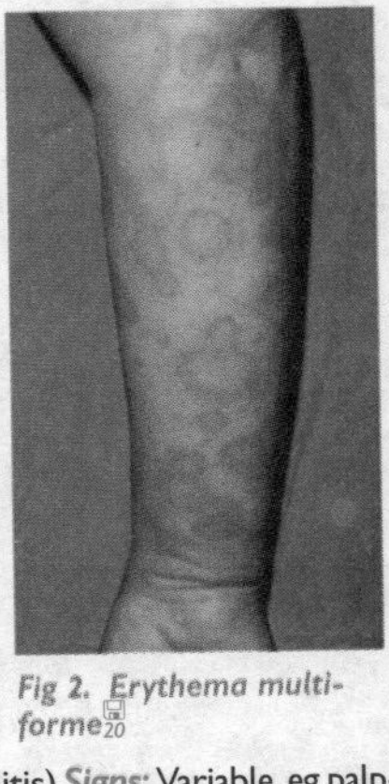

Fig 2. Erythema multiforme [20]

Cutaneous vasculitis (capillaritis/venulitis/arteriolitis) **Signs:** Variable, eg palpable purpura, eg on legs; nodules; ulcers; livedo reticularis. **Causes:** Ideopathic (often); drugs (thiazides); neoplasia; systemic vasculitis, eg polyarteritis nodosum (PAN), Henoch-Schönlein purpura (vasculitic rash on legs/buttocks ± arthralgia, abdominal pain & glomerulonephritis); Wegener's granulomatosus.

Livedo reticularis Red net-like discolouration of venules, eg on legs. Cold triggers it. It may become permanent. **Causes:** Pregnancy[2]; RA; SLE; PAN; lymphoma; TB; polymyositis; Raynaud's; Sneddon's syndrome of cerebral infarction; obstruction (cryoglobulins; sticky platelets; Ca^{2+}↑; intra-arterial injection; cholesterol emboli; homocystinuria). ♀/♂>1.

Fig 3. Livedo reticularis [23]

1 Maetzel D 2005 *Parasitol Res* **95** 5 This study was conducted in the German city of Bonn.
2 D'cruz 2005 *An Rheu Dis* **64** 147 Livedo is associated with miscarriage even if antiphospholipid -ve.

Connective tissue and related diseases and the skin

Lupus erythematosus **(LE):** 2 types: *chronic cutaneous lupus erythematosus* (discrete chronic inflammatory plaques with scarring, atrophy, ANA -ve). Systemic lupus (SLE, 5%)—ANA +ve. Decreasing exposure to the sun, topical steroids, and antimalarials (eg hydroxychloroquine) help.
Subacute cutaneous(LE): Widespread, non-scarring round or psoriasis-like plaques in photodistribution. ANA +ve or Ro/La +ve.
Acute systemic lupus erythematosus (SLE): Specific malar induration forming butterfly rash or widespread indurated erythema of upper trunk.
Non-specific cutaneous LE phenomenon: Vasculitis, alopecia, oral ulcers, palmar erythema, periungual erythema, Raynaud's phenomenon.
Dermatomyositis: Inflammatory disease of striated muscles with a heliotrope rash (red/purple erythema of lids); scaly red plaques over neck, trunk and extensor extremities; periungual erythema; telangiectasia of nail folds; Gottron's papules (violet flat-topped papules on knuckles)—association with malignancy (typically lung or breast). 24 6 images
CREST: Scleroderma/morphea with: Calcinosis cutis; Raynaud's; oEsophageal dysmotility; Sclerodactyly; Telangiectasia. Typically anti-centromere +ve.
Sarcoidosis *Hypopigmented areas, waxy deposits* (biopsy shows non-caseating granulomata). ***Plaques*** are red/violet, indurated, and shiny, eg on face and extremities. They may become annular in shape and the centre of the plaque may become atrophic. If seen with telangiectatic vessels use the term angiolupoid. ***Lupus pernio*** comprises chronic sarcoid plaques eg on nose, ears, lips, and cheeks. Permanent scarring can occur. Granulomatous infiltration of nasal mucosa and respiratory tract may precede nasal septum destruction. Examine the hands: bulbous, sausage-shaped fingers signify underlying bone cysts. ***Darier–Roussy subcutaneous nodules*** may be seen on arms and legs. These are typically non-tender. Fish-like ichthyosiform sarcoidosis presents as dark polygonal scaly patches on the legs. Verruciform (warty) lesions, erythroderma, oral lesions, nail dystrophy, and scarring alopecia may complicate the already elaborate picture. 25

Paraneoplastic skin phenomena 26

Acanthosis nigricans: Flexural skin is like dark velvet. Seen with gastric ca, Hodgkin's lymphoma (also: obesity; acromegaly, Cushing's, DM, thyroid). 27
Amyloidosis: Purpura ('raccoon eyes' if periorbital), macroglossia; low voltage ECG, nephrosis, carpal tunnel syndrome, neuropathy. Its malignant associations include myeloma, lymphoma, and endometrial cancer. 28
Paraneoplastic pemphigus: (Leukaemias, etc, mainly). In 45% of cases, isolated mouth lesions are present before the malignancy manifests. Non-haematological neoplasms comprise 16% of cases (eg melanoma; mesenchymal sarcomas; basal cell carcinoma; bronchogenic carcinoma.) 29
Erythroderma Chronic erythema and scale involving >50% of the skin; may be caused by lymphoreticular malignancy and cutaneous T-cell lymphoma.
Acquired ichthyosis: Generalized, dry scaly skin; recent onset can point to underlying lymphoma or carcinoma—as one poor lost soul said: "Pay no attention to the dry scales which discolour my skin, nor to the way my flesh is wasted away." (Dante, *Purgatorio*). 30
Pruritus: See p 586. 31 11 images
Hypertrichosis lanuginosa (An increase in downy lanugo hair); associated with ca lung, bladder, gallbladder, rectum, colon, uterus and breast.

Skin diagnoses not to be missed

Solar (actinic) keratoses occur on sun-exposed skin, as pre-malignant, crumbly yellow-white scaly crusts, as a result of dysplastic intra-epidermal proliferation of atypical keratinocytes. ***UK prevalence:*** If 40yrs old, 21%; if 70yrs old, 52%. ***Natural history:*** May regress/recur. ***ΔΔ:*** Bowen's, psoriasis, seborrhoeic wart, BCC; if in doubt, biopsy. ***Treatment:*** See BOX. ***Prevention:*** Education; hats; sunscreens ± ↓dietary fat—but enough vitamin A. 32 33

Basal cell carcinoma (BCC=**rodent ulcer**, fig 1) Typically, pearly nodule with rolled telangiectatic edge usually on the face. Metastases are very rare. It is locally destructive if left untreated. Lesions on trunk can appear as red scaly plaques with raised smooth edge. ***Cause:*** UV exposure. ***Treatment:*** Excision is best; radiotherapy if big lesion in the elderly. Cryotherapy ± curettage can be used in non-critical sites. 34

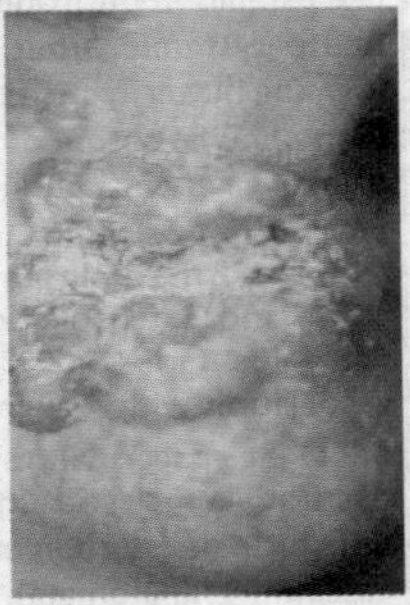

Fig 1. BCC on the nose

Kaposis sarcoma (p 607).

Bowen's disease Slow-growing red scaly plaque, eg on lower leg. ***Histology:*** Full-thickness dysplasia (carcinoma *in situ*). Infrequently progresses to squamous cell cancer. ***℞:*** Cryo; topical 5-FU (BOX); photodynamic therapy. 35 36

Leprosy Rare; suspect in any hypopigmented anaesthetic skin lesion.

Leukoplakia (p 606). 37 12 images **Lentigos** (p 587) **Melanoma** (p 592).

Metastatic cancer Skin metastases are uncommon but well recognized in association with carcinomas of breast, kidney, and lung. Non-Hodgkin's lymphoma and leukaemia can also metastasize to the skin. Metastases are usually firm, rather inflammatory lesions; often on the scalp or trunk.

Mycosis fungoides (Skin CD4 T-cell lymphoma). There may be a long history of undiagnosed well-defined red scaly plaques on trunk/limbs, and eventually patients may succumb to unrelated disease. Treatments include potent topical steroids, PUVA (p 595) and electron beam therapy. Leukaemic phase (Sezary syndrome) is associated with erythroderma and circulating Sezary cells 38 [n=213]—and deletions on chromosome 10q.[1]

Paget's disease of the nipple is a cutaneous sign of intraductal breast cancer. It presents as a unilateral, red, scaly, or crusted nipple, which is often itchy. ***Diagnosis:*** Biopsy. The chief differential diagnosis is eczema. ►Don't diagnose nipple eczema without at least considering a biopsy. ***Surgery:*** Mastectomy or lesser surgery ± radiotherapy. 39 40

Squamous cell carcinoma Presents as a persistently ulcerated or crusted firm irregular lesion. Usually found on sun-exposed sites, eg ears; dorsa of hands; bald scalp—here it may develop in a pre-existing actinic keratosis (below). Also related to smoking (on the lower lip) and chronic inflammation, eg venous leg ulcers. ***℞:*** Excision. Metastases are relatively rare, but more frequent at some sites, eg the ears. 41 30 images

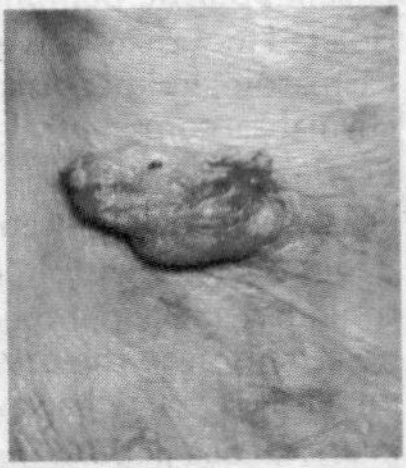

Fig 2. Squamous cell cancer

Syphilis Isolated painless genital ulcers (1° chancre). Pityriasis rosea-like copper-coloured rashes affecting trunk, limbs, palms, and soles (2° syphilis). Are other venereal diseases (STD) present? 42

1 Wain E 2005 *Genes Chromosomes Cancer* **42** 184

Options in solar keratoses (None is of proven superiority)

- *Cryotherapy.* After any cryo warn that blisters may form afterwards; they may be burst, repeatedly, with a sterile needle; advise using an antiseptic cream to prevent infection, and aspirin for pain, in adults.
- Daily 5% *5-FU (fluorouracil) cream*, with this sequence of events: erythema→vesiculation→erosion→ulceration (red and sore)→necrosis→healing epithelialization. This inflammatory response is in pre-actinic lesions: healthy skin is unharmed. Using pulsed therapy (eg with gaps of a week or more) reduces this inflammatory problem.
- *3% diclofenac gel* (Solaraze®) is effective (mechanism unknown); used twice daily for 2 months, it is well tolerated. RCT [43] [N=98] RCT [44] [N=96]
  Side-effects: Dry skin and rash at the application site. Expect ≥75% clearance of any actinic keratosis within 90 days—in ≥75% of patients. [45]
- 5% imiquimod 3 times a week for 6 weeks may be tried to enhance cell mediated immunity via induction of interferon-α. [46] [47]

Moles and melanomas

Malignant melanoma ♀/♂ ≈ 1.3:1. *UK incidence:* ≥10/100,000/yr (↑in the last 20yrs by ~300% in ♂ and ~200% in ♀). 5-yr survival is rising (now >80%). ~4% have a family history of melanoma. ***Mortality:*** 1.9/100,000/yr in UK.[48]

Causes: Intermittent UV exposure and sunburn is correlated, whereas high occupational sun exposure seems to be inversely associated. 66% are related to BRAF gene missense mutations (T→A 'mis-spelling').[49]

Signs: Most arise in normal skin, a few in dysplastic naevi. *'The Glasgow 7'*: major—Change in: **1** Size (in either vertical or horizontal plane). **2** Shape **3** Colour. Minor: **4** Diameter >7mm **5** Inflammation **6** Oozing/bleeding **7** Itch/odd sensation. Always have a high index of suspicion for changing moles, particularly if the edge is irregular and the pigmentation varies in any mole. ►Any lesion with one major feature should be considered for excision. Any minor features add to the suspicion. Differential diagnosis: benign melanocytic lesions; nonmelanocytic pigmented lesions (eg seborrhoeic keratoses—common in those >50yrs; they feel greasy, and look as though they have been stuck on). Benign moles tend to be <5mm across, with uniform colour and shape, whereas early melanomas frequently are different shades of brown, black, red, or even blue.

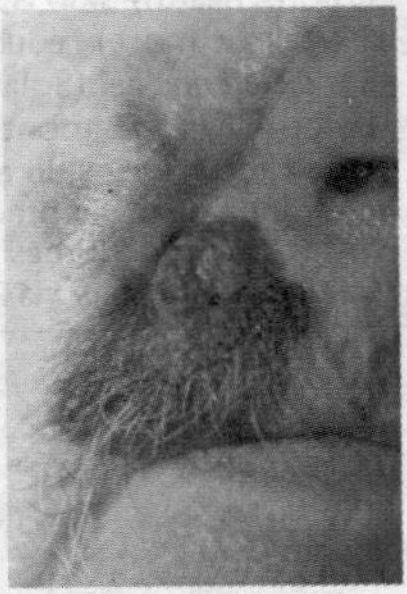

Fig 1. Malignant melanoma

Treatment Consider excision biopsy with a *margin of normal skin* for *any* unusual, growing, or changing pigmented lesion. If histology shows melanoma, read the report carefully: prognosis depends on completeness of excision and tumour thickness ('Breslow thickness' is a major prognostic sign). Tumours less than 1mm thick have a disease-free 5yr survival of >90%, while those thicker than 4mm have only a 50% 5yr disease-free survival rate.[1] Melanomas must be completely excised eg with 1cm of normal skin around the lesion for every millimetre of depth, up to 3cm (there is no evidence for wider excision). Don't do incisional biopsies on possible melanomas. *Metastatic melanoma:* multi-drug chemotherapy gives a transitory response in 10-30%.[50]

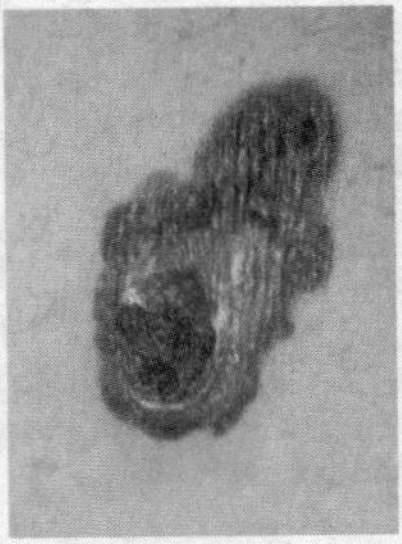

Fig 2. Malignant melanoma

Early diagnosis is vital—everyone should know what an early melanoma looks like, and know how to get prompt expert help.[51] 103 images

Pigmented naevi/moles It is normal to have benign pigmented naevi/moles on the skin. 3% of us have ≥2 congenital pigmented naevi present at birth; by late teenage years, most have 20–50 small naevi. As patients mature, naevi gradually involute so that in old age, benign pigmented naevi are relatively rare on the skin surface. Most naevi are not pre-malignant. Lesions which are less than 5mm in diameter and have a uniform colour and outline do not require to be excised for medical reasons unless there is a clear history of growth or change.[52] 22 images The benign ***halo naevus*** occurs most often on the back of young adults. The 'white' halo is not a sinister feature and results from destruction of melanocytes by a lymphocytic infiltrate.[53]

1 **TNM staging** is complex; note that melanoma thickness and ulceration but not level of invasion are used in the *T* category (except for *T1*); the number of metastatic nodes rather than gross dimensions is used in the *N* category; the site of distant metastases and *LDH*↑ are used in the *M* category.

Skin sensitivity to ultraviolet (UV) light

We all have a genetic skin type which determines sensitivity to UV.

Skin type	Burn/tan	Those affected
I	Always burns easily, never tans	Caucasians (many celts)
II	Always burns, tans minimally	Caucasians
III	Sometimes burns, always tans	Caucasians
IV	Rarely burns, always tans well	Caucasians
V	Rarely burns, always tans deeply	Dark-skinned (Latin, Indian, etc)
VI	Never burns, tans if +++exposure	Afro-Americans

This helps predict individual susceptibility for development of skin cancers and manifestations of photo-ageing. While persons in groups I-II are at highest risk, most skin cancers cluster in type II & III people: type I people know from experience to stay out of the sun. How to determine type:[54]
When you first go out in the sun each summer do you sunburn?
If so, do you always burn? Easily? Do you ever blister when you burn?
Can you tan? Does it take a long time or do you tan easily?
Do you develop a deep tan or just a shade beyond your normal colour?

History & examination ►Don't just diagnose today's melanoma. You need to prevent tomorrow's by educating the whole family: sun exposure in childhood is a strong determinant of melanoma risk.[55] Public education should aim to protect children primarily by sun avoidance and protective clothing (and sunscreens—but these may be less effective).[56]

Tailor your advice to your patient's risk. Those with highest risk may benefit from professional skin exam every 6–12 months. Would you like information about harmful effects of solar radiation? Ask about family and personal history of freckles/melanomas, and past sun exposure, esp. exposure that caused blistering. Do you use sun-screens? Do you practice safe-skin techniques & skin self-examination? Are your jobs/hobbies out-door? Are you pregnant? (moles darken during pregnancy). Is hair colour red or blond? Are the eyes blue? Note number and type of all moles (examine all over). NB: melanoma colours are often not all blacks: if melanomas incite inflammation, pink-reds may appear. If the immune response is active, areas of regression with dermal scarring appear as white or greys, depending on residual pigment.[57] [58] [59]

When to refer Think of ABCD: asymmetric lesions, border irregularity, colour irregularity, and diameter >6mm. Refer if ≥3—or if there is a clear spontaneous change in any of A, B, C, or D—or itching, pain, or bleeding.

Sunscreens and melanoma prevention The SPF (sun protection factor) indicates how long an individual can be exposed to sunshine without burning, eg SPF8 means that an individual can stay out in the sun 8 times longer than the time it would normally take them to burn. This time will vary depending on the individual's skin type. The SPF refers only to UVB protection. Many sunscreens now contain UVA-blocking agents. These are graded on a 'star-rating', which as yet, is not internationally standardized.

Sunscreens protect by blocking light (eg titanium dioxide) or by absorbing light by photochemical reaction (eg benzophenones; cinnamates).

The melanoma paradox 'Sun exposure is associated with *increased* survival from melanoma'.[60] (n=528) Why?* One of sunshine's best effects is to ↑vitamin D, which has anti-neoplastic effects (↑cell differentiation and apoptosis, and ↓angiogenesis and metastases).[61] The annual number of premature deaths from lack of UVB exposure is reported to be 21,700 for white Americans (1400 if black)[62] —considerably more than the 8000 deaths from melanoma.[63] This is due to fewer deaths from other cancers (bladder, oesophagus, kidney, lung, pancreas, rectum). What does this mean? Not that we should abandon limitation to sun exposure—but that we should exercise scepticism, and be open to new (and provisional) data and ideas.

Psoriasis

Psoriasis is a common chronic inflammatory skin condition affecting ~2% of Caucasians of any age, peaking in the 20s (type 1) and 50s (type 2). ♂/♀ ≈ 1:1

There are two pathologies: ***epidermal proliferation*** (with abnormal differentiation) and T-cell driven ***inflammatory infiltration*** of the dermis and epidermis. The signal to hyperproliferation is (partly) tumour necrosis factor (TNF-α—which is why infliximab, below, is a logical therapy).

30% of patients have a family member with psoriasis.[1] If both parents have psoriasis, the risk of their offspring being affected is ~50%. Infections (esp. streptococci) and drugs such as β-blockers, lithium, and antimalarials are recognized triggers. *Histology:* Epidermal keratinocyte hyperproliferation, parakeratosis, and intraepidermal neutrophil microabscesses (of Munro).[64]

Signs Look for symmetrical well-defined red plaques with silvery scale, on extensor aspects of the elbows, knees, scalp, and sacrum. Flexures (axillae, groins, submammary areas, and umbilicus) also frequently affected but lesions are non-scaly. ***Nail changes*** (in 50%; fig 1): pitting, onycholysis (separation from nail-bed), thickening and subungual hyperkeratosis. ***Small plaques*** (guttae) are seen in the young (especially if associated with concurrent streptococcal infection).[65] 9 images ***Pustular variants*** (sterile) can affect the palms & soles.[66] 22 images ***Generalized (erythrodermic) psoriasis*** (and generalized pustular psoriasis) may cause severe systemic upset (fever, ↑ WCC, dehydration)—also triggered by rapid withdrawal of systemic steroids.

Other signs: Köbner phenomenon (p 584); Auspitz sign: pinpoint bleeding when scale removed; pepper pot nail pitting and 'grease-spots'.

Systemic signs 7% develop arthropathy, which can be of 5 types:

1 Asymmetrical oligomonoarthritis [67] 6 images
2 Predominant DIP joints
3 Rheumatoid-like polyarthritis (sero-ve)
4 Arthritis mutilans (severe, destructive)
5 Psoriatic spondylitis

Differential diagnosis Eczema; fungal infection (solitary or few lesions; asymmetrical; expanding); mycosis fungoides (asymmetrical lesions, minimal scaling, biopsy required); seborrhoeic dermatitis (may co-exist).

Management Education is vital as control, not cure, is the practical aim. Remove possible triggers (streptococcal infection, drugs); factors such as stress and alcohol may also aggravate condition. Topical drugs are the mainstays of treatment for most patients. *Tar:* Messy ointments are best avoided unless patients are admitted for treatment; 'clean' preparations are available (eg Alphosyl®, applied twice daily). *Dithranol:* Available in creams for use in short-contact regimens (applied carefully to affected skin then washed off after 20-30min): start at low concentrations (0.1%) and increase as tolerated (eg 0.25%, 0.5%, 1%). SE: burning (avoid in flexures); staining (avoid on face). *Calcipotriol/tacalcitol*: (vit D analogues): avoid use in calcium metabolism disorders; small risk of hypercalcaemia if large amounts used on extensive inflamed skin (use calcipotriol up to twice-daily; max 75g per week). Tacalcitol may be applied once daily before going to bed (max 5g/day, and only up to two 12-week courses/yr). For flexural disease, topical steroid/antibiotic/antifungal preparations can be useful (*Trimovate*®). *NB:* Methotrexate helps psoriatic arthropathy.[68] Combining calcipotriol with betamethasone dipropionate cream 0.05% (eg Dovobet®) can be used once-daily,[2] and is a good way of reducing psoriasis and improving quality of life.[69]

1 *Am J Hum Genet* 2005 **76** 164 *PSORS1* is at 6p21.3. HLA associations: *HLA-CW6, HLA-B13, B17, DR7*.
2 In stable plaque psoriasis, apply to <30% of body surface for ≤ 4 weeks; max 15g/day or 100g/wk.

Agents to consider in recalcitrant psoriasis

Tazarotene (a topical retinoid): for mild to moderate psoriasis affecting <10% skin surface. Apply once daily. Avoid in pregnancy. Wash hands after use. Avoid contact with: eyes, face, intertriginous areas, hair-covered scalp, eczematous or inflamed skin; avoid exposure to UV light/PUVA etc. Don't use emollients or cosmetics within 1h of tazarotene.

Phototherapy: Narrow-band UVB (TL-01): 3 × weekly for 6 weeks; avoid if history of photosensitivity; most suitable for guttate/small plaque psoriasis. PUVA: UVA + oral/topical psoralen; suitable for extensive large plaque disease (oral psoralen) and localized psoriasis (topical psoralen); limit total dose to 1000J/150 treatments to avoid excessive skin ageing and risk of skin cancer (especially squamous cell carcinoma); can be combined with oral retinoids (re-PUVA) to ↓light dose needed to clear lesions.

Oral drugs: Severe psoriasis often needs oral drugs. ►Liaise with an expert.

Methotrexate: 10–25mg/week PO; most useful in elderly patients; best avoided in younger patients in view of long-term risk of hepatic fibrosis.

Ciclosporin: 2.5–5mg/kg/day PO; usefulness often limited by side-effects (hypertension; renal dysfunction).

Acitretin: Oral retinoid; useful for moderate to severe disease; side-effects: teratogenic; dry skin and mucosae; ↑lipids; glucose↑; ↑LFTs (reversible). Check lipids and glucose—and LFT at start, then every 1–2 weeks for 2 months, then every 3 months. In the UK, use is limited to hospitals. Starting dose: 25–30mg/24h PO; typical maintenance dose: 25–50mg/day; adjusted according to response). Exclude pregnancy, and avoid donating blood for >1yr and pregnancy until >2yrs after the last dose.

Hydroxycarbamide (=hydroxyurea): 0.5–1.5g/24h PO. Main SE: marrow suppression.[70]

Parenteral cytokine inhibitors/monoclonal antibodies: *Etanercept* (25mg SC, twice-weekly for ≤24wks) is licensed in adult plaque psoriasis unresponsive to other systemic agents. It is validated by 3 randomized trials.[RCT 71] This tumour necrosis factor (TNF-α) inhibitor can also help joint symptoms in psoriatic arthropathy (and ↓radiographic progression).[72] It is usually well tolerated. *SE:* vomiting, oesophagitis, cholecystitis, pancreatitis, *GI* bleeds, myocardial or cerebral ischaemia, emboli, BP ↑↓, dyspnoea, demyelination, seizures. It is used by specialists only. *Infliximab* is an alternative.[RCT 73]

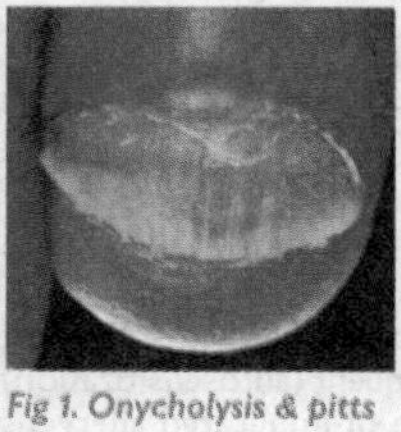

Fig 1. Onycholysis & pitts

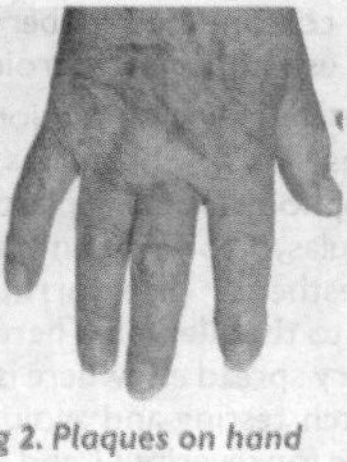

Fig 2. Plaques on hand

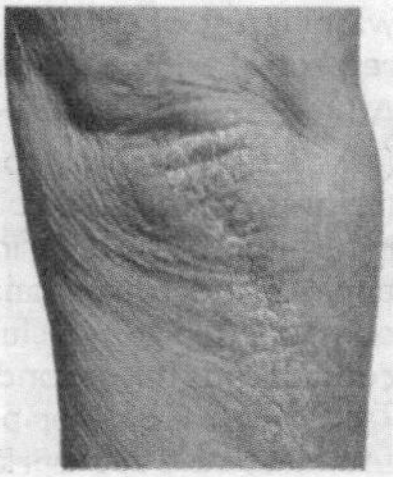

Fig 3. Psoriasis of elbow

Eczema (dermatitis)

Acute eczema presents as a rash with less scale and less well-demarcated than psoriasis. Eczema may be atopic, hypersensitive (type VI), or be caused by irritants or venous stasis. See also discoid eczema (p 586). Different types may co-exist. Ask about work, hobbies, and other exposures to allergens. 74 350 images

Atopic eczema *Causes:* multifactorial: *Genetic:* a family history of atopy is common (70%); Overactive TH2 lymphocytes produce IL4 & IL5, stimulating IgE production. *Infection*: *Staphs* colonises lesions and toxins act as a superantigen. *Allergens:* ↑IgE is common. *RAST* (radioallergosorbent testing) identifies specific antigens, eg house dust mite or animal dander. *Diet:* Some atopic children have significant food allergies, eg dairy products ± egg which can exacerbate eczema. Although infantile eczema is common (~2% of UK infants), most grow out of it before 13 years of age. *Treatment:*

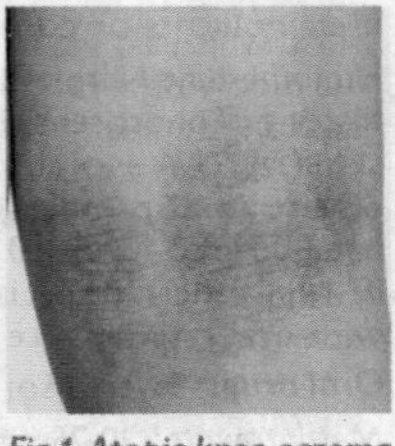

Fig 1. Atopic knee eczema

- Explain that management involves control, not cure. Patients will have dry skin (xerosis), which itches and is susceptible to irritant substances, so emollients are vital (used liberally—even when eczema is less active). They treat dryness and act as a barrier. Ditto for bath emollients—eg oilatum or Aveeno® (oat oils). Use soap substitutes such as emulsifying ointment.
- *Emollients* (use at least twice a day). In severe eczema, greasy emollients are best, eg emulsifying ointment, eg 50/50 emulsifying ointment and liquid paraffin (~£3/week); Epaderm® costs ~£7/week. In less severe eczema, less greasy preparations are more acceptable, eg Diprobase® (~£7/week).
- Daily topical steroids for active sites; being greasy, ointment is better than creams. Strength depends on severity, site, and patient's age. *Face, flexures & groins:* 1-2.5% hydrocortisone. Potency of clobetas***one*** 0.05% (Eumovate®) is ***one*** step above base (can cause vision↓ so use on face for <1wk). 75 *Elsewhere:* Get control in ≤7 days with higher-potency betamethasone 0.1% ointment. Reduce strength & frequency soon (betamethasone 0.025% = Betnovate RD®). Clobetas***o̲l̲*** (Dermovate®) is very (j**o̲l̲**ly) potent; use briefly only on thick skin (∵ skin thinning, telangiectasia, and adrenal suppression).

Irritant dermatitis We are all susceptible to irritants. Hands are often affected; redness ± weeping precedes dry fissuring. *Common irritants:* detergents, soaps, oils, solvents, alkalis; water (if repeated). It often affects bar staff and cleaners. *Treatment:* Avoid all irritants if possible. Good hand care (soap substitutes; regular use of emollients; careful drying of hands after washing; use of cotton or cotton-lined rubber gloves for dry and wet work respectively; intermittent use of topical steroids for acute flare-ups).

Allergic contact dermatitis (Type IV reaction). Common allergens: nickel (jewellery, watches, coins, keys); chromates (cements, leather); lanolin (creams, cosmetics); colophony (sticking plasters, glues, ink); rubber (foam in furniture); plants (primulas); topical neomycin/framycetin; topical antihistamines and topical anaesthetics (haemorrhoid creams). The pattern of contact often gives a clue to the allergen. There is often sharp cut-off where contact ends but secondary spread elsewhere is frequent (autosensitization). *Treatment:* Consider patch testing and avoidance of implicated allergens; topical steroid appropriate for severity (↓ and stop as the condition settles).

Adult seborrhoeic dermatitis This common red, scaly rash affects scalp (dandruff), eyebrows, nasolabial folds, cheeks, and flexures. Cause: eg overgrowth of skin yeasts (*Malassezia*). It can be very severe if HIV+ve. *℞:* Mild topical steroid/anti-fungal preparations, eg Daktacort®; ketoconazole cream or shampoo. Treat intermittently, depending on disease activity.

Helping children with atopic eczema[1]

- Dry skin is itchy, so scratching is a big problem; it may become a habit, so distraction therapies can help, and star charts act as encouragement.
- Dermatology nurses play a big role in providing practical support for parents ('he will grow out of it: it won't be like this forever'). They can show how to apply treatments and occlusive dressings, eg stockingette suits, which aid emollient absorption, and prevent drying and scratching.
- Turn down the central heating (it is very drying).
- Sedating antihistamines may be helpful, eg hydroxyzine or alimemazine. High doses may be needed in breaking the itch-scratch cycle, and in enabling the whole family to get a good night's sleep.
- Encourage joining a national eczema association (in UK, 020 7388 4097).
- Discourage elimination diets. Only occasionally is there a clear trigger (eg confirm a dairy allergy with a RAST test; if +ve, get a dietician's help).
- Reducing exposure to house dust mite may help (high filtration vacuuming of mattresses, limiting of carpet use; gortex mattress covers).

Non-steroidal immunomodulation Twice-daily pimecrlimus 1% cream and tacrolimus 0.03% ointment ***may*** have a role in those >2yrs old, used sparingly, twice-daily on any skin, including face & flexures, for ≤3 weeks (usually by a dermatologist, when topical steroids have failed or skin thinning would be a problem—see NICE). Stop if no effect after 2 weeks. SE: pruritus, burning, acne (*not* skin atrophy). One advantage is an ability to carry on producing benefits even after treatment stops.[76] [77] [78] *Cautions:* Infection at treatment site; UV exposure. *CI:* Generalized erythroderma; pregnancy; breastfeeding. *SE:* Burning/tingling, pruritus, erythema, folliculitis, acne, herpes simplex infection, ↑sensitivity to hot and cold, alcohol intolerance. NB: tacrolimus ointment is said to be more effective with faster onset of action than pimecrolimus cream in atopy (safety profiles are similar).[RCT 79]

Preventing infantile eczema[80]

Despite the numerous studies on possible benefits of breastfeeding, the issue remains controversial: one meta-analysis suggests that exclusive breastfeeding for the 1st 3 months of life is associated with less atopic eczema in children with a 1st degree relative with atopy.[MET 81]

Using antigen avoidance diets in high-risk women during pregnancy has little effect[82] but during lactation this might 'substantially reduce her child's risk of developing atopic eczema, but better trials are needed'. If a mother wants to try antigen avoidance, point out that it may not work; at present there is not enough evidence for us to try persuading neutral mothers.[83] Supplementing prenatal diets with fish oil (n-3PUF) may prevent allergies.[RCT 84]

If breastfeeding is impossible, many try soya milk, but this doesn't work. Good blind trials show that a better alternative is a milk in which the protein (casein) is hydrolysed (eg Nutramigen® or Pregestimil®).[RCT 85] [N=595]
Reducing exposure to house-dust mite: High-filtration vacuuming of mattresses; acaricidal sprays, eg *benzyltannate*; Gore-tex® mattress covering; washing bedding at 55°C. NB: meta-analyses doubt the efficacy of these.[MET 86]

Williams diagnostic criteria for atopic eczema[87]

A child must have an itchy skin (or parents report scratching) + ≥3 of:
- Onset before 2yrs old (this criterion is not used if child <4yrs old).
- History of skin crease involvement (including cheeks if <10yrs old)
- History of generally dry skin.
- Personal history of other atopy or history of atopy in 1st degree relative.
- Flexural dermatitis or on cheeks/forehead and outer side of limbs if <4yrs.

1 See *NHS HTA systematic review* www.ncchta.org & Cochrane reviews

Skin infections

Fungi The superficial mycoses are the commonest of human fungal infections—and are limited to skin, hair, nails, and mucous membranes. They include dermatophytes (ringworm), superficial candidosis, and Pityrosporum infections. Three genera of dermatophytes affect humans: Trichophyton, Microsporum, and Epidermophyton and can be spread from man to man (anthropophilic) eg *T. rubrum*, animal to man (zoophilic) (eg *M. canis*) or soil to man (geophilic), eg *M. gypseum*. A dermatophyte infection is a round, scaly, itchy lesion whose edge is more inflamed than its centre. It is called tinea followed, in Latin, by the part affected, eg tinea pedis (foot); cruris (groins); capitis (scalp); unguium (nail); corporis (body). Infection caused by yeasts of the Candida genus (eg *C. albicans*) are common, particularly in the immunocompromised (colonization→invasion→dissemination, *OHCM* p 613). Skin infections are often pink and moist, and there may be satellite lesions. Sites involved by candida: mouth, vagina, glans, skin folds/toe web; nail areas. Other yeasts causing infection include *Pityrosporum ovale* and *orbiculare* in seborrhoeic dermatitis, and *Malassezia furfur* in Pityriasis versicolor (multiple hypo- or hyperpigmented scaly macules on the upper trunk and back). ***Diagnosis:*** Skin scrapings are taken by scraping from the edge (active margin) of the lesion, with a blunted scalpel. Hair-pulls and nail clippings should be taken and specimens collected in folds of black paper (contrasting with the white scrapings). A Wood's light which causes fluorescence in some fungal infections can help diagnosis, and suggest areas for scrapings. Microscopy (potassium hydroxide added to scrapings helps dissolve keratin) and culture (takes 6 weeks) also helps. Skin swabs should be taken if candidosis is suspected. ***Treating fungi:***

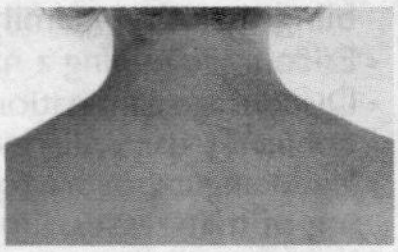

Fig 1. Tina corporis

Fig 2. Close-up view

- ***Dermatophyte infections:*** Skin—terbinafine or imidazole creams (eg clotrimazole) applied twice daily for 14 days. Scalp—oral griseofulvin or terbinafine for children for 2 weeks. Nails—oral terbinafine for 3 months if treatment is desired, after explaining about side-effects (headache; dizziness; taste disturbance; arthralgia; liver failure; psychiatric illness; vertigo) and interactions (β-blockers; antidepressants).
- ***Candida:*** Mouth—nystatin (eg pastilles, sucked 4 times a day for 1 week); Vagina—imidazole cream ± pessary (eg Gyno-Daktarin Combipack®).
- ***Pityriasis versicolor:*** Selenium sulfide shampoo (as a lotion; alternate nights for 2wks, washed off in morning) or twice-daily topical imidazole creams.

Bacteria

- ***Impetigo:*** Superficial *Staph aureus* infection, common in children and often starting around the nose and face. *Clinical features:* Honey-coloured crusts on erythematous base; lesions often well-defined and superficial flaccid blisters sometimes seen. *Treatment:* Topical fusidic acid, or systemic antibiotics (eg flucloxacillin 125mg/6h PO, in a child).
- ***Erysipelas:*** Sharply defined superficial infection caused by streptococcus. Often affects the face (unilateral). Associated with fever, leukocytosis. *Treatment:* Systemic penicillin (see below).
- ***Cellulitis:*** Deeper streptococcal infection with systemic upset & lymphadenopathy, less well-defined than erisipelas and often affecting the legs. Commonest organisms: β-haemolytic streps ± staphs. *Treatment:* ►Elevate the legs. Benzylpenicillin 600mg/6h *IV* (or penicillin V 500mg/4–6h PO) + flucloxacillin 500mg/6h PO. If penicillin-allergic, try erythromycin 500mg/12h PO.

Common viral infections of the skin

Warts Cause: human papillomavirus (HPV) infection of keratinocytes. Large numbers of lesions often seen in the immunosuppressed, eg transplant patients. *Common warts:* Most common in children and young adults; often resolve spontaneously but individual lesions can be stubbornly persistent. Treatment is either expectant (wait-and-see) or destructive: topical salicylic acid paints (keratolytic); liquid nitrogen cryotherapy (if the child is >6–8yrs old); stubborn lesions are occasionally treated with intralesional bleomycin ± lasers.88 28 images

Plantar warts: Large confluent lesions (mosaic warts) are often resist repeated treatments. Warts are infectious and excision is best avoided. After abrading the wart, salicylic acid (eg 26%) is sometimes tried, under an occlusive plaster, eg as Occlusal®. Cryo: double freeze-thaw cycles are more effective than single cycles (but not for hand warts).89 Recalcitrant warts may respond to photodynamic therapy; use is non-standard.90 NB: schools expect children to wear verruca socks for swimming. One uncontrolled study supports this: public shower users were at greater risk for plantar warts than were locker room users who did not use communal showers.91 92 image

Plane warts: Flat skin-coloured or brown lesions; tend to Köbnerise (p 584) in scratch marks; they often resist treatment.93 3 images

Genital warts (condylomata acuminata): Usually treated with cryo ± podophyllin (avoid in pregnancy: teratogenic) or imiquimod cream. Also screen for other sexually transmitted diseases. Women with genital warts (or whose partners have them) need a yearly cervical smear (HPV 16 & 18 contribute to cervical cancer, p 272).94 4 images

Molluscum contagiosum *(pox virus)* These pink papules have umbilicated central punctum. White material can be expressed and microscoped to confirm the diagnosis (molluscum bodies). Common in children. They resolve spontaneously (but this may take months). Gentle cryo may be tried. It is more common in atopic eczema.95 9 images

Herpes simplex Gingivostomatitis or *recurrent genital or peri oral.* infection, triggered by fevers, sunlight, immunosuppression. Eruption often preceded by symptoms of burning/itching. *Signs:* Grouped painful vesicles on erythematous base which heal without scarring. *Treatment:* Often none needed. Topical aciclovir may prevent or reduce severity of recurrences. Systemic treatment is indicated in certain circumstances (immunosuppressed; frequent recurrent genital herpes). There is evidence that Bell's palsy may be related to recurrent herpes infection.96 4 images

Herpes zoster (shingles) Varicella-zoster virus becomes dormant in dorsal root ganglia. Recurrent infection affects one or more dermatomes (esp. immunosuppressed, when it may become generalized). Pain and malaise may precede eruption. *Signs:* Polymorphic eruption (red papules, vesicles pustules, and crusting). May heal with scarring and development of post-herpetic neuralgia. *℞:* If mild, none may be needed. More severe disease or infection in immunosuppressed requires early treatment with systemic treatment, eg aciclovir 800mg 5×/day PO for 7 days (SE: confusion; LFT↑; urea↑)—or famciclovir 250mg/8h PO for 7 days (SE: headache, confusion).97 32 images

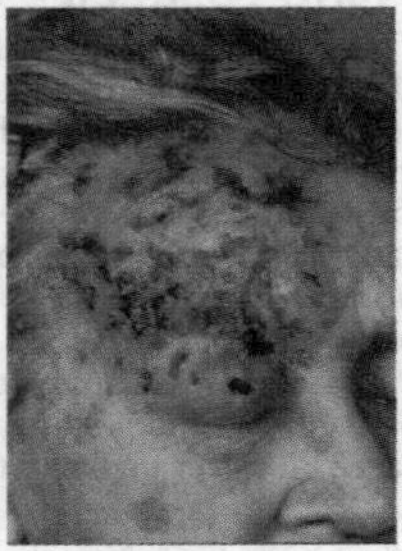

Fig 1. Ophthalmic zoster

Acne vulgaris

This is an inflammatory disorder of the pilosebaceous follicle. It is almost universal amongst teenagers, affecting the face, neck, upper chest, and back.

Cause *Comedone (whitehead & blackhead) formation* is the central abnormality in acne and is due to an abnormality of keratinization/desquamation within the follicle, leading to a blockage of secretions. ↑*Sebum production:* This is regulated by androgens and CRH—►see p 583. Most individuals with acne do not have excessive androgens but their sebaceous glands may be more sensitive to the actions of androgens. *Propionobacterium acnes: P. acnes* is a normal skin commensal that flourishes in the anaerobic conditions within the blocked follicle. It is the inflammatory response to this bacterial proliferation which causes the typical inflamed lesions of acne.

Signs (Face, trunk) Comedones; papules; pustules; nodules; cysts; scars.

Differential diagnosis Acne rosacea—no comedones; diffusely red nose, cheeks, chin, and forehead; telangiectasia; flushing, especially after alcohol.

Management Dispel some of the myths about acne—it is NOT due to lack of washing, eating sweets/chocolate, etc. Treatment will depend on severity.

Mild acne (mainly comedones, mainly on the face): topical therapies (singly or in combination): benzoyl peroxide (as low a strength as is effective, eg 2.5%; if higher, it may irritate); azelaic acid (max 10g/day; treat for no longer than 6 months); roll-on antibiotics (clindamycin as Dalacin T®).

Moderate acne (inflammatory lesions, face ± chest, back): try erythromycin 500mg/12h PO for ≳4–6 months (better than micocycline) with topical benzoyl peroxide (start with 2.5%, not 5% or 10% to avoid irritation).[RCT 98] Any topical antibiotic must be the same as the oral drug to avoid drug resistance, eg erythromycin PO + benzamycin gel® (benzoyl peroxide 5% + erythromycin 3%). These antibiotic gels are said to 'improve quality of life', but are 3-times the price of benzoyl peroxide and offer scant advantage.[RCT 99]

Severe acne (nodules, cysts, scarring): the synthetic retinoid isotretinoin is the drug of choice (eg 0.5–1mg/kg/day for 16 weeks). Highly significant improvements are seen in virtually all patients. 60–70% will have no further recurrences. SE: teratogenic (sexually active women must use effective contraception during and for 1 month after treatment); dryness of skin, lips, mucosae, myalgia, headache (benign intracranial hypertension reported); psychotic depression;[1] hepatitis; ↑lipids.[100] Alternative (if ♀): co-cyprindiol (Dianette®); CI: personal or family history of thrombo-embolism.

Other putative indications for isotretinoin: Moderate acne not responding to antibiotics; presence of scarring and severe psychological problems.

Acne rosacea

This chronic relapsing/remitting facial disorder of unknown cause typically affects fair-skinned people—with chronic flushing[2] triggered by alcohol or spicy foods preceding characteristic fixed erythema (chin, nose, cheeks, forehead), telangiectasia, papules, and pustules. In males, rhinophyma (swelling + soft tissue overgrowth of the nose) may occur. Recurrent severe flares can lead to lymphoedema. *Eye associations:* Blepharitis (scaling and irritation at base of eyelashes); conjunctivitis; rarely, keratitis. *℞:* Avoid irritants & sun overexposure. 0.75% metronidazole gel 12hrly for 8wks helps mild to moderate disease ± oxytetracycline 500mg/12h PO.[101] Once skin has settled, discontinue, and restart as needed. (NB: long-term use of minocycline can cause blue/grey pigmentation of exposed sites and, very rarely, hepatitis).[102]

1 Barak Y 2005 *Int Clin Psychopharmacol* **20** 39. Either a personal history of obsessive-compulsive disorder, neurological insult or family history of a major psychiatric illness were present in all cases.
2 *Flushing ΔΔ:* Menopause; alcohol; food intolerances; toxins; drugs (nicotinic acid, bromocriptine, tamoxifen, cyproterone acetate, ciclosporin); mastocytosis (p 602); carcinoid; pheochromocytoma.

Drug eruptions

10% of hospital patients develop a drug eruption during their admission, so it is important to know which drugs typically cause problems, and to understand how to manage these problems. Drug reactions can be classified according to various criteria, eg immunological (IgE type I response to penicillin) or non-immunological (teratogenicity from retinoids); histological features, eg lichenoid; clinical features.

Types of clinical reaction *Maculopapular* or *exanthematous:* (fig 1) This is the typical type of drug eruption. *Clinical features:* Macular erythema and red papules, particularly affecting trunk. There may be associated fever and eosinophilia. *Drugs:* Penicillins; cefalosporins; anti-epileptics.

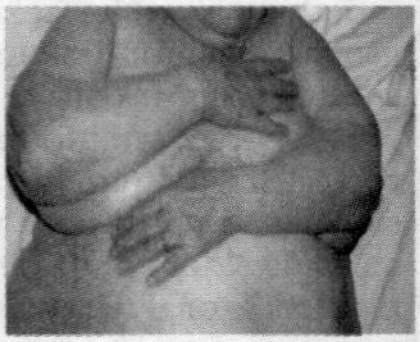

Fig 1. Penicillin rash

Urticaria:[1] *Signs:* Weals (fig 2 on p 584); rapid onset after taking drug ± association with angio-oedema/anaphylaxis. This can result from both immunological and non-immunological mechanisms. *Drugs:* Morphine and codeine cause direct mast cell degranulation; penicillins and cefalosporins trigger IgE responses; NSAIDs; ACE-i.

Exfoliative dermatitis: Signs: Widespread erythema and dermatitis; erythroderma. *Causative drugs:* Sulfonamides; allopurinol; carbamazepine; gold.

Erythema multiforme major (Stevens–Johnson syndrome): The more severe variants of erythema multiforme are usually due to drugs. *Signs:* Target lesions and polymorphic erythema, eg with blistering mucosae (conjunctivae, oral, labial, genital) if severe. *Drugs:* Sulfonamides; anticonvulsants.

Toxic epidermal necrolysis (TEN) is an extreme end of the erythema multiforme/Stevens-Johnson syndrome (SJS) spectrum. *Signs:* Widespread erythema followed by epidermal necrosis with loss of large sheets of epidermis. Mucosae severely affected. Mortality: ~30%. Manage in a dermatology or burns unit. *Drugs:* Sulfonamides; anticonvulsants; penicillins; allopurinol; NSAIDs.

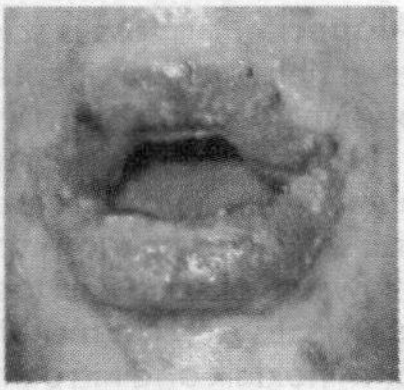

Fig 2. TEN/Stevens-Johnson

Lichenoid: Clinical features: There are clinical features which show some similarity to lichen planus but are rarely typical of idiopathic lichen planus. *Drugs implicated:* β-blockers; thiazides; gold; antimalarials.

Management A clear history of the onset and duration of the rash is essential. Record *all* drugs taken (herbal remedies, etc). Stop the likely offender. If the clinical diagnosis is in doubt, a prick test or skin biopsy may be helpful but is not always so. In order to confirm the suspicion of drug sensitivity, some advocate rechallenge with the suspected drug once the patient has recovered. While this may be the ideal, re-challenge may be dangerous (beware erythroderma and anaphylaxis). Not unreasonably, patients may also object to this. 103 Many drug rashes need no intervention. Symptoms such as dryness or itch may be helped by regular emollients. Very itchy rashes, eg lichenoid or dermatitic, may need short courses of topical steroids. Urticaria: prompt antihistamine with IV hydrocortisone/IM adrenaline (=epinephrine, p 237) if anaphylaxis. More severe eruptions, eg erythema multiforme are best managed by specialists. There is debate as to the efficacy of oral prednisolone in both conditions.

1 Other triggers of ***acute urticaria***: Animals; rubber; shellfish; nuts; dairy products; stings; viruses.
Chronic urticaria: Food additives; autoantibodies which attack mast cells, which release histamine.

Miscellaneous skin disorders

Lichen planus This is an itchy disorder (cause unknown), occurring at any age (uncommon in the very young and old). ***Signs:*** The eruption consists of flat-topped purple papules with white lacy markings on the surface (known as Wickham's striae). The flexor aspects of the wrists, forearms, ankles and legs are commonly affected. Typical lesions at other sites include scalp (scarring alopecia), nails (longitudinal ridges), tongue, mouth (lacy white areas on inner cheeks), and genitals (annular lesions). Lesions often arise at sites of trauma. Usually persists for 6-18 months. Treatment is symptomatic: moderate to potent topical steroids are helpful for severe itch. Occasionally, severe disease warrants the use of oral steroids. Clobetasol ointment (in the mouth eg on tape,[104] or fluticasone spray) is probably better than oral steroids.[RCT 105]

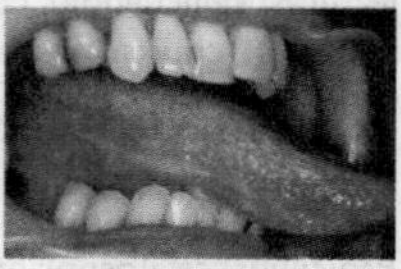
Fig 1. Tongue lichen

Haemangiomas ***Strawberry naevae*** occur in neonates, as a rapidly enlarging red spot. Most go by the age of 5-7 years. No treatment is required unless a vital function is impaired, eg obscuring vision.

Pyogenic granuloma: This is a lesion which is thought to arise as a result of minor trauma, typically occurring on fingers. It appears a moist red lesion which grows rapidly and often bleeds easily. *Treatment:* Curettage.

Pityriasis rosea This is common, often affecting young adults, and may have a viral cause (eg herpes hominis viruses HHV-6 & HHV-7).[106] A rash is preceded by a herald patch (ovoid red scaly patch with a prominent scaly edge, similar to but larger than later lesions). Tends to affect the neck, trunk, and proximal limbs. It is self-limiting; no treatment is needed.[107] 10 images

Alopecia Hair loss is *scarring* or *non-scarring*. Non-scarring causes may be reversible, but scarring alopecia implies irreversible loss. Scalp disorders may be signs of skin elsewhere: (look for signs of lichen planus, and *SLE*).

Non-scarring alopecia: *nutritional* (Fe or Zn deficiency); *androgenic* (♀ & ♂) *autoimmune* (alopecia areata: smooth round patches of hair loss on scalp; hairs like exclamation marks are a typical feature; often spontaneously regrows; total scalp hair loss = alopecia totalis; total body hair loss = alopecia universalis—its treatment is difficult: consider topical or intralesional steroids, or minoxidil, or dinitrochlorobenzene); *telogen effluvium* (shedding of telogen phase hairs after period of stress, eg childbirth, surgery, severe illness).

Scarring alopecia: lichen *planus; discoid lupus erythematosus; trauma.*

Blistering disorders *Infection* (eg herpes); *insect bites* (eg on legs); *drugs* (ACE-i; furosemide); *trauma/friction*; *Zn↓*; *autoimmune blistering disorders (*ABD*)*, eg ***pemphigoid***—the chief ABD in the elderly—due to IgG autoantibodies to basement membrane components (bullous pemphigoid antigens 1 & 2). *Signs of pemphigoid:* Tense blisters on an urticated base. Skin biopsy: (+ve immunofluorescence; linear IgG and C3 along the basement membrane). ℞: clobetasol propionate cream 40g/day is better than oral steroids.[108] [N=341]

Pemphigus affects younger people than pemphigoid (>40yrs) and is due to IgG autoantibodies against desmosomal components (desmoglein 1 & 3). This leads to acantholysis (keratinocytes separate from each other). Drugs may cause it, eg ACE-i, NSAID, phenobarbital, L-dopa. *Signs:* Flaccid blisters which rupture easily to leave widespread erosions. The oral mucosa is often affected early. Diagnosis is confirmed by skin biopsy with positive immunofluorescence (intercellular IgG giving a crazy-paving effect). *Treatment:* Prednisolone (60-80mg/day PO, may be life-long in low doses).[109]

Photosensitivity For classification of susceptibility to ultraviolet, see p 593. Photosensitivity denotes conditions triggered by light (eg solar urticaria;

polymorphic light eruption). Photoaggravation describes disorders worsened by light but are not due to abnormal sensitivity to light (eg recurrent herpes labialis; rosacea). Photosensitivity can occur to visible light, UVA (320–400nm) or UVB (290-320nm). ►Usually a *careful history* allows accurate diagnosis:

- A rash every summer, for example, suggests that UV has a role.
- How long does the rash take to appear? Within 30min suggests solar urticaria; polymorphic light eruption may take days to appear.
- Itching suggests polymorphic light eruption or solar urticaria.
- Face rashes, including the V of the neck, but sparing periorbital skin.
- The dorsum of the hands and the arms are other typical sites.
- As hands are usually relaxed in the semi-flexed position, skin around DIP joins is less affected than that around the knuckles and PIP joints.
- Is there a family history? If so, refer to genophotodermatologist. Is it xeroderma pigmentosum, Bloom's syndrome, or Cockayne's syndrome?
- Pain (± family history) suggests erythropoietic protoporphyria (sun may hurt so much that a child quickly avoids it, so there is pain but no rash).
- Was the rash related to starting a drug (eg nalidixic acid)? See below.
- Are there papules: this suggests polymorphic light eruption.
- Any blisters or linear marks where plants have scratched the skin (phyto-photodermatitis from furocoumarins)? Ask about hobbies/work. [110] images

Polymorphic light eruption: This is a common idiopathic disorder typically affecting young women in spring. After light exposure, itchy red papules, vesicles, and plaques develop on exposed sites, often improving over the summer due to a phenomenon called 'hardening'. ***Treatment:*** Sun-avoidance; sun-protection (high factor UVA + UVB sunscreen); desensitization by phototherapy; strong topical steroids ± brief course of oral prednisolone. [RCT 111] [N=10]

Porphyria cutanea tarda: (The commonest porphyria) The primary abnormality is hypofunction of the liver enzyme uroporphyrinogen decarboxylase. *Causes/triggers:* certain alleles of the haemochromatosis gene; HIV; hepatitis C; alcohol; oestrogen. *Signs:* Vesicles/bullae in sun-exposed sites, hypertrichosis, hyperpigmentation, skin fragility, and scarring (milia). *Tests:* ↑LFTs; ↑ferritin; ↑urine, plasma, and faecal porphyrins. *Management:* Remove precipitants; sun-avoidance; sun-protection; regular venesection until ferritin in normal range; chloroquine. [112]

Systemic lupus erythematosus: (*OHCM* p 422) Light exposure often triggers erythematous rashes, with systemic flare. A variant of lupus, subacute LE, is associated with marked photosensitivity and anti-Ro antibodies.

Drugs are a major cause of photosensitivity, so ... ►*look up details of all drugs taken.* Frequent offenders: thiazides (sunburn-like or lichenoid eruptions); tetracyclines/sulfonamides (sunburn-like); tricyclics; phenothiazines (dermatitic eruption); NSAIDs; amiodarone (sunburn-like eruptions). It may take months to settle, after drug withdrawal.

Ordinary urticaria *Acute:* Rash (eg to latex etc, p 584, fig 1) lasts <6wks. Skin prick or blood RAST tests (p 596) may be useful. ***Chronic:*** Typically idiopathic, or seen with collagen, thyroid or sinus disease. Antibodies may be directed to mast-call IgE receptors (causing degranulation, p 610). **Physical urticaria** is caused within minutes by an external trigger, eg heat, cold, exercise, or trauma (dermatographism). **Contact urticaria** arises eg on contact with food, insect bites, or pet saliva. **Urticaria pigmentosa:** p 610. **Urticarial vasculitis** causes non-migratory rash with fever ± purpura ± arthralgia, eg in sicca syndrome or SLE). *Rx:* Antihistamine, eg loratadine 10mg/day ± chlorphenamine 4mg at night. Ketotifen may help adults (1mg/12h [113]) and children. [114] [115] Gastric/CNS H_2 blockers (ranitidine; doxepin 10mg/8h PO [116]) may help too. Avoid stress and triggers, and antihistamine or steroid creams (may be a trigger).

Skin disorders in old age

Typical causes
• Gravity/stasis • Neuropathy • Vascular: venous 75%; arterial 10%; mixed 15% • Trauma
Rarer causes
• Pyoderma gangrenosum eg with Crohn's; UC) • Sickle-cell disease • Vasculitis (SLE, rheumatoid arthritis; syphilis) • Vasculitis (eg SLE). • Cryoglobulinaemia • Leishmaniasis

Leg ulcers (fig 1) *Causes:* Typically *venous hypertension* from damaged valves of the deep venous system (eg 2° to DVT). This causes superficial varicosities and skin changes (lipodermatosclerosis = induration, pigmentation and inflammation of the skin of the lower leg). Minimal trauma typically over the medial malleolus causes ulcers. *Management:* The only effective treatment is compression, ideally in community leg ulcer clinics. Ulcers heal more quickly with occlusive dressings which absorb exudate and improve comfort. Treat varicose eczema with emollients and a short course of moderately potent topical steroids. Consider patch testing if unresponsive. Bacterial colonization doesn't require treatment ***unless*** streptococcal or pseudomonal, *or* there are clear signs of cellulitis/infection (↑pain and tenderness, fever, erythema or lymphangitis). Four-layer compression bandaging should be applied by trained nursing staff, to produce a pressure of 40mmHg at the ankle. Do Dopplers before this to exclude arterial disease (make sure the ankle–brachial pressure index is >0.8, *OHCM* p 490). Ulcers which do not heal on adequate treatment for 3 months should be investigated further (eg biopsy for malignancy). Once the ulcer has been healed, compression hosiery should be worn. Grade III stockings are the ideal but many find them uncomfortable; grade II is a reasonable compromise.

Asteatotic eczema (eczema craquelé) Commoner in the elderly, this particularly affects the lower legs with a dry eczema which polygonally fissures into a crazy-paving pattern. Emollients and soap substitutes help.[117]

Pruritus is a common complaint in the elderly. *Primary skin causes: Eczema; scabies* (can have an atypical appearance in the elderly); *pemphigoid/pre-pemphigoid eruptions*; *asteatotic eczema*; *generalized xerosis*. *Medical causes: Anaemia*; *polycythaemia*; *lymphoma*; *solid neoplasms*; *hepatic* and *renal failure*; *hypo-* and *hyperthyroidism*; *diabetes (candidiasis)*. In the absence of a primary skin disorder, these should be excluded by appropriate investigations.

Pressure sores If made immobile by age, or CNS problems (stroke, cord lesions), uninterrupted pressure on skin may lead to ulceration, and extensive, painful, subcutaneous destruction—eg on the sacrum, heel, or greater trochanter. Protein malnutrition, arteriopathy, and old age make the condition more likely to occur, particularly if nursing care is poor. They are a big problem. Cost: >£800 million/yr.[118] A full-thickness sacral sore causes much misery and extends hospital stay by 6 months, and costs >£30,000. ►This should make prevention a central preoccupation, not just on long-stay geriatric wards, but in *all* acute wards—where most pressure sores start. Nurse education, ↑staff numbers, and nursing comatose patients prone (with a prone-head support system) may help.[119] Don't rely on special mattresses![RCT 120]

Staging	*Stage I:*	Non-blanching erythema over intact skin.
	Stage II:	Partial thickness skin loss, eg shallow crater.
	Stage III:	Full thickness skin loss, extending into fat.
	Stage IV:	Destruction of muscle, bone, or tendons.

Prevalence: ~7% of inpatients have pressure sores; >70% are over 70yrs old. Up to 85% of paraplegic patients have pressure sores.

Complications: Osteomyelitis; pyoarthrosis. *Further information:* NICE.

Treatment and prevention of pressure sores

- Prevent the condition getting worse (see below).
- Improve nutrition. Insulin if hyperglycaemic.
- Treat systemic infection with antibiotics.
- Dress the area. There is no convincing evidence from randomized trials which favours any one type of dressing.
- Vascular reconstruction, if needed, and if practicable.
- Split thickness skin grafts.
- Neurosensory myocutaneous flap surgery.

Prevention

- Find an interested, knowledgeable nurse to educate the patient.
- Proper positioning, with regular turning (eg every 2h, see p 768 & p 776, alternating between supine, and right or left lateral position). Use pillows to separate the legs.
- Functional electrical stimulation can prevent sores in paraplegics, by inducing the buttocks to change shape, and by improving blood flow. A good randomized trial (*N*=44 patients aged ~85yrs with hip fracture) showed that a DeCube® mattress with removable cubes for provision of rest for pressure points can halve the incidence of pressure sores.[RCT 121]

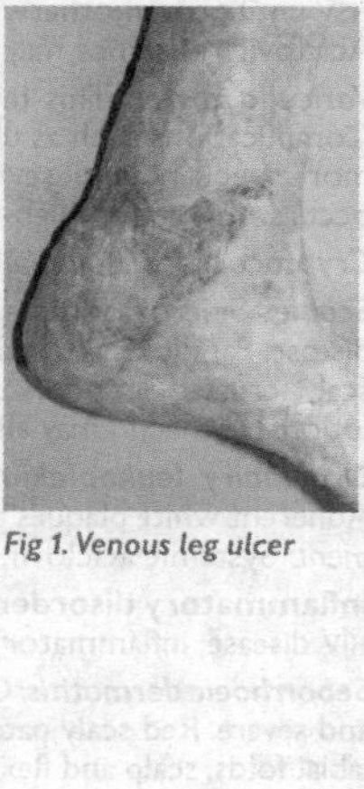

Fig 1. Venous leg ulcer

Skin disorders in HIV disease

There are many cutaneous manifestations of HIV disease, due to both infectious and non-infectious conditions. With the introduction of the protease inhibitor group of drugs and the advent of early treatment with triple therapy regimens, it is likely that some of the conditions described below will become less common in the HIV positive population.

Infections: HIV positive individuals are more prone not only to infections common in the general population but also to infections with organisms which do not usually cause disease in immunocompetent individuals (commensal organisms). In an HIV positive patient, any new lesion should be considered as possibly due to infection with an unusual organism.

HIV: Seroconversion is associated with an acute mononucleosis type illness, usually accompanied by a non-specific maculopapular eruption affecting the upper trunk, associated with lymphadenopathy, malaise, headache, and fever.

Thrush may be severe, disseminated, treatment-resistant, involving the posterior pharynx and oesophagus. *℞:* Topical nystatin; systemic imidazoles.

Molluscum contagiosum: Lesions tend to develop on the face and genitals. Management can be difficult: cryotherapy, topical retinoids, cautery, and curettage may be tried. *Differential diagnosis:* Disseminated cryptococcosis.

Herpes simplex virus infection: This can be increasingly troublesome as HIV progresses. Painful ulcers and erosions develop, particularly around the mouth and genitals. Any ulcerated or eroded area should be considered as HSV until proven otherwise. *Management:* High-dose aciclovir (oral or IV). Aciclovir resistance may develop and foscarnet is an alternate treatment.

Varicella zoster: This may occur early in HIV, with atypical presentation. Complications such as ulceration and post-herpetic neuralgia appear to be more frequent and severe. In advanced disease, disseminated infection occurs. *Treatment:* High-dose aciclovir (IV if systemic disease).

Cryptococcosis: Looks like facial molluscum contagiosum. *℞:* Fluconazole.

Scabies: Severe variants, eg crusted scabies are more common in advanced HIV disease. Paradoxically, patients may not complain of severe itch. A widespread scaly, crusted eruption occurs (highly infectious). *Treatment:* Permethrin lotion. Ivermectin may also be of benefit (but side-effects may be serious).

Oral hairy leukoplakia: (Epstein–Barr virus infection of oral mucosa) Adherent white plaques are seen on the lateral aspects of the tongue. *Treatment:* Systemic aciclovir. 122

Inflammatory disorders Despite the immunosuppression associated with HIV disease, inflammatory cutaneous conditions occur frequently.

Seborrhoeic dermatitis: Common in later stages of HIV, it may be widespread and severe. Red scaly patches typically affect hair-bearing areas, eg the nasolabial folds, scalp and flexures. *℞:* Topical (or systemic) imidazoles.

Psoriasis: Treatment: Standard therapies (p 594, dithranol; calcipotriol; UV). Treatment of HIV will often improve psoriasis.

Eosinophilic folliculitis: The cause of this condition is unknown and it occurs frequently as HIV progresses. Itchy follicular papules and pustules affect the face, chest, and back. Treatments are often unsatisfactory but include topical steroids; phototherapy; antihistamines.

Drug reactions: These occur more commonly in HIV patients and particular culprits include co-trimoxazole (maculopapular eruptions; erythema multiforme; toxic epidermal necrolysis, fig 2 on p 601); dapsone; foscarnet (ulceration); zidovudine (nail + mucosal pigmentation).

Neoplasia and HIV

HIV disease is associated with a significantly increased risk of certain types of malignancy, eg lymphoma, cervical carcinoma. Common skin cancers (eg basal cell carcinomas, fig 1 on p 590) are also seen with HIV.

Kaposi's sarcoma (KS): Cause: HHV-8 (herpes hominis virus). It is HIV-associated. Here, sero-prevalence of HHV-8 is higher in men who have sex with men when compared with the other groups such as bisexuals/heterosexuals (32% *vs* 10%).[1] Oral transmission through deep kissing (with copious exchange of saliva) is thought to be an important means of transmission in both HIV+ve and -ve individuals.

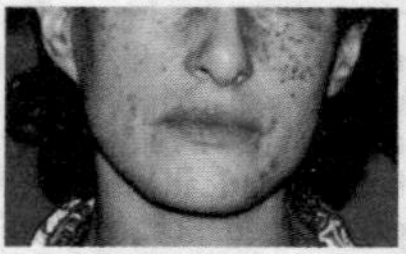

Fig 1. Kaposi's sarcoma (varicelliform eruption)

Not all KS is HIV associated. Before the HIV pandemic, it was recognized eg in people living in Southern Europe, the Middle East and Africa.

Signs: Purple macules, papules, nodules, and plaques affecting limbs, face, and oral mucosa.

Differential: Bacillary angiomatosis (Bartonella species); pyogenic granuloma.

Treatment: Cryotherapy; intralesional vincristine; radiotherapy; treatment of HIV disease (protease inhibitors).

1 2005 *Sex Transm* Dis **32** 57 *PCR* is one way of detecting *HHV-8*

Infestations

Scabies (*Sarcoptes scabei*) This is a common disorder particularly affecting children and young adults, and spreads within families or those living in close contact. The ♀ mite digs a burrow and lays eggs which hatch as larvae. The itch and subsequent rash is probably due to allergic sensitivity to the mite or its products. ***Signs:*** Markedly itchy papular eruption affecting the fingerwebs (esp. first), wrist flexures, axillae, abdomen (esp. around umbilicus and waistband area), buttocks, and groins (itchy red penile or scrotal papules are virtually diagnostic). In young infants, the palms and soles are characteristically involved. The eruption is usually excoriated and becomes eczematized. Scabies mites can sometimes be extracted from burrows and visualized microscopically; eggs can be visualized from skin scrapings.

Management: A good explanation (verbal + written) will aid concordance between the patient's and the doctor's requirements, and will promote the chances of successful cure. A suitable anti-scabetic should be prescribed (malathion, permethrin). Preparations are applied to all areas of the skin, from the neck down for 24h. Areas which are washed during this period (eg hands) should have treatment re-applied. ALL members of a household should be treated at the same time, even if asymptomatic. The rash and symptom of itch will take a few weeks to settle, occasionally longer. A suitable anti-pruritic such as crotamiton cream (which also has anti-scabetic activity) can be useful during this period. *Example of written advice:*

- Take a warm bath and soap the skin all over.
- Scrub the fingers and nails with a firm brush. Dry your body.
- Apply malathion 0.5% liquid (Derbac-M®, not if pregnant or <6 months old) from the neck down (include the head in those <2yrs old). Remember to paint *all* parts, including the soles.
- Wash off after 24h. If you wash your hands before 24h is up, reapply the liquid to the parts you have washed.
- Use fresh pillow cases and sheets, if you have any.
- Treatment may worsen itch for 2 weeks—so use calamine lotion.
- Warnings: avoid the eyes.

Note: one or two doses of ivermectin 200μg/kg PO may be effective in recalcitrant scabies (eg with HIV) on a named patient basis.

Headlice (*Pediculus humanus capitis*) This is a common problem among schoolchildren, with lice being spread by head to head contact. The louse is 3mm long and has legs adapted to cling onto hair shafts. The eggs (nits) are bound firmly to the scalp hairs and when empty appear white. ***Clinical features:*** Itch and a papular eruption on the nape of the neck are common. ***Management:*** Resistance to treatment has become a problem and many health boards operate a rotation policy of treatments. Sometimes the only option is meticulous combing (after applying conditioner to the hair). One new option with initial success in >90% of patients is the application of a thin film with suffocates lice, over 8h, and can then be shampooed off (Nuvo®).[124]

Crab lice (*Phthiriasis pubis*) These are usually sexually transmitted and affect the pubic hairs. The eyebrows, eyelashes, and axillae may also be involved. ***Management:*** Topical malathion to all affected (or potentially affected) areas. Evidence of other sexually transmitted disease should be sought. All sexual contacts should also be treated.

Flea* bites (*Pulicidae*) spread plague, typhus, cat-scratch disease. The animal (eg cat or dog) which spreads the flea may not itch or scratch itself. Flea bites cause a papular urticaria in a sensitized individual. Treatment: de-flea pets; de-flea household carpets and soft-furnishings.

Treating head lice

- Only treat living, moving, lice.
- Treatment courses entail 2 applications of >50mL of lotion', 1 week apart.
- Do contact tracing; treat confirmed infections with the same agent.
- In choosing which agent, use the 'mosaic model', to avoid prolonged use of the same agent. Be guided by local patterns of resistance. Try malathion alcoholic lotion (aqueous if young or atopic), then permethrin, then carbaryl (only the latter needs a GP prescription in UK: it is a potential carcinogen). Allow to dry and wash off after 12h, and wet-comb.
- Shampoo formulations rarely work.
- Families should do wet hair 'detection combing' 2–3 days after the 2nd application, to check on cure.
- Don't use insecticides as prophylaxis.
- Lice on pillowcases can be killed by heating the pillowcase by immersion in water at > 60°C, by a hot wash, or by 15mins in a hot clothes dryer. [125]
- Prophylaxis: in typical 'cases' (urban girl aged 4–11) regular combing with early intervention may work.

If drugs fail (often the case), use mechanical methods. Dry-on pediculocides which suffocate (not poison) lice are under investigation and look promising and less toxic. [126]

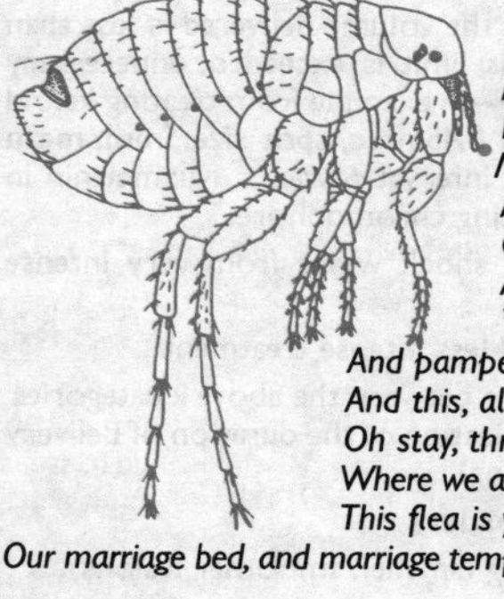

The flea

Mark but this flea, and mark in this
How little that which thou deny'st me is;
Me it suck'd first, and now sucks thee,
And in this flea our two bloods mingled be;
Confess it; this cannot be said
A sin, or shame, or loss of maidenhead,
Yet this enjoys before it woo,
And pamper'd swells with one blood made two,
And this, alas, is more than we can do.
Oh stay, three lives in one flea spare,
Where we almost, nay more than married are:
This flea is you and I, and this
Our marriage bed, and marriage temple is. John Donne, to his lover *circa* 1600.

Mast cell disorders

Mastocytosis (urticaria pigmentosa) There are too many mast cells in the skin (± other organs), eg in nests or as a single mastocytoma. These release histamine, leukotrienes, and heparin (this has systemic effects) and proteases (which have local effects). Adults usually express activating mutations of the stem cell factor receptor 'c-kit'.[127]

Skin lesions in adults are typically red-brown macules/papules which urticate if scratched (Darier's sign) and are extremely itchy. Systemic features: headache, palpitations, syncope, flushing, wheeze, diarrhoea, hepatosplenomegaly, osteoporosis, osteosclerosis, anaemia, eosiniophilia, and, rarely, mast cell leukaemia.[128]

Diagnosis: Skin biopsy; ↑urinary histamine, and ↑histamine metabolites.

Tests: Urinary histamine may be ↑ (helps if no skin signs). Labs may also report *N'*-methylhistamine (MH) and *N'*-methylimidazoleacetic acid (MIMA).

Differential diagnoses: Sarcoidosis; histiocytosis.

Treatment: Avoid triggers (eg aspirin, heat, cold). H_1 and H_2 antihistamines; disodium cromoglycate. Nd:YAG lasers have been tried.[129]

Lasers in dermatology

Lasers (light amplification by stimulated emission of radiation) have an increasing role, and it is worth knowing who may benefit from them. The destructive energy of lasers can be concentrated in time and space, and the light's wavelength can be adjusted to match the target lesion. Energy can be selectively taken up by targets as long as the volume delivered is less than the target's capacity to absorb it. If this limit is exceeded, unnecessary destruction is caused. Variables to specify—an example from treating keloid scars: wavelength 585nm, pulse duration 0.45msec, spot size 5mm, mean fluence per pulse 7Joules/cm^2, treatment interval: 6 weeks. NB: melanin in dark skins may be a problematic competing chromophore.

Photoacoustic damage is produced by shock waves from very intense energy delivered over picoseconds.

Photocoagulation implies less rapid, and less intense treatment.

Selective photothermolysis is somewhere between the above 2 categories. It may produce minimum scarring. Modification of the duration of delivery is possible (Q-switching and mode-locking).

Examples of laser-treatable skin disorders

Port wine stain: Best treated when young (smaller, smoother lesions).

Tuberous sclerosis: Angiofibromata (misnamed adenoma sebaceum) can cover much of the face.

Strawberry naevi: These do *not* need treatment, unless they fail to resolve spontaneously. If they ulcerate, get expert advice.

Flat, pigmented lesions: These are problematic because it is essential to know that they are benign.

Tattoos: If multicoloured, multiple wavelengths must be used.

Scars: Raised, red, nodular *keloid scars* may appear ugly (and itchy); lasers can help somewhat. *Acne scars* (atrophic or 'ice-pick'): randomized comparisons of CO_2 *vs* YAG laser are needed.[130]

Using *formal* descriptions for decision support

Formal descriptions of skin lesions are vital for computer 'diagnosis'. Here we give a language and 3 examples from the *Dermis* decision support system.[1]

Number of skin lesions '*Single*' means a localized skin lesion, surrounded by normal skin. Ask about change in size or pigmentation. '*Multiple*': up to 20 lesions, each surrounded by normal skin. All are of same type and surface.

Rash Any single or multiple large area(s) of abnormal skin, parts of which have appeared at differing times or >20 multiple lesions. A rash is symmetrical if distributed to much the same extent on both sides of the body.

Lesion size If there is one main type of lesion present, record *average size*. If there are several main types of lesion present of different sizes then record *various sizes*. If there are large plaques of abnormal skin containing other types of lesion then record the plaque size.

Lesion(s)/rash colour Record colours under clear white light.

Shape Record the general shape of the particular lesion or multiple similar lesions. Which fits best? *Round, oval, linear* (if takes the form of a line) *irregular* when no particular shape; *pedunculated lesion* if on a stalk that is narrower at the base; an *umbilicated lesion* has a central round depression on its surface.

Border definition *Well defined* if can draw a line round the abnormal skin; if able to draw a line around parts only, record '*distinct/indistinct*'. If no clear border record *'indistinct'*. *Annular* implies ring-shaped. '*Has an active edge*' means the edge appears more coloured, scaly or diseased than centre'.

Vascular features of abnormal skin *Erythema:* reddening that blanches on pressure. *Purpura:* Red/purple/brown stain that does not blanche. *Telangiectasia:* Dilated superficial vessels.

Duration of lesion or rash This is the time since the disease was first noticed, irrespective of any periods of remission.

Itching of abnormal skin *Mild; Moderate* if sufficiently annoying for the patient to seek help. *Severe* when itching keeps the patient awake at night.

Palpation of abnormal skin On palpating a lesion or rash record as: '*soft*' if easily compressible (like lips); '*firm*' if slightly compressible, like tip of nose. '*Hard*' if incompressible, like forehead. '*Rough*' if like sand-paper.

Feed this language into a database-algorithm to yield probability data

3 cases:	Case 1: male, 20yrs	Case 2: male, 22yrs	Case 3: female, 40yrs
1st onset	6 months ago	<6 months ago	>1 year ago
Lesion number	multiple lesions	multiple lesions	multiple lesions
Location	arm(s), leg(s)	arm(s), leg(s)	arm(s), leg(s)
Type	plaques & papules	papule, erosion	Plaque
Size	20–29mm	20–29mm	20–29mm
Border	definite border	variable border	definite border
Colour	pink	pink, red	pink, red
Surface	scale	normal	atrophic
Itch	mild	mild	Severe
Vascular	erythema	erythema	erythema; telangiectasia
Probability	plaque psoriasis **96%** others **3%**	discoid eczema **93%** other eczema **5%**	necrobiosis lipoidica **99%** Others **1%**

Dermis images for the likeliest diagnosis in cases 1–3. If >90%, a good working diagnosis may be to hand. <40% is a 'poor match', so 'refer to clinic'.

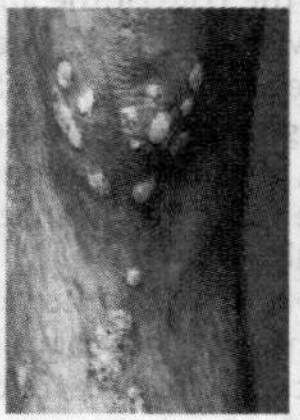

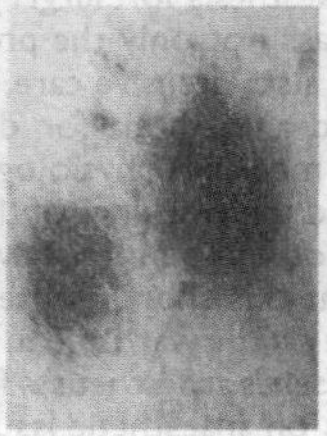

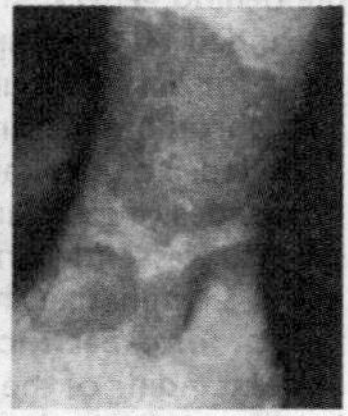

1 *Dermis* Brooks G, Ashton R *Brit J Dermatol* 127 614 Try the software at www.webmentorlibrary.com

9 Anaesthesia

Other relevant pages: Pain relief in labour (p 66); resuscitation after delivery (p 107); neonatal ITU (p 108); ventilating neonates (p 110); major injury (p 726); choosing the correct dose of lidocaine (=lignocaine) according to body weight (p 729); pain relief in children (p 718); Bier's block (p 742).

Introduction

Anaesthesia has evolved from humble origins in 1842 when CW Long gave ether, but he failed to report this landmark in the relief of pain. Then, in 1844, Horace Wells used nitrous oxide for tooth extraction, and in 1846 WTG Morton gave the first surgical anaesthetic with ether. It is now a highly sophisticated specialty in its own right. While the triad of anaesthesia (hypnosis, analgesia, and muscle relaxation) remains the fundamental principle behind general anaesthesia for surgery, the role of the anaesthetist has expanded to encompass not only the provision of ideal operating conditions for surgery, but also intensive care, resuscitation, alleviation of acute and chronic pain, and anaesthesia for diagnostic procedures. A detailed knowledge of general medicine, physiology, pharmacology and the physical properties of gases and the workings of the vast array of anaesthetic equipment are essential, in order to practise well.

►We emphasize that this short chapter is no substitute for a specialist text or for experience on the ward and in theatre. The main aim is to enable understanding of the issues anaesthetists face, and to prepare one's mind for intelligent discussions on anaesthetic issues.

Pre-operative care

Aims—***To ensure that patients:*** • Get the right surgery • Are happy and pain-free • Are as fit as possible • Have individualized decisions on type of anaesthesia/analgesia taking into account risks, benefits, and wishes.

The pre-operative visit Have the symptoms, signs or patient's wishes changed? If so, inform the surgeon. Assess cardiovascular and respiratory systems, exercise tolerance, existing illnesses, drug therapy, and allergies. Assess past history—of myocardial infarction, diabetes, asthma, hypertension, rheumatic fever, epilepsy, jaundice. Assess any specific risks—eg is the patient pregnant? Any dental problems, or history of GI reflux (or vomiting propensity) making 'rapid sequence induction' essential—see p 626? Have there been any anaesthetic problems (nausea, DVT)? Has he had a recent GA?

Family history Ask about malignant hyperpyrexia (p 628); dystrophia myotonica (*OHCM* p 398); porphyria; cholinesterase problems; sickle-cell disease (test if needed). Does the patient have any specific worries?

Drugs Ask about allergy to any drug, antiseptic, plaster, and latex.

ACE inhibitors: No special action required.

Anticoagulants: Know the indication; do INR; switch warfarin to heparin 24h pre-op. Avoid epidural/spinal blocks. Beware regional anaesthesia.

Anticonvulsants: Give the usual dose up to 1h before surgery. Give drugs IV (or by NGT) post-op, until able to take oral drugs. Sodium valproate: an IV form is available (give the patient's usual dose). Phenytoin: give IV slowly (<50mg/min). IM phenytoin absorption is unreliable.

Antibiotics: Neomycin, aminoglycosides, colistin & tetracycline prolong neuromuscular blockade, even *depolarizing* neuromuscular blockers.

Beta-blockers: Continue up to and including the day of surgery as this precludes a labile cardiovascular response.

Contraceptive Pill: See *BNF*. Stop 4 weeks before major (or leg) surgery.

Digoxin: Continue up to and *including* morning of surgery. Check for toxicity and do plasma K^+. Suxamethonium ↑serum K^+ by ~1mmol/L, and can lead to ventricular arrhythmias in the fully digitalized.

Diuretics: Beware hypokalaemia. Do U&E.

HRT: Stop before hip surgery; use heparin thromboprophylaxis + stockings.

Insulin: Stop insulin on day of surgery and start a GIK infusion (glucose, potassium, and insulin). See *OHCM* p 458 & *OHCM* p 783.

Levodopa: Possible arrhythmias when the patient is under GA.

Lithium: Check if recent level; non-depolarizing muscle relaxants may be potentiated. Beware post-op toxicity ± U&E imbalance: p 354.

Monoamine oxidase inhibitors: Get expert help as interaction with narcotics and anaesthetics may lead to hypotensive/hypertensive crisis. Newer selective MAOIs are safer.

Ophthalmic drugs: Anticholinesterases used to treat glaucoma (eg ecothiopate iodine) may cause sensitivity to, and prolong duration of, drugs metabolized by cholinesterases, eg suxamethonium.

Steroids: If the patient is on or has recently taken steroids at an equivalent of >10mg prednisolone per day give extra cover for the peri-operative period (p 616).

Tricyclics: These enhance adrenaline (=epinephrine), exerting anticholinergic effects causing tachycardia, arrhythmias and low BP.

Pre-operative examination and tests

It is the anaesthetist's duty to assess suitability for anaesthesia. Be alert to chronic lung disease, BP↑, arrhythmias, and murmurs (endocarditis prophylaxis needed?—p 166). In rheumatoid arthritis do a lateral cervical spine x-ray to warn about atlanto-axial instability. Post-op chest infections are *six times* more likely in smokers. Stopping smoking even 1 day pre-op is of benefit.

The *ward doctor* assists with a good history and examination—but should not be responsible for consent. DoH guidelines are that the consenting doctor must be capable of the procedure or have been specially trained.[1] NB: consent is needed for orchidectomy in orchidopexy procedures; thyroidectomy patients need to be warned about of nerve damage risk, and those having prostate surgery should be warned about retrograde ejaculation. Other concerns for the house officer to address include:

- DVT prophylaxis (p 706)
- Frozen section (tell pathology)
- Perioperative antibiotics
- Bowel preparation
- Skin preparation
- On-table x-rays
- Post-op physio

Tests Be guided by the history and examination.

- FBC, ward test for blood glucose, and U&E—especially important if the patient is: –On diuretics –A diabetic –A burns victim –Has hepatic or renal disease –Starved –In ileus –Parenterally fed. No tests may be needed for young fit adults having day-case surgery.
- If Hb <10g/dL tell anaesthetist. Investigate/treat as appropriate.
- Group & save for all major surgery; crossmatch according to local Blood Transfusion Service guides, depending on pre-op Hb and type of surgery.
- Tests: LFT in jaundice, malignancy, or alcohol abuse. Amylase if needed.
  Blood glucose in diabetic patients (*OHCM* p 470).
  Drug levels as appropriate (eg digoxin).
  Clotting studies in liver disease, DIC, massive blood loss, already on warfarin or heparin. Contact lab as special bottles are needed.
  HIV, HBsAg in high-risk patients—after appropriate counselling.
  Sickle test in those from Africa, West Indies, or Mediterranean area—and others whose origins are in malarial areas (including most of India).
  Thyroid function tests in those with thyroid disease.
- CXR: if known cardiorespiratory disease, pathology or symptoms.
- ECG: those with poor exercise tolerance, angina etc, BP↑, past rheumatic fever/Kawasaki's (p 646), age >50 (high incidence of 'silent' ischaemia).

Preparation ►Fast the patient: Clear fluids (including black tea or coffee) up to 2 hours pre-op, food 6 hours.

Use nasogastric tube as indicated: insert *before* induction to avoid risk of aspiration *at* induction. (Technique: *OHCM* p 743.) Catheterize as indicated.

ASA score (≈health at the time of surgery) ASA=American Soc. of Anesthesiologists

1 Normally healthy.
2 Mild systemic disease, but with no limitation of activity.
3 Severe systemic disease that limits activity; not incapacitating.
4 Incapacitating systemic disease which poses a threat to life.
5 Moribund. Not expected to survive 24h even with operation.

There is a slot for ASA numbers on most anaesthetic charts; the prefix e denotes *emergencies*. NB: in most (but not all) studies ASA correlates with morbidity.

1 Use only words the patient understands. Ensure he believes your facts and can retain pros and cons long enough to inform his decision. Make sure his choice is free from pressure from others. A patient may complain if: • He is unaware of what will happen • He has not been offered all options • He was sedated at the time of consent • He changed his mind • He was not told a treatment was experimental • A 2nd opinion has been denied • Details of prognosis were glossed over.

Patient-centred anaesthesia

Being patient-centred means more than just doing something for someone rather than yourself or a third party (such as a surgeon). The patient-centred anaesthetist will not only do a good technical job but will also score highly in those subjective areas of particular importance to patients. These are centred around ***physical comfort*** and ***respect***. In one study, ***ratings for information provision, involvement***, and ***emotional support*** were rated significantly less important than physical comfort and respect.[1] Ratings did not differ very much vis à vis inpatient *vs* day surgery, surgical service, type of anaesthetic, or anaesthetist.[2] Physical comfort may centre around needle-less induction of anaesthesia and good peri-operative care in non-frightening surroundings.[3] Also, avoiding nausea/vomiting are top priorities whenever these possibilities are explained.[4]

Patient-centred anaesthesia cannot flourish in a vacuum: if the whole context of care is patient-centred the need for anaesthetic care itself may be less. For example, in obstetrics where there is a one-to-one relationship between the midwife and the mother, the need for epidurals is about 50% less (and the 2nd stage of labour is shorter) then when less personal methods are used.[5]

One way to improve patient-centred anaesthesia is to control distractions in the anaesthetic work-place. Time-and-motion studies show that it is very easy for anaesthetists to get distracted by over-attention to monitoring equipment and other more extraneous interruptions.[6] Exactly how to do this in busy NHS practice is a challenge.

Patients can be confused by an uncertain locus of responsibility. In some cultures (eg in Japan) chief responsibility for perioperative care is the surgeon's. In other cultures, responsibility is shared—with confusing results unless the surgeon and the anaesthetist co-operate closely.[7]

1 Information booklets *do* have a valuable role, and can increase patient satisfaction.

Premedication

The patient should be aware of what will happen, where he will waken and how he will feel. Premedication aims to allay anxiety and contribute to a smooth induction of anaesthesia by decreasing secretions (much less important than when ether was used), promoting amnesia, analgesia, and decreasing vagal reflexes. *Timing:* 2h pre-op for oral drugs; 1h pre-op if IM.

Examples for the 70kg man
- Lorazepam 1-2.5mg PO.
- Temazepam 10-30mg PO.
- Diazepam 5mg PO.

Some anaesthetists still use the traditional IM premeds. Examples:
- Morphine 10mg IM and, more rarely, atropine 0.6mg IM.

Examples for children
- Midazolam 0.5mg/kg (tastes bitter so often put in Calpol®).
- Always use oral premeds in children as first choice.
- Local anaesthetic creams: tetracaine 4% (Ametop®; apply content of the tube 45mins before inserting IVI) is more popular than EMLA® as it does not vasoconstrict. ►The presence of the mother at induction is more powerful than any premed in reducing anxiety.[8]

Specific premedications
- Antibiotic prophylaxis (a single dose at induction is best, *OHCM* p 448).
- Bronchodilators, eg salbutamol nebulizer.
- Nitrate, eg as patch or IVI eg in cardiac surgery.
- Steroids, eg minor operations: 100mg of IM hydrocortisone 1h pre-op and 6h post-op. Major operations hydrocortisone 100mg/6h IM—if adrenal insufficiency or adrenal surgery, or steroid therapy within last 3 months with over 10mg of prednisolone per day.
- For reflux either ranitidine or omeprazole 40mg night before and 2 hours pre-op. In emergency Caesareans, ranitidine can be given IV just before induction with 30mL of sodium citrate PO.[9]
- Pre-op clonidine can ↓post-op analgesia requirement and prevent haemodynamic instability caused by the pneumoperitoneum during laparoscopic cholecystectomy. Its use is nonstandard.[10]

Common reasons for cancellation
- Upper respiratory or recent viral illness if still symptomatic.
- Recent myocardial infarction (eg within last 3 months).
- Patient not adequately fasted.
- U&E imbalance (particularly K^+); anaemia.
- Inadequate preparation (results not available, not crossmatched).
- Patient not in optimum condition—eg poor control of drug therapy (digoxin, thyroxine, phenytoin); exacerbation of illness.
- Undiagnosed or untreated hypertension or uncontrolled atrial fibrillation (heart rate > 100/min).
- Insufficient ITU beds, staff, or theatre time or other logistical problems.

Equipment

Careful checking of equipment is vital before any anaesthetic or sedation procedure. The essentials are an anaesthetic machine plus:
- Tipping bed or trolley (in case of vomiting)
- High-volume suction with rigid (Yankauer) and flexible suction catheters (several)
- Reliable oxygen supply, capable of delivering 15L/min
- Self-inflating bag with oxygen reservoir, non-rebreathing valve and compatible mask (a bag-valve-mask system)
- Oropharyngeal, nasopharyngeal, and laryngeal mask airways
- A range of anatomical face mask sizes
- Endotracheal tubes (range) and introducer/bougie
- Anaesthetic circuits
- Laryngoscope with range of blade sizes, spare bulbs, and batteries
- Intravenous infusion cannula and fluids
- 'Crash cart' and resuscitation drugs and anaesthetic gases
- Defibrillator
- Monitoring equipment, eg pulse oximeter & end-tidal CO_2 monitor (p628).

Inhalational agents

These are the vapours which in clinically useful concentrations help to maintain anaesthesia and decrease awareness. In the UK they are generally added to the fresh gas flow by passing a fraction of the carrier gas (N_2O/O_2 or oxygen and air) through a plenum vaporizer.

Halothane This gas has little analgesic effect. It decreases cardiac output (vagal tone ↑, leading to bradycardia, vasodilation, and hypotension). It sensitizes the myocardium to catecholamines (beware in patients with arrhythmias & surgical infiltration with local anaesthetic and adrenaline (epinephrine)). Halothane has been replaced by safer inhalational agents, due to the rare but serious complication of postoperative hepatitis.

Isoflurane This is a halogenated ether. Theoretically, induction should be quick, but isoflurane is irritant, so coughing, laryngospasm, or breath-holding may complicate the onset of anaesthesia.

Sevoflurane This is a fluorogenated ether which is well tolerated, and the agent of choice for inhalational induction of general anaesthesia with low blood/gas solubility.

Desflurane is another halogenated ether, with a pungent smell and rapid onset of anaesthesia and quick recovery. Meta-analyses of trials in which the duration of anaesthesia was <3h indicate that patients receiving either desflurane or sevoflurane did not have significant differences in time to be discharged from the recovery unit, or in nausea/vomiting frequency. Patients receiving desflurane followed commands, were extubated, and were oriented 2 minutes earlier than those receiving sevoflurane—but this may not be significant clinically. Also, desflurane needs a special vaporizer.

Stopping inhalation reverses all the above effects (except for hepatitis resulting from drug metabolism).

Equipment

Careful checking of equipment is vital before any anaesthetic or sedative procedure. The essentials are an anaesthetic machine plus:

- Tilting bed or trolley (in case of vomiting).
- High-volume suction with rigid Yankauer/long suction catheters. [11]
- Reliable oxygen supply, capable of delivering 15L/min.
- Self-inflating bag with oxygen reservoir, non-rebreathing valve, and compatible mask (a 'bag-valve-mask' system).
- Oropharyngeal, nasopharyngeal, and laryngeal mask airways.
- A range of anatomical face mask sizes.
- Endotracheal tubes (range) and catheter mount.
- Anaesthetic circuit.
- Laryngoscope with range of blade sizes, spare bulbs, and batteries.
- Intravenous infusion cannulae and fluids.
- Anaesthetic and resuscitation drugs and anaesthetic gases.
- Defibrillator.
- Monitoring equipment (eg pulse oximeter ± end tidal CO_2 monitor, p 628).

Inhalational agents

These are the vapours which in clinically useful concentrations help to maintain anaesthesia and decrease awareness. In Britain they are generally added to the fresh gas flow by passing a fraction of the carrier gas (N_2O/O_2 or oxygen enriched air) through a plenum vaporizer.

Halothane This gas has little analgesic effect. It decreases cardiac output (vagal tone ↑, leading to bradycardia, vasodilation, and hypotension). It sensitizes the myocardium to catecholamines (beware in patients with arrhythmias; surgical infiltration with local anaesthetic and adrenaline/epinephrine). Halothane has been replaced by safer inhalational agents, due to the rare but serious complication of postoperative hepatitis.

Isoflurane This is a halogenated ether. Theoretically induction should be quick, but isoflurane is irritant, so coughing, laryngospasm, or breath-holding may complicate the onset of anaesthesia.

Sevoflurane This is a halogenated ether which is well-tolerated. It is the agent of choice for inhalation induction of general anaesthesia with low blood:gas solubility.

Desflurane is another halogenated ether with a pungent smell, rapid onset of anaesthesia, and quick recovery. Meta-analyses of trials in which the duration of anaesthesia was ≤3h indicate that patients receiving either desflurane or sevoflurane did not have significant differences in time to be discharged from the recovery unit, or in nausea/vomiting frequency. Patients receiving desflurane followed commands, were extubated, and were oriented ≥1 minute earlier than those receiving sevoflurane.[1] But this may not be significant clinically. Also, desflurane needs a special vaporizer.

Stopping inhalation reverses all the above effects—except for hepatitis resulting from drug metabolism.

1 Macario A 2005 *Am J Health Syst Pharm* **62** 63

The ideal (but imaginary) IV anaesthetic agent

The ideal IV agent would be stable in solution, be water-soluble and have a long shelf-life. It would be painless when given IV, non-irritant if injected extravascularly (with a low incidence of thrombosis) with some pain (as a warning) if given intra-arterially.

- It should act rapidly within one arm–brain circulation.
- Recovery should be quick and complete with no hangover effect.
- It should provoke no excitatory phenomena.
- Analgesic properties are advantageous.
- Respiratory and cardiovascular effects should be minimal.
- It should not interact with other anaesthetic agents.
- Hypersensitivity reactions are not ideal.
- There should be no post-op phenomena, eg nausea or hallucination.

Commonly used IV anaesthetic agents

Propofol This phenol derivative is the most widely used IV anaesthetic agent and is formulated in soya oil and egg phosphatide.

- Dose example: 2mg/kg IVI at 2–4mg/kg. It is often used in day-case surgery. Rapid injection may cause cardiovascular depression (↓BP) and respiratory depression can occur when combined with IV narcotics. For sedation: 1–4mg/kg/h IVI. It acts and is metabolized quickly. It is used in induction and maintenance of GA, and for sedation during regional anaesthesia, short procedures, and as a sedative in ITU. Cautions: egg allergy, fits; dose depends partly on premed use: with midazolam premeds, propofol requirements are less by up to 20%.
- Its good recovery characteristics and antiemetic effect make it popular.
- Once opened, use ampoules or discard, because of the risk of bacterial growth. Propofol in rubber-capped vials has antibacterial properties.
- Pain on injection occurs in up to 40% of patients. This can be minimized by either adding a small amount of lidocaine (= lignocaine) (2mL of 1%) to the propofol, or by pre-injection of local anaesthetic.

Thiopental sodium (=thiopentone) When mixed with water to give a 2.5% solution this barbiturate is stable for 24–48h, so make it up daily. It has a rapid onset of action (arm-brain circulation time about 30sec). Effects last 3–5min. Awakening is due largely to redistribution, not metabolism. Some 30% of the injected dose is still present in the body after 24h, giving rise to the hangover effect. Patients must not drive, operate machinery etc within 24h. 10mL of 2.5% solution contains 250mg. Dose eg 4–6mL of 2.5% solution, but less in the elderly and the premedicated, and more in children who generally require 5mg/kg (but some children need much less, eg 2mg/kg); subsequent doses are cumulative. Note: thiopental sodium interacts with other drugs, eg increase dose in those who consume much alcohol. Fast induction of GA: it is also a potent anticonvulsant.

Contraindications: • Airway obstruction • Barbiturate allergy • Fixed cardiac output states • Hypovolaemia/shock • Porphyria.

Problems: Intra-arterial injection produces pain and blanching of the hand/limb below the level of injection due to arterial spasm, followed by ischaemic damage and gangrene. Frequently follows inadvertent brachial artery puncture in the antecubital fossa. Treatment:

- Leave the needle in the artery and inject a vasodilator, eg papaverine.
- Heparinization; ask an experienced colleague to perform a brachial plexus or stellate ganglion block. (This should cause vasodilatation and analgesia.)
- Prevent further thrombus forming.
- Give pain relief—and postpone surgery unless desperate.

Extravascular injection causes severe pain and local necrosis: infiltrate with hyaluronidase 1500U dissolved in 1mL water through the cannula.

The ideal (but imaginary) IV anaesthetic agent

The ideal IV agent would be stable in solution, be water-soluble and have a long shelf-life. It would be painless when given IV; non-irritant if injected extravascularly (with a low incidence of thrombosis) with some pain (as a warning) if given intra-arterially.
- It should act rapidly within one arm–brain circulation.
- Recovery should be quick and complete with no hangover effect.
- It should provoke no excitatory phenomena.
- Analgesic properties are advantageous.
- Respiratory and cardiovascular effects should be minimal.
- It should not interact with other anaesthetic agents.
- Hypersensitivity reactions are not ideal.
- There should be no post-op phenomena, eg nausea or hallucinations.

Commonly used IV anaesthetic agents

Propofol This phenol derivative is the most widely used IV anaesthetic agent and is formulated in soya oil and egg phosphatid.
- ***Dose example:*** 2mg/kg IVI at 2–4mg/sec. It is often used in day-case surgery. ►Rapid injection can cause cardiovascular depression (↓BP), and respiratory depression can occur when combined with IV narcotics. For sedation: 1.5–4.5mg/kg/h IVI. It acts and is metabolized quickly. It is used in induction and maintenance of GA, and for sedation during regional anaesthesia, short procedures, and as a sedative in ITU. CI: the extremities of age; egg allergy. NB: dose depends partly on premed use: with midazolam premeds, propofol requirements are less by up to 20%.[12]
- Its good recovery characteristics and anti-emetic effect make it popular.
- Once opened, use ampoules or discard, because of the risk of bacterial growth. Propofol in rubber-capped vials has antibacterial properties.
- Pain on injection occurs in up to 40% of patients. This can be minimized by either adding a small amount of lidocaine (=lignocaine) (2mL of 1%) to the propofol, or by pre-injection of local anaesthetic.

Thiopental sodium ($t_{½}$=11h) When mixed with water to give a 2.5% solution this barbiturate is stable for 24–48h, so make it up daily. It has a rapid onset of action (arm–brain circulation time about 30sec). Effects last 3–8min. Awakening is due largely to redistribution, not metabolism. Some 30% of the injected dose is still present in the body after 24h, giving rise to the hangover effect. Patients must not drive, operate machinery etc within 24h. One mL of 2.5% solution contains 25mg/mL. *Dose:* eg 4–6mL of 2.5% solution (3–5mg/kg, but less in the elderly and the premedicated, and more in children who generally require 6–7mg/kg, but some children need much less, eg 2mg/kg.) Subsequent doses are cumulative. Note: thiopental sodium interacts with other drugs eg increase dose in those who consume much alcohol. Uses: induction of GA; it is also a potent anticonvulsant.

Contraindications: • Airway obstruction • Barbiturate allergy • Fixed cardiac output states • Hypovolaemia/shock • Porphyria.

►Problems: Intra-arterial injection produces pain and blanching of the hand/limb below the level of injection due to arterial spasm, followed by ischaemic damage and gangrene—frequently following inadvertent brachial artery puncture in the antecubital fossa. ***Treatment:***

1. Leave the needle in the artery and inject a vasodilator, eg papaverine.
2. Perform, or ask an experienced colleague to perform, brachial plexus or stellate ganglion block. (This should dilate vessels and ↓ischaemia.)
3. Heparin IV to stop thrombus forming.
4. Give pain relief—and postpone surgery unless desperate.

Extravascular injection causes severe pain and local necrosis. Infiltrate with hyaluronidase 1500iu dissolved in 1mL water through the cannula.

Other IV anaesthetic agents (See p 620)

Etomidate ($t_{½}$=3.5h) This is a carboxylated imidazole. It is used as an induction agent. *Dose:* 0.1–0.3mg/kg. Histamine release is not a feature; rapidity of recovery and cardiovascular stability are; therefore it is suitable for day-case surgery, the elderly, and those with compromised cardiovascular systems. Be aware that this may induce involuntary muscle movements, nausea, and adrenal suppression.

Ketamine[1] (an N-methyl-d-aspartate receptor antagonist, used mainly for paediatric anaesthesia) *Dose:* 0.5–2mg/kg; $t_{½}$=2.2h. This is a phencyclidine derivative. There may be delay before onset of sleep. Hypertonus and salivation are problems, but there is some maintenance of laryngeal reflexes (do not rely on this). Recovery is slow. Emergence phenomena are troublesome (delirium, hallucinations, nightmares; all made worse if the patient is disturbed during recovery). Cardiac output is unchanged or increased. It is a good 'on site' or 'in the field' agent, as it can be given IM and produces profound analgesia without compounding shock. ►Avoid in the hypertensive patient, those with a history of stroke, or raised intracranial pressure (further ↑ produced), patients with a recent penetrating eye injury (risk of ↑ intra-ocular pressure), and psychiatric patients. Avoid adrenaline (epinephrine) infiltrations. It is uncommonly used in developed countries, probably the most widely used anaesthetic drug in developing countries. In the UK, the Home Office classifies it as a class C drug (like cannabis) as it is prone to misuse ('Special-K').

Ideal weight and drug dosages To avoid excessive dosage in obese patients it may be best to calculate the dose on the basis of ideal body-weight (IBW). ***In males***, IBW = 50kg + 2.3kg for each inch over 5 feet tall. ***In females***, IBW = 45.5kg+2.3kg for each inch over 5 feet tall. See www.globalrph.com

Anaesthesia

1 Elia N 2005 *Pain* **113** 61

Neuromuscular blockers

►Never give a muscle relaxant in the presence of a compromised airway.

These drugs act on the post-synaptic receptors at the NMJ (neuromuscular junction). There are two main groups:

1 Depolarizing agents eg suxamethonium (=succinylcholine, Scoline®). These drugs depolarize the post-synaptic membrane, causing paralysis by inhibiting the normal membrane polarity. They are partial agonists for acetylcholine and cause initial fasciculation, liberating K^+, enough to raise the plasma K^+ by ~0.5-1.0mmol/L (avoid in paraplegia and burns!), myoglobin and creatine kinase. Beware that K^+ liberation is increased with multiple sclerosis, Guillain–Barré, stroke, and crush injury. Suxamethonium increases intra-ocular pressure (eg increase risk of vitreous extrusion). 30% of patients get post-operative muscle pains. Suxamethonium is an ideal intubating agent: it has a rapid onset, a short duration of action (2-6min), and produces good relaxation. Note: a second dose, if required, should be preceded by atropine, as the vagotonic effects of suxamethonium can lead to profound bradycardia. Beware suxamethonium (Scoline®) apnoea (p 628). Dose of suxamethonium: eg 1-1.5mg/kg IV. Bradycardia related to the 1st dose is an occasional problem in children.

2 Non-depolarizing agents These drugs compete with acetylcholine at the NMJ—but without producing initial stimulation (see suxamethonium above). Repeated doses may be given without atropine. Their action can be reversed by anticholinesterases (neostigmine). They are used during balanced anaesthesia to facilitate IPPV and surgery. Length of action and side-effects will govern anaesthetists' choices. Examples of the more common agents are:

Vecuronium: Lasting 20-30min, it is used if cardiovascular stability is important. No ganglion-blocking effect. *Dose:* 80-100μg/kg IV then 20-30μg/kg IV as needed. Starting dose for infants ≤4 months: 10-20μg/kg. If over 5 months, as adult dose, but high intubation dose may not be needed for the age group between 5 months and 1 year. Known as the 'cleanest' of these three agents due to least histamine release.

Atracurium: Lasting ~20min this causes histamine release so avoid in asthma. Metabolism is by Hoffman Elimination (spontaneous molecular breakdown), so it is the drug of choice in renal and liver failure.
Dose: 300-600μg/kg IV then 100-150μg/kg IV as needed.

Pancuronium: Long acting (~1h), vagal blockade and sympathomimetic action. *Dose:* 50-100μg/kg IV then 10-20μg/kg IV as needed. (No longer used in some anaesthetic practice.)

Other non-depolarizing agents in use include cisatracurium, rocuronium (fastest onset of the non-depolarizing drugs), and mivacurium.

Note on neuromuscular blockers in those with myasthenia In general, these patients are resistant to suxamethonium and very sensitive to non-depolarizing relaxants (action may be prolonged: lower doses may be needed). Warn patients that mechanical ventilation may be needed post-op. Liaise closely with a senior anaesthetist. A small dose of atracurium is most commonly used.

Practical conduct of anaesthesia: I

The practitioner administering the anaesthetic is responsible for the suitability of the surroundings, the adequacy of the available equipment, and his own competence to deal with potential complications. Equipment must be checked before even the shortest anaesthetic procedure.

Induction May be gaseous or IV (IM possible with ketamine).

Gaseous
- Either start with nitrous oxide, oxygen 60%:40% mixture. In children, it is less frightening to start with a hand cupped from the end of the circuit onto the face than to apply the mask direct to face.
- Or, give sevoflurane in oxygen according to patient's age and clinical state for rapid induction of general anaesthesia.
- Monitor vital signs closely as the time factor separating a struggling child from a flaccid, apnoeic, overdosed child is short.
- Establish IV access when and where appropriate, as soon as asleep.

Indications for gaseous induction:
- Some patients with airway obstruction (actual or potential, eg foreign body, tumour, or abscess).
- At the patient's request.
- Difficult IV access.

Intravenous
- Establish IV access.
- A sleep-inducing dose of, eg thiopental (=thiopentone) sodium, is injected after a 2mL test dose to detect inadvertent arterial cannulation (p 629).
- Beware: Stimulation before anaesthesia is established can have drastic consequences (vomiting, breath-holding, laryngospasm). Remember, noise is a stimulus too.

Airway control This is maintained either by holding a mask onto the face, by inserting a laryngeal mask airway, or by intubation (p 627). To prevent airway obstruction, standard chin lift and/or jaw thrust manoeuvres are used. It may be facilitated by the use of an airway adjunct (eg oropharyngeal or nasopharyngeal). Insertion of an airway adjunct may produce vomiting or laryngospasm.

Ensure the patient is adequately anaesthetized, as laryngoscopy and endotracheal intubation can produce a harmful adrenergic stress response with adverse increases in pulse and BP. Concurrent short acting opiates or esmolol IV can attenuate this in a dose-dependent way.

Practical conduct of anaesthesia: I

The practitioner administering the anaesthetic is responsible for the suitability of the surroundings, the adequacy of the available equipment, and his own competence to deal with potential complications. Equipment *must* be checked before even the shortest anaesthetic procedure.

Induction May be gaseous or IV (IM possible with ketamine).

Gaseous:

- Either start with nitrous oxide: oxygen 60%:40% mixture. In children, it is less frightening to start with a hand cupped from the end of the circuit onto the face than to apply the mask direct to face.
- Or give sevoflurane in oxygen according to patient's age and clinical state for rapid induction of general anaesthesia.
- Monitor vital signs closely, as the time factor separating a struggling child from a flaccid, apnoeic, overdosed child is short.
- Establish IV access when and where appropriate, as soon as asleep.

Indications for gaseous induction:

- Some patients with airway obstruction (actual or potential, eg foreign body, tumour, or abscess).
- At the patient's request.
- Difficult IV access.

Intravenous:

- Establish IV access.
- A sleep-inducing dose of, eg thiopental (=thiopentone) sodium, is injected after a 2mL test dose to detect inadvertent arterial cannulation (p 620).
- Beware! Stimulation before anaesthesia is established can have drastic consequences (coughing, breath-holding, laryngospasm). Remember, noise is a stimulus too.

Airway control This is maintained either by holding a mask onto the face, by inserting a laryngeal mask airway, or by intubation (p 627). To prevent airway obstruction, standard chin lift and/or jaw thrust manoeuvres are used. It may be facilitated by the use of an airway adjunct (eg oropharyngeal, or nasopharyngeal). Insertion of an airway adjunct may produce vomiting or laryngospasm.

Ensure the patient is adequately anaesthetized, as laryngoscopy and endotracheal intubation can produce a harmful *adrenergic stress response* with adverse increases in pulse and BP. Concurrent short-acting opiates or esmolol IVI can attenuate this in a dose-dependent way.[MET 13]

Mechanical ventilation

Indications: Ventilators are used in anaesthesia when there is an operative need for muscle paralysis, or when muscle paralysis is part of a balanced general anaesthetic for a long operation. (Ventilators are used in intensive care for ventilatory support in reversible acute respiratory failure—this is a different topic: see eg p 110.)

Modes:

- Whenever surgeons open the pleural cavity to operate on the heart, lungs, or oesophagus, *intermittent positive pressure ventilation* is required (IPPV). These ventilators have controls to alter the respiratory rate, the tidal volume, and the pressure necessary to inflate the lungs. Other controls may be available to adjust the inspiratory time, the inspiratory flow wave form, the end tidal pause, and the I:E ratio (I:E means the ratio of inspiratory to expiratory time).
- Some ventilators deliver ***synchronized intermittent mandatory ventilation*** which allows the patient to start breathing spontaneously when paralysis wears off, providing assistance if these breaths are inadequate. These are less common in theatre, and more often used in intensive care units.
- Specialized patterns of ventilation are not commonly available using ventilators designed for operating theatre use.

►It is mandatory for ventilators to have disconnect, high pressure, and oxygen failure alarms.

The practical conduct of anaesthesia: II

Intubation This is needed for protection of the airway in:

- Risk of vomiting/aspiration of gastric contents (eg reflux oesophagitis, abdominal disease, major trauma, non-fasted, hiatus hernia, pregnancy).
- Management of difficult airways. If difficulty is suspected, ensure senior help is available/consider fibreoptic or awake intubation.
- Head and neck surgery, where masks clutter the operative field.
- Where muscle paralysis facilitates surgery, eg abdominal surgery.

►Paralyzed patients cannot breathe—and so require ventilation.

Intubation requires good muscle relaxation:

- Deep anaesthesia in the spontaneously breathing patient.
- Use of short- or long-acting muscle relaxant.

Short-acting: (suxamethonium, typically 1mg/kg IV) Uses: • If risk of vomiting ↑. • When difficulty with intubation is anticipated. • If the intention is to let the patient breathe spontaneously via the ET tube.

Long-acting: Numerous available, eg vecuronium 0.1mg/kg IV. They take longer to provide suitable conditions for intubation. Remember it will be at least 20min before breathing recommences, so *if there is any doubt as to the ability to maintain a patent airway, then a short-acting (or even no) muscle relaxant is more appropriate.*

Rapid sequence induction Used where the risk of vomiting is high (eg trauma, non-fasted, pregnancy >15 weeks' gestation, hiatus hernia).

- Pre-oxygenate with 100% oxygen for 3min to provide an O_2 reservoir in the lungs for use during the period of induced apnoea.
- Cricoid pressure on induction (firm backward pressure on cricoid cartilage occluding oesophagus may stop gastric reflux to larynx).
- Short-acting muscle relaxant is given immediately after induction. The trachea is intubated, and the cuff of the ET tube inflated.
- Once the ET tube is correctly positioned, cricoid pressure may be released, and a volatile agent added to maintain anaesthesia.

Maintenance of anaesthesia

1. Volatile agent added to N_2O/O_2 mixture as before. Either spontaneously breathing or ventilation, with or without opiates. If the patient is ventilated, muscle relaxants are generally used.
2. High-dose opiates with mechanical ventilation.
3. IV infusion anaesthesia, eg propofol ± opiates. *Maintenance dose of propofol:* 4–12mg/kg/h IVI. SE: anaphylaxis.

Whatever the technique, the dose and concentration of each drug used is adjusted according to the level of anaesthesia achieved versus the desired level (determined by monitoring vital signs—eg pulse, BP, signs of sympathetic stimulation such as sweating, pupillary dilatation, lacrimation etc).

End of anaesthesia Change inspired gases to 100% oxygen only, then:

- Discontinue any infusions of anaesthetic drugs.
- Reverse muscle paralysis with neostigmine (~2.5mg in adults) + an anticholinergic to prevent its muscarinic side-effects (bradycardia, salivation), eg atropine 1.2mg IV (or glycopyrronium 500μg—preferred with neostigmine).
- Once spontaneously breathing, put the patient in the recovery position (p 799). Before the ET tube is removed the mouth and oropharynx should be cleared under direct vision. Then administer oxygen by face mask.
- If there are no problems, transfer to the recovery room, but be prepared to reassess the patient at any time.

Intubation technique

Preparation is the key word. Always assess neck mobility, (arthritis, ankylosing spondylitis, goitre etc) pre-op. Beware the obese, short-necked, chinless patient with protruding teeth!

- ET tube sizes (mm internal diameter, ID): 8.5 in adult ♂, 7.5 in ♀. Children:
  ID = [age in years/4] + 4.0mm (*neonate = 3–3.5mm*)
  Length (oral) = [age/2] + 12.5cm
  Length (nasal) = [age/2] + 14.5cm
  Broselow tape-measures are said to be more accurate.[14]
- Lubricate the tube, and check that its cuff and the laryngoscope work.
- Position the patient with neck flexed and head extended using a pillow ('sniffing the morning air').
- Hold the laryngoscope in the left hand; open the mouth with the right.
- Slide the laryngoscope blade down the right side of the tongue into the vallecula (area between tongue and epiglottis), guarding the lip and teeth with the fingers of your right hand.
- Lift the laryngoscope blade upwards and away from yourself. DO NOT lever on the teeth or you may damage them.
- Lift the epiglottis from view: the cords should become visible. When they are, insert the tube with your right hand (anatomy—p 567).
- Once the cuff of the endotracheal tube is beyond the cords, remove the laryngoscope; ask the assistant to inflate the cuff to prevent air leak.
- Attach to the circuit. Gently inflate lungs. Watch the chest move. Do both sides move equally? Is the abdomen moving and not the chest?
- Auscultate both sides of chest. Is air entry equal? Fix the tube with a tie.
- Confirm correct placement with capnography (detects CO_2, p 628).

►Remember: *if in doubt, take it out.* It is safer to re-intubate than to risk leaving a tube in the oesophagus happily inflating the stomach. Tubes may slip down a main bronchus (usually right). If so, withdraw, until both sides of the chest move equally, and air entry is equal (so avoiding collapse in the unventilated lung, or pneumothorax on the overventilated side).

If you are having problems intubating: ►Adequate oxygenation is top priority. • Get help • Blind nasal and fibreoptic intubation are options, if experienced • If you find you need another dose of suxamethonium, give atropine first, to prevent bradycardia • Consider a laryngeal mask (below).

Laryngeal mask airway (LMA, a half-way house between a simple airway and an endotracheal tube.) It is used in 50% of elective UK surgery, and in cardiac arrests where a skilled intubator is not present. It consists of a tube with a cuff designed to sit over the larynx. A cuff takes ~30mL of air (depends on size). It is more efficient than masks (eg if arthritis prevents the neck extension needed by masks).

During its use, nasogastric aspiration of air is occasionally needed (and usually only if used with IPPV). Advantages are that *no laryngoscope is needed* (no damage to teeth or cord stimulation), and *ease of insertion*. Lubricate the cuff, and slide over the palate, so the device sits over the larynx. Learn the method at the bedside. It is available in a range of sizes from 1.0 to 5.0 (in the UK, available eg via Intavent (01628 594500). It is safe and effective.[15]

Specialized LMAs can assist with difficult intubation (eg the Intubating Laryngeal Mask Airway, LMA),[16] and allow air and fluid to be aspirated from the stomach (eg the Proseal®).

If unable to intubate? ►►Learn *beforehand* about location and use of equipment such as the combitube or cricothyrotomy kit (*OHCM* p 756).

Monitoring during anaesthesia

Monitoring begins prior to induction of anaesthesia and continues throughout. ►*A warm, pink, and well-perfused patient is the aim.* Sweating and lacrimation invariably indicate something is wrong: ***Respiration:*** Rate, depth (IPPV if inadequate). ***BP:*** Intra-arterial in long cases. ***T °:*** Particularly important in infants. (Large surface area to body mass may lead to hypothermia.) A warm environment, warming blankets, and warming IV fluid, are important in long cases. ***Pulse oximetry:*** Computes pulse rate and arterial O_2 saturation, but does not obviate need for manual pulse checks. ***ECG:*** Reveals rate, arrhythmias, and ischaemia. ***CVP:*** Helps differentiate hypovolaemia from ↓cardiac function. Insert when large blood loss is anticipated, or in unstable patients. ***Capnography*** and ***Inspired gas analysis*** are essential. A low end tidal CO_2 warns of a displaced endotracheal tube, emboli, and more. Also monitor neuromuscular status and ventilator pressures. End-tidal volatile agent concentration may also be monitored.

Bispectral Index (BIS) EEG monitoring helps measure of the depth of GA.

Some complications of anaesthesia

►***The commonest respiratory complication is airway obstruction from loss of muscle tone in the soft palate ('swallowing the tongue').***

Atelectasis and pneumonia Atelectasis is best seen on CT (not CXRs). It starts within minutes of induction, and is partly caused by using 100% O_2. ℞: good pain relief aids coughing. Arrange physio + antibiotics (*OHCM* p 173).

Laryngospasm The cords are firmly shut. Treat with 100% oxygen. Attempt to ventilate. It may be necessary to paralyze and intubate.

Bronchospasm Ensure oxygenation. If intubated, check tube position (carina stimulation may be the cause: withdraw tube slightly). Check for pneumothorax. (Increase concentration of volatile agent if he is 'light'.) Salbutamol 250μg eg by IV, aminophylline (p 165) + hyperventilation with 100% O_2. If persistent, give hydrocortisone 100mg IV and consider epinephrine (=adrenaline, 1-10mL up to 0.1mL/kg of 1:10,000 IV). **Anaphylaxis** See p 237.

Shivering ± hypothermia Preventable with 'space blankets', and may be treated by radiant heat and pethidine for shivering (0.3mg/kg slowly IV). Be aware that shivering increases O_2 consumption 5-fold.

Scoline apnoea (Abnormal cholinesterase) ventilate until power returns.

Malignant hyperpyrexia (Autosomal dominant). Rapidly rising temperature (>2°C/h) is precipitated by eg halothane or suxamethonium. Masseter spasm may be the first indication, then tachycardia, mottling, hypercarbia, hyperkalaemia, arrhythmias, hypoxaemia, and acidosis.

Treatment: • Get senior help; stop all precipitants and stop surgery. • Hyperventilate with O_2. • Active cooling (ice packs, cold IVI). • Take to ITU • Dantrolene 1mg/kg IV bolus; repeat as needed till up to 10mg/kg given. • Mannitol for myoglobinuria. • Correct acidosis (sodium bicarbonate). • Treat any hyperkalaemia (*OHCM* p 825; children p 176 this book) • Encourage diuresis • Insulin • Steroids, eg hydrocortisone 100mg IV. • Phenotype relatives (muscle biopsy response to halothane and caffeine). • Get a Medicalert® bracelet, and a letter to give to future anaesthetists.

Awareness This is most distressing for patients. Neuromuscular blockade makes its diagnosis difficult; the BIS monitor (above) may ↓incidence. ***Prevalence:*** Much less than 1% even in emergency/obstetric anaesthesia (here doses used are minimized, to avoid shock). It is still rarer in other contexts (eg 0.2%).

Sedation

Definition: Sedation is an induced depression in conscious level, during which verbal contact is maintained with the patient.

Doctors in many specialties may be called to provide [illegible] sedation. The doctor giving the sedation may not be also responsible for performing any procedure [illegible] the role [illegible] is to ensure that the sedation is adequate, and to monitor the patient's airway, breathing, and circulation. Sedation is not a short cut to avoid formal anaesthesia, and it does not excuse the patient from an appropriate work-up or assessment [illegible]. Monitoring is mandatory, and should include pulse oximetry.

It is easy for sedation to become general anaesthesia with its attendant risks (see p 626). The loss of the eyelash reflex (gently stroking of the upper eyelashes produces blinking) is a good guide to the onset of general anaesthesia.

[illegible] after GA may persist for months: it is unknown whether lesser forms of anaesthesia can do this [illegible].

Agents

- **Midazolam:** Initial adult dose: 2mg IV over 1min (1mg if elderly). Further 0.5–1mg may be needed after 2min. Usual range 2.5–7.5mg (elderly 1–3.5mg). [illegible] functional.
- In some circumstances (eg manipulation of large joints, painful dressing changes), a narcotic analgesic may be used in addition (eg morphine in [illegible]). Shorter acting opioids such as fentanyl or small incremental doses of ketamine may be administered.
- [illegible] is an option: [illegible] via a face mask.

Recovery from anaesthesia

Ensure the [illegible] during [illegible]:

- Give O_2 [illegible]
- [illegible] hypoxaemia [illegible]
- Monitor pulse and BP.
- Keep the patient warm.
- Look for [illegible] — check with [illegible] for [illegible] with [illegible] care of airway [illegible] adequate analgesia.
- Return the patient to the ward when you are satisfied with his cardiovascular and respiratory status and [illegible].
- Give clear instructions on post-operative fluid regimes, [illegible] oxygen therapy, [illegible] and [illegible].
- Post-op vomiting is [illegible] ([illegible] eg [illegible]).

[illegible] unless [illegible].

[illegible] analgesia [illegible] with [illegible] opioids, with [illegible].

[illegible] also [illegible] respiratory [illegible].

[illegible]

Sedation

Definition: Sedation is an induced reduction in conscious level, during which verbal contact is maintained with the patient.

Doctors in many specialties may be required to administer sedation. The doctor giving the sedation *must not* be also responsible for performing any procedure (such as manipulation of a dislocated joint). His sole responsibility is to ensure that the sedation is adequate, and to monitor the patient's airway, breathing, and circulation. Sedation is not a short cut to avoid formal anaesthesia, and it does not excuse the patient from an appropriate work-up or reasonable fasting. Monitoring is mandatory, and should include pulse oximetry.

It is easy for sedation to become general anaesthesia, with its attendant risks (see p 628). The loss of the 'eyelash reflex' (gentle stroking of the upper eyelashes to produce blinking) is a good guide to the onset of general anaesthesia.

In the elderly, ↓cognition after GA may persist for months: it is unknown whether lesser forms of anaesthesia can obviate this.[17]

Agents

- Midazolam: Initial adult dose 2mg IV over 1min (1mg if elderly). Further 0.5–1mg IV as needed after 2min. Usual range 3.5–7.5mg (elderly max 3.5mg). SE: psychomotor function↓.[18]
  In some circumstances (eg manipulation of large joint; painful dressing changes) a narcotic analgesic may be used in addition (eg morphine in 1–2mg aliquots IV, or shorter acting opioids such as fentanyl), or small incremental doses of ketamine may be administered.
- Diazepam (as emulsion = Diazemuls®): initial adult dose 2.5–10mg IV over 4min via a large vein.

Recovery from anaesthesia

- Ensure same monitoring as *during* anaesthesia.
- 40% O_2 via a face mask for >15min to assist with any respiratory depression or ventilation/perfusion mismatch.[1]
- Monitor pulse and BP.
- Keep the patient warm.
- Look for hypoventilation (?inadequate reversal—check with nerve stimulator; narcosis—reverse opiates with naloxone—*cautiously* to minimize pain; check for airway obstruction, eg from bleeding tonsil). Ensure adequate analgesia.
- Return the patient to the ward when you are satisfied with his cardiovascular and respiratory status and pain relief.
- Give clear instructions on post-operative fluid regimens, blood transfusions, oxygen therapy, pain relief, and physiotherapy.
- Post-op vomiting is partly preventable by a 5-HT_3 antagonist eg granisetron, or dexamethasone.

  Metoclopramide is less good.[19] [MET 20] [MET 21]

  Epidural local anaesthetics ↓GI paralysis compared with systemic or epidural opioids, with comparable pain relief.[22]

  Epidurals may also ↓post-op risk of respiratory failure.[RCT 23]

1 For a short duration (<5mins) while very soluble nitrous oxide is diffusing out of the circulation into the alveoli, the concentration of O_2 in alveolar gas will be falling (diffusion hypoxia).

Local anaesthesia

All regional techniques may lead to loss of consciousness or loss of airway and so require the same facilities, expertise, and precautions as for general anaesthesia (eg full resuscitation facilities and patient fasted).

Local anaesthesia is used either alone or to supplement general anaesthesia: the aim is to prevent or reduce nerve conduction of painful impulses to higher centres (via the thalamus), where the perception of pain occurs. (Action is by a membrane-stabilizing effect, impairing membrane permeability to sodium, so blocking impulse propagation.)

Types of local anaesthesia (LA) Amides:

1 Lidocaine (=lignocaine) $t_{1/2}$≈2h, max dose in typical healthy adult: 3mg/kg up to 200mg (500mg with epinephrine, but use with caution).

2 Prilocaine $t_{1/2}$≈2h. Moderate onset. The dose is 3-6mg/kg; 400mg is the maximum dose in adults (600mg if used with felypressin). Very low toxicity, so it is the drug of choice for Bier's block (IV regional anaesthesia).

3 Bupivacaine (levobupivacaine)[1] $t_{1/2}$≈3h. Slow onset and prolonged duration. Contraindicated in intravenous regional anaesthesia (Bier's block). (NB: levobupivacaine is a newer less cardiotoxic local analgesic, otherwise similar in action to bupivacaine.) For dose see BNF.

4 Ropivacaine $t_{1/2}$≈1.8h. Dose see BNF. Less cardiotoxic than bupivacaine. Less motor block when used epidurally. Contraindicated for regional anaesthesia and paracervical block in obstetrics.

Note 0.5% solution=5mg/mL; 1% solution=10mg/mL. So for a 70kg man, the max dose of lidocaine is 20mL of 1% or 10mL of 2% solution. NB: lidocaine injections are less painful if they are warm, or at lower concentrations.

Certain commercially available preparations contain adrenaline (=epinephrine): these should be used with extreme caution, as systemic effects from the adrenaline may arise and prove hazardous, especially in CVS disease or ↑BP.

• Adrenaline (epinephrine) is ABSOLUTELY contraindicated in digital or penile blocks and around the nose or ears (the ischaemia produced may cause gangrene.)

Esters (infrequently used now.)

1 Cocaine. Very high toxicity. Short duration of action. Used as a paste preparation for anaesthesia and vasoconstriction prior to nasal intubation or nasal surgery.

2 Tetracaine $t_{1/2}$≈1h. Slow onset. High toxicity. Drops for topical anaesthesia to eye (the eye must be covered with a patch following use) and now topically as an alternative to EMLA®.

Toxicity From excess dose, too rapid absorption, or direct IV injection.

Features: Perioral tingling; numb tongue; anxiety; lightheadedness; tinnitus; seizures; apnoea; collapse; direct myocardial depression; coma.

Treatment: Ensure oxygenation.

• Hypotension: try IV fluids first, then consider ephedrine 3mg IV as a slow bolus (may be repeated every 3–4min to a total of 30mg).

• Convulsions: thiopental (=thiopentone) sodium or benzodiazepines, eg IV Diazemuls® 2.5–5mg, or midazolam 1mg boluses. Intubation/IPPV will probably also be needed.

• CVS collapse: full resuscitation, ie intubation, adrenaline (=epinephrine), atropine, and cardiac massage as required.

Anaphylaxis (p 237) Occurs more commonly with the esters, but can occur with amides. A 2mL test dose can detect possible allergic reactions, but not anaphylaxis (and can warn of inadvertent intravascular injection).

1 Racemic bupivacaine contains D- and L-isomers; the D-isomer may cause cardiac problems. 2 Non-enantiomeric molecules having the same formula but 2 possible mirror-image structures (enantiomers). A racemic mixture contains equal amounts of both enantiomers ... the S-isomer (L-enantiomer) to the R-[illegible]

Local anaesthesia

►All regional techniques may lead to loss of consciousness or loss of airway, and so require the same facilities, expertise, and precautions as for general anaesthesia (eg full resuscitation facilities and patient fasted).

Local anaesthesia is used either alone or to supplement general anaesthesia, the aim is to prevent or reduce nerve conduction of painful impulses to higher centres (via the thalamus), where the perception of pain occurs. (Action is by a membrane-stabilizing effect, impairing membrane permeability to sodium, so blocking impulse propagation.)

Types of local anaesthesia (LA) ***Amides:***

1 Lidocaine (=lignocaine) $t_{½}$=2h; max dose in typical healthy adult=3mg/kg up to 200mg (500mg with epinephrine, but use with caution).
2 Prilocaine $t_{½}$=2h. Moderate onset. The dose is 3-5mg/kg. (400mg is the maximum dose in adults; 300mg if used with felypressin.) Very low toxicity, so it is the drug of choice for Bier's block (IV regional anaesthesia).
3 Bupivacaine (levobupivocaine[1]) $t_{½}$=3h. Slow onset and prolonged duration. Contraindicated in intravenous regional anaesthesia (Bier's block). (NB: levobupivacaine is a newer less cardiotoxic local analgesic, otherwise similar in action to bupivacaine.) For dose see *BNF*.
4 Ropivacaine $t_{½}$=1.8h. Dose: see *BNF*. Less cardiotoxic than bupivacaine. Less motor block when used epidurally. Contraindicated for regional anaesthesia and paracervical block in obstetrics.

Note: 0.5% solution=5mg/mL. 1% solution=10mg/mL. So for a 70kg man, the max dose of lidocaine is 20mL of 1% or 10mL of 2% solution. NB: lidocaine injections are less painful if they are *warm*, or at lower concentrations.

Certain commercially available preparations contain adrenaline (=epinephrine); these should be used with extreme caution, as systemic effects from the adrenaline may arise and prove hazardous, especially in CVS disease or ↑BP.

►*Adrenaline (epinephrine) is ABSOLUTELY contraindicated in digital or penile blocks, and around the nose or ears.* (Ischaemia produced may cause gangrene.)

Esters (Infrequently used now.)

1 Cocaine. Very high toxicity. Short duration of action. Used as a paste preparation for anaesthesia and vasoconstriction prior to nasal intubation or nasal surgery.
2 Tetracaine $t_{½}$=1h. Slow onset. High toxicity. *Drops* for topical anaesthesia to eye (the eye must be covered with a patch following use), and now *topically* as an alternative to EMLA®.

Toxicity From excess dose, too rapid absorption, or direct IV injection.

Features: Perioral tingling; numb tongue; anxiety; lightheadedness; tinnitus; seizures; apnoea; collapse; direct myocardial depression; coma.

Treatment: Ensure oxygenation.

- Hypotension: try IV fluids first, then consider ephedrine 5mg IV as a slow bolus (may be repeated every 3–4min to a total of 30mg).
- Convulsions: thiopental (=thiopentone) sodium, or benzodiazepines, eg IV Diazemuls® 2.5-5mg, or midazolam 5mg boluses. Intubation/IPPV will probably also be needed.
- CVS collapse: full resuscitation, ie intubation, adrenaline (=epinephrine), atropine, and cardiac massage as required.

Anaphylaxis (p 237) Occurs more commonly with the esters, but can occur with amides. A 2mL test dose can detect possible allergic reactions, but not anaphylaxis (and can warn of inadvertent intravascular injection).

1 Racemic mixtures contain D & L isomers; the D isomer may cause cardiac problems. NB: stereoisomerism describes molecules having the same formula but a 2 possible mirror-image structures (enantiomers). R (rectus) enantiomers rotate light to the right; S (sinister) enantiomers to the left.

Local and neuraxial anaesthesia: techniques

(Local blocks see [illegible])

- Explain the procedure [illegible] co-operation [illegible]. Obtain informed consent.

1 Infiltration: Use a small gauge needle [illegible] lidocaine [illegible] [illegible] [illegible] [illegible] through infiltrated [illegible] edges of [illegible] less pain [illegible]

2 Topical: [illegible] lidocaine [illegible] spray [illegible] prior to [illegible]

3 Nerve blocks: [illegible] [illegible] stimulation [illegible]

Femoral nerve block: [illegible] femoral sheath. Useful for [illegible] femur.

- [illegible] the inguinal ligament [illegible] femoral artery [illegible] iliac spine [illegible] femoral artery.
- Insert [illegible] below the ligament [illegible] and again on [illegible] position [illegible] with a nerve stimulator.
- Aspiration test, then inject eg 0.25% bupivacaine, 20–30mL.

Spinal anaesthesia

- Insert IV cannula and [illegible] crystalloid [illegible]
- Sit or left lateral position [illegible]
- Infiltrate skin with 1% lidocaine [illegible]
- Insert a [illegible] spinal needle at L3–4 [illegible] ensure that all the needle [illegible]
- Inject [illegible] bupivacaine [illegible] solution that falls by gravity [illegible] the height of block [illegible]
- Position patient [illegible] unilateral block [illegible]
- [illegible] BP may fall [illegible]

A [illegible] drug concentration [illegible] sympathetic block [illegible] motor blockade [illegible] lower limb [illegible]

Absolute contraindications to spinal anaesthesia

- Coagulopathy [illegible] (risk [illegible] cord [illegible])
- Local sepsis (risk [illegible])
- [illegible]
- Raised intracranial pressure
- Unwilling or uncooperative patient
- [illegible]

Relative contraindications to spinal anaesthesia

- [illegible]
- [illegible]
- Spinal deformity or previous surgery
- [illegible]

Local and neuraxial anaesthesia: techniques

(►Bier's block: see p 742)

►Explain the procedure (co-operation helps). Obtain informed consent.

1 ***Infiltration:*** Use a small gauge needle. Lidocaine (=lignocaine) 0.5% is the most common agent. Frequent aspiration is important. Remember: after initial injection, subsequent injections through infiltrated areas hurt less. Likewise, infiltration through the cut edges of a laceration is less painful than through the skin.

2 ***Topical:*** Tetracaine to eye. Lidocaine 4% spray to cords prior to intubation (nil by mouth for 4h afterwards avoids aspiration).

3 ***Nerve blocks:*** Lidocaine (=lignocaine) 1-2%, prilocaine 0.5%, or bupivacaine (levobupivacine) 0.25%. Nerve stimulation increases success rate. It is now believed that it is the *volume* of the anaesthetic agent used, rather than the concentration *per se*, that improves anaesthesia.

Femoral nerve block Direct injection or catheter placement into the femoral sheath. Useful for fractured femur.

- Mark out the inguinal ligament (pubic tubercle to the anterior superior iliac spine). Palpate, and mark, the femoral artery.
- Insert short-bevel needle (insulated if nerve stimulator is used) 1cm lateral to the artery, just below the ligament. A 'click' is felt on traversing the skin, and again on traversing the fascia lata. Find the position either by eliciting paraesthesia, or with a nerve stimulator.
- Aspiration test, then inject eg 0.375% bupivacaine, 20-30mL.

Spinal anaesthesia

- Insert IV cannula and infuse 300-500mL crystalloid. Check BP.
- Sitting or left lateral position. Surgical scrub; gown & gloves. Prepare back.
- Infiltrate skin with 1-2mL 1% lidocaine (=lignocaine).
- Insert a 22-25G spinal needle at L3/4 space (ie below spinal cord). Free flow of CSF confirms correct placement. Rotate the needle through 180° to ensure that all the needle aperture is in (avoids patchy blocks).
- Inject 1-3mL 0.5% Marcain Heavy® (bupivacaine + dextrose, a hyperbaric solution that falls by gravity. This allows the height of block to be varied by posture.) Note—much less LA is required during pregnancy.
- Position patient to achieve low, high, or unilateral block.
- Monitor BP—may fall; if so, give crystalloid ± vasopressors (eg ephedrine 5mg IV repeated as needed (p 632), or phenylephrine 50-100μg).

A small total drug concentration is required—producing sympathetic blockade (vasodilation, hypotension); sensory blockade (numbness); and finally motor blockade (reduction or absence of lower limb power).

Absolute contraindications to spinal anaesthesia:

- Anticoagulant states (risk pressure damage to cord from bleed).
- Local sepsis (risk of introducing infection to CSF).
- Shock or hypovolaemic states (effective reduction in circulating volume due to vasodilatation).
- Raised intracranial pressure.
- Unwilling or unco-operative patient.
- Fixed output states (eg mitral and aortic stenosis).

Relative contraindications to spinal anaesthesia:

- Neurological disease—procedure may be blamed for change in state.
- Ischaemic heart disease.
- Spinal deformity or previous surgery.
- Bowel perforation (theoretical risk of ↑parasympathetic activity, peristalsis and peritoneal soiling).

Extradural (epidural) anaesthesia RCT 24

Insertion of indwelling catheter allows prolonged instillation of LA and/or opiates. Larger volumes of LA are required than with spinal anaesthesia. Lumbar most common site, but cervical/thoracic possible (needs great skill).

- Use aseptic technique, with patient sitting, or in the left lateral position.
- Do BP. Infuse 300–500mL crystalloid.
- L3/4 commonest site. Infiltrate with 1–2mL 0.5% lidocaine (=lignocaine).
- Insert 16G Touhy needle until held firm in ligamentum flavum (~2–3cm).
- 'Loss of resistance' technique finds epidural space: 10mL 0.9% saline via Touhy needle is difficult to inject while in ligaments, but once in the epidural space, sudden loss of resistance enables easy injection.
- Fine-bore epidural catheter threaded, needle withdrawn, and catheter placed to needle depth plus 3–5cm.
- Aspiration test prior to 2mL test done. Wait 3min.
- Inject required dose, eg 10mL 0.25% plain bupivacaine in 5mL aliquots.
- Secure catheter in place.
- Monitor BP every 5min for 15min (slower onset than spinal, therefore hypotension takes longer to be revealed).

Complications of epidural anaesthesia:

- Dural puncture. CSF leak may not be obvious, hence the importance of test dose. (Ward tests for glucose will be +ve on fluid appearing during injection if CSF present.) Push oral fluids, with caffeine. Nurse flat. Prescribe analgesics for headaches, laxatives to prevent constipation and straining. Blood patch is usually necessary if headache persists longer than 24–48h. *Inform a consultant.*
- Vessel puncture and injection. Treat with oxygen, IVI, pressor drugs, atropine if bradycardia (due to block of sympathetic outflow to heart T2–4), and remember the ABC of basic resuscitation.
- Hypoventilation. Due to motor block of intercostals. May or may not require control of ventilation.
- 'Total spinal'—ie injection of a large epidural dose into the CSF. Marked hypotension. Apnoea. Loss of consciousness. Treatment: IPPV. Treat hypotension. ►Death will occur from asphyxia if treatment is not prompt.
- Epidural haematoma or abscess formation: aim for early diagnosis—as this helps prevent big CNS deficits. MET 25
- Patchy or unilateral block.
- Nerve root damage.

NB: in obstetric practice (p 66) there is no excess risk of caesarean section.[1]

Caudal (sacral epidural)

- Left lateral position.
- Palpate sacral hiatus (~4–5cm above the tip of the coccyx). This is often not easy. Another method is to palpate the posterior superior iliac spines: the line joining them forms the base of an equilateral triangle with the sacral hiatus at the apex.
- Insert 21G block needle perpendicular to skin through the sacrococcygeal membrane, into the sacral canal. A 23G needle may be useful for infants.
- Aspirate, and inject up to 20mL 0.5% bupivacaine in the adult.
- If the injection is difficult (there should be no resistance), or swelling occurs, then the needle is in the wrong place—so **stop!** Withdraw the needle and start again.

Indications:

- Provides anaesthesia for the sacral region.
- Useful, eg in scrotal surgery, low cavity forceps (needs experience because of risk of injecting into baby's head), hernias or haemorrhoids.

1 Wong C 2005 *N Engl J Med* **352** 655 RCT

Pain

John Keats, the best known medical student to die of unrequited love, demonstrated that the life of the spirit entails the capacity to feel pain—but, as usual, Nature has been over-generous in endowing us with this capacity—so making the treatment of pain paramount: analgesia promotes wellbeing, sleep, and the honeyed indolence preceding recovery or the easeful passage into oblivion. We tend to think simplistically about pain, assuming that when pain is submitted to us we must respond with something analgesic or anaesthetic—but there are other approaches.[1]

Remember also that pain relief aids physiotherapy (allowing coughing and mobility), preventing pneumonia.

Pain exacerbates hypo/hyperventilation, hypertension, and tachycardia.

Methods of analgesia (See *OHCM* p 454 and *OHCM* p 438.)

1 *Oral:* • Paracetamol 0.5–1g/6h. • NSAIDs: diclofenac 50mg/8h (remember danger of GI bleed; cover with ranitidine or misoprostol; caution in asthma). Effects on renal function are minimal if pre-op U&E is normal.[26] Tramadol 50–100mg/4–6h PO/IV. Less side-effects than morphine, but less potent. • Opioids, eg Oromorph® solution. NB: most opiates are poorly absorbed from the gut.

2 *Sublingual:* Buprenorphine (an uncommonly used synthetic opiate; 'controlled' drug): 0.4mg/6h sublingually, or fentanyl drops.

3 *Inhalational:* Nitrous oxide/oxygen (Entonox®), useful for labour pains, changing dressings, and physiotherapy.

4 *Intramuscular:* Morphine eg 10mg IM; children 0.2mg/kg IM. Pethidine 25–100mg IM is alternative. (Doses for typical healthy adults.)

5 *Intravenous:* Boluses or continuous infusion. Opiates (as above). Patient Controlled Analgesic (PCA). The patient can give himself boluses, and if this is sufficient, no background infusion of opiates is necessary. Remember to programme maximum dose limit!

6 *Regional anaesthesia (RA):* p 634. Epidurals (opiates, or LA, boluses or continuous infusion). Many techniques used (intercostal nerve, brachial plexus, femoral nerve blocks). Coeliac plexus ablation with alcohol may give 6-months' pain relief in upper GI carcinoma. Some meta-analyses of RA for hip surgery find marginal benefits, eg fewer deaths and DVTs.[MET 27]

7 ***Transcutaneous fentanyl patches.***

8 ***Transcutaneous nerve stimulation:*** (TNS) see p 67.

Chronic pain

- Epidural steroids for chronic backache.
- Nerve blocks: either temporary (LA) or permanent (neurolytic drugs eg alcohol, phenol). Trigeminal nerve, spinal nerve, autonomic blocks (eg stellate ganglion, coeliac plexus).
- Radiofrequency lesions produce localized damage within the nervous system to block conduction.
- Subcutaeneous narcotic ± antiemetics continuously, by syringe driver.
- Hypnosis.
- Acupuncture.

Pain in children See p 718 for narcotic and other analgesia in painful conditions such as sickle-cell disease. For burns, see p 730. For post-op relief, see p 172. For pain relief in casualty: see p 718.

Quality in anaesthesia

Deming's definition: quality is meeting customer requirements at a price they are willing to pay. On this view, anaesthesia has various customers rating its quality: surgeons, hospitals, payers, and patients. These groups may have conflicting requirements. www.cja-jca.org/cgi/content/full/48/1/6
The most important customer is the patient, and their chief requirement is pain relief—but don't focus on this narrowly. Patients are also very keen to have a friendly anaesthetist explaining what to expect. This is the chief area of disparity between what anaesthetists think patients should want and what they actually want. A holistic approach to anaesthesia does not regard these tasks as separate: they are complimentary.

EBM in anaesthesia: possible limitations

In anaesthesia research, surrogate or intermediate outcomes predominate as the end-points which is a weakness when the results serve as the evidence on which to base clinical decisions. More importantly, in interventions requiring skill, dexterity, and dynamic decision-making, do not assume that equally good outcomes are achievable by all, by the simple application of the results of EBM.[28]

[1] *That some stream of lightning*
From the old man in the skies
Can burn out that suffering
No right-taught man denies.

But a coarse old man am I,
I choose the second-best,
I forget it all awhile
Upon a woman's breast.

Daybreak and a candle-end, WB Yeats

10 Unusual eponymous syndromes

To have *any* disease is unfortunate, but to have a rare disease is doubly so: the patient must often wait for ages for a diagnosis, and then he must contend with his physician's lifelong morbid interest in him.

For syndromes relevant to *general medicine* and *surgery*, see *OHCM* p 718.

Alport's syndrome X-linked or autosomal recessive sensorineural deafness, with pyelonephritis, haematuria, & renal failure (glomerulonephritis + basket weaving of basement membrane). The X-linked forms are caused by mutations in COL4A5 genes that encode the α5-chain of type-IV collagen. Typical age at death (♂): 20–30yrs.[1]

Asperger's syndrome Autistic features (p 394) *without* autistic aloneness or linguistic difficulty. It is less severe than autism. It is possible to teach better recognition of emotions and how to predict emotional responses.[2]

Bardet–Biedl syndrome Retinal dystrophy, IQ↓, hypogonadism, obesity (± polydactyly) + renal abnormalities (calyceal clubbing or blunting, calyceal cysts or diverticula, fetal lobulation). Absence of paraparesis distinguishes it from the Laurence-Moon-Biedl syndrome, p 648. ♂/♀ ≈47:41. Genetic locus: 16q13–q21 (recessive). A higher incidence is found in Newfoundland (1:17,500 *vs* 1:160,000 elsewhere).[3][4]

Batten's syndrome (Juvenile neuronal ceroid lipofuscinoses) ↑Apoptosis of photoreceptors & neurones from defects in the CLN3 gene causes vision↓, childhood dementia, fits, ataxia, spasticity, athetosis, dystonia, and early death (in teens). ***Tests:*** Lipopigments in lymphocytes & urine.[5]

Becker's muscular dystrophy This is sex-linked like Duchenne's, but later onset, slower progression, and more calf enlargement in adolescence. Heart involvement occurs (~50%). ***Cause:*** Eg lysine to glutamine dystrophin gene mutation (Xp-21 defects). ***℞:*** A few respond to steroids: try and see, under expert guidance; monitor plasma creatine kinase).[6][7]

Beckwith–Wiedemann syndrome ***Signs:*** Large tongue and kidneys, hemihypertrophy, microcephaly, hypoglycaemia, and omphalocoele, plus early feeding difficulties. Risk of neoplasia: 8%: half of these are Wilms' tumours (p 133). Genes involved are at the 11p15 locus; their dysregulation can allow too much insulin-like growth factor 2 to be made.[8]

Bourneville's disease (Tuberous sclerosis; epiloia=epilepsy, low intelligence + adenoma sebaceum) There are multi-organ calcified hamartomatous tubers. Autosomal^{dom}: loci on 9q34 (TSC1, making *harmatin*) & 16p13 (TSC2 makes *tuberin*; mutations here are most serious). Prognosis: often benign.

- ***CNS/eye:*** Subependymal giant cell astrocytoma*, fits, hydrocephalus, periventricular calcification, ↓IQ; retinal nodules* & achromatic patches.
- ***Skin:*** Hypomelanic macules (Wood's lamp +ve)*, adenoma sebaceum (warty nasolabial angiofibromas*; fig 1), *café-au-lait* spots, butterfly rash, periungual fibromas*, sacral plaques (Shagreen patches, like shark skin), skin tags.
- ***Mouth:*** Pitted tooth enamel, gingival fibromas.
- ***Eye:*** Phakomata (white or yellow retinal tumours; present in ~50%).
- ***Bone:*** Sclerotic lesions, phalangeal cysts, hypertelorism.
- ***Kidney:*** Angiomyolipomas*, multiple cysts, haematuria.
- ***Teeth; hair:*** Pitted enamel; gingival fibromas; white lock.
- ***Lungs:*** Honeycomb lung, pneumothorax, 'muscular hyperplasia of lung'.
- ***Heart:*** Rhabdomyomas*, BP↑, cardiomyopathy, haemopericardium.
- ***Lymph nodes:*** Lymphangiomyomatosis*, Castleman tumour.
- ***Bowel:*** Polyps ± Peutz-Jeghers, *OHCM* p 732.
- ***Liver & peritoneum:*** Carney's complex (p 699). ***Also:*** Precocious puberty.

Diagnosis: Try to get 2 major features (*), or 1 major and 2 minor.[9]

Tests: Fundoscopy, skull views, CT/MRI, EEG, heart and renal ultrasound.

The hidden faces of Jack, some gunpowder—and a spark

We are surrounded by eponyms commemorating the Great and the Good, from the Reith Lectures and the Booker prize, to the 100 degree proof of Jack Daniels and Johnnie Walker. Medical eponyms are pickled in something almost as intoxicating: the hidden recesses of our minds. We store away the bizarre, the fearsome, and the mundane—and then, years later, as if playing some dreadful game of snap, we match these features with the person sitting in front of us, and say:'Dandy-Walker!' or 'Prader-Willi!' Here we deal a pack and a half (84 cards) to play with, plus a few jokers, and fascinating and frightening games they can be. But as the years go by we wonder more and more about the people behind the eponyms. We read about these quacks and geniuses—but it is always rather unsatisfying: history shows us everything except the one thing we want to see: the spark that made these eponymous characters truly original. We resign ourselves to the fact that we can only ever see one face of the jack. More years pass and inexplicable events teach us that we all have hidden faces we never directly see or know. *So the possibility arises that these hidden faces are regarding each other.* That is the sensation we have on conjuring with the names of Dandy and Walker and the rest: a sensation that we are not alone—that we are *accompanied.*

Whether we are connoisseurs of Jonnie Walker or Dandy-Walker and its diagnosis, we are relying on hidden processes going on in the dark over many years, to give us the spirit that burns with a steady flame when we are mixed with gunpowder—and that spark. This 'steady flame' is the old definition of alcoholic proof above 100°.[1] It is also our reward for having transformed raw knowledge into something illuminating, by the hidden processes of fermentation and distillation.

When entertaining the diagnosis of a rare disease...

- Ask whether other members of the family have been affected.
- Draw up a family pedigree (as per *OHCM* p 35).
- Have there been unexplained miscarriages or stillbirths in the family?
- Who is now pregnant (may become so) in the family? In your hands you may hold vital information or vital clues which need to get to the right person at the right time. That person may not be the person who is in front of you now. Get consent from your patient to talk to the whole family, and for referral for genetic counselling (p 154).
- Is prenatal diagnosis available? If this is a critical issue, don't rely on the judgment of a single expert. Keep on asking, as the field of prenatal tests is constantly enlarging.
- Once a diagnosis is made, don't assume that the disease is untreatable today just because it was last year. Search Medline (p 504) and find out what's changed. Get in touch with a patient's group.

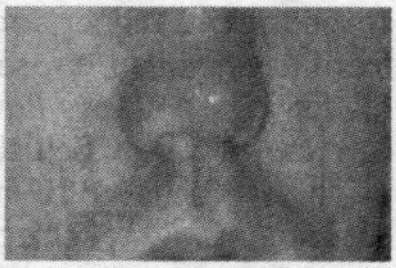

Fig 1. Tuberose sclerosis (angiofibromatal adenoma sebaceum)

1 Spirits were once graded by the ***gunpowder test:*** a mixture of water and alcohol 'proved' itself if one could pour it on gunpowder and a spark could induce it to burn with a steady flame. If it did not, the liquor was too weak. A 'proven' liquor was defined as 100 degrees proof (100°).

Briquet's syndrome (Fat file syndrome) Hypochondria (p 334) + somatization with >13 unexplained symptoms in various organs (see BOX).

Bruton sex-linked♂ agammaglobulinaemia (tyrosine kinase gene mutation) Infections + arthropathy + absent Peyer's patches, tonsils & appendix.

Buchanan's syndrome A single artery arises out of the base of the heart, supplying pulmonary *and* systemic vasculature. The aorta may be divided. There is cyanosis from birth. Surgical correction is possible.

Capgras syndrome A delusion that a friend has been replaced by an exact double, who is an impostor. *Cause*: Psychosis; head injury; B_{12}↓; watershed cerebral infarct; right occipitotemporal lesion; pituitary tumour.[11]

Castleman's disease Angiofollicular lymph node hyperplasia + benign vascular mediastinal tumour. *2 types:* Hyaline vascular and plasma cell type (causes fever, anaemia, weight↓). Development of frank lymphoma is rare. POEMS syndrome may be present (BOX).[12]

Chediak–Higashi syndrome Immunodeficiency ± albinism, photophobia, nystagmus on exposure to light, weakness, tremor, fever, platelets↓, liver↑, ± lymphoma. WBCs contain big peroxidase granules. *Cause:* 1q43 mutation. Fatal in 90% by 10yrs of age without marrow transplantation.[13]

Conradi–Hünermann syndrome (Chondrodysplasia punctata) Saddle nose, nasal hypoplasia, frontal bossing, short stature, stippled epiphyses, optic atrophy, cataracts, IQ↓, flexural contractures. *Cause:* Genetic or effects of warfarin given during the 1st trimester of pregnancy.[14]

Cornelia De Lange syndrome Short stature + abnormally shaped head with brows meeting in the midline ± hirsutism, low-set ears, widely spaced teeth, Simian (single) palmar crease, IQ↓, seizures, self-harm, abnormal temporal lobes. Autosomal dominant, sporadic in 99%.[15]

Corrigan's syndrome This is congenital aortic regurgitation.

Cotard's syndrome (nihilistic delusions) We deny our existence, or believe we are rotting, or we demand burial, thinking we are a corpse. *Nihil* is Latin for nothing; a good nihilist will *annihilate* all trace of himself, *leaving only such trace upon earth as smoke leaves in air, or foam in water.* Dante Alighieri *Inferno XXIV* 50
Cause: Depression, alcohol, syphilis, parietal lobe lesion, or just being born, for *there is in everyone a deep instinct which is neither that of destruction, nor that of creation. It is simply the longing to resemble nothing.* Albert Camus

Crigler–Najjar syndrome Jaundice ± CNS signs appear in the 1st days of life due to ↓gluconyl transferase activity (?from homozygosity for G71R & Y486D genes). *Treatment:* Liver transplant before irreversible kernicterus.[16]

Dandy–Walker syndrome Congenital obstruction of the foramina of Luschka and Magendi leads to progressive enlargement of the head, congested scalp veins, bulging fontanelle, separation of the cranial sutures, papilloedema, bradycardia. *Treatment:* Drain the CSF into a body cavity.

De Clerambault's syndrome (Etomania) The patient is deluded that someone of a higher social status is in love with her. She derives satisfaction from having been 'chosen', and may make trouble by publicizing her view of his feelings. ►*Always have a chaperone!* Homoerotomania may be complicated by Fragoli delusions (eg the love object of a teenage boy was a neighbour believed by him to be his father). Stalking is one manifestation. *Associations:* IQ↓; schizophrenia; mania; left frontal lobe lesion.[17]

Diamond–Blackfan syndrome (erythrogenesis imperfecta) ↓Erythroid production (Hb↓, platelets↑, MCV↑) causes pallor ± limb anomalies. *Cause:* ?sporadic deletions on 19q13.[18] Steroids ± marrow transplant are tried—or stem-cell transplant from a donor embryo created by IVF (pre-implantation genetic diagnosis confirms HLA matching).[19] See BOX.

Helping people with Briquet's syndrome

- Give time—don't dismiss these patients as 'just the "worried well"'.
- Explore with the patient the factors perpetuating the illness (disordered physiology, misinformation, unfounded fears, misinterpretation of sensations, unhelpful 'coping' behaviour, social stressors).
- Agree a management plan which focuses on each issue and makes sense to the patient's holistic view of him or herself.
- Treat any depression (p 342); consider cognitive therapy; make the patient feel understood, broaden the agenda, negotiating a new understanding of symptoms including psychosocial factors.[20] BMJ 2005 330 4

Castleman's lymph node hyperplasia with POEMS syndrome

POEMS syndrome entails: **p**eripheral neuropathy, **o**rganomegaly/hyperplasia, **e**ndocrinopathy, a **m**onoclonal paraprotein, and **s**kin lesions. Interleukin-6 excess is also a feature of Castleman's disease, so also look for PUO and chronic inflammatory symptoms ± failure to thrive. Children with unexplained chronic inflammatory symptoms may need detailed soft tissue tests to reveal associated vascular tumours.

Cloning our wives

In idle moments, we might think that it would be very useful to clone our wives. This is exactly what men with Capgras syndrome have accomplished. But could we really cope with this in our own case? Men with Capgras syndrome get very destabilized by not knowing who they are talking to—the genuine wife or fake one.[21] It is an example of a delusion called the 'clonal pluralization of identities'.[22] As such, it is the best example we have of a purely metaphysical disease. When a man with Capgras syndrome asks his wife with all solicitude: '*How are we to-day?*'—he means *every word* he utters. And he never knows the answer.

Creating donor embryos to donate stem-cells: good idea?

Bishops, authors, harmless bigots and philosophers like to sound off about the morals of creating embryos, brothers, and sisters for the express purpose of providing spare parts—in this case, an umbilical cord for harvesting of stem-cells—to populate the failing marrow of a 6-year old with Diamond-Blackfan syndrome. To create a new human in this way is thought to be using people as means, not ends. Proponents of this argument seem to ignore the requirement on them to state what *would* be a 'good enough' reason to create an embryo. Behind the expression 'a much hoped-for baby' lies a raft of reasons most parents would rather not look at in too much detail: the hope is often unconsciously selfish (who will look after me in my old age?). Yet when parents have a very specific and altruistic motive—they are questioned remorselessly. What patient-centred ethics teaches is that special circumstances require special sensitivity. Anyone witnessing parents taking these sorts of decisions will be well aware that concepts such as 'designer babies' are unhelpful (and in any case guarded against by the Human Fertilization and Embryology Authority).

PATIENT-CENTRED ETHICS

Di George's syndrome Absent thymus, small parathyroids, anaemia, lymphopenia, hypocalcaemia, cell-mediated immune deficiency, and seizures. Most are associated with a monosomy for a region of chromosome 22q11. It is related to the velo-cardiofacial syndrome of multiple anomalies, cleft palate, heart defects, cognitive defects, and a characteristic face.[23]

Di Guglielmo's disease (erythromyelosis) Dysplastic RBCs infiltrate liver, spleen & heart. Hb↓; MCV↔; WCC↓, platelets↓; LDH & B_{12}↑. Immunoperoxidase stains show antihaemoglobin antibody. Transfusions are needed.[24]

Duchenne's muscular dystrophy presents in boys of 1-6yrs, with a waddling, clumsy gait. Gower's manoeuvre: on standing, he uses his hands to climb up his legs. Distal girdle muscles are affected late; selective wasting causes calf pseudohypertrophy. Later wheelchairs are needed (eg at 9-12yrs). Scoliosis and many chest infections occur. Aim to maintain walking (eg using knee–ankle–foot orthoses). Spinal fixation (Luque operation) or bracing helps scoliosis. Prednisolone 0.75mg/kg/24h helps, but doesn't allow wheelchair abandoning.[25] There is progressive hypoventilation: the cause of death in ~70%. Vital capacity of <700mL is a bad sign. Extending life by ventilation is unlikely to increase its quality. ***Creatine kinase*** is ↑; measure this in all boys who are not walking by 1½yrs, so that genetic advice may be given (sex-linked recessive). ***Muscle biopsy:*** Abnormal fibres surrounded by fat & fibrous tissue. ***Mortality:*** 75% are dead by 20yrs; 5% are alive after 50yrs. ~80% of carrier ♀ have abnormal chemistry. Prenatal screening is available.

Ebstein's anomaly A congenital defect with downward displacement of the tricuspid valve (± deformed leaflets) atrializing the right ventricle. There may be no symptoms, or cyanosis, clubbing, triple rhythm, systolic, and diastolic murmurs. It is to be associated with other cardiac malformations. ***Tests:*** ECG: tall *P* waves, ↑*P–R* interval; right bundle branch block.[26]

Edwards syndrome Trisomy 18, our 2nd commonest trisomy; Down's is 1st; ♀:♂ ≈2:1. *Signs:* rigid baby + limb flexion, odd low-set ears, receding chin, proptosis, rockerbottom feet, cleft lip/palate, ± umbilical/inguinal hernia; short sternum makes nipples look widely separated. Fingers cannot be extended; the index finger overlaps the 3rd digit. Girls survive longer (mean 10 months).[27]

Ehlers–Danlos syndrome (EDS) Bennett's paradox: the woman at a drag ball is the true impostor for, unlike everyone else, she is what she seems. So with EDS which does not behave like a connective tissue disease *because it really is one* (a true disease of collagen). Other 'connective tissue diseases' are really diseases of something else. EDS causes soft, hyperelastic, poor-healing, easily bruising skin ± aneurysms or GI bleeds/perforation + loose, hypermobile joints ± flat feet. There are 6 types. Type II, eg, is caused by COL52A mutations, while in type IV COL381 mutations upset encoding of type III collagen. See figures.

Eisenmenger's syndrome A congenital heart defect which is at first associated with a left to right shunt may lead to pulmonary hypertension and shunt reversal. If so, cyanosis develops (± heart failure and chest infections), and Eisenmenger's syndrome is present.[28]

Erb's scapulohumeral dystrophy ♀:♂ ≈1:1. ***Onset:*** 1-6 decades. *Early sign:* Cannot raise hands above head, then (in order): deltoid→erector spinae→ trunk muscles→pelvic girdle→thigh muscles. Lifespan is shortened.

Fallot's tetrad Pulmonary stenosis, overriding aorta, interventricular defect, RVH. ***Signs:*** Cyanosis as ductus closes, dyspnoea, faints, squatting at play, clubbing, thrills, absent pulmonary part of S_2, harsh systolic murmur at left sternal base. ***Tests:*** FBC: Hb↑. CXR: wooden shoe heart contour + RVH. ECG: RVH; MRI. ***Prognosis:*** 86% 32yrs survival after corrective surgery. 'Total repair' entails VSD closure and removal of the pulmonary stenosis: it may result in normal life, with driving possible, if no syncopal attacks.

X-linked muscular dystrophies

1 Duchenne's muscular dystrophy (severe)
2 Becker muscular dystrophy (benign)
3 Emery–Dreifuss muscular dystrophy (benign; early contractures)
4 McLeod syndrome (benign with acanthocytes)
5 Scapuloperoneal (rare).

Myotonic dystrophy & other autosomal muscular dystrophies

1 Myotonic dystrophy (autosomal dominant; Steinert disease)
2 Congenital myotonic dystrophy
3 Facioscapulohumeral muscular dystrophy (Landouzy–Dejerine p 468)
4 Autosomal recessive Duchenne-like limb-girdle dystrophy of early childhood
5 Late-onset (Erb-type) autosomal recessive limb-girdle dystrophy (usually scapulohumeral; rarely pelvifemoral)
6 Autosomal dominant limb-girdle dystrophy
7 Oculopharyngeal muscular dystrophy
8 Distal myopathies
9 Non-progressive myopathies. www.homepages.hetnet.nl/~b1beukema/ziekspieren.html

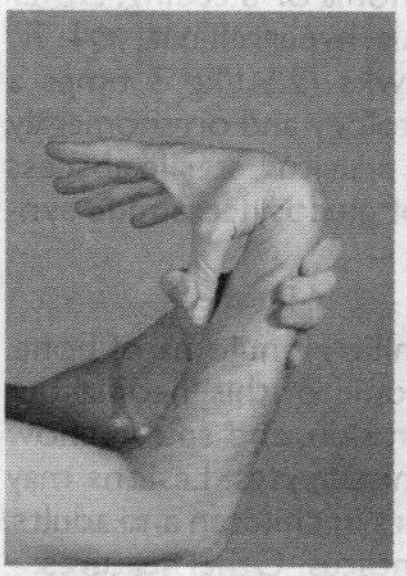

Fig 1. Hypermobile thumb Ehlers–Danlos syndrome

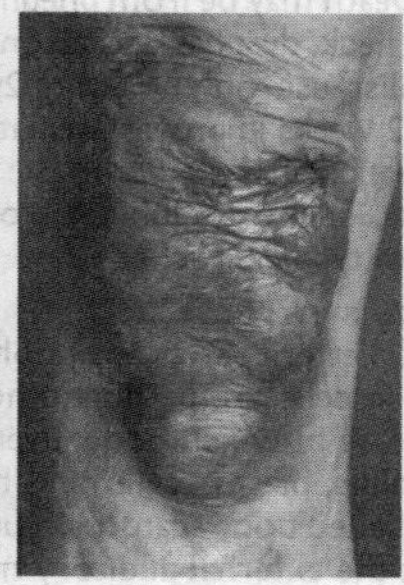

Fig 2. Skin on knee in Ehlers–Danlos syndrome

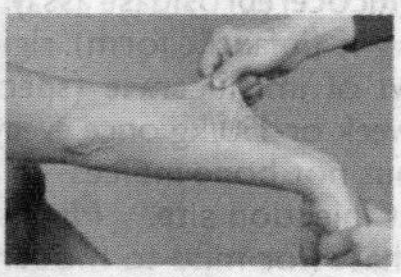

Fig 3. Elastic skin in Ehlers–Danlos syndrome

Post-op problems: •Residual VSD + pulmonary hypertension, if big •Ventricular tachycardia •Complete heart block •Right ventricular aneurysm •SBE (risk is low-ish) •Dilated cardiomyopathy •Pulmonary or aortic regurgitation. NB: when pregnant (may be unproblematic), do careful fetal echo.[29]

Fanconi anaemia Autosomal recessive progressive marrow failure + absence of radii, thumb hypoplasia, syndactyly, missing carpal bones, skin pigmentation, microsomy, microcephaly, strabismus, cryptorchidism, IQ↓, deafness, short stature, and ↑risk of malignancy. *Survival:* 70% at 5yrs post-marrow transplant (umbilical cord blood stem cells are also tried, p 641). There are 8 groups: FA-A to FA-H. FAA and FAC genes are the commonest.[30]

Galeazzi fracture Radius shaft fracture with distal ulna subluxation.

Ganser syndrome Disorientation plus pseudodementia with 'approximate answering', eg in answer to 'What is the colour of the chair in the corner?' it might be answered: 'What corner? I don't know what a corner is. I don't see a chair...' Absurd remarks only occur as answers to questions. Intellectual deficit is inconstant (hence the 'pseudo'). Hysteria, hallucinations, and fluctuating consciousness are common. It may follow head injury.[31]

Gaucher's syndrome (autosomal recessive) The glucocerebrosidase gene is on chromosome 1q21; mutations here cause Gaucher's, the commonest lysosomal storage disease. Glucosylceramide accumulates in macrophage lysosomes (producing Gaucher's cells), causing face & leg pigmentation and organomegaly, with marrow & CNS infiltration. *Diagnosis:* Skin fibroblast glucocerebrosidase assay. Death may be from pneumonia or bleeding. *Other signs* (infantile form): rigid neck, dysphagia, catatonia, hyperreflexia, IQ↓. *℞:* IVI of imiglucerase (specialist use only): 60U/kg/2wks (2.5U/kg 3 times a week or 15U/kg once every 2 weeks improves haematology and organomegaly, but not bone indices—in Gaucher's type I & III). SE: pruritus, sterile abscess at injection site.[32] Miglustat is an oral inhibitor of glucosylceramide synthase (for mild to moderate type I Gaucher's).

Hand–Schüller–Christian syndrome (Langerhans' cell histiocytosis) Synonyms: histiocytosis X, Letterer-Siwe eosinophilic granuloma of bone. Monoclonal Langerhans-like cells are pathognomonic of this 'neoplastic', destructive, infiltrative disease in which bone, liver, skin, and spleen show lytic aggregates of eosinophils, plasma cells, and histiocytes. Lesions may show on a ^{99}Technetium-labelled bone scan. It occurs in children and adults, eg starting with a polyp at the external auditory meatus. Other features:

•Fever	•Dyspnoea	•Bone pain	•Failure to thrive
•Scalp lumps	•Cord compression	•Skin erosions	•Pustular eczema-like rash
•Proptosis	•Ear discharge	•Liver/spleen↑	•Lymphadenopathy ± fits
•Stomatitis	•Platelets↓	•Anaemia	•Honeycomb lung

A lethal 'leukaemia' picture is seen in infants. *Treatment:* Bone surgery, steroids, cytotoxics, and radiotherapy may induce remissions.[33] [34]

Hartnup's disease is an autosomal recessive involving a transporter for monoamino-monocarboxylic acids (gene on 11q13). Skin is thick, scaly, and hyperpigmented where exposed to light. *Signs:* ↓Rashes, nystagmus, ataxia, bruxism (teeth grinding), diplopia, insomnia, reflexes↑. Presentation in adults is rare. *Treatment:* Give nicotinamide and B vitamins.[35] [36]

Hunter's syndrome (Mucopolysaccharidosis II) Iduronate sulfatase (IDS) deficiency (X-linked recessive, but a new mutation in 33% so usually ♂), producing deafness, IQ↓, short stature, chronic diarrhoea, an unusual face, joint stiffness, and hepatosplenomegaly (like Hurler's disease, p 646 but almost always without corneal clouding, and pursuing a milder course). *Diagnosis:* Serum iduronate sulfatase↓; DNA sequencing of IDS gene.[37] *Typical age at death:* Later childhood; survival into the 30s is possible. *Pathology:* Alterations at the IDS locus, mostly missense mutations.[38]

Huntington's chorea Autosomal dominant; progressive motor, cognitive, and emotional symptoms with loss of GABA-ergic neurons in the neostriatum—owing to expansion of CAG repeats in the huntingtin gene. Those without Huntington's have <35 repeats; penetrance is incomplete at 36–39 repeats; 40+ means the disorder is inevitable (≥50 CAG repeats means no signs until they may pass. Huntington's is earlier in children due to paternal transmission; 36–39 CAG repeats means a penetrance of 40+ is certain). 10% get Huntington's disease in their 20s; long enough. Early findings: Abnormal visual reaction time, unable to suppress saccades; often mild chorea (fidgety, incoordination), odd, unpurposeful movements. Later: Rigidity, voluntary movements impaired; dysarthria; cognitive impairment is found until chorea starts. Abnormal ocular saccades may inconsistently indicate imminent, manifest symptoms. Signs: Personality change, self-neglect, apathy, clumsiness, fidgets, fleeting grimaces (may be mistaken for normal signs) → dementia, death. Clinical diagnosis: Careful testing as symptoms may only start after progression has finished. Genetic tests are confirmatory (counselling is vital).

Hunt's syndrome (Ramsay Hunt) causing cerebral ischaemia. The acute neuromuscular cause of ... unless given pyridostigmine (30mg/8h under specialist control).

Hurler's syndrome (mucopolysaccharidosis I) Apparent after 6 months of normal growth, there is physical & mental decline, hydrocephalus, thickened skin, hepatosplenomegaly, corneal clouding and nodules over scapulae. There is deficiency of α-L-iduronidase, hence blocking degradation of dermatan sulfate and heparan sulfate, causing excess mucopolysaccharides in urine, cartilage, periosteum, tendons, valves, meninges, and cornea. Tests: Skull X-ray: thick vault, synostoses, frontal sinuses and deformed pituitary fossa. Marrow: Metachromatic Reilly bodies in lymphocytes. Death is often by 10yrs.

Holt–Oram syndrome (Congenital syndrome): Dyspnoea + keratosis + normal ...

Ivemark's syndrome This is the association of congenital asplenia with cardiac abnormalities; septal defects (± pulmonary valve atresia or stenosis).

Kartagener's syndrome Primary ciliary dyskinesia (PCD) leads to bronchiectasis, sinusitis, and infertility (in some). Visceral (situs inversus—i.e. major internal organs are mirrored from normal; hence heart on the right). Otitis media and salpingitis are frequent. Tests: Saccharin test: Slows in nasal mucociliary transit. Sweat test; PCD must be considered in cases of bronchiectasis, with ultrastructural analysis that interfaces with dynein of cilia (tails).

Kawasaki disease Suspect this in anyone <5yrs old with ≥5 days of fever + lymphadenopathy (≥1.5cm, often single) + bilateral non-purulent conjunctival injection, dry, red, fissured lips; strawberry tongue; oral erythema; erythema; swelling of hands/feet & desquamation; polymorphous exanthema. Coronary artery aneurysms may occur (commonest in the UK in childhood, as a cause of acquired heart disease). It may be a reaction to infection. Tests: ESR/CRP↑, platelets↑, bilirubin↑, AST↑, albumin↓, urine: leucocytes, RBCs. Stevens–Johnson syndrome, measles, streptococcal infection, and rickettsial infection may mimic it. Rx: Intravenous immunoglobulin (IVIG, 2g/kg as a single infusion) usually causes rapid (≤48h) improvement. If not, plasma exchange may help. Follow-up: monitor echocardiography: aspirin reduces platelet aggregation. Echo (if coronary aneurysms) may be indicated. Dispensing aspirin (low dose) and coronary angiography (see Image 4).

Klinefelter's syndrome (XXY or XXXY; polysomy Y; variable Leydig cell defects). A common cause of hypogonadism (male hypogonadism, affecting ~1:1000 births); may present in adolescence with psychiatric problems, ↓libido, gynaecomastia, ↓sexual maturation. Associations: DM, ↓stature, ↓learning, osteoporosis. Androgens and surgery for gynaecomastia may help. Lifespan is normal, but the arm span may exceed the body length by ≥6cm.

Huntington's chorea Autosomal dominant triad of progressive motor, cognitive, and emotional symptoms with loss of spiny neurones in the neostriatum—owing to excessive triplet (CAG) repeats in the huntingtin gene. Those without Huntington's have <28 repeats. ***Penetrance:*** A large number of repeats means the disease is more likely. 29–35 CAG repeats means no signs but they may pass Huntington's to their children due to paternal meiotic instability. 36–39 CAG repeats means ↓penetrance. If >40 CAG repeats, 100% get Huntington's disease if they live long enough. ***Early findings:*** ↓Auditory & visual reaction times (needs special equipment) then mild chorea (flitting, jerky movements), odd extraocular movements, ↑reflexes, ↓rapid alternating movements. Unpredictable motor impairment is found until chorea starts. Abnormal ocular saccades may inconsistently indicate imminent manifest signs. ***Late signs:*** Personality change, self-neglect, apathy, clumsiness, fidgets, fleeting grimaces (may be mistaken for mannerisms), chorea, and dementia.

Ethical dilemmas surround testing, as symptoms may only start after procreation has finished. Careful pre-test counselling is vital.[39]

Hunt's syndrome (Pyridoxine cerebral deficiency) Intractable neonatal fits cause death unless given pyridoxine (50 mg IV under EEG control).

Hurler's syndrome (Mucopolysaccharidosis 1h) After a few months of normal growth, there is physical & mental decline, hydrocephalus, thickened skin, hirsutism, coxa valga, and nodules over scapulae. There is deficiency of α-L-iduronidase, hence blocking degradation of dermatan sulfate and heparan sulfate, causing excess mucopolysaccharides in urine, cartilage, periosteum, tendons, valves, meninges, and cornea. ***Tests:*** Skull x-ray: thickened bone, absent frontal sinuses and deformed pituitary fossa. Marrow: Metachromatic Reilly bodies in lymphocytes. Death is often at ≤10yrs.

Hutchinson's triad (Congenital syphilis) Deafness + keratitis + pointed teeth.

Ivemark's syndrome This is the association of congenital asplenia with ostium primum atrial septal defects (± pulmonary valve atresia or stenosis).

Kartagener's syndrome Primary ciliary akinesia (PCA) leads to bronchiectasis, sinusitis, ♂ infertility + situs inversus (transposed heart & abdominal organs—an odd effect of ↓ciliary function). Otitis media and salpingitis are frequent. ***Tests:*** ECG: inverted P-waves in lead I, reversed R-wave progression. Mutations in dyneins (DNAI1) can cause PC4 (these are large multisubunit ATPases that interact with microtubules to make cilia beat).[40]

Kawasaki's disease Suspect this in anyone <9yrs old with T°↑ for ≥5 days + neck lymphadenopathy (>1.5cm across), dry fissured lips, arthralgia, palmar erythema, red eyes (uveitis), diarrhoea, strawberry tongue, or, later, finger-tip desquamation + swelling of hands/feet ± jaundice. ►*Coronary arteritis* (similar to PAN) ± *infarction* may occur (commoner than rheumatic fever as a cause of acquired heart disease). It may be a reaction to infection. ***Tests:*** ESR/C-reactive protein↑; bilirubin↑, AST↑, α_2-globulin↑, platelets↑. ΔΔ: Stevens-Johnson syndrome, measles, streps, infectious mononucleosis. ***R:*** Immunoglobulin 2g/kg as a single IVI dose *usually* causes rapid (diagnostic) improvement.[41] If not, plasma exchange may help. ***Follow-up:*** Echo; 3D coronary magnetic resonance angiography accurately defines aneurysms (non-invasive alternative when transthoracic echo quality is insufficient, and coronary angiography is too invasive).[42]

Klinefelter's syndrome (XXY or XXYY polysomy + variable Leydig cell defect) A common cause of ♂ hypogonadism (small firm testes; small penis; 1:2000 births) may present at adolescence with psychopathy, cognition↓, libido↓, gynaecomastia, ↓sexual maturation. *Associations:* T_4↓, diabetes, asthma, ?oncogenesis. Androgens and surgery for gynaecomastia may help. Lifespan is normal, but the arm span may exceed the body length by 10cm.[43]

Klippel–Feil syndrome (Autosomal dominant or recessive; candidate gene on chromosome 8) Congenital fusion of cervical vertebrae, nystagmus, deafness, and CNS signs. Mirror movements are said to occur if voluntary movements in a limb are involuntarily mimicked by another.

Landouzy–Déjérine (fascioscapulohumeral 4q35) **muscular dystrophy** Weakness of the shoulder muscles, eg on combing the hair appears at 12–14yrs of age. There is difficulty in closing the eyes, sucking, blowing, and whistling. Scapulae wing and the lips pout, and the facial expression is ironed out. Adult myoglobin is reduced and fetal myoglobin & sarcolemmal nuclei are increased. Inheritance: often autosomal dominant.

Laurence–Moon syndrome The patient is usually a boy who presents with night blindness progressing to visual loss from retinitis pigmentosa. It is distinct from Bardet–Biedl syndrome (there is paraplegia, but no polydactyly and obesity). Other signs: scant body hair, azoospermia, IQ↓, renal anomalies (calyceal clubbing, cysts, or diverticula; fetal lobulation; end-stage renal failure in 15%). Inheritance: autosomal recessive.

Leber's hereditary optic atrophy There is risk of myopathy + neuropathy mostly affecting males with acute or subacute bilateral visual loss and central scotoma. A mutation (G→A in mitochondrial DNA coding for a dehydrogenase enzyme has been proposed (a type of cytoplasmic inheritance).

Lesch–Nyhan syndrome Hypoxanthine-guanine phosphoribosyl transferase (HGPRT) lack leads to hyperuricaemia in boys (X-linked—only fully expressed if ♂), with orange crystals in the nappy, then motor delay, IQ↓ (eg <65), torsion spasms, clonus, choreoathetosis, hypotonia, and fits. Compulsive, agitated, self-mutilation (lip/finger biting, head banging, face scratching—may be unilateral) then follow, gout, renal colic, and megaloblastic anaemia. Smiling aggression to others may occur. The chief defect might be 'pain-consciousness' perhaps related to dopamine hyperinnervation of D_1 receptors in cingulum bundle projections. Death is usually before 25yrs from renal failure or infection. *Treatment:* Good hydration (urine flow↑). Allopurinol prevents urate stones, but not CNS signs. It has been necessary to remove teeth to stop lip mutilation.

Lewy-body dementia Characterized by Lewy-bodies in brainstem and cortex, and a fluctuating but persisting cognitive impairment, parkinsonism, hallucinations, and visuoperceptual deficits. It is a common type of dementia. Lewy bodies are eosinophilic intracytoplasmic neuronal inclusion bodies; there is overlap between Lewy-body dementia and Alzheimer's and Parkinson's diseases, making treatment hard as antiparkinsonian agents can precipitate delusions, and antipsychotics worsen parkinsonism.

Li–Fraumeni syndrome Families are highly susceptible to multiple malignancy at an early age. As well as being devastating for the families, it is of great interest to geneticists as families inherit a germ-line nonsense or oncogene-like missense mutation in one p53 allele.

Lutembacher's syndrome Secondary ASD + mitral stenosis—a rare, possibly fortuitous combination, unless iatrogenic, ie valvuloplasty.

Martin–Bell (fragile X) syndrome (semi-dominant; prevalence: 1:5000) This is the commonest form of inherited cognitive impairment, and is one of the commonest single-gene disorders. It is caused by a stretch of CGG-repeats within the fragile X gene which increases in length as it is transmitted from generation to generation. Once the repeat exceeds a threshold length, no fragile X protein is produced and disease results. *Other features:* Large testes, big forehead, a big jaw, facial asymmetry, long ears, and a short temper. *Tests:* Prenatal tests are possible. Screening could be general or of high-risk groups (eg families with >1 retarded ♂); screening for carrier status leads to labelling and stigmatization, and is rejected by some families.

Klippel–Feil syndrome (Autosomal dominant or recessive; candidate KFS gene on chromosome 8) Congenital fusion of cervical vertebrae, nystagmus, deafness and CNS signs. *Mirror movements* are said to occur if *voluntary* movements in a limb are *involuntarily* mimicked by another.

Landouzy–Dejerine (fascioscapulohumeral 4q35) muscular dystrophy Weakness of the shoulder muscles, eg on combing the hair, appears at 12-14yrs of age. There is difficulty in closing the eyes, sucking, blowing, and whistling. Scapulae wing and the lips pout, and the facial expression is 'ironed out'. Adult myoglobin is reduced and fetal myoglobin & sarcolemma nuclei are increased. Inheritance: often autosomal dominant.[44,45]

Laurence–Moon syndrome The patient is usually a boy who presents with night blindness progressing to visual loss from retinitis pigmentosa. It is distinct from Bardet-Biedl syndrome (there is paraplegia, but no polydactyly and obesity). Other signs: scant body hair, azoospermia, IQ↓, renal anomalies (calyceal clubbing, cysts, or diverticula; fetal lobulation; end-stage renal failure in 15%). Inheritance: autosomal recessive.

Leber's hereditary optic atrophy There is ↑risk of neoplasia + neuropathy mostly affecting males, with acute or subacute bilateral visual loss and central scotoma. A mutation (G→A) in mitochondrial DNA coding for a dehydrogenase enzyme has been proposed (a type of cytoplasmic inheritance).

Lesch–Nyhan syndrome ↓Hypoxanthine-guanine phosphoribosyl transferase (PP-ribose-P) leads to hyperuricaemia in boys (X-linked ∴ only fully expressed if ♂) with orange crystals in the nappy, then motor delay, IQ↓ (eg <65), torsion spasms, clonus, choreoathetosis, hypotonia, and fits. Compulsive, agitated, self-mutilation (foot biting, head banging, face scratching—may be unilateral) then follow gout, renal colic, and megaloblastic anaemia. Smiling aggression to others may occur. The chief defect might be ↓pain-consciousness *perhaps* related to dopaminergic denervation of D_1 receptors in cingulum bundle projections. Death is usually before 25yrs, from renal failure or infection. *Treatment:* Good hydration (urine flow↑). Allopurinol prevents urate stones, but not CNS signs. It has been necessary to remove teeth to stop lip mutilation.

Lewy-body dementia Characterized by Lewy-bodies in brainstem *and* cortex, and a fluctuating but persisting cognitive impairment, parkinsonism, hallucinations, and visuoperceptual deficits. It is a common type of dementia. Lewy bodies are eosinophilic intracytoplasmic neuronal inclusion bodies; there is overlap between Lewy-body dementia and Alzheimer's and Parkinson's diseases, making treatment hard as antiparkinsonian agents can precipitate delusions, and antipsychotics worsen parkinsonism.[46]

Li–Fraumeni syndrome Families are highly susceptible to multiple malignancy at an early age. As well as being devastating for the families, it is of great interest to geneticists as families inherit a germ-line nonsense or oncogene-like missense mutation in one *p*53 allele.

Lutembacher's syndrome Secundum ASD + mitral stenosis—a rare, possibly fortuitous conjunction, unless iatrogenic, at valvuloplasty.[47]

Martin–Bell (fragile X) syndrome (Semi-dominant; prevalence: 1:5700) This is the commonest form of inherited cognitive impairment, and is one of the commonest single-gene disorders. It is caused by a stretch of CGG-repeats within the fragile X gene, which increases in length as it is transmitted from generation to generation. Once the repeat exceeds a threshold length, no fragile X protein is produced and disease results. *Other features:* Large testes, high forehead, a big jaw, facial asymmetry, long ears, and a short temper. *Tests:* Prenatal tests are possible. Screening could be general or of high-risk groups (eg families with >1 retarded ♂). Screening for carrier status leads to labelling and stigmatization, and is rejected by some families.[48]

Li–Fraumeni syndrome, *p*53, and the guardian of the genome

*p*53 is a tumour-suppressor gene (chromosome 17p13.1; encoding nuclear phosphoprotein, a transcription factor allowing passage through the cell cycle). In this syndrome, as only one allele is affected, development is normal until a spontaneous mutation affects the other allele. Somatic mutation of *p*53 occurs at both alleles in 50–80% of spontaneous human cancers. Cells with a *p*53 mutation do not pause in G1 (a phase in which DNA repair takes place, and faulty DNA purged), but proceed straight to S1 (DNA replication), which is why *p*53 protein is known as the 'guardian of the genome'.

Note that tumours are associated with more than one syndrome, eg adrenocortical tumours are associated with familial cancer syndromes such as the Beckwith–Wiedemann and Li-Fraumeni syndromes, the Carney complex (p 699), multiple endocrine neoplasia type 1, congenital adrenal hyperplasia, and the McCune-Albright syndrome (p 650).[49]

McCune–Albright syndrome Polyosteotic fibrous dysplasia of bone, irregular areas of skin pigmentation and facial asymmetry ± precocious puberty.

Meckel's diverticulum *Prevalence:* ≤2%. ≤2 inches long, and >2 feet from the ileocaecal valve (antemesenteric aspect of ileum), it contains gastric and pancreatic tissue, and may be the cause of occult GI pain and bleeding (brick red stools, or dark becoming bright). This is a leading cause of rectal bleeding (± GI obstruction) in children. *Diagnosis*: radioisotope scan; laparotomy.

Monteggia fracture Fracture of proximal ⅓ of ulna, with angulation + radial head subluxation, caused forced pronation. Open reduction/plating aids good alignment (5 weeks in plaster), so as not to impair pronation. Wait for full union (~12 weeks) before normal arm use.[50]

Morquio's syndrome (Mucopolysaccharidosis IV) Defective degradation of keratin sulfate (it is excreted in the urine) causes stature↓; deafness; weakness; a coarse, broad mouth; widely spaced teeth; pectus carinatum; aortic regurgitation—but not mental retardation. Autosomal recessive.

Moyamoya disease Vascular disease at the Circle of Willis causes strokes or TIAs (alternating hemiplegia, dyspraxia, headache). The typical patient is a Japanese girl, with triggering infection (eg tonsillitis) or hyperventilation (CO_2↓ causes vasoconstriction). Digital subtraction angiography shows collateral vessel formation 'like a puff of smoke'. MRI/CT shows multiple infarctions in watershed areas. Bypass surgery may be possible.[51]

Niemann–Pick disease Autosomal recessive neurovisceral lysosomal lipid storage disorder[52] in which, after years of normal growth, there is physical and mental decline, wasting ± hepatosplenomegaly from abnormal metabolism of sphingomyelin. Psychosis may be the 1st sign. Other signs: brown skin patches; a cherry red spot on the macula; AST↑. There are 5 types; eg, type D is caused by a G3097→T transversion in NPC1 gene.[53]

Noonan syndrome Hypertrophic cardiomyopathy, VSD/ASDs, bruising (APTT↑; ↓factors VIII, XI, XII), ptosis, down-slanting eyes, low-set ears, webbed neck. Height, IQ, and hearing are↓, but not severely. ~50% have germ-line PTPN11 mutations (± associated neuroblastoma[et al]).[54] ***Prevalence:*** 1:5000.

Othello syndrome (Morbid jealousy) A lover believes, against all reason, that his beloved is being sexually unfaithful, thinking that she is plotting against him, or deliberately making him impotent. He may engage a detective to spy on her, and obsessively examine her underwear for signs of sexual activity. It may be primary or from alcohol, schizophrenia, neurosis, or depression. ►Get psychiatric help: it may be deadly. 'Without my having seen Albertine…there would flash from my memory some vision of her with Gisèle in an attitude which had seemed innocent to me at the time; it was enough now to destroy the peace of mind I had managed to recover, I had no longer any need to go and breath dangerous germs outside, I had, as Cottard would have said, supplied my own toxin'. Marcel Proust: *ch 2 of Sodome & Gomorre*

Patau's syndrome (Trisomy 13) The head and eyes are small: ± defects such as absent corpus callosum and a single ventricle. Heart lesions, polycystic kidneys and cleft lip/palate are common. Hands show flexion contractures ± polydactyly with narrow fingernails. ***Prevalence:*** 1/7500 births.

Pick's dementia This often presents later than Alzheimer's disease—eg with character change associated with frontal lobe signs such as gross tactlessness. Lack of restraint may lead to stealing, practical jokes, and unusual sexual adventures. Social graces are replaced by fatuous euphoria and jargon dysphasia, before intellectual and CNS deterioration occurs.

Pierre Robin syndrome Neonatal difficulty in feeding and breathing due to micrognathia (short chin) ± cleft palate or eye abnormality. Prevent the tongue slipping back by nursing on the belly (chest elevated on a pillow).

Hyper-endocrinopathies, McCune–Albright syndrome, and the Taiwanese giant

In the McCune–Albright syndrome, precocious puberty is not the only endocrinopathy: hyperthyroidism and Cushing's have also been reported. In the case of the 'Taiwanese giant' (an unfortunate name) excess growth hormone production has also been found.[55] Deformities, fractures, and pain further complicate the picture (sometimes ameliorated by IV pamidronate). The craniofacial fibrous dysplasia may encroach on the optic nerve, causing visual problems. GnRH analogues have been used (experimentally) to treat the precocious puberty.[56]

The cause may be a mutation of the GNAS 1 gene coding the α subunit of the stimulatory guanine-nucleotide binding protein, G-protein, which activates adenylate cyclase (∴ ↑intracellular cyclic AMP).[57]

Pompe's glycogen storage disease (type II) ↓Lysosomal $\alpha_{1,4}$-glucosidase activity leads to weakness and failure to thrive in early (or later) life. IQ↓ and chest infections occur. Glycogen accumulates in heart; muscle; liver; CNS; kidney; adrenals. Few survive beyond infancy. Mutations include: a G residue insertion in exon 16 (InsG2242), a deletion of 20 nucleotides in exon 4 delta, and a nonsense mutation in exon 16 (G2237A-Trp746Stop).[58]

Prader–Willi syndrome *Cause:* Loss of the paternal contribution of the proximal part of the long arm of chromosome 15 (15q11–q13, deletion, disomy, and imprinting mutations). *Prevalence:* 1:25,000. *Signs:* Hypotonia, epilepsy, failure to thrive, and sleepiness. The child usually has blue eyes and blond hair. Later, hyperphagia (eg eating dog biscuits, or shop-lifting food), obesity, hypogonadism, short stature, hyperglycaemia, cor pulmonale, and sleep apnoea occur. Toddlers may be passive, autistic, or introverted may go on to show unstable mood disorder. Those who are extrovert may develop psychosis. *Tests:* EEG: slow spike & wave activity.[59]

Ramsay Hunt syndrome (Herpes zoster oticus) Severe otalgia, usually in the elderly, precedes facial nerve palsy. Zoster vesicles appear around the ear, in the deep meatus (± soft palate & tonsillar fossa). There may be vertigo and sensorineural deafness which are both slow to resolve.[60]

Rett disorder A neurodevelopmental disorder of repetitive hand wringing with loss of purposeful hand use, eg at 2-3yrs old, with mental and motor regression ± partial seizures ± autism (p 394) ± arrhythmias ± and apneustic/ Valsalva breathing). MECP2 gene mutations are the cause in ~70% (X-linked; lethal to the male fetus).[61][62] Diagnosis (DSM IV) is complex. It is similar to cretinism and fragile X (p 648) as there are defects in activity-dependent neuronal plasticity (how neuronal activity shapes new circuits) causing faulty intracellular signalling pathways with failure of linking of cell surfaces with nuclear events for gene expression (signalling pathways so disrupted are involved in learning, memory, and behaviour as well as in 'synaptic proliferation and pruning' occurring during normal development).[63]

Reye's syndrome *Presentation:* Vomiting, fever, hypotonia, stupor/coma, liver failure. It may have an infectious cause and/or be related to aspirin, anti-emetic or antihistamine use by children. Median age of onset:[uk] 14 months. *Tests:* Glucose↓; transaminases↑; blood ammonium↑ (levels correlate with survival); INR↑. Liver biopsy: swollen, pleomorphic mitochondria (ATP↓, gluconeogenesis & ureagenesis↓). *ΔΔ:* Inherited metabolic disorders (IMD).

Russell Silver syndrome Asymmetrical growth/hemihypertrophy with small stature and precocious puberty. Association: Wilms'. Aberrant genomic imprinting may be to blame. In imprinting, DNA sequences have conditional behaviour depending on if it is maternally or paternally inherited. The idea is that there is some imprint put on the DNA in the mother's ovary or in the father's testes which marks that DNA as being maternal or paternal, and influences expression in their progeny.[64]

Shakhonovich's syndrome (Hypokalaemic periodic paralysis) Attacks precipitated by: stress, menstruation, cold, large carbohydrate meals, rest after exercise, or liquorice, eg with flaccid paralysis, spreading up from the legs. Eye movements, swallowing, and speech are unaffected. Recovery is over 1-24h. Typical age: 7-21yrs. During attacks muscles feel firmer than usual. Reflexes are diminished. There are mis-sense mutations on the CACNA1S (type 1) and SCN4A genes (type 2), where arginine is mostly replaced eg by histidine. The mutation is in the voltage sensor of the transmembrane segment of calcium channels (type 1) and sodium channels (type 2).[65] Oral or intravenous potassium can help. Acetazolamide can ↓ frequency of attacks. *Tests:* Serum K^+ and phosphorus usually fall during attacks; urate may rise. Glycosuria may be present. WCC↑.[66]

Prader–Willi syndrome and epigenetic proof of existentialism

Human chromosome 15q11-q13 is a critical region for Prader–Willi syndrome (PWS) and Angelman syndrome (AS, a totally different syndrome of ataxia and hypotonia).[67] PWS results from loss of expression of paternally expressed genes and AS of maternally expressed genes *from the same locus*. How do the genes know where they come from? They bear an imprint of their origin. This is *genetic imprinting*—an example of *epigenetics*—ie transgenerationally-transmissible functional changes in the genome that can be altered by environmental events and do not involve an alteration of DNA sequences.

What we expose our genes to today may be influencing the lives our grandchildren can lead. Mice models show that this can be inherited down unlimited generations. In humans we know that certain permanent reactions to stress such as increased glucocorticoid receptor sensitivity following a terrorist outrage (for example) can be inherited down at least one generation.[68] Another example of the environment controlling genomic events is the association of Beckwith–Wiedemann syndrome (11p15 deletion) with embryos which have been stored and treated in certain unusual ways during IVF. Furthermore, changes in our diet may activate certain pathways leaving an imprint which is passed on to the next generation (Kaati's hypothesis is supported by data on harvest yields in Overkalix in northern Sweden: a propensity to diabetes is inherited only if there is a surfeit of food during the time leading up to one's *grandfather's* puberty).[69,70]

A cardinal precept of genetics has always been that we cannot choose what we pass on to the next generation. But epigenetics opens up an unlimited dialogue between genes and our environment. It is likely to be the case that we can be responsible *by free choice* whether a gene is turned on or off (eg by exposing ourselves to pesticides or smoke)—and this turning-off may be inherited in an unchanging way. ►*We need to nurture our own genome carefully for future generations.* Does this mean that we have a duty to be happy and lead a stress-free life? We do not know. What we *do* know is that the existentialists have a point—it is as if we are all now responsible for everything forever. And this knowledge may itself be stressful. By confronting this stress and making free choices we can authenticate our dialogue with our genes.

Staging and treatment of Reye's syndrome

The point of staging is to recognize stage 2 (or worse) which should prompt rapid referral to a tertiary centre with facilities for monitoring ICP (eg with subarachnoid bolts) and intra-arterial pressure. Stage 2 criteria: inappropriate verbalizing, combative or stuporose, normal posture, purposeful or non-purposeful response to pain, sluggish pupillary responses, intact eye reflex.

Management: ►Correct hypoglycaemia; set up a *continuous* IVI of 10–15% glucose. Fluid restriction; do blood glucose every 2h; give vitamin K 0.25mg/kg slowly IV (monitor prothrombin time); lower ICP—see p 200. Aim for 40mmHg cerebral perfusion pressure (= systolic BP minus ICP). Control fever and seizures.

Mortality: ~31%. Since abandoning aspirin in children, incidence has fallen to ≤1–6 patients/yr/10^6 children <16yrs. www.nejm.org/content/1999/0340/0018/

Still's disease This juvenile chronic arthritis subtype (JCA) presents with systemic upset in a prepubertal girl with: mono- or poly-articular synovitis, cartliage erosion, ± fevers, pericarditis, iridocyclitis, pneumonitis (lung biopsy specific), lymphadenopathy, splenomegaly. It is a rare cause of toe walking (ie on tip-toes; other causes are a short Achilles tendon; habit; muscle contractures; cerebral palsy).[71] Rheumatoid factor is -ve.[72] *Other subgroups:* juvenile ankylosing spondylitis; psoriatic arthritis and ulcerative colitis-associated arthritis; juvenile-onset rheumatoid arthritis (here Rh factor +ve, and less likely to present as systemic upset).

Adult-onset Still's disease (AOSD): diagnostic criteria—all of: daily fever >39°C; arthralgia/arthritis; Rh factor *and* antinuclear factor -ve *plus any* 2 of: WCC >15 × 10^9/L; rash; serositis (pleural or pericardial); hepatosplenomegaly; lymphadenopathy—*provided* that endocarditis, leukaemia and sarcoidosis are excluded. As with all rheumatology, classification is muddled, and unexpected complications may occur (DIC, liver failure; renal failure; amyloid; cardiac tamponade; sterile endocarditis; peritonitis). ***Tests:*** WCC↑; ESR↑; mild anaemia; ferritin↑; LFT↑; albumin↓; echo.[73] ***Treatment:*** Mild exercise; then rest for 1h each day. If hips are affected, physiotherapy aims to prevent contractures by encouraging extension (eg lying prone on the floor to watch TV). Splinting, traction, and non-weight-bearing exercises are tried. Hot baths help morning stiffness. Give aspirin, up to 80mg/kg/day PO pc to give levels <250mg/L (beware liver & CNS toxicity). Alternative: naproxen 5mg/kg/12h PO pc. If there is severe systemic disturbance, prednisolone 0.5mg/kg/day may be used. In unremitting destructive disease, consider penicillamine, gold, hydroxychloroquine, and infliximab (in those with AOSD; SE include serious infections, eg TB & pneumonia). Surgery may be needed to conserve joint function.[74]

Sydenham's chorea (St Vitus dance) This may start with emotional lability and a preference for being alone (± attention span↓). Next comes purposeless movement, exaggerated by tension, and disappearing on sleep, with clumsiness, grimacing, a darting lizard's tongue and unclear speech (*OHCM* p 66). It is part of rheumatic fever (in <5%, p 166), and may be the *only* feature, appearing up to 6 months after clinical and lab signs of streptococcal infection have abated. The term **PANDAS** (pediatric autoimmune neuropsychiatric disorder associated with streptococcus) denotes a putative subset of obsessive-compulsive disorder and Tourette's syndrome (*OHCM* p 724) that bears some resemblance to Sydenham's chorea.[75] *ΔΔ:* Wilson's disease, juvenile Huntington's, thyrotoxicosis, SLE, polycythaemia, Na^+↓, hypoparathyroidism, kernicterus, encephalitis lethargica, subdural haematoma, alcohol, phenytoin, neuroleptics, hereditary chorea, neuroacanthosis. ***℞:*** (if desired) carbamazepine; sodium valproate.[76]

Syme's amputation An amputation immediately proximal to the ankle.

Tay–Sachs disease This is an autosomal recessive gangliosidosis (type I) which affects ~1:4000 Ashkenazic Jewish births. It is a disease of grey matter. There is reduced lysosomal hexosaminidase A. Low levels of enzyme are detectable in carriers. Children are normal until ~6 months old, when developmental delay, photophobia, myoclonic fits, hyperacusis and irritability occur. Ophthalmoscopy: cherry-red spot at macula. Death usually occurs at 3-5yrs of age. Prenatal diagnosis may be made by amniocentesis.

Tolosa–Hunt syndrome A lesion in the superior orbital fissure produces unilateral ophthalmoplegia with disordered sensation (1st branch of V).

Treacher–Collins' syndrome Lower lid notching, oblique palpebral fissures, flattening of malar bones ± hypoplastic zygoma. If these are associated with mandibular defects, ear defects, and deafness, it is called Franceschetti's syndrome. Mutations in the TCOF1 gene may be to blame.

Turner's syndrome (X0 karyotype or mosaic, eg 45X/46,XX or 45,X/47,XXX.) ***Prevalence:*** 1:2500 girls. ***The Patient:*** Girls typically lack a sex chromosome, and this is associated with short stature (<130cm) ±, hyper-convex nails, wide carrying angle (cubitus valgus), inverted nipples, broad chest, ptosis, nystagmus, webbed neck, coarctation of the aorta, left heart defects, leg lymphoedema. Gonads are rudimentary/absent and puberty may not occur. ***Typical mode of death:*** Heart disease. ℞: Somatropin (human GH; 0.6–2U/kg/week SC, or in divided nightly doses) adds a median of 5.1cm to final stature (6.4cm if GH + oxandrolone ≤0.1mg/kg/day); don't give if epiphyses are fused. NB: GH may prolong the physiological state of insulin resistance observed in normal puberty (resultant hyperinsulinaemia may ↑anabolic effects of insulin on protein metabolism during puberty).[77] If hypogonadic, HRT, eg 2mg estradiol valerate + levonorgestrel 75µg at night, can start at 13yrs. ***Associations:*** Crohn's disease; chronic liver disease.[78] [79]

Ulysses syndrome After the Trojan war, Ulysses (the Latin name for Odysseus), King of Ithaca had many dangerous, and perhaps pointless adventures before he returned to his starting place. Similarly, many of our incurable patients start out with a problem, and end with much the same problem, after many dangerous and pointless tests have advanced their case not one iota. All this because none of us have been brave enough to say: "There is nothing we can do". It is always easier to order another scan or perform some daring operation, and Ulysses syndrome describes this over-investigation. But Homer, who was the first to describe Ulysses syndrome, offers us a tantalizing ambiguity: 'Ithaca has given you the beautiful voyage. Without her you would never have taken the road. And if you find her poor, Ithaca has not defrauded you…' Why not? Because the journey teaches our patients the one thing that has eluded us: namely wisdom.

Von Gierke's syndrome (type Ia glycogen storage disease; GSD 1a) is the most common and severe glycogenosis. ***Inheritance:*** Autosomal recessive (glucose-6-phosphatase↓ ∴ G6Pase gene mutation). ***Signs:*** Hepatomegaly, kidney enlargement, growth retardation, hypoglycaemia, lactic acidaemia, hyperuricaemia, failure to thrive, lumbar lordosis, hyperlipidaemia, adiposity, xanthomata over joints and buttocks, and a tendency to bleed. ***Complication:*** Hepatic adenoma; hepatocellular carcinoma.[80]

Werner's syndrome (WS; progeria) is characterized by precocious ageing after puberty, with diabetes, cataracts and scleroderma-like skin changes. The complex molecular and cellular phenotypes of WS involve features of genomic instability and accelerated replicative senescence. The gene involved (WRN) was recently cloned, and its gene product (WRNP) is a helicase. Helicases play important roles in a variety of DNA transactions, including DNA replication, transcription, repair, and recombination, and in WS unwinding of DNA pairs is disordered.[81] [82]

Winkler's disease p 538.

Wiskott–Aldrich syndrome is a severe X-linked primary immunodeficiency (p 198) with eczema, recurrent infections, autoimmune disorders, IgA nephropathy, and risk of haematopoietic malignancies. Platelets are too few and too small. Without marrow transplant, most will die before adulthood. DNA linkage helps with prenatal diagnosis. The responsible gene's protein is called Wiskott-Aldrich syndrome protein. Prenatal tests include direct gene analysis with single strand conformation polymorphism (SSCP) and heteroduplex formation (HD).[83]

11 Orthopaedics and trauma

Relevant pages in other chapters Any medical or surgical illness from acute abdomen to zoster may present to the Emergency Department. So every page here and in *OHCM* has relevance. ▸See *Pre-hospital care* (p 790–1). ▸Rheumatology chapter (*OHCM* p 408). ▸▸Childhood poisoning, p 190–3; (adults, *OHCM* p 826–7).

Internet orthopaedics www.worldortho.com; textbook: www.medmedia.com/med.htm.
www.trauma.org/imagebank/imagebank.html

▸Many detailed treatments are described in this chapter, and it is not envisaged that the inexperienced doctor will try them out except under appropriate supervision. The importance of enlisting early expert help (either at once or, if appropriate, by calling the patient back to the next morning's clinic) cannot be overemphasized.

'All these hags'

Once, after a stay in hospital with a fracture, a patient who was not quite as deaf as she was supposed to be, told one of us (JML) how she had overheard a newly arrived orthopaedic surgeon say to the Ward nurse "What are we going to do with all these hags?" As he progressed down the ward, turning first to the left and then to the beds on the right, his mood became morose, then black—as if he was getting angry that all these 'hags' were clogging up his beds, preventing his scientific endeavours. But what was really happening, my patient suspected, was that, as he turned to left and right, he was really nodding goodbye to his humanity, and, dimly aware of this, he was angry to see it go. On this view, these rows of hags were like buoys in the night, marking his passage out of our world. We all make this trip. Is there any way back? The process of becoming a doctor takes us away from the very people we first wanted to serve. Must medicine take the brightest and the best and turn us into quasi monsters?

The answer to these questions came unexpectedly in the months that followed: sheer pressure of work drove this patient's observations out of my mind. It was winter, and there was 'flu. In the unnatural twilight of a snowy day I drifted from bed to bed in a stupor of exhaustion with a deepening sense of a collapse that could not be put off…It was all I could do to climb into bed: but when I awoke, I found I had somehow climbed into a patient's bed, who had kindly moved over to make space for me, and was now looking at me with concern in her eyes. Herein lay the answer: the hag must make room for the doctor, and the doctor must make room for the hag: *we are all in the same bed.*

*A&E nomenclatures

A&E stands for Accident & Emergency; the word *accident* is often dropped, and ***emergency medicine*** has emerged as a speciality in its own right—which centres on the 'knowledge and skills required for the prevention, diagnosis, and management of the acute and urgent aspects of illness and injury affecting patients of all age groups with a full spectrum of physical and behavioural disorders. It is a specialty in which time is critical'. [1]

The neck

⏩If you suspect a cervical spine injury, immobilize the neck with hard-collar, sandbags,[1] and tape. NB: if very restless, use hard collar only, as otherwise the neck is vulnerable when the body moves on an immobilized head.

Examination The posture of the neck and any bone tenderness are noted. The range of movement ts: flexion; extension (mainly atlanto-occipital joint); rotation (mainly atlanto-axial joint); lateral flexion (whole of cervical spine). Rotation is the movement most commonly affected. The arms are examined for weakness that might signify root lesions (elbow flexion C5; wrist extension C6; elbow extension C7; finger flexion (grip) C8; finger abduction (intrinsics) T1). Reflexes are examined: biceps C5; supinator C6; triceps C7. Nerve root testing, including dermatomes are illustrated on p 765. If cord compression is suspected examine the lower limbs for signs of this (p 772)—eg upgoing plantars, hyperreflexia.

Investigation ⏩In major trauma, the first radiograph to do after resuscitation is a cross-table lateral of the cervical spine. All seven cervical vertebrae must be seen, along with the C7-T1 junction: do not accept an incomplete image—'swimmers' view of C7-T1 may be needed.

►A cross-table lateral in the best hands will miss ≤15% of injuries.

When examining the image, follow 4 simple steps (ABCS):

1 ***Alignment:*** •Anterior vertebral bodies •Posterior vertebral bodies •Posterior spinal canal •Spinous processes.
- Atlas-dens interval (ADI, fig 1)—normal = <3mm (adults); <5mm (children).
- A step of >3mm is abnormal (<25% = unifacet; >50% = bifacet dislocation).
- 40% of <7yr-olds have anterior displacement C2 on C3 (in this pseudo- or physiological subluxation, the posterior spinal line is maintained).

2 ***Bone contour:*** Trace around each vertebra individually.
- Anterior/posterior height difference of >3mm (implies *wedge fracture*). In general <25% difference is stable and >25% difference is unstable.
- Pedicles/spinous processes (*hangman's/clayshoveller's* fracture, fig 2).
- Avulsion fractures of the vertebral body (*Teardrop* fractures).

3 ***Cartilages:*** The disc space margins should be parallel (>11° is abnormal).

4 ***Soft tissues:*** Check soft tissue shadows:
- Retropharyngeal soft tissues—C1-C3 <3mm; C4-C7 <1 vertebral body.
- Spinous process separation (interspinous ligament rupture). Spiral CT can help diagnose fractures here.[2]

Other views and investigations

- Open mouth 'peg' view (OMV)
  - Odontoid peg fractures (type I = tip; type II = base; type III = body).
  - C1 fractures (TOTAL lateral mass overhang—normal is <8mm).
- CT is used to image areas not adequately assessed on plain films.
- MRI is used to assess ligamentous disruption, disc prolapse, and the neural elements (spinal cord and nerve roots).

►Epiphyses in children can be mistaken for fractures.

Spinal cord injury without radiological abnormality (SCIWORA) is a condition in which there is a neurological deficit (ie spinal cord injury) in the absence of a lesion on plain radiographs. It most commonly occurs in paediatric cervical spine injuries and is treated in the same manner as a spinal fracture with appropriate immobilization and referral.

1 If there is marked kyphosis, avoid hard collars to stabilize the spine, as the extension produced may be more than is natural for the patient: so collars may *cause* spinal injury.

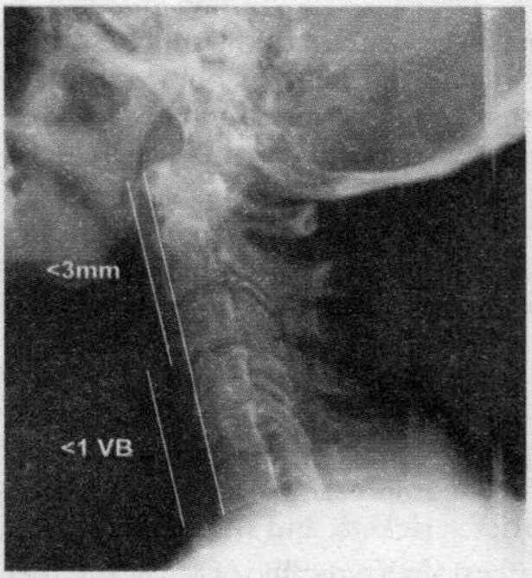

Fig 1. Landmarks in neck imaging.

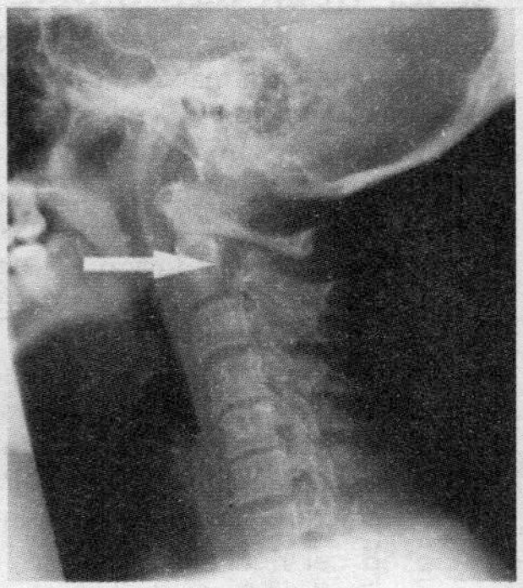

Fig 2. Spinus process fracture. Lateral radiograph of the cervical spine showing a fracture through the pedicles of the C2 vertebra—a hangman's fracture.

Other neck pathologies

Cervical spondylosis (See *OHCM* p 396.) Degeneration of the annulus fibrosus and bony spurs narrow the spinal canal and intervertebral foramina causing neck and arm pain with paraesthesiae—sometimes with myelopathy (spastic weakness, and, later, incontinence). Images and treatment: see *OHCM*.

Cervical spondylolisthesis: This is displacement of one vertebra upon the one below. ***Causes:***

1 Congenital failure of fusion of the odontoid process with the axis, or fracture of the odontoid process (skull, atlas, and odontoid process slip forward on axis).

2 Inflammation softens the transverse ligament of the atlas (eg rheumatoid or complicating throat infections), so the atlas slips forward upon the axis.

3 Instability after injuries. The most important consequence of spondylolisthesis is the possibility of spinal cord compression. Treatments used include traction, immobilization in plaster jackets, and spinal fusion.

Prolapsed cervical disc Central protrusions (typically of C5,6 & C6,7) may give symptoms of spinal cord compression (p 772; refer to neurosurgeon). Posterolateral protrusions may cause a stiff neck, pain radiating to the arm, weakness of muscles affected by the nerve root, and depressed reflexes. ***Tests:*** MRI is the preferred image. ***Treatment*** is with NSAIDs, and a collar. As pain subsides, physiotherapy may help to restore mobility. Surgery is occasionally indicated, in the light of CT/MRI findings.

Cervical rib Congenital development of the costal process of the C7 vertebra is often asymptomatic but may cause thoracic outlet compression. Similar symptoms with no radiological abnormality is called a scalenus or 1st rib syndrome. Thoracic outlet compression involves the lowest trunk of the brachial plexus (p 766) ± the subclavian artery. Pain or numbness may be felt in hand or forearm (often on the ulnar side); there may be hand weakness and muscle wasting (thenar or hypothenar). ***Diagnosis:*** Weak radial pulse ± forearm cyanosis. Radiographs may not reveal cervical ribs, as symptoms may be caused by fibrous bands. Arteriography may show subclavian compression. ***Treatment:*** Physiotherapy to strengthen the shoulder elevators may improve symptoms, but rib removal or band division may be needed.

Spasmodic torticollis (cervical dystonia) The commonest adult focal dystonia. Episodes of sudden-onset of a stiff painful neck with torticollis are due to trapezius and sternocleidomastoid spasm. ***Causes:*** Genetic; trauma. ***Treatment:*** If not self-limiting, heat, manipulation, relaxants, and analgesia may help. If severe, wearing a collar may help initial discomfort but may prolong symptoms. Botulinum toxin (p 460) may help for 4 months. Adjuncts: anticholinergics, benzodiazepines, baclofen.[3]

Infantile torticollis This may result from birth damage to sternocleidomastoid. ***Typical age:*** 6–36 months. ***Signs:*** Tilted head (ear nearer shoulder on affected side). ♂:♀ ≈3:2. There is retarded facial growth on the affected side, hence facial asymmetry. Early, there is a tumour-like thickening in the muscle (may be palpable). ***Differential:*** Spasmus nutans (head-nodding; torticollis; nystagmus); acquired late-infancy torticollis from rare CNS disorders (eg gangliocytoma). If there is an associated muscle mass, biopsy may be reassuring by showing a benign fibrous lesion.[4]

Treatment: Self-limiting in 97%. If persistent, physiotherapy helps by lengthening the muscle; division at its lower end is more drastic.[5]

The shoulder

The shoulder

Anatomically, the glenohumeral joint is lax, depending on surrounding rotator cuff muscles for stability—ie the sheath of tendons of subscapularis (internal rotation) infraspinatus (external rotation), and teres minor (external rotation + extension). Biceps' long head traverses the cuff, attaching to the top of the glenoid cavity.

History Any trauma? *Where* is the pain: shoulder? Neck? Does shoulder movement make it worse? (if all movements worsen pain, suspect arthritis or capsulitis; if only some movements, suspect impingement). General health OK? (If aches and pains all over, is it fibromyalgia or polymyalgia?)

Examination Strip to waist. To assess glenohumeral movement, feel the lower half of the scapula to estimate degrees of scapular rotation over the thorax. Half the range of normal abduction is achieved by scapula movement. Test *abduction* by raising hands from the sides sideways to above the head; *flexion* by raising hands forwards and upwards; *extension* by backward movement of elbows; *external rotation* by holding elbows against the sides flexed at 90° and moving the hands outwards (normal 80°); and *internal rotation* by placing the back of the hand against the lumbar spine and moving the elbows forward; an easier test is to assess how far behind her back she can reach: 'imagine you are doing up a bra at the back'.

The muscles used for movement at the shoulder joint

- *Flexion* (forward movement): pectoralis major, deltoid, coracobrachialis.
- *Extension:* deltoid (latissimus dorsi, pectoralis major, and teres major begin the extension if the shoulder starts out flexed).
- *Abduction:* supraspinatus (for first 15°); deltoid thereafter.
- *Adduction*: pectoralis major, latissimus dorsi, teres major, subscapularis.
- *Medial rotation*: pec. major, deltoid, latissimus dorsi, teres major, subscapularis.
- *Lateral rotation:* deltoid, teres minor, infraspinatus.

NB: rotator cuff muscles are most important in rotation: subscapularis, teres minor, infraspinatus (supraspinatus is also part of the rotator cuff).

Scapula movement on the chest wall NB: serratus anterior prevents 'winging' of the scapula as pressure is placed on the outstretched hand.

- *Elevation*: (shrug shoulders) levator scapulae, trapezius
- *Depression*: serratus anterior, pectoralis minor
- *Forward action* (eg punch): serratus anterior; pectoralis major
- *Retraction (brace shoulders)*: trapezius, rhomboid.

Recurrent dislocation of the shoulder (For initial dislocation, see p 738.) There are 2 types: ***Atraumatic:*** (5%) The patient is often a teenager with no history of trauma, but having general joint laxity. Remember BRAA: *b*ilateral; treat by *r*ehabilitation; *a*traumatic; dislocates in *a*ll directions.

Traumatic: Dislocation is usually anterior (sometimes inferior, rarely posterior) and secondary to trauma (may be mild). Remember BUST: *B*ankart lesion (see below); *u*nidirectional; *s*urgical treatment; *t*raumatic. Abduction + lateral rotation of the arm (eg donning a coat) may cause dislocation. The capsule is attached to the neck of scapula but detached from the glenoid labrum (Bankart lesion). There may be a posterolateral 'dent' in the humeral head (seen on radiographs with arm medially rotated). Treatment: (open or arthroscopic) in Bankart repair (sew capsule back to glenoid); the Putti-Platt operation (the subscapularis tendon is shortened) is less commonly done.[6]

With the rarer recurrent posterior dislocation, the capsule is torn from the back of the neck of scapula, the humeral dent is superomedial, and it is abduction & medial rotation which causes dislocation (eg seizure). ***Treatment:*** Surgery—if prompt closed reduction fails.[7]

Recurrent *subluxation* is also recognized (disabling and difficult to treat).

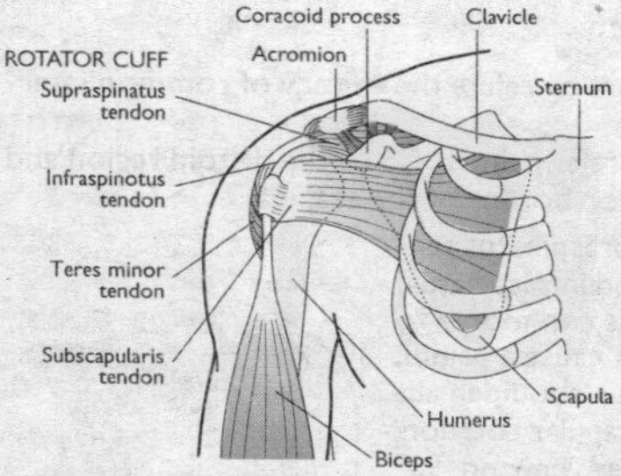

Fig 1. Shoulder anatomy (without deltoid).

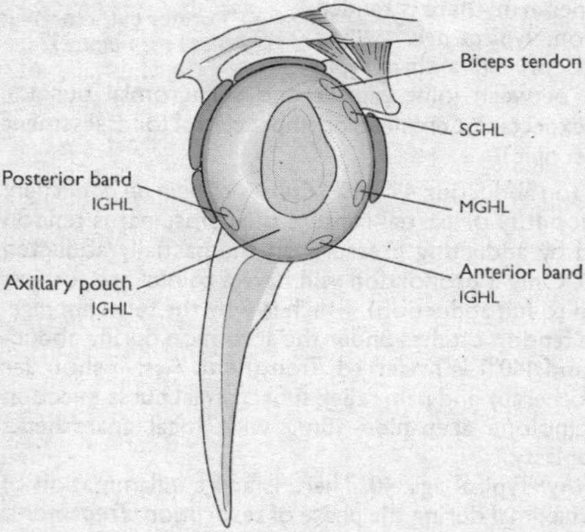

Fig 2. The glenoid surface of the gleno-humeral joint, showing the glenohumeral ligaments (GHL)—superior (SGHL), medial (MGHL), and inferior (IGHL).

The painful shoulder

'There is little evidence to support or refute the efficacy of common interventions for shoulder pain...'[MET 10]

Remember that the neck may refer pain via C5 to the deltoid region and via C6, C7, and C8 to the superior border of the scapula.

Rotator cuff tears Tears in supraspinatus tendon (or adjacent subscapularis and infraspinatus) may be from degeneration, or, less commonly, to a sudden jolt or fall. Partial tears cause a painful arc (below); complete tears limit shoulder abduction to the 45–60° given by scapular rotation. If the arm is passively abducted beyond 90° deltoid's contribution to abduction comes into play, which is then possible from this point. Full-range *passive* movement is present. Pain is felt at the shoulder-tip and upper arm; there is tenderness under the acromion. *Typical age:* >40yrs. ***Tests:*** Ultrasound, MRI, or MRI-arthrography reveals communication between joint capsule and subacromial bursa.[12] ***Treatment:*** *Incomplete:* expectant. *Complete:* prompt referral for assessment for repair (open/arthroscopic).

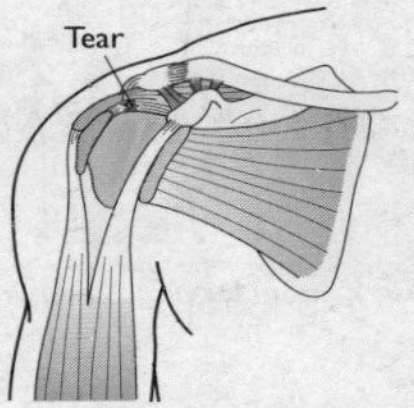

Fig 1. Rotator cuff tear.[11] *(See p 662 for names.)*

Painful arc syndrome (on abducting 45°–160°) *Causes of pain on abduction:*

1 ***Supraspinatus tendinopathy*** or partial rupture of supraspinatus tendon gives pain reproduced by adducting pressure on the partially abducted arm. Typical age: 35–60. Only a proportion will have a painful arc (others have increasing pain up to full abduction), which is why the term *impingement syndrome* (as the tendon catches under the acromion during abduction between, eg 70° and 140°) is preferred. ***Treatment:*** Active shoulder movement with physiotherapy and pain relief; subacromial bursa injection of steroid, eg triamcinolone acetonide 40mg with local anaesthetic; arthroscopic acromioplasty.

2 ***Calcifying tendinopathy:*** Typical age: 40. There is acute inflammation of supraspinatus. Pain is maximal during the phase of resorption. ***Treatment:*** Physiotherapy; NSAIDs; steroid injection; rarely, excision of calcium.

3 ***Acromioclavicular joint osteoarthritis (AC joint OA):*** This is common. Try steroid injections or excision of the lateral end of the clavicle.

Tendinopathy of long head of biceps Pain is felt in the anterior shoulder and is characteristically worse on forced contraction of biceps. ***Treatment:*** Pain relief; hydrocortisone injection to the tendon may give relief but risks tendon rupture. Technique: p 710.

Rupture of long head of biceps Discomfort occurs after 'something has gone' when lifting or pulling. A 'ball' appears in the muscle on elbow flexion. ***Treatment:*** Repair is rarely indicated as function remains.

Frozen shoulder (adhesive capsulitis) may follow modest injury in older people. Pain may be severe and worse at night (eg unable to lie on one side). Active and passive movement range is reduced. Abduction↓ (<90°) ± external rotation↓ (<30°). It may be associated with cervical spondylosis (more global restriction of movement). ***Treatment:*** NSAIDs, intra-articular steroid, physiotherapy, manipulation. Meta-analyses of randomized trials are said not to support any one option, but they did not include Der Windt's trial which strongly favoured injections. Resolution may take years.[13]

Shoulder osteoarthritis This is not so common as hip or knee OA. Good success rates are being achieved by joint replacement—complications: infection, dislocation, loosening, periprosthetic humeral/glenoid fractures, nerve injury, prosthetic fracture; ectopic ossification.[14]

The elbow

[illegible]

The elbow

The normal range of flexion and extension at the elbow is 0–150°. With the elbow flexed, supination and pronation of 90° should be possible. A 100° arc in each plane is required for acceptable upper limb function, ie 30°–130° extension/flexion and 50°–50° pronation/supination.[15] Pain at the elbow and middle outer aspect of the arm may radiate from the shoulder.

Tennis elbow There is inflammation where the common extensor tendon arises from the lateral epicondyle of the humerus (lateral epicondylitis—better named as a teno-periostitis) ± rupture of aponeurotic fibres. This is usually caused by strain. ***Presentation:*** Pain is worst when the tendon is most stretched (wrist and finger flexion with hand pronated). Pain is felt at the front the lateral condyle. Ask the patient to extend the wrist, and then pull on the hand to elicit pain. ***Radiography:*** Nonspecific. ***Treatment:*** Pain often subsides in time, but some favour injection of the tendon origin (p 710).[RCT 16] If this fails, physiotherapy may help, or an epicondylitis brace; with severe disability, excision of the diseased part of the common extensor origin and repair of the extensor mechanism gives relief in 80% of recalcitrant disease. Meta-analyses are equivocal on the best form of treatment.[MET 17]

Golfer's elbow This is medial humeral epicondylitis. It is less common than tennis elbow. Steroid injection may help, but be wary of the ulnar nerve; the brachial artery is also nearby.[18]

Student's elbow This is a traumatic bursitis following pressure on the elbows, eg while engrossed in a long book. There is pain and swelling behind the olecranon. Other causes are septic and gouty bursitis (look for tophi). The bursa should be aspirated (send fluid for Gram stain and microscopy for crystals). Traumatic bursitis may then be injected with hydrocortisone. Septic bursitis should be formally drained.

Ulnar neuritis Osteoarthritic or rheumatoid narrowing of the ulnar groove and constriction of the ulnar nerve as it passes behind the medial epicondyle, or friction of the ulnar nerve due to cubitus valgus (a possible sequel to childhood supracondylar fractures) can cause fibrosis of the ulnar nerve and ulnar neuropathy. ***Presentation:*** Sensory symptoms usually occur first, eg ↓ sensation over the little finger and medial half of ring finger. Patients may experience clumsiness of the hand and weakness of the small muscles of the hand innervated by the ulnar nerve (adductor pollicis, interossei, abductor digiti minimi and opponens digiti minimi). ***Tests:*** Nerve conduction studies will confirm the site of the lesion. ***Treatment:*** Operative release of the nerve to lie in a new channel in front of the elbow.

Deformities ***Cubitus valgus:*** The normal degree of valgus ('carrying angle') at the elbow is 10° in ♂, and 15° in ♀. Fractures at the lower end of the humerus or interference with the lateral epiphyseal growth plate may cause the angle to be greater. As a result ulnar neuritis and osteoarthritis may occur. Treat if necessary. Association: Turner's.

Cubitus varus: This may occur after poorly reduced supracondylar fractures.

Osteoarthritis of the elbow Osteochondritis dissecans and fractures involving the joint are risk factors. ***Tests:*** Flexion, extension and forearm rotation may be impaired. ***Treatment:*** Operation is rarely indicated but operative procedures include: removal of loose bodies, debridement, radial head excision, and joint replacement.

The wrist and hand

The wrist and hand

Dupuytren's contracture Progressive, painless fibrotic thickening of the palmar fascia (aponeurosis) with skin puckering and tethering. ***Causes/ associations:*** Multifactorial, eg genetic (autosomal dominant), alcoholism, antiepileptics, Peyronie's disease, knuckle pads. Ring and little fingers are chiefly affected (± plantar fascia). It is often bilateral and symmetrical. As thickening occurs there may be MCP joint flexion. If interphalangeal joints are affected the hand may be quite disabled. Surgery (eg fasciectomy) aims to remove affected palmar fascia and hence prevent progression. As a guide, if he cannot place his palm flat on a flat surface (*Hueston's* table-top test) surgical referral is wise. There is tendency for recurrence. Try to avoid finger amputations.[19]

Ganglia These smooth, multilocular jelly like swellings are bulges of synovium, eg at the wrist. They communicate with joint capsules or tendon sheaths. ***Treatment*** is not needed unless they cause pain or pressure (eg on median or ulnar nerve at wrist, or lateral popliteal nerve at the knee). They may disappear spontaneously. Local pressure may disperse them (traditionally a blow from a Bible). Aspiration via a wide-bore needle may work, or they may be dissected out; problems include painful scars, neurovascular damage (esp. in volar wrist ganglia), and recurrence.[20]

De Quervain's syndrome (stenosing tenovaginitis) There is pain over the styloid process of the radius and thickening of the tendons of abductor pollicis longus and extensor pollicis brevis. Pain is worst when these tendons are stretched (eg lifting a teapot) and is elicited by forced adduction and flexion of the thumb into the palm. (Finckelstein's sign). Pain is more proximal than that from osteoarthritis of the first carpometacarpal joint. ***Cause:*** unknown but it commonly follows activities involving much use of the tendons (eg wringing clothes). ***Treatment:*** First try NSAIDs or hydrocortisone injection around the tendons in their sheaths. If injection (p 710) and rest fail to relieve, decompression of the tendons is provided by deroofing or splitting the tendon sheaths. >80% do well post-op.[21,22]

Trigger finger (tendon nodules) Disproportion of the tendon to its sheath giving a fixed flexion deformity. Ring and middle fingers are most commonly affected, and the thumb especially in babies and children. Full extension of the affected digit cannot be achieved by the muscles of the hand, and if aided by the other hand, a 'click' may be felt in the flexor tendon. As extension occurs, the nodule moves with the flexor tendon, but then becomes jammed on the proximal side of the pulley, and has to be flicked straight, so producing triggering. Nodules are associated with rheumatoid arthritis. ***Treatment:*** Unless the patient is a child, or has renal failure or diabetes, steroid injection into the region of the nodule, under low pressure, but not into the nodule itself (eg 1mL of Depomedrone® + lidocaine) may be tried. Risk of recurrence is high, so surgery may be needed (eg as an 'office procedure' to release the 'A1' pulley).[23,24]

Volkmann's ischaemic contracture Follows interruption of the brachial artery near the elbow (eg after supracondylar fracture of humerus, p 740). Muscle necrosis (especially flexor pollicis longus and flexor digitorum profundus) results in contraction and fibrosis causing a flexion deformity at wrist and elbow, with forearm pronation, wrist flexion, thumb flexion & adduction, digital metacarpophalangeal joint extension, and interphalangeal joint flexion. Suspect if a damaged arm is blue, with no radial pulse, and passive finger extension is painful (this is the crucial sign). ***Treatment:*** Remove constricting splints, warm other limbs (promote vasodilatation). If pulse doesn't return within 30min, explore the artery. *Treating contractures:* release of compressed nerves ± tendon lengthening and transfers to restore lost function.[25]

Examination of the back

Examination of the back

History The commonest orthopaedic complaint is back pain. Attention should be paid to the nature of the pain, exacerbating and relieving factors, and the history of onset. It is important to know if bowel or bladder function is affected (this signifies cord or cauda equina compression and should set your alarm bells ringing loudly: refer at once). With low back pains it is not uncommon for pain to radiate down the leg (sciatica): such pain may be accompanied by root signs (see below).

Examination With the patient standing and wearing only bra & pants inspect the back for abnormality and palpate for local tenderness and deformity. Movements assessed are *forward flexion* (stretch forward to touch toes with knees straight—look to see how much movement is due to back flexion and how much by flexion at the hips—with back flexion the back has a gently rounded contour. Look for a rib lump, a sign of scoliosis); *extension* (arch spine backwards); *lateral flexion* (lean sideways so hand moves down corresponding thigh) and *rotation* (keep pelvis fixed but move shoulders round to each side in turn). Movement at the costovertebral joints is assessed by the difference in chest expansion between maximal inspiration and expiration (normal: 5cm). Iliac crests are grasped by the examiner and compressed to move sacroiliac joints and see if this reproduces the pain. ***Note:*** On bending fully forwards, expansion of a line drawn from 10cm above L5 to 5cm below it by <5cm is firm and quantifiable evidence of movement restriction.

Compare leg length; quantify discrepancy and muscle wasting (measure thigh and calf circumference), for weakness, sensory loss, and normal reflexes (knee jerk is mainly L4, ankle jerk S1, plantars should be down-going).

Straight leg raising *Why?* To test for a mechanical cause of sciatic pain. ***How?*** Keeping the knee extended, lift the patient's leg off the couch and note the angle to which the leg can be raised before eliciting pain. If <45°, Lasègue's sign is said to be positive. ***Mechanism?*** This stretches the sciatic nerve and causes root pain (a characteristic lancinating pain distributed in the relevant dermatome, and made worse by coughing or sneezing). ***Alternatively:*** The method described above often elicits pain in the hypersensitive nerve root. Alternatively sit the patient up in bed with legs out in front. This can be done while examining another system, and may prove pain-free.

Other parts of the body examined These are the iliac fossae (important in days when tuberculous psoas abscesses were common), abdomen, pelvis and rectum, and major arteries. The commonest tumours to metastasize to bone are: breast, bronchus, kidney, thyroid, and prostate so it may be relevant to examine these.

Tests In acute low back pain, tests are not usually needed in the first 2 weeks. FBC, CRP (infection), ESR (if high, think of metastases or myeloma, and do electrophoresis ± bone marrow), alkaline phosphatase (high in Paget's disease and tumours), calcium. In the absence of trauma, MRI is the gold-standard imaging investigation and is sometimes available in primary care. Radioisotope scanning is a non-specific investigation but may reveal 'hot spots' of tumour or pyogenic infection.

Kyphosis and scoliosis

Causes of kyphosis
• Osteoporosis • Spina bifida • Calvé's & Scheuermann's osteochondritis (p 704). • Cancer; wedge fractures • Tuberculosis; polio • Paget's disease • Ankylosing spondylitis

Kyphosis is spinal cervical flexion deformity typically with slight extension (lordosis), the thoracic spine flexed, and lumbar spine again extended. Treat the underlying cause if indicated. NB: congenital kyphosis is much less common than congenital scoliosis, but is more serious, as cord compression and paraplegia sometimes develop rapidly, eg during adolescence.

Scoliosis This is lateral spinal curvature with secondary vertebral rotation. The chief cause is muscle spasm (eg with sciatica). Classification:

- Congenital (failure of formation or segmentation).
- Idiopathic (this is seen both in infants and adolescents).
- Neuromuscular (neuropathic, eg UMN/LMN lesion or myopathic eg cerebral palsy or muscular dystrophy).
- Syndromic (eg Marfan's, *OHCM* p 730, or neurofibromatosis, *OHCM* p 402).
- Other (eg tumour, infection, trauma).

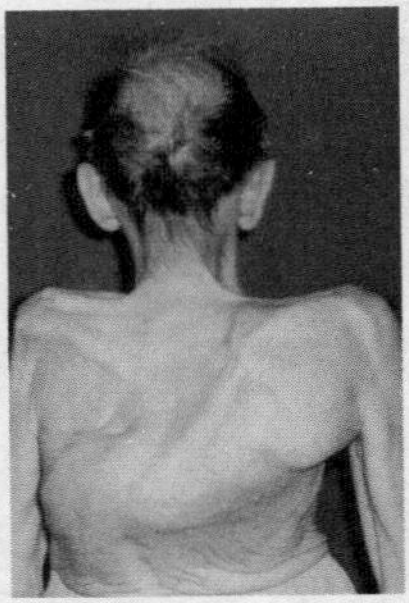

Fig 1. Kyphoscoliosis

Idiopathic scoliosis There is lateral curvature of the thoracic or lumbar spine >10°. Adolescent idiopathic scoliosis (AIS) is the most common spinal deformity; girls are more often affected than boys—and they are often taller than their peers at presentation (but not ultimately). Complications in later life revolve around pain, cosmesis, and impaired lung function. Thoracic problems tend to give more severe deformity than lumbar. Rib deformity causes a characteristic hump on the convex side of the curve which becomes manifest on asking the patient to bend forwards. Curvature increases while the affected person continues to grow, so usually the earlier the onset the worse the deformity. Since the advent of screening, scoliosis has been detected in 1.5-3%; of these only ~6% progress: the younger the child, the more the risk of progression—double curves progress more than single curves. Thoracolumbar or lumbar curves progress the least. Treatment is needed in 2.75/1000 screened. Where curvatures are <45-50° and growth is completed, or <29° if growth is in progress, the situation is monitored regularly: eg every 3 months during growth, and every 8 months thereafter.[1] When curvatures are progressing, attempts to halt it may be made using a Boston or Milwaukee distraction-derotation brace (particularly for double curves, or if the apex of the curve is higher than the 8th thoracic vertebra[1]) until the child is old enough for any spinal surgery that may be indicated. NB: it can be hard to persuade a child to wear a brace for the ≥20h/day that is optimal!—bracing will not correct the deformity but has a role in slowing/preventing curve progression. Surgery involves deformity correction with spinal fusion and stabilization (pedicle screws and longitudinal rods). The most feared complication of spinal surgery, paralysis, has reduced with the advent of intra-operative spinal cord monitoring, and occurs in 0.23%.

►When scoliosis in youth gives pain (especially at night), exclude osteoid osteoma, osteoblastoma, spondylolisthesis, and spinal tumours.

1 Boston braces worn for >18h/day *do* prevent progression of large curves at a mean of 9.8 years after bracing is discontinued: J Wiley 2000 *Spine* **25** 2326

Causes of back pain

Causes of back pain

Sinister back pain: ►p 678

Backache is often from low back strain or degenerative disease. ***Local pain*** is typically deep and aching (from soft tissue and vertebral body irritation). ***Radicular pain*** is stabbing, and is caused by compression of the dorsal nerve roots. Radicular pain projects in a dermatomal distributions. *Other causes:* retroperitoneal (duodenal ulcer, pancreas ca, aneurysm; pain is often lumbodorsal and spine movements pain-free & full); neoplasia (eg myeloma), infection, disc lesions, arthritis, and osteoporosis/osteomalacia.

Mechanical pain The spine is a complex series of articulations, with spongy discs between vertebral bodies acting as shock absorbers, and a multitude of articulating facet joints. Problems in one part affect function of the whole, and spasm of vertebral muscles can cause much pain. Upright posture provokes big forces on the spine, eg when lifting and discs may rupture (if young), vertebrae fracture (elderly) or soft tissues tear (low back strain). NB: with low back strain the exact mechanism may be elusive; if there are no sinister features (p 676) take time to explain the diagnosis and management (p 676); radiography if unimproved eg at 6 weeks.

Danger signs of cauda equina compression
►►Saddle-area sensation ↓
►►Incontinence/retention of faeces or urine
►►Poor anal tone (do PR)
►►Paralysis ± sensory loss
Do neuroimaging *today*.

Disc prolapse Lumbar discs are those most likely to rupture (esp. the lowest 2). Typically, one is seized by severe pain on coughing, sneezing, or twisting a few days after back strain (onset may be insidious). Pain may be confined to the lower lumbar area (lumbago), or may radiate to buttock or leg (sciatica) if the herniated nucleus pulposus compresses a nerve root. ***Signs:*** Forward flexion (p 670) and extension limited, ± lateral flexion—unilaterally and inconstantly. With L5–S1 prolapse, S1 root compression causes calf pain, weak foot plantar flexion, ↓sensation (pinprick) over sole of foot and back of calf, and ↓ankle jerk. With L4–5 prolapse, hallux extension is weak and sensation↓ on outer dorsum of foot. If lower lumbar discs prolapse centrally, cauda equina compression (p 772) may occur.

Tests: MRI (or CT) if intervention is contemplated, eg cauda equina compression, or if rest fails and symptoms are severe, with CNS signs such as reflex or sensory changes, or muscle wasting.

Treating disc prolapse: Brief rest and early mobilization + pain relief (p 676) is all that is needed in 90% (± physiotherapy). Discectomy is needed in cauda equina syndrome, progressive muscular weakness, or continuing pain. 27 40 trials

Spondylolisthesis There is displacement (usually forward) of one lumbar vertebra upon the one below. ***Causes:*** Spondylolysis (defect in pars interarticularis of neural arch); congenital malformation of articular processes, osteoarthritis of posterior facet joints (older folk). Onset of pain with or without sciatica is often in adolescence. ***Diagnosis*** is by plain radiographs. ***Treatment*** may involve wearing a corset, or nerve release and spinal fusion.

Lumbar spinal stenosis (LSS) and lateral recess stenosis

Facet joint osteoarthritis (the only synovial joints in the back) may produce generalized narrowing of the lumbar spinal canal or simply of its lateral recesses. Unlike the pain of lumbar disc prolapse, this causes:

- Pain worse on walking with aching and heaviness in one or both legs causing the person to stop walking ('spinal claudication').
- Pain on extension. • Negative straight leg raising test. • Few CNS signs.

Tests: MRI (CT and myelography are less good options).

Treatment: Canal decompression (removing its posterior wall) gives good results if NSAIDs, epidural steroid injections, and corsets (to prevent exaggerating the lumbar lordosis of standing) fail to help.

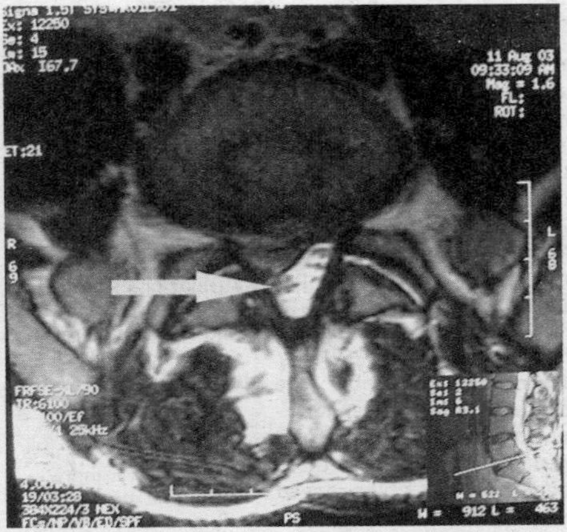

Fig 1. Axial MRI image at the L5/S1 level showing a right-sided para-central disc prolapse. Observe the displaced nerve roots within the CSF-filled dural sac (arrow). (CSF is white on this T2 weighted MRI)

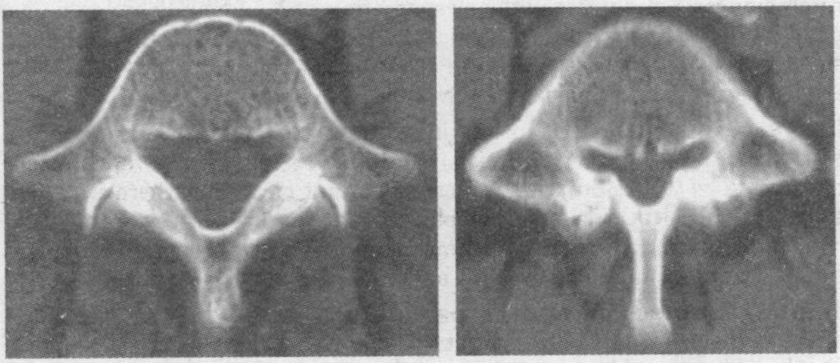

Fig 2. Cross-section CT images at L5, one with spinal stenosis. Observe the difference in spinal canal shape and dimensions caused by osteoarthritis of the facet joints posterolaterally. Factors contributing to spinal stenosis: disc prolapse, spondylolisthesis, and congenitally short pedicles. Identify the spinal canal contents at this level, including the thecal sac and the two L5 nerve root sheaths that occupy the lateral recesses.

Notes on the cauda equina

The spinal cord tapers to its end, the conus medullaris, at L1. Lumbar and sacral nerve roots arising from the conus medullaris form the cauda equina. These spinal nerve roots separate in pairs, exiting laterally through the nerve root foramina, providing motor and sensory innervation of the legs and pelvic organs. Compression may be from extrinsic tumours, primary tumours, spondylosis, spinal stenosis, achondroplasia, fluorosis, central disk herniation, abscess, or tuberculoma.[28]

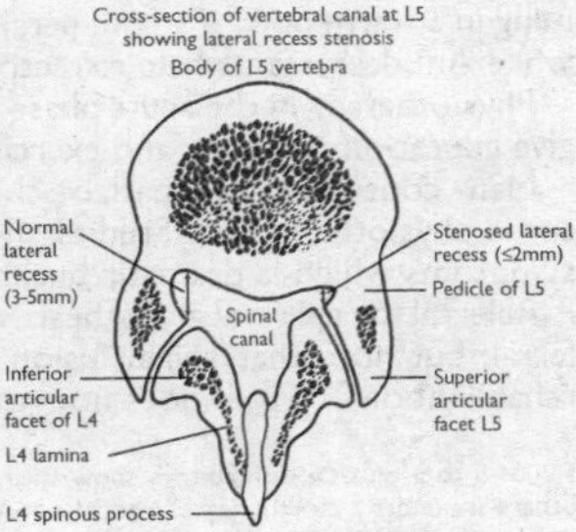

Fig 3. L5 cross-section: lateral recess stenosis.

Management of low back pain

Back pain is common. 80% of the Western population suffer it at some stage in their lives. 50/1000 industrial workers have time off work because of it each year. In the UK it accounts for 11 million lost working days/yr (£3.8 billion/yr in lost production). A GP expects 20 people per 1000 on her list to consult with it each year, of whom ~10% are referred to hospital. Fewer than 10% of those referred to a specialist will have surgery. Physiotherapy may be carried out in hospital or general practice.

Most back pain is self-limiting: of those attending GPs, 70% are better after 3 weeks, 90% by 6 weeks, irrespective of treatment. But remember: the cause of back pain can be sinister—cancer, infection, or cord or cauda equina compression—and an approach is needed that detects these promptly. Age is important: only 3% of those aged between 20 and 55 have 'spinal pathology' (tumour, infection, inflammatory disease) compared with 11% of those <20yrs, and 19% >55yrs. ►Pain brought on by activity and relieved by rest is *rarely* sinister. Refer those with any suggestion of cord or cauda equina compression (p 772), or with deteriorating unilateral signs *at once*. If cancer or infection is suspected, refer promptly. ►Do FBC, ESR, LFT etc whenever pain lasts >3wks, whatever the age.

Backache is sinister if:

- ≤20 or ≥55 years old
- Violent trauma
- Alternating sciatica (both legs involved)
- Bilateral sciatica
- Weak legs
- Weight loss
- ESR↑ (>25mm/h)
- Taking oral steroids
- Progressive, continuous, non-mechanical pain
- Systemically unwell
- Drug abuse or HIV +ve
- Spine movement in all directions painful
- Local bony tenderness
- CNS deficit at more than one root level
- Pain or tenderness of thoracic spine
- Bilateral signs of nerve root tension
- Past neoplasia

Imaging In general, don't do imaging such as CT/MRI before doing blood tests (LFT, FBC, ESR, electrophoesis)—and reserve for when symptoms are chronic, ie >4 weeks duration (unless significant trauma or there are alarm symptoms, see BOX). Plain radiographs correlate poorly with symptoms and irradiate gonads. ~25% of asymptomatic adults show degenerative changes on plain films of the lumbar spine, and 50% have bulging discs.[29]

Treating biomechanical back pain 'Get on with your life within the limits of the pain' gives better results than physiotherapy with lateral bending exercises. Avoid bed-rest after the 1st 48h (a board under the mattress helps). Avoid slouching. Advise on avoiding back stress: how to rise from lying, avoid stooping, bending, lifting, and low chairs.[30] RCT[31] [N=52]

Analgesia breaks the pain-muscle spasm cycle (paracetamol, ≤4g/24h PO, ± NSAID, eg diclofenac, combined with gastroprotective misoprostol, eg as Arthrotec®).[1] Opioids may be needed at first. Warmth helps, as does swimming in a warm pool. If spasm persists, try diazepam 2mg/8h PO for a short while. Antidepressants help refractory pain, but not level of functioning. MET[32]

Physiotherapy in the acute phase can ↓pain and spasm. In convalescence, give education on lifting and exercises to strengthen the back muscles.

Many consult an osteopath or chiropractor for manipulation (as done by some physiotherapists). Studies show manipulation can produce relief of symptoms which is dramatic but may not be longlasting.[33]

Referral for epidural anaesthesia, and corsets may help + orthopaedic referral; but note that spinal fusion is probably not better than intensive rehabilitation RCT[34] if pain does not resolve.

1 2004-5 data on COX-2 inhibitors show their role is uncertain (some have been withdrawn and others are under a cloud); heart SE are also↑. And COX-2 inhibitor peptic SEs may be more serious than standard NSAIDs. Arthrotec® (eg 50mg/12h after food) is a good choice as its gastric protective properties (misoprostol) translate into ↓mortality. ►Avoid in fertile women. Alternative: nabumetone 1g PO at night; in severe pain 0.5-1g in morning as well; elderly 0.5-1g daily. In one study, the adjusted odds of death for Arthrotec® was 1.4 and 3 for naproxen. Ashworth 2004 *J Rheumatol* 2004 **31** 951

Why do some people get intractable back pain?

39% of adults have, or have had, an intermittent chronic back problem, and much energy is expended on frequently fruitless searches for the causes listed opposite. Imaging may be non-specific (subclinical disc protrusion, facet joint arthritis, or minor spondylosis). Risk factors for chronicity:

- Smoking
- Psychological morbidity
- Low income/social class
- Co-existing cardio-respiratory disease
- Poor work conditions
- Number of children (for women *and* men)

Be cautious of blaming sitting at work for chronic back pain. Meta-analyses do not find in favour of this popular association.[35]

Vascular problems may underlie chronicity (hence associations with smoking and heart disease), and pain may be maintained by involvement of the sympathetic chain, which may mediate hyperaesthesia, hyperpathia (excess pain from minor noxious stimuli), allodynia (pain from minor skin stimulation)—but surgical sympathectomy often only provides temporary relief. This implies central neuromodulation of stimuli producing a complex regional pain syndrome. Dorsal horn receptor fields may expand and have their thresholds changed by peripheral injury, so pain is more intense, and appreciated over a wider area than simple anatomy would predict.[36]

Specific and sometimes sinister back pain

Typical causes ***15–30yrs:*** Prolapsed disc, trauma, fractures, ankylosing spondylitis (*OHCM* p 419), spondylolisthesis (L5 shifts forward on S1), pregnancy. ***>30yrs:*** Prolapsed disc, cancer (lung, breast, prostate, thyroid, kidney). ***>50yrs:*** Degenerative, osteoporosis, Paget's, malignancy, myeloma. Lumbar artery atheroma (which may itself cause disc degeneration).

Rarer causes: Spinal stenosis (bony encroachment); cauda equina tumours; spinal infection (usually staphylococcal, also *Proteus*, *E. coli*, *Salmonella typhi*, TB). Often no systemic signs of infection.

Spinal tumours These may be of spinal cord, meninges, nerves, or bone. They may be primary, secondary, lymphoma, or myeloma. They may compress the cord, causing pain, lower motor neurone signs at the level of lesion, upper motor neurone signs and sensory loss below; bowel and bladder dysfunction. Peripheral nerve function may be impaired resulting in pain along the course of the nerve, weakness, hyporeflexia & ↓sensation (p 764). With cauda equina involvement there is often urinary retention ± saddle anaesthesia. When the deposit is in the spinal canal and if there is no bone involvement, there may be no pain, just long tract signs. When bones of the back are involved there is progressive constant pain and local destruction of bone. Metastases tend to affect cancellous bone, but focal lesions cannot be seen on radiographs until 50% of bone mass is lost. There may be much muscle spasm and local tenderness to percussion. Bone collapse may result in deformity, or cause cord or nerve compression. ***Tests:*** Plain radiographs; CT; MRI; isotope bone scans; bone biopsy.

In those with past cancer and current back pain, it is best to do a bone scan first, with plain radiographs of any hot spots suggesting metastases.

Pyogenic spine infections This is a notoriously difficult diagnosis as all signs of infection may be absent (eg no fever, tenderness, or WCC↑), although the ESR is often raised. It may be secondary to other septic foci. Pain occurs, and movement is restricted by spasm. It is usually an infection of the disc space (discitis). ***Risk factors:*** Diabetes mellitus, immunosuppression, urinary surgery, or catheterization. Half the infections are staphylococcal; *Proteus, E. coli, Salmonella typhi* and TB also occur. ***Tests:*** Radiographs shows bone rarefaction or erosion, joint space narrowing ± subligamentous new bone formation. Technetium bone scans and MRI are better. ***Treatment:*** As for osteomyelitis elsewhere (p 696), resting the back with bed rest, brace, or plaster jacket. Surgery may be needed.

Spinal TB Rare in those born in the West, this tends to affect young adults, giving pain, and stiffness of all back movements. ESR↑. Abscesses and cord compression may occur (Pott's paraplegia). Radiographs show narrow disc spaces and local osteoporosis early, with bone destruction leading to wedging of vertebrae later. In the thoracic spine, paraspinal abscesses may be seen on radiographs, and kyphosis on examination; with lower thoracic or lumbar involvement abscess formation may be related to psoas muscle in the flank, or in the iliac fossa. MRI (not CT) is the ideal way to delineate cord compression. Treatment is anti-TB drugs (eg for 1yr; p 160) with abscess drainage. Fixation + bone grafting, or metal rods, plates, or wires needs highly specialized services. If a syrinx (tubular cavity) has developed, complete neural recovery is not expected.[37]

Central disc protrusion This neurosurgical emergency is suggested by bilateral sciatica, perineal or 'saddle' anaesthesia and disturbance of gut or bladder function. ►*Prompt decompression may prevent leg paralysis.*

Diagnostic triage: which group encompasses your patient?

Simple lumbar pain	*Nerve root pain*	*Possibly sinister features*
Aged 20-55 with 'mechanical' backache, eg caused by twisting and worse on moving	One leg hurting more than the back	Pain unrelated to mechanical events
Patient well in himself; no fever no weight loss	Radiation to foot/ toes	Thoracic pain ± deformity
	Hip flexion reproduces the pain in the leg	Past history, eg HIV; TB neoplasia, or steroid use
	Localized neurological signs	Widespread CNS signs
		Weight loss; fever; unwell; no pain, but long tract signs

►Signs demanding immediate (same-day) referral: gait or sphincter disturbance; saddle anaesthesia—these suggest cauda equina compression.

Evidence on management: see www.rcgp.org.uk/clinspec/guidelines/backpain/

Hip history and examination

(For hip prostheses, see p 706.)

The movements examined at the hip are described in fig 1. Internal rotation is often the first movement to be restricted by hip disease.[38]

Questions Are activities of daily living affected?—walking distance, ability to climb stairs (only one at a time possible?), difficulty getting out of low chairs. Remember that pain in the knee may be referred from the hip.

Measurements Apparent leg length disparity (with the lower limbs parallel and in line with the trunk) is called either 'apparent shortening' (eg due to pelvic tilt or fixed adduction deformity—which gives the apparent shortening on that side) or 'apparent lengthening' (eg due to fixed hip abduction). In these cases, there is no true disparity, as detected by measuring between the anterior superior iliac spine and medial malleolus on each side with the pelvis held square and the lower limbs held equally adducted or abducted.

Fixed deformity Joint or muscle contractures prevent limbs from being put in the neutral position. With fixed adduction deformity, the angle between the limb and the transverse axis of the pelvis (line between both anterior superior iliac spines) is <90° but with fixed abduction deformity it is >90°. Fixed flexion deformity is detected by ***Thomas' test:*** Feel for lumbar lordosis[1] under the side on which fixed flexion deformity is suspected. If none is present, there is no flexion deformity (provided both legs are resting flat on the table). If lordosis is present, flex the sound side maximally (knee to chest). At the end point of flexion, you will feel his lumbar spine press against your hand as the lumbar lordosis straightens out. If there is a fixed flexion deformity, the leg opposite the one being flexed will rise a few degrees off the table, as it is being pulled up as the pelvis rotates. Push down on the thigh of the side being tested to help check whether or not it has been pulled off the table. The angle through which the thigh is raised is the angle of fixed flexion. (NB: to assess the full range of extension, have the patient assume the prone position on the table and then extend the hip.)[39]

The Trendelenburg test This tests the stability of the hip and the ability to support the pelvis when standing on one leg. In this state, it is normal for the pelvis to rise on the side of the lifted leg. A +ve test is when the pelvis falls on the side of the lifted leg. ***Causes:*** **1** Abductor muscle paralysis (gluteus medius and minimus); **2** Upward displacement of the greater trochanter (severe coxa vara or dislocated hip); **3** Absence of a stable fulcrum (eg ununited fractures of the neck of the femur).

Gait Those with unstable or painful hips use a stick on the opposite side from affected hip. (The reverse is true for knees.)

Other joints to examine Spine, knee, sacroiliac joints/pelvis.

Coxa vara This is the term used to describe a hip in which the angle between the neck and the shaft of femur is less than the normal 125°. ***Causes:*** Congenital; slipped upper femoral epiphysis; fracture (trochanteric with malunion, ununited fractures of neck of femur); due to softening of bones (rickets, osteomalacia, Paget's disease). ***Consequences:*** True shortening of limb; Trendelenburg 'dip' on walking makes the affected person limp.

1 Lordosis is lumbar spine anterior convexity (to give a 'hollow back')—when viewed from the side

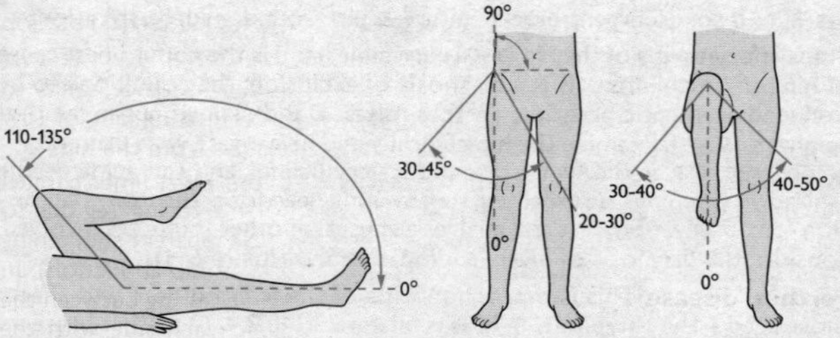

Fig 1. Ball and socket (eg hip) joints have 3 axes of movement: *flexion–extension (left); ab–ad–duction (middle); and external & internal rotation. External rotation of the ball in the socket is achieved by movement of the shin across the midline, as in the diagram (40–50°). After trauma, a hip at rest in external rotation is likely to be fractured; if in internal rotation dislocation is more likely.*

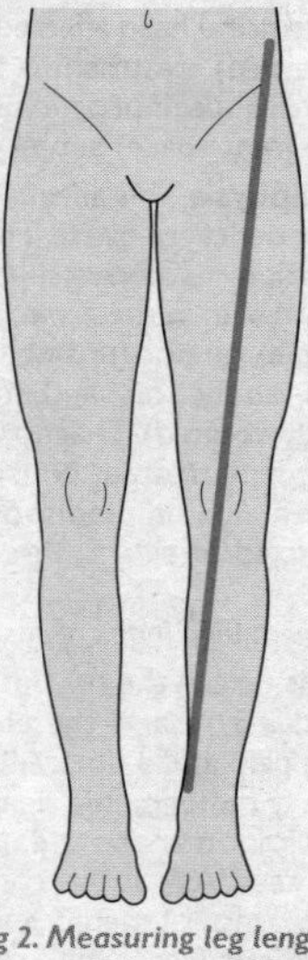

Fig 2. Measuring leg length

Painful hips in children

►When a child complains of pain in the knee, examine the hip.
►Is T°↑? If so, do urgent blood culture & ultrasound-guided aspiration.

Transient synovitis of the hip (TSOH; 'irritable hip')[1] is the commonest cause of hip pain in children. It is a diagnosis of exclusion; the conditions to be excluded are: septic arthritis; Perthes' disease; and slipped upper femoral epiphysis (SUFE). Examine the hip clinically and investigate with plain radiographs, FBC, ESR, and CRP. Ultrasound is very helpful, and can guide needle aspiration when pus is suspected, so obviating need for arthrotomy. Admission for observation, rest and analgesia is usual. If other joints are involved, consider the diagnosis of juvenile idiopathic arthritis (p 654).

Perthes' disease This is osteochondritis of the femoral head and affects those aged 3-11yrs (typically 4–7). It is bilateral in 10%. ♂/♀ ≈ 4:1. It presents with pain in hip or knee and causes a limp. On examination all movements at the hip are limited. Early radiographs ± MRI show widening of the joint space. Later there is a decrease in size of the femoral head with patchy density. Later still, there may be collapse and deformity of the femoral head with new bone formation. Severe deformity of the femoral head risks early arthritis. The younger the patient the better the prognosis. For those with less severe disease (<½ the femoral head affected on lateral radiographs, and joint space depth well preserved) treatment is bed rest until pain-free, followed by radiographic surveillance. If prognosis poorer (>½ femoral head affected, narrowing of total joint space) surgery may be indicated.[41]

Slipped upper femoral epiphysis This affects those aged 10-16yrs. 20% are bilateral. ♂/♀ ≈3:1. 50% of patients are obese. There is displacement through the growth plate with the epiphysis always slipping down and back. It usually presents with limping and pain in the groin, anterior thigh, or knee. Can the patient weightbear (stable) or not (unstable)?[42]

On examination flexion, abduction, and medial rotation are limited (eg lying with foot externally rotated). Diagnosis is by a lateral radiograph (may look normal on AP). If untreated, consequences may be avascular necrosis of femoral head or malunion predisposing to arthritis. Minor epiphyseal slips are carefully fixed *in situ*. Severe slips may require femoral osteotomy.[43]

►*Symptoms may be mild: have a high index of suspicion if in correct age group.*

Tubercular arthritis This is rare in the UK, but worldwide there is a resurgence of TB. Children aged 2-5yrs and the elderly are most commonly affected. The symptoms are pain and a limp. All hip movements cause pain and muscle spasm. ***Tests:*** Early radiographic sign: rarefaction of bone. Subsequently there is fuzziness of joint margins and narrowing of the joint space. Later bony erosion may be seen. Ask about contacts. Check ESR, CXR, and Mantoux test (*OHCM* p 566). Synovial membrane biopsy confirms the diagnosis of TB arthritis. ***Treatment*** (eg of hip): rest + anti-TB drugs (p 160), given by experienced personnel. Arthrodesis may be needed if much joint destruction has occurred.

1 Protocols exist for assessment of TSOH, occasionally a Perthes' patient slips through

Developmental dysplasia of the hip

Developmental dysplasia of the hip DDH (eg hip dislocation)

1.3% of neonates have unstable hips or subluxation. A hip may be normal at birth, and become abnormal later. Incidence (UK): 2 per 1000 live births. ♀/♂ ≈6:1; left hip/right hip incidence ≈ 4:1 (bilateral in ⅓).

At-risk babies:
• Breech birth • Caesar for breech • Other malformations • Positive family history • Birth weight↑ • Oligohydramnios • Primip/older mother • Postmaturity

Diagnosis Examine hips of all babies in the 1st days of life and at 6 weeks. With *well trained, well supported staff* this prevents later dysplasia.[44] ►Be alert to DDH throughout child surveillance (p 150).

Click test of Ortolani: With the baby supine and relaxed, flex the hips to 90° and knees fully. Place your middle finger over the greater trochanter, and thumb on inner thigh opposite the lesser trochanter. Diagnose a dislocated hip if slow hip abduction produces a palpable (often audible) jerk or jolt (ie more than a click)—as the femoral head slips back into the acetabulum. ***The Barlow manoeuvre:*** With the pelvis stabilized by one hand, abduct each hip in turn by 45°. Forward pressure by the middle finger causes the femoral head to slip into the acetabulum if the hip is dislocated. If the femoral head slips over the posterior lip of acetabulum and straight back again when pressure is exerted by the thumb it is 'unstable' (ie dislocatable not dislocated). Use both tests but avoid repetitions (may *induce* instability/dislocation). NB: both tests are problematic, missing up to ⅔ of those later needing surgery.

In older children signs may be: delay in walking, abnormal waddling gait (affected leg is shorter), asymmetric thigh creases (extra crease on the affected side), and inability to fully abduct the affected hip. With bilateral involvement the perineum appears wide and lumbar lordosis is increased.

Ultrasound is the image of choice, as it is non-invasive and dynamic. In a large series (Nottingham) 40/1000 babies had evidence of instability on routine ultrasound screening; only 3/1000 required treatment. Routine ultrasound screening for DDH remains controversial.

Treatment If neonatal examination suggests instability, use double nappies; reassess at 3 weeks. If still a problem, splint the hips in moderate abduction for 3 months (eg the Pavlik harness). Excess abduction may case avascular necrosis of the head of femur. *From 6–18 months* an examination-under-anaesthetic (EUA), arthrogram and closed reduction is performed followed by a period of immobilization in a hip spica. Open reduction is sometimes required if closed techniques fail. *After 18 months* (delayed presentation) open reduction is required with corrective femoral/pelvic osteotomies to maintain joint stability.

Club foot

Neonatal club foot (talipes equinovarus; ♂:♀ >1:1). The foot deformity consists of: **1** Inversion; **2** Adduction of forefoot relative to hindfoot; **3** Equinus (plantarflexion). The foot cannot be passively everted and dorsiflexed through the normal range. Treatment begins within 1 week of birth with weekly foot manipulations, holding it strapped or splinted in position between manipulations. The knee is flexed 90° in a splint to stop the baby drawing up his foot. If treatment has not corrected the foot by ~3 months, operative reduction is carried out. If this does not work, operations on soft tissues and/or bones of the foot may be carried out later (from 2 years).

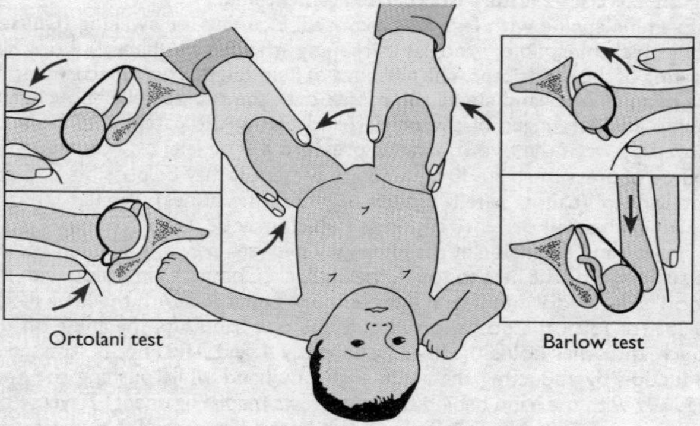
Ortolani test
Barlow test

Knee history and examination

►*Pain in the knee may be referred from the hip.* So examination must include the hip. Does internal hip rotation hurt?—so revealing hip pathology.

Ask about trauma, pain, swelling, mobility, locking, clicking, and giving way (eg on exercise—a feature of cruciate ligament injury).

Examine supine with legs fully exposed. Examine for swelling (***Causes:*** Bone thickening, fluid, synovial thickening—this feels 'rubbery'). Look for wasting of the quadriceps. The presence of fluid can be confirmed by placing the palm of one hand above the patella over the suprapatellar pouch, and thumb and forefinger of the other hand below the patella. Fluid can be moved between the two (hydraulic pressure will be felt) by alternating the source of pressure. If 30-40mL fluid are present it may be possible to feel a 'patellar tap' (ballott patella against neighbouring bones). Patellar taps are absent with small or tense effusions (which may be up to 120mL).

Flexion and extension at the knee vary between persons. Flexion should be sufficient for the heel to touch the buttock. Compare extension with the 'good' side. Medial and lateral ligaments are examined with the knee flexed 20-30° (to relax the posterior capsule), as one hand lifts the ankle off the couch, the other holds the knee just slightly flexed. The knee is stressed in abduction by abducting the ankle with one hand while pushing the knee medially with the hand behind the knee (tests medial ligament). Reverse the pressures to give adducting force to test lateral ligament. If these ligaments are torn the knee joint opens more widely when the relevant ligament is tested (compare knees against each other).

Test the cruciate ligaments with the knee 90° flexed, with the foot placed on couch with you sitting on it (to anchor the tibia). Place your fingers interlocking behind the knee clasping the sides of leg between the thumbs (each tip on a femoral condyle). With quadriceps relaxed, assess anteroposterior glide of tibia on femur (normal ~0.5cm). The anterior cruciate ligament prevents anterior glide; the posterior prevents posterior glide. Excessive glide in one direction (compare knees) suggests damage to the relevant ligament. Examination should also be performed in 20° of flexion (Lachman's test). A more sensitive test to determine if symptoms are really due to cruciate ligament damage (can be asymptomatic) is the 'pivot shift test': flex the knee, then put it in valgus; now extend it. If the anterior cruciate is ruptured, the knee jumps smartly forwards. (Often hard to elicit, unless very relaxed or under general anaesthesia.)

McMurray's rotation test is an unreliable way of detecting pedunculated tears of menisci. The knee is flexed, the tibia laterally rotated on the femur, then the knee is extended with tibia kept rotated. This is repeated with varying degrees of knee flexion, and then again with the tibia medially rotated on the femur. This manoeuvre is designed to jam the free end of a pedunculated meniscus in the joint—a click being felt and heard and pain experienced by the patient as the jammed tag is released as the knee is straightened. This test may not detect bucket-handle tears (p 752). Note: normal knees commonly produce patellar clicks. Simply eliciting joint-line tenderness may be a more valid test when combined with a history of mechanical locking.

Arthroscopy Arthroscopes enable internal structures of the knee to be seen and a definite diagnosis may be made. They also enable a wide range of operations to be done as day-case surgery. May be combined with MRI.

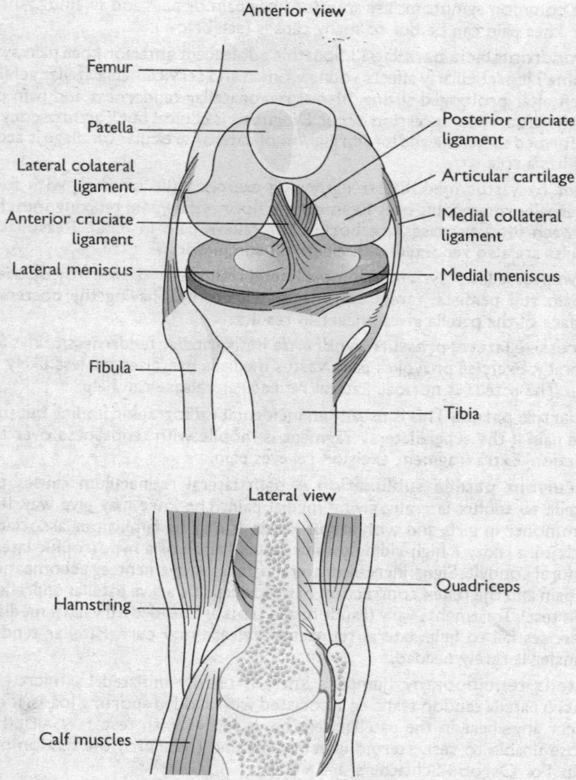

Fig 1. The anatomy of the knee—seen from in front. 45

Pain in the knee

The common symptoms are anterior knee pain or pain and swelling. Anterior knee pain can be due to many causes (see below).

Chondromalacia patellae ('Idiopathic adolescent anterior knee pain syndrome') It particularly affects young women and servicemen. Patellar aching is felt after prolonged sitting. Medial retropatellar tenderness and pain on patellofemoral compression occur. ***Diagnosis*** is clinical but if arthroscopy is performed softening and/or fibrillation of patellar articular cartilage is seen. MRI has a role.[46]

Treat by vastus medialis strengthening exercises (lie on back with foot externally rotated; lift heel 10cm off the floor × 500/24h, relaxing muscles between lifts—exercises are boring but relieve pain in 80%). Reasonable results are also reported with electrical stimulators.[47]

If symptoms last >1yr, arthroscopic lateral retinacular release may be tried. If pain still persists, rarely consider patellectomy. Shaving the posterior surface of the patella gives uncertain results.

Excessive lateral pressure syndrome Retropatellar tenderness/pain is felt laterally. Exercise provokes pain. Vastus medialis exercises are less likely to help. The patella is normal. Lateral retinacular release can help.

Bipartite patella This is usually an incidental radiographic finding but may give pain if the superolateral fragment is mobile with tenderness over the junction. Extra fragment excision relieves pain.[48]

Recurrent patella subluxation A tight lateral retinaculum causes the patella to sublux laterally giving medial pain. The knee may give way. It is commoner in girls and with valgus knees. It may be familial, or associated with joint laxity, a high-riding patella (*patella alta*), or a hypotrophic lateral femoral condyle. Signs: increased lateral patellar movement, eg accompanied by pain and the reflex contraction of quadriceps (ie a +ve patellar apprehension test). Treatments vary (randomized trials are needed). If vastus medialis exercises fail to help, lateral retinacular release may cure. Patellar tendon transfer is rarely needed.[49]

Patella tendinopathy (Jumper's knee) is usually initiated by micro- or macro patella tendon tears, eg associated with sudden sporting loads. It can occur anywhere in the patellar tendon. It settles with rest ± NSAIDs. For those unable to rest, steroid injection around (not into) the tendon may help. For Osgood-Schlatter's, see p 704.[50]

Iliotibial tract syndrome Synovium deep to the iliotibial tract is inflamed as it rubs on the lateral femoral condyle (which is tender). Common in runners, it settles with rest, NSAIDs or steroid injection.[51]

Medial shelf syndrome The synovial fold above the medial meniscus is inflamed. Pain is superomedial. There may be brief locking of the knee (mimics a torn meniscus). *Diagnosis:* Arthroscopy. *Treatment:* Rest, NSAIDs, local steroid injection; or division of the synovial fold arthroscopically.

Hoffa's fat pad syndrome Think of this in those with meniscus or ligament-type symptoms when investigation shows they are intact. MRI may show a hypertrophic Hoffa pad impinging between the articular surfaces of the joint. This causes pain under the patella. There may be hydrarthrosis or haemarthrosis (from arteriole rupture). Extending a bent knee while putting pressure on the patellar tendon margins elicits a strong pain and a defensive behaviour.[52]

Results of meta-analyses in knee osteoarthritis

(NB: knee OA is the commonest joint disease in Europe)

- Paracetamol and quadriceps-strengthening exercises are helpful. (EULAR)[1]
- Weight loss in women ↓risk of getting OA symptoms.[53] [n=796]
- Trials comparing NSAIDs are often flawed because the drugs compared tend not to be used in comparable doses, as expressed as a fraction of the maximum daily dose.[54] 16 trials
- There seems to be little benefit from intra-articular steroid injections beyond a placebo effect (but this is substantial and quite long-lasting). Some trials report benefits which last a week or so.[RCT 55] [N=98] Injecting high molecular weight hyaluronan appears to be safe and effective in a meta-analysis done in 1995, but 3 later trials showed no overall benefit at 2–5 months (subgroup analysis shows there may be benefit in those with the severest symptoms).[56]
- Transcutaneous electrical nerve stimulation (TENS) for knee osteoarthritis is a noninvasive modality in physiotherapy. Different modes of TENS setting (high rate and strong burst mode) show significant benefit in relief of pain and stiffness over placebo.[57] 7 trials
- Knee replacement is often the treatment of choice. But 21% of patients are still getting knee pain one or more years post-op. Significant complications include preventable thromboembolism. Intermittent pneumatic compression devices and low molecular weight heparin are significantly better than warfarin and aspirin in preventing DVT. Incidence of asymptomatic PE: 11.7% for aspirin, 8.2% for warfarin, and 6.3% for pneumatic compression group. (Numbers of symptomatic PEs are too small to produce reliable statistics.)[58]
- Post-op aseptic loosening and other problems requiring revision are a problem in 9% over 5yrs for unicompartmental prostheses (7% over 4yrs for bicompartmental prostheses). Serious infections may be less in those centres doing many procedures.[59]

1 **Key reference:** EULAR European Task Force 2000 Ann Rheu Dis **59** 936

Knees that swell

Arthritis Knee swelling may occur with any arthritic process. Osteoarthritis particularly affects the posterior patella and the medial compartment, so tending to varus deformity. Treatment is usually with NSAIDs, knee support (Tubigrip®), weight loss, local steroid injections, knee replacement (p 706), or osteotomy (corrects varus deformity). If these fail or are unsuitable, some may benefit from augmentation of the synovial fluid within the joint.[1] Rest pain (or pain while driving) which is relieved by movement suggests patellofemoral compartment problems. Simply pulling the patella medially using tape (Leukotape®, Beiersdorf) may reduce pain by 25%.

Rheumatoid, gout and septic arthritis all affect the knee. Remember that a unilaterally swollen knee may be a septic arthritis. Diagnosis is made on the basis of aspiration, so avoid steroid injections prior to this (p 708).

Meniscal cysts ***Typical patient:*** A young man. Swelling is variable. Pain may be felt over the joint line. Lateral cysts are commoner than medial. Swelling is maximal on knee flexion to ~60° (less noticeable at full flexion). The meniscus is often torn radially (an otherwise unusual direction) so there may be knee clicking and giving way. ***Diagnosis:*** MRI. ***Histology:*** Myxoid degeneration. ***Treatment:*** Arthroscopic decompression relieves pain.[60]

Ligament tears, meniscus lesions, patellar dislocation See p 752.

Osteochondritis dissecans An osteochondral fragment separates from underlying bone. ***Cause:*** Unknown. ***Typical site:*** Lateral side of the medial femoral condyle. ***Typical patient:*** Young adult/adolescent. ***Symptoms:*** Pain after exercise with intermittent knee swelling. Locking may occur. ***Radiography:*** Look for articular surface defects. ***Treatment:*** None, initially, as spontaneous healing can occur. The osteochondral fragment maybe pinned in place. Loose bodies maybe removed and the defect drilled to promote fibro-cartilage formation. The condition predisposes to arthritis.[61]

Loose bodies These cause knee locking (*all* movements may be jammed unlike locking from torn menisci when only extension is limited). Also, there is effusion and swelling. ***Diagnosis:*** Plain films ± ultrasound (helps show if fragments are intra-articular).[62] ***Differential:*** Tophi (gout).[63] ***Causes:*** Osteochondritis dissecans (up to 3 loose bodies), osteoarthritis (≤10 loose bodies), chip fractures of joint surfaces (≤3 loose bodies) or synovial chondromatosis (>50 loose bodies). When locking is a problem, loose bodies are best removed. This can often be done arthroscopically.

Bursitis There are 16 bursae around the knee. The most commonly affected are the prepatellar bursa ('housemaid's knee') where swelling over the anterior inferior patella is due to inflammation and fluid in the bursa due to friction (kneeling); the infrapatellar bursa (Vicar's knee—they kneel more upright), and the semi-membranous bursa in the popliteal fossa (a popliteal cyst which differs from the 'Baker's cyst' which is a herniation from the joint synovium). Prepatellar bursae may be aspirated, have hydrocortisone injected to decrease recurrence, or, if very persistent, may need excision. Pain may be relieved by topical NSAIDs. Aspiration distinguishes friction bursitis from infective suppurative bursitis, which needs drainage and antibiotics, eg flucloxacillin 250mg/6h PO (adult dose).[RCT 64]

1 This technique involves a 5-week course (2mL/wk) of high molecular weight intra-articular hyaluronan derivatives (eg Synvisc®). Any effusion is drained to dryness. A 5-week course may be repeated at 6 months. Trials are few, but at least some benefit is likely, if all standard alternatives are contra-indicated, eg NSAIDs: see *Drug Ther Bul* 1999 **37** 71; SE: transient pain; knee swelling; synovitis. See p 637. According to one meta-analysis (J Fam Pract 2005 758-67) intra-articular viscosupplementation is quite effective up to 10 weeks after the last injection, but not at 15-22 weeks. Pain relief is augmented by adding 1mL triamcinolone to the 1st and 4th injection (Rheumetol Int 2005 Feb 10).

A journey on foot

By the time we get down to the foot our anatomical interest is flagging but on close inspection we would never have believed, my dear José, that so much glory could fit into a shoe.[1] Feet made for walking are really quite old (4–7 million years—according to Sterkfontein Man's remains).[2] The significant thing about these old feet is that they can and did take us anywhere. We left off swinging from tree to tree in an African forest, and began quite a journey—on foot.

Ankle examination 25° of extension (dorsiflexion) and 30° of flexion are the normal at the talocrural joint. Inversion and eversion are effected at the subtalar and midtarsal joints. Toes should have between 60° and 90° extension. Note any callosities. Examine the arches. Watch as the toes are lifted off the ground, and on standing on tiptoe. Examine gait and shoes (normal wear pattern is medially under ball of foot posterolaterally at heel).

Hallux valgus The big toe deviates laterally at the metatarsophalangeal joint. Biomechanical forces, pointed shoes and wearing of heels forcing the forefoot forward probably promote deformity. Pressure of the metatarsophalangeal joint against the shoe leads to bunion formation. Secondary arthritis in the joint is common. Bunion pads and plastic wedges between great and second toes may relieve pain, but severe deformity requires surgery. Many different operations are used. Broadly, in the absence of MTP joint OA the deformity is corrected with a metatarsal osteotomy. End-stage MTP joint OA (*hallux rigidus*) is treated with arthrodesis (fusion).

Pes planus (**flat feet**) The arch of the foot is low. There may be valgus and eversion foot deformity. Flat feet are normal when a child is learning to walk. The medial arch develops over the next few years. If flat feet persist, no action is needed if the medial arch restores itself on standing on tiptoe. In most, it is asymptomatic but occasionally it is painful (especially 'peroneal spasmodic flat foot' in which the heel is held everted and the medial border of the foot held flat to the ground; here attempts to invert the hind foot induces painful peroneal muscle spasm). Exercises, faradic foot stimulation and medial shoe heel wedges may not yield much benefit. With the spasmodic type, hindfoot fusion can be needed for pain relief. Prevention: studies of feet in India show that going barefoot until 6 years old keeps feet healthy. Pain and limitations in sport tend to be post-op complications (eg after the Viladot procedure), so don't advise surgery lightly.

Pes cavus Accentuated longitudinal foot arches which do not flatten with weight-bearing may be idiopathic, or from spina bifida, cerebral palsy, or old polio. Claw toes may occur, as weight is taken on metatarsal heads when walking (hence causing pain). Other symptoms: difficulty with shoes, foot fatigue, mobility↓, ankle instability/sprains, callosities. If foot used to be normal, refer to a neurologist. Is there muscular dystrophy, Charcot–Marie–Tooth disease, syringomyelia, Friedreich's ataxia, or a spinal tumour? MRI may help.

If orthoses and custom footwear fail surgical procedures include (if vascular supply is good): soft-tissue releases, tendon transfers, arthrodesis.

Lesser toe deformities *Hammertoes*: These are extended at the MTP joint, hyperflexed at the PIP joint and extended at the DIP joint. Second toes are most commonly affected. *Claw toes*: Extended at the MTP joint but flexed at both PIP and DIP joints. The operative treatment for both hammer and claw toes is metatarsal shortening (flexible deformity) or PIP joint arthrodesis (fixed deformity). *Mallet toes*: flexion deformity of the DIP joint in isolation treated with flexor tenotomy (flexible deformity) or DIP joint arthrodesis (fixed deformity).

1 Gabriel García Márquez 1989 *The General in His Labyrinth*.
2 Toumaï man is 7 million years old.

A journey on foot

By the time we get down to the foot, our anatomical interest is flagging, but on close inspection *we would never have believed, my dear José, that so much glory could fit into a shoe.*[1] Feet made for walking are really quite old (~4–7 million years—according to Sterkfontein Man's remains).[2] The significant thing about these old feet is that they can *and did* take us anywhere. We left off swinging from tree to tree in an African forest, and began quite a journey—on foot.

Ankle examination 25° of extension (dorsiflexion) and 30° of flexion are the norm at the tibiotalar joint. Inversion and eversion are effected at the subtalar and midtarsal joints. Toes should have between 60° and 90° extension. Note any callosities. Examine the arches. Watch as the toes are lifted off the ground, and on standing on tiptoe. Examine gait and shoes (normal wear pattern is medially under ball of foot, posterolaterally at heel).

Hallux valgus The big toe deviates laterally at the metatarsophalangeal joint. Biomechanical forces, pointed shoes and wearing of heels forcing the forefoot forward probably promote deformity. Pressure of the metatarsophalangeal joint against the shoe leads to bunion formation. Secondary arthritis in the joint is common. Bunion pads and plastic wedges between great and second toes may relieve pain, but severe deformity requires surgery. Many different operations are used. Broadly, in the absence of MTP joint OA the deformity is corrected with a metatarsal osteotomy. End-stage MTP joint OA (***Hallux rigidus***) is treated with arthrodesis (fusion).

Pes planus (flat feet) The arch of the foot is low. There may be valgus and eversion foot deformity. Flat feet are normal when a child is learning to walk. The medial arch develops over the next few years. If flat feet persist, no action is needed if the medial arch restores itself on standing on tiptoe. In most, it is asymptomatic but occasionally it is painful (especially 'peroneal spasmodic flat foot' in which the heel is held everted and the medial border of the foot held flat to the ground. Here, attempts to invert the hind foot induces painful peroneal muscle spasm). Exercises, faradic foot stimulation, and medial shoe heel wedges may not yield much benefit. With the spasmodic type, hindfoot fusion can be needed for pain relief. Prevention: studies of feet in India show that going barefoot until 6 years old keeps feet healthy. Pain and limitations in sport tend to be post-op complications (eg after the Viladot procedure), so don't advise surgery lightly.[65]

Pes cavus Accentuated longitudinal foot arches which do not flatten with weight-bearing may be idiopathic, or from spina bifida, cerebral palsy, or old polio. Claw toes may occur, as weight is taken on metatarsal heads when walking (hence causing pain). ***Other symptoms:*** difficulty with shoes, foot fatigue; mobilty↓; ankle instability/sprains; callosities. *If foot used to be normal, refer to a neurologist.* Is there muscular dystrophy, Charcot–Marie–Tooth disease, syringomyelia, Friedreich's ataxia, or a spinal tumour? MRI may help.

If orthoses and custom footwear fail surgical procedures include (if vascular supply is good): soft-tissue releases, tendon transfers, arthrodesis.[66]

Lesser toe deformities •*Hammertoes*: These are extended at the MTP joint, hyperflexed at the PIP joint and extended at the DIP joint. Second toes are most commonly affected. •*Claw* toes: Extended at the MTP joint but flexed at both PIP and DIP joints. The operative treatment for both hammer and claw toes is metatarsal shortening (flexible deformity) or PIP joint arthrodesis (fixed deformity). •*Mallet toes*: Flexion deformity of the DIP joint in isolation treated with flexor tenotomy (flexible deformity) or DIP joint arthrodesis (fixed deformity).

1 Gabriel Gacía Marquez 1989 *The General in His Labyrinth*
2 Toumaï man is 7 million years old.

Classification of severity of hallux valgus deformity

	Hallux valgus angle (HVA)	Intermetatarsal angle (IMA)
Normal	< 15	<9
Mild	15–20	9–11
Moderate	20–40	11–18
Severe	>40	>18

NB: sources vary 67

Surgery: (May be problematic[1,2]) Mild and moderate deformities maybe corrected with a distal metatatarsal osteotomy (eg Mitchell's or Chevron osteotomy). Severe deformities also require correction of the intermetatarsal angle (eg Scarf osteotomy).

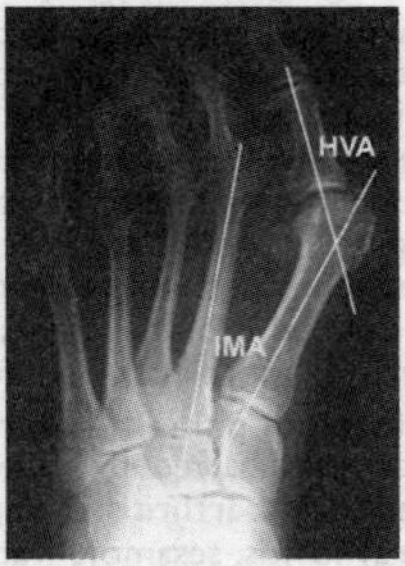

Fig 1. Weightbearing AP image showing a hallux valgus deformity and the hallux valgus angle (HVA) and intermetatarsal angle (IMA).

1 A Zembsch 2000 *Clin Orthop* **376** 183

2 *Cochrane Database Syst Rev* CD 000964

The painful foot

►Look at a wet footprint (and wear on the shoe sole) to assess functional anatomy of the loaded foot. Many of the conditions mentioned in 'the foot' (p 692) can be painful. Other causes of pain are mentioned here.

Young people Children rarely complain of foot pain: if they complain of pain in the soles think of a foreign body. Shoe pressure on a prominent navicular bone, or sometimes an accessory bone, or a prominent postero-superior os calcis may require surgical trimming. Osteochondritis (p 702) of foot bones may be the cause (diagnose by radiography).

Metatarsus primus varus: 1st metatarsal angulation towards the midline. Typical patients: teenagers. It may be familial. If deformity is great, a metatarsal or wedge osteotomy may be tried. 68

Ingrowing toenails (Typically the big toe.) Incorrect nail cutting ± pressure of shoes predispose to the lateral nail digging into its fleshy bed, which reacts by becoming heaped up infection-prone 'proudflesh'. ***Conservative treatment*** involves tucking cotton-wool soaked in surgical spirit under the proudflesh and awaiting nail growth (then cut it straight with edges protruding beyond flesh margins). Antibiotics *may* help the young. 69 Recurrent infections may require surgery. ***Simple nail avulsion*** plus ***phenol*** to the nail bed is better than ***simple excision*** without use of phenol (but there may be more post-op infection). MET 70

Adult forefoot pain (metatarsalgia) Increased pressure on the metatarsal heads causes pain. *Treat* by insole supports. Treatment by surgery other than for rheumatoid arthritis is unpredictable. Other causes of metatarsalgia include synovitis, sesamoid fracture, and injury.

Morton's metatarsalgia Pain is from pressure on an interdigital neuroma between the metatarsals (eg from fashion shoes). Pain usually radiates to the lateral side of one toe, and the medial side of its neighbour (eg toes 3 & 4). A compression test of the affected web space is quite specific. MRI is helpful. Neuroma excision may be needed. 71

March (stress) fractures occur in the shaft of the 2nd or 3rd metatarsals and may follow excessive walking. Radiographs may be normal (radionuclide bone scans are more discriminating). Treatment is expectant. If pain is severe, a plaster cast while awaiting healing may help.

Pain in the heel *Causes:* (✓ means *may* respond to steroid injec)

- Diseases of the calcaneum
- Rupture of calcaneal tendon (p 712)
- Postcalcaneal bursitis (back of heel)
- Plantar fasciitis* 72 ✓
- Arthritis of the subtalar joint
- Calcaneal paratendinopathy ✓
- Tender heel pad ✓

MRI may have a role in undiagnosed heel pain (eg from occult stress fractures). 73 Apart from calcaneal diseases and tendon rupture, conservative treatment (eg shoe alteration to prevent rubbing) may help. If not, with postcalcaneal bursitis the bursa may be surgically removed.

Corns These focal friction-dependent hyperkeratotic intradermal nodules develop on the foot at bony pressure points (eg the top of hammertoes), which stop keratinized skin cells coming to the surface. A bursa-like structure may form around these islands. They are more likely if there is a neuropathy (eg diabetes). Unlike calluses they have a central core of keratin, occur only on the foot, and cause pain. 74 **Management:** *Optimize footwear* (not too tight or loose, ± an instep); *chiropody* (± softening with *salycylic acid*)—or *excize the corn* (try to remove its core without causing bleeding), or, more radically, remove the culprit bone too (eg hammertoe condylectomy). 75

* If proximal planar fasciitis doesn't respond to injections, extracorporeal shockwave therapy is a reasonable alternative to surgery.

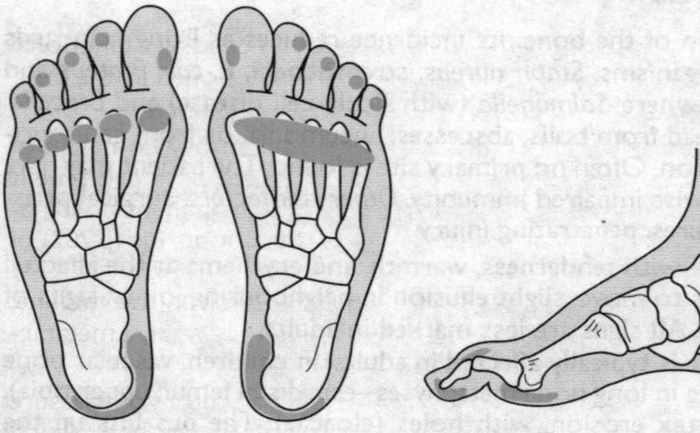

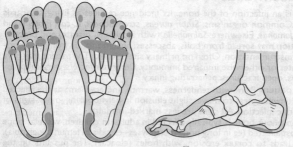

Fig 1. Pressure points in a foot with hammertoe. 76

Osteomyelitis

This is an infection of the bone. Its incidence reduces as living standards rise. Common organisms: *Staph aureus*, streptococci, *E. coli*, *Proteus* and *Pseudomonas*. Elsewhere: *Salmonella* (with sickle-cell disease) and *Brucella*. Infection may spread from boils, abscesses, pneumonia, or from genitourinary instrumentation. Often no primary site is found. The patient may have diabetes or otherwise impaired immunity. *Other risk factors:* surgical prostheses, open fractures, penetrating injury.[77]

The patient Pain—with tenderness, warmth, and erythema at the affected part; unwillingness to move; slight effusion in neighbouring joints; signs of systemic infection. All signs are less marked in adults.

Cancellous bone is typically affected in adults; in children, vascular bone is most affected (eg in long bone metaphyses—esp. distal femur, upper tibia). This leads to cortex erosion, with holes (cloacae). The pus lifts up the periosteum causing death of the original bone (sequestrum). Continued bone formation by the elevated periosteum forms an involucrum. Pus may discharge into joint spaces or via sinuses to skin.

Tests ESR/CRP↑, WCC↑. Blood culture (+ve in 60%). MRI is sensitive and specific (88% and 93%, *vs* 61% and 33% for isotope scans)—and avoids ionizing radiation. But isotope scans are still sometimes needed.[1] Radiographic changes are not apparent for 10–14 days but then show haziness ± loss of density of affected bone, then subperiosteal reaction, and later, sequestrum and involucrum. Infected cancellous bone shows less change.

Treatment Drain abscesses and remove sequestra by open surgery. Culture all sequestra. Antibiotic: vancomycin 1g/12h and cefotaxime 1g/12h IVI until the organism and its sensitivities are known. Continue for 6 weeks. Alternative treatments for adults are fusidic acid or clindamycin. Ciprofloxacin 500mg/8–12h PO is suitable for *Pseudomonas* osteomyelitis but be guided by sensitivities and a microbiologist. In children, prevalence of *Haemophilus influenzae* osteomyelitis is reducing due to the HiB vaccination.

Complications of osteomyelitis Septic arthritis; fractures; deformity.

Chronic osteomyelitis Poor treatment results in pain, fever, and sinus suppuration with ± long remissions. Radiographs show thick irregular bone. Treatment involves radical excision of sequestra, skeletal stabilization, 'dead-space' management (often needs plastic surgical input) and treatment with antibiotics (as above, modified according to sensitivities) for ≥12 weeks.

Complications: Amyloid, squamous carcinoma development in sinus track.

Bone TB (eg vertebral body) 1–3% of all TB; incidence is rising, rare in UK. ***Spread:*** Haematogenous or via nearby nodes. ***Signs:*** Local pain, swelling, and 'cold abscess' formation ± joint effusion are common. With joint involvement there is pain, swelling, pain on movement and muscle wasting. Also: weight↓; malaise; fever; lethargy. ***Differential:*** Malignancy; other infections; gout; rheumatoid. ***Imaging:*** Radiographic changes: bone rarefaction, periostitis changes, cyst formation. Later: loss of joint space, erosions, bony ankylosis. Also look for soft tissue swellings (abscess; tenosynovitis/bursitis). MRI is especially useful in analysing soft tissue changes. Bone scans may be useful in diagnosing dactylitis (a feature of childhood TB). ***Other tests:*** Aspirated pus is creamy and may be positive on culture or ZN stain. ESR↑, Mantoux +ve. CXR. HIV tests. ***Treatment:*** Drain abscesses, immobilize affected large joints. Standard 6-month courses (*OHCM* p 566) of eg isoniazid (300mg/day), rifampicin (600mg/day) and pyrazinamide (1.5g/day) may not be long enough. Late arthroplasty or arthrodesis is needed for gross joint destruction.[78]

1 Links: 2001 or newer includes J Auletta *Cl Inf Dis* **32** 9

Bone tumours

Tumours present with pain, swelling, or pathological fracture. Bone is a common site for secondaries (eg from breast, bronchus, prostate, kidney). Primary bone neoplasia is rare (~5 per million population/yr). They often present with non-mechanical pain (like backache) followed by swelling. Delays in diagnosis are common. Radiological features suggestive of bone tumours include: bone destruction, new bone formation, soft tissue swelling, and periosteal elevation. Metastases are blood-borne and usually arise first in the lungs. Treatment of these rare and highly aggressive tumours is best carried out in multidisciplinary specialist treatment centres.

Giant cell tumour (osteoclastoma): this histologically 'benign' primary skeletal neoplasm (with unpredictable biological aggressiveness) is commonest in young adults. It occurs around epiphyses (esp. knee). The tumour is osteolytic and often slowly progressive, sometimes resulting in pathological fracture. Treatment is by curettage and thorough curettage resulting in 75% cure. Recurrences are usually treated by wide excision. Metastasis is rare.

Ewing's sarcoma This malignant round-cell tumour of long bones (typically diaphysis) and limb girdles, usually presents in adolescents. Radiographs show bone destruction, concentric layers of new bone formation ('onion peel' sign) and a soft tissue mass. MRI is helpful. Typically those with Ewing's sarcoma have a t11:22 chromosomal translocation. Chemotherapy, bone resection, and limb salvage surgery, or radiotherapy cures ~half. The key adverse prognostic factor is metastases at diagnosis (5-year recurrence-free survival is 22% vs 55% if no metastases at diagnosis).

Osteosarcoma Primary osteosarcoma typically affects adolescents and arises towards the end of long bones (typically the knee) in the metaphysis. Secondary osteosarcoma may arise in bone affected by Paget's disease or after irradiation. Radiography shows destruction and new bone formation, often with marked periosteal elevation (sunray spiculation and Codman's triangle respectively). Treatment: resection + chemotherapy, eg doxorubicin and cisplatin in 3-week cycles for 18 weeks (safer and as good as multi-drug regimens). A cure rate of ~50% is achievable. Vigorous treatment of metastatic disease may be worthwhile.

Chondrosarcoma may arise de novo or from malignant transformation of chondromas. It is usually associated with pain or swelling and presents in the axial skeleton of the middle-aged. 'Popcorn' calcification is typical on radiography. MRI/CT will better define tumour extent. They don't respond to chemotherapy or radiotherapy, so treatment is by excision. Inadequate surgery is accompanied by local recurrence, often of a higher grade of malignancy. The cure rate is ~70%.

Malignant fibrous histiocytoma (The rarest primary bone tumour) arises in middle age, often at the site of previous bone abnormality (eg bone infarcts). Treatment is as for osteosarcoma.

Chordomas arise from notochord remnants in the spine and are typically sacral, and quite big before a diagnosis is made. Bladder & bowel sphincter problems may occur. Radical surgery ± pre-op radiotherapy cures ~20%. The others may have a slow and difficult demise.

Surgical reconstruction (after excising a bone tumour) involves replacing affected bone with a metal and polyethylene endoprosthesis—as an alternative to amputation. Excellent and durable reconstruction is possible using massive endoprostheses or bone allografts. 85% of patients now have limb salvage following chemotherapy for primary bone tumours.

Bone tumours

Tumours present with pain, swelling or pathological fracture. Bone is a common site for secondaries (eg from breast, bronchus, prostate, kidney). Primary bone neoplasia is rare: 6 per million population/year. They all present with non-mechanical pain (like toothache) followed by swelling. Delays in diagnosis are common. Radiological features suggestive of bone tumours include: bone destruction, new bone formation, soft tissue swelling, and periosteal elevation. Metastases are blood-borne and usually arise first in the lungs. Treatment of these rare and highly aggressive tumours is best carried out in multidisciplinary specialist treatment centres.

Giant cell tumour (osteoclastoma); this histologically 'benign', primary skeletal neoplasm with unpredictable biological aggressiveness, is commonest in young adults. It occurs around epiphyses (esp. knee). The tumour is osteolytic and often slowly progressive, sometimes resulting in pathological fracture. Treatment is by detailed and thorough curettage resulting in 75% cure. Recurrences are usually treated by wide excision. Metastasis is rare.

Ewing's sarcoma This malignant round-cell tumour of long bones (typically diaphysis) and limb girdles, usually presents in adolescents. Radiographs show bone destruction, concentric layers of new bone formation ('onion-peel' sign) and a soft tissue mass. MRI is helpful. Typically those with Ewing's sarcoma have a t11:22 chromosomal translocation. Chemotherapy, bone resection, and limb salvage surgery or radiotherapy cures ~half. The key adverse prognostic factor is metastases at diagnosis (5-year recurrence-free survival is 22%—*vs* 55% if no metastases at diagnosis).[79] [n=975]

Osteosarcoma Primary osteosarcoma typically affects adolescents and arises towards the end of long bones (typically the knee), in the metaphysis. Secondary osteosarcomas may arise in bone affected by Paget's disease or after irradiation. ***Radiography:*** Bone destruction and new bone formation, often with marked periosteal elevation (sunray spiculation and Codman's triangle respectively). ***Treatment:*** Resection + chemotherapy, eg doxorubicin and cisplatin in 3-week cycles for 18 weeks (safer, and as good as multi-drug regimens).[80] A cure rate of ~50% is achievable. Vigorous treatment of metastatic disease may be worthwhile.

Chondrosarcoma may arise *de novo* or from malignant transformation of chondromas. It is usually associated with pain or a lump and presents in the axial skeleton of the middle-aged. 'Popcorn calcification' is typical on radiography. MRI/CT will better define tumour extent. They don't respond to chemotherapy or radiotherapy, so treatment is by excision. Inadequate surgery is accompanied by local recurrence, often of a higher grade of malignancy. The cure rate is ~70%.[81]

Malignant fibrous histiocytoma (The rarest primary bone tumour) arise in middle age, often at the site of previous bone abnormality (eg bone infarcts). Treatment is as for osteosarcoma.[82]

Chordomas arise from notochord remnants in the spine and are typically sacral, and quite big before a diagnosis is made. Bladder & bowel sphincter problems may occur. Radical surgery + pre-op radiotherapy cure <20%. The others may have a slow and difficult death.[83]

Surgical reconstruction (after excising a bone tumour) involves replacing affected bone with a metal and polyethylene endoprosthesis— as an alternative to amputation. Excellent and durable reconstruction is possible using massive endoprostheses or bone allografts. 85% of patients now have limb salvage following chemotherapy for primary bone tumours.

Benign tumours ***Osteoid osteoma*** occur most commonly in long bones of males 10–25yrs old, and cause severe pain. They appear as local cortical sclerosis on radiographs. ***Treatment:*** CT guided biopsy and radiofrequency ablation. NB: In young adults, any bone pain responding to aspirin within 15min could be caused by an osteoid osteoma. A radionuclear scan can confirm or exclude.

Chondroma: These benign cartilaginous tumours may arise from bone surfaces or within the medulla (enchondromata). They may cause local swelling or fracture. ***Treatment*** is rarely needed, except to exclude malignancy (chondrosarcoma). NB: Carney's syndrome is gastric leiomyosarcoma, plus pulmonary chondroma plus a non-adrenal paraganglioma.[84]

Osteochondromas are the most common benign bone tumour. ***Treatment:*** Remove if causing symptoms (typically pressure on adjacent structures). Any osteochondroma continuing to grow after skeletal maturity should be removed because of the risk of malignancy (arises rarely in solitary osteochondromas but in up to 10% of patients with hereditary multiple exostoses—an autosomal dominant inherited condition).

Fibrous dysplasia of bone is a developmental abnormality where bone is not properly formed. May lead to pain and increased risk of fracture. Surgical stabilization is sometimes needed. In the polyostotic form biphosphonates may help relieve symptoms.

Soft tissue sarcomas (STS) are uncommon (about 1500/yr in UK) but can arise in any mesenchymal tissue, taking origin from fat, muscle etc; they present as a painless mass, increasing in size. Risk factors include neurofibromatosis type 1 and previous radiotherapy. ***Diagnosis:*** Any lump that has any of the following features:

- Bigger than 5cm
- Increasing in size
- Deep to the deep fascia
- Painful

Should be considered malignant until proved otherwise. *Imaging* with MRI followed by needle biopsy at a specialist sarcoma unit is recommended. Pathological diagnoses include rhabdomyosarcoma (most common in children), liposarcoma, leiomyosarcoma, fibrosarcoma etc. Gene expression profiling is helping to improve diagnosis and indicate tumours which may respond to chemotherapy. ***Treatment*** is by surgical excision with wide margins followed by radiotherapy for most cases. Metastases most frequently arise in the lungs. Most adult STS are not sensitive to chemotherapy but it may be used for metastatic disease. ***Prognosis*** is related to histological grade, size and depth of the tumour. High grade, large, deep tumours have <50% 5 year survival. STS in children often respond well to chemotherapy and survival is better.

Gastro-intestinal stromal tumours (GIST) are rare submucosal tumours arising principally in the upper GI tract. Frequently misdiagnosed in the past they are characterised by typical expression of the KIT protein (also known as CD117) which can be identified with antibodies. Initial treatment is with surgery but about half will recur and spread to the liver. Targeted therapy with Imatinib has proved effective in controlling this disease.

This page own much to Rob Grimer FRCS, whom we thank.

Congenital disorders of bone & cartilage[1]

Osteogenesis imperfecta (Adair-Dighton syndrome) Skeletal dysplasia with abnormal bone density causing brittle, fragile bones. There are 4 types:

I Blue sclerae with deafness but little deformity (defective formation of type I collagen; autosomal dominant).
II Lethal perinatal form with many fractures and dwarfism (recessive).
III Fractures at birth + progressive deformity; blue or white scleral hue; dentinogenesis imperfecta common (enamel separates from defective dentine, leaving teeth transparent or discoloured; recessive).
IV Fragile bones, white sclerae after infancy; autosomal dominant.

Radiographs: Many fractures, osteoporotic bones with thin cortex, and bowing deformity of long bones. ***Histology:*** Immature unorganized bone with abnormal cortex. ***Treatment:*** Prevent injury. Osteotomies may correct deformity. Intramedullary rods are sometimes used in long bones.

Achondroplasia Reduced growth of cartilaginous bone (membranous bone growth is OK) from mutations eg in the fibroblast growth factor receptor 3 (FGFR3) gene. Affected babies have large heads, normal trunk length, short limbs and fingers all the same length. Adults are dwarfed with ↑lumbar lordosis, bow legs, and shortened proximal arms and legs. ***Radiographs:*** Short bones with wide epiphyses. Growth hormone has been tried.

Craniocleidodysostosis Those affected have a flat face, a globular skull, absent clavicles ± wide perineum (if coxa vara). ***Radiographs:*** Midline frontal bone suture; deficient clavicles; wide pubic symphysis; coxa vara. Coxa vara is correctable, if needed, by osteotomy. Life expectancy is normal.

Hereditary multiple exostoses (HME≈diaphyseal aclasis) is a commonish autosomal dominant disorder in which certain proteins accumulate in the Golgi apparatus leading to cartilage-capped tumours (exostoses/osteochondromata) developing from affected cartilage nests at the end of long bones. These point away from the near-by joint. If severe, bones are broad and badly modelled, causing short stature as well as forearm, knee, and ankle deformity. Beware of malignant transformation to chondrosarcomas[2] or osteosarcomas. HME is usually caused by defects in various EXT genes which encode enzymes catalyzing biosynthesis of heparan sulfate, an important component of the extracellular matrix. Although genetic linkage analysis has identified 3 loci at 8q24, 11p 11-13, and 19p (genes EXT1, EXT2, & EXT3), most HME is attributed to missense or frameshift mutations in genes encoding 746- and 718-aa proteins, which are expressed in many human tissues. ***Treatment:*** Removal of symptom-producing exostoses.

Ollier's (Maffucci's) enchondromatosis is a nonhereditary disease characterized by multiple central (medullary) cartilaginous radiolucent bone tumours of unknown pathogenesis. It usually involves the extremities with a unilateral predominance. Sarcoma transformation may occur. Small bones of hands, feet, upper tibia, and lower femur are chiefly affected. Whole-body MRI detects associated haemangiomas & gliomas.

Osteopetrosis Lack of differentiation between cortex and medulla of bone results in very hard dense 'marble' bones that are brittle. Anaemia and thrombocytopenia may result from decreased marrow space. Deafness and optic atrophy can result from compression of cranial nerves. Lack of remodelling preserves variations of ossific density causing the characteristic 'bone within a bone' appearance. www.skiagram.com/margaret/338-1552-1641440.jpg

1 *See* Neurofibromatosis (*OHCM* p 390), Marfan's (*OHCM* p 730), Ehlers-Danlos & Morquio's, p 746.
2 ***Cartilage tumour classification:*** Is the lesion benign or malignant? Is the lesion a pure or impure cartilaginous tumour? Is the epicentre of the lesion intraosseous, juxtacortical, or in the soft tissues? The most common benign tumours are enchondroma, osteochondroma, chondroblastoma, and chondromyxoid fibroma. Chondrosarcoma is malignant.

Developmental bone biology

Because bone is ossified, we tend to think of it as the architectural rock around which our living tissues are constructed. But bone maintenance and development is a highly dynamic and regulated process sensitive to a wide variety of hormones, inflammatory mediators, growth factors, and genetic influences which become aberrant whenever there are deletions, insertions, and missense mutations.[88] The concept of a *master gene* is useful here—to indicate how genes relate and interact. Master genes encode proteins that can control other genes by directly binding to their DNA. For example, transcription factor Osf2 (osteoblast specific transcription factor 2) gene is thought to serve as a master gene regulating expression of other genes, allowing mesenchymal stem cells to differentiate into osteoblasts. Osf2 maps close to a chromosomal locus on chromosome 6p21 (thought to be important eg in cleidocranial dysostosis). NB: master genes make a mockery of genes *vs* environment issues. One gene is an environment for another, and the effects of each may be catastrophic in some environments or negligible in others.

Osteochondritis

Osteochondritis juvenilis (osteochondrosis) is a condition of unknown origin in which bony centres of children or adolescents become temporarily softened, resulting in deformation secondary to pressure. After a variable period of time (often about 2 or 3 years) the bone hardens again in its new, deformed shape.

The Patient The age at which these changes occur depends on which bone is affected, as it is usually at the time of development of the bony nucleus. The main symptom is local pain. ***Radiographs:*** Initial increase in density of the bony nucleus; followed by patchy appearances (as affected bone is resorbed) and flattening; then normal texture returns but deformity is maintained. The long-term consequence is degenerative arthritis.

Name of osteochondritis	***Site affected:***
Perthe's disease (p 682)	Hip
Scheuermann's disease	Vertebral ring epiphyses
Köhler's disease	Navicular bone
Kienböck's disease	Lunate bone (in adults)
Freiberg's disease	Head of 2nd or 3rd metatarsal

Treatment Often none is necessary but large joints may need protection (eg with a plaster cast).

Scheuermann's kyphosis This is the commonest cause of kyphosis in 13–16-yr-olds. It is an autosomal dominant. The normal ossification of ring epiphyses of several thoracic vertebrae is affected. Deforming forces are greatest at their anterior border, so vertebrae are narrower here, causing kyphosis. During the active phase, vertebrae may be tender. ***Radiographs:*** Irregular vertebral endplates, Schmorl's nodes and ↓disc space ± anterior wedging. Schmorl's nodes are herniations of the intervertebral disc through the vertebral end-plate. ***Treatment:*** If posture control (eg standing during lessons rather than sitting) and exercises (eg swimming) fails, physiotherapy ± spinal braces can help. Surgery may be tried for severe kyphosis (>75°) with curve progression, refractory pain, or neurologic deficit.[89] & http://web.idirect.com/~xray/ced/ced00079.htm

Köhler's disease Children affected are 3–5-yr-olds. Pain is felt in the mid-tarsal region and they limp. There may be navicular tenderness. ***Radiographs:*** Dense, deformed bone. ***Treatment:*** Symptomatic: resting the foot or wearing a walking plaster. ***Prognosis:*** Excellent.[90]

Kienböck's disease Pain is felt over the lunate (esp. during active wrist movement). Grip is impaired due to pain. ***Radiographs:*** Dense lunate with a little depth reduction early; more marked flattening later. Osteoarthritis is a consequence. ***Treatment:*** ***Early:*** Try wrist splinting for 3 months; *later:* lunate excision with prosthesis implantation. Once arthritis is established lunate excision does not help.

Freiberg's infarction This may be classed as an osteochondritis dissecans (p 704), eg of the 2nd metatarsal head, presenting as forefoot pain around puberty, in girls. There may be microfractures at the junction of the metaphysis and the growth plate ***Radiographs:*** Epiphysis of a metatarsal head becomes granular, fragmented and flattened. ***Treatment:*** Good shoes ± metatarsal pad. Limit activity for 4–6 weeks. If severe, consider removal of affected bone with bone grafting or interpositional arthroplasty and use of a walking plaster.

Osteochondritis-like conditions

Calvé's vertebra (like Scheuermann's disease, p702, but rarer) Typically in a thoracic vertebra (if neck or atlas, torticollis may result). Histology may show eosinophilic granuloma. Typical age: 2–10yrs. *Symptoms:* Pain and tenderness over the affected vertebra; slight kyphosis.

Radiographs: Dense, flattened vertebral body with disc space preserved. Bone scan: Hyperactive spot. ΔΔ: Sarcoma; osteomyelitis; TB.

Treatment: Bed rest ± plaster-cast immobilization.

Osgood–Schlatter's disease This tibial tuberosity apophysitis and traction of quadriceps on domus affects children (8–14yrs; boys:girls ≈3:1). The pain below the knee is worse on strenuous activity and quadriceps contraction (lift straight leg against resistance). The tuberosity looks big, and is tender.

Radiographs: Tibial tuberosity enlargement (± fragmentation). Its diagnosis is clinical, not simply radiological. The cause may be strain on the developing tuberosity. MRI shows the tendinopathy.

Treatment: Rest. Some advocate ice + compresses.

Plaster cast immobilization for 6 weeks may be needed. Tibial tubercle excision has been recommended if the above fail.

Sinding Larsen's disease Traction tendinopathy with calcification in the proximal attachment of the patellar tendon, which may be partially avulsed. Symptoms/treatment are similar to Osgood–Schlatter's disease (above), but the onset tends to be 1–2yrs earlier.

Sever's disease This common calcaneal apophysitis is probably from strained attachment of the Achilles tendon. It is usually self-limiting. Typical age: 8–13yrs. There is pain behind the heel (bilateral in 60%) ± limping, and tenderness over the lower posterior calcaneal tuberosity.

Radiographs: Often normal.

Treatment: Physiotherapy and heel raise. If needed, a below-knee walking plaster may give pain relief. Most are well after 8 weeks.

Osteochondritis dissecans See p690 for knee osteochondritis. Other sites: elbow, hip, ankle. *Cause:* A loose body is formed (1–3cm across) from a convex joint surface when a segment of subchondral bone and cartilage becomes avascular and separates from underlying bone. Adolescents or young adults experience early aching and effusions after use, and sudden painful locking or giving if the pieces have separated to make loose bodies.

Radiographs: Look for lucent areas in a piece about to separate, the defect from which the piece has separated, and loose bodies after separation.

Treatment: Expectant, ± removal of loose bodies. Closed wedge osteotomy may lead to revascularization (eg capitellum).

Avascular necrosis (osteonecrosis) Sites of infarction: hip (commonest), knee, shoulder. *Imaging* (MRI is best): Sclerotic or porotic bone, flattening of joint surface, and osteochondral fragments.

Local causes: Trauma (eg fractured neck of femur) & secondary to rheumatoid; severe osteoarthritis; psoriatic arthropathy or neuropathic joints.

Systemic: Thalassaemia; sickle-cell (+ other causes of microembolism, eg platelets in thalassaemia); SLE; steroids (eg post-transplant); hypercoagulable states; dyslipidaemias; alcoholism; pancreatitis; diabetes; big burns; radiation; diving accidents (p574); Cushing's; & Gaucher's disease.

Treatment: Immobilization; analgesia; for hips, arthroplasty.

Osteochondritis-like conditions

Calvé's vertebra (Like Scheuermann's disease, p 702, but rarer.) Typical site: a thoracic vertebra (if neck or atlas, torticollis may result). Histology: Look for eosinophilic granulomata. Typical age: 2-10yrs. Symptoms: Pain and ± tenderness over the affected vertebra; slight kyphosis.

Radiographs/CT/MRI: Dense, flattened vertebral body with disc space preserved. *Bone scan:* Hyperactive spot. ΔΔ: Sarcoma; osteomyelitis.

Treatment: Bed rest ± plaster-cast immobilization.[91]

Osgood–Schlatter's disease This tibial tuberosity apophysitis and quadriceps tendonitis affects children 10-14yrs old. ♂/♀ ≈ 3 : 1. The pain below the knee is worse on strenuous activity and quadriceps contraction (lift straight leg against resistance). The tuberosity looks big, and is tender.

Radiographs: Tibial tuberosity enlargement (± fragmentation). NB: diagnosis is clinical, not simply radiological. The cause may be strain on the developing tuberosity. MRI shows the tendonitis.

Treatment: Rest. Some advocate ice compresses.[92]

Plaster cast immobilization for 6 weeks may be needed. Tibial tubercle excision has been recommended if the above fail.[93]

Sinding Larsen's disease Traction tendinopathy with calcification in the proximal attachment of the patellar tendon, which may be partially avulsed. Symptoms, treatment are similar to Osgood-Schlatter's disease (above), but the onset tends to be 1-2yrs earlier.[94]

Sever's disease This common calcaneal apophysitis is probably from strained attachment of the Achilles tendon. It is usually self-limiting. Typical age: 8-13yrs. There is pain behind the heel (bilateral in 60%) ± limping, and tenderness over the lower posterior calcaneal tuberosity.

Radiographs: Often normal.

Treatment: Physiotherapy and heel raise. If needed, a below knee walking plaster may give pain relief. Most are well after 5 weeks.[95]

Osteochondritis dissecans See p 690 for knee osteochondritis. Other sites: elbow, hip, ankle, talus. A loose body is formed (1-3cm across) from a convex joint surface when a segment of subchondral bone and cartilage becomes avascular and separates from underlying bone. Adolescents or young adults experience early aching and effusions after use, and sudden painful locking of joints once pieces have separated to make loose bodies.

Radiographs: Look for lucent areas in a piece *about* to separate, the defect from which the piece *has* separated, and loose bodies *after* separation.

Treatment: Expectant ± removal of loose bodies. Closed wedge resection may lead to revascularization (eg capitellum).[96]

Avascular necrosis (osteonecrosis) ***Sites of infarction:*** Hip (commonest), knee, shoulder. ***Imaging:*** (MRI is best) Sclerotic or porotic bone due to infarction; joint surface odd, osteochondral fragments.[97]

Local causes: Trauma (eg fractured neck of femur); secondary to rheumatoid, severe osteoarthritis, psoriatic arthropathy, or neuropathic joints.

Systemic: Thalassaemia, sickle-cell (+ any cause of microthrombi, eg platelets↑ in leukaemia), NSAIDs/steroids (eg post-transplant), SLE, scleroderma, SBE, dyslipidaemia, alcoholism, pancreatitis, diabetes, big burns, radiation, diving accidents (p 814), Cushing's & Gaucher's diseases.[98]

Treatment: Immobilization; analgesia; for hips, arthroplasty.[99]

Joint replacement

Joint replacement has been used for >40yrs. Each year, 46,000 hips and 35,000 knees are replaced in the UK (knees are overtaking hips).

Hip replacement The usual indication for operation is pain (surgery for fixed flexion deformity affecting walking is less successful). It's rare to replace osteoarthritic hips. These patients are usually elderly. Rheumatoid arthritis (RA) is the next most common indication (patients are often in their 30s or 40s). Other conditions which may result in replacement are: avascular necrosis of head of femur, congenitally dislocated hip, fractured neck of femur.

Many prostheses are available but most consist of a metal femoral component with an intramedullary stem usually held in place by bone cement and a plastic acetabular component. Early success of operation occurs in 95%. Early complications include thromboembolism (1%), dislocation (3%), deep infection (≤1%), fracture (1%), sciatic palsy (1%), limb-length discrepancy (5%) and death (0.1–0.2%).

Later problems of loosening or infection are heralded by return of pain. If plain radiographs are inconclusive in the case of loosening, arthrography or technetium scans may reveal increased bone activity. Suspected sepsis should be investigated by white cell count, ESR, and gallium scan. Scans are unreliable within 6 months of operation. Revision arthroplasty is more successful for loosening than for infection. 10yr results for the original kind have been revised. Be cautious in recommending replacement to those in their 60s who are likely to cause excessive wear of the prosthesis. Excess weight should be lost as this also contributes to wear. Earlier replacement is urged for rheumatoid arthritis as joints tend to be grossly affected younger—and excessive delay may result in surgery upon very porotic osteoporotic bone.

Central migration of the prosthesis via perforation of the medial acetabular wall is a rare cause of external iliac artery & bladder injury. Hip resurfacing is an evolving technology that is indicated for active individuals under 65yrs old who have severe arthritis. It remains an experimental procedure as there is currently no medium- to long-term clinical data.

Knee replacement The knee is more complicated than the hip, and designs for replacements have altered greatly: from joint-stemmed hinge mechanisms, to short-stemmed articulations. The usually used indications for knee replacement are pain, or disturbing sleep, or making housebound. Pain correlates poorly with radiological signs. Success rate: ~95% joint survival at 10yrs (better than hips). Revision rates are similar. Quality of life can be transformed, even if >80yrs old.

Other joints Joint spacers are used in finger joints for rheumatoid, with success. Elbow replacements are beginning to show some success. Shoulder replacement success rates are approaching those of knees.

Preventing thromboses DVT occurs in >25% of major orthopaedic events, but fatal PE in only 0.1–0.25%. Low-molecular-weight heparin (LMWH) halves DVT rate and lowers risk of fatal pulmonary embolism (PE) by 2/3 in major orthopaedic surgery. Low-molecular-weight heparin (LMWH) is preferable to ordinary heparin. CI: Uncontrolled bleeding/risk of bleeding (eg peptic ulcer), endocarditis, children. Dose example: dalteparin 2500U SC pre-op and at 8h post-op then 5000U once daily for 1 week, or longer. Fondaparinux, 2.5mg/day, may be better than enoxaparin. DVT prophylaxis may need continuing for 1 month post-op. NB: if the rate of fatal PE is low (<0.1%) in some centres, prophylaxis may not be warranted.

Joint replacement

Joint replacement has been used for 30yrs. Each year 40,000 hips and 15–20,000 knees are replaced in the UK (knees are overtaking hips).

Hip replacement The usual indication for operation is pain (surgery for fixed flexion deformity affecting walking is less successful). 75% are to replace osteoarthritic hips. These patients are usually elderly. Rheumatoid arthritis (RA) is the next most common indication (patients are often in their 30s or 40s). Other conditions which may result in replacement are: avascular necrosis of head of femur; congenitally dislocated hip; fractured neck of femur.

Many prostheses are available but most consist of a metal femoral component with an intramedullary stem usually held in place by bone cement, and a plastic acetabular component. Early success of operation occurs in 90%. Early complications include: thrombo-embolism (4%), dislocation (3%), deep infection (2%), fracture (1%), nerve palsy (1%), limb-length discrepancy (1%), and death (0.4–0.7%).[100]

Later problems of loosening or infection are heralded by return of pain. If plain radiographs are inconclusive in the case of loosening, strontium or technetium scans may reveal increased bone activity. Suspected sepsis should be investigated by white cell count, ESR, and gallium scan. Scans are not reliable within 8 months of operation. Revision arthroplasty is more successful for loosening than for infection. By 9–10yrs post-op 11% of implants have been revised. Be cautious in recommending replacement to those in their 60s who are likely to cause excessive wear of the prosthesis. Excess weight should be lost as this also contributes to usage. Earlier replacement is used for rheumatoid arthritis as joints tend to be grossly affected younger—and excessive delay may result in surgery upon very rarefied osteoporotic bone.

Central migration of the prosthesis via perforation of the medial acetabular wall is a rare cause of external iliac artery & bladder injury.[MET 101] Hip resurfacing is an evolving technology that is indicated for active individuals under 65yrs old who have an end-stage arthropathy. It remains an "experimental" procedure as there is currently no medium- to long-term clinical data.[102]

Knee replacement The knee is more complicated than the hip, and designs for replacements have altered greatly, from long-stemmed hinge mechanisms, to short-stemmed articulations currently used. Indications for knee replacement: pain at rest, or disturbing sleep, or making housebound. Pain correlates poorly with radiological signs. Success rate: 95%. Joint survival: 90% last 15yrs (better than hips). Revision rates are similar. Quality of life can be transformed, even if >80yrs old.[103]

Other joints Joint spacers are used in finger joints for rheumatoid, with success. Elbow replacements are beginning to show some success. Shoulder replacement success rates are approaching those of knees.

Preventing thromboses DVT occurs in >2/3; of major orthopaedic events, but fatal PE in only 0.1–0.2%.[104] [n=130000] Low-molecular weight heparin (LMWH) halves DVT rate and lowers risk of fatal pulmonary embolus (PE) by 2/3. In major orthopaedic surgery, low-molecular weight heparin (LMWH) is preferable to ordinary heparin. CI: uncontrolled bleeding/risk of bleeding (eg peptic ulcer); endocarditis; children. *Dose example:* dalteparin 2500U 2h pre-op and at 12h post-op, then 5000U once/day for 1 week. In knees, fondaparinux 2.5mg/day may be better than enoxaparin.[105] [N=1049] DVT/PE prophylaxis may need continuing for 1 month post-op. NB: if the rate of fatal PE is low (~0.1%), in some centres prophylaxis may not be warranted.[106]

Infected hip and knee prostheses

This may be a disastrous complication of joint replacement—presenting with pain, fever, or ESR↑. Sinus formation may relieve pockets of pus. Gallium scintigraphy may help make the diagnosis. Get expert help from radiologists, an orthopaedic surgeon specializing in the problem, and a consultant in infectious diseases.

Treatment: Early on, debridement + antibiotics may be enough.[107] Later, with loosening of components, radical debridement must include removal of all prosthetic material, as well as any involved bone and soft tissue. Sometimes reconstruction by exchange arthroplasty works, eg for less virulent infections. Antibiotics may be needed for months. Patient selection is vital, eg those without draining sinuses, without immunocompromise, and with adequate bone quality after debridement.[108]
The Mayo Clinic reports a 13% failure rate with a 2-stage reconstruction.
Another alternative may be the removal of all foreign material and allowing ankylosis to occur, ie a Girdlestone pseudarthrosis, for the hip.

SBE-style antibiotic prophylaxis ± antibiotic-impregnanted cement?

- ***Dentistry-associated prosthesis infection*** with oral bacteria is very rare and risks of antibiotics are palpable (>500 penicillin-caused deaths/yr, in the USA), and SBE-style prophylaxis is not recommended.
- *Colonoscopy + polypectomy* may be more risky than dentistry; some recommend prophylaxis, if <6 months since replacement.[109]
- The best prophylaxis might be achieved with a combination of gentamicin-impregnated cement (on its own, unreliable), systemic antibiotics for >24h, and surgical enclosure. However, the additional cost of the surgical enclosure may prove too expensive in some areas. Reimplantation need not require use of cement: hydroxyapatite coated total prostheses are an alternative.[110] [111]

Joint injection and aspiration

Joint aspirations *Diagnostic role:* Any blood, crystals, or pus? [MET 112] *Therapeutic role:* For tense effusions, septic effusions, and haemarthroses.

Steroid injections to inflamed joints, bursae, or tendon sheaths aim to ↓inflammation and relieve pain, perhaps by ↓prostaglandin synthesis, stabilizing mast cells, or ↓tissue calcification, or increasing vascularization and permeability of synovium. ***Side-effects:*** Skin atrophy (hydrocortisone acetate is safer than triamcinolone), haemarthrosis, facial flushing, urticaria, Charcot's arthropathy, post-injection flare syndrome (synovitis with fever), paresis, and septic arthritis (≤1 in 14,000 injections). www.clinicalevidence.org ►*It is essential that steroids are not used in septic conditions* and, if any doubt at all exists, results of synovial fluid culture should be awaited. Remember the possibility of tuberculous synovitis—especially in immigrant populations. Repeated injections are more dangerous: beware ligamentous laxity, joint instability, calcification, or rupture of tendons.

Preparations are available: *hydrocortisone acetate* (cheapest, shortest acting), *methylprednisolone*, and *triamcinolone*. They may be mixed with 1% lidocaine. When triamcinolone is used for injecting near short tendons, 10mg strength is preferred to 40mg as tendon rupture has been reported after the latter. Despite our best intentions 'joint' injections often fail to meet their target (50% in one study in which contrast material was also injected); those off-target are less likely to relieve symptoms. [113]

Conditions responding reasonably well to steroid injection Localized subdeltoid bursitis; supraspinatus, infraspinatus, and subscapular tendinopathy; shoulder arthritis; tennis and golfer's elbow, arthritis of elbow, radioulnar, acromioclavicular, and sternoclavicular joints; ganglia; trigger fingers; strains of collateral and cruciate ligaments of knee; suprapatellar, infrapatellar, and Achilles tendinopathy; plantar fasciitis; traumatic arthritis of metatarsophalangeal joints; and sesamo-first-metatarsal joint.

Preparation Check that you have swabs, needles, and sterile bottles. For aspiration of viscid fluid (eg haemarthrosis) use 19G needle. For the larger joints use a 21G (green, in the NHS) needle, and for fingers and toes a 23G (blue) needle. Locate joint margins carefully before cleansing with chlorhexidine in 5% spirit or surgical spirit, and once the skin is cleansed use scrupulous aseptic no-touch technique. Remember that antiseptics and local anaesthetics take 3min to work; even then, the skin is clean but not sterile. Samples for microbiology should be sent in sterile containers, those for cytology or crystal examination in heparinized or FBC containers.

Knee joint (►see p 689) The patient lies with knee supported slightly flexed and muscles relaxed. Palpate the joint space behind patella either medially or laterally. Insert a needle horizontally between the patella and femur. Slight resistance is felt on traversing the synovial membrane; it should be possible to aspirate fluid, and injection fluid should flow easily. ***Usual doses:*** 50mg hydrocortisone acetate, 40mg methylprednisolone, 20mg triamcinolone hexacetonide. Repeat injections should be longer than 3 months apart. If injection is used for prepatellar bursitis, give 25mg hydrocortisone acetate into the most tender spot.

The ankle Plantar flex foot slightly, palpate joint margin between extensor hallucis longus (lateral) and tibialis anterior (medial) tendons just above tip of medial malleolus. Inject 25mg hydrocortisone acetate into the joint.

Synovial fluid in health and disease

Aspiration of synovial fluid is used primarily to look for infectious or crystal (gout and pseudogout) arthropathies.

	Appearance	*Viscosity*[114]	*WBC/mm*^{3}	*Neutrophils*
Normal	Clear, colourless	High	<200	<25%
Noninflammatory[1]	Clear, straw	High	<5000	<25%
Haemorrhagic[2]	Bloody, xanthochromic	Variable	<10,000	<50%
Acute inflammatory[3]	Turbid, yellow	Decreased		
• Acute gout			~14,000	~80%
• Rheumatic fever			~18,000	~50%
• Rheumatoid Arthritis			~16,000	~65%
Septic	Turbid, yellow	Decreased		
• TB			~24,000	~70%
• Gonorrhoeal			~14,000	~60%
• Septic (non-gonococcal)[4]			~65,000	~95%

For inflammatory causes of arthritis: Synovial fluid WBC >2000/mm^3 is 84% sensitive (84% specific); synovial fluid neutrophil count >75% is 75% sensitive (92% specific). ►NB: not all labs are equally skillful.[MET 115]

1 Eg, degenerative joint disease, trauma.
2 Eg, tumour, haemophilia, trauma.
3 Includes eg Reiter's, pseudogout, SLE etc.
4 Includes staphs, streps, Lyme, and *Pseudomonas* (eg post-op).

Joint injections—continued

Shoulder injection Because shoulder pain from soft tissue causes is common (*lifetime incidence:* ~10%), and because the pain can be long-lasting (only 23% resolve within a month), this is one of the most commonly injected joints, but we do not know *who* to inject or *when* in their illness, because trials are few, and the best ones cast doubt on the benefit of *any* injection. ***Anterior approach:*** (for aspiration, synovitis, frozen shoulder) seat the patient with arm relaxed by side of his chest. Feel the space between head of humerus and glenoid cap about 1cm below coracoid process. Insert a 21-gauge green needle into the joint space (enters joint space when almost up to its hilt) and inject 25–50mg hydrocortisone acetate. Be sure not to go medial to the coracoid process. ***Lateral approach:*** (subacromial bursitis, painful arc syndrome) inject 25–50mg hydrocortisone acetate with lidocaine just below lateral tip of acromion, pointed downwards and advanced medially. If the needle is withdrawn from touching the head of humerus with slight pressure on the plunger, a drop in pressure is felt as the bursa is entered. Painful arc pain may be reproduced. A second injection may be given after >48h.

Tennis elbow 25mg hydrocortisone acetate with 1mL lidocaine is injected with force to area of maximal tenderness over lateral humeral condyle moving to and fro down to bone several times. A second injection may be needed, eg after 2 weeks. Warn the patient that symptoms may worsen briefly after the injection has been given. (Avoid triamcinolone and Depo-Medrone®: as injections are superficial, fat necrosis may occur.)

Elbow joint injection With elbow flexed at 90°, inject 25mg hydrocortisone acetate between proximal head of radius (locate by rotating patient's hand) and lateral epicondyle by lateral approach (needle 90° to skin), or posteriorly between olecranon and lateral epicondyle.

Biceps tendinopathy is worsened by externally rotating the arm. Insert needle parallel to tendon (if resistance, it is in the tendon: withdraw a bit); inject 25mg hydrocortisone acetate into tendon sheath and 25mg into joint.

Wrist injection Inject 25mg hydrocortisone acetate 1-1.5cm deep between extensor tendons of ring and little fingers between ulnar head and lunate.

De Quervain's tenosynovitis Extensor pollicis brevis and abductor pollicis longus tendons, eg on traversing the extensor retinaculum on the dorsal wrist, may cause a tender swelling (p 668). With needle almost parallel to skin pointing proximally, inject 25mg hydrocortisone acetate slowly just distal or proximal to the radial styloid, at the site of maximum tenderness. If needle in tendon, injection is difficult so withdraw until easy flow occurs.

Carpal tunnel Place the hand comfortably palm up. Inject 25mg hydrocortisone acetate at 90° through the distal transverse skin crease of the palmar surface of the wrist closer to the hamate than the trapezium—ie a few mm to the ulnar side flexor carpi radialis. Other techniques are also used. Sometimes the needle enters the median nerve causing sudden pain in the fingers—so reposition the needle. If the first injection fails, consider repeating with 10-20mg triamcinolone. A splint worn for the next few days may mitigate symptoms which can occur at the time of injection.

Trigger finger Insert needle at proximal finger skin crease parallel to flexor tendon, pointing towards palm. Palpate tendon thickening in palm and proceed as for De Quervain's.

First carpometacarpal joint of thumb Avoiding radial artery, inject 25mg hydrocortisone acetate at base of first metacarpal at 1cm depth in anatomical snuffbox (aim at base of little finger).

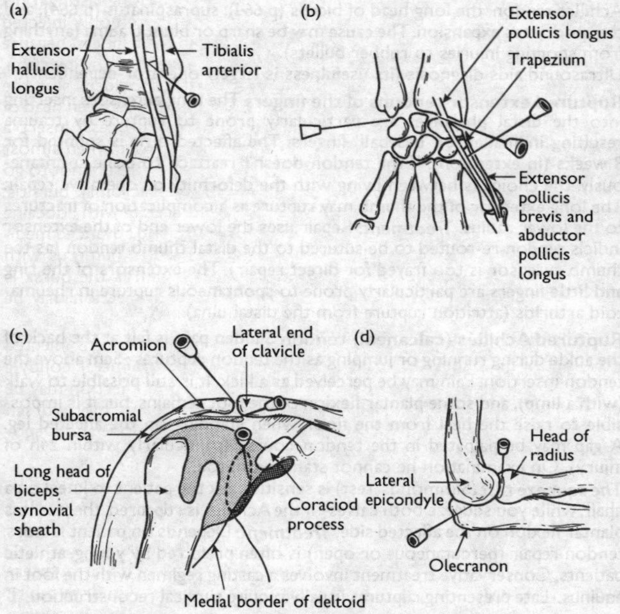

(a) Dorsal aspect of the right ankle indicating anatomical landmarks.

(b) Dorsal aspect of the right wrist indicating anatomical landmarks.

(c) Diagrammatic representation of the anterior aspect of the right shoulder region. The stippled areas indicate synovial membranes of the subacromial bursa and the glenohumeral joints.

(d) The right elbow, flexed.[116]

Tendon rupture and injury

The main tendons to rupture are the extensor tendons of the fingers, the Achilles tendon, the long head of biceps (p 664), supraspinatus (p 664), and the quadriceps expansion. The cause may be sharp or blunt trauma (anything from sporting injuries to rubber bullets).[117]
Ultrasound aids diagnosis (its usefulness is largely operator-dependent).

Ruptured extensor tendons of the fingers The long extensors inserting into the distal phalanges are particularly prone to rupture by trauma resulting in 'mallet' or 'baseball' fingers. The affected digit is splinted for 8 weeks (in extension). If the tendon doesn't reattach to bone spontaneously, the choice is between living with the deformity or operative repair. The long extensor of the thumb may rupture as a complication of fractures to the lower radius. ***Treatment:*** Repair uses the lower end of the extensor indicis tendon re-routed to be sutured to the distal thumb tendon (as the thumb extensor is too frayed for direct repair). The extensors of the ring and little fingers are particularly prone to spontaneous rupture in rheumatoid arthritis (attrition rupture from the distal ulna).

Ruptured Achilles (calcaneal) tendon Sudden pain is felt at the back of the ankle during running or jumping as the tendon ruptures ~5cm above the tendon insertion. Pain may be perceived as a kick. It is still possible to walk (with a limp), and some plantar flexion of the foot remains, but it is impossible to raise the heel from the floor when standing on the affected leg. A gap may be palpated in the tendon course (particularly within 24h of injury). On examination he cannot stand on tiptoe.
The squeeze test (Simmonds' test) is sensitive: ask the patient to kneel on a chair, while you squeeze both calves—if the Achilles is ruptured, there is less plantar flexion on the affected side. ***Treatment:*** Depends on patient factors: tendon repair (percutaneous or open) is often preferred by young, athletic patients. Conservative treatment involves a casting regimen with the foot in equinus. Late presenting ruptures usually require surgical reconstruction.[MET 118]

Ruptured quadriceps expansion Injury may be direct (eg a blow) or indirect (stumbling causing sudden contraction of the apparatus). The quadriceps expansion encloses the patella and inserts into the tibial tuberosity as the patellar tendon. ***Non-traumatic causes:*** Pseudogout; Wilson's disease; renal failure with hyperparathyroidism.[119] ***Treatment:*** Rupture can occur at the site of quadriceps insertion to the patella, through the patella by fracture, or by avulsion of the patellar tendon from the tibial tuberosity. In all cases where the extensor mechanism is disrupted (the patient cannot perform a straight leg raise) surgery is mandatory. After repair, a plaster cylinder is worn for some weeks then intensive physiotherapy helps regain knee function. Many have persistent weakness and difficulty returning to higher level sporting activities.[120]

Tenosynovitis Tendons and surrounding synovium may become locally inflamed (possibly from strain) thereby causing pain, eg supraspinatus tendinopathy and bicipital tendinopathy (p 664), or De Quervain's (p 668). Acute frictional synovitis at the wrist is another example, with swelling over the wrist and thumb extensors. If palpation doesn't detect crepitus, at some sites, stethoscope auscultation reveals sounds like bronchial breathing.[1]
Treatment: In wrist tenosynovitis, a splint for 3 weeks (leaving the fingers free) may be needed to allow inflammation to subside.

1 R Adler 1999 *NEJM* **340** 156 —'Bronchial breathing' on the painful right arch on great toe flexion with 'vesicular'-type breathing on the unaffected left side.

Nerve compression syndromes

For brachial plexus and peripheral nerve lesions, see p 756, p 758 & p 762.

Carpal tunnel syndrome This is the commonest cause of hand paraesthesiae; it is due to compression of the median nerve as it passes under the flexor retinaculum. Pregnancy, the Pill, myxoedema, lunate fracture, (rarely) rheumatoid arthritis, cardiac failure, or being premenstrual may all increase compression. *Clinical features* are of median nerve distribution.
- Tingling or pain are felt in the thumb, index finger, and middle finger.
- When the pain is at its worst, the patient characteristically dangles or shakes the wrist to bring about relief. Pain is especially common at night and after repetitive actions. Affected persons may experience clumsiness. Early on there may be no signs. Later there is:
- Wasting of the thenar eminence • ↓Sensation over the lateral 3½ fingers. Lateral palmar sensation is spared as the supply (the palmar cutaneous branch of the median nerve) does not pass through the tunnel.
- Phalen's test: holding the wrist hyperflexed for 1 min reproduces the symptoms. (This is more reliable than Tinel's test—tapping over the tunnel to produce paraesthesiae. Note: Phalen = flexing, Tinel = tapping.)

Tests: Nerve conduction studies are not usually needed (and may be wrong).

Treatment: Steroid injection (p 710). Symptom relief beyond one month compared to placebo is unproven. Wrist splints worn at night may relieve nocturnal pain. Fairly permanent results are obtained from decompression by flexor retinaculum division.

Ulnar nerve compression at the elbow This is described on p 656.

Radial tunnel syndrome (Posterior interosseus nerve compression) This radial nerve branch is sometimes compressed on passing through the supinator muscle (eg after forearm fracture or excessive exercise). Patients experience weakness of the thumb and fingers. Examination may reveal weakness of long finger extensors and short and long extensors of the thumb, but no sensory loss. *Treatment* after trauma is surgical decompression and spring-loaded splints to extend fingers.

Anterior interosseus nerve compression This median nerve branch may be compressed under the fibrous origin of flexor digitorum sublimis, causing weakness of pinch and pain along the forearm's radial border. Examination shows weakness of the long thumb flexor and flexor profundus to the index and middle fingers. *Treatment* is surgical decompression.

Ulnar nerve compression at the wrist Uncommon. Loss may be motor or sensory. Diagnose by electrophysiology. Treat by surgical decompression.

Meralgia paraesthetica If the lateral cutaneous nerve of the thigh is compressed (on leaving the pelvis just medial to the anterior superior iliac spine, eg by tight jeans), pain and paraesthesiae may be felt over the upper outer thigh. Sensation may be ↓ over this area. It is usually self-limiting, and can occur in pregnancy. *Treatment:* Corticosteroid and local anaesthetic injection at the anterior superior iliac spine gives unpredictable results. Complete or partial pain relief was found in 77% after decompression and in 82% after transection of the nerve.

Common peroneal compression Nerve compression against the head of fibula (eg plaster casts, thin patients lying unconscious, proximal fibula fracture, squatting, obstructed labour) causes inability to dorsiflex the foot. Sensation may be ↓ over the dorsum of the foot. *Tests:* electrophysiology. *Treatment:* Most recover spontaneously but surgical decompression may be needed (eg if 3 months' duration without improvement). Physiotherapy and splint until foot-drop recovers.

Nerve compression syndromes

For brachial plexus and peripheral nerve lesions, see p 766, p 716 & p 762.

Carpal tunnel syndrome ►This is the commonest cause of hand pain at night. It is is due to compression of the median nerve as it passes under the flexor retinaculum. Pregnancy, the Pill, myxoedema, lunate fracture (rare), rheumatoid arthritis, cardiac failure, or being premenstrual may all increase compression. ***Clinical features*** are of median nerve distribution:

- Tingling or pain are felt in the thumb, index finger, and middle finger.
- When the pain is at its worse, the patient characteristically flicks or shakes the wrist to bring about relief. Pain is especially common at night and after repetitive actions. Affected persons may experience clumsiness. Early on there may be no signs. Later there is:
- Wasting of the thenar eminence & ↓sensation over the lateral 3½ fingers.
- Lateral palmar sensation is spared as its supply (the palmar cutaneous branch of the median nerve) does not pass through the tunnel.
- Phalen's test: holding the wrist hyperflexed for 1–2min reproduces the symptoms. (This is more reliable than Tinel's test—tapping over the tunnel to produce paraesthesiae. Note: Phalen's flexing, Tinel's tapping.)

Tests: Nerve conduction studies are not usually needed (and may be -ve).

Treatment: Carpal injection: p 710. (Symptom relief beyond one month compared to placebo is unproven.)[121] Wrist splints worn at night may relieve nocturnal pain. More permanent results are obtained from decompression by flexor retinaculum division.

Ulnar nerve compression at the elbow This is described on p 666.

Radial tunnel syndrome (Posterior interosseus nerve compression) This radial nerve branch is sometimes compressed on passing through the supinator muscle (eg after forearm fracture or excessive exercise). Patients experience weakness of the thumb and fingers. ***Examination*** may reveal weakness of long finger extensors, and short and long extensors of the thumb, but no sensory loss. ***Treatment*** after trauma is surgical decompression and springed splints to extend fingers.[122]

Anterior interosseus nerve compression This median nerve branch may be compressed under the fibrous origin of flexor digitorum sublimis, causing weakness of pinch and pain along the forearm's radial border. Examination shows weakness of the long thumb flexor and flexor profundus to the index and middle fingers. ***Treatment*** is surgical decompression.

Ulnar nerve compression at the wrist Uncommon. Loss may be motor or sensory. ***Diagnose*** by electrophysiology. ***Treat*** by surgical decompression.

Meralgia paraesthetica If the lateral cutaneous nerve of the thigh is compressed (on leaving the pelvis just medial to the anterior superior iliac spine, eg by tight jeans), pain and paraesthesiae may be felt over the upper outer thigh. Sensation may be ↓ over this area. It is usually self-limiting, and can occur in pregnancy. ***Treatment:*** Cortisone and local anaesthetic injection at the anterior superior iliac spine gives unpredictable results. Complete or partial pain relief was found in 72% after decompression and in 82% after transection of the nerve.[123]

Common peroneal compression Nerve compression against the head of fibula (eg plaster casts, thin patients lying unconscious, proximal fibula fracture, squatting, obstructed labour) causes inability to dorsiflex the foot. Sensation may be ↓ over the dorsum of the foot. ***Tests:*** Electrophysiology. ***Treatment:*** Most recover spontaneously but surgical decompression may be needed (eg if 3 months elapse without improvement). Physiotherapy and splint until foot-drop recovers.[124]

Soft tissue injuries

Correct management of soft tissue injuries reduces pain, recovery time and subsequent disability.

Treatment in the first 24 hours: 'RICE'

*R*est: A splint or plaster cast may help.

*I*ce: Cold is anaesthetic and a vasoconstrictor. Apply ice packs (eg a packet of frozen peas wrapped in a cloth) or cold compresses intermittently for <10min at a time, to avoid cold injury.

*C*ompression: Strapping restricts swelling and further bleeding.

*E*levation: Ideally elevate the affected part above the heart to improve drainage from the affected part and to reduce pain.

Rehabilitation Passive stretching to maintain joint mobility and muscle length, then progressive active exercise until the full range and strength of movement is restored, eg wobbleboards for ankles. Sportsmen must then retrain to full fitness. Also consider NSAIDs, rubefacients, and ultrasound.

Sports injuries Many sports injuries can be prevented.

- Is the patient preparing the body for activity with a proper warm-up? Inadequate warm-up increases the risk of injury.
- Cooling-down is also important in reducing muscle soreness.
- Is protective equipment being worn?
- Many acute and chronic injuries are caused by unsuitable equipment, faulty technique, or unwise training schedules—advice from a professional coach can be invaluable.

Common patterns of injury in sport: 'Shin splints'—shin soreness, common in unfit runners on hard surfaces and due to muscle tears, mild anterior compartment syndrome or stress fracture; knee pain—most causes on p 688; ligamentous ankle injury (p 754); plantar fasciitis (p 694); stress fractures such as march fracture—suspect with increasing bony pain despite normal radiographs (radionuclide scans are more discriminating); Achilles tendon problems; tennis elbow (p 666).

Overuse phenomena

Overuse phenomena at work (*Work-related upper limb injury = occupational overuse syndrome = isometric contraction myopathy = repetitive strain injury = RSI*) Activity requiring repetitive actions, particularly those associated with prolonged muscle contraction, may lead to chronic symptoms. Employers have a duty to provide a safe working environment and well-designed chairs and tools, and frequent short breaks. Changes of posture and activity help to reduce work-related upper limb injury (this term is preferred to repetitive strain injury). The cost of these injuries in suffering, and hours lost from work, is considerable as treatment of established symptoms is often difficult and may necessitate change in employment—if one is available.

Compensation is a vexed issue, and recent Court judgments have gone in favour of the employers in some instances, and in favour of patients in others. Some people argue that the condition does not exist as a separate medical entity emphasizing lack of histopathology. It should be noted that this is not a prerequisite for a disease (see *Sudden infant death*, p 148)—and in any case histopathology *is* sometimes demonstrable. Treatments tried include splinting (may prolong the problem), physiotherapy, β-blockers for relaxation, and the Alexander technique for posture re-education.

Those who use vacuum cleaners, assemble cars, or play stringed instruments may all develop overuse phenomena.

Testing peripheral nerve motor functions

Nerve root	*Muscle*	*Test—by asking the patient to:*
C3,4	Trapezius	Shrug shoulder (via accessory nerve) www.bartleby.com/107/206.html
C4,5	Rhomboids	Brace shoulder back.
C5,6,7	serratus anterior	Push arm forward against resistance.
C5,6	pectoralis major (clavicular head)	Adduct arm from above horizontal, and push it forward.
C6,7,8	pectoralis major (sternocostal head)	Adduct arm below horizontal.
C5,6	Supraspinatus	Abduct arm the first 15°.
C5,6	Infraspinatus	Externally rotate arm, elbow at side.
C6,7,8	latissimus dorsi	Adduct arm from horizontal position.
C5,6	Biceps	Flex supinated forearm.
C5,6	Deltoid	Abduct arm between 15° and 90°.
The radial nerve		
C6,7,8	Triceps	Extend elbow against resistance.
C5,6	Brachioradialis	Flex elbow with forearm half way between pronation and supination.
C5,6	extensor carpi radialis longus	Extend wrist to radial side with fingers extended.
C6,7	Supinator	Arm by side, resist hand pronation.
C7,8	extensor digitorum	Keep fingers extended at MCP joint.
C7,8	extensor carpi ulnaris	Extend wrist to ulnar side.
C7,8	abductor pollicis longus	Abduct thumb at 90° to palm.
C7,8	extensor pollicis brevis	Extend thumb at MCP joint.
C7,8	extensor pollicis longus	Resist thumb flexion at IP joint.
Median nerve		
C6,7	pronator teres	Keep arm pronated against resistance.
C6,7	flexor carpi radialis	Flex wrist towards radial side.
C7,8,T1	flexor digitorum sublimis	Resist extension at PIP joint (while you fix his proximal phalanx).
C8,T1	flexor digitorum profundus I & II	Resist extension at the DIP joint of index finger.
C8,T1	flexor pollicis longus	Resist thumb extension at interphalangeal joint (fix proximal phalanx).
C8,T1	abductor pollicis brevis	Abduct thumb (nail at 90° to palm).
C8,T1	opponens pollicis	Thumb touches base of 5th finger-tip (nail parallel to palm).
C8,T1	1st and 2nd lumbricals	Extend PIP joint against resistance with MCP joint held hyperextended.
Ulnar nerve		
C7,8,T1	flexor carpi ulnaris	Flex wrist towards ulnar side.
C7,C8	flexor digitorum profundus III and IV	Fix middle phalanx of little finger, resist extension of distal phalanx.
C8,T1	dorsal interossei	Abduct fingers (use index finger).
C8,T1	palmar interossei	Adduct fingers (use index finger).
C8,T1	adductor pollicis	Adduct thumb (nail at 90° to palm).
C8,T1	abductor digiti minimi	Abduct little finger.
C8,T1	flexor digiti minimi	Flex the little finger at MCP joint.

The musculocutaneous nerve (C5–6) This may be injured at the brachial plexus, causing weakness of biceps, coracobrachialis, and brachialis. Forearm flexion is weak. There may be some loss of sensation.

Sources: MRC *Handbook* & www.rad.washington.edu/atlas AND www.medmedia.com/05/324.htm

Nerve root	*Muscle*	*Test—by asking the patient to:*
L**4**,**5**, S1	gluteus medius and minimus (superior gluteal nerve)	Internal rotation at hip, hip abduction.
L5, S1,2	gluteus maximus (inferior gluteal nerve)	Extension at hip (lie prone).
L2,**3**,4	adductors (obturator nerve)	Adduct leg against resistance.
Femoral nerve		
L1,2,3	iliopsoas	Flex hip with knee flexed and lower leg supported: patient lies on back.
L2,3	sartorius	Flex knee with hip external rotated.
L2,3,4	quadriceps femoris	Extend knee against resistance.
Obturator nerve		
L2,3,4	Hip adductors	Adduct the leg.
Inferior gluteal nerve		www.rad.washington.edu/atlas2/gluteusmaximus.html
L5,S1,S2	Gluteus maximus	Hip extension.
Superior gluteal nerve		www.rad.washington.edu/atlas2/gluteusmedius.html
L4,5,S1	Gluteus medius	Abduction and internal rotation of hip.
Sciatic nerve (including the common peroneal* and tibial nerve)		
*L**4**,5	tibialis anterior	Dorsiflex ankle.
*L**5**,S1	extensor digitorum longus	Dorsiflex toes against resistance.
*L**5**,S1	extensor hallucis longus	Dorsiflex hallux against resistance.
*L**5**,S1	peroneus longus & brevis	Evert foot against resistance.
*L5,S1	extensor digit. brevis	Dorsiflex hallux (muscle of foot).
L5 **S1**,2	hamstrings	Flex knee against resistance.
L4,5	tibialis posterior	Invert plantarflexed foot.
S1,2	gastrocnemius	Plantarflex ankle joint.
L5,**S1**,2	flexor digitorum longus	Flex terminal joints of toes.
S1,2	small muscles of foot	Make sole of foot into a cup.

Quick screening test for muscle power

Shoulder	Abduction	C5	Hip	Flexion	L1-2
	Adduction	C5-7		Extension	L5-S1
Elbow	Flexion	C5-6	Knee	Flexion	S1
	Extension	C7		Extension	L3-4
Wrist	Flexion	C7-8	Ankle	Dorsiflexion	L4
	Extension	C7		Plantarflexion	S1-2
Fingers	Flexion	C7-8; Extension C7			
	Abduction	T1			

The UK MRC scale objectifies strength (reasonably well):

Grade 0 No muscle contraction ***Grade 3*** Active movement against gravity
Grade 1 Flicker of contraction ***Grade 4*** Active movement against resistance
Grade 2 Some active movement ***Grade 5*** Normal power

Grade 4–, 4, and 4+ describes movement against slight, moderate, and strong resistance. Dynamometers help quantify strength. 125 [n=30]
Remember to test proximal muscle power: ask the patient to sit from lying, to pull you towards himself, and to rise from squatting. ►Also, observe walking (easy to forget, even if the complaint is of walking difficulty!)

NB: Root numbers in **bold** indicate that that root is more important than its neighbour. ►Sources vary in ascribing particular nerve roots to muscles—and there is some biological variation in individuals. The above is a reasonable compromise, and is based on the MRC guidelines.

Reducing pain in A&E

►All patients must be asked specifically if they require pain relief. Clinical assessment is expedited by relieving pain. Patients in pain must be given high priority and should be seen by a doctor as soon as possible. They should be reassured that their pain will be relieved promptly. No acute pain is uncontrollable. If systemic analgesia is required, select the analgesic most appropriate to the type of pain. In pleuritic or musculoskeletal pain, aspirin is often more efficacious than a narcotic. NB: There are NO contraindications to narcotic analgesia (other than well defined allergy which is very rare). If in doubt—TREAT!

Adjuncts: Splint and elevate fractures and dislocations; RICE (p 715). ***Local anaesthesia:*** Local infiltration of wounds with 0.5-1 % lidocaine; digital nerve block in finger injuries; femoral nerve block for fractured shaft of femur. ***Non-narcotic systemic analgesia:*** *Paracetamol* 1g/4h; *aspirin* 600mg ± *codeine* 15-30mg/3-4h. NB: avoid dextropropxyphene (owing to dysphoria). NSAID: *ibuprofen* 400-800mg/8h PO. Ketorolac is an injectable NSAID: 10-30mg IM or 10mg IV over 1min, then 5mg every 5min to a maximum of 30mg (if aged >65, max dose is 10mg). *Tramadol* is a synthetic opioid analgesic that has weak agonist activity at mu opiate receptors and inhibits serotonin and noradrenaline reuptake in the spinal cord. Tramadol dose: 50mg/4h PO. ***Gas:*** *Entonox*® is a 50% mixture of nitrous oxide in O_2. It is self-administered by patients using a demand valve system and can provide a good level of analgesia for short procedures or when awaiting other forms of analgesia. ***Ketamine*** is a dissociative agent which can be used in subanaesthetic doses (ie: 0.25mg/kg IV) to provide analgesia. It should be used only under the authority of a consultant.

Narcotic analgesia must be given IV or IVI (IM is too slow and unpredictable). *Morphine* dose: 50-100μg/kg, eg 2.5-7.5mg IV slowly. Further increments should be titrated to the patient's response, initially at 5min intervals. Respiratory depression is unlikely with careful titration. ►There is no defined maximum dose. A typical total dose is 10-20mg. Don't give metoclopramide (≤10mg IV) *routinely* as vomiting is uncommon.

Fentanyl (1-2μg/kg, eg 50-100μg IV) is useful for short procedures requiring conscious sedation (cardioversion, reduction of dislocated shoulder) especially in combination with midazolam.

Children with trauma needing pain relief White coats can be very frightening. Toys, friendliness, and a simple explanation of what is going to happen go a long way to avoid creating a lifelong fear of doctors.

- Do you need to suture a wound? Consider the alternatives (p 728).
- Do you need to inject local anaesthetic? Consider needle-free alternatives. It is rarely worth an injection for a single suture.
- If suturing or other painful procedures are unavoidable, consider sedation: morphine, fentanyl, or ketamine (p 802) are the agents of choice. Ketamine is a potent, short-acting analgesic at 3-10mg/kg. The injectable formulation can be used orally in a flavoured drink. It is a class C drug (UK).

Explain gently to the child and the parents what you are going to do. Wrap the child in a blanket. Enlist enough nurses to hold the child and immobilize the part you are suturing. Warn the parents of possible distress. If they prefer not to be present, try to sit them out of earshot! Showing the child the result in a mirror, offering a big bandage, and giving an 'I was brave' badge can help. GA is rarely justified; if it is, the wound should probably be sutured by a plastic surgeon.

Gunshot and other penetrating injuries

Murders by handguns (Typical annual figures) Australia 13; UK 08; Sweden 36; USA 13 220. There are 4 cardinal rules in managing these injuries:

- All but superficial wounds need exploration under GA to repair or exclude damage to deep structures (and for debridement). Get expert help as it is all too easy to do further damage.
- Even minimal surface injury may hide much deep injury, depending on the weapon used, the mechanism of injury, and bullet speed.
- Most victims are young and have good reserves. Therefore cardiorespiratory decompensation indicates severe injury.
- If the weapon (eg knife) is still in situ do not remove it until the patient is on the operating table—the danger is exsanguination.

Define and record each injury. Note that low velocity bullets leave dirty tracks, requiring exploration, excision, and delayed closure. High velocity weapons (eg military rifles) are extraordinarily destructive due to the temporary cavity caused by the missile. Ruthless and massive debridement is essential. Tetanus prophylaxis: p 720.

Chest injury Penetration of the chest may damage pleura, lung, great vessels, heart, mediastinum, diaphragm, and abdominal contents. The commonest injury is haemopneumothorax from damage to lung & chest wall. This requires a large (adult 32 gauge) chest drain. Any deterioration or cardiac arrest demands prompt thoracotomy. Wounds of intercostal vessels, great vessels, or heart can cause massive haemorrhage. If drainage is initially 1500mL or >200mL/h, thoracotomy is needed.

- Sucking chest wounds must be closed at once, eg by vaseline gauze pad sealed on 3 sides, only (acts as flutter valve)—complete the seal on chest drain insertion. Relieve tension pneumothorax by needling the chest on the side of the suspected lesion before inserting a 32G chest drain (p 794), or doing radiographs (delay may be fatal).
- Respiratory embarrassment due to pain, flail chest, or diaphragmatic injury requires intubation and ventilation. Insert a chest drain—there is a chance of a tear to lung, bronchus, or chest wall.

Cardiac tamponade 1% of deep chest injuries involve the heart.

Diagnosis: Beck's triad: rising venous pressure, falling BP, and a small quiet heart (± pulsus paradoxus). JVP may not be visible if there is hypovolaemia. Pericardial aspiration is life-saving and diagnostic (take bloods before definitive anterolateral thoracotomy).

Procedure Insert an 18G needle to the left of the xiphisternum. Aim at the left shoulder (but with the needle angled downwards at 45° to the horizontal).

All these patients need: Crossmatching of 6 units of blood. Then:

- At least one large-bore IV cannula for vigorous fluid replacement.
- Monitoring: vital signs; blood gases; CVP; ECG monitoring.
- Underwater chest drain immediately to hand, and facilities for immediate thoracotomy (esp if any deterioration or a cardiac arrest).

Abdominal injuries All but the most superficial will need admission and exploration (never just observe).

Limb injury Nerves, tendons, and vessels are endangered. Test each of these in good light. Testing pulses (their presence doesn't exclude vessel injury), sensation and swelling. Any damage found will need formal surgical repair. Direct pressure will stop most bleeding. Do not use a tourniquet—it may be mechanically damaging and you may forget to take it off.

▸▸Gunshot and other penetrating injuries

Murders by handguns: (Typical annual figures) Australia 13; UK 33; Sweden 36; USA 13,220. There are 4 cardinal rules in managing these injuries:

- ▸All but superficial wounds need exploration under GA to repair or exclude damage to deep structures (and for debridement). Get expert help as it is all too easy to do further damage.
- ▸Even minimal surface injury may hide much deep injury, depending on the weapon used, the mechanism of injury, and bullet speed.
- ▸Most victims are young and fit with good reserves. Therefore cardiorespiratory decompensation indicates severe injury.
- ▸If the weapon (eg knife) is still *in situ*, do not remove it until the patient is on the operating table—the danger is exsanguination.

Define and record each injury. Note that low velocity bullets leave dirty tracks, requiring exploration, excision, and *delayed* closure. High velocity weapons (eg military rifles) are extraordinarily destructive due to the temporary cavity caused by the missile. Ruthless and massive debridement is essential. Tetanus prophylaxis: p 728.

Chest injury Penetration of the chest may damage pleura, lung, great vessels, heart, mediastinum, diaphragm, and abdominal contents. The commonest injury is haemopneumothorax from damage to lung & chest wall. This requires a large (adult: 32 gauge) chest drain. Any deterioration or cardiac arrest demands prompt thoracotomy. Wounds of intercostal vessels, great vessels, or heart can cause massive haemorrhage: if drainage is initially >1500mL, or >300mL/h, thoracotomy is needed.

Sucking chest wounds must be closed at once, eg by Vaseline® gauze pads sealed on 3 sides only (acts as flutter valve)—complete the seal on chest drain insertion. ▸▸Relieve tension pneumothorax by needling the chest on the side of the suspected lesion *before* inserting a 32G chest drain (*OHCM* p 798) or doing radiographs (delay may be fatal).

Respiratory embarrassment due to pain, flail chest, or diaphragmatic injury requires intubation and ventilation. Insert a chest drain if there is any chance of a tear to lung, bronchus, or chest wall.

Cardiac tamponade 15% of deep chest injuries involve the heart.

Diagnosis: Beck's triad: rising venous pressure, falling BP, and a small, quiet heart (± pulsus paradoxus). NB: JVP may not be visible if there is hypovolaemia. ▸▸Pericardial aspiration is life-saving and diagnostic (and buys time before definitive anterolateral thoracotomy).

Procedure: Insert an 18G needle to the left of the xiphoid. Aim at the left shoulder, but with the needle angled downwards at 45° to the horizontal.

All these patients need: Crossmatching of ≥6 units of blood, THEN:

- At least one large-bore IV cannula for vigorous fluid replacement.
- Monitoring: vital signs; blood gases; CXR; ECG monitoring.
- ITU care with a chest drain immediately to hand, and facilities for immediate thoracotomy (eg if any deterioration, or a cardiac arrest).

Abdominal injuries All but the most superficial will need admission, and exploration, never just observation. See p 760.

Limb injury Nerves, tendons, and vessels are endangered, so examine limbs in good light, testing *pulses* (their presence doesn't exclude arterial injury), *sensation* and *sweating*. Any damage found will need formal surgical repair. Direct pressure will staunch bleeding. Do not use a tourniquet: it may augment ischaemic damage, and you may forget to take it off.

The Glasgow Coma Scale (GCS)

This gives a reliable, objective way of recording the conscious state of a person. It can be used by medical and nursing staff for initial and continuing assessment. It has value in predicting ultimate outcome. 3 types of response are assessed:

• **Best motor response** This has 6 grades:

6 *Carrying out request* ('obeying command'): The patient does simple things you ask (beware of accepting a grasp reflex in this category).

5 *Localizing response to pain*: Put pressure on the patient's finger nail bed with a pencil then try supraorbital and sternal pressure: purposeful movements towards changing painful stimuli is a 'localizing' response.

4 *Withdraws to pain*: Pulls limb away from painful stimulus.

3 *Flexor response to pain*: Pressure on the nail bed causes abnormal flexion of limbs: decorticate posture.

2 *Extensor posturing to pain*: The stimulus causes limb extension (adduction, internal rotation of shoulder, pronation of forearm): decerebrate posture.

1 *No response to pain*.

NB: record the best response of any limb.

• **Best verbal response** This has 5 grades:

5 *Oriented*: The patient knows who he is, where he is and why, the year, season, and month.

4 *Confused conversation*: The patient responds to questions in a conversational manner but there is some disorientation and confusion.

3 *Inappropriate speech*: Random or exclamatory articulated speech, but no conversational exchange.

2 *Incomprehensible sounds*: Moaning but no words.

1 *None*.

NB: record level of best speech.

• **Eye opening** This has 4 grades:

4 *Spontaneous eye opening*.

3 *Eye opening in response to speech*: Any speech, or shout, not necessarily request to open eyes.

2 *Eye opening to response to pain*: Pain to limbs as above.

1 *No eye opening*.

An overall score is made by summing the score in the 3 areas assessed, eg no response to pain + no verbalization + no eye opening = 3.

Severe injury: GCS ≤8; moderate injury: GCS 9–12; minor injury: GCS 13–15.

Note: an abbreviated coma scale, AVPU, is sometimes used in the initial assessment ('primary survey') of the critically ill:

• A = alert
• V = responds to vocal stimuli
• P = responds to pain
• U = unresponsive

The Glasgow Coma Scale (GCS)

This gives a reliable, objective way of recording the conscious state of a person. It can be used by medical and nursing staff for initial and continuing assessment. It has value in predicting ultimate outcome. 3 types of response are assessed:

- **Best motor response** This has 6 grades:

  6 ***Carrying out request ('obeying command'):*** The patient does simple things you ask (beware of accepting a grasp reflex in this category).

  5 ***Localizing response to pain:*** Put pressure on the patient's finger nail bed with a pencil then try supraorbital and sternal pressure: purposeful movements towards changing painful stimuli is a 'localizing' response.

  4 ***Withdraws to pain:*** Pulls limb away from painful stimulus.

  3 ***Flexor response to pain:*** Pressure on the nail bed causes abnormal flexion of limbs: decorticate posture.

  2 ***Extensor posturing to pain:*** The stimulus causes limb extension (adduction, internal rotation of shoulder, pronation of forearm): decerebrate posture.

  1 ***No response to pain.***

NB: record the best response of any limb.

- **Best verbal response** This has 5 grades.

  5 ***Oriented:*** The patient knows who he is, where he is and why, the year, season, and month.

  4 ***Confused conversation:*** The patient responds to questions in a conversational manner but there is some disorientation and confusion.

  3 ***Inappropriate speech:*** Random or exclamatory articulated speech, but no conversational exchange.

  2 ***Incomprehensible speech:*** Moaning but no words.

  1 ***None.***

NB: record level of best speech.

- **Eye opening** This has 4 grades.

  4 ***Spontaneous eye opening.***

  3 ***Eye opening in response to speech:*** Any speech, or shout, not necessarily request to open eyes.

  2 ***Eye opening to response to pain:*** Pain to limbs as above.

  1 ***No eye opening.***

An overall score is made by summing the score in the 3 areas assessed, eg: no response to pain + no verbalization + no eye opening = 3.

Severe injury, GCS ≤8; moderate injury, GCS 9-12; minor injury, GCS 13-15.

Note: an abbreviated coma scale, **AVPU**, is sometimes used in the initial assessment ('primary survey') of the critically ill

- A = **a**lert
- V = responds to **v**ocal stimuli
- P = responds to **p**ain
- U = **u**nresponsive

Drowning

Worldwide, half a million drowning deaths occur yearly: most are children. Boys are at especial risk. Drowning is second only to road accidents as the leading cause of death in those aged 1–14yrs.

Most drownings occur in drunk adults, or in children who are poorly supervised near water. It is quite common for a toddler to bath with a slightly older sibling 'in charge', after realizing that as the child can sit up, he can also save himself from drowning should he topple over.

In communities wealthy enough to have many private swimming pools, there are summertime spates of drownings. An adult is temporarily distracted and leaves the garden, and on return finds a corpse in the pool. When such a child is brought to A&E the chief concerns are:

1 Cervical injury **2** Hypothermia **3** Asphyxia **4** Pulmonary oedema.

Management Focus on airway, breathing, and circulation.

- Immobilize the cervical spine as you open the airway—there may have been trauma here.
- Clear vomit from mouth. Vomiting is common (much water is ingested).
- If pulseless, start cardiopulmonary resuscitation.
- Expect BP to drop after leaving the water and be sure to transport in the horizontal position, and keep cardiovascular lability to a minimum.
- Intubate; pre-oxygenate with 100% O_2. If hypothermic, this can induce VF.
- Use 100% O_2—water in alveoli dilutes surfactant, causing atelectasis.
- Do Glasgow Coma Scale, p 722. If <4 prognosis is poor.
- Monitor ECG. Defibrillate if VF (p 239). For the first shock, give 2J/kg body weight (~20J at 9 months; 40J at 4yrs; 60J at 8yrs; and 80J at 12yrs). Defibrillation often fails until core T° >30°C. Heroic measures have been used without clearly affecting outcome—eg gastric, core rewarming (warm-water immersion, warm IV fluids at 40°C, breathing heated humidified gas), peritoneal dialysis, thoracotomy for heart irrigation, or heart bypass).
- Monitor core T° & CNS signs. Cerebral oedema may occur suddenly in first 24h: no evidence supports use of dexamethasone. Hypothermia is common if T° <34°C: monitor rectal T° often and rewarm using high ambient T°.
- Circulatory support may be needed to counter rewarming vasodilatation.
- Measuring left atrial pressure helps guide IV fluid; too much will ↑ICP.
- Pass a nasogastric tube to relieve gastric distension.
- Check blood gases, and pH. Get expert advice on the treatment of acidosis.

Effects of asphyxia and fresh water overload The child usually swallows large amounts of water before final aspiration. This leads to gastric distension, vomiting and further aspiration. Acute respiratory distress syndrome can occur, leading to the major villain: hypoxaemia—hence cerebral oedema and ↑ICP. To combat these, steroids and antibiotics are sometimes given, but without proof of efficacy. As the raised intracranial pressure (ICP) is due to cell death (cytotoxic oedema), steroids do not lower ICP (unlike the vasogenic oedema seen with space-occupying lesions).

The diving reflex Children retain this useful adaptation to our earlier aquatic way of life. As cold water hits the face, the pulse slows and blood is diverted from limbs and muscles to vital areas (brain, kidney). Cold further reduces the metabolic rate. This is the physiological explanation for remarkable stories of recovery from prolonged (eg 70min) cold immersion. It is also the reason why resuscitation of a seemingly dead child must continue for 40min before death is declared.

▸▸Drowning

Worldwide, half a million drowning deaths occur yearly: most are children.[1] Boys are at especial risk. Drowning is second only to road crashes as the leading cause of death in those aged 1-40yrs.

Most drownings occur in drunk adults, or in children who are poorly supervised near water. It is quite common for a toddler to bath with a slightly older sibling 'in charge'—the mother thinking that as the child can sit up, he can also save himself from drowning should he topple over.

In communities wealthy enough to have many private swimming pools there are summertime spates of drownings. An adult is temporarily distracted and leaves the garden, and, on return, finds a corpse in the pool. When such a child is brought to A&E the chief concerns are:
1 Cardiac arrest **2** Hypothermia **3** Acidaemia **4** Pulmonary oedema.

Management focuses on **a**irway, **b**reathing and **c**irculation:
- Immobilize the cervical spine as you open the airway—there may have been trauma here.
- Clear vomit from mouth. Vomiting is common (much water is ingested).
- If pulseless, start cardiopulmonary resuscitation.
- Expect BP to drop after leaving the water, and be sure to transport in the horizontal position, and keep cardiovascular instability to a minimum.[126]
- Intubate (pre-oxygenate with 100% O_2; if hypothermic, this can induce VF). Use 100% O_2—water in alveoli dilutes surfactant, causing atelectasis.
- Do Glasgow Coma Scale, p 722; if <6 prognosis is poor.
- Monitor ECG. Defibrillate if VF (p 239). For the first shock, give ~2joules/kg body weight (~20J at 9 months, 40J at 4yrs, 60J at 8yrs, and 80J at 12yrs). Defibrillation often fails until core T° > 30°C. Heroic measures have been tried without clearly affecting outcome[127]—eg rapid core rewarming (warm-water immersion, warm IV fluids at 40°C, breathing heated humidified gas,[128] peritoneal dialysis, thoracotomy for heart irrigation, or heart bypass).
- Monitor core T° & CNS signs. Cerebral oedema may occur suddenly in first 24h: no evidence supports use of dexamethasone or barbiturate coma.
- If T° < 35°C, monitor rectal T° often and rewarm using high ambient T°. Circulatory support may be needed to counter rewarming vasodilatation. Measuring left atrial pressure helps guide IV fluid: too much will ↑ICP.
- Pass a nasogastric tube to relieve gastric dilatation.
- U&E, blood gases, and Hb. Get expert advice on the problem of acidosis.

Effects of asphyxia and fresh water overload The child usually swallows large amounts of water before final aspiration. This leads to gastric dilatation, vomiting, and further aspiration.[129] Acute respiratory distress syndrome can occur, leading to the major villain, hypoxaemia—hence cerebral oedema and ↑ICP. To combat these, steroids and antibiotics are sometimes given, but without proof of efficacy. As the raised intracranial pressure (ICP) is due to cell death (cytotoxic oedema), steroids do not lower ICP (unlike the vasogenic oedema seen with space-occupying lesions).

The diving reflex Children retain this useful adaptation to our earlier aquatic way of life. As cold water hits the face, the pulse slows and blood is diverted from limbs and muscles to vital areas (brain, kidney). Cold further reduces the metabolic rate. This is the physiological explanation for remarkable stories of recovery from prolonged (eg 20min) total immersion. It is also the reason why resuscitation of a seemingly dead child must continue for 40min before death is declared.

1 R Brenner 2002 *BMJ* **i** 1050

Preventing death by drowning

In richer parts of the world, drownings in garden ponds are getting commoner, while those in natural freshwater sites are declining. Toddlers have the highest drowning rates—so prevention must target toddlers:

- Constant supervision of infants in baths by adults. Even brief moments away, eg to answer the door-bell, can be disastrous.
- Isolation fencing that *surrounds* the pool, separating it from the home.
- Not swimming alone or in remote, unguarded sites.
- Training of the public in basic life support. If given promptly, neurological outcomes are better.[130]

▸▸Major injury, including blunt chest injury

On news of major trauma, summon experienced help (eg senior traumatologist). Remember ABC (*a*irway, *b*reathing, *c*irculation; BOX). If breathing spontaneously, give *all* patients O_2 at 15L/min through tight-fitting mask with reservoir. *Quality of breathing:* stridor (± voice change) indicates a sternoclavicular fracture/posterior dislocation—get expert help at once as intubation may be difficult owing to tracheal compression, until the dislocation is reduced—by extending the shoulders, and grasping the clavicle with a clamp (eg towel clip) and manually reducing the fracture. Cover & seal open chest wounds on 3 sides only. ▸▸*Is there a tension pneumothorax?* Urgent treatment: chest needling on the side with ↓breath sounds; other signs are:

- Air hunger + respiratory distress
- Pulse↑; BP↓
- Tracheal deviation
- Breath sounds↓ on one side
- Cyanosis
- Neck vein distension

Relieve by inserting a needle (2nd intercostal space, mid-clavicular line).

- Apply pressure and elevation to any actively bleeding part.
- Crossmatch; glucose stix; 2 wide-bore saline IVs (femoral catheter or saphenous cutdown anterior to medial malleolus if no IV access). 131
- Take systolic BP. If <90mmHg and blood loss is the probable cause, give colloid (Haemaccel®) fast IV until BP↑, pulse↓, urine flows (>30mL/h; catheterize at leisure—exclude urethral injury first) and crossmatched blood arrives (▸ask for group-compatible blood—only takes 5-10min).
- Remove clothes (large scissors). *What are the injuries?* Do *circumferential burns* need escharotomy to ↓laryngeal pressure? Any *surgical emphysema* (chest drain needed?). Is there a *flail chest* (a segment has no bony continuity with thorax, with paradoxical respiration)? The main problem is the injured lung (sensitive to *over* and *under* resuscitation; intubate & ventilate).
- *Assume spinal instability.* Before imaging, keep immobile (sandbags, collar, tape; CT is the best method if high/moderate risk for cervical fracture). 132
- Do level-of-consciousness (AVPU, p 722) + ECG (ST & conduction problems ≈ myocardial damage: extent is revealed via direct inspection by thoracic surgeon).
- Falling BP + rising JVP and a quiet heart = cardiac tamponade: ▸see p 720.
- Examine all peripheral pulses. 30% of fractures are missed in resus rooms; Image cervical spine (p 768) + pelvis. *Skull radiographs waste time.* If intraperitoneal bleeding is suspected, see p 760. Do blood gases & CXR; *implications:*
  - If free air, needle the chest (or formal chest drain) for pneumothorax.
  - If persistent large pneumothorax after chest drain suspect bronchial tear.
  - # of ribs 1-3≈?airway/big vessel injury[1]
  - Ribs 9-12≈?abdominal trauma
  - # of >2 ribs in 2 places≈?flail chest
  - CXR fluid level≈haemothorax[2]
  - Bowel gas in chest≈?diaphragm injury
  - Diaphragm contour↓≈?rupture
  - Coils of NGT in chest≈?diaphragm injury
  - Liver raised≈?diaphragm injury
  - # of sternum≈?myocardial contusion
  - Mediastinal air≈lung barotrauma
  - Respiratory distress + CXR OK≈?aspiration
  - # of scapula≈?airway injury
  - Wide mediastinum≈?aortic rupture[1]
  - Tracheal deviation≈aortic injury[1]
  - Deviation of oesophagus≈?aortic rupture[1]
  - No aortic knob≈?ruptured aorta[1]
- Chart pulse, BP + pupil size every few mins. If pupils unequal, summon neurological help; give 20% mannitol 1g/kg (5mL/kg) IV (↑cerebral blood flow).
- Head-to-toe exam ('secondary survey'). Glasgow Coma Scale (p 722).
- If fits occur give 10mg diazepam IV followed by 40mg in 500mL 5% dextrose infused at ~100mL/h if they continue (children: 0.3mg/kg IV, then 50μg/kg/h IVI)—beware apnoea.
- In near-drowning or smoke inhalation, consider early high-dose methylprednisolone (30mg/kg IV); also in lung contusion (ventilate if S_AO_2 <90%).
- Give *tetanus toxoid* booster ± *human anti-tetanus immunoglobulin* (p 728).
- Get experienced help in prioritizing treatment for each specific injury.

1 Have a low threshold for contrast-enhanced aorta CTs, especially if deceleration injury: ATLS 6e, 135

Adult basic life-support algorithm

This algorithm assumes that only one rescuer is present, with no equipment. (If a defibrillator is to hand, get a rhythm readout, and defibrillate, as needed, as soon as possible.)

Remove yourself and the casualty from obvious dangers

↓

Check responsiveness (shake and shout)

↓

Open the airway (head tilt; chin lift)

↓

Check breathing (look, listen, feel; if breathing, place in recovery position)

↓

Give 2 breaths (have up to 5 goes at giving 2 rescue breaths sufficient to raise the chest)

↓

Assess for signs of life for 10sec only (look for signs of circulation; now phone for help at once)

↙ ↘

Circulation present: Continue rescue breathing

No circulation: compress chest give breaths (100 compressions/min at ratio of 15:2 with ventilations. Spend <10sec to check circulation, eg carotid pulse, every min

Send for health as soon as possible

Managing the airway

- You open the airway by tilting the head and lifting the chin—but only do this if there is no question of spinal trauma.
- Use a close-fitting mask if available, held in place by thumbs pressing downwards either side of the mouthpiece; palms against cheeks.

Chest compressions

- Cardiopulmonary resuscitation (CPR) involves compressive force over the lower sternum with the heel of the hands placed one on top of the other, directing the weight of your body through your verticle, straight, arms.
- Depth of compression: ~4cm.
- Rate of compressions: 100/min.

2 Appears as an opaque hemithorax if the CXR is supine. See www.resus.org.uk/pages/blsalgo.pdf *Definitive control rather than normalization of plasma volume is the aim in bleeding*[ATLS] For practising dynamic ATLS with shifting scenarios see www.trauma.org/resus/moulage/moulage.html

Wound management

Principles of management Where possible, convert dirty ragged wounds into clean wounds that can be reconstructed simply—eg by waiting for healing by secondary intention (may be suitable for small wounds in inconspicuous areas—or perform primary closure by suturing or other means. Other more complex options in the reconstructive ladder include grafts, flaps, tissue expansion and tissue engineering and require specialist care.

Important points in the management of wounds

1 Irrigation, irrigation, and more irrigation with 0.9% saline. It is vital to clean the wound well as soon as possible particularly if the patient is going to be referred to specialist care that could incur further delay.

2 Infiltrate with lidocaine (=lignocaine; blocks voltage gated Na channels to prevent depolarization) 4mg/kg plain or 7mg/kg with adrenaline. See opposite. Lidocaine is a vasodilator (∴ increases its own systemic clearance).
- Adrenaline is used where vasoconstriction to reduce bleeding is useful and if the predicted dose of lidocaine needed would exceed 4mg/kg. 1 in 200,000 adrenaline is most suitable for daily use (1:1000 is 1mg/mL). 1% lidocaine=10mg/mL (to get from % to concentration multiply by 10).
- Use the minimum strength for job. Local anaesthesia (LA) will still work at dilute concentrations but will need to wait for longer; for suturing 0.5% provides a good effect with less toxicity.
- Reduce the pain of injection by using a fine needle eg insulin syringe, warming the LA and injecting slowly. Bicarbonate may be added.
- Wait for anaesthetic (3 minutes) and vasoconstrictor effect (7minutes).

3 Remove debris, foreign bodies and necrotic tissue; very ragged or shelved skin edges may need to be trimmed. Avoid excessive tissue resection on face where better healing possible. Abrasions need to be scrubbed thoroughly otherwise permanent tattooing will occur.

4 Use absorbable dermal sutures (vicryl or PDS) to bring skin edges together and avoid skin tension. Use interrupted monofilament (nylon or prolene) on the skin in most cases for optimal apposition 6'0 for the face, 5'0 or thicker for other areas - very thick sutures are not needed as the strength of repair lies in the deeper layer. Avoid skin tension and wound inversion. Vicryl Rapide® or other absorbables may be considered as skin sutures in non-cosmetic areas—the suture knots can be brushed away after a week.

5 Remove sutures at the correct time to minimize risk of unsightly permanent stitch marks: face 5 days, upper limb 7–10 days.

Alternatives to sutures (to avoid need for removal) Steristrips® are good for non-hairy skin that is not likely to get moist/wet. Avoid too much traction when applying as it may cause blistering in fragile skin. It may be combined with buried dermal absorbable sutures (esp in children).

Glues eg Histoacryl®, use a blue needle (gauge 23) to accurately place on top of accurately apposed and dried skin edges. Watch for the exothermic reaction. Avoid getting glue into the wound as it is cytotoxic. Up to one minute of manipulating time is available.

Antibiotics Prophylaxis for fresh wounds is not required unless there is obvious risk eg direct inoculation with animal bites etc.

Tetanus Prophylaxis is vital. A full course (3 vaccinations in infancy + 2 boosters in pre-school and as teenager) provide good immunity. So vaccinate those who have not completed their schedule and where there is uncertainty.[1] Human immunoglobulin is for wounds that are prone to cause tetanus eg involving manure or extensive necrosis (give vaccine and Ig in different arms).

1 A full adult course if unimmunized would be 0.5mL of 'combined tetanus & low-dose diphtheria and inactivated polio vaccine' IM repeated × 2 at monthly intervals with boosters at 10 & 20yrs.

We thank Prof Tor Chiu for this page.

Calculating lidocaine (lignocaine) doses 133

0.25% lidocaine =	1.12mL/kg
0.5%	0.56mL/kg
1%	0.28mL/kg
2%	0.14mL/kg

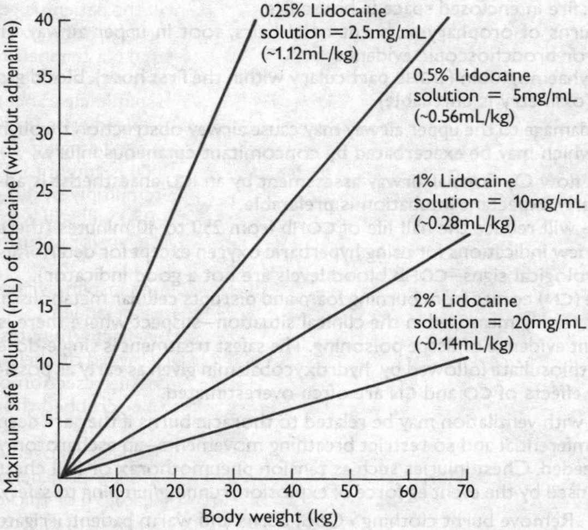

Maximum safe volume of plain lidocaine (=lignocaine) according to body weight. Maximum safe dose of lidocaine *without adrenaline:* (=epinephrine) 3mg/kg; *with adrenaline:* 7mg/kg. ***Use different strengths for different jobs:*** 0.25–0.5% for infiltration & intravenous regional anaesthesia; 1% for nerve blocks, epidural anaesthesia, and intravenous regional anaesthesia; 2% for nerve blocks.

▸▸Major burns: emergency treatment

The majority of burns are minor; non-specialist staff will see very few major burns. Their task should be to ensure the rapid and safe transfer to Burns units (with ITU resources and access to burn surgery) experienced in their care. Staff should be familiar with ATLS and EMSB protocols.(Early Management of Severe Burns) 134

Airway and breathing Inhalational injury can occur by many mechanisms: thermal, chemical/acids, irritant or systemic effects. Direct damage to lung parenchyma is rare. Risk of inhalational injury is best judged by clinical assessment—have a high index of suspicion (there is no single diagnostic sign).

- History: fire in enclosed space ie house fire
- Signs: burns of oropharynx, burnt nasal hairs, soot in upper airway or sputum or bronchoscopic evidence
- Carboxyhaemoglobin (COHb particulary within the first hour), blood gas results (oximetry is unreliable)

Thermal damage to the upper airway may cause airway obstruction through oedema which may be exacerbated by concomitant cutaneous injury.

Give high flow O_2. Formal airway assessment by an ICU anaesthetist is advisable. Early expectant intubation is preferable.

- 100% O_2 will reduce the half life of COHb from 250 to 40 minutes (there are very few indications for using hyperbaric oxygen except for deteriorating neurological signs—COHb blood levels are not a good indicator).
- Cyanide (CN) comes from burning foam and disrupts cellular metabolism. It is not readily measured in the clinical situation—suspect where there is persistent evidence of tissue poisoning. The safest treatment is single-dose sodium thiosulfate followed by hydroxycobalamin given as early as possible. The effects of CO and CN are often overestimated.

Difficulty with ventilation may be related to thoracic burns if they are deep and circumferential and so restrict breathing movements—an escharotomy may be needed. Chest injuries such as tension pneumothorax or flail chest may be caused by the event eg force of explosion, running/jumping to safety.

First Aid: • Remove burnt clothing • Cool burns and warm patient: irrigate with cool water for 10-20 minutes • Can use clingfilm in thermal burns (do not wrap circumferentially) • Cooling gels/masks simple to use especially for the face, but have the most effect when left exposed to the air. • Chemical burns need continued irrigation.

Circulation: Insert 2 large-bore IV cannulae even if you have to go through burnt skin. The estimation of burn surface areas (BSA) is important as the size of the burn injury reflects magnitude of inflammatory reaction; subsequent fluid shifts may lead to shock if uncorrected (occurs over hours rather than minutes as in actual haemorrhage). The aim of fluid 'resuscitation' in burns is to anticipate and prevent shock.

Burn surface area (BSA) Use ***rule of 9s (BOX)*** or:

- A burn chart—eg Lund and Browder.
- Serial halves: 'half burnt/half not' (particularly for pre-hospital assessment).

Wallace rule of nines

- Arm (all over) 9%
- Leg (all over) 18%
- Front 18%
- Back 18%
- Head (all over) 9%
- Genitals/perineum 1%
- Palm and fingers (one side of the hand) 1%

Fluids There are several commonly used formulae for fluid administration—Parklands is often preferred to formulae using colloids (Muir & Barclay) but the actual dangers of the latter are probably overestimated particularly in uncomplicated patients. The administration of colloid is generally regarded as being safe after the 1st day (when capillary permeability recovers) but is not always given; similarly blood is advocated by some but rarely given.

Parklands Volume of Hartmanns (mL)=4×body weight (kg) × BSA (%). ½ is given in the 1st 8h; the other ½ in the next 16. Time of injury is taken as the start time and with any delay, the deficit needs to be calculated and given.

Do not confuse the formulae: Muir & Barclay uses about half the volume but in the form of colloid. Use the appropriate fluid with the formula. All formula represent starting points: tailor continuing fluids to the response. The patient should be catheterised as the best single measure is the urine output – aim for more than 0.5mL/kg/hour. The temperature gradient (core and periphery) is used in some units to measure peripheral perfusion.

Burn depth This implications for healing/scarring but assessment can be difficult particularly for intermediate thickness burns. Many burns especially scalds are mixed depth. Also, burns can continue to evolve for up to 48 hours. For the emergency department, the most important apect of assessing burn depth is erythema (simple redness with no signs of skin damage, eg blisters or oedema) should not be counted as it does not represent any significant pathological damage. It will lead to overestimation of the injury. Full thickness burns can cause constriction if circumferential.

- Full thickness burns are white/grey/black, thick and insensate
- Superficial burns are painful, red and have blisters.

Decompression Full thickness burns are tough and inflexible; if circumferential, they can have a tourniquet-like effect and hinder breathing or limb circulation. Also, big volumes of crystalloid may lead to marked soft tissue swelling. In such cases, **decompression** which may include escharotomy (incising burns along prescribed lines) as well as fasciotomy may be needed. It is rarely needed at once, and contrary to some advice, it is best performed under controlled conditions ie in operating theatre and under GA.

Transfer and dressings There is no need for anything fancy. Simple cleaning of the wound with sterile 0.9% saline is adequate. Blisters should be left alone unless tense and causing pain.

- Apply cool wet dressings for pain relief.
- Using Clingfilm® covered with blankets to keep warm is adequate.
- Hands (and feet) can be put into clean plastic bags, and should be elevated.
- Analgesia should be adequate; use IV opiates if necessary, titrated to comfort. Tetanus prophylaxis is given as necessary.

Paediatric burns Standard estimation of area cannot be applied: Wallace's rule of nines needs to be modified, burn charts are most reliable. There is a lower threshold to begin resuscitation (10% BSA).

- Maintenance fluids are given, and a higher urine output is needed: >1mL/kg/h.
- Keep warm as there is a greater tendency to hypothermia.
- Be alert to possibility of non-accidental injury.

Because of advances in wound management in specialized burns centres eg autologous split-thickness skin grafts ± cultured fetal skin fibroblasts) even 95% burns are survivable by 50% of children.[1] 135

1 Scott P 2005 *Lancet* **366** 788

We thank Prof Tor Chiu for this page.

Fractures

Seven key questions
• How many fractures? • Can I see all the bone? • What is broken? • Are the bones normal? • Any trapped air? • Any foreign body? • More plain films needed (IVU, CT, arteriogram)?

Description

- Site: bone fractured; part of bone (proximal, shaft, distal etc)
- Obliquity: transverse; short oblique; spiral; multi-fragmentary
- Displacement: angulation; translation; rotation
- Soft tissues: open/closed; neurovascular status; compartment syndrome.

Clinical features Pain; loss of function; tenderness; deformity; swelling; crepitus; soft tissues.

Fracture healing A rule-of-thumb for fracture healing is given by the 'rule-of-3s'. A *closed, paediatric, metaphyseal, upper limb* fracture is the simplest and will heal in 3 weeks. Any 'complicating factor' doubles the fracture-healing time i.e. adult; diaphyseal; lower limb; open injury. For example an *adult (6), diaphyseal (12) forearm* fracture may take 12 weeks (3 months) to heal. Likewise an *open (6), adult (12), diaphyseal (24), tibia (48)* may be expected to take 48 weeks (almost one year!) to heal.

Salter and Harris classification of epiphyseal injury (See diagram)

I Seen in babies or pathological conditions (eg scurvy).
II The commonest.
III There is a displaced fragment.
IV Union across the growth plate may interfere with bone growth.
V Compression of the epiphysis causes deformity and stunting.

Treatment ►► Correct shock (eg colloid IVI, 500mL/30min, until systolic BP >100mmHg); give blood if >1-1.5 litres lost, or continued bleeding. Monitor BP/15min, urine output (± CVP). Stop bleeding (may need open surgery).

- Relieve pain (eg morphine 10mg/4h IM or 1-2mg aliquots IV if shocked).
- Sterile cover (eg Betadine®-soaked) over protruding bones and torn skin.
- Prevent infection: eg cloxacillin 500mg IM/IV + benzylpenicillin 600mg IV/IM; tetanus toxoid (0.5mL IM) if needed.

Ways of managing fractures: Immobilize and reduce the part (if needed, p 734), eg using a plaster of Paris cast. The problem with this method is that 'fracture disease' follows immobilization—muscle atrophy, stiff joints, and osteoporosis—so anything speeding return of function may be beneficial.[1] If possible, fractures involving joint articulations should be treated by open reduction, accurate reconstruction of the joint surfaces, and fixation, such that immediate movement can occur. Otherwise, secondary osteoarthritis is inevitable. Prompt ***internal fixation:*** eg with plates (~10 screw-holes), nails (Küntscher) or wires (Kirschner)—of all fractures in those with polytrauma leads to large reductions in serious complications (fat embolism, acute respiratory distress syndrome), as well as lessening the time during which mechanical ventilation is needed. 136

External fixation uses screws into bone, a bar, and a means (clamps) of attaching the bar to the screws to align and engage the fractured cortices. The screws may be driven through the bone and out of the far side of the limb, so that a second bar can add stability. Further rigidity is afforded by another set of screws at 90° to the first set. Because the intervention is away from the field of injury, this method is very useful when there are burns, loss of skin and bone, or an open fracture.

1 J Busse 2002 *CMAJ* **166** 437 meta-analysis; it's nonstandard; healing may be speeded by ~64 days.

Fixation

Fixation options

- Kirschner wires
- Cannulated screws
- Staples
- Self-tapping screws
- Osteosynthesis lag screws
- Herbert headless screws 137
- Absorbable pins
- T-screws

Screw insertion to unite the fragments typically begins with temporary wire or bone clamp fixation. A pilot hole is then drilled into bone, which must be substantial enough to support the screw head. Both near and far cortices are drilled with the pilot drill. Countersinking decreases incidence of stress risers and micro-fractures of the bone as the head of the screw compresses into the near cortex. The pilot hole is measured to aid selection of the best length of screw. Distal threads have a smaller diameter than proximal threads to give thread cutting action for self-tapping screws. Have eg 2 threads of the screw exiting the far cortex to assure that the largest threads of the screw purchase the far cortex. (Add eg 2mm to the pilot measurement.)

Lag screw technique: An oversized countersunk hole is drilled through the near cortex. The distal portion of the hole is drilled with a diameter corresponding to the core diameter of the screw. As the screw tightens its distal end engages the threaded hole of the distal fragment. The undersurface of the screw head contacts the countersink hole and pulls the distal fragment against the proximal fragment causing compression. A lag effect can only occur if the screw can pass freely through the gliding hole. Lag screws are most appropriate for oblique fractures. 138

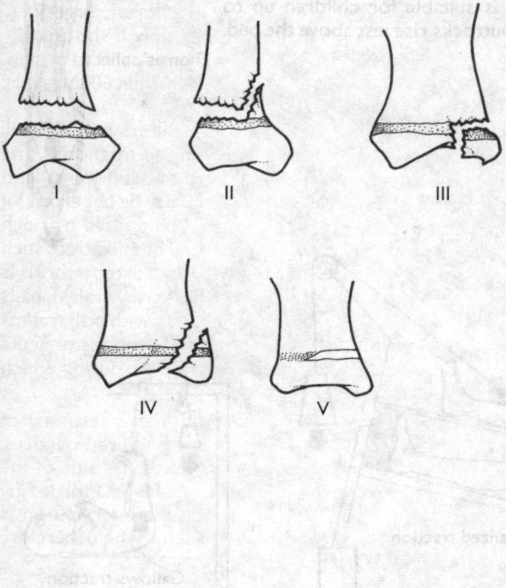

Fracture reduction and traction

A displaced fragment needs realignment (reduction) unless function and appearance of the limb are satisfactory. For example, a small displacement acceptable in a fracture of the femoral shaft might not be acceptable in the radius, where it could interrupt supination. Reduction also allows freeing of any structures trapped between bone ends. Accurate reduction aids revascularization (vital in subcapital fractures of the femur) and prevents later degeneration if fractures involve joints. Internal and external fixation has removed the need for much traction in adults, but it is still used for children.

Methods of reduction ***Manipulation*** under anaesthesia (most cases). ***Traction*** may be used for subcapital femur fractures or spinal injury. ***Open reduction*** aids accuracy, eg before internal fixation (p 732).

The next problem is to hold the reduction in place (using traction or fixation) during healing—which takes from 2 weeks (babies) to >12 weeks (p 732).

Skin traction uses adhesive strapping to attach the load to the limb. The problems are that the load cannot be very great, and that sensitivity to the adhesive may develop.

Skeletal traction Using a pin through bone, bigger forces can be employed (eg Steinmann pin, Gardner-Wells, or Crutchfield skull calipers).

Fixed traction The Thomas' splint.

Balanced traction (below) The weight of the patient balances against the load.

Gallows traction is suitable for children up to 2 years of age. The buttocks rise just above the bed.

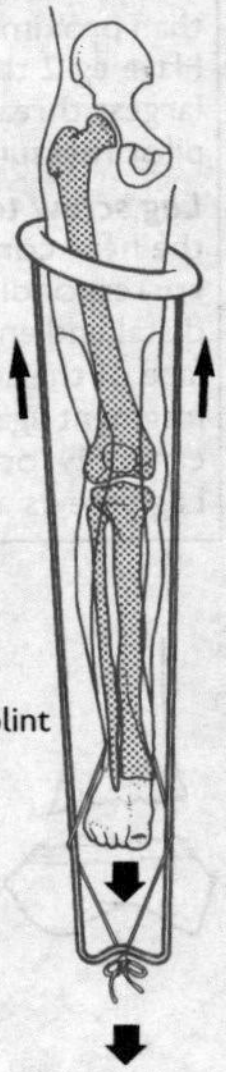

Thomas' splint

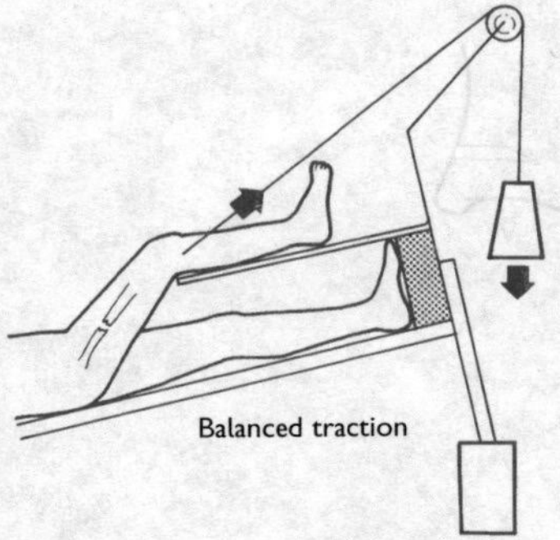

Balanced traction

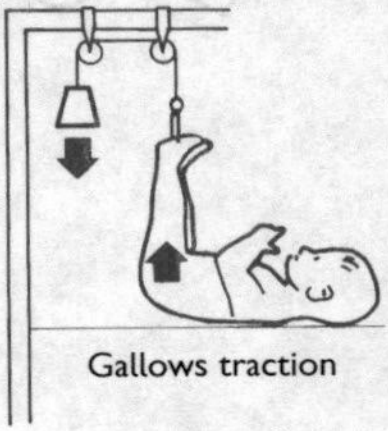

Gallows traction

Complications from fractures

Healing: Haematoma → vascular granulation tissue → subperiosteal osteoblasts' calcification → bone matrix → endochondral ossification → organic matrix → woven bone (callus) → lamellar bone → fracture union.

Fat embolism typically occurs on day 3–10. Signs: confusion, dyspnoea, ↓PaO₂, fits, coma, ARDS, petechial rash. CXR/CT: small subpleural nodular opacities. Take to ITU • Get expert help • Correct shock • Monitor CVP & urine output • Treat respiratory failure (OHCM p 182). Aim for early mobilization. Early fixation of fractures is preventive.

Crush syndromes and compartment syndromes are a cause of ischaemia; also fluid loss, DIC, and myoglobin release cause tubular necrosis (dialysis may be needed). Correct hypovolaemia vigorously. Watch urine output and plasma K⁺. A limb's own dead weight, when immobile or in coma, may cause crush injury. Compartment syndromes are vicious circles of pressure → vascular occlusion → hypoxia → ↑oedema → ↑pressure. Look for tell-tale signs of redness, mottling, blisters, swelling, and pain on passive muscle stretch. Compartment syndrome is both a limb- and life-threatening emergency. Avoiding delay requires vigilance and perhaps intracompartmental pressure measurement (reference ranges for relevance are controversial). Prompt fasciotomy is life/limb-saving.

Late complications

- **Wound sepsis** (early wound cleansing is vital). Infection also complicates ~8% of closed fractures if internal fixation is used.
- **Failure of fixation** (eg plates or nails break, or dislodge).
- **Joint stiffness**, contractures, malalignment (malunion).
- **Algodystrophy** (see Box): joint stiffness and patchy **osteoporosis**.
- **Psychological problems in mobilizing** (eg 'compensation neurosis').
- **Non-union:** this is deemed to have occurred when there is no evidence of progression towards healing (clinical/radiological).
- **Delayed union** is when the fracture has not healed within the time reasonably expected for that fracture. *Causes of delay:*
  - A fracture in a bone which has finished growing.
  - Poor blood supply (eg lower tibia) or avascular fragments (eg scaphoid).
  - Comminuted/infected fractures, grafts, open reduction/internal fixation.
  - Generalized disease (eg malignancy, infection).
  - Distraction of bone ends by muscle, open reduction, external fixation prevents this. Note: osteoporosis & old age don't necessarily delay union.

Management of non-union: Broadly, a non-union will have occurred as a result of inadequate/abnormal biology or mechanics. Management is therefore aimed at optimizing the biology (infection, blood supply, bone graft) or the mechanics (skeletal stabilization).

Fracture complications

Immediate
- Internal bleeding
- External bleeding
- Organ injury, eg brain
- Nerve or skin injury
- Vessel injury (limb ischaemia)

Later—local
- Skin necrosis/gangrene
- Pressure sores
- Infection
- Non-/delayed union

Later—general
- Venous or fat embolism
- Pulmonary embolism
- Pneumonia
- Renal stones

Complications from fractures

Fracture complications
Immediate:
• Internal bleeding
• External bleeding
• Organ injury, eg brain
• Nerve or skin injury
• Vessel injury (limb ischaemia)
Later—local:
• Skin necrosis/gangrene
• Pressure sores
• Infection[1]
• Non- or delayed union
Later—general:
• Venous or fat embolism
• Pulmonary embolism
• Pneumonia
• Renal stones

Healing Haematoma→vascular granulation tissue→subperiosteal osteoblast stimulation→bone matrix→endochondral ossification→deformable woven bone (callus)→lamellar bone→fracture union.

Fat embolism typically occurs on day 3–10. Signs: confusion, dyspnoea, P_aO_2↓, fits, coma, T°↑, petechial rash, CXR/CT: small subpleural nodular opacities. 139 ▸▸Take to ITU ▸▸Get expert help ▸▸Correct shock ▸▸Monitor CVP & urine output. ▸▸Treat respiratory failure (*OHCM* p 192). Aim for early mobilization. Early fixation of fractures is preventive.

Crush syndromes and compartment syndromes are a cause of ischaemia; also fluid loss, DIC, and myoglobin release cause tubular necrosis (dialysis may be needed). Correct hypovolaemia vigorously. Watch urine output and plasma K^+. A limb's own dead weight when immobile or in coma, may cause crush injury/compartment syndrome—a vicious cycle of pressure→vascular occlusion→hypoxia →necrosis→pressure↑. Look for tell-tale signs of redness, mottling, blisters, swelling, and pain on passive muscle stretching. ▸▸Compartment syndrome is both a limb- and life-threatening emergency. Avoiding delay requires vigilance and perhaps intracompartmental pressure measurement (reference ranges for intervention are controversial). *Prompt* fasciotomy is life-/limb-saving. 140

Late complications

- ***Wound sepsis*** (early wound cleaning is vital). Infection also complicates ~8% of closed fractures if internal fixation is used.[1]
- ***Failure of fixation*** (eg plates or nails break, or dislodge).
- ***Joint stiffness***, contractures, malalignment (malunion).
- ***Algodystrophy*** (see BOX): joint stiffness and patchy osteoporosis.
- ***Psychological problems in mobilizing*** (eg 'compensation neurosis').
- ***Non-union:*** this is deemed to have occurred when there is no evidence of progression towards healing (clinical/radiological).
- ***Delayed-union*** is when the fracture has not healed within the time reasonably expected for *that* fracture p 732. *Causes of delay:*
  - A fracture in a bone which has finished growing.
  - Poor blood supply (eg lower tibia) or avascular fragment (eg scaphoid).
  - Comminuted/infected fractures, eg after open reduction/internal fixation.
  - Generalized disease (eg malignancy, infection).
  - Distraction of bone ends by muscle; open reduction ± internal fixation prevents this. NB: osteoporosis ± old age don't necessarily delay union.

Management of non-union: Broadly, a non-union will have occurred as a result of inadequate/abnormal biology or mechanics. Management is therefore aimed at optimizing the biology (infection, blood supply, bone graft) or the mechanics (skeletal stabilization).

1 Ceftriaxone 2g IV at induction halves infection risk

Algodystrophy

Synonyms
Sudeck's atrophy/osteodystrophy
Reflex sympathetic dystrophy; sympathetically maintained pain syndrome
Post-traumatic sympathetic atrophy;
Shoulder-hand syndrome
Minor causalgia (causalgia means burning pain)
Post-traumatic painful osteoporosis
Complex regional pain syndrome type I

Definitions 'A complex disorder of pain, sensory abnormalities, abnormal blood flow, sweating, and trophic changes in superficial or deep tissues.' The central event may be loss of vascular tone or supersensitivity to sympathetic neurotransmitters. The 1994 systematic criteria for definitive diagnosis are given below,[1] but are of uncertain validity.[MET 141]

Presentation This may follow weeks or months after an insult—which may be minor trauma, a fracture, zoster, or myocardial infarction. Lancinating pain (which may have a trigger point) in a limb accompanies vasomotor instability. The limb may be cold and cyanosed, or hot and sweating (locally). Temperature sensitivity may be heightened. The skin of the affected part may be oedematous—and later becomes shiny and atrophic. Hyperreflexia, dystonic movements, and contractures may occur.

Note that it is not the traumatized area where the symptoms occur: rather, it is some neighbouring area.

There are no systemic signs (no fever, tachycardia, or lymphadenopathy).

Timid, neurotic personalities are particularly affected—perhaps because of poor mobilization following the initial insult.

Tests Patchy osteoporosis on radiography, but no joint space narrowing (thinning of cartilage); bone scintigraphy shows characteristic uniform uptake.

Treatment Refer to a pain clinic. Standard painkillers often have little effect. Consider physiotherapy and NSAIDs. Calcitonin and postganglionic sympathetic blockade (guanethidine or bretylium) have advocates. Ultimately, the condition is self-limiting.

1 Continuing pain which is disproportionate to any inciting event with reports of at least one ***symptom*** in each of these 4 categories: Sensory; vasomotor; sudomotor/oedema; motor/trophic—***and*** at least one ***sign*** in 2 or more of the above categories. www.stoppain.org/for_professionals/archive/pain_jul99.html#assessment

Trauma to the arm

Fracture of the clavicle This is common in the young, eg from a fall on an outstretched arm (which in the elderly would be more likely to cause a Colles' fracture). A broad sling support for 3 weeks is usually all that is needed. Fractures at the lateral end may need internal fixation.

Scapula and acromion fractures These represent high-energy transfer injuries, so assess carefully to exclude other injuries.

Acromioclavicular joint dislocations These rarely require anything more than sling support and early mobilization. A small number (<5%) have persistent symptoms and require surgery.

Fracture of the humeral neck Often these are impacted and stable; if there is displacement there is risk to the brachial plexus and axillary artery. Manipulation or open reduction may be needed if there is displacement of the upper humeral epiphysis (in children) or if there is co-existing shoulder dislocation. Fractures of the head itself may result in 2–4 fragments. If ≥3, internal fixation is likely to be needed.

Fracture of the humerus shaft This is often caused by a fall on an outstretched arm. Marked displacement often makes the diagnosis easy. Radial nerve injury may cause wrist-drop. Splinting with metal gutter-shaped splints and support from the wrist to the neck (collar and cuff sling) usually gives satisfactory reduction. Immobilize for 8–12 weeks.

Anterior shoulder dislocation may follow a fall on an arm or shoulder (fig 1). ***Signs:*** Loss of shoulder contour (flattening of deltoid), an anterior bulge from the head of the humerus, which may also be palpated in the axilla. Check pulses and nerves (including the axillary nerve supplying sensation over lower deltoid area) pre- and post-op. Before reduction, do radiography (*is there a fracture too?*)—unless this is a case of recurrent dislocation, when just a post-reduction image may be needed.

Relieve pain (eg intra-articular local anaesthetic, parenteral opioid, Entonox® through the procedure). Methods of reduction:

Treatment by simple reduction: Apply longitudinal traction to the arm in abduction, and replace the head of the humerus by gentle pressure.

Kocher's method: • Flex the elbow and put traction on the arm.
• Apply forced external rotation and adduction of the point of the elbow across the chest while the arm is flexed at the shoulder.
• Now apply internal rotation, so that the volar aspect of the forearm lies on the chest. Risk: fractures of the humerus.

Surgery may be needed for young athletic patients or recurrent dislocation (eg Bankart repair and capsular shift).

Posterior dislocation of the shoulder is rare and presents with a limitation of external rotation. It may be hard to diagnose from an anteroposterior radiograph ('light-bulb' appearance of humeral head); lateral radiographs are essential. Refer to an orthopaedic surgeon. www.ncemi.org/cse/cse0905.htm

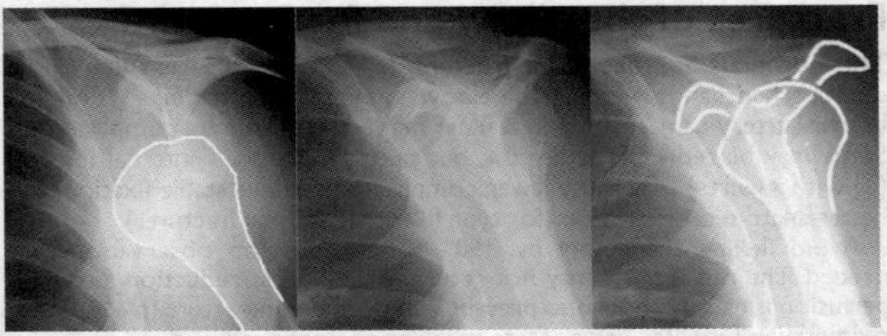

Anterior dislocation of the shoulder and a post-reduction image that is copied and highlighted. The dislocation can be painful, so positioning is difficult for the radiographer. These are attempted lateral views of the scapula. After reduction, the head of the humerus lies in the centre of the 'Y' with the coracoid process anterior and the acromion posterior.

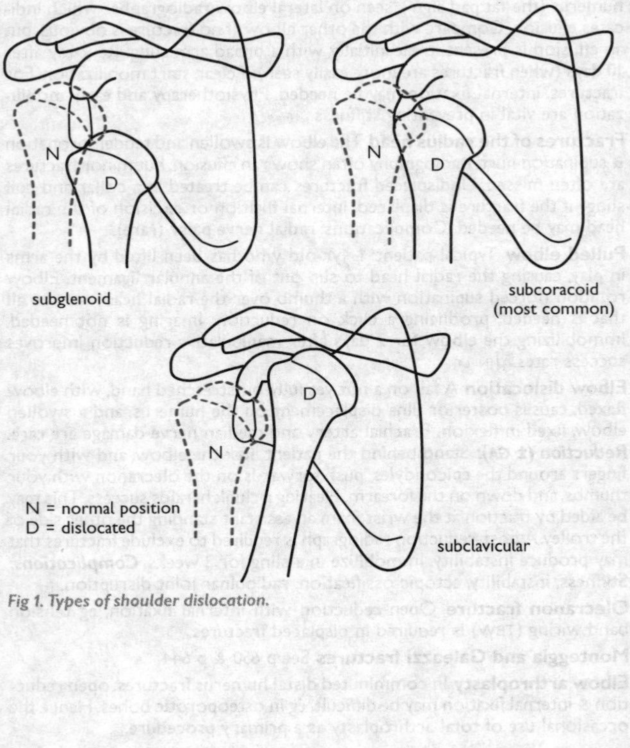

Fig 1. Types of shoulder dislocation.

Fractures of the elbow and forearm

The humerus ***Supracondylar fracture:*** (eg a child who has fallen on an outstretched hand). Keeping the elbow in extension after injury prevents brachial artery damage. Median & ulnar nerve palsies are rare complications. Some may be reducible under GA, but open reduction & internal fixation (eg with K-wires) may cause fewer complications, more stable fixation, and better anatomical reduction (for type III supracondylar fractures).[142]

Avoid flexing the elbow by >90°. Careful post-op observations are needed. The radial pulse may not return for 24h post-reduction, but limb perfusion is usually enough to prevent Volkmann's contracture (p 668). Pulse oximetry ± Doppler helps assess vascular compromise.

Fracture of the medial condyle: These may require surgery if manipulation fails to bring about satisfactory reduction.

Fracture of the lateral condyle: Surgical fixation will be required. Complications: cubitus valgus and ulnar nerve palsy.

T-shaped intercondylar humerus fracture: This is a supracondylar fracture with a break between the condyles. The presence of a fracture is suggested by the hoisting of the sail-shaped fat pad on the anterior aspect of the distal humerus (the 'fat pad sign'), seen on lateral elbow radiographs—which indicates effusion. Compare with the other elbow. If no fracture is obvious, but an effusion is present, treat initially with a broad arm sling. Re-x-ray after 10 days (when fractures are more easily seen): if clear, start mobilization. For fractures, internal fixation may be needed. Physiotherapy and early mobilization are vital in preventing stiffness.[143] [n=30]

Fractures of the radius head The elbow is swollen and tender; pronation & supination hurt. Radiography often shows an effusion, but minor fractures are often missed. Undisplaced fractures can be treated in a collar and cuff sling—if the fracture is displaced, internal fixation or excision of the radial head may be needed. Complications: radial nerve palsy (rare).

Pulled elbow Typical patient: 1–4yr-old who has been lifted by the arms in play, causing the radial head to slip out of the annular ligament. Elbow rotation (forced supination with a thumb over the radial head) may be all that is needed, producing a click on reduction. Imaging is not needed. Immobilizing the elbow for 2 days after manipulative reduction improves success rates.[RCT 144] [N=64]

Elbow dislocation A fall on a not yet fully outstretched hand, with elbow flexed, causes posterior ulna displacement on the humerus, and a swollen elbow, fixed in flexion. Brachial artery and median nerve damage are rare. ***Reduction (± GA):*** Stand behind the patient, flex the elbow, and with your fingers around the epicondyles, push forwards on the olecranon with your thumbs, and down on the forearm. Hearing a clunk heralds success. This may be aided by traction at the wrist from an assistant standing the other side of the trolley. A post-reduction radiograph is required to exclude fractures that may produce instability. Immobilize in a sling for 3 weeks. ***Complications:*** Stiffness, instability, ectopic ossification, radioulnar joint disruption.[145]

Olecranon fracture Open reduction with internal fixation, eg tension band wiring (TBW) is required in displaced fractures.

Monteggia and Galeazzi fractures See p 650 & p 644.

Elbow arthroplasty In comminuted distal humerus fractures, open reduction & internal fixation may be difficult, eg in osteoporotic bones. Hence the occasional use of total arthroplasty as a primary procedure.[146]

Classifying supracondylar fractures

There are 2 chief categories: *extension* (95%) and *flexion* types. Gartland has classified extension fractures thus:

- Type I: non-displaced fractures
- Type II: displaced with intact posterior cortex
- Type III: posterior displacement—which is unstable.[147] IIIA is posteromedial and threatens the radial nerve. Type IIIB is posterolateral and threatens the median nerve (esp. the anterior interosseous branch, which innervates deep flexors to the index finger as well as flexor pollicis longus; it is an entirely motor nerve—so injury is easily missed).[148]

Reduction of a fracture of the distal radius (Colles' type)

View before reduction (radius shown alone in lateral view only)

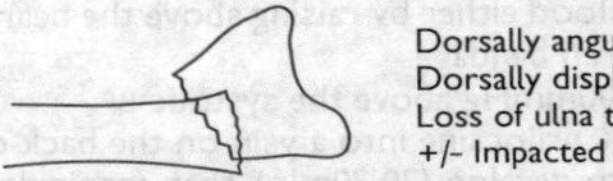

1. Traction should be applied to the hand with an assistant to provide counter-traction at the elbow. The fracture can often be felt to disimpact with 'clunk'.
2. Exaggerate the dorsal angulation while maintaining distal traction. This is most easily done by keeping both thumbs on the dorsal fracture line. The intact dorsal periosteum will prevent over-distraction.

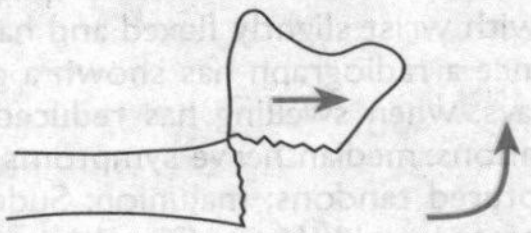

3. Correct dorsal and radial angulation, again maintaining distal traction. Aim for anatomical alignment.

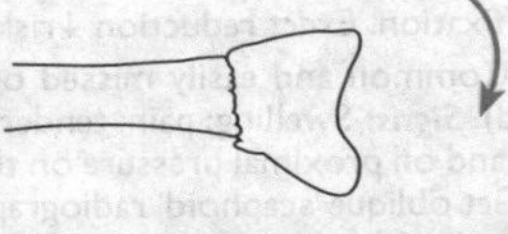

4. Apply plaster of Paris (POP), moulded to provide 3-point pressure. Traction should be maintained while the POP is applied. This is most easily done by pulling on the ring and little finger against counter traction. This applies both palmar and ulnar forces.

►An inability to achieve a good position may indicate soft tissue interpositioning.

►Finding good staff with experience saves remanipulating in theatre.

Fractures and dislocations of the wrist

Distal radial fractures—eg Colles' (common in osteoporotic postmenopausal ladies who fall on an outstretched hand). There is backward angulation and displacement producing a 'dinner-fork' wrist deformity when viewed in pronation (the fingers are the prongs). Avulsion of the ulna styloid process may also occur. If there is much displacement reduction is needed (esp. if backward and proximal shift of the distal fragment). In comminuted fractures, cast immobilization can be supplemented with pins and plaster technique and external fixators—or internal fixation.[149]

Treatment: Bier's block (regional anaesthesia)—method:[150] [N=142]
▸▸Never use bupivacaine for a Bier's block (cardiotoxic if the cuff is inadvertently deflated). The use of a double cuff is controversial—a properly applied and checked tourniquet should suffice.

1 Place a loose tourniquet around the upper arm.
2 Empty the arm of blood either by raising above the heart for 1 min or by the use of an esmarch bandage.
3 Inflate the cuff to 100mmHg above the systolic BP.
4 Inject 30–40mL 0.5% prilocaine into a vein on the back of the hand.
5 Allow anaesthetic to develop (20–30min), then manipulate the fracture.
6 30min after the injection deflate the tourniquet. NB: Sudden early release of prilocaine into the circulation can cause fits. Other methods such as direct infiltration of the haematoma (haematoma block) are less effective. The alternative is general anaesthesia.

The manipulation: Prepare a plaster back slab up to the knuckles. Ask an assistant to hold the elbow. Apply traction to disimpact the fragment and push it forwards, and towards the ulnar side. Keeping the arm under traction, apply the slab, with wrist slightly flexed and hand in ulnar deviation. Support in a sling, once a radiograph has shown a good position. Check radiologically in 5 days, when swelling has reduced. The plaster is then completed. Complications: median nerve symptoms (should resolve after good reduction); ruptured tendons; malunion; Sudeck's atrophy (p 737). NB: a right Colles' plaster is unlikely to affect driving.[151]

Smith's fracture (Distal radius, radial fragment angled *forward*). Manipulate, with the forearm in full supination. Fixation is commonly needed.

Bennett's fracture Carpometacarpal fracture/dislocation of thumb. *R:* percutaneous wire fixation. *Exact* reduction ↓risk of future OA.[152]

Scaphoid fracture (Common and easily missed on radiography; results from falls on the hand). ***Signs:*** Swelling; pain; tender 2cm distal to Lister's tubercle of the radius, and on proximal pressure on the extended thumb or index finger. ***Images:*** Get oblique 'scaphoid' radiography. If -ve, and fracture is likely, long-axis CT is wise (also identifies unstable fractures). If unavailable, put in plaster and x-ray at 2 weeks, when the fracture may be visible. Non-displaced fractures involving the waist or the proximal pole are often treated with immobilization in a long-arm thumb-spica cast for several weeks, then in a short-arm thumb-spica cast until union. Percutaneous cannulated Acutrak screw fixation allows the patient to return to work earlier but does not affect the long-term outcome.[153]

Complications: As the nutrient artery enters distally, there may be avascular necrosis of the proximal fragment, causing late wrist degeneration.

Wrist dislocation (eg scapho-lunate or luno-triquetral) May be anterior or posterior. Manipulation and often open reduction, and plaster immobilization eg for 6 weeks. Median nerve compression may occur.[154]

A-P views

Normal

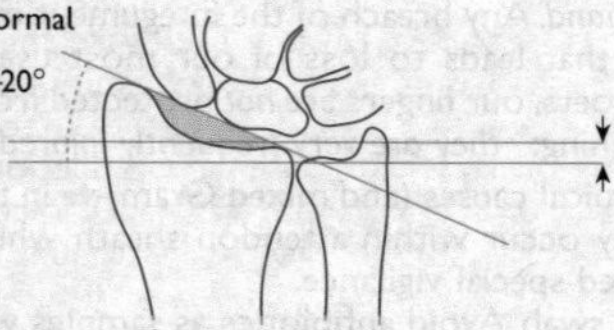

The articular surface of the radius is level with, or proud of, the ulna and is tilted towards the ulna.

Unacceptable reductions

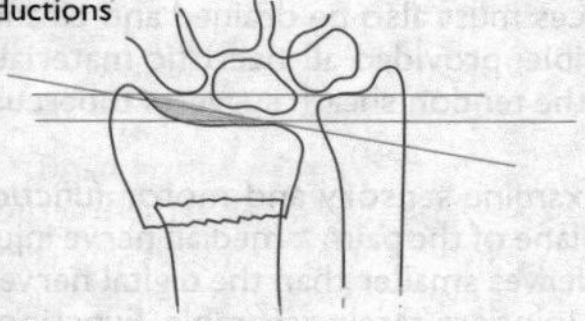

Note loss of radial length and reduction in ulnar tilt of the radius.

Lateral views

Normal

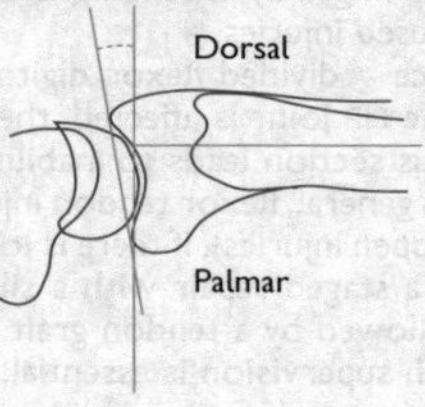

Acceptable

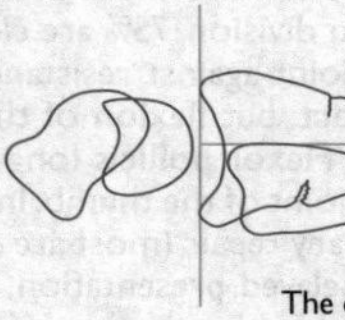

The distal radial articular surface is vertical

Unacceptable

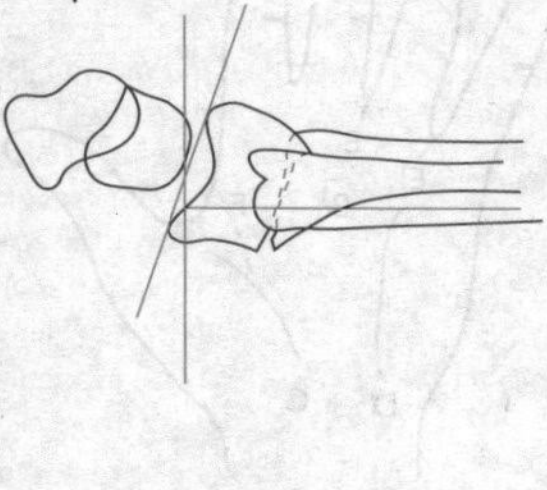

The distal radius surface is dorsally angulated. If allowed to heal in this position it will cause a marked restriction in function.

Injuries to the hand

►*There are no minor injuries to the hand.* Any breach of the integument may be the start of a chain of events that leads to loss of our most useful appendage. Contrary to beliefs of poets, our fingers are *not* protected from accidents by an invisible ring of shining:* *they are very frequently injured.*

Infections Streps and staphs are typical causes (and mixed Gram -ve in the immunocompromised). Spread may occur within a tendon sheath which may slough. Injuries in diabetics need special vigilance.
Treatment: If pus is present, take a swab. Avoid antibiotics as samples will be taken during surgery. Under GA and tourniquet control, the bloodless field is explored. If necessary, the synovial sheath is excised at its proximal end. Local collections of pus can occur in tendon sheaths or palmar spaces. Surgical drainage ± irrigation is indicated. Any abscess (eg paronychial or subcutaneous) or infected fascial spaces must also be drained and cleaned. Sometimes primary suturing is possible, provided all necrotic material is removed. A chronic 'cold' abscess of the tendon sheath suggests tuberculosis. Enlist expert help early. 155

Nerve injury (see p 716 & p 762) Examine sensory and motor function. Inability to lift the thumb out of the plane of the palm ≈ median nerve injury (failure of abductor pollicis brevis). Nerves smaller than the digital nerve at the level of the distal interphalangeal joint are rarely reparable. Function is better if the injury is to a nerve subserving a single modality (motor or sensory), as regenerating fibres simply grow down the nearest neural tube (at ~1mm/day) irrespective of distal function. Let an expert decide the method of repair: primary, secondary, or nerve graft. 156

Tendon injuries Failure to raise the affected finger by extending the MCP joint ≈ extensor tendon division. 75% are *closed* injuries. 157
Failure to flex the DIP joint against resistance ≈ divided flexor digitorum profundus. If this is intact, but flexion of the PIP joint is affected, there is division of superficialis. Flexor pollicis longus section leads to inability to flex the interphalangeal joint of the thumb. In general, flexor tendon injuries are best treated by primary repair (most are *open* injuries). If there is loss of tendon substance, or delayed presentation, a staged repair with a silastic implant to keep the tendon sheath open, followed by a tendon graft, may be needed. Intensive hand physiotherapy with supervision is essential.

Hand incisions: A, pulp space drainage; B & B[1], lavage of flexor tendons; C, drainage of radial bursa; D, drainage of the ulnar bursa; E & E[1], for the mid-palmar space; F, drainage of the thenar space.

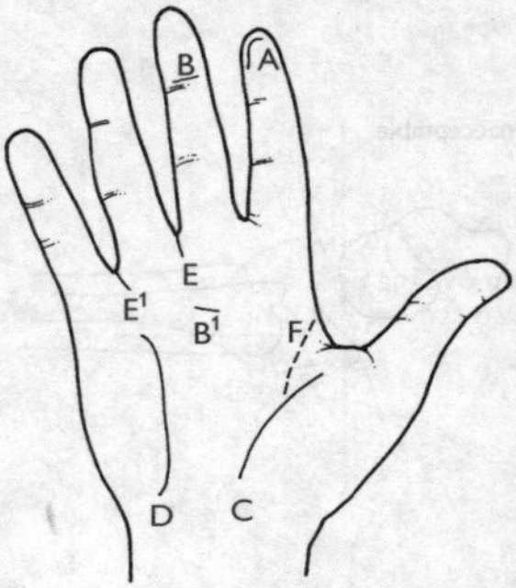

*Stephen Spender 1985 *To My Daughter* Complete Works, Faber

* *BRIGHT clasp of her whole hand around my finger*
My daughter, as we walk together now.
All my life I'll feel a ring invisibly
Circle this bone with shining ...

Limb surgery in bloodless fields

This may be achieved with pneumatic tourniquets, which must have adequate width and curve, and be applied for as brief a time as possible.[158]

'***Bruner's rules***': These minimize risk of ischaemic limb changes.

- Width of tourniquet: 10cm for the arm; 15cm for legs.
- Apply to the upper arm, or mid/upper thigh.
- Use ≥2 layers of orthopaedic wool to provide adequate padding (make sure it does not get wet with the skin preparation fluid, which should be aqueous, so that if wetting happens inadvertently, 'burns' do not occur).
- Inflation—arm: 50–100mmHg above systolic BP; leg: double systolic.
- Deflation—must be within 2h.
- Re-application after only brief reperfusion is inadvisable.[159]
- Avoid heating the limb (cooling is better, if feasible).[160]
- Apply only with the utmost caution to an unhealthy limb.
- Ensure the apparatus is calibrated weekly, and is well maintained.
- Document duration and pressure of tourniquet use.

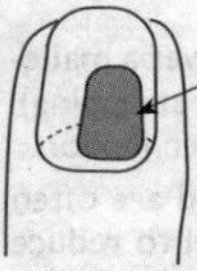

Sub-ungual haematoma
Release with needle by 'drilling' down—twiddling it between finger and thumbs; *or* by heating a paper clip to white heat and burning a hole through the nail.

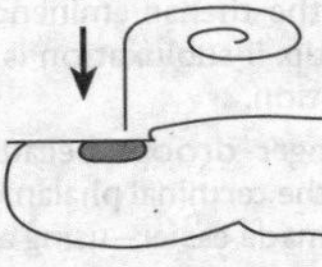

If left, the blood does not clot for up to 24hrs, therefore there is a throbbing pain due to pressure. This sometimes works (relieving the pressure) up to 2 days after the original injury.

Beware: subungual lacerations to the nail bed

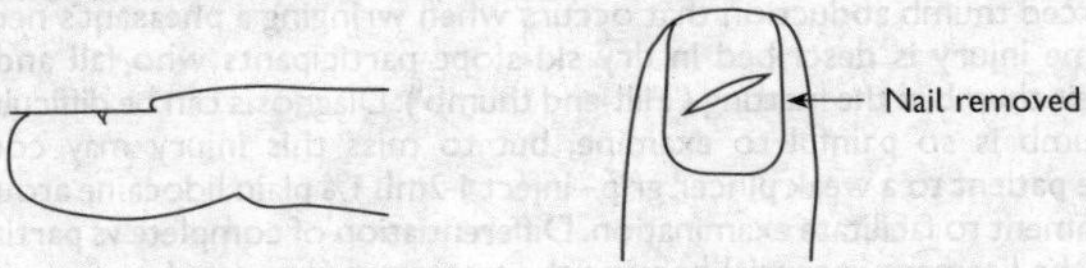

Remove the nail first—then stitch.
Also remove nail if there is nail avulsion.

Fractures in the hand

Metacarpal fractures These only need manipulation if there is gross displacement or angulation. The 5th metacarpal is most commonly involved, often from a punching injury. Immobilization for up to 10 days in a wool & crêpe bandage may be all that is needed, with finger movement encouraged after 2-3 days. Closed reduction + cast immobilization is also used.[161]

Longer periods of splinting in plaster or 'boxing glove' bandage can cause a stiff hand. Refer any fractures with obvious rotational deformity (a clinical, not a radiological decision), as this can be disable. Rotational fractures disclose themselves by producing a rotation of the fingers (flex the fingers and look at all the nails end on); they usually require operative fixation (plate & screws), as do fractures of ≥2 metacarpals. ►Beware wounds overlying metacarpophalangeal joints (often from the teeth of the punched victim, so they are contaminated bites, and may communicate with the joint).

Fractures of the proximal phalanx Spiral or oblique fractures occurring at this site are likely to be associated with a rotation deformity—and this must be corrected. Often, the only way to do this accurately is by open reduction and fixation, eg with a single compression screw.[162]

Middle phalanx fractures Manipulate these; splint in flexion over a malleable metal splint, strapping the finger to its neighbour (buddy strapping). The aim is to control rotation, which interferes with later finger flexion.

Distal phalanx fractures may be caused by crush injuries and are often open. If closed, symptoms may be relieved by trephining the nail to reduce swellings. Split skin grafts from the thenar eminence may be needed for partial amputations of the finger tip. If subluxation is a problem, joint stiffness may be avoided by open fixation.[163]

Mallet finger The tip of the finger droops because of avulsion of the extensor tendon's attachment to the terminal phalanx. If the avulsed tendon includes a piece of bone, union is made easier—using a special splint, eg with 0° of extension. Use for 6 weeks.[164] [n=37]

Interphalangeal arthrodesis may be needed if active extension remains limited. Poorer outcome is associated with delay in splinting, and if >50yrs old.

Gamekeeper's thumb This is so-called because of the rupture of the ulnar collateral ligament of the metacarpophalangeal joint of the thumb during the forced thumb abduction that occurs when wringing a pheasant's neck. The same injury is described in dry ski-slope participants who fall and catch their thumb in the matting ('Hill-end thumb'). Diagnosis can be difficult as the thumb is so painful to examine, but to miss this injury may condemn the patient to a weak pincer grip—inject 1-2mL 1% plain lidocaine around the ligament to facilitate examination. Differentiation of complete *vs* partial tears of the ligament is crucial because the treatment for complete tears is surgical. Radiographic evaluation will detect a bony avulsion fragment.

Partial tears (clinically stable), or those associated with undisplaced avulsion fractures of the proximal phalanx, can be adequately treated using simple shortarm thumb spica casting.

Nail avulsion

1. Warn the patient the nail may not regrow or regrow properly.
2. Ring block the finger and test it is numb.
3. Push one jaw of a small straight clamp down one side of the nail at its edge.
4. Close the clamp firmly . Warn the patient to look away.
5. Turn the clamp on its long axis as if opening a sardine can. The nail will wrap round the clamp and peel off its nail bed.
6. Having repaired the nailbed, dress the wound with some paraffin gauze, tucking some into the pocket at the base of the nailbed.

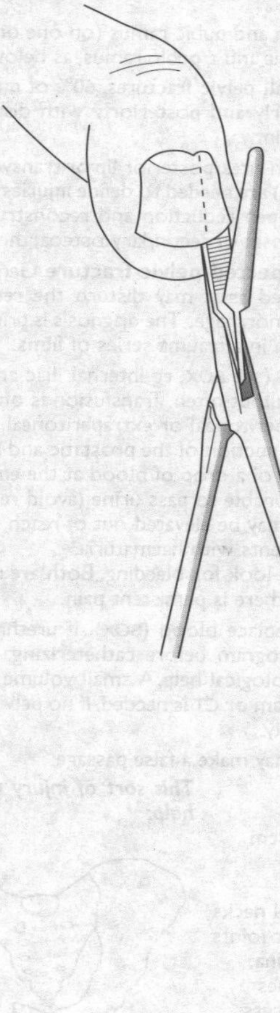

Pelvic fractures

Rang's aphorism: *The pelvis is like a suit of armour: after damage there is much more concern about its contents than about the structure itself.* Owing to the ring structure of the pelvis, single fractures are often stable and just need a few weeks rest. In contrast, ≥2 fractures in the pelvis (with one above the level of the hip) renders the ring unstable and is a serious injury, with internal injuries in 25%. The force producing the fracture maybe antero-posterior (AP), lateral compression (LC) or vertical shear. Signs to look for include bruising, perineal or scrotal haematoma, and blood at the urethral meatus.

Examples: Fractures of the ilium and pubic ramus (on one or both sides); fracture through a sacroiliac joint and a pubic ramus, as below.

Malgaigne's fracture (20% of all pelvic fractures, 60% of unstable ones): disruption of the pelvis anteriorly and posteriorly with displacement of a fragment containing the hip joint.

Acetabular fractures Common sites: posterior lip or transverse. Two 45° oblique radiographs (± CT scans) are needed to define injuries exactly (easy to miss on x-ray). Treatment: open reduction and reconstruction of the articular surface—to delay the onset of secondary osteoarthritis.

Examining patients with suspected pelvic fracture Gentle palpation of the iliac crests is discouraged as it may disturb the retroperitoneal haematoma, so exacerbating haemorrhage. The diagnosis is principally made from the pelvis radiograph taken in a trauma series of films.

Complications •Haemorrhage (see BOX, eg internal iliac artery). Check foot pulses, BP, CVP, and urine output often. Transfusion is often needed.
- Bladder rupture—may be intraperitoneal or extraperitoneal.
- Urethral rupture, often at the junction of the prostatic and membranous parts in males. The appearance of a drop of blood at the end of the urethra is suggestive. He may be unable to pass urine (avoid repeated tries). On rectal exam, the prostate may be elevated out of reach. NB: CT is the image of choice in trauma patients with haematuria.
- Vaginal and rectal perforation—look for bleeding. Both are rare.
- Trapping of the sciatic nerve—there is persistent pain.

Treatment Relieve pain and replace blood (BOX). If urethral rupture is suspected, check with a urethrogram before catheterizing; a suprapubic catheter may be needed. Get urological help. A small volume of urine suggests bladder rupture. A cystogram or CT is needed. If no pelvic fluid is seen on CT, bladder rupture is unlikely. 165 166

Avoid urethral catheters: they may make a false passage.

Reassuring signs on a pelvis radiograph:
- Symphysis pubis separation <1cm
- Integrity of superior & inferior rami
- Integrity of acetabula & femoral necks
- Symmetry of ilium & sacroiliac joints
- Symmetry of the sacral foramina, eg by evaluating the arcuate lines
- No fracture of transverse process of L5

This sort of injury needs expert help:

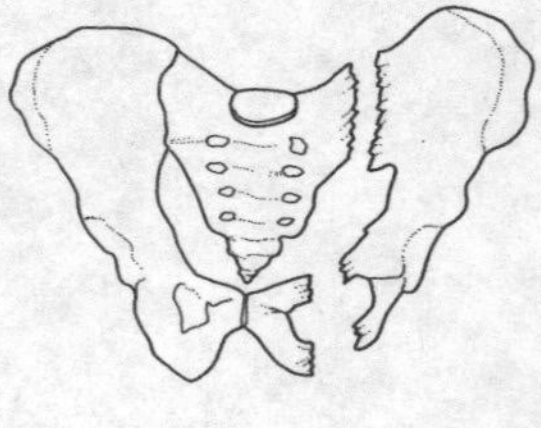

Shock with pelvic fracture

- This carries a mortality of 14-55% (towards the higher end if base excess on arterial blood gas analysis is ≤-5).[167][168] [n=660]
- *Is the patient pregnant?* This poses big problems, eg ↑pelvic blood flow.
- Resuscitate vigorously and meticulously: p 726.
- Ways to reduce blood loss: avoid manipulations of the pelvis. Internally rotate both lower legs to close an 'open-book' fracture. Apply a pelvic binder. Suspend the patient in a pelvic sling promptly. The patient lies supine with the pelvis over the sling's webbing, which exerts upward and medial (thereby compressing) traction via weights and runners suspended above the bed. Traction is also applied to the legs. Surgical reconstruction may then be undertaken.
- Alternative: external fixation frame.[169]
- Look for associated abdominal and pelvic injury. In one series of pelvic fractures there were splenic lesions (37%), diaphragm (21%) and bladder ruptures (24%), liver lacerations (19%), urethra lesions (17%), intestinal lesions (17%), and ruptures of the kidney (9%).[170]
- Sometimes diagnosis is hard. Prompt spiral CT identifies those needing a special procedure, such as angiographic embolization.[171]
- Ordering of interventions matters—eg laparotomy if indicated, intra-operative fixation, followed by postoperative embolization.[172]
- Inter-disciplinary cooperation is vital—and must be practised.

Injury to the hip and femur

Incomplete or impacted femoral head fractures may present with coxa valgus; complete fracture with dislocation may present with coxa varus.

Intracapsular fractures occur just below the femoral head. This often causes external rotation and leg adduction. The injuring force may be trivial and the patient may be able to walk (but with difficulty). As the medial femoral circumflex artery supplies the head via the neck, ischaemic necrosis of the head may occur, particularly if there is much displacement. Femur fractures fill 20% of all UK orthopaedic beds. The incidence is rising (~1:100/yr in females aged 75–84). Mortality: 50%.

Treatment: Assess vital signs. Treat shock with Haemaccel®, but beware incipient heart failure. If present, monitor CVP.

- Relieve pain (eg morphine 0.2mg/kg IM+prochlorperazine 12.5mg IM).
- Images: a good quality lateral is essential to make the diagnosis if there is impaction or little displacement. 5% can be missed unless CT is used.
- Prepare for theatre: FBC, U&E, CXR, ECG, crossmatch 2U, consent. Tell the anaesthetist about any drugs the patient is taking.
- Sort out any medical problems before embarking on surgery.
- If displacement is minimal, multiple screw fixation *in situ*. In displaced fractures the head is excised and a prosthesis inserted. [173]

Intertrochanteric-extracapsular fractures (between greater & lesser trochanters). They occur in a younger age group and, as blood supply is adequate, non-union is rarer. ***Treatment:*** Dynamic hip screw (DHS) fixation. The principle of the DHS is to stabilize the fracture but allow compression by sliding. Surgery is associated with ↓length of hospital stay and improved rehab. [MET 174] [175]

Femoral shaft fracture ►Is the femoral artery torn? (Look for swelling and check distal pulses.) Sciatic nerve injury may also occur. The proximal bone fragment is flexed by iliopsoas, abducted by gluteus medius, and laterally rotated by gluteus maximus. The lower fragment is pulled up by the hamstrings and adducted (with lateral rotation) by the adductors. ***Treatment:*** Typically, this is with a locked intramedullary nail introduced proximally over a guide wire that is manipulated across the fracture under fluoroscopic control. This allows early mobilization. Alternative: manipulation under anaesthesia (exact reduction is not needed) with fixed traction with a Thomas knee splint, or skeletal traction, or sliding traction, with the thigh supported on a frame, or a cast brace with a hinge at the knee (this permits early weight bearing). Union takes 3–4 months.

Condylar fractures & tibial plateau fractures Being intra-articular, these demand accurate joint reconstruction to minimize later OA.

Posterior hip dislocation (eg to front-seat passengers if the knee strikes the dashboard). Feel for the femoral head in the buttock. The leg is flexed, adducted, and short. The sciatic nerve may be lacerated, stretched, or compressed; early MRI diagnosis may prevent later equinus foot deformity. ***Treatment:*** Reduction under GA, by lifting the femoral head back into the joint. Traction for 3 weeks promotes joint capsule healing. [176]

Fracture of the acetabulum This is described on p 748.

▸▸Emergency management of open fractures: the 6 'As'

1 *Assessment*—neurovascular status, soft tissues and photograph wound (reduces number of wound inspections)
2 *Antisepsis*—cover wound with large antiseptic-soaked dressing
3 *Alignment*—align fracture and splint (also provides analgesia by reducing fracture site movement)
4 *Anti-tetanus*—check status and immunize appropriately
5 *Antibiotics*—intravenous 3rd generation cephalosporin (± metronidazole if wound grossly contaminated)
6 *Analgesia*—intravenous opiate analgesia titrated to effect

Gustilo classification of open fractures[177]

Type I *Low-energy* wounds <1cm long, eg caused by bone piercing skin.

Type II *Low-energy* wounds >1cm, causing moderate soft tissue damage.

Type III All *high-energy* injuries irrespective of wound size. Type IIIA fractures have *adequate* local soft-tissue coverage. Type IIIB have *inadequate* local soft-tissue coverage. Type IIIC implies arterial injury needing repair.

Preventing hip fractures

- Prevent falls: eg good lighting, less sedation, & keep-fit programmes.
- Teach exercise and balance training, eg with Tai Chi[1] classes for the elderly). This lessens fear of falling, and can halve rates of multiple falls.[178]
- Prevent osteoporosis: eg exercise, bisphosphonates.
- Ensure good vitamin D intake (plasma levels ≥30nmol/L; esp. in northern climes). A lack of vitamin D and calcium is associated with hip fracture whether or not patients are osteoporotic.[179]
- Meta-analyses suggest that hip protectors decrease risk of hip fracture in selected populations at high risk. Acceptability by users remains a problem, due to discomfort and practicality.[MET 180]

The following may prevent complications after hip injury

- Early mobilization to prevent thromboembolism.
- Co-ordinated multidisciplinary inpatient rehabilitation.[MET 181]
- Good nutrition—but meta-analyses do not provide much support for specific multi-nutritional commercial food supplements.[MET 182]

1 The Chinese characters for Tai Chi Chuan can be translated as the 'Supreme Ultimate Force'—an odd concept, one might think, to find in village halls—until one combines this with the Chinese concept of yin-yang—the dynamic duality (male/female, active/passive, dark/light, forceful/yielding, etc.) seen in *all* things. Think of Tai Chi as meditation combined with mobile yoga sequenced into sets of movements inspired as much from the animal kingdom as from martial arts traditions—as the movements are gracefully smooth as birds in flight. In Chinese philosophy and medicine there exists the concept of 'chi', a vital force that animates the body. One aim of Tai Chi is to circulate 'chi' within the body to promote health and vitality. Another aim of Tai Chi is to foster a calm and tranquil mind, focused on the precise execution of movements. www.chebucto.ns.ca/Philosophy/Taichi/what.html

Injuries of the lower leg

The patella Lateral dislocation results from a blow to the side of the knee, causing a tear in the medial capsule and the quadriceps aponeurosis, typically in the young. Knee flexion is limited. Sudden contraction of quadriceps may snap the patella transversely, whereas direct force may produce a multiple 'star-shaped' fracture (undisplaced within the quadriceps tendon). *Recurrent dislocation* may be related to developmental abnormalities around the knee.

The knee ***Injury to a collateral ligament*** is common in sport. ***Signs:*** Effusion ± tenderness over affected ligaments. Rest is needed, then firm support. If there is full rupture, varus and valgus straining opens the joint if the knee is held in 10° flexion (and if the knee is held in extension, if a cruciate ligament is also torn). Surgery to isolated medial collateral ligaments is rarely needed.[183]

Anterior cruciate tears: Typically follow posterior blows to the tibia, or rotation injury, with the foot fixed to the ground. ***Signs:*** Effusion; haemarthrosis; +ve 'draw' sign (immobilize the patient's leg by sitting on his foot, and then with the knee in 90° flexion, grip the upper tibia, and try to draw it towards you, away from the femur; the reverse 'set back' suggests a posterior cruciate tear—eg in car crashes as the knee strikes the dashboard.) Do a 'pivot shift test' (p 686). Examination under GA may be needed. ***Treatment:*** This is problematic. 3 weeks' rest and physio may help. In high demand athletes or ↑knee instability, consider ligament reconstruction (autograft).

Semilunar cartilage (meniscal) tears: Medial cartilage tears (eg 'bucket-handle') follow twists to a flexed knee (eg in football). Adduction + internal rotation causes lateral cartilage tears. Extension is limited (knee locking) as the displaced segment lodges between femoral and tibial condyles. The patient must stop what he is doing, and can only walk on tiptoe, if at all. The joint line is tender, and McMurray's test is +ve (p 686). If the 'handle' of the 'bucket' becomes free at one end ('parrot beak' tear), the knee suddenly gives way, rather than locking. MRI gives tear location, morphology, length, depth, and stability, and helps predict tears requiring repair.[184]

Occult bone injury: If MRI/x-rays are -ve, don't put everything down to 'minor problems with the meniscus'. Detailed MRI (STIR[1] +dynamic contrast to show periosteal oedema)[185] may show: • Subchondral fracture eg of the posterior margin of the medial tibial condyle.[186] • Stress fracture (intramedullary and periosteal oedema with high signal intensity)[187] • Tibial plateau oedema.

Tibia fracture *Avulsion fractures* of the intercondylar region often occur with anterior cruciate injury. Arthroscopic reduction may be tried.[188] Sliding traction, or surgery with open elevation of the joint surface may be needed. Open shaft fractures are common as there is so little anterior covering tissue. Tearing the nutrient artery may cause non-union in lower tibia fractures.

With *closed fractures*, operative or non-operative management depends on variable patient (eg kneeling occupation) and fracture (eg stability) factors.

Open fractures: see management of open fractures (p 751).

Isolated fibular fracture A supportive dressing may be sufficient.

Pretibial lacerations The shin (esp. if elderly) has poor blood supply. It is vulnerable to flap wounds, eg caused by steps of buses. ***Treatment:*** Try hard to iron out *all* the flap, repositioning it carefully: an ideal tool is the wrong end of a Vacutainer® needle, sheathed in rubber. The important thing is to prevent tension (tension→breakdown→plastic surgery)—so skin closure with adhesive strips (eg Steristrip®), which can be loosened if the tissues swell, is better than sutures. Dress the wound and advise a support bandage, and leg elevation. Review to check for infection, wound tension, and necrosis.

1 STIR = Short TI Inversion Recovery MRI (has specific timing to suppress the signal from fat).

Managing skin flap on the shin

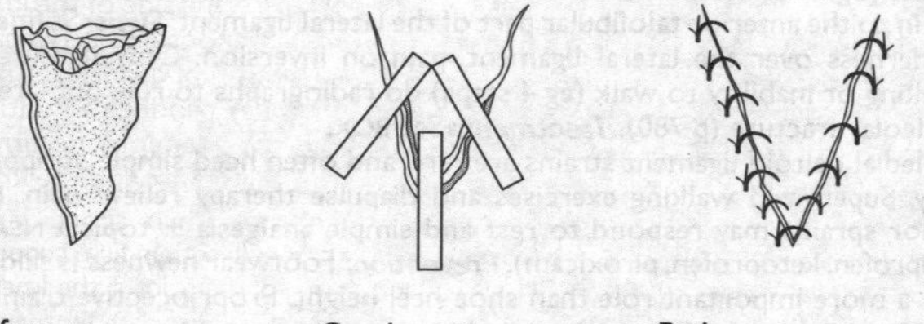

Before
Flap retracts back

Good
No tension in flap.
Held with adhesive sutures.

Bad
Flap stretched tight and likely to necrose.

Bone marrow contusions reveal the mechanism of injury

Bone marrow contusions are often seen on knee trauma MRIs. These osseous injuries result from a direct blow, from compression from impact from adjacent bones, or from traction from avulsion injury. The distribution of oedema gives valuable clues to associated soft-tissue injuries.

5 contusion patterns are associated with soft-tissue injuries in the knee:

1 Pivot shift injury: oedema involves the posterolateral tibial plateau and the midportion of the lateral femoral condyle.

2 Dashboard injury: oedema is in the anterior aspect of the proximal tibia.

3 Hyperextension results in the 'kissing' contusion pattern involving the anterior aspect of the proximal tibia and distal femur.

4 The clip injury results in a big area of oedema in the lateral femoral condyle and a small area of oedema involving the medial femoral condyle.

5 Lateral patellar dislocation causes oedema involving the inferomedial patella and the lateral femoral condyle (anteriorly).

So you can infer the mechanism of injury by patterns of oedema, and hence predict which specific soft-tissue abnormalities are present.[189]

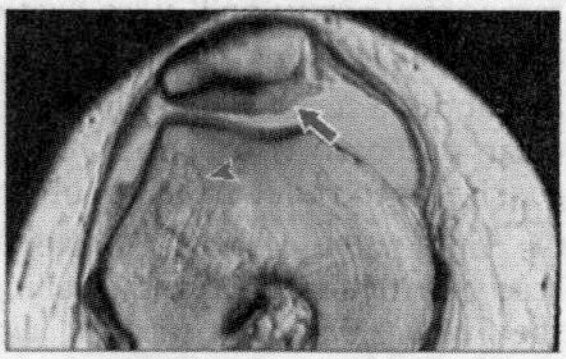

Axial view fat-suppressed fast-spin echo MRI in patella dislocation injury. Full thickness chondral fracture (arrow) of the medial patella facet is seen as an area of increased signal intensity. Bone contusion oedema of the subjacent marrow (arrow-head) involving the lateral femoral condyle was caused by impaction of the patella against the epicondyl.[190]

Ankle and foot strains, and fractures

Ankle ligament strains Twisting inversion accounts for the common strain to the anterior talofibular part of the lateral ligament. ***Signs:*** Stiffness, tenderness over the lateral ligament, pain on inversion. Only if there is swelling or inability to walk (eg 4 steps) do radiographs to rule out lateral malleolar fracture (p 780). ***Treatment:*** See BOX.

Medial deltoid ligament strains are rare, and often need simple strapping only. Supervized walking exercises and diapulse therapy relieve pain. NB: minor sprains may respond to rest and simple analgesia ± topical NSAID (ibuprofen, ketoprofen, piroxicam). ***Prevention:*** Footwear newness is said to play a more important role than shoe-heel height. Proprioceptive training can ↓incidence of ankle sprains in athletes.[191]

Malleolar and metatarsal fractures Either malleolus may be fractured by the above injuries. Rotation causes oblique lateral malleolar fracture (hard to see except on lateral radiographs), or a proximal fracture of the 5th metatarsal (avulsion by peroneus brevis). ***Treatment:*** Unstable or displaced fractures require surgery. Stable or minimally displaced fractures maybe treated non-operatively in a cast.

Dupuytren's fracture: *Distal* fibula fracture + distal rupture of tibiofibular ligament ± fracture of the back of the lower end of the tibia (trimalleolar) with lateral displacement of the talus. ***Treatment:*** Open reduction+screw fixation if >⅓ of the joint surface is involved; no full weight-bearing for 7wks.

Maisonneuve's fracture: *Proximal* fibula fracture + syndesmosis rupture, and medial malleolus fracture or deltoid ligament rupture. If 2 bones dislocate where no true joint exists, the term diastasis is used. ►Always examine the proximal fibula with 'ankle sprains'. Treatment of Maisonneuve's fracture is operative, with restoration of the ankle mortise and placement of one or two suprasyndesmotic screws.[192] [n=26]

Lisfranc fracture-dislocation at the 1st tarsometatarsal joint: A commonly missed fracture in multitrauma patients, it can also occur by stepping awkwardly off a kerb. It may cause compartment syndrome of the medial foot (± later arthritis and persistent pain).[193] ***Images:*** *Plain x-rays:* look for widening of the gap between the medial cuneiform and the base of the 2nd metatarsal. Because of the overlapping bones, subluxations can be hard to see. CT helps.[194] ***℞:*** Achieve *precise* anatomic reduction. Open reduction and temporary screw or K-wire fixation may be best.[195] [n=31]

Other fractures *Fractured neck of talus* can occur after forced dorsiflexion, and is a serious injury because interruption of vessels may lead to avascular necrosis of the body of the talus. *Treatment:* Displaced fractures require open reduction and internal fixation (ORIF).

Os calcis fractures (often bilateral, following serious falls; look for associated spinal fracture). *Signs:* swelling; bruising; inability to weight bear. ►*Does the fracture enter the subtalar joint?* Only opt for conservative treatment in extra-articular fractures, or minor displaced intra-articular fractures in nonambulatory patients. Otherwise, get *expert* surgery. Anatomic reduction is achievable in >50% of even 3-part fractures.[196]

Mid-tarsal (eg calcaneocuboid) dislocation produces a painful, swollen foot. The navicula proximal articular surface may not articulate with the talus. *Treatment:* Early manipulation + plaster cast for, eg 7 weeks.[197]

2nd metatarsal march fracture follows stress, eg from marching. *Signs:* inconstant. *Imaging:* bone scan hot spot. ***℞:*** plaster cast for 6 weeks.[198]

Fractures of the toes: Simple protective dressings usually suffice.

Treating ankle inversion trauma when there is no fracture

- Compression bandage, or below-knee plaster if there is much swelling.
- Rest with leg elevation.
- Ankle movements (especially dorsal extension).[199]
- Weight-bearing as soon as the pain allows. A few days later, when pain and swelling subside, examine to detect lateral ligament rupture.
- If you suspect ligament rupture, consider stress radiographs (GA may be needed). Look for talar tilt ± anterior talar displacement, in comparison to the unaffected side.[200] Be sceptical of the result: meta-analyses paint a pessimistic picture of reliability.[MET 201]
- If cost allows, MRI is a non-invasive and accurate way to evaluate injured lateral collateral ligaments.[202] [n=44]
- Treat *simple lateral ankle ligament tears* non-operatively. Use surgery for *dislocated bone avulsions* and *chondral or osteochondral fracture*.
- *Conservative treatment of ligament rupture:* immobilization of fibular ligaments with as little compromise of ankle joint function as possible, and rehabilitation with muscle strengthening and proprioception training.
- Recurrent instability may require reconstructive surgery.
- At surgery, ligament stumps are reapproximated in anatomic position, reinforced with local tissue if needed.[203]

Classification of malleolar fractures:

There is the ***Weber*** and the ***AO*** system. The AO system is detailed in the figure.*

A Transverse fibula fracture (#) at or below joint line.

B Spiral fibula # starting at the joint line ± medial injury.

C1 Oblique fibula # above a ruptured tibiofibular ligament + medial injury.

C2 Maisonneuve's fracture, only the fibular fracture is more proximal.

*Both systems have problems.[204] [205]

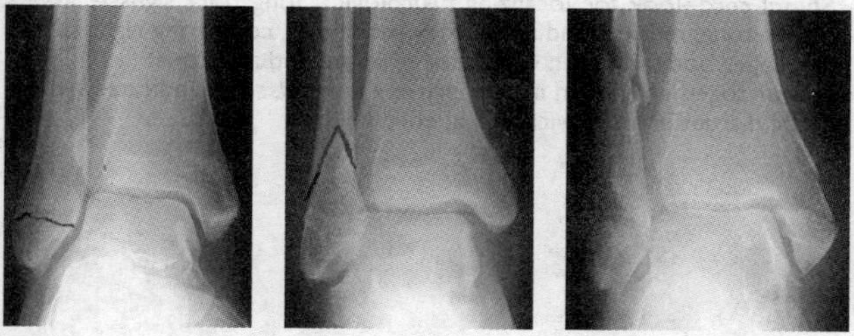

▸▸Head injury

In the UK, manage according to NICE guidelines. A summary follows.[206]

Definition Any trauma to the head other than superficial injury to the face.

Emergency care As always, treat ABCs—Airway, Breathing, and Circulation.

▸▸Note pupil sizes and reactivity.

▸▸Give O_2 and treat shock.

▸▸Protect the cervical spine.

▸▸Do not neglect other injuries. Primary brain damage occurs with the initial trauma. The clinical imperative is to prevent or ameliorate secondary brain injury, ie further neuronal death.

Ask about: Time and mechanism of injury

- Trends in consciousness level.
- Symptoms of co-existent medical conditions (especially epilepsy, diabetes). Any alcohol or drugs? ***On examination:*** Look for:
- Palpate ***scalp & skull*** for evidence of compound or depressed fracture.
- Examine the ***facial bones*** including orbits and middle third.
- Examine ***cervical spine*** for tenderness, deformity, and abnormal neurology.
- Check ***ears & nose*** for bleeding or CSF leaks. The presence of these or blood behind the tympanic membrane may indicate a fractured base of skull. Bruising over the mastoid (Battle's sign) and periorbital bruising ('Raccoon eyes') are late and unreliable signs of fractured base of skull.

Neurological assessment Write full notes; record times.

- Assess the ***Glasgow Coma Score*** (GCS, p 722) *accurately* and *repeatedly*. Record all 3 parameters (*Motor*, *Eyes*, and *Verbal*). If there is a difference between the sides, record the better result. If there is the possibility of a spinal injury, check for a response such as grimacing to a painful stimulus applied above the clavicles. Assess and record any contribution to mental status from alcohol or other drugs.
- ***Pupils***—check size and reactivity every few mins until stable. Unequal pupils are less important if conscious, but a grave sign in coma.
- ***Spinal cord***—look for localizing neurological long tract signs ie: assess power, tone, reflexes, and all sensory modalities, comparing right side *vs* left, upper body *vs* lower. Check for priapism and anal tone.
- ***Low BP*** together with an inappropriately ***low pulse*** rate indicates sympathetic disruption in cervical spinal cord injury.

Investigating and managing head injury patients

Imaging	Head (CT scan) if:	Cervical spine (X-ray/CT) if:
Clinical indicators	• GCS <13 at any time • Open or depressed skull or basal skull fracture • Post-traumatic fit • Focal CNS deficit • >1 episode of vomiting • Retrograde amnesia >½h	*Patients with neck pain or tenderness + one of:* • GCS <15 • Extremity paraesthesiae • Focal CNS deficit *Patient non-compliance* • Age >65years
Risk factor indicators	• Age >65 years • Coagulopathy • Suspicious mode of injury	• Suspicious mode of injury

⏩If +ve CT, GCS <15, or significant symptoms or signs, you must admit 'under a consultant with specialist training in managing head injured patients.' Those not fulfilling the admission criteria maybe discharged with a *head injury information sheet.* Tertiary referral to a neurosurgical service should be according to agreed local guidelines/policy.

▶▶Injuries to the face and neck

►*If there is airway obstruction, summon expert help promptly.* Remove blood, loose (or false) teeth, and vomit from the mouth. Lie in the semi-prone position to prevent obstruction from a swollen injured tongue, but always beware of cervical spine trauma with injuries above the clavicle. If the pharynx is swelling or there is fracture of the larynx, try gentle intubation. If impossible, do cricothyrotomy (*OHCM* p 756), then tracheostomy. Blood aspiration is prevented by direct pressure to the bleeding site.

Lacerations of the face Clean meticulously. Alignment of the tissues must be exact to produce a good cosmetic result.

- Complex lacerations: Is there a plastic surgeon available?
- Dog bites: give antibiotic cover (eg co-amoxiclav 1 tab/8h PO).
- Rugby player's ear: aspirate haematoma (repeat every few days) and then strap orthopaedic felt pressure pads against the head. Ruptured ear drum: advise against letting water into the meatus.
- Avulsed teeth may be replaced (p 786). If inhaled, do expiratory CXR. Bleeding socket: bite on adrenaline (=epinephrine)-soaked pads, or use sutures.
- Eye injury, nose fractures, and nose bleeds: see p 453, p 558, & p 560.

Mandible injury ***Signs:*** Local tenderness and swelling; jaw malocclusion; a mobile fragment; bone may protrude into the mouth in open fractures; if comminuted, the tongue may cause airway problems.

Diagnosis: Orthopantogram (OPG) radiographs. Enlist expert dental help.

Treatment of dislocations: Place your (gloved) thumbs over the back teeth and press downwards, while at the same time levering the chin upwards with your fingers (both hands). Consider midazolam sedation: titrate up to 0.07mg/kg IV: start with 2mg over 30sec, max 1.5mg if elderly—antidote: flumazenil 0.2mg IV over 15sec, then 0.1mg every 60sec, max 1mg total.

Blows to the chin may cause fracture at the impact site, or indirect fractures near the temporomandibular joint.

Fractures: Open reduction + internal fixation with miniplates is better than wiring teeth together for 6 weeks. Try to arrange this for a daytime consultant list, rather than at night. Complicated fractures may benefit from lag[1] screw osteosynthesis. 207 Complications: infection; non-union. 208 [n=492]

'Whiplash' injury is cervical strain caused by sudden neck extension with rebound flexion. It is common, often in rear-end crashes. Hyperextension causes the damage—to the anterior musculoligamentous structures. Subsequent protective muscle spasm causes pain and stiffness, which may be severe. ***Treatment:*** Prompt active moblilization (if tolerated), eg with gentle stretching and posture control. Aim to prevent chronicity and 'disuse syndrome'. If symptoms last for >1yr, they are likely to be permanent. 209 [N=97]

►Do not rely on plain radiographs to rule out facet joint fractures. They are more likely if the neck is rotated at the time of forced extension. Here it may be wise to ask a senior colleague if CT is indicated.

Other car-crash neck sprains (Seen in ⅓ of car users soon after crashes.) Symptoms may be delayed—and persist for years. The best treatment may be to give NSAIDs, a cervical collar, and review in the next clinic, with referral for immediate physiotherapy if symptoms warrant this. Explain to the patient that head restraints *are* helpful—the usual mistake is that they are adjusted too low.

1 Lag compression anneals the fracture line under compressive force, giving rigid fixation and coupling of the fractured fragments to promote fusion.

Bony injuries to the face

The face forms a shock absorber which protects the brain from injury. The most common fractures to the facial bones lie along 2 hoops, from ear to ear. One is formed by the zygomatic arch, body, infraorbital rim and nose. The other is formed by the mandible.

Major blunt trauma can cause a fracture to the entire middle third of the face, which has been classified by Le Fort, but since the advent of seat belts these are less common.

Zygoma fractures

The Arch: Before swelling arrives, there is a depression in front of the ear and lateral excursions or opening of the mandible may be limited and painful. A suitable radiograph is the submentovertex view (SMV).

The complex: The body of the zygoma has 4 extensions: (i) Frontozygomatic, (ii) Arch, (iii) Maxillary buttress in the mouth, (iv) Infraorbital rim. Fractures may be palpated at these points, or disproportionately severe pain elicited on palpation. A suitable radiograph is an occipito mental view (OM). Lateral views have no place.

Orbital floor injuries Blunt trauma around the eye can cause fracture to the orbital floor. Imaging: CT is best, but OM views may show trap door sign in the maxillary sinus. ***Clinical exam for periorbital trauma:***

- Check zygomatic arch by assessing range of mandibular lateral excursions and opening. Also palpate over the arch which lies just under the skin and compare with the unaffected side.
- Patient sitting, doctor standing above and behind, place index fingers on the cheeks and look down from above for asymmetry.
- Check orbital floor:
  - diplopia on upward gaze suggests entrapment of orbital contents.
  - enopthalmos.
  - numbness in the distribution of the infraorbital nerve suggests fracture.
- Small risk of retrobulbar haemorrhage—catastrophic if missed:
  - severe pain at back of eye
  - proptosis
  - loss of visual acuity
  - prompt exam is essential.

NB: If the eye is very swollen, application of a rubber glove filled with ice is invaluable, especially if you ask a specialist to travel to check patient, they can no more open a swollen eye than you. ***Treatment:*** Unless vision↓, or there is significant risk of infection, admission on presentation is not mandatory: an appointment at the next fracture clinic will be adequate. If in doubt, consult with the relevant specialist. Explain about not blowing the nose in fractures in continuity with the maxillary sinus (risks periorbital emphysema and infection).

Medicolegal: Facial injuries commonly result from assault. Your notes may be used in criminal injuries claims, or as evidence in court. Often the individual is drunk and abusive, and it is late, and you are busy, but you must take a few minutes to make accurate notes (use a ruler) with diagrams. Other people will definitely take time to study and criticize what you have written. Don't forget photographs if assault is particularly serious or children involved. Document that the patient has given, or refused, permission for statements to be made to the police or legal professionals (the medical notes are confidential).

▸▸Abdominal injury[1]

Penetrating injuries mostly require prompt laparotomy/laparoscopy. Assess degree of penetration (if uncertain) under local anaesthetic, by extending the wound, if necessary. Ask for expert assistance with this. Laparotomy is indicated if the posterior rectus sheath is breached.

Blunt trauma Deceleration forces may tear bowel from mesentery, liver from vena cava, or bladder from bladder neck. After blunt trauma abdomen and chest may be sites of hidden blood loss—*always* consider intra-abdominal bleeding or pelvic fracture (p 748) if BP↓ and no source of loss is found.

Key questions: *Are vital signs stable?* and *Is laparotomy needed?* (BP↓; GI, GU, or PR bleeding; evisceration; +ve ultrasound or peritoneal lavage). Liver, spleen, and kidneys are chiefly at risk—but remember the pancreas (amylase↑; injury may be missed by CT/ultrasound; endoscopy may be needed).

Tests CVP measurements, CT, and ultrasound may all mislead. There is no substitute for monitoring vital signs and examining the abdomen *often*. In the young and fit, signs of shock may take time to appear. Systolic BP doesn't fall consistently until ≥30% of blood volume is lost. *Radiographic implications:*[1]

- Lower rib fracture (?liver/spleen trauma)
- Pelvic fracture (?rectal injury)
- Spine fracture (?renal or pancreas trauma)
- Free gas (rupture)
- Bowel displaced (?haemoperitoneum)

Signs of organ damage ***Ruptured spleen:*** Suggested by shock, abdominal tenderness, and distension, left shoulder-tip pain, overlying rib fracture.

Any visceral injury may cause bruising in the flanks, absent bowel sounds, and muscular spasm. ***GU injury*** is suggested by haematuria.

Management Maintain airway; ensure adequate ventilation. Give high-flow O_2 (12–15L/min). Treat shock (p 726). Crossmatch blood. Then:

1 If the patient does not respond quickly, take straight to theatre for exploratory laparotomy (after urgent CXR to rule out pneumothorax and after passing of a nasogastric tube).

2 Baseline tests: pulse, BP, respirations, temperature, urine output.

3 Look for signs of GU injury:
- Blood at the urethral tip, signifying ruptured urethra.
- Test the urine. Is there frank or microscopic haematuria?
- Do a rectal exam to assess bowel integrity, presence of blood, or high-riding prostate (this suggests bladder neck injury).

If any suspicious signs, seek urological help to plan urethral repair. Rarely, GU trauma needs ureteroureterostomy, ureteroneocystostomy, or even kidney autotransplantation.

4 Consider peritoneal lavage (BOX, p 761) or LIF diagnostic tap.

5 Arrange a prompt exploratory laparotomy if there is:
- Shock (eg ruptured spleen)
- Penetration to unknown extent
- Peritonism (ruptured viscus)
- Pneumoperitoneum

A non-functioning kidney on IVU is a *relative* indication. *Don't* deny analgesia on finishing your assessment, simply for fear of masking signs.

6 ***Blood tests:*** FBC (raised WCC may occur in ruptured spleen), U&E, amylase.

7 ***Radiology:*** All with serious blunt trauma (eg RTA) need radiographs of cervical spine, chest, and pelvis as part of their primary assessment. Abdominal images are part of the secondary assessment: consider these along with IVU, thoracolumbar spine, and other injured sites.

1 ATLS *Manual* 6e, page 270 ISBN 1-880696-10-X

Diagnostic peritoneal lavage (DPL)

Indications DPL is used to assist in the diagnosis of significant intra-abdominal injury following trauma, particularly when abdominal examination by palpation is unreliable (spinal injury; neuromuscular blocking drugs; head injury; alcohol) or difficult to interpret (pelvic, lower rib and lumbar spine fractures may produce abdominal pain and muscle guarding). It may be used to determine the cause of unexplained hypotension following trauma. It should be performed by the surgeon who is responsible for any subsequent operation.

Focused abdominal ultrasound for trauma (FAST) or DPL? FAST-trained surgeons achieve accuracy of >90% in detecting intraperitoneal fluid from the outset.[210] But liver & spleen tears and free fluid can still be missed.[211] Therefore, don't rely on ultrasound; CT may be required.[212] [n=938]

CT may be difficult to interpret if there has not been enough time to opacify the bowel with oral contrast. It is good for lacerations of the spleen, liver, and kidneys. In a stable patient, CT may allow close observation of the patient, instead of, for example, splenectomy.

In children CT & U/S is preferred to DPL.

Contraindications The need for urgent laparotomy is an *absolute* contraindication—*don't delay for DPL*. Relative contraindications: late pregnancy, cirrhosis, known coagulation disorder.

Technique

- The bladder and stomach must be empty, so pass a urinary catheter (not if urethral trauma) and a nasogastric tube.
- Use strict asepsis and clean the abdomen in the midline below the umbilicus. Inject lidocaine (=lignocaine) *with epinephrine* (*=adrenaline*) ⅓ of the way between the umbilicus and the symphysis, in the midline (epinephrine limits false positives from abdominal wall bleeding).
- Incise down to peritoneum, then grasp the peritoneum with 2 artery forceps and lift clear of the bowel.
- Incise the peritoneum and pass a dialysis catheter into the pelvis.
- Aspirate for blood—if >5mL, DPL is positive. If <5mL, run in 10mL/kg of warm normal saline. Leave for 5-10min, then allow fluid to drain by hanging the bag below the level of the abdomen.

Interpretation Lavage fluid *must* be sent to the laboratory. Do not rely on naked eye appearance. ***Red cells:*** $>10^5/mm^3$ is positive. ***White cells:*** $>500/mm^3$ is positive. A positive result requires exploratory laparotomy. False negatives occur with retroperitoneal haemorrhage.

Complications Haemorrhage; organ perforation ± peritonitis; infection.

Principal source: *Advanced Trauma Life Support*, American College of Surgeons

Injury to nerves and arteries

Nerve injury classification ***Neurapraxia*** implies temporary loss of nerve conduction often via ischaemia following pressure (eg to the lateral popliteal nerve as it crosses the neck of the fibula, see below). In mixed nerves, the motor modality is the more vulnerable component. ***Axonotmesis*** entails damage to the nerve fibre but the endoneural tube is intact, providing guidance to the regrowing nerve. Good recovery is the rule. Growth rate is ~3mm/day. ***Neurotmesis*** means division of the whole nerve. As there is no guidance from the endoneural tube, regrowing fibrils cause a traumatic neuroma if they are unable to bridge the gap. The current surgical standard is epineural repair with nylon sutures. To span gaps that primary repair cannot bridge without excess tension, nerve-cable interfascicular autografts are used. Results of nerve repair are fair (at best), with ~50% of regaining useful function. There is much current research regarding drugs, immune system modulators, enhancing factors, and entubulation chambers.[213]

Median nerve (C5–T1) The nerve of *grasp*. Injury above the cubital fossa causes inability to flex the interphalangeal joints of the index finger on clasping the hands (Ochner's test); inability to flex the terminal phalanx of the thumb (flexor pollicis longus); loss of sensation over the thenar half of the hand.

If the lesion is at the wrist, the only muscle reliably affected is abductor pollicis brevis. Test it by holding the hand palm up. Can the patient raise the thumb out of the plane of the hand? The area of sensory loss is smaller than that for higher lesions.

Ulnar nerve (C8–T1) This is the nerve of finger abduction and adduction (among other roles). One subtle sign of an ulnar nerve lesion is inability to cross the fingers in the 'good luck' sign. Injury level determines severity of the claw deformity. In a low lesion of the ulnar nerve, there will be more clawing of the 4th and 5th fingers compared to a higher, more complete lesion at the elbow. This is the ***ulnar paradox***, and comes about because higher lesions paralyse flexors too (eg flexor digitorum profundus, FDP).[214] ***Froment's paper sign:*** On holding a piece of paper between thumb and finger (both hands), there is flexion of the thumb's distal phalanx on trying to pull apart (flexor pollicis longus, is recruited to overcome adductor pollicis weakness). Sensory loss is over the little finger, and a variable area of the ring finger.

Radial nerve (C5–T1) This is the nerve of extension of the elbow, wrist, and fingers. It opens the fist. Injury will produce wrist-drop. Test for this with the elbow flexed and the forearm pronated. Sensory loss is variable, always including the dorsal aspect of the root of the thumb.

Sciatic nerve (L4–S2) Complete lesions will affect all muscles below the knee, and sensation below the knee laterally.

Lateral popliteal (common peroneal) nerve (L4–S2) Lesions lead to equinovarus with inability to dorsiflex the foot and toes. Sensory loss is over the dorsum of the foot.

Tibial nerve (S1–3) Loss causes calcaneovalgus and inability to stand on tiptoe or invert the foot. Sensory loss over the sole.

Injuries to arteries Bleeding is usually controllable by pressure and elevation of the part. After any injury in which an artery may have been damaged, examine distal pulses carefully. If they are not felt, do not assume that this is due to spasm, but request expert help. Surgical exploration with end-to-end suture, or reversed vein grafts may be needed. The prognosis is not so bad if there are good collaterals (eg to the femoral artery, compared with the popliteal artery). *Complications:* gangrene, contractures, traumatic aneurysms, and arteriovenous fistulae.

Sensory relearning after median nerve repair: the Lundborg–Rosén metaphor

Tactile gnosis: This is tested by 2-point discrimination and tactile recognition of objects. Restoration of tactile gnosis in the hand is the main challenge of median nerve repair. It is easy to point out that touch is a major way we interact with our world. More subtle is how the brain performs ***cross-modal interpretation*** of our world—ie integrating touch, sound, and vision, and producing meaning out of this integration. Loss of one modality is not a simple case of subtraction, but gives rise to complex compensatory mechanisms. Interpretation of textures, for example, is not usually regained after major injury to a nerve trunk in adults, but there is more plasticity in children: here, cortical remodelling allows meaningful interpretation from mis-connected regrown axons. Best results of repair are seen before the age of 10yrs. By 18yrs, there has been a rapid decline in relearning ability. There is an unexplained temporary increase in learning ability in the late twenties. This pattern, intriguingly, follows that of our ability to learn a new language. So the notion that the problem after nerve injury/repair is that '***the hand is speaking a new language to the brain***' is more than an metaphor; accepting this metaphor leads to the idea that education and training are vital to successful nerve repair.215

Median nerve anatomy It arises from C5, C6, C7, C8, & T1 as a condensation of lateral & medial cords of brachial plexus (p 766). It crosses medial to the brachial artery in antecubital fossa. It has no branches above the elbow. ~5cm distal to elbow it gives off its anterior interosseous branch (motor to FPL, FDP index finger & pronator quadratus). The palmar cutaneous branch (sensory to thenar skin) arises ~5cm proximal to wrist and overlies the flexor retinaculum. The recurrent motor branch to the thenar muscles arises at the distal end of carpal tunnel. ***The median nerve is motor to*** PT (pronator teres), FCR (flexorcarpi radialis), PL (palmaris longus), FDS (flexor digirorum superficialis), LOAF (radial 2 lumbricals, opponens pollicis, abductor pollicis, flexor pollicis brevis). ***Sensation:*** Radial 3-and-a-half digits.

M=median nerve; 4 tendons abutt it: *South-west:* FCR flexor carpi radialis. *South:* FDP=flexor digitorum profundis. *South-east:* FDS flexor digitorum sublimis for the index finger (f). *East:* FDS for middle f.

Under the dome of the flexor retinaculum are 4 other tendons: two touch capitate (cap) ie, FDP for the middle & ring fingers. FDP for the little finger touches the hamate (ham). Above it is FDS for the ring finger; next to this is the little finger's FDS.

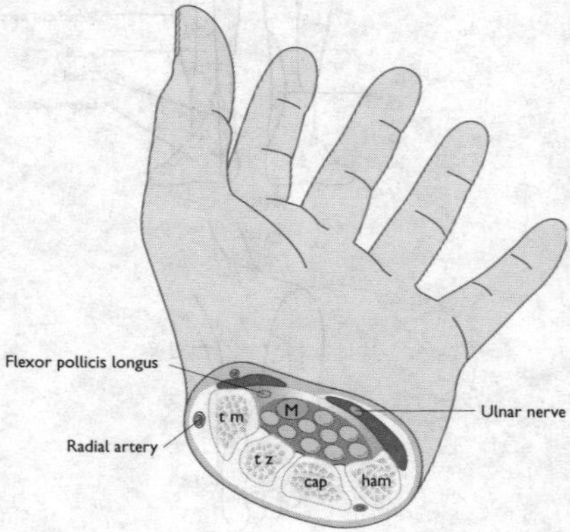

tm=trapezium bone
tz=trapezoid bone 216

Dermatomes

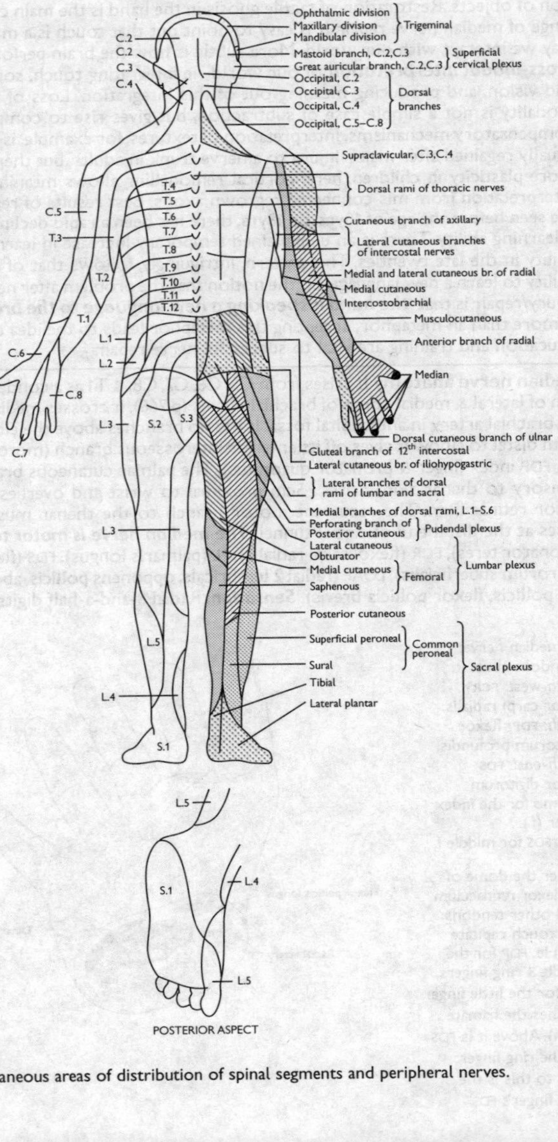

Cutaneous areas of distribution of spinal segments and peripheral nerves.

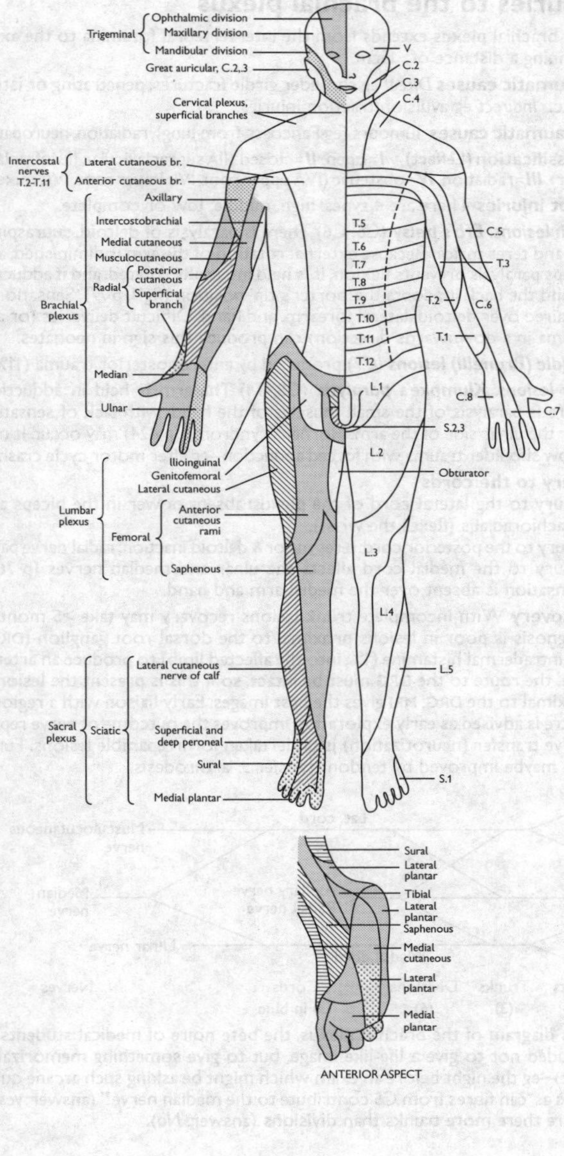

ANTERIOR ASPECT

Injuries to the brachial plexus

The brachial plexus extends from the intervertebral foramina to the axilla spanning a distance of ~15cm.

Traumatic causes *Direct* eg shoulder girdle fractures, penetrating or iatrogenic. *Indirect* eg avulsion/traction injuries.

Atraumatic causes Tumours (eg Pancoast, from lung), radiation, neuropathy.

Classification (Leffert) ***I***=open. ***II***=closed (IIA supraclavicular, IIB infraclavicular). ***III***=radiation. ***IV***=obstetric (IVA upper root, IVB lower root, IVC mixed).

Root injuries There are 4 types: high, middle, low or complete.

High lesions: Erb's palsy (C5, C6) There is paralysis of deltoid, supraspinatus, and teres major. Because external rotation of the arm is diminished, and biceps paralysis prevents flexion, it is held internally rotated, and if adducted behind the back it adopts the 'porter's tip' position (fig 1, p 77). Sensation is impaired over deltoid, lateral forearm, and hand. Difficult deliveries (or any trauma in a downwards direction) can produce this sign in neonates.

Middle (Brunelli) lesions (C7) produced by anteroposterior trauma (11%).[1]

Low lesions: Klumpke's paralysis (C8, T1) The arm is held in adduction. There is paralysis of the small muscles of the hand, with lack of sensation over the ulnar side of the arm. Horner's syndrome (p 424) may occur. It may follow shoulder trauma with forced abduction—eg after motor cycle crashes.

Injury to the cords

- Injury to the lateral cord of the plexus: absent power in the biceps and brachioradialis (flexes the wrist).
- Injury to the posterior cord: teres major & deltoid inaction; radial nerve palsy.
- Injury to the medial cord affects the ulnar and median nerves (p 762). Sensation is absent over the medial arm and hand.

Recovery With incomplete trunk lesions recovery may take >5 months. Prognosis is poor in lesions proximal to the dorsal root ganglion (DRG). For intradermal histamine (1%, into the affected limb) to produce an arterial flare, the route to the DRG must be intact, so if this is present the lesion is proximal to the DRG. MRI gives the best images. Early liaison with a regional centre is advised as early exploration improves the outcome of nerve repair. Nerve transfer (neurotization) is undertaken for irreparable lesions. Function maybe improved by tendon transfer ± arthrodesis.

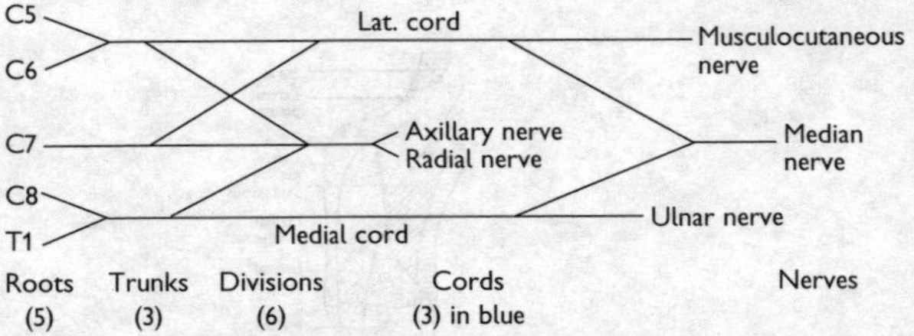

This diagram of the brachial plexus, the bête noire of medical students, is included not to give a life-like image, but to give something memorizable (just)—eg the night before an exam which might be asking such arcane questions as 'can fibres from C5 contribute to the median nerve?' (answer: *yes*)—or are there more trunks than divisions (answer: *No*).

1 A 4th type of brachial plexus injury. Brunelli GA & Brunelli GR 1992 *Ital J Orthop Traumatol* 1992 **18** 389-93

Spinal cord injury—the first day

At the site of the accident Spinal injury should be assumed to be present in any serious accident and in all accidents when the nature of the injuring force is not known, and the patient is unconscious. This does not mean that the patient cannot be moved into the recovery position (protection of the airway is always the first priority)—but all movement should be planned, keeping the head in neutral; the patient may be log-rolled into a semi-prone position (not lateral), see p [illegible]. For immobilization, see p 796.

Radiology Don't rely on portable equipment if possible: take to the radiology department, supervising all movements and the removal of sandbags and collars oneself, if possible. With plain radiographs, the lateral view is often the most revealing; do oblique views if the C7–T1 junction is not visible. Anterior vertebral displacement of <½ the diameter of the vertebral body suggests unilateral facet dislocation. Greater displacements indicate bilateral (unstable) facet dislocations. Look for the soft tissue shadow of a paravertebral haematoma if bony signs are minimal. Other views: anteroposterior (AP) with an open mouth view of the odontoid process; AP view of C3–7 and thoracic, lumbar & sacral injuries are usually shown on AP and lateral films. If there is an anomaly and unsure about it, discuss with the radiologist how to show it best. CT is preferred to x-rays of the cervical spine in some dedicated trauma centres. MRI shows fractures, subluxations, disc disruption and protrusion, and cord contusion—and helps establish prognosis.

Respiratory insufficiency Check vital capacity repeatedly. If <500–600mL, intubation and ventilation will be needed. Monitor blood gases. Intubation may produce vagal bradycardia, so give atropine 0.3–0.6mg IV before intubation and airway suction.

Fluid balance There is likely to be hypotension below the lesion (sympathetic interruption). This is not due to hypovolaemia, and it is dangerous to give large volumes of fluid. Usually no oral fluids for 48h and while ileus persists. If abdominal distension causes respiratory embarrassment, pass a nasogastric tube.

The skin Turn every 2h between supine and right and left lateral positions. The Stoke Mandeville bed does this electronically. Use pillows to separate the legs and maintain a lumbar lordosis.

Steroid treatment Methylprednisolone 30mg/kg IV stat (within 8h of trauma) followed by 5.4mg/kg/h IV for 23h is known to significantly improve subsequent recovery. The maintenance dose can be extended to 48h if treatment is started >3h from injury.

Early surgical decompression Get expert advice on removing damaging bone and disc fragments. (Later internal fixation may also be used.)

Anticoagulation Enoxaparin 40mg/24h SC; start warfarin later.

The bladder Pass a 12 gauge silicone Foley balloon catheter before the bladder volume exceeds 500mL. Overstretching under anaesthesia can delay the return of automatic bladder function; see p [illegible].

Arrange early and expert transfer to a spinal injury unit.

Skeletal traction will be needed for cervical injuries. Spring-loaded Gardner–Wells skull calipers are preferable to Crutchfield calipers, which need incisions.

Spinal cord injury—the first day

At the site of the accident Spinal injury should be assumed to be present in any serious accident, and in all accidents when the nature of the injuring force is not known, and the patient is unconscious. This does not mean that the patient cannot be moved into the recovery position (protection of the airway is always the first priority)—but all movement should be planned. Keeping the head in neutral, the patient may be 'log-rolled' into a semi-prone position (not lateral, see p 799). For immobilization, see p 798.

Radiology Don't rely on mobile equipment; if possible, take to the radiology department, supervising all movements and the removal of sandbags and collars. Do CT if possible.[218] With plain radiographs, the lateral view is often the most revealing; do oblique views if the C7–T1 junction is not visible. Anterior vertebral displacement of <½ the diameter of the vertebral body suggests unilateral facet dislocation. Greater displacements indicate bilateral (unstable) facet dislocations. Look for the soft-tissue shadow of a paravertebral haematoma if bony signs are minimal. *Other views:* anteroposterior (AP) with an open mouth view of the odontoid process ± AP view of C2–T1 area. Thoracic, lumbar, & sacral injuries are usually shown on AP and lateral films. If there is an area you are unsure about, discuss with the radiographer how to show it better. CT is preferred to x-rays of the cervical spine in some dedicated trauma centres. MRI shows fractures, subluxations, disc disruption and protrusion, and cord contusion—and helps establish prognosis.[1]

Respiratory insufficiency Check vital capacity repeatedly. If <500–600mL, intubation and ventilation will be needed. Monitor blood gases. Intubation may produce vagal bradycardia, so give atropine 0.3–0.6mg IV before intubation and airway suction.

Fluid balance There is likely to be hypotension below the lesion (sympathetic interruption). This is not due to hypovolaemia, and it is dangerous to give large volumes of fluid. Use IV not oral fluids for 48h and while ileus persists. If abdominal distension causes respiratory embarrassment, pass a nasogastric tube.

The skin Turn every 2h between supine and right and left lateral positions. The Stoke Manderville bed does this electronically. Use pillows to separate the legs and maintain a lumbar lordosis.

Steroid treatment ►Methylprednisolone 30mg/kg IV stat (within 8h of trauma) followed by 5.4mg/kg/h IVI for 23h is known to significantly improve subsequent recovery. The maintenance dose can be extended to 48h if treatment is started >8h from injury.[219]

Early surgical decompression Get expert advice on removing damaging bone & disc fragments. (Late internal fusions may also be tried.)

Anticoagulation Heparin 5000U/8h SC. Start warfarin later.

The bladder Pass a 12-gauge silicone 5mL balloon catheter before the bladder volume exceeds 500mL (overstretching of detrusor can delay the return of automatic bladder function). See p 774.

►Arrange early and expert transfer to a spinal injuries unit.

Skeletal traction will be needed for cervical injuries. Spring-loaded Gardner-Wells skull calipers are preferable to Crutchfield calipers, which need incisions.

Does this patient have a spinal cord injury?

In any unexplained trauma, suspect cord injury if:[220]

- Responds to pain only above clavicle.
- Dermatomal pattern of sensory loss.
- Breathing—diaphragmatic without use of accessory respiratory muscles.
- Muscles—hypotonic, including reduced anal tone (do a PR).
- Reflexes—hyporeflexic.
- Absence of movement in both legs.
- Slow pulse and ↓BP, but in the presence of normovolaemia.
- Priapism[1] or urinary retention.
- Unexplained ileus.
- Clonus in an unconscious trauma patient without decerebrate rigidity.
- Poikilothermia (poor temperature regulation).

How complete is the injury? ASIA scale   ASIA=american spinal injury association

A=complete; no sensory or motor function in sacral segments S4–S5.

B=incomplete; sensory but not motor function preserved below the neurological level, and extending through sacral segments S4–S5.

C=incomplete; motor function preserved below the level, most key muscles weaker than grade 3 (ie no movement against gravity).

D=incomplete; motor function preserved below the level; most key muscles are stronger than grade 3, ie active movement against gravity.

E=normal motor and sensory function.

What are the mechanisms of injury?

Primary injury (immediate) is easy to understand: within seconds, the cord expands to occupy the entire diameter of the spinal canal. Glutamate floods out of neurons, overexciting their neighbours. Calcium floods in, leading to the formation of toxic free radicals.

Secondary injury (delayed, eg unfolding over weeks) is a response to release of neurotoxins and apoptosis (cell death) which may spread up to 4 segments away from the trauma site. www.trauma.org

1 Priapism is when pathologic stimuli (eg cervical cord lesions) cause prolonged erection (>4h), or when normal stimuli occur under pathologic circumstances—eg stasis from sickle-cell disease or leukemia with leukostaisis (WCC↑↑) cause prolonged erections. As it can cause permanent damage, get help. Bilateral shunting between the corpus cavernosum and corpus spongiosum may be needed.

Priapism is named after Priapus, the son of Aphrodite (the goddess of love). He, though, is ugly in most depictions—with a penis so large that he is generally relegated to the position of a scarecrow in the fields. From this position he is happy to be the god of gardens, bees, goats, sheep—and fertility.

Images of cord pathology

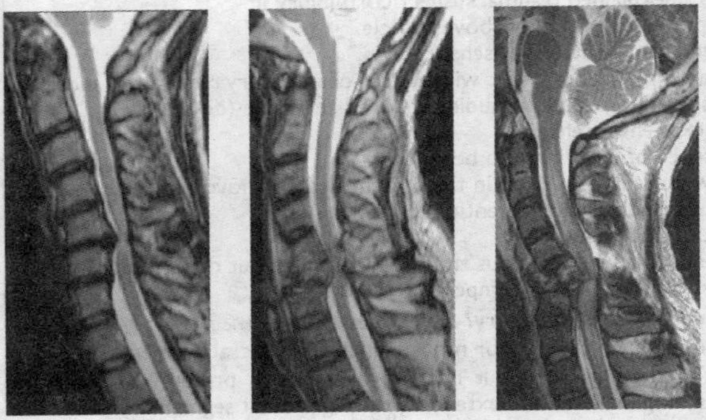

Because of different technical settings, MRI images can be called **T1** or **T2** weighted. These images can be recognized as **T2** weighted because the CSF is white. Compression of the cord has occurred as a result of a disc protrusion, a metastatic deposit, and trauma.

Cord injury—function and functional anatomy

The tightest fit between cord and canal is in the thoracic spine; this region also has the poorest blood supply. These factors explain why thoracic lesions are more likely to be complete than cervical or lumbar lesions. Ischaemic injury often spreads below the level of the mechanical injury. For the segment of the cord involved with injury at a specific vertebra, see below.

Cord compression may be due to bone displacement, disc prolapse, local tumour, or abscess. Root pain (p 670) and lower motor neurone signs occur at the level of the lesion with upper motor neurone signs and sensory changes below the lesion (spastic weakness, brisk reflexes, upgoing plantars, loss of co-ordination, joint position sense, vibration sense, temperature and pain). Cord anatomy is such that 'dorsal column' sensation (fine touch, joint position sense, vibration sense) are affected on the same side as the lesion, but spinothalamic tract interruption affects pain and temperature sensation for the opposite side of the body 2–3 dermatomic levels lower than the affected sensory level. As the cord ends at L1, compression at this vertebral level affects information in the cord relating to lower dermatomes. To determine the cord level affected behind a given vertebra, add the number in blue to that of the vertebra concerned: thus C2+1; T1–6+2; T7–9+3. T10 has L1 and L2 levels behind it. T11 has L3 and 4. L1 has sacral and coccygeal segments. It can be difficult to determine the level. MRI will help clarify this.

Lower lumbar problems can cause cauda equina compression (p 672) characterized by muscular pain, dermatomal sensory changes (if the lower sacral dermatomes are affected the genitals are anaesthetic) and retention of urine ± faeces. These signs indicate urgent neurosurgical referral with imaging to confirm or exclude a tumour or extradural abscess.

Spinal shock (BP↓ but no tachycardia): there is areflexia and flaccid paralysis of all segments and muscles innervated below the level affected with areflexia and retention of urine. A stage of reorganization then occurs (reflex emptying of bladder and rectum; sweating). Later flexion at hip and knee may be induced by stimuli (frequently cold), often with emptying of the bladder and rectum (Head and Riddoch's mass reflexes). The legs may become permanently fixed in a drawn up position with dorsiflexion of the ankles (spastic paraplegia in flexion). Over months, tendon reflexes return and proprioceptive stimuli give rise to mass extension.

Paraplegia/quadriplegia Levels fluctuate, so examine often.

Raises elbow to horizontal: deltoid C5	Flexes hip: iliopsoas L2
Flexes forearm: biceps C6	Extends knee: quadriceps L3
Extends forearm: triceps C7	Dorsiflexes ankle: tibialis anterior L4
Flexes wrist and fingers C8	Plantarflexes ankle: gastrocnemius S1
Spreads fingers T1	

Segment injury as guide to possible subsequent function

C4 Can use electric chairs with chin control type with mouthstick; use a Possum (environmental control system) to turn on lights & open doors.

C5 With special devices, he can feed, wash face, comb hair, and help with dressing the upper body. He may be able to push a wheelchair along the flat if pushing gloves are worn, and there are capstan rims on the wheels. The NHS will supply an electric wheelchair (indoor use only). Unable to transfer from wheelchair to toilet.

C6 Still needs assistance with feeding and washing. Dresses top half of body, helps dress lower half. Can drive with hand controls.

C7 Can transfer, dress, feed himself.

C8 Independent wheelchair life.

Cord injury—function and functional anatomy

The 'tightest fit' between cord and canal is in the thoracic spine; this region also has the poorest blood supply. These facts explain why thoracic lesions are more likely to be complete than cervical or lumbar lesions. Ischaemic injury often spreads below the level of the mechanical injury. For the segment of the cord involved with injury at a specific vertebra, see below.

Cord compression may be due to bone displacement, disc prolapse, local tumour, or abscess. Root pain (p 670) and lower motor neurone signs occur at the level of the lesion with upper motor neurone signs and sensory changes below the lesion (spastic weakness, brisk reflexes, upgoing plantars, loss of co-ordination, joint position sense, vibration sense, temperature and pain). Cord anatomy is such that dorsal column sensibilities (light touch, joint position sense, vibration sense) are affected on the same side as the insult, but spinothalamic tract interruption affects pain and temperature sensation for the opposite side of the body 2-3 dermatome levels lower than the affected sensory level. As the cord ends at L1, compression at this vertebral level affects information in the cord relating to lower dermatomes. To determine the cord level affected behind a given vertebra, add the number in blue to that of the vertebra concerned, thus: C2-7: ***+1***. T1-6: **+2**. T7-9: ***+3***. T10 has L1 and L2 levels behind it; T11 has L3 and 4, L1 has sacral and coccygeal segments. It can be difficult to determine the level: MRI will help clarify this.

Lower lumbar problems can cause cauda equina compression (p 674) characterized by muscular pain, dermatomal sensory changes (if the lowest sacral dermatomes are affected the genitals are anaesthetic), and retention of urine ± faeces. ►*These signs indicate urgent neurosurgical referral with imaging* eg to confirm or exclude a tumour or extradural abscess.

Spinal shock (BP↓ but no tachycardia.) There is anaesthesia and flaccid paralysis of all segments and muscles innervated below the level affected with areflexia and retention of urine. A 'stage of reorganization' then occurs (reflex emptying of bladder and rectum; sweating). Later, flexion at hip and knee may be induced by stimuli (notably cold), often with emptying of the bladder and rectum (Head and Riddoch's mass reflexes). The legs may become permanently fixed in a drawn up position, with dorsiflexion of the ankles (spastic paraplegia in flexion). Over months, tendon reflexes return, and proprioceptive stimuli give rise to 'mass extension'.

Paraplegia/quadriplegia levels Levels fluctuate, so examine often.

Raises elbow to horizontal: *deltoid* **C5**
Flexes forearm: *biceps* **C6**
Extends forearm: *triceps* **C7**
Flexes wrist and fingers **C8**
Spreads fingers **T1**
Flexes hip *iliopsoas* **L2**
Extends knee *quadriceps* **L3**
Dorsiflexes ankle *tibialis anterior* **L4**
Plantarflexes ankle *gastrocnemius* **S1**

Segment injury—a guide to possible subsequent function

- C4 Can use electric chairs with chin control; type with mouthstick; use a 'Possum' environmental control system to turn on lights & open doors.
- C5 With special devices, he can feed, wash face, comb hair, and help with dressing the upper body. He may be able to push a wheelchair along the flat, if pushing gloves are worn, and there are capstan rims on the wheels. The NHS will supply an electric wheelchair (indoor use only). Unable to transfer from wheelchair to toilet.
- C6 Still needs a strap to aid feeding and washing. Dresses top half of body; helps dress lower half. Can drive with hand controls.
- C7 Can transfer, dress, feed himself.
- C8 Independent wheelchair life.

Restoring lost function: is it possible?[1]

The following is not a list of well-tried treatment options: the field is too new. The following is more a way of thinking about cord injury, and preparing our minds for discussions with experts. Most patients prioritize their wishes for restoration of functions in this order: bowel and bladder control; sexual function; hand function; breathing. Options might be:

- Glutamate receptor blockers to limit secondary injury (p 768-9).
- Anti-apoptotic agents, eg NT-3 (neurotrophin-3), BDNF (brain-derived neurotrophic factor), and ICE-protease (interleukin-1β-converting enzyme) inhibitors.
- Chemical prevention of action potential dissipation from demyelinated areas ± agents to remyelinate axons.
- Blocking natural inhibitors of regeneration, eg IN-1 (inhibitor neutralizing antibody).
- Promotion of axonal regeneration—eg BDNF & NT-3, (see above). Note that guidance of axons must be arranged, eg via guidance molecules such as netrins, cell adhesion molecules, and specific matrix proteins.
- Replacement of lost cells (cloned embryonic stem cells are one option; use of endogenous progenitor cells is another option).

Often these options seem a long way off, but note that only 10% of damaged neurones need to be replaced to enable useful locomotion.

1 Restoring function after cord injury *Neurologist* 2003 **9** 1 & J McDonald 2002 *Lancet* **359** 417

Spinal cord injury: genitourinary aspects

One major problem is urinary incontinence and reflex detrusor activity (after acontractility in the period of spinal shock) and the presence of residual urine. This predisposes to infection and ureteric reflux. These are major causes of renal failure, morbidity, and mortality.

The method of bladder drainage In the first weeks after cord injury use suprapubic or intermittent urethral catheterization with a 12 or 14 FG Nelaton® catheter, with strict asepsis. Culture the urine every week, and aim to eradicate infection (particularly important with *Proteus* which induces stones in infected alkaline urine). In some patients it may be possible to induce voiding by tapping the suprapubic area for ~20sec. Initially, catheterization is still necessary to drain the residual urine, but when this is <80mL (on 3 consecutive occasions), discontinue the catheter. If this does not occur, and particularly if the detrusor is non-contractile (conus medullaris or cauda equina injury), intermittent self-catheterization (eg with a silver catheter in women) may be used, as soon as the patient can sit. If reflex voiding occurs, propantheline 15–30mg/8–12h PO 1h ac may reduce detrusor activity and obviate the need for wearing drainage devices continuously. The elderly may require an indwelling silicone catheter, with 6-weekly changes. Weekly washouts (eg Suby-G®) may prevent stones. Aim for an output of >3litres/day. Use clamps to achieve volumes of 300mL. Artificial sphincters are available for acontractile bladders.

Complications *Urinary infection:* This may be prevented by a high fluid intake, ensuring effective bladder emptying, and acidification of the urine (eg ascorbic acid 1g/6h PO).

Detrusor-sphincter dyssynergia: The external urethral sphincter fails to relax or actively contracts during detrusor contraction. There is poor bladder emptying and vesicoureteric reflux, predisposing to pyelonephritis, hydronephrosis, and renal failure. It is wise to do U&E, creatinine, and IVU as early baseline tests. ***Treatment:*** Endoscopic external sphincterotomy.

Autonomic dysreflexia: In those with lesions above the sympathetic outflow (ie above T1) bladder distension (eg with a blocked catheter) results in sympathetic overactivity below the level of the lesion. There is vasoconstriction and hypertension (may cause strokes). The patient has a pounding headache, and blotchy skin above the lesion. The carotid baroreceptors are stimulated causing reflex vagal bradycardia, but the signals which would normally produce relieving vasodilatation and normotension are unable to pass down the cord. Other stimuli which may produce this effect include UTI, calculi, labour, and ejaculation. ***Treatment:*** Remove the cause; give nifedipine (10mg—bite the capsule) with glyceryl trinitrate 0.5mg. Phentolamine 5–10mg IV is an alternative. Sphincterotomy may prevent attacks.

On-demand urination There have been encouraging trials in those with ASIA-A lesions (p 768–9) of the Brindley-Finetech Vocare implantable bladder system which activates anterior sacral nerve roots to regulate bladder and large bowel and urethral/anal contraction. This leads to cost savings (fewer catheters), fewer UTIs, and a better life.[221]

Sexual function

►*Sexual counselling is an integral part of rehabilitation.* It is important in itself, but we should recognize that sexuality interacts with important determinants of our patient's quality of life, eg levels of dependency, aggression, self-esteem, and autonomy.[222]

We should enlist expert help, but we can all counter myths that disabled men cannot sexually satisfy able-bodied women; and that the cord-injured cannot have intercourse. Don't be shy and don't be shocked: for help with discussing sexual issues, see p 328. ►Given a knowing and patient partner, most persons with spinal injury can enjoy a satisfying sex life.[223] [224]

Be aware that sexuality encompasses more than physical attractiveness and penile–vaginal intercourse. With spinal cord injury, use of sexual imagery and concentration on body areas that retain sensation have especial importance, as does a certain inventiveness and readiness to experiment.[225]

When helping these patients it is important to distinguish sexual drive and sexual satisfaction from fertility and parenting needs. Both need addressing in a systematic way within the broader contexts of psychosocial, emotional, and relationship aspects—and also in terms of cognitive-genital dissociation, perceived sexual disenfranchisement, and sexual rediscovery. Cognitive-genital dissociation may take various forms, eg indicating that for some, sexual activity is more like watching a graphic movie than engaging in a physical experience.[226] It is equally important to assess the partner's needs and responses to the injury. This takes time.[227]

Do not concentrate on physical aspects alone: nevertheless it may be helpful to familiarize yourself with some statistics, and to emphasize that individuals vary. In some studies, locomotor impairment and dysreflexia were more frequently given as causes of reduced sexual pleasure than specific sexual dysfunctions.[228]

In women, only 17% with complete lower motor neurone dysfunction affecting the S2–S5 spinal segments can achieve orgasm, compared with 59% of women with other levels and degrees of injury.

In men with lesions between T6 and L5, 75% can expect improvement in erections with use of sildenafil.[229] [230]

Fertility issues in men centre around performance, and sperm quality which may be reduced by scrotal hyperthermia, retrograde ejaculation, prostatic fluid stasis, and testicular denervation. Electro-ejaculation and intracytoplasmic sperm injection have a useful role.

In women, pregnancy rates vary from ~10% to 60%.[231]

Cord injury—OT, physio, and nursing aspects

The occupational therapist (OT) is a key person in maximizing the levels of achievement outlined above. She is also in a position to arrange a home visit with a member of the spinal injuries team, and a community liaison nurse or social worker. The aim is to construct a plan with local social services and the local domiciliary occupational therapist, so that the patient's (and his family's) hopes can be realized to the fullest extent. She can arrange the necessary home modifications, and give invaluable professional advice about the level of independence which is realistic to strive for. As ever, the aims of the occupational therapist extend into augmenting self-esteem, and helping the patient come to terms with loss of role, and loss of confidence, and to mitigate the effects of disability by arranging for as much purposeful activity as possible, both in the realms of work and leisure. She will also be able to make plans for acquiring of social skills to assist the patient in his or her new way of life.

Nursing & physiotherapy ***The chest:*** Regular physio with coughing and breathing exercises prevents sputum retention and pneumonia which are likely to follow diaphragmatic partial paralysis (eg C3–4 dislocation). If the lesion is above T10 segmental level, there is no effective coughing.

The straight lift: (for transferring patients) One attendant supports the head with both hands under the neck so that the head lies on the arms. 3 lifters standing on the same side insert their arms under the patient, one at a time, starting at the top. After the lift, withdraw in the reverse order.

The log-roll: (Learn from observation.) 3 lifters stand on the same side of the patient. The one near the head has both arms under the patient's trunk and over the patient's further arm; the 2nd has one arm under the legs and the other arm holds the patient's iliac crest. The 3rd lifter supports the calves. A 4th person controls the head and neck, and gives the command to turn. The patient is then gently rolled laterally, with pillows to support the lumbar curve and to keep the position stable.

Posture: Place joints in a full range of positions. Avoid hyperextensions. Keep the feet flexed at 90° with a pillow between soles and bed-end.

Bowels: From the second day of injury gentle manual evacuation using plenty of lubricant is needed. A flatus tube may be helpful in relieving distension once the ileus of spinal shock has passed.

Wheelchairs: The patient should be kept sitting erect; adjust the footplates so that the thighs are supported on the wheelchair cushion and there is no undue pressure on the sacrum. Regular relief of pressure on the sacral and ischial areas is vital. Independence in transferring to bed or toilet will be a suitable aim for some patients with paraplegia. Expert skill is needed in assigning the correct wheelchair for any particular patient.

Standing and walking: Using a 'tilt table', or the Oswestry standing frame with trunk support straps, the tetraplegic patient can gain the upright posture. If the level of injury is at L2–4, below-knee calipers and crutches will enable walking to take place. If the lesion is at T1–8, 'swing to gait' may be possible. The crutches are placed a short distance in front of the feet. By leaning on them and pushing down with the shoulders, both legs may be lifted and moved forwards together.

Sport: Consider archery, darts, snooker, table tennis, and swimming for those with paraplegia. Many other sports may also be suitable.

Personal qualities in therapists are almost as important as exact anatomic lesion. There may be big mood swings from euphoria to despair as the patient accustoms himself to his loss and his new body image.

Vegetative states

Persistent vegetative state is a term coined to describe the behaviour of severely brain-damaged people who show sleep-awake behaviour, but in whom there is absent cognition and awareness. The term is something of a misnomer, because its presence does not imply permanence (recovery of cognition may occur up to 5yrs after the original insult)—and it has nothing to do with vegetables.

Persistent vegetative states are rare, and liable to misdiagnosis by non-specialist neurologists and neurosurgeons—perhaps because diagnosis depends on history and examination—requiring careful, repeated assessment and the taking into account of observations made by family and carers. ▶The harder you look, the more likely you are to find signs of active cognition, so negating the diagnosis of a vegetative state.

One method of showing awareness and cognition is by demonstrating communication, eg by following a simple request to press a buzzer or to look at a named object. These switches are particularly suited to those who can only manage a tiny amount of voluntary movement. Other ways of communicating include listener scanning: the therapist goes through A–Z slowly, and the patient buzzes when the required letter is reached. It may take weeks or months to establish that the patient can communicate. Rancho scale assessment establishes the level of cognition, from confused and inappropriate (level 5) to purposeful and appropriate (level 8).

Causes Trauma, anoxia, vascular causes, encephalitis.

Management Seek expert rehabilitation help. While waiting for any recovery, aim to provide vigorous nursing care to maintain nutrition, and to prevent pressure sores, and tracheostomy and muscle contracture complications. No drugs are known to help, although there is anecdotal evidence that bromocriptine may help. Randomized trials indicate that multimodal stimulation (arousal programmes) help. These programmes involve stimulation of all senses every 15min for up to 11h per day.

Once it is agreed that there will be no recovery (a difficult issue) discussions about withdrawing active treatment and nutrition raise difficult ethical questions—which are only partly mitigated if the patient has an advance directive (an unlikely event). Ethicists, medical specialists, nurses, physiotherapists, judges, and the family must all be allowed to have their say. None is infallible.

Vegetative states

"I seemed to have been asleep nearly all my life."
"...But when did you wake up?"
"I don't know that I ever did, or ever have". *Sons & Lovers*, 274

'Persistent vegetative state' is a term coined to describe the behaviour of severely brain damaged people who show sleep-awake behaviour, but in whom there is absent cognition and awareness. The term is something of a misnomer, because its presence does not imply permanence (recovery of cognition may occur up to 5yrs after the original insult)—and it has nothing to do with vegetables.

Persistent vegetative states are rare, and liable to misdiagnosis by non-specialist neurologists and neurosurgeons—perhaps because diagnosis depends on history and examination—requiring careful, repeated assessment and the taking into account of observations made by family and carers. ►*The harder you look, the more likely you are to find signs of active cognition, so negating the diagnosis of a vegetative state.*

One method of showing awareness and cognition is by demonstrating communication, eg by following a simple request to press a buzzer or to look at a named object. These switches are particularly suited to those who can only manage a tiny amount of voluntary movement. Other ways of communicating include listener scanning: the therapist goes through A–Z slowly, and the patient buzzes when the required letter is reached. It may take weeks or months to establish that the patient can communicate. Rancho scale assessment establishes the level of cognition—from confused-and-inappropriate (level 5) to purposeful-and-appropriate (level 8).

Causes Trauma, anoxia, vascular causes, encephalitis.

Management Seek expert rehabilitative help. While waiting for any recovery, aim to provide vigorous nursing care to maintain nutrition, and to prevent pressure sores, and tracheostomy and muscle contracture complications. No drugs are known to help, although there is anecdotal evidence that bromocriptine may help. Randomized trials indicate that multimodal stimulation (arousal programmes) help. These programmes involve stimulation of all senses every 15min for up to 11h per day.

Once it is agreed that there will be no recovery (a difficult issue), discussions about withdrawing active treatment and nutrition raise difficult ethical questions—which are only partly mitigated if the patient has an advance directive (an unlikely event). Ethicists, medical specialists, nurses, physiotherapists, judges, and the family must all be allowed to have their say. None is infallible.

Does he need a radiograph?

The aim is to provide information that will alter management, without exposing patients to unnecessary radiation. The following is based on the advice of the UK Royal College of Radiologists and other bodies.

Presenting conditions: Twisting injury of foot or ankle: A radiograph is indicated if patients cannot bear weight—and it is said not to be indicated if he can weight-bear on the affected ankle, and if tenderness and swelling are confined to a ligament, or are absent—but all rules have exceptions, and, on occasion, we all have patients walk on a fractured ankle.

Crush injury to the terminal phalanx of a digit: A radiograph is not indicated in localized closed injury provided there is pain-free movement at the distal interphalangeal joint.

Injury to the cervical spine: if any of these are present, imaging is needed:
- Neurological exam reveals a focal deficit
- Spine exam reveals tenderness (posterior midline)
- Alteration in consciousness
- Intoxication
- Distracting injuries; the mechanism of injury.

The Canadian CT head rule: CT is only required for minor head injury if one of the following is present:
- Glasgow coma scale <15 at 2h post-injury
- Suspected open or depressed skull fracture
- Any sign of basal skull fracture (haemotympanum, raccoon eyes, CSF otorrhoea/rhinorrhoea, Battle's sign—see p756)
- Amnesia before impact of >30min
- Dangerous mechanism (pedestrian struck by car, car occupant ejected, fall from a height of >1m or 5 stairs).[1]

Possible neck injury in minor head injury: A radiograph is not indicated if fully conscious and there are no symptoms or signs related to the neck.

Nose injury: Imaging in A&E is not indicated in simple nasal injury.

Rib injury: Only a posteroanterior CXR is indicated if you suspect a pneumothorax; rib views are not needed in uncomplicated blunt injury.

Lumbar spine pain: Avoid early radiography (in <6 weeks) if there are no CNS factors suggesting serious disease, eg trauma, fever, weight↓, anaemia, ESR↑ (so do blood tests first). Each examination = 2.2mSv (=110 chest radiographs; the sievert is the SI unit of radiation absorbed by biological tissues—its abbreviation is Sv), which may be expected to cause 16 malignancies/yr in the UK at current rates of exposure. It is impossible to protect the ovaries.

Abdominal pain: Plain films are rarely needed; request only an erect chest film in suspected gastrointestinal perforation. Erect abdominal films are generally not indicated in most patients with abdominal pain.

Foreign bodies: Always do radiography if the presence of glass is possible (glass is usually radiopaque).

Note: Lumbar spine radiographs deliver a significant dose of radiation to the gonads—similarly for skull and facial radiographs to the eyes.

These guidelines yield substantial savings in costs and in patients' waiting times, without compromising patient care.

1 Ottawa rules; see www.ohri.ca/programs/clinical_epidemiology/OHEU.asp

Does he need a radiograph?

The aim is to provide information that will alter management, without exposing patients to unnecessary radiation. The following is based on the advice of the UK Royal College of Radiologists, and other bodies.

Presenting conditions ***Twisting injury of foot or ankle:*** A radiograph is indicated if patients cannot bear weight; one is said *not* to be indicated if he can weight-bear on the affected ankle, and if tenderness and swelling are confined to a ligament, or are absent—but all rules have exceptions, and, on occasion, we've all seen patients walk on a fractured ankle.[1]

Crush injury to the terminal phalanx of a digit: A radiograph is not indicated in localized closed injury, provided there is pain-free movement at the distal interphalangeal joint.

Injury to the cervical spine: If any of these are present, imaging is needed:[232]

- Neurological exam reveals a focal deficit.
- Spine exam reveals tenderness (posterior midline).
- Alteration in consciousness.
- Intoxication.
- Distracting forces as the mechanism of injury.

The Canadian CT head rule: CT is only required for minor head injury if one of the following is present:[233]

- Glasgow coma scale <15 at 2h post-injury.
- Suspected open or depressed skull fracture.
- Any sign of basal skull fracture (haematotympanum, racoon eyes, CSF otorrhoea/rhinorrhoea, Battle's sign—see p 756).
- Amnesia before impact of >30min.
- Dangerous mechanism (pedestrian struck by car; car occupant ejected, fall from a height of >1m, or downstairs).

'Possible' neck injury in minor head injury: A radiograph is not indicated if fully conscious and there are no symptoms or signs related to the neck.

Nose injury: Imaging in A&E is not indicated in simple nasal injury.

Rib injury: Only a posteroanterior CXR is indicated if you suspect a pneumothorax; rib views are not needed in uncomplicated blunt injury.

Lumbar spine pain: Avoid early radiographs (in 1st 6wks) if there are no CNS factors suggesting serious disease, eg trauma, fever, weight↓, anaemia, ESR↑ (so do blood tests first). Each examination=2.2mSv (=40 chest radiographs; the sievert is the SI unit of radiation absorbed by biological tissues—its abbreviation is Sv), which may be expected to cause 16 malignancies/yr in the UK at current rates of exposure. It is impossible to protect the ovaries.

Abdominal pain: Plain films are rarely needed; request *only* an erect chest film in suspected gastrointestinal perforation. Erect abdominal films are generally not indicated in most patients with abdominal pain.

Foreign bodies: Always do radiography if the presence of glass is possible (glass is usually radiopaque).

Note: Lumbar spine radiographs deliver a significant dose of radiation to the gonads—similarly for skull and facial radiographs to the eyes.

These guidelines yield substantial savings in costs and in patients' waiting times, without compromising patient care.

1 Otowa rules, see: www.ohri.ca/programs/clinical_epidemiology/OHDEC/ankle_rule/default.asp

Appropriate use of Emergency Departments

From our point of view the ideal scenario is to have a pristine, remarkably but empty trauma department with the doctors and nurses occupying themselves (decorously) in the coffee room—occasionally being called out by paramedics to save a few lives in a brief display of energy and technical brilliance. This is not how the public sees Emergency Departments: if in shock having just run over a neighbour's pet, they need some attention now. All Emergency Departments are abused—because it is always doctors who define what abuse is. Up to 70% of users have been deemed inappropriate in some studies. This figure dwindles towards nothingness if abuse is defined as those consultations where all 3 parties to the visit on reflection, concur that it was inappropriate: the doctor, the patient & family, and the patient's GP (who may have sent them).

Overcrowding and exit-block: This is a major problem in Emergency Departments the world over—partly reflecting centrally determined reductions in acute bed provision and availability, and partly reflecting access problems for populations seeking prompt help with immediate (and, sometimes, chronic) problems. If the inpatient side of a hospital is full, patients will stack up in Emergency Departments awaiting admission. If overcrowding is cumulative, ambulances may be redirected to other hospitals (adding to delay and danger) and patients with genuine needs may catastrophically decide they can do without any more nudging for help.

How to cope with inappropriate attendance

- Triage by a trained nurse is one way to reduce inappropriate attendance (in the UK, triage is mandatory): is this condition life-threatening, urgent, semi-urgent, or is delay acceptable? These are the chief categories. If the most urgent patients are seen first, patients who do not really need to be in the department can wait for ages, and many will begin to drift away. Note that if long waits become essential because of dealing with life-threatening conditions, this should be explained to patients (under the terms of the UK health charter—and as a matter of common courtesy).
- Another way to reduce unnecessary spending is to have primary care facilities within the Emergency Department, or, more radically, to have GPs as the casualty officers—because they use resources more sparingly and are used to dealing with mismatches between patient's expectations and reality. Is this expectation borne out in practice? In one earlier randomized study of patient contacts with the Emergency Department in Dublin, GPs, ie GPs treating people with semi-urgent problems investigated less (by 18%), referred to other hospital services less (by 37%), admitted fewer patients (45%) and prescribed more often (43%). There were no differences in measures of outcome. It is not clear whether the more economical style of the GPs was to do with being a GP, or whether the reason was that these doctors were older and more experienced than their emergency department counterparts.

Risk management strategy when overwhelmed by the work to be done:
- Prioritize the waiting tasks and then concentrate on the task in hand.
- At times you may feel you are working at a pace that is faster than is comfortable. This is part of continuous learning, and as you get better this unease will abate. Look on it as practice for emergency situations where quick decisions are vital. Working faster does not necessarily mean making more errors.
- Have good techniques of clinical decision-making, which you continuously refine. Start with something like the system on p 445.
- Keep the goal in mind: What to do for the best for this patient.

1 BMJ 2002 324 58

Appropriate use of Emergency Departments

From our point of view, the ideal scenario is to have a pristine, ever-ready but empty trauma department with the doctors and nurses educating themselves (etcetera) in the coffee room, occasionally being called out by paramedics to save a few lives in a brief display of energy and technical brilliance. This is not how the public sees our role. If in shock having just run over a hedgehog some people feel they need attention *now*. All Emergency Departments are abused—because it is always doctors who define what abuse is. Thus up to 70% of users have been deemed inappropriate in some studies. This figure dwindles towards nothingness if abuse is defined as those consultations where all 3 parties to the visit, on reflection, concure that it was inappropriate: the doctor, the patient ± family; and the patient's GP (who may have sent them).

Overcrowding and 'exit-block'[1] This is a major problem in Emergency Departments the world over—partly reflecting centrally determined reductions in acute bed provision and availability, and partly reflecting access problems for populations seeking prompt help with immediate (and, sometimes, chronic) problems. If the inpatient side of a hospital is full, patients will stack up in Emergency Departments, awaiting admission. If overcrowding is cumulative, ambulances may be redirected to other hospitals (adding to delay and danger) and patients with genuine needs may, catastrophically, decide they cannot wait any more hours for help.

How to cope with inappropriate attendance

- ***Triage*** by a trained nurse is one way to reduce inappropriate attendance. (In the UK, triage is mandatory.) Is this condition ***life-threatening, urgent, semi-urgent*** or is ***delay acceptable***? These are the chief categories. If the most urgent patients are seen first, patients who do not really need to be in the department can wait for ages, and many will begin to drift away. Note that if long waits become essential because of dealing with life-threatening conditions, this should be explained to patients (under the terms of the UK health charter—and as a matter of common courtesy).
- Another way to reduce unnecessary spending is to have primary care facilities within the Emergency Department, or, more radically, to have GPs as the casualty officers—because they use resources more sparingly and are used to dealing with mismatches between patient's expectations and reality. Is this expectation borne out in practice? In one careful randomized study of patient-contacts with the Emergency Department in Dublin (N=4684), GPs treating people with semi-urgent problems investigated less (by 20%) referred to other hospital services less (by 39%), admitted fewer patients (45%) and prescribed more often (43%): there were no differences in measures of outcome. It is not clear whether the more economical style of the GPs was to do with being a GP, or whether the reason was that these doctors were older and more experienced than their emergency department counterparts.

Risk management strategy when overwhelmed by the work to be done:

- Prioritize the waiting tasks and then concentrate on the task in hand.
- At times you may feel you are working at a pace that is faster than is comfortable. This is part of 'continuous learning', and as you get better this unease will abate. Look on it as practice for emergency situations where quick decisions are vital. Working faster does not necessarily mean making more errors.
- Have good techniques of clinical decision making, which you continue to refine. Start with something like the system on p 533.
- Keep the goal in mind *What to do for the best for this patient.*

1 D Fatovich 2002 *BMJ* i 958

Bites, stings and foreign bodies

Mammal bites All animal bites are contaminated, especially those of humans: human bites, everything that comes out of the human mouth is poison. Clean well with soap and water, debriding if needed (see p 716). Avoid suturing unless cosmetically essential. Give antibiotics covering anaerobes unless very trivial and not high risk (risk ↑ if: >50yrs, asplenic, immunosuppressed/compromised, has alcoholic liver disease, or the wound is to hand or foot), eg co-amoxiclav 1 tab/8h PO (clindamycin 300mg/6h PO if allergic to penicillin, but beware pseudomembranous colitis). Cat bites, from cats may look trivial, as they look; they carry *Pasteurella multocida*, strep, and fusobacteria. Is tetanus prophylaxis needed? Consider rabies if bitten outside UK. If post-exposure rabies prophylaxis: phone the UK Central Public Health Lab/Health Protection Agency (020 8200 6868; after hours: 020 8200 4400).

Snake bites Of the only poisonous snake (the adder), bites very rarely lethal. Identify the species if possible and move the patient to hospital at once. Treat shock, monitor for clotting time (with venom; treat coagulation), and watch for renal failure, respiratory paralysis, and local tissue necrosis. Indications for antivenom treatment include systemic envenoming as signalled by hypotension, WCC, marked local swelling which is spreading beyond the wrist and ankle more than 1h after the bite (for bites at these locations). Give European viper venom antiserum (see BNF) IV over 15 mins. Use the same dose for children. It may be repeated after 1h if there is no improvement. Have adrenaline (epinephrine) to hand (p 237). If the bite is from a foreign snake or spider, the relevant antivenom may be found in the UK at Liverpool Hospital Pharmacy, Liverpool (0151 525 3611). Information on identification and treatment is available.[1] Avoid tourniquets, incisions, and sucking the wound (but a bandage of the limb may help contain venom).

Lesser weever fish stings (*Echiichthys vipera*) eg in barefoot bathers. It is not serious, and may be relieved by immersion of the leg for 5–20min in water which is as hot as can be tolerated (eg ≤45°C).

Scorpion venom Signs: pain, hypersalivation, ↑BP. Lidocaine 1% at the site relieves pain. Antidotes prepared from animal antisera are effective against some species of scorpions.[2] Prazosin (p 144) can lessen some effects. [illegible]

Bee stings Scrape out with a knife or credit card quickly; pheromones released from the expiring bee will attract more bees. You may well be able to pin them down. Keep calm. A single sting almost never kills you (risk ~1 in 11 000 000) but fatalities are more likely if you get >200 stings (but >1000 is survivable). Cool calamine lotion may help itch. Give antihistamines for severe swelling. Anaphylaxis, p 237.

Air gun pellets These are common, and can be hard to remove. Deaths have occurred, eg when a pellet passes through the eye. Get 2 radiographic views to pinpoint the foreign body. If it has just penetrated the skin, inject local anaesthetic carefully so that you can still palpate it. If you cannot remove it easily, leave it: it is far better than risk extensive tissue destruction trying to find it; many are left without trouble. Subcutaneously, any which have penetrated deeply, must be sought.

Other foreign bodies Always do radiography if there may be glass in a wound. Tiny shards may be left in situ. Even large shards can be hard to find during exploration under GA so remove (also true for metal items or plastic ones (U)). Always do plain radiography for a high-velocity injury: ie a foreign body that cannot be seen (eg grinding/hammering injury).

Heimlich manoeuvre and back blows see p 795.

[1] [illegible]
[2] [illegible]

Bites, stings and foreign bodies

Mammal bites All animal bites are contaminated, especially those of human animals: *everything that comes out of the human mouth is poison.*[1] Clean well with soap and water, debriding if needed. See p 746. ►Avoid suturing unless cosmetically essential. Give antibiotics covering anaerobes unless very trivial and not high-risk (risk↑ if: ♀, >50yrs, asplenic, immunosuppressed/compromised, has alcoholic liver disease, or the wound is to hand or foot), eg co-amoxiclav 1tab/8h PO (clindamycin 300mg/6h PO if allergic to penicillin but beware pseudomembranous colitis). NB: bites from cats may not be as trivial as they look: they carry *Pasteurella multocida*, streps, and fusibacteria. Is tetanus prophylaxis needed? Consider rabies if bitten outside UK. (Post-exposure rabies prophylaxis: phone the UK Central Public Health Lab/Health Protection Agency, 020 8200 6868; after hours, 020 8200 4400.) 234

Snake bites Britain's only poisonous snake, the adder, is very rarely lethal. Identify the species if possible and move the patient to hospital at once. Treat shock, monitor clotting time (many venoms are anticoagulant), and watch for renal failure, respiratory paralysis, and tissue necrosis. Indications for antivenom treatment include systemic envenoming, as signalled by hypotension, WCC raised—as well as local envenoming which is spreading beyond the wrist and ankle more than 4h after the bite (for bites in these locations). Give European viper venom antiserum (see *BNF*) 1 vial IV over 15 mins. Use the same dose for children. It may be repeated after 1h, if there is no improvement. Have adrenaline (=epinephrine) to hand (p 237). If the bite is from a foreign snake or spider, the relevant antivenom may be found in the UK at Fazakerley Hospital Pharmacy, Liverpool (0151 525 5980). Information on identification and treatment is available.[2] ►Avoid tourniquets, incisions, and sucking the wound (but a bandage to the limb may help confine venom).

Lesser weever fish stings (*Echiicthys vipera*)—eg in barefoot UK bathers. It is not serious, and may be relieved by immersion of the leg for 5-20min in water which is as hot as can be tolerated (eg <45°C).

Scorpion venom Signs: BP ↓ or ↑, renal failure, LVF. Lidocaine SC at the site relieves pain. Antidotes prepared from animal antisera are effective against some species of scorpion. 235 Prazosin 236 & L-carnitine 660mg/8h PO *may* help. 237

Bee stings Scrape out with a knife or credit card *quickly*. Pheromones released from the expiring bee will attract more bees. You may well be able to outrun them if you see them coming. NB: although always fatal to the bee, a single sting almost never kills you (risk <1 in 1,000,000)—but fatalities are more likely if you get >200 stings (but >1000 is survivable). Ice ± calamine lotion help itch. Give antihistamines for severe swelling/itch. Anaphylaxis, p 237.

Airgun pellets These are common, and can be hard to remove. Deaths have occurred, eg when a pellet enters brain through the eye. Get 2 radiographic views to position the foreign body. If it has just penetrated the skin, inject local anaesthetic carefully so that you can still palpate it: if you cannot remove it easily, leave it *in situ* rather than risk extensive tissue destruction trying to find it; give antibiotics. Pellets tracking subcutaneously, or which have penetrated deeply, must be sought.

Other foreign bodies ►Always do radiography if there may be glass in a wound. Tiny shards may be left *in situ*. Even large shards can be hard to find, needing exploration under GA to remove (also true for needles/pins stuck in the sole). ►Always do orbit radiography for a high-velocity metallic foreign body, that cannot be seen (eg grinding/hammering injury).

Heimlich manoeuvre and back blows See p 795.

1 John Steinbeck 1945 *Cannery Row*, Minerva, 410
2 Oxford: 01865 220968/741166; Liverpool: 0151 708 9393; London: 0207 1 635 9191

Coin ingestion

If symptomatic, arrange chest & neck radiograph (AP and lateral, to differentiate GI and respiratory tract location). Abdominal films may be needed. If below diaphragm, let it pass. If in upper $^1/_3$ of oesophagus, remove it with an endoscope. Make sure that there are no more foreign bodies before removing the scope; if lower, repeat radiography after 12–24h. If the coin is still in the oesophagus, remove endoscopically under GA.

Common minor procedures

►When in doubt, ask the trauma nurse: she will have seen it all before

'I've hammered my finger, doctor' This usually causes a subungual haematoma—relieved by expressing the blood through a hole trephined in the nail, using a 19G needle. No force is needed: simply twiddle the needle vertically on the nail: cutting edge will make a suitable hole (p 745).

'I've swallowed a fish bone and it's stuck' Always examine the throat and tonsils carefully. Often the bone has only grazed the mucosa. Use a good light, and grip the tongue with gauze to move it out of the way before removing any visible bones with forceps. If you fail, refer to ENT.

'My fish hook has barbed my finger' Infiltrate with plain lidocaine (=lignocaine), and push the hook on through the finger—provided no important structures are in its path. Once the barb is through, cut it off. Remove the hook by the way it entered.

'My tooth has been knocked out' Try to replace permanent teeth. Send deciduous teeth to the tooth fairy. If the former, after the patient sucks it clean (do not use water) transport in milk—or reinsert it, stabilizing with finger pressure (or biting). Go to a dentist for splinting.

Plaster 'back slabs' (for undisplaced forearm fractures).
- Remove anything which impairs finger circulation (eg rings).
- Protect yourself and your patient with a plastic apron.
- Measure the length for the back slab—from knuckles to just below elbow, so that the fingers and elbow will remain mobile.
- Cut a piece of plaster-impregnated bandage 5 times longer than the desired length. Fold it into 5-ply. (Fig ①, OPPOSITE)
- Cut off one corner so that it does not impinge on the thumb.
- Cut a wedge off the other end—the wedge's thick end being on the same side as the thumb. This aids elbow movement. ②
- Roll stockinette over the forearm, to well above the elbow.
- Wind a roll of wool padding over the stockingette (turns must overlap by 50%, so protecting flesh from the hard plaster). ③
- Immerse the plaster bandage in tepid water and apply it to the dorsum of the arm—without pitting it with your finger tips. ④
- Reflect the stockinette down from the elbow and up from the wrist making comfortable top and bottom ends to the plaster. ⑤
- Place a bandage right around the forearm to keep everything in place, securing its end with a strip of wet plaster). ⑥
- Setting takes place over 4min: sooner if warm water is used.
- Put the arm in a sling for 1 day—after which encourage movement of shoulder, elbow, and fingers to prevent stiffness.

►*Cautions for the patient:* **1** Return immediately to A&E if the fingers go blue, swell, or you cannot move them. **2** Do not get the plaster wet. **3** Do not lift heavy weights with the hand.

How to remove a tight ring from a swollen finger Wind some cotton tape around the finger, advancing towards the ring. When it is reached, thread the tape through it. Grasp this end of the tape and unwind. This levers the ring over the PIP joint. If not, try using a ring cutter (not for brass or steel).

'I've caught my penis in my zip, doctor' Failing simple measures (copious lubrication with mineral oil), the most elegant solution to this is to cut out the bridge from the slider of the zip with strong wire-cutters as shown in the diagrams. The zip then falls apart and all that is needed is a new zip. (Beware the bridge flying off at speed: hold gauze by it.)

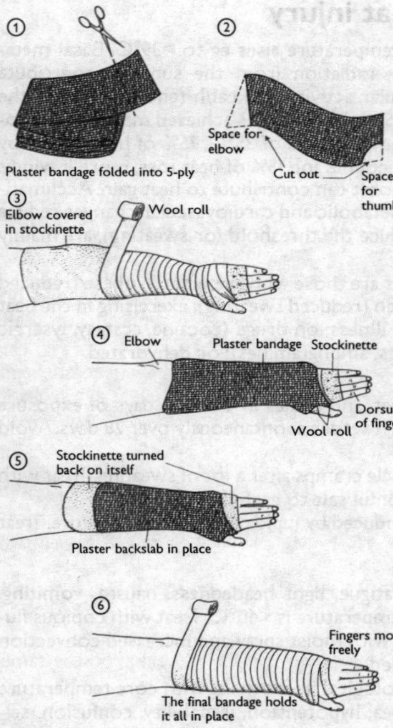
1
Plaster bandage folded into 5-ply
2
Space for elbow
Cut out
Space for thumb
3
Elbow covered in stockinette
Wool roll
4
Elbow
Plaster bandage
Stockinette
Dorsum of fingers
Wool roll
5
Stockinette turned back on itself
Plaster backslab in place
6
Fingers move freely
The final bandage holds it all in place

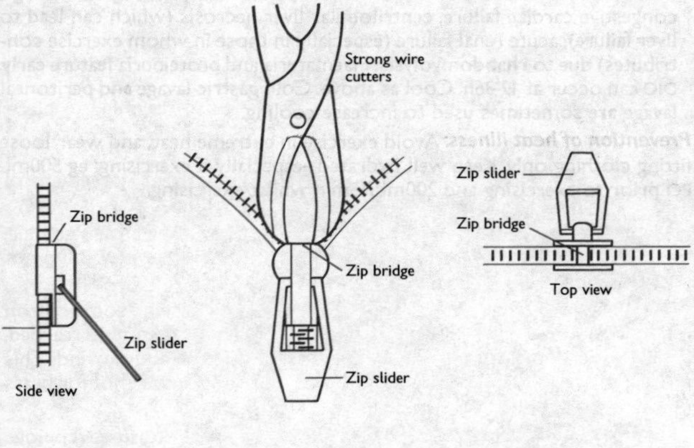
Strong wire cutters
Zip bridge
Zip slider
Side view
Zip bridge
Zip slider
Zip slider
Zip bridge
Top view

Heat exhaustion/heat injury

This occurs when core body temperature rises eg to >39°C. Basal metabolic rate produces 100kcal/h; radiation from the sun can contribute 300kcal/h, and strenuous muscular activity 900kcal/h (enough to raise the core temperature by 1°C every 5min). Cooling is achieved mainly by evaporation. Above environmental temperatures of 35°C, 75% of heat loss is by sweating. Convection usually accounts for 15% of heat loss, more if windy, but if the environment is very hot it can contribute to heat gain. Acclimatization to a hot environment (metabolic and cardiovascular changes reduce body core temperature and reduce the threshold for sweating), are mainly completed by 7-12 days.

Those at risk from heat illness are those who are: elderly; obese (reduced cardiovascular reserves); children (reduced sweating); exercising in the heat (eg soldiers); with acute febrile illness; on drugs (cocaine, ecstasy, lysergic acid diethylamide—LSD, tricyclics, amphetamines); or dehydrated.

Forms of heat illness

- Oedema: swelling of hands, feet, and ankles in the first days of exposure (worse after long-haul flights). It settles spontaneously over 28 days. Avoid diuretics.
- Heat cramps: painful large muscle cramps after a lot of sweating. Treat with oral rehydration (half teaspoonful salt to each litre of water).
- Heat tetany: hyperventilation induced by rapid change in temperature. Treat as for usual hyperventilation.
- Heat syncope.
- Heat exhaustion: weakness, fatigue, light headedness, nausea, vomiting, cramps, pilo-erection. Core temperature is <40°C. Treat with copious fluids eg 1litre/h PO; and cooling with moist spray and increased convection (fan). Rarely, IV fluids are needed.
- Heat stroke: this is acute neurological impairment with core temperature ≥40°C. Tachycardia, tachypnoea, hypotension, irritability, confusion, seizures (± hyponatraemia), and coma may occur. Skin may be hot and dry. Mortality: ~10%. Complications include persistant neurological damage, congestive cardiac failure, centrilobular liver necrosis (which can lead to liver failure), acute renal failure (especially in those in whom exercise contributes) due to rhabdomyolysis. Haematuria and proteinuria feature early, DIC can occur at 12-36h. Cool as above. Cold gastric lavage and peritoneal lavage are sometimes used to increase cooling.[238]

Prevention of heat illness: Avoid exercise in extreme heat, and wear loose fitting clothing only. Keep well hydrated—especially if exercising; eg 500mL PO prior to exercising and 200mL/15min whilst exercising.

Electrocution

This accounts for 1000 deaths per year in the USA. Lightning strikes kill between 150 and 300 people per year and seriously injure 1000–1500. Utility workers and those working with electricity lines are the most commonly affected. Injuries within the home are usually due to using improperly earthed appliances or using electrical appliances near water. Alternating current is more dangerous than direct current of the same magnitude.

- Ensure the source of current is turned off before attempting rescue.
- Tetanic muscle spasm may make it impossible for the victim to let go of the source.
- Use paradoxical triage: resuscitate the apparently 'dead' before attending to the living. Using standard resuscitation techniques, resuscitate long and aggressively—remarkable recoveries have been reported.
- Assume blunt trauma (stabilize the spine).
- If there are burns, more fluid replacement is required than for normal thermal burns (7mL/kg/% rather than the standard 4mL/kg/%).
- Treat arrythmias conventionally.
- Nerves preferentially conduct electrical current resulting in preferential damage to them when other tissues remain intact.

12 Pre-hospital immediate care

Relevant pages in other chapters:
Glasgow Coma Scale (p 722); Child Coma Scale (p 201); cardiorespiratory arrest (p 238–9 & *OHCM* p 766–7); drowning (p 724); burns (p 730); pneumothorax (*OHCM* p 194); asthma (p 164).

Sources The best text we have found is *Pre-hospital Medicine* by Greaves & K Porter, 1999, Arnold, ISBN 0 340 67656 6. ***EBM and pre-hospital care:*** See F Bunn *et al* 2001 Report of WHO pre-hospital care steering committee.

Definition Pre-hospital *Immediate Care* is the provision of skilled medical help at the scene of an accident or medical emergency, or while in transit to hospital. The Diploma in Immediate Medical Care is a benchmark for professional standards in this area (nurses, doctors, and paramedics may apply).

History Baron Dominique Larrey, Napoleon's Surgeon Marshall, may have provided the first skilled help at the scene with his *ambulances volantes* ('flying ambulances'), and was the first to apply the principle of triage—to sort the injured into priorities for treatment (p 796–7).

Note The aim of this chapter is not to provide a full account of the care of *any* patient prior to hospitalization—this is by-and-large the province of the general practitioner. Rather, our aim here is to highlight those circumstances when doctor and paramedic can work together effectively to save life.

►'Accidents' are in fact predictable and preventable

Road crashes affect 1 in 4 people in their lifetime. Each day ~3000 people die and 30,000 people are seriously injured on the world's roads. They are the chief cause of death in those <45yrs; most deaths in the 15-19 age group are preventable.

In the UK, road deaths have fallen since 1966 despite a >50% ↑ in numbers of vehicles. There are 3500 deaths/yr and ≤45,500 serious injuries/yr in the UK. Data analysis shows little impact on the rate of decline in fatal accidents in the UK from the seat-belt law (1983). One reason may be ***risk compensation***—ie safety improvements are transferred by drivers into increased speed or recklessness—illustrating that public health experts must recognize our complex emotional and cognitive reactions to safety issues.[1,2]

Air bags also give a complex picture. They reduce fatalities, but front seat children without a seat belt and infants in passenger-side rear-facing car seats are at risk of fatal injury. Burns, high-frequency hearing loss, corneal and retinal injuries also occur.[3,4]

Casualty rates per 100 million vehicle km are similar for cyclists (~200 deaths/yr) and motorcyclists (~500 deaths/yr). Age factors: babies are rarely killed as their *risk exposure* is less. Deaths fall in middle age, rising again before falling in old age. In children, death rates are higher in lower social classes and in more deprived socioeconomic areas.[5]

Alcohol is a major factor in >10% of preventable crashes. 20% of drivers and 36% of pedestrians killed have blood alcohol levels >the legal limit of 80mg/100mL (17.4mmol/L). This rises to 50% of drivers and 73% of pedestrians killed between 10pm & 4am. There is evidence that older drivers compensate for alcohol-impaired performance by driving carefully; young drivers can compensate in this way, but may choose not to do so (peer group pressure or a delight in risk-taking).

Benzodiazepines, antidepressants, antihistamines, and mobile phone use also contribute to road crashes, and it is important that patients are advised not to drive while on these.[6]

If a patient has epilepsy or diabetes with hypoglycaemic attacks (or is otherwise unfit to drive, p 526) it is his duty to inform the licensing authorities, and the doctor's duty to request him to do so.

Prevention A vital cognitive shift occurs if the word *accident* is replaced by *preventable occurrence*, implying that accidents are predictable. They typically happen because of laziness, haste, ignorance, bad design, false economy, and failure to apply existing knowledge—and *safety education can* change behaviour.[RCT 7]

Schemes can help young drivers who abuse alcohol, eg the *Driver improvement system for traffic violators*, and re-education by driving instructors. Psychotherapy helps more than lectures. Health education posters picturing tragic consequences to a girl- or boyfriend are successful.

Laws can save lives (roadworthiness of cars, drunken-driving and seat-belt laws, speed restrictions, speed cameras[1])—particularly when infringement leads to re-education (speed-awareness courses) rather than punishment (fine plus licence endorsement).[8]

Another effective way of reducing alcohol-related road crashes is to provide good lighting at difficult bends or junctions. Injury in homes may be prevented by such simple measures as child-proof containers, putting holes in polythene bags, using toughened glass throughout the home, and using cooking pans with handles turned in away from toddlers.

1 Pilkington P 2005 *BMJ* 330 331 (speed cameras do prevent accidents, but studies are not that good)

Accident statistics (UK)

Every year about 13,000 people are killed in accidents in Great Britain. This includes 1000 children.

UK deaths[1,2] and other injuries

On the roads	
Deaths	3500
Serious injuries	40,000
Less serious injuries	261,400
Children's deaths	270
Children seriously injured	~7000
Deaths in those >65yrs old	1004
Home-based accidents	
Deaths	4066
Other injuries	224,000
Injuries in gardens, drives and pathways	388,000
Deaths at work	376
Injuries at work (~45,000 are serious)	1,500,000

Accidents in the home Old people are particularly at risk. Over half the males and three-quarters of females who die from accidents in their homes were 65 years old or older. About half of those old ladies falling and fracturing their femur will be dead in 6 months (p 750). The commonest cause of accidental death in children is suffocation; in the 15–44 age group it is poisoning, and in the over-45s the chief cause is falls.

Hospital attendances for accidents 7.5 million people/year in the UK attend an accident and emergency department following an 'accident'. 350,000 (4.7%) of these are admitted. One-third of accidents occur in the home, and one-quarter are in those under 5yrs old.

Many more receive treatment from their general practitioner.

Accidents in children

- ~10,000 children are permanently disabled by accidents each year.
- Accidents cause 1 child in 5 to attend the A&E department each year.
- Accidents are the commonest cause of death among children aged 1–14yrs, and they cause half of all deaths in those aged 10–14yrs.
- School age children (4–14yrs) in road crashes restrained with a seat belt are 2–10 times as safe as unbelted children, and were at least as well protected as adults wearing seat belts.[2]

Useful contacts and addresses:

- British Safety Council, 62 Chancellors Road, London W6 9RS (UK).
- Construction Health and Safety Group, St Ann's Road, Chertsey, Surrey KT16 9AT (UK); tel. 020 8741 1231.
- Scottish Chamber of Safety, Heriot-Watt University, Riccarton, Currie, Edinburgh EH14 4AS (UK).
- *Injury Prevention* (full-text) http://ip.bmjjournals.com/current.shtml-ORIGINAL_ARTICLES

1 Royal Society for the Prevention of Accidents (RoSPA), 353 Bristol Rd, Birmingham B5 7ST (tel. UK 0121 248 2000) 2 APLS group *Advanced Paediatric Life Support*, BMA

Basic life support (BLS)[1]

Synonyms Artificial Respiration; cardiopulmonary resuscitation (CPR).

Definition BLS is the provision of life support—expired air (your own) ventilation + external chest compression, without any equipment.

SAFE approach

- As you approach the patient shout for help (pointing to an individual if possible, to activate him or her).
- Approach him with care—are there any hazards to yourself (p 800)?
- Free the patient from immediate danger.
- Evaluate the patient's ABC (see below).

The SAFE approach
Shout for help
Approach with care
Free from danger
Evaluate ABC (Airway, Breathing, Circulation)

Establish unresponsiveness Shake gently by the shoulder while stabilizing the forehead with the other hand. Ask 'Are you all right?' If he responds, put in the recovery position (p 799)—if not, check for breathing.

Breathing Open and clear the airway (finger-sweep; remove dental plate or loose false teeth—leave a well-fitting set otherwise the mouth collapses making expired air ventilation difficult). If breathing, put in the recovery position; if not, go to get help now. On return, open the airway and give 2 rescue breaths (slow inflations, just enough to make the chest rise—and achieve a tidal volume of ~400–500mL).

Circulation Feel the carotid pulse for up to 10s (can be difficult and other signs of circulation may also be used). If felt, give 10 rescue breaths, then go for help. If no pulse, give 15 chest compressions (lower ⅓ of sternum, 2 finger's breadth above xiphisternum); depress by ⅓ of the chest's diameter, a rate of ~100/min.

Children (1–8yrs) Same sequence, but use one hand one finger breadth above xiphisternum (rate 100/min). Avoid blind finger sweep—may impact foreign body in conical upper airway. Do look into the airway for easily removable foreign body. See p 238.

Infants (<1yr) If not breathing, give 5 rescue breaths, then check pulse (use brachial pulse as the neck is very short). If no pulse, give 20 cycles of 1:5 ventilations-to-compressions (compression rate 100/min) then go for help—take the baby with you and continue BLS while phoning for help. Avoid blind finger sweeps.

See p 238 for the algorithm of the European guidelines for basic and advanced life support.

1 BLS by a doctor is defined [illegible] of the bystander [illegible] for the individual [illegible].

▸▸Basic life support (BLS)

Synonyms Artificial Respiration; cardiopulmonary resuscitation (CPR).

Definition BLS is the provision of life support—expired air (your own) ventilation + external chest compression, without any equipment.

SAFE approach

- As you approach the patient shout for help (pointing to an individual if possible, to activate him or her).
- Approach him with care—are there any hazards to yourself (p 800)?
- Free the patient from immediate danger.
- Evaluate the patient's 'ABC' (see below).

The SAFE approach
Shout for help
Approach with care
Free from danger
Evaluate ABC (Airway, Breathing, Circulation)

Establish unresponsiveness Shake gently by the shoulder while stabilizing the forehead with the other hand. Ask 'Are you all right?' If he responds, put in the recovery position (p 799)—if not, check for breathing.

Breathing Open and clear the airway (finger sweep; remove dental plate or *loose* false teeth—leave a well-fitting set, otherwise the mouth collapses making expired air ventilation difficult). If breathing, put in the recovery position; if not, go to get help *now*. On return, open the airway, and give 2 rescue breaths (slow inflations, just enough to make the chest rise—and achieve a tidal volume of ~400-500mL).

Circulation Feel the carotid pulse for up to 10s (can be difficult, and other signs of circulation may also be used). If felt, give 10 rescue breaths, then go for help. If no pulse, give 15 chest compressions (lower ⅓ of sternum, 2 fingers' breadth above xiphisternum); depress by ⅓ of the chest's diameter, a rate of ~100/min).

Children (1–8yrs) Same sequence, but use one hand one finger breadth above xiphisternum (rate 100/min). Avoid blind finger sweep—may impact foreign body in conical upper airway; do look into the airway for easily removable foreign body. See p 238.

Infants (<1yr) If not breathing, give 5 rescue breaths, *then* check pulse (use brachial pulse as the neck is very short). If no pulse, give 20 cycles of 1:5 ventilations-to-compressions (compression rate 100/min) *then* go for help—take the baby with you and continue BLS while phoning for help. Avoid blind finger sweeps.

►See p 238 for the algorithm of the European guidelines for basic and advanced life support.[1]

1 BLS by soldiers is deemed inappropriate on the battlefield if the victim has no vital signs

▸▸Choking

Respiratory obstruction by choking on a foreign body is not an infrequent cause of death—which may be prevented by performing the Heimlich manoeuvre. If the person who is choking is conscious and standing, first ask him to bend forward and cough. If this fails, get behind him, and with your arms encircle his abdomen, mid-way between umbilicus and xiphoid process. One hand makes a fist, positioned thumb-to-abdomen. The other hand grasps this fist, and with a sharp movement presses it up and into the abdomen, to dislodge the foreign body. If the victim is already comatose, this manoeuvre can be accomplished with him lying on his back—using the heel of the hand to press with, rather than a fist. Repeated thrusts may be needed. In adults, sweep the mouth with a finger to remove the foreign body.

▸Do not perform this manoeuvre on small children, instead use back blows (below) and chest thrusts (similar to cardiac compressions).

Complications (Rare) If applied incorrectly, direct trauma to abdominal viscera may result ± thrombosis of an abdominal aortic aneurysm or dislodgement of thrombus causing bilateral acute leg ischaemia.[10]

Back blows These are no better, and no worse, than the Heimlich manoeuvre in relieving foreign body obstruction. Neither should be taught or practised to the exclusion of the other. Alternate 5 back blows with 5 abdominal/chest thrusts. Use the heel of the hand to strike forcefully between the scapulae, with the patient leaning forwards.

▸▸Road crashes[1]—1: assessment and triage

If you are the first on the scene, the following page (which assumes a highly organized response) will seem impossible on a dark night, alone. So the first priority is to get help. You may be surprised in how short a time it all becomes organized to give the picture described below. Requesting the fire service when dialing emergency services may be the quickest way to get a dozen trained first-aiders to the scene with unrivalled skill in extrication.

The distribution of trauma deaths is trimodal–*immediate* (aortic deceleration injury; severe head injury), *early* (hypoxia and hypovolaemia), and *delayed* (sepsis; multiple organ failure). Prevention (speed restriction; road lighting; seat-belt laws; no drunken-driving; air bags) is better than cure–and medical intervention is too late for the immediate deaths.

Priorities at the scene These are command, safety, communications, assessment, triage, treatment, and evacuation.

Command: Once in attendance the doctor is responsible for the provision of all medical care. He will work closely with the ambulance service, but will have supplementary skills (eg providing potent IV analgesia).

Safety: Yourself First ensure your own safety (do not approach fire or chemical hazards (p 800) until the fire service have made the area safe; wear high-visibility clothing, and carry gloves/eye protection/ear defenders). The scene If first to arrive, park obliquely behind the incident ('fend off') and leave hazard lights/green beacon on. The casualties Remove from any immediate danger; protect from further injury during extrication (eg cover with blanket when windows broken). ▸Check for a hidden victim, eg under a car or over a wall.

Communications: Liaise with police (they are in overall command), fire service (for any hazards; they can remove the casualty quickly if he is about to die, or in a very controlled manner, eg if an isolated spinal injury), and ambulancemen (identify if they have extended skills; use appropriately). Speak to the receiving hospital by radio or telephone (p 804, radio procedure), and relay the number and severity of casualties.

Assessment: Relate vehicle damage to potential injuries in the casualty ('reading the wreckage'). Is the casualty trapped–relative (cannot move a broken arm to open the door), or absolute (eg feet caught in pedals)?

Triage: From the French *trier*, to sift or sort (coffee beans), this process sorts casualties into priorities for treatment. Divide into *Immediate* (colour-code RED, will die in a few minutes if no treatment, eg obstructed airway, tension pneumothorax); *Urgent* (YELLOW, may die in 1-2h if no treatment, eg hypovolaemia); and *Delayed* (GREEN, can wait, eg minor fractures). Those who will certainly die are labelled *Expectant*—to treat them may delay you helping the salvageable, who then die unnecessarily (BLUE, but not all triage labels have this colour–use GREEN). Do not forget to label the dead (WHITE or BLACK), otherwise emergency personnel may repeatedly take a doctor to the same victim, so wasting time and resources. Note that alcohol or drug abuse (eg cannabis[11,12]) which may have caused the accident in the first place may make assessing of casualties much harder.

Note that triage is dynamic. It starts with a brief-look assessment (see OPPOSITE), but later may involve a detailed examination. Priorities (and label colour) will change while awaiting, and after treatment.

1 I Roberts 2002 *BMJ* i 402—RTA (road traffic accident) is a misnomer: most result from speed and carelessness, and are all too predictable, rather than being truly accidental

How to triage[1]

This is a simple system: its main virtue is *speed*. All casualties should be reassessed when time and resources allow. Go through the following sequence until you arrive at a triage priority (in CAPITALS below)—assign its colour label to the casualty and move immediately to the next. Do NOT stop to treat, or you will surrender control of the incident.

1 • Can the patient walk?

Yes → DELAYED (Code with green label)
No → check for breathing …

2 • Is the patient breathing?

No → open the airway
Are they breathing now?
Yes → IMMEDIATE (Red)
No → DEAD (White)
Yes → count or estimate the rate (eg over 15sec)
<10 to >30 per minute → IMMEDIATE (Red)
10–30 per minute → check the circulation …

3 • Check the circulation

Capillary refill >2sec (or pulse >120) → IMMEDIATE (Red)
Capillary refill <2sec (or pulse <120) → URGENT (Yellow)

1 Advanced Life Support Group *Major Incident Medical Management & Support: the Practical Approach*, London, BMA Publishing—also ATLS *Manual* 6e, p409 ISBN 1-880696-10-X

Equipment

In your car boot carry the following minimum equipment:

Oropharyngeal airway(s)	Dressings	Bandages
IV cannulae (14G+16G)	IV fluid (eg Haemaccel®)	Giving set
Sticky tape	Scissors + Torch	Fire extinguisher

You should give a high priority to making yourself safe and visible, eg: reflective jacket, hard hat, Wellington boots.

Extra equipment Cervical collars; Mini-Trach II® (cricothyrotomy kit); chest drain set; sutures; local anaesthetic; analgesia; splints; stethoscope (more a badge of office than a useful tool owing to noise).

▸▸First aid treatment

A: ***Airway:*** Remove false teeth and any vomit. Lie in the lateral position. If trapped in a car, continue to manually stabilize head and neck when a rigid collar is applied. Extricate on to a spinal board, and immobilize the head and neck with foam headblocks and securing straps.

B: ***Breathing:*** If spontaneous, give O_2 at 15L/min via tight fitting face mask with reservoir. If not breathing, ventilate mouth-to-mouth.[13] If available give 100% O_2 via bag-valve-mask and intubate the trachea.[1] If *tension pneumothorax* suspected (cyanosis, engorged neck veins, shifted trachea), pierce chest with a large IV cannula in 2nd interspace in the mid-clavicular line, on the side from which the trachea is deviated. If there is an *open chest wound*, cover with an Asherman chest seal (adhesive disc with central rubber flutter valve).[14]

C: ***Circulation:*** Is there a pulse? If not, start external cardiac massage. (Survival from traumatic cardiac arrest with no vital signs at the accident scene approaches 0%.) If there is bleeding, this will almost always be stopped by pressure and elevation of the part. Avoid tourniquets: these are often forgotten and left on too long. Insert 2 large IV cannulae (eg antecubital fossae 14G or 16G; secure these well and splint the arm, eg Armlok®) and start fluid resuscitation (eg Haemaccel®). A policeman or fireman makes a willing drip-stand. Ensure that the cannula is not pulled out when the patient is moved. Suspected internal bleeding and fractures of long bones indicate that IV fluid is needed, as blood loss may be considerable (fractured pelvis 2L, femur 1L, tibia, ankle and fractures of several ribs ~½L each). Splinting (eg one leg to the other) helps reduce blood loss as well as relieving pain. NB: the ATLS target is definitive haemorrhage control, rather than plasma volume normalization.

D: ***Disability:*** Assess responsiveness rapidly with AVPU:

A = Alert
V = responds to Vocal stimuli
P = responds to Pain
U = Unresponsive

E: ***Exposure*** = head-to-toe exam (secondary survey), but is often not practical outside hospital. Reassess ABC; quantify coma level (adult Glasgow Coma Scale, p 722; child, p 201). Remember to give analgesia (p 802).

Transport: Keep the injured warm. Procedures can be performed in moving ambulances (eg IV cannulation) if the patient can be extricated quickly.

1 Rapid sequence intubation (RSI) is as do-able in the field as in hospital

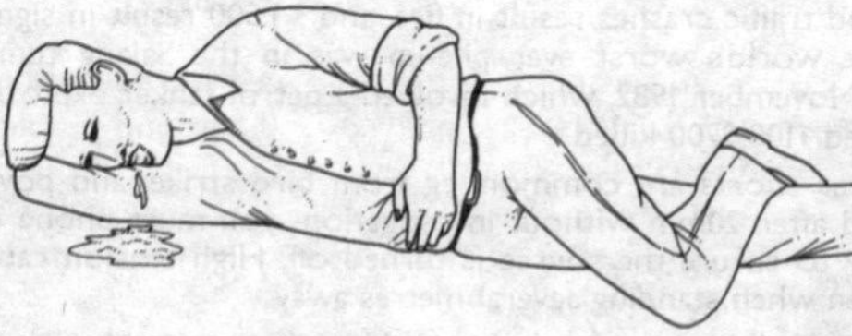

The above is one way of positioning the unconscious so vomit is not inhaled and the cervical spine is kept supported in the midline—minimizing risk of spinal cord injury. It helps if there are 2-3 people to 'log-roll' the casualty into this position, so that the neck is never out of alignment with the body. There have been reports of neurovascular risk to the arm supporting the head, so other positions are being tried, but none has been formally validated.

'Scoop and run'—or 'stay and play'?

'Scoop and run' refers to rapid evacuation of casualties to a trauma centre (or A&E department); 'stay and play' entails detailed resuscitation at the scene of trauma. In deciding which is better, take the following into account.

- There is no single answer for all circumstances. Local geography plays a part, as does the fitness of the casualty. Only experience can tell which option is most appropriate—and luck may well play its part too.
- 'Scoop and run' and 'stay and play' are two ends of a spectrum of activity. Often a minimal amount of resuscitation can be done without causing too much delay—ie: get the best of both worlds.[15]
- Penetrating chest injuries have been studied in a pseudo-randomized trial (*N*=289; full randomization was impossible but 'scoop and run' operated for one day, and 'stay and play' for the next). This showed that the balance of benefit probably lies in 'scoop and run' for this type of injury. Fluid resuscitation aiming for normotension without an operating theatre to hand may be dangerous, as clot may be displaced by the rising BP—with subsequent fatal haemorrhage, which could only have been prevented by major surgery. In this study, 70% in the delayed-resuscitation group survived, compared with 62% who received immediate fluid resuscitation. Duration of hospital stay was shorter for survivors in the delayed-resuscitation group. But note that the results only achieved significance when pre-op and post-op deaths were pooled, and that rates of complications were similar in the two groups (eg respiratory distress syndrome, coagulopathy, wound infection, and pneumonia).[16][17] [n=598]

Road crashes—2: hazards and extrication

Hazards

Fire: <5% of road traffic crashes result in fire, and <1:500 result in significant burns. The world's worst ever pile-up was in the Salang tunnel, Afghanistan, in November 1982, which involved a petrol tanker explosion with an estimated 1100-2700 killed.

Electricity: Power shorts are common, eg from bird strike, and power may be restored after 20min without investigation—you must phone the power company to ensure the source is turned off. High tension cables can be lethal even when standing several metres away.

Rail: An electrified rail may be short circuited by a bar carried by the fire service, or the operating rail authority. Remember that cutting power does not stop diesel locomotives that may also operate on the same line: trains may be stopped by signal lights, red flags, or a series of charges placed on the rail—the noise warns the driver.

Chemical: Lorries carrying hazardous loads are required to display an orange 'HAZCHEM' board (see OPPOSITE). This contains information on how to fight a fire, what protective equipment to wear, if the chemical can be safely washed down the storm drains, and whether to evacuate the area (TOP LEFT); a United Nations (UN) product identification number of four digits (MIDDLE LEFT)—eg 1270 = petrol; a pictorial hazard diamond warning (TOP RIGHT); and an emergency contact number (BOTTOM). A white plate means the load is non-toxic. The European 'Kemler' plate contains only the UN product number (BOTTOM) and a numerical hazard code (TOP—note repeated number means intensified hazard).

As a concession to freight carriers, mixed loads of <500kg need only be identified by a plain orange square at the front and rear.

To obtain information about the chemical at the scene of an accident look at the transport emergency card (TREM card) carried in the driver's cab; the fire service will be linked with CHEMDATA—a computer database at the national chemical information centre at Harwell; alternatively phone a Poison's Information Centre (eg 0207 635 9191), or the company.

►*Do not* approach a chemical incident until declared safe by the fire service.

Principles of extrication

- Stabilize the vehicle where it lies—movement may exacerbate injury.
- Make the vehicle safe—switch off ignition; immobilize the battery; swill away any petrol.
- Identify the time-critical patient—some will die unless rapidly removed from the vehicle, at whatever cost.
- Read the wreckage—relate the damage of the vehicle to potential injuries: steering wheel deformed = chest injury; dashboard intrusion = patella/femur fracture ± posterior dislocation of the hip. Bodies are softer than metal: major bodywork distortion = major injury.
- The easiest way to enter a car is through the door—try this before removing the windscreen or the roof!
- Remove the wreckage from the casualty, not the casualty from the wreckage; don't try to manouevre the casualty through too small a hole.
- Don't move from one entrapment situation straight into another—if necessary spend a short time stabilizing the patient before moving into the back of the ambulance.

Danger labels

Pre-hospital analgesia

Why should I give pain relief? There are more than humanitarian reasons for giving analgesia. Catecholamines released with pain may further reduce peripheral perfusion and oxygen delivery in hypovolaemic shock, and increase myocardial oxygen demand following myocardial infarction.

When do I give pain relief? Unless all hope of life and rescue has been abandoned, the priorities of securing an airway and stabilizing the cervical spine, maintaining ventilation, and optimizing the circulation always come before analgesia. The effects of any drugs must be weighed against their potential side-effects (respiratory depression; sedation).

How do I relieve pain? ***Psychological:*** Beecher noted in 1944 at Anzio[1] that soldiers were indifferent to serious injury. This is unlikely in road crashes; a soldier is released from war horrors by his injuries, but a crash victim is just beginning his nightmare. Reassurance that 'the doctor is here' is important.

Splintage: Simple splints can be improvised from clothing; an uninjured leg can splint the injured one. Inflatable air splints are not very robust, although are light and easy to apply. Box splints (fold around the limb) are popular but poorly accommodate a deformed limb, when a vacuum splint (full of tiny beads) is better. Traction splints should be used for a fractured femur: they also reduce blood loss, morbidity, and mortality (the Thomas splint reduced mortality of open fractured femur from 80% to 20% in World War I).

Gaseous: Nitrous oxide provides comparable analgesia to 10mg morphine. It is mixed with 50% O_2 as Entonox® or Nitronox® in blue cylinders with a white top. It separates at -6°C (O_2 on top). *Do not* use in decompression sickness, p 814, or pneumothorax (may tension).

Opioids: Morphine is the gold standard. Give in small aliquots (1-2mg) IV. Don't give IM if poor peripheral perfusion might result in erratic absorption. Naloxone (0.4-1.2mg IV) must be available at all times. Nalbuphine is a synthetic prescription-only opioid: it is increasingly used by paramedics. Nalbuphine dose: small aliquots, up to 10-20mg slowly IV, repeated after 30min if needed; for a child the max dose is 0.3mg/kg. As a partial antagonist, it will compete with any morphine given later.[18]

NSAIDs: IM NSAIDs (diclofenac 75mg IM, repeated once only, at 30min if needed, or ketorolac 10mg IM stat then 10-30mg/2-6h as needed, max 60-90mg/day) has a role in musculoskeletal pain—and it doesn't entail monitoring for sedative effects; it isn't recommended for children.[19] Ketorolac can be given IV over ≥15sec; avoid in: hypovolaemia; labour; asthma.

Ketamine: This is a potent, short-acting analgesic at 0.25-0.5mg/kg IV. At higher doses it can be used as sole anaesthetic agent (2mg/kg IV will produce 5-10min of surgical anaesthesia); 'emergence delirium' is common unless a benzodiazepine (midazolam ~2mg IV) is also given.[20]

Sedation: An anxious or aggressive patient is often in pain or hypoxic. Reassurance, a clear airway with supplemental oxygen and analgesia is better than sedation, although this is needed rarely: give small aliquots of midazolam (p 630, up to 1.5mg in elderly—have flumazenil to hand).

Local anaesthesia: Peripheral nerve blocks aid release of a trapped limb. Femoral nerve block is most used and provides complete analgesia (anaesthesia) for femoral fractures (less effective for low shaft fracture). Locate the artery in the groin and put 10-20mL 1% plain lidocaine (=lignocaine) in a fan shape *lateral* to the artery. Aspirate frequently to avoid intravascular injection. Maximum dose <3mg/kg or 0.28mL/kg of 1%.

1 Anzio, 33 miles south of Rome, was a crucial Allied beachhead in the recapturing of that 'Eternal City' (5/6/44)

Communications

The radio net. A radio 'user' is identified by a call sign. Messages are usually passed through a central controller (call sign 'control', or zero) without being able to hear other users—two frequency simplex. But on some nets, all users can hear and talk directly to each other—single frequency simplex.

Acquiring a 'radio voice'. This takes practice. Rhythm should be steady; speed is slower than normal speech; volume—do not shout or whisper; pitch should be raised (the voice is then clearer). Remember RSVP.

Using a radio. Switch on and check battery light (switch off to change battery). Listen on the frequency, or look at the 'channel busy' light, before talking, as you do not want to interrupt the message. Wait ½ sec after pressing the transmit button before speaking, or the first word/syllables are lost. Release the transmit button after speaking, or you will prevent others from transmitting. VHF radios have a longer range than UHF.

Messaging. To initiate say the receiver's call sign then your own, say 'over' to indicate when the receiver should reply. To continue a message always start with your own call sign when you speak. To end a transmission say 'out'.

Example: 'Zero from Mike One, message, over.'
'Zero, go ahead, over.'
'Mike One moving now to new location, out.'

Remember that anyone can be listening: don't be a comic ('Send the vomit over, over'), don't swear, address by appointment rather than name.

Key words. Spell long or difficult words using the NATO phonetic alphabet (see OPPOSITE) (you do not want an empty box when you asked for 'Entonox'). Long numbers (eg 6-figure grid references) are given whole then digit by digit (eg 1000 = 'one thousand figures one-zero-zero-zero'). 'Roger' or 'OK' means 'message understood'. 'Say again' means repeat the message ('Repeat' is the order for artillery to fire again and is avoided at least on military networks!). ETA/ETD are common abbreviations for estimated time of arrival/departure. Avoid radio gibberish (roger/ten four/over and out, etc.; negative and positive for yes and no).

Telephone. Mobile telephones are useful for pre-hospital communication. However, in major incidents all cells are rapidly utilized, often by the press, so in the UK, on application to the Cabinet Office, the telephone may be registered to operate on a number of restricted cells in cases where the system is overloaded—this is ACCess OverLoad Control (ACCOLC).

Rank structure

Epaulette	For police	For fire	For ambulance
1 pip	Inspector	Station Officer	Officer band 1
2 pips	Chief Inspector	Asst. Divisional Officer	Officer band 2
Crown	Superintendent		
Laurel 'U'		Asst. Senior Officer	
Laurel 'U' around pip		Divisional Officer	

UK fire service helmets:

Colour	Black bands	Rank
Yellow	Nil	Firefighter
Yellow	1 thin	Leading fireman
Yellow	2 thin	Sub-officer
White	1 thin	Station Officer
White	1 thick	Assistant Divisional Officer
White	1 thick (19mm), 1 thin (12mm)	Divisional Officer

Communications

The radio net A radio user is identified by a 'call sign'. Messages are usually passed through a central controller (call sign 'control', or 'zero') without being able to hear other users—'two frequency simplex'; but on some nets all users can hear and talk directly to each other—'single frequency simplex'.

Acquiring a 'radio voice' This takes practice. *Rhythm* should be steady; *speed* is slower than normal speech; *volume*—do not shout or whisper; *pitch* should be raised if the voice is gruff. Remember: 'RSVP'.

Using a radio Switch on and check battery light (switch off to change battery). Listen (single frequency) or look at the 'channel busy' light (two frequency)—you do not want to interrupt any message. Wait 1-2sec after pressing the transmit button before speaking, or the important first few words are lost. Release the transmit button after speaking, or you will prevent others from transmitting. VHF radios have a longer range than UHF.

Messaging To *initiate* say the receiver's call sign then your own. Say 'over' to indicate when the receiver should reply. To *continue* a message always start with your own call sign when you speak. To *end* a transmission say 'out'.

Example: 'Zero from Mike One, message over.'
'Zero, go ahead over.'
'Mike One, moving now to new location out.'

Remember that anyone can be listening: don't be a comic ('Send the rover over, over'); don't swear; address by appointment rather than name.

Key words Spell long or difficult words using the NATO phonetic alphabet (see OPPOSITE)—you do not want an 'empty box' when you asked for 'Entonox'. Long numbers (drug dose; grid reference) are given whole, then digit by digit (eg 1000 = 'one thousand, figures one-zero-zero-zero'). 'Roger' or 'OK' means you have understood; 'say again' means repeat the message ('Repeat' is the order for artillery to fire again and is avoided, at least on military networks!). ETA/ETD are common abbreviations for estimated time of arrival/departure. Avoid radio gibberish ('roger dodger/ten four/over and out'; 'negative' and 'positive' for 'yes' and 'no').

Telephone Mobile telephones are useful for pre-hospital communication. However, in major incidents all cells are rapidly utilized (often by the press). In the UK, on application to the Cabinet Office the telephone may be registered to operate on a number of restricted cells in cases where the system is overloaded—this is ACCess OverLoad Control (ACCOLC).

Rank structure 21

Epaulette	*For police*	*For fire*	*For ambulance*
2 pips	Inspector	Station Officer	Officer band 1
3 pips	Chief inspector	Asst. Divisional Officer	Officer band 2
Crown	Superintendent		
Laurel 'U'		Asst. Senior Officer	
Laurel 'U' around pip		Divisional Officer	

UK fire service helmets: 22

Colour	*Black bands*	*Rank*
Yellow	Nil	Firefighter
Yellow	1 thin	Leading fireman
Yellow	2 thin	Sub-officer
White	1 thin	Station Officer
White	1 thick	Assistant Divisional Officer
White	1 thick (18mm), 1 thin (12mm)	Divisional Officer

The NATO phonetic alphabet

ALPHA	BRAVO	CHARLIE	DELTA
ECHO	FOXTROT	GOLF	HOTEL
INDIA	JULIET	KILO	LIMA
MIKE	NOVEMBER	OSCAR	PAPA
QUEBEC	ROMEO	SIERRA	TANGO
UNIFORM	VICTOR	WHISKEY	XRAY
YANKEE	ZULU		

Radio procedure—number pronunciation

1 WUN
2 TOO
3 THUREE
4 FOWER
5 FIYIV
6 SIX
7 SEVEN
8 ATE
9 NINER

▸▸The major incident

Planning For a hospital to be prepared to cope with multiple casualties there must be planning. Each hospital will produce a detailed *Major Incident Plan*, but additionally the tasks of key personnel can be distributed on individual *Action Cards*.

At the scene A medical incident officer (MIO) will be requested from Hospital or BASICS scheme (British Association for Immediate Care—usually GPs). Mobile medical teams (eg A&E senior doctor/surgeon + anaesthetist + 2 to 4 nurses) should come from hospitals not accepting the main casualties. BASICS doctors should be requested to the scene by radio via the ambulance station). Further BASICS doctors make valuable treatment officers, as they arrive.

Safety: Is paramount—your own and others. Be visible (luminous monogrammed jacket) and wear protective clothing where appropriate (safety helmet; waterproofs; boots; respirator in chemical environment).

Triage: See p 796.

Communications: Are essential—and frequently an area where improvements are needed.[23] The police are in overall control of the scene. Each emergency service will dispatch a control vehicle and will have a designated incident officer for liaison. Support medical staff from hospital report to the medical incident officer: his job is to assess then communicate to the receiving hospital the number and severity of casualties, to assess need for further medical teams, to oversee triage (p 797) and treatment (with the Ambulance Incident Officer). He must resist temptation to treat casualties as this compromises his role.

Equipment: Must be portable (in small cases/backpacks) and include: triage labels, intubation[1] and cricothyrotomy equipment; intravenous fluids (colloid); bandages and dressings; chest drain (plus flutter valve); amputation kit (when required ideally two doctors should concur); drugs—*analgesic:* morphine; *anaesthetic:* ketamine (p 802); *specific antidote* if a chemical threat; cardiac resuscitation drugs; drugs to cover common medical emergencies: eg GTN spray, salbutamol inhaler; limb splints; defibrillator/monitor; ± pulse oximeter; 'comfort bag' for staff and others (£1 coins, sweets, toilet paper, etc).

Evacuation: Remember: with immediate treatment on scene, the priority for evacuation may be reduced (eg a tension pneumothorax—RED—relieved can wait for evacuation—becomes YELLOW), but those who may suffer by delay at the scene must go first (eg unconscious closed head injury; myocardial infarct). Send any severed limbs to the same hospital as the patient, if possible keeping them on ice (not *in* ice as freezing harms tissues).

At the hospital a 'major incident' is declared (eg if >10 serious injuries). A control room is established and the medical coordinator ensures staff have been summoned, nominates a triage officer and supervises the best use of inpatient beds, intensive care, and theatre resources. When the incident is declared clear of casualties, the major incident may still continue for some time at the hospital.[24]

1 It is wise to include a Broselow tape-measure for giving child tube sizes relative to height—more reliable than (age in years + 16) divided by 4.

When do major incidents become complex emergencies?

- If the context involves administrative, political, or economic anarchy.
- If the incident sparks a self-perpetuating chain of violence.
- If the incident is not a random event, but focused on one ethnic group.
- If competition for wholly inadequate resources compounds their inadequacy.
- If the incident leads to displacement of children.
- If the incident promotes a state of war.[25]

Helicopter transport

►It is often better to spend 30min transporting serious injuries to a well-resourced trauma centre with consultants standing by, than to spend 10min transporting such a person to a small hospital where the most skilled help is not *immediately* available. If the small hospital has to transfer the casualty to a trauma centre, no significant savings may have been made compared with immediate helicopter transfer to the centre.[26]

The importance of helicopters for casualty rescue/transport is increasingly recognized—but be aware of limitations. Helicopters may be used for transporting casualties to hospital, or for interhospital transfer. ***Advantages:*** Speed over long distances; access to remote areas; delivery of highly trained doctors and special equipment to the scene—eg ready to intubate, paralyze and ventilate, and give mannitol IVI if head injury.[27] ***Disadvantages:***

- Mid-air crashes in air ambulances have occurred, and are hard to survive.
- Noise and general stress, leading to anxiety and disorientation, and hampering communication—reassure and provide with a headset.
- Vibration exacerbating bleeding and pain from fracture sites.
- Cold—beware in those hypothermic rescues from sea or mountain.
- Problems related to altitude; aircraft limitations, eg weather, landing site, limited carriage space (especially if additional medical personnel).
- Police craft don't allow ECG monitor/oximeter due to magnetic radiation.
- Many published reports of the advantages of air ambulances lack rigour.

The gains of helicopter transfer depend on how many severe injuries occur. One UK study concluded that only ~13 lives would be saved per year in London if it was reserved for the severest cases (ISS >15, p 810) in lesser trauma, there is evidence that outcome is *less* good.[28]

Helicopter safety • Always approach from the front of the aircraft, in full view of the pilot. Secure loose items, eg headgear.

- Do not enter/leave the rotor disc area without permission (thumbs up signal from pilot). Lower your head in the rotor disc area.
- Do not touch the winch strop/cable until the earthing lead has contacted the ground. Also, be sure to avoid the tail rotor.
- Make sure no-one is smoking within 50m of the aircraft.

Problems of altitude Hypoxia is unlikely unless there is cardiac or lung disease, anaemia, shock or chest trauma, as helicopters rarely fly high enough to produce a significant fall in P_aO_2.

Reduction in atmospheric pressure results in an expansion of enclosed gases on ascent. This produces pain in blocked sinuses, expansion of a pneumothorax, abdominal wound dehiscence (avoid flying for 10 days post surgery if possible) and renewed bleeding from a peptic ulcer. Remember drips may slow down.

On descent, beware of endotracheal tube cuffs and military antishock trousers (MAST*) deflating significantly (particularly if applied at altitude eg on hillside). Rapid descent may induce barotrauma.

Specific problems • Decompression sickness (p 814): if air is breathed under pressure (divers), nitrogen dissolves in blood and tissues. On rapid ascent after a dive the nitrogen will come out of solution as bubbles, producing joint pains ('the bends') ± urticaria, CNS defects and shortness of breath. ►Do not fly if dived <30m within last 12h or >30m within 24h.

- Ischaemic chest pain or infarction is not a contraindication to flying.
- Psychiatric illness (eg mania) may preclude safe air transport.
- Burns >20% need preflight nasogastric tube insertion (prevents gas expansion of an ileus) ± in-flight pressure-controlled ventilation.[29]

***MAST (=medical anti-shock trousers)**

MAST inflation may impair breathing & ventricular function.[30] They have proved deleterious in those with moderate hypotension (systolic BP 50–90mmHg) who face only a short ride to a hospital, especially those with thoracic injuries. MAST's role in severe shock or long pre-hospital transport times remains unclear. In severe shock, improvement in BP and oxygenation to the heart and CNS may override any negative effects of continued haemorrhage.[31]

Trauma scoring

Essence Trauma scoring can be used at the roadside to predict the probability of survival (Ps), and thus the severity of injury, which may influence where to take the patient (nearby district general hospital, regional hospital, or Trauma Centre?). Retrospectively, physiological data may be combined with an anatomical injury score to compare performance (expected *vs* actual survivors) between hospitals. NB: trauma scoring in children is problematic. See expert literature.[1]

Trauma Score (TS): The original score introduced in 1981 in USA to allow paramedics to make an objective decision on whether patient needed Trauma Centre facilities. Measures respiratory rate + effort; systolic BP; capillary refill; Glasgow Coma Scale (GCS). Maximum score 16. Score ≤13 means mortality ≥10%—USA take to Level 1 Trauma Centre; UK take to large hospital and alert trauma team en route.

Revised Trauma Score (RTS): Measures respiratory rate, systolic BP, and GCS only: other parameters were found to be poorly reproducible on analysis of a large North American database. Each parameter has values coded to give score of 0–4. These scores are multiplied by a weighting coefficient, then added together to produce the RTS—it is not a suitable roadside tool. RTS has a more reliable correlation with Ps than does TS.

Triage Revised Trauma Score (TRTS): This uses the same coded values of respiratory rate, systolic BP, and GCS from the RTS, but a fall by one point in any parameter is taken as significant (thus TRTS ≤11 is significant). This is the most useful pre-hospital trauma triage tool.

Limitations: These scoring systems are not validated for the very young or elderly; up to 20% may have severity underestimated on their initial assessment (if attended rapidly, before physiological decompensation).

Injury Severity Score (ISS) TS, RTS, and TRTS use physiological variables to predict Ps. Anatomical injury (data from operation or postmortem notes) can also be used—injuries are scored from 1 (minor) to 6 (fatal) using tables from the Abbreviated Injury Scale (AIS). The body is divided into 6 regions and the 3 highest scores from different regions are squared and added. Maximum score is 75 (5 squared × 3) since AIS6 in any body region is fatal—and therefore awarded a score of 75. ISS correlates closely with Ps. ISS ≥16 implies mortality ≥10% and is termed 'major trauma'.

Limitations: Injuries can be difficult to code; isolated head injury with AIS of 3 has high mortality, but is excluded from 'major trauma' outcome analysis.

TRISS methodology Trauma audit programmes are established in USA & UK—*Major Trauma Outcome Study* (MTOS). TRISS is a complex formula combining RTS, ISS, age, and whether blunt or penetrating trauma. It is poor at predicting individual outcome, but allows comparison of overall performance between hospitals, or the same hospital following, say, introduction of trauma teams. ASCOT (*a severity characterization of trauma*) is newer but not necessarily better. Similarly, TRISS has been combined with physiological categorizations (SAPS-II)[2] to improve reliability.

Z & M statistics compare outcome in different populations. *Z* measures the difference between the actual and predicted number of deaths. *M* (the 'injury severity match') compares the range of injury severity to the main database—if *M* <0.88, *Z* is invalid.

1 D Potoka 2001 *J Ped Surg* **36** 106 See also
2 SAPS = Simplified Acute Physiology Score (SAPS); see A Reiter 2004 *J Trauma* **57** 375

Blast injury

Blast injury may be encountered in domestic (eg gas explosion) or industrial (eg mining) accidents, or as the result of a terrorist bomb/terrorist attacks. Worldwide, it is responsible for 15,000 injured or killed in the last 20 years, and most casualties are from primus. Death may occur without any obvious external injury, often due to air emboli, the correct cause first being recognized by Pierre Jars in 1758 in an explanation of the 'blast wave'. Explosions cause injury in seven ways:

1 Blast wave A transient (milliseconds) wave of overpressure expands rapidly away from the point of explosion, its intensity inversely proportional to the distance cubed. It produces (a) cellular disruption at the air–tissue interface (spalling), ie perforated eardrums at 100kPa, blast lung, and (b) shearing forces along tissue planes (submucosal/subserosal haemorrhage), (c) re-expansion of compressed trapped gas: bowel perforation, fatal air embolism (coronary artery or cerebral).

2 Blast lung is often delayed (up to 48h). It is rare in survivors—only 0.6%. Suspect it if there is a perforated drum, but this is **not** a prerequisite (as position of drum in relation to blast wave is critical). Intra-alveolar haemorrhage causes adult respiratory distress syndrome (ARDS p 170). Most patients who survive immediate injury regain good lung function within a year.

3 Blast wind Air displaced by the explosion will totally disrupt a body in the immediate vicinity. Others may suffer traumatic amputations. Others can be carried by the wind with deceleration injuries on landing. Glass, wood, stones, and other objects are also carried and act as secondary missiles.

4 Missiles Penetration or laceration from missiles are by far the commonest injuries. Missiles arise from the bomb (casing or incorporated fragments—nails, nuts, and bolts) or are secondary (as above, glass and wood particularly).

5 Flash burns These are usually superficial and occur on exposed skin (hands/face) in those close to explosions.

6 Crush injuries result from falling masonry.

7 Psychological Acute fear and panic is the aim of the terrorist. Later chronic intrusive thoughts, anxiety, and poor concentration may form the basis of a post-traumatic stress disorder (p 347). This may be augmented by repeated watchings of the event on TV/video.

Treatment Approach the same as any major trauma with priority to airway and cervical spine control, breathing and circulation with haemorrhage control. Rest and observe any suspected of exposure to significant blast, but without other injury. Sudden death or renal failure may follow release of a limb after prolonged crush (hyperkalaemia and myoglobinuria); ensure continuous ECG and adequate hydration. Facial burns may compromise airway, which should be secured by intubation or surgical airway. Psychological support will be required.

Blast injury

Blast injury may be encountered in domestic (eg gas explosion) or industrial (eg mining) accidents, or as the result of a terrorist bomb. Terrorism worldwide is responsible for 15,000 injured or killed in the last 20 years and most casualties are from bombs. Death may occur without any obvious external injury, often due to air emboli, the correct cause first being recognized by Pierre Jars in 1758 as a 'dilatation d'air' (ie blast wave). Explosions cause injury in seven ways:

1 **Blast wave** A transient (milliseconds) wave of overpressure expands rapidly away from the point of explosion, its intensity inversely proportional to the distance cubed. It produces: (a) cellular disruption at air-tissue interface ('spalling'), ie perforated ear-drum at 100kPa, 'blast lung' at 175kPa; (b) shearing forces along tissue planes: submucosal/subserosal haemorrhage; (c) re-expansion of compressed trapped gas: bowel perforation, fatal air embolism (coronary artery or cerebral).

2 **Blast lung** is often delayed (up to 48h). It is **rare** in survivors—only 0.6%. Suspect it if there is a perforated drum, but this is **not** a prerequisite (as position of drum in relation to blast wave is critical). Intra-alveolar haemorrhage causes acute respiratory distress syndrome (*OHCM* p 190). Most patients who survive lung blast injury regain good lung function within a year.[37] [n=11]

3 **Blast wind** Air displaced by the explosion will totally disrupt a body in the immediate vicinity. Others may suffer avulsive amputations. Bodies can be carried by the wind with deceleration injuries on landing. Glass, wood, stones, and other objects are also carried and act as secondary missiles.[38]

4 **Missiles** Penetration or laceration from missiles are by far the commonest injuries. Missiles arise from the bomb (casing or preformed fragment—nails, nuts, and bolts), or are secondary (as above, glass and wood particularly).

5 **Flash burns** These are usually superficial and occur on exposed skin (hands/face) in those close to explosion.

6 **Crush** Injuries result from falling masonry.

7 **Psychological** Acute fear and panic is the aim of the terrorist. Later, chronic intrusive thoughts, anxiety, and poor concentration may form the basis of a post-traumatic stress disorder (p 347). This may be augmented by repeated watchings of the event on TV/Video.[39]

Treatment Approach the same as any major trauma with priority to airway and cervical spine control, breathing, and circulation with haemorrhage control. Rest and observe any suspected of exposure to significant blast, but without other injury. Sudden death or renal failure may follow release of a limb after prolonged crush (hyperkalaemia and myoglobinuria): ensure continuous ECG and adequate hydration. Facial burns may compromise airway, which should be secured by intubation or surgical airway. Psychological support will be required.

Diving accidents

Thousands go diving every year for recreation. Because of speedy world travel, complications of diving may present to doctors miles from diving centres: for this reason we all need to be familiar with the contraindications and complications of diving, whatever our specialty. Do not underestimate the stress of diving: a depth change of 7m produces changes in ambient pressure equal to a trip from sea level to the top of Everest!

Contraindications to diving •Lung diseases •Pneumothorax history
•Migraine + vomiting attacks •Epilepsy •Angina; arrhythmias
•Otitis (media or externa) •Ménière's disease •Perforated ear drum
•Hypoglycaemia risk (eg DM) •Pregnancy •Bleeding disorders
•Patent foramen ovale[1]

Complications of diving •Barotrauma •Decompression sickness
•Drowning (p 724) •Air embolism •Pulmonary oedema
•Marine bites or stings (p 784) •Hypothermia •Nitrogen narcosis
•Surface accidents (boating)

Decompression sickness Nitrogen is more soluble in lipid than in water so as N_2 tension increases, it accumulates in CNS, marrow and fat. Symptoms appear from 1 to 36h after surfacing. Risk factors: multiple dives, ignoring proper decompression stops, rapid ascent, previous decompression sickness, alcohol ingestion, subsequent ascent to high altitude (p 808).

Presentation: •Vomiting •Mood changes •Deafness; nystagmus
•Throbbing muscle/joint pains •Cough; chest pain •Fits; CNS signs
•Migrating skin mottling/rashes •Cyanosis; shock •Cognitive changes
•Pruritus; paraesthesiae •Osteonecrosis •Headache

Management: Speed of response is vital. If recompression starts ≤30min after the onset of symptoms, 80% will respond; if 6h delay, only 50% respond. If air embolism is suspected, place on the left side and give 100% O_2 (15L/min through tight-fitting facemask with reservoir). Seek expert help.[2] Transfer to a hyperbaric facility. If airlift needed, maximally pressurize the cabin, if the route does not allow flying at sea-level. Transport the breathing apparatus and the diving partner (will give the history, but may himself also be at risk). If there is hypothermia, expect BP to drop after leaving the water, and be sure to transport in the horizontal position, and keep cardiovascular instability to a minimum.

Preventing diving accidents •Augment swimming fitness.
•Avoid dehydration (no alcohol or caffeine for ≥24h before the dive).
•Do the deepest part of the dive first. Time your ascent.
•Plan no-stop dive profiles (ie avoid decompression stops).
•Make a safety stop at 6m. Avoid remaining under water for longer than is recommended by decompression tables or dive computers.
•Rest before the dive, and keep warm during the dive.
•After the dive avoid sitting still for long periods (decreases regional blood flow and nitrogen removal). Avoid boarding aircraft for about 24h.
•No diving if pregnant: there is (uncertain) risk to the fetus as right-to-left shunting diverts blood from the lungs—which are the best filters of micro-bubbles. (The role of the placenta in this task is unknown.)

1 See M Knauth 1997 BMJ i 689 & 701 [illegible] In this cerebral MRI study in 160 asymptomatic scuba divers, found many [illegible] lesions (taken to mean [illegible] damage) associated with a patent foramen ovale (or other shunts allowing paradoxical embolism of venous nitrogen bubbles) [illegible] after ascent from [illegible] bubbles are normally filtered by the lungs).
2 Telephone numbers: UK Hyperbaric Medicine Unit, Aberdeen, Royal Infirmary [illegible]; Royal Navy [illegible]; diving diseases research centre [illegible]. USA: Diving Accident Network [illegible] or US Navy [illegible] or Air Force [illegible].

Diving accidents

Thousands go diving every year for recreation. Because of speedy world travel, complications of diving may present to doctors miles from diving centres: for this reason we all need to be familiar with the contraindications and complications of diving, *whatever* our specialty. Do not underestimate the stress of diving: a depth change of 7m produces changes in ambient pressure equal to a trip from sea level to the top of Everest.[1]

Contraindications to diving
- Migraine + vomiting attacks
- Otitis (media or externa)
- Hypoglycaemia risk (eg DM)
- Patent foramen ovale[1]
- Lung diseases
- Epilepsy
- Ménière's disease
- Pregnancy
- Pneumothorax history
- Angina; arrhythmias
- Perforated ear drum
- Bleeding disorders

Complications of diving
- Drowning (p 724)
- Marine bites or stings (p 784)
- Surface accidents (boating)
- Barotrauma
- Air embolism
- Hypothermia
- Decompression sickness
- Pulmonary oedema
- Nitrogen narcosis

Decompression sickness Nitrogen is more soluble in lipid than in water, so as N_2 tension increases, it accumulates in CNS, marrow and fat. Symptoms appear from 1 to 36h after surfacing. Risk factors: multiple dives, ignoring proper decompression stops, rapid ascent, previous decompression sickness, alcohol ingestion, subsequent ascent to high altitude (p 808).

Presentation:
- Vomiting
- Throbbing muscle/joint pains
- Migrating skin mottling/rashes
- Pruritus; paraesthesiae
- Mood changes
- Cough; chest pain
- Cyanosis; shock
- Osteonecrosis
- Deafness/nystagmus
- Fits; CNS signs
- Cognitive changes
- Headache

Management: Speed of response is vital. If recompression starts ≤30min after the onset of symptoms, 80% will respond; if 6h delay, only 50% respond. If air embolism is suspected, place on the left side and give 100% O_2 (15L/min through tight-fitting face mask with reservoir). Seek expert help. Transfer to a hyperbaric facility.[2] If airlift needed, maximally pressurize the cabin, if the route does not allow flying at sea-level. Transport the breathing apparatus and his diving partner (will give the history, but may himself also be at risk). If there is hypothermia, expect BP to drop after leaving the water, and be sure to transport in the horizontal position, and keep cardiovascular instability to a minimum.

Preventing diving accidents
- Augment swimming fitness.
- Avoid dehydration (no alcohol or caffeine for >24h before the dive).
- Do the deepest part of the dive first. Time your ascent.
- Plan 'no-stop' dive profiles (ie avoid decompression stops)
- Make a safety stop at 6m. Avoid remaining under water for longer than is recommended by decompression tables or dive computers.
- Rest before the dive, and keep warm during the dive.
- After the dive avoid sitting still for long periods (decreases regional blood flow and nitrogen removal). Avoid boarding aircraft for about 24h.
- No diving if pregnant: there is (uncertain) risk to the fetus as right-to-left shunting diverts blood from the lungs—which are the best filters of microbubbles. (The role of the placenta in this task is unknown.) 40

1 See M Knauth 1997 *BMJ* i 689 & 701 »This careful MRI study in 160 asymptomatic scuba divers found many CNS lesions (?akin to multi-infarct dementia) associated with a patent foramen ovale (or other shunt) allowing paradoxical embolism of venous nitrogen bubbles (venous bubbles occur after ascent from as little as 3m (these bubbles are normally filtered by the lungs).

2 *Telephone numbers:* UK: Hyperbaric Medicine Unit's Aberdeen Royal Infirmary 01224 681818; Royal Navy: 07831 151523; diving diseases research centre: 01752 209999 USA: Diving Accident Network (919 684 8111) or US Navy 904 234 4351 or Air Force (512 538 3281 or 512 536 3278)

The last page

It is a pleasure to end this work with a chapter which is really a new beginning: the patient on his way to hospital. So far we have concentrated on what we can bring to the patient; but now let us turn to what the patient brings to us. All too often time and circumstance lead us to the view that patients are tireless devourers of our energies, and that for all practical purposes, we must go on giving until we die, or give up the unequal struggle with Nature and her diseases. This is to ignore the view that patients can be a source of nutrition: not just in the sense of providing us with our daily bread and butter, but also in the sense of nourishing our personalities. They do this by telling us about ourselves. You may think that you are kind and wise, or clumsy and inadequate, and it takes our patients to disabuse us of these illusions, and to show us that some days we are good, and some days we are bad. Thanks to our patients, we never stay the same. After practising medicine for a decade or two, our minds become populated by the ghosts of former patients, beckoning us, warning us, reminding us of the things we cannot control—and the ideals to which we aspire. We are lucky to work in a profession in which experience counts for more than knowledge, and it is to augment this thirst for experience that we urge our readers to turn away from learning by rote: let us read novels, cultivate our friends, travel far and wide—and try to keep forever curious, for then, if we are lucky, we stand to gain that priceless therapeutic asset: a rich and compassionate personality, and we will be all the more inclined to reformulate this tiresome and inconvenient patient who now confronts us into a lovable series of imperfecions, which match and reflect, and reveal our own characteristics.

Index

Entries in **Bolder type** denote emergency topics. ►To look up a drug, look up the disease you want to treat.

A

E

G

H

I

J

K

M

N

O

P

Q

R

S

U

V

W

X

Y

Z

Reference intervals—biochemistry

*See p222 for **children** and p15 for **obstetric reference intervals***

►*All laboratory discourse is probabilistic.* ►Drugs may interfere with any chemical method; as these effects may be method-dependent, it is difficult for us to be aware of all possibilities. If in doubt, discuss with the lab.

Substance	***Specimen***	***Normal value***	***Your hospital***
Adrenocorticotrophic hormone	P	<80ng/L	
Alanine aminotransferase (ALT)	P	5–35IU/L	
Albumin	P¶	35–50g/L	
Aldosterone	P**	100–500pmoL/L	
Alkaline phosphatase	P¶	30–300IU/L (adults)	
α-fetoprotein	S	<10kU/L	
α-amylase	P	0–180 Somogyi U/dL	
Angiotensin II	P**	5–35pmol/L	
Antidiuretic hormone (ADH)	P	0.9–4.6pmol/L	
Aspartate transaminase	P	5–35IU/L	
Bicarbonate	P¶	24–30mmol/L	
Bilirubin	P	3–17μmol/L (0.25–1.5mg/100/mL)	
Calcitonin	P	<0.1μg/L	
Calcium (ionized)	P	1.0–1.25mmol/L	
Calcium (total)	P¶	2.12–2.65mmol/L	
Chloride	P	95–105mmol/L	
*Cholesterol (see p654)	P	3.9–7.8mmol/L	
VLDL (see p654)	P	0.128–0.645mmol/L	
LDL	P	1.55–4.4mmol/L	
HDL	P	0.9–1.93mmol/L	
Cortisol	P	a.m. 450–700nmol/L midnight 80–280nmol/L	
Creatine kinase (CK)	P	♂ 25–195IU/L; ♀ 25–170	
Creatinine (*related to lean body mass*)	P¶	70–≤150μmol/L	
Ferritin	P	12–200μg/L	
Folate	S	2.1μg/L	
Follicle-stimulating hormone (FSH)	P/S	2–8U/L (luteal): ovulatory peak 8–15 follicular phase, & ♂: 0.5–5 postmenopausal: >30	
Gamma-glutamyl transpeptidase	P	♂ 11–51; ♀ 7–33IU/L	
Glucose (fasting)	P	3.5–5.5mmol/L	
Glycated (glycosylated) haemoglobin	B	5–8%	
Growth hormone	P	<20mU/L	
Iron	S	♂ 14–31μmol/L; ♀ 11–30	
Lactate dehydrogenase (LDH)	P	70–250IU/L	
Lead	B	<1.8mmol/L	
Luteinizing hormone (LH)	P/S	premenopausal: 3–13U/L follicular: 3–12 ovulatory peak: 20–80 luteal: 3–16 postmenopausal: >30	
Magnesium	P	0.75–1.05mmol/L	
Osmolality	P	278–305mosmol/kg	
Parathyroid hormone (PTH)	P	<0.8–8.5pmol/L	
Phosphate (inorganic)	P	0.8–1.45mmol/L	
Potassium	P	3.5–5.0mmol/L	
Prolactin	P	♂ <450u/L; ♀ <600U/L	
Prostate specific antigen	P	0–4 nanograms/mL	
Protein (total)	P	60–80g/L	
Red cell folate	B	0.36–1.44μmol/L (160–640μg/L)	
Renin (erect/recumbent)	P**	2.8–4.5/1.1–2.7pmol/mL/h	

Sodium	P¶	135–145mmol/L
Thyroid-binding globulin (TBG)	P	7–17mg/L
Thyroid-stimulating hormone (TSH) **NR** widens with age	P	0.5–5.7mU/L
Thyroxine (T_4)	P	70–140nmol/L
Thyroxine (free)	P	9–22pmol/L
Total iron binding capacity	S	54–75μmol/L
Triglyceride	P	0.55–1.90mmol/L
Tri-iodothyroinine (T_3)	P	1.2–3.0nmol/L
Urea	P¶	2.5–6.7mmol/L
Urate	P¶	♂ 210–480μmol/L ♀ 150–390μmol/L
Vitamin B_{12}	S	0.13–0.68nmol/L (>150ng/L)

Arterial blood gasses

pH: 7.35–7.45 P_aCO_2: 4.7–6.0kPa

P_aO_2: >10.6kPa   Base excess: ± 2 mmol/L

NB: 7.6mmHg = 1kPa (atmospheric pressure≈100kPa)

* Desired upper limit of cholesterol would be <5mmol/L.

** The sample requires special handling: contact the laboratory.

¶ Range is significantly different in pregnancy, see p15.

Keys: P = plasma (heparin bottle); S = serum (clotted; no anticoagulant); B = whole blood (edetic acid—EDTA—bottle); IU = international unit ♂ = male; ♀ = female.

Haematology—reference intervals

Measurement	*Reference interval*	*Your hospital*
White cell count (WCC)	$4.0–11.0 \times 10^9/L$	
Red cell count	♂ $4.5–6.5 \times 10^{12}/L$ ♀ $3.9–5.6 \times 10^{12}/L$	
Haemoglobin	♂ 13.5–18.0g/dL ♀ 11.5–16.0g/dL	
Packed red cell volume (PCV) or haematocrit	♂ 0.4–0.54 l/L ♀ 0.37–0.47 l/L	
Mean cell volume (MCV)	76–96fl	
Mean cell haemoglobin (MCH)	27–32pg	
Mean cell haemoglobin concentration (MCHC)	30–36g/dL	
Neutrophils	$2.0–7.5 \times 10^9/L$; 40–75% WCC	
Lymphocytes	$1.3–3.5 \times 10^9/L$; 20–45% WCC	
Eosinophils	$0.04–0.44 \times 10^9/L$; 1–6% WCC	
Basophils	$0.0–0.10 \times 10^9/L$; 0–1% WCC	
Monocytes	$0.2–0.8 \times 10^9/L$; 2–10% WCC	
Platelet count	$150–400 \times 10^9/L$;	
Reticulocyte count	0.8–2.0% $25–100 \times 10^9/L$;	
Erythrocyte sedimentation rate	depends on age (*OHCM* p670)	
Activated partial thromboplastin time (VIII, IX, XI, XII)	35–45 seconds	
Prothrombin time (factors I, II, VII, X)	10–14 seconds	

Internat. ratio (INR)	Clinical state (see *OHCM* p648–9)
2.0–3.0	Treating DVT, pulmonary emboli (treat for 3–6 months)
2.5–3.5	Embolism prophylaxis in atrial fibrillation, see *OHCM* p649
3.0–4.5	Recurrent deep vein thrombosis and pulmonary embolism; arterial disease including myocardial infarction; arterial grafts; cardiac prosthetic valves (if caged ball aim for 4–4.9) and grafts.